NATIONAL ROAD ATLAS BRITAIN

George Philip

CONTENTS

Key Map 1

Maps of Great Britain 2-64
General Scale 1 inch = 5 miles

Maps of Approaches to London 65-72
Scale ¾ inch = 1 mile

Maps of Central London 73-80
Scale 5 inches = 1 mile

Town Plans 81-112

81 Aberdeen
81 Bath
82-4 Birmingham
85 Blackpool
85 Bolton
86 Bournemouth
86-7 Bradford
87 Brighton
88 Bristol
89 Cambridge
89 Canterbury
90 Cardiff
89 Cheltenham
89 Chester
91 Coventry
91 Croydon
92 Derby
92 Dundee
92 Durham
93 Edinburgh
92 Exeter
94 Glasgow
95 Gloucester
95 Kingston upon Hull
96 Leeds
97 Leicester
97 Lincoln
98 Liverpool
99-100 Manchester
101 Middlesbrough
101 Milton Keynes
102-103 Newcastle
103 Newport (Gwent)
103 Northampton
103 Norwich
104 Nottingham
105 Oxford
105 Peterborough
105 Plymouth
106 Portsmouth
106 Reading
107 Rochester and the Medway Towns
107 Salisbury
108 Scarborough
108 Sheffield
109 Shrewsbury
109 Southampton
110 Southend
111 Stoke-on-Trent
110 Stratford-upon-Avon
112 Swansea
111 Torquay
112 Windsor
112 York

Index to Maps of Great Britain 1-48

Index to Maps of London 49-61

The representation in this atlas of a road or track is not evidence of the existence of a right of way.

British Library Cataloguing in Publication Data
RAC national road atlas Britain.
1. Great Britain— Road maps
912'.41 G1812.21.P2

ISBN 0-540-03290-5

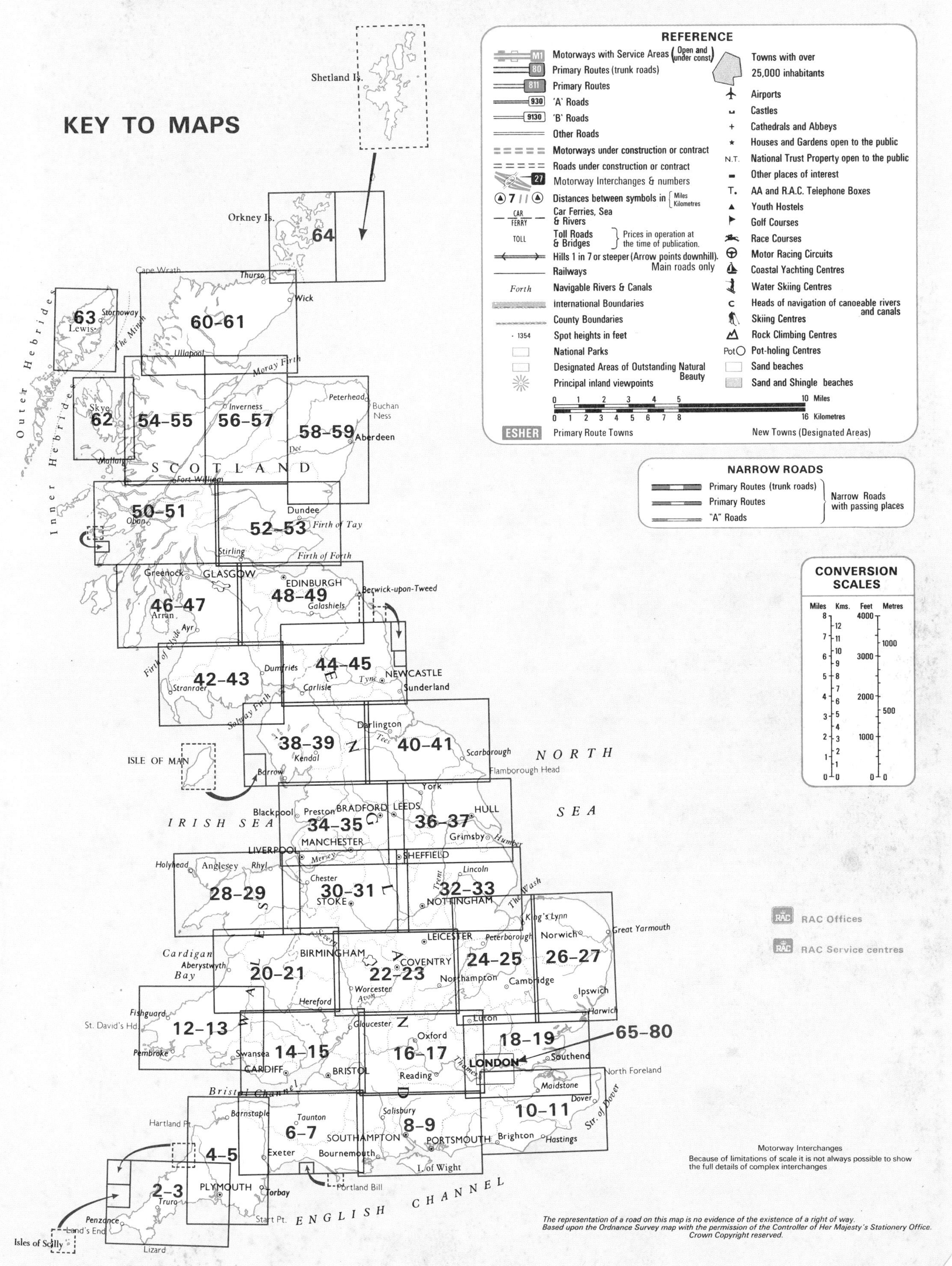

KEY TO MAPS
REFERENCE
Motorways with Service Areas (Open and under const.)
Primary Routes (trunk roads)
Primary Routes
'A' Roads
'B' Roads
Other Roads
Motorways under construction or contract
Roads under construction or contract
Motorway Interchanges & numbers
Distances between symbols in Miles / Kilometres
Car Ferries, Sea & Rivers
Toll Roads & Bridges
Prices in operation at the time of publication.
Hills 1 in 7 or steeper (Arrow points downhill). Main roads only
Railways
Navigable Rivers & Canals
International Boundaries
County Boundaries
Spot heights in feet
National Parks
Designated Areas of Outstanding Natural Beauty
Principal inland viewpoints
ESHER Primary Route Towns
Towns with over 25,000 inhabitants
Airports
Castles
Cathedrals and Abbeys
Houses and Gardens open to the public
N.T. National Trust Property open to the public
Other places of interest
AA and R.A.C. Telephone Boxes
Youth Hostels
Golf Courses
Race Courses
Motor Racing Circuits
Coastal Yachting Centres
Water Skiing Centres
Heads of navigation of canoeable rivers and canals
Skiing Centres
Rock Climbing Centres
Pot-holing Centres
Sand beaches
Sand and Shingle beaches
New Towns (Designated Areas)
10 Miles
16 Kilometres
NARROW ROADS
Primary Routes (trunk roads)
Primary Routes
"A" Roads
Narrow Roads with passing places
CONVERSION SCALES
Miles Kms. Feet Metres
RAC Offices
RAC Service centres
Shetland Is.
Orkney Is.
Outer Hebrides
Inner Hebrides
SCOTLAND
ENGLAND
WALES
NORTH SEA
IRISH SEA
ISLE OF MAN
ENGLISH CHANNEL
64
63
60-61
62
54-55
56-57
58-59
50-51
52-53
46-47
48-49
42-43
44-45
38-39
40-41
34-35
36-37
28-29
30-31
32-33
20-21
22-23
24-25
26-27
12-13
14-15
16-17
18-19
65-80
6-7
8-9
10-11
4-5
2-3
Motorway Interchanges
Because of limitations of scale it is not always possible to show the full details of complex interchanges
The representation of a road on this map is no evidence of the existence of a right of way.
Based upon the Ordnance Survey map with the permission of the Controller of Her Majesty's Stationery Office.
Crown Copyright reserved.

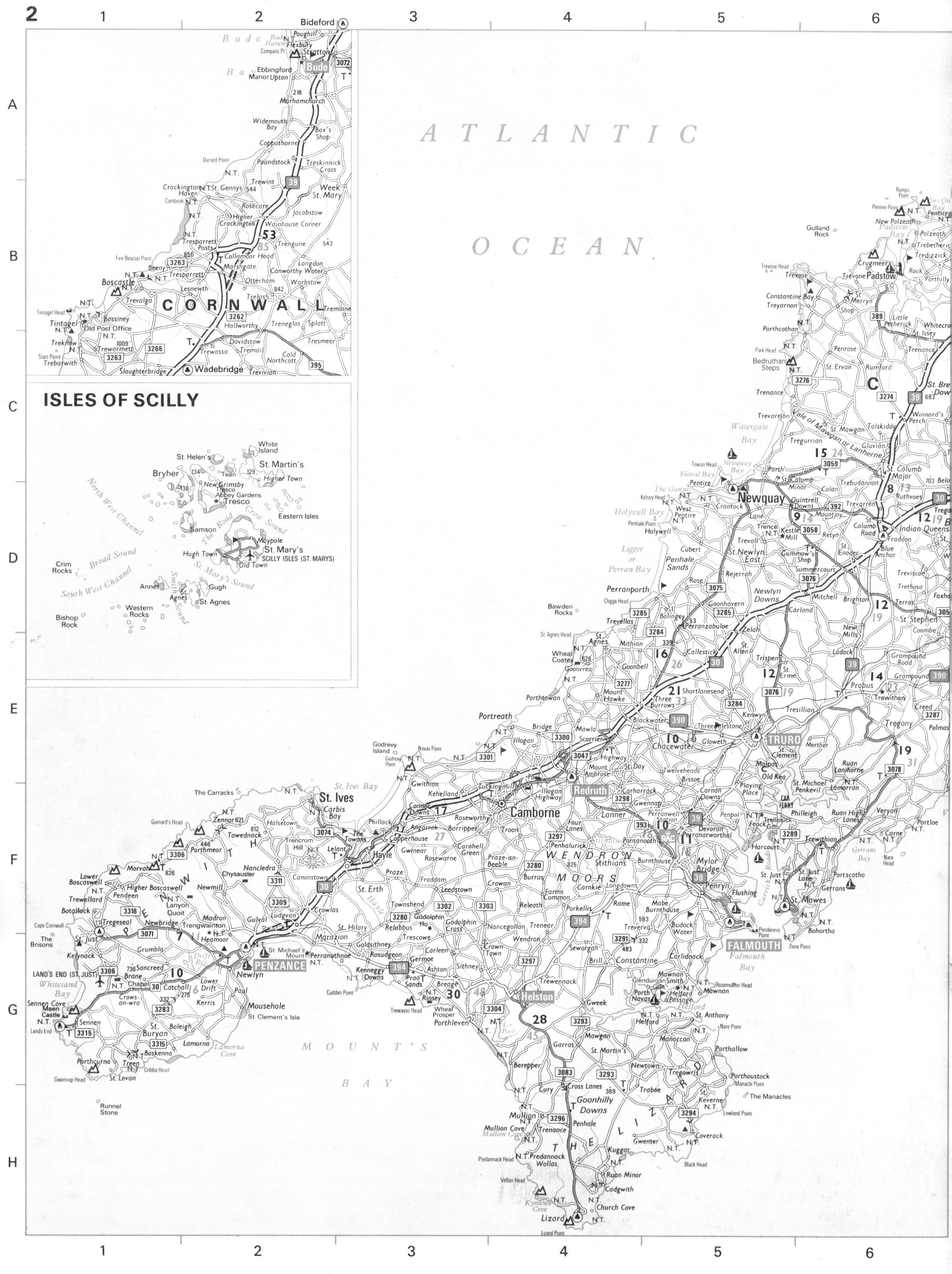
ATLANTIC
OCEAN
CORNWALL
ISLES OF SCILLY
Bideford
Bude
Stratton
Flexbury
Poughill
Marhamchurch
Widemouth Bay
Box's Shop
Coppathorne
Poundstock
Treskinnick Cross
Crackington Haven
St. Gennys
Week St. Mary
Rosecare
Jacobstow
Wainhouse Corner
Tresparrett Posts
Trengune
Collamoor Head
Boscastle
Beeny
Tresparrett
Marshgate
Otterham
Canworthy Water
Warbstow
Lesnewth
Trevalga
Tintagel
Bossiney
Old Post Office
Tremaine
Treneglos
Splatt
Hallworthy
Davidstow
Tremail
Tresmeer
Treknow
Trewarmett
Trebarwith
Trewassa
Cold Northcott
Slaughterbridge
Wadebridge
Trevivian
White Island
St. Helen's
St. Martin's
Higher Town
Bryher
Tean
New Grimsby
Tresco
Abbey Gardens
Eastern Isles
Samson
Moypole
St. Mary's
SCILLY ISLES (ST. MARYS)
Hugh Town
Old Town
North West Channel
Broad Sound
Crow Sound
The Road
St. Mary's Sound
Smith Sound
South West Channel
Crim Rocks
Annet
Gugh
St. Agnes
Western Rocks
Bishop Rock
Padstow
Trevone
St. Merryn
Constantine Bay
Treyarnon
Porthcothan
Bedruthan Steps
St. Ervan
Rumford
St. Issey
Little Petherick
Trenance
St. Mawgan
Talskiddy
Watergate Bay
Vale of Mawgan or Lanherne
Newquay
St. Columb Major
St. Columb Minor
Porth
Pentire
Crantock
Holywell Bay
Holywell
West Pentire
Quintrell Downs
Kestle Mill
Trevarren
Indian Queens
Fraddon
St. Newlyn East
Ligger or Perran Bay
Penhale Sands
Cubert
Rejerrah
Summercourt
Mitchell
Newlyn Downs
Perranporth
Bolingey
Perranzabuloe
Goonhavern
Zelah
Carland
St. Agnes
Mithian
Callestick
St. Allen
Trispen
Wheal Coates
Goonbell
Shortlanesend
Porthtowan
Mount Hawke
Three Burrows
Probus
Grampound
Tresillian
Trewithen
Tregony
Portreath
Bridge
Mawla
Scorrier
Blackwater
Threemilestone
Kenwyn
Illogan
Chacewater
Gloweth
TRURO
Merther
St. Clement
Malpas
Old Kea
Godrevy Island
Navax Point
St. Ives Bay
St. Ives
Carbis Bay
Gwithian
Kehelland
Tuckingmill
Pool
Redruth
Carharrack
Camborne
Illogan Highway
Connor Downs
Roseworthy
Barripper
Phillack
Hayle
Lelant
Copperhouse
Angarrack
Gwinear
Carnhell Green
Praze-an-Beeble
Troon
Four Lanes
Lanner
Gwennap
Stithians
Perranwell Station
Ponsanooth
Devoran
Penryn
Mylor Bridge
Flushing
FALMOUTH
Falmouth Bay
Pendennis Point
St. Mawes
St. Just in Roseland
Gerrans
Portscatho
Veryan
Zennor
Towednack
Halsetown
Trencrom Hill
Porthmeor
Morvah
Chysauster
Nancledra
Canonstown
St. Erth
Praze
Fraddam
Leedstown
Crowan
WENDRON MOORS
Lower Boscaswell
Higher Boscaswell
Pendeen
Trewellard
Botallack
Newmill
Lanyon Quoit
Madron
Trengwainton
Heamoor
Gulval
Ludgvan
Crowlas
St. Hilary
Relubbus
Godolphin Cross
Townshend
Releath
Porkellis
Carnkie
Rame
Mabe Burnthouse
Budock Water
Cape Cornwall
The Brisons
St. Just
Tregeseal
Newbridge
Kelynack
Grumbla
PENZANCE
Newlyn
Marazion
St. Michael's Mount
Perranuthnoe
Goldsithney
Rosudgeon
Germoe
Trescowe
Nancegollan
Wendron
Trenear
Crowntown
Sithney
Helston
Constantine
Seworgan
Brill
Carlidnack
Mawnan Smith
Mawnan
Port Navas
Helford Passage
LAND'S END (ST. JUST)
Whitesand Bay
Sancreed
Brane
Chapel
Catchall
Lower Drift
Drift Res.
Crows-an-wra
Kerris
Paul
Mousehole
St. Clement's Isle
Sennen Cove
Maen Castle
Sennen
Lands End
St. Buryan
Boleigh
Lamorna
Lamorna Cove
Boskenna
Porthcurno
Treen
St. Levan
Gwennap Head
Runnel Stone
Kenneggy Downs
Praa Sands
Ashton
Breage
Rinsey
Cudden Point
Trewavas Head
Wheal Prosper
Porthleven
Loe Pool
MOUNT'S BAY
Gweek
Helford
St. Anthony
Manaccan
Mawgan
Garras
St. Martin's
Newtown
Porthallow
Porthoustock
Manacle Point
The Manacles
Berepper
Cury
Cross Lanes
Goonhilly Downs
Trabee
Tregowris
St. Keverne
Mullion
Mullion Cove
Penhale
Trenance
Coverack
Gwenter
THE LIZARD
Kuggar
Predannack Wollas
Predannack Head
Ruan Minor
Cadgwith
Vellan Head
Kynance Cove
Church Cove
Lizard
Lizard Point
Black Head
Nare Point
Rosemullion Head
Zone Point
Bohortha
Carrick Roads
CAR FERRY
Feock
Penpol
Playing Place
Carnon Downs
Bissoe
Twelveheads
St. Day
Mount Ambrose
Ruan Lanihorne
St. Michael Penkevil
Lamorran
Philleigh
Ruan High Lanes
Trewithian
Portloe
Gerrans Bay
Nare Head
Gulland Rock
Trevose Head
Trevose
Crugmeer
Polzeath
New Polzeath
Pentireglaze
Rock
Padstow Bay
Towan Head
Fistral Bay
Newquay Bay
Kelsey Head
Penhale Point
Bawden Rocks
St. Agnes Head
Gurnard's Head
The Carracks
Godrevy Point

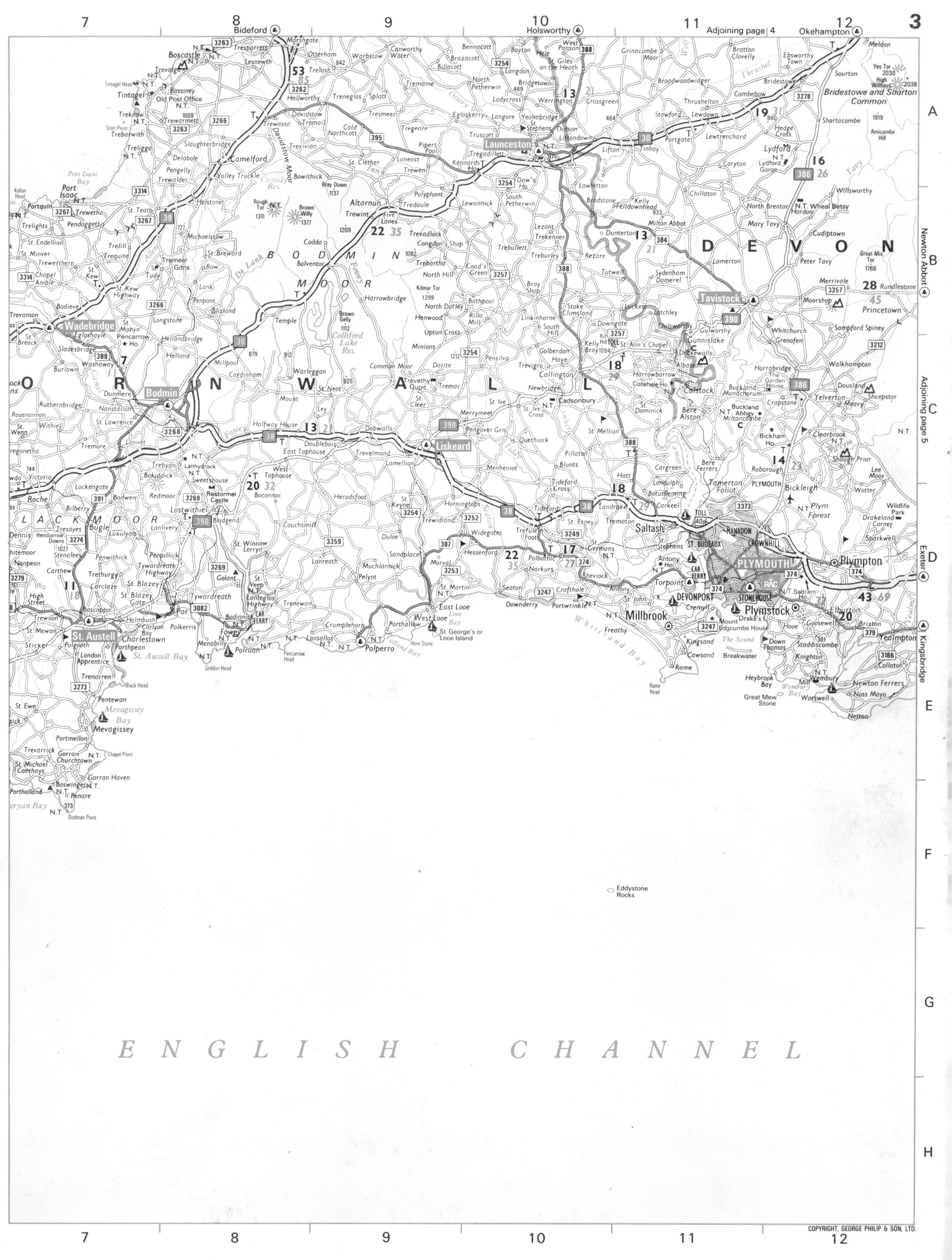

3
Bideford
Holsworthy
Adjoining page 4
Okehampton
Newton Abbot
Adjoining page 5
Exeter
Kingsbridge
C O R N W A L L
D E V O N
B O D M I N M O O R
ENGLISH CHANNEL
Boscastle
Tintagel
Bossiney
Old Post Office
Trebarwith
Camelford
Delabole
Port Isaac
Port Isaac Bay
Portquin
Trelights
St. Endellion
St. Minver
Wadebridge
Egloshayle
St. Breock
Burlawn
Washaway
Bodmin
Lanivet
Lanhydrock
Lostwithiel
Restormel Castle
Bugle
Luxulyan
Par
Tywardreath
St. Blazey
Charlestown
St. Austell
St. Austell Bay
Polgooth
London Apprentice
Pentewan
Mevagissey
Mevagissey Bay
Portmellon
Gorran Churchtown
Gorran Haven
Chapel Point
Boswinger
Penare
Portholland
Dodman Point
Black Head
Gribbin Head
Fowey
Polruan
Golant
Lerryn
St. Winnow
Lanteglos Highway
Lansallos
Polperro
Pelynt
Duloe
Sandplace
Morval
East Looe
West Looe
Looe Bay
St. George's or Looe Island
Talland Bay
Hessenford
Widegates
Seaton
Downderry
Portwrinkle
Craftholе
Sheviock
Antony
Torpoint
Millbrook
Freathy
Whitesand Bay
Kingsand
Cawsand
Rame
Rame Head
Cremyll
Mount Edgcumbe House
Drake's I.
The Sound
Breakwater
Plymouth
PLYMOUTH
DEVONPORT
STONEHOUSE
ST. BUDEAUX
CROWNHILL
MANADON
Plymstock
Plympton
Saltash
St. Stephens
Landrake
Trematon
St. Germans
Tideford
Liskeard
Dobwalls
Doublebois
East Taphouse
West Taphouse
Boconnoc
St. Neot
St. Cleer
Tremar
Darite
Common Moor
Minions
Upton Cross
Henwood
North Darley
Rilla Mill
Bathpool
Kilmar Tor 1299
Brown Willy 1377
Rough Tor 1311
Bolventor
Altarnun
Five Lanes
Trewint
Colliford Lake Res.
Warleggan
Cardinham
Temple
Blisland
St. Breward
Michaelstow
Helstone
St. Teath
Davidstow Moor
Davidstow
Launceston
Lewannick
Polyphant
South Petherwin
North Petherwin
Egloskerry
Werrington
St. Giles on the Heath
Lifton
Lewdown
Stowford
Bridestowe
Bridestowe and Sourton Common
Sourton
Meldon
Yes Tor 2030
High Willhays 2038
Lydford
Lydford Gorge
Brentor
North Brentor
Mary Tavy
Peter Tavy
Milton Abbot
Lamerton
Tavistock
Gunnislake
Calstock
Cotehele Ho.
Bere Alston
Bere Ferrers
Callington
Kelly Bray
Stoke Climsland
South Hill
Pensilva
St. Ive
Menheniot
Quethiock
St. Mellion
Pillaton
Landulph
Botusfleming
Tamerton Foliot
Roborough
Bickleigh
Buckland Monachorum
Buckland Abbey
Yelverton
Horrabridge
Whitchurch
Sampford Spiney
Walkhampton
Dousland
Meavy
Sheepstor
Princetown
Merrivale
Great Mis Tor 1768
Rundlestone
Shaugh Prior
Plym Forest
Wotter
Lee Moor
Sparkwell
Drakeland Corner
Wildlife Park
Elburton
Brixton
Yealmpton
Staddiscombe
Down Thomas
Knighton
Wembury
Heybrook Bay
Wembury Bay
Great Mew Stone
Worswell
Newton Ferrers
Noss Mayo
Netton
Collaton
Eddystone Rocks
COPYRIGHT, GEORGE PHILIP & SON, LTD.

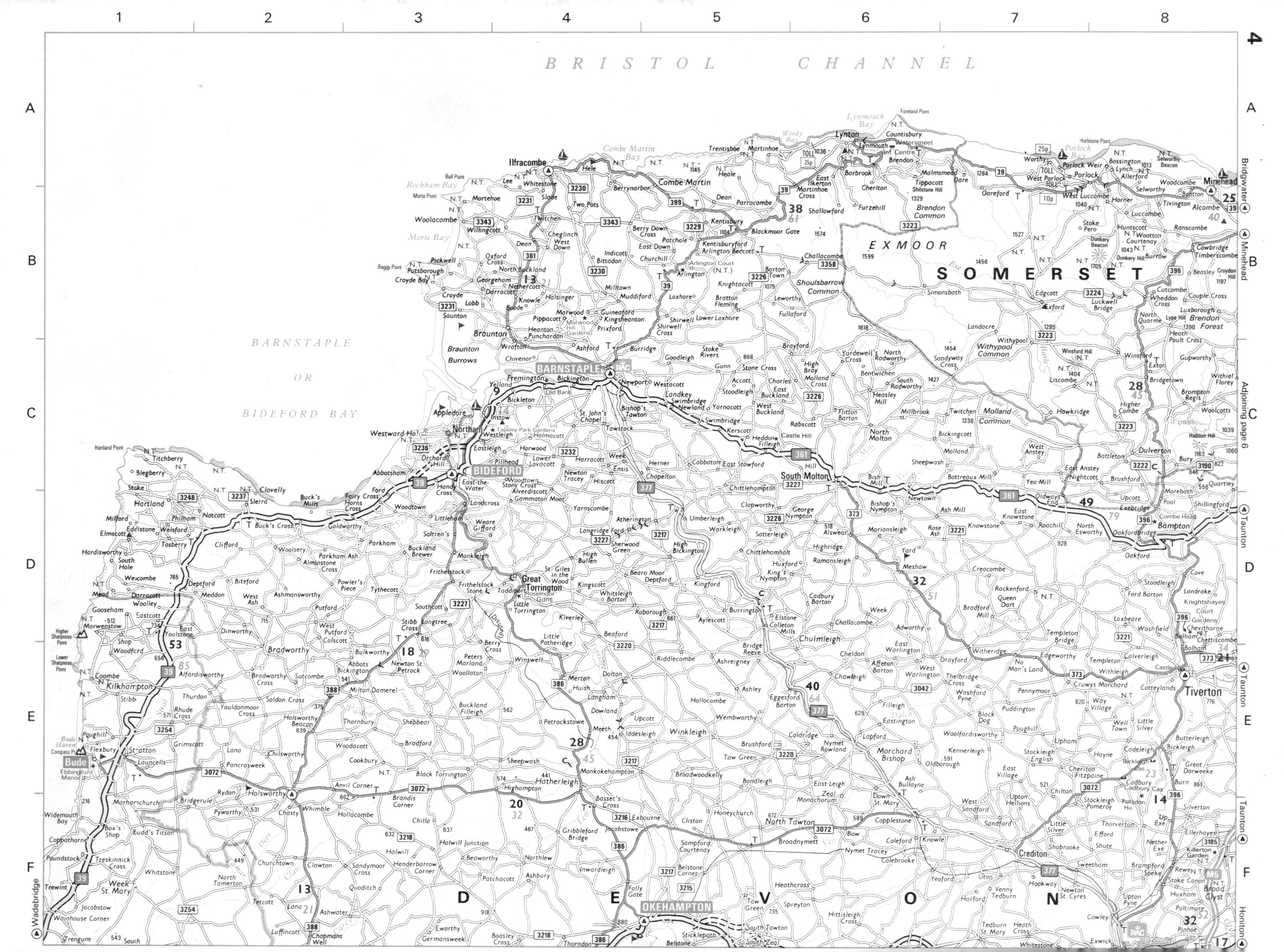

Bridgwater
Minehead
Adjoining page 6
Taunton
Taunton
Taunton
Honiton
Wadebridge
BRISTOL CHANNEL
BARNSTAPLE OR BIDEFORD BAY
EXMOOR
SOMERSET
DEVON
Ilfracombe
Combe Martin
Lynton
Lynmouth
Porlock
Minehead
Dulverton
Tiverton
Crediton
South Molton
Chulmleigh
BARNSTAPLE
BIDEFORD
Northam
Appledore
Westward Ho!
Braunton
Great Torrington
Holsworthy
Bude
OKEHAMPTON
North Tawton
Hartland
Clovelly
Kilkhampton
Bradworthy
Hatherleigh
Winkleigh
Morchard Bishop
Rackenford
Exford
Woolacombe
Saunton
Croyde Bay
Morte Bay
Rockham Bay
Lynmouth Bay
Porlock Bay
Combe Martin Bay
Hartland Point
Bull Point
Morte Point
Baggy Point
Foreland Point
Hurlstone Point
Shoulsbarrow Common
Withypool Common
Molland Common
Brendon Common
Braunton Burrows

Adjoining page 6
Adjoining page 3
Exmouth
Bodmin
St. Austell

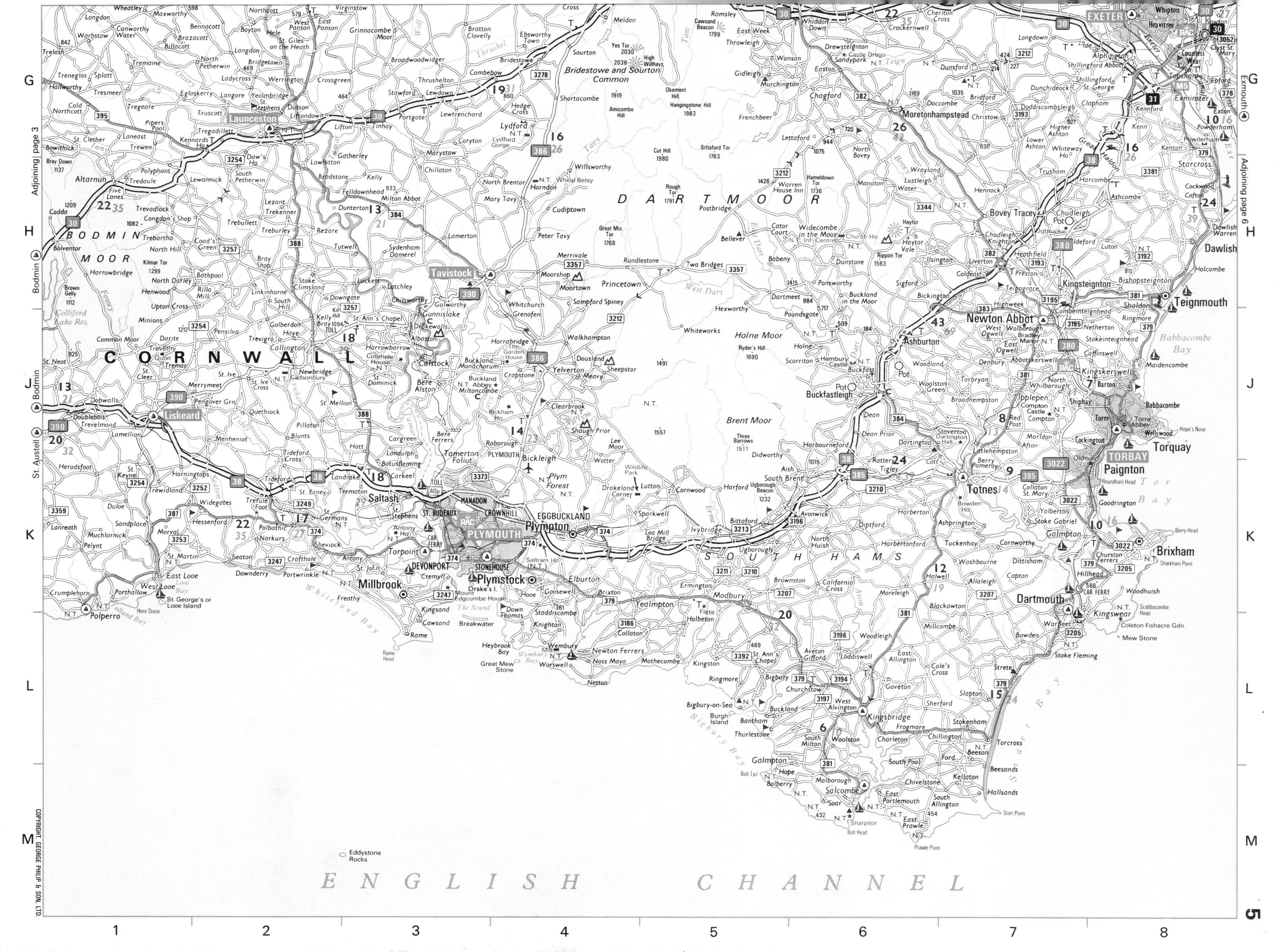

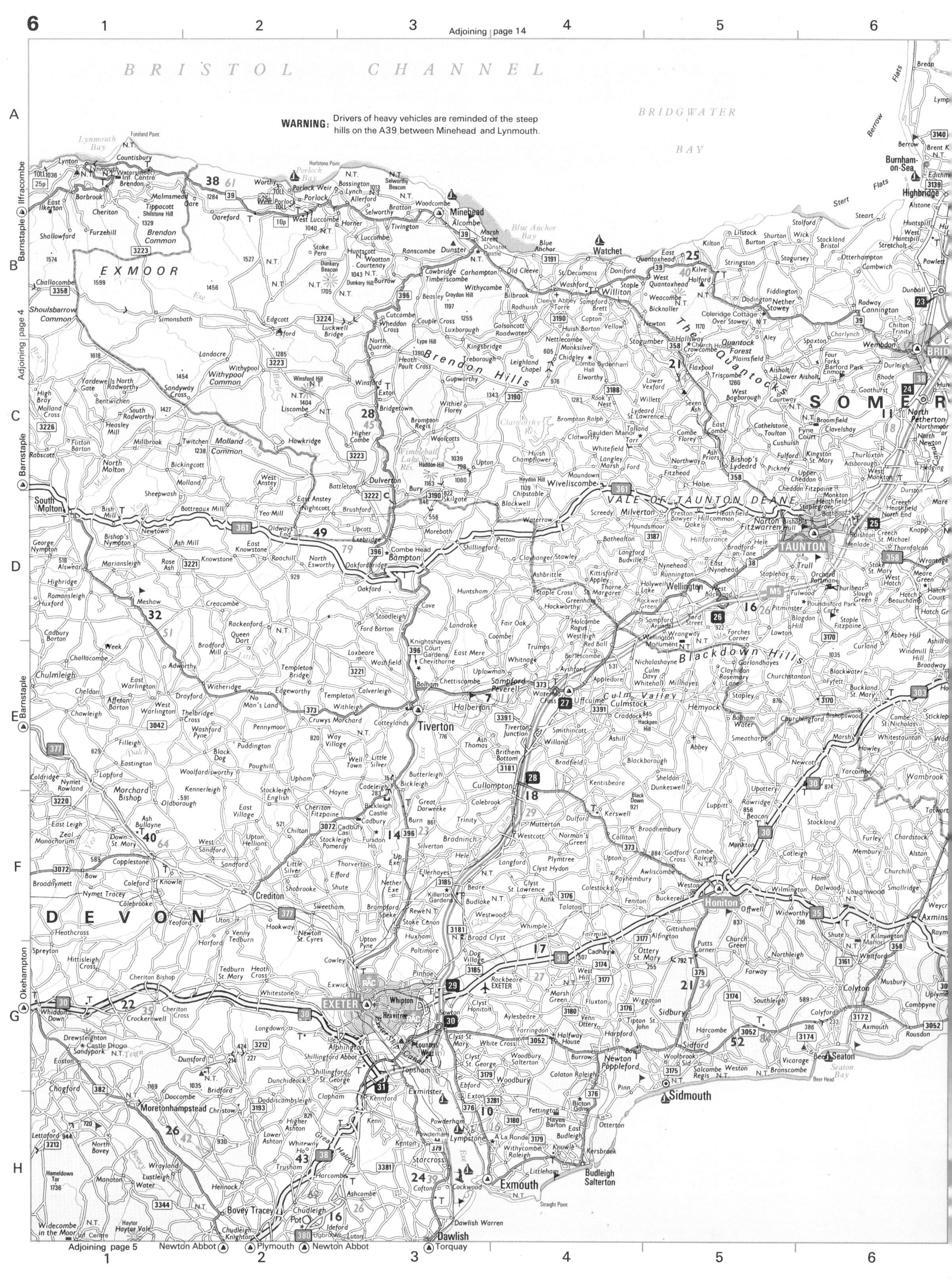

6
Adjoining page 14
BRISTOL CHANNEL
BRIDGWATER BAY
WARNING: Drivers of heavy vehicles are reminded of the steep hills on the A39 between Minehead and Lynmouth.
EXMOOR
Brendon Hills
The Quantocks
VALE OF TAUNTON DEANE
Blackdown Hills
Culm Valley
SOMER
DEVON
Minehead
Watchet
Burnham-on-Sea
Highbridge
Taunton
Wellington
Tiverton
Cullompton
Honiton
Exeter
Exmouth
Sidmouth
Budleigh Salterton
Dawlish
Crediton
South Molton
Dulverton
Bampton
Moretonhampstead
Bovey Tracey
Axminster
Seaton
Adjoining page 4
Adjoining page 5
Barnstaple
Ilfracombe
Okehampton
Newton Abbot
Plymouth
Torquay

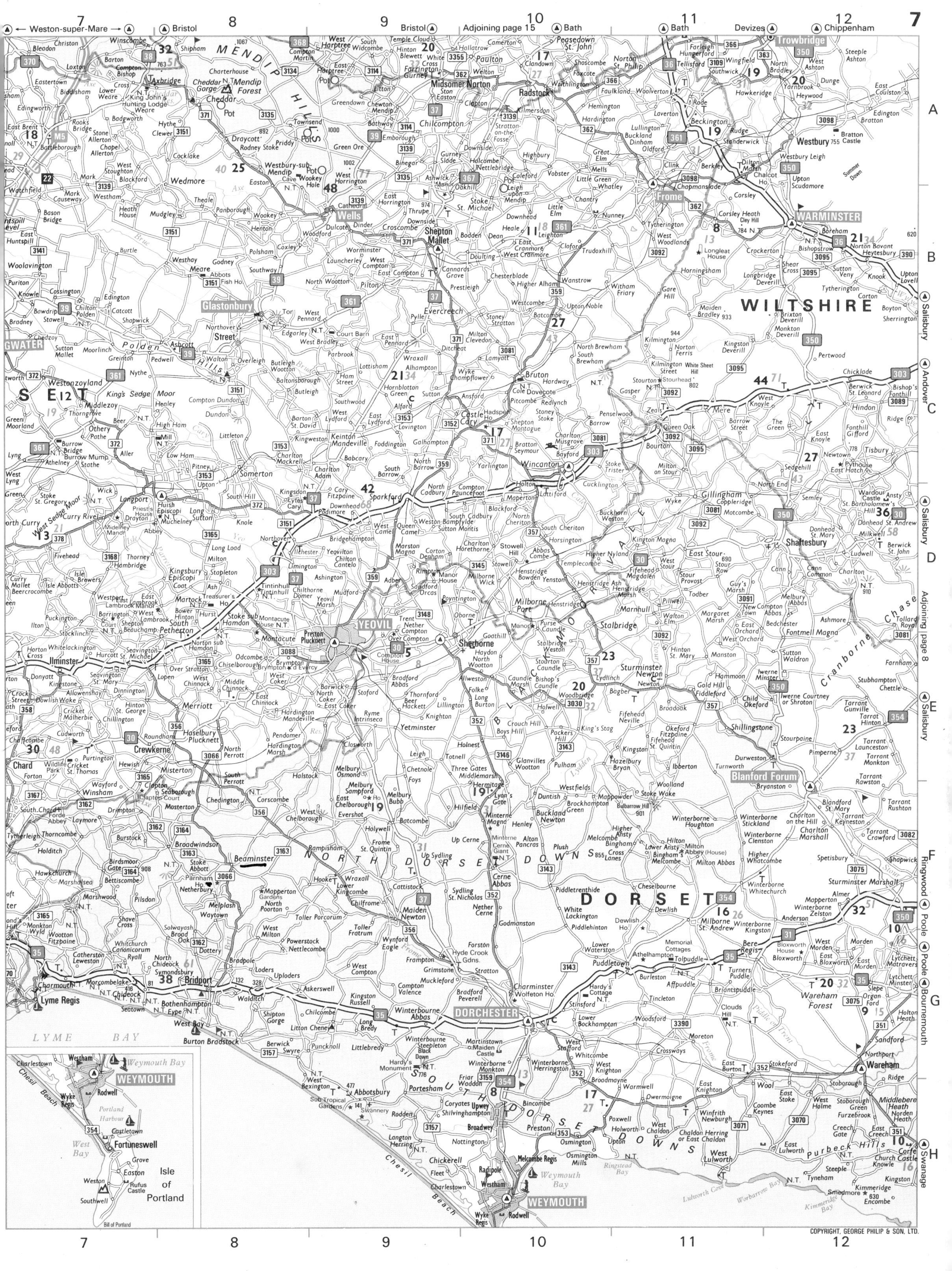

7
8
9
10
11
12
Weston-super-Mare
Bristol
Adjoining page 15
Bath
Devizes
Chippenham
A
B
C
D
E
F
G
H
Salisbury
Andover
Adjoining page 8
Ringwood
Poole
Bournemouth
Swanage
MENDIP HILLS
WILTSHIRE
DORSET
NORTH DORSET DOWNS
SOUTH DORSET DOWNS
Cranborne Chase
Purbeck Hills
LYME BAY
Chesil Beach
Isle of Portland
Bill of Portland
Weymouth Bay
Glastonbury
Wells
Frome
Trowbridge
WARMINSTER
Shepton Mallet
Midsomer Norton
Radstock
Westbury
Street
Somerton
Langport
Ilminster
Chard
Crewkerne
Beaminster
Bridport
Lyme Regis
YEOVIL
Sherborne
Wincanton
Bruton
Castle Cary
Gillingham
Shaftesbury
Sturminster Newton
Blanford Forum
DORCHESTER
WEYMOUTH
Wareham
Fortuneswell
COPYRIGHT, GEORGE PHILIP & SON, LTD.

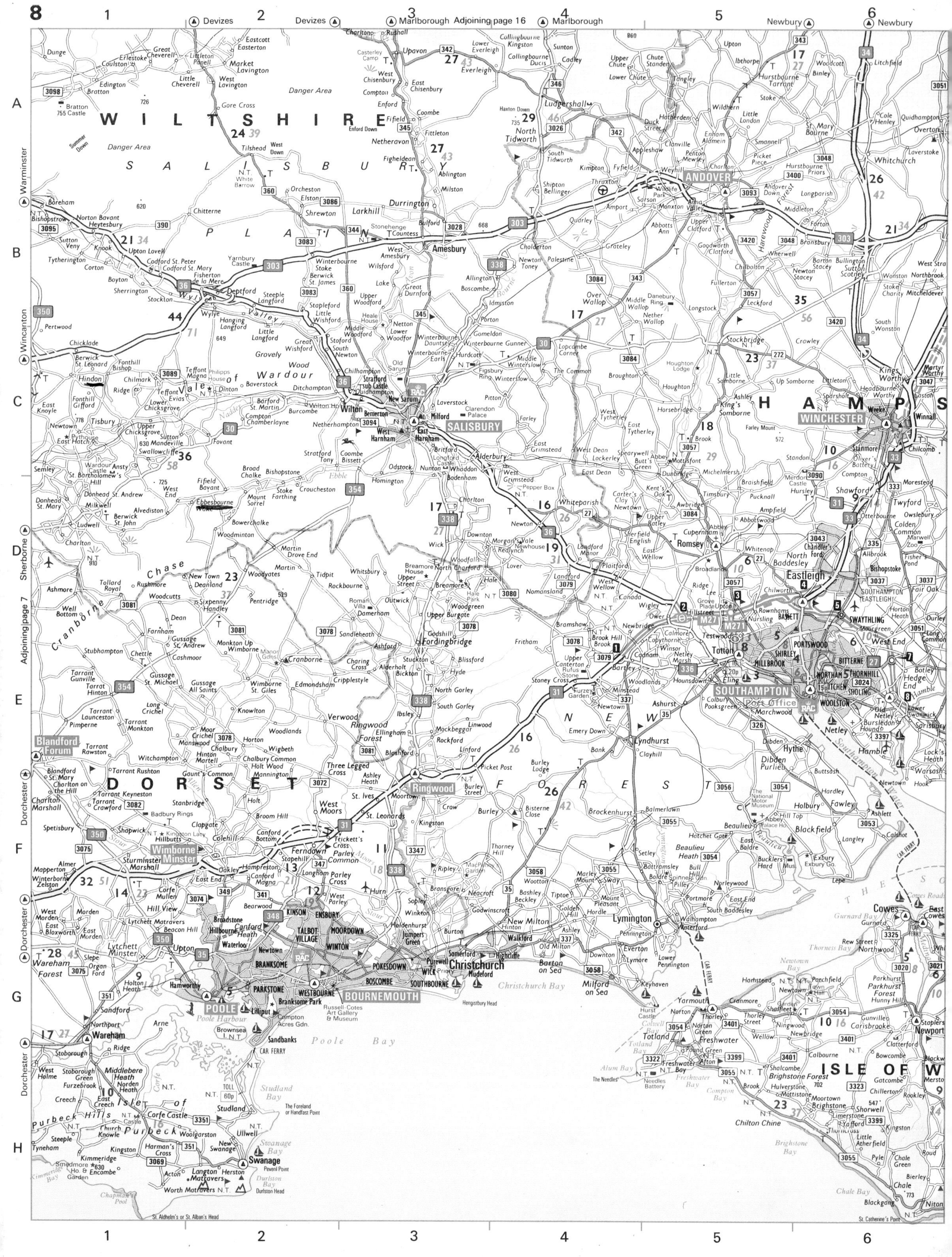
Devizes
Devizes
Marlborough
Adjoining page 16
Marlborough
Newbury
Newbury
Warminster
Wincanton
Sherborne
Adjoining page 7
Dorchester
Dorchester
Dorchester
Dorchester
WILTSHIRE
SALISBURY PLAIN
Danger Area
Vale of Wardour
Cranborne Chase
DORSET
HAMPSHIRE
NEW FOREST
ISLE OF WIGHT
Isle of Purbeck
Purbeck Hills
ANDOVER
WINCHESTER
SALISBURY
SOUTHAMPTON
Eastleigh
Romsey
Ringwood
Fordingbridge
Amesbury
Wilton
Blandford Forum
Wimborne Minster
Wareham
POOLE
BOURNEMOUTH
Christchurch
Lymington
Lyndhurst
New Milton
Swanage
Cowes
Newport
Yarmouth
Totland
Freshwater
Poole Harbour
Poole Bay
Christchurch Bay
Studland Bay
Swanage Bay
Compton Bay
Brighstone Bay
Chale Bay
Hengistbury Head
The Needles
Stonehenge
St. Alban's Head
St. Catherine's Point

Newbury
7
Reading
8
Reading
Staines
9
Adjoining page 17
10
11
London
12
A
B
C
D
E
F
G
H
Sevenoaks
Horsham
Adjoining page 10
Horsham
Brighton
Brighton
BASINGSTOKE
Aldershot
Farnborough
Fleet
FARNHAM
GUILDFORD
Godalming
Farncombe
Alton
Haslemere
Petersfield
Midhurst
Petworth
Pulborough
Billingshurst
Cranleigh
Shottermill
Hindhead
Liphook
Liss
S U R R E Y
W E S T
S U S S E X
H I R E
South Downs
New Alresford
Bishop's Waltham
Wickham
Waterlooville
Cowplain
Havant
Emsworth
CHICHESTER
Arundel
Littlehampton
Rustington
WORTHING
BOGNOR REGIS
Selsey
Selsey Bill
Hayling Island
South Hayling
FAREHAM
Gosport
PORTSMOUTH
SOUTHSEA
Portsea Island
Spithead
Ryde
Sandown
Shanklin
Ventnor
Bembridge
Brading
GHT
CAR FERRY
CAR FERRY TO CHERBOURG, CHANNEL IS. & ST. MALO
Port Office
Forest of Bere
7
8
9
10
11
12

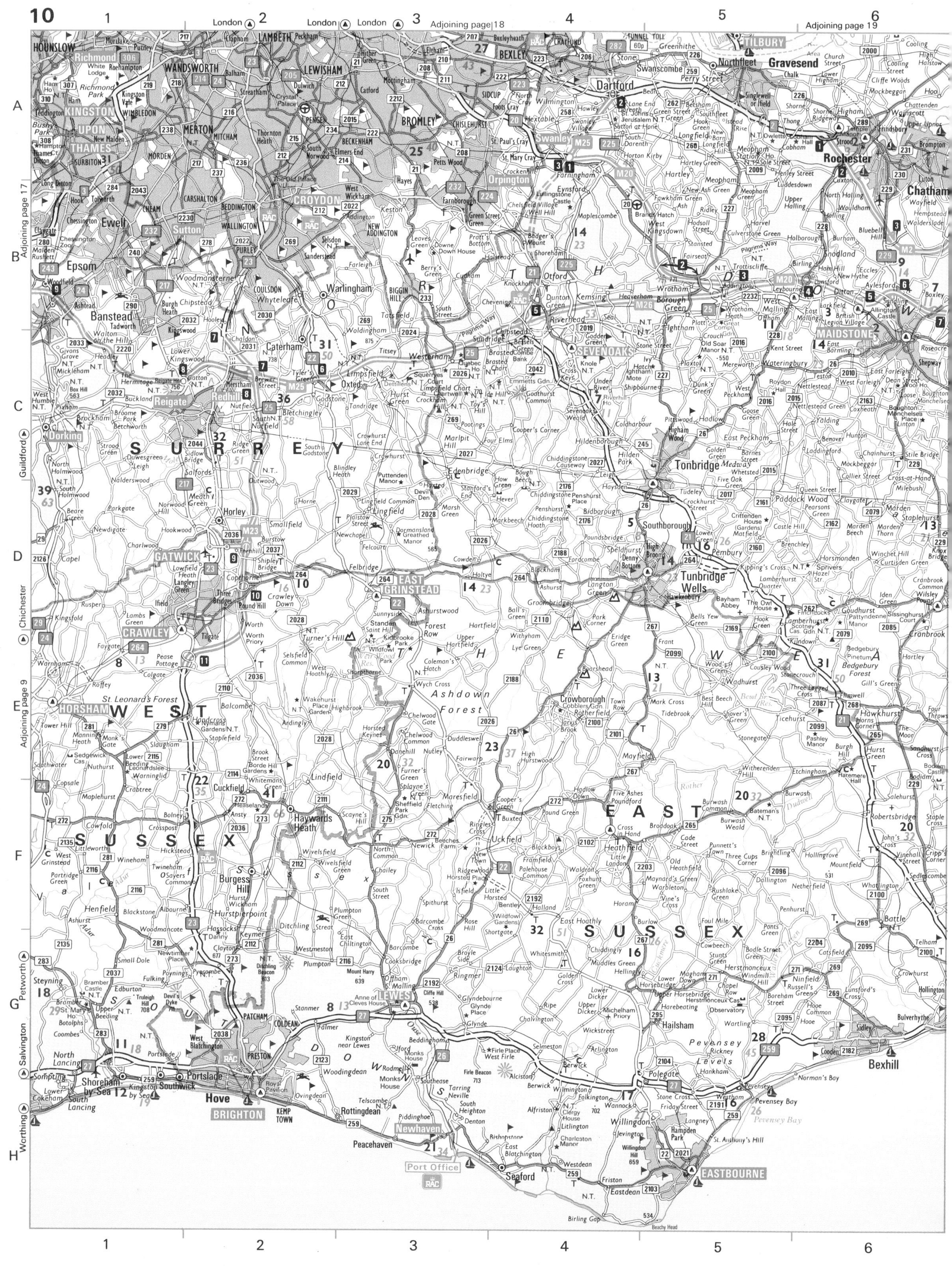
London
Adjoining page 18
Adjoining page 19
Adjoining page 17
Adjoining page 9
Guildford
Chichester
Petworth
Salvington
Worthing
TUNNEL TOLL 60p
TILBURY
Gravesend
Northfleet
Dartford
Swanscombe
Rochester
Chatham
Strood
HOUNSLOW
Richmond
WANDSWORTH
LAMBETH
LEWISHAM
BEXLEY
Bexleyheath
Crayford
KINGSTON UPON THAMES
MERTON
MITCHAM
MORDEN
SURBITON
CROYDON
BROMLEY
CHISLEHURST
SIDCUP
BECKENHAM
Orpington
Swanley
Farningham
Epsom
Ewell
Sutton
CARSHALTON
PURLEY
COULSDON
Warlingham
BIGGIN HILL
Banstead
Caterham
Westerham
Oxted
Limpsfield
Reigate
Redhill
Dorking
SEVENOAKS
Otford
Kemsing
Wrotham
Borough Green
West Malling
MAIDSTONE
SURREY
Tonbridge
Southborough
Tunbridge Wells
Edenbridge
Lingfield
Horley
GATWICK
Crawley
EAST GRINSTEAD
Forest Row
Ashdown Forest
Crowborough
Wadhurst
Mayfield
Pembury
Paddock Wood
Goudhurst
Cranbrook
Hawkhurst
HORSHAM
St. Leonard's Forest
WEST SUSSEX
Cuckfield
Haywards Heath
Burgess Hill
Hurstpierpoint
Uckfield
Heathfield
EAST SUSSEX
Battle
Bexhill
Hailsham
Pevensey Levels
Pevensey Bay
Polegate
EASTBOURNE
Beachy Head
Birling Gap
Seaford
Newhaven
Peacehaven
Rottingdean
LEWES
BRIGHTON
Hove
Portslade
Southwick
Shoreham-by-Sea
Lancing
Steyning
Henfield
Port Office

Adjoining page 19

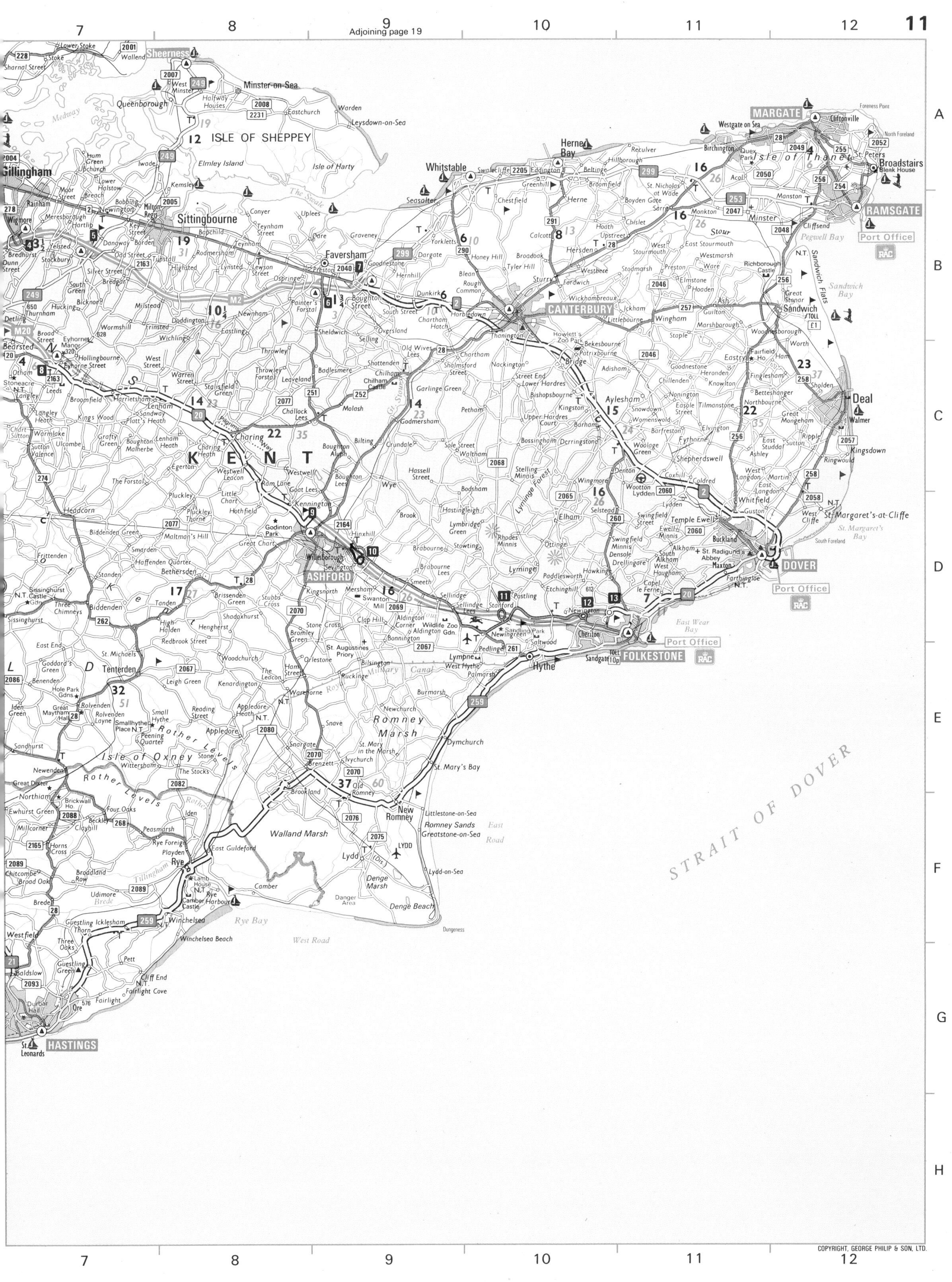

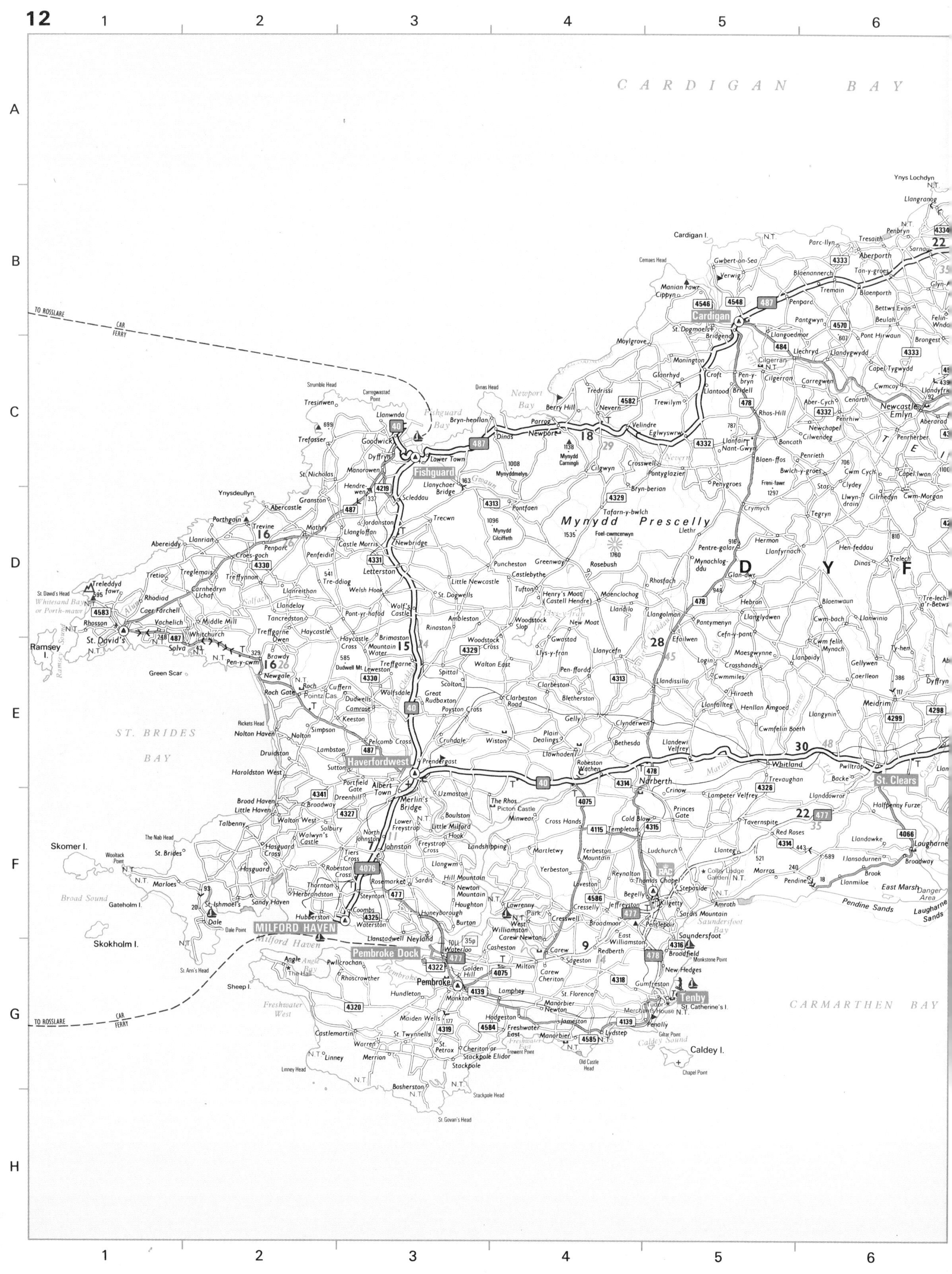

1
2
3
4
5
6
A
B
C
D
E
F
G
H
CARDIGAN BAY
TO ROSSLARE
CAR FERRY
Ynys Lochdyn
N.T.
Llangranog
Penbryn
4334
22
Cardigan I.
Parc-llyn
Tresaith
Aberporth
Sarnau
Cemaes Head
Gwbert-on-Sea
Verwig
4333
Tan-y-groes
Blaenannerch
Glyn-
Manian Fawr
Cippyn
Tremain
Blaenporth
4546
4548
487
Penparc
Bettws Evan
Cardigan
Pantgwyn
Beulah
Felin-Wnda
St. Dogmaels
Bridgend
4570
Llangoedmor
601
Pont Hirwaun
Brongest
Moylgrove
484
Llechryd
Llandygwydd
Monington
Cilgerran
Croft
Capel Tygwydd
Glanrhyd
Pen-y-bryn
Carregwen
Cwmcoy
Strumble Head
Carregwastad Point
Dinas Head
Newport Bay
Tredrissi
Llantood
Bridell
Cenarth
Newcastle Emlyn
Tresinwen
Llanwnda
Fishguard Bay
Berry Hill
Nevern
4582
Trewilym
478
Rhos-Hill
Aber-Cych
4332
Aberarad
699
Bryn-henllan
Velindre
Eglwyswrw
Penrhiw
Penrherber
40
Dinas
Parrog
Newport
18
29
787
Llanfair Nant-Gwyn
Newchapel
Cilwendeg
Trefosser
Goodwick
487
1138
Mynydd Carningli
4332
Boncath
Dyffryn
Lower Town
Fishguard
1008
Mynyddmelyn
Cilgwyn
Crosswell
Nevern
Pontyglazier
Blaen-ffos
Penrieth
706
Cwm Cych
Capel Iwan
St. Nicholas
Manorowen
Hendre-wen
4219
337
Llanychaer Bridge
163
Gwaun
Bryn-berian
Penygroes
Freni-fawr
1297
Bwlch-y-groes
Star
Clydey
Ynysdeullyn
Granston
Scleddau
4313
4329
Llwyn-drain
Cilrhedyn
Cwm-Morgan
Abercastle
Pontfaen
Tafarn-y-bwlch
Crymych
Porthgain
Trevine
Mathry
Jordanston
Trecwn
1096
Mynydd Cilciffeth
Mynydd Prescelly
Llethr
Tegryn
16
Llangloffan
1535
Foel-cwmcerwyn
1760
810
Abereiddy
Llanrian
26
Penparc
Castle Morris
Newbridge
Hermon
Llanfyrnach
Hen-feddau
Tretio
Treglemais
Croes-goch
4330
Penfeidir
4331
Letterston
Puncheston
Greenway
Rosebush
916
Pentre-galar
Mynachlog-ddu
D
Y
F
Dinas
Trelech
Treleddyd fawr
Treffynnon
Carnhedryn Uchaf
541
Tre-ddiog
Little Newcastle
Castlebythe
Rhosfach
Glan-dwr
St. David's Head
595
Whitesand Bay or Porth-mawr
Rhodiad
Solfach
Llanreithan
Welsh Hook
Tufton
Henry's Moat (Castell Hendre)
Maenclochog
948
Hebron
Blaenwaun
Tre-lech-a'r-Betws
4583
Caer Farchell
Llandeloy
Pont-yr-hafod
Wolf's Castle
St. Dogwells
Llandilo
Llangolman
Llanglydwen
Cwm-bach
Llanwinio
Rhosson
Middle Mill
Tancredston
Haycastle
Ambleston
Woodstock Slop
New Moat
Pantymenyn
Cefn-y-pant
Ramsey I.
Ramsey Sound
St. David's
Vachelich
Whitchurch
Treffgarne Owen
Brimaston
Rinaston
Llys-y-fran
Gwastad
Efailwen
Cwm felin Mynach
Ty-hen
248
487
Solva
329
Haycastle Cross
Mountain Water
15
Woodstock Cross
4329
Llys-y-fran
Llanycefn
28
Maesgwynne
Llanboidy
Gellywen
Green Scar
Pen-y-cwm
Brawdy
16
585
Dudwell Mt.
Treffgarne
Leweston
Walton East
Pen-ffordd
45
Login
Crosshands
Caerlleon
386
Dyffryn
Newgale
4330
Spittal
4313
Cwmmiles
117
Roch
Cuffern
Scolton
Clarbeston
Llandissilio
Hiraeth
Meidrim
Roch Gate
Pointz Cas.
Wolfsdale
Dudwells
Great Rudbaxton
Clarbeston Road
Bletherston
Llanfallteg
Henllan Amgoed
4299
4298
Rickets Head
Camrose
Keeston
40
Poyston Cross
Llangynin
ST. BRIDES BAY
Nolton Haven
Nolton
Simpson
Gelly
Clynderwen
Druidston
Lambston
487
Pelcomb Cross
Crundale
Wiston
Plain Dealings
Bethesda
Llandewi Velfrey
Cwmfelin Boeth
30
48
Haverfordwest
Prendergast
Llawhaden
Robeston Wathen
478
Whitland
Pwlltrap
St. Clears
Haroldston West
Sutton
Portfield Gate
Albert Town
40
4314
Narberth
Trevaughan
Backe
Broad Haven
4341
Dreenhill
Merlin's Bridge
Uzmaston
The Rhos
4075
Crinow
Lampeter Velfrey
4328
Llanddowror
Little Haven
Broadway
4327
Picton Castle
Boulston
Minwear
Cold Blow
Princes Gate
22
477
Halfpenny Furze
Talbenny
Walton West
Solbury
North Johnston
Lower Freystrop
Little Milford
Cross Hands
4115
Templeton
4315
35
Tavernspite
Red Roses
4066
The Nab Head
St. Brides
Walwyn's Castle
Hasguard Cross
Johnston
Freystrop Cross
Hook
Landshipping
Martletwy
Yerbeston Mountain
Ludchurch
Llanteg
4314
443
Llandawke
Laugharne
Skomer I.
Wooltack Point
Tiers Cross
Robeston Cross
4076
Llangwm
Yerbeston
Reynalton
Colby Lodge Garden
521
240
589
Llansadurnen
Broadway
N.T.
Marloes
Hasguard
Thornton
Rosemarket
Sardis
Hill Mountain
Newton Mountain
Loveston
Thomas Chapel
Marros
Pendine
18
Brook
Llanmiloe
East Marsh
Danger Area
Broad Sound
Gateholm I.
93
20
St. Ishmael's
Sandy Haven
Herbrandston
Steynton
477
Houghton
Lawrenny
Park
4586
Cresselly
Jeffreyston
477
Begelly
Kilgetty
Stepaside
Amroth
Pendine Sands
Laugharne Sands
Dale
Dale Point
Hubberston
Coombs
Honeyborough
Burton
West Williamston
Cresswell
Broadmoor
Pentlepoir
Sardis Mountain
Saundersfoot Bay
MILFORD HAVEN
4325
Waterston
Carew Newton
East Williamston
Skokholm I.
Milford Haven
Llanstadwell
Neyland
35p
TOLL
Waterloo
Cosheston
9
4316
Saundersfoot
Pembroke Dock
477
Carew
Sageston
14
Redberth
478
Broadfield
Monkstone Point
Angle
Angle Bay
Pwllcrochan
The Hall
4322
Golden Hill
4075
Milton
Carew Cheriton
4318
New Hedges
St. Ann's Head
Rhoscrowther
Pembroke
Sheep I.
Hundleton
Pembroke
4139
Lamphey
St. Florence
Gumfreston
Tenby
Freshwater West
4320
Monkton
Manorbier Newton
Tudor Merchants House
St. Catherine's I.
CARMARTHEN BAY
Maiden Wells
177
Hodgeston
Jameston
4139
Penally
Castlemartin
St. Twynnells
4319
4584
Freshwater East
Manorbier
4585
Lydstep
Giltar Point
Caldey Sound
Warren
St. Petrox
Cheriton or Stackpole Elidor
Trewent Point
Freshwater East
Caldey I.
Linney
Merrion
Stackpole
Old Castle Head
Chapel Point
Linney Head
Bosherston
Stackpole Head
St. Govan's Head

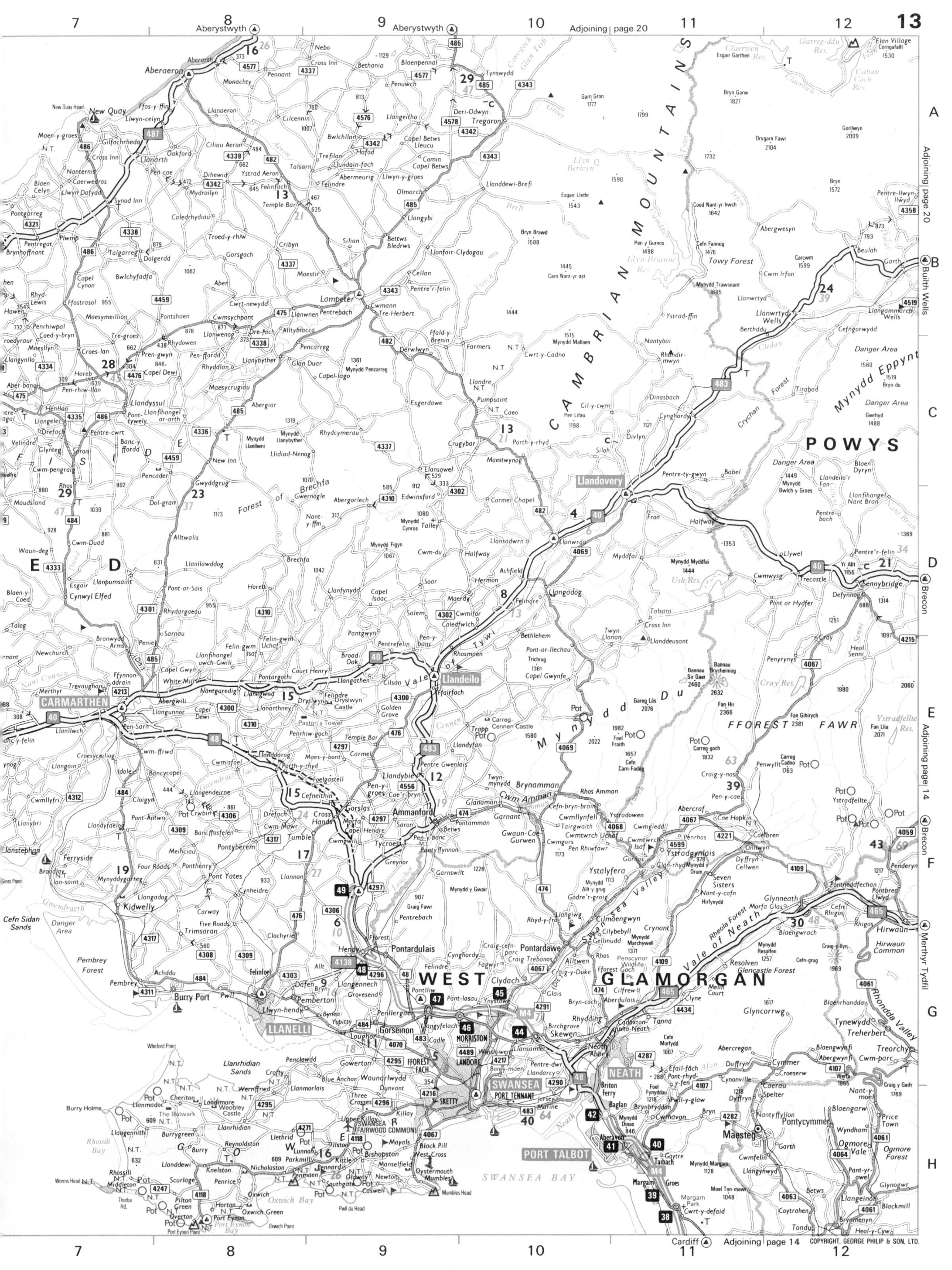

CAMBRIAN MOUNTAINS
POWYS
WEST GLAMORGAN
DYFED
Mynydd Du
FFOREST FAWR
Mynydd Eppynt
Forest of Brechfa
Towy Forest
Crychan Forest
Vale of Tywi
Vale of Neath
Swansea Valley
Rhondda Valley
Rheola Forest
Glencastle Forest
SWANSEA BAY
Aberaeron
New Quay
New Quay Head
Llanarth
Tregaron
Lampeter
Llandyssul
Llanybyther
Pumpsaint
Llandovery
Llandeilo
CARMARTHEN
Ammanford
Brynamman
Kidwelly
Pembrey
Pembrey Forest
Burry Port
LLANELLI
Gorseinon
Pontardulais
Pontardawe
Ystalyfera
Ystradgynlais
Glynneath
Hirwaun
Resolven
Clydach
Morriston
Landore
SWANSEA
SKETTY
PORT TENNANT
Neath
NEATH
Briton Ferry
Skewen
PORT TALBOT
Aberavon
Taibach
Margam
Maesteg
Pontycymmer
Treherbert
Treorchy
Cwm-parc
Blaengwynfi
Cymmer
Ogmore Vale
Ogmore Forest
Llangeinor
Blackmill
Tondu
Mumbles
Mumbles Head
Oystermouth
Black Pill
Bishopston
Port Eynon
Port Eynon Point
Oxwich
Oxwich Bay
Oxwich Point
Rhossili
Rhossili Bay
Worms Head
Burry Holms
Whiteford Point
Llanrhidian
Llanrhidian Sands
Reynoldston
Cefn Sidan Sands
Ferryside
Llanstephan
Trecastle
Sennybridge
Defynnog
Beulah
Llanwrtyd Wells
Abergwesyn
Cwm Irfon
Llangammarch Wells
Garth
Llangadog
Llanwrda
Llandeusant
Usk Res.
Cray Res.
Llyn Brianne Res.
Claerwen Res.
Caban Coch Res.
Garreg-ddu Res.
Elan Village
Danger Area
Talley
Edwinsford
Abergorlech
Brechfa
Carreg-Cennen Castle
Dryslwyn Castle
Paxton's Tower
Fan Hir
Bannau Brycheiniog
Bannau Sir Gaer
Fan Gihirych
Fan Llia
Ystradfellte
Penderyn
Craig-y-nos
Abercraf
Penwyllt
Adjoining page 20
Adjoining page 14
Builth Wells
Brecon
Merthyr Tydfil

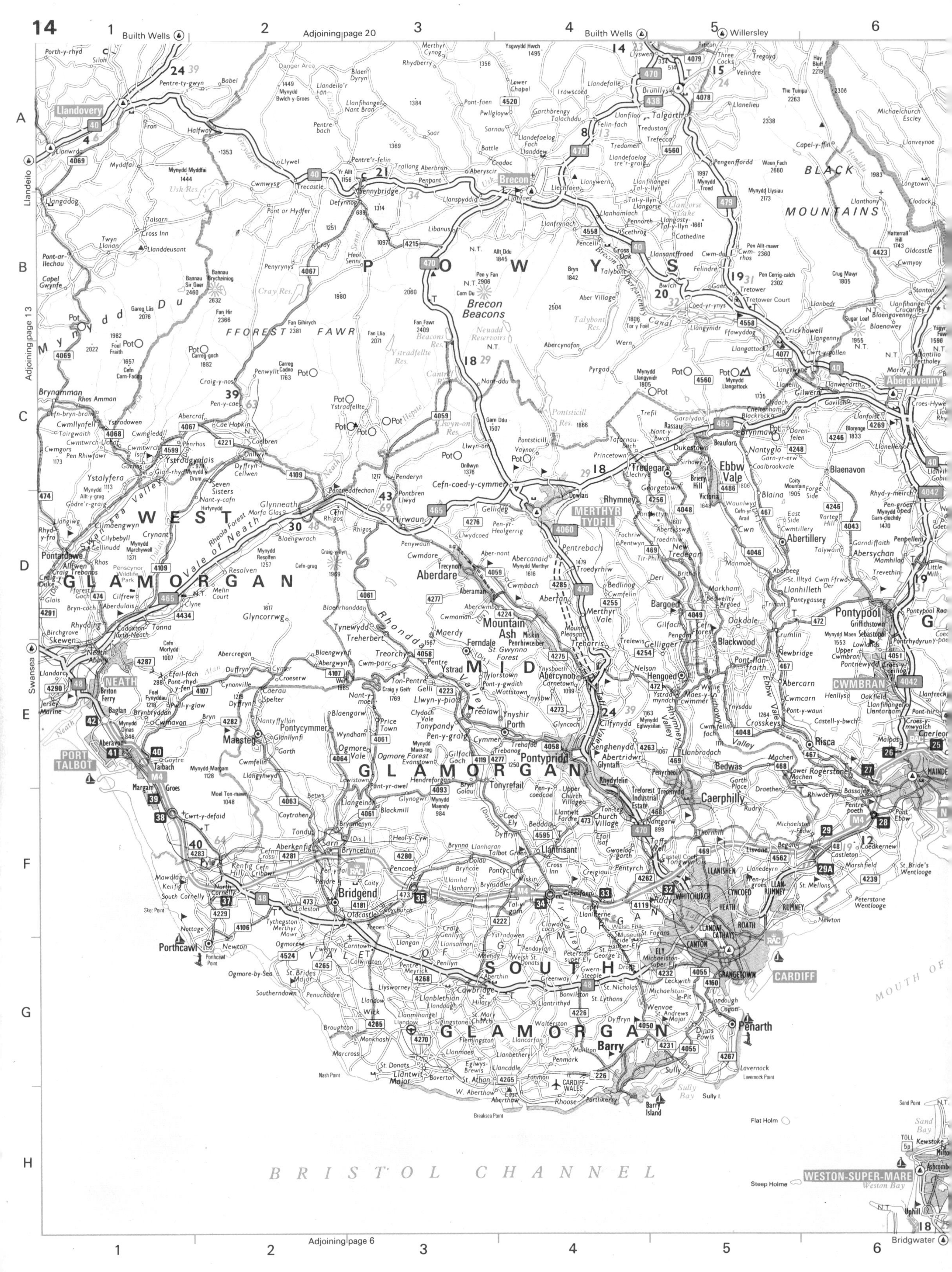

Builth Wells
Adjoining page 20
Builth Wells
Willersley
Llandeilo
Adjoining page 13
Swansea
Adjoining page 6
Bridgwater
1
2
3
4
5
6
A
B
C
D
E
F
G
H
Llandovery
Brecon
Abergavenny
MERTHYR TYDFIL
NEATH
PORT TALBOT
CWMBRAN
CARDIFF
WESTON-SUPER-MARE
P O W Y S
BLACK MOUNTAINS
Brecon Beacons
FFOREST FAWR
Mynydd Du
WEST GLAMORGAN
MID GLAMORGAN
SOUTH GLAMORGAN
VALE OF GLAMORGAN
Vale of Neath
Rhondda Valley
Swansea Valley
BRISTOL CHANNEL
MOUTH OF
Sennybridge
Trecastle
Talgarth
Crickhowell
Tredegar
Ebbw Vale
Rhymney
Aberdare
Mountain Ash
Pontypridd
Caerphilly
Blackwood
Pontypool
Risca
Bridgend
Maesteg
Porthcawl
Pyle
Cowbridge
Llantrisant
Barry
Barry Island
Penarth
Llantwit Major
Pontardawe
Ystradgynlais
Glynneath
Hirwaun
Merthyr Vale
Treharris
Bargoed
Hengoed
Porth
Tonypandy
Treorchy
Abertillery
Blaenavon
Bedwas
Newport
Taibach
Aberavon
Briton Ferry
Skewen
Neath Abbey
Llanishen
Whitchurch
Llandaff
Cathays
Canton
Ely
Grangetown
Heath
Roath
Rumney
Llanrumney
Cyncoed
Sully
Lavernock
Flat Holm
Steep Holme
Sand Point
Sand Bay
Kewstoke
Weston Bay
Uphill
Cardiff-Wales
Rhoose
Breaksea Point
Nash Point
Sker Point
Porthcawl Point
Ogmore-by-Sea
Southerndown
St. Athan
Llanmaes
Dinas Powis
Wenvoe
Radyr
Taffs Well
Nantgarw
Pentyrch
Penarth

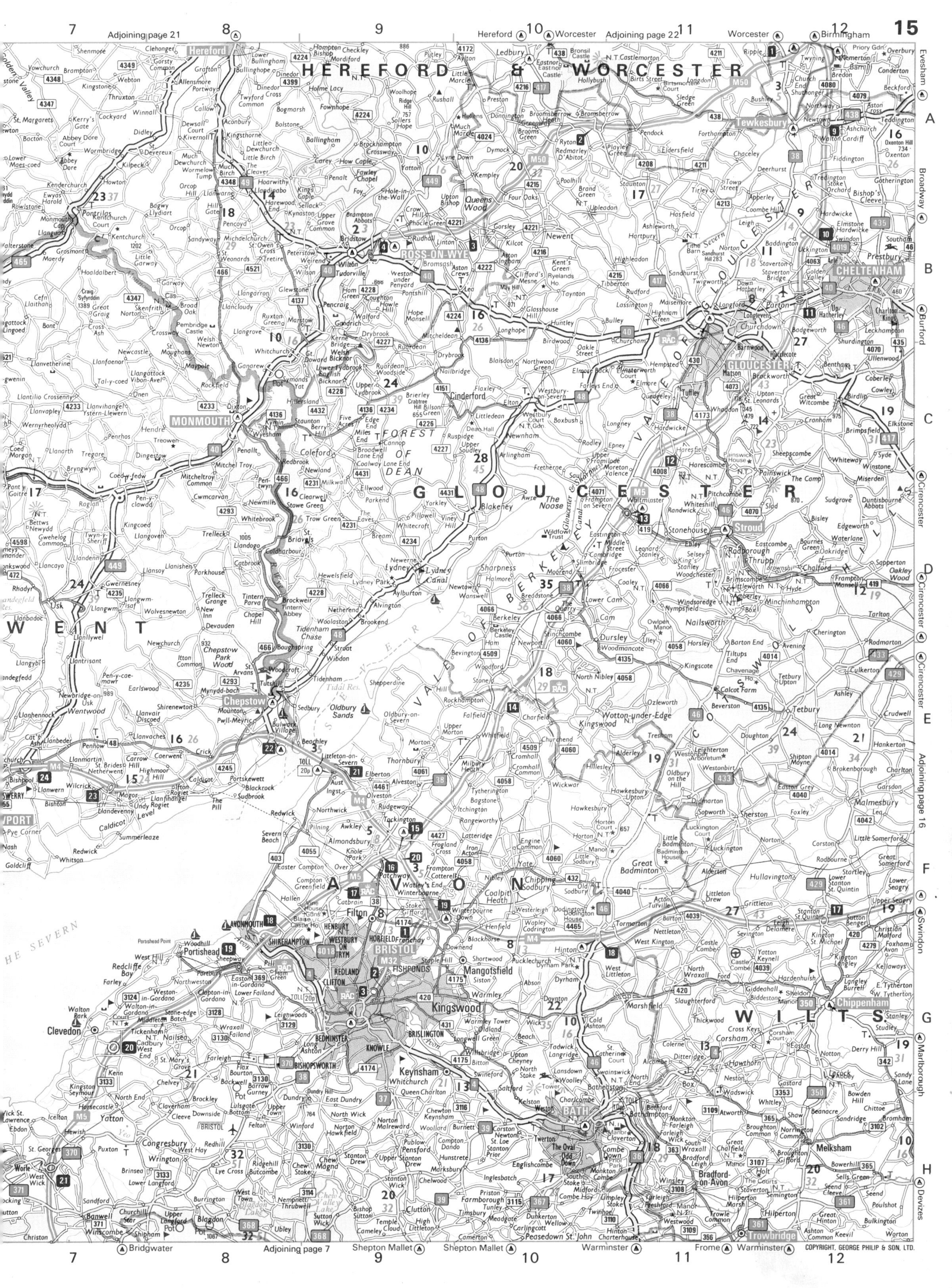

15
Adjoining page 21
Hereford
Worcester
Adjoining page 22
Birmingham
Evesham
Broadway
Burford
Cirencester
Adjoining page 16
Swindon
Marlborough
Devizes
Bridgwater
Adjoining page 7
Shepton Mallet
Warminster
Frome
HEREFORD & WORCESTER
GLOUCESTER
GWENT
AVON
WILTS.
FOREST OF DEAN
VALE OF BERKELEY
COTSWOLD HILLS
SEVERN
THE SEVERN
Hereford
Ross-on-Wye
Monmouth
Chepstow
Tewkesbury
Cheltenham
Gloucester
Stroud
Bristol
Avonmouth
Kingswood
Bath
Chippenham
Trowbridge
Clevedon
Portishead
Ledbury
Newent
Cinderford
Lydney
Coleford
Tetbury
Malmesbury
Dursley
Wotton-under-Edge
Thornbury
Keynsham
Melksham
Corsham
Bradford-on-Avon
Nailsworth
Yate
Chipping Sodbury
COPYRIGHT, GEORGE PHILIP & SON, LTD.

1 Evesham · Stratford-upon-Avon 2 · Evesham · Adjoining page 22 3 · Warwick · Stratford-upon-Avon 4 · Adjoining page 23 · 5 · Banbury 6

A B C D E F G H · Gloucester · Stroud · Adjoining page 15 · Stroud · Bath · Chippenham · Severn Bridge · Cheltenham · Chippenham · Frome

GLOUCESTER
OXFORD
WILTSHIRE
BERKSHIRE
HAMPSHIRE
CHELTENHAM
CIRENCESTER
SWINDON
OXFORD
NEWBURY
Marlborough
Hungerford
Devizes
VALE OF WHITE HORSE
MARLBOROUGH DOWNS
BERKSHIRE DOWNS
Vale of Pewsey

1 Salisbury · 2 Andover · Salisbury · 3 Salisbury · Adjoining page 8 4 · Andover 5 · Winchester 6

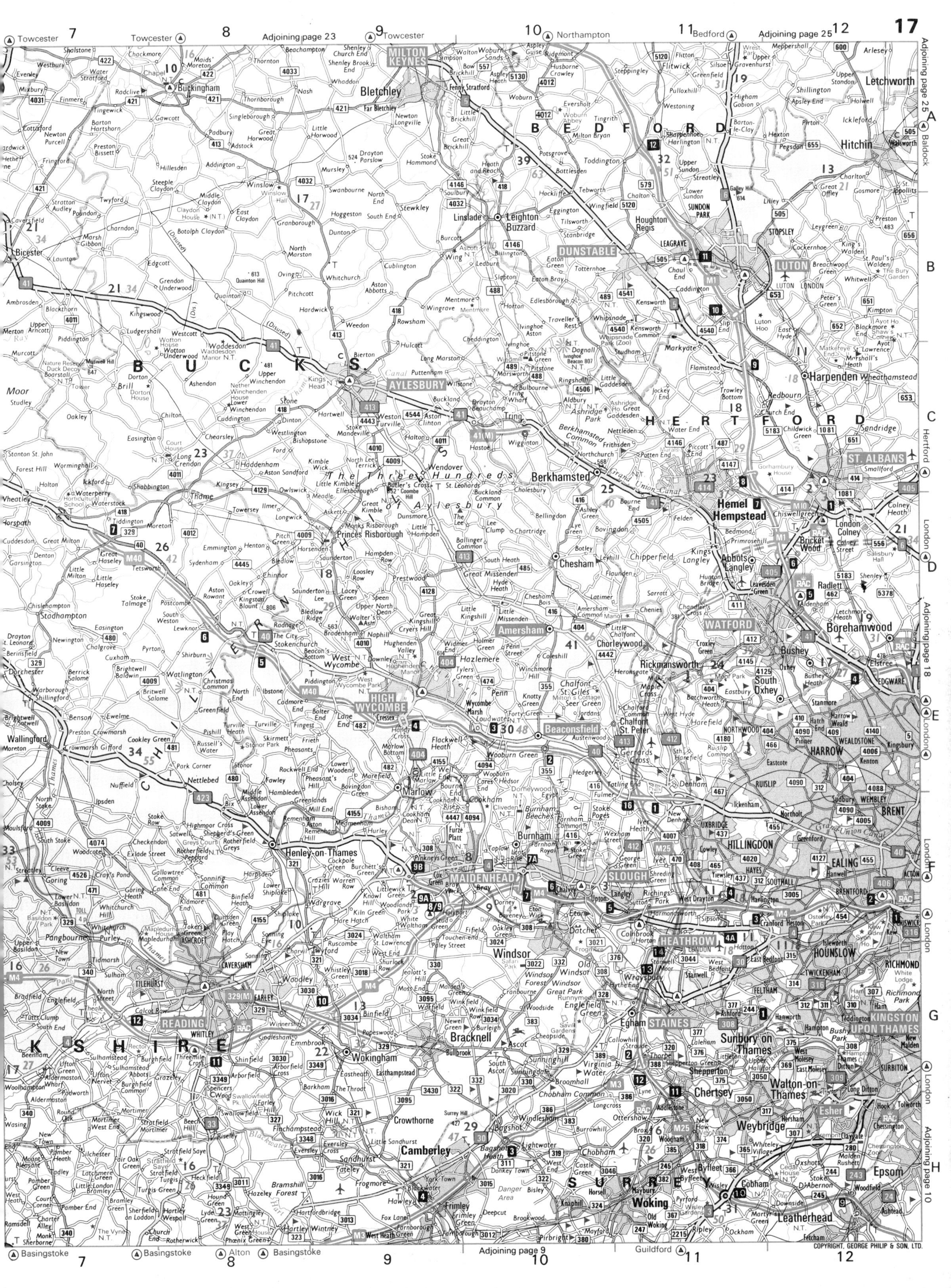
Towcester 7
Towcester 8
Adjoining page 23
9 Towcester
10 Northampton
11 Bedford
Adjoining page 25 12
Adjoining page 25
Baldock
Hertford
London
Adjoining page 18
London
London
London
Adjoining page 10
A
B
C
D
E
F
G
H
BEDFORD
BUCKS.
HERTFORD
CHILTERN
SURREY
KSHIRE
MILTON KEYNES
Bletchley
Buckingham
Leighton Buzzard
Dunstable
Luton
Letchworth
Hitchin
Harpenden
Aylesbury
Tring
Berkhamsted
Hemel Hempstead
St. Albans
Watford
Borehamwood
Chesham
Amersham
High Wycombe
Beaconsfield
Princes Risborough
Thame
Rickmansworth
Harrow
Wembley
Brent
Hillingdon
Ealing
Marlow
Maidenhead
Slough
Windsor
Henley-on-Thames
Reading
Wokingham
Bracknell
Heathrow
Staines
Hounslow
Richmond
Kingston upon Thames
Surbiton
Sunbury on Thames
Walton-on-Thames
Chertsey
Weybridge
Esher
Epsom
Leatherhead
Woking
Camberley
Wallingford
Basingstoke 7
Basingstoke 8
Alton
Basingstoke
9
Adjoining page 9 10
Guildford 11
12
COPYRIGHT, GEORGE PHILIP & SON, LTD.

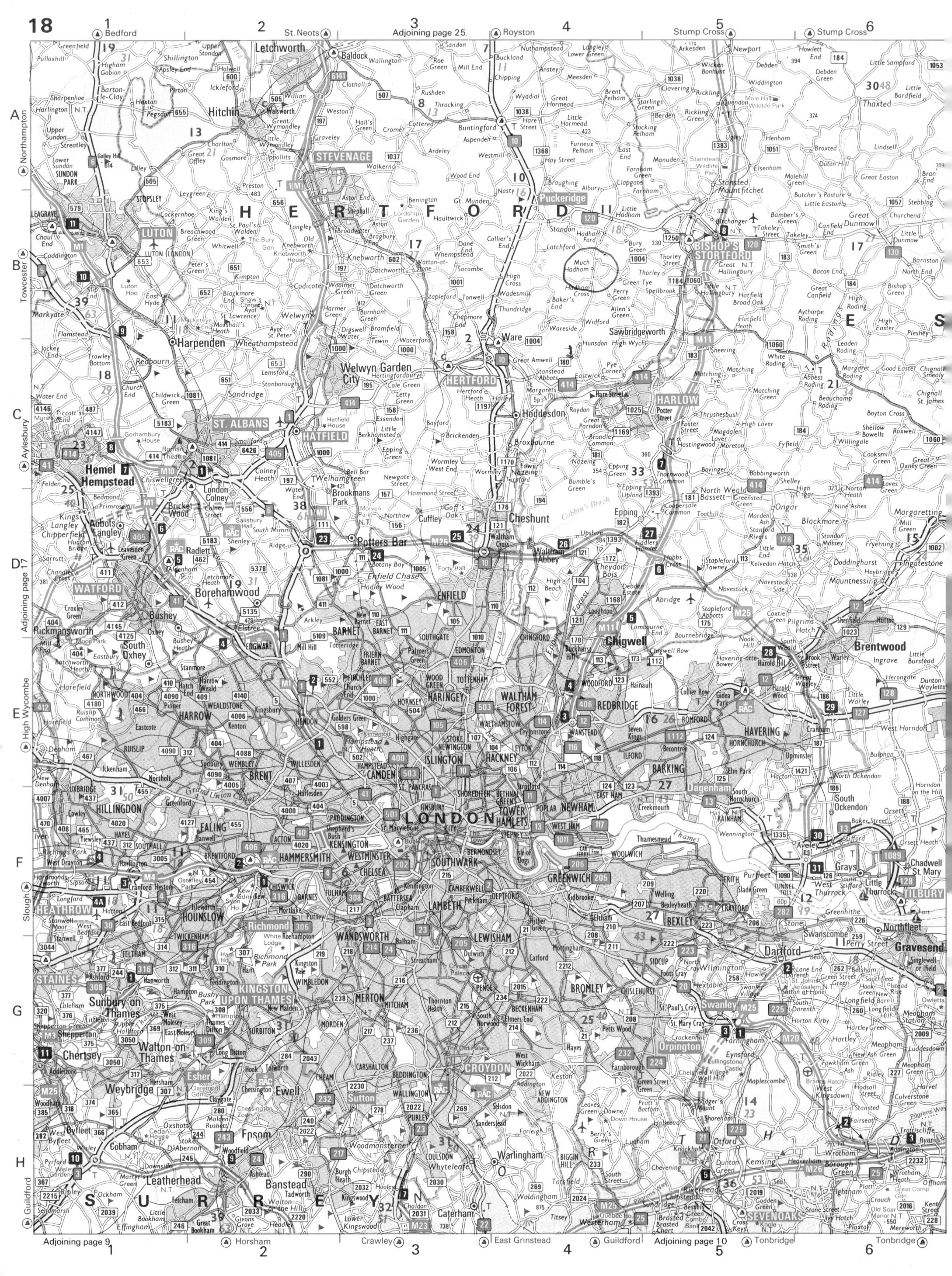

18
Bedford
St. Neots
Adjoining page 25
Royston
Stump Cross
Stump Cross
Northampton
Towcester
Aylesbury
Adjoining page 17
High Wycombe
Slough
Guildford
Adjoining page 9
Horsham
Crawley
East Grinstead
Guildford
Adjoining page 10
Tonbridge
Tonbridge
H E R T F O R D
E S
S U R R E Y
Letchworth
Hitchin
Baldock
STEVENAGE
LUTON
Harpenden
Welwyn Garden City
HERTFORD
Ware
Puckeridge
BISHOP'S STORTFORD
Stansted Mountfitchet
Thaxted
Great Dunmow
Sawbridgeworth
HARLOW
ST. ALBANS
HATFIELD
Hemel Hempstead
WATFORD
Borehamwood
Potters Bar
Cheshunt
Hoddesdon
Waltham Abbey
Epping
Ongar
Brentwood
ENFIELD
Chigwell
HARROW
WALTHAM FOREST
REDBRIDGE
HAVERING
ROMFORD
BARKING
Dagenham
HILLINGDON
EALING
BRENT
CAMDEN
ISLINGTON
HACKNEY
LONDON
NEWHAM
TOWER HAMLETS
KENSINGTON
HAMMERSMITH
WESTMINSTER
SOUTHWARK
GREENWICH
HOUNSLOW
HEATHROW
Richmond
WANDSWORTH
LAMBETH
LEWISHAM
BEXLEY
Dartford
Gravesend
TILBURY
Grays
STAINES
KINGSTON UPON THAMES
MERTON
BROMLEY
CROYDON
Sutton
Orpington
Swanley
Epsom
Leatherhead
Weybridge
Walton-on-Thames
Esher
Caterham
SEVENOAKS

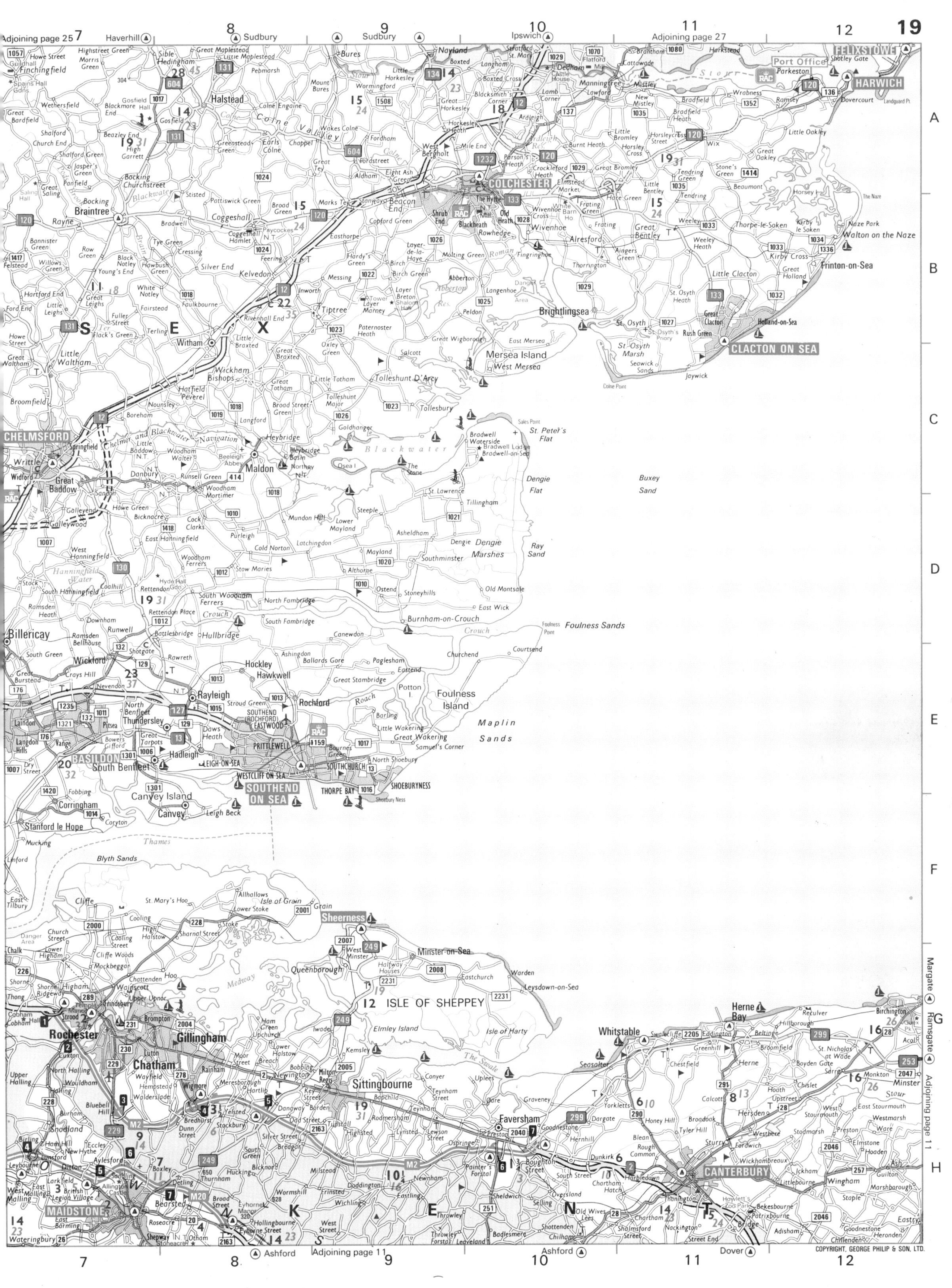

19
Adjoining page 25
Haverhill
Sudbury
Ipswich
Adjoining page 27
Adjoining page 11
Ashford
Dover
Margate
Ramsgate
Adjoining page 11
7
8
9
10
11
12
A
B
C
D
E
F
G
H
FELIXSTOWE
HARWICH
Port Office
Parkeston
Dovercourt
Manningtree
Mistley
Dedham
Stratford St. Mary
Nayland
Bures
Sible Hedingham
Halstead
Finchingfield
Colne Valley
Colne Engaine
Earls Colne
Wakes Colne
West Bergholt
Boxted
Langham
Mile End
Ardleigh
COLCHESTER
Elmstead Market
Wivenhoe
Alresford
Rowhedge
Brightlingsea
St. Osyth
Great Clacton
Holland-on-Sea
CLACTON ON SEA
Jaywick
Frinton-on-Sea
Walton on the Naze
Kirby Cross
Thorpe-le-Soken
Great Bentley
Weeley
Little Clacton
Tendring
Great Oakley
Little Oakley
Ramsey
Wix
Bradfield
Lawford
Braintree
Rayne
Bocking
Coggeshall
Kelvedon
Feering
Silver End
Witham
Tiptree
Messing
Marks Tey
Stanway
Copford Green
Birch
Layer-de-la-Haye
Abberton
Peldon
Mersea Island
West Mersea
East Mersea
Salcott
Tolleshunt D'Arcy
Tollesbury
Goldhanger
Heybridge
Maldon
Blackwater
Osea I.
Bradwell Waterside
Bradwell-on-Sea
St. Peter's Flat
Dengie Flat
Buxey Sand
St. Lawrence
Tillingham
Steeple
Mundon Hill
Asheldham
Dengie
Dengie Marshes
Southminster
Mayland
Althorne
Ray Sand
Burnham-on-Crouch
Crouch
Foulness Sands
Foulness Island
Maplin Sands
Chelmer and Blackwater Navigation
CHELMSFORD
Writtle
Springfield
Great Baddow
Danbury
Woodham Walter
Woodham Mortimer
Hatfield Peverel
Wickham Bishops
Terling
Little Waltham
Broomfield
Galleywood
East Hanningfield
West Hanningfield
Hanningfield Water
Rettendon
South Woodham Ferrers
North Fambridge
South Fambridge
Hullbridge
Runwell
Billericay
Wickford
Rawreth
Hockley
Hawkwell
Rochford
Rayleigh
Canewdon
Paglesham
Great Stambridge
Potton I.
Great Wakering
Little Wakering
North Shoebury
SHOEBURYNESS
THORPE BAY
SOUTHCHURCH
PRITTLEWELL
WESTCLIFF ON SEA
SOUTHEND ON SEA
LEIGH-ON-SEA
Hadleigh
Thundersley
Benfleet
South Benfleet
Canvey Island
Canvey
Leigh Beck
BASILDON
Laindon
Pitsea
Vange
Corringham
Fobbing
Stanford le Hope
Coryton
Mucking
Thames
Blyth Sands
Cliffe
Allhallows
Isle of Grain
Grain
Sheerness
Minster-on-Sea
Queenborough
Eastchurch
Warden
Leysdown-on-Sea
ISLE OF SHEPPEY
Elmley Island
Isle of Harty
The Swale
Medway
Hoo
Rochester
Strood
Chatham
Gillingham
Rainham
Brompton
Sittingbourne
Milton Regis
Faversham
Whitstable
Seasalter
Herne Bay
Herne
Reculver
Birchington
Minster
Monkton
Sturry
CANTERBURY
Harbledown
Chartham
Bridge
Wingham
Boughton Street
Dunkirk
Newington
Teynham
Detling
Bearsted
MAIDSTONE
Aylesford
Snodland
Hollingbourne
Eastling
Doddington
Selling
E
S
S
E
X
K
E
N
T
COPYRIGHT, GEORGE PHILIP & SON, LTD.

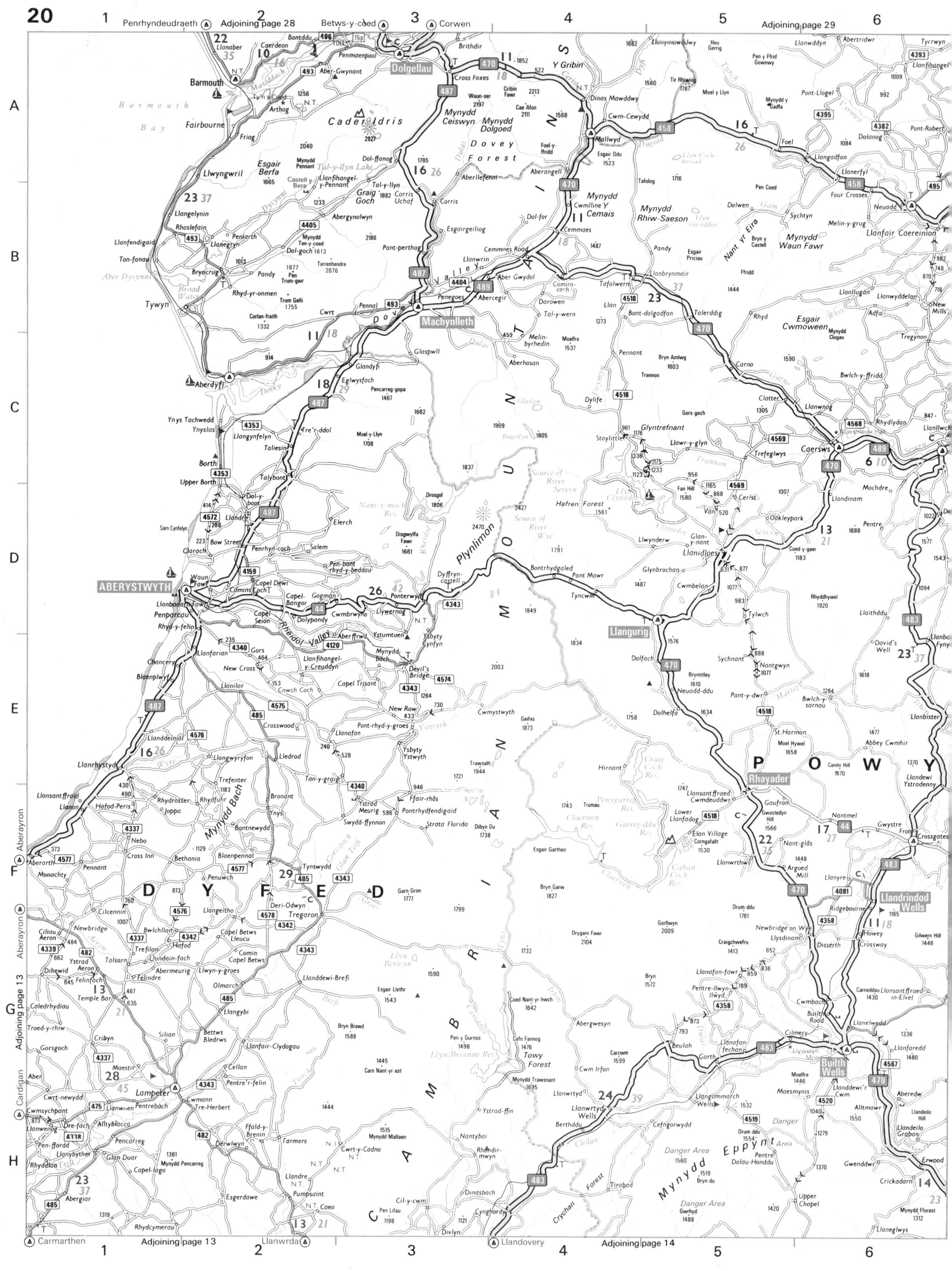

Penrhyndeudraeth
Adjoining page 28
Betws-y-coed
Corwen
Adjoining page 29
Barmouth
Barmouth Bay
Fairbourne
Dolgellau
Cader Idris
Y Gribin
Dinas Mawddwy
Mallwyd
Llwyngwril
Tywyn
Aberdyfi
Machynlleth
Dovey Forest
Corris
Carno
Caersws
Llanfair Caereinion
Llanidloes
Llangurig
Plynlimon
Source of River Severn
Source of River Wye
Hafren Forest
Talybont
Borth
Ynyslas
Aberystwyth
Devil's Bridge
Ponterwyd
Rheidol Valley
Rhayader
Elan Village
Llandrindod Wells
Newbridge on Wye
Builth Wells
Llanwrtyd Wells
Eppynt
Danger Area
Mynydd Eppynt
Towy Forest
Tregaron
Lampeter
Aberaeron
Llanon
Llanrhystyd
Strata Florida
Pontrhydfendigaid
Llyn Brianne Res.
Cambrian Mountains
Dyfed
Powys
Llandovery
Adjoining page 14
Carmarthen
Adjoining page 13
Llanwrda
Cardigan
Aberayron

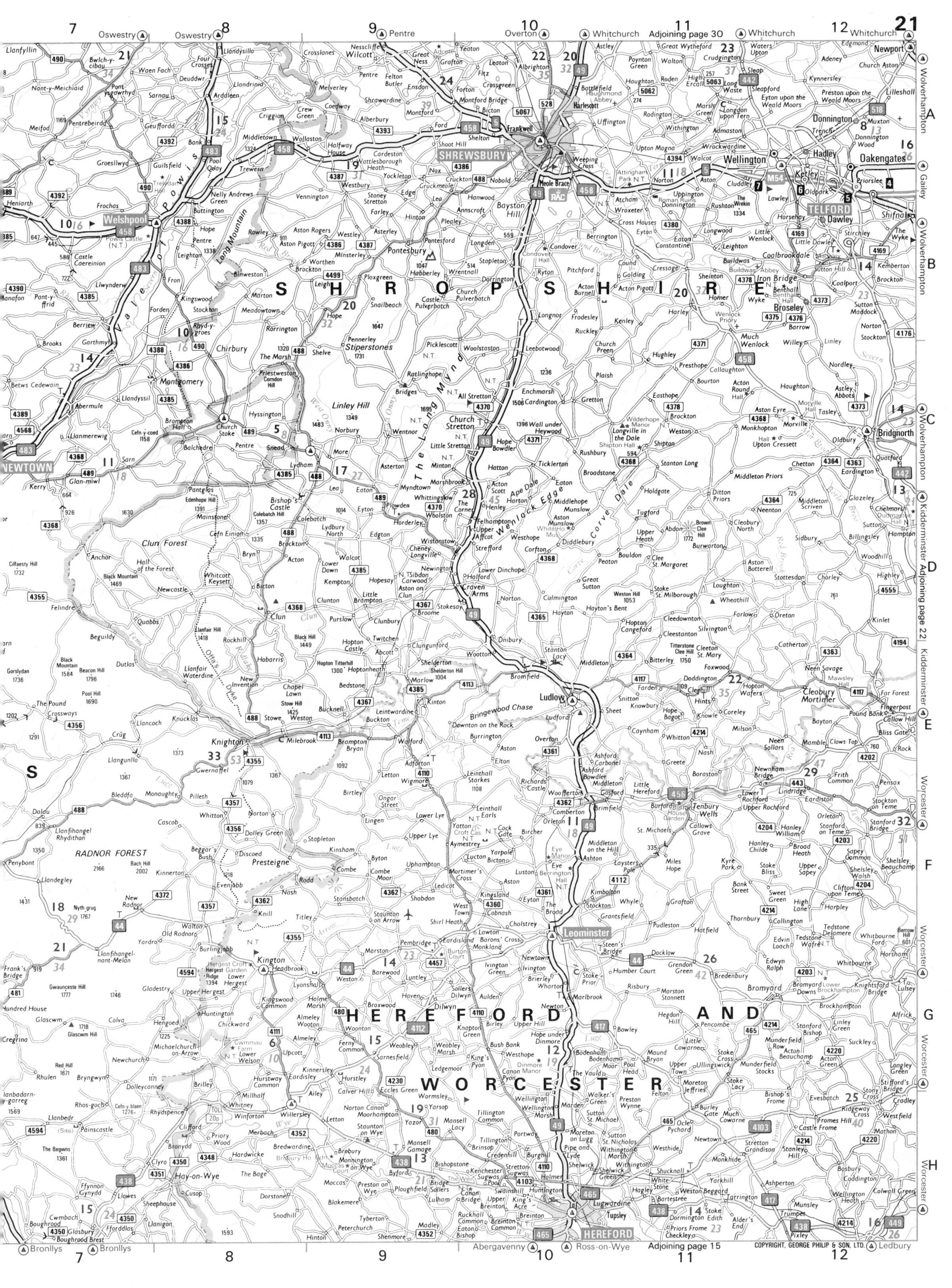
7
8
9
10
11
12
A
B
C
D
E
F
G
H
Oswestry
Pentre
Overton
Whitchurch
Adjoining page 30
Wolverhampton
Gailey
Kidderminster
Adjoining page 22
Worcester
Bronllys
Abergavenny
Ross-on-Wye
Adjoining page 15
Ledbury
SHROPSHIRE
HEREFORD AND WORCESTER
SHREWSBURY
TELFORD
Welshpool
NEWTOWN
Leominster
HEREFORD
Ludlow
Bridgnorth
Wellington
Oakengates
Newport
Donnington
Dawley
Iron Bridge
Much Wenlock
Church Stretton
Craven Arms
Bishop's Castle
Montgomery
Clun
Knighton
Presteigne
Kington
Hay-on-Wye
Tenbury Wells
Bromyard
Cleobury Mortimer
Long Mountain
The Long Mynd
Wenlock Edge
Clun Forest
RADNOR FOREST
Stiperstones
Linley Hill
Bringewood Chase
Corve Dale
Ape Dale
Vale of Powis
COPYRIGHT, GEORGE PHILIP & SON, LTD.

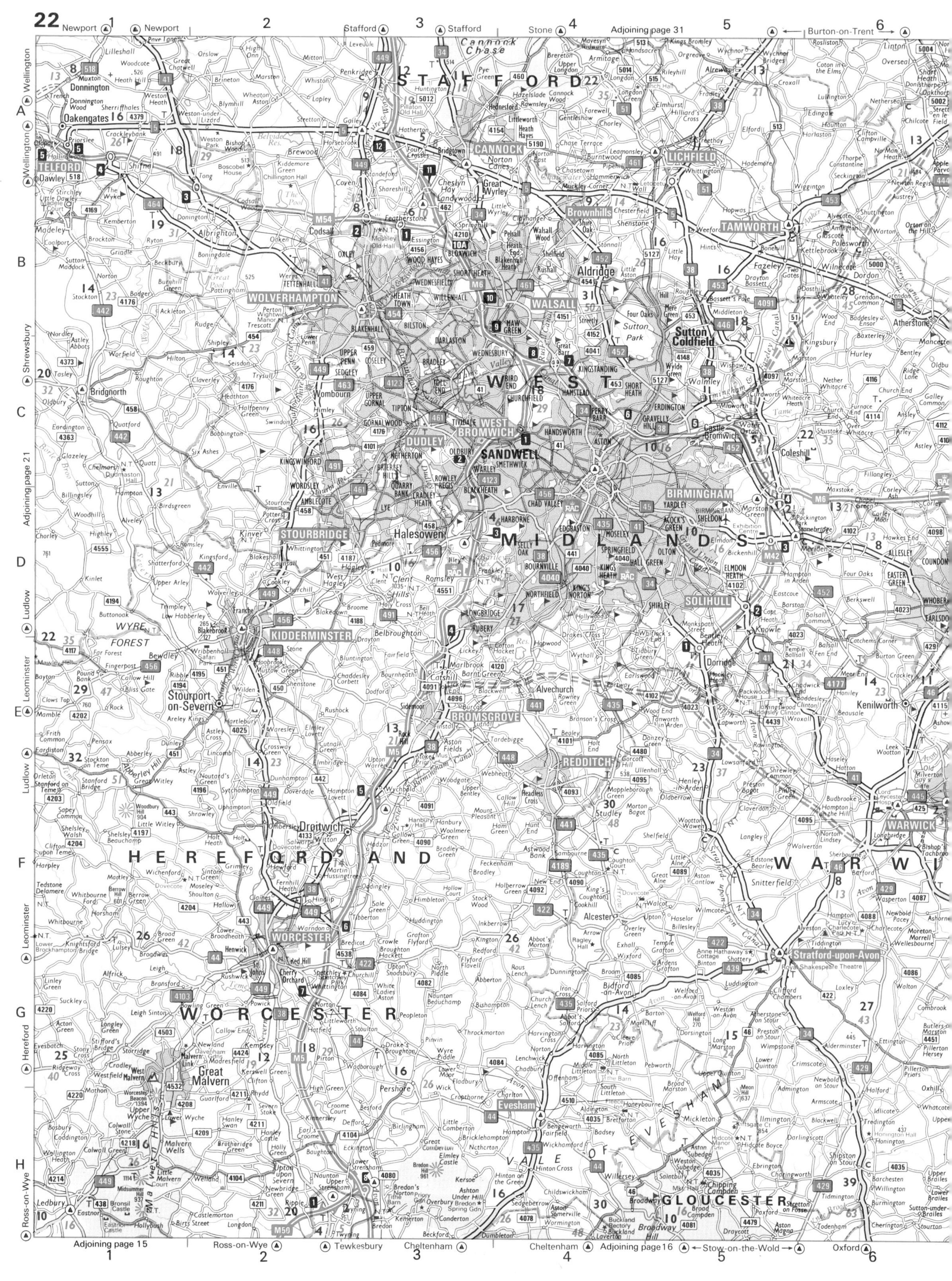
Newport
Newport
Stafford
Stafford
Stone
Adjoining page 31
Burton-on-Trent
Wellington
Wellington
Shrewsbury
Adjoining page 21
Ludlow
Leominster
Ludlow
Leominster
Hereford
Ross-on-Wye
Adjoining page 15
Ross-on-Wye
Tewkesbury
Cheltenham
Cheltenham
Adjoining page 16
Stow-on-the-Wold
Oxford
STAFFORD
Cannock Chase
TELFORD
Oakengates
Donnington
Dawley
Madeley
CANNOCK
LICHFIELD
Brownhills
TAMWORTH
WOLVERHAMPTON
WALSALL
Aldridge
Sutton Coldfield
Sutton Park
Bridgnorth
WEST MIDLANDS
DUDLEY
WEST BROMWICH
SANDWELL
BIRMINGHAM
SOLIHULL
Coleshill
Atherstone
STOURBRIDGE
Halesowen
KIDDERMINSTER
WYRE FOREST
Bewdley
Stourport-on-Severn
BROMSGROVE
REDDITCH
Alvechurch
Kenilworth
WARWICK
Droitwich
HEREFORD AND WORCESTER
WORCESTER
Great Malvern
Malvern Wells
Alcester
Stratford-upon-Avon
Royal Shakespeare Theatre
Pershore
Evesham
VALE OF EVESHAM
GLOUCESTER
Ledbury
Broadway
WARWI

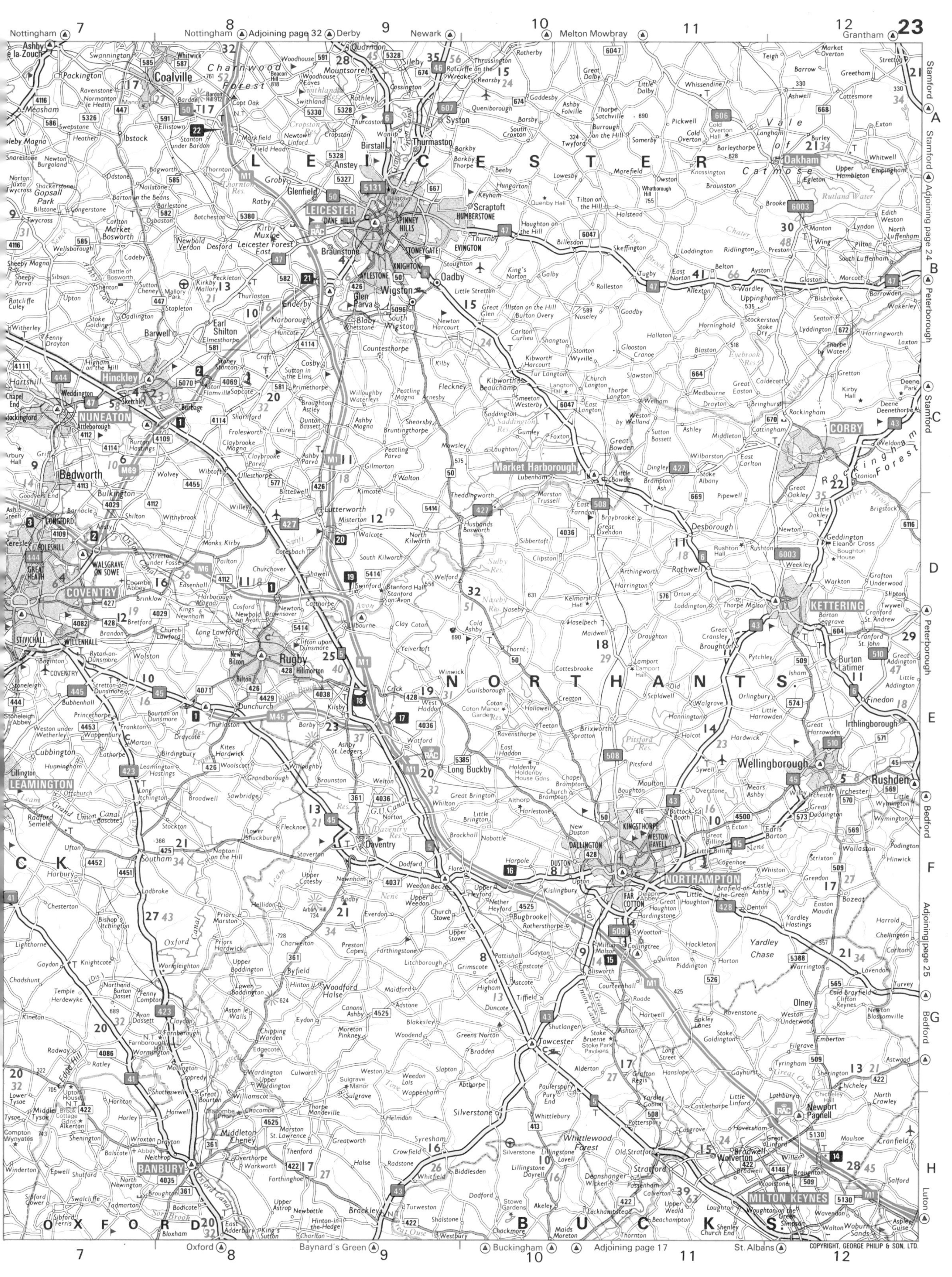
Nottingham
Nottingham
Adjoining page 32
Derby
Newark
Melton Mowbray
Grantham
Stamford
Stamford
Adjoining page 24
Peterborough
Stamford
Peterborough
Adjoining page 25
Bedford
Bedford
Luton
Oxford
Baynard's Green
Buckingham
Adjoining page 17
St. Albans
L E I C E S T E R
N O R T H A N T S.
B U C K S.
O X F O R D
Vale of Catmose
Charnwood Forest
Rockingham Forest
Yardley Chase
Whittlewood Forest
Rutland Water
Coalville
LEICESTER
Oakham
Hinckley
NUNEATON
Bedworth
COVENTRY
Rugby
LEAMINGTON
Market Harborough
CORBY
KETTERING
Wellingborough
Rushden
NORTHAMPTON
Daventry
Towcester
BANBURY
MILTON KEYNES
Newport Pagnell
Wolverton
Stratford
Brackley
Uppingham
Oadby
Wigston
Lutterworth
Desborough
Rothwell
Burton Latimer
Irthlingborough
Long Buckby
Silverstone
Olney
COPYRIGHT, GEORGE PHILIP & SON, LTD.

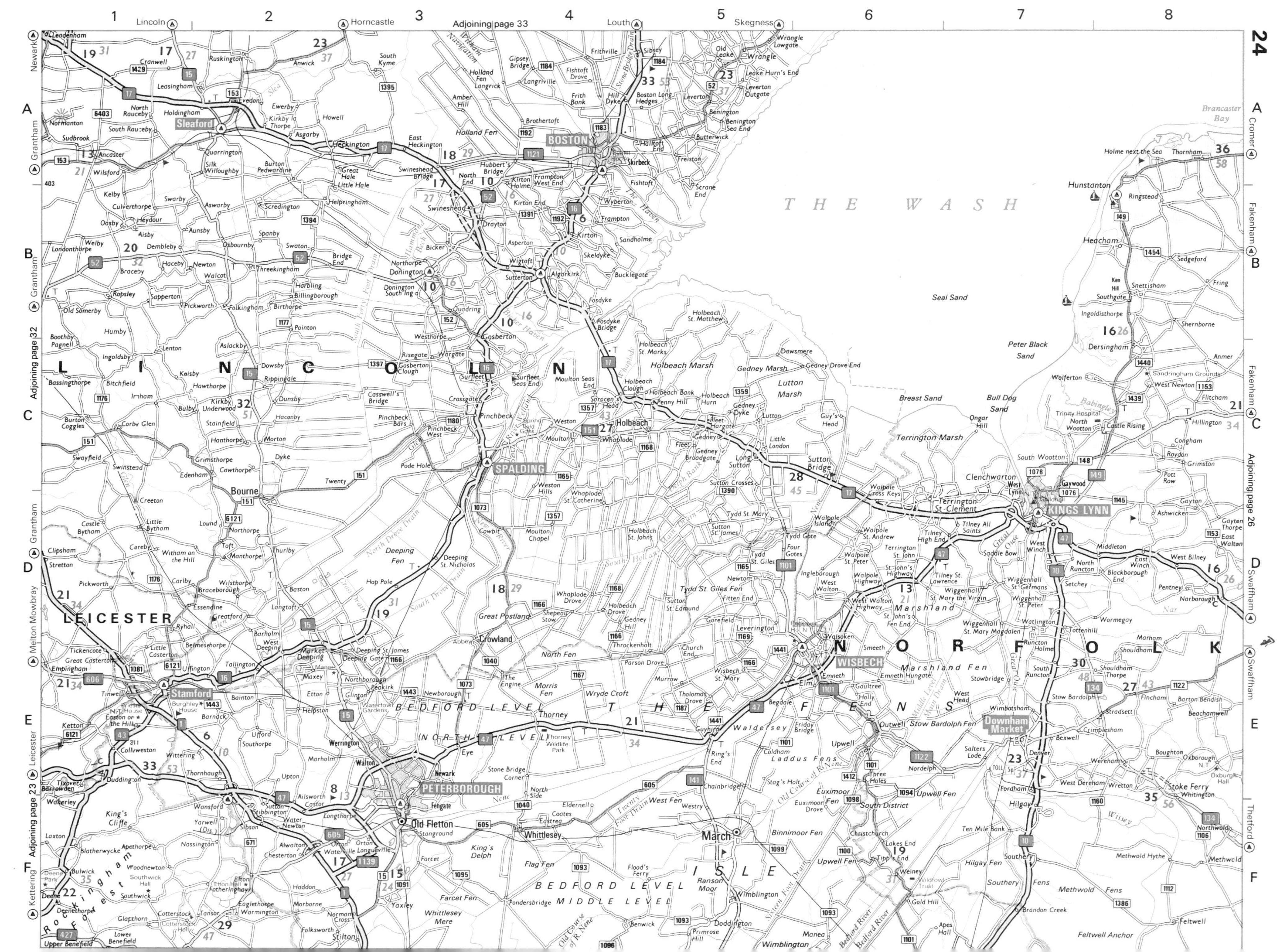
Lincoln
Horncastle
Adjoining page 33
Louth
Skegness
Cromer
Fakenham
Adjoining page 26
Swaffham
Thetford
Newark
Grantham
Adjoining page 32
Melton Mowbray
Leicester
Adjoining page 23
Kettering
THE WASH
LINCOLN
NORFOLK
THE FENS
ISLE
LEICESTER
BEDFORD LEVEL
NORTH LEVEL
BEDFORD MIDDLE LEVEL
Marshland
Marshland Fen
KINGS LYNN
BOSTON
SPALDING
WISBECH
PETERBOROUGH
Downham Market
Sleaford
Stamford
Hunstanton
Heacham
Dersingham
Holbeach
Long Sutton
Sutton Bridge
March
Whittlesey
Crowland
Bourne
Market Deeping
Old Fletton
Peter Black Sand
Bull Dog Sand
Seal Sand
Breast Sand
Terrington Marsh
Lutton Marsh
Holbeach Marsh
Gedney Marsh
Brancaster Bay

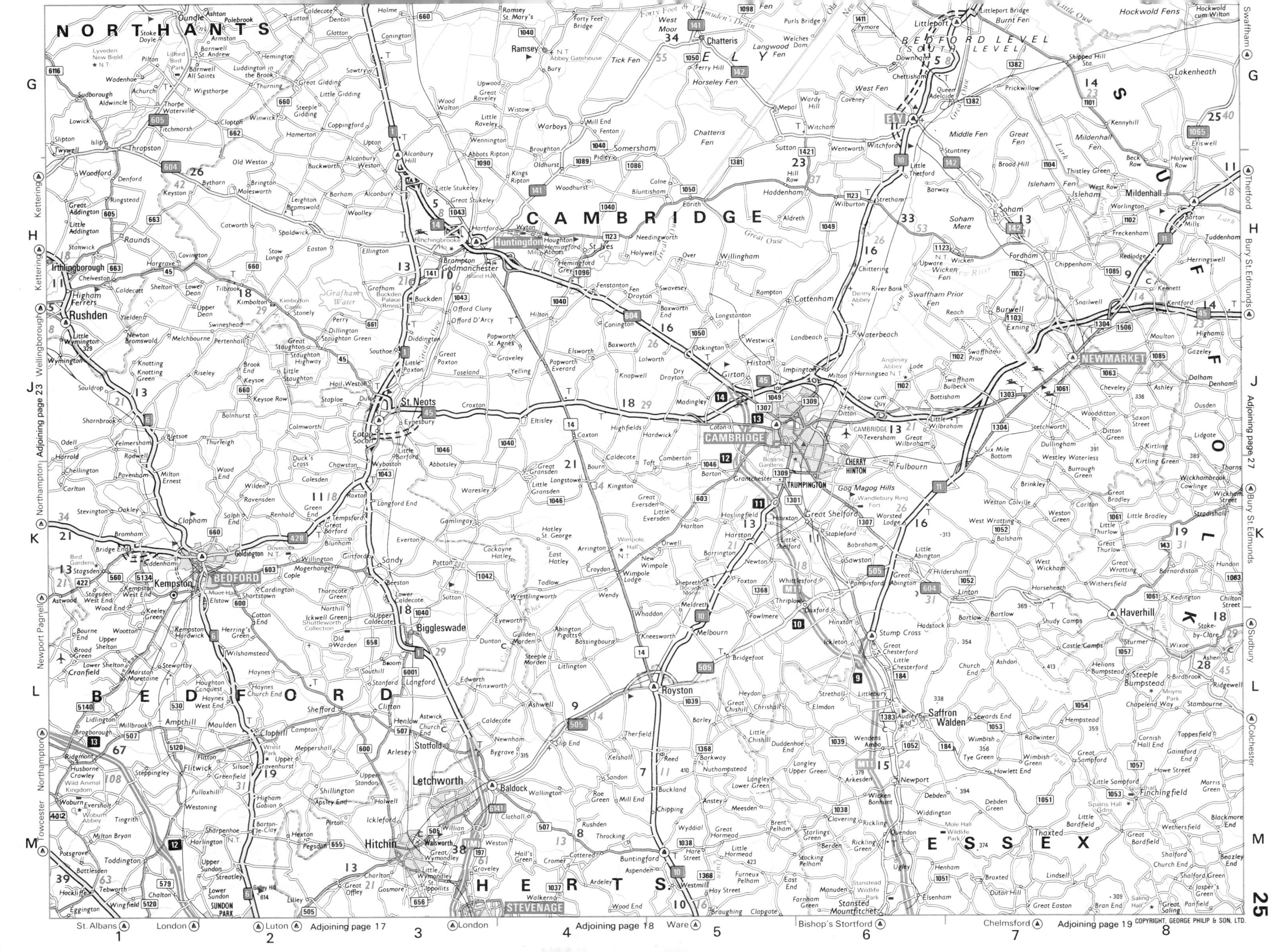

NORTHANTS
CAMBRIDGE
BEDFORD
HERTS
ESSEX
SUFFOLK
Swaffham
Thetford
Bury St.Edmunds
Adjoining page 27
Bury St.Edmunds
Sudbury
Colchester
St. Albans
London
Luton
Adjoining page 17
London
Adjoining page 18
Ware
Bishop's Stortford
Chelmsford
Adjoining page 19
Kettering
Kettering
Wellingborough
Adjoining page 23
Northampton
Newport Pagnell
Northampton
Towcester

NORTH SEA
1
2
3
4
5
6
7
8
A
B
C
D
E
F
Hunstanton
King's Lynn
Adjoining page 24
Wisbech
Brancaster Bay
Holkham Bay
Salt Marshes
Wells-next-the-Sea
Blakeney
Sheringham
Cromer
Mundesley
Holt
Fakenham
North Walsham
Aylsham
Reepham
Swaffham
East Dereham
NORFOLK
THE BROADS
NORWICH
Wymondham
Attleborough
Acle
Caister-on-Sea
GREAT YARMOUTH
Gorleston on Sea
LOWESTOFT
Beccles
Bungay
Halvergate Marshes
Danger Area
BRECKLAND

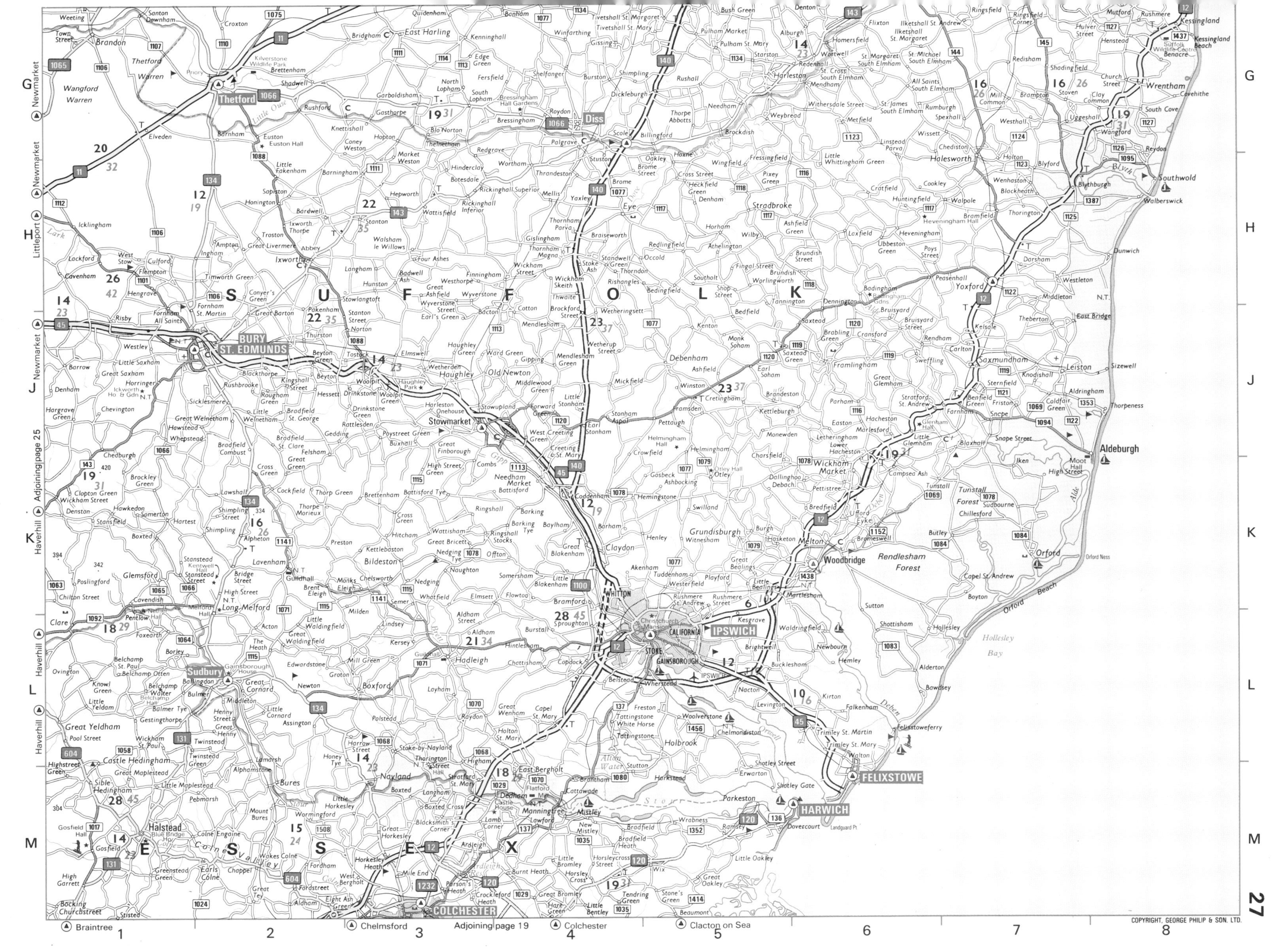
G
H
J
K
L
M
1
2
3
4
5
6
7
8
SUFFOLK
ESSEX
IPSWICH
FELIXSTOWE
HARWICH
COLCHESTER
BURY ST. EDMUNDS
Sudbury
Stowmarket
Diss
Thetford
Aldeburgh
Southwold
Woodbridge
Halstead
Hadleigh
Saxmundham
Framlingham
Eye
Halesworth
Kessingland
Adjoining page 19
Adjoining page 25
Colchester
Chelmsford
Braintree
Clacton on Sea
Haverhill
Newmarket
Littleport
COPYRIGHT, GEORGE PHILIP & SON, LTD.

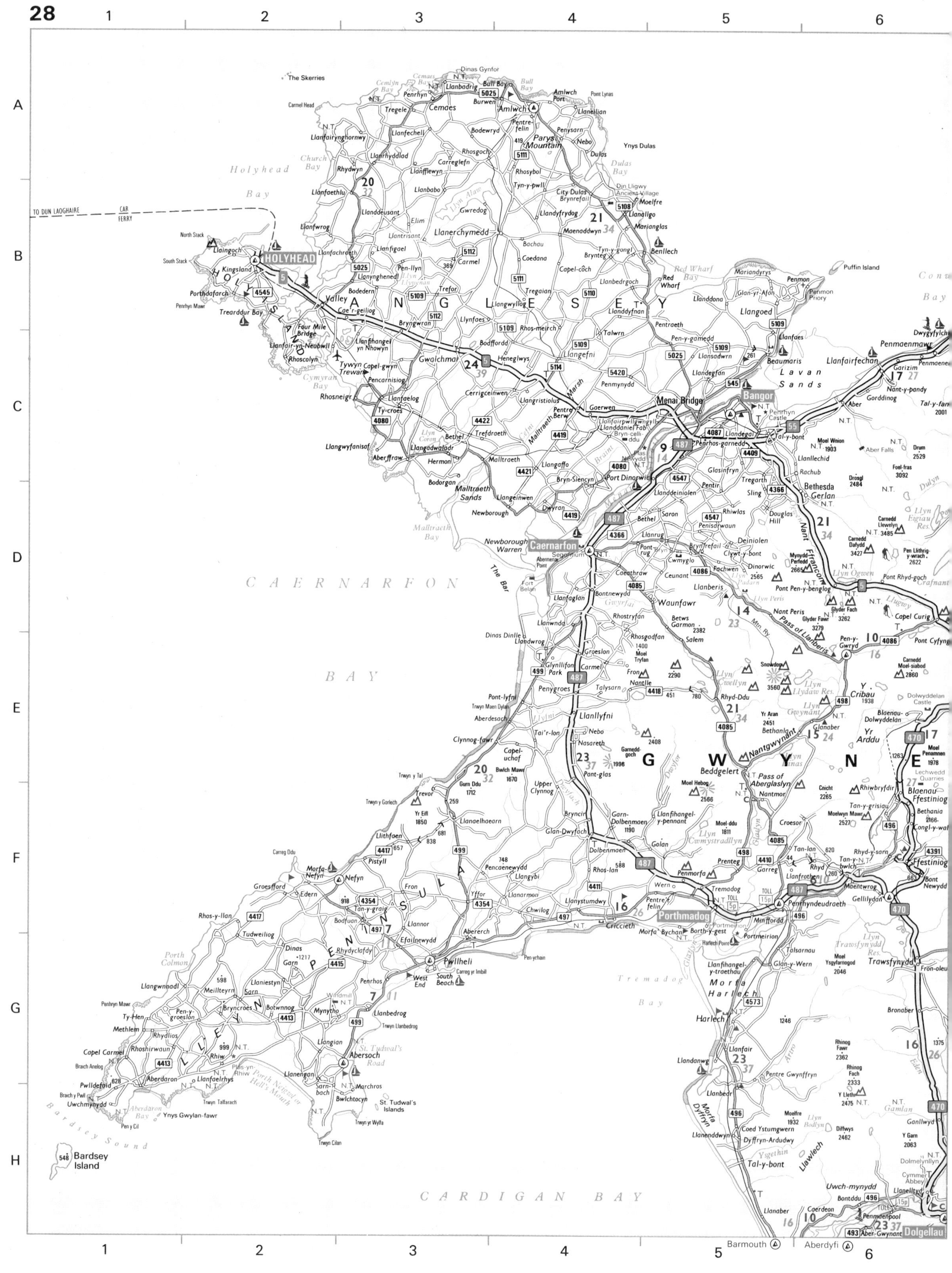

Adjoining page 34

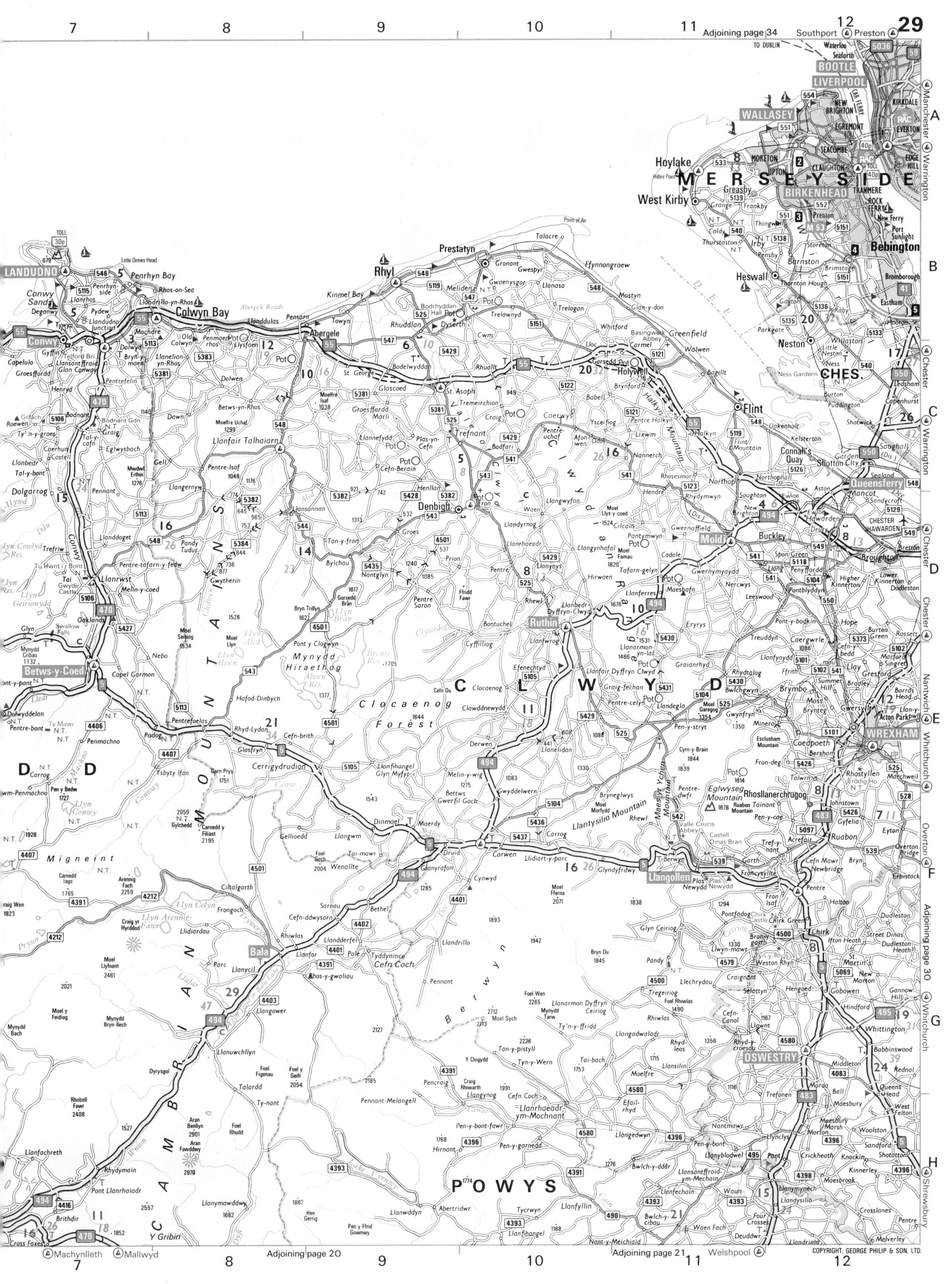

Adjoining page 30
Adjoining page 20
Adjoining page 21

Adjoining page 34

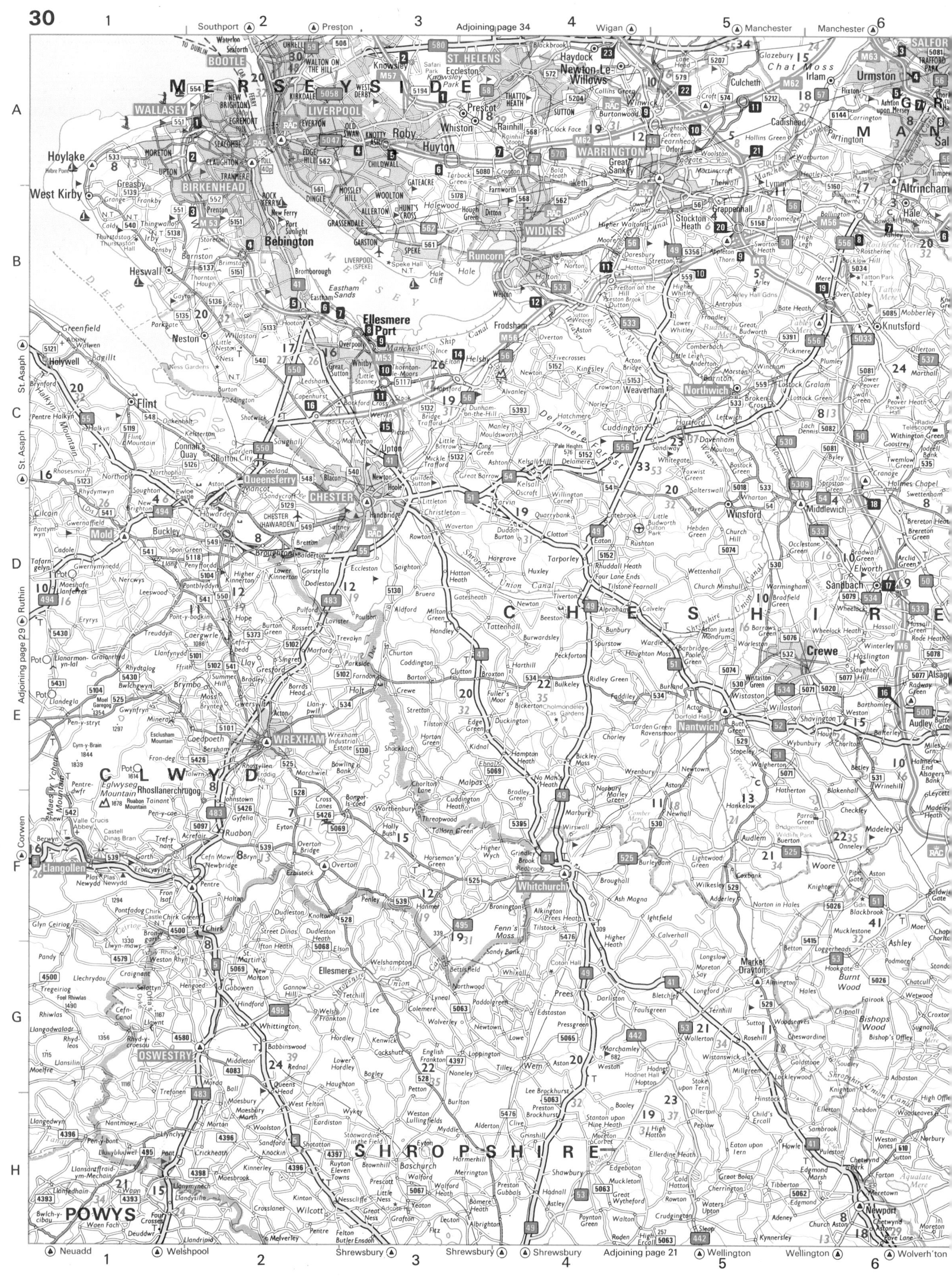

Adjoining page 29

Adjoining page 21

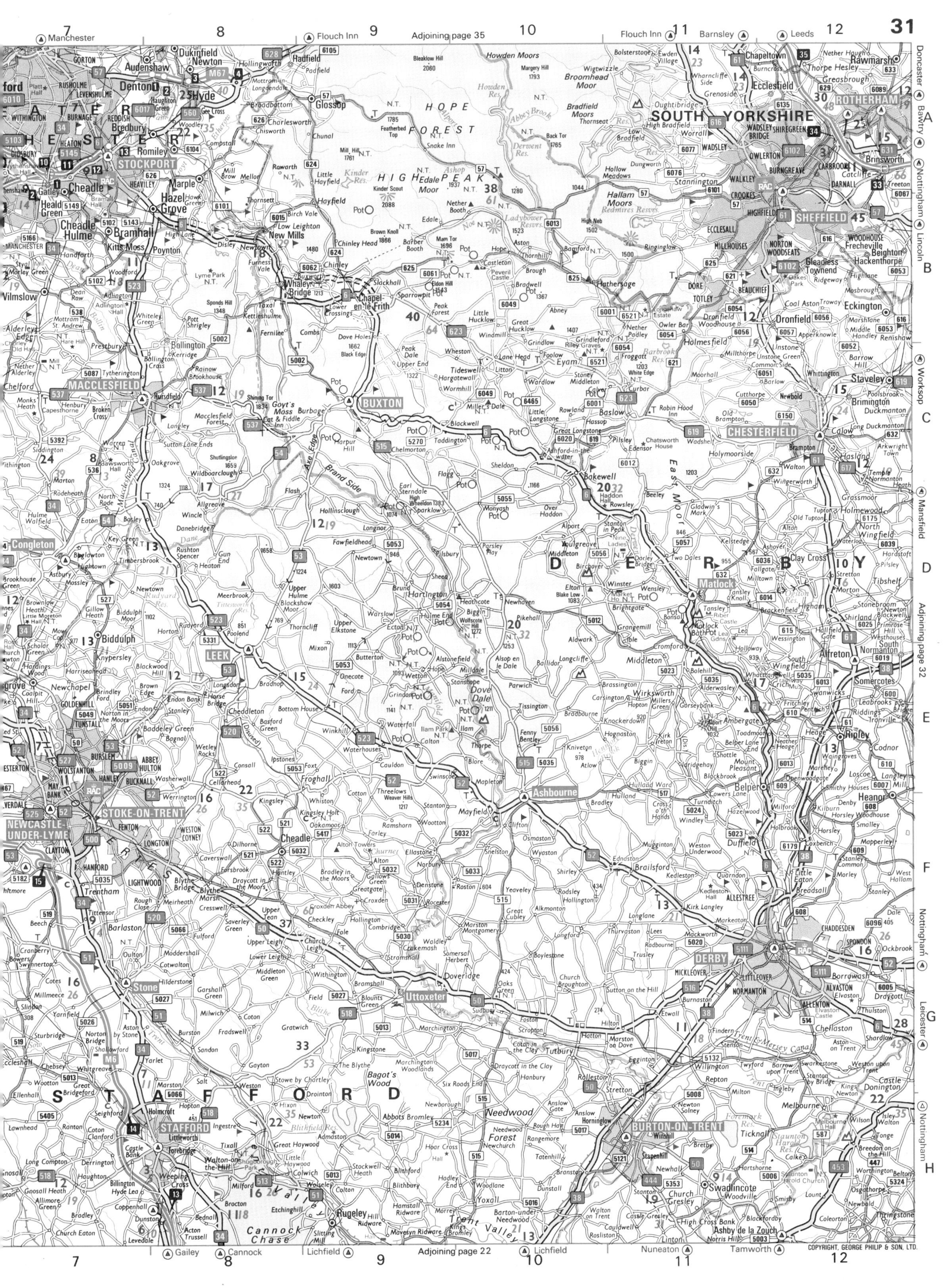

Adjoining page 35
Adjoining page 32
Adjoining page 22

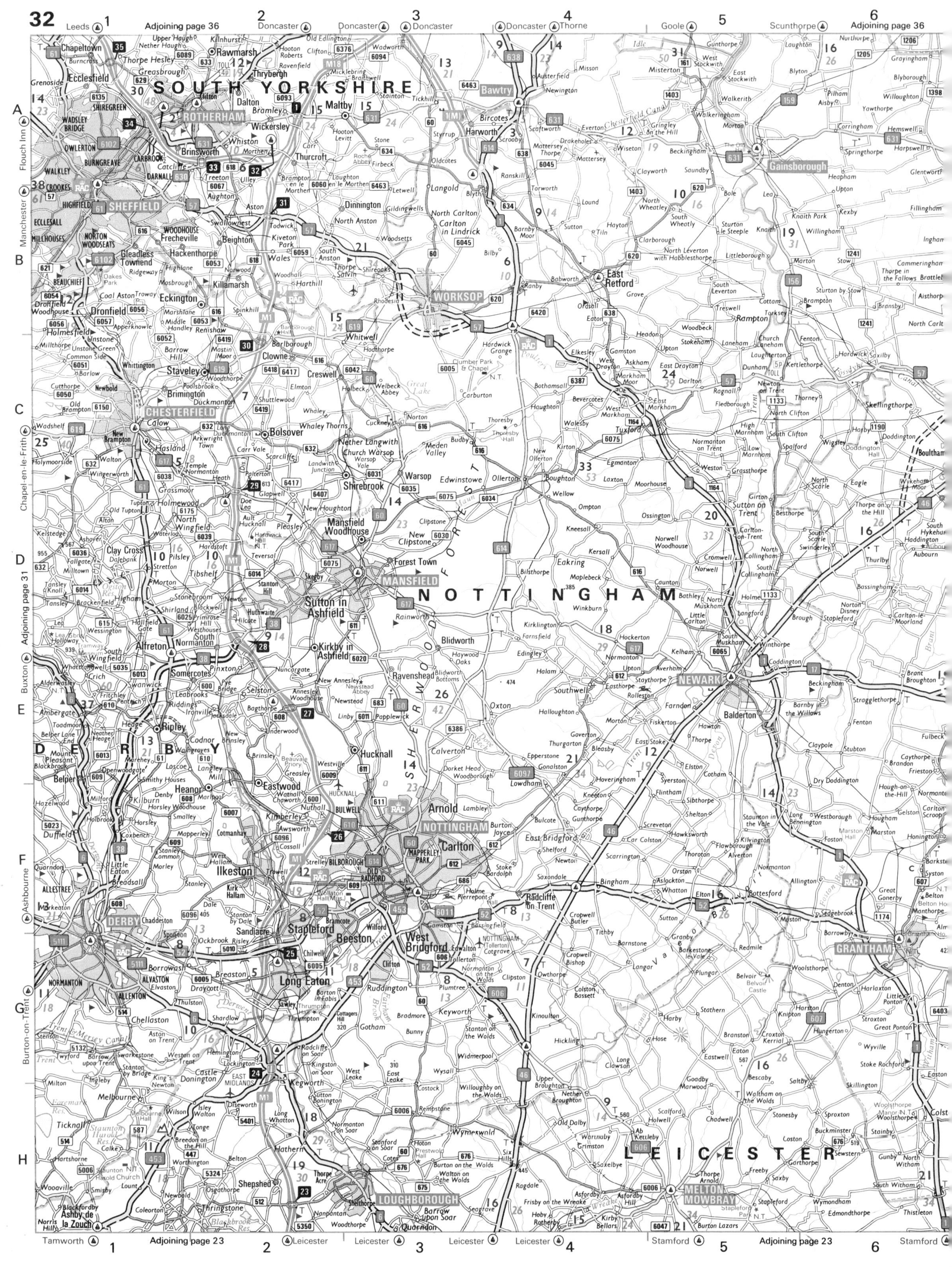
SOUTH YORKSHIRE
NOTTINGHAM
DERBY
LEICESTER
SHEFFIELD
ROTHERHAM
CHESTERFIELD
WORKSOP
MANSFIELD
NOTTINGHAM
DERBY
NEWARK
GRANTHAM
LOUGHBOROUGH
MELTON MOWBRAY
Gainsborough
Bawtry
East Retford
Sutton in Ashfield
Long Eaton
Ilkeston
Stapleford
Beeston
West Bridgford
Arnold
Carlton
Hucknall
Eastwood
Heanor
Ripley
Alfreton
Belper
Bolsover
Staveley
Dronfield
Eckington
Maltby
Ashby de la Zouch
Shepshed
Flouch Inn
Manchester
Chapel-en-le-Frith
Adjoining page 31
Buxton
Ashbourne
Burton-on-Trent

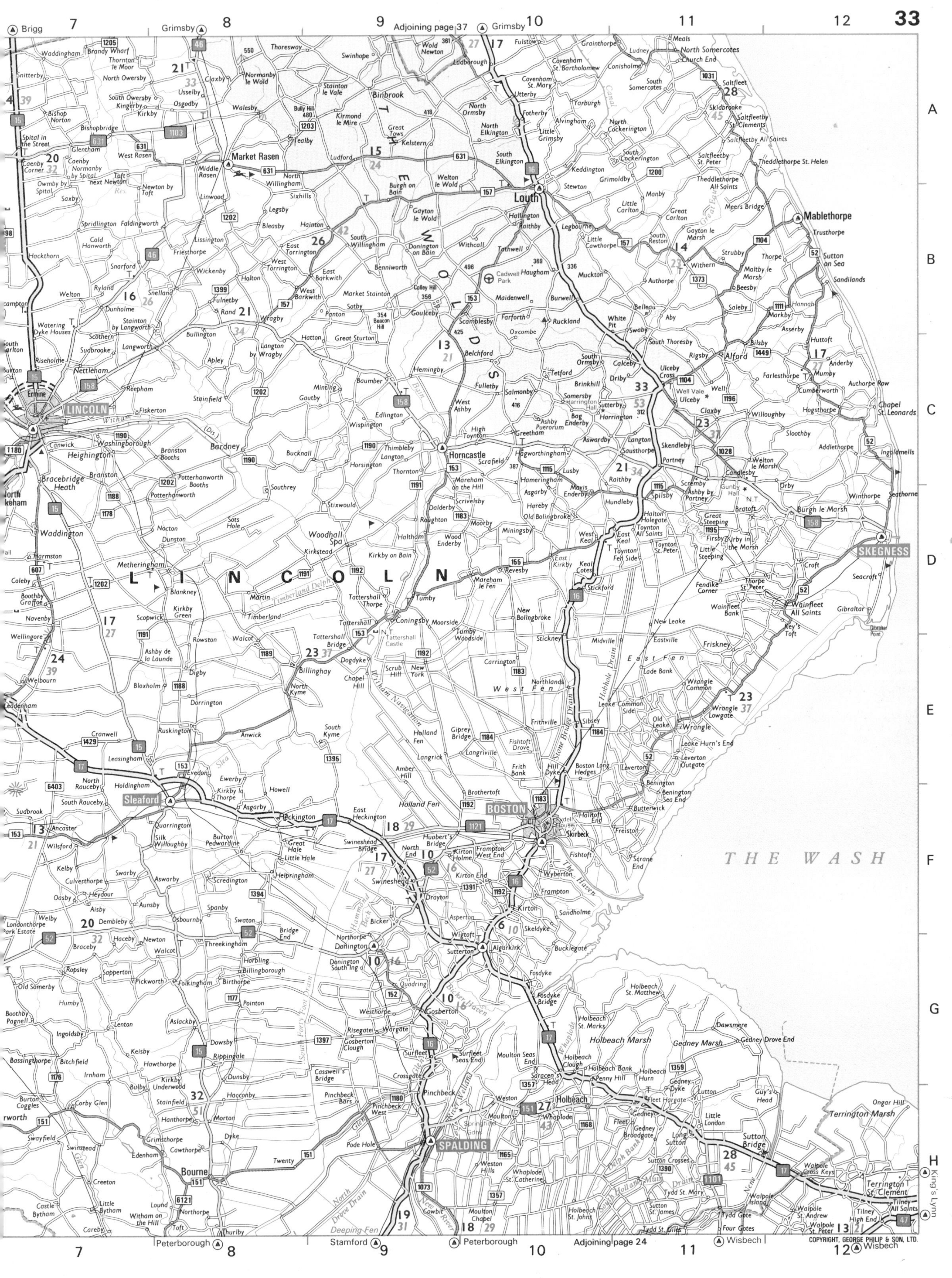
33
Brigg
Grimsby
Adjoining page 37
Grimsby
Peterborough
Stamford
Peterborough
Adjoining page 24
Wisbech
Wisbech
King's Lynn
COPYRIGHT, GEORGE PHILIP & SON, LTD.
LINCOLN
THE WASH
W O L D S
East Fen
West Fen
Holland Fen
Holbeach Marsh
Gedney Marsh
Terrington Marsh
Witham Navigation
Timberland Delph
Stone Bridge Drain
Hobhole Drain
South Forty Foot Drain
The Haven
North Drove Drain
New River
River Welland
Deeping Fen
Market Rasen
Louth
Mablethorpe
Sutton on Sea
Alford
Horncastle
Woodhall Spa
Coningsby
Tattershall
Skegness
Wainfleet All Saints
Boston
Sleaford
Spalding
Holbeach
Long Sutton
Sutton Bridge
Bourne
Donington
Heckington
Billinghay
Navenby
Waddington
Bracebridge Heath
Heighington
Washingborough
Nettleham
Welton
Wragby
Binbrook
Ludford
North Somercotes
Saltfleet
Grainthorpe
Fulstow
Ludborough
Utterby
Legbourne
Burgh le Marsh
Ingoldmells
Chapel St. Leonards
Anderby
Huttoft
Spilsby
Stickney
Sibsey
Frithville
Kirton
Sutterton
Algarkirk
Fosdyke
Swineshead
Gosberton
Pinchbeck
Surfleet
Moulton
Weston
Whaplode
Fleet
Gedney
Tydd St. Mary
Walpole St. Andrew
Walpole St. Peter
Terrington St. Clement
Tilney All Saints
Ruskington
Cranwell
Leasingham
Ancaster
Wilsford
Folkingham
Morton
Rippingale
Dowsby
Castle Bytham
Little Bytham
Corby Glen
Swinstead
Edenham
Thurlby

Adjoining page 38
Adjoining page 39

Adjoining page 30

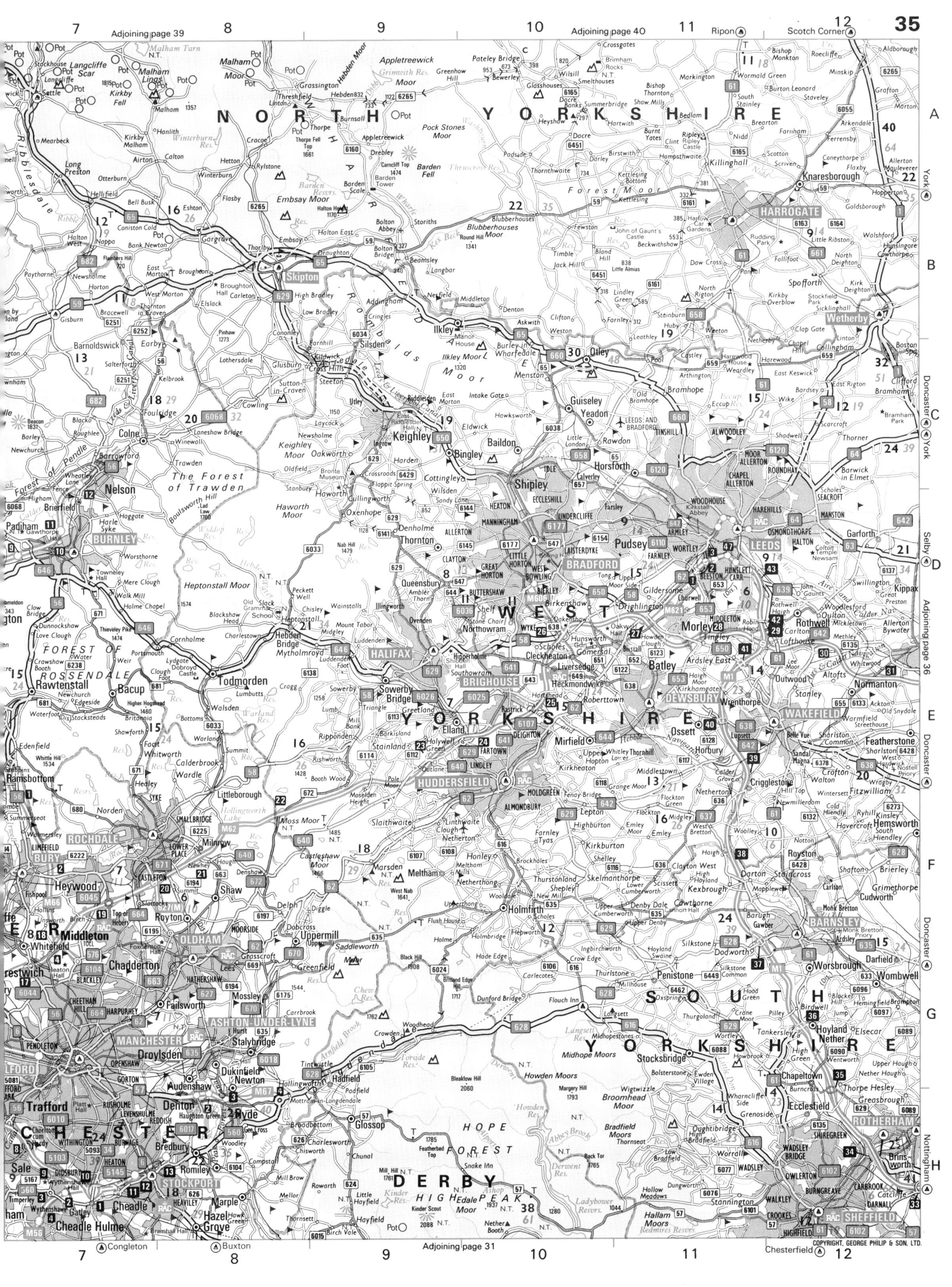

Adjoining page 39
Adjoining page 40
Ripon
Scotch Corner
NORTH YORKSHIRE
WEST YORKSHIRE
SOUTH YORKSHIRE
CHESTER
DERBY
York
Doncaster
Selby
Adjoining page 36
Nottingham
Congleton
Buxton
Adjoining page 31
Chesterfield
Harrogate
Knaresborough
Skipton
Wetherby
Otley
Ilkley
Keighley
Bingley
Shipley
Bradford
Leeds
Pudsey
Morley
Halifax
Brighouse
Dewsbury
Wakefield
Huddersfield
Barnsley
Rotherham
Sheffield
Burnley
Nelson
Colne
Rochdale
Bury
Oldham
Manchester
Stockport
Trafford
Ashton-under-Lyne
Todmorden
Hebden Bridge
Holmfirth
Penistone
Stocksbridge
Glossop
HOPE FOREST
HIGH PEAK
Forest of Rossendale
The Forest of Trawden
Rombalds Moor
COPYRIGHT, GEORGE PHILIP & SON, LTD.

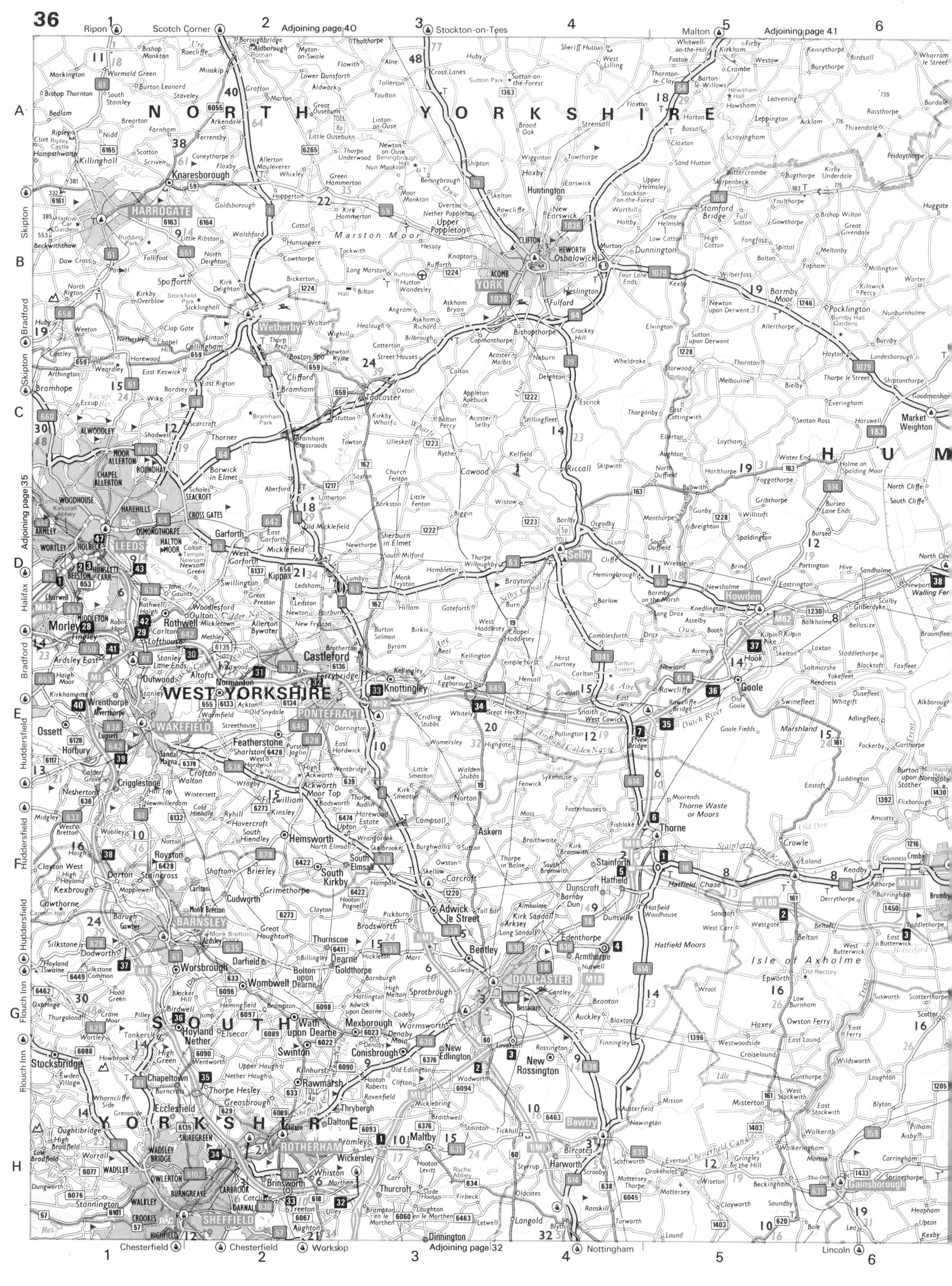

Ripon
Scotch Corner
Adjoining page 40
Stockton-on-Tees
Malton
Adjoining page 41
NORTH YORKSHIRE
WEST YORKSHIRE
SOUTH YORKSHIRE
HUM
Skipton
Bradford
Adjoining page 35
Halifax
Huddersfield
Flouch Inn
Chesterfield
Worksop
Adjoining page 32
Nottingham
Lincoln
Boroughbridge
Aldborough
Knaresborough
HARROGATE
Wetherby
Tadcaster
YORK
Marston Moor
Huntington
Osbalawick
Heslington
Fulford
Bishopthorpe
Stamford Bridge
Pocklington
Market Weighton
Selby
Howden
Goole
LEEDS
Morley
Castleford
PONTEFRACT
Knottingley
WAKEFIELD
Ossett
Horbury
Featherstone
Hemsworth
South Kirkby
Adwick le Street
Bentley
DONCASTER
Thorne
Hatfield
Crowle
Isle of Axholme
Epworth
BARNSLEY
Wombwell
Mexborough
Conisbrough
Swinton
Rawmarsh
ROTHERHAM
SHEFFIELD
Stocksbridge
Chapeltown
Ecclesfield
Maltby
Bawtry
Harworth
Tickhill
Dinnington
Gainsborough
Hatfield Moors
Thorne Waste or Moors
Marshland
Selby Canal
Aire and Calder Navig.
Dutch River
Chesterfield Canal
Stainforth and Keadby Canal
Ouse
Aire
Trent
Idle

Adjoining page 41
Scarborough
BRIDLINGTON
Hilderthorpe
Bridlington Bay
NORTH SEA
Driffield
Nafferton
Skipsea
North Frodingham
Hornsea
Hornsea Bridge
Hornsea Mere
Leven Canal
Mappleton
Beverley
Cottingham
NEWLAND
SCULCOATES
STONEFERRY
SUTTON-ON-HULL
MARFLEET
KINGSTON UPON HULL
Hessle
Humber Br.
Hedon
Withernsea
Patrington
Aldbrough
HOLDERNESS
HUMBERSIDE
YORKSHIRE WOLDS
Barton-upon-Humber
New Holland
Foulholme Sands
MOUTH OF THE HUMBER
Sunk Island Sands
Spurn Head
Kilnsea
Immingham
GRIMSBY
Cleethorpes
SCUNTHORPE
Brigg
Caistor
Louth
Market Rasen
Binbrook
Humberston
LINCOLN
Lincoln
Boston
Adjoining page 33
COPYRIGHT, GEORGE PHILIP & SON, LTD.

Adjoining page 43
Adjoining page 44
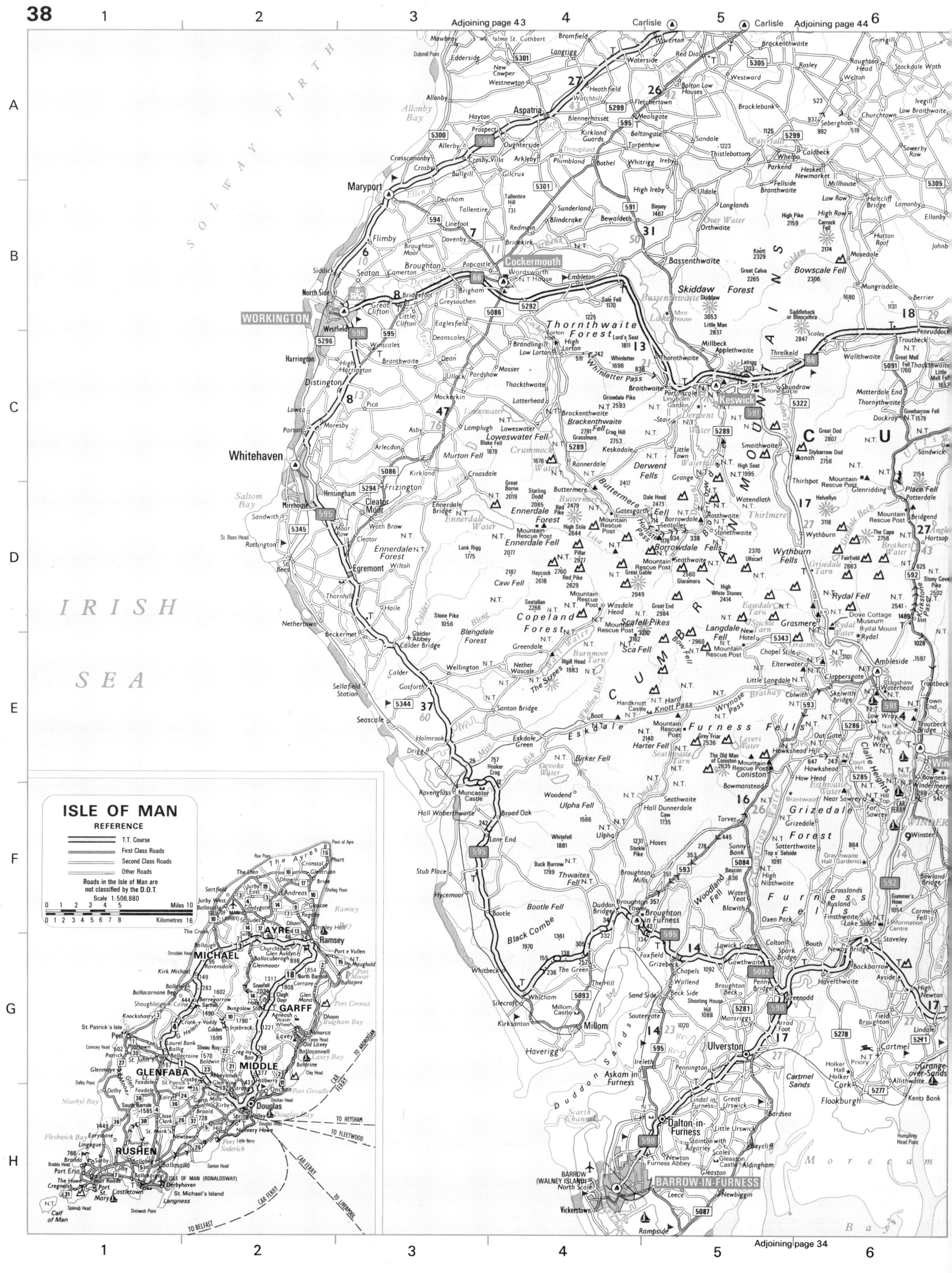

Adjoining page 34

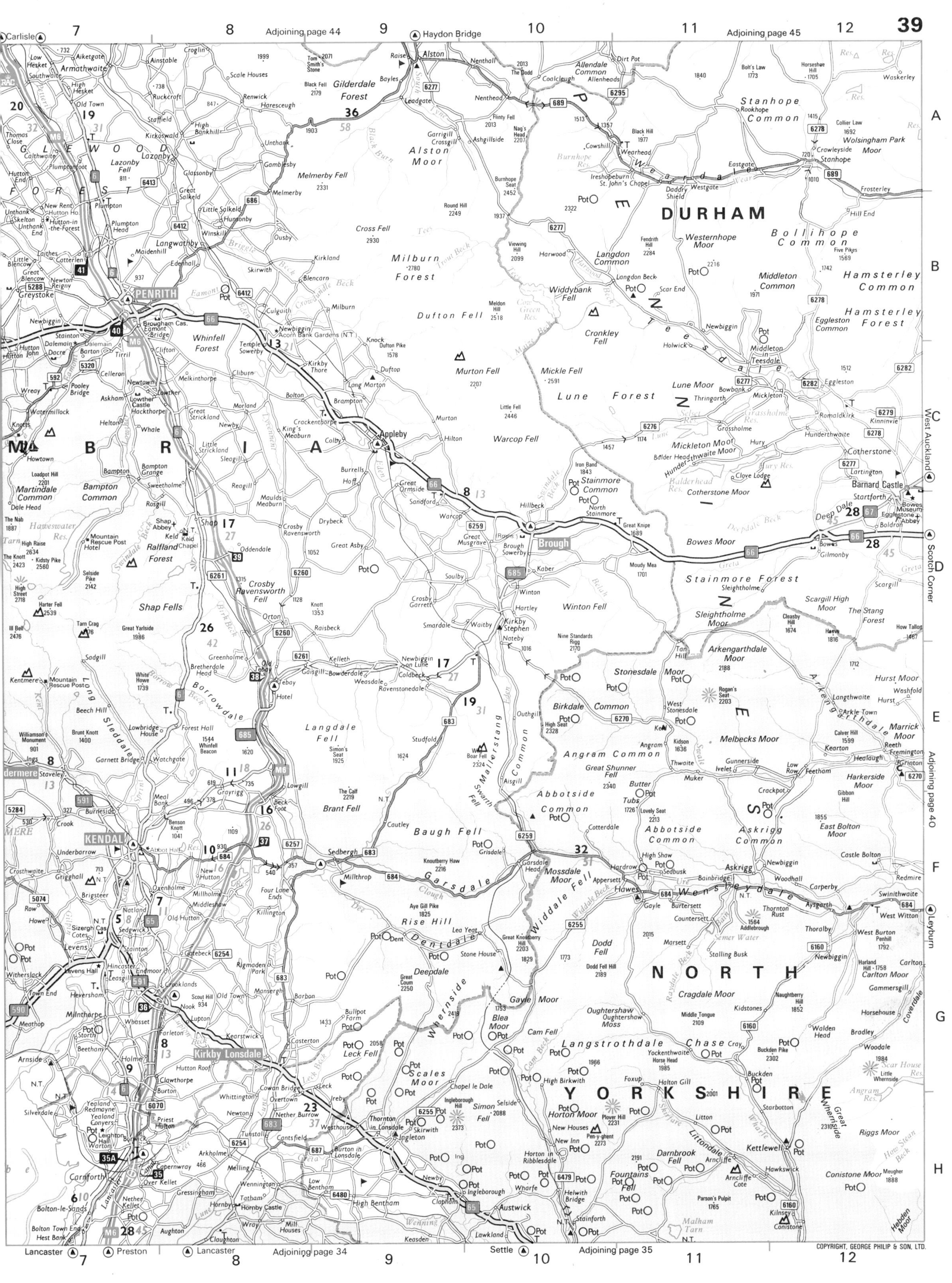

Carlisle
Adjoining page 44
Haydon Bridge
Adjoining page 45
7
8
9
10
11
12
A
B
C
D
E
F
G
H
West Auckland
Scotch Corner
Adjoining page 40
Leyburn
Lancaster
Preston
Lancaster
Adjoining page 34
Settle
Adjoining page 35
COPYRIGHT, GEORGE PHILIP & SON, LTD.
DURHAM
NORTH YORKSHIRE
PENNINES
CUMBRIA
GLEWOOD FOREST
PENRITH
KENDAL
Kirkby Lonsdale
Brough
Appleby
Alston
Alston Moor
Gilderdale Forest
Melmerby Fell
Cross Fell
Milburn Forest
Dufton Fell
Murton Fell
Mickle Fell
Lune Forest
Warcop Fell
Stanhope Common
Stanhope
Weardale
Bollihope Common
Hamsterley Common
Hamsterley Forest
Westernhope Moor
Middleton Common
Langdon Common
Widdybank Fell
Cronkley Fell
Teesdale
Middleton in Teesdale
Lune Moor
Mickleton Moor
Cotherstone Moor
Barnard Castle
Stainmore Common
Bowes Moor
Stainmore Forest
Winton Fell
Kirkby Stephen
Sleightholme Moor
Arkengarthdale Moor
Stonesdale Moor
Birkdale Common
Angram Common
Melbecks Moor
Abbotside Common
Askrigg Common
Wensleydale
Hawes
Askrigg
Baugh Fell
Garsdale
Sedbergh
Dentdale
Rise Hill
Deepdale
Dodd Fell
Cragdale Moor
Langstrothdale Chase
Whernside
Scales Moor
Leck Fell
Simon Fell
Horton Moor
Fountains Fell
Darnbrook Fell
Littondale
Kettlewell
Wharfe
Whinfell Forest
Bampton Common
Martindale Common
Haweswater Res.
Ralfland Forest
Shap Fells
Shap
Crosby Ravensworth Fell
Borrowdale
Long Sleddale
Langdale Fell
Brant Fell
Mallerstang Common
Lancaster Canal
Carnforth
Kirkby Lonsdale
Ingleton
Austwick
Clapham
High Bentham
Wennington

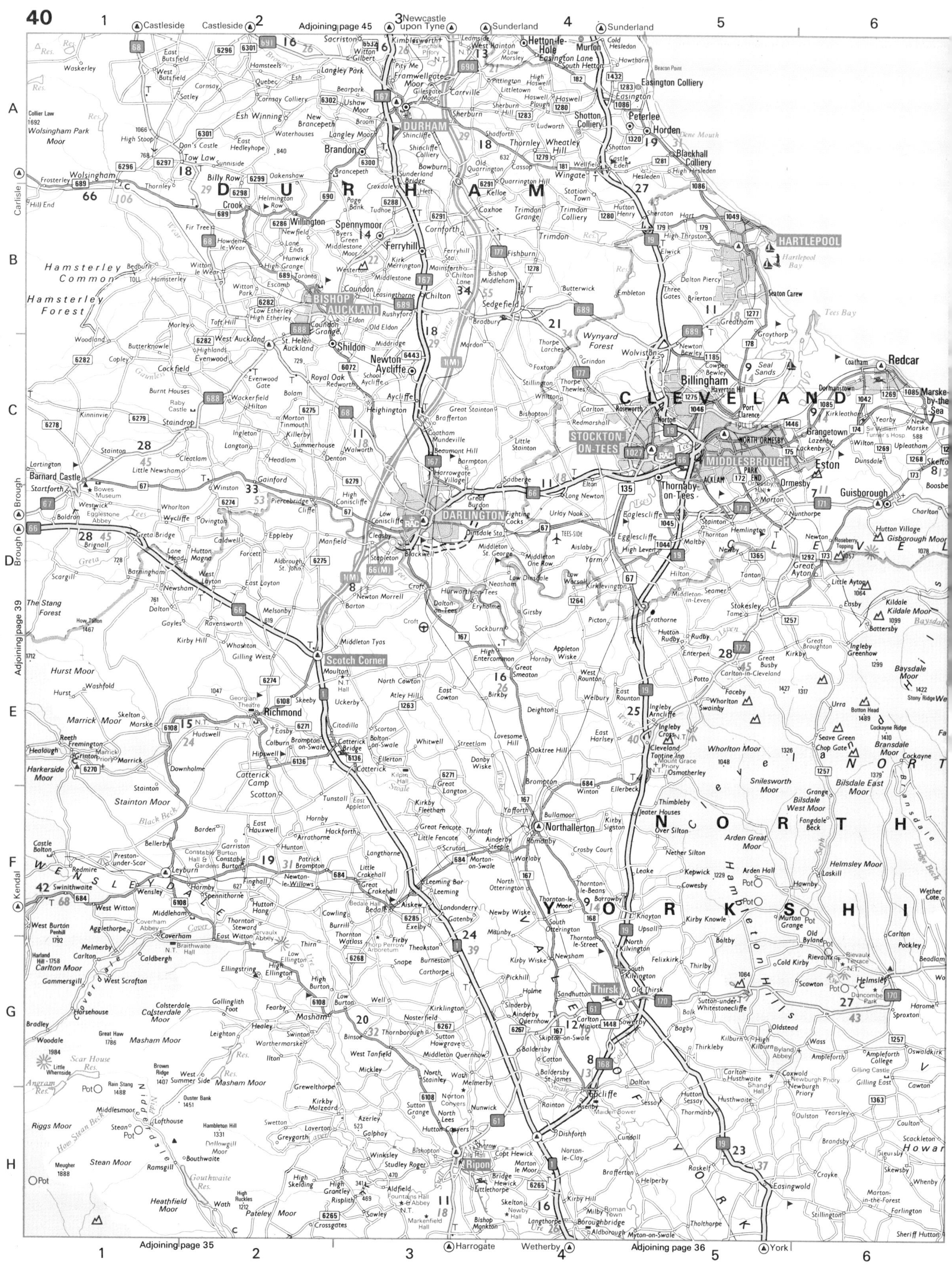
Adjoining page 45
Adjoining page 39
Adjoining page 35
Adjoining page 36
Castleside
Newcastle upon Tyne
Sunderland
Carlisle
Brough
Kendal
Harrogate
Wetherby
York
DURHAM
CLEVELAND
NORTH YORKSHIRE
DURHAM
HARTLEPOOL
BISHOP AUCKLAND
STOCKTON-ON-TEES
MIDDLESBROUGH
DARLINGTON
Scotch Corner
Thirsk
Ripon
Sacriston
Kimblesworth
Hetton-le-Hole
Murton
Easington Lane
South Hetton
Easington Colliery
Easington
Peterlee
Horden
Blackhall Colliery
Hesleden
High Hesleden
Wingate
Wheatley Hill
Thornley
Shotton Colliery
Haswell
Sherburn
Shincliffe
Langley Moor
Brandon
Esh Winning
Cornsay Colliery
Tow Law
Wolsingham
Frosterley
Hamsterley Common
Hamsterley Forest
Wolsingham Park Moor
Waskerley
Satley
Crook
Billy Row
Willington
Spennymoor
Ferryhill
Coundon
Shildon
Newton Aycliffe
Sedgefield
Trimdon
Fishburn
Cornforth
Coxhoe
Kelloe
Cassop
Bowburn
Sheraton
Hart
Elwick
Dalton Piercy
Seaton Carew
Greatham
Tees Bay
Seal Sands
Billingham
Redcar
Coatham
Dormanstown
Marske-by-the-Sea
Kirkleatham
Grangetown
Eston
Normanby
Ormesby
Guisborough
Thornaby-on-Tees
Acklam
Eaglescliffe
Yarm
Middleton St. George
Great Ayton
Stokesley
Hutton Rudby
Ingleby Greenhow
Kildale
Baysdale Moor
Bransdale Moor
Bilsdale West Moor
Bilsdale East Moor
Osmotherley
Ingleby Arncliffe
Whorlton Moor
Snilesworth Moor
Arden Great Moor
Helmsley Moor
Helmsley
Rievaulx
Hambleton Hills
Northallerton
Romanby
Brompton
Thornton-le-Beans
Thornton-le-Moor
Kirby Wiske
Sowerby
Topcliffe
Dishforth
Asenby
Boroughbridge
Aldborough
Easingwold
Ampleforth
Coxwold
Kilburn
Bedale
Leeming Bar
Leeming
Masham
Leyburn
Wensley
Middleham
Coverham
Richmond
Catterick
Catterick Camp
Catterick Bridge
Scotton
Brompton-on-Swale
Barnard Castle
Startforth
Bowes Museum
Greta Bridge
Staindrop
Raby Castle
Gainford
Piercebridge
Winston
Cockfield
Evenwood
West Auckland
St. Helen Auckland
Heighington
Aycliffe
Croft
Hurworth-on-Tees
Middleton Tyas
Hurst Moor
Marrick Moor
Harkerside Moor
Stainton Moor
Wensleydale
Carlton Moor
Masham Moor
Pateley Moor
Heathfield Moor
Stean Moor
Riggs Moor
Nidderdale
Pateley Bridge
Fountains Hall & Abbey
Studley Roger
Bishop Monkton
Markenfield Hall
Newby Hall
Sutton-under-Whitestonecliffe
Vale of York

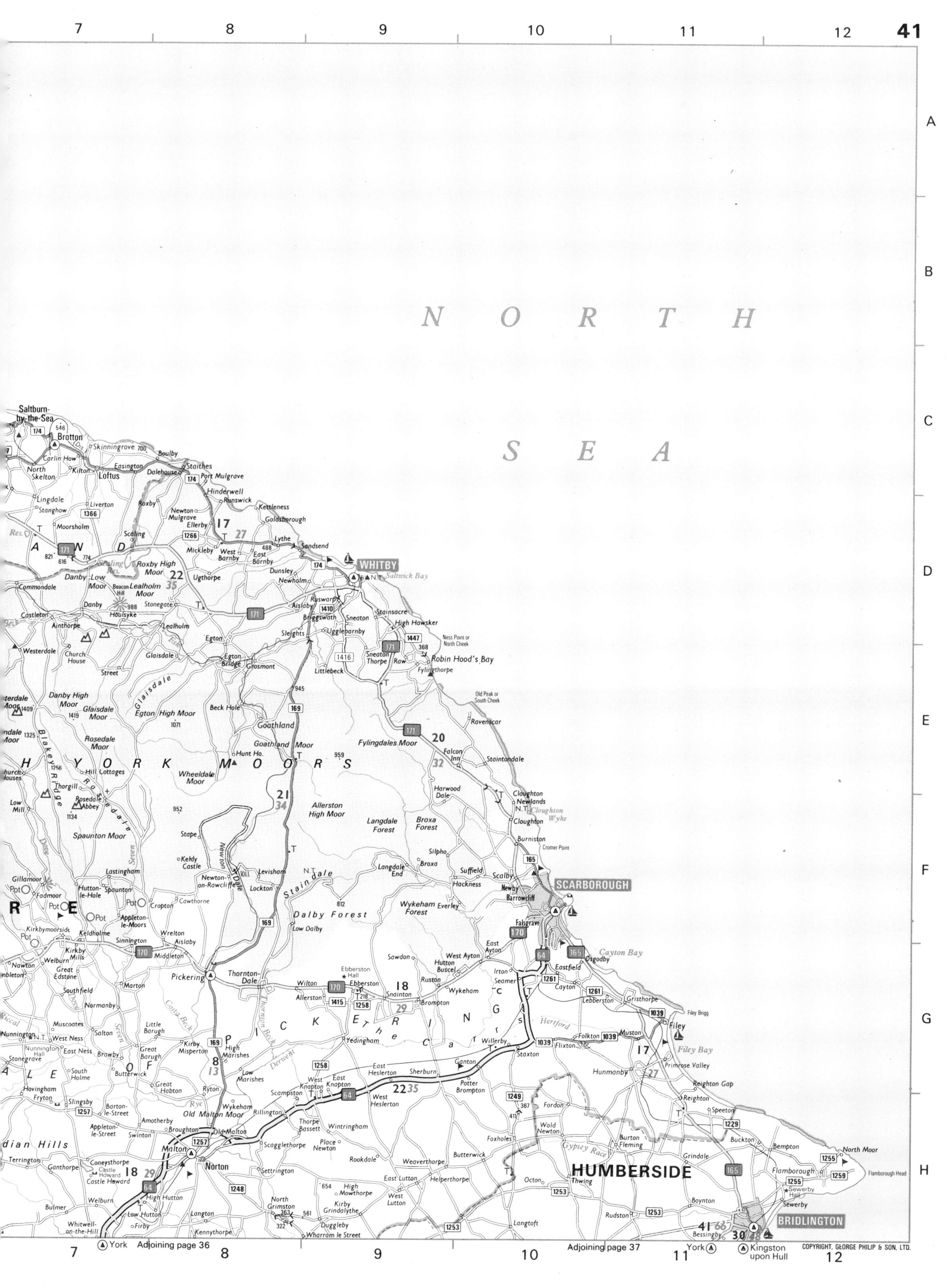

Adjoining page 36
Adjoining page 37

Adjoining page 47

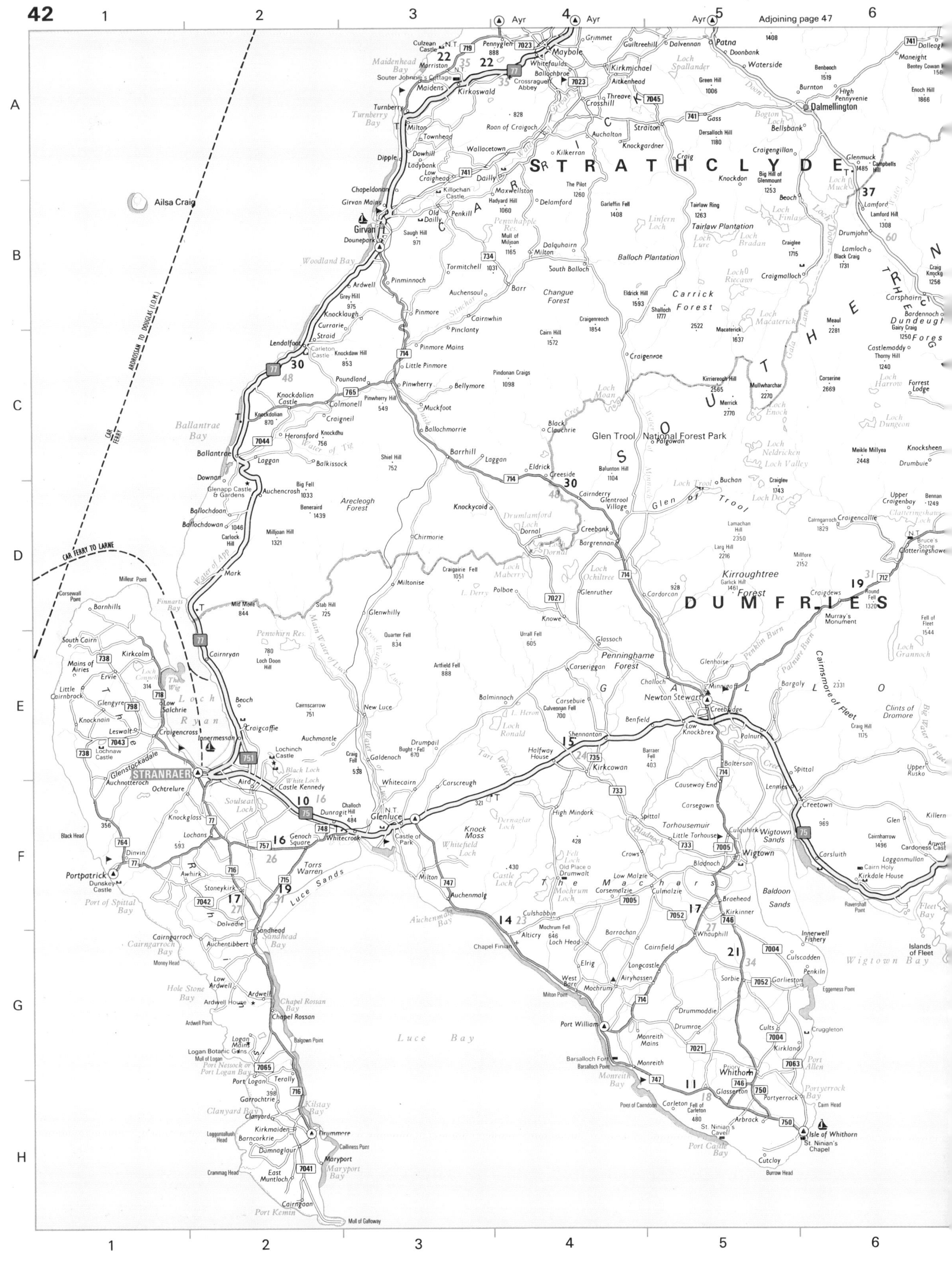

1 2 3 4 5 6
A B C D E F G H

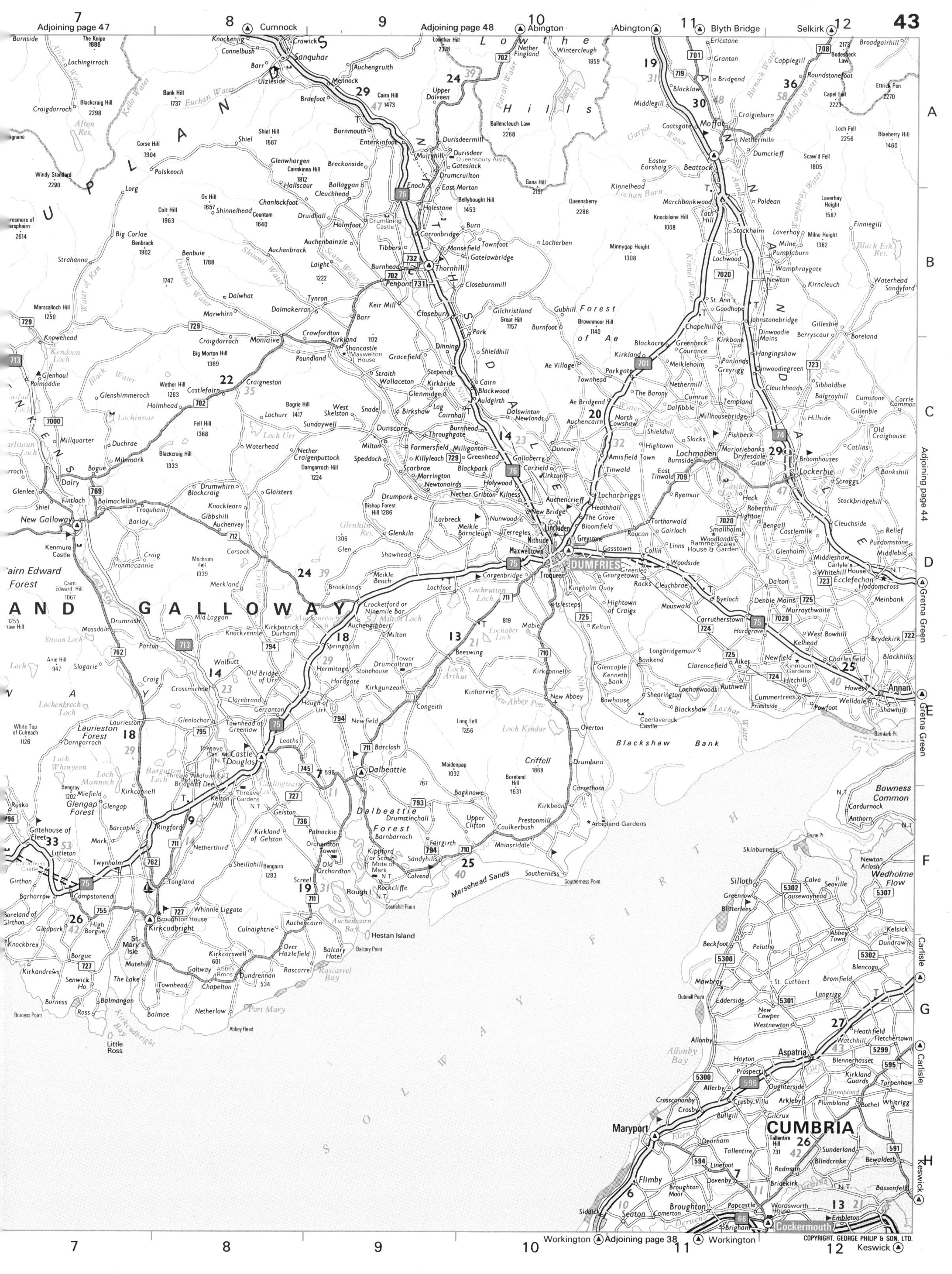
Adjoining page 47
Cumnock
Adjoining page 48
Abington
Blyth Bridge
Selkirk
Adjoining page 44
Gretna Green
Carlisle
Keswick
Workington
Adjoining page 38
Lowther Hills
UPLAND
DUMFRIES AND GALLOWAY
NITHSDALE
ANNANDALE
CUMBRIA
SOLWAY FIRTH
Blackshaw Bank
Forest of Ae
Dalbeattie Forest
Laurieston Forest
Glengap Forest
Cairn Edward Forest
Sanquhar
Thornhill
Moffat
Beattock
Lockerbie
Lochmaben
Ecclefechan
Annan
DUMFRIES
Castle Douglas
Dalbeattie
Kirkcudbright
New Galloway
Dalry
Moniaive
Gatehouse of Fleet
Maryport
Aspatria
Silloth
Cockermouth
Abbey Town
Allonby
Flimby
Seaton
Crossmichael
Kirkbean
Hestan Island
Little Ross
Mersehead Sands
Southerness
Arbigland Gardens
Caerlaverock Castle
Criffell
Auchencairn
Rockcliffe
Kippford
Penpont
Closeburn
Auldgirth
Holywood
Kirkpatrick Durham
Crocketford or Ninemile Bar
New Abbey
Kirkconnell
Templand
Johnstonebridge
St. Ann's
Bowness Common
Wedholme Flow
Allonby Bay
Kirkcudbright Bay
Auchencairn Bay
Rascarrel Bay
Port Mary
Abbey Head
Balcary Point
Borness Point
Grune Pt.
Dubmill Point
COPYRIGHT, GEORGE PHILIP & SON, LTD.

Adjoining page 48 Selkirk Selkirk Adjoining page 49 Lauder Kelso

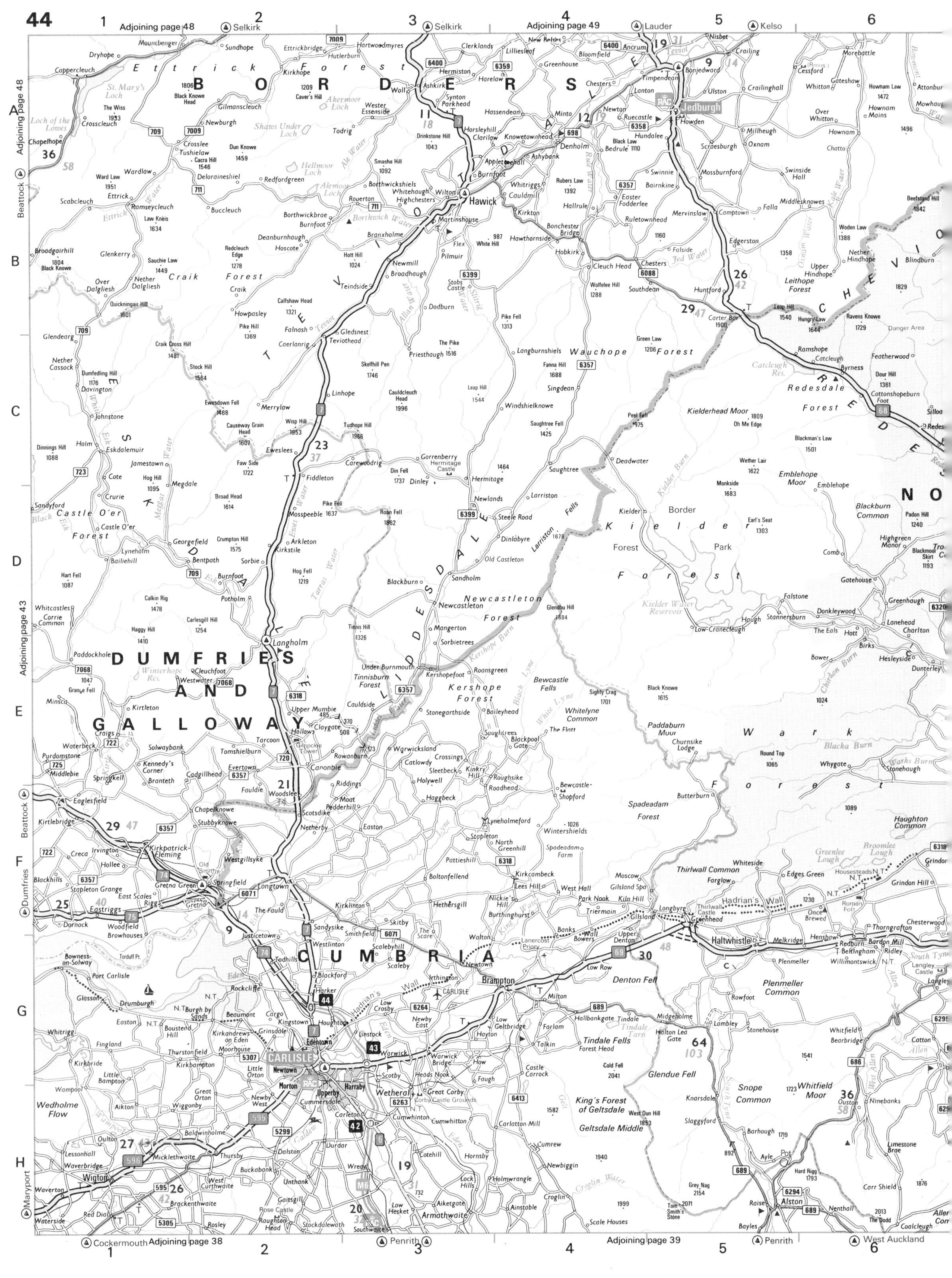

Adjoining page 49

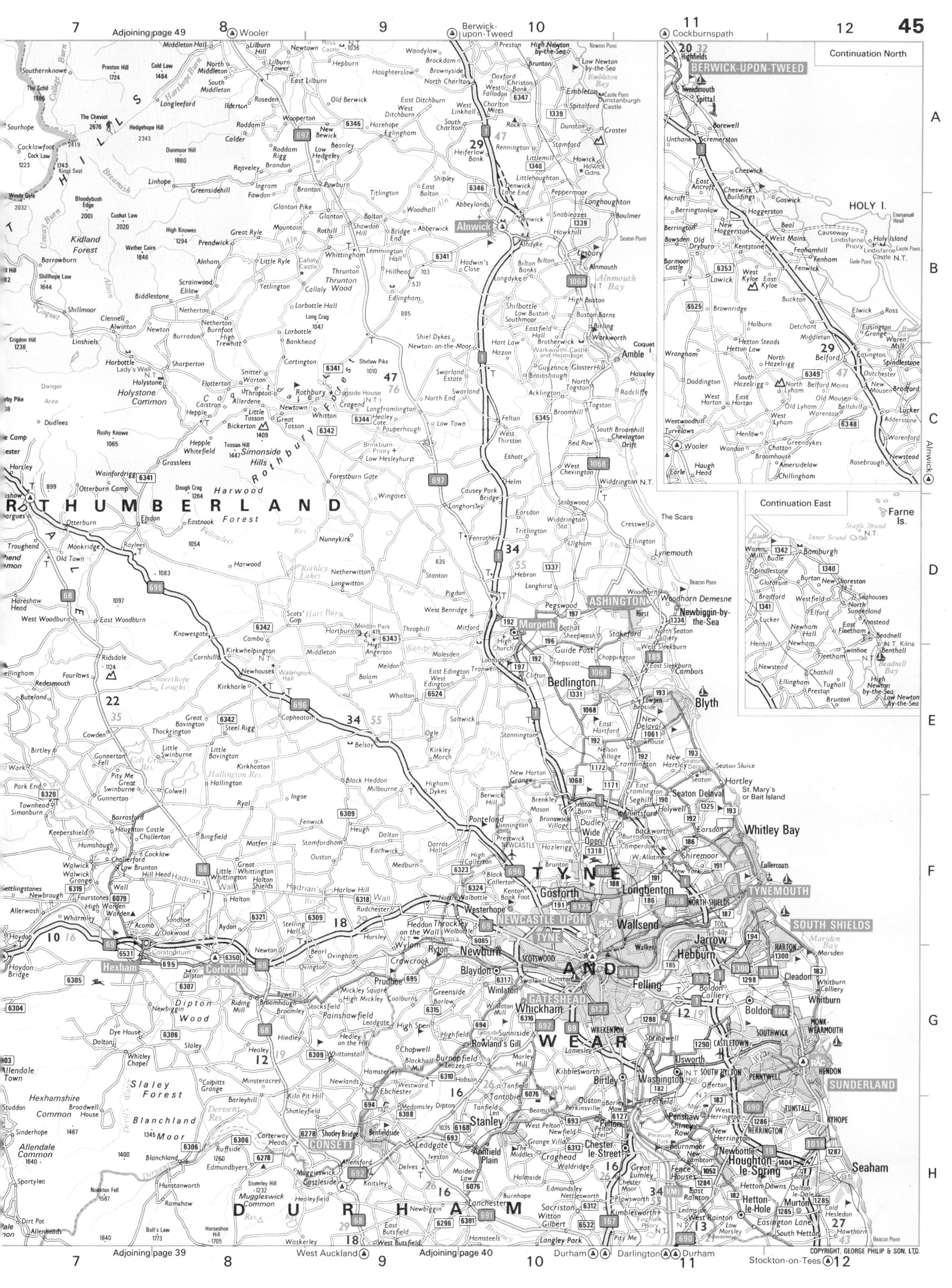

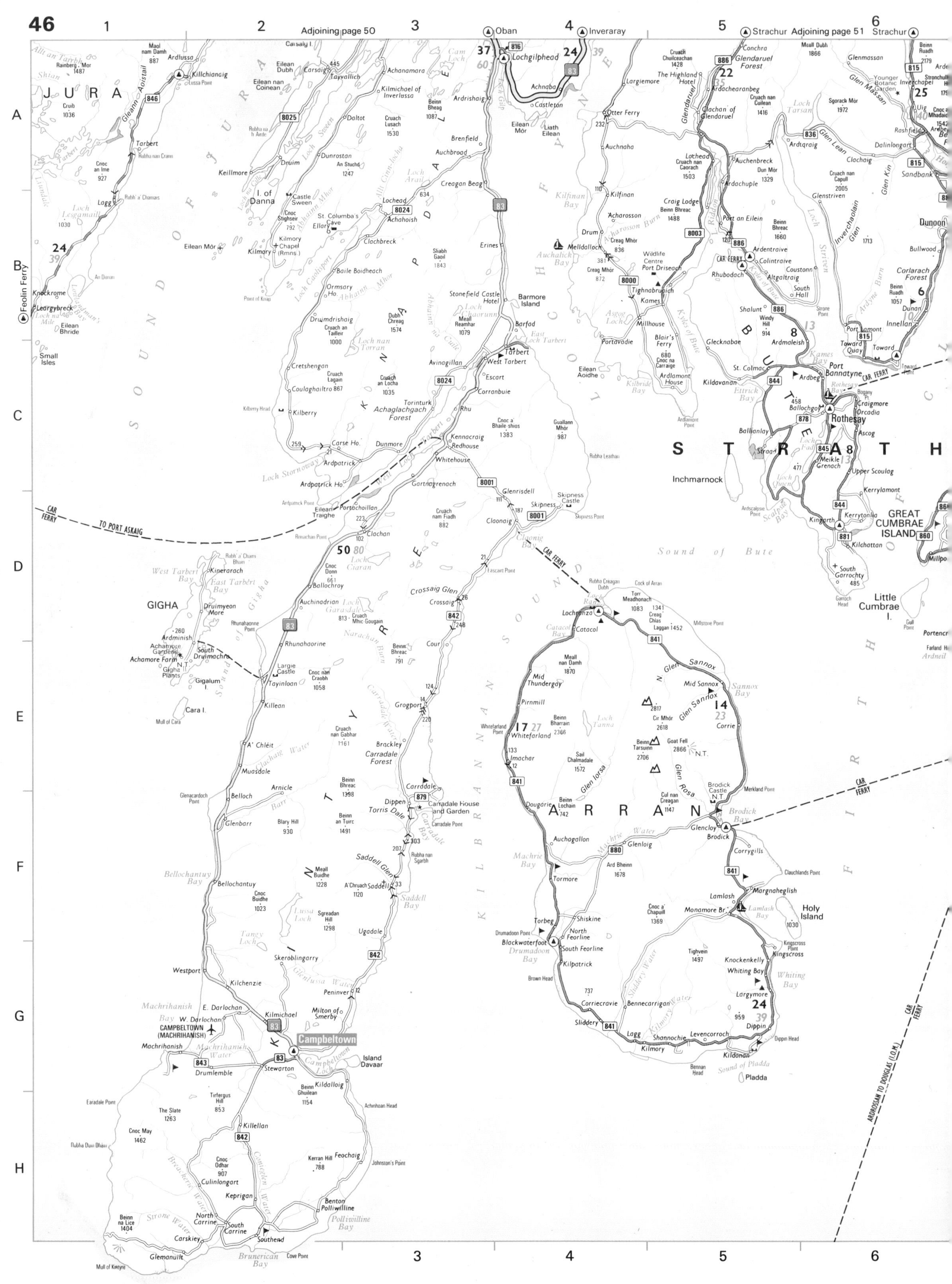

1
2
Adjoining page 50
3
Oban
4
Inveraray
5
Strachur
Adjoining page 51
Strachur
6
JURA
Killchianaig
Ardlussa
Maol nam Damh 887
Rainberg Mór 1487
Cruib 1036
Gleann Aoistail
Tarbert
Lagg
Loch Lesgamail 1030
Cnoc an Ime 927
SOUND OF JURA
Eilean Mór
Feolin Ferry
Knockrome
Leargybreck
Eilean Bhride
Small Isles
Carsaig
Tayvallich
Eilean Dubh
Eilean nan Coinean
Achanamara
Kilmichael of Inverlussa
Dunrostan
An Stuchd 1247
Daltot
Cruach Lusach 1530
Keillmore
Druim
I. of Danna
Castle Sween
Cnoc Stighseir 792
Kilmory
Kilmory Chapel (Rmns.)
Ellary
St. Columba's Cave
Lochead
Achahoish
Clachbreck
Baile Boidheach
Ormsary Ho.
Drumdrishaig
Cruach an Tailleir 1000
Loch nan Torran
Dubh Chreag 1574
Cretshengan
Cruach Lagain
Coulaghailtro 867
Cruach an Locha 1035
Kilberry
Kilberry Head
Carse Ho.
Ardpatrick
Ardpatrick Ho.
Loch Stornoway
Dunmore
KNAPDALE
Torinturk
Achaglachgach Forest
Sliabh Gaoil 1843
Lochgilphead
Ardrishaig
Achnaba
Castleton
Eilean Mór
Liath Eilean
Beinn Bheag 1087
Brenfield
Auchbroad
Creagan Beag
Erines
Stonefield Castle Hotel
Barmore Island
Meall Reamhar 1079
Barfad
East Loch Tarbert
Tarbert
West Tarbert
Avinagillan
Escart
Corranbuie
Rhu
Kennacraig
Redhouse
Whitehouse
West Loch Tarbert
Gartnagrenach
Cnoc a' Bhaile-shios 1383
Guallann Mhór 987
Cruach nam Fiadh 882
Glenrisdell
Skipness
Skipness Castle
Skipness Point
Claonaig
Portachoillan
Eilean Traighe
Clachan
Rubh' a' Chairn Bhain
Kinerarach
West Tarbert Bay
East Tarbert Bay
GIGHA
Druimyeon More
Ardminish
Achamore Gardens N.T.
Achamore Farm
Gigha Plants
South Druimachro
Gigalum I.
Cara I.
Mull of Cara
CAR FERRY
TO PORT ASKAIG
Loch Ciaran
Cnoc Donn 661
Ballochroy
Auchinadrian
Loch Garasdale
Cruach Mhic-Gougain 813
Rhunahaorine
Rhunahaorine Point
Largie Castle
Tayinloan
Cnoc nan Craobh 1058
Killean
Beinn Bhreac 791
Crossaig Glen
Crossaig
Cour
Grogport
Cruach nan Gabhar 1161
A' Chleit
Muasdale
Brackley
Carradale Forest
Belloch
Arnicle
Glenbarr
Beinn Bhreac 1398
Carradale
Dippen
Torris Dale
Carradale House and Garden
Carradale Point
Beinn an Tuirc 1491
Blary Hill 930
Bellochantuy Bay
Bellochantuy
Meall Buidhe 1228
Saddell Glen
A' Chruach 1120
Saddell
Saddell Bay
Cnoc Buidhe 1023
Sgreadan Hill 1298
Ugadale
Skeroblingarry
Westport
Kilchenzie
Peninver
Milton of Smerby
Machrihanish Bay
E. Darlochan
W. Darlochan
CAMPBELTOWN (MACHRIHANISH)
Kilmichael
Campbeltown
Machrihanish
Drumlemble
Stewarton
Island Davaar
Beinn Ghuilean 1154
Kildalloig
Tirfergus Hill 853
The Slate 1263
Cnoc Moy 1462
Killellan
Cnoc Odhar 907
Kerran Hill 788
Feochaig
Culinlongart
Keprigan
North Carrine
South Carrine
Beinn na Lice 1404
Benton
Polliwilline
Polliwilline Bay
Southend
Carskiey
Glemanuilt
Mull of Kintyre
Brunerican Bay
Cove Point
KINTYRE
KILBRANNAN SOUND
Otter Ferry
Largiemore
Auchnaha
Kilfinan
Kilfinan Bay
Acharosson
Drum
Melldalloch
Creag Mhór 836
Auchalick Bay
Creag Mhór 872
Wildlife Centre
Port Driseach
Tighnabruaich
Kames
Millhouse
Asgog Loch
Portavadie
Blair's Ferry
Cnoc na Carraige 680
Ardlamont House
Kilbride Bay
Eilean Aoidhe
Kyles of Bute
Conchra
Glendaruel Forest
Cruach Chuilceachan 1428
The Highland Hotel
Ardachearanbeg
Clachan of Glendaruel
Cruach nan Cuilean 1416
Lothead
Cruach nan Caorach 1503
Auchenbreck
Dun Mór 1329
Ardachuple
Craig Lodge
Beinn Bhreac 1488
Port an Eilein
Ardentraive
Colintraive
Rhubodach
Altgaltraig
Coustonn
South Hall
Beinn Bhreac 1660
Meall Dubh 1866
Glenmassan
Glen Massan
Younger Botanic Garden
Sgorach Mór 1972
Loch Tarsan
Ardtaraig
Glen Lean
Clachaig
Cruach nan Capull 2005
Glenstriven
Loch Striven
Inverchaolain Glen
Dalinlongart
Sandbank
Dunoon
Bullwood
Corlarach Forest
Beinn Ruadh 1057
Dunan
Innellan
Port Lamont
Toward Quay
Toward
Toward Point
Inverchapel
Rashfield
BUTE
Shalunt
Windy Hill 914
Ardmaleish
Kames Bay
Port Bannatyne
Ardbeg
Glecknabae
St. Colmac
Kildavanan
Ettrick Bay
Ballochgoy
Rothesay
Rothesay Bay
Craigmore
Orcadia
Ascog
Ballianlay
Straad
Loch Fad
Meikle Grenach
Loch Quien
Upper Scoulag
Kerrylamont
Scalpsie Bay
Kingarth
Kerrytonlia
Inchmarnock
STRATH
GREAT CUMBRAE ISLAND
Kilchattan
South Garrochty 485
Garroch Head
Little Cumbrae I.
Millport
Sound of Bute
FIRTH OF CLYDE
ARRAN
Lochranza
Loch Ranza
Catacol
Catacol Bay
Cock of Arran
Torr Meadhonach 1083
Creag Chlas
Laggan 1452
Millstone Point
Meall nan Damh 1870
Glen Sannox
Mid Sannox
Sannox Bay
Mid Thundergay
Pirnmill
Beinn Bharrain 2366
Loch Tanna
Cir Mhór 2618
Glen Sannox
Corrie
Whitefarland
Whitefarland Point
Imachar
Beinn Tarsuinn 2706
Goat Fell 2866 N.T.
Sail Chalmadale 1572
Glen Iorsa
Glen Rosa
Brodick Castle N.T.
Merkland Point
Dougarie
Beinn Lochain 742
Cul nan Creagan 1147
Brodick Bay
Glencloy
Brodick
Machrie Water
Auchagallon
Glenloig
Machrie Bay
Ard Bheinn 1678
Corrygills
Clauchlands Point
Tormore
Lamlash
Margnaheglish
Lamlash Bay
Holy Island 1030
Monamore Br.
Cnoc a' Chapuill 1369
Torbeg
Shiskine
Drumadoon Point
Blackwaterfoot
North Feorline
South Feorline
Drumadoon Bay
Brown Head
Kilpatrick
Tighvein 1497
Kingscross Point
Kingscross
Knockenkelly
Whiting Bay
Largymore
Corriecravie
Bennecarrigan
Sliddery
Lagg
Kilmory
Shannochie
Levencorroch
Dippin
Dippin Head
Kildonan
Bennan Head
Sound of Pladda
Pladda
CAR FERRY
ARDROSSAN TO DOUGLAS (I.O.M.)
A
B
C
D
E
F
G
H

Adjoining page 51
Adjoining page 52
Adjoining page 48

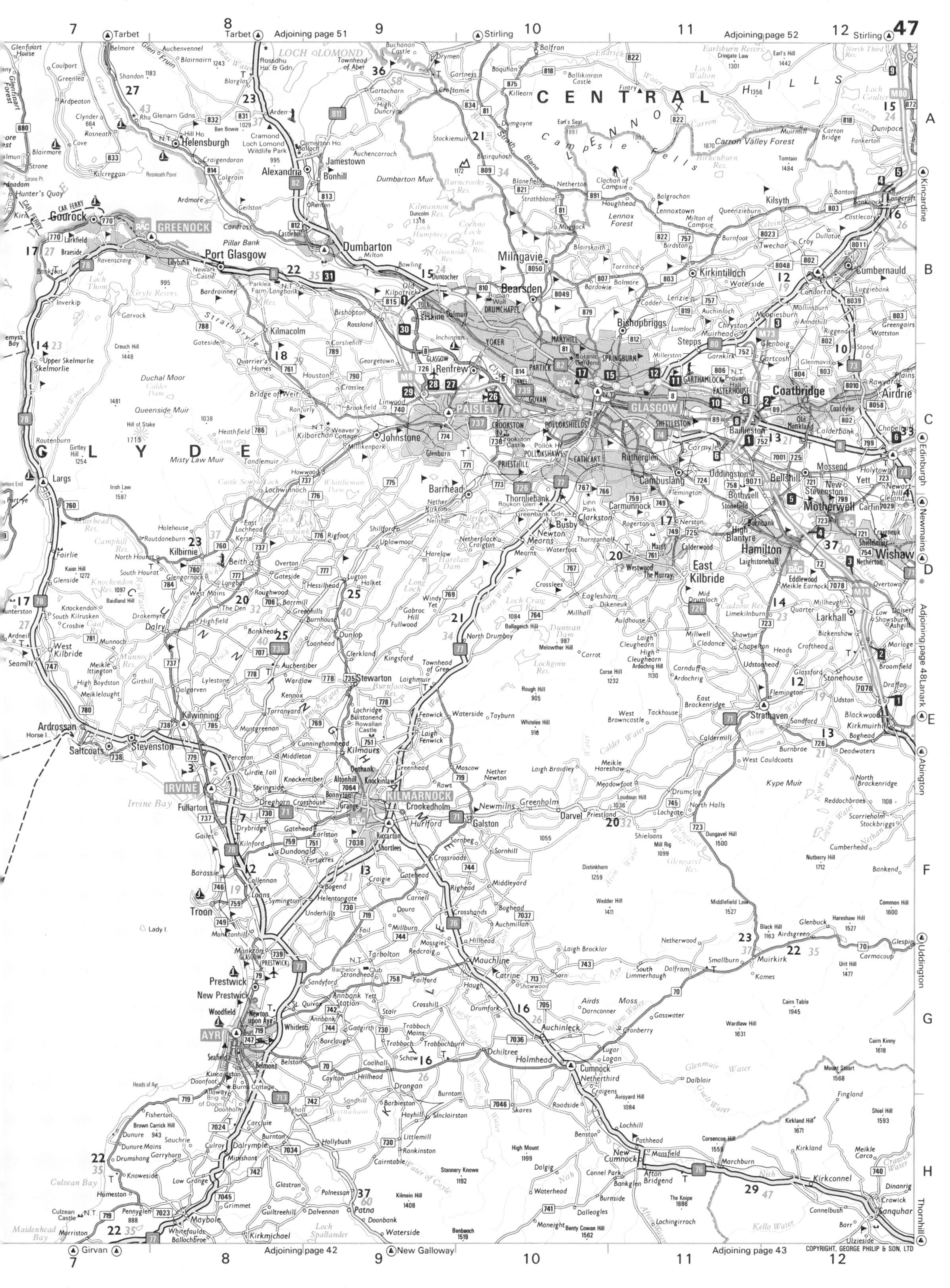

Adjoining page 42
Adjoining page 43

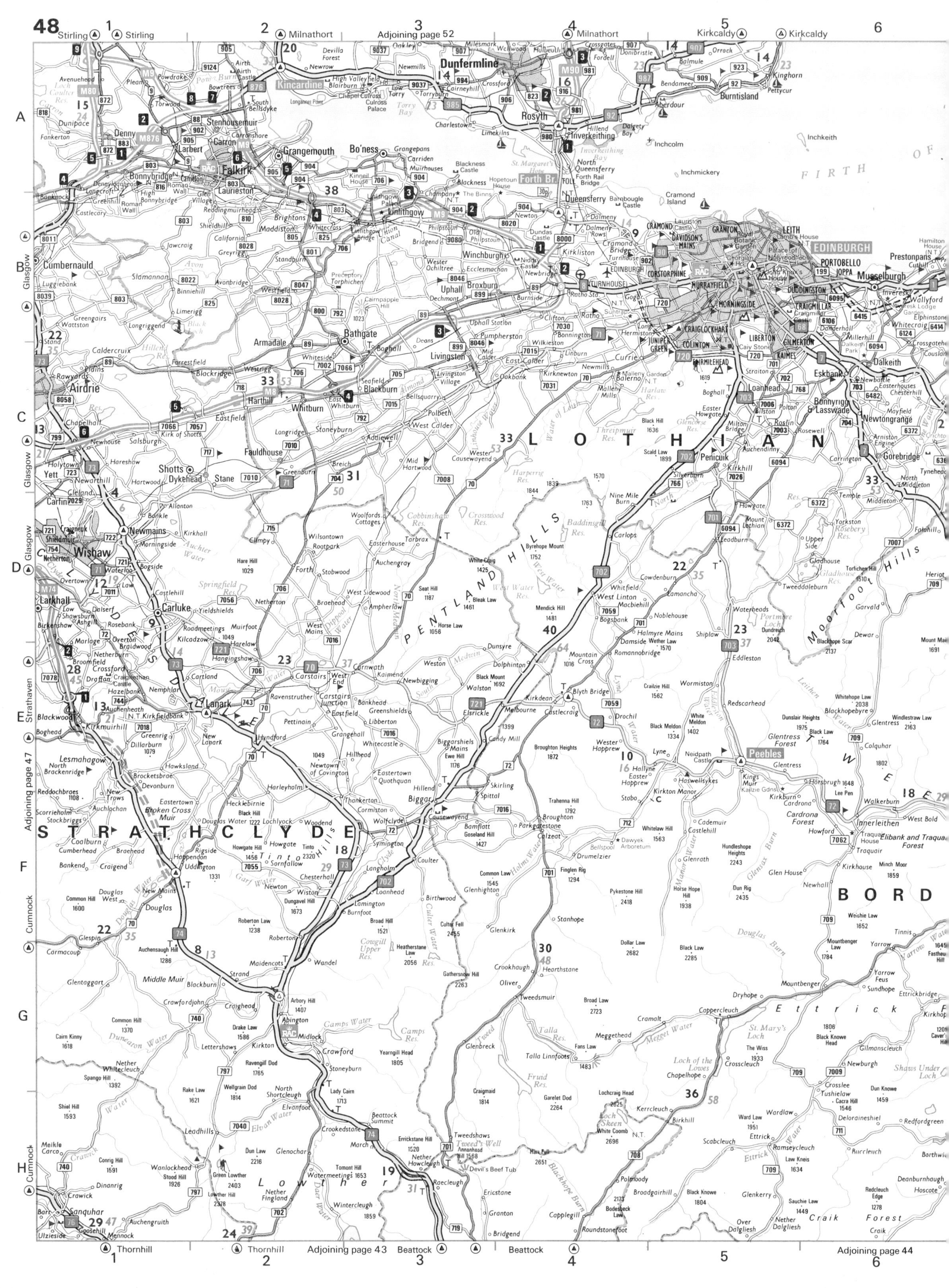
A
B
C
D
E
F
G
H
Glasgow
Strathaven
Adjoining page 47
Cumnock
Dunfermline
Rosyth
Inverkeithing
Kincardine
Burntisland
Kinghorn
Aberdour
Inchkeith
Inchcolm
Inchmickery
FIRTH OF
Forth Br.
Queensferry
Cramond Island
Grangemouth
Bo'ness
Falkirk
Larbert
Denny
Stenhousemuir
Carron
Bonnybridge
Linlithgow
Cumbernauld
Airdrie
EDINBURGH
LEITH
GRANTON
PORTOBELLO
JOPPA
Musselburgh
Prestonpans
Dalkeith
Eskbank
Bonnyrigg & Lasswade
Newtongrange
Gorebridge
Penicuik
Loanhead
CORSTORPHINE
MURRAYFIELD
MORNINGSIDE
CRAIGLOCKHART
COLINTON
LIBERTON
GILMERTON
DUDDINGSTON
CRAIGMILLAR
Winchburgh
Broxburn
Uphall
Livingston
Bathgate
Armadale
Whitburn
Blackburn
West Calder
Fauldhouse
Shotts
Harthill
Wishaw
Newmains
Carluke
Larkhall
Lanark
Carstairs
Biggar
Lesmahagow
Douglas
Abington
Crawford
Leadhills
Wanlockhead
Sanquhar
Peebles
Innerleithen
West Linton
Carlops
Tweedsmuir
LOTHIAN
PENTLAND HILLS
Moorfoot Hills
STRATHCLYDE
Tinto Hills
Lowther
TWEED
BORD
Ettrick
Craik Forest

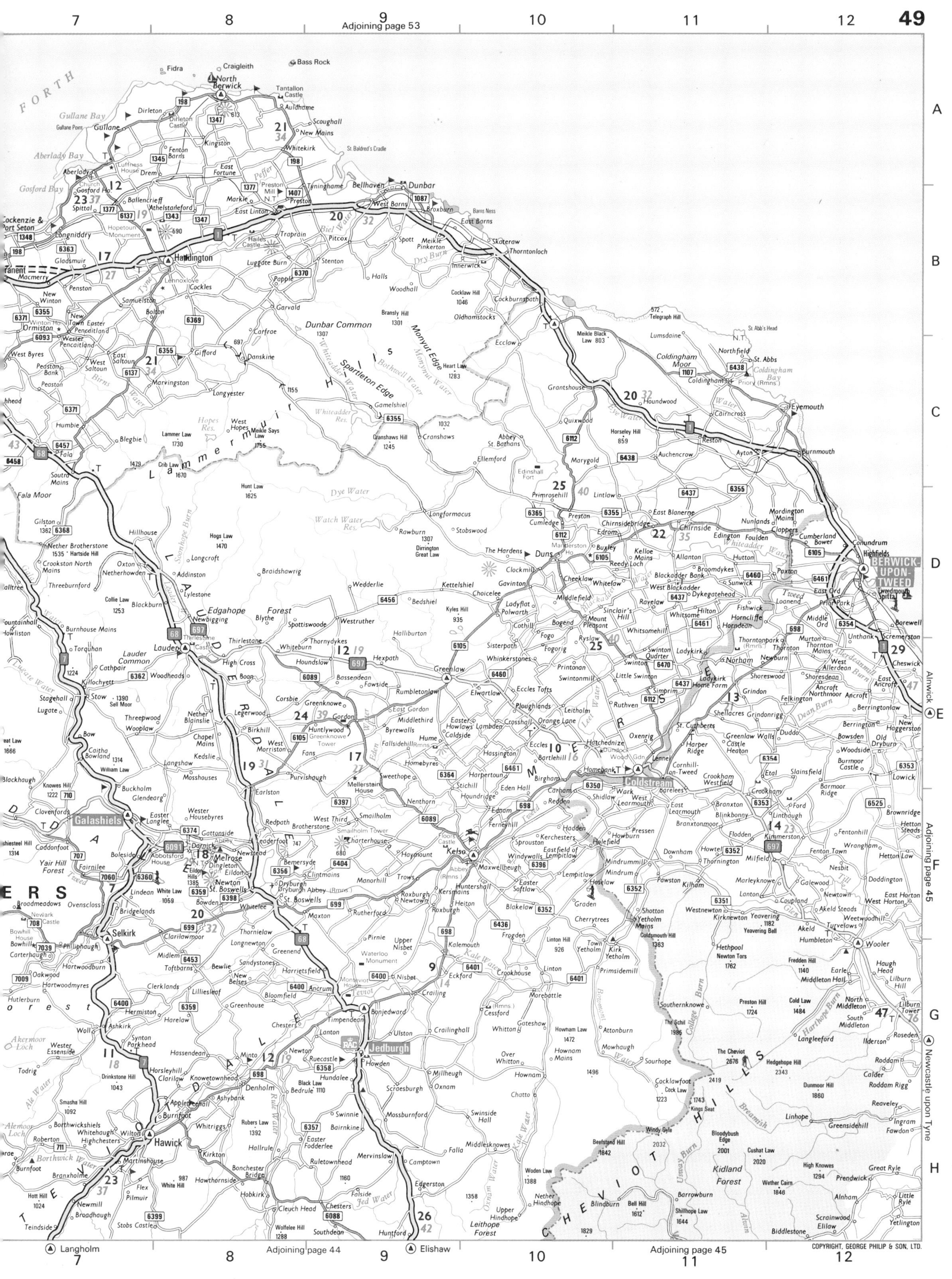
49
Adjoining page 53
Adjoining page 44
Adjoining page 45
Alnwick
Newcastle upon Tyne
Langholm
Elishaw
FORTH
Bass Rock
Craigleith
Fidra
North Berwick
Tantallon Castle
Auldhame
Scoughall
New Mains
Whitekirk
St. Baldred's Cradle
Gullane Bay
Gullane Point
Gullane
Dirleton
Dirleton Castle
Fenton Barns
Kingston
Aberlady Bay
Aberlady
Luffness House
Drem
East Fortune
Gosford Bay
Gosford Ho
Spittal
Ballencrieff
Athelstaneford
Preston Mill
Tyninghame
Bellhaven
Dunbar
Markle
Preston
East Linton
West Barns
Broxburn
Barns Ness
East Barns
Cockenzie & Port Seton
Longniddry
Hopetoun Monument
Hailes Castle
Traprain
Biel Water
Pitcox
Spott
Meikle Pinkerton
Skateraw
Thorntonloch
Gladsmuir
Haddington
Tranent
Macmerry
Penston
Lennoxlove
Cockles
Luggate Burn
Popple
Stenton
Halls
Dry Burn
Innerwick
Woodhall
Cocklaw Hill
Cockburnspath
New Winton
Samuelston
Bolton
Garvald
Dunbar Common
Bransly Hill
Oldhamstocks
Winton Ho
Ormiston
New Town
Easter Pencaitland
Wester Pencaitland
Carfrae
Monynut Edge
Telegraph Hill
St. Abb's Head
Lumsdaine
Meikle Black Law
Ecclaw
West Byres
Pencaitland
Pedston Bank
West Saltoun
East Saltoun
Gifford
Danskine
Spartleton Edge
Bothwell Water
Monynut Water
Heart Law
Coldingham Moor
Northfield
St. Abbs
Coldingham
Coldingham Bay
Priory (Rmns)
Peaston
Marvingston
Longyester
Gamelshiel
Grantshouse
Houndwood
Eyemouth
Whiteadder Res.
Humbie
Hopes Res.
West Hopes
Meikle Says Law
Cranshaws Hill
Cranshaws
Quixwood
Eye Water
Horseley Hill
Cairncross
Reston
Blegbie
Lammer Law
Lammermuir
Abbey St. Bathans
Ayton
Burnmouth
Auchencrow
Marygold
Fala
Crib Law
Soutra Mains
Ellemford
Edinshall Fort
Fala Moor
Hunt Law
Dye Water
Primrosehill
Linthlaw
Gilston
Longformacus
Watch Water Res.
Rawburn
Stobswood
Preston
Cumledge
Chirnsidebridge
East Blanerne
Nunlands
Mordington Mains
Hillhouse
Soonhope Burn
Hogs Law
Dirrington Great Law
The Hardens
Duns
Manderston Ho
Edrom
Chirnside
Edington
Foulden
Clappers
Cumberland Bower
Conundrum
Highfields
Nether Brotherstone
Hartside Hill
Crookston North Mains
Longcroft
Oxton
Netherhowden
Addinston
Braidshawrig
Clockmill
Buxley
Kelloe Mains
Allanton
Hutton
Whiteadder Water
Paxton
BERWICK-UPON-TWEED
Threeburnford
Lylestone
Wedderlie
Kettelshiel
Gavinton
Cheeklaw
Whitelaw
Blackadder Bank
Broomdykes
Sunwick
Tweedmouth
Spittal
Collie Law
Blackburn
Edgahope
Forest
Bedshiel
Choicelee
Ladyflat
Polwarth
Middlefield
West Blackadder
Dykegatehead
East Ord
Newbigging
Blythe
Spottiswoode
Westruther
Kyles Hill
Cothill
Bogend
Sinclair's Hill
Rayelaw
Whitsome
Hilton
Fishwick
Loanend
Horncliffe
Horndean
Middle Ord
Prior Park
Borewell
Burnhouse Mains
Halliburton
Mount Pleasant
Whitsomehill
Scremerston
Torquhan
Lauder
Thirlestane
Thirlestane Castle
Whiteburn
Thornydykes
Hexpath
Sisterpath
Fogo
Ryslaw
Swinton Quarter
Ladykirk
Thorntonpark
Thornton
Murton
Thornton Mains
Unthank
Cheswick
Lauder Common
Cathpair
High Cross
Houndslow
Greenlaw
Whinkerstones
Fogorig
Printonan
Swinton
Norham
Newburn
West Allerdean
Allerdean Burn
Boon
Bassendean
Fawside
Rumbletonlaw
Swintonmill
Little Swinton
Shoreswood
Shoresdean
East Ancroft
Ancroft Northmoor
Ancroft
Woodheads
Killochyett
Stow
Sell Moor
Corsbie
Greenknowe
Elwartlaw
Eccles Tofts
Simprim
Ladykirk Home Farm
Grindon
Felkington
Stagehall
Lugate
Legerwood
Gordon
East Gordon
Easter Howlaws
Lambden
Crosshall
Ploughlands
Leitholm
Ruthven
Shellacres
Grindonrigg
Dean Burn
Berringtonlaw
Nether Blainslie
Threepwood
Wooplaw
Birkhill
Huntlywood
Greenknowe Tower
Middlethird
Byrewalls
Caldside
Orange Lane
Leet Water
St. Cuthberts
Berrington
New Haggerston
Caitha Bowland
William Law
Chapel Mains
Kedslie
West Morriston
Fans
Fallsidehill
Hume
Eccles
Bartlehill
Hatchednize
Oxenrig
Harper Ridge
Greenlaw Walls
Castle Heaton
Duddo
Bowsden
Old Dryburn
Langshaw
Mosshouses
Purvishaugh
Homebyres
Mellerstain House
Sweethope
Harpertoun
Hassington
Dundock Wood Gdn
Lennel
Cornhill-on-Tweed
Etal
Slainsfield
Woodside
Burnmoor Castle
Lowick
Blackhaugh
Knowes Hill
Buckholm
Glendearg
Earlston
Stichill
Eden Hall
Birgham
Homebank
Coldstream
Crookham Westfield
Crookham
Barmoor Ridge
Clovenfords
Galashiels
Easter Langlee
Wester Housebyres
Redpath
Brotherstone
West Third
Smailholm
Nenthorn
Houndridge
Ednam
Carham
Redden
Wark
West Learmouth
Shidlaw
East Learmouth
Branxton
Branxtonmoor
Blinkbonny
Ford
Linthaugh
Brownridge
Hetton Steads
Gattonside
Darnick
Leaderfoot
Smailholm Tower
Charterhouse
Floors Castle
Ferneyhill
Hadden
Kerchesters
Sprouston
Pressen
Howburn
Flodden
Kimmerston
Fentonhill
Wrangham
Caddonfoot
Yair Hill Forest
Fairnilee
Boleside
Abbotsford House
Melrose
Newstead
Bemersyde
Haymount
Kelso
Windywalls
Eastfield of Lempitlaw
Helefield
Mindrummill
Downham
Howtel
Thornington
Milfield
Fenton Town
Hetton Law
Eildon Hills
Dingleton
Eildon
Clintmains
Manorhill
Trows
Maxwellheugh
Lempitlaw
Mindrum
Marleyknowe
Galewood
Doddington
Lindean
White Law
Newton St. Boswells
Dryburgh
Dryburgh Abbey (Rmns)
Roxburgh Newtown
Kersmains
Huntershall
Easter Softlaw
Hoselaw
Pawston
Kilham
Lanton
Coupland
Newtown
East Horton
West Horton
Broadmeadows
Ovenscloss
Bridgelands
Bowden
Whitelee
St. Boswells
Heiton
Roxburgh
Blakelaw
Graden
Shotton
Yetholm Mains
Westnewton
Kirknewton
Yeavering
Yeavering Bell
Akeld Steads
Akeld
Weetwoodhill
Newark Castle
Selkirk
Philiphaugh
Clarilawmoor
Maxton
Rutherford
Thornielaw
Cherrytrees
Coldsmouth Hill
Humbleton
Turvelaws
Wooler
Bowhill House
Bowhill
Carterhaugh
Longnewton
Greenend
Pirnie
Upper Nisbet
Kalemouth
Frogden
Linton Hill
Town Yetholm
Kirk Yetholm
Hethpool
Newton Tors
Fredden Hill
Haugh Head
Oakwood
Hartwoodburn
Midlem
Toftbarns
Sandystones
Waterloo Monument
Kale Water
Crookhouse
Linton
Primsidemill
Earle
Middleton Hall
Lilburn Hill
Hartwoodmyres
Bewlie
New Belses
Harrietsfield
Monteviot House
Nisbet
Eckford
Clerklands
Lilliesleaf
Bloomfield
Ancrum
Teviot
Crailing
Cessford
Morebattle
Southernknowe
College Burn
Preston Hill
Cold Law
North Middleton
Lilburn Tower
Hutlerburn
Greenhouse
Hermiston
Ashkirk
Harelaw
Chesters
Timpendean
Bonjedward
Gateshaw
Whitton
Attonburn
The Schil
South Middleton
Hartope Burn
Roseden
Woll
Synton
Akermoor Loch
Wester Essenside
Parkhead
Lanton
Ulston
Crailinghall
Howman Law
Langleeford
Ilderton
Hassendean
Minto
Newton
Ruecastle
RAC
Jedburgh
Over Whitton
Hownam Mains
Mowhaugh
The Cheviot
Hedgehope Hill
Roddam
Todrig
Horsleyhill
Clarilaw
Knowetownhead
Howden
Millheugh
Sourhope
Calder
Roddam Rigg
Drinkstone Hill
Denholm
Black Law
Bedrule
Hundalee
Oxnam
Hownam
Cocklawfoot
Cock Law
Dunmoor Hill
Ale Water
Appletreehall
Ashybank
Rule Water
Scraesburgh
Chatto
Reaveley
Smasha Hill
Burnfoot
Kings Seat
Linhope
Ingram
Fawdon
Alemoor Loch
Borthwickshiels
Whitehaugh
Wilton
Rubers Law
Whitriggs
Swinnie
Bairnkine
Mossburnford
Swinside Hall
Windy Gyle
Breamish
Greensidehill
Robertson
Highchesters
Hawick
Hallrule
Easter Fodderlee
Kirkton
Falla
Middlesknowes
Beefstand Hill
Bloodybush Edge
Cushat Law
Great Ryle
Borthwick Water
Martinshouse
Bonchester Bridge
Ruletownhead
Mervinslaw
Camptown
Woden Law
Kidland Forest
High Knowes
Prendwick
Branxholme
Flex
Pilmuir
White Hill
Hawthornside
Hobkirk
Falside
Edgerston
Oxnam Water
Nether Hindhope
Barrowburn
Wether Cairn
Alnham
Little Ryle
Hott Hill
Newmill
Broadhaugh
Cleuch Head
Chesters
Jed Water
Upper Hindhope
Blindburn
Bell Hill
Shillhope Law
Scrainwood
Elilaw
Teindside
Stobs Castle
Wolfelee Hill
Southdean
Huntford
Leithope Forest
Biddlestone
Yetlington
CHEVIOT HILLS
LAMMERMUIR HILLS
LAUDERDALE
MERSE
TEVIOTDALE
COPYRIGHT, GEORGE PHILIP & SON, LTD.

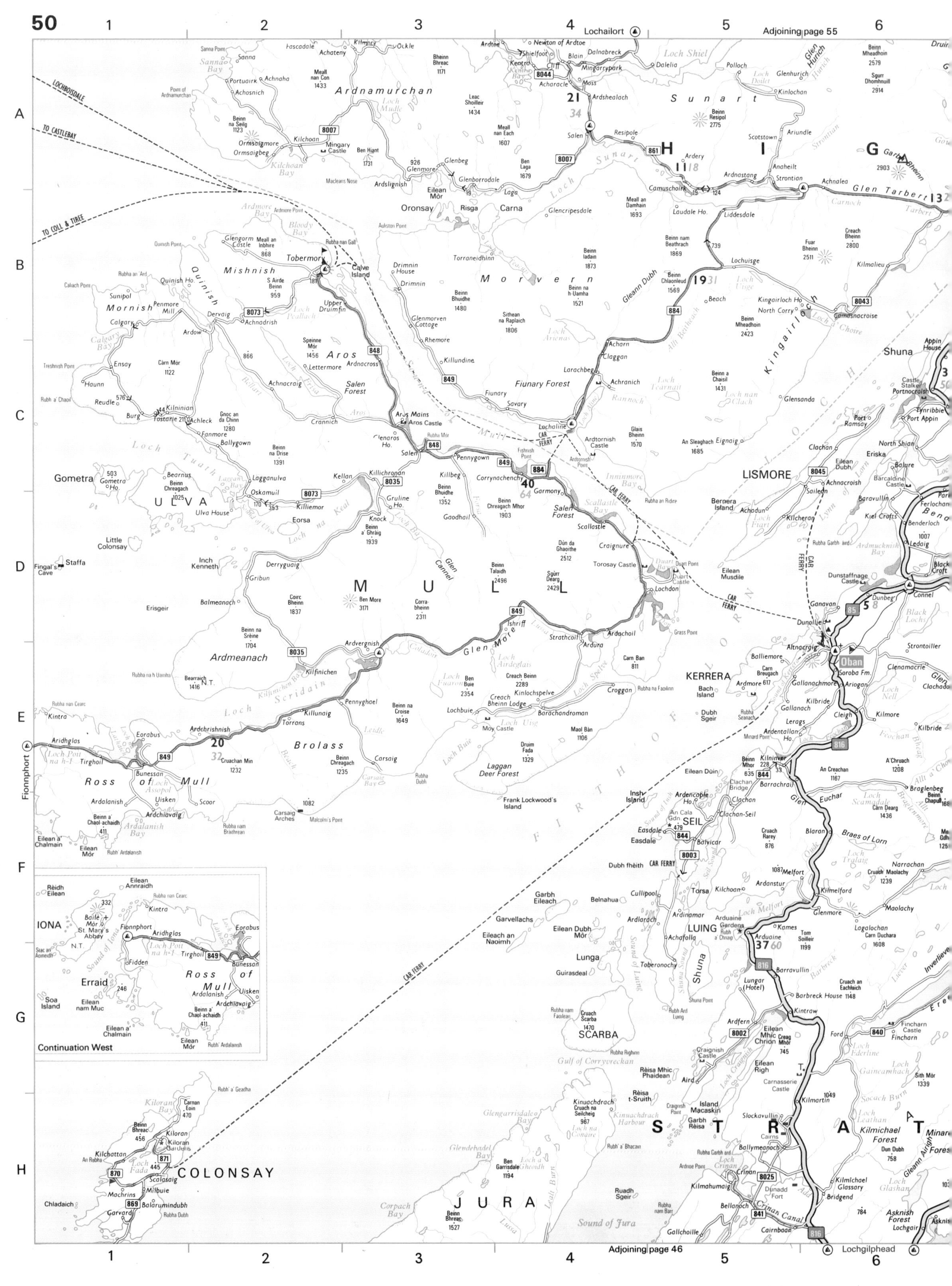
1 2 3 4 5 6
A B C D E F G H
Lochailort
Adjoining page 55
Adjoining page 46
Lochgilphead
Sanna Point
Sanna
Sanna Bay
Fascadale
Achateny
Kilmory
Ockle
Portuairk
Achnaha
Point of Ardnamurchan
Achosnich
Meall nan Con 1433
Ardnamurchan
Bheinn Bhreac 1171
Leac Shoilleir 1434
Loch Mudle
Beinn na Seilg 1123
Ormsaigmore
Ormsaigbeg
Kilchoan
Kilchoan Bay
Mingary Castle
Ben Hiant 1731
LOCHBOISDALE
TO CASTLEBAY
TO COLL & TIREE
Macleans Nose
Ardslignish
Glenmore
Glenbeg
Glenborrodale
Eilean Mòr
Oronsay
Risga
Carna
Meall nan Each 1607
Ben Laga 1679
Laga
Loch Sunart
Glencripesdale
Ardtoe
Newton of Ardtoe
Shielfoot
Kentra
Kentra Bay
Blain
Mingarrypark
Dalnabreck
Acharacle
Moss
Ardshealach
Salen
Resipole
Loch Shiel
Dalelia
Polloch
Glen Hurich
Glenhurich
Loch Doilet
Kinlochan
Sunart
Beinn Resipol 2775
Scotstown
Ariundle
Strontian
Anaheilt
Ardnastang
Ardery
Camuschoirk
Laudale Ho.
Liddesdale
Achnalea
Glen Tarbert
Carnoch
Tarbert
Beinn Mheadhoin 2579
Sgurr Dhomhnuill 2914
Garbh Bheinn 2903
Meall an Damhain 1693
Ardmore Bay
Ardmore Point
Bloody Bay
Aulistori Point
Quinish Point
Glengorm Castle
Meall an Inbhire 868
Rubha nan Gall
Tobermory
Calve Island
Mishnish
Quinish
Quinish Ho.
S Airde Beinn 959
Rubha an 'Ard
Caliach Point
Sunipol
Mornish
Penmore Mill
Dervaig
Achnadrish
Loch Peallach
Upper Druimfin
Calgary
Calgary Bay
Ardow
Drimnin House
Drimnin
Beinn Bhuidhe 1480
Torraneidhinn
Morvern
Beinn Iadain 1873
Beinn na h-Uamha 1521
Beinn nam Beathrach 1869
Glenmorven Cottage
Rhemore
Sithean na Raplaich 1806
Loch Arienas
Killundine
Fiunary Forest
Fiunary
Savary
Gleann Dubh
Beinn Chlaonleud 1569
Lochuisge
Loch Uisge
Beach
Fuar Bheinn 2511
Creach Bheinn 2800
Kilmalieu
Kingairloch Ho.
North Corry
Camasnacroise
Beinn Mheadhoin 2423
Kingairloch
Loch a' Choire
Acharn
Claggan
Larachbeg
Achranich
Loch Tearnait
Rannoch
Beinn a Chaisil 1431
Loch nan Clach
Glensanda
Treshnish Point
Ensay
Haunn
Càrn Mòr 1122
Speinne Mòr 1456
Aros
Lettermore
Ardnacross
Salen Forest
Achnacraig
Loch Frisa
Rubh' a' Chaoil
Reudle
Burg
Kilninian
Tostarie
Achleck
Gnoc an da Chinn 1280
Crannich
Aros Mains
Aros Castle
Lochaline
Mull
CAR FERRY
Ardtornish Castle
Ardtornish Point
Glais Bheinn 1570
An Sleaghach 1685
Eignaig
Fanmore
Ballygown
Loch Tuath
Beinn na Drise 1391
Glenaros Ho.
Salen
Rubha Mòr
Pennygown
Fishnish Point
Killbeg
Corrynachenchy
Garmony
Gometra
Gometra Ho.
Beàrnus
Beinn Chreagach 1025
Lagganulva
Oskamuil
Kellan
Killichronan
ULVA
Ulva House
Killiemor
Gruline Ho.
Knock
Loch na Keal
Eorsa
Beinn Bhuidhe 1352
Gaodhail
Beinn Chreagach Mhor 1903
Salen Forest
Scallastle Bay
Scallastle
Innimmore Bay
Rubha an Ridire
Bernera Island
Achadun
Loch Fiart
Kilcheran
LISMORE
Clachan
Eilean Dubh
Achnacroish
Sailean
Port Ramsay
Eriska
North Shian
Balure
Barcaldine Castle
Baravullin
Ferlochan
Kiel Crofts
Benderloch
Ledaig
Shuna
Appin House
Castle Stalker
Portnacroish
Tynribbie
Port Appin
Little Colonsay
Fingal's Cave
Staffa
Inch Kenneth
Beinn a' Ghràig 1939
Glen Cannel
Craignure
Dùn da Ghaoithe 2512
Torosay Castle
Duart Bay
Duart Point
Duart Castle
Eilean Musdile
Rubha Garbh aird
Ardmucknish Bay
Dunstaffnage Castle
Connel
Black Crofts
Derryguaig
Gribun
MULL
Beinn Talaidh 2496
Sgùrr Dearg 2429
Lochdon
Erisgeir
Balmeanach
Coirc Bheinn 1837
Ben More 3171
Corra-bheinn 2311
Ishriff
Ardachoil
Grass Point
Ganavan
Dunbeg
Dunollie
Black Lochs
Beinn na Srèine 1704
Ardvergnish
Glen More
Strathcoil
Ardura
Carn Ban 811
Altnacraig
Oban
Soroba Fm.
Strontoiller
Clenamacrie
Ardmeanach
Loch Airdeglais
Ballimore
Carn Breugach
Gallanachmore
Ariogan
Rubha na h Uamha
Bearraich 1416
N.T.
Kilfinichen
Kilfinichen Bay
Loch Scridain
Loch Fuaron
Ben Buie 2354
Creach Beinn 2289
Kinlochspelve
Loch Spelve
Croggan
Rubha na Faoilinn
KERRERA
Ardmore
Bach Island
Kilbride
Gallanach
Loch Nell
Rubha nan Cearc
Kintra
Pennyghael
Killunaig
Beinn na Croise 1649
Lochbuie
Creach Bheinn Lodge
Barachandroman
Dubh Sgeir
Lerags
Cleigh
Kilmore
Fionnphort
Aridhglas
Eorabus
Ardchrishnish
Torrans
Moy Castle
Loch Uisg
Maol Bàn 1106
Ardentallan Ho.
Minard Point
Kilbride
Feochan
Loch Poit na h-I
Tirghoil
Ross of Mull
Bunessan
Loch Assopol
Brolass
Beinn Chreagach 1235
Carsaig
Cruachan Min 1232
Loch Buie
Druim Fada 1329
Laggan Deer Forest
Eilean Dùin
Beinn Mhor 635
Kilninver
An Creachan 1167
A'Chruach 1208
Braglenbeg
Beinn Chapull
Ardalanish
Uisken
Scoor
Carsaig Bay
Rubha Dubh
Frank Lockwood's Island
Insh Island
Clachan Bridge
Clachan
Barrachrail
Glen Euchar
Loch Scamadale
Càrn Dearg 1436
Beinn a' Chaol-achaidh 411
Ardchiavaig
Ardalanish Bay
Carsaig Arches
Malcolm's Point
Rubha nam Braithrean
Ardencople Ho.
An Cala Gdn.
SEIL
Clachan-Seil
Easdale
Balvicar
Cruach Rarey 876
Blarcan
Braes of Lorn
Eilean a' Chalmain
Eilean Mòr
Rubh' Ardalanish
FIRTH OF LORN
Dubh fhèith
CAR FERRY
Melfort
Loch Tralaig
Narrachan
Cruach Maolachy 1239
Eilean Annraidh
Rèidh Eilean
Rubha nan Cearc
Kintra
IONA
Baile Mòr
St. Mary's Abbey
Fionnphort
Aridhglas
Eorabus
Stac an Aoineidh
N.T.
Sound of Iona
Fidden
Tirghoil
Erraid
Soa Island
Eilean nam Muc
Eilean a' Chalmain
Continuation West
Garbh Eileach
Garvellachs
Eileach an Naoimh
Belnahua
Cullipool
Ardinamar
Ardlarach
Achafolla
LUING
Eilean Dubh Mòr
Lunga
Toberonochy
Guirasdeal
Shuna
Shuna Point
Torsa
Kilchoan
Ardanstur
Kilmelford
Glenmore
Maolachy
Arduaine Gardens
Rubh' a Chnaip
Kames
Arduaine
Tom Soilleir 1199
Lagalochan
Carn Duchara 1608
Barravullin
Lunga (Hotel)
Barbreck House
Cruach an Eachlaich 1148
Rubha nam Faoilean
Cruach Scarba 1470
SCARBA
Rubh Ard Luing
Kintraw
Ardfern
Eilean Mhic Chrion
Creag Mhòr 745
Fincharn Castle
Fincharn
Ford
Loch Ederline
Rubha Righinn
Gulf of Corryvreckan
Craignish Castle
Rèisa Mhic Phaidean
Aird
Eilean Righ
Carnasserie Castle
Loch Gaineamhach
Sìth Mòr 1339
Kiloran Bay
Carnan Eoin 470
Rubh' a' Geadha
Glengarrisdale Bay
Kinuachdrachd
Cruach na Seilcheig 967
Loch na Conaire
Kinuachdrachd Harbour
Rèisa t-Sruith
Island Macaskin
Garbh Rèisa
Kilmartin
Slockavullin
Socach Burn
Loch Leathan
Kilmichael Forest
Dun Dubh 758
Beinn Bhreac 456
Kiloran
Kiloran Gardens
Kilchattan
An Rabha
Loch Fada
Scalasaig
COLONSAY
Machrins
Milbuie
Balarumindubh
Chladaich
Garvard
Rubha Dubh
Glendebadel Bay
Ben Garrisdale 1194
Loch a' Gheodh
Rubh' a' Bhacain
STRATH
Cairns
Ballymeanoch
Rubha Garbh ard
Ardnoe Point
Loch Crinan
Crinan
Kilmahumaig
Dunadd Fort
Kilmichael Glassary
Bridgend
Loch Glashan
Ruadh Sgeir
JURA
Corpach Bay
Beinn Bhreac 1527
Lussa
Sound of Jura
Rubha nam Barr
Bellanoch
Crinan Canal
Gallchoille
Cairnbaan
784
Asknish Forest
Lochgair
8044 8007 861 19 124 8043 8073 848 849 884 8035 8073 8045 85 816 844 8003 8002 840 870 871 869 8025 841

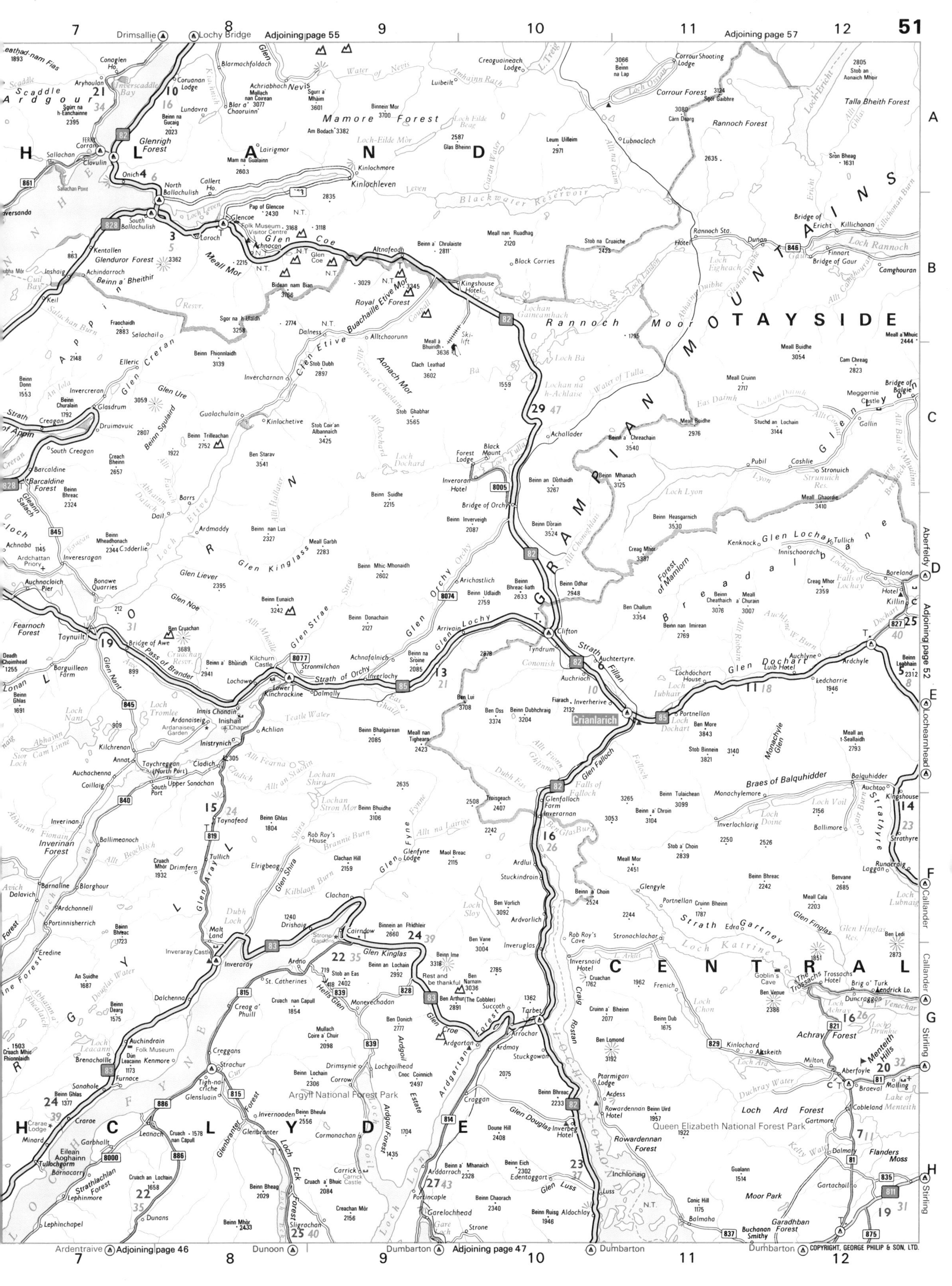
Drimsallie
Lochy Bridge
Adjoining page 55
Adjoining page 57
Adjoining page 46
Adjoining page 47
Adjoining page 52
Ardentraive
Dunoon
Dumbarton
Aberfeldy
Lochearnhead
Callander
Stirling
H
L
A
N
D
Ardgour
Conaglen Ho.
Aryhoulan
Inverscaddle Bay
Coruanan Lodge
Blarmachfoldach
Glen Nevis
Achriabhach
Mullach nan Coirean
Blar a' Chaoruinn
Sgurr a' Mhaim 3601
Mamore Forest
Binnein Mor 3700
Am Bodach 3382
Water of Nevis
Luibeilt
Amhainn Rath
Creaguaineach Lodge
L. Treig
Beinn na Lap 3066
Corrour Shooting Lodge
Loch Ossian
Corrour Forest
Sgor Gaibhre 3124
Càrn Dearg 3080
Rannoch Forest
Talla Bheith Forest
Stob an Aonaich Mhoir 2805
Loch Ericht
Sgùrr na h-Eanchainne 2395
Lundavra
Beinn na Gucaig 2023
Glenrigh Forest
Corran
Sallachan
Clovulin
Onich
Lairigmor
Mam na Gualainn 2603
Kinlochmore
Kinlochleven
Loch Eilde Mòr
Glas Bheinn 2587
Ciaran Water
Leum Uilleim 2971
Allt na Caim
Lubnaclach
Sròn Bheag 1631
Sallachan Point
North Ballachulish
Callert Ho.
Leven
Blackwater Reservoir
Loch Leven
South Ballachulish
Pap of Glencoe 2430
Glencoe
Folk Museum
Visitor Centre
Laroch
Achnacon
Glen Coe
N.T.
Meall Mor
Kentallen
Glendurror Forest
Achindarroch
Beinn a' Bheithir
Cuil Bay
Jnshaig
Keil
Bidean nam Bian 3766
Altnafeadh
Beinn a' Chrulaiste 2811
Meall nan Ruadhag 2120
Black Corries
Stob na Cruaiche 2423
Rannoch Sta.
Hotel
Dunan
Bridge of Ericht
Killichonan
Loch Rannoch
Finnart
Bridge of Gaur
Camghouran
Loch Eigheach
Kingshouse Hotel
Royal Forest
Buachaille Etive Mor
Lochan Gaineamhach
Rannoch Moor
TAYSIDE
Meall a' Mhuic 2444
Meall Buidhe 3054
Cam Chreag 2823
Fraochaidh 2883
Salachail
Sgor na h-Ulaidh 3258
Dalness
Alltchaorunn
Meall à Bhuiridh 3636
Ski-lift
Glen Etive
Glen Creran
Elleric
Beinn Fhionnlaidh 3139
Stob Dubh 2897
Aonach Mor
Clach Leathad 3602
Loch Bà
Lochan na h-Achlaise
Water of Tulla
GRAMPIAN MOUNTAINS
Meall Cruinn 2717
Bridge of Balgie
Meggernie Castle
Gallin
Glen Lyon
Beinn Donn 1553
Invercreran
Beinn Churalain 1792
Glasdrum
Creagan
Strath of Appin
Glen Ure
Gualachulain
Kinlochetive
Inverchamnan
Stob Coir' an Albannaich 3425
Stob Ghabhar 3565
Achallader
Beinn a' Chreachain 3540
Meall Buidhe 2976
Stuchd an Lochain 3144
Druimavuic
South Creagan
Beinn Sgulaird
Beinn Trilleachan 2752
Ben Starav 3541
Loch Dochard
Black Mount
Forest Lodge
Loch Tulla
Beinn Mhanach 3125
Pubil
Cashlie
Stronuich
Loch Lyon
Barcaldine
Barcaldine Forest
Beinn Bhreac 2324
Creach Bheinn 2657
Inveroran Hotel
Beinn an Dòthaidh 3267
Meall Ghaordie 3410
Barrs
Dail
Loch Etive
Beinn Suidhe 2215
Bridge of Orchy
Beinn Inverveigh 2087
Beinn Dòrain 3524
Beinn Heasgarnich 3530
Ardmaddy
Achnaba
Beinn nan Lus 2327
Meall Garbh 2283
Glen Kinglass
Creag Mhor 3387
Kenknock
Glen Lochay
Tullich
Innischoarach
Ardchattan Priory
Inveresragan
Beinn Mheadhonach 2344
Cadderlie
Glen Liever 2395
Beinn Mhic-Mhonaidh 2602
Arichastlich
Beinn Udlaidh 2759
Beinn Bhreac-liath 2633
Beinn Odhar 2948
Forest of Mamlorn
Breadalbane
Boreland
Falls of Lochay
Creag Mhor 2359
Hotel
Killin
Auchnacloich Pier
Bonawe Quarries
Glen Noe
Beinn Eunaich 3242
Glen Strae
Glen Orchy
Beinn Cheathaich 3076
Meall a' Churain 3007
Ben Challum 3354
Beinn nan Imirean 2769
Fearnoch Forest
Taynuilt
Bridge of Awe
Ben Cruachan 3689
Cruachan Resr.
Beinn Donachain 2127
Arrivain
Glen Lochy
Clifton
Tyndrum
Strath Fillan
Auchtertyre
Auchlyne
Glen Dochart
Ardchyle
Deadh Choimhead 1255
Barguillean Farm
Beinn a' Bhùiridh 2941
Kilchurn Castle
Stronmilchan
Achnafalnich
Beinn na Sròine 2085
Inverlochy
Strath of Orchy
Cononish
Auchriach
Lochdochart House
Luib Hotel
Ledcharrie 1946
Beinn Leabhain 2312
Pass of Brander
Lochawe
Lower Kinchrackine
Dalmally
Eas Ghaill
Ben Lui 3708
Fiarach
Inverherive 2132
Ben Oss 3374
Beinn Dubhchraig 3204
Crianlarich
Portnellan
Loch Dochart
Loch Iubhair
Ben More 3843
Beinn Ghlas 1691
Loch Nant
Loch Tromlee
Innis Chonain
Ardanaiseig
Inishail
Chapel
Achlian
Teatle Water
Beinn Bhalgairean 2085
Meall nan Tighearn 2423
Stob Binnein 3821
Monachyle Glen
Meall an t-Seallaidh 2793
Kilchrenan
Annat
Taychreggan
Cladich
Inistrynich
North Port
South Port
Upper Sonachan
Allt an Stacain
Lochan Shira
Dubh Eas
Glen Falloch
Falls of Falloch
Braes of Balquhidder
Monachylemore
Balquhidder
Auchtoo
Kingshouse
Auchachenna
Coillaig
Lochan Stron Mor
Beinn Bhuidhe 3106
Troisgeach 2407
Glenfalloch Farm
Inverarnan
Beinn Tulaichean 3099
Beinn a' Chroin 3104
Inverlochlarig
Loch Doine
Loch Voil
Ballimore
Strathyre
Inverinan
Inverinan Forest
Taynafead
Beinn Ghlas 1804
Rob Roy's House
Brannie Burn
Allt na Lairige
Ben Glas Burn
Stob a' Choin 2839
Ballimeanoch
Tullich
Glen Aray
Cruach Mhòr 1932
Drimfern
Elrigbeag
Glen Shira
Clachan Hill 2159
Glenfyne Lodge
Glen Fyne
Maol Breac 2115
Ardlui
Stuckindroin
Meall Mor 2451
Beinn Bhreac 2242
Benvane 2685
Runacraig
Laggan
Barnaline
Blarghour
Dalavich
Ardchonnell
Portinnisherrich
Beinn Bhreac 1723
Kilblaan Burn
Clachan
Drishaig 1240
Dubh Loch
Malt Land
Cairndow
Binnein an Fhidhleir 2660
Loch Sloy
Ben Vorlich 3092
Ardvorlich
Beinn a' Choin 2524
Glengyle
Portnellan
Cruinn Bheinn 1787
Meall Cala 2203
Loch Lubnaig
Eredine
Inveraray Castle
Inveraray
Strone Gardens
Glen Kinglas
Ben Vane 3004
Inveruglas
Rob Roy's Cave
Stronachlachar
Strath Gartney
Glen Finglas
Glen Finglas Res.
Ben Ledi 2873
An Suidhe 1687
Douglas Water
Ardno
Stob an Eas 2402
St. Catherines
Hells Glen
Beinn an Lochain 2992
Beinn Ime 3318
Rest and be thankful
Ben Narnain 3036
Inversnaid Hotel
Cruachan 1762
L. Arklet
Loch Katrine
CENTRAL
Goblin's Cave
The Trossachs
Trossachs Hotel
Brig o' Turk
Lendrick Lo.
Ben Venue 2386
Duncraggan
L. Venachar
Dalchenna
Creag a' Phuill
Cruach nan Capull 1854
Monevechadan
Ben Arthur (The Cobbler) 2891
Succoth
Tarbet
Craig Rostan
Frenich
Loch Chon
Beinn Dearg 1575
Ben Donich 2777
Glen Croe
Ardgartan
Arrochar
Cruinn a' Bheinn 2077
Beinn Dub 1675
Loch Achray
Achray Forest
Loch Drunkie
Menteith Hills
Auchindrain
Folk Museum
Loch Leacann
Dùn Leacainn
Kenmore
Brenachoille
Furnace
Cruach Mhic Fhionnlaidh 1503
Creggans
Strachur
Mullach Coire a' Chuir 2098
Lochgoilhead
Ardgoil Estate
Ardmay
Stuckgowan
Ben Lomond 3192
Kinlochard
Altskeith
Loch Ard
Milton
Aberfoyle
Braeval
Malling
Lake of Menteith
Sanahole
Beinn Ghlas 1377
Tigh-na-criche
Glensluain
Beinn Lochain 2306
Drimsynie
Corrow
Cnoc Coinnich 2497
Argyll National Forest Park
Ardgartan Forest
Craggan
Beinn Bhreac 2233
Ptarmigan Lodge
Ardess
Rowardennan Hotel
Beinn Uird 1957
Duchray Water
Loch Ard Forest
Cobleland
Gartmore
Crarae Lodge
Crarae
Minard
Leanach
Cruach nan Capull 1578
Glenbranter
Glenbranter Forest
Invernoaden
Beinn Bheula 2556
Cormonachan
Loch Goil
Ardgoil Forest
Doune Hill 2408
Glen Douglas
Inverbeg Hotel
Loch Lomond
Rowardennan Forest
Queen Elizabeth National Forest Park
Eilean Aoghainn
Garbhalt
Tullochgorm
Barnacarry
Strathlachlan Forest
Cruach an Lochain 1658
Beinn Bheag 2029
Loch Eck
Carrick Castle
Cruach a' Bhuic 2084
Beinn a' Mhanaich
Arddarroch 2328
Beinn Eich 2302
Edentaggart
Glen Luss
Inchlonaig
Gualann 1514
Dalmary
Flanders Moss
Gartachoil
Lephinmore
Lephinchapel
Dunans
Beinn Mhòr 2433
Sligrachan
Creachan Mòr 2156
Portincaple
Garelochhead
Beinn Chaorach 2340
Strone
Beinn Ruisg 1946
Aldochlay
Luss
Conic Hill 1175
Balmaha
Buchanan Smithy
Garadhban Forest
Moor Park
COPYRIGHT, GEORGE PHILIP & SON, LTD.

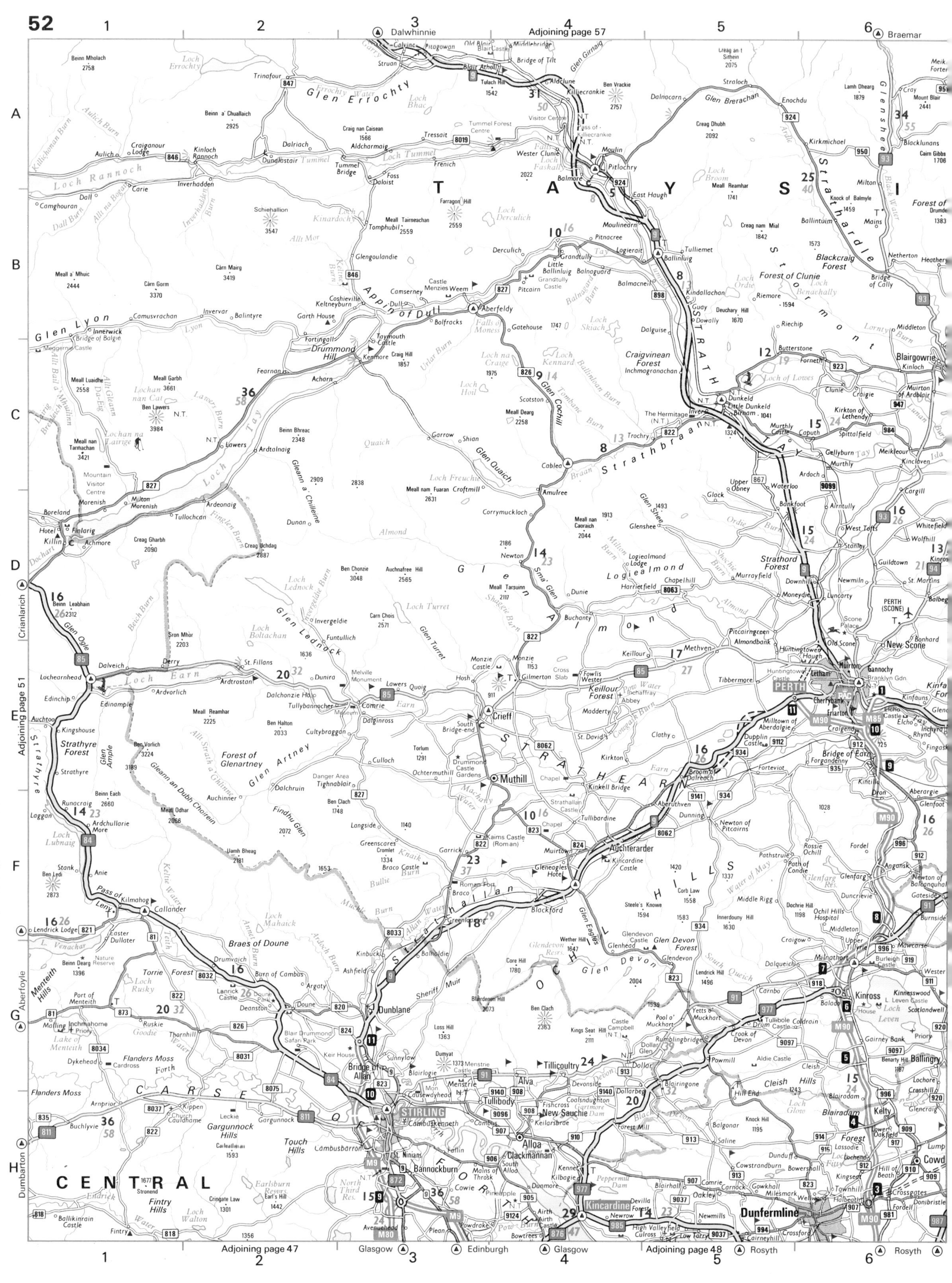
1
2
3
4
5
6
Dalwhinnie
Braemar
A
B
C
D
E
F
G
H
Beinn Mholach 2758
Loch Errochty
Trinafour
Glen Errochty
Errochty Water
Calvine
Pitagowan
Old Blair
Blair Castle
Middlebridge
Struan
Blair Atholl
Bridge of Tilt
Glen Girnaig
Tulach Hill 1542
Aldclune
Killiecrankie
Ben Vrackie 2757
Dalnacarn
Glen Brerachan
Straloch
Enochdu
Creag an t-Sithein 2075
Lamh Dhearg 1879
Cray
Mount Blair 2441
Glenshee
Meikle Forter
Loch Bhac
Beinn a' Chuallaich 2925
Craig nan Caisean 1566
Tummel Forest Centre
Visitor Centre
Pass of Killiecrankie
Creag Dhubh 2092
Kirkmichael
Blacklunans
Cairn Gibbs 1706
Aulich Burn
Craiganour Lodge
Kinloch Rannoch
Dalriach
Aldcharmaig
Tressait
Loch Tummel
Wester Clunie
Loch Faskally
Moulin
Pitlochry
Aulich
Dunalastair
Tummel Bridge
Foss
Frenich
Dalcist
Balmore
Loch Rannoch
Carie
Inverhadden
Dall
Camghouran
Dall Burn
Allt na Bogair
Inverhadden Burn
Schiehallion 3547
Loch Kinardochy
Tomphubil
Meall Tairneachan 2559
Farragon Hill 2559
Loch Derculich
East Haugh
Loch Broom
Meall Reamhar 1741
Strathardle
Milton
Knock of Balmyle 1459
Ballintuim
Mains
Forest of Drumderg 1383
TAYSIDE
Allt Mor
Glengoulandie
Derculich
Pitnacree
Moulinearn
Logierait
Ballinluig
Tulliemet
Creag nam Mial 1842
Blackcraig Forest
Netherton
Bridge of Cally
Heatheryhaugh
Meall a' Mhuic 2444
Càrn Gorm 3370
Càrn Mairg 3419
Keltie Burn
Castle Menzies
Weem
Camserney
Appin of Dull
Grandtully
Little Ballinluig
Balnaguard
Grandtully Castle
Pitcairn
Balmacneil
Kindallachan
Forest of Clunie
Loch Ordie
Loch Benachally
Riemore
Glen Lyon
Camusvrachan
Invervar
Balintyre
Garth House
Coshieville
Keltneyburn
Dull
Aberfeldy
Bolfracks
Falls of Moness
Gatehouse
Guay
Dowally
Deuchary Hill 1670
Riechip
Stormont
Middleton
Lornty Burn
Innerwick
Bridge of Balgie
Meggernie Castle
Fortingall
Drummond Hill
Taymouth Castle
Kenmore
Craig Hill 1857
Urlar Burn
Loch na Craige 1975
Loch Kennard
Loch Skiach
Craigvinean Forest
Inchmagranachan
Butterstone
Forneth
Loch of Lowes
Blairgowrie
Kinloch
Meall Luaidhe 2558
Meall Garbh 3661
Lochan nan Cat
Ben Lawers 3984
Fearnan
Acharn
Loch Hoil
Glen Cochill
Scotston
Tombane Burn
Dunkeld
Little Dunkeld
Birnam
The Hermitage (N.T.)
Inver
Clunie
Craigie
Muirton of Ardblair
Kirkton of Lethendy
Lunan Burn
Meall nan Tarmachan 3421
Lochan na Lairige
Lawers
Ardtalnaig
Beinn Bhreac 2348
Quaich
Garrow
Shian
Meall Dearg 2258
Trochry
Strathbraan
Murthly Castle
Caputh
Spittalfield
Gellyburn
Meikleour
Murthly
Kinclaven
Mountain Visitor Centre
Loch Tay
Gleann a' Chilleine
Loch Freuchie
Croftmill
Meall nam Fuaran 2631
Glen Quaich
Cablea
Amulree
Braan
Upper Obney
Waterloo
Ardoch
Cargill
Boreland
Morenish
Milton Morenish
Ardeonaig
Tullochcan
Finglen Burn
Hotel
Finlarig
Killin
Achmore
Dochart
Creag Gharbh 2090
Creag Uchdag 2887
Dunan
Almond
Corrymuckloch
Meall nan Caoraich 2044
Glack
Glen Shee
Glenshee
Bankfoot
Airntully
West Tofts
Whitefield
Wolfhill
Stanley
Ben Chonzie 3048
Auchnafree Hill 2565
Newton
Glen Almond
Sma' Glen
Logiealmond Lodge
Logiealmond
Strathord Forest
Guildtown
St. Martins
Crianlarich
Beinn Leabhain 2312
Glen Ogle
Loch Lednock
Invergeldie Burn
Glen Lednock
Invergeldie
Fintullich
Carn Chois 2571
Loch Turret
Meall Tarsuinn 2117
Shaggie Burn
Dunie
Harrietfield
Chapelhill
Murrayfield
Downhill
Moneydie
Luncarty
Newmiln
PERTH (SCONE)
Balbeggie
Beich Burn
Sron Mhor 2203
Loch Boltachan
Glen Turret
Buchanty
Pitcairngreen
Almondbank
Scone Palace
Old Scone
New Scone
Bonhard
Dalveich
Derry
St. Fillans
Loch Earn
Ardtrostan
Ardvorlich
Dunira
Melville Monument
Lawers
Quoig
Monzie Castle
Monzie
Gilmerton
Cross Slab
Fowlis Wester
Keillour
Methven
Keillour Forest
Inchaffray Abbey
Pow Water
Huntingtower
Huntingtower Castle
Tibbermore
Letham
PERTH
Muirton
Gannochy
Branklyn Gdn.
Cherrybank
Kinfauns
Lochearnhead
Edinchip
Edinample
Dalchonzie Ho.
Tullybannocher
Comrie
Earn
Museum
Hosh
Crieff
Madderty
Friarton
Auchtoo
Kingshouse
Strathyre Forest
Meall Reamhar 2225
Ben Halton 2033
Cultybraggan
Dalginross
South Bridge-end
Strathearn
St. David's
Cowgask Burn
Clathy
Milltown of Aberdalgie
Craigend
Elcho Castle
Elcho
Inchyra
Rhynd
Fingask
Glen Ampul
Ben Vorlich 3224
Forest of Glenartney
Glen Artney
Torlum 1291
Drummond Castle Gardens
Culloch
Ochtermuthill
Muthill
Kirkton
Dupplin Castle
Bridge of Earn
Forgandenny
Strathyre
Gleann an Dubh Choirein
Danger Area
Tighnablair
Dalchruin
Chapel
Kinkell Bridge
Broom of Dalreach
Forteviot
Kintillo
Dron
Aberargie
Glenfoot
Beinn Each 2660
Runacraig
Auchinner
Meall Odhar 2066
Ben Clach 1748
Findhu Glen
Machany Water
Strathallan Castle
Tullibardine
Aberuthven
Dunning
Newton of Pitcairns
Laggan
Ardchullarie More
Loch Lubnaig
Langside
Kaims Castle (Roman)
Chapel
Greenscares
Cromlet
Rossie Ochill
Fordel
Garrick
Muirtown
Auchterarder
Kincardine Castle
Pathstruie
Path of Condie
Glenfarg
Stank
Ben Ledi 2873
Anie
Uamh Bheag 2181
Braco Castle
Knaik Burn
Gleneagles Hotel
Ochil Hills
Water of May
Glenfarg Res.
Arngask
Newton of Balcanquhal
Pass of Kilmahog
Kilmahog
Leny
Callander
Roman Fort
Braco
Blackford
Glen Eagles
Corb Law 1558
Middle Rigg
Duncrievie
Dochrie Hill 1198
Ochil Hills Hospital
Gateside
Burnside
Lendrick Lodge
Loch Venachar
Easter Dullater
Loch Mahaick
Greenloaning
Strathallan
Steele's Knowe 1594
Innerdouny Hill 1630
Middleton
Braes of Doune
Ardoch Burn
Kinbuck
Balhaldie
Wether Hill 1647
Glendevon Castle
Glen Devon Forest
Glenhead
Glendevon
Glendevon Resrs.
Craigow
Upper Tillyrie
Mawcarse
Beinn Dearg 1396
Nature Reserve
Torrie Forest
Drumvaich
Burn of Cambus
Ashfield
Sheriff Muir
Core Hill 1780
Glen Devon
OCHIL HILLS
South Queich
Dalqueich
Milnathort
Burleigh Castle
Wester
Menteith Hills
Loch Rusky
Lanrick Castle
Doune Park
Deanston
Argaty
Doune
Dunblane
Blairdenon Hill 2073
2004
Lendrick Hill 1496
Carnbo
Kinross
Kinnesswood
L. Leven Castle
Port of Menteith
Inchmahome Priory
Ruskie
Goodie
Thornhill
Blair Drummond Safari Park
Keir House
Loss Hill 1363
Ben Clach 2363
Castle Campbell (N.T.)
Kings Seat Hill 2111
Yetts o' Muckhart
Pool o' Muckhart
Tullibole Castle
Drum
Coldrain
Balado
Loch Leven
Scotlandwell
Malling
Lake of Menteith
Flanders Moss
Cardross
Forth
Sunnylaw
Dumyat
Menstrie Castle
Tillicoultry
Dollar
Dollar Glen
Rumblingbridge
Crook of Devon
Gairney Bank
Priory
Dykehead
Bridge of Allan
Blairlogie
Alva
Devonside
Powmill
Aldie Castle
Cleish
Ballingry
Flanders Moss
Arnprior
CARSE OF FORTH
Kippen
Church
Cauldhame
Menstrie
Causewayhead
Tullibody
Fishcross
Coalsnaughton
Gartmore Dam
Dollarbeg
Blairingone
Cleish Hills
Hill End
Loch Glow
Lochore
Crosshill
Buchlyvie
Leckie
Gargunnock
STIRLING
Cambuskenneth
Cambus
New Sauchie
Keilarsbrae
Forest Mill
Knock Hill 1195
Balgonar
Blairadam Forest
Kelty
Glencraig
Gargunnock Hills
Carleatheran 1593
Touch Hills
Cambusbarron
St. Ninians
Fallin
Alloa
Clackmannan
Saline
Lassodie
Lochend
Lumphinnans
Cowdenbeath
Dumbarton
CENTRAL
Stronend 1677
Bannockburn
Mains of Throsk
South Alloa
Kennet
Kilbagie
Peppermill Dam
Cowstrandburn
Bowershall
Hill of Beath
Endrick
Earlsburn Resrs.
Earl's Hill 1442
Cringate Law 1301
North Third Res.
Cowie
Pineapple
Dunmore
Kincardine
Blairhall
Comrie
Oakley
Carnock
Gowkhall
Milesmark
Wellwood
Kingseat
Townhill
Halbeath
Crossgates
Donibristle
Fintry Hills
Loch Walton
Airth
Airth Castle
Newrow
Devilla Forest
High Valleyfield
Culross
Low Torry
Newmills
Dunfermline
Crossford
Cairneyhill
Fordell
Ballikinrain Castle
Fintry
Plean
Powdrake
Pow Burn
Bowtrees
Avenuehead
1356
Adjoining page 51
Aberfoyle
Glasgow
Edinburgh
Rosyth

Adjoining page 59

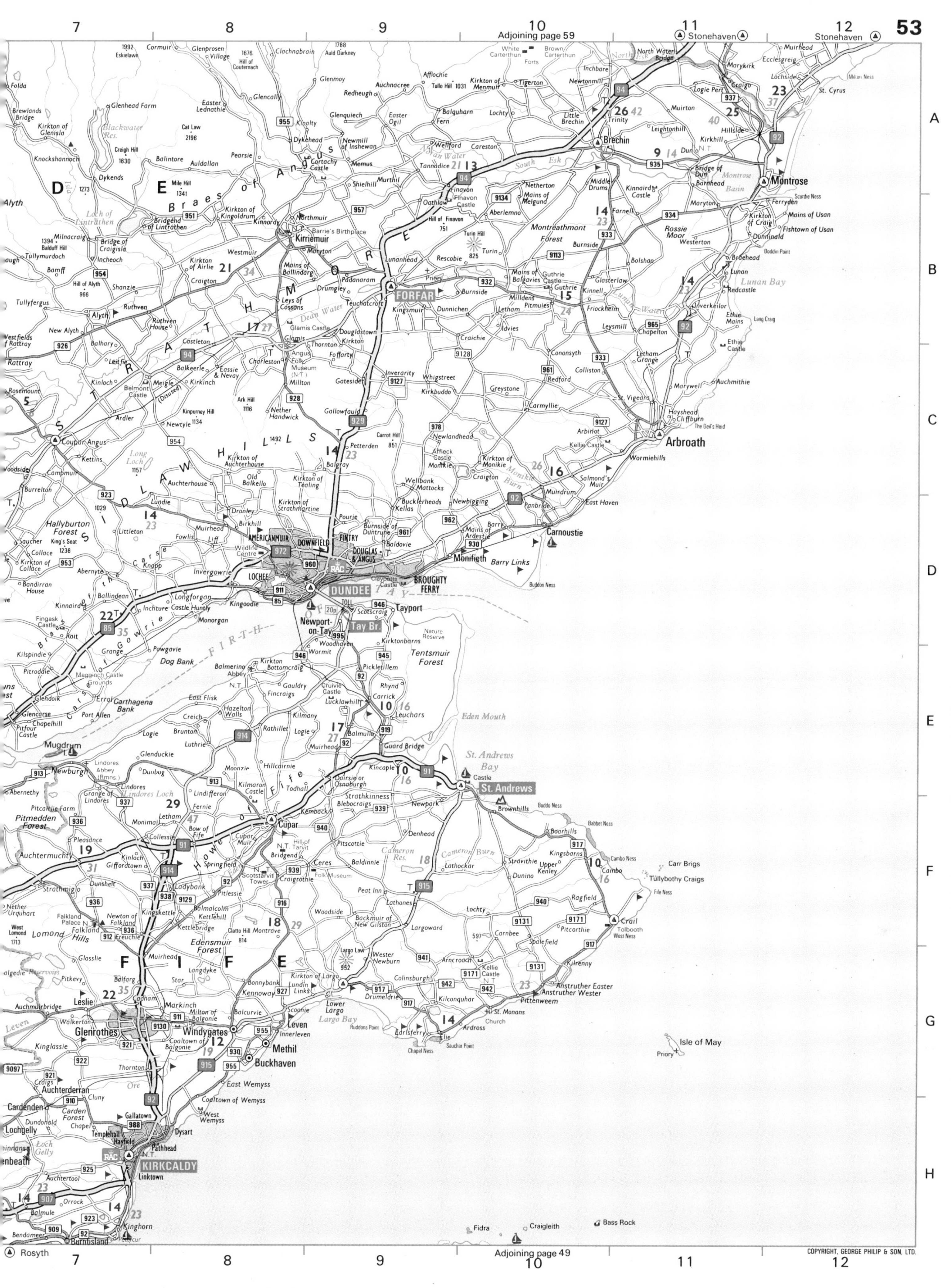

Adjoining page 49

Adjoining page 60
Adjoining page 56

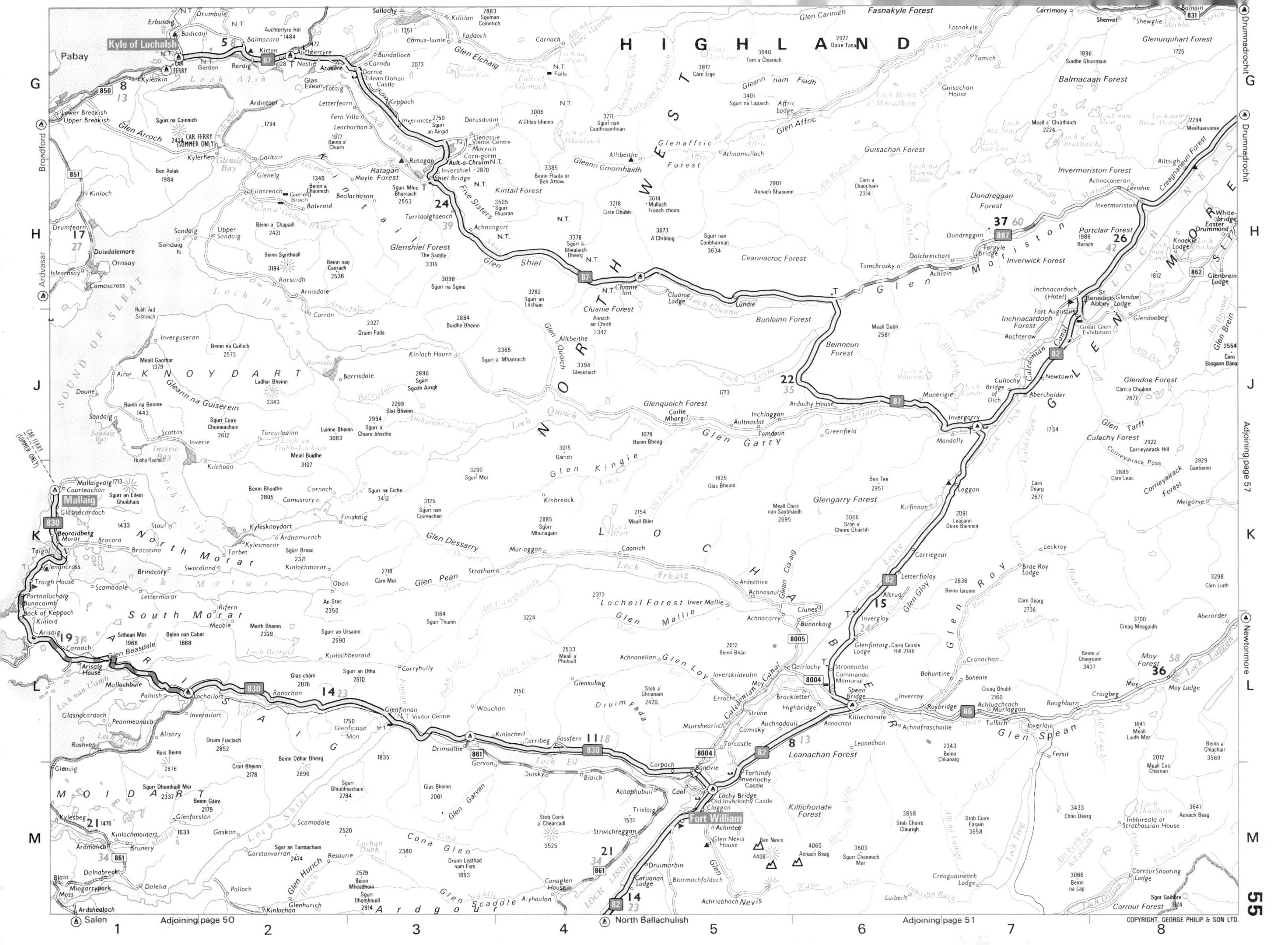

Adjoining page 50

Adjoining page 51

Adjoining page 57

Adjoining page 60
Lairg
Adjoining page 61
The Mound
Adjoining page 54
Gorstan
Cannich
Adjoining page 58
Keith
Rhynie
NORTH SEA
MORAY FIRTH
CROMARTY FIRTH
EASTER ROSS
BLACK ISLE
LAICH O' MORAY
GRAMPIAN
Beauly Firth
Dornoch Firth
Burghead Bay
Nigg Bay
The Bar
Lossiemouth
Branderburgh
Elgin
Burghead
Findhorn
Kinloss
Forres
Nairn
Auldearn
Ardersier
Fort George
Cromarty
Invergordon
Alness
Dingwall
Conon Bridge
INVERNESS
Fortrose
Rosemarkie
Tain
Dornoch
Bonar Bridge
Portmahomack
Tarbat Ness
Wilkhaven
Rothes
Charlestown of Aberlour
Craigellachie
Culloden Forest
Glen of Rothes
Strath Rusdale
Cawdor
Dava
Strathnairn
Strathdearn Forest
Lochindorb
The Aird
Beauly
Kiltarlity
Muir of Ord
Whiteness Sands
Dornoch Sands
Clashmore Wood
Monaughty Forest
Elchies Forest
Altyre Woods
Darnaway Forest
Culbin Forest
Millbuie Forest

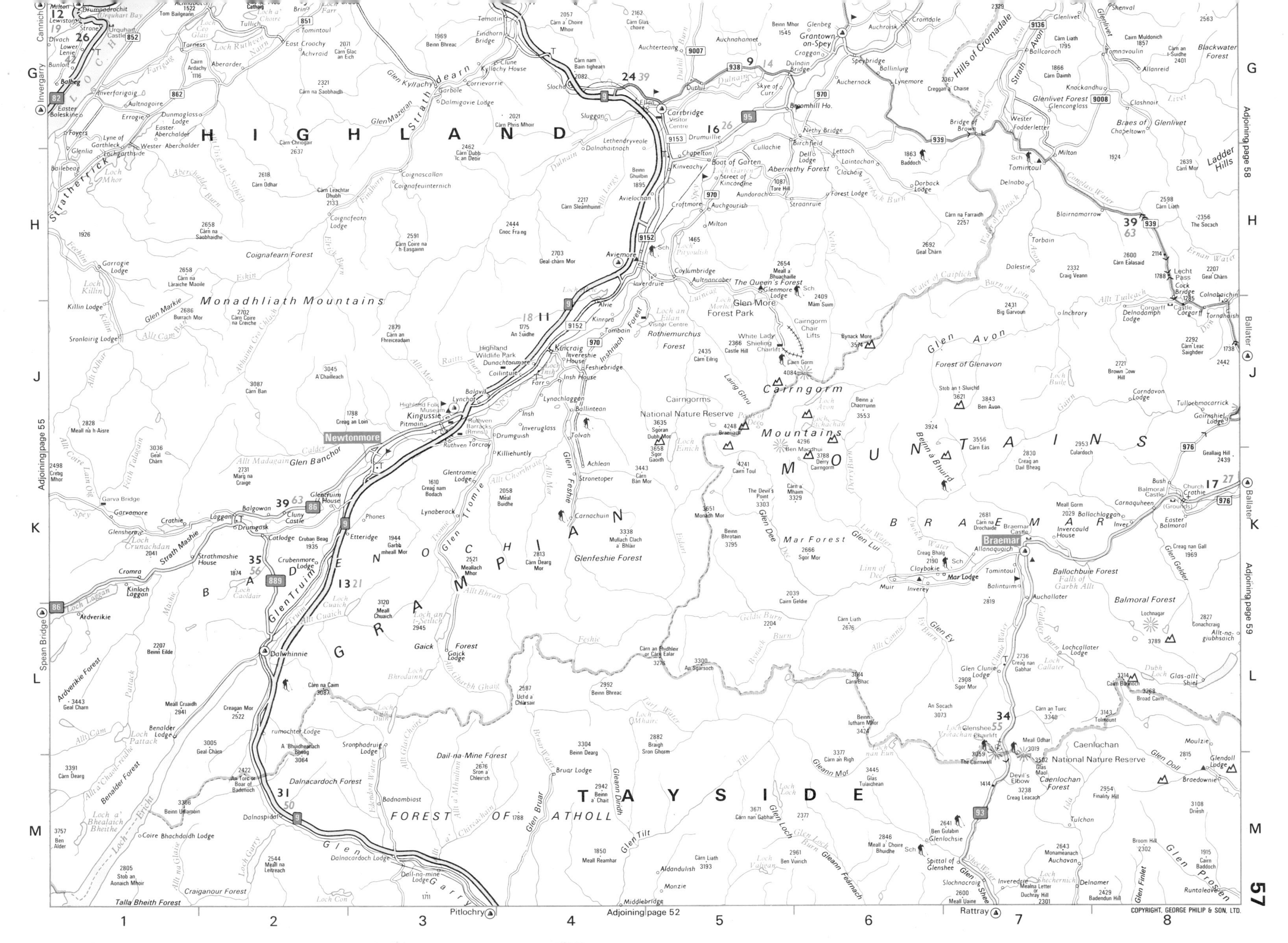
Adjoining page 58
Adjoining page 59
Adjoining page 55
Adjoining page 52
Ballater
Rattray
Pitlochry
Spean Bridge
Invergarry
COPYRIGHT, GEORGE PHILIP & SON, LTD.
G
H
J
K
L
M
1
2
3
4
5
6
7
8
H I G H L A N D
T A Y S I D E
G R A M P I A N
M O U N T A I N S
Monadhliath Mountains
Cairngorm Mountains
Cairngorms National Nature Reserve
Glen More Forest Park
Rothiemurchus Forest
Abernethy Forest
Mar Forest
Glenfeshie Forest
Gaick Forest
Forest of Atholl
Forest of Glenavon
Glenlivet Forest
Coignafearn Forest
Balmoral Forest
Ballochbuie Forest
Caenlochan National Nature Reserve
Caenlochan Forest
Dalnacardoch Forest
Dail-na-Mine Forest
Talla Bheith Forest
Craiganour Forest
Ardverikie Forest
Benalder Forest
Braemar
Newtonmore
Kingussie
Aviemore
Carrbridge
Grantown-on-Spey
Tomintoul
Dalwhinnie
Kincraig
Nethy Bridge
Boat of Garten
Glenlivet
Hills of Cromdale
Ladder Hills
Lecht Pass
Cock Bridge
Corgarff Castle
Balmoral Castle
Crathie Church
Inverey
Glen Feshie
Glen Dee
Glen Lui
Glen Ey
Glen Shee
Spittal of Glenshee
Devil's Elbow
Glen Gelder
Glen Tilt
Glen Bruar
Glen Garry
Glen Truim
Glen Banchor
Glen Tromie
Glen Avon
Glen Doll
Glen Prosen
Strath Mashie
Loch Laggan
Loch Ericht
Ben Macdhui
Braeriach
Cairn Gorm
Beinn à Bhuird
Ben Avon
Lairig Ghru
Highland Wildlife Park
Ruthven Barracks

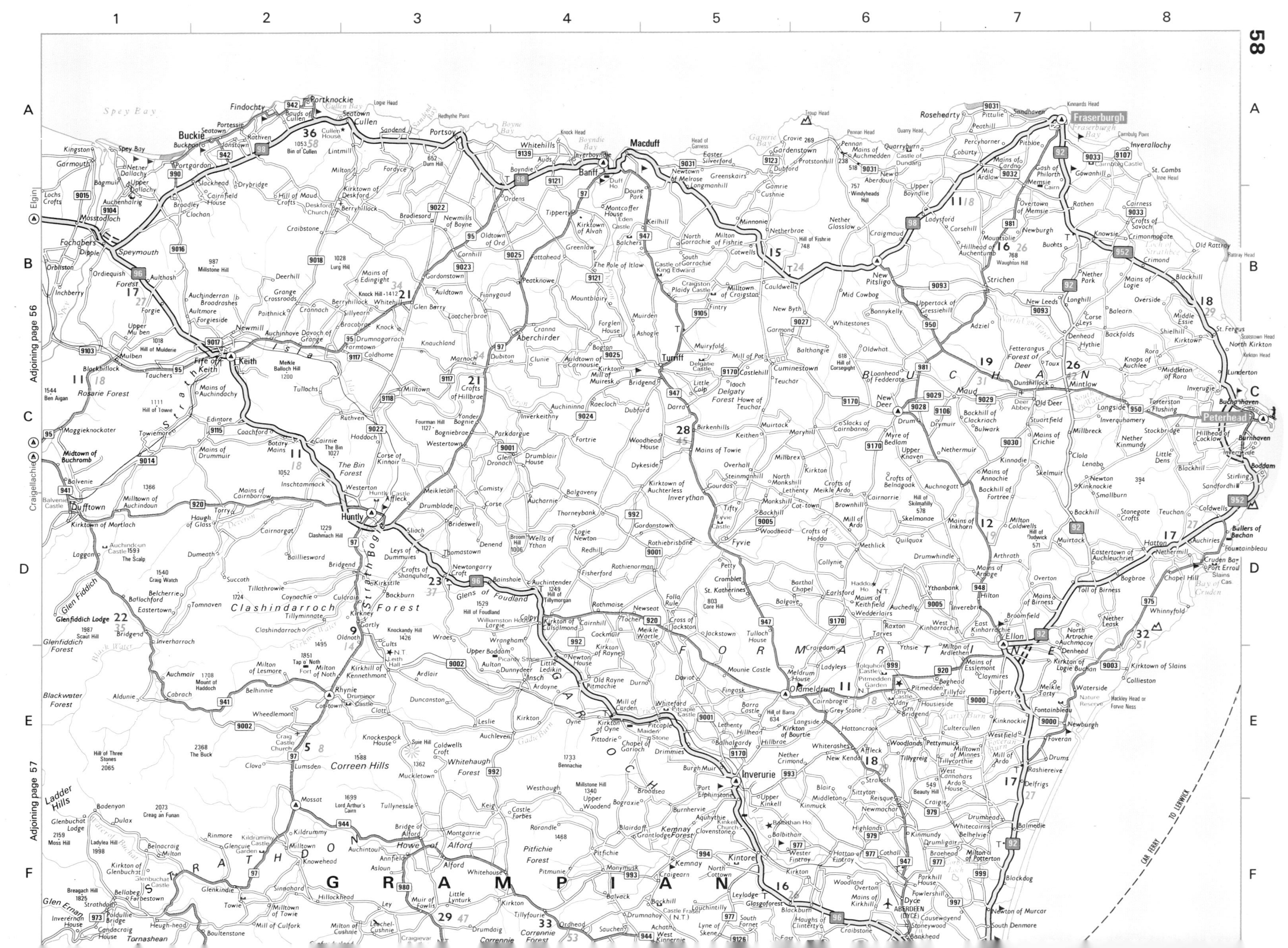

1
2
3
4
5
6
7
8
A
B
C
D
E
F
Adjoining page 56
Adjoining page 57
Elgin
Craigellachie
Spey Bay
Findochty
Portknockie
Cullen Bay
Seatown
Cullen
Logie Head
Sandend
Portsoy
Boyne Bay
Knock Head
Whitehills
Boyndie Bay
Macduff
Banff
Gamrie Bay
Troup Head
Pennan Head
Quarry Head
Rosehearty
Sandhaven
Kinnairds Head
Fraserburgh
Fraserburgh Bay
Cairnbulg Point
Inverallochy
St. Combs
Buckie
Portgordon
Kingston
Garmouth
Mosstodloch
Fochabers
Keith
Fife of Keith
Rosarie Forest
Dufftown
Huntly
Aberchirder
Turriff
New Pitsligo
Strichen
New Deer
Maud
Mintlaw
Old Deer
Longside
Peterhead
Boddam
Crimond
Rattray Head
St. Fergus
Cruden Bay
Port Erroll
Hatton
Ellon
Newburgh
Oldmeldrum
Fyvie
Inverurie
Kintore
Kemnay
Alford
Insch
Rhynie
Clashindarroch Forest
Correen Hills
Glen Fiddich
Glenfiddich Lodge
Glenfiddich Forest
Blackwater Forest
Ladder Hills
Strathbogie
FORMARTINE
BUCHAN
GARIOCH
STRATHDON
GRAMPIAN
Howe of Alford
Pitfichie Forest
Bennachie
Dyce
ABERDEEN
Balmedie
Foveran
Collieston
Car Ferry to Lerwick

ABERDEEN
OLD ABERDEEN
Stonehaven
Inverbervie
Johnshaven
Montrose
Brechin
Forfar
Kirriemuir
Laurencekirk
Banchory
Aboyne
Ballater
Tarland
Torphins
Peterculter
Portlethen
Newtonhill
Lunan Bay
Glen Esk
Glen Clova
Glen Muick
Forest of Birse
Forest of Glentanar
Fetteresso Forest
Drumtochty Forest
Howe of the Mearns
Montreathmont Forest
DEESIDE
TAYSIDE
Braes of Angus
Adjoining page 53
Adjoining page 57
Dundee
Arbroath
Coupar Angus
Crathie
Rattray
Grantown-on-Spey

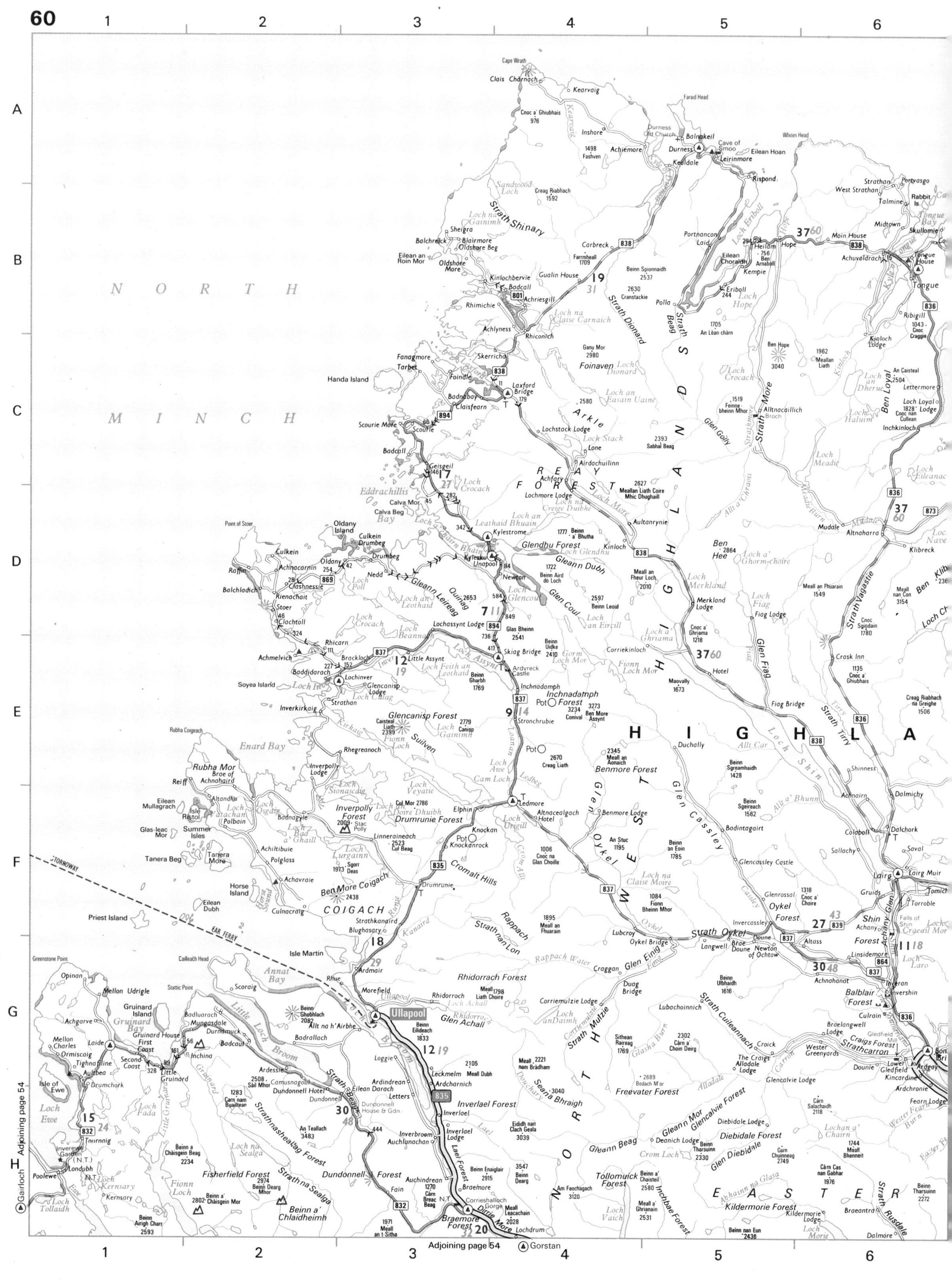

Adjoining page 54

Adjoining page 64

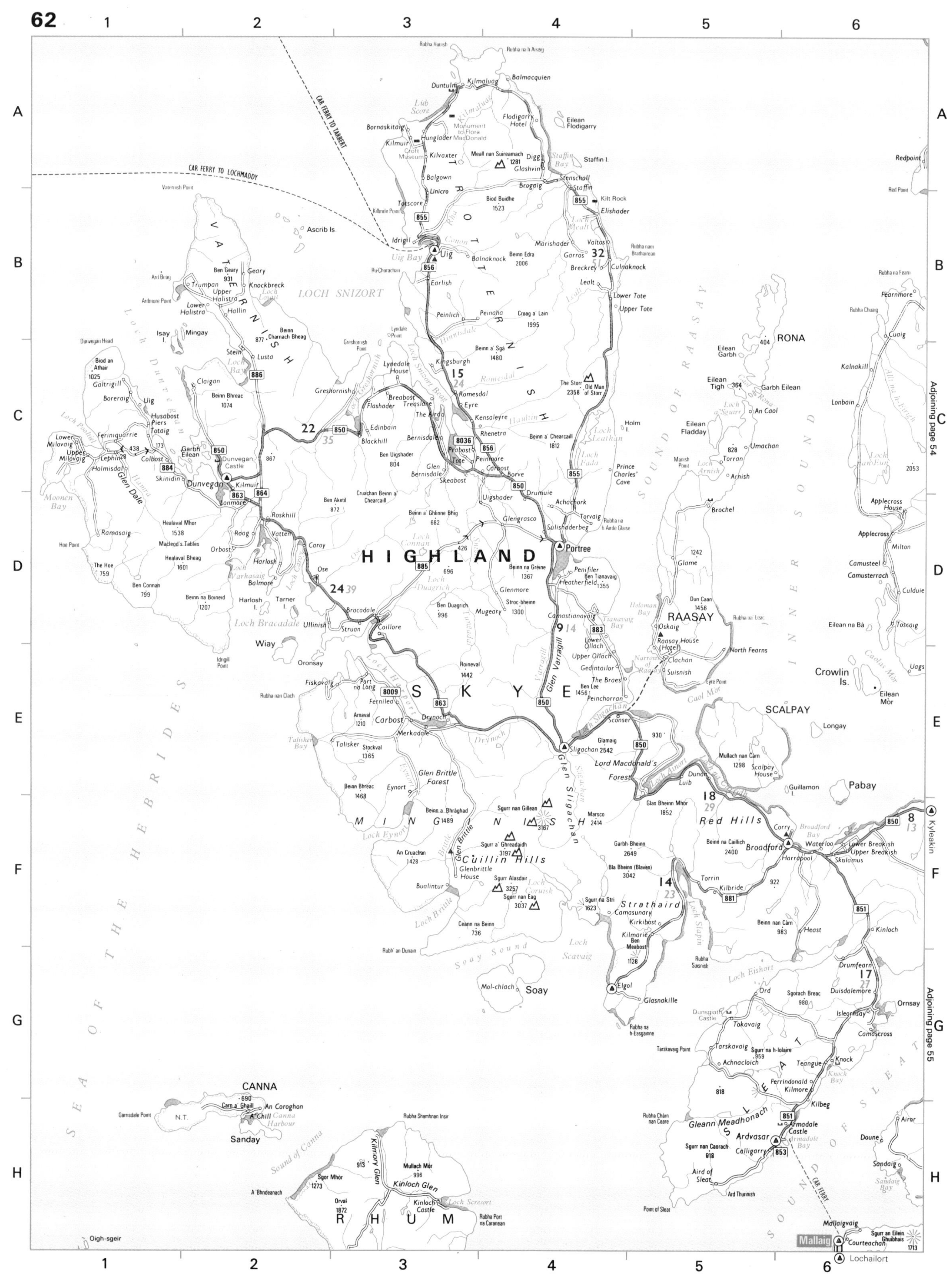

Adjoining page 54
Adjoining page 55

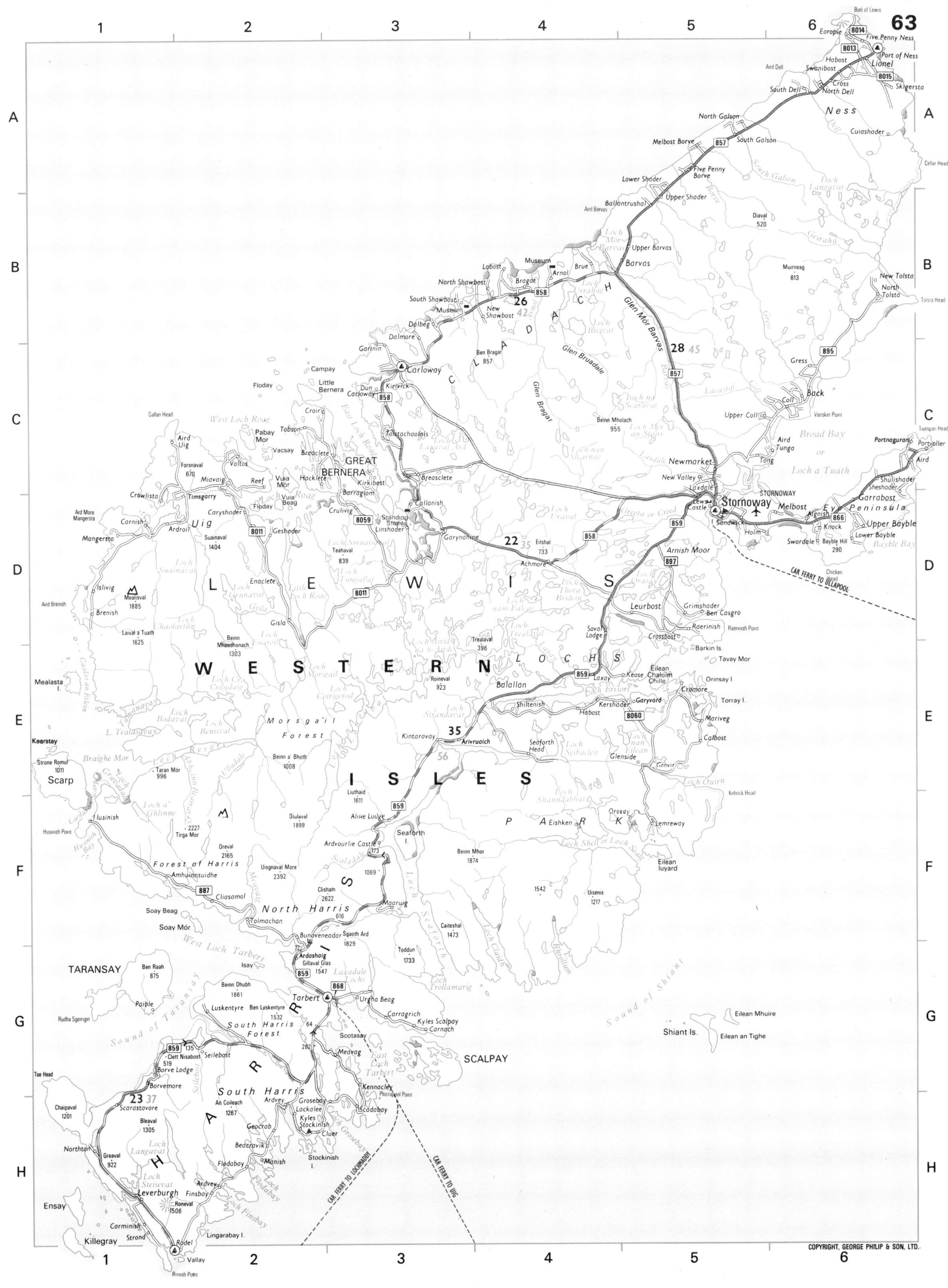

Butt of Lewis
Eoropie
8014
8013
Five Penny Ness
Port of Ness
Habost
Lionel
Aird Dell
Swanibost
8015
Cross
North Dell
South Dell
Skigersta
Ness
North Galson
Cuiashader
Melbost Borve
857
South Galson
Cellar Head
Five Penny Borve
Lower Shader
Upper Shader
South Galson
Loch Langavat
Ballantrushal
Aird Barvas
Diaval 520
Geiraha
Loch Mòr Barvas
Upper Barvas
Barvas
Museum
Arnol
Brue
Labost
Bragar
Muirneag 813
New Tolsta
North Tolsta
Tolsta Head
North Shawbost
858
South Shawbost
Museum
New Shawbost
26
42
L
A
D
A
C
H
Loch Urrahag
Loch Breivat
Glen Mòr Barvas
Dalbeg
Dalmore
Garinin
Carloway
Ben Bragar 857
Glen Bruadale
28
45
857
895
Gress
Campay
Little Bernera
Floday
Dun Carloway
Kirivick
858
C
Glen Bragar
Loch na Scaravat
Lacastal
Coll
Back
Gallan Head
West Loch Roag
Croir
Tobson
Pabay Mor
Vacsay
East Loch Roag
Tolstachaolais
Loch Lasavat Ard
Beinn Mholach 955
Loch Mòr an Stairr
Upper Coll
Vatisker Point
Aird Uig
Forsnaval 670
Valtos
Breaclete
GREAT BERNERA
Hacklete
Kirkibost
Breasclete
Loch nan Sgarnag
Laxdale
Newmarket
Aird Tunga
Broad Bay or Loch a Tuath
Tong
Tiumpan Head
Portnaguran
Portvoller
Aird
Crowlista
Timsgarry
Miavaig
Reef
Vuia Mòr
Vuia Beag
Floday
Barraglom
Callanish
Crulivig
8059
Standing Stones
Linshader
New Valley
Laxdale
Lews Castle
Stornoway
STORNOWAY
Melbost
Eye Peninsula
Shulishader
Sheshader
Garrabost
Ard More Mangersta
Carnish
Uig
Ardroil
Caryshader
Gesbader
8011
Suainaval 1404
Mangersta
Loch Suainaval
Teahaval 839
Garynahine
22
35
Eitshal 733
Loch Urraval
858
859
Greeta or Creed
Sandwick
Holm
Aignish
866
Knock
Upper Bayble
Lower Bayble
Swordale
Bayble Hill 290
Bayble Bay
Arnish Moor
897
Achmore
Chicken Head
CAR FERRY TO ULLAPOOL
Islivig
Mealisval 1885
L
E
W
I
S
Enaclete
Loch Grunavat
Little Loch Roag
Loch Tungavat
8011
Loch Orasay
Leurbost
Grimshader
Ben Casgro
Aird Brenish
Brenish
Loch Chaolartan
Gisla
Loch Thota Bridein
Loch nam Falcan
Raerinish
Raerinish Point
Laival a Tuath 1625
Beinn Mhaodhonach 1303
Loch Fuaroid
Gisla
Loch Trealaval
Soval Lodge
Crossbost
Barkin Is.
Trealaval 396
Tavay Mor
W
E
S
T
E
R
N
L
O
C
H
S
Mealasta I.
Loch Croistean
Loch Morsgail
Roineval 923
859
Laxay
Keose
Eilean Chaluim Chille
Orinsay I
Balallan
Loch Erisort
Garyvard
Cromore
Torray I.
Loch Corrigerod
Shiltenish
Habost
Kershader
8060
Loch Bodavat
Loch Strandavat
Mariveg
L. Tealasdavat
Loch Benisval
Morsga'il Forest
Kintaravay
35
Arivruaich
Seaforth Head
Loch Sgibacleit
Calbost
Kearstay
Loch Resort
Glenside
Loch nan Eilean
Gravir
Strone Romul 1011
Braighe Mor
Beinn a' Bhoth 1008
56
Scarp
Taran Mór 996
I
S
L
E
S
Loch Ouirn
Kebock Head
Liuthaid 1611
Loch Shanndabhat
Loch a' Ghlinne
859
Orosay
Hushinish
Aline Lodge
P
A
R
K
Eishken
Lemreway
Husinish Point
Hushinish Bay
2227
Tirga Mor
Oiulaval 1899
Ardvourlie Castle
Seaforth I.
Loch Shell or Loch Sealg
Oreval 2165
Beinn Mhor 1874
Eilean Iuyard
Forest of Harris
Amhuinnsuidhe
Uisgnaval More 2392
1069
F
1542
Uisenis 1217
887
Cliasamol
Clisham 2622
North Harris
Maaruig
Soay Beag
616
Soay Mór
Tolmachan
Sgaoth Ard 1829
Caiteshal 1473
Loch Claidh
Loch Seaforth
West Loch Tarbert
Bunaveneadar
Ardhasaig
Toddun 1733
Isay
TARANSAY
Ben Raah 875
Gillaval Glas 1547
859
Laxadale Lochs
Loch Trollamarig
Sound of Shiant
Beinn Dhubh 1661
Tarbert
868
Urgha Beag
Paible
Luskentyre
Ben Luskentyre 1532
Carragrich
Eilean Mhuire
Kyles Scalpay
Rudha Sgeirigin
Sound of Taransay
South Harris Forest
64
Carnach
Shiant Is.
Eilean an Tighe
Scotasay
282
859
135
Clett Nisabost
Seilebost
Meavag
SCALPAY
519
Borve Lodge
East Loch Tarbert
Toe Head
Borvemore
South Harris
Kennacley
Plocrapool Point
23
37
Chaipaval 1201
Scarastavore
An Coileach 1267
Ardvey
Grosebay
Lackalee
Scadabay
Bleaval 1305
Kyles Stockinish
Cluer
Loch Grosebay
Geocrab
Northton
Loch Langavat
Bedersvik
Greaval 922
Manish
Stockinish I.
H
Flodabay
Loch Steisevat
Ardvey
Finsbay
Loch Flodabay
CAR FERRY TO LOCHMADDY
CAR FERRY TO UIG
Leverburgh
Roneval 1506
Ensay
Loch Finsbay
Carminish
Strond
Lingarabay I.
Killegray
Rodel
Vallay
Renish Point

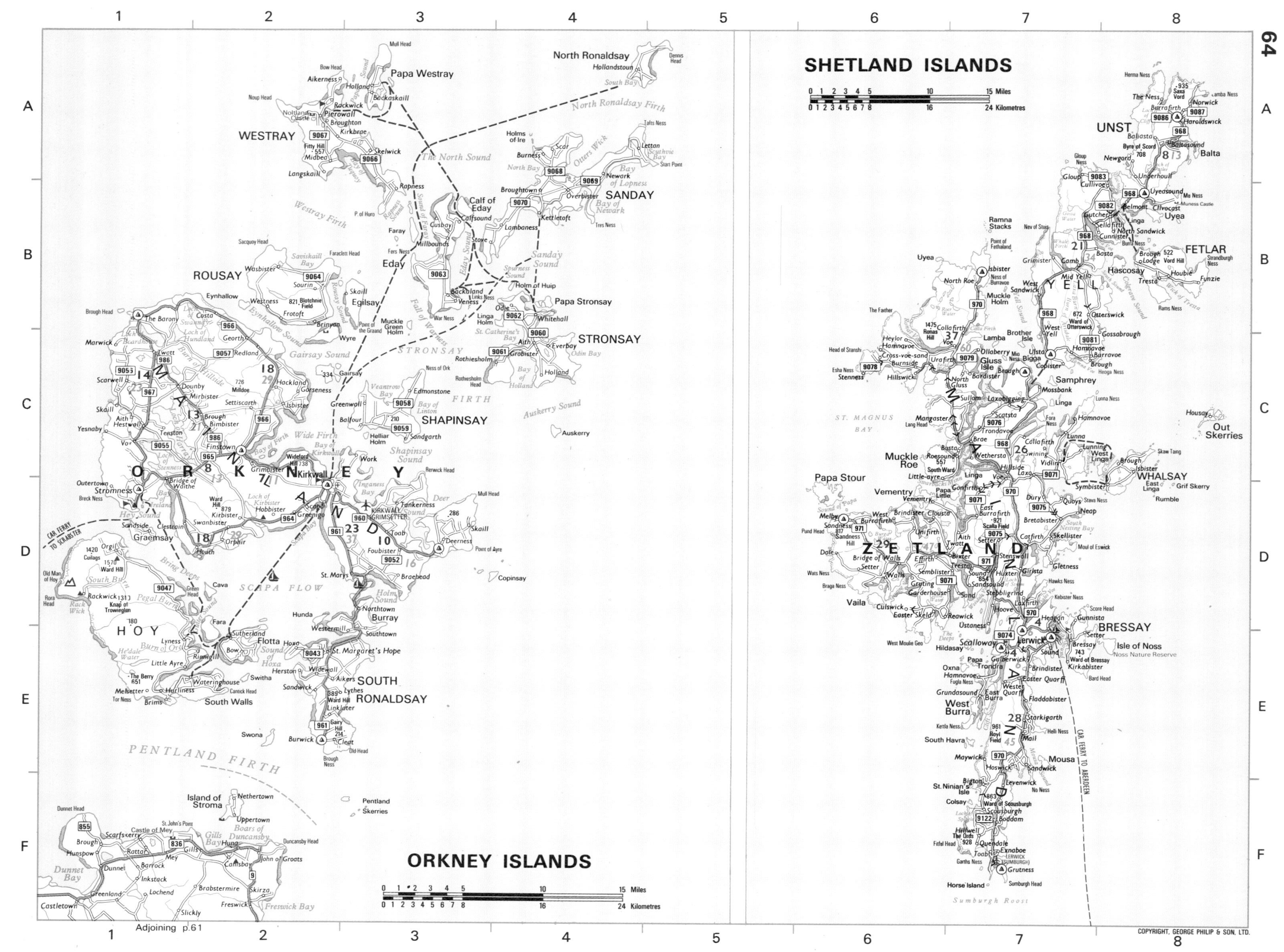

Adjoining p.61

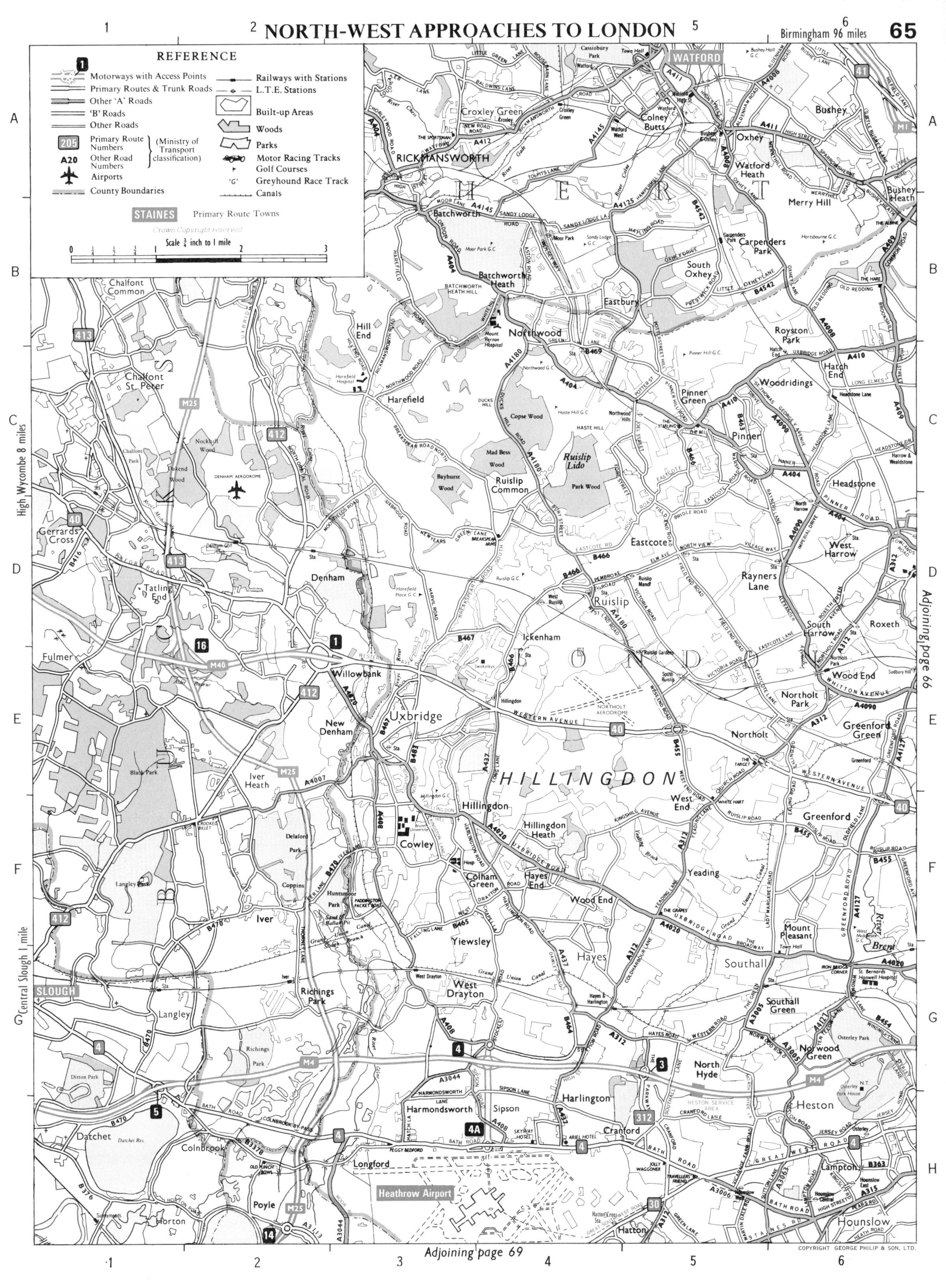
Birmingham 96 miles
REFERENCE
Motorways with Access Points
Primary Routes & Trunk Roads
Other 'A' Roads
'B' Roads
Other Roads
Primary Route Numbers
Other Road Numbers
(Ministry of Transport classification)
Airports
County Boundaries
Railways with Stations
L.T.E. Stations
Built-up Areas
Woods
Parks
Motor Racing Tracks
Golf Courses
Greyhound Race Track
Canals
STAINES
Primary Route Towns
Crown Copyright reserved
Scale ¾ inch to 1 mile
WATFORD
Croxley Green
Colney Butts
Oxhey
Bushey
RICKMANSWORTH
Watford Heath
Merry Hill
Bushey Heath
Batchworth
Carpenders Park
South Oxhey
Batchworth Heath
Eastbury
Chalfont Common
Hill End
Northwood
Royston Park
Hatch End
Chalfont St. Peter
Woodridings
Harefield
Pinner Green
Pinner
Copse Wood
Mad Bess Wood
Bayhurst Wood
Ruislip Common
Ruislip Lido
Park Wood
Headstone
DENHAM AERODROME
Gerrards Cross
Eastcote
West Harrow
Tatling End
Denham
Rayners Lane
Ruislip
South Harrow
Roxeth
Ickenham
Fulmer
Willowbank
Wood End
Northolt Park
Uxbridge
New Denham
NORTHOLT AERODROME
Northolt
Greenford Green
Black Park
Iver Heath
HILLINGDON
West End
Hillingdon
Greenford
Hillingdon Heath
Cowley
Delaford Park
Langley Park
Colham Green
Hayes End
Yeading
Wood End
Iver
Mount Pleasant
Yiewsley
Hayes
Southall
SLOUGH
West Drayton
Richings Park
Langley
Southall Green
Norwood Green
Osterley Park
North Hyde
Harlington
Heston
Harmondsworth
Sipson
Datchet
Colnbrook
Cranford
Longford
Lampton
Heathrow Airport
Poyle
Horton
Hatton
Hounslow
High Wycombe 8 miles
Central Slough 1 mile
Adjoining page 66
Adjoining page 69
COPYRIGHT GEORGE PHILIP & SON, LTD.

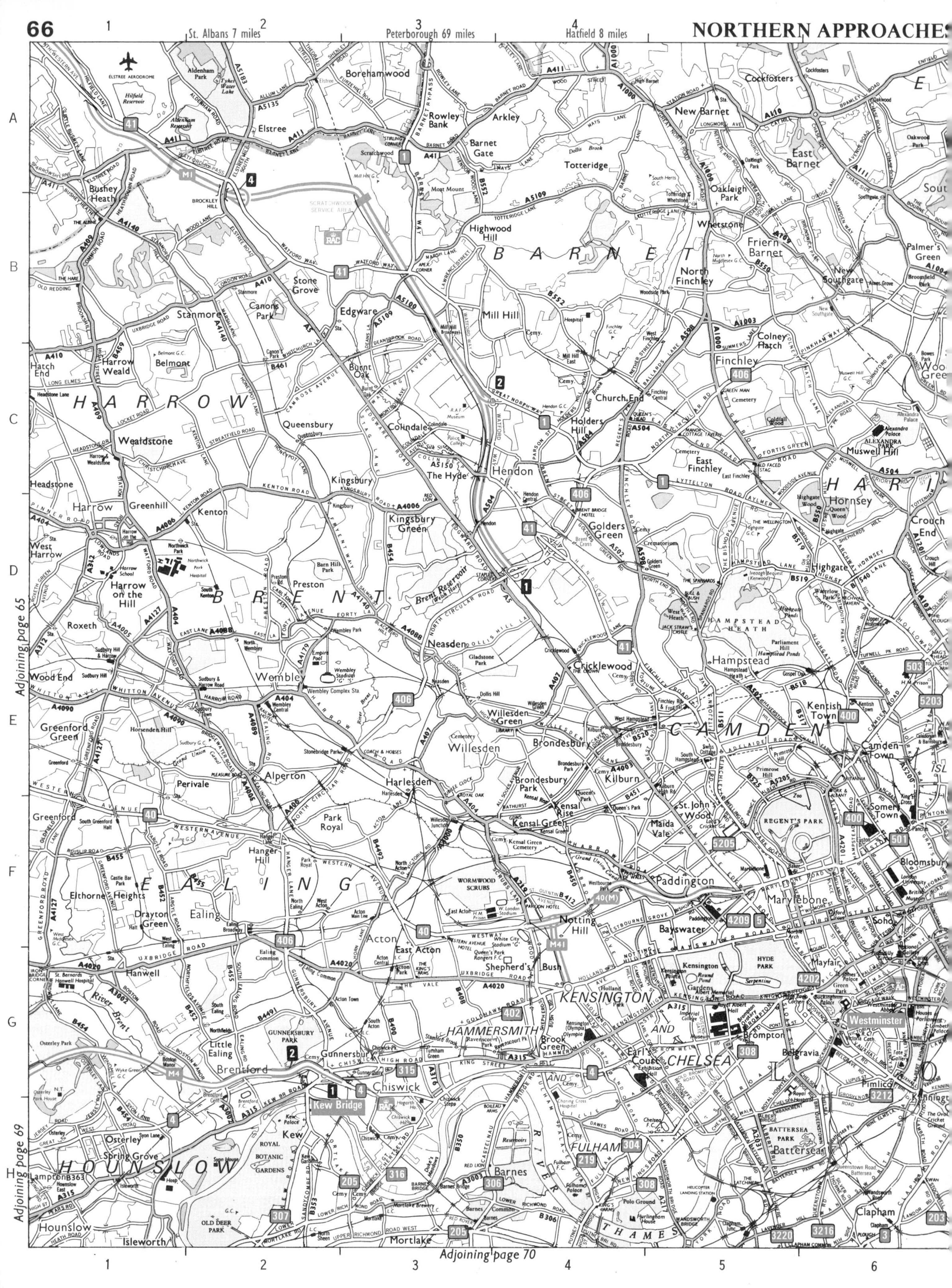

St. Albans 7 miles
Peterborough 69 miles
Hatfield 8 miles
Adjoining page 65
Adjoining page 69
Adjoining page 70
ELSTREE AERODROME
Aldenham Park
Borehamwood
Cockfosters
Rowley Bank
Arkley
New Barnet
Elstree
Barnet Gate
Totteridge
East Barnet
Oakleigh Park
Bushey Heath
Highwood Hill
Whetstone
Friern Barnet
Palmer's Green
BARNET
North Finchley
New Southgate
Stone Grove
Stanmore
Canons Park
Edgware
Mill Hill
Colney Hatch
Harrow Weald
Belmont
Burnt Oak
Finchley
Hatch End
HARROW
Queensbury
Colindale
Church End
Holders Hill
Wealdstone
Hendon
The Hyde
East Finchley
Muswell Hill
Kingsbury
HARINGEY
Headstone
Harrow
Greenhill
Kenton
Kingsbury Green
Hornsey
Golders Green
Crouch End
West Harrow
Highgate
Harrow on the Hill
Preston
BRENT
Brent Reservoir
Roxeth
Neasden
HAMPSTEAD HEATH
Wood End
Wembley
Cricklewood
Hampstead
Kentish Town
Greenford Green
Willesden Green
CAMDEN
Willesden
Brondesbury
Camden Town
Alperton
Harlesden
Brondesbury Park
Kilburn
Perivale
St. John's Wood
Greenford
Park Royal
Kensal Green
Maida Vale
REGENT'S PARK
Somers Town
Hanger Hill
Bloomsbury
EALING
Paddington
Marylebone
Elthorne Heights
WORMWOOD SCRUBS
Drayton Green
Ealing
Notting Hill
Bayswater
Soho
Acton
East Acton
HYDE PARK
Mayfair
Hanwell
Shepherd's Bush
KENSINGTON
Westminster
River Brent
HAMMERSMITH
AND
CHELSEA
Brompton
Belgravia
GUNNERSBURY PARK
Little Ealing
Gunnersbury
Brook Green
Earl's Court
Brentford
Chiswick
Pimlico
Kennington
Kew Bridge
Kew
Osterley
ROYAL BOTANIC GARDENS
FULHAM
BATTERSEA PARK
Battersea
Spring Grove
HOUNSLOW
RIVER THAMES
Barnes
Polo Ground
Clapham
OLD DEER PARK
Hounslow
Isleworth
Mortlake

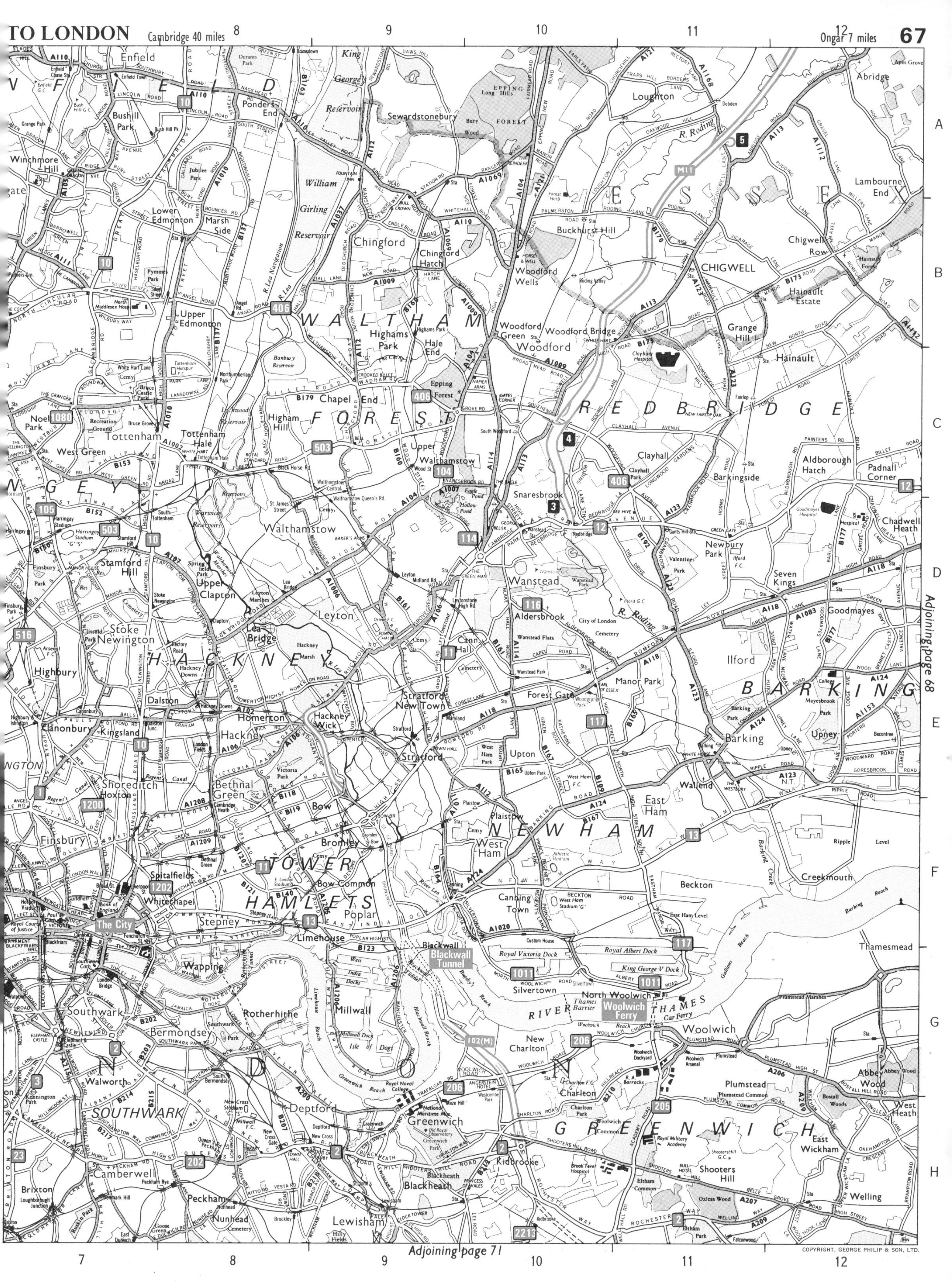

TO LONDON
Cambridge 40 miles
Ongar 7 miles
67
Adjoining page 68
Adjoining page 71
COPYRIGHT, GEORGE PHILIP & SON, LTD.
Enfield
Bushill Park
Winchmore Hill
Ponders End
Lower Edmonton
Upper Edmonton
Sewardstonebury
King George's Reservoir
William Girling Reservoir
Chingford
Chingford Hatch
Epping Forest
Loughton
Buckhurst Hill
Woodford Wells
Woodford Green
Woodford Bridge
Woodford
Chigwell
Chigwell Row
Abridge
Lambourne End
Hainault
Hainault Estate
Grange Hill
Essex
Waltham Forest
Highams Park
Hale End
Chapel End
Higham Hill
Tottenham
Tottenham Hale
West Green
Noel Park
Haringey
Walthamstow
Upper Walthamstow
Snaresbrook
Redbridge
Clayhall
Barkingside
Aldborough Hatch
Padnall Corner
Chadwell Heath
Newbury Park
Seven Kings
Goodmayes
Ilford
Barking
Upney
Stamford Hill
Upper Clapton
Stoke Newington
Lea Bridge
Leyton
Wanstead
Aldersbrook
Cann Hall
Manor Park
Forest Gate
Hackney
Highbury
Canonbury
Kingsland
Dalston
Homerton
Hackney Wick
Stratford New Town
Stratford
Upton
East Ham
Wallend
Shoreditch
Hoxton
Bethnal Green
Bow
Bromley
Plaistow
Newham
West Ham
Finsbury
Spitalfields
Whitechapel
Tower Hamlets
Bow Common
Poplar
Stepney
Limehouse
The City
Wapping
Canning Town
Beckton
Creekmouth
Thamesmead
Blackwall
Blackwall Tunnel
Royal Victoria Dock
Royal Albert Dock
King George V Dock
Silvertown
North Woolwich
Woolwich Ferry
River Thames
Millwall
Isle of Dogs
Rotherhithe
Southwark
Bermondsey
Walworth
Camberwell
Deptford
Greenwich
New Charlton
Charlton
Woolwich
Plumstead
Abbey Wood
West Heath
East Wickham
Shooters Hill
Welling
Kidbrooke
Blackheath
Lewisham
Brixton
Peckham
Nunhead
Ripple Level
Barking Reach

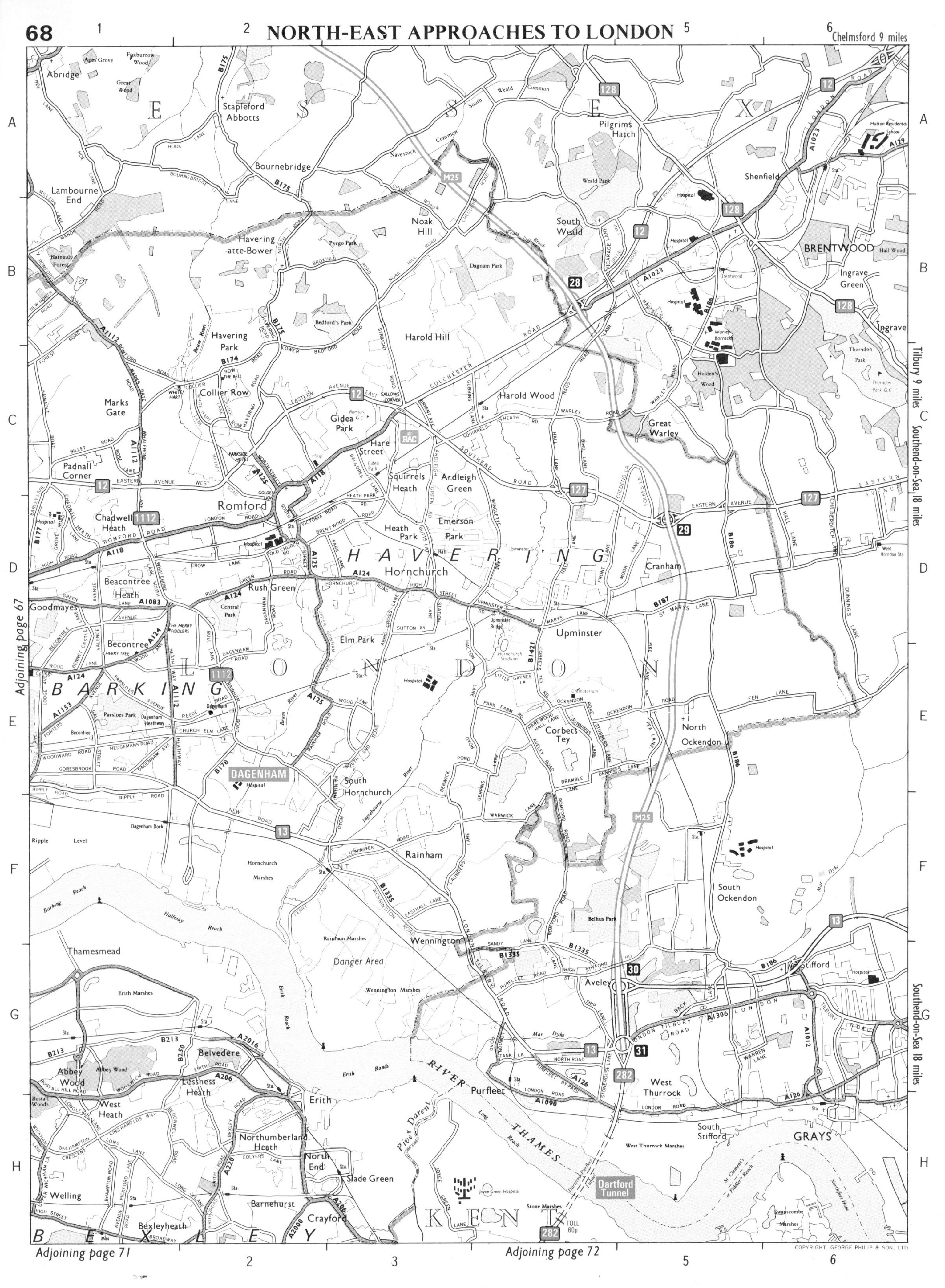

Adjoining page 71
Adjoining page 72

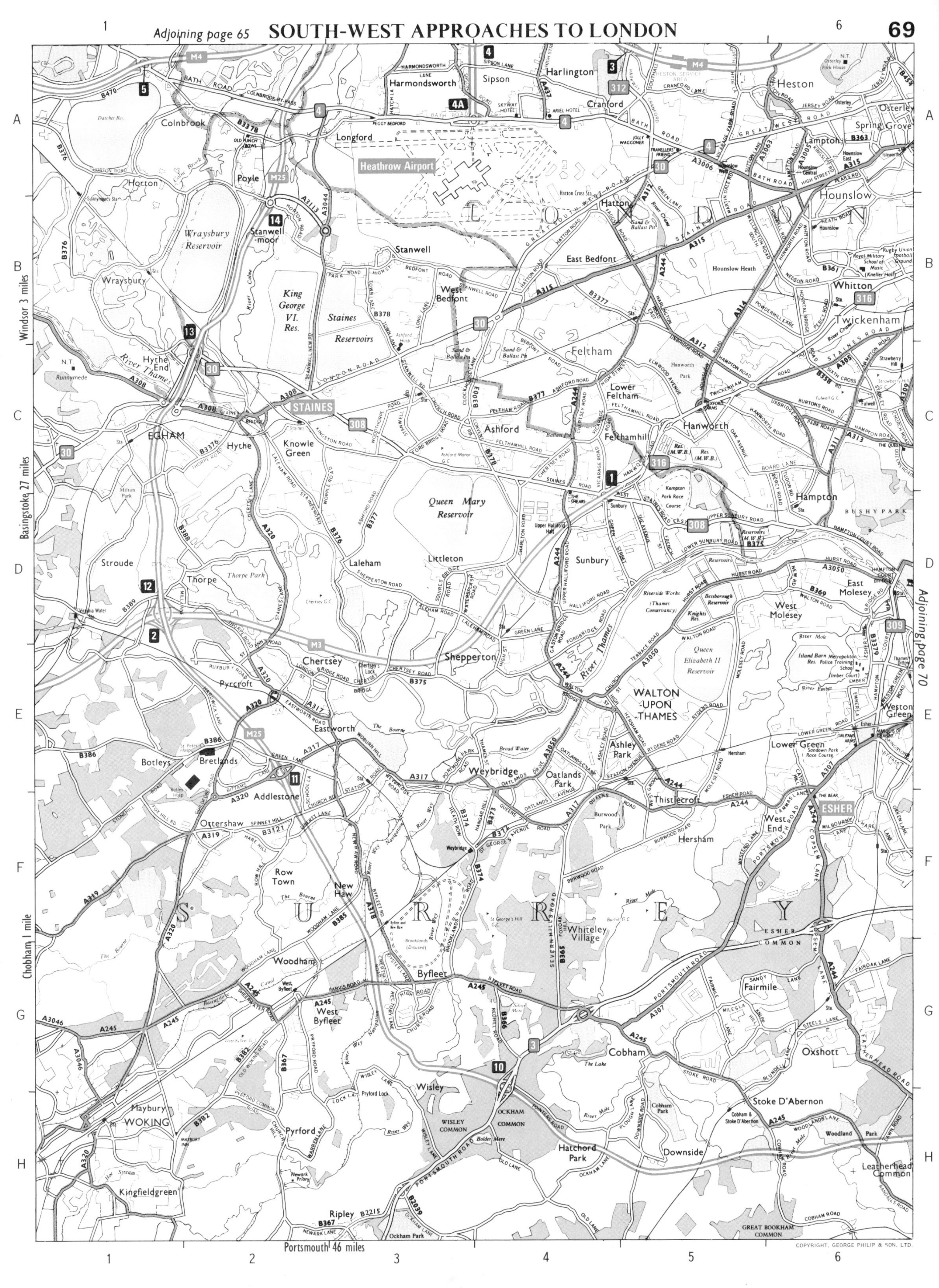
Windsor 3 miles
Basingstoke 27 miles
Chobham 1 mile
Portsmouth 46 miles
Adjoining page 70
Heathrow Airport
Harmondsworth
Sipson
Harlington
Cranford
Heston
Osterley
Spring Grove
Lampton
Hounslow
Colnbrook
Longford
Horton
Poyle
Wraysbury Reservoir
Stanwell-moor
Stanwell
East Bedfont
Wraysbury
King George VI. Res.
Staines Reservoirs
West Bedfont
Whitton
Twickenham
Hythe End
River Thames
Feltham
Lower Feltham
STAINES
EGHAM
Hythe
Knowle Green
Ashford
Feltham hill
Hanworth
Queen Mary Reservoir
Hampton
BUSHY PARK
Stroude
Laleham
Littleton
Sunbury
Thorpe
Thorpe Park
East Molesey
West Molesey
Queen Elizabeth II Reservoir
Chertsey
Shepperton
Pyrcroft
WALTON -UPON THAMES
Eastworth
Botleys
Bretlands
Weybridge
Oatlands Park
Ashley Park
Lower Green
Weston Green
Addlestone
Thistlecroft
ESHER
Ottershaw
Hersham
West End
Row Town
New Haw
S U R R E Y
Whiteley Village
ESHER COMMON
Woodham
Byfleet
Fairmile
West Byfleet
Cobham
Oxshott
Wisley
Stoke D'Abernon
Maybury
WOKING
Pyrford
WISLEY COMMON
OCKHAM COMMON
Hatchford Park
Downside
Leatherhead Common
Kingfieldgreen
Ripley
Ockham Park
GREAT BOOKHAM COMMON
M4
M25
M3
A30
A308
A320
A315
A244
A317
A3050
A245
A3
A307
A319
B376
B375
B377
B378
B3377
B365
B367
B382
B386
B389

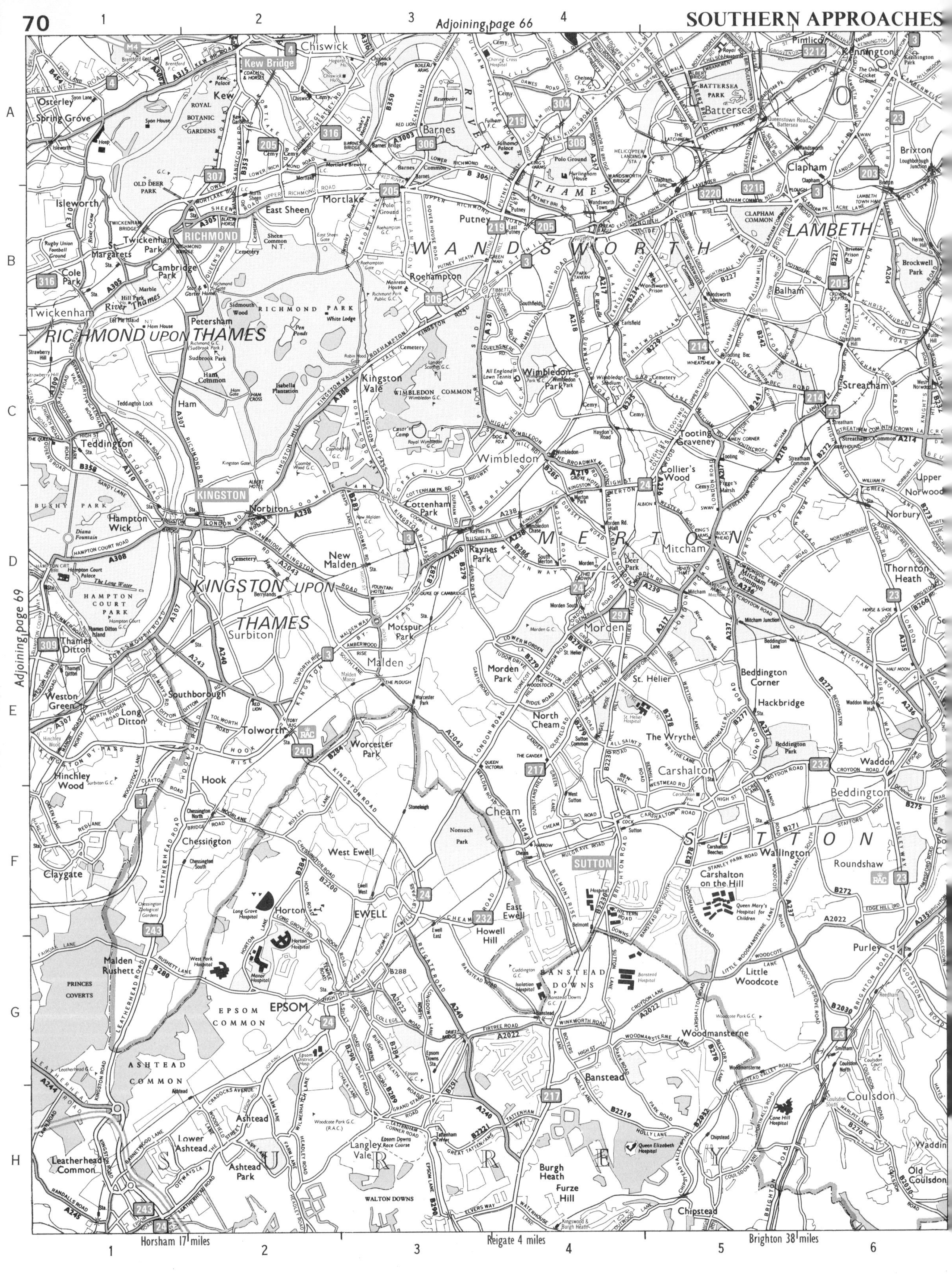

Adjoining page 66
Adjoining page 69
Horsham 17 miles
Reigate 4 miles
Brighton 38 miles
Chiswick
Kew Bridge
Kew
ROYAL BOTANIC GARDENS
Osterley
Spring Grove
Isleworth
OLD DEER PARK
Barnes
Mortlake
East Sheen
Putney
Pimlico
Kennington
Battersea
BATTERSEA PARK
Brixton
Clapham
CLAPHAM COMMON
LAMBETH
WANDSWORTH
Twickenham
St. Margarets
Twickenham Park
Cambridge Park
RICHMOND
Cole Park
RICHMOND PARK
Petersham
RICHMOND UPON THAMES
Roehampton
Balham
Brockwell Park
Kingston Vale
WIMBLEDON COMMON
Wimbledon Park
Streatham
Ham
Teddington
Wimbledon
Tooting Graveney
Collier's Wood
BUSHY PARK
Hampton Wick
KINGSTON
Norbiton
Cottenham Park
MERTON
Mitcham
Norbury
Upper Norwood
New Malden
Raynes Park
Thornton Heath
KINGSTON UPON THAMES
HAMPTON COURT PARK
Surbiton
Thames Ditton
Motspur Park
Morden
Malden
Morden Park
St. Helier
Beddington Corner
Hackbridge
Weston Green
Southborough
Long Ditton
Tolworth
Worcester Park
North Cheam
The Wrythe
Carshalton
Waddon
Hinchley Wood
Hook
Cheam
Beddington
Nonsuch Park
Chessington
West Ewell
SUTTON
SUTTON
Wallington
Roundshaw
Claygate
Horton
EWELL
East Ewell
Howell Hill
Carshalton on the Hill
Malden Rushett
PRINCES COVERTS
EPSOM COMMON
EPSOM
BANSTEAD DOWNS
Little Woodcote
Purley
Woodmansterne
ASHTEAD COMMON
Banstead
Coulsdon
Ashtead
Lower Ashtead
Leatherhead Common
Ashtead Park
Langley Vale
Burgh Heath
Furze Hill
WALTON DOWNS
Chipstead
Old Coulsdon
SURREY

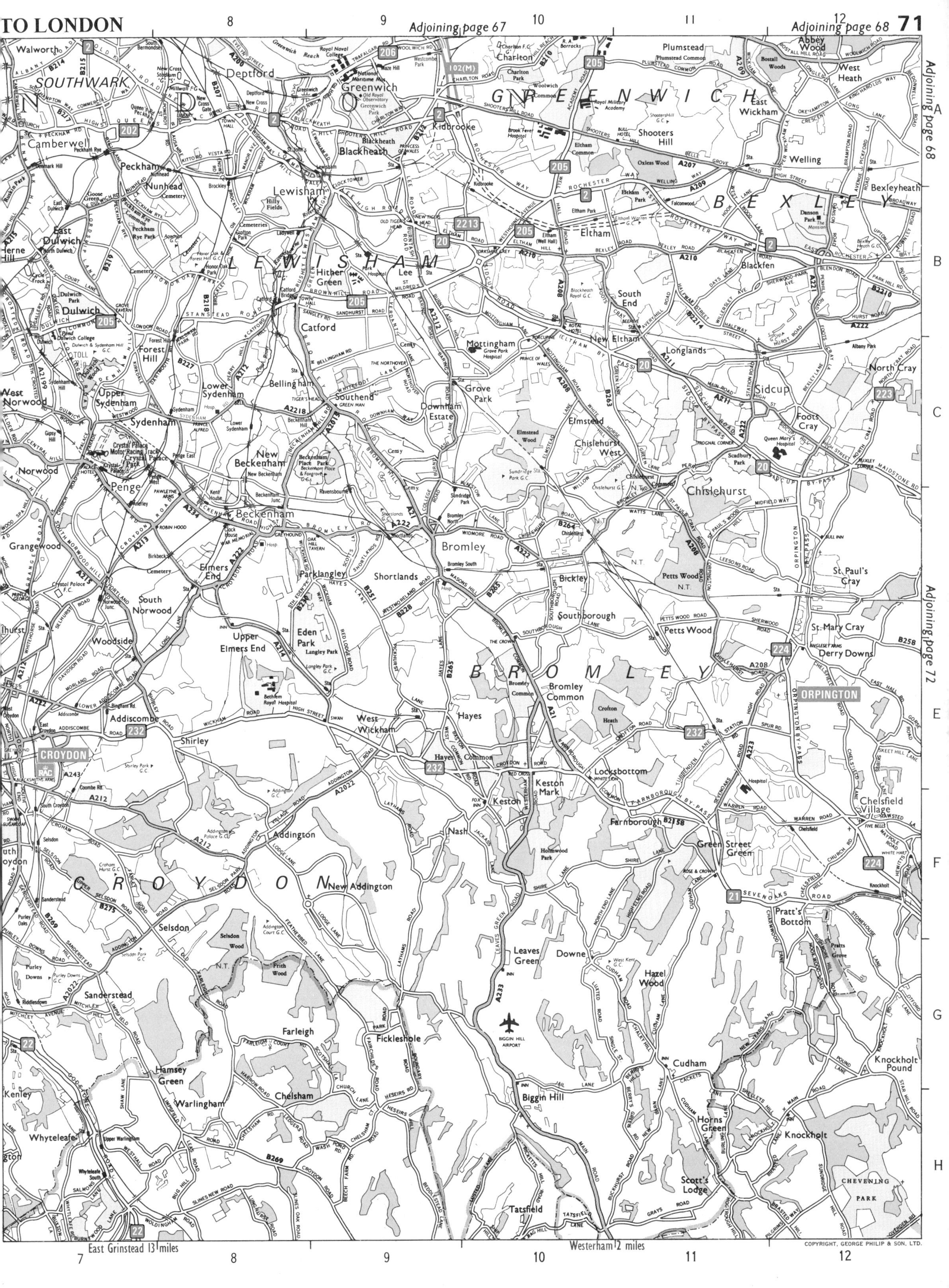

Adjoining page 67
Adjoining page 68
Adjoining page 72
8
9
10
11
12
A
B
C
D
E
F
G
H
SOUTHWARK
GREENWICH
LEWISHAM
BEXLEY
BROMLEY
CROYDON
Walworth
Deptford
Greenwich
Charlton
Plumstead
Abbey Wood
West Heath
Camberwell
Peckham
Nunhead
Kidbrooke
Blackheath
East Wickham
Shooters Hill
Welling
Bexleyheath
Lewisham
Eltham
East Dulwich
Dulwich
Hither Green
Lee
Blackfen
South End
Catford
Forest Hill
Mottingham
New Eltham
Longlands
Sidcup
North Cray
Foots Cray
Upper Sydenham
Lower Sydenham
Bellingham
Southend
Grove Park
Downham Estate
Elmstead
Chislehurst West
Sydenham
West Norwood
Norwood
New Beckenham
Penge
Chislehurst
Beckenham
Bromley
Grangewood
Elmers End
Shortlands
Parklangley
Bickley
St. Paul's Cray
South Norwood
Southborough
Petts Wood
St. Mary Cray
Derry Downs
Woodside
Upper Elmers End
Eden Park
Hayes
Bromley Common
Addiscombe
Shirley
West Wickham
Hayes Common
ORPINGTON
CROYDON
Locksbottom
Keston Mark
Keston
Nash
Chelsfield Village
Addington
Farnborough
Green Street Green
New Addington
Selsdon
Pratt's Bottom
Leaves Green
Downe
Hazel Wood
Sanderstead
Farleigh
Fickleshole
Cudham
Knockholt Pound
Hamsey Green
Warlingham
Chelsham
Biggin Hill
Kenley
Whyteleafe
Horns Green
Knockholt
Scott's Lodge
Tatsfield
CHEVENING PARK
BIGGIN HILL AIRPORT
East Grinstead 13 miles
Westerham 2 miles

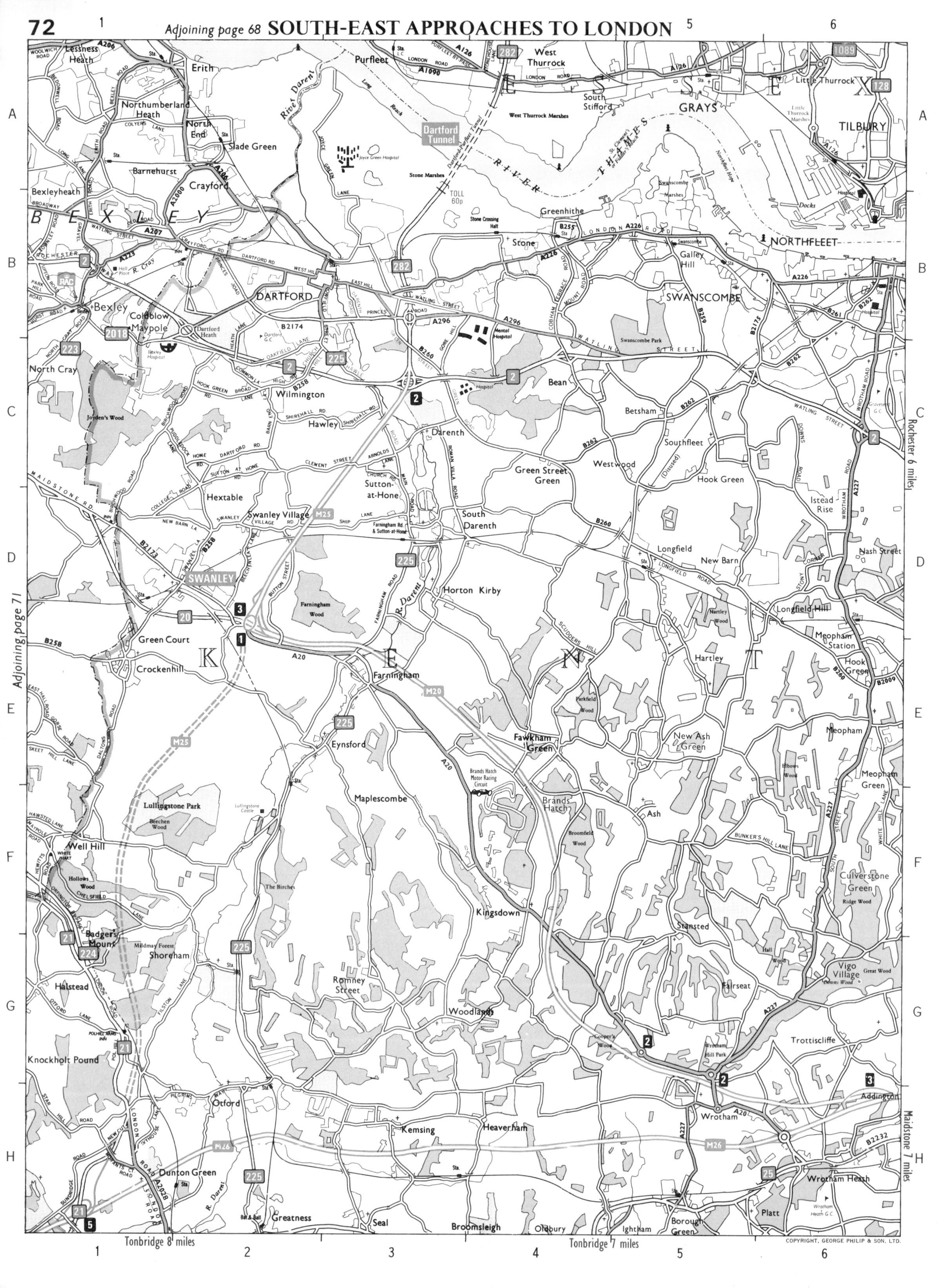
Lessness Heath
Erith
Purfleet
West Thurrock
Little Thurrock
Northumberland Heath
North End
Slade Green
Barnehurst
Crayford
Bexleyheath
Dartford Tunnel
Joyce Green Hospital
Stone Marshes
West Thurrock Marshes
South Stifford
GRAYS
TILBURY
RIVER THAMES
Swanscombe Marshes
Greenhithe
Stone Crossing Halt
Stone
NORTHFLEET
Galley Hill
SWANSCOMBE
Swanscombe Park
BEXLEY
Bexley
Coldblow
Maypole
Dartford Heath
DARTFORD
Dartford G.C.
Bexley Hospital
Mental Hospital
North Cray
Wilmington
Bean
Betsham
Joyden's Wood
Hawley
Darenth
Southfleet
Westwood
Green Street Green
Hook Green
Hextable
Sutton-at-Hone
Swanley Village
South Darenth
Istead Rise
Farningham Rd. & Sutton-at-Hone
Longfield
New Barn
Nash Street
SWANLEY
Farningham Wood
Horton Kirby
Longfield Hill
Hartley Wood
Meopham Station
Green Court
Crockenhill
KENT
Farningham
Hartley
Hook Green
Parkfield Wood
Fawkham Green
New Ash Green
Meopham
Eynsford
Brands Hatch Motor Racing Circuit
Maplescombe
Brands Hatch
Ash
Elbows Wood
Meopham Green
Lullingstone Park
Lullingstone Castle
Beechen Wood
Broomfield Wood
Well Hill
Hollows Wood
The Birches
Culverstone Green
Ridge Wood
Kingsdown
Stansted
Badgers Mount
Mildmay Forest
Shoreham
Hall Wood
Vigo Village
Great Wood
Halstead
Romney Street
Fairseat
Woodlands
Trottiscliffe
Knockholt Pound
Cooper's Wood
Wrotham Hill Park
Addington
Otford
Wrotham
Kemsing
Heaverham
Dunton Green
Wrotham Heath
Greatness
Seal
Broomsleigh
Oldbury
Ightham
Borough Green
Platt
Wrotham Heath G.C.
Rochester 6 miles
Maidstone 7 miles
Adjoining page 71
Tonbridge 8 miles
Tonbridge 7 miles
COPYRIGHT, GEORGE PHILIP & SON, LTD.

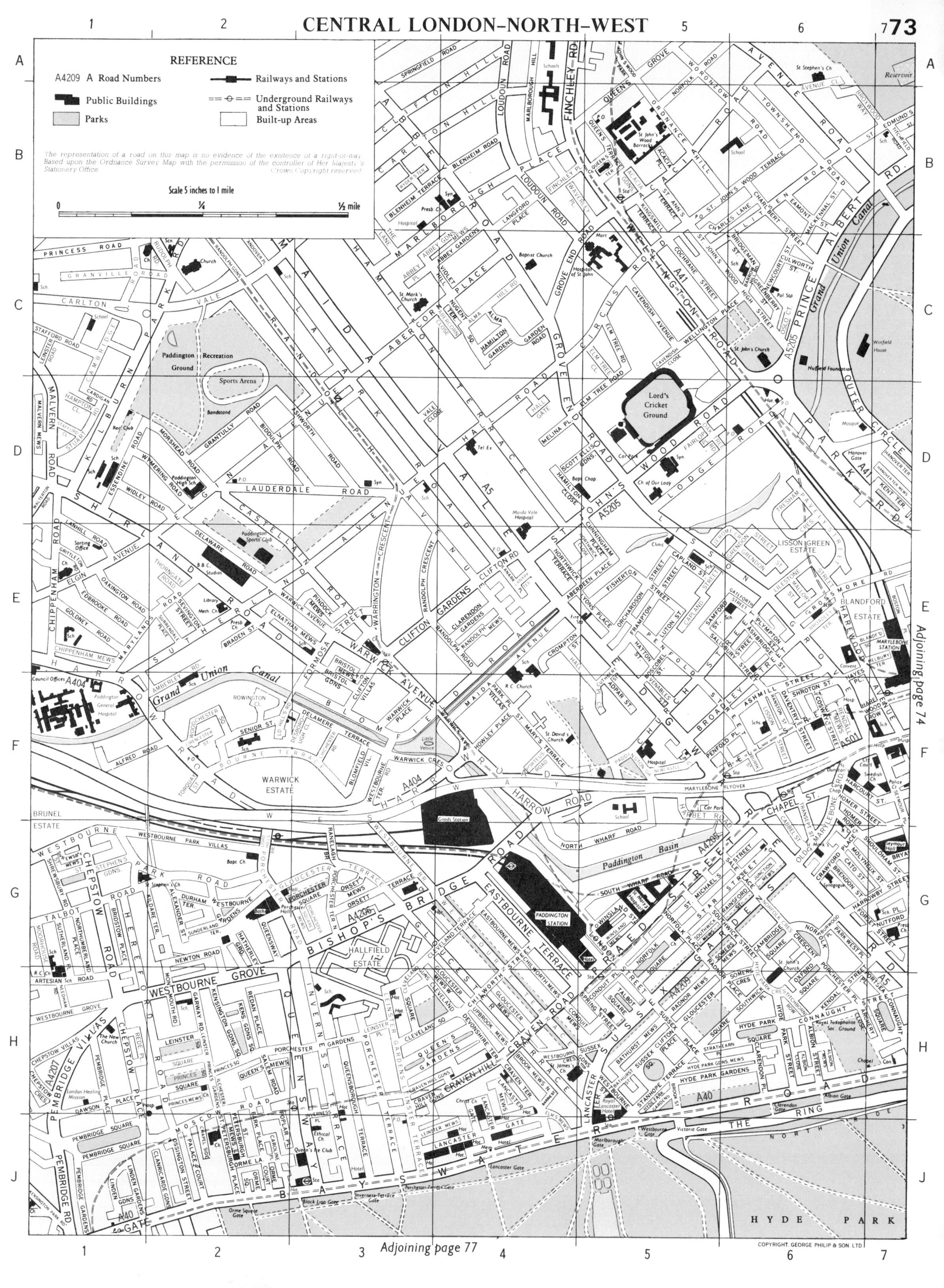

Adjoining page 74

Adjoining page 77

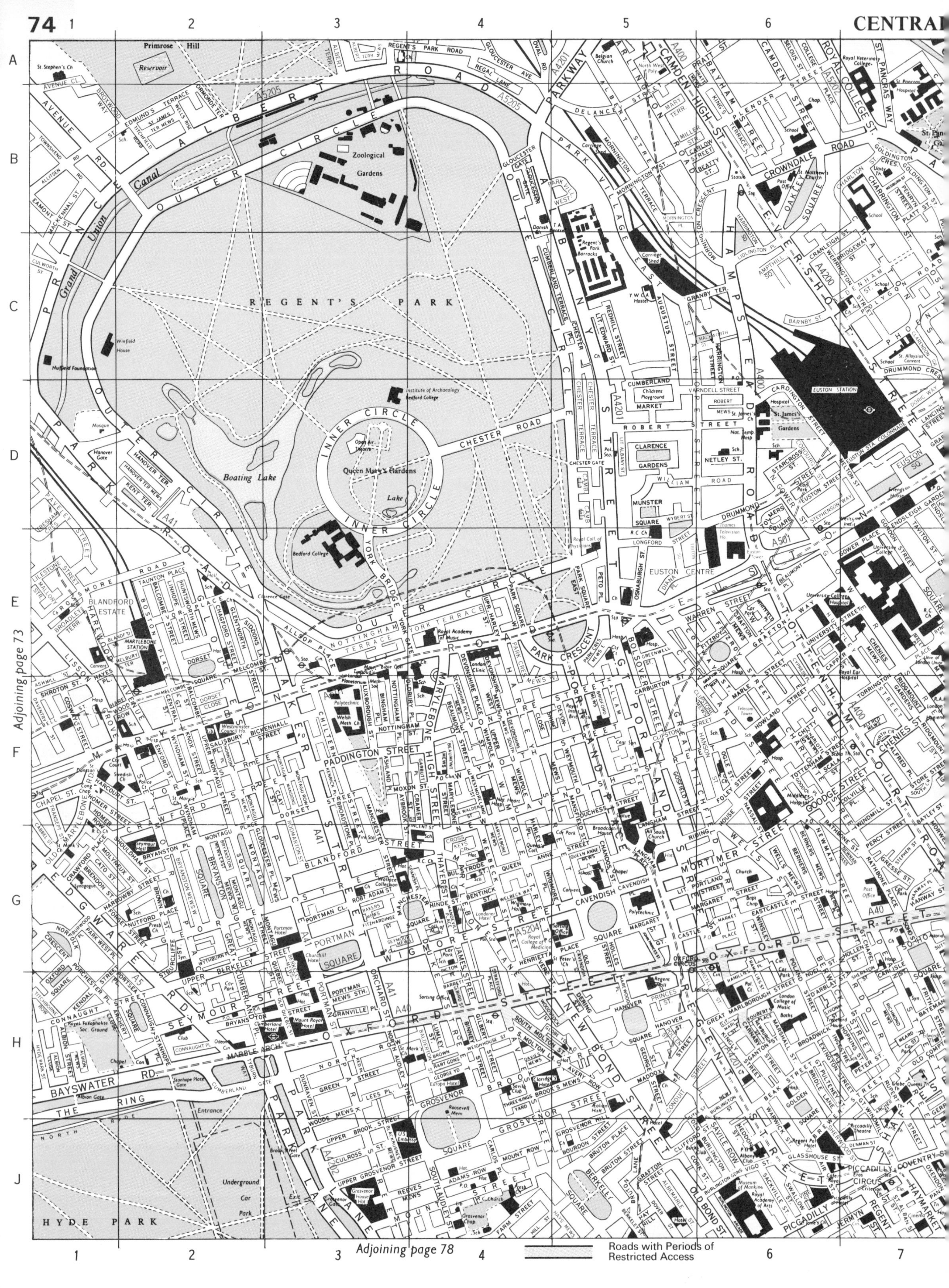

Adjoining page 73

Adjoining page 78

Roads with Periods of Restricted Access

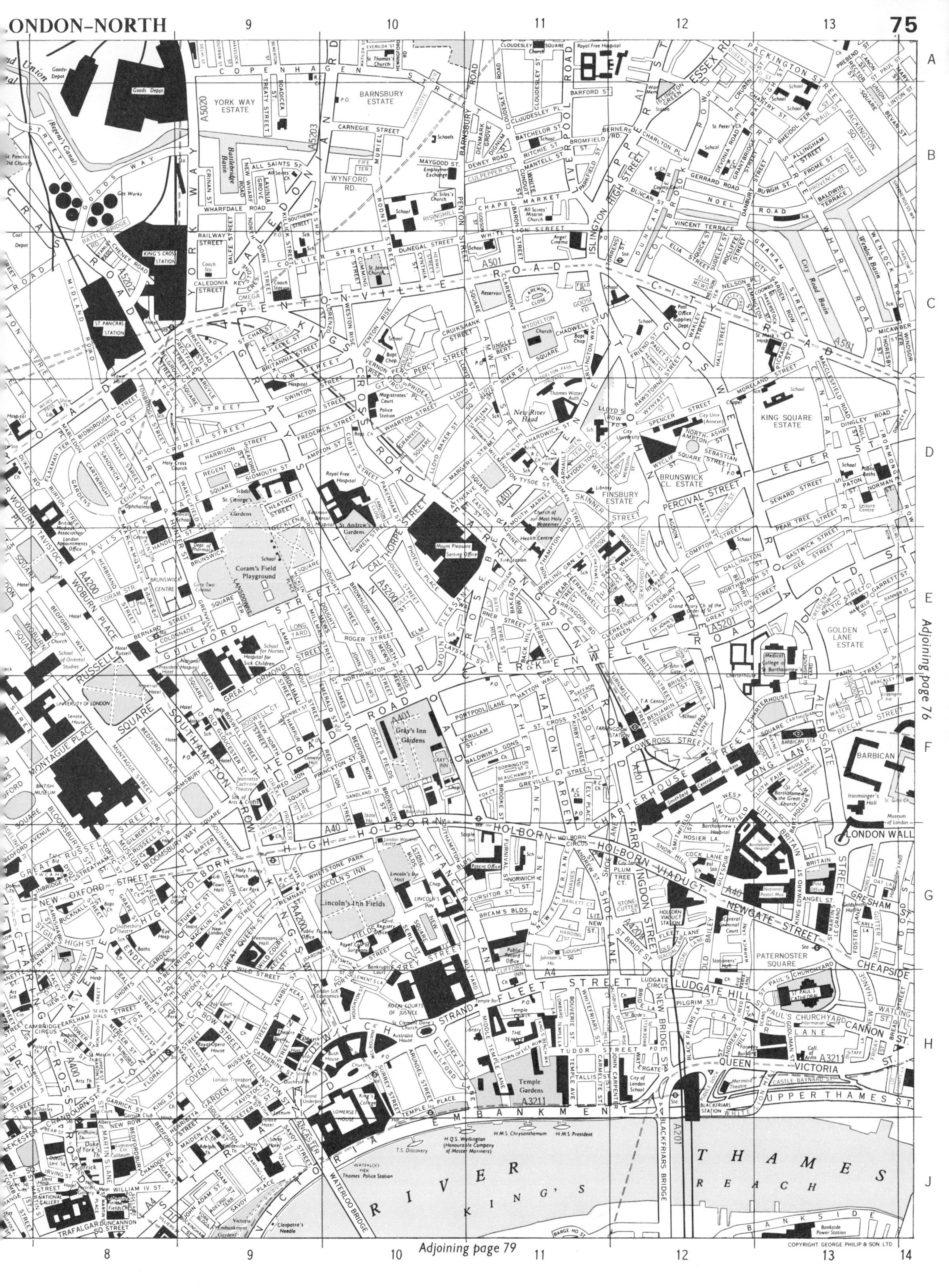

Adjoining page 76

Adjoining page 79

8 9 10 11 12 13 14

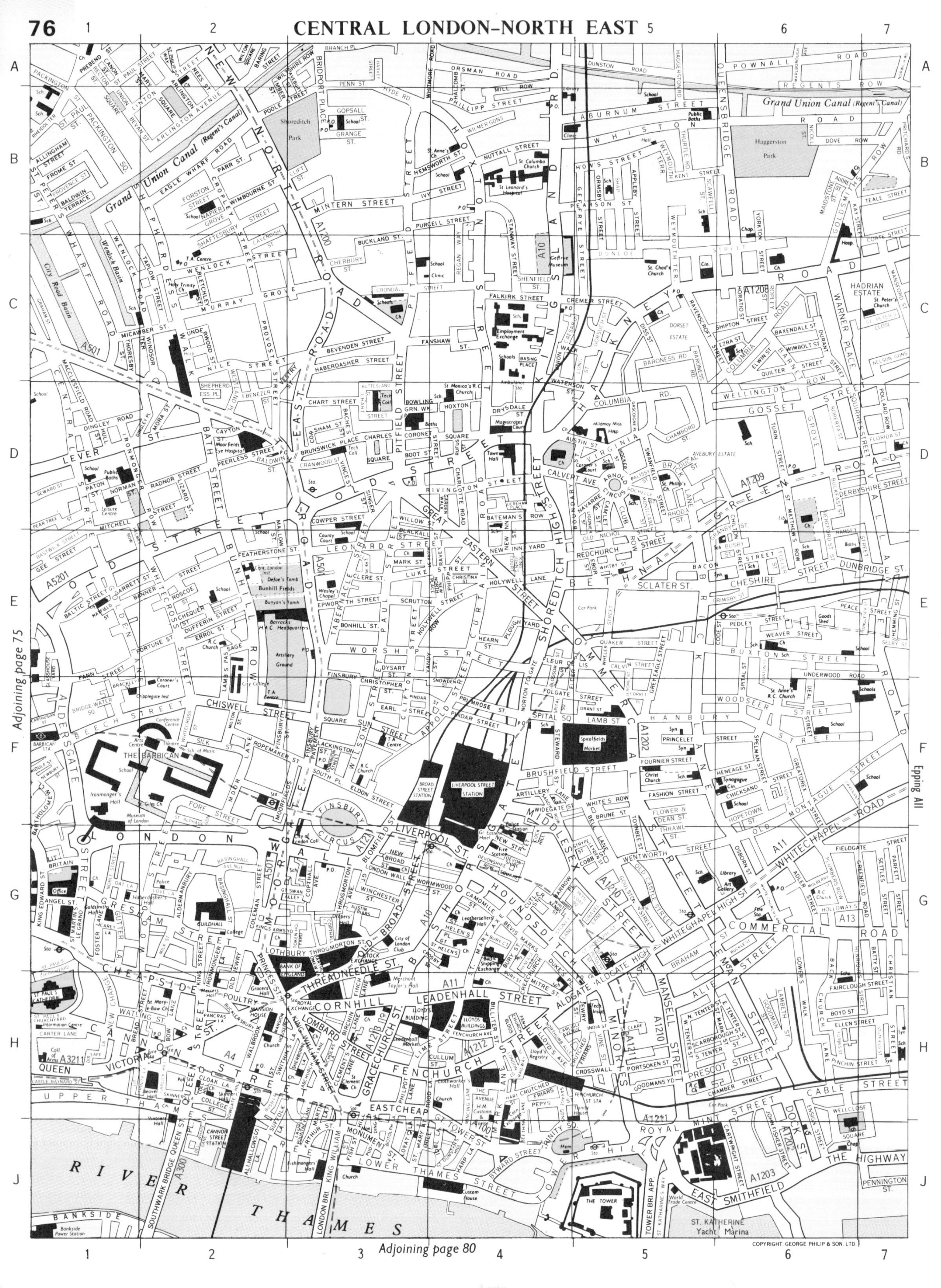
76
CENTRAL LONDON–NORTH EAST
1
2
5
6
7
A
B
C
D
E
F
G
H
J
Adjoining page 75
Epping A11
Adjoining page 80
COPYRIGHT, GEORGE PHILIP & SON, LTD.
Grand Union Canal (Regent's Canal)
Shoreditch Park
Haggerston Park
City Road Basin
Wenlock Basin
NEW NORTH ROAD
EAST ROAD
CITY ROAD
OLD STREET
KINGSLAND RD.
HACKNEY ROAD
BETHNAL GREEN ROAD
SHOREDITCH HIGH STREET
COMMERCIAL STREET
BISHOPSGATE
HOUNDSDITCH
WHITECHAPEL ROAD
WHITECHAPEL HIGH ST.
COMMERCIAL ROAD
CABLE STREET
THE HIGHWAY
EAST SMITHFIELD
ROYAL MINT STREET
LOWER THAMES STREET
UPPER THAMES STREET
QUEEN VICTORIA STREET
CANNON STREET
CHEAPSIDE
LONDON WALL
ALDERSGATE STREET
MOORGATE
FINSBURY CIRCUS
LIVERPOOL ST.
THREADNEEDLE ST.
CORNHILL
LEADENHALL STREET
FENCHURCH ST.
EASTCHEAP
GRACECHURCH ST.
KING WILLIAM STREET
LOMBARD ST.
POULTRY
GRESHAM STREET
CHISWELL STREET
BUNHILL ROW
BUNHILL FIELDS
Artillery Ground
THE BARBICAN
BARBICAN STA
Museum of London
St. Paul's Cathedral
BANK OF ENGLAND
ROYAL EXCHANGE
Mansion House
Guildhall
BROAD STREET STATION
LIVERPOOL STREET STATION
Spitalfields Market
CANNON STREET STATION
FENCHURCH STREET STA
THE TOWER
TOWER HILL
TOWER BRI. APP.
ST. KATHERINE Yacht Marina
World Trade Centre
Custom House
Bankside Power Station
BANKSIDE
SOUTHWARK BRIDGE
LONDON BRI.
RIVER THAMES
MINORIES
ALDGATE
ALDGATE HIGH ST.
MANSELL STREET
LEMAN STREET
PRESCOT STREET
HANBURY STREET
BRICK LANE
HOXTON STREET
PITFIELD STREET
GOLDSMITHS ROW
HADRIAN ESTATE
DORSET ESTATE
AVEBURY ESTATE
A10
A11
A13
A100
A1200
A1202
A1208
A1209
A1210
A1211
A1212
A1213
A1203
A501
A5201
A3211
A300
A4
A501

Adjoining page 73

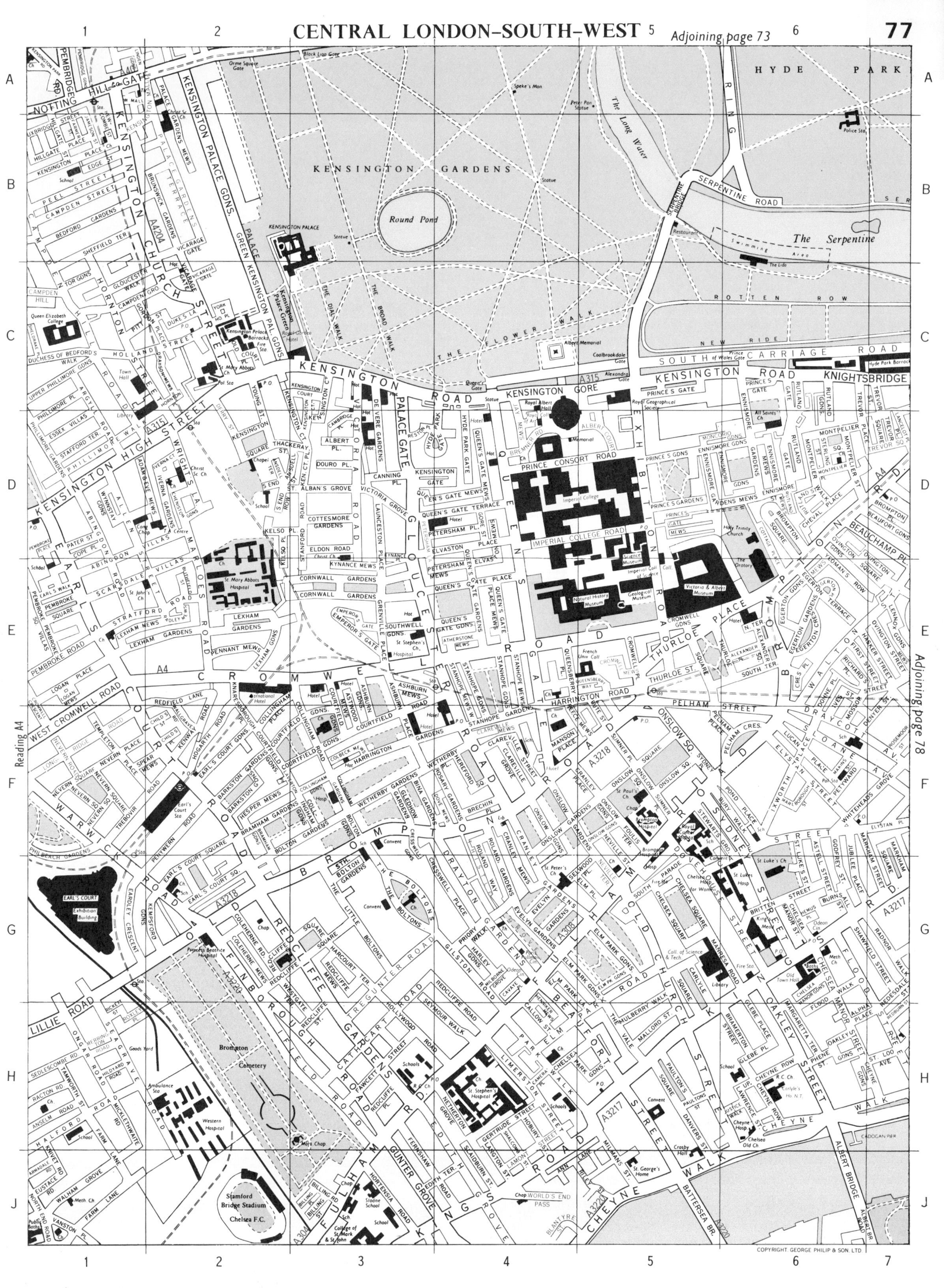

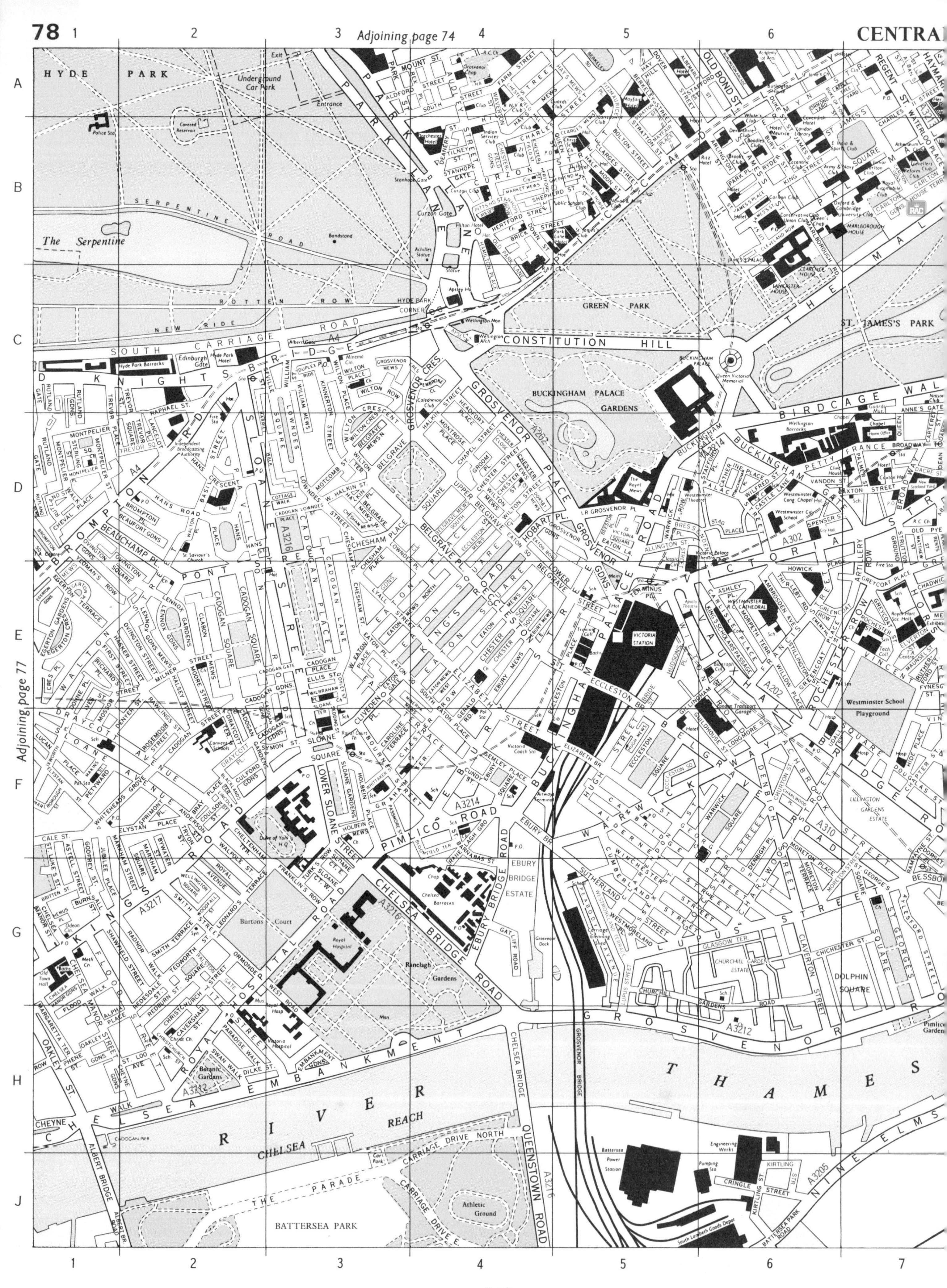
78
CENTRA
Adjoining page 74
Adjoining page 77
HYDE PARK
The Serpentine
SERPENTINE ROAD
ROTTEN ROW
NEW RIDE
SOUTH CARRIAGE ROAD
Underground Car Park
Covered Reservoir
Police Sta
Bandstand
Achilles Statue
HYDE PARK CORNER
Hyde Park Barracks
Edinburgh Gate
Albert Gate
KNIGHTSBRIDGE
PARK LANE
CURZON ST
PICCADILLY
OLD BOND ST
REGENT ST
HAYMARKET
PALL MALL
THE MALL
GREEN PARK
CONSTITUTION HILL
ST. JAMES'S PARK
BUCKINGHAM PALACE
BUCKINGHAM PALACE GARDENS
Queen Victoria Memorial
BIRDCAGE WALK
Wellington Barracks
GROSVENOR PLACE
GROSVENOR CRES
BELGRAVE SQUARE
EATON SQUARE
LOWNDES SQUARE
CADOGAN PLACE
SLOANE STREET
SLOANE SQUARE
CADOGAN SQUARE
PONT ST
BROMPTON ROAD
BEAUCHAMP PL
WALTON STREET
KING'S ROAD
VICTORIA STATION
VICTORIA STREET
BUCKINGHAM PALACE ROAD
VAUXHALL BRIDGE ROAD
Westminster Cathedral
Westminster School Playground
LILLINGTON GARDENS ESTATE
PIMLICO ROAD
EBURY BRIDGE ROAD
EBURY BRIDGE ESTATE
CHELSEA BRIDGE ROAD
Chelsea Barracks
Burtons Court
Royal Hospital
Ranelagh Gardens
ROYAL HOSPITAL ROAD
CHELSEA EMBANKMENT
GROSVENOR ROAD
CHURCHILL GARDENS ESTATE
DOLPHIN SQUARE
Pimlico Gardens
RIVER THAMES
CHELSEA REACH
CHELSEA BRIDGE
GROSVENOR BRIDGE
Battersea Power Station
QUEENSTOWN ROAD
BATTERSEA PARK
CARRIAGE DRIVE NORTH
THE PARADE
Athletic Ground
ALBERT BRIDGE
NINE ELMS
South Lambeth Goods Depot
A4
A202
A3214
A3216
A3217
A3212
A302
A310
A3205
1
2
3
4
5
6
7
A
B
C
D
E
F
G
H
J

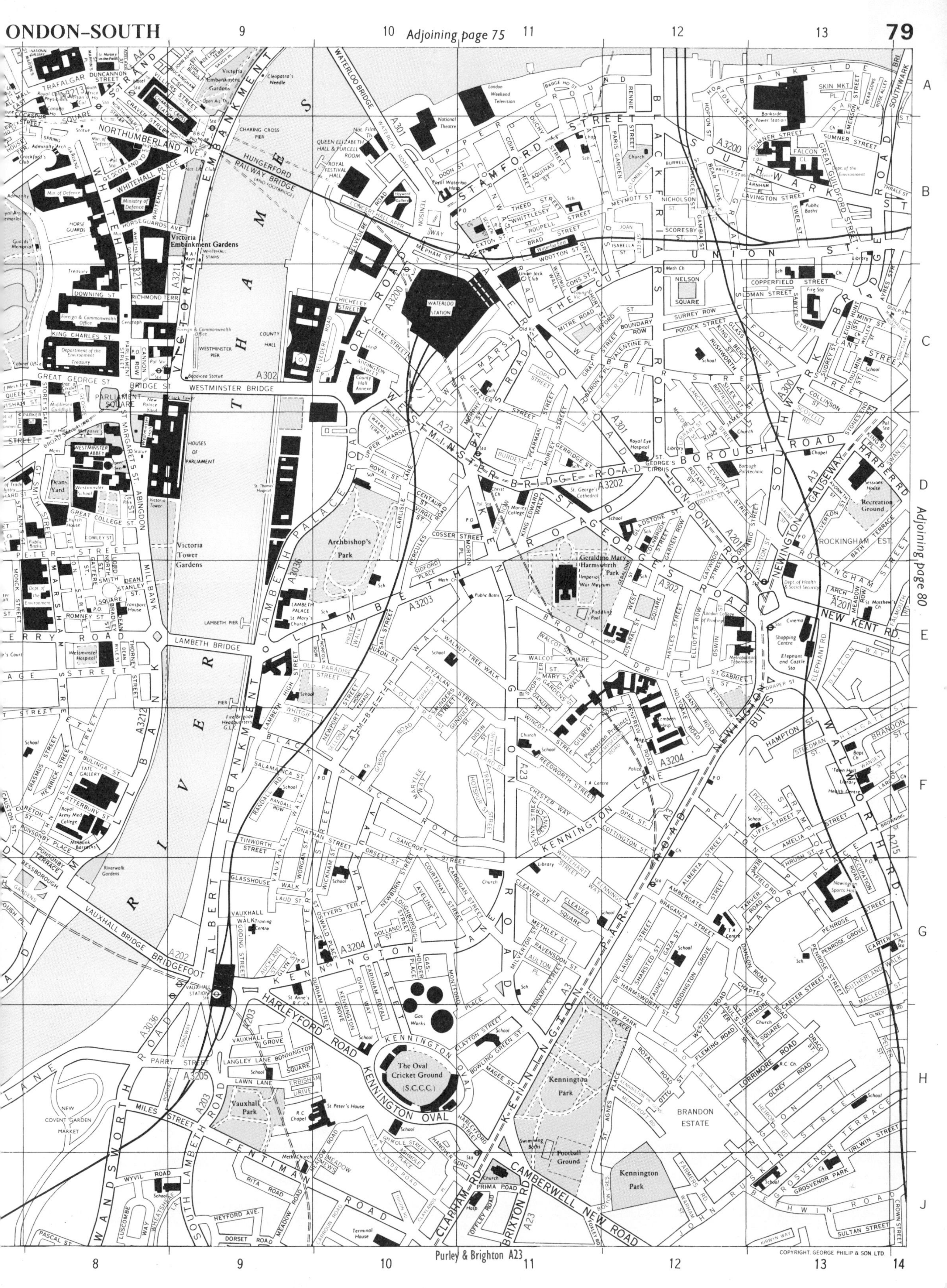
9
10
11
12
13
A
B
C
D
E
F
G
H
J
Adjoining page 80
TRAFALGAR
DUNCANNON STREET
NORTHUMBERLAND AVE.
WHITEHALL
WHITEHALL PLACE
HORSE GUARDS AVE.
HORSE GUARDS
Treasury
DOWNING ST.
RICHMOND TERR.
Foreign & Commonwealth Office
KING CHARLES ST.
Department of the Environment Treasury
GREAT GEORGE ST.
PARLIAMENT SQUARE
BRIDGE ST.
WESTMINSTER BRIDGE
WESTMINSTER ABBEY
Deans Yard
Westminster School
GREAT COLLEGE ST.
ABINGDON
PETER STREET
MARSHAM STREET
HORSEFERRY ROAD
LAMBETH BRIDGE
Westminster Hospital
MILLBANK
TATE GALLERY
ATTERBURY ST.
Royal Army Med College
Millbank Barracks
Riverwalk Gardens
VAUXHALL BRIDGE
VAUXHALL BRIDGEFOOT
VAUXHALL STATION
WANDSWORTH ROAD
SOUTH LAMBETH ROAD
NEW COVENT GARDEN MARKET
Victoria Embankment Gardens
VICTORIA EMBANKMENT
HUNGERFORD RAILWAY BRIDGE
HOUSES OF PARLIAMENT
Victoria Tower Gardens
RIVER THAMES
ALBERT EMBANKMENT
WATERLOO BRIDGE
National Theatre
London Weekend Television
QUEEN ELIZABETH HALL & PURCELL ROOM
ROYAL FESTIVAL HALL
COUNTY HALL
WATERLOO STATION
YORK ROAD
STAMFORD STREET
UPPER GROUND
THE CUT
WATERLOO ROAD
BLACKFRIARS ROAD
SOUTHWARK STREET
UNION ST.
BANKSIDE
Bankside Power Station
SOUTHWARK BRIDGE ROAD
BOROUGH ROAD
ST. GEORGE'S CIRCUS
WESTMINSTER BRIDGE ROAD
LAMBETH ROAD
St. George's Cathedral
Geraldine Mary Harmsworth Park
Imperial War Museum
Archbishop's Park
LAMBETH PALACE
LAMBETH PALACE ROAD
KENNINGTON ROAD
BROOK DRIVE
LONDON ROAD
NEWINGTON CAUSEWAY
NEW KENT RD.
Elephant and Castle Sta
Shopping Centre
NEWINGTON BUTTS
WALWORTH RD.
KENNINGTON LANE
KENNINGTON PARK ROAD
HARLEYFORD ROAD
The Oval Cricket Ground (S.C.C.C.)
KENNINGTON OVAL
Gas Works
Vauxhall Park
Kennington Park
Football Ground
BRANDON ESTATE
CAMBERWELL NEW ROAD
CLAPHAM RD.
BRIXTON ROAD
FENTIMAN ROAD
MILES STREET
PARRY STREET
GROSVENOR PARK
Recreation Ground
ROCKINGHAM EST.

Adjoining page 76

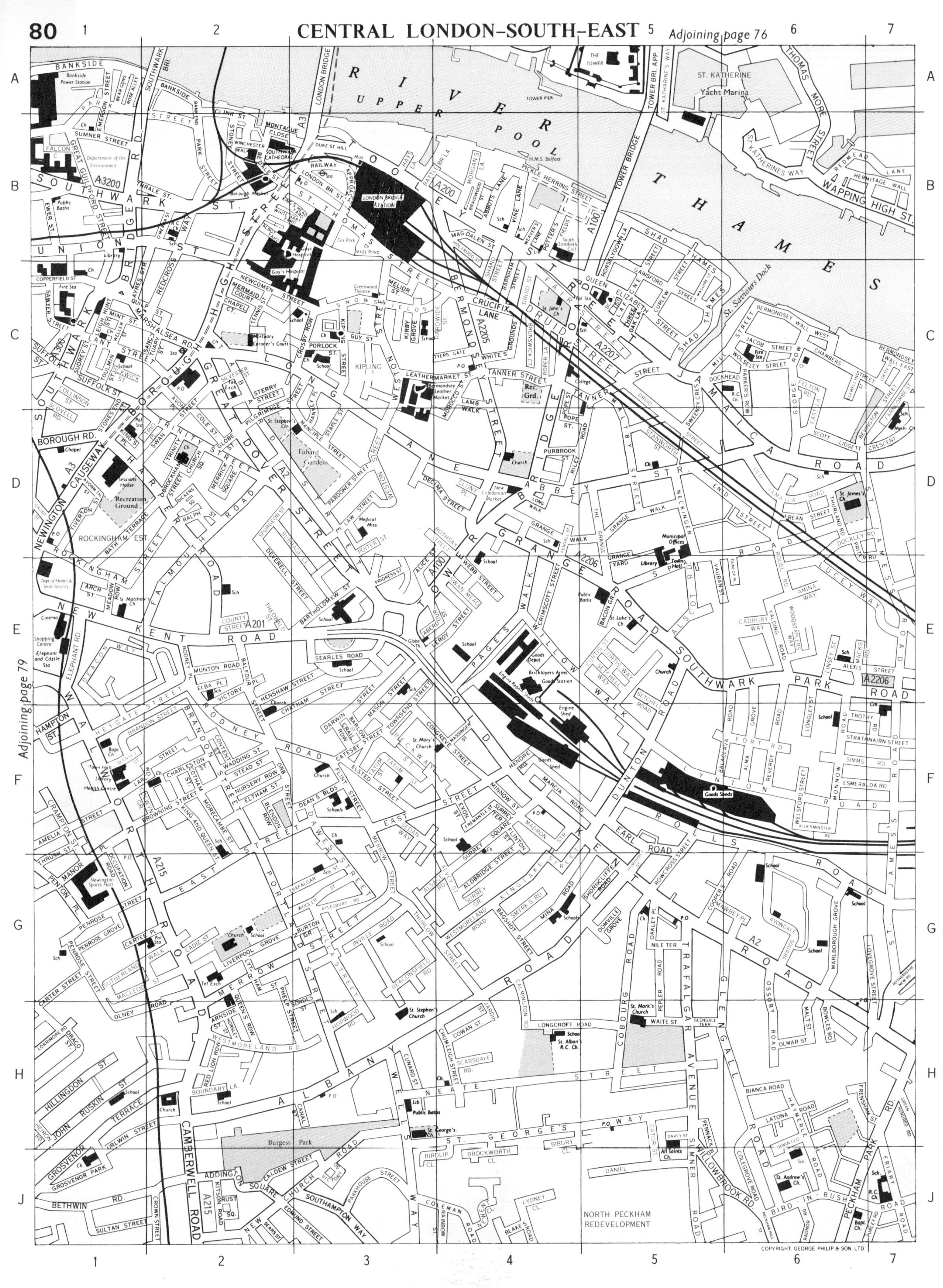

Adjoining page 79

REFERENCE

TOWN MAPS / CITY MAPS

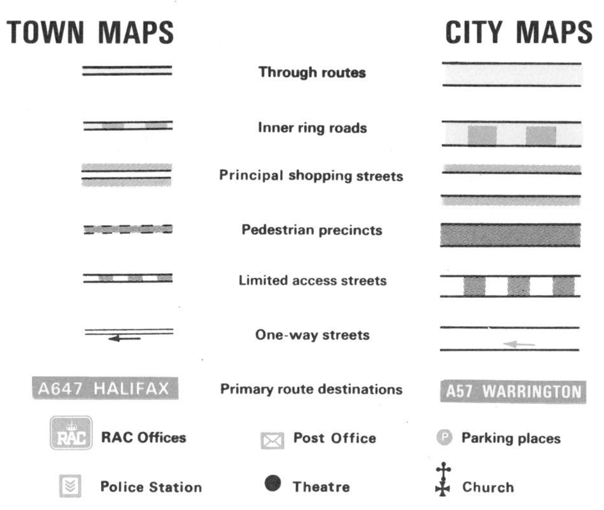

APPROACH MAPS

MOTORWAYS
with interchanges numbered on principal motorways

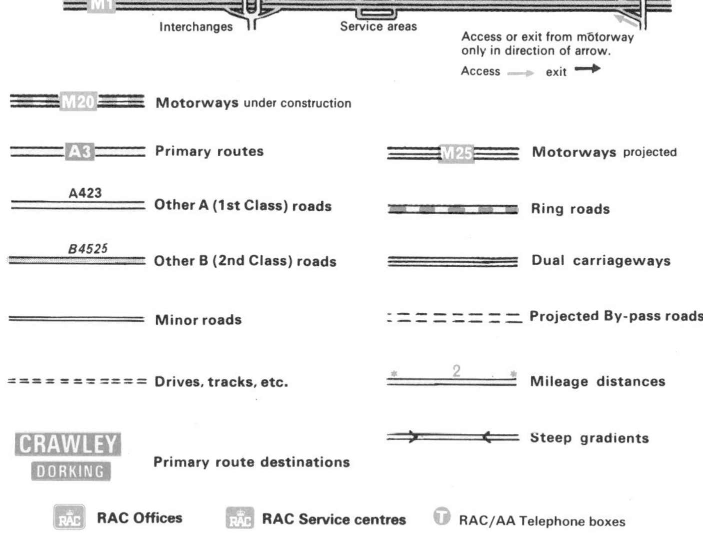

Scale 1 : 100 000 (1·6 miles to 1 inch)

0 1 2 3 4 5 miles
0 8 kilometres

PLACES OF INTEREST

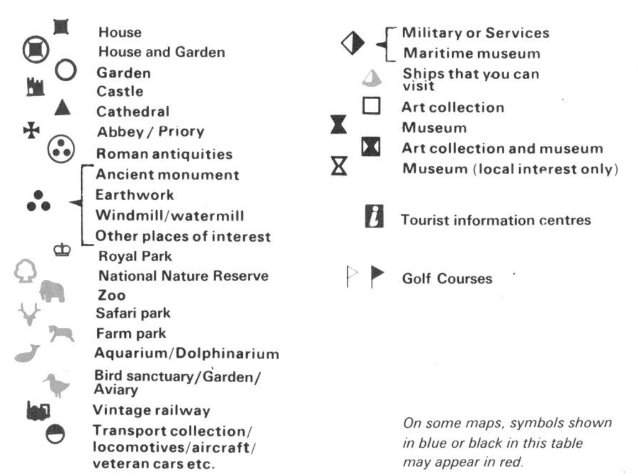

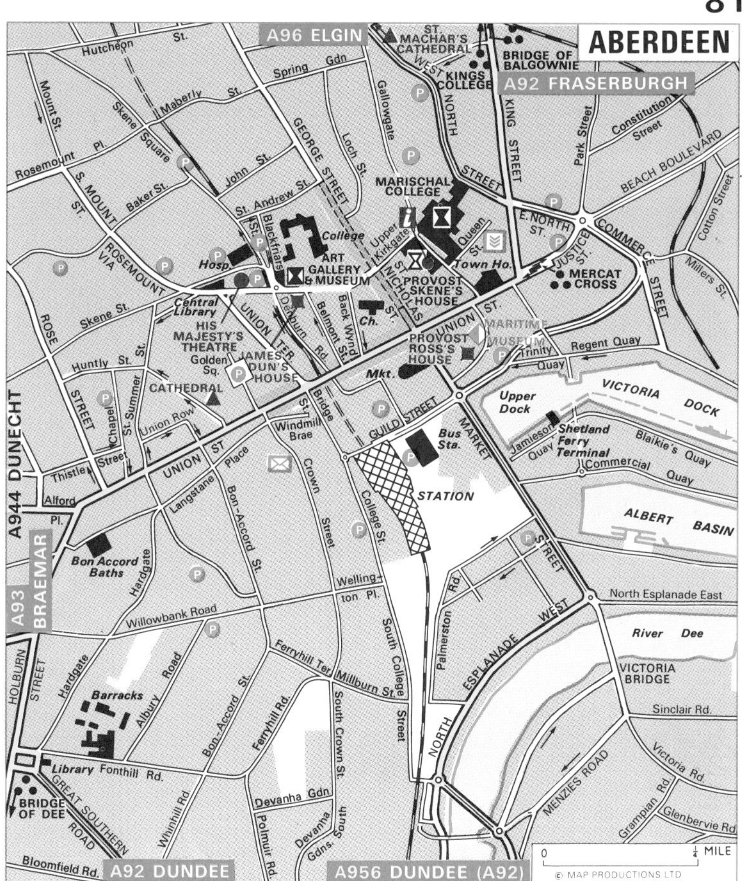

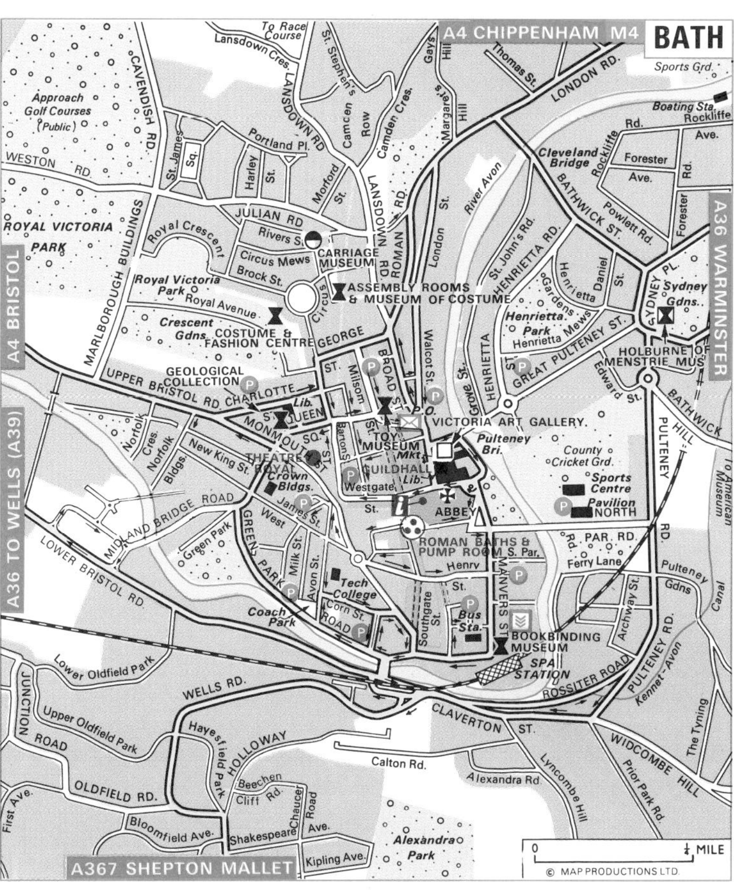

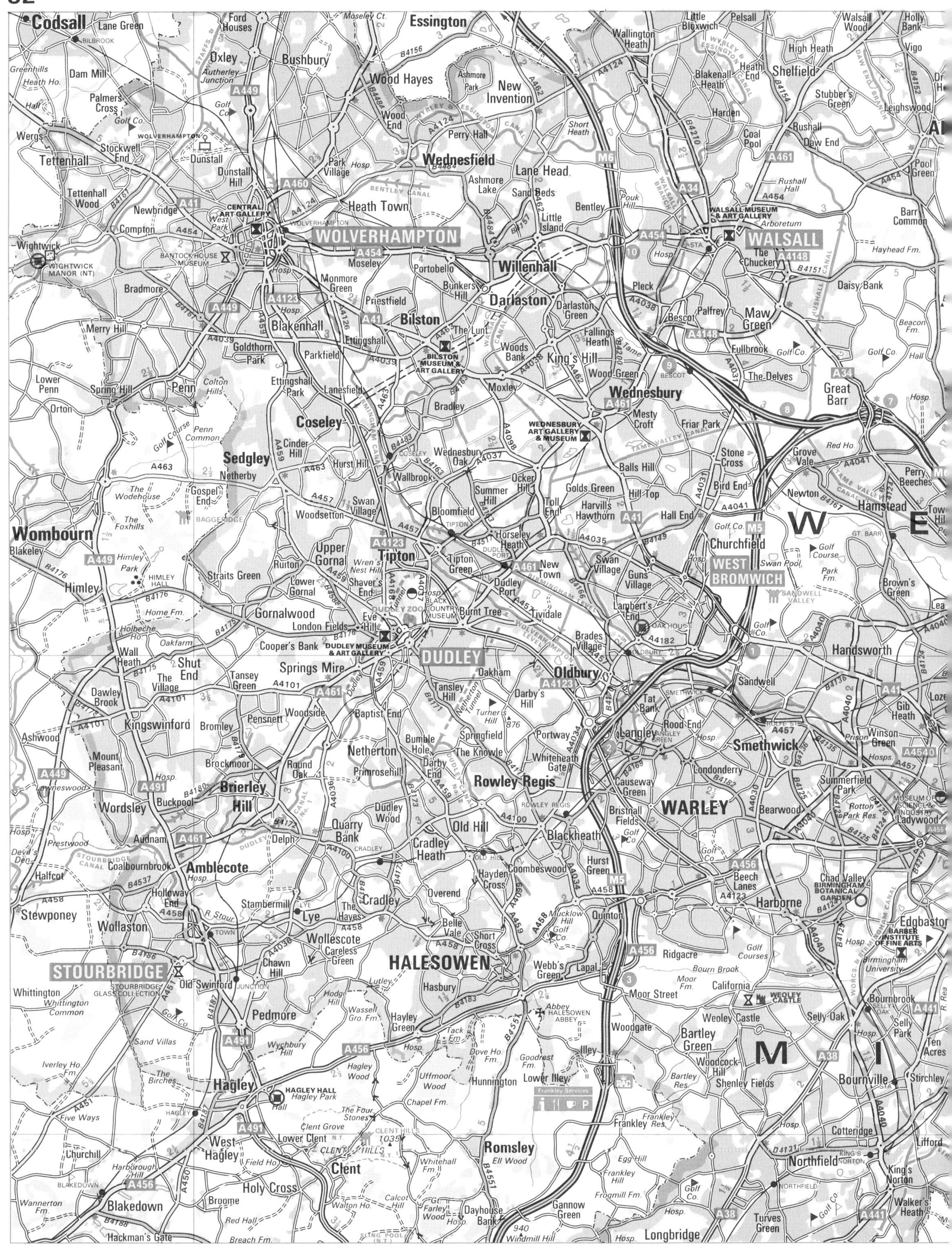
Codsall
Lane Green
Bilbrook
Ford Houses
Essington
Oxley
Bushbury
Wood Hayes
New Invention
Wallington Heath
Little Bloxwich
Pelsall
Walsall Wood
High Heath
Shelfield
Wergs
Tettenhall
Stockwell End
Dunstall
Wednesfield
Perry Hall
Short Heath
Lane Head
Tettenhall Wood
Newbridge
Central Art Gallery
Heath Town
Bentley
Walsall Museum & Art Gallery
WOLVERHAMPTON
WALSALL
Wightwick
Wightwick Manor (NT)
Compton
Bantock House Museum
Moseley
Portobello
Willenhall
The Chuckery
Bradmore
Monmore Green
Priestfield
Bilston
Darlaston
Pleck
Bescot
Palfrey
Maw Green
Merry Hill
Blakenhall
Goldthorn Park
Ettingshall
The Lunt
Bilston Museum & Art Gallery
Kings Hill
Wood Green
Fullbrook
The Delves
Lower Penn
Penn
Spring Hill
Orton
Ettingshall Park
Lanesfield
Moxley
Bradley
Wednesbury
Great Barr
Coseley
Sedgley
Cinder Hill
Wednesbury Art Gallery & Museum
Mesty Croft
Friar Park
Penn Common
Netherby
Hurst Hill
Wallbrook
Wednesbury Oak
Ocker Hill
Stone Cross
Balls Hill
Grove Vale
Red Ho.
Gospel End
The Wodehouse
Swan Village
Summer Hill
Golds Green
Hill Top
Bird End
Perry Beeches
Newton
Hamstead
Woodsetton
Bloomfield
Tipton
Toll End
Harvills Hawthorn
Hall End
Wombourn
Blakeley
Upper Gornal
Horseley Heath
Churchfield
Himley Park
Himley
Himley Hall
Straits Green
Ruiton
Wren's Nest Hill
Tipton Green
New Town
Swan Village
Guns Village
WEST BROMWICH
Sandwell Valley
Brown's Green
Lower Gornal
Shaver's End
Dudley Port
Dudley Zoo
Black Country Museum
Burnt Tree
Tividale
Gornalwood
London Fields
Eve Hill
Lambert's End
Oak House
Home Fm.
Holbeche Ho.
Oakfarm
Wall Heath
Cooper's Bank
Dudley Museum & Art Gallery
DUDLEY
Brades Village
Oldbury
Handsworth
Shut End
The Village
Tansey Green
Springs Mire
Oakham
Sandwell
Dawley Brook
Kingswinford
Bromley
Pensnett
Woodside
Baptist End
Tansley Hill
Darby's Hill
Turner's Hill
Tat Bank
Rood End
Gib Heath
Ashwood
Mount Pleasant
Netherton
Bumble Hole
Springfield
The Knowle
Portway
Langley
Langley Green
Smethwick
Winson Green
Brockmoor
Round Oak
Primrosehill
Darby End
Whiteheath Gate
Londonderry
Lawnswood
Brierley Hill
Rowley Regis
Causeway Green
Summerfield Park
Wordsley
Buckpool
Dudley Wood
Quarry Bank
Old Hill
Bristnall Fields
WARLEY
Bearwood
Rotton Park Res.
Ladywood
Museum of Science & Industry
Audnam
Delph
Cradley Heath
Blackheath
Prestwood
Coalbournbrook
Amblecote
Hurst Green
Halfcot
Holloway End
Stambermill
Lye
Cradley
Overend
Hayden Cross
Coombeswood
Beech Lanes
Chad Valley
Birmingham Botanical Garden
Harborne
Stewponey
Wollaston
The Hayes
Belle Vale
Quinton
Mucklow Hill
Edgbaston
Wollescote
Careless Green
Short Cross
Barber Institute of Fine Arts
STOURBRIDGE
Chawn Hill
HALESOWEN
Webb's Green
Lapal
Ridgacre
Birmingham University
Whittington
Whittington Common
Stourbridge Glass Collection
Old Swinford
Lutley
Hasbury
Moor Street
California
Weoley Castle
Bournbrook
Pedmore
Wassell Gro. Fm.
Hayley Green
Abbey
Halesowen Abbey
Woodgate
Bartley Green
Selly Oak
Selly Park
Sand Villas
Wychbury Hill
Dove Ho. Fm.
Goodrest Fm.
Illey
Woodcock Hill
Shenley Fields
Bournville
Stirchley
Ten Acres
Iverley Ho. Fm.
The Birches
Hagley
Hagley Hall
Hagley Wood
Uffmoor Wood
Hunnington
Lower Illey
Frankley Services
Chapel Fm.
Five Ways
The Four Stones
Clent Grove
Lower Clent
Clent Hills
Frankley
Frankley Res.
Cotteridge
Lifford
Churchill
West Hagley
Clent
Romsley
Northfield
King's Norton
Harborough Hill
Field Ho.
Whitehall Fm.
Ell Wood
Egg Hill
Frankley Hill
Blakedown
Holy Cross
Broome
Calcot Hill
Gt. Farley Wood
Dayhouse Bank
Frogmill Fm.
Gannow Green
Wannerton Fm.
Walton Ho.
Walker's Heath
Red Hall
Turves Green
Hackman's Gate
Breach Fm.
Sling Pool (N.T.)
Windmill Hill
Longbridge
M6
M5
A449
A460
A41
A454
A4123
A4039
A459
A463
A461
A4148
A34
A4041
A4035
A457
A4101
A491
A458
A456
A4040
A4540
A38
A441
A4124
A451
A450

APPROACHES TO BIRMINGHAM

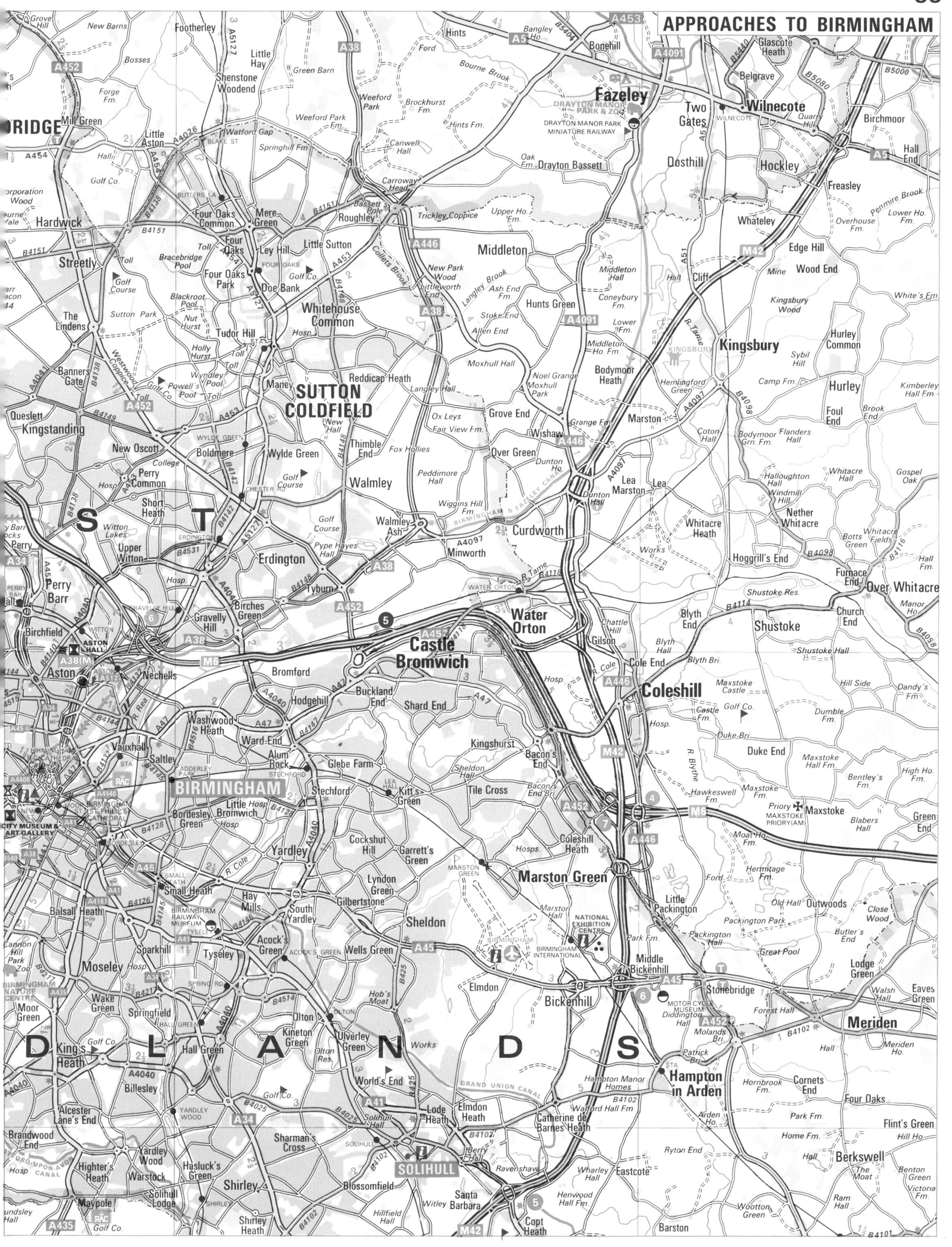

BIRMINGHAM
A34 WALSALL
A38(M) TO M6 Int. 6 GRAVELLY HILL
A41 WOLVERHAMPTON M5 Int. 1
A47 TO M6 Int. 5
A457 DUDLEY
A456 KIDDERMINSTER
A45 COVENTRY, BIRMINGHAM AIRPORT NATIONAL EXHIBITION CENTRE
A41 WARWICK
A34 STRATFORD-UPON-AVON
A38 WORCESTER
A441 REDDITCH
A435 EVESHAM
ASTON
NEW TOWN ROW
BROOKFIELDS
DUDDESTON
VAUXHALL DUDDESTON
BORDESLEY
LADYWOOD
EDGBASTON
SPARK BROOK
BALSALL HEATH
CALTHORPE PARK
EDGBASTON GOLF COURSE
EDGBASTON POOL
CITY CENTRE OFFICE
57 North Court
Birmingham, B2 4XJ
MILE
© MAP PRODUCTIONS LTD

APPROACHES TO BLACKPOOL

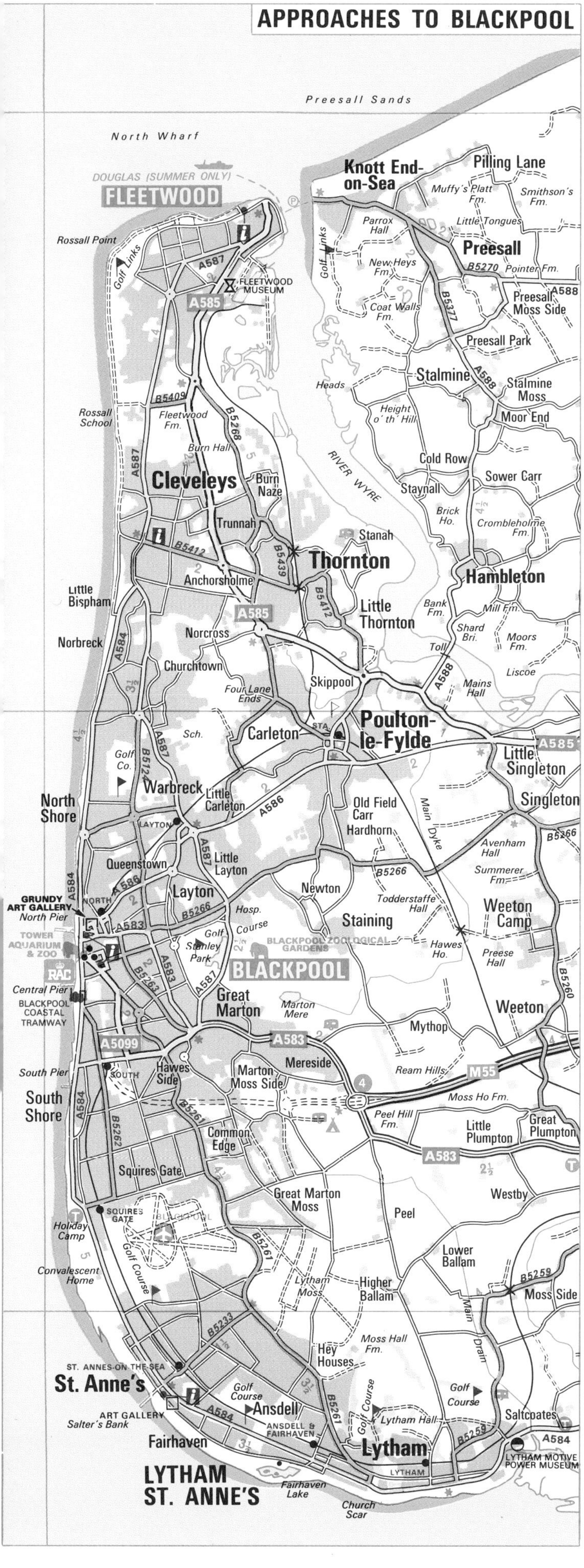

Preesall Sands
North Wharf
DOUGLAS (SUMMER ONLY)
FLEETWOOD
Rossall Point
Golf Links
A587
FLEETWOOD MUSEUM
A585
Knott End-on-Sea
Pilling Lane
Muffy's Platt Fm.
Smithson's Fm.
Parrox Hall
Little Tongues
Preesall
B5270
Pointer Fm.
New Heys Fm.
A588
Preesall Moss Side
Coat Walls Fm.
B5377
Preesall Park
Stalmine
Stalmine Moss
Heads
A588
Height o' th' Hill
Moor End
Rossall School
Fleetwood Fm.
B5409
B5268
Burn Hall
RIVER WYRE
Cold Row
Sower Carr
Cleveleys
Burn Naze
Staynall
Brick Ho.
Crombleholme Fm.
Trunnah
Stanah
B5412
B5439
Thornton
Hambleton
Anchorsholme
Little Bispham
B5412
Little Thornton
Bank Fm.
Mill Fm.
A585
Shard Bri.
Moors Fm.
Norbreck
Norcross
Toll
A584
Churchtown
A588
Liscoe
Skippool
Four Lane Ends
Mains Hall
Sch.
Carleton
STA.
Poulton-le-Fylde
A585
Golf Co.
A587
B5124
Little Singleton
Warbreck
Little Carleton
A586
Singleton
North Shore
Old Field Carr
Hardhorn
Main Dyke
B5266
LAYTON
Avenham Hall
A587
Little Layton
Queenstown
Summerer Fm.
Newton
B5266
Layton
A586
Todderstaffe Hall
GRUNDY ART GALLERY
North Pier
A583
B5266
Hosp.
Staining
Weeton Camp
Golf Course
Stanley Park
BLACKPOOL ZOOLOGICAL GARDENS
Hawes Ho.
Preese Hall
TOWER AQUARIUM & ZOO
RAC
B5263
A583
A587
BLACKPOOL
B5260
Central Pier
BLACKPOOL COASTAL TRAMWAY
Great Marton
Marton Mere
Weeton
A5099
A583
Mythop
South Pier
SOUTH
Hawes Side
Mereside
Ream Hills
M55
South Shore
A584
Marton Moss Side
4
Moss Ho Fm.
B5261
Peel Hill Fm.
Little Plumpton
Great Plumpton
B5262
Common Edge
A583
Squires Gate
Westby
Great Marton Moss
SQUIRES GATE
Peel
Holiday Camp
B5261
Golf Course
Lower Ballam
Convalescent Home
Lytham Moss
Higher Ballam
B5259
Moss Side
Main Drain
B5233
Moss Hall Fm.
Hey Houses
ST. ANNES-ON-THE-SEA
St. Anne's
Golf Course
Golf Course
Golf Course
Ansdell
A584
ART GALLERY
Salter's Bank
Lytham Hall
Saltcoates
ANSDELL & FAIRHAVEN
B5261
B5259
A584
Fairhaven
Lytham
LYTHAM MOTIVE POWER MUSEUM
LYTHAM
LYTHAM ST. ANNE'S
Fairhaven Lake
Church Scar

BLACKPOOL

A584 FLEETWOOD (A587)
A586 LANCASTER (A6)
North Station
Banks St.
Gorton St.
Elizabeth St.
Coleridge Rd.
George St.
Collingwood Av.
B5266 FLEETWOOD (A587)
Springfield Rd.
Dickson Rd.
Buchanan St.
Cocker St.
Cookson St.
Caunce Street
Caunce St.
DEVONSHIRE RD.
London Rd.
GRUNDY ART GALL.
Queen St.
Charles St.
Milbourne St.
Granville
PROMENADE
Tramway
NORTH PIER THEATRE
TALBOT RD.
Abingdon St.
Topping St.
King St.
Grosvenor St.
Talbot Sq.
CLIFTON
ST.
NEWTON DR.
ROAD
NORTH PIER
Birley St.
Market St.
Corporation St.
Church
CHURCH
CHURCH STREET
WHITEGATE DRIVE
Bryan Rd.
WINTER GDNS THEATRE & OPERA HOUSE
Regent Rd.
PARK ROAD
Leamington Road
Leicester Rd.
Liverpool Rd.
Lincoln Rd.
RAC
Bank Hey St.
Victoria St.
Adelaide St.
Alfred St.
Sth. King St.
Forest Gate
BLACKPOOL TOWER
AQUARIUM & ZOO
Coronation St.
Charnley Rd.
HORNBY ROAD
Albert Rd.
Hull St.
CENTRAL DR.
Vance Rd.
HORNBY ROAD
Read's Avenue
Breck Road
Road
Manor Rd.
Gorse Rd.
Bonny St.
Livingstone Rd.
Palatine
Ripon Rd.
St. Albans Rd.
Woodland Grove
LOUIS TUSSAUD'S WAXWORKS
Read's Avenue
Palatine Rd.
Ribble Rd.
Sutton Pl.
Clinton Av.
PARK
Salisbury Rd.
Gloucester Av.
Cumberland Ave.
CENTRAL PIER THEATRE
Chapel Street
Kent Road
Ibbison St.
Freckleton St.
DRIVE
Westmoreland Av.
A583 PRESTON M55
CENTRAL PIER
Foxhall Road
Dale Street
Somerset Av.
ROAD
Keswick Rd.
Westmoreland Av.
Lune Grove
THE GOLDEN MILE
Princess St.
Kent Rd.
Saltash Av.
Condor Grove
Blackpool Borough Rugby Grd.
Road
GRASMERE
Thornber Gro.
Knox Gro.
Rigby Road
Tyldesley Rd.
CENTRAL DRIVE
Lune Grove
Gro.
St. Vincent Av.
SEAFRONT TRAMWAY
Coach Sta.
Queen Victoria Road
Levens Gro.
ROAD
Grove
Sharow Gro.
SOUTH PIER THEATRE
Recreation Ground
Condor
LYTHAM R.
MODEL RAILWAY
Blackpool F.C.
SOUTH PIER
A584 LYTHAM ST. ANNE'S
0 ¼ MILE
© MAP PRODUCTIONS LTD

BOLTON

A666 BLACKBURN
Gaskell St.
Duke St. North
Cotton Mills
Turnton Street
Street
Phoenix St.
HIGHER BR. ST.
KAY STREET
WINDLEY ST.
Kent St.
School Hill
Falcon St.
ROAD
FOLDS
Vernon Street
Duke St.
WAY
Davenport
Street
Lum Street
Craddock St.
Bleach Works
A673 CHORLEY
ST. GEORGES RD.
TOPP
ST. GEORGES RD.
ST. GEORGE'S
Mill Hill St.
KESTOR ST.
River Tonge
Chorley
Bark
St.
ART GALLERY
BOW
Bark St.
Street
Market Hall
BRIDGE ST.
BANK ST.
BURY
Old Road
Bolton Royal Infirmary
MARSDEN RD.
KNOWSLEY ST.
River Croal
Churchgate
Bury
NEW
RD.
A58 BURY
DEANSGATE
St. Peter's Ch.
Devon St.
R. Croal
DEANSGATE
Victoria Sq.
ART GALLERY
CASTLE STREET
SPA ROAD
Crown Court
Black Horse St.
Civic Centre
Town Hall
Octagon Theatre
Library, Art Gallery & Museum
Chancery La.
BRADSHAWGATE
Breightmet St.
Dorset Street
MOOR LA.
Bus Sta.
Shiffnall St.
River St.
BRADFORD
Chadwick St.
Market Hall
RAC
MOOR ST.
Bromwich Street
New St.
GREAT
Dawes St.
NEWPORT ST.
BRIDGEMAN PL.
COLLEGE WAY
TRINITY ST.
TRINITY ST.
LWR. BRIDGEMAN
ST. PETERS WAY
Westbrook St.
A676 ST. HELENS (A58) M61
Bolton Institute of Technology
Crook St.
MANCHESTER RD.
Technical College
Iron Works
Trinity St. Station
Orlando St.
A666 MANCHESTER M62, M63
Ramsbottom St.
DERBY ST.
Fletcher St.
Pilkington Street
Street
Monica Gr.
Thynne St.
ORLANDO
MANCHESTER ROAD
M61
Rothwell St.
Bridgeman St.
Coe St.
Sidney St.
Street
Street
Street
Bolton Wanderers Football Ground
A579 WARRINGTON
Lumsden Street
Street
Fletcher Street
Street
Lever St.
Nelson St.
ROAD
Slaterfield
Bridgeman
Recreation Ground
Grecian St.
Lever
High St.
0 ¼ MILE
© MAP PRODUCTIONS LTD

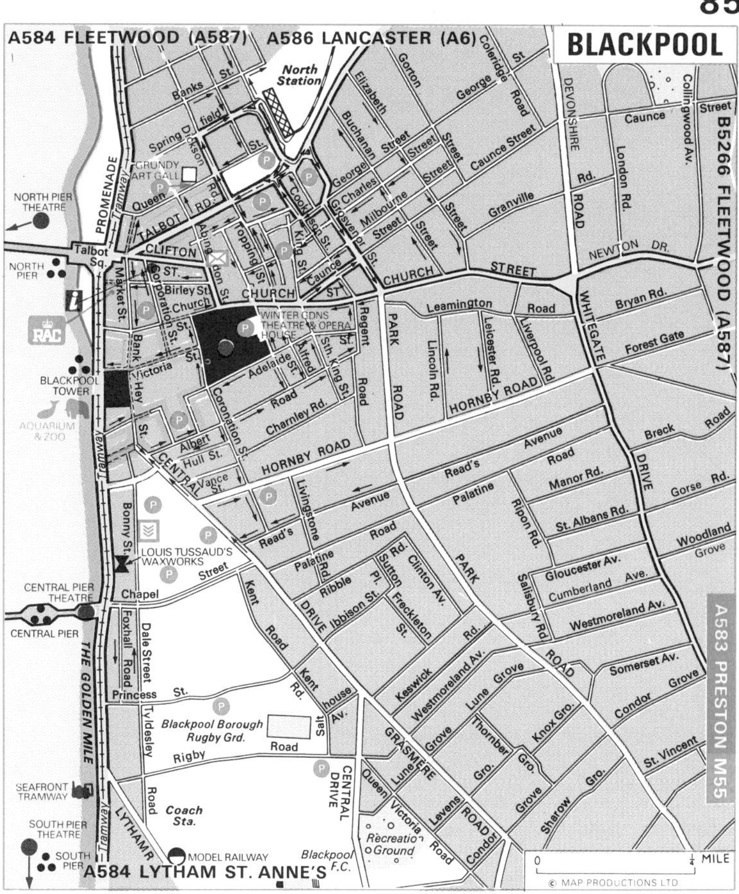

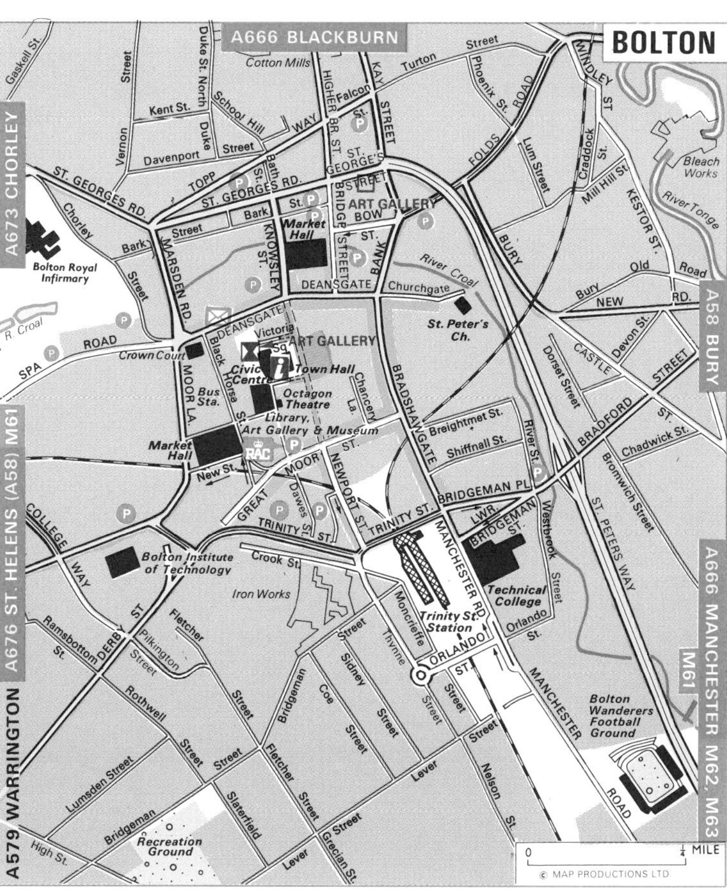

APPROACHES TO BOURNEMOUTH
Wimborne Minster
Oakley
Leigh Park
Merley Tropical Bird Gardens
Merley Ho.
Canford Magna
Canford Park
Moortown Fm.
Hampreston
Knighton
Dudsbury
Longham
Parley Common
E. Parley Common
Moors R.
Bournemouth (Hurn)
Parley Cross
East Parley
West Parley
Parley Green
Avon Common
River Avon
Avon Tyrrell Fm.
Shirley
Ripley
Poors Common
Court Fm.
Bransgore
Harrow Lo.
Sopley
North Bockhampton
Middle Bockhampton
Neacroft
Godwinscroft
Sopley Common
Sopley Park
Hurn
Merritown
West Hurn
Bearwood
Bear Cross
Ensbury
R. Stour
Berry Hill
Eastlands Fm.
Golf Course
Broadstone
CANFORD
HEATH
Golf Course
Kinson
Northbourne
Red Hill
Muscliff
Mill Throop
Hurn Ct.
Blackwater
Town Common
St. Catherine's Hill
Winkton
South Bockhampton
Waterditch
Hillbourne
Darby's Corner
Haymoor Bottom
West Howe
East Howe
Ensbury Park
Holdenhurst
Winkton Common
Burton
Waterloo
Hosp.
Moordown
Charminster
Jumper's Common
Talbot Village
Wallisdown
Rossmore
Talbot Heath
Winton
Little Down
Golf Co.
Queen's Park
Red House Museum & Art Gallery
Iford Bri.
Iford
Somerford
R. Mude
Fleet's Corner
Newtown
Oakdale
Stanley Green
Christchurch Castle (AM)
Christchurch Priory
Purewell
Tucktonia Aquarium
Christchurch
Holes Bay
Sterte
Branksome
Meyrick Park
Golf Co.
Hosps.
Pokesdown
Tuckton
Wick
Stanpit
Mudeford
Poole
Longfleet
Parkstone
Big Four Railway Museum & Model Centre
Russell-Cotes Art Gallery & Museum
Rothesay Museum
Christchurch Harbour
Guildhall Museum
Boating Lake
Poole Park Zoo
Branksome Park
Westbourne
Pier
Boscombe
Southbourne
Warren Hill
Scaplens Court
Poole Pottery
Parkstone Bay
Bournemouth
Hengistbury Head
Lower Hamworthy
Poole Maritime Museum
Poole Quay Aquarium
Pier
Luscombe Valley
Lilliput
Golf Co.
Canford Cliffs
Compton Acres
Branksome Chine
The Chines
Canford Cliffs Chine
Main Channel
POOLE HARBOUR
Flag Head Chine
The Villa
Brownsea Island
Castle
Poole Head
POOLE BAY
Furzey I.
Nth. Haven Pt.
Sandbanks
Sth. Haven Pt.
Shell Bay
Green I.
South Deep
Cleavel Pt.
A348
B3073
B3074
A349
A341
A3049
A35
A350
A347
A3060
A338
A3049
B3063
B3059
B3347
B3065
B3369
A337
A35

BOURNEMOUTH
Transport & Rural Museum
Central Drive
St. Anthony's Road
St. Winifred's Road
Wimborne Road
Lansdowne Road
Wellington Road
Beechey Road
Ophir Road
Portchester Road
Wellington Way
Ascham Rd
A338 RINGWOOD
Recreation Ground
Golf Course
St. Valerie Road
Meyrick Park
Central Drive
Braidley Road
Cavendish Road
County Cricket Grd.
North Road
Park Rd.
Wessex
Bournemouth Sta.
St. Paul's Road
Dean Park Rd.
Horseshoe Common
Wessex Way
Madeira Road
Lansdowne Rd. S.
Holdenhurst
Christchurch Rd
A35 SOUTHAMPTON
A35 POOLE
Durrant Rd
St. Stephen's Road
Town Hall
Bourne Avenue
Richmond Hill
Underpass
Big 4 Railway Museum
Yelverton Rd.
Old Christchurch Road
Glen Fern Rd.
Lorne Park Rd.
Stafford Rd.
College & Library
Upper Central Gardens
The Square
The Triangle
Avenue Rd
St. Peter's Road
St. Peter's Ch
Upper Hinton Rd
Hinton Road
Bath Road
Gervis Road
Meyrick Rd.
Grove Road
Commercial Road
Terrace Rd
Upper Terrace Rd
Cranborne Rd
Lower Central Gardens
Bus & Coach Sta.
Westover Road
Playhouse Theatre
Russell Cotes Rd.
East Overcliff Drive
Cliff Lift
To Boscombe Pier
Winter Gardens
Priory Rd.
Exeter Rd
Pavilion
Beach Office
Zig-Zag
Undercliff Drive
Russell-Cotes Art Gallery & Museum
West Hill Road
Tregonwell Rd.
St. Michael's Road
Beacon Rd.
Pier Parade
Rothesay Museum
Promenade
West Cliff
Cliff Lift
Zig-Zag
West Undercliff Promenade
International Centre
Bournemouth Pier
Pier Theatre
0 ½ MILE
© MAP PRODUCTIONS LTD

APPROACHES TO BRADFORD
A650
Gilstead Moor
Priestthorpe
Bingley
Gilstead
Bracken Hall
Baildon
Tong Park
Tarn
Kirklands
Charlestown
Baildon Green
Shipley Glen Tramway
Thackley End
Thackley
Beck Foot Golf Co.
Cottingley Bri.
Mill
Nab Wood
Saltaire
Cottingley Park
Moor Head
Windhill
Apperley Bridge
Idle
Cottingley
Greengates
Shipley
Cottingley Moor
New Brighton
Bunkers Hill
Wrose
Idle Moor
Bank Top
Shay Gate
Sandy Lane
Noon Nick
Heaton Royds
Frizinghall
Bolton Woods
Eccleshill
A658
Chellow Heights
Heaton
Bradford Art Gallery & Museum
Bolton
Bradford Industrial Museum
Daisy Hill
A6177
Undercliffe
Allerton
Infmy
Girlington
Manningham
Scar Hill
Golf Co.
Aldersley Fm.
Four Lane Ends
Forster Square
Cathedral
Thornbury
Lower Grange
Thornton
Crossley Hall
A647
Laisterdyke
Leventhorp Hall
Birks
Lidget Green
Coll.
Exchange
Chat Hill
Scholemoor
National Museum of Photography, Film & Television
Bradford
Hosp.
Clayton
Great Horton
Little Horton
Bolling Hall
Bowling
Dudley Hill
Golf Co.
Clayton Heights
West Bowling
Bowling Park
A650
Tong Street
Old Dolphin
Hosp.
Wibsey
Slack Side
Bierley
Odsal Top
Golf Co.
Tofthaw
East Bierley
A6036
Shelf
Buttershaw
A641
Low Moor
B6146
B6144
B6269
B6145
B6147
B6380
A644
A6038
A6037
A6176
B6381
A6181
A657
B6151

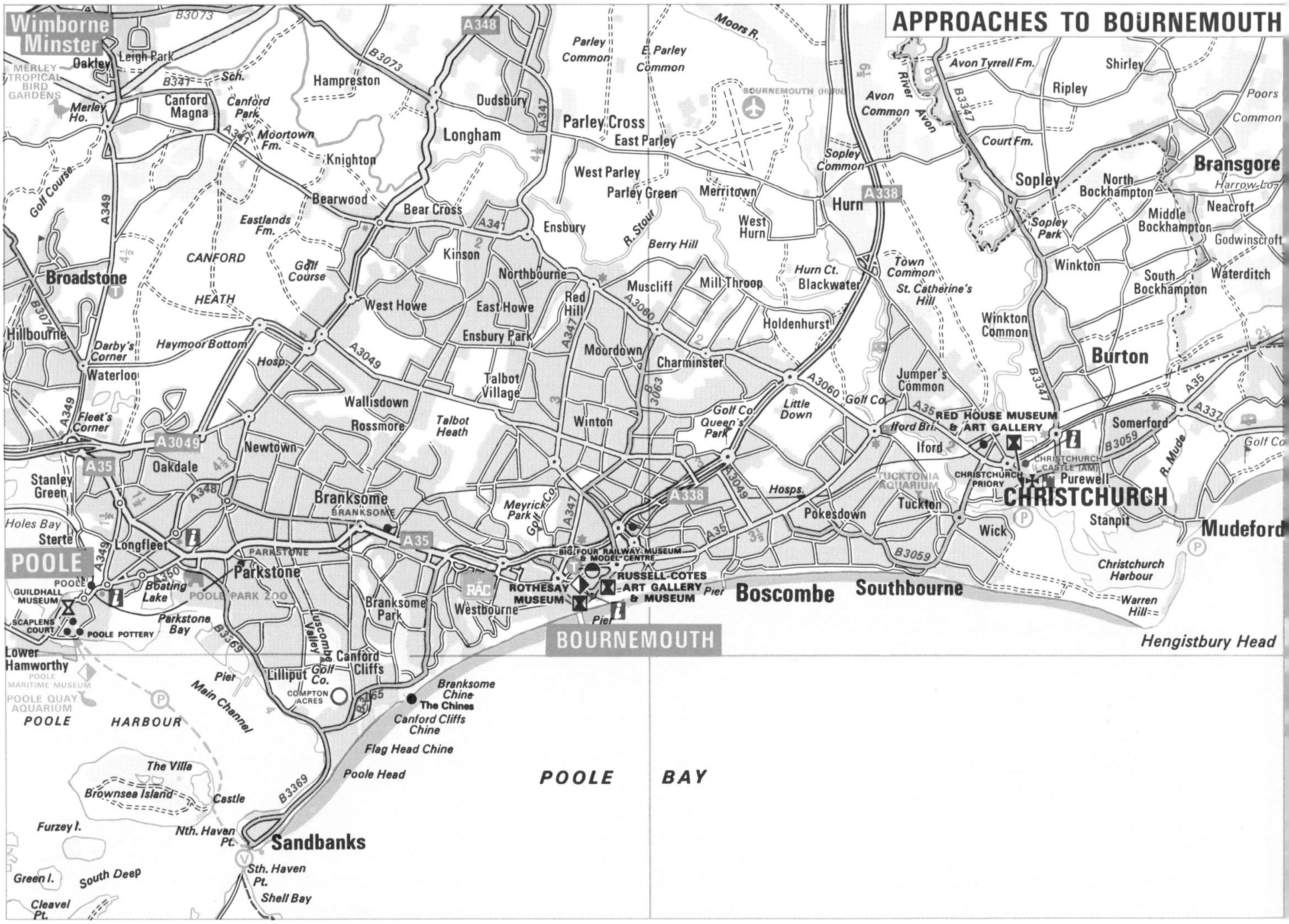

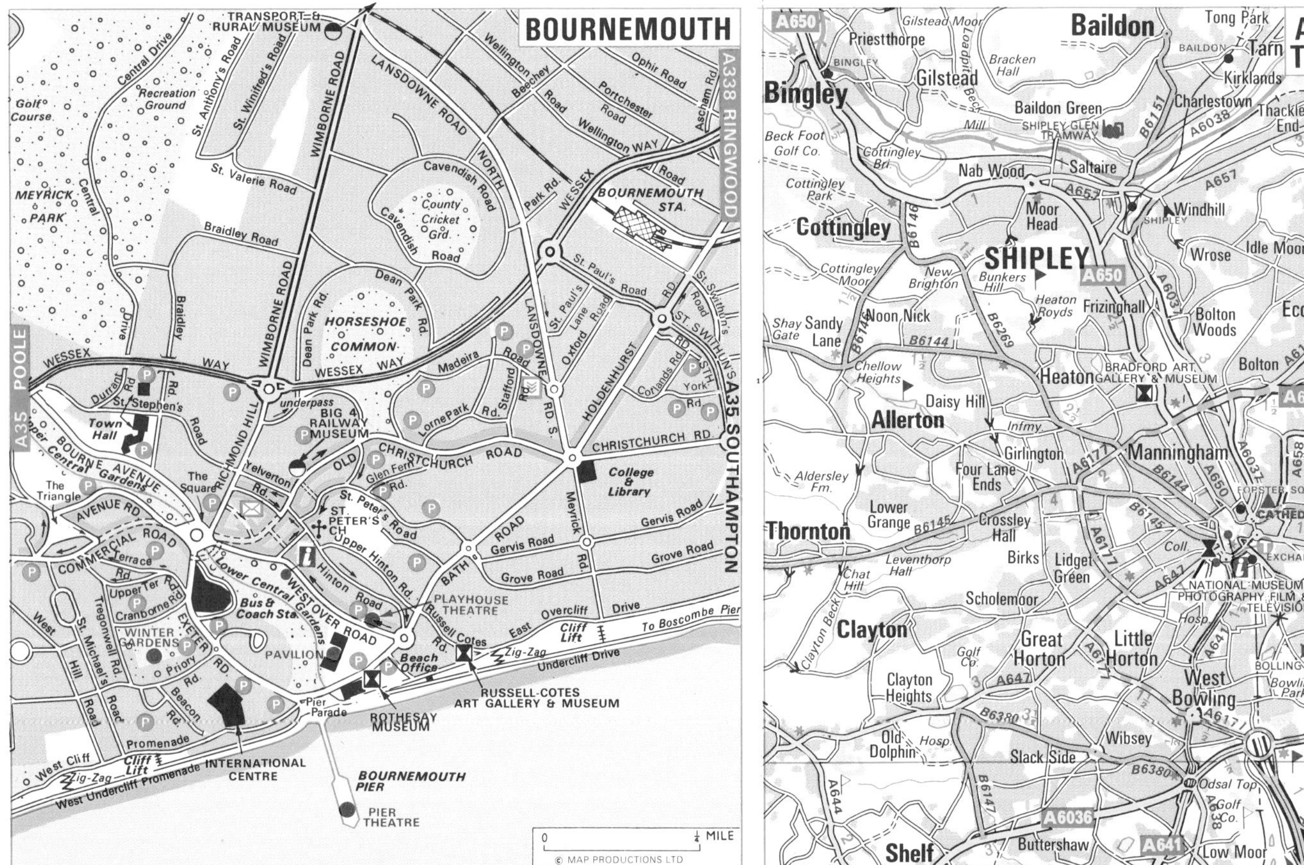

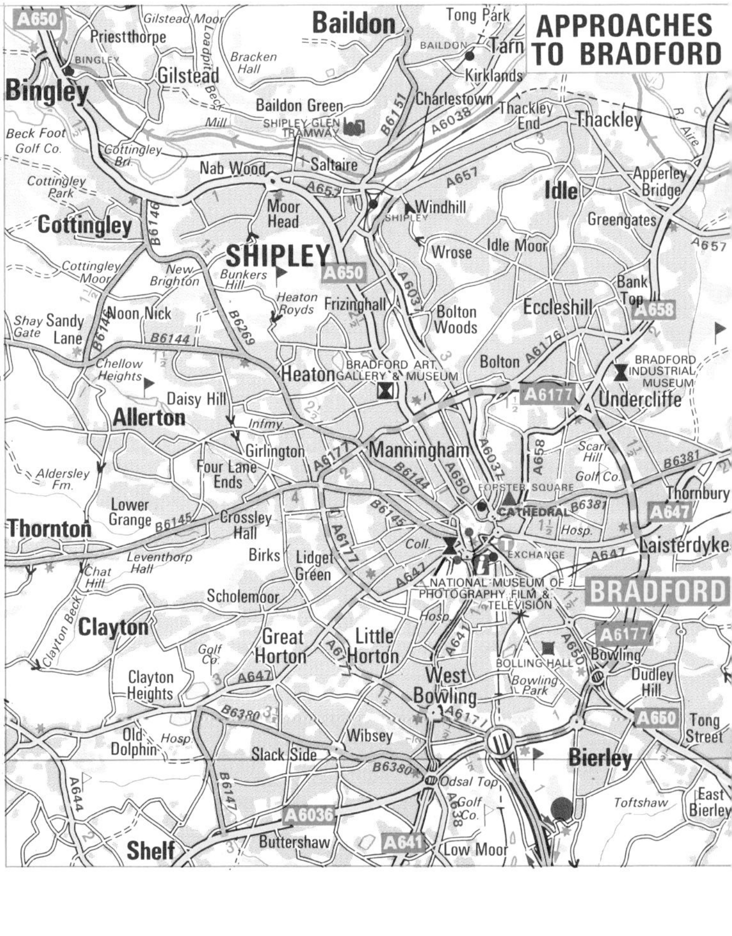

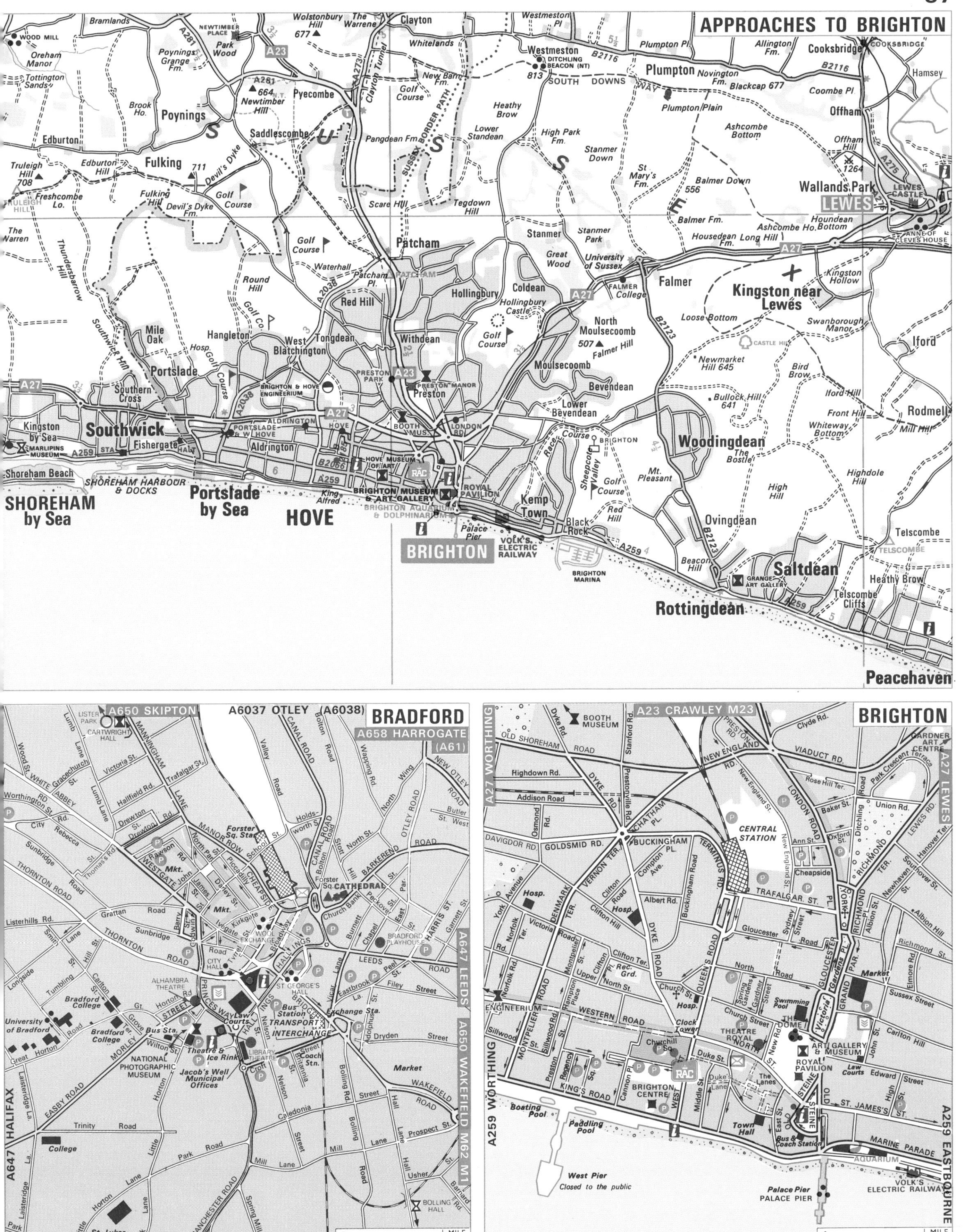
APPROACHES TO BRIGHTON
Bramlands
WOOD MILL
Oreham Manor
Tottington Sands
NEWTIMBER PLACE
Park Wood
Poynings Grange Fm.
Wolstonbury Hill 677
The Warrene
Clayton
Whitelands
Clayton Tunnel
Westmeston Pl
Westmeston
DITCHLING BEACON (NT)
813
B2116
Plumpton Pl
Plumpton
Novington Fm.
Blackcap 677
Allington Fm.
Cooksbridge
COOKSBRIDGE
Hamsey
Coombe Pl
Offham
Brook Ho.
Poynings
A281
664
Newtimber Hill
Pyecombe
New Barn Fm.
Golf Course
SOUTH DOWNS WAY
Heathy Brow
Plumpton Plain
Ashcombe Bottom
Edburton
Saddlescombe
Pangdean Fm.
SUSSEX BORDER PATH
Lower Standean
High Park Fm.
Stanmer Down
Offham Hill
1264
A275
Truleigh Hill 708
Edburton Hill
Fulking
711
Devil's Dyke
St Mary's Fm.
Balmer Down 556
Wallands Park
LEWES CASTLE
LEWES
Freshcombe Lo.
Fulking Hill
Devil's Dyke Fm.
Golf Course
Scare Hill
Tegdown Hill
Balmer Fm.
Ashcombe Ho.
Houndean Bottom
The Warren
Thundersbarrow Hill
Golf Course
Waterhall
Patcham
Stanmer
Stanmer Park
Great Wood
University of Sussex
Housedean Fm.
Long Hill
A27
ANNE OF CLEVES HOUSE
Patcham Pl.
PATCHAM
Hollingbury
Coldean
FALMER College
Falmer
Kingston near Lewes
Kingston Hollow
Round Hill
A2038
Red Hill
Hollingbury Castle
North Moulsecoomb 507
B2123
Loose Bottom
Swanborough Manor
Southwick Hill
Golf Co.
Mile Oak
Hangleton
West Blatchington
Tongdean
Withdean
Golf Course
Falmer Hill
CASTLE HILL
Iford
Portslade
Hosp.
Golf Course
PRESTON PARK
A23
Moulsecoomb
Newmarket Hill 645
Bird Brow
A27
Southern Cross
BRIGHTON & HOVE ENGINEERIUM
PRESTON MANOR
Preston
Bevendean
Iford Hill
Bullock Hill 641
Rodmell
Lower Bevendean
Front Hill
Mill Hill
Kingston by Sea
Southwick
PORTSLADE & W. HOVE
ALDRINGTON
HOVE
BOOTH MUS.
LONDON RD
Race Course
BRIGHTON
Whiteway Bottom
MARLIPINS MUSEUM
Fishergate
Aldrington
Woodingdean
The Bostle
A259
HOVE MUSEUM OF ART
Sheepcote Valley
Mt. Pleasant
Highdole Hill
Shoreham Beach
SHOREHAM HARBOUR & DOCKS
B2066
ROYAL PAVILION
Golf Course
High Hill
SHOREHAM by Sea
Portslade by Sea
King Alfred
BRIGHTON MUSEUM & ART GALLERY
BRIGHTON AQUARIUM & DOLPHINARIUM
Kemp Town
Red Hill
HOVE
Palace Pier
Black Rock
Ovingdean
BRIGHTON
VOLK'S ELECTRIC RAILWAY
Telscombe
TELSCOMBE
BRIGHTON MARINA
Beacon Hill
GRANGE ART GALLERY
Saltdean
Heathy Brow
Telscombe Cliffs
Rottingdean
Peacehaven
BRADFORD
A650 SKIPTON
A6037 OTLEY (A6038)
A658 HARROGATE (A61)
LISTER PARK
CARTWRIGHT HALL
MANNINGHAM LANE
Lumb Lane
Wood St.
WHITE ABBEY RD
Gracechurch St.
Victoria St.
Trafalgar St.
Hallfield Rd.
Drewton Rd.
Worthington St.
City Rd.
Rebecca St.
Sunbridge Rd
Thomas's Rd
THORNTON ROAD
Rawson Rd
Mkt.
WESTGATE
John St.
James St.
Mkt.
MANOR ROW
North Par.
Forster Sq. Sta.
School St.
Piccadilly
Darley St.
CHEAPSIDE
Valley Road
CANAL ROAD
Bolton Road
Holdsworth St.
North Wing
Wapping Rd
OTLEY ROAD
NEW OTLEY ROAD
Butler St. West
Stott Hill
North St.
BARKEREND ROAD
Forster Sq.
CATHEDRAL
Church Bank
Peckover St.
East Par.
HARRIS ST.
Garnett St.
Listerhills Rd.
Grattan Road
Sunbridge
Barry St.
Godwin St.
Ivegate
Kirkgate
WOOL EXCHANGE
HALL INGS
Burnett St.
Chapel St.
BRADFORD PLAYHOUSE
Smith St.
Lane
Hill St.
THORNTON ROAD
CITY HALL
Tyrrel St.
LEEDS ROAD
Longside Lane
Tumbling Hill St.
Carlton St.
ALHAMBRA THEATRE
PRINCES WAY
Law Courts
ST GEORGE'S HALL
Eastbrook La.
Peel St.
Filey Street
Bradford College
Gt. Horton Rd
Bus Station
TRANSPORT INTERCHANGE
Exchange Sta.
Vicar Lane
Dryden Street
University of Bradford
Bradford College
Grove
Bus Sta.
Wilton St.
Theatre & Ice Rink
LIBRARY THEATRE
Coach Stn.
Britannia St.
Adolphus St.
Great Horton Road
NATIONAL PHOTOGRAPHIC MUSEUM
MORLEY ST.
Jacob's Well Municipal Offices
Croft St.
Nelson St.
Market
WAKEFIELD ROAD
Lasterdyke La.
EASBY ROAD
Horton
Street
Caledonia
Bolling Rd.
Hall Lane
Trinity Road
Prospect St.
College
Park Road
Mill Lane
Lane
Little Horton Lane
MANCHESTER ROAD
Spring Mill St.
Usher St.
BOLLING HALL
Barnard Rd.
St. Lukes
Park Avenue
A647 HALIFAX
A641 HUDDERSFIELD
A647 LEEDS
A650 WAKEFIELD M62 M1
0 ¼ MILE
© MAP PRODUCTIONS LTD
BRIGHTON
A23 CRAWLEY M23
BOOTH MUSEUM
Dyke Rd.
Stanford Rd.
PRESTON RD
Clyde Rd.
GARDNER ART CENTRE
OLD SHOREHAM ROAD
NEW ENGLAND RD.
VIADUCT RD.
Highdown Rd.
Addison Road
Prestonville Rd.
DYKE RD
New England St.
LONDON ROAD
Rose Hill Ter.
Park Crescent Terrace
Baker St.
Union Rd.
Ditchling Road
LEWES RD
Osmond Rd.
DAVIGDOR RD.
GOLDSMID RD.
SCHATHAM PL.
BUCKINGHAM PL.
CENTRAL STATION
Ann St.
Oxford St.
RICHMOND TER.
Hanover Ter.
Southover St.
Compton Ave.
Buckingham Road
TERMINUS RD.
Cheapside
YORK PL.
Newhaven St.
York Avenue
Hosp.
Clifton Road
Albert Rd.
TRAFALGAR ST.
Albion St.
Albion Hill
Norfolk Ter.
DENMARK TER.
VERNON TER.
Clifton Hill
Hosp.
DYKE ROAD
Gloucester Road
Sydney Street
GLOUCESTER PL.
RICHMOND PL.
Richmond St.
Victoria Road
Montpelier Rd.
Clifton Ter.
Rec. Grd.
QUEEN'S ROAD
North Road
Elmore Rd.
Norfolk Rd.
Upper North St.
GRAND PAR.
Market
Sussex Street
MONTPELIER ROAD
Hampton Place
Church St.
Hosp.
Spring Gardens
Gardner St.
Swimming Pool
Victoria Gardens
ENGINEERIUM
WESTERN ROAD
Clock Tower
Church Street
THE DOME
Carlton Hill
Sillwood Rd
Sillwood St.
THEATRE ROYAL
NORTH ST.
New Rd
ART GALLERY & MUSEUM
Churchill Sq.
Duke St.
Preston St.
Regency Sq.
Duke's Lane
ROYAL PAVILION
John St.
Law Courts
Edward Street
Cannon Pl.
BRIGHTON CENTRE
Middle St.
West St.
The Lanes
OLD STEINE
High St.
KING'S ROAD
East St.
ST. JAMES'S ST.
Boating Pool
Paddling Pool
Town Hall
Bus & Coach Station
MARINE PARADE
AQUARIUM
West Pier
Closed to the public
Palace Pier
PALACE PIER
VOLK'S ELECTRIC RAILWAY
A27 WORTHING
A259 WORTHING
A27 LEWES
A259 EASTBOURNE
0 ¼ MILE
© MAP PRODUCTIONS LTD

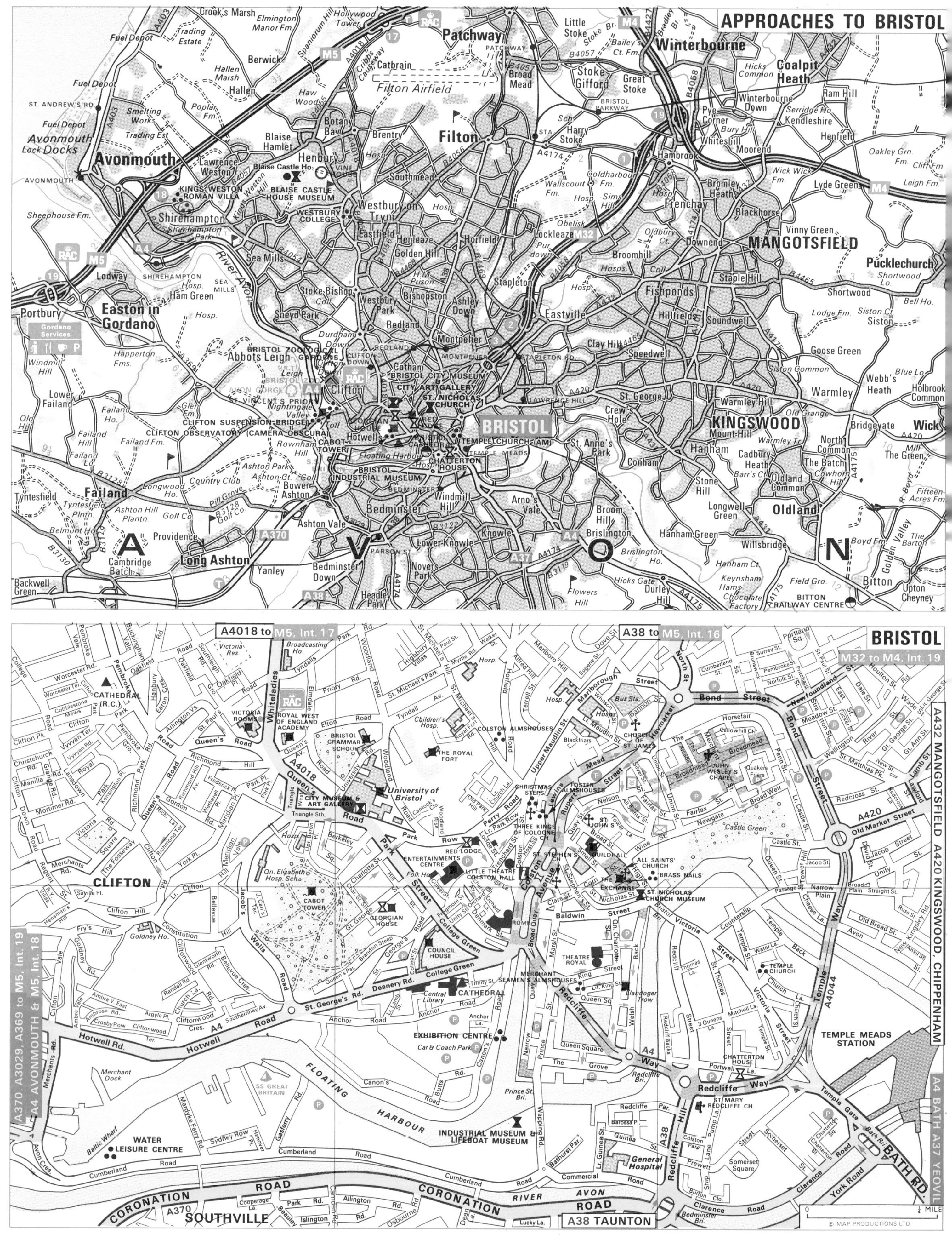
APPROACHES TO BRISTOL
Avonmouth
Shirehampton
Patchway
Winterbourne
Coalpit Heath
Filton
Henbury
Westbury on Trym
MANGOTSFIELD
Pucklechurch
Fishponds
Kingswood
BRISTOL
Clifton
Bedminster
Long Ashton
Failand
Easton in Gordano
Portbury
A V O N
BRISTOL
CLIFTON
CATHEDRAL
CABOT TOWER
GEORGIAN HOUSE
COUNCIL HOUSE
UNIVERSITY of Bristol
CITY MUSEUM & ART GALLERY
THEATRE ROYAL
ST. MARY REDCLIFFE CH
TEMPLE MEADS STATION
INDUSTRIAL MUSEUM & LIFEBOAT MUSEUM
FLOATING HARBOUR
SS GREAT BRITAIN
WATER LEISURE CENTRE
CORONATION ROAD
SOUTHVILLE
A38 TAUNTON
A4018 to M5, Int. 17
A38 to M5, Int. 16
M32 to M4, Int. 19
A432 MANGOTSFIELD A420 KINGSWOOD, CHIPPENHAM
A4 BATH A37 YEOVIL
A370, A3029, A369 to M5, Int. 19
A4 AVONMOUTH & M5, Int. 18
© MAP PRODUCTIONS LTD

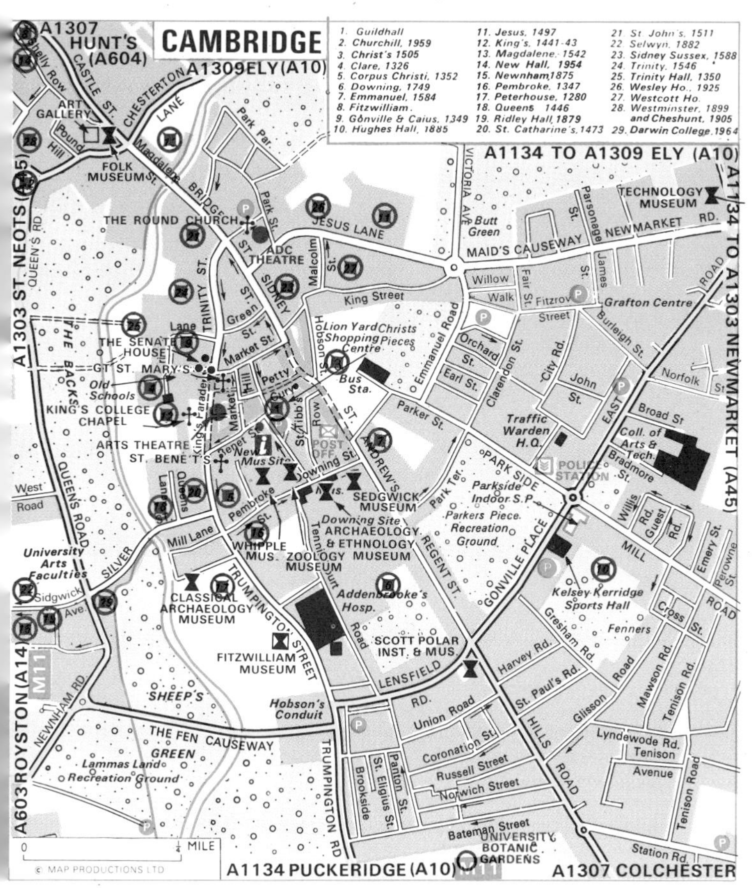
CAMBRIDGE
1. Guildhall
2. Churchill, 1959
3. Christ's 1505
4. Clare, 1326
5. Corpus Christi, 1352
6. Downing, 1749
7. Emmanuel, 1584
8. Fitzwilliam.
9. Gonville & Caius, 1349
10. Hughes Hall, 1885
11. Jesus, 1497
12. King's, 1441-43
13. Magdalene, 1542
14. New Hall, 1954
15. Newnham 1875
16. Pembroke, 1347
17. Peterhouse, 1280
18. Queens, 1446
19. Ridley Hall 1879
20. St. Catharine's, 1473
21. St. John's, 1511
22. Selwyn, 1882
23. Sidney Sussex, 1588
24. Trinity, 1546
25. Trinity Hall, 1350
26. Wesley Ho., 1925
27. Westcott Ho.
28. Westminster, 1899 and Cheshunt, 1905
29. Darwin College, 1964
A1307 HUNT'S (A604)
A1309 ELY (A10)
A1134 TO A1309 ELY (A10)
A1134 TO A1303 NEWMARKET (A45)
A1303 ST. NEOTS (A45)
A603 ROYSTON (A10)
A1134 PUCKERIDGE (A10)
A1307 COLCHESTER
ART GALLERY
FOLK MUSEUM
THE ROUND CHURCH
ADC THEATRE
JESUS LANE
TECHNOLOGY MUSEUM
NEWMARKET RD.
MAID'S CAUSEWAY
Butt Green
King Street
Grafton Centre
THE SENATE HOUSE
GT. ST. MARY'S
Old Schools
KING'S COLLEGE CHAPEL
ARTS THEATRE
ST. BENET'S
Lion Yard Shopping Centre
Christs Pieces
Bus Sta.
Emmanuel Road
Parker St.
Traffic Warden H.Q.
Coll. of Arts & Tech.
POLICE STATION
Parkside Indoor S.P.
Parkers Piece Recreation Ground
SEDGWICK MUSEUM
Downing Site ARCHAEOLOGY & ETHNOLOGY MUSEUM
WHIPPLE MUS.
ZOOLOGY MUSEUM
Addenbrooke's Hosp.
SCOTT POLAR INST. & MUS
Kelsey Kerridge Sports Hall
Fenners
University Arts Faculties
CLASSICAL ARCHAEOLOGY MUSEUM
FITZWILLIAM MUSEUM
SHEEP'S GREEN
Hobson's Conduit
THE FEN CAUSEWAY
Lammas Land Recreation Ground
LENSFIELD RD.
TRUMPINGTON STREET
TRUMPINGTON ROAD
REGENT ST.
GONVILLE PLACE
HILLS ROAD
MILL ROAD
Mill Lane
Silver St.
QUEEN'S ROAD
THE BACKS
NEWNHAM RD.
Union Road
Coronation St.
Russell Street
Norwich Street
Bateman Street
UNIVERSITY BOTANIC GARDENS
Station Rd.
© MAP PRODUCTIONS LTD

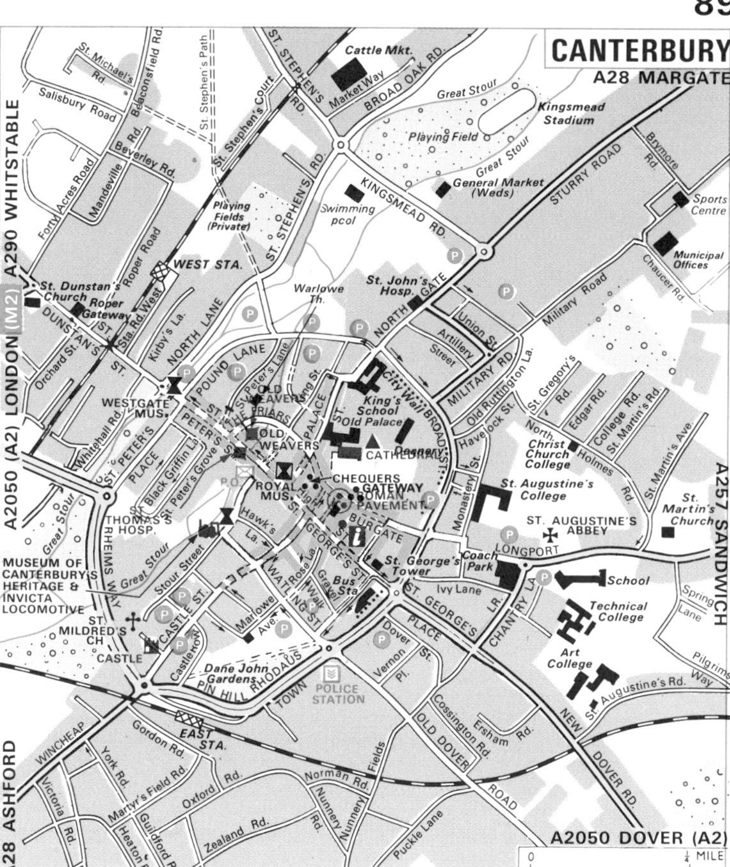
CANTERBURY
A28 MARGATE
A290 WHITSTABLE
A2050 (A2) LONDON (M2)
A28 ASHFORD
A257 SANDWICH
A2050 DOVER (A2)
Cattle Mkt.
Kingsmead Stadium
Playing Field
General Market (Weds)
Swimming pool
Playing Fields (Private)
WEST STA.
St. Dunstan's Church
Roper Gateway
St. John's Hosp.
Municipal Offices
Sports Centre
WESTGATE MUS.
King's School
Old Palace
CATHEDRAL
OLD WEAVERS
ROYAL MUS.
CHEQUERS
GATEWAY
ROMAN PAVEMENT
Christ Church College
St. Augustine's College
ST. AUGUSTINE'S ABBEY
THOMAS'S HOSP.
St. George's Tower
Coach Park
Bus Sta.
School
Technical College
Art College
MUSEUM OF CANTERBURY'S HERITAGE & INVICTA LOCOMOTIVE
ST. MILDRED'S CH
CASTLE
Dane John Gardens
PIN HILL
RHODAUS TOWN
POLICE STATION
EAST STA.
OLD DOVER RD.
NEW DOVER RD.
WINCHEAP
Military Road
STURRY ROAD
LONGPORT
© MAP PRODUCTIONS LTD

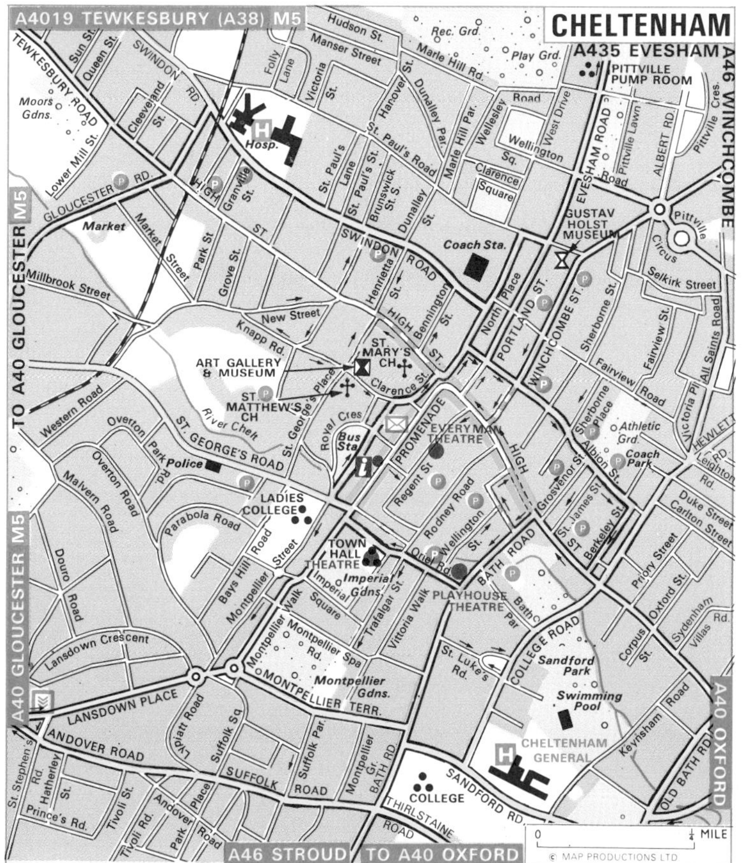
CHELTENHAM
A4019 TEWKESBURY (A38) M5
A435 EVESHAM
A46 WINCHCOMBE
TO A40 GLOUCESTER M5
A40 GLOUCESTER M5
A40 OXFORD
A46 STROUD
TO A40 OXFORD
PITTVILLE PUMP ROOM
Hosp.
Market
Coach Sta.
GUSTAV HOLST MUSEUM
ART GALLERY & MUSEUM
ST. MARY'S CH
ST. MATTHEW'S CH
Police
Bus Sta.
EVERYMAN THEATRE
LADIES COLLEGE
TOWN HALL
THEATRE
Imperial Gdns.
PLAYHOUSE THEATRE
Montpellier Gdns.
Sandford Park
Swimming Pool
CHELTENHAM GENERAL
COLLEGE
PROMENADE
HIGH ST.
ST. GEORGE'S ROAD
SWINDON ROAD
EVESHAM ROAD
PORTLAND ST.
WINCHCOMBE ST.
BATH ROAD
LANSDOWN PLACE
MONTPELLIER TERR.
SUFFOLK ROAD
ANDOVER ROAD
SANDFORD RD.
THIRLSTAINE RD.
OLD BATH RD.
COLLEGE ROAD
© MAP PRODUCTIONS LTD

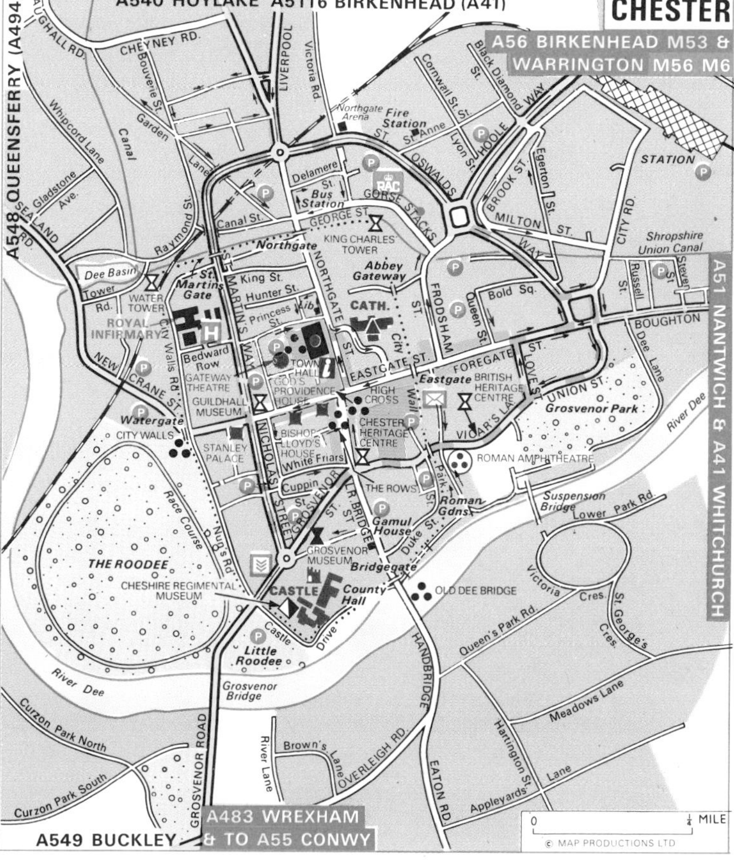
CHESTER
A540 HOYLAKE
A5116 BIRKENHEAD (A41)
A56 BIRKENHEAD M53 & WARRINGTON M56 M6
A548 QUEENSFERRY (A494)
A51 NANTWICH & A41 WHITCHURCH
A549 BUCKLEY
A483 WREXHAM & TO A55 CONWY
STATION
Fire Station
Bus Station
KING CHARLES TOWER
Northgate
Abbey Gateway
CATH.
WATER TOWER
St. Martin's Gate
ROYAL INFIRMARY
GATEWAY THEATRE
GUILDHALL MUSEUM
GOD'S PROVIDENCE HOUSE
TOWN HALL
HIGH CROSS
Eastgate
BRITISH HERITAGE CENTRE
Watergate
CITY WALLS
STANLEY PALACE
BISHOP LLOYD'S HOUSE
CHESTER HERITAGE CENTRE
White Friars
THE ROWS
Roman Gdns.
ROMAN AMPHITHEATRE
Grosvenor Park
Suspension Bridge
Gamul House
GROSVENOR MUSEUM
Bridgegate
THE ROODEE
CHESHIRE REGIMENTAL MUSEUM
CASTLE
County Hall
OLD DEE BRIDGE
Little Roodee
Grosvenor Bridge
River Dee
Shropshire Union Canal
FOREGATE ST.
EASTGATE ST.
BOUGHTON
GROSVENOR ROAD
HANDBRIDGE
EATON RD.
© MAP PRODUCTIONS LTD

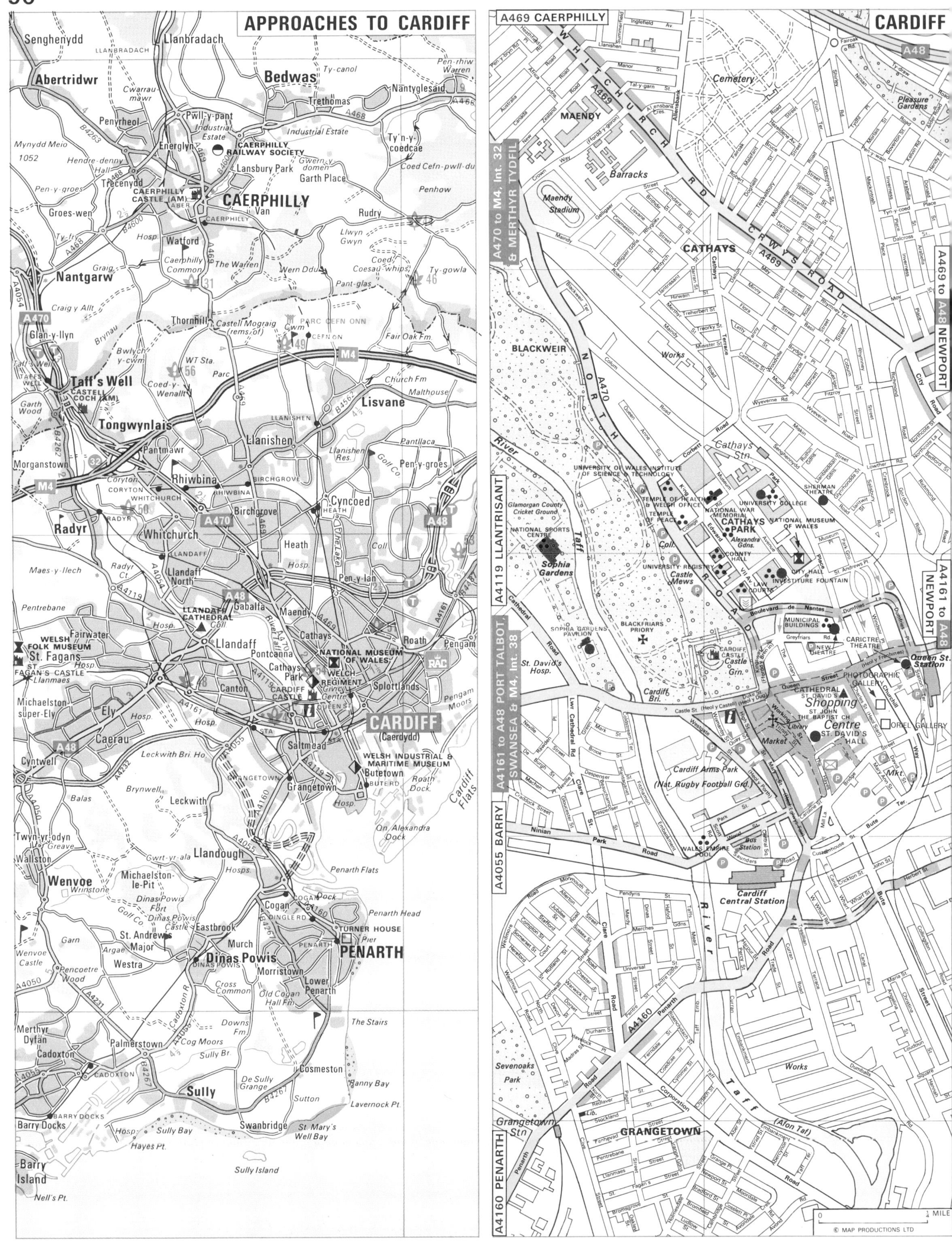
APPROACHES TO CARDIFF
CARDIFF
A469 CAERPHILLY
A470 to M4, Int. 32 & MERTHYR TYDFIL
A4119 LLANTRISANT
A4161 to A48 PORT TALBOT, SWANSEA & M4, Int. 38
A4055 BARRY
A4160 PENARTH
A469 to A48 NEWPORT
A4161 to A48 NEWPORT
Senghenydd
Llanbradach
Abertridwr
Bedwas
Trethomas
Nantyglesaid
Penyrheol
Pwll-y-pant
Energlyn
CAERPHILLY RAILWAY SOCIETY
Lansbury Park
Garth Place
Trecenydd
CAERPHILLY CASTLE (AM)
CAERPHILLY
Rudry
Groes-wen
Watford
Nantgarw
Thornhill
Glan-y-llyn
Taff's Well
Tongwynlais
Lisvane
Llanishen
Pantmawr
Rhiwbina
Morganstown
Radyr
Whitchurch
Cyncoed
Birchgrove
Heath
Llandaff North
Pen-y-lan
Gabalfa
Maendy
Cathays
Roath
Pengam
LLANDAFF CATHEDRAL
Llandaff
WELSH FOLK MUSEUM
St. Fagans
ST. FAGAN'S CASTLE
Fairwater
Pontcanna
NATIONAL MUSEUM OF WALES
WELSH REGIMENT
Splottlands
Canton
CARDIFF CASTLE
Ely
Michaelston-super-Ely
Caerau
Cyntwell
CARDIFF (Caerdydd)
Saltmead
WELSH INDUSTRIAL & MARITIME MUSEUM
Butetown
Grangetown
Leckwith
Llandough
Wenvoe
Michaelston-le-Pit
Cogan
Penarth Head
TURNER HOUSE
PENARTH
Dinas Powis
St. Andrews Major
Eastbrook
Murch
Morristown
Lower Penarth
Westra
Palmerstown
Cadoxton
Sully
Cosmeston
Lavernock Pt.
Barry Docks
Sully Bay
Swanbridge
St. Mary's Well Bay
Sully Island
Barry Island
Nell's Pt.
MAENDY
Barracks
Maendy Stadium
Cemetery
CATHAYS
BLACKWEIR
Cathays Stn
UNIVERSITY OF WALES INSTITUTE OF SCIENCE & TECHNOLOGY
TEMPLE OF HEALTH & WELSH OFFICE
TEMPLE OF PEACE
NATIONAL WAR MEMORIAL
CATHAYS PARK
UNIVERSITY COLLEGE
NATIONAL MUSEUM OF WALES
SHERMAN THEATRE
Glamorgan County Cricket Ground
NATIONAL SPORTS CENTRE
Sophia Gardens
COUNTY HALL
UNIVERSITY REGISTRY
Castle Mews
CITY HALL
LAW COURTS
INVESTITURE FOUNTAIN
Boulevard de Nantes
MUNICIPAL BUILDINGS
NEW THEATRE
CARICTRE THEATRE
Queen St. Station
SOPHIA GARDENS PAVILION
BLACKFRIARS PRIORY
CARDIFF CASTLE
Castle Grn.
St. David's Hosp.
Cardiff Bri.
CATHEDRAL ST. DAVID'S
ST. JOHN THE BAPTIST CH.
Shopping Centre
ST. DAVID'S HALL
PHOTOGRAPHIC GALLERY
ORIEL GALLERY
Market
Cardiff Arms Park (Nat. Rugby Football Grd.)
WALES EMPIRE POOL
Bus Station
Cardiff Central Station
River Taff (Afon Taf)
Sevenoaks Park
Grangetown Stn
GRANGETOWN
Works
0 1/4 MILE
© MAP PRODUCTIONS LTD

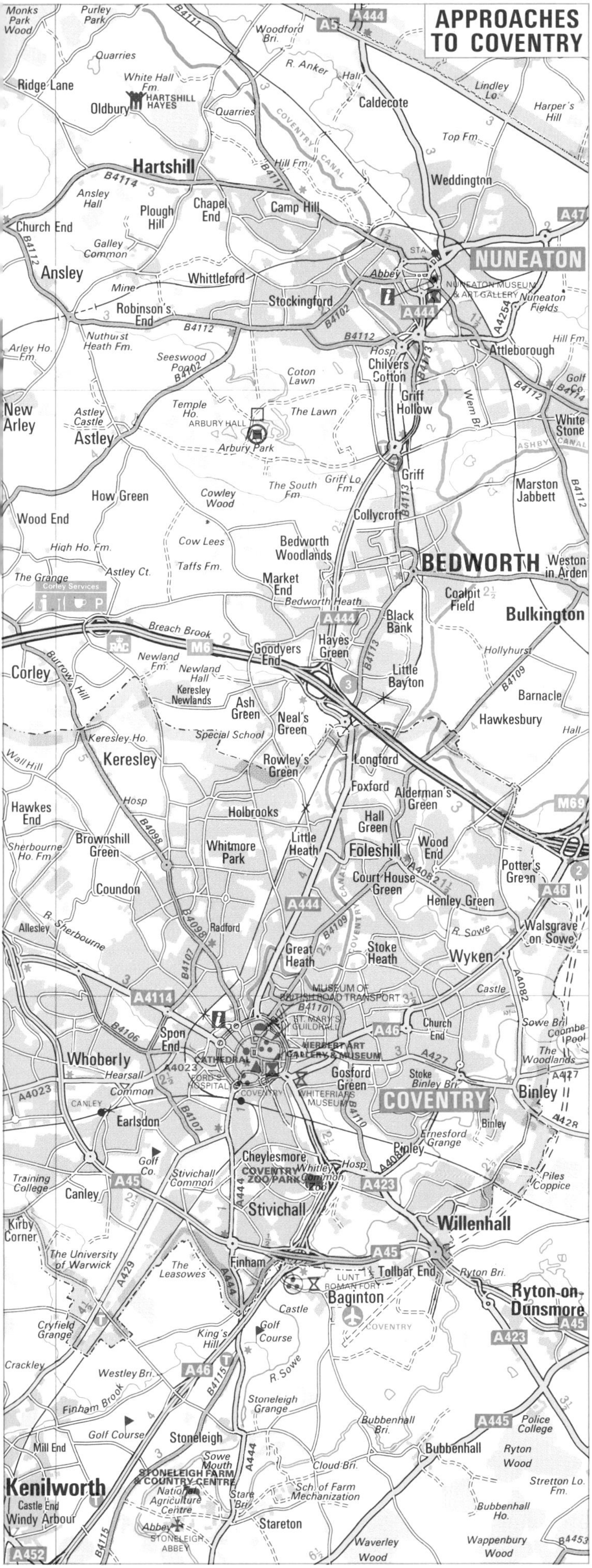

APPROACHES TO COVENTRY
Monks Park Wood
Purley Park
Woodford Bri.
R. Anker
Quarries
Ridge Lane
White Hall Fm.
HARTSHILL HAYES
Oldbury
Caldecote
Lindley Lo.
Harper's Hill
Top Fm.
COVENTRY CANAL
Hartshill
Hill Fm.
Weddington
Ansley Hall
Plough Hill
Chapel End
Camp Hill
Church End
Galley Common
NUNEATON
Ansley
Mine
Whittleford
Abbey
NUNEATON MUSEUM & ART GALLERY
Nuneaton Fields
Robinson's End
Stockingford
Nuthurst Heath Fm.
Arley Ho. Fm.
Seeswood Pool
Attleborough
Hill Fm.
Chilvers Coton
Coton Lawn
Griff Hollow
New Arley
Astley Castle
Temple Ho.
The Lawn
ARBURY HALL
Arbury Park
White Stone
Astley
ASHBY CANAL
Griff
How Green
Cowley Wood
The South Fm.
Griff Lo. Fm.
Marston Jabbett
Wood End
Collycroft
High Ho. Fm.
Cow Lees
Bedworth Woodlands
BEDWORTH
Weston in Arden
The Grange
Astley Ct.
Taffs Fm.
Market End
Corley Services
Bedworth Heath
Coalpit Field
Bulkington
Black Bank
Breach Brook
Newland Fm.
Goodyers End
Hayes Green
Hollyhurst
Corley
Newland Hall
Keresley Newlands
Little Bayton
Barnacle
Ash Green
Neal's Green
Hawkesbury
Keresley Ho.
Special School
Keresley
Rowley's Green
Longford
Hawkes End
Foxford
Alderman's Green
Holbrooks
Hall Green
Sherbourne Ho. Fm.
Brownshill Green
Whitmore Park
Little Heath
Foleshill
Wood End
Potter's Green
Court House Green
Coundon
Henley Green
Allesley
R. Sherbourne
Radford
Great Heath
Stoke Heath
Walsgrave on Sowe
Wyken
MUSEUM OF BRITISH ROAD TRANSPORT
Castle
Spon End
ST. MARY'S GUILDHALL
Church End
Sowe Bri.
Coombe Pool
Whoberly
CATHEDRAL
HERBERT ART GALLERY & MUSEUM
The Woodlands
Hearsall Common
Gosford Green
Stoke Bri.
Binley
FORD'S HOSPITAL
WHITEFRIARS MUSEUM
COVENTRY
Canley
Earlsdon
Ernesford Grange
Cheylesmore
COVENTRY ZOO PARK
Whitley Common
Training College
Stivichall Common
Piles Coppice
Canley
Stivichall
Willenhall
Kirby Corner
The University of Warwick
Finham
The Leasowes
LUNT ROMAN FORT
Tollbar End
Ryton Bri.
Ryton-on-Dunsmore
Baginton
Cryfield Grange
Castle
Golf Course
King's Hill
Crackley
Westley Bri.
R. Sowe
Finham Brook
Stoneleigh Grange
Bubbenhall Bri.
Police College
Golf Course
Stoneleigh
Mill End
Bubbenhall
Ryton Wood
Sowe Mouth
Cloud Bri.
STONELEIGH FARM & COUNTRY CENTRE
National Agriculture Centre
Stare Bri.
Sch of Farm Mechanization
Stretton Lo. Fm.
Kenilworth
Castle End
Windy Arbour
Stareton
Bubbenhall Ho.
Abbey
STONELEIGH ABBEY
Waverley Wood
Wappenbury Wood
M6
M69
A444
A5
A47
A46
A4114
A4023
A45
A423
A427
A428
A429
A445
A452
A4082
B4111
B4114
B4112
B4102
B4113
B4109
B4098
B4107
B4106
B4110
B4115
B4453

COVENTRY
A4170 TAMWORTH (B4098)
A444 NUNEATON M6
A4114 BIRMINGHAM (A45) M42
A46 LEICESTER (M69)
A428 RUGBY
A46 WARWICK & TO A423 BANBURY
A4023 REDDITCH
A444 ROYAL LEAMINGTON SPA
Naul's Mill Park
Playing Field
Bablake Sch.
Lake
Middleborough Rd.
ABBOTS LA.
RADFORD RD.
COUNDON RD.
HOLYHEAD RD.
RINGWAY
COVENTRY AND WARWICKSHIRE
Swanswell Pool
CITY WALLS & GATES
MUSEUM OF BRITISH ROAD TRANSPORT
APOLLO THEA.
Coach Park
Bus Sta.
BELGRADE THEA.
St. John's Hosp.
CORPORATION ST.
LADY GODIVA STATUE
HOLY TRINITY CH.
CATHEDRAL
Baths
Sports Centre
LANCHESTER POLYTECHNIC
BOND'S HOSP.
ST. JOHN THE BAPTIST CH.
Library
ST. MARY'S HALL
Art Faculty
Market
Precinct
Council Ho.
HERBERT ART GALLERY & MUSEUM
Gulson Hosp.
CHRIST CH. SPIRE
FORD'S HOSP.
Police H.Q.
CHEYLESMORE MANOR HO.
TOY MUSEUM
MARTYR'S MEM.
THEA.
Technical College
Queen's Rd.
COVENTRY STA.
SPENCER PARK
King Henry V111 School
Top Green
Quarryfield La.
0 ¼ MILE
© MAP PRODUCTIONS LTD

CROYDON
A235 TO CENTRAL LONDON (A23)
A212 SYDENHAM
MAYDAY HOSPITAL
A236 MITCHAM
A222 BECKENHAM
A232 ORPINGTON
A232 SUTTON
A235 TO REDHILL (A23)
M23
ST. JAMES'S ROAD
LR. ADDISCOMBE ROAD
Leslie Grove
Hosp.
West Croydon Sta.
Bus Sta.
WELLESLEY ROAD
Sydenham Rd.
Lansdowne Rd.
WHITGIFT CENTRE
WHITGIFT HOSPITAL
East Croydon Sta.
ADDISCOMBE RD.
Wandle Park
PARISH CHURCH
ARCHBISHOP'S PALACE
Town Hall
Katharine St.
Mint Walk
Croydon College
FAIRFIELD HALLS
ARNHEM GALLERY
FAIRFIELD RD.
ASHCROFT THEATRE
Park Hill Rec. Ground
OLD TOWN
THE CROYDON FLYOVER
DUPPAS HILL
COOMBE RD.
PARK LANE
SOUTH END
0 ½ MILE
© MAP PRODUCTIONS LTD

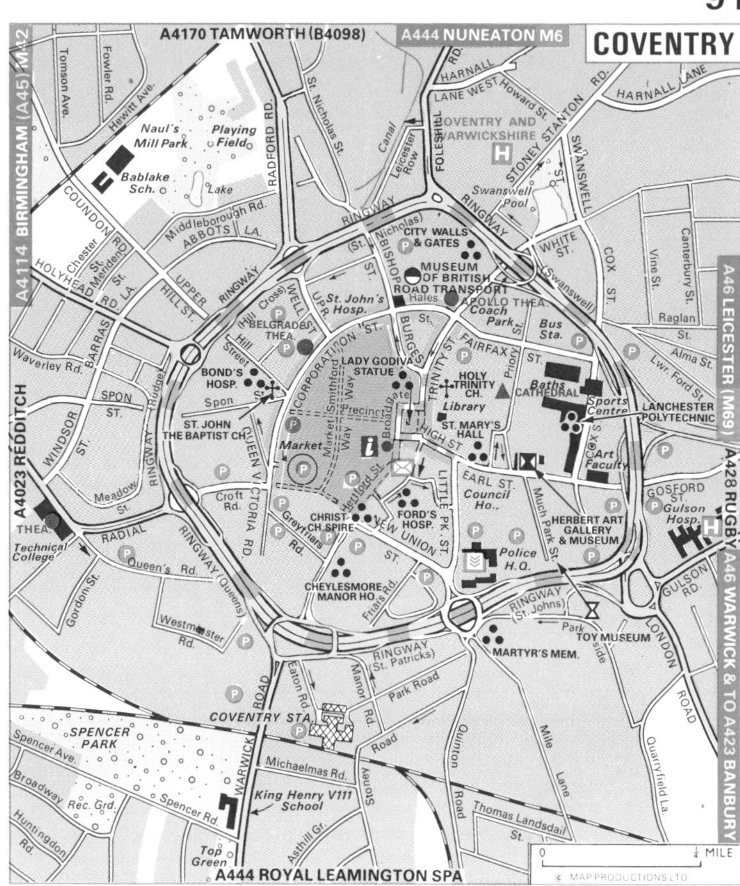

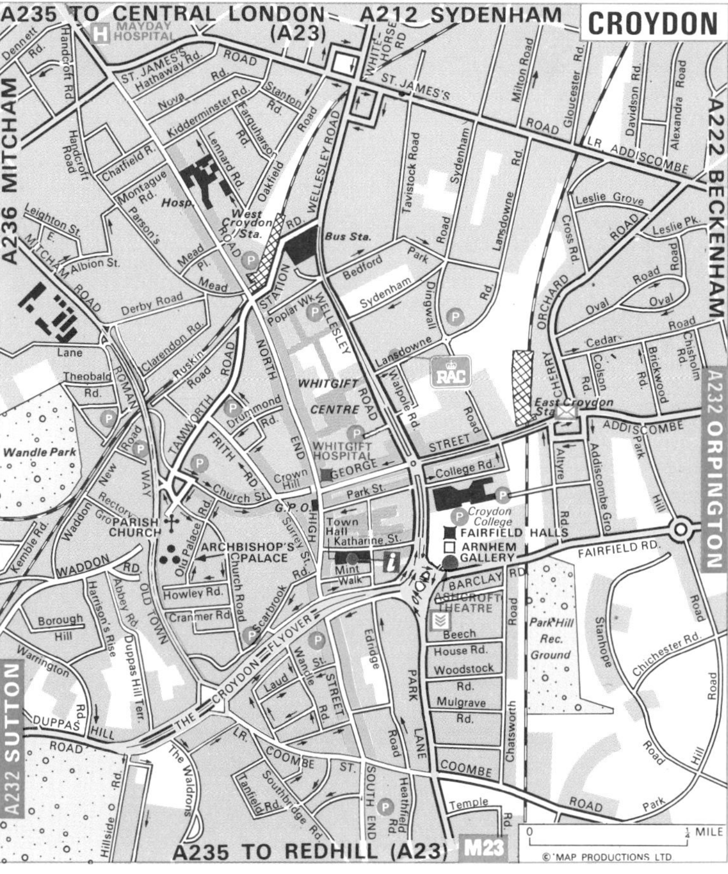

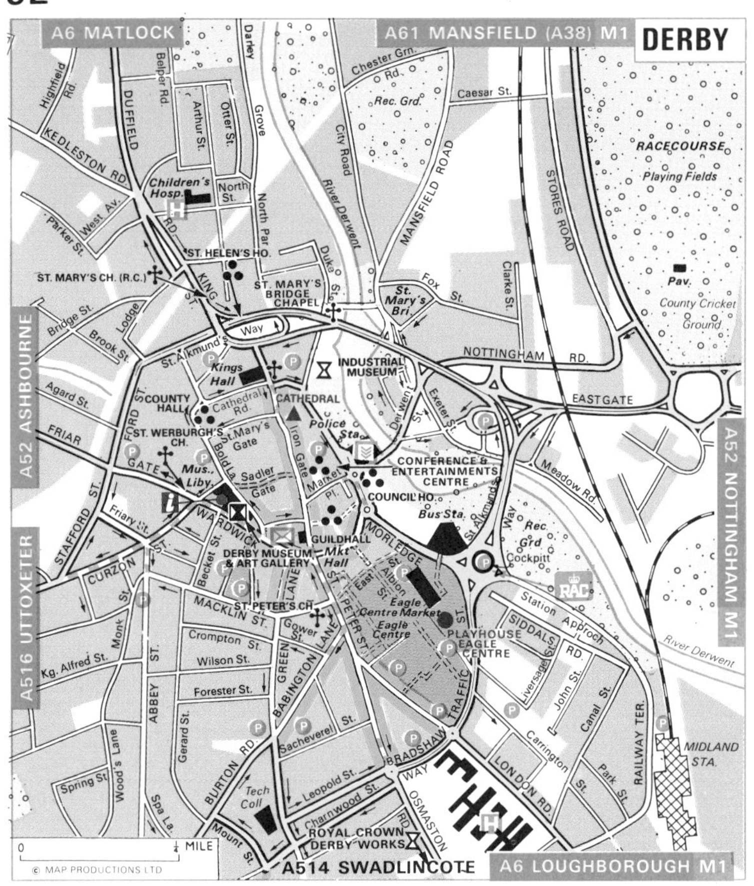
DERBY
A6 MATLOCK
A61 MANSFIELD (A38) M1
A52 ASHBOURNE
A516 UTTOXETER
A52 NOTTINGHAM M1
A514 SWADLINCOTE
A6 LOUGHBOROUGH M1
RACECOURSE
Playing Fields
County Cricket Ground
Pav.
Children's Hosp.
ST. HELEN'S HO.
ST. MARY'S CH. (R.C.)
ST. MARY'S BRIDGE CHAPEL
St. Mary's Bri.
INDUSTRIAL MUSEUM
Kings Hall
CATHEDRAL
COUNTY HALL
ST. WERBURGH'S CH.
Mus. Liby.
Police Sta.
CONFERENCE & ENTERTAINMENTS CENTRE
COUNCIL HO.
Bus Sta.
GUILDHALL
DERBY MUSEUM & ART GALLERY
Mkt Hall
ST. PETER'S CH.
Eagle Centre Market
Eagle Centre
PLAYHOUSE EAGLE CENTRE
Rec Grd
Cockpitt
Tech Coll
ROYAL CROWN DERBY WORKS
MIDLAND STA.
River Derwent
NOTTINGHAM RD.
EASTGATE
MORLEDGE
STORES ROAD
MANSFIELD ROAD
City Road
FRIAR GATE
WARDWICK
CURZON ST.
MACKLIN ST.
ABBEY ST.
BURTON RD
BABINGTON LANE
GREEN LANE
ST. PETER'S ST.
TRAFFIC ST.
SIDDALS RD.
LONDON RD.
OSMASTON RD.
RAILWAY TER.
BRADSHAW WAY
KEDLESTON RD.
DUFFIELD RD.
STAFFORD ST.
0 ¼ MILE
© MAP PRODUCTIONS LTD

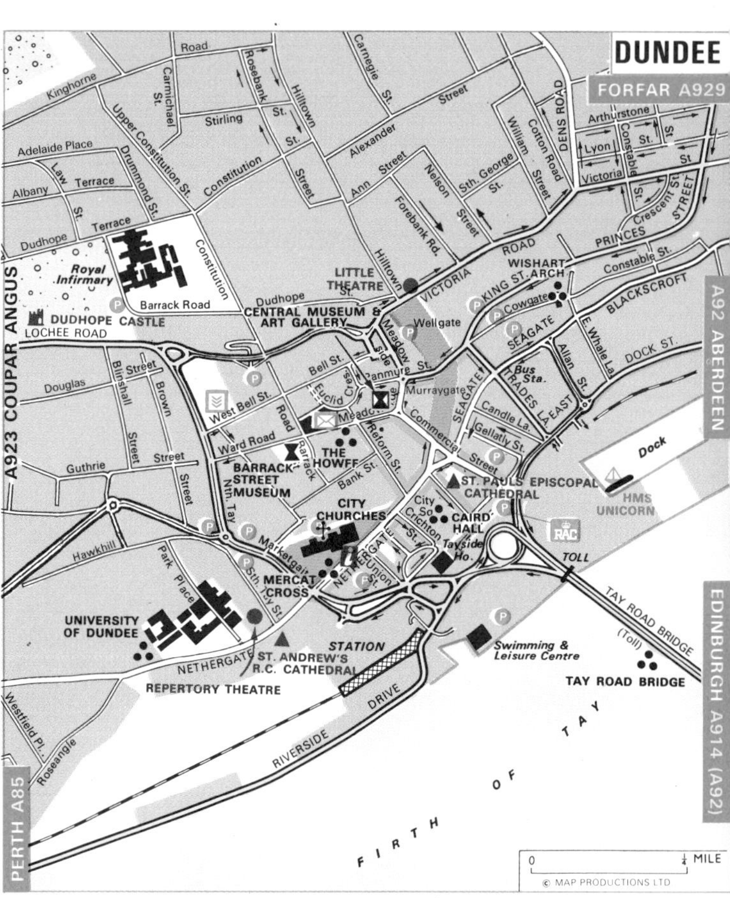
DUNDEE
FORFAR A929
A92 ABERDEEN
EDINBURGH A914 (A92)
A923 COUPAR ANGUS
PERTH A85
Royal Infirmary
Barrack Road
DUDHOPE CASTLE
LOCHEE ROAD
LITTLE THEATRE
CENTRAL MUSEUM & ART GALLERY
VICTORIA ROAD
KING ST. ARCH
WISHART ARCH
BLACKSCROFT
Wellgate
Murraygate
SEAGATE
Bus Sta.
DOCK ST.
Dock
HMS UNICORN
THE HOWFF
BARRACK STREET MUSEUM
CITY CHURCHES
ST. PAUL'S EPISCOPAL CATHEDRAL
CAIRD HALL
City Sq.
Tayside Ho.
MERCAT CROSS
NETHERGATE
UNIVERSITY OF DUNDEE
ST. ANDREW'S R.C. CATHEDRAL
REPERTORY THEATRE
STATION
Swimming & Leisure Centre
TAY ROAD BRIDGE
TOLL
RIVERSIDE DRIVE
FIRTH OF TAY
Hawkhill
Perth Road
Constitution
PRINCES STREET
0 ¼ MILE
© MAP PRODUCTIONS LTD

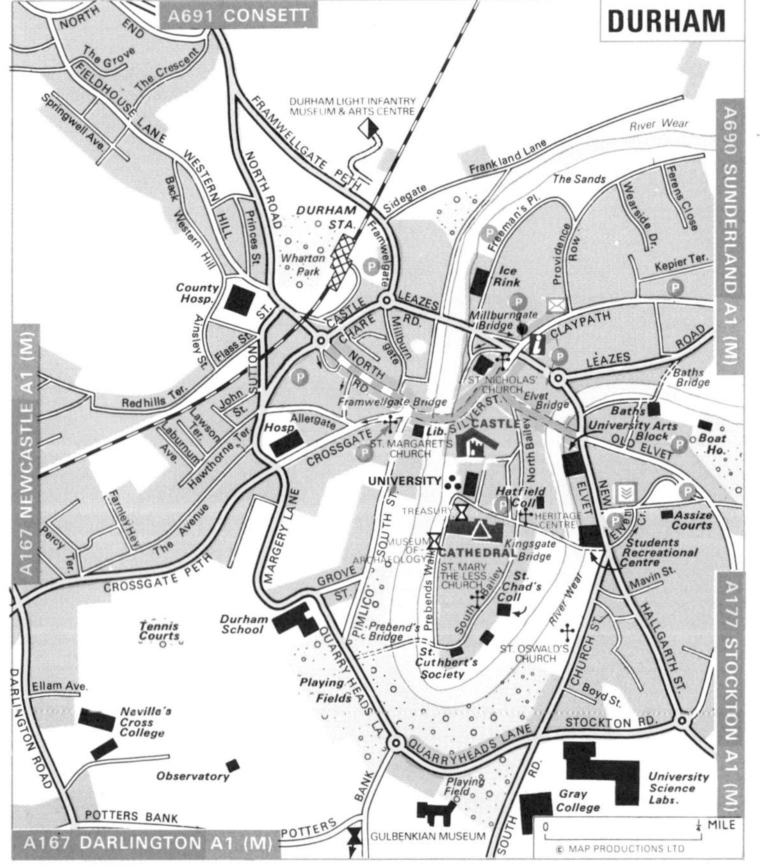
DURHAM
A691 CONSETT
A690 SUNDERLAND A1 (M)
A177 STOCKTON A1 (M)
A167 NEWCASTLE A1 (M)
A167 DARLINGTON A1 (M)
DURHAM LIGHT INFANTRY MUSEUM & ARTS CENTRE
River Wear
DURHAM STA.
Wharton Park
County Hosp.
Hosp.
Ice Rink
Millburngate Bridge
CLAYPATH
ST. NICHOLAS' CHURCH
Framwellgate Bridge
Elvet Bridge
Baths
Baths Bridge
Lib.
CASTLE
ST. MARGARET'S CHURCH
University Arts Block
Boat Ho.
UNIVERSITY
Hatfield Coll.
TREASURY
HERITAGE CENTRE
MUSEUM OF ARCHAEOLOGY
CATHEDRAL
ST. MARY THE LESS CHURCH
Kingsgate Bridge
Assize Courts
Students Recreational Centre
St. Chad's Coll.
Prebend's Bridge
ST. OSWALD'S CHURCH
St. Cuthbert's Society
Tennis Courts
Durham School
Playing Fields
Neville's Cross College
Observatory
Playing Field
Gray College
University Science Labs.
GULBENKIAN MUSEUM
QUARRYHEADS LANE
STOCKTON RD.
HALLGARTH ST.
CROSSGATE PETH
MARGERY LANE
NORTH ROAD
DARLINGTON ROAD
POTTERS BANK
0 ¼ MILE
© MAP PRODUCTIONS LTD

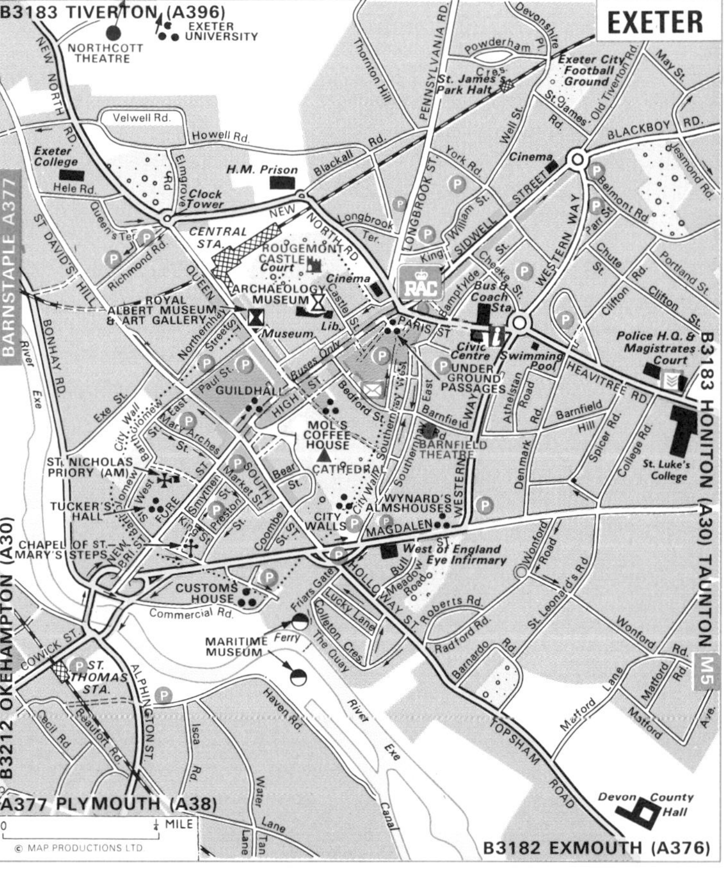
EXETER
B3183 TIVERTON (A396)
EXETER UNIVERSITY
NORTHCOTT THEATRE
BARNSTAPLE A377
B3183 HONITON (A30) TAUNTON M5
B3212 OKEHAMPTON (A30)
A377 PLYMOUTH (A38)
B3182 EXMOUTH (A376)
Exeter City Football Ground
St. James's Park Halt
BLACKBOY RD.
Exeter College
H.M. Prison
Clock Tower
CENTRAL STA.
ROUGEMONT CASTLE Court
ARCHAEOLOGY MUSEUM
Cinema
ROYAL ALBERT MUSEUM & ART GALLERY
Museum
Lib.
Bus & Coach Sta.
Civic Centre
UNDER GROUND PASSAGES
Swimming Pool
Police H.Q. & Magistrates Court
St. Luke's College
GUILDHALL
MOL'S COFFEE HOUSE
CATHEDRAL
BARNFIELD THEATRE
HEAVITREE RD
ST. NICHOLAS PRIORY (AM)
TUCKER'S HALL
CHAPEL OF ST. MARY'S STEPS
CITY WALLS
WYNARD'S ALMSHOUSES
MAGDALEN ST.
West of England Eye Infirmary
CUSTOMS HOUSE
MARITIME MUSEUM
Ferry
ST. THOMAS STA.
River Exe
Canal
TOPSHAM ROAD
Devon County Hall
ALPHINGTON ST.
COWICK ST.
SIDWELL STREET
WESTERN WAY
0 ¼ MILE
© MAP PRODUCTIONS LTD

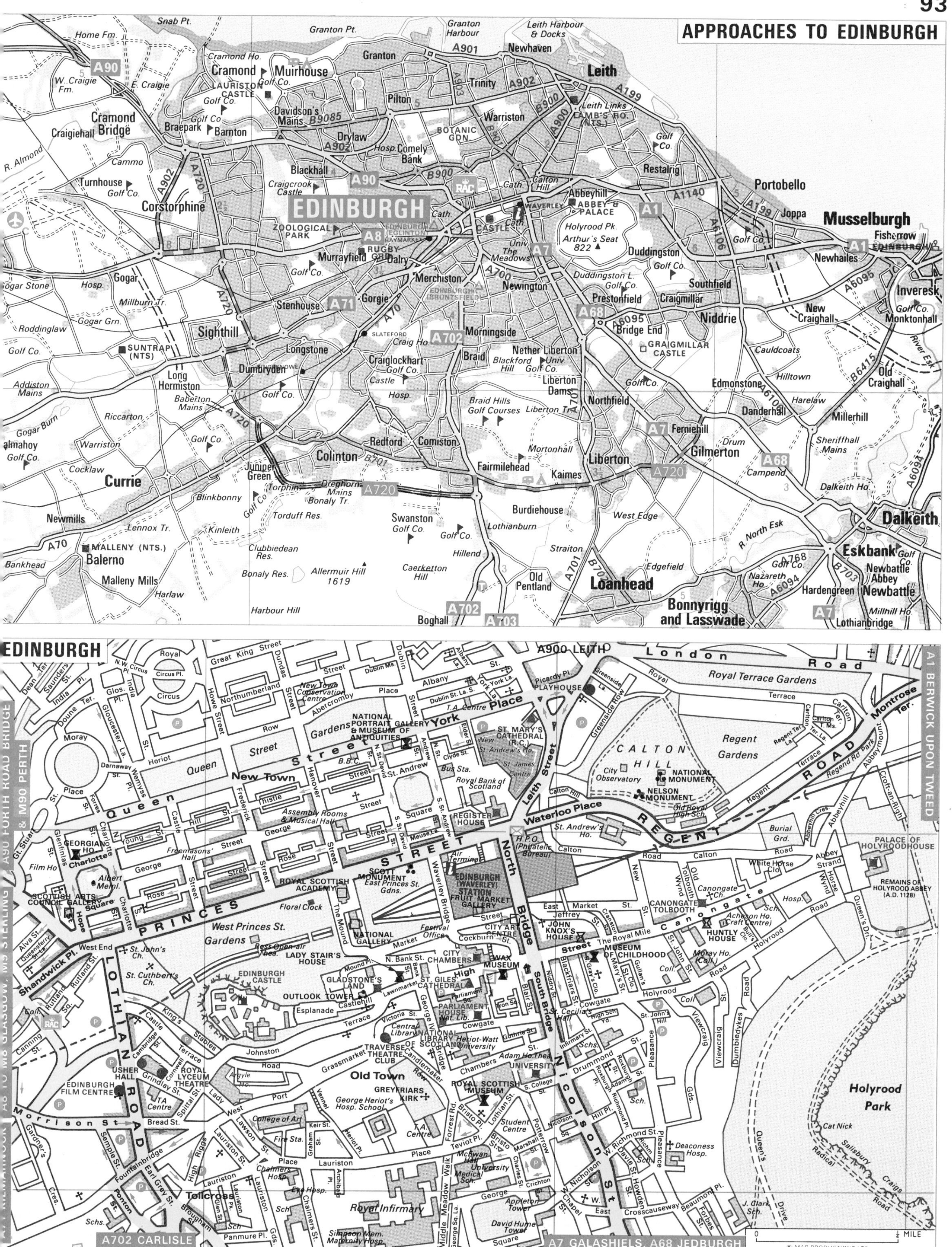
EDINBURGH
Leith
Portobello
Musselburgh
Dalkeith
Loanhead
Bonnyrigg and Lasswade
Currie
Balerno
Corstorphine
Cramond Bridge
Colinton
Liberton
Gilmerton
Newhaven
Granton
Morningside
Newington
Inveresk
Eskbank
Newbattle
Holyrood Park
PRINCES STREET
Old Town
New Town
A1 BERWICK UPON TWEED
A702 CARLISLE
A7 GALASHIELS, A68 JEDBURGH
© MAP PRODUCTIONS LTD

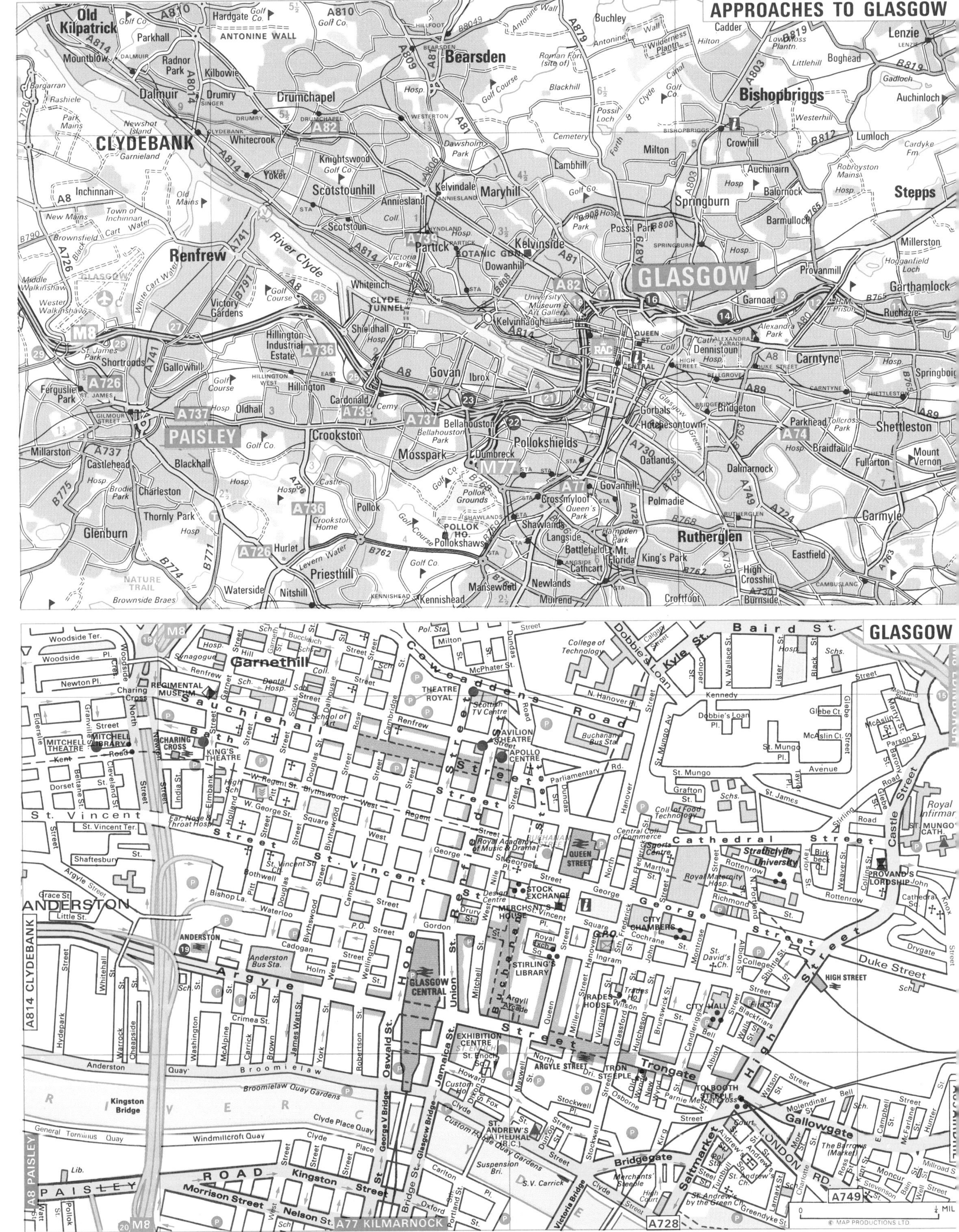
APPROACHES TO GLASGOW
GLASGOW
CLYDEBANK
PAISLEY
Renfrew
Bearsden
Bishopbriggs
Rutherglen
Stepps
Lenzie
Old Kilpatrick
Dalmuir
Drumchapel
Scotstounhill
Maryhill
Springburn
Kelvinside
Partick
Govan
Pollokshields
Shettleston
Carntyne
Cathcart
Pollokshaws
River Clyde
ANTONINE WALL
A8 PAISLEY
A814 CLYDEBANK
A77 KILMARNOCK
Sauchiehall Street
St. Vincent Street
Argyle Street
George Street
Cathedral Street
High Street
Gallowgate
Trongate
Buchanan Street
Hope Street
Renfield Street
Broomielaw
GLASGOW CENTRAL
QUEEN STREET
ANDERSTON
Garnethill
© MAP PRODUCTIONS LTD

GLOUCESTER
A38 TEWKESBURY
A40 CHELTENHAM M5
A417 CIRENCESTER
A40 ROSS-ON-WYE
TO A38 BRISTOL
A430 TO A38 BRISTOL M5
CATHEDRAL
GUILDHALL
STATION
GLOUCESTERSHIRE ROYAL HOSPITAL
BLACKFRIARS
THE PARK
HULL
A1079 YORK
A165 BRIDLINGTON
A1033 HEDON
A1105 SELBY (A63) M62
A63 SELBY M62
HUMBER BRIDGE
PARAGON STATION
GUILDHALL
WILBERFORCE HOUSE
FERENS ART GALLERY
TOWN DOCKS MUSEUM
Victoria Pier
RIVER HUMBER
© MAP PRODUCTIONS LTD
APPROACHES TO HULL
Woodmansey
Walkington
Cottingham
Willerby
Kirk Ella
West Ella
Anlaby
Anlaby Park
Swanland
Welton
Melton
North Ferriby
Hessle
Skidby
Little Weighton
Sutton-on-Hull
Stoneferry
Sculcoates
Summergangs
Newland
Dunswell
Wawne
Swine
Coniston
Bilton
Marfleet
KINGSTON UPON HULL
HUMBER BRIDGE
ROTTERDAM ZEEBRUGGE

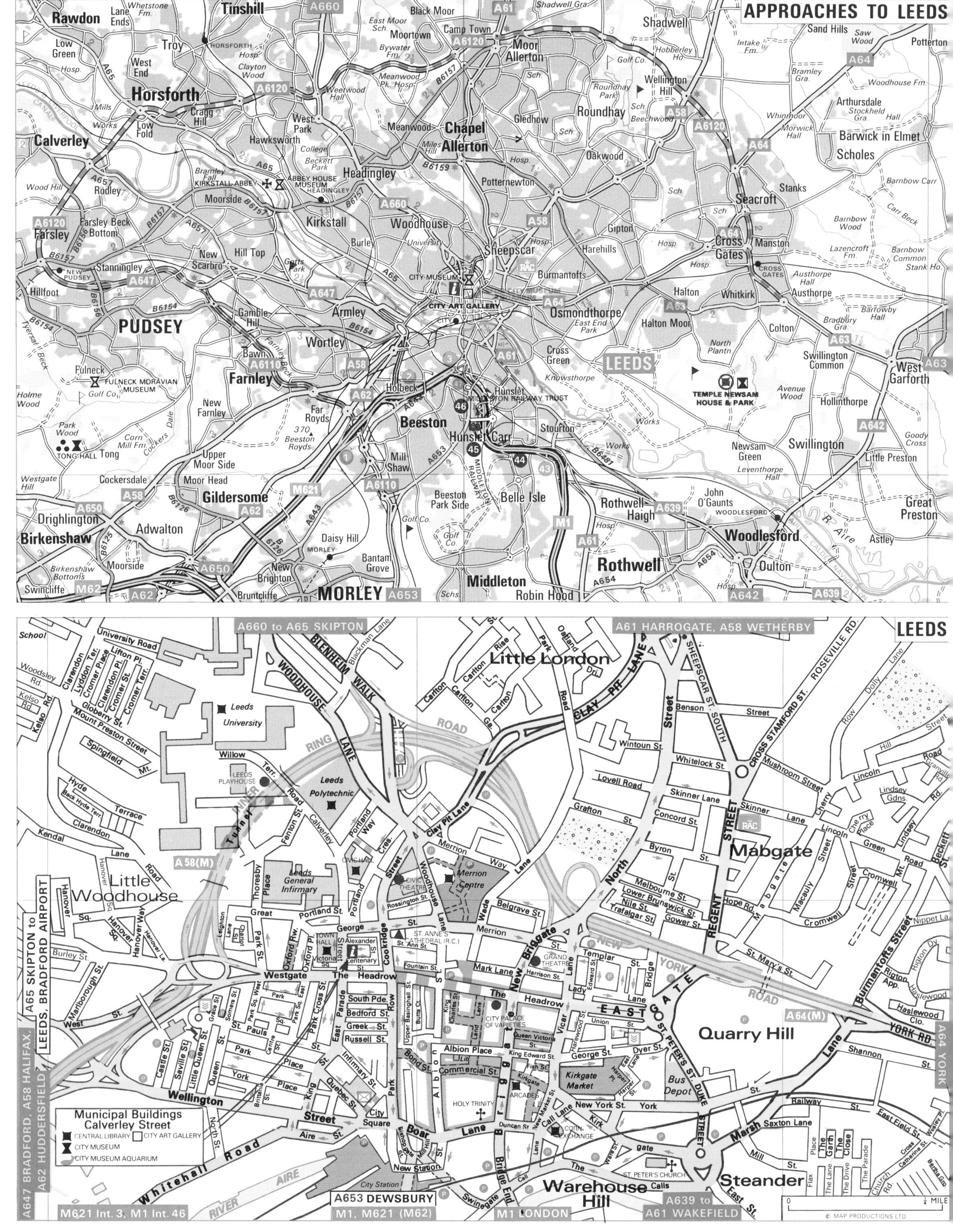
APPROACHES TO LEEDS
Rawdon
Lane Ends
Whetstone Fm.
Tinshill
A660
Black Moor
A61
Shadwell Gra
Shadwell
Sand Hills
Saw Wood
Potterton
Low Green
Troy
HORSFORTH
Hosp.
Clayton Wood
East Moor Sch.
Moortown
Bywater Fm.
Camp Town
A6120
Moor Allerton
Intake Fm.
Hobberley Ho.
Golf Co.
A64
Bramley Gra.
Woodhouse Fm.
West End
Horsforth
A6120
Meanwood Pk. Hosp.
Weetwood Hall
B6157
Wellington Hill
Roundhay Park
Arthursdale
Stockheld Gra.
Hall
Mills
Works
Cragg Hill
Low Fold
West Park
Meanwood
Chapel Allerton
Gledhow
Roundhay
Sch.
Beechwood
A58
A6120
Whinmoor
Morwick Hall
Barwick in Elmet
Calverley
Hawksworth
College
Beckett Park
Miles Hill
Oakwood
A64
Scholes
Bramley Fall
KIRKSTALL ABBEY
ABBEY HOUSE MUSEUM
HEADINGLEY
Headingley
B6159
Potternewton
Hosp.
Barnbow Carr
Wood Hill
Rodley
A657
Moorside
B6157
Sch
Seacroft
Stanks
Carr Beck
A6120
Farsley Beck Bottom
Farsley
Kirkstall
A660
Woodhouse
A58
Gipton
Sch.
Barnbow Wood
B6157
NEW PUDSEY
New Scarbro
Hill Top
Gotts Park
Burley
University
Sheepscar
Hosp
Harehills
Hosp.
Cross Gates
Manston
Lazencroft Fm.
Barnbow Common
Stank Ho.
Stanningley
A647
A65
CITY MUSEUM
RAC
Burmantofts
Hosp.
CROSS GATES
Austhorpe Hall
Hillfoot
A647
CITY MUSEUM
Halton
Whitkirk
Austhorpe
B6154
CITY ART GALLERY
A64
Osmondthorpe
A63
Barrowby Hall
PUDSEY
Gamble Hill
Armley
East End Park
Halton Moor
Colton
Bradbury Gra.
B6154
B6154
Wortley
Tyersal Beck
Farnley Beck
Bawn
A6110
A58
A61
Cross Green
LEEDS
North Plantn
A63
Swillington Common
West Garforth
A63
Fulneck
FULNECK MORAVIAN MUSEUM
Farnley
Holbeck
Hunslet
MIDDLETON RAILWAY TRUST
Knowsthorpe
TEMPLE NEWSAM HOUSE & PARK
Avenue Wood
Hollinthorpe
Holme Wood
Golf Co.
New Farnley
A62
Far Royds
Beeston
Stourton
Works
A642
Park Wood
370
Beeston Royds
Hunslet Carr
Works
Newsam Green
Swillington
Goody Cross
TONG HALL
Tong
Corn Mill Fm.
Cockers Dale
Upper Moor Side
Mill Shaw
A653
MIDDLETON RAILWAY
B6481
Leventhorpe Hall
Little Preston
Westgate Hill
Cockersdale
Moor Head
M621
A6110
Beeston Park Side
Belle Isle
John O'Gaunts
A58
Gildersome
A62
A643
Rothwell Haigh
A639
WOODLESFORD
Great Preston
A650
Drighlington
B6126
Golf Co.
M1
R. Aire
Birkenshaw
Adwalton
B6125
Daisy Hill
Golf Co.
Hosp
A61
Woodlesford
Astley
MORLEY
Bantam Grove
Rothwell
A654
Oulton
Birkenshaw Bottoms
Moorside
A650
New Brighton
A654
Swincliffe
M62
A62
Bruntcliffe
MORLEY
A653
Middleton
Schs
Robin Hood
Hosp
A642
A639
LEEDS
A660 to A65 SKIPTON
A61 HARROGATE, A58 WETHERBY
School
University Road
Woodsley Rd.
Clarendon Ter.
Lyddon Ter.
Cromer Place
Lifton Pl.
Clarendon Pl.
Cromer Terr.
Kelso Rd.
Globerry St.
Mount Preston Street
Leeds University
Blenheim Walk
Woodhouse Lane
Blackman Lane
Little London
Carlton
Carlton Rise
Carlton Gs.
Park
Oatland
Dri.
Clay Pit Lane
Road
Sheepscar St. South
Roseville Rd.
Benson
Street
Row
Dolly
Lane
Street
Wintoun St.
Spingfield Mt.
Willow Terr. Road
LEEDS PLAYHOUSE
Ring Road
Leeds Polytechnic
Whitelock St.
Cross Stamford St.
Mushroom Street
Lincoln
Hill
Road
Lovell Road
Skinner Lane
Lindsey Gdns.
Rd.
Hyde Terrace
Back Hyde Terr.
Clarendon
Inner
Tunnel
Fenton St.
Calverley
Portland Way
Clay Pit Lane
Grafton
Concord St.
Skinner
Lane
RAC
Cherry
Cherry Place
Lincoln
Lindsey
Kendal
Lane
Road
A 58(M)
CIVIC HALL
Cres.
Merrion
Way
Lane
Byron
Street
Mabgate
Green
Road
Beckett St.
Hanover
Little Woodhouse
Thoresby Place
Leeds General Infirmary
Portland
Street
CIVIC THEATRE
Woodhouse Lane
Merrion Centre
North
St.
St.
Melbourne St.
Lower Brunswick St.
Nile St.
Trafalgar St.
Gower St.
Hope Rd.
Mabgate
Macaulay
Cromwell
Street
Cromwell
Mt.
Hanover Sq.
Hanover Way
Hanover La.
Great
Rossington St.
Portland St.
Wade
Belgrave St.
Brigate
Regent
Nippet La
A65 SKIPTON to LEEDS, BRADFORD AIRPORT
Burley St.
Leighton Lane
Chorley
Park St.
Oxford Rw.
Oxford Pl.
TOWN HALL
Victoria Sq.
Alexander St.
Centenary St.
Cookridge
George
St.
ST. ANNE'S CATHEDRAL (R.C.)
St. Ann St.
Merrion
St.
New
GRAND THEATRE
Templar
St.
Bridge
St. Mary's St.
Rigton Dv.
Rigton App.
Burmantofts Street
Fountain St.
Mark Lane
Harrison St.
Edward St.
Lady
Lane
York
Road
Haslewood
Marlborough St.
Westgate
The
Headrow
Park
South Pde.
Bedford St.
Greek St.
Russell St.
Row
Upper Basinghall St.
Butts Ct.
King Charles St.
The
Headrow
Land Lane
CITY PALACE OF VARIETIES
Queen Victoria St.
Vicar
Harewood St.
Union
St.
East
Gate
St. Peter's St.
Quarry Hill
A64(M)
Haslewood Clo.
York Rd.
A64 York
West
St.
Grace St.
Somers St.
Park Sq. West
Park Sq.
Park Sq. East
St. Pauls
St.
Park Cross St.
East Parade
Park
Centre St.
Place
Albion Place
King Edward St.
George St.
Dyer St.
Shannon
Lane
St.
A647 BRADFORD, A58 HALIFAX
A62 HUDDERSFIELD
Castle St.
Saville St.
Little Queen St.
Queen St.
York
Place
Britannia St.
King St.
Quebec St.
Infirmary St.
Park
Bond St.
Albion
Commercial St.
Fish St.
Kirkgate Market
Harper St.
East St.
Harper St.
Bus Depot
Duke
St.
Railway
St.
East Field St.
Wellington
Street
City Square
HOLY TRINITY
ARCADES
Kirkgate
New Market St.
Call Lane
New York St.
York
Kirk
gate
Saxton Lane
Street
Municipal Buildings Calverley Street
CENTRAL LIBRARY
CITY ART GALLERY
CITY MUSEUM
CITY MUSEUM AQUARIUM
North St.
Aire St.
Boar Lane
Duncan St.
CORN EXCHANGE
Marsh
Place
The Garth
The Close
Cross Catherine St.
Whitehall Road
Bishopsgate St.
Mill Hill
New Station
Bridge End
Warsheet
The
Calls
ST. PETER'S CHURCH
Mill
St.
Flax
The Lane
The Drive
The Parade
Church Rd.
River Aire
City Station
A653 DEWSBURY
Swinegate
Call
Warehouse Hill
Steander
A639 to A61 WAKEFIELD
East St.
0
¼ MILE
M621 Int. 3, M1 Int. 46
M1, M621 (M62)
M1 LONDON
© MAP PRODUCTIONS LTD.

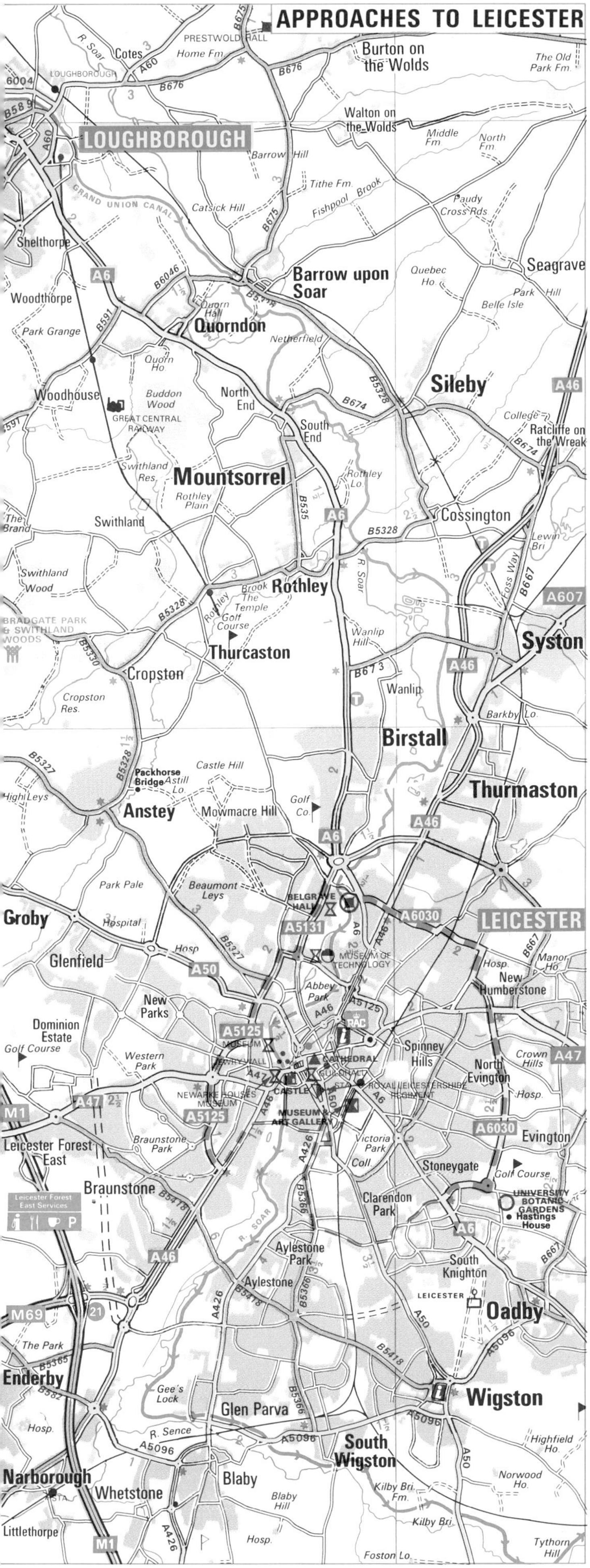

APPROACHES TO LEICESTER

APPROACHES TO LEICESTER
LOUGHBOROUGH
Burton on the Wolds
Walton on the Wolds
Prestwold Hall
Cotes
Home Fm.
The Old Park Fm.
Barrow Hill
Middle Fm.
North Fm.
Tithe Fm.
Fishpool Brook
Catsick Hill
Paudy Cross Rds.
GRAND UNION CANAL
Shelthorpe
Barrow upon Soar
Quebec Ho.
Seagrave
Park Hill
Belle Isle
Woodthorpe
Quorn Hall
Quorndon
Park Grange
Netherfield
Quorn Ho.
Sileby
Woodhouse
Buddon Wood
GREAT CENTRAL RAILWAY
North End
South End
College
Ratcliffe on the Wreak
Swithland Res.
Mountsorrel
Rothley Lo.
Rothley Plain
Cossington
The Brand
Swithland
Lewin Bri.
Swithland Wood
Rothley
The Temple
Golf Course
BRADGATE PARK & SWITHLAND WOODS
Thurcaston
Wanlip Hill
Syston
Cropston
Cropston Res.
Wanlip
Barkby Lo.
Birstall
Packhorse Bridge
Castle Hill
Astill Lo.
High Leys
Anstey
Mowmacre Hill
Golf Co.
Thurmaston
Park Pale
Beaumont Leys
BELGRAVE HALL
Groby
Hospital
LEICESTER
Glenfield
Hosp
MUSEUM OF TECHNOLOGY
Manor Ho.
Hosp.
New Humberstone
Abbey Park
New Parks
Dominion Estate
Golf Course
Western Park
Spinney Hills
Crown Hills
North Evington
Hosp.
JEWRY WALL
CATHEDRAL
GUILDHALL
ROYAL LEICESTERSHIRE REGIMENT
NEWARKE HOUSES MUSEUM
CASTLE
MUSEUM & ART GALLERY
Leicester Forest East
Braunstone Park
Victoria Park
Coll.
Evington
Stoneygate
Golf Course
Braunstone
UNIVERSITY BOTANIC GARDENS
Hastings House
Clarendon Park
Leicester Forest East Services
Aylestone Park
South Knighton
Aylestone
LEICESTER
Oadby
The Park
Enderby
Gee's Lock
Glen Parva
Wigston
Hosp.
R. Sence
South Wigston
Highfield Ho.
Narborough
Whetstone
Blaby
Blaby Hill
Norwood Ho.
Kilby Bri. Fm.
Kilby Bri.
Littlethorpe
Hosp.
Foston Lo.
Tythorn Hill
A6
A46
A607
A6030
A5131
A5125
A50
A47
A426
M1
M69
B676
B675
B6046
B591
B5328
B674
B535
B673
B5330
B5327
B667
B5366
B5418
B582
B5365
A5096

LEICESTER

A50 BURTON-UPON-TRENT M1
A6 LOUGHBOROUGH
A46 NEWARK-ON-TRENT
LEICESTER
A47 PETERBOROUGH
A6 MARKET HARBOROUGH
A47 HINCKLEY
A46 COVENTRY (M69) M1
A426 RUGBY
A50 N HAMPTON (A508)
St. Margaret's Church
Bus Sta.
All Saints' Church
Swimming Baths
CLOCK TOWER
HAYMARKET THEA.
HUMBERSTONE GATE
ST. NICHOLAS CH.
JEWRY WALL
JEWRY WALL MUSEUM
CATHEDRAL
GUILDHALL
CORN EXCH
Market
MUSEUM OF COSTUME
Town Hall
P.O.
Police Sta.
LITTLE THEA.
ST. MARY DE CASTRO CH.
CASTLE
Trinity Hosp.
The Magazine Gateway
ROYAL LEICESTER REGIMENT MUSEUM
NEWARKE HOUSES MUSEUM
Polytechnic
PHOENIX THEA.
Lib.
Civic Centre
LONDON ROAD STA.
Crown Cts.
MUSEUM & ART GALLERY
Fielding Johnson Hosp.
ROYAL INFIRMARY
Leicester Royal Infirmary
GRANBY HALLS
Rec. Ground
UNIVERSITY
DE MONTFORT HALL
Leicester City Football Ground
UPPERTON RD.
WALNUT ST.
0 ¼ MILE
© MAP PRODUCTIONS LTD

LINCOLN

A1102 TO A15
A15 HULL
A46 GRIMSBY (A18)
LINCOLN
A158 SKEGNESS
A57 GAINSBOROUGH (A156)
A46 NEWARK-ON-TRENT
A15 SLEAFORD
ROYAL LINCOLNSHIRE REGIMENT MUS.
Ellis Mill
NEWPORT ARCH
MUS. OF LINCOLNSHIRE LIFE
BISHOP'S PALACE
Cricket Grd.
Rugby Football Grd.
Assize Courts
CASTLE
EXCHEQUER GATE
CATHEDRAL
Priory Gate
CATHEDRAL TREASURY
Potter Gate
AARON THE JEW'S HO.
JEWS HOUSE
CARDINAL'S HAT
USHER GALLERY
COUNTY HOSP
County Office
City Hall
Arboretum
THEATRE ROYAL
CITY & COUNTY MUSEUM
National Cycle Mus.
LOWER WESTGATE
Draw Bridge
HIGH BRIDGE
Stonebow
St. Swithin's Church
ST. BENEDICT'S CH.
ST. MARY-LE-WIGFORD CH.
Mkt.
Anglian Water Offices
Bus Sta. (City)
River Witham
CENTRAL STA.
Bus Sta. (Rural)
GUILDHALL
0 ¼ MILE
© MAP PRODUCTIONS LTD

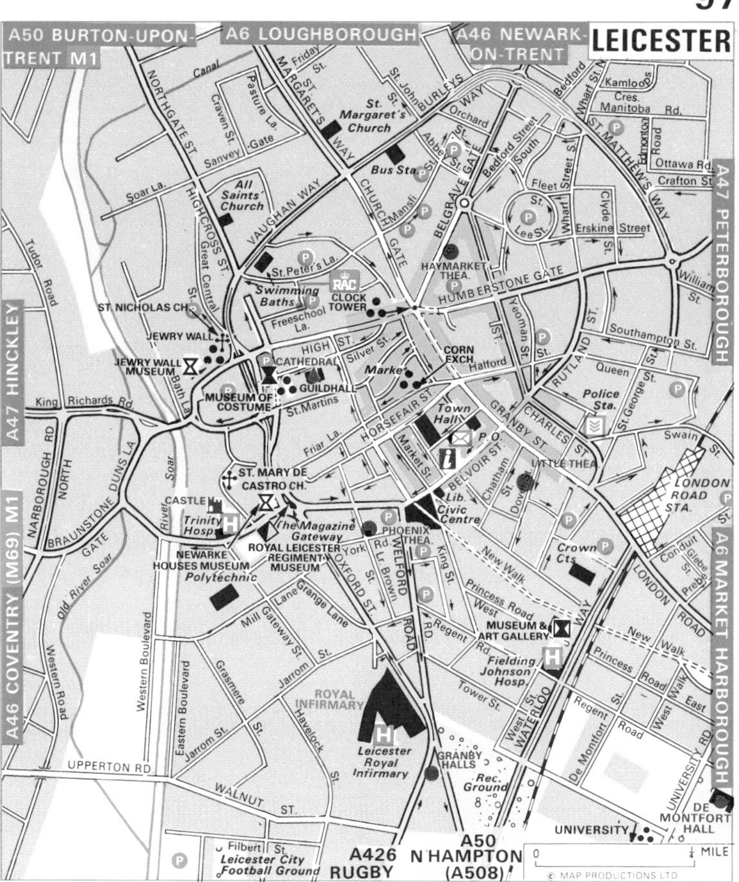

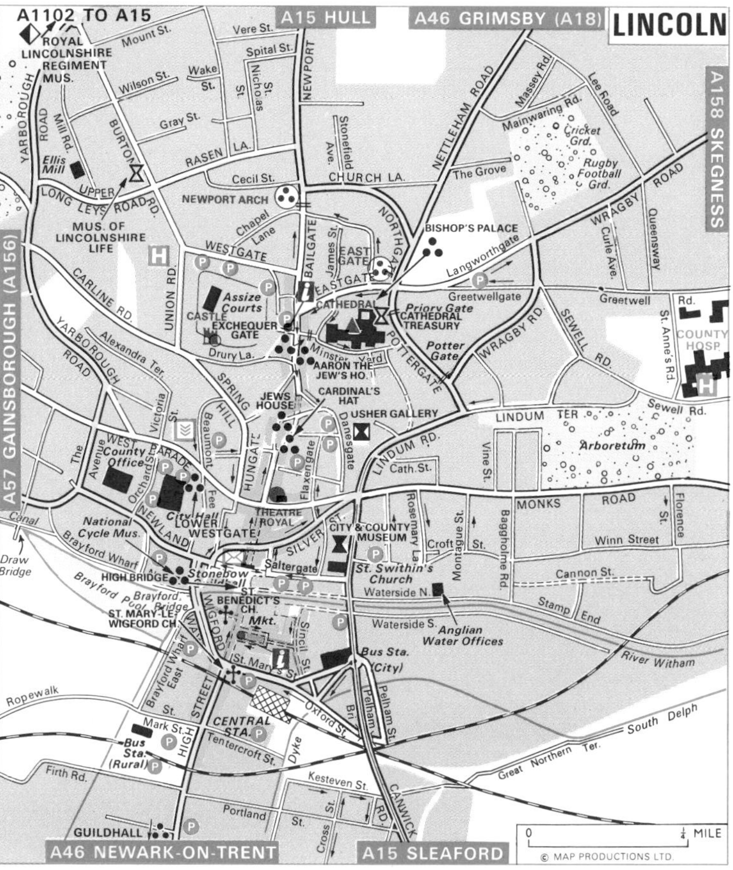

LIVERPOOL
A59 PRESTON
A580 MANCHESTER
M6
A57 WARRINGTON (M62)
A565 SOUTHPORT
BIRKENHEAD
A562 WIDNES
A561 WIDNES (A562)
LIME ST. STA.
R.C. CATHEDRAL
CATHEDRAL
LIVERPOOL DOCKS
MAP PRODUCTIONS LTD
APPROACHES TO LIVERPOOL
ORMSKIRK
Aughton
Maghull
Lydiate
Aintree
KIRKBY
Knowsley
CROSBY
Waterloo
Seaforth
Litherland
BOOTLE
WALLASEY
New Brighton
Egremont
Liscard
Moreton
Bidston
Upton
Greasby
Woodchurch
BIRKENHEAD
Tranmere
Rock Ferry
BEBINGTON
Port Sunlight
RIVER MERSEY
LIVERPOOL
Kirkdale
Everton
Anfield
Walton on the Hill
Norris Green
West Derby
Old Swan
Edge Hill
Wavertree
Childwall
Dingle
Mossley Hill
Aigburth
Allerton
Garston
Grassendale
Woolton
Gateacre
Halewood
Hunt's Cross
Roby
Huyton
Prescot
Fazakerley
Orrell
Knotty Ash
Broad Green

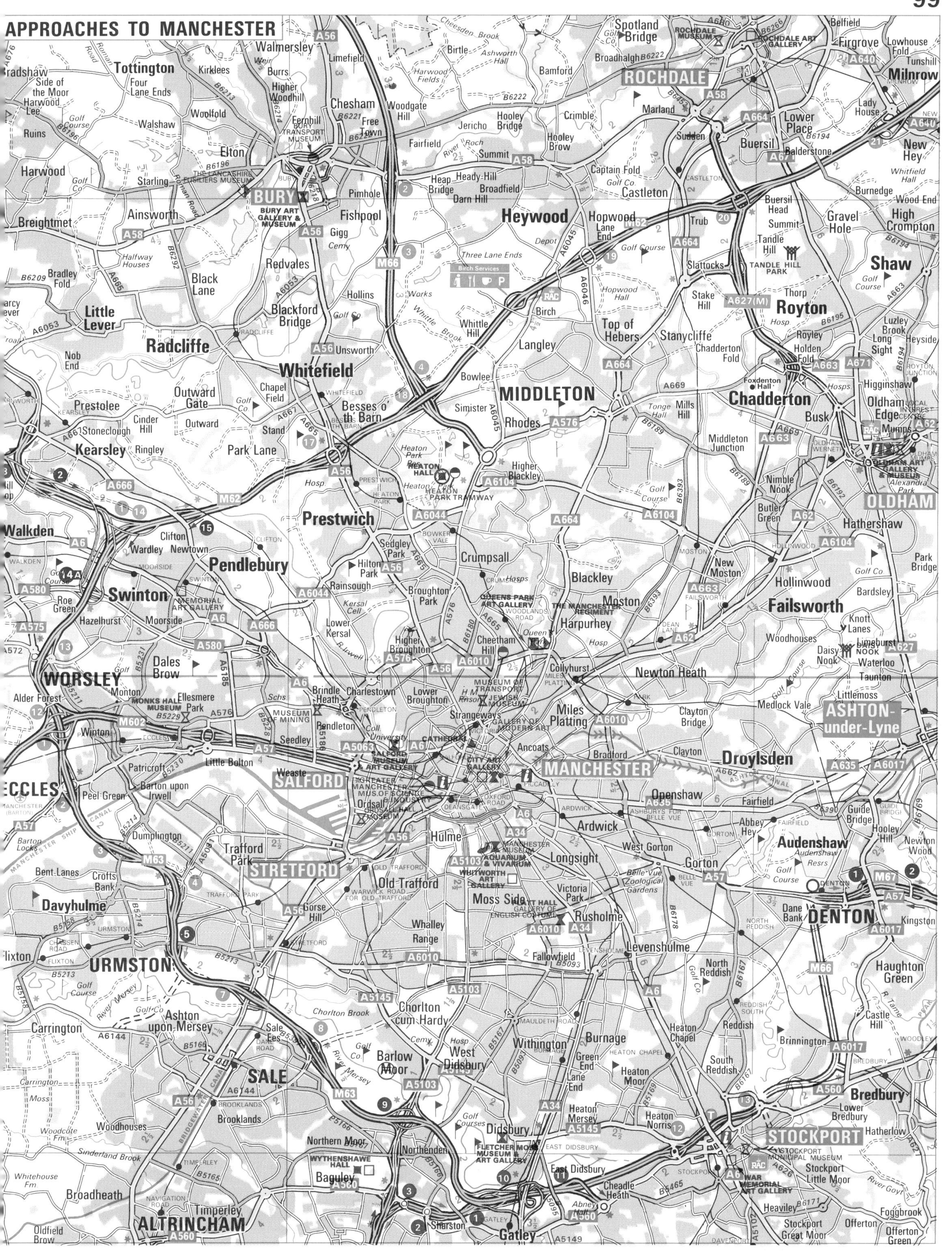
APPROACHES TO MANCHESTER
Walmersley
Tottington
Kirklees
Limefield
Birtle
Ashworth Hall
Bamford
Spotland Bridge
ROCHDALE MUSEUM
ROCHDALE ART GALLERY
Belfield
Firgrove
Lowhouse Fold
Tunshill
Milnrow
Side of the Moor
Harwood Lee
Four Lane Ends
Burrs
Higher Woodhill
Harwood Fields
Broadhalgh
ROCHDALE
Chesham
Woodgate Hill
Walshaw
Woolfold
Fernhill
BURY TRANSPORT MUSEUM
Free Town
Jericho
Hooley Bridge
Crimble
Marland
Lady House
Ruins
Elton
Fairfield
Summit
Hooley Brow
Sudden
Lower Place
Buersil
Balderstone
New Hey
Harwood
THE LANCASHIRE FUSILIERS MUSEUM
Starling
BURY
BURY ART GALLERY & MUSEUM
Pimhole
Heap Bridge
Heady-Hill
Broadfield
Darn Hill
Captain Fold
Castleton
Whitfield Hall
Burnedge
Wood End
Breightmet
Ainsworth
Fishpool
Gigg
Heywood
Hopwood
Lane End
Trub
Buersil Head
Summit
Gravel Hole
High Crompton
Halfway Houses
Redvales
Three Lane Ends
Tandle Hill
TANDLE HILL PARK
Bradley Fold
Black Lane
Birch Services
Slattocks
Shaw
Hollins
Hopwood Hall
Stake Hill
Thorp
Royton
Little Lever
Blackford Bridge
Whittle Hill
Birch
Top of Hebers
Stanycliffe
Radcliffe
Unsworth
Langley
Chadderton Fold
Royley
Holden Fold
Luzley Brook
Long Sight
Heyside
Nob End
Whitefield
Bowlee
Foxdenton Hall
Higginshaw
Prestolee
Outward Gate
Chapel Field
Besses o' th' Barn
Simister
MIDDLETON
Tonge Hall
Mills Hill
Chadderton
Busk
Oldham Edge
Mumps
Stoneclough
Cinder Hill
Outward
Stand
Rhodes
Middleton Junction
Kearsley
Ringley
Park Lane
Heaton Park
HEATON HALL
HEATON PARK TRAMWAY
Higher Blackley
Nimble Nook
OLDHAM ART GALLERY & MUSEUM
Alexandra Park
OLDHAM
Butler Green
Walkden
Clifton
Prestwich
Hathershaw
Wardley
Newtown
Sedgley Park
Crumpsall
New Moston
Park Bridge
Pendlebury
Hilton Park
Blackley
Hollinwood
Swinton
MEMORIAL ART GALLERY
Rainsough
Broughton Park
QUEENS PARK ART GALLERY
THE MANCHESTER REGIMENT
Moston
Bardsley
Failsworth
Roe Green
Hazelhurst
Moorside
Kersal Cell
Lower Kersal
Harpurhey
Knott Lanes
Woodhouses
Higher Broughton
Cheetham Hill
Daisy Nook
Waterloo
Dales Brow
WORSLEY
Collyhurst
Newton Heath
Taunton
Alder Forest
Monton
MONKS HALL MUSEUM
Ellesmere Park
MUSEUM OF MINING
Brindle Heath
Charlestown
Lower Broughton
MUSEUM OF TRANSPORT
JEWISH MUSEUM
Littlemoss
Medlock Vale
ASHTON-under-Lyne
Winton
Pendleton
Strangeways
GALLERY OF MODERN ART
Miles Platting
Clayton Bridge
Seedley
University
CATHEDRAL
Ancoats
Bradford
Clayton
Droylsden
Patricroft
Little Bolton
SALFORD MUSEUM & ART GALLERY
CITY ART GALLERY
MANCHESTER
ECCLES
Barton upon Irwell
Weaste
SALFORD
GREATER MANCHESTER MUS. OF SCIENCE & INDUSTRY
Openshaw
Fairfield
Guide Bridge
Peel Green
Ordsall
ORDSALL HALL MUSEUM
Ardwick
Abbey Hey
Hooley Hill
Newton Wood
Dumplington
Hulme
MANCHESTER MUSEUM
AQUARIUM & VIVARIUM
Audenshaw
Audenshaw Resrs
Barton Locks
Trafford Park
West Gorton
Gorton
Longsight
Belle Vue Zoological Gardens
Bent Lanes
Crofts Bank
STRETFORD
Old Trafford
WHITWORTH ART GALLERY
Victoria Park
Denton
Dane Bank
DENTON
Kingston
Davyhulme
Moss Side
GALLERY OF ENGLISH COSTUME
Rusholme
Gorse Hill
Whalley Range
Flixton
URMSTON
Fallowfield
Levenshulme
North Reddish
Haughton Green
Chorlton cum Hardy
Chorlton Brook
Ashton upon Mersey
Carrington
Sale
Withington
Burnage
Reddish
Castle Hill
Heaton Chapel
Brinnington
Barlow Moor
West Didsbury
Green End
Heaton Moor
South Reddish
SALE
Lane End
Bredbury
Lower Bredbury
Carrington Moss
Brooklands
Heaton Mersey
Heaton Norris
Woodhouses
Woodcote Fm
Northern Moor
Didsbury
FLETCHER MOSS MUSEUM & ART GALLERY
STOCKPORT
Hatherlow
Sinderland Brook
WYTHENSHAWE HALL
Northenden
East Didsbury
STOCKPORT MUNICIPAL MUSEUM
Stockport Little Moor
Whitehouse Fm
Baguley
Cheadle Heath
WAR MEMORIAL ART GALLERY
Broadheath
Timperley
Abney Hall
Heaviley
Foggbrook
ALTRINCHAM
Sharston
Gatley
Stockport Great Moor
Offerton
Offerton Green
Oldfield Brow
M62
M66
M63
M602
M67
A56
A58
A6
A57
A34
A664
A627(M)
A663
A62
A6104
A6010
A5103
A5145
A560
A6017
A635

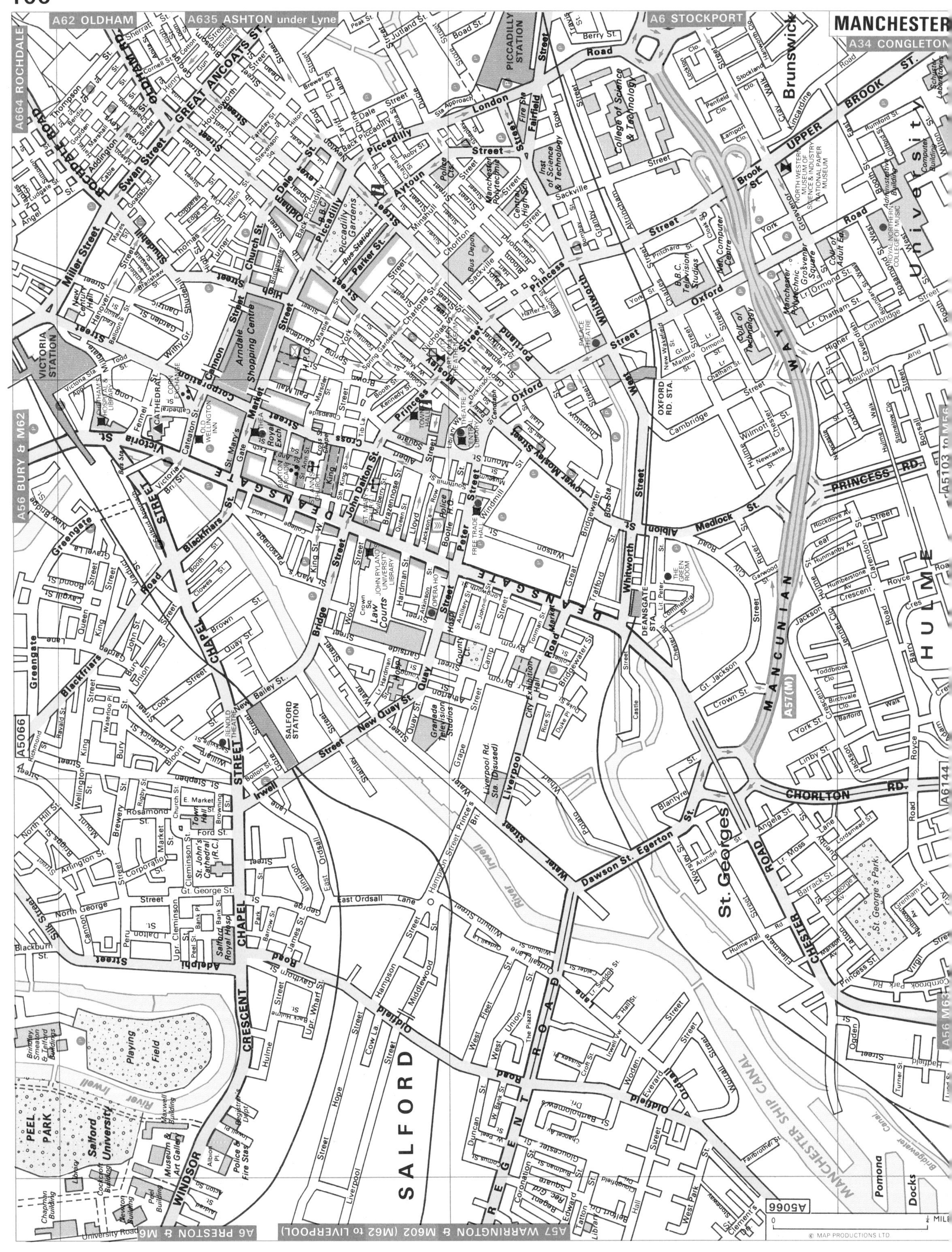
MANCHESTER
A62 OLDHAM
A635 ASHTON under Lyne
A6 STOCKPORT
A34 CONGLETON
A664 ROCHDALE
A56 BURY & M62
A5066
A6144
A5103 to M56
A56 M63
A6 PRESTON & M6
A57 WARRINGTON & M602 (M62 to LIVERPOOL)
PICCADILLY STATION
VICTORIA STATION
SALFORD STATION
OXFORD RD. STA.
DEANSGATE STA.
Liverpool Rd. Sta. (Disused)
Brunswick
University
HULME
SALFORD
St. Georges
PEEL PARK
Salford University
Playing Field
River Irwell
MANCHESTER SHIP CANAL
Bridgewater Canal
Pomona
Docks
College of Science & Technology
Inst. of Science & Technology
Manchester Polytechnic
Arndale Shopping Centre
CATHEDRAL
CORN EXCHANGE
CHETHAM'S HOSPITAL & LIBRARY
OLD WELLINGTON INN
TOWN HALL
CITY ART GALLERY
THE ATHENAEUM
LIBRARY THEATRE
CENTRAL LIBRARY
PALACE THEATRE
FREE TRADE HALL
OPERA HO.
JOHN RYLANDS UNIVERSITY LIBRARY
Law Courts
Crown Sq.
Granada Television Studios
B.B.C. Television Studios
Nat. Computer Centre
Coll. of Technology
Coll. of Adult Ed.
ROYAL NORTHERN COLLEGE OF MUSIC
Administrative Building
Computer Building
NORTH WESTERN MUSEUM OF SCIENCE & INDUSTRY
NATIONAL PAPER MUSEUM
Schuster Laboratories
THE GREEN ROOM
Piccadilly Gardens
Bus Station
Bus Depot
Police
St. John's Cathedral (R.C.)
Salford Royal Hosp.
Museum & Art Gallery
Police & Fire Stas.
Registrar's Dept.
Library
Chapman Building
Newton Building
Peel Building
Cockcroft Building
Brindley, Smeaton & Telford Buildings
Maxwell Building
PICCADILLY
MANCUNIAN WAY
A57(M)
DEANSGATE
CHAPEL STREET
CRESCENT
WINDSOR
REGENT ROAD
CHESTER ROAD
CHORLTON RD.
PRINCESS RD.
UPPER BROOK ST.
GREAT ANCOATS ST.
OLDHAM RD.
ROCHDALE ROAD
Oxford Road
Oxford Street
Portland Street
Whitworth Street
Whitworth Street West
Market Street
Corporation Street
Cross Street
Mosley Street
Princess Street
Peter Street
Quay Street
Water Street
Liverpool Road
Dawson St.
Egerton St.
Oldfield Road
Blackfriars
Greengate
Stanley
0
1/4 MILE
© MAP PRODUCTIONS LTD

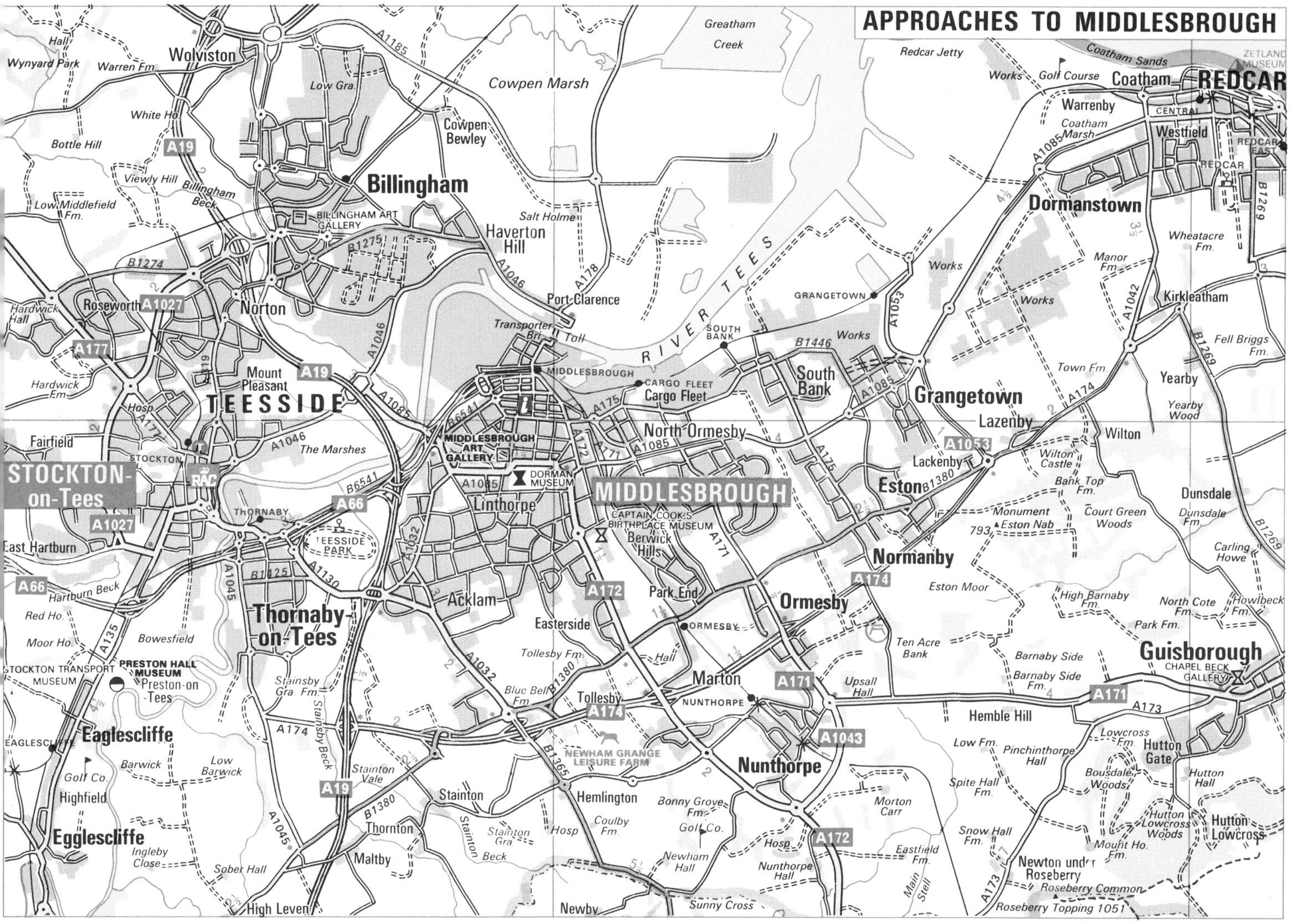
APPROACHES TO MIDDLESBROUGH
Wolviston
Wynyard Park
Warren Fm.
Greatham Creek
Cowpen Marsh
Cowpen Bewley
Redcar Jetty
Coatham Sands
Golf Course
Coatham
REDCAR
Warrenby
Coatham Marsh
Westfield
Billingham
BILLINGHAM ART GALLERY
Haverton Hill
Salt Holme
Dormanstown
Wheatacre Fm.
Kirkleatham
Fell Briggs Fm.
Port Clarence
Transporter Br.
RIVER TEES
GRANGETOWN
SOUTH BANK
Norton
Roseworth
Hardwick Hall
Mount Pleasant
TEESSIDE
MIDDLESBROUGH
CARGO FLEET
Cargo Fleet
South Bank
Grangetown
Lazenby
Yearby
Wilton
Wilton Castle
North Ormesby
Fairfield
STOCKTON-on-Tees
The Marshes
MIDDLESBROUGH ART GALLERY
DORMAN MUSEUM
MIDDLESBROUGH
Lackenby
Eston
Bank Top Fm.
Dunsdale
Linthorpe
CAPTAIN COOK'S BIRTHPLACE MUSEUM
Berwick Hills
THORNABY
TEESSIDE PARK
Monument
Eston Nab
Court Green Woods
East Hartburn
Normanby
Hartburn Beck
Acklam
Park End
Eston Moor
High Barnaby Fm.
North Cote Fm.
Howlbeck Fm.
Thornaby-on-Tees
Ormesby
Easterside
Ten Acre Bank
Park Fm.
Guisborough
CHAPEL BECK GALLERY
Bowesfield
Tollesby Fm.
Barnaby Side
STOCKTON TRANSPORT MUSEUM
PRESTON HALL MUSEUM
Preston-on-Tees
Stainsby Gra Fm.
Marton
Upsall Hall
Tollesby
NUNTHORPE
Hemble Hill
Eaglescliffe
NEWHAM GRANGE LEISURE FARM
Nunthorpe
Low Fm.
Pinchinthorpe Hall
Hutton Gate
Barwick
Low Barwick
Stainton Vale
Golf Co.
Highfield
Stainton
Hemlington
Bonny Grove Fm.
Morton Carr
Spite Hall Fm.
Hutton Lowcross Woods
Hutton Lowcross
Egglescliffe
Thornton
Coulby Fm.
Snow Hall Fm.
Mount Ho. Fm.
Ingleby Close
Maltby
Newham Hall
Eastfield Fm.
Sober Hall
Nunthorpe Hall
Newton under Roseberry
Roseberry Common
High Leven
Newby
Sunny Cross
Roseberry Topping 1051

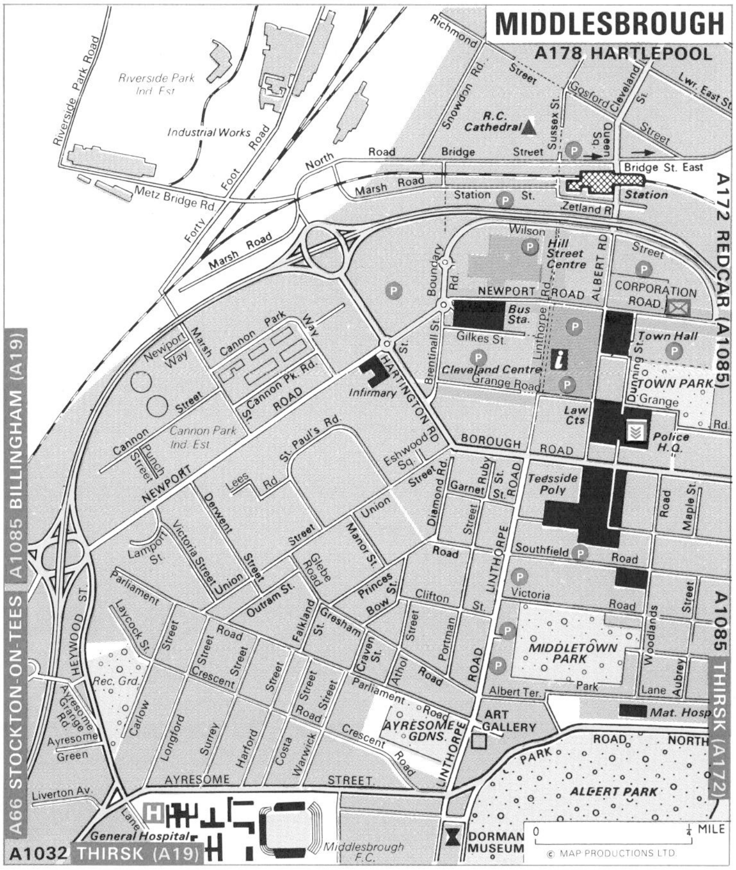
MIDDLESBROUGH
A178 HARTLEPOOL
Riverside Park Ind. Est
Industrial Works
R.C. Cathedral
Bridge St. East
Station
A172 REDCAR (A1085)
Hill Street Centre
CORPORATION ROAD
Bus Sta.
Town Hall
Cleveland Centre
TOWN PARK
Infirmary
Law Cts
Police H.Q.
Cannon Park Ind. Est
Teesside Poly
A1085 THIRSK (A172)
MIDDLETOWN PARK
Mat. Hosp
ART GALLERY
AYRESOME GDNS.
ALBERT PARK
A66 STOCKTON-ON-TEES A1085 BILLINGHAM (A19)
General Hospital
Middlesbrough F.C.
DORMAN MUSEUM
A1032 THIRSK (A19)
© MAP PRODUCTIONS LTD.

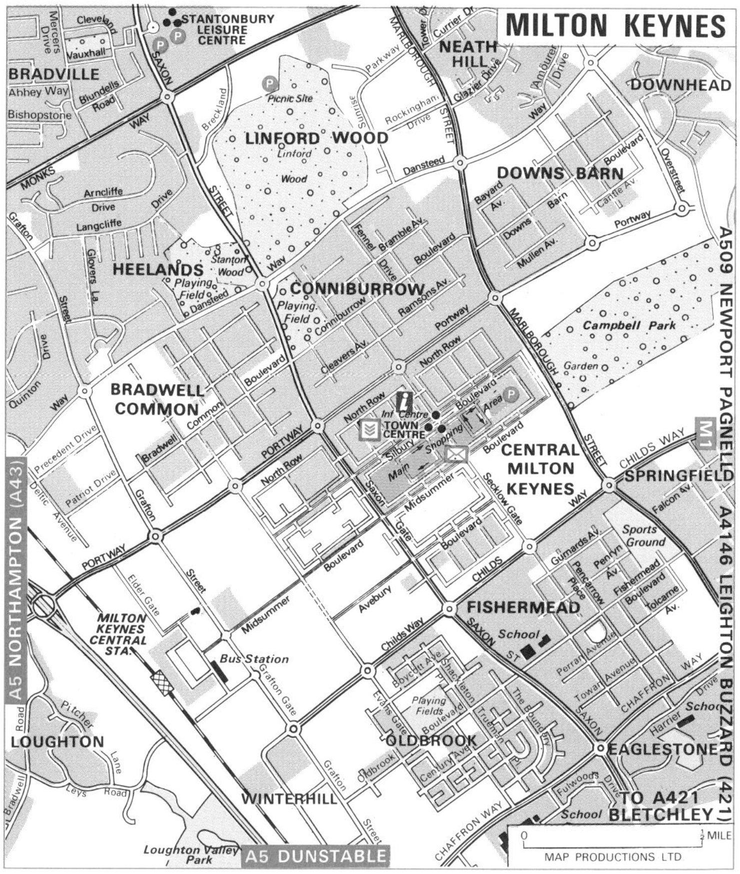
MILTON KEYNES
STANTONBURY LEISURE CENTRE
NEATH HILL
BRADVILLE
DOWNHEAD
LINFORD WOOD
DOWNS BARN
A509 NEWPORT PAGNELL
HEELANDS
CONNIBURROW
Campbell Park
BRADWELL COMMON
TOWN CENTRE
CENTRAL MILTON KEYNES
SPRINGFIELD
A4146 LEIGHTON BUZZARD (421)
A5 NORTHAMPTON (A43)
FISHERMEAD
MILTON KEYNES CENTRAL STA.
Bus Station
OLDBROOK
EAGLESTONE
LOUGHTON
WINTERHILL
TO A421 BLETCHLEY
Loughton Valley Park
A5 DUNSTABLE
MAP PRODUCTIONS LTD

APPROACHES TO NEWCASTLE

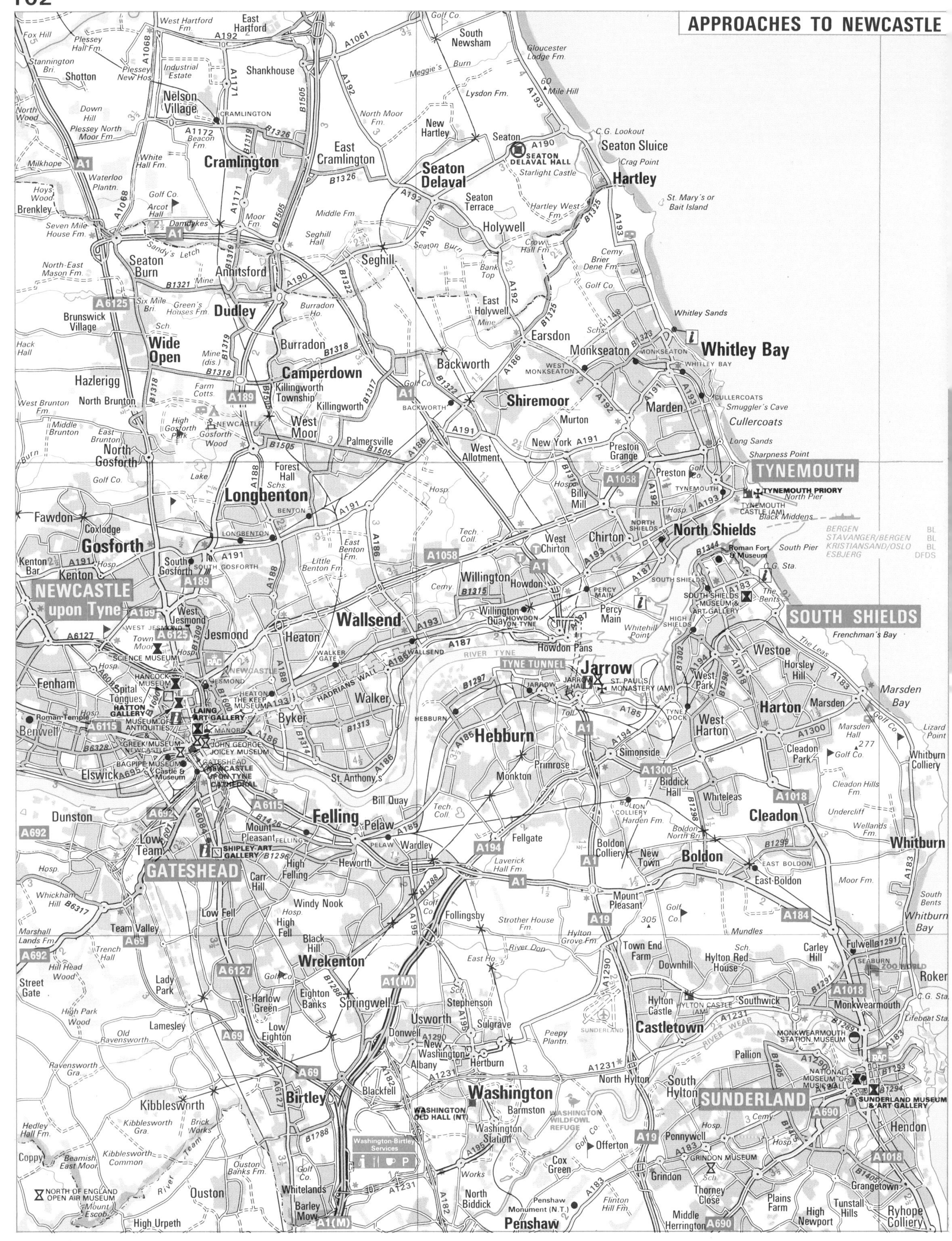

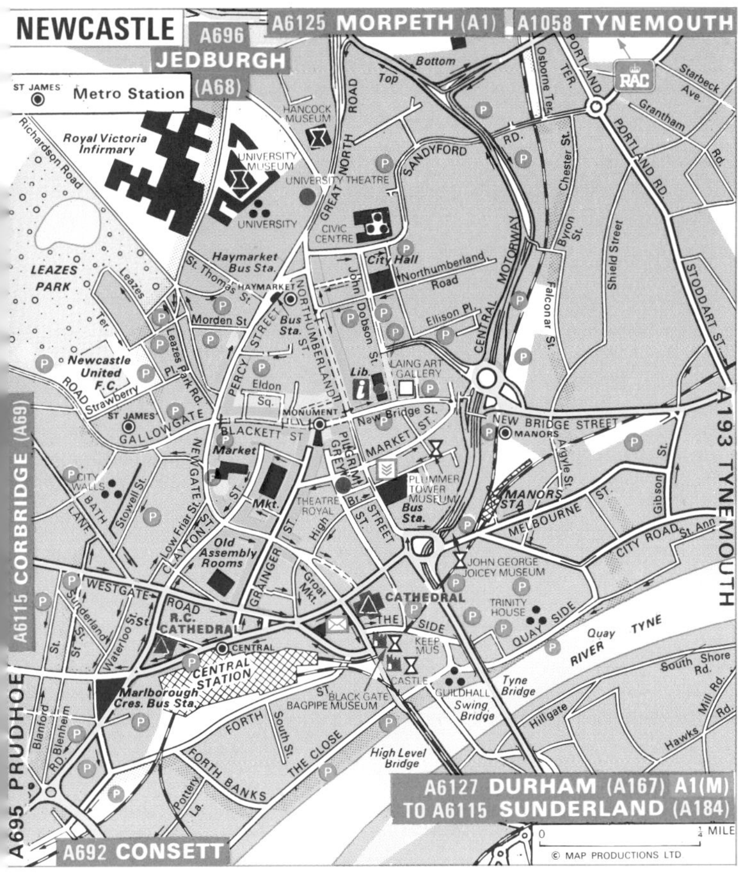
NEWCASTLE
A696 JEDBURGH (A68)
A6125 MORPETH (A1)
A1058 TYNEMOUTH
Metro Station
Royal Victoria Infirmary
HANCOCK MUSEUM
UNIVERSITY MUSEUM
UNIVERSITY THEATRE
UNIVERSITY
SANDYFORD
CIVIC CENTRE
City Hall
Haymarket Bus Sta.
LEAZES PARK
Newcastle United F.C.
HAYMARKET
Bus Sta.
LAING ART GALLERY
Lib
MONUMENT
New Bridge St.
NEW BRIDGE STREET
MANORS
ST JAMES
GALLOWGATE
BLACKETT ST
Market
CITY WALLS
Mkt.
PLUMMER TOWER MUSEUM
MANORS STA.
MELBOURNE ST.
CITY ROAD
THEATRE ROYAL
Bus Sta.
Old Assembly Rooms
JOHN GEORGE JOICEY MUSEUM
TRINITY HOUSE
CATHEDRAL
R.C. CATHEDRAL
CENTRAL
CENTRAL STATION
KEEP MUS.
CASTLE
GUILDHALL
BLACK GATE BAGPIPE MUSEUM
QUAY SIDE
RIVER TYNE
Tyne Bridge
Swing Bridge
High Level Bridge
Marlborough Cres. Bus Sta.
FORTH BANKS
THE CLOSE
A193 TYNEMOUTH
A6115 CORBRIDGE (A69)
A695 PRUDHOE
A692 CONSETT
A6127 DURHAM (A167) A1(M)
TO A6115 SUNDERLAND (A184)
© MAP PRODUCTIONS LTD

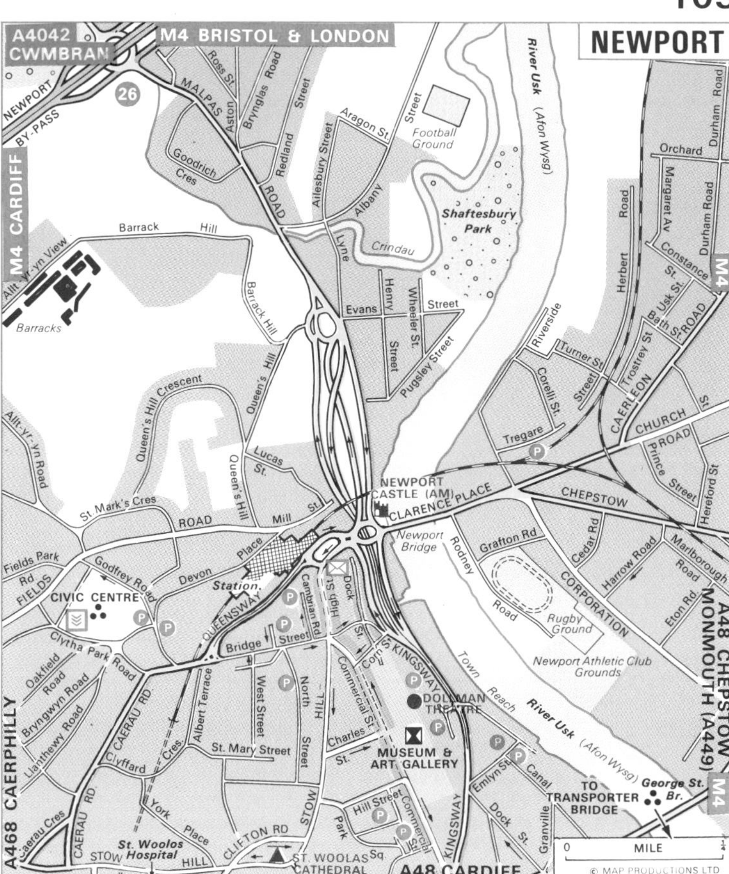
NEWPORT
A4042 CWMBRAN
M4 BRISTOL & LONDON
NEWPORT BY-PASS
M4 CARDIFF
26
MALPAS ROAD
Football Ground
River Usk (Afon Wysg)
Shaftesbury Park
Barrack Hill
Barracks
Queen's Hill Crescent
Crindau
CAERLEON ROAD
CHURCH ROAD
CHEPSTOW ROAD
NEWPORT CASTLE (AM)
CLARENCE PLACE
Newport Bridge
Rugby Ground
Newport Athletic Club Grounds
CORPORATION ROAD
CIVIC CENTRE
Station
QUEENSWAY
KINGSWAY
DOLMAN THEATRE
MUSEUM & ART GALLERY
St. Mary Street
St. Woolos Hospital
ST. WOOLOS CATHEDRAL
CLIFTON RD
TO TRANSPORTER BRIDGE
George St. Br.
A48 CHEPSTOW MONMOUTH (A449)
M4
A468 CAERPHILLY
A48 CARDIFF
MILE
© MAP PRODUCTIONS LTD

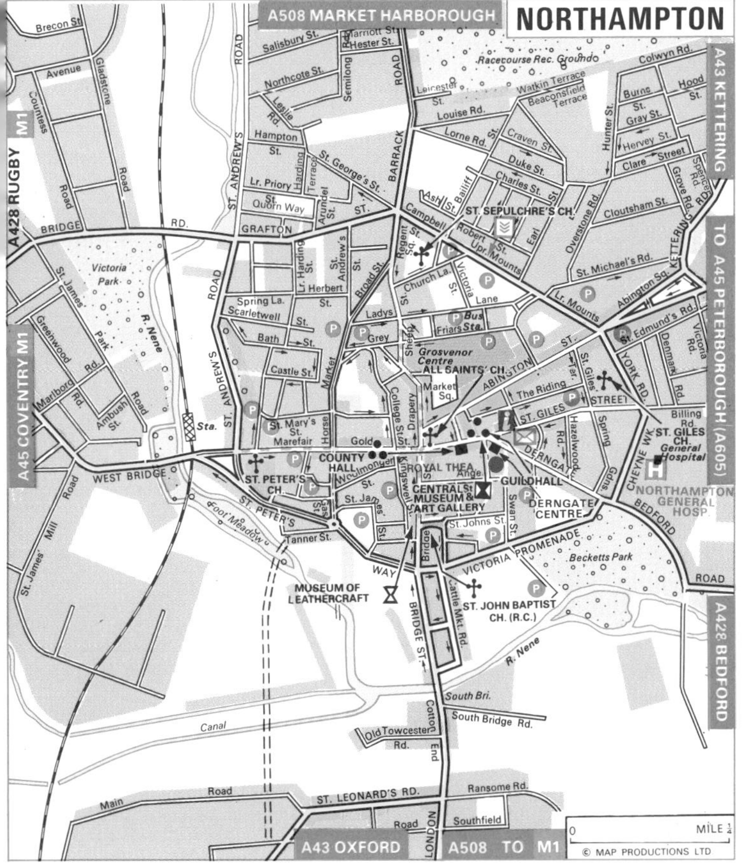
NORTHAMPTON
A508 MARKET HARBOROUGH
Racecourse Rec. Grounds
A43 KETTERING
M1
A428 RUGBY
ST. SEPULCHRE'S CH.
GRAFTON
Victoria Park
R. Nene
TO A45 PETERBOROUGH (A605)
Bus Sta.
Grosvenor Centre
ALL SAINTS' CH.
ABINGTON STREET
ST. GILES STREET
ST. GILES CH.
General Hospital
A45 COVENTRY M1
Sta.
ST. PETER'S CH.
COUNTY HALL
ROYAL THEA.
CENTRAL MUSEUM & ART GALLERY
GUILDHALL
DERNGATE CENTRE
NORTHAMPTON GENERAL HOSP.
WEST BRIDGE
VICTORIA PROMENADE
Becketts Park
MUSEUM OF LEATHERCRAFT
ST. JOHN BAPTIST CH. (R.C.)
BRIDGE ST.
R. Nene
Canal
ST. LEONARD'S RD.
A428 BEDFORD
A43 OXFORD
A508 TO M1
MILE
© MAP PRODUCTIONS LTD

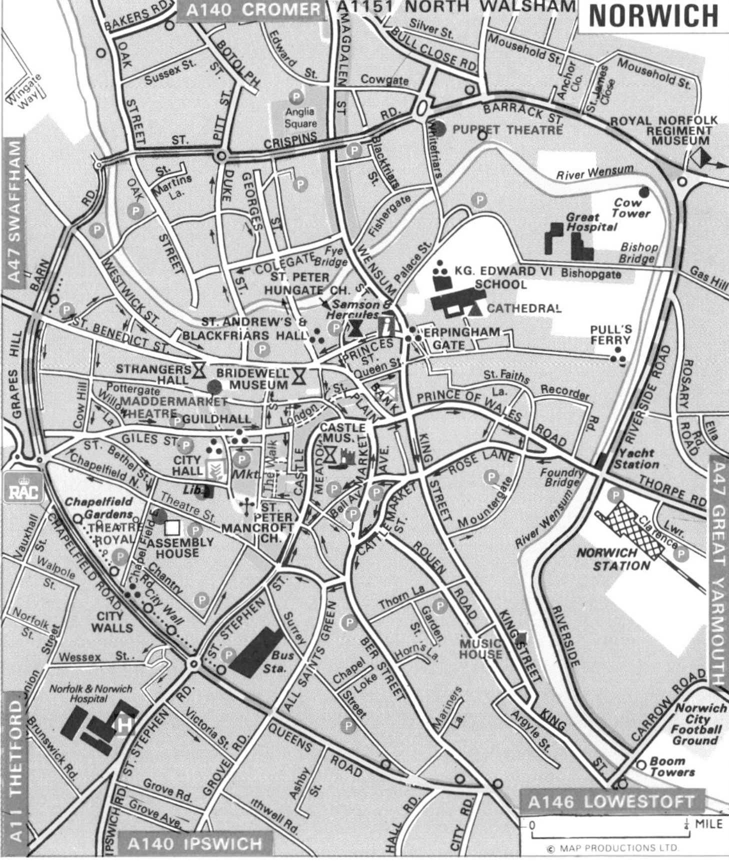
NORWICH
A140 CROMER
A1151 NORTH WALSHAM
BARRACK ST
PUPPET THEATRE
ROYAL NORFOLK REGIMENT MUSEUM
River Wensum
Cow Tower
Great Hospital
Bishop Bridge
A47 SWAFFHAM
ST. PETER HUNGATE CH.
KG. EDWARD VI SCHOOL
CATHEDRAL
ST. ANDREW'S & BLACKFRIARS HALL
Samson & Hercules
ERPINGHAM GATE
PULL'S FERRY
STRANGERS HALL
BRIDEWELL MUSEUM
MADDERMARKET THEATRE
GUILDHALL
CASTLE MUS.
PRINCE OF WALES ROAD
CITY HALL
Mkt.
Lib.
Chapelfield Gardens
THEATRE ROYAL
ASSEMBLY HOUSE
ST. PETER MANCROFT CH.
Yacht Station
NORWICH STATION
THORPE RD
CITY WALLS
Bus Sta.
MUSIC HOUSE
Norfolk & Norwich Hospital
Norwich City Football Ground
Boom Towers
A47 GREAT YARMOUTH
A11 THETFORD
A140 IPSWICH
A146 LOWESTOFT
MILE
© MAP PRODUCTIONS LTD

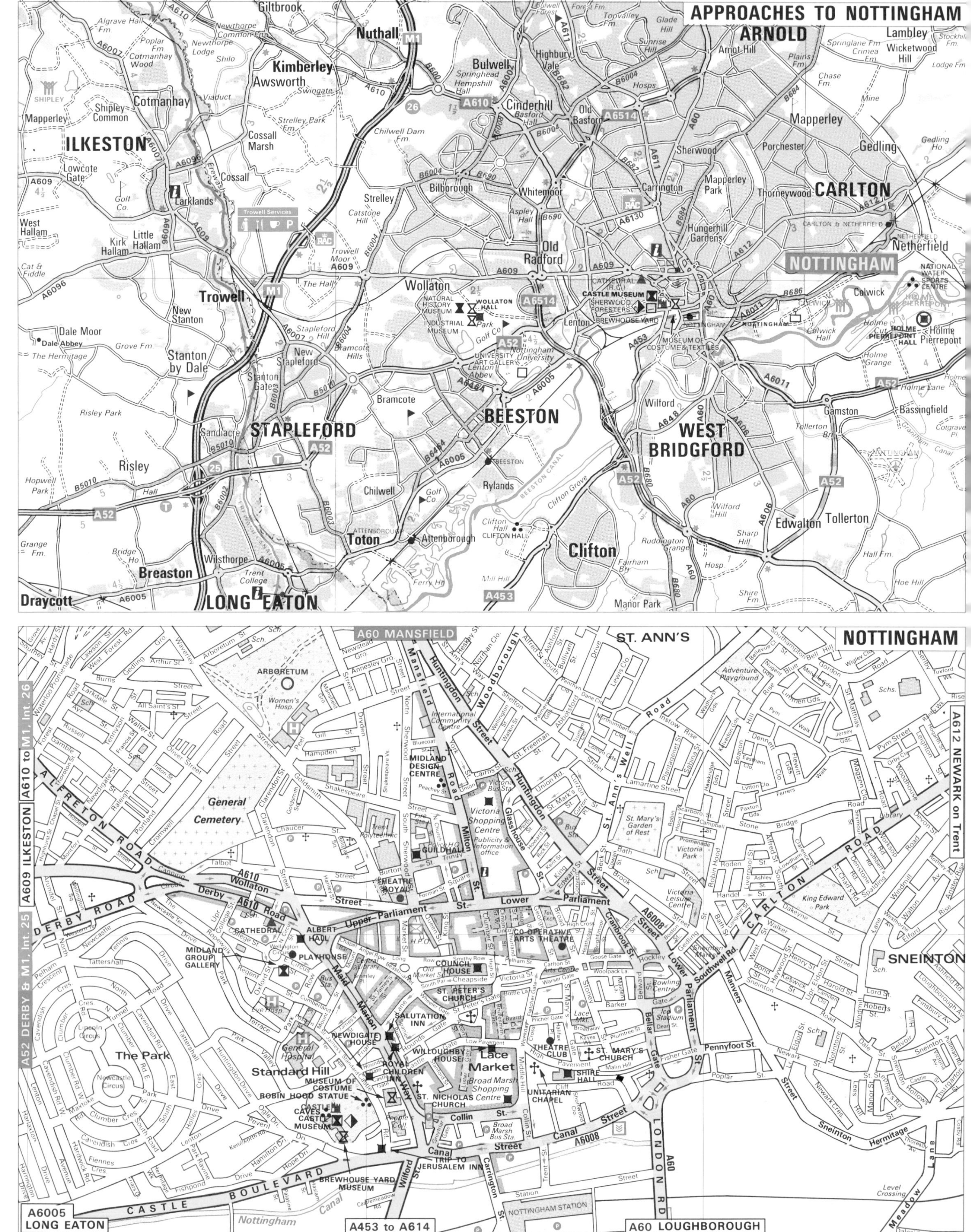
APPROACHES TO NOTTINGHAM
ARNOLD
Lambley
Giltbrook
Nuthall
Kimberley
Awsworth
Bulwell
Cinderhill
Highbury Vale
Old Basford
Sherwood
Mapperley
Gedling
Cotmanhay
Shipley Common
Mapperley
ILKESTON
Cossall Marsh
Cossall
Larklands
Trowell Services
Strelley
Bilborough
Whitemoor
Carrington
Mapperley Park
Thorneywood
CARLTON
Netherfield
Hungerhill Gardens
Old Radford
NOTTINGHAM
West Hallam
Kirk Hallam
Little Hallam
Trowell
Wollaton
WOLLATON HALL
NATURAL HISTORY MUSEUM
INDUSTRIAL MUSEUM
CASTLE MUSEUM
SHERWOOD FORESTERS
BREWHOUSE YARD
MUSEUM OF COSTUME & TEXTILES
Lenton
Colwick
Holme Pierrepont
HOLME PIERREPONT HALL
NATIONAL WATER SPORTS CENTRE
Dale Moor
Dale Abbey
New Stanton
Stanton by Dale
Stapleford Hill
New Stapleford
Bramcote Hills
Bramcote
UNIVERSITY ART GALLERY
Nottingham University
Lenton Abbey
BEESTON
STAPLEFORD
Sandiacre
Risley
Risley Park
Chilwell
Rylands
Wilford
WEST BRIDGFORD
Gamston
Bassingfield
Tollerton
Edwalton
Wilford Hill
Sharp Hill
Clifton
Clifton Hall
Toton
Attenborough
Wilsthorpe
Trent College
Breaston
Draycott
LONG EATON
Ruddington Grange
Manor Park
BEESTON CANAL
NOTTINGHAM
ST. ANN'S
A60 MANSFIELD
ARBORETUM
General Cemetery
MIDLAND DESIGN CENTRE
Victoria Shopping Centre
Trent Polytechnic
GUILDHALL
THEATRE ROYAL
CATHEDRAL
ALBERT HALL
PLAYHOUSE
MIDLAND GROUP GALLERY
CO OPERATIVE ARTS THEATRE
COUNCIL HOUSE
ST. PETER'S CHURCH
SALUTATION INN
NEWDIGATE HOUSE
ROYAL CHILDREN INN
WILLOUGHBY HOUSE
Lace Market
Broad Marsh Shopping Centre
ST. NICHOLAS CHURCH
THEATRE CLUB
ST. MARY'S CHURCH
SHIRE HALL
UNITARIAN CHAPEL
MUSEUM OF COSTUME
ROBIN HOOD STATUE
CASTLE CAVES
CASTLE MUSEUM
TRIP TO JERUSALEM INN
BREWHOUSE YARD MUSEUM
The Park
Standard Hill
General Hospital
Victoria Park
Victoria Leisure Centre
King Edward Park
SNEINTON
St. Mary's Garden of Rest
NOTTINGHAM STATION
A610 to M1, Int. 26
A609 ILKESTON
A52 DERBY & M1, Int. 25
A612 NEWARK on Trent
A6005 LONG EATON
A453 to A614
A60 LOUGHBOROUGH
CASTLE BOULEVARD
ALFRETON ROAD
DERBY ROAD
CARLTON ROAD
LONDON RD
Canal Street
Mansfield Road
Huntingdon Street
Lower Parliament Street
Upper Parliament Street

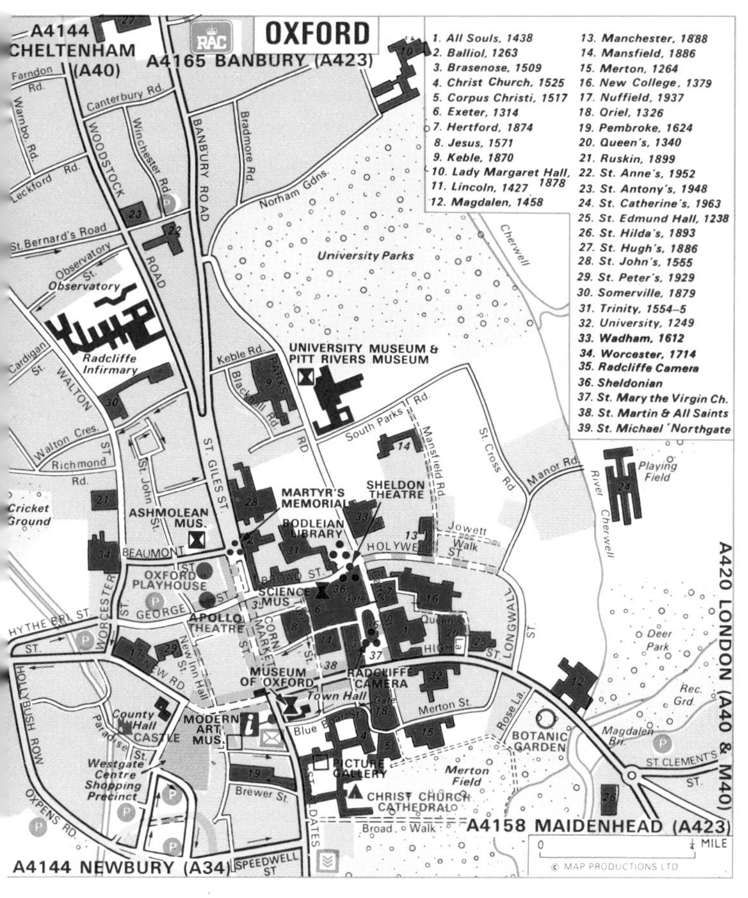
OXFORD
A4144 CHELTENHAM (A40)
A4165 BANBURY (A423)
1. All Souls, 1438
2. Balliol, 1263
3. Brasenose, 1509
4. Christ Church, 1525
5. Corpus Christi, 1517
6. Exeter, 1314
7. Hertford, 1874
8. Jesus, 1571
9. Keble, 1870
10. Lady Margaret Hall, 1878
11. Lincoln, 1427
12. Magdalen, 1458
13. Manchester, 1888
14. Mansfield, 1886
15. Merton, 1264
16. New College, 1379
17. Nuffield, 1937
18. Oriel, 1326
19. Pembroke, 1624
20. Queen's, 1340
21. Ruskin, 1899
22. St. Anne's, 1952
23. St. Antony's, 1948
24. St. Catherine's, 1963
25. St. Edmund Hall, 1238
26. St. Hilda's, 1893
27. St. Hugh's, 1886
28. St. John's, 1555
29. St. Peter's, 1929
30. Somerville, 1879
31. Trinity, 1554–5
32. University, 1249
33. Wadham, 1612
34. Worcester, 1714
35. Radcliffe Camera
36. Sheldonian
37. St. Mary the Virgin Ch.
38. St. Martin & All Saints
39. St. Michael Northgate
University Parks
St. Observatory
Radcliffe Infirmary
UNIVERSITY MUSEUM & PITT RIVERS MUSEUM
ASHMOLEAN MUS.
MARTYR'S MEMORIAL
SHELDON THEATRE
BODLEIAN LIBRARY
OXFORD PLAYHOUSE
APOLLO THEATRE
SCIENCE MUS.
MUSEUM OF OXFORD
RADCLIFFE CAMERA
Town Hall
County Hall
CASTLE
MODERN ART MUS.
Westgate Centre Shopping Precinct
PICTURE GALLERY
CHRIST CHURCH CATHEDRAL
BOTANIC GARDEN
Merton Field
Deer Park
Playing Field
Cricket Ground
A420 LONDON (A40 & M40)
A4158 MAIDENHEAD (A423)
A4144 NEWBURY (A34)
© MAP PRODUCTIONS LTD

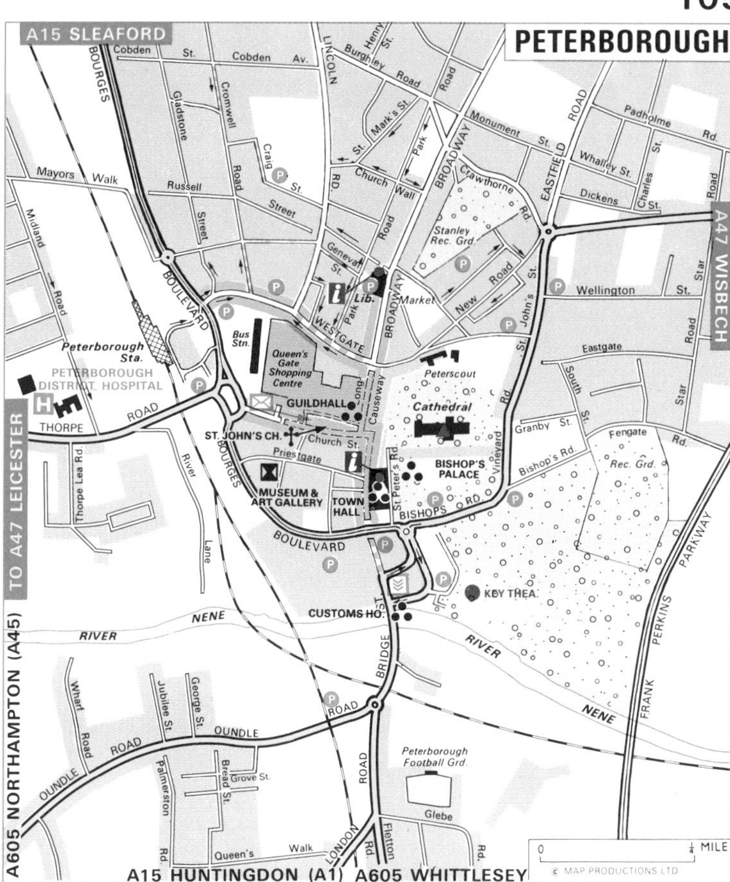
PETERBOROUGH
A15 SLEAFORD
A47 WISBECH
TO A47 LEICESTER
A605 NORTHAMPTON (A45)
A15 HUNTINGDON (A1)
A605 WHITTLESEY
Peterborough Sta.
PETERBOROUGH DISTRICT HOSPITAL
Queen's Gate Shopping Centre
GUILDHALL
Cathedral
ST. JOHN'S CH.
MUSEUM & ART GALLERY
TOWN HALL
BISHOP'S PALACE
KEY THEA.
CUSTOMS HO.
RIVER NENE
Peterborough Football Grd.
Stanley Rec. Grd.
Rec. Grd.
© MAP PRODUCTIONS LTD

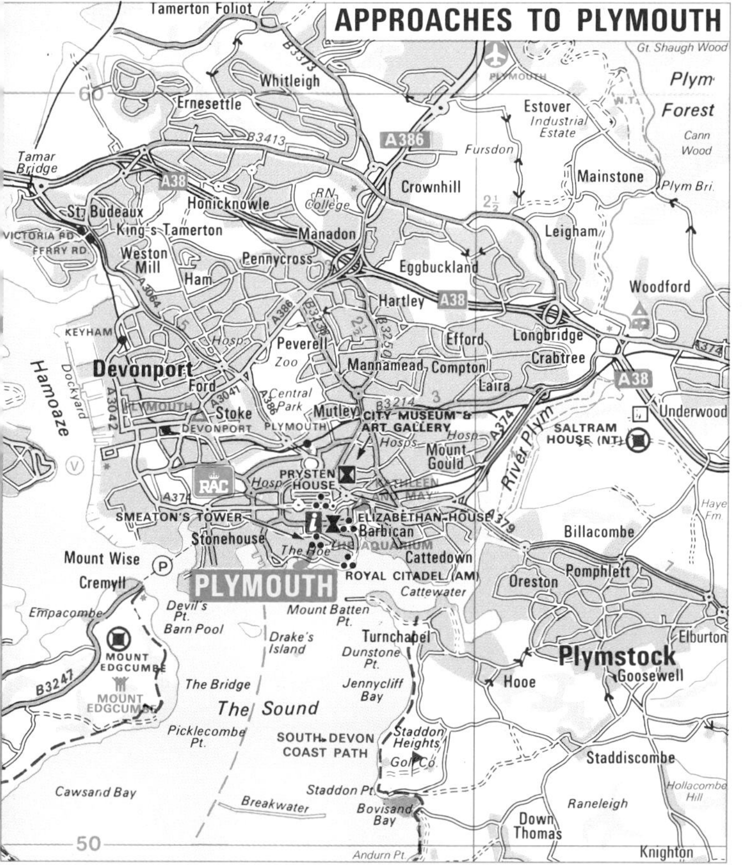
APPROACHES TO PLYMOUTH
Tamerton Foliot
Whitleigh
Ernesettle
Estover Industrial Estate
Plym Forest
Tamar Bridge
St. Budeaux
Crownhill
Mainstone
Honicknowle
King's Tamerton
Manadon
Leigham
Weston Mill
Pennycross
Eggbuckland
Woodford
Hartley
Longbridge
Devonport
Peverell
Efford
Crabtree
Hamoaze
Mannamead
Compton
Laira
Stoke
Mutley
CITY MUSEUM & ART GALLERY
Mount Gould
River Plym
SALTRAM HOUSE (NT)
Underwood
PRYSTEN HOUSE
SMEATON'S TOWER
ELIZABETHAN HOUSE
Stonehouse
Barbican
Billacombe
Mount Wise
Cattedown
Oreston
Pomphlett
Cremyll
PLYMOUTH
ROYAL CITADEL (AM)
Mount Batten Pt.
Turnchapel
Plymstock
Elburton
MOUNT EDGCUMBE
Drake's Island
Hooe
Goosewell
The Sound
SOUTH DEVON COAST PATH
Staddiscombe
Cawsand Bay
Breakwater
Bovisand Bay
Down Thomas
Knighton

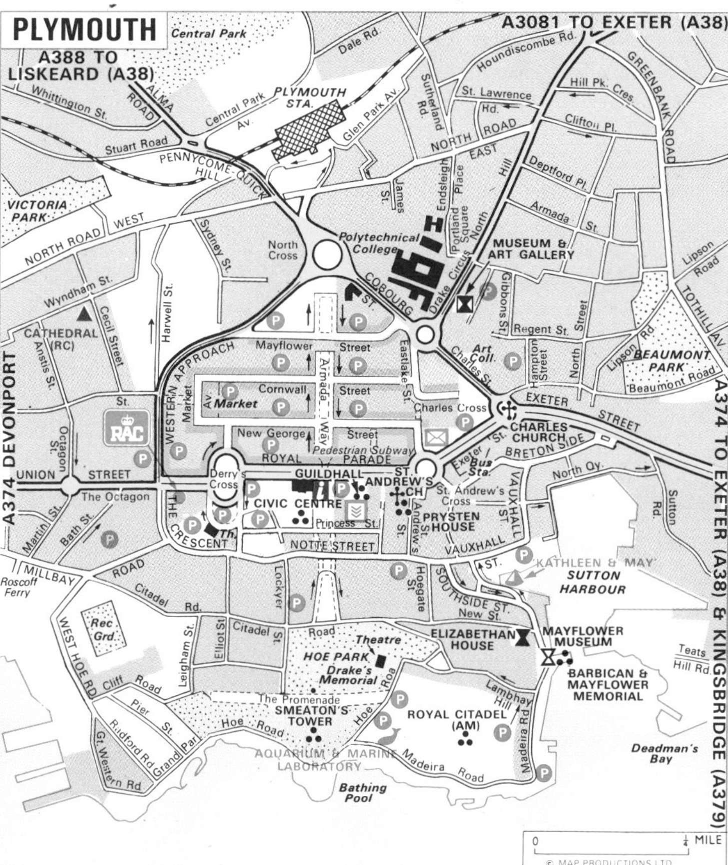
PLYMOUTH
A388 TO LISKEARD (A38)
A3081 TO EXETER (A38)
Central Park
PLYMOUTH STA.
VICTORIA PARK
Polytechnical College
MUSEUM & ART GALLERY
CATHEDRAL (RC)
Art Coll.
BEAUMONT PARK
A374 DEVONPORT
A374 TO EXETER (A38) & KINGSBRIDGE (A379)
Market
CHARLES CHURCH
GUILDHALL
ST. ANDREW'S CH.
CIVIC CENTRE
PRYSTEN HOUSE
KATHLEEN & MAY
SUTTON HARBOUR
ELIZABETHAN HOUSE
MAYFLOWER MUSEUM
BARBICAN & MAYFLOWER MEMORIAL
HOE PARK
Drake's Memorial
Theatre
SMEATON'S TOWER
ROYAL CITADEL (AM)
AQUARIUM & MARINE LABORATORY
Bathing Pool
Deadman's Bay
Roscoff Ferry
© MAP PRODUCTIONS LTD

APPROACHES TO PORTSMOUTH

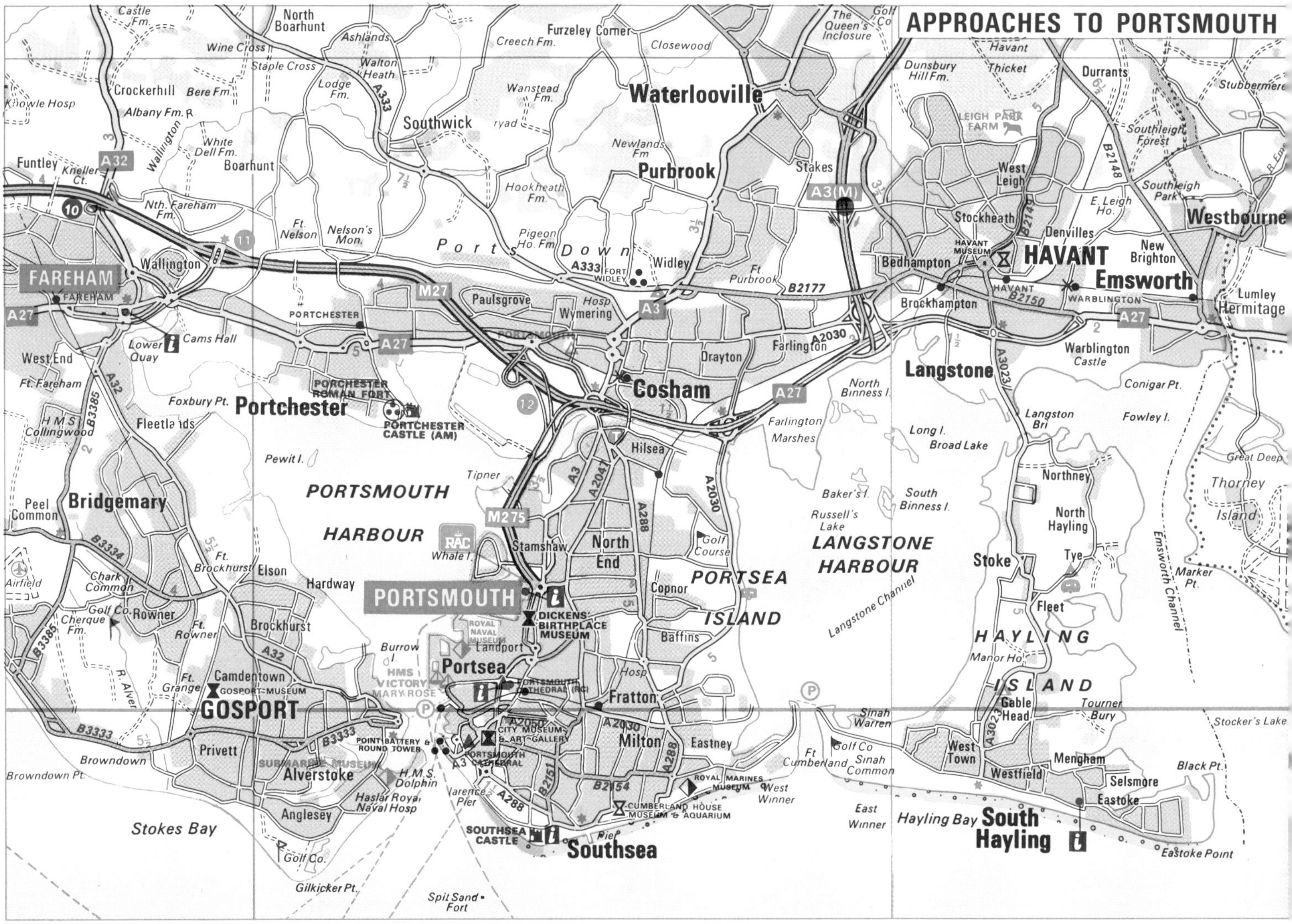

Waterlooville
Purbrook
Southwick
Boarhunt
North Boarhunt
Fareham
Wallington
Portchester
Portchester Castle (AM)
Portchester Roman Fort
Paulsgrove
Wymering
Cosham
Drayton
Farlington
Bedhampton
HAVANT
Emsworth
Westbourne
West Leigh
Stockheath
Denvilles
Leigh Park Farm
Brockhampton
Warblington
Warblington Castle
Langstone
Hilsea
Stamshaw
North End
Copnor
Baffins
Fratton
Milton
Eastney
Portsea
PORTSMOUTH
PORTSMOUTH HARBOUR
PORTSEA ISLAND
LANGSTONE HARBOUR
HAYLING ISLAND
North Hayling
Stoke
Fleet
West Town
Mengham
South Hayling
Eastoke
Eastoke Point
Hayling Bay
Southsea
Southsea Castle
GOSPORT
Bridgemary
Rowner
Brockhurst
Elson
Hardway
Camdentown
Privett
Alverstoke
Anglesey
Stokes Bay
Gilkicker Pt.
Browndown
Spit Sand Fort
Ports Down
Dickens' Birthplace Museum
Royal Naval Museum
HMS Victory
Mary Rose
Gosport Museum
City Museum & Art Gallery
Portsmouth Cathedral
Cumberland House Museum & Aquarium
Royal Marines Museum

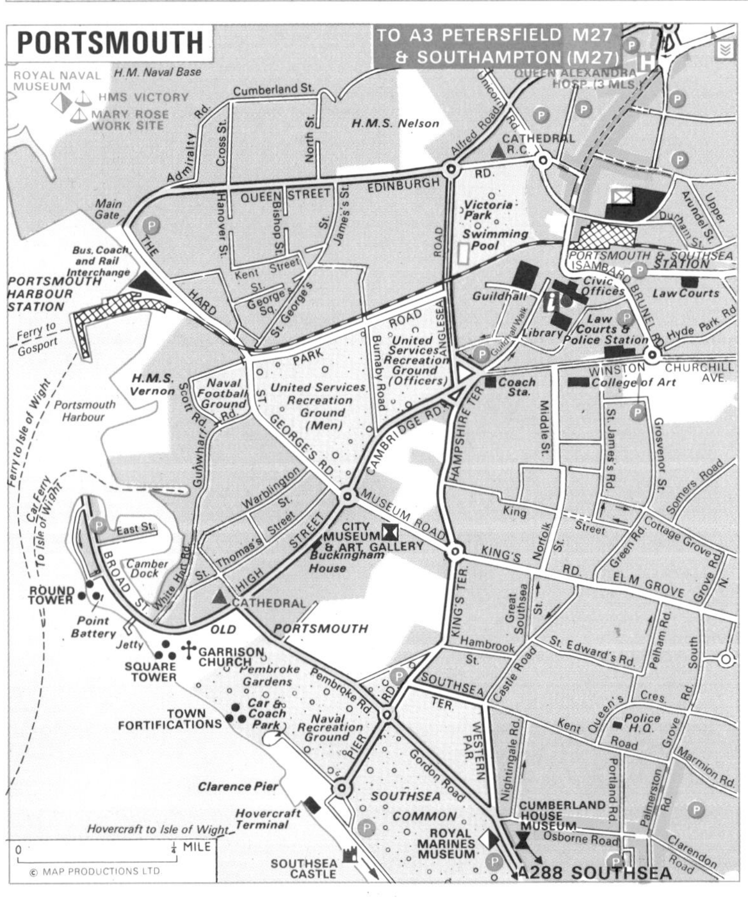

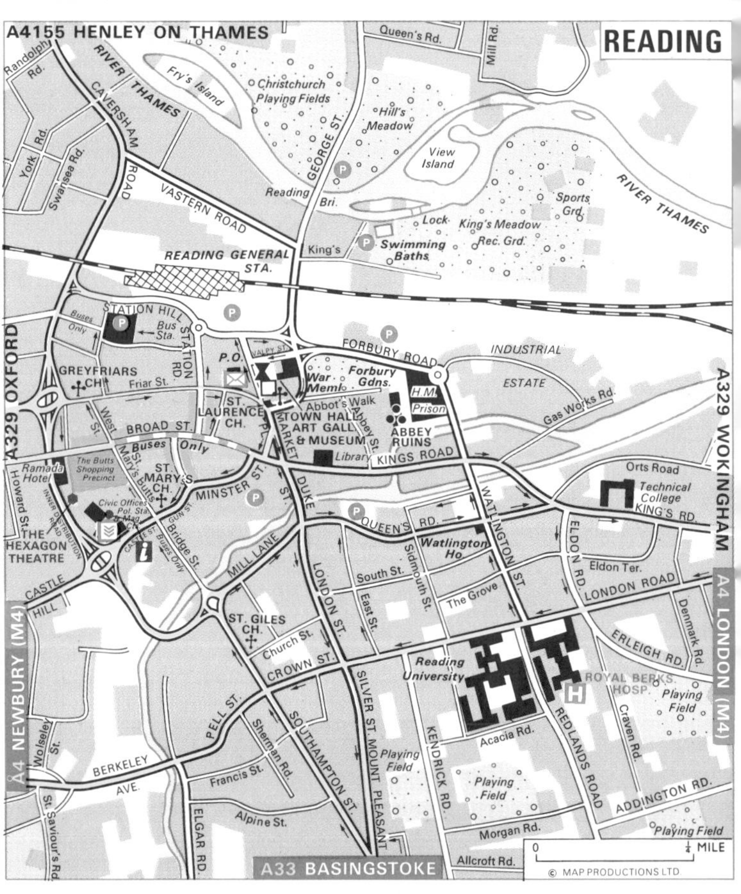

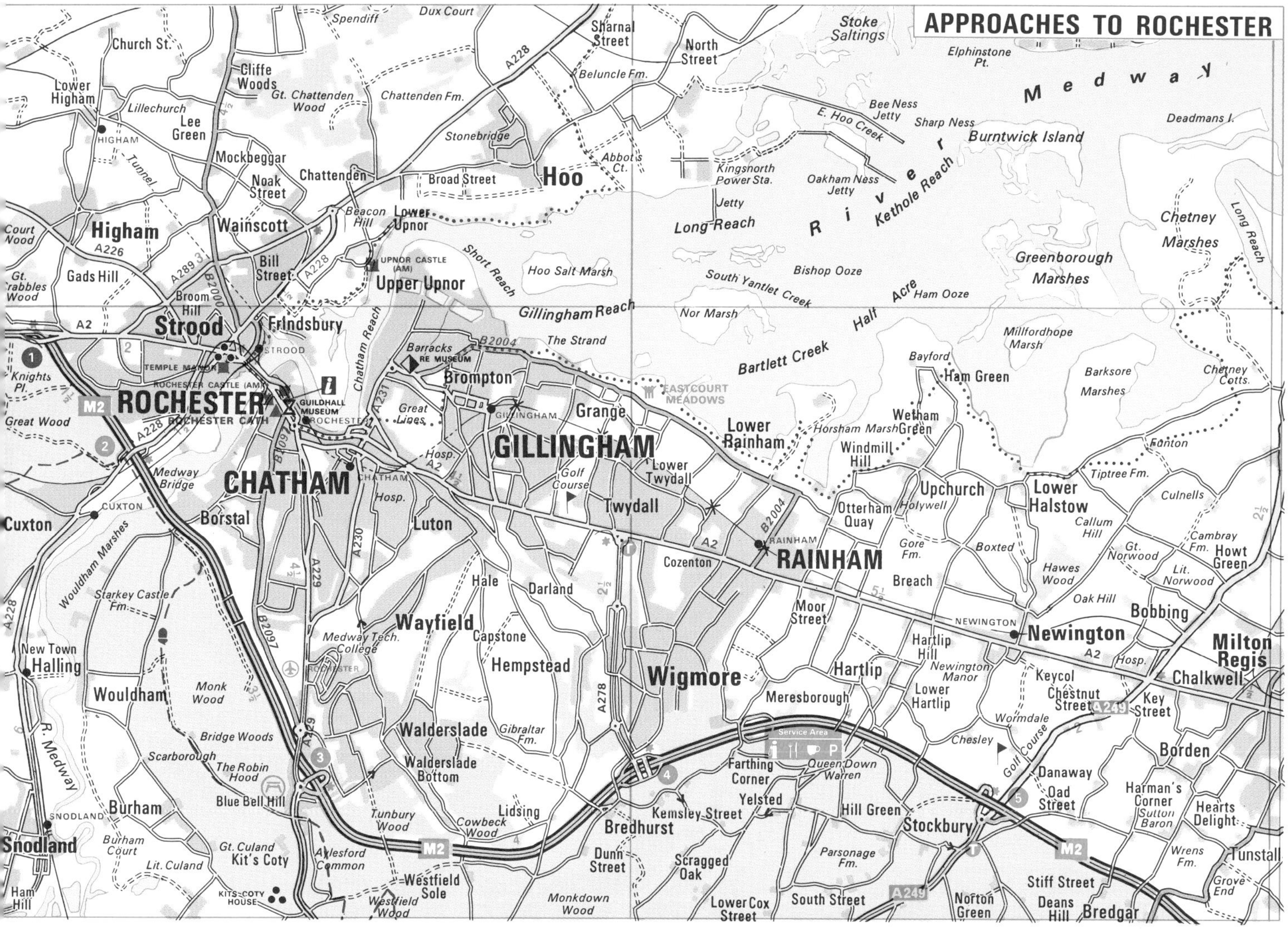
APPROACHES TO ROCHESTER
Stoke Saltings
Elphinstone Pt.
River Medway
Deadmans I.
Bee Ness Jetty
Sharp Ness
Burntwick Island
E. Hoo Creek
Kethole Reach
Kingsnorth Power Sta.
Oakham Ness Jetty
Jetty
Long Reach
Chetney Marshes
Greenborough Marshes
Bishop Ooze
South Yantlet Creek
Ham Ooze
Half Acre
Nor Marsh
Millfordhope Marsh
Bartlett Creek
Bayford
Ham Green
Barksore Marshes
Chetney Cotts.
Spendiff
Dux Court
Sharnal Street
North Street
Church St.
Cliffe Woods
Gt. Chattenden Wood
Chattenden Fm.
Belunce Fm.
Lower Higham
Lillechurch
Lee Green
Higham
Tunnel
Stonebridge
Mockbeggar
Noak Street
Chattenden
Broad Street
Hoo
Abbots Ct.
Court Wood
Higham
Wainscott
Beacon Hill
Lower Upnor
Upnor Castle (AM)
Short Reach
Hoo Salt Marsh
Gads Hill
Bill Street
Upper Upnor
Gt. Crabbles Wood
Broom Hill
Strood
Frindsbury
Gillingham Reach
The Strand
A2
A226
A289
A228
B2000
B2004
Knights Pl.
Temple Manor
Rochester Castle (AM)
Guildhall Museum
Rochester
Rochester Cath
Chatham Reach
Barracks
RE Museum
Brompton
Eastcourt Meadows
M2
Great Wood
Great Lines
Gillingham
Grange
Lower Rainham
Horsham Marsh
Wetham Green
Windmill Hill
Fonton
Tiptree Fm.
Medway Bridge
Chatham
Hosp.
Golf Course
Lower Twydall
Twydall
Upchurch
Holywell
Otterham Quay
Lower Halstow
Callum Hill
Culnells
Cuxton
Borstal
Luton
A230
A231
A229
A278
Cozenton
Rainham
Gore Fm.
Boxted
Cambray Fm.
Howt Green
Gt. Norwood
Lit. Norwood
Hawes Wood
Wouldham Marshes
Starkey Castle Fm.
Hale
Darland
Breach
Oak Hill
Moor Street
Bobbing
Newington
Milton Regis
B2097
New Town
Halling
Medway Tech. College
Wayfield
Capstone
Hempstead
Wigmore
Hartlip Hill
Hartlip
Newington Manor
Lower Hartlip
Keycol
Chestnut Street
Hosp.
Chalkwell
Key Street
Wouldham
Monk Wood
Rochester
Meresborough
Wormdale
A249
Walderslade
Gibraltar Fm.
Service Area
Chesley
Golf Course
Borden
R. Medway
Bridge Woods
Scarborough
The Robin Hood
Walderslade Bottom
Farthing Corner
Queen Down Warren
Danaway
Oad Street
Harman's Corner
Sutton Baron
Hearts Delight
Snodland
Burham
Blue Bell Hill
Tunbury Wood
Lidsing
Cowbeck Wood
Kemsley Street
Yelsted
Hill Green
Stockbury
Bredhurst
Burham Court
Gt. Culand
Kit's Coty
Lit. Culand
Aylesford Common
Westfield Sole
Dunn Street
Scragged Oak
Parsonage Fm.
Stiff Street
Wrens Fm.
Tunstall
Grove End
Ham Hill
Kits Coty House
Westfield Wood
Monkdown Wood
Lower Cox Street
South Street
Norton Green
Deans Hill
Bredgar

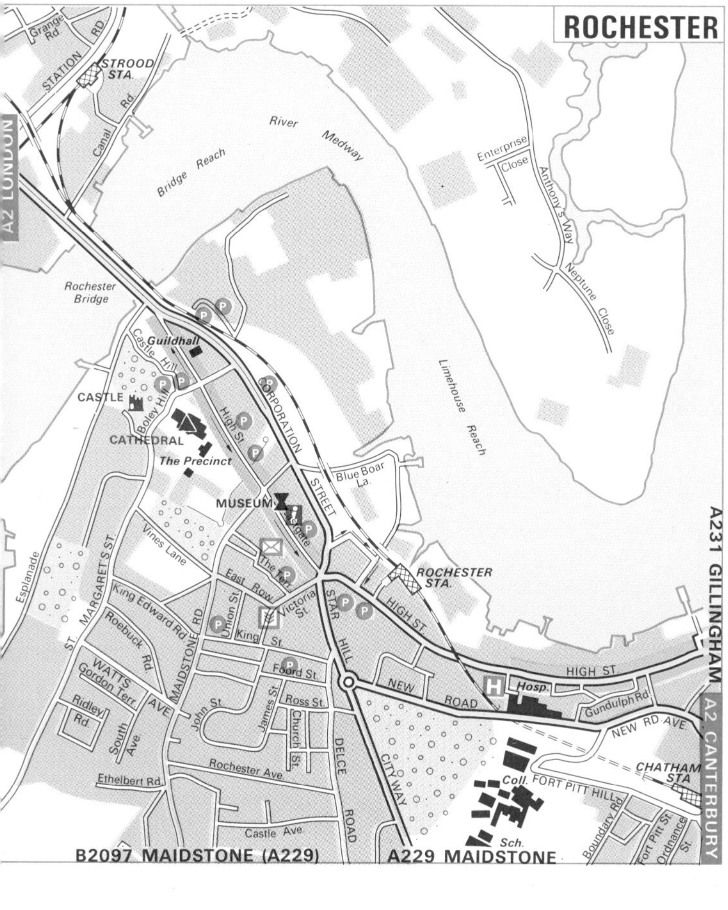
ROCHESTER
Strood Sta.
Station Rd.
Canal Rd.
River Medway
Bridge Reach
Enterprise Close
Anthony's Way
Neptune Close
Limehouse Reach
Rochester Bridge
Guildhall
Castle Hill
Castle
Boley Hill
High St.
Corporation Street
Cathedral
The Precinct
Blue Boar La.
Museum
Esplanade
Vines Lane
St. Margaret's St.
East Row
The Ter.
Victoria St.
Rochester Sta.
King Edward Rd.
Roebuck Rd.
Union St.
King St.
Star Hill
High St.
Watts Ave.
Gordon Terr.
Maidstone Rd.
Foord St.
New Road
Hosp.
High St.
Gundulph Rd.
Ridley Rd.
South Ave.
John St.
James St.
Ross St.
Church St.
New Rd. Ave.
Rochester Ave.
Delce Road
City Way
Coll.
Fort Pitt Hill
Chatham Sta.
Ethelbert Rd.
Castle Ave.
Sch.
Boundary Rd.
Fort Pitt St.
Ordnance St.
A2 London
A231 Gillingham
A2 Canterbury
B2097 Maidstone (A229)
A229 Maidstone

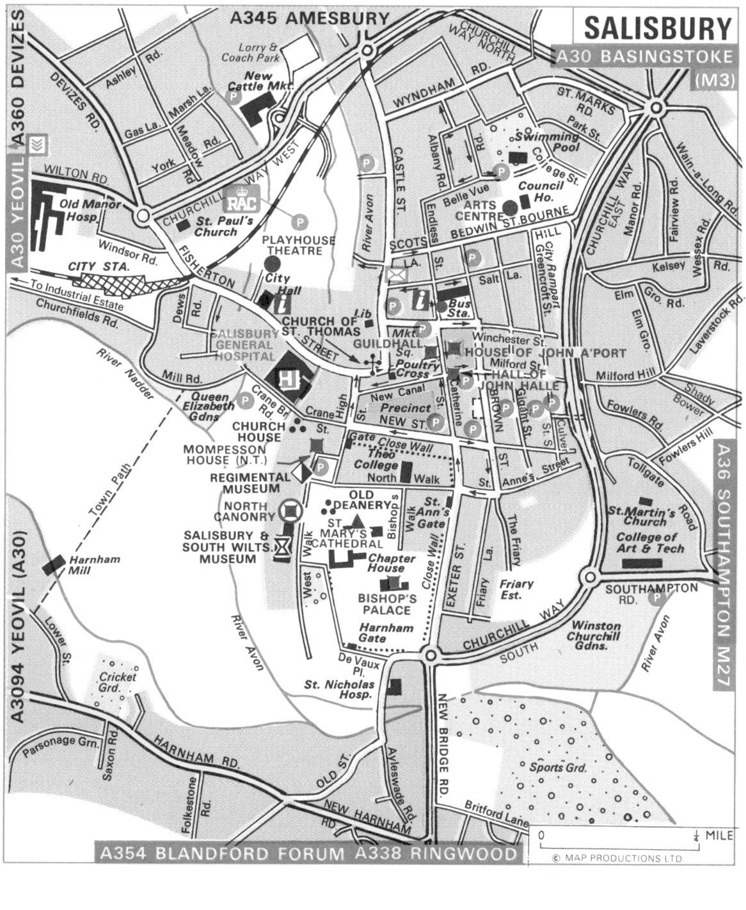
SALISBURY
A345 Amesbury
A30 Basingstoke (M3)
A360 Devizes
Lorry & Coach Park
New Cattle Mkt.
Churchill Way North
Devizes Rd.
Ashley Rd.
Marsh La.
Gas La.
Meadow Rd.
York Rd.
Wyndham Rd.
St. Marks Rd.
Park St.
Swimming Pool
College St.
Council Ho.
Wilton Rd.
Churchill Way West
Old Manor Hosp.
St. Paul's Church
Arts Centre
Bedwin St.
Bourne Hill
Playhouse Theatre
Castle St.
Albany Rd.
Belle Vue
Endless St.
River Avon
Churchill Way East
Manor Rd.
Fairview Rd.
Wain-a-Long Rd.
Wessex Rd.
Kelsey Rd.
A30 Yeovil
Windsor Rd.
City Sta.
Fisherton St.
City Hall
Scots La.
Salt La.
City Rampart
Greencroft St.
Elm Gro. Rd.
To Industrial Estate
Churchfields Rd.
Dews Rd.
Church of St. Thomas
Lib.
Bus Sta.
Salisbury General Hospital
Guildhall
Winchester St.
House of John A'Port
Milford St.
Hall of John Halle
Laverstock Rd.
Milford Hill
River Nadder
Mill Rd.
Crane Br. Rd.
Poultry Cross
New Canal
Catherine St.
Brown St.
Gigant St.
Culver St.
Shady Bower
Fowlers Rd.
Fowlers Hill
Queen Elizabeth Gdns
Church House
Crane St.
Precinct
New St.
Mompesson House (N.T.)
Gate
Close Wall
Theo College
North Walk
St. Ann's Street
Tollgate Road
Regimental Museum
Old Deanery
North Canonry
St. Mary's Cathedral
St. Ann's Gate
The Friary
St. Martin's Church
College of Art & Tech
Town Path
Salisbury & South Wilts. Museum
West Walk
Bishop's Walk
Chapter House
Close Wall
Exeter St.
Friary La.
Friary Est.
Harnham Mill
A3094 Yeovil (A30)
Bishop's Palace
Harnham Gate
River Avon
Churchill Way South
Southampton Rd.
Winston Churchill Gdns.
Lower St.
De Vaux Pl.
St. Nicholas Hosp.
Cricket Grd.
Parsonage Grn.
Saxon Rd.
Harnham Rd.
Old St.
New Bridge Rd.
Sports Grd.
Folkestone Rd.
New Harnham Rd.
Ayleswade Rd.
Britford Lane
A36 Southampton M27
0 ¼ Mile
A354 Blandford Forum
A338 Ringwood
© Map Productions Ltd

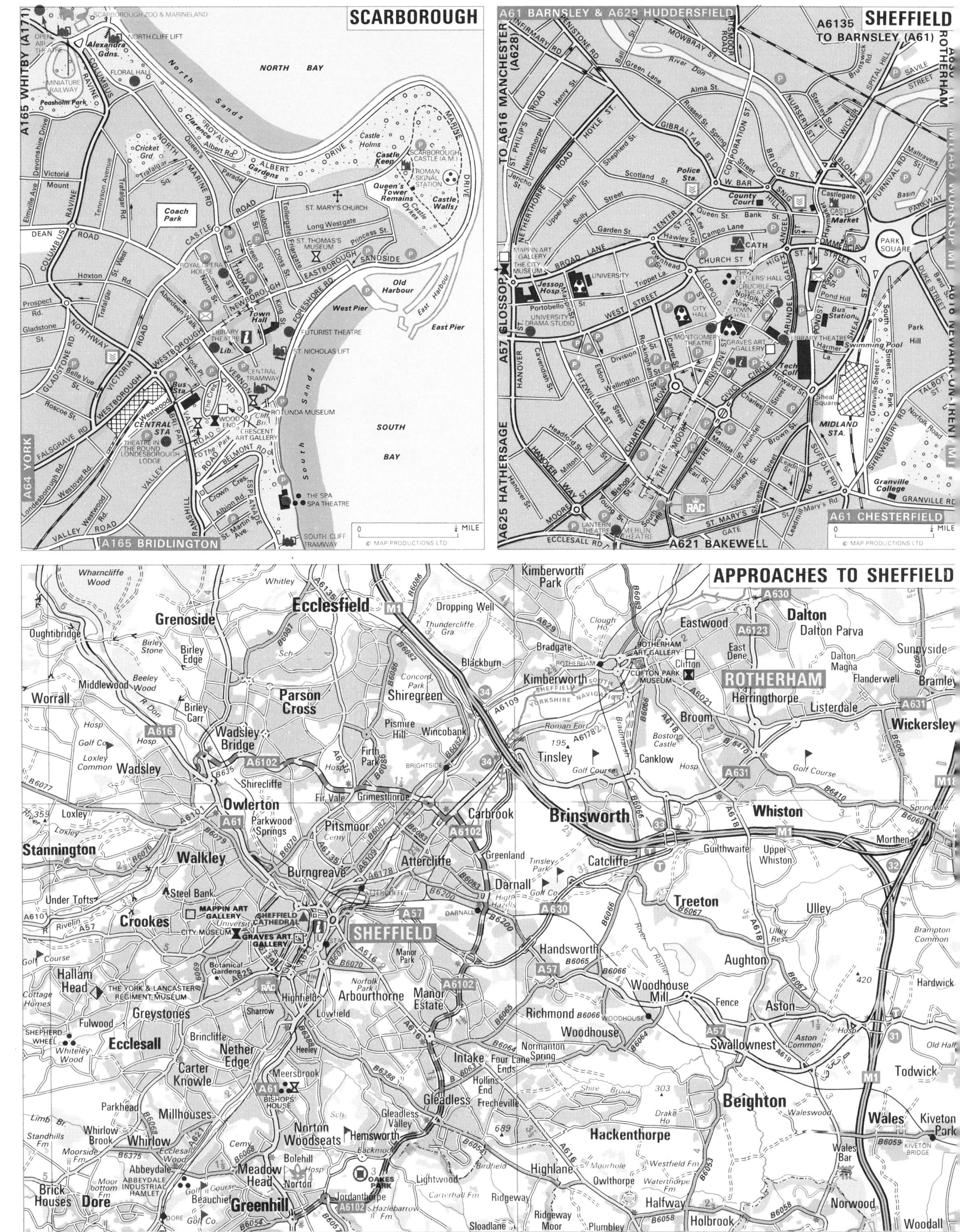
SCARBOROUGH
NORTH BAY
North Sands
A165 WHITBY (A171)
Alexandra Gdns.
NORTH CLIFF LIFT
FLORAL HALL
MINIATURE RAILWAY
Peasholm Park
Castle Holms
Castle Keep
SCARBOROUGH CASTLE (A.M.)
ROMAN SIGNAL STATION
Queen's Tower Remains
Castle Walls
ST. MARY'S CHURCH
Long Westgate
ST. THOMAS'S MUSEUM
SANDSIDE
Old Harbour
West Pier
East Pier
East Harbour
Coach Park
ROYAL OPERA HOUSE
Town Hall
FUTURIST THEATRE
LIBRARY THEATRE
Lib.
ST. NICHOLAS LIFT
CENTRAL TRAMWAY
ROTUNDA MUSEUM
CRESCENT ART GALLERY
WOOD END
CENTRAL STA
THEATRE IN THE ROUND LONDESBOROUGH LODGE
Bus Sta.
SOUTH BAY
South Sands
THE SPA
SPA THEATRE
SOUTH CLIFF TRAMWAY
A64 YORK
A165 BRIDLINGTON
0 ½ MILE
© MAP PRODUCTIONS LTD
SHEFFIELD
A61 BARNSLEY & A629 HUDDERSFIELD
A6135 TO BARNSLEY (A61)
A630 ROTHERHAM
TO A616 MANCHESTER (A628)
A57 GLOSSOP
A625 HATHERSAGE
A621 BAKEWELL
A61 CHESTERFIELD
A616 NEWARK-ON-TRENT M1
A57 WORKSOP M1
River Don
PARK SQUARE
Police Sta.
County Court
CATH
Castlegate
CASTLE Market
MAPPIN ART GALLERY
THE CITY MUSEUM
UNIVERSITY
Jessop Hosp.
UNIVERSITY DRAMA STUDIO
CUTLERS' HALL
CRUCIBLE THEATRE
CITY HALL
TOWN HALL
MONTGOMERY THEATRE
GRAVES ART GALLERY
LIBRARY THEATRE
Tech Coll
Bus Station
Swimming Pool
Park Hill
Sheaf Square
MIDLAND STA.
Granville College
RAC
LANTERN THEATRE
MERLIN THEATRE
0 ½ MILE
© MAP PRODUCTIONS LTD
APPROACHES TO SHEFFIELD
Wharncliffe Wood
Ecclesfield
Grenoside
Oughtibridge
Dropping Well
Thundercliffe Gra
Kimberworth Park
Eastwood
Dalton
Dalton Parva
Sunnyside
Bradgate
ROTHERHAM ART GALLERY
Clifton
CLIFTON PARK MUSEUM
ROTHERHAM
Kimberworth
Blackburn
Parson Cross
Shiregreen
Herringthorpe
Listerdale
Wickersley
Worrall
Middlewood
Birley Edge
Birley Carr
Wadsley Bridge
Wincobank
Broom
Tinsley
Canklow
Wadsley
Firth Park
Owlerton
Shirecliffe
Fir Vale
Grimesthorpe
Carbrook
Brinsworth
Whiston
Stannington
Walkley
Pitsmoor
Parkwood Springs
Burngreave
Attercliffe
Catcliffe
Upper Whiston
Morthen
Crookes
MAPPIN ART GALLERY
SHEFFIELD CATHEDRAL
CITY MUSEUM
GRAVES ART GALLERY
SHEFFIELD
Darnall
Treeton
Ulley
Hallam Head
THE YORK & LANCASTER REGIMENT MUSEUM
Greystones
Ecclesall
Handsworth
Woodhouse Mill
Aughton
Arbourthorne
Manor Estate
Richmond
Woodhouse
Swallownest
Aston
Todwick
Nether Edge
Carter Knowle
Intake
Gleadless
Beighton
Hackenthorpe
Wales
Kiveton Park
Millhouses
Whirlow
Norton
Woodseats
Hemsworth
Meadow Head
Highlane
Dore
Greenhill
Brick Houses
Beauchief
Jordanthorpe
Lightwood
Ridgeway
Halfway
Holbrook
Norwood
Woodall
Plumbley
Sloadlane

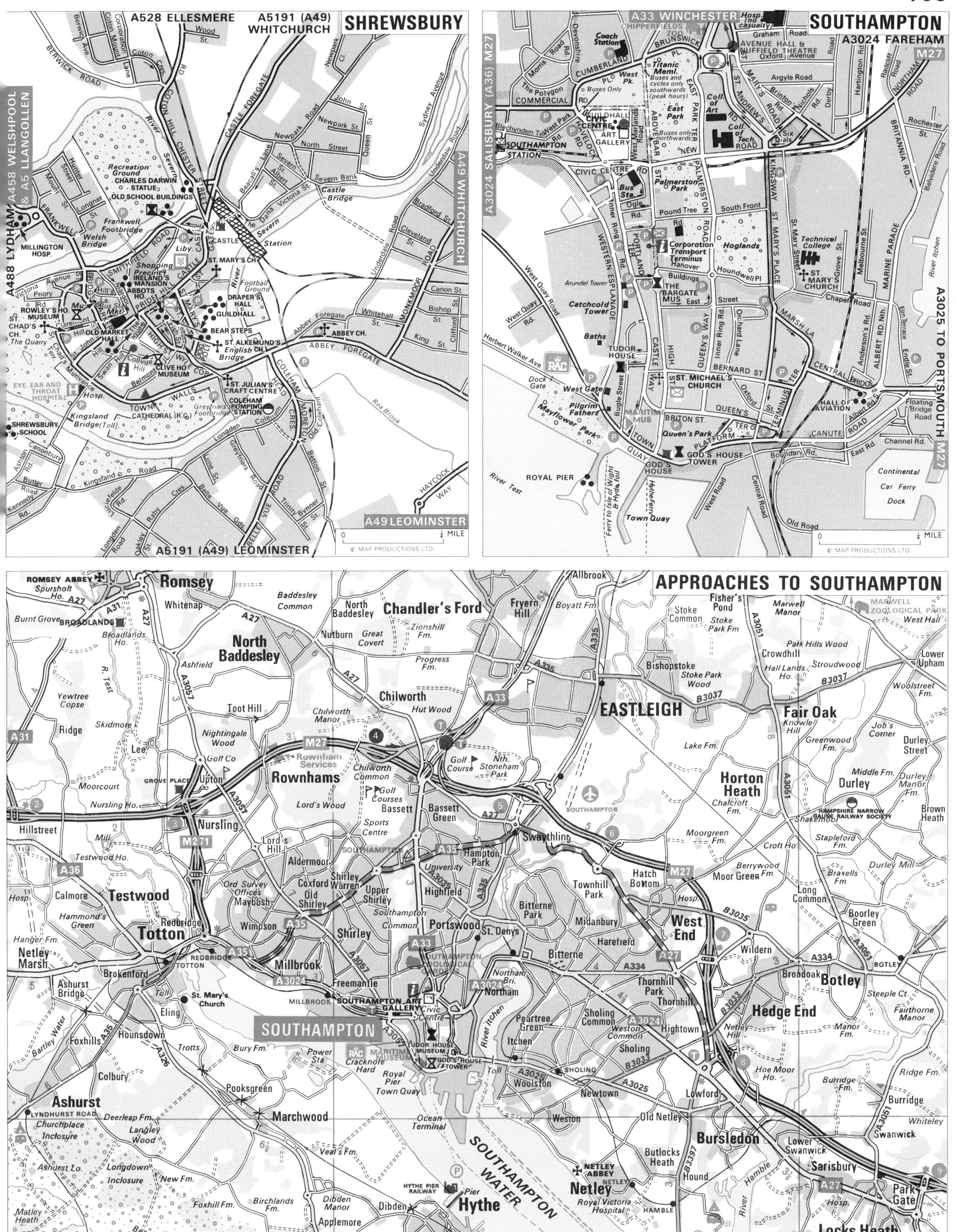
SHREWSBURY
SOUTHAMPTON
APPROACHES TO SOUTHAMPTON
A528 ELLESMERE
A5191 (A49) WHITCHURCH
A49 WHITCHURCH
A49 LEOMINSTER
A5191 (A49) LEOMINSTER
A488 LYDHAM
A458 WELSHPOOL & A5 LLANGOLLEN
A33 WINCHESTER
A3024 FAREHAM
A3024 SALISBURY (A36) M27
A3025 TO PORTSMOUTH M27
© MAP PRODUCTIONS LTD.
© MAP PRODUCTIONS LTD.

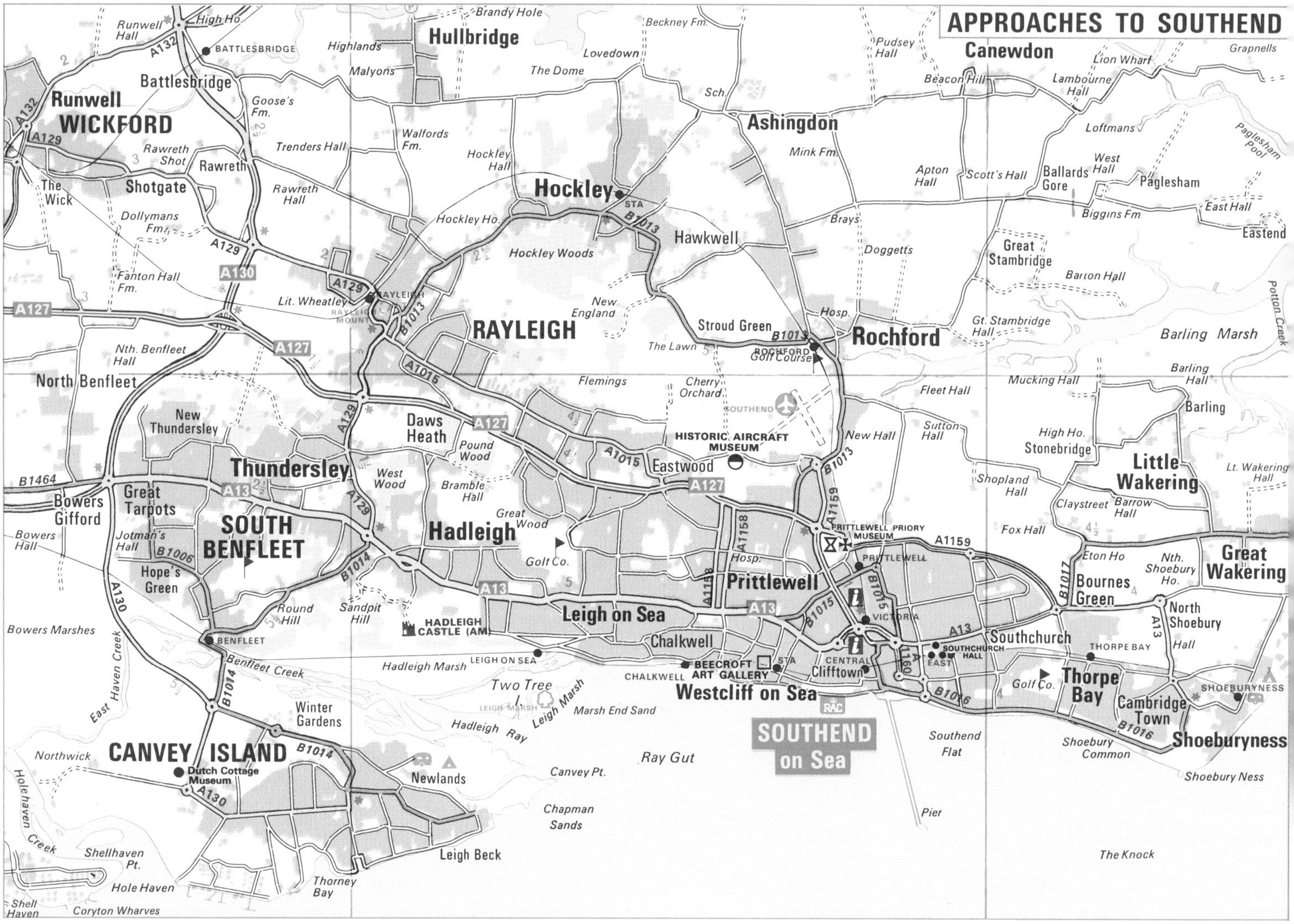

APPROACHES TO SOUTHEND
Runwell Hall
High Ho.
Brandy Hole
Hullbridge
Beckney Fm.
Pudsey Hall
Canewdon
Grapnells
Battlesbridge
Highlands
Malyons
Lovedown
The Dome
Beacon Hill
Lion Wharf
Lambourne Hall
Runwell
WICKFORD
Goose's Fm.
Sch.
Ashingdon
Loftmans
Paglesham Pool
Rawreth Shot
Trenders Hall
Walfords Fm.
Hockley Hall
Mink Fm.
Rawreth
Shotgate
The Wick
Rawreth Hall
Hockley
Apton Hall
Scott's Hall
Ballards Gore
West Hall
Paglesham
East Hall
Dollymans Fm.
Hockley Ho.
Biggins Fm
Eastend
Hawkwell
Brays
Doggetts
Great Stambridge
Fanton Hall Fm.
Hockley Woods
Barton Hall
Lit. Wheatley
RAYLEIGH
New England
Hosp.
Gt. Stambridge Hall
Potton Creek
RAYLEIGH MOUNT
Stroud Green
Rochford
Barling Marsh
Nth. Benfleet Hall
The Lawn
ROCHFORD Golf Course
North Benfleet
Flemings
Cherry Orchard
Mucking Hall
Barling Hall
Fleet Hall
SOUTHEND
Barling
New Thundersley
Daws Heath
New Hall
Sutton Hall
High Ho.
Stonebridge
Pound Wood
HISTORIC AIRCRAFT MUSEUM
Little Wakering
Thundersley
West Wood
Eastwood
Lt. Wakering Hall
Shopland Hall
Bramble Hall
Claystreet
Barrow Hall
Bowers Gifford
Great Tarpots
SOUTH BENFLEET
Great Wood
PRITTLEWELL PRIORY MUSEUM
Fox Hall
Bowers Hall
Jotman's Hall
Hadleigh
PRITTLEWELL
Eton Ho
Nth. Shoebury Ho.
Great Wakering
Hope's Green
Golf Co.
Hosp.
Prittlewell
Bournes Green
Round Hill
Sandpit Hill
HADLEIGH CASTLE (AM)
Leigh on Sea
VICTORIA
North Shoebury
Bowers Marshes
BENFLEET
Chalkwell
SOUTHCHURCH HALL
Southchurch
THORPE BAY
Hall
LEIGH ON SEA
CENTRAL
EAST
Hadleigh Marsh
BEECROFT ART GALLERY
STA
Clifftown
Golf Co.
Thorpe Bay
Benfleet Creek
Two Tree
CHALKWELL
Westcliff on Sea
Cambridge Town
SHOEBURYNESS
East Haven Creek
Winter Gardens
LEIGH MARSH
Leigh Marsh
Marsh End Sand
Hadleigh Ray
SOUTHEND on Sea
Southend Flat
Shoeburyness
Northwick
CANVEY ISLAND
Ray Gut
Shoebury Common
Dutch Cottage Museum
Newlands
Canvey Pt.
Shoebury Ness
Holehaven Creek
Chapman Sands
Pier
Shellhaven Pt.
Leigh Beck
The Knock
Hole Haven
Thorney Bay
Shell Haven
Coryton Wharves
A132
A129
A130
A127
A13
A1015
A1013
A1159
A1158
A1017
A1016
A1160
B1013
B1014
B1006
B1015
B1464

SOUTHEND
A127 LONDON & SOUTHEND AIRPORT
Southend United F.C.
Gainsborough
Shakespeare Dr.
WEST ST.
Colchester Rd.
VICTORIA AVENUE
Tickfield
Crowborough
Tunbridge
Kenway
Glenhurst Rd.
SUTTON ROAD
Ruskin
Sycamore
Tennyson Av.
Browning Av.
Byron Av.
Bournemouth Park
Redstock Rd.
Dryden Av.
North Road
Tudor Rd.
Salisbury
Harcourt Av.
Carnarvon Rd.
CIVIC CENTRE
Southend Stadium
Stadium Rd.
North
Central
South
Chelmsford Av.
Boston
Baxter Avenue
Maldon
Swanage Rd.
St. Ann's Rd.
Wimborne
Sweyne Av.
Library
Guildford Rd.
Milton St.
Victoria Sta.
Boscombe
BRADLEY
DOWSETT AV.
Chichester
A13 TILBURY
Balmoral Rd.
Hamlet Ct.
LONDON ROAD
Bus Sta.
SOUTHCHURCH
A13 SHOEBURYNESS
St. John's Rd.
St. Helen's Rd.
Park Rd.
Queens
Princes
Ashburnham Rd.
Napier Ave.
Elmer Ave.
Warrior Sq.
Tyrrel Dr.
Lancaster Gdns
Canewdon Rd.
Milton
Whitegate
Elmer Appr.
Central Sta.
Tylers Av.
St. Vincent's Rd.
Hamlet
Clifftown Rd.
HIGH ST.
Baltic Av.
York
York
ART GALLERY
Scratton Rd.
Clarence Rd.
Bus Sta.
Heygate Av.
Cambridge Rd.
Alexandra
Alexandra St.
Church Rd.
Westcliff Parade
Clifftown Par.
Royal Ter.
Hartington Rd.
Pleasant Rd.
Cliffs Pav.
Cliff Lift
Lucy Rd.
Pier Hill
Marine Par.
WESTERN ESPLANADE
RAC
Boating Pool
Dolphinarium
THAMES ESTUARY
Southend Pier
0 ¼ MILE
© MAP PRODUCTIONS LTD.

STRATFORD UPON AVON
A34 BIRMINGHAM
Golf Course
Avenue Farm Industrial Estate
Clopton Road
Benson Rd.
Park Rd.
BIRMINGHAM ROAD
Maybrook Ind. Estate
District Council Office
A46 WARWICK (A429)
Timothy's Bridge Road
Avon Ind. Estate
Maidenhead Road
Avenue Rd.
Rowley Cres.
Welcombe Rd.
Canal
Masons Road
Town Football Ground
Western Rd.
St. Gregory's Rd.
WARWICK ROAD
A422 WORCESTER
Lodge Road
R.C. Church
Clarence Road
Fire Station
Shakespeare St.
Great William St.
Tyler St.
Canal
Swimming Pool
STATION
MOTOR MUSEUM
Payton St.
ALCESTER RD.
STRATFORD HOSPITAL
ARDEN ST.
JUDITH SHAKESPEARE'S HOUSE
Mansell St.
GUILD ST.
Bus Sta.
BRIDGEWAY
Moat House Hotel
College
Old People's Home & Clinic
SHAKESPEARE'S BIRTHPLACE
Meer St.
Council Off.
WOOD ST.
BRIDGE ST.
Albany Rd.
HARVARD HO.
SHAKESPEARE MON.
Willows
GROVE RD.
Masons Ct.
Heritage Theatre
CLOPTON BRIDGE
NASH'S HO.
TOWN HALL
TIDDINGTON RD.
Scholars
NEW PLACE
ROYAL SHAKESPEARE THEATRE
Ely St.
Chapel La.
Tramway Br.
ANNE HATHAWAY'S COTTAGE
TUSSAUD'S WAXWORKS
Boat Club
GUILDHALL GUILD CHAPEL & SCHOOL
PICTURE GALLERY
Shottery
SHAKESPEARE INSTITUTE
ALMSHOUSES
Cricket Ground
A422 BANBURY
The
Rd.
Orchard Way
HALL'S CROFT
THE OTHER PLACE
Ferry
Children's Playground
Tramway Walk
SHIPSTON ROAD
Bridgetown R.
A439 EVESHAM (A435)
EVESHAM RD.
Brookvale Rd.
Broad St.
West St.
Narrow La.
Bull St.
College St.
Old Town
Southern La.
Sanctus St.
HOLY TRINITY CH.
Rec. Ground
Garrick Way
Cherry
College La.
Holton St.
Ryland St.
Lock
Borden Pl.
Orchard
Sanford Rd.
Paddock Lane
Hartford Rd.
Weirs
River Avon
A34 OXFORD
& TO A46 CHELTENHAM
0 ¼ MILE
© MAP PRODUCTIONS LTD

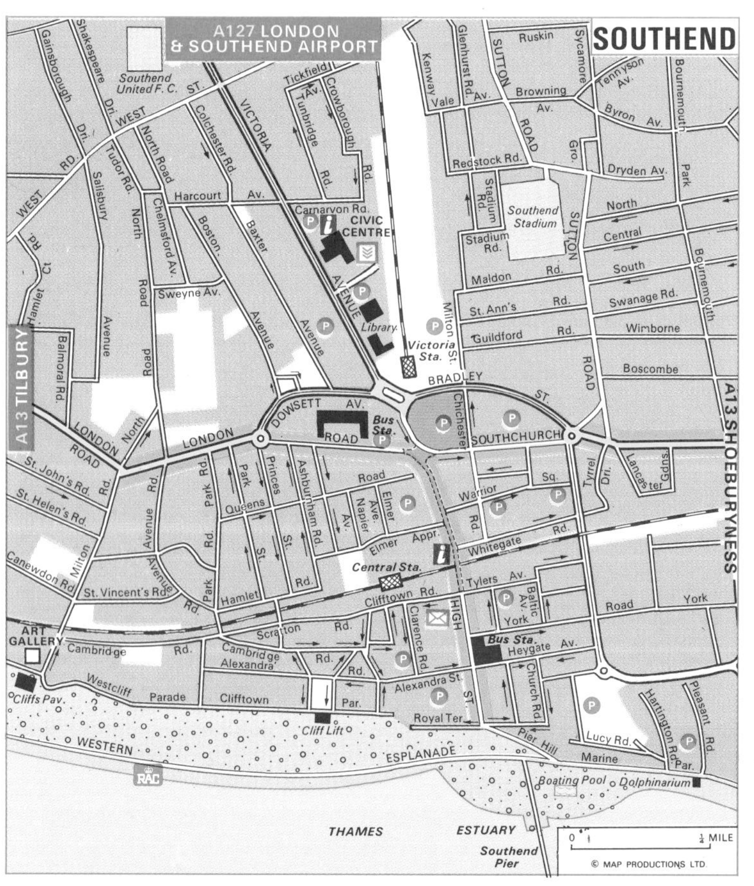

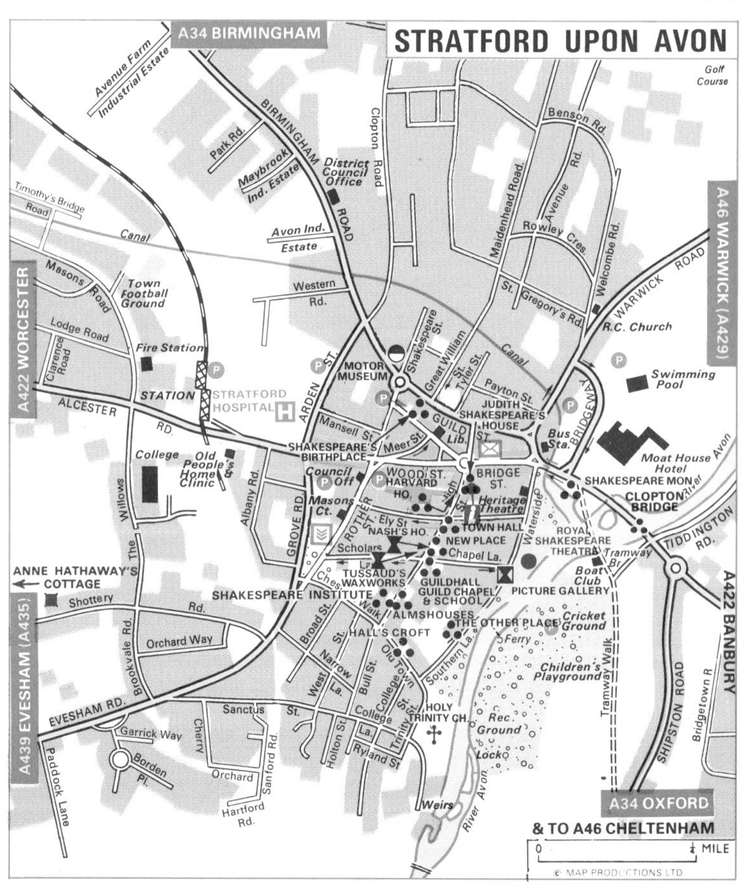

STOKE ON TRENT

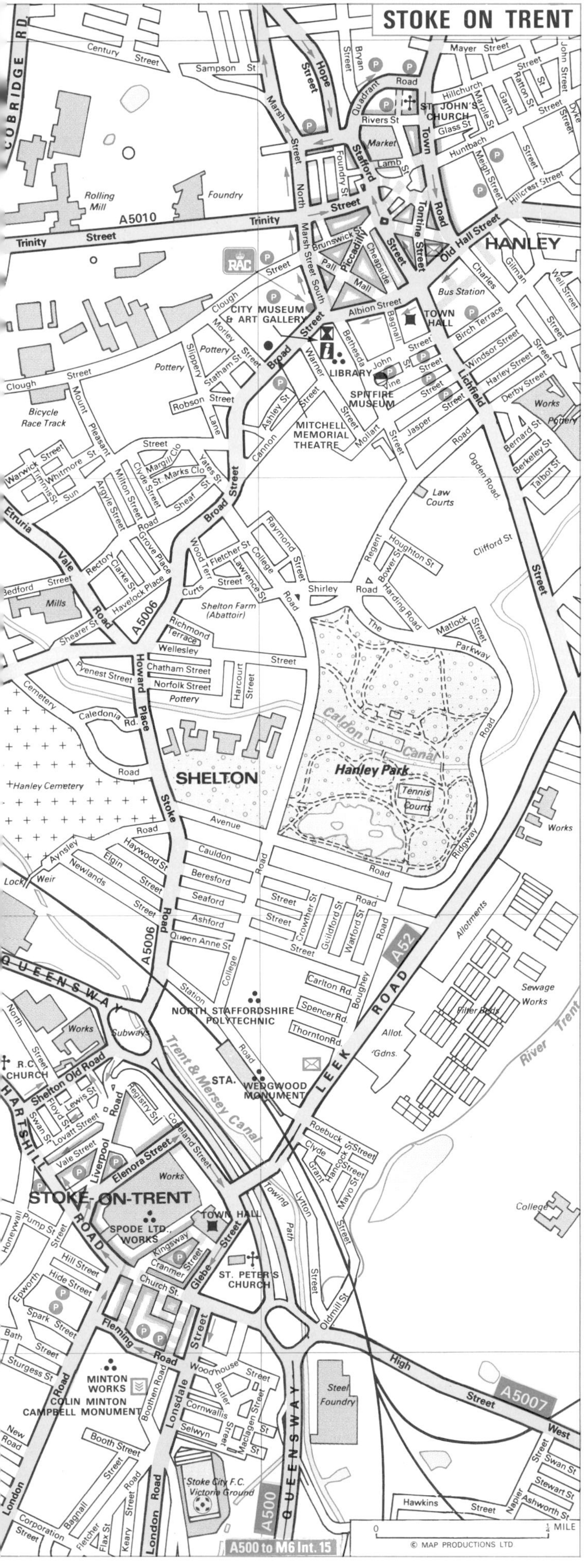

HANLEY
SHELTON
STOKE-ON-TRENT
Hanley Park
Caldon Canal
Trent & Mersey Canal
River Trent
QUEENSWAY
LEEK ROAD
A5010
A5006
A52
A5007
A500
Trinity Street
Broad Street
Stoke Road
Howard Place
Lichfield Street
Hope Street
Town Road
Piccadilly
Albion Street
Clough Street
Etruria Vale Road
Shelton Old Road
Hartshill Road
High Street
London Road
Fleming Road
Glebe Street
Rolling Mill
Foundry
Bicycle Race Track
Hanley Cemetery
CITY MUSEUM & ART GALLERY
TOWN HALL
LIBRARY
SPITFIRE MUSEUM
MITCHELL MEMORIAL THEATRE
Bus Station
Law Courts
Shelton Farm (Abattoir)
NORTH STAFFORDSHIRE POLYTECHNIC
WEDGWOOD MONUMENT
ST. JOHN'S CHURCH
ST. PETER'S CHURCH
R.C. CHURCH
SPODE LTD. WORKS
MINTON WORKS
COLIN MINTON CAMPBELL MONUMENT
Stoke City F.C. Victoria Ground
Sewage Works
Steel Foundry
A500 to M6 Int. 15
0 ½ MILE
© MAP PRODUCTIONS LTD

APPROACHES TO STOKE ON TRENT

TORQUAY

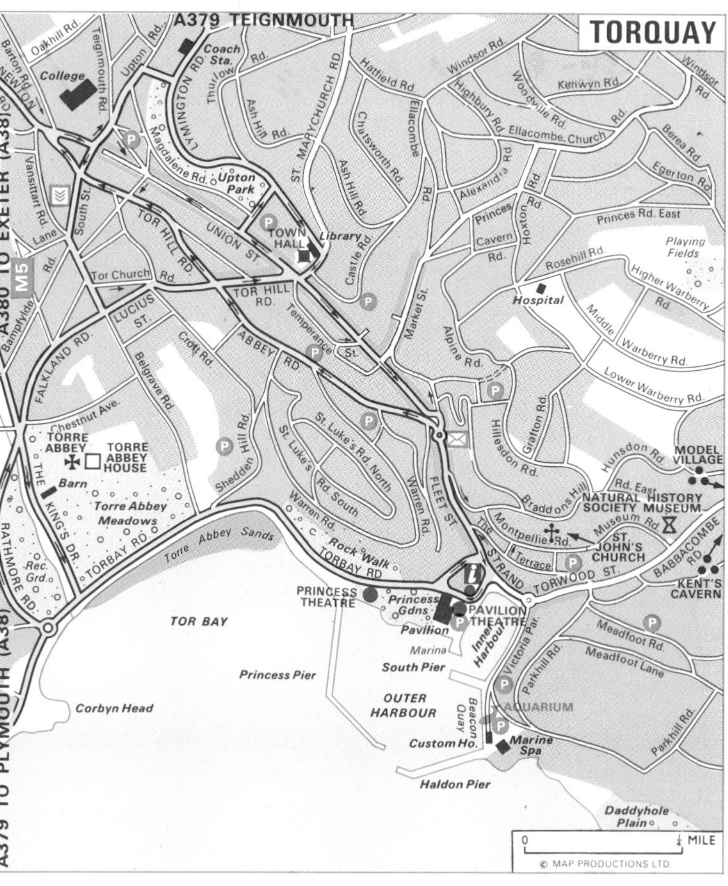

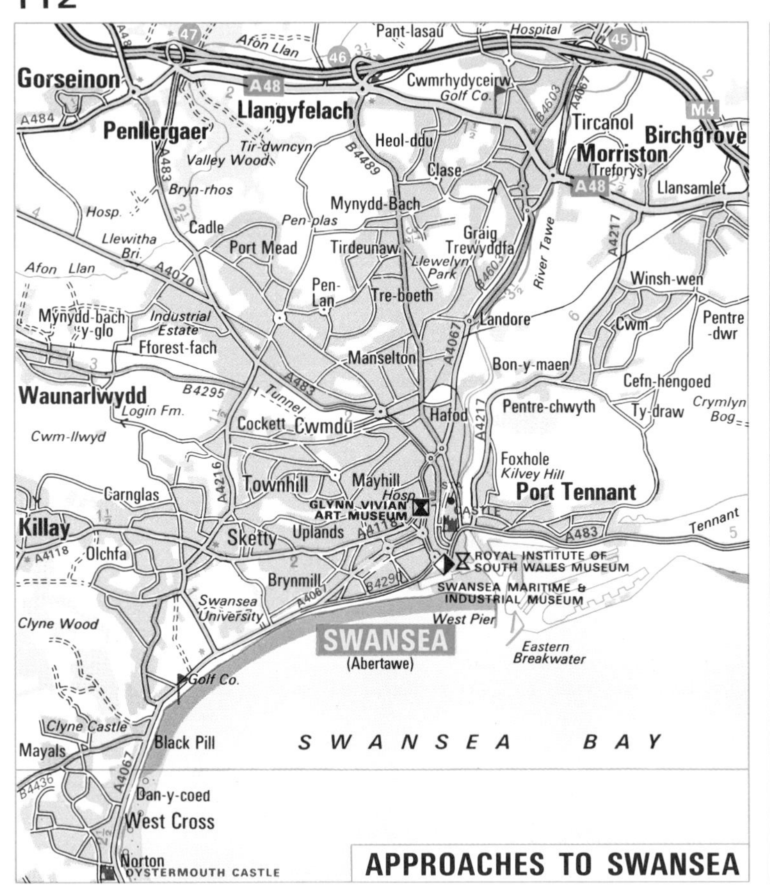
APPROACHES TO SWANSEA
Gorseinon
Penllergaer
Llangyfelach
Pant-lasau
Cwmrhydyceirw
Tircanol
Morriston
(Treforys)
Birchgrove
Llansamlet
Heol-ddu
Clase
Mynydd-Bach
Tir-dwncyn
Valley Wood
Bryn-rhos
Cadle
Port Mead
Tirdeunaw
Graig Trewyddfa
Llewelyn Park
Pen-Lan
Tre-boeth
River Tawe
Winsh-wen
Mynydd-bach-y-glo
Industrial Estate
Fforest-fach
Landore
Cwm
Pentre-dwr
Manselton
Bon-y-maen
Cefn-hengoed
Waunarlwydd
Login Fm.
Cwm-llwyd
Cockett
Cwmdu
Hafod
Pentre-chwyth
Ty-draw
Crymlyn Bog
Foxhole
Kilvey Hill
Carnglas
Townhill
Mayhill
Port Tennant
Killay
Olchfa
Sketty
Uplands
GLYNN VIVIAN ART MUSEUM
CASTLE
ROYAL INSTITUTE OF SOUTH WALES MUSEUM
SWANSEA MARITIME & INDUSTRIAL MUSEUM
Brynmill
Swansea University
West Pier
Eastern Breakwater
Clyne Wood
SWANSEA
(Abertawe)
Golf Co.
Clyne Castle
Mayals
Black Pill
SWANSEA BAY
Dan-y-coed
West Cross
Norton
OYSTERMOUTH CASTLE

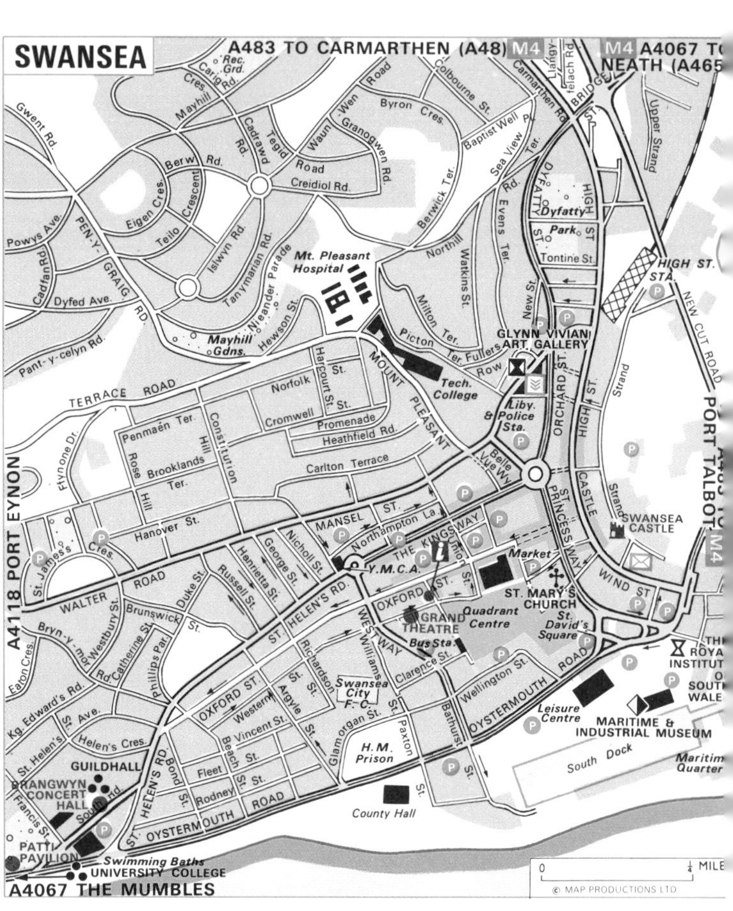
SWANSEA
A483 TO CARMARTHEN (A48)
A4067 TO NEATH (A465)
Mt. Pleasant Hospital
Mayhill Gdns.
Tech. College
GLYNN VIVIAN ART GALLERY
Liby. & Police Sta.
TERRACE ROAD
MOUNT PLEASANT
Carlton Terrace
HIGH ST. STA.
PORT TALBOT
SWANSEA CASTLE
Y.M.C.A.
THE KINGSWAY
Market
ST. MARY'S CHURCH
Quadrant Centre
St. David's Square
GRAND THEATRE
Bus Sta.
Swansea City F.C.
H.M. Prison
County Hall
Leisure Centre
MARITIME & INDUSTRIAL MUSEUM
South Dock
Maritime Quarter
GUILDHALL
BRANGWYN CONCERT HALL
PATTI PAVILION
Swimming Baths
UNIVERSITY COLLEGE
A4118 PORT EYNON
A4067 THE MUMBLES
0 ½ MILE
© MAP PRODUCTIONS LTD

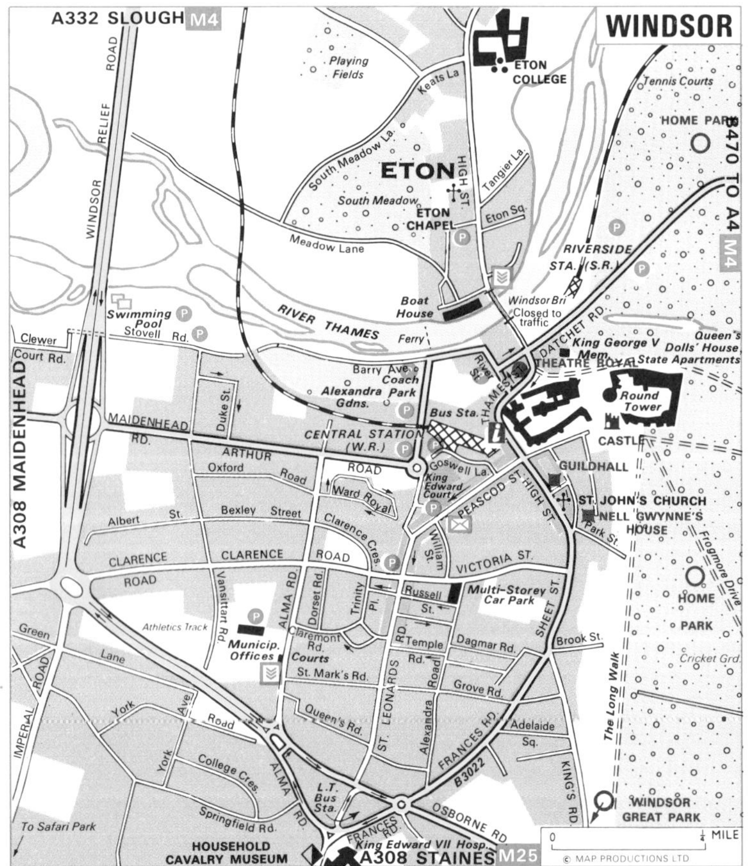
WINDSOR
A332 SLOUGH
ETON COLLEGE
Playing Fields
Tennis Courts
HOME PARK
B470 TO A4
ETON
South Meadow
ETON CHAPEL
Meadow Lane
RIVERSIDE STA. (S.R.)
Boat House
Windsor Br. Closed to traffic
Swimming Pool
RIVER THAMES
King George V Mem.
THEATRE ROYAL
Queen's Dolls' House
State Apartments
Alexandra Park Gdns.
Bus Sta.
CENTRAL STATION (W.R.)
Round Tower
CASTLE
GUILDHALL
ST. JOHN'S CHURCH
NELL GWYNNE'S HOUSE
A308 MAIDENHEAD
Multi-Storey Car Park
Athletics Track
Municip. Offices
Courts
The Long Walk
Cricket Grd.
To Safari Park
L.T. Bus Sta.
HOUSEHOLD CAVALRY MUSEUM
King Edward VII Hosp.
A308 STAINES
WINDSOR GREAT PARK
0 ½ MILE
© MAP PRODUCTIONS LTD

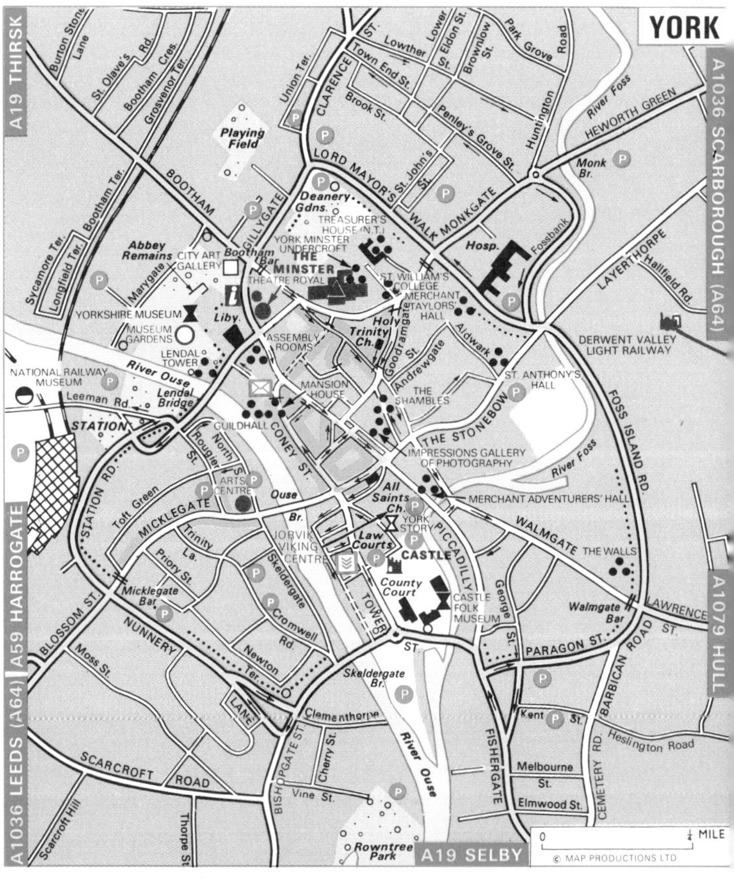
YORK
A19 THIRSK
A1036 SCARBOROUGH (A64)
Playing Field
BOOTHAM
LORD MAYOR'S WALK
MONKGATE
Deanery Gdns.
TREASURER'S HOUSE (N.T.)
YORK MINSTER UNDERCROFT
THE MINSTER
Abbey Remains
CITY ART GALLERY
Bootham Bar
THEATRE ROYAL
ST. WILLIAM'S COLLEGE
MERCHANT TAYLORS' HALL
Hosp.
YORKSHIRE MUSEUM
MUSEUM GARDENS
LENDAL TOWER
Liby.
ASSEMBLY ROOMS
Holy Trinity Ch.
NATIONAL RAILWAY MUSEUM
River Ouse
Lendal Bridge
MANSION HOUSE
THE SHAMBLES
ST. ANTHONY'S HALL
DERWENT VALLEY LIGHT RAILWAY
STATION
GUILDHALL
THE STONEBOW
IMPRESSIONS GALLERY OF PHOTOGRAPHY
MERCHANT ADVENTURERS' HALL
ARTS CENTRE
All Saints Ch.
YORK STORY
JORVIK VIKING CENTRE
Law Courts
CASTLE
County Court
CASTLE FOLK MUSEUM
THE WALLS
Micklegate Bar
Walmgate Bar
A59 HARROGATE
A1036 LEEDS (A64)
A1079 HULL
Skeldergate Br.
Rowntree Park
A19 SELBY
0 ½ MILE
© MAP PRODUCTIONS LTD

INDEX

INDEX TO SECTIONAL MAP OF GREAT BRITAIN

ABBREVIATIONS

Beds. – *Bedfordshire*
Berks. – *Berkshire*
Bucks. – *Buckinghamshire*
Cambs. – *Cambridgeshire*
Cas. – *Castle*
Ches. – *Cheshire*
Co. – *County*
Com. – *Common*
Corn. – *Cornwall*
Cumb. – *Cumbria*
Derby. – *Derbyshire*
Dumf. & Gall. – *Dumfries & Galloway*
Dur. – *Durham*
E. – *East*
E. Sussex – *East Sussex*
Glos. – *Gloucestershire*
Gt. – *Great*
Grn. – *Green*
Hants. – *Hampshire*
Heref. & Worcs. – *Hereford & Worcester*
Hth. – *Heath*
Herts. – *Hertfordshire*
Ho. – *House*
Humber. – *Humberside*
I.o.M. – *Isle of Man*
I.o.W. – *Isle of Wight*
Junc. – *Junction*
Lancs. – *Lancashire*
Leics. – *Leicestershire*
Lincs. – *Lincolnshire*
Lo. – *Lodge*
London – *Greater London*
Manchester – *Greater Manchester*
Mid Glam. – *Mid Glamorgan*
Norf. – *Norfolk*
N. – *North*
N. Yorks. – *North Yorkshire*
Northants. – *Northamptonshire*
Northumb. – *Northumberland*
Notts. – *Nottinghamshire*
Oxon. – *Oxfordshire*
Salop. – *Shropshire*
Som. – *Somerset*
S. – *South*
S. Glam. – *South Glamorgan*
S. Yorks. – *South Yorkshire*
Staffs. – *Staffordshire*
Sta. – *Station*
Suff. – *Suffolk*
War. – *Warwickshire*
W. – *West*
W. Glam. – *West Glamorgan*
W. Mid. – *West Midlands*
W. Sussex – *West Sussex*
W. Yorks. – *West Yorkshire*
W. Isles. – *Western Isles*
Wilts. – *Wiltshire*

32 Ab Kettleby **H 4**
7 Abbas Combe **D 10**
22 Abberley **E 1**
19 Abberton, Essex **B 10**
22 Abberton, Heref. & Worcs **G 3**
45 Abberwick **B 9**
18 Abbess Roding **C 6**
6 Abbey **E 5**
15 Abbey Dore **A 7**
6 Abbey Hill **D 6**
31 Abbey Hulton **E 7**
49 Abbey St. Bathans **C 10**
32 Abbey Town **F 12**
34 Abbey Village **E 5**
20 Abbeycwmhir **E 6**
38 Abbeylands, I.o.M. **G 2**
45 Abbeylands, Northumb. **B 10**
34 Abbeystead **B 4**
4 Abbots Bickington **E 3**
31 Abbots Bromley **H 9**
17 Abbots Langley **D 11**
15 Abbots Leigh **G 8**
22 Abbot's Morton **G 4**
25 Abbots Ripton **G 3**
22 Abbot's Salford **G 4**
7 Abbotsbury **H 9**
4 Abbotsham **C 3**
5 Abbotskerswell **J 7**
25 Abbotsley **K 3**
8 Abbotswood **D 5**
8 Abbots Ann **B 5**
21 Abcott **E 9**
21 Abdon **D 11**
13 Aber, Dyfed **B 8**
28 Aber, Gwynedd **C 6**
13 Aberarth **A 8**
20 Aber Gwydol **B 3**
28 Aber-Gwynant **H 6**
14 Aber Village **B 4**
13 Aberaeron **A 8**
14 Aberaman **D 3**
20 Aberangell **A 4**
57 Aberarder, Highland **G 2**
55 Aberarder, Highland **L 8**
52 Aberargie **F 6**
13 Aberavon **H 11**
13 Aber-banc **C 7**
14 Aberbeeg **D 5**
14 Aberbran **A 3**
14 Abercanaid **D 4**
14 Abercarn **E 5**
12 Abercastle **D 2**
20 Abercegir **B 4**
55 Aberchalder **J 7**
58 Aberchirder **B 4**
13 Abercraf **F 11**
14 Abercrave **C 2**
14 Abercregan **E 2**
14 Abercwmboi **D 3**
12 Abercych **C 6**
14 Abercynafon **C 4**
14 Abercynon **E 4**
14 Aberdare **D 3**
28 Aberdaron **H 1**
59 Aberdeen **G 7**
28 Aberdesach **E 4**
48 Aberdour **A 5**
20 Aberdovey **C 2**
13 Aberdulais **G 11**
20 Aberedw **H 6**
12 Abereiddy **D 2**
28 Abererch **G 3**
14 Aberfan **D 4**
52 Aberfeldy **B 3**
28 Aberffraw **C 3**
20 Aberffrwd **E 2**
36 Aberford **C 2**
51 Aberfoyle **G 12**
13 Abergarwed **G 11**
14 Abergavenny **C 6**
29 Abergele **B 9**
13 Abergiar **C 8**
13 Abergorlech **D 9**
20 Abergwesyn **G 4**
13 Abergwili **E 8**
14 Abergwynfi **E 2**
20 Abergynolwyn **B 2**
20 Aberhosan **C 4**
14 Aberkenfig **F 2**
49 Aberlady **A 7**
53 Aberlemno **B 10**
20 Aberllefenni **A 3**
20 Abermeurig **G 1**
21 Abermule **C 7**
13 Abernant, Dyfed **E 7**
14 Aber-nant, Mid Glam. **D 3**
53 Abernethy **E 7**
53 Abernyte **D 7**
12 Aberporth **B 6**
28 Abersoch **G 3**
14 Abersychan **D 6**
14 Aberthin **G 3**
14 Abertillery **D 5**
14 Abertridwr, Mid Glam. **E 4**
29 Abertridwr, Powys **H 9**
14 Abertysswg **D 5**
52 Aberuthven **F 5**
14 Aberyscir **A 3**
20 Aberystwyth **D 2**
16 Abingdon **D 6**
9 Abinger Common **B 12**
9 Abinger Hammer **A 12**
48 Abington **G 2**
25 Abington Pigotts **L 4**
16 Ablington, Glos. **C 2**
8 Ablington, Wilts. **A 3**
31 Abney **B 10**
59 Aboyne **H 3**
34 Abram **G 5**
56 Abriachan **F 1**
18 Abridge **D 5**
15 Abson **G 10**
23 Abthorpe **G 10**
33 Aby **B 11**
21 Acaster Malbis **C 4**
36 Acaster Selby **C 3**
4 Accott **C 5**
34 Accrington **D 6**
62 Achachork **D 4**
50 Achadun **D 5**
50 Achafolla **F 5**
61 Achagary **B 7**
46 Achahoish **B 3**
51 Achallader **C 10**
46 Achamore Farm **E 1**
54 Achanalt **D 6**
46 Achanamara **A 3**
56 Achandunie **C 2**
60 Achany **F 6**
55 Achaphubuil **M 5**
50 Acharacle **A 4**
50 Acharn, Highland **C 4**
52 Acharn, Tayside **C 2**
61 Acharole **C 11**
46 Acharosson **B 4**
50 Achateny **A 3**
58 Achath **F 5**
61 Achavanich **C 11**
56 Achavraat **E 5**
60 Achavraie **F 2**
13 Achddu **G 8**
61 Achentoul **D 8**
60 Achfary **C 4**
60 Achfrish **F 6**
60 Achgarve **G 1**
60 Achiemore, Kyle of Durness, Highland **A 4**
61 Achiemore, Highland **B 9**
62 A'Chill **H 2**
60 Achiltibuie **F 2**
61 Achina **B 7**
51 Achindarroch **B 7**
55 Achintee, Highland **M 5**
54 Achintee, Highland **F 3**
54 Achintraid **F 2**
55 Achlain **H 6**
57 Achlean **K 4**
50 Achleck **C 1**
46 A'Chleit **E 2**
51 Achlian **E 8**
55 Achluachrach **L 7**
60 Achlyness **B 4**
60 Achmelvich **E 2**
52 Achmore, Central **D 1**
54 Achmore, Highland **F 2**
63 Achmore, W. Isles **D 4**
51 Achnaba, Strathclyde **D 7**
46 Achnaba, Strathclyde **A 4**
57 Achnabat **G 2**
60 Achnacarnin **D 2**
55 Achnacarry **L 5**
62 Achnacloich **G 5**
51 Achnacon **B 8**
50 Achnacraig **C 2**
50 Achnacroish **C 6**
50 Achnadrish **B 2**
51 Achnafalnich **E 9**
55 Achnafraschoille **L 6**
56 Achnaggaron **C 2**
50 Achnaha **A 2**
60 Achnahanat **G 6**
50 Achnalea **A 6**
61 Achnaluachrach **F 7**
55 Achnanellan **L 5**
60 Achnanerain **F 6**
55 Achnangart **H 3**
55 Achnasaul **K 5**
54 Achnasheen **D 5**
54 Achnashellach **E 4**
56 Achnastank **F 8**
50 Achosnich **A 2**
50 Achranich **C 4**
61 Achreamie **A 9**
51 Achriabhach **A 8**
60 Achriesgill **B 4**
61 Achrimsdale **F 9**
61 Achtoty **B 7**
25 Achurch **G 1**
60 Achuvoldrach **B 6**
61 Achvaich **G 7**
57 Achvraid, Highland **G 2**
56 Achvraid, Highland **F 2**
61 Ackergill **B 12**
40 Acklam, Cleveland **C 5**
36 Acklam, N. Yorks. **A 5**
22 Ackleton **B 1**
45 Acklington **C 10**
36 Ackton **E 2**
36 Ackworth Moor Top **F 2**
26 Acle **D 7**
22 Acock's Green **D 5**
11 Acol **A 11**
45 Acomb, Northumb. **F 7**
36 Acomb, N. Yorks. **B 4**
15 Aconbury **A 8**
34 Acre **E 6**
9 Acre Street **F 9**
29 Acrefair **F 12**
30 Acton, Cheshire **E 5**
8 Acton, Dorset **H 1**
18 Acton, London **F 2**
21 Acton, Salop **D 8**
27 Acton, Suffolk **L 2**
30 Acton Bridge **C 4**
21 Acton Beauchamp **G 12**
21 Acton Burnell **B 10**
21 Acton Green **G 12**
30 Acton Park **E 2**
21 Acton Pigott **B 11**
21 Acton Round **C 11**
21 Acton Scott **C 10**
31 Acton Trussell **H 8**
15 Acton Turville **F 11**
30 Adbaston **G 6**
7 Adber **D 9**
30 Adderley **F 5**
45 Adderstone **C 12**
48 Addiewell **C 3**
35 Addingham **B 9**
17 Addington, Bucks. **A 8**
10 Addington, Kent **B 5**
18 Addington, London **G 4**
49 Addinston **D 8**
17 Addlestone **H 11**
33 Addlethorpe **C 12**
36 Adel **C 1**
30 Adeney **H 5**
20 Adfa **B 6**
21 Adforton **E 9**
11 Adisham **C 11**
16 Adlestrop **A 3**
36 Adlingfleet **E 6**
31 Adlington, Ches. **B 7**
34 Adlington, Lancs. **F 5**
21 Admaston, Salop. **A 11**
31 Admaston, Staffs. **H 9**
22 Admington **G 5**
17 Adstock **A 8**
23 Adstone **G 9**
9 Adversane **D 12**
56 Advie **F 7**
36 Adwick le Street **F 3**
36 Adwick upon Dearne **G 3**
4 Adworthy **D 6**
58 Adziel **B7**
43 Ae Bridgend **C 10**
43 Ae Village **C 10**
4 Affeton Barton **E 6**
58 Affleck, Grampian **D 3**
58 Affleck, Grampian **E 6**
7 Affpuddle **G 11**
55 Affric Lodge **G 5**
29 Afonwen **C 10**
5 Afton, Devon **J 7**
8 Afton, I.o.W. **G 5**
47 Afton Bridgend **H 11**
40 Agglethorpe **F 1**
38 Agneash **G 2**
63 Aignish **D 6**
37 Aike **C 8**
64 Aikerness **A 2**
64 Aikers **E 2**
43 Aiket **E 11**
39 Aiketgate **A 7**
44 Aikton **H 1**
21 Ailey **G 9**
24 Ailsworth **F 2**
40 Ainderby Steeple **F 4**
19 Aingers Green **B 11**
34 Ainsdale **F 2**
39 Ainstable **A 7**
34 Ainsworth **F 6**
41 Ainthorpe **D 7**
34 Aintree **G 3**
42 Aird, Dumf & Gall. **F 2**
50 Aird, Strathclyde **G 5**
63 Aird, W. Isles **C 6**
62 Aird of Sleat **H 5**
63 Aird of Tunga **C 6**
63 Aird Uig **C 2**
60 Airdachuilinn **C 4**
47 Airdrie **C 12**
47 Airdsgreen **F 12**
61 Airdtorrisdale **B 7**
54 Airigh-drishaig **F 1**
36 Airmyn **E 5**
52 Airntully **D 6**
55 Airor **J 1**
52 Airth **H 4**
35 Airton **A 7**
42 Airyhassen **G 4**
33 Aisby, Lincs. **F 7**
32 Aisby, Lincs. **A 6**
39 Aisgill **E 10**
5 Aish **K 6**
6 Aisholt **C 5**
40 Aiskew **F 3**
40 Aislaby, N. Yorks. **D 4**
41 Aislaby, N. Yorls. **G 8**
41 Aislaby, N. Yorks. **D 8**
32 Aisthorpe **B 6**
64 Aith, Orkney Is. **C 4**
64 Aith, Shetland Is. **D 7**
64 Aith Hestwall **C 1**
42 Aitkenhead **A 4**
56 Aitnoch **F 5**
49 Akeld **F 12**
49 Akeld Steads **F 12**
23 Akeley **H 10**
27 Akenham **K 5**
3 Albaston **C 11**
21 Alberbury **A 9**
12 Albert Town **E 3**
10 Albourn **F 1**
22 Albrighton, Salop. **B 2**
30 Albrighton, Salop. **H 4**
27 Alburgh **G 6**
27 Alburgh Street **G 5**
18 Albury, Herts. **B 4**
9 Albury, Surrey **A 12**
26 Alby Hill **B 5**
56 Alcaig **D 1**
22 Alcester **F 4**
10 Alciston **G 4**
6 Alcombe, Som. **B 3**
15 Alcombe, Wilts. **G 11**
25 Alconbury **H 3**
25 Alconbury Hill **G 3**
25 Alconbury Weston **H 3**
47 Aldandulish **M 5**
26 Aldborough, Norf. **B 5**
40 Aldborough, N. Yorks. **H 4**
16 Aldbourne **G 4**
37 Aldbrough, **C 10**
40 Aldbrough St John **D 2**
17 Aldbury **C 10**
52 Aldcharmaig **A 3**
34 Aldcliffe **A 3**
52 Aldclune **A 4**
27 Aldeburgh **J 8**
26 Aldeby **F 7**
18 Aldenham **D 1**
8 Alderbury **C 3**
26 Alderford **D 4**
15 Alderley **E 11**
31 Alderley Edge **B 7**
17 Aldermaston **H 7**
17 Aldermaston Wharf **G 7**
22 Alderminster **G 6**
21 Alder's End **H 11**
8 Alderholt **E 3**
9 Aldershot **A 10**
16 Alderton, Glos. **A 1**
23 Alderton, Northants **G 10**
30 Alderton, Salop **H 4**
27 Alderton, Suffolk **L 6**
15 Alderton, Wilts **F 11**
31 Alderwasley **E 11**
40 Aldfield **H 3**
30 Aldford **D 3**
19 Aldham, Essex **A 9**
27 Aldham, Suffolk **L 3**
27 Aldham Street **L 3**
56 Aldie **B 3**
9 Aldingbourne **F 10**
38 Aldingham **H 5**
22 Aldington **H 4**
11 Aldington Corner **D 9**
57 Aldochlay **H 10**
43 Aldoth **G 12**
25 Aldreth **H 5**
22 Aldridge **B 4**
27 Aldringham **J 7**
16 Aldsworth **C 3**
58 Aldunie **E i**
31 Aldwark, Derby **D 10**
36 Aldwark, N. Yorks. **A 2**
9 Aldwick **F 10**
25 Aldwincle **G 1**
16 Aldworth **F 6**
47 Alexandria **A 9**
6 Aley **B 5**
4 Alfardisworthy **E 2**
6 Alfington **F 5**
9 Alfold **C 11**
9 Alfold Crossways **C 11**
58 Alford, Grampian **F 3**
33 Alford, Lincs. **C 11**
7 Alfold, Somerset **C 9**
32 Alfreton **E 1**
22 Alfrick **G 1**
10 Alfriston **H 4**
24 Algarkirk **B 4**
7 Alhampton **C 9**
63 Aline Lodge **F 3**
55 Alisary **L 1**
36 Alkborough **E 6**
23 Alkerton **H 7**
11 Alkham **D 11**
30 Alkington **F 4**
31 Alkmonton **F 10**
16 All Cannings **H 2**
27 All Saints, South Elmham **G 6**
21 All Stretton **C 10**
60 Alladale Lodge **G 5**
5 Allaleigh **K 7**
57 Allanaquoich **K 7**
56 Allanfearn **E 3**
56 Allangrange Mains **E 2**
49 Allanton **D 11**
8 Allbrook **D 6**
45 Allendale Town **G 7**
39 Allenheads **A 10**
18 Allen's Green **B 4**
45 Allensford **H 9**
15 Allensmore **A 8**
31 Allenton **G 12**
48 Allenton **D 1**
7 Aller **C 7**
43 Allerby **H 11**
45 Allerdene **C 8**
6 Allerford **B 3**
41 Allerston **G 9**
36 Allerthorpe **B 5**
30 Allerton, Merseyside **B 3**
35 Allerton, W. Yorks. **D 10**
36 Allerton Bywater **D 2**
36 Allerton Mauleverer **A 2**
45 Allerwash **F 7**
22 Allesley **D 6**
31 Allestree **F 11**
23 Allexton **B 11**
31 Allgreave **D 8**
19 Allhallows **F 8**
54 Alligin Shuas **D 2**
31 Allimore Green **H 7**
32 Allington, Lincs. **F 6**
8 Allington, Wilts. **B 4**
16 Allington, Wilts. **H 2**
38 Allithwaite **G 6**
52 Alloa **H 4**
43 Allonby **G 11**
47 Alloway **H 8**
7 Allowenshay **E 7**
13 Allt **G 9**
55 Alltbeithe, Highland **G 4**
55 Alltneithe, Highland **J 4**
51 Alltchaorunn **B 9**
20 Alltmawr **H 6**
60 Alltnacaillich **C 5**
57 Allt-na-giubhsaich **L 8**
60 Allt na h'Airbhe **G 3**
55 Alltsigh **H 8**
13 Alltwalis **D 8**
13 Alltwen **G 10**
13 Alltyblacca **B 8**
7 Allweston **E 10**
32 Alma Park Estate **F 6**
21 Almeley **G 9**
21 Almeley Wooton **G 9**
7 Almer **F 12**
36 Almholme **F 4**
30 Almington **G 5**
4 Alminstone Cross **D 2**
52 Almondbank **E 5**
15 Almondbury **F 10**
15 Almondsbury **F 9**
45 Alndyke **B 10**
36 Alne **A 3**
56 Alness **C 2**
45 Alnham **B 8**
45 Alnmouth **B 10**
45 Alnwick **B 10**
27 Alphamstone **M 2**
27 Alpheton **K 2**
5 Alphington **G 8**
31 Alport **D 10**

30 Alpraham D 4
19 Alresford B 10
22 Alrewas A 5
30 Alsager E 6
30 Alsagers Bank E 6
31 Alsop en le Dale E 10
44 Alston, Cumb. H 5
6 Alston, Devon F 6
16 Alstone, Glos. A 1
6 Alstone, Som. B 6
31 Alstonefield E 9
4 Alswear D 6
60 Altandhu E 2
61 Altanduin E 8
3 Altarnun B 9
60 Altass G 6
46 Altgaltraig B 5
34 Altham D 6
19 Althorne D 9
36 Althorpe F 6
42 Alticry G 4
61 Altnabea E 10
61 Altnabreac Stn. C 9
56 Altnacardich E 1
60 Altnacealgach Hot. F 4
50 Altnacraig E 6
51 Altnafeadh B 9
60 Altnaharra D 6
35 Altofts E 12
32 Alton, Derby D 1
9 Alton, Hants. B 8
31 Alton, Staffs. F 9
16 Alton Barnes H 2
7 Alton Pancras F 10
16 Alton Priors H 2
47 Altonhill E 9
30 Altrincham A 6
55 Altrua K 6
51 Altskeith G 11
52 Alva G 4
30 Alvanley C 4
31 Alvaston G 12
22 Alvechurch E 4
22 Alvecote B 6
8 Alvediston D 1
22 Alveley D 1
4 Alverdiscott C 4
9 Alverstoke F 7
32 Alverton F 5
16 Alvescot D 4
15 Alveston, Avon E 9
22 Alveston, War. F 6
9 Alverstone G 7
57 Alvie J 4
33 Alvingham A 10
15 Alvington D 9
24 Alwalton F 2
45 Alwinton B 7
35 Alwoodley C 11
53 Alyth B 7
60 Amatnatua G 5
33 Amber Hill E 9
15 Amberley, Glos. D 11
9 Amberley, W. Sussex E 11
31 Ambersgate E 11
45 Amble C 11
22 Amblecote D 2
35 Ambler Thorn D 9
38 Ambleside E 6
12 Ambleston D 3
17 Ambrosden B 7
36 Amcotts F 6
53 Americanmuir D 8
17 Amersham D 10
17 Amersham Com. D 10
45 Amersidelaw C 12
8 Amesbury B 3
63 Amhuinnsuidhe F 2
22 Amington B 6
43 Amisfield Town C 11
28 Amlwch A 4
28 Amlwch Port A 4
13 Ammanford F 9
41 Amotherby H 7
8 Ampfield D 5
48 Ampherlaw D 3
40 Ampleforth G 6
40 Ampleforth Coll. G 6
16 Ampney Crucis D 2
16 Ampney St. Mary D 2
16 Ampney St. Peter D 2
8 Amport B 4
25 Ampthill L 1
27 Ampton H 2
12 Amroth F 5
52 Amulree C 4
62 An Caol C 5
62 An Coroghon H 2
50 Anaheilt A 5
54 Anancaun C 4
33 Ancaster F 7
21 Anchor D 7
49 Ancroft E 12
49 Ancroft Northmoor E 12
49 Ancrum G 9
33 Anderby C 12
7 Anderson F 12
30 Anderton C 5
8 Andover B 5
8 Andover Down B 5
16 Andoversford B 1
38 Andreas F 2
52 Angansk F 6
2 Angarrak F 3
44 Angerton G 1
12 Angle G 2
38 Anglers' Hotel D 3
28 Anglesey C 4
9 Angmering F 12
9 Angmering-on-Sea F 12
39 Angram, N. Yorks. E 11
36 Angram, N. Yorks. B 3
52 Anie F 1
56 Ankerville B 4
37 Anlaby D 8
24 Anmer C 8
8 Anna Valley B 5
43 Annan E 12
54 Annat, Highland D 3
51 Annat, Strathclyde E 7
47 Annathill B 12
47 Annbank G 9
47 Annbank Station G 9
32 Annesley Woodhouse E 2
58 Annfield F 3
45 Annfield Plain H 10
45 Annitsford F 11
21 Annscroft B 10
45 Annstead D 12
7 Ansford C 10
22 Ansley C 6
31 Anslow H 10
31 Anslow Gate H 10
9 Anstey, Hants. B 8
25 Anstey, Herts. M 5
23 Anstey, Leics. A 9
53 Anstruther Easter G 10
53 Anstruther Wester G 10
23 Ansty, War. D 7
10 Ansty, W. Sussex F 2
8 Ansty, Wilts. C 1
9 Anthill Common E 8
43 Anthorn F 12
26 Antingham B 6
3 Antony D 11
4 Anvil Corner E 2
33 Anwick E 8
42 Anwoth F 6
24 Apes Hall F 6
24 Apethorpe F 1
33 Apley C 8
32 Apperknowle B 1
15 Apperley B 11
39 Appersett F 10
50 Appin House C 6
39 Appleby, Cumbria C 9
37 Appleby, Humber. F 7
22 Appleby Magna A 6
22 Appleby Parva A 6
54 Applecross E 1
54 Applecross House E 1
4 Appledore, Devon C 3
6 Appledore, Devon E 4
11 Appledore, Kent E 8
11 Appledore Heath E 8
16 Appleford E 6
8 Appleshaw A 4
38 Applethwaite C 5
40 Appleton, N. Yorks. E 4
16 Appleton, Oxon. D 5
36 Appleton Roebuck C 3
30 Appleton Thorn B 5
41 Appleton-le-Moors F 7
41 Appleton-le-Street H 7
49 Appletreehall H 8
35 Appletreewick A 9
6 Appley D 4
34 Appley Bridge F 4
9 Apse Heath H 7
18 Apsley End A 1
9 Apuldram F 9
58 Aquhythie F 5
54 Araid D 2
54 Aranarff F 3
59 Arbeadie H 4
56 Arabella B 4
53 Arbirlot C 10
17 Arborfield G 8
17 Arborfield Cross G 8
42 Arbrack H 5
53 Arbroath C 11
59 Arbuthnott K 5
56 Archiestown E 8
30 Arclid Green D 6
46 Ardachearanbeg A 5
50 Ardachoil D 4
46 Ardachuple A 5
55 Ardachvie K 5
51 Ardanaiseig E 8
54 Ardaneaskan F 2
50 Ardanstur F 5
54 Ardarroch F 2
46 Ardbeg C 6
60 Ardcharnich G 3
60 Ardchiavaig F 1
51 Ardchonnell F 7
50 Ardchrishnish E 2
52 Ardchullarie More F 1
51 Ardchyle E 12
53 Ardcross G 10
51 Arddarroch H 9
21 Arddleen A 8
50 Ardelanish F 1
18 Ardeley A 3
55 Ardelve G 2
47 Arden A 8
40 Arden Hall F 5
50 Ardencaple Ho. F 5
22 Ardens Grafton G 5
50 Ardentallan Ho. E 5
46 Ardentraive B 5
52 Ardeonaig D 2
50 Ardery A 5
51 Ardess H 10
60 Ardessie G 2
50 Ardfern G 5
51 Ardgartan G 10
60 Ardgay G 6
63 Ardhasig G 2
54 Ardheslaig D 2
50 Ardinamar F 5
60 Ardindrean G 3
10 Ardingly E 2
16 Ardington E 5
55 Ardintoul G 2
58 Ardlair E 3
46 Ardlamont House C 5
50 Ardlarach F 5
27 Ardleigh M 3
53 Ardler C 7
16 Ardley A 6
51 Ardlui F 10
46 Ardlussa A 2
51 Ardmaddy D 8
60 Ardmair G 3
46 Ardmaleish C 6
51 Ardmay G 10
46 Ardminish E 2
55 Ardmolich M 1
61 Ardmore, Highland H 7
50 Ardmore, Strathclyde E 5
47 Ardmore, Strathclyde B 8
50 Ardnacross C 3
47 Ardnadam A 7
56 Ardnagrask E 1
55 Ardnamurach K 2
50 Ardnastang A 5
47 Ardneil D 7
51 Ardno G 8
58 Ardo House E 7
52 Ardoch C 6
47 Ardochrig E 11
61 Ardochu F 7
55 Ardochy House J 6
50 Ardow B 2
58 Ardoyne E 4
46 Ardpatrick C 3
46 Ardpatrick House C 3
47 Ardpeaton A 7
46 Ardrishaig A 3
63 Ardroil D 1
56 Ardross Castle B 2
47 Ardrossan E 7
50 Ardshealach A 4
35 Ardsley G 12
35 Ardsley East E 11
50 Ardslignish A 3
52 Ardtalnaig C 2
46 Ardtaraig A 5
50 Ardtoe A 4
52 Ardtrostan E 2
50 Arduaine F 5
56 Ardullie C 1
50 Ardura E 4
62 Ardvasar H 5
50 Ardvergnish E 3
57 Ardverikie L 1
63 Ardvey, Loch Finsbay H 2
63 Ardvey,
Loch Stockinish H 2
51 Ardvorlich,
Strathclyde F 10
52 Ardvorlich, Tayside E 1
63 Ardvourlie Castle F 3
52 Ardwell, Dumf. & Gall. G 2
42 Ardwell, Strathclyde B 3
22 Areley Kings E 2
9 Arford B 9
52 Argaty G 2
14 Argoed D 5
20 Argoed Mill F 5
51 Arichastlich D 10
50 Aridhglas F 1
54 Arinacrinachd D 1
50 Ariogan E 6
55 Arisaig L 1
55 Arisaig House L 1
50 Ariundle A 5
36 Arkendale A 2
25 Arkesden M 6
39 Arkholme H 8
39 Arkle Town E 12
43 Arkleby H 12
44 Arkleton D 2
18 Arkley D 2
36 Arksey F 4
32 Arkwright Town C 2
15 Arle B 12
38 Arlecdon C 3
25 Arlesey L 3
21 Arleston A 12
30 Arley, Cheshire B 5
22 Arley, War. C 6
15 Arlingham C 10
4 Arlington, Devon B 5
10 Arlington, E. Sussex G 4
16 Arlington, Glos. C 2
4 Arlington Beccott B 5
61 Armadale, Highland B 8
48 Armadale, Lothian C 2
62 Armadale Castle H 6
39 Armathwaite A 7
26 Arminghall E 5
22 Armitage A 4
35 Armley D 11
22 Armscote H 6
25 Armston G 2
36 Armthorpe G 4
39 Arncliffe H 11
39 Arncliffe Cote H 11
53 Arncroach G 10
8 Arne G 1
23 Arnesby C 9
46 Arnicle F 2
55 Arnisdale H 2
62 Arnish C 5
48 Arniston Engine C 6
63 Arnol B 4
37 Arnold, Humber. C 9
32 Arnold, Notts. F 3
52 Arnprior H 1
39 Arnside G 7
50 Aros Mains C 3
38 Arrad Foot G 5
37 Arram C 8
40 Arrathorne F 2
9 Arreton G 7
25 Arrington K 4
51 Arrivain D 10
51 Arrochar G 10
22 Arrow F 4
56 Artafallie E 2
35 Arthington C 11
23 Arthingworth D 11
20 Arthog A 2
58 Arthrath D 7
9 Arundel E 11
51 Aryhoulan A 7
38 Asby C 3
37 Asby cum Fenby G 10
46 Ascog C 6
17 Ascot G 10
16 Ascott-under-
Wychwood B 4
40 Asenby H 4
32 Asfordby H 4
32 Asfordby Hill H 4
33 Asgarby, Lincs. D 10
24 Asgarby, Lincs. A 2
11 Ash, Kent B 11
10 Ash, Kent B 5
7 Ash, Somerset D 8
9 Ash, Surrey A 10
4 Ash Bullayne E 6
23 Ash Green D 7
30 Ash Magna F 4
4 Ash Hill D 6
6 Ash Priors C 5
6 Ash Thomas E 3
9 Ash Vale A 10
16 Ashampstead F 6
27 Ashbacking K 5
31 Ashbourne F 10
6 Ashbrittle D 4
5 Ashburton J 6
4 Ashbury, Devon F 4
16 Ashbury, Oxon. F 4
37 Ashby F 7
33 Ashby by Partney D 11
33 Ashby de la Launde E 7
31 Ashby de la Zouch H 12
26 Ashby Dell E 8
23 Ashby Folville A 10
23 Ashby Magna C 9
23 Ashby Parva C 8
33 Ashby Puerorum C 10
23 Ashby St. Ledgers E 9
26 Ashby St. Mary E 6
15 Ashchurch A 12
14 Ashcombe, Avon H 6
6 Ashcombe, Devon H 3
7 Ashcott C 8
17 Ashcroft F 8
25 Ashdon L 7
9 Ashe A 7
19 Asheldham D 9
25 Ashen L 8
17 Ashendon C 8
52 Ashfield, Central G 3
13 Ashfield, Dyfed D 10
27 Ashfield, Suffolk J 5
27 Ashfield Green H 6
4 Ashford, Devon C 4
8 Ashford, Hants. E 3
11 Ashford, Kent D 9
17 Ashford, Surrey G 11
21 Ashford Bowdler E 10
21 Ashford Carbonel E 10
16 Ashford Hill H 6
31 Ashford-in-the-
Water C 10
47 Ashgill D 12
39 Ashgillside A 10
6 Ashill, Devon E 4
26 Ashill, Norfolk E 2
6 Ashill, Somerset D 6
19 Ashington, Essex E 8
45 Ashington, Northumb. D 10
7 Ashington, Som. D 9
9 Ashington, W. Sussex E 12
49 Ashkirk G 7
8 Ashlett F 6
15 Ashleworth B 11
25 Ashley, Cambs. J 8
30 Ashley, Cheshire B 6
4 Ashley, Devon E 5
15 Ashley, Glos. E 12
8 Ashley, Hants C 5
8 Ashley, Hants G 4
11 Ashley, Kent C 11
23 Ashley, Northants. C 11
30 Ashley, Staffs. F 6
17 Ashley Green D 10
8 Ashley Heath F 3
16 Ashmansworth H 5
4 Ashmansworthy D 2
7 Ashmore D 12
16 Ashmore Green G 6
22 Ashorne F 6
32 Ashover D 1
22 Ashow E 6
21 Ashperton H 11
5 Ashprington K 7
4 Ashreigney E 5
10 Ashtead B 1
30 Ashton, Cheshire C 4
2 Ashton, Cornwall G 3
21 Ashton,
Heref. & Worcs. F 10
23 Ashton, Northants. G 11
25 Ashton, Northants. G 2
15 Ashton Common H 12
16 Ashton Keynes E 2
34 Ashton-in-Makerfield G 5
22 Ashton under Hill H 3
35 Ashton under Lyne G 8
34 Ashton-upon-Mersey H 6
15 Ashton Watering G 8
8 Ashurst, Hants. E 5
10 Ashurst, Kent D 4
10 Ashurst, W. Sussex F 1
10 Ashurstwood D 3
4 Ashwater F 3
25 Ashwell, Herts. L 4
23 Ashwell, Leics. A 12
26 Ashwellthorpe F 4
7 Ashwick A 9
24 Ashwicken D 8
49 Ashybank H 8
38 Askam in Furness G 4
36 Askern F 3
7 Askerswell G 9
39 Askham C 7
36 Askham Bryan B 3
36 Askham Richard B 3
50 Asknish H 6
39 Askrigg F 11
35 Askwith B 10
24 Aslackby C 2
26 Aslacton F 4
32 Aslockton F 5
58 Asloun F 3
43 Aspatria G 12
18 Aspenden A 4
23 Aspley Guise H 12
17 Aspley Heath A 10
34 Aspull F 5
36 Asselby D 5
33 Asserby B 12
27 Assington L 2
56 Assynt House C 2
31 Astbury D 7
23 Astcote G 10
21 Asterley B 9
21 Asterton C 9
16 Asthall C 4
16 Asthall Leigh C 4
22 Astley,
Heref. & Worcs. E 1
30 Astley, Salop. H 4
22 Astley, War. C 6
21 Astley Abbots C 12
34 Astley Bridge F 6
22 Astley Cross E 2
34 Astley Green G 6
17 Aston, Berks. F 9
30 Aston, Cheshire E 5
30 Aston, Cheshire B 4
29 Aston, Clwyd C 12
31 Aston, Derby B 10
21 Aston,
Heref. & Worcs. E 10
21 Aston,
Heref. & Worcs. F 10
18 Aston, Herts. B 3
16 Aston, Oxon. D 4
30 Aston, Salop. G 4
21 Aston, Salop A 11
32 Aston, S. Yorks B 2
30 Aston, Staffs. F 6
31 Aston, Staffs. G 7
22 Aston, W. Midlands C 4
17 Aston Abbotts B 9
21 Aston Botterell D 11
22 Aston Cantlow F 5
17 Aston Clinton C 9
15 Aston Crews B 10
15 Aston Cross A 12
18 Aston End B 3
21 Aston Eyre C 12
22 Aston Fields E 3
23 Aston Flamville C 8
15 Aston Ingham B 10
30 Aston juxta Mondrum D 5
23 Aston le Walls G 8
16 Aston Magna A 3
21 Aston on Clun D 9
31 Aston on Trent G 12
21 Aston Pigott B 9
21 Aston Rogers B 9
17 Aston Rowant D 8
17 Aston Sandford C 8
22 Aston Somerville H 4
22 Aston Subedge H 5
16 Aston Tirrold F 6
16 Aston Upthorpe E 6
25 Astwick L 3
25 Astwood K 1
22 Astwood Bank F 4
24 Aswarby B 2
33 Aswardby C 10
21 Atcham B 11
27 Athelington H 5
7 Athelney C 7
49 Athelstaneford B 8
4 Atherington, Devon D 5
9 Atherington,
W. Sussex F 11
22 Atherstone B6
22 Atherstone on Stour G 5
34 Atherton G 5
55 Athnamulloch G 5
40 Atley Hill E 3
31 Atlow E 10
54 Attadale F 3
26 Attleborough, Norfolk F 3
23 Attleborough, War. C 7
26 Attlebridge D 4
59 Atton K 1
49 Attonburn G 10
37 Atwick B 9
15 Atworth H 11
32 Aubourn D 6
51 Auchachenna E 7
46 Auchagallon F 4
57 Auchallater K 7
42 Auchalton A 4
57 Auchavan M 7
46 Auchbroad A 3
58 Aucheldy D 6
43 Auchenbainzie B 9
59 Auchenblae J 5
43 Auchenbrack B 8
46 Auchenbreck A 5
43 Auchencairn,
Dumf. & Gall. C 10
43 Auchencairn,
Dumf. & Gall. F 9

47 Auchencarroch A 9
42 Auchencrosh D 2
49 Auchencrow C 11
48 Auchendinny C 5
43 Auchengibbert D 9
48 Auchengray D 3
43 Auchengruith A 9
58 Auchenhairig B 1
48 Auchenheath E 1
42 Auchenmalg F 3
42 Auchensoul B 3
42 Auchentibbert G 2
47 Auchentiber E 8
47 Auchenvennel A 8
43 Auchenvey D 8
57 Auchernack G 6
57 Auchgourish H 5
46 Auchinadrian D 2
58 Auchinderran B 2
51 Auchindrain G 6
54 Auchindrean B 6
58 Auchinhove B 2
58 Auchininna C 4
47 Auchinleck G 10
47 Auchinloch B 11
52 Auchinner F 2
58 Auchintender D 4
59 Auchintoul, Grampian G 4
58 Auchintoul, Grampian F 3
58 Auchiries D 8
58 Auchleven E 4
48 Auchlochan F 1
59 Auchlossan G 3
60 Auchlunachan H 3
59 Auchlunies G 6
51 Auchlyne E 12
58 Auchmacoy D 7
42 Auchmantle E 2
47 Auchmillan F 10
53 Auchmithie C 11
53 Auchmuirbridge G 7
59 Auchmull K 3
51 Auchnacloich Pier D 7
50 Auchnacraig D 4
55 Auchnadaull L 5
52 Auchnafree D 3
56 Auchnagallin F 6
58 Auchnagatt C 7
46 Auchnaha A 4
57 Auchnahannet G 5
56 Auchnahillin F 3
42 Auchnotteroch F 1
59 Aucholzie H 1
51 Auchrioch E 10
57 Auchroisk G 6
59 Auchronie J 2
52 Auchterarder F 4
55 Auchteraw J 7
53 Auchterderran H 7
53 Auchterhouse C 8
53 Auchtermuchty F 7
54 Auchterneed D 8
57 Auchterteang G 5
53 Auchtertool H 7
51 Auchtertyre, Central E 10
56 Auchtertye, Grampian D 7
55 Auchtertyre, Highland G 2
52 Auchtoo E 1
61 Auckingill B 12
36 Auckley G 4
58 Auckmair E 1
35 Audenshaw G 8
30 Audlem F 5
30 Audley E 6
25 Audley End L 6
58 Auds A 4
36 Aughton, Humber. C 5
34 Aughton, Lancs. G 3
39 Aughton, Lancs. H 8
32 Aughton, S. Yorks. B 2
16 Aughton, Wilts. H 3
53 Auldallan A 8
56 Auldearn D 5
21 Aulden G 10
43 Auldgirth C 10
49 Auldhame A 8
47 Auldhouse D 11
58 Auldtown B 3
58 Auldtown of Carnousie C 4
52 Aulich A 1
32 Ault Hucknall D 2
55 Ault-a-chruinn H 3
60 Aultanrynie D 4
60 Aultbea G 1
54 Aultdearg C 7
56 Aultfearn E 1
54 Aultgowrie E 8
54 Aultgrishan A 1
54 Aultguish Inn C 7
58 Aulthash B 1
61 Aultiphurst A 8
58 Aultmore B 1
57 Aultnagoire G 1
56 Aultnamain Inn B 2
57 Aultnancaber H 5
55 Aultnaslat J 5
58 Aulton E 3
59 Aultonrea H 1
57 Aundorach H 5
6 Aunk F 4
24 Aunsby B 1
15 Aust E 9
17 Austenwood E 10
36 Austerfield H 4
22 Austrey B 6
39 Austwick H 10
33 Authorpe B 11
33 Authorpe Row C 12
16 Avebury G 2
18 Aveley F 6
15 Avening E 12
32 Averham E 5
5 Aveton Gifford L 6
57 Avielochan H 5
57 Aviemore H 4
46 Avinagillan C 3
16 Avington, Berks. G 5
9 Avington, Hants. C 7
56 Avoch D 3
16 Avon F 1
15 Avon, Co. F 9
23 Avon Dassett G 7
48 Avonbridge B 2
15 Avonmouth F 8
5 Avonwick K 6
8 Awbridge D 5
42 Awhirk F 2
15 Awkley F 9
6 Awliscombe F 5
15 Awre D 10
32 Awsworth F 2
7 Axbridge A 8
9 Axford, Hants. B 7
16 Axford, Wilts. G 3
6 Axminster F 6
6 Axmouth G 6
40 Aycliffe C 3
45 Aydon F 8
15 Aylburton D 9
44 Ayle H 5
6 Aylesbeare G 4
17 Aylesbury C 9
37 Aylesby F 9
4 Aylescott D 5
10 Aylesford B 6
11 Aylsham C 11
23 Aylestone B 9
26 Aylmerton B 5
26 Aylsham C 5
15 Aylton A 9
21 Aymestrey F 9
16 Aynho A 6
18 Ayot St. Lawrence B 2
18 Ayot St. Peter B 2
47 Ayr G 8
39 Aysgarth F 12
6 Ayshford E 4
38 Ayside G 6
23 Ayston B 12
18 Aythorpe Roding B 6
49 Ayton C 11
40 Azerley H 3
5 Babbacombe J 8
30 Babbinswood G 2
7 Babcary C9
13 Bw C 11
29 Babell C 11
7 Babington A 10
25 Babraham K 6
32 Babworth B 4
28 Bachau B 4
63 Back C 6
55 Back of Keppcoh L 1
57 Backaland B 3
64 Backaskaill A 3
38 Backbarrow G 6
58 Backburn D 3
12 Backe E 6
58 Backfolds B 8
30 Backford C 3
30 Backford Cross C 3
58 Backhill, Grampian D 5
58 Backhill, Grampian F 5
58 Backhill, Grampian D 7
58 Backhill of Clackriach C 7
58 Backhill of Fortree D 7
59 Backhill of Trustach H 4
61 Backies F 8
53 Backmuir of New Gilston F 9
15 Backwell G 8
45 Backworth F 11
18 Bacon End B 6
26 Baconsthorpe B 4
15 Bacton, Heref. & Worcs. A 7
26 Bacton, Norfolk B 6
27 Bacton, Suffolk J 3
35 Bacup E 7
54 Badachro B 2
61 Badanloch Lodge D 8
54 Badavanich D 5
16 Badbury F 3
23 Badby F 9
60 Badcall, Highland G 2
60 Badcall, Loch Inchard, Highland B 4
22 Baddersley Clinton E 5
31 Baddeley Green E 8
22 Baddesley Ensor B 6
60 Baddidarach E 2
15 Baddington B 12
56 Baddock D 4
58 Badenyon F 1
7 Badford Peverell G 10
22 Badger B 1
10 Badger's Mount B 4
15 Badgeworth B 12
7 Badgworth A 7
55 Badicaul G 1
27 Badingham H 6
60 Badintagairt F 5
11 Badlesmere C 9
60 Badluarach G 2
60 Badnabay C 3
60 Badnagyle F 2
57 Badnambiast M 3
56 Badnonan F 5
60 Badrallach G 2
22 Badsey H 4
9 Badshot Lea A 10
36 Badsworth F 2
27 Badwell Ash H 3
33 Bag Enderby C 10
7 Bagber E 11
40 Bagby G 5
16 Bagendon C 1
29 Bagillt C 11
23 Baginton E 7
13 Baglan H 10
30 Bagley G 3
31 Bagnal E 8
16 Bagnor G 5
17 Bagshot, Surrey H 10
16 Bagshot, Wilts. H 4
15 Bagstone F 10
26 Bagthorpe, Norf. B 1
32 Bagthorpe, Notts. E 2
23 Bagworth A 8
15 Bagwy Llydiart B 8
35 Baildon C 10
46 Baile Boidheach B 2
50 Baile Mor F 1
57 Bailebeag H 1
44 Baileyhead E 3
44 Bailiehill D 1
47 Baillieston C 11
58 Bailliesward D 2
39 Bainbridge F 11
58 Bainshole D 4
24 Bainton, Cambs. E 2
37 Bainton, Humberside B 7
44 Bairnkine B 5
18 Baker Street F 6
18 Baker's End B 4
44 Bakethin D 4
31 Bakewell C 10
29 Bala G 8
52 Balado G 6
63 Balallan E 4
50 Balarumindubh H 1
57 Balavil J 8
57 Balbeg G 1
52 Balbeggie D 6
58 Balbithan F 5
56 Balblair, Highland E 1
56 Balblair, Highland C 3
43 Balcary G 9
21 Balchedre C 8
58 Belchers B 4
60 Balchladich D 2
56 Balchraggan F 1
58 Balchrick B 3
10 Balcombe E 2
53 Balcurvie G 8
39 Balder Head C 11
40 Baldersby G 4
40 Baldersby St. James G 4
34 Balderstone D 5
30 Balderton D 2
53 Baldinnie F 9
25 Baldock M 3
53 Baldovie D 9
38 Baldrine G 2
11 Baldslow G 7
38 Baldwin G 2
44 Baldwinholme H 2
30 Baldwins Gate F 6
26 Bale B 3
58 Balearn B 8
48 Balerno C 4
59 Balfeith K 5
59 Balfield K 3
64 Balfour C 3
47 Balfron A 10
58 Balgaveny D 4
43 Balgerran E 8
52 Balgonar H 5
58 Balgove D 6
57 Balgowan K 2
62 Balgown A 3
53 Balgray C 9
43 Balgrayhill C 12
47 Balgrochan B 11
54 Balgy D 2
52 Balhaldie G 3
58 Balhalgardy E 5
18 Balham G 3
53 Balharry C 7
64 Baliasta A 8
61 Baligill A 8
56 Balintore, Highland B 4
53 Balintore, Tayside A 7
56 Balintraid C 3
57 Balintuim K 7
52 Balintyre B 2
40 Balk E 5
53 Balkeerie C 8
36 Balkholme D 6
42 Balkissock C 2
30 Ball G 2
16 Ball Hill H 5
38 Ballabeg H 1
38 Ballacannell G 2
38 Ballacarnane Beg G 1
57 Ballachlaggan K 8
59 Ballachrosk H 1
38 Ballacraine G 1
38 Ballacuberagh G 2
43 Ballaggan B 9
38 Ballajora G 3
38 Ballakaigan H 1
38 Ballaleigh G 1
42 Ballantrae C 2
63 Ballantrushal B 5
19 Ballards Gore E 9
38 Ballasalla, I.o.M. F 2
38 Ballasalla, I.o.M. H 1
59 Ballater H 1
38 Ballaugh G 2
57 Ballcorah G 7
49 Ballencrieff B 7
46 Ballianlay C 5
50 Balliemore E 5
38 Ballig G 1
52 Balikinrain Castle H 1
51 Ballimcanoch F 7
51 Ballimore F 12
56 Ballindalloch F 7
53 Ballindean D 7
27 Ballingdon L 2
17 Ballinger Com. D 10
15 Ballingham A 9
52 Ballingry G 6
57 Ballinluig, Highland G 6
52 Ballinluig, Tayside B 5
57 Ballintean J 4
52 Ballintuim B 6
42 Ballminnoch E 4
56 Balloan E 2
56 Balloch, Highland E 3
47 Balloch, Strathclyde A 9
59 Ballochan H 3
42 Ballochbroe A 4
42 Ballochdoan D 2
42 Ballochdowan D 2
58 Ballochford D 1
46 Ballochgoy C 6
42 Ballochmorrie C 3
46 Ballochroy D 2
59 Ballogie H 3
9 Balls Cross D 11
10 Ball's Green D 4
50 Ballygown C 2
50 Ballymeanoch H 5
55 Balmacara G 2
43 Balmaclellan D 7
52 Balmacneil B 5
53 Balmacolm F 8
62 Balmacquien A 4
43 Balmae G 7
51 Balmaha H 11
50 Balmaneach D 2
43 Balmeanach G 7
58 Balmedie F 7
53 Balmerino E 8
8 Balmerlawn F 5
54 Balmore, Highland F 7
62 Balmore, Skye, Highland D 2
47 Balmore, Strathclyde B 11
52 Balmore, Tayside A 4
56 Balmuchy B 4
53 Balmule H 7
53 Balmullo E 9
56 Balmungie D 3
59 Balnaboth K 1
56 Balnabruaich C 3
56 Balnabual E 3
61 Balnacoil F 8
54 Balnacra E 3
56 Balnacraig F 1
56 Balnafoich F 2
56 Balnagall B 4
56 Balnageith D 6
59 Balnagowan G 2
52 Balnaguard B 4
56 Balnaguisich C 2
55 Balnain G 8
60 Balnakeil A 5
62 Balnaknock B 3
56 Balnapaling C 4
59 Balquharn L 2
51 Balquhidder E 12
22 Balsall E 6
22 Balsall Common D 6
23 Balscote H 7
25 Balsham K 7
64 Baltasound A 8
30 Balterley E 6
42 Baltersan E 5
32 Balterton E 5
58 Balthangie C 6
7 Baltonsborough C 8
50 Balure C 6
58 Balvack F 4
56 Balvaird D 1
58 Balvenie C 1
50 Balvicar F 5
55 Balvraid, Highland H 2
56 Balvraid, Highland F 4
34 Bamber Bridge E 4
18 Bamber's Green B 6
45 Bamburgh D 12
53 Bamff B7
48 Bamflatt F 3
31 Bamford B 10
39 Bampton, Cumbria C 7
6 Bampton, Devon D 3
16 Bampton, Oxon. D 4
39 Bampton Grange C 7
55 Banavie M 5
23 Banbury H 8
13 Bancffosfelen F 8
59 Banchory, Grampian G 7
59 Banchory, Grampian H 4
13 Bancycapel E 7
12 Bancyfelin E 6
13 Banc-c-ffordd C 7
53 Bandirran House D 7
58 Banff A 4
28 Bangor C 5
30 Bangor-Is-coed F 3
27 Banham G 4
8 Bank, Hants. E 4
21 Bank, Powys A 8
35 Bank Newton B 8
21 Bank Street F 11
43 Bankend, Dumf & Gall E 11
48 Bankend, Strathclyde F 1
47 Bankfoot, Strathclyde B 7
52 Bankfoot, Tayside D 5
47 Bankglen H 11
58 Bankhead, Grampian F 6
59 Bankhead, Grampian G 4
45 Bankhead, Northumb. B 8
47 Bankhead, Strathclyde D 8
48 Bankhead, Strathclyde E 3
47 Banknock B 12
44 Banks, Cumb. F 4
34 Banks, Lancs. E 3
43 Bankshill C 12
26 Banningham C 5
19 Bannister Green B 7
52 Bannockburn H 3
10 Banstead B 1
5 Bantham L 5
47 Banton B 12
15 B anwell H 7
11 Bapchild B 8
50 Barachandroman E 4
47 Barassie F 8
50 Baravullin D 6
56 Barbaraville C 3
31 Barber Booth B 9
47 Barbieston H 9
39 Barbon G 8
50 Barbreck House G 5
4 Barbrook A 6
23 Barby E 9
51 Barcaldine C 7
43 Barcaple F 7
22 Barchesten H 6
47 Barclaugh G 9
43 Barclosh E 9
10 Barcombe G 3
10 Barcombe Cross F 3
40 Barden F 2
35 Barden Scale A 9
42 Bardennoch B 6
64 Bardister C 7
61 Bardnabeinne G 7
33 Bardney C 8
23 Bardon A 8
44 Bardon Mill G 6
47 Bardowie B 10
47 Bardrainney B 8
38 Bardsea H 5
35 Bardsey C 12
27 Bardwell H 2
49 Barelees F 11
21 Barewood G 9
46 Barfad B 4
26 Barford, Norfolk E 4
22 Barford, War. F 6
16 Barford St. John A 5
8 Barford St. Martin C 2
16 Barford St. Michael A 5
11 Barfreston C 11
42 Bargaly E 5
14 Bargoed D 5
42 Bargrennan D 4
51 Barguillean Farm E 7
25 Barham, Cambs. H 2
11 Barham, Kent C 10
27 Barham, Suffolk K 4
43 Barharrow F 7
24 Barholm D 2
44 Barhough H 5
23 Barkby A 9
23 Barkby Thorpe A 9
32 Barkestone le Vale G 5
17 Barkham G 9
18 Barking, London E 5
27 Barking, Suffolk K 4
27 Barking Tye K 4
35 Barkisland E 9
32 Barkston, Lincs. F 6
36 Barkston, N. Yorks. D 3
25 Barkway M 5
31 Barlaston F 7
43 Barlay D 7
32 Barlborough C 2
36 Barlby D 4
23 Barlestone B 8
25 Barley, Herts. L 5
35 Barley, Lancs. C 7
45 Barley Mow H 11
45 Barleyhill H 8
23 Barleythorpe A 11
19 Barling E 9
32 Barlow, Derby C 1
36 Barlow, N. Yorks. D 4
45 Barlow, Tyne & Wear G 9
36 Barmby Moor B 5
36 Barmby on the Marsh D 5
26 Barmer B 1
49 Barmoor Castle E 12
49 Barmoor Ridge E 12
20 Barmouth A 2
40 Barmpton C 3
37 Barmston A 9
43 Barmurrie D 7
51 Barnacarry H 7
24 Barnack E 2
23 Barnacle D 7
51 Barnaline F 7
39 Barnard Castle C 12
25 Barnardiston K 8
43 Barnbarroch F 9
36 Barnburgh G 3
26 Barnby F 8
36 Barnby Dun F 4
32 Barnby in the Willows E 6
32 Barnby Moor B 4
42 Barncorkrie H 2
18 Barnes F 2
10 Barness Street C 5
18 Barnet D 3
37 Barnetby le Wold F 8
26 Barney B 3
27 Barnham, Suffolk G 2
9 Barnham, W. Sussex F 11
26 Barnham Broom E 4
59 Barnhead L 4
56 Barnhill D 7
42 Barnhills D 1
40 Barningham, Dur. D 1
27 Barningham, Suff. H 3
37 Barnoldby le Beck G 10
35 Barnoldswick C 7

9 Barns Green C 12
16 Barnsley, Glos. D 2
35 Barnsley, S. Yorks. F 12
4 Barnstaple C 4
18 Barnston, Essex B 6
30 Barnston, Merseyside B 1
32 Barnstone G 4
22 Barnt Green E 4
30 Barnton C 5
25 Barnwell All Saints G 2
25 Barnwell St. Andrew G 2
15 Barnwood C 11
21 Barons' Cross G 10
47 Barr, Dumf. & Gall. H 12
43 Barr, Dumf. & Gall. B 9
42 Barr, Strathclyde B 4
58 Barra Castle E 5
42 Barrachan G 4
50 Barrachrail E 5
63 Barraglom D 3
45 Barrasford F 7
50 Barravullin G 5
38 Barregarow G 2
47 Barrhead D 10
42 Barrhill C 3
25 Barrington, Cambs. K 5
7 Barrington, Som. D 7
2 Barripper F 3
55 Barrisdale J 3
47 Barrmill D 8
61 Barrock A 11
34 Barrow, Lancs. C 6
23 Barrow, Leics. A 12
21 Barrow, Salop. B 12
7 Barrow, Som. C 10
27 Barrow, Suffolk J 1
15 Barrow Gurney G 8
37 Barrow Haven E 8
32 Barrow Hill C 1
32 Barrow-in-Furness H 5
34 Barrow Nook G 3
7 Barrow Street C 11
37 Barrow-upon-Humber E 8
32 Barrow-upon-Soar H 3
31 Barrow-upon-Trent G 12
45 Barrowburn B 7
32 Barrowby G 6
41 Barrowcliff F 10
23 Barrowden B 12
35 Barrowford C 7
30 Barrows Green D 5
51 Barrs D 8
14 Barry, S. Glam. G 4
53 Barry, Tayside D 10
23 Barsby A 10
26 Barsham F 7
22 Barston D 5
21 Bartestree H 11
58 Barthol Chapel D 6
30 Barthomley E 6
49 Bartlehill E 10
8 Bartley E 4
25 Bartlow L 7
7 Barton, Avon A 7
25 Barton, Cambs. K 5
30 Barton, Cheshire E 3
39 Barton, Cumbria C 7
5 Barton, Devon J 8
16 Barton, Glos. B 2
34 Barton, Lancs. C 4
34 Barton, Lancs. F 2
40 Barton, N. Yorks. D 3
22 Barton, War. G 4
24 Barton Bendish E 8
26 Barton Common C 7
15 Barton End E 11
17 Barton Hartshorn A 7
32 Barton in Fabis G 2
23 Barton-in-the-Beans B 7
25 Barton-le-Clay M 2
25 Barton Mills H 8
8 Barton-on-Sea G 4
16 Barton-on-the-Heath A 4
7 Barton St. David C 8
23 Barton Seagrave D 12
8 Barton Stacey B 6
4 Barton Town B 5
41 Barton-le-Street H 7
36 Barton-le-Willows A 5
31 Barton-under-
Needwood H 10
37 Barton-upon-Humber E 8
35 Barugh F 11
63 Barvas B 5
25 Barway H 6
23 Barwell B 8
7 Barwick E 9
36 Barwick in Elmet C 2
30 Baschurch H 3
23 Basecote F 7
31 Basford Green E 8
34 Bashall Eaves C 6
8 Bashley F 4
17 Basildon, Berks F 7
19 Basildon, Essex E 7
9 Basing A 8
9 Basingstoke A 7
31 Baslow C 11
7 Bason Bridge B 7
14 Bassaleg F 6
49 Bassendean E 9
38 Bassenthwaite B 5
4 Basset's Cross F 4
8 Bassett D 5
22 Bassett's Pole B 5
25 Bassingbourn L 4
23 Bassingfield F 3
32 Bassingham D 6
33 Bassingthorpe G 7
64 Basta B 7
24 Baston D 2
26 Bastwick D 7
18 Batchworth Heath E 1
7 Batcombe, Dorset F 9
7 Batcombe, Som. B 10
30 Bate Heath B 5
15 Bath H 10
15 Bathampton H 11
15 Bathealton D 4
15 Batheaston G 11
15 Bathford H 11
48 Bathgate B 3
32 Bathley D 5
3 Bathpool, Corn. B 10
6 Bathpool, Som. D 6
7 Bathway A 9
35 Batley E 11
16 Batsford A 3
40 Battersby D 6
18 Battersea F 3
27 Battisford K 4
27 Battisford Tye K 3
10 Battle, E. Sussex F 6
34 Battle, Powys A 3
7 Battleborough A 7
21 Battlefield A 10
19 Battlesbridge D 8
17 Battlesden A 10
6 Battleton C 3
8 Battramsley F 5
9 Batt's Corner B 9
58 Bauds of Cullen A 2
22 Baughton H 2
17 Baughurst H 7
59 Baulds H 4
16 Baulking E 4
33 Baumber C 9
16 Baunton D 1
8 Baverstock C 2
26 Bawburgh E 5
26 Bawdeswell C 3
7 Bawdrip B 7
27 Bawdsey L 6
32 Bawtry A 4
34 Baxenden E 6
22 Baxterley B 6
9 Baybridge D 7
38 Baycliff H 5
16 Baydon F 4
18 Bayford, Herts. C 3
7 Bayford, Som. C 10
39 Bayles A 9
27 Baylham K 4
16 Baynards' Green A 6
21 Bayston Hill B 10
21 Bayton E 12
15 Beach, Avon G 10
50 Beach, Highland B 5
23 Beachampton H 11
24 Beachamwell E 8
15 Beachley E 9
19 Beacon End A 9
8 Beacon Hill, Dor. G 1
9 Beacon Hill, Surrey B 10
17 Beacon's Bottom E 9
17 Beaconsfield E 10
63 Beacravik H 2
40 Beadlam G 6
45 Beadnell D 12
4 Beaford D 4
45 Beal, Northumb. B 12
36 Beal, N. Yorks. E 3
55 Bealachasan H 3
7 Beaminster F 8
45 Beamish H 10
35 Beamsley B 9
10 Bean A 5
15 Beanacre H 12
45 Beanley A 9
4 Beara Moor D 4
44 Bearbridge G 6
6 Beare F 3
10 Beare Green D 1
45 Bearl G 9
22 Bearley F 5
50 Bearnus C 1
40 Bearpark A 3
47 Bearsden B 10
11 Bearsted C 7
8 Bearwood F 2
6 Beasley B 3
43 Beattock A 11
18 Beauchamp Roding C 6
32 Beauchief B 1
14 Beaufort C 5
8 Beaulieu F 5
56 Beauly E 1
28 Beaumaris C 5
44 Beaumont, Cumb. G 2
19 Beaumont, Essex A 11
40 Beaumont Hill C 3
22 Beausale E 6
9 Beauworth C 7
4 Beaworthy F 3
19 Beazley End A 7
30 Bebington B 2
45 Bebside E 11
26 Beccles F 7
34 Becconsall E 3
39 Beck Foot F 8
41 Beck Hole E 8
25 Beck Row H 8
38 Beck Side G 5
22 Beckbury B 1
18 Beckenham G 4
38 Beckermet D 3
43 Beckfoot G 11
16 Beckford A 1
16 Beckhampton G 2
32 Beckingham, Lincs. E 6
32 Beckingham, Notts. A 5
7 Beckington A 11
8 Beckley, Hants. F 4
16 Beckley, Oxon. C 6
11 Beckley, E. Sussex F 7
35 Beckwithshaw B 11
18 Becontree E 5
40 Bedale F 3
40 Bedburn B 1
7 Bedchester D 12
14 Beddau F 4
28 Beddgelert E 5
10 Beddingham G 3
18 Beddington G 3
27 Bedfield J 5
25 Bedford K 2
25 Bedfordshire, Co. K 2
9 Bedhampton E 8
27 Bedingfield H 5
35 Bedlam A 11
45 Bedlington E 10
14 Bedlinog D 4
15 Bedminster G 9
17 Bedmond D 11
31 Bednall H 8
49 Bedrule H 8
49 Bedshiel D 9
21 Bedstone E 9
14 Bedwas E 5
14 Bedwellty D 5
23 Bedworth C 7
23 Beeby A 10
9 Beech, Hants. B 8
31 Beech, Staffs. F 7
17 Beech Hill, Berks. H 8
39 Beech Hill, Cumb. E 7
34 Beech Hill, Manchester F 4
16 Beechingstoke H 2
16 Beedon F 6
16 Beedon Hill F 6
37 Beeford B 9
31 Beeley C 11
37 Beelsby G 9
17 Beenham G 7
2 Beeny B 1
6 Beer, Devon G 6
7 Beer, Somerset C 7
7 Beer Hackett E 9
7 Beercrocombe D 7
5 Beesands M 7
33 Beesby B 11
5 Beeson L 7
25 Beeston, Beds. K 3
30 Beeston, Cheshire D 4
26 Beeston, Norfolk D 2
32 Beeston, Notts. G 3
35 Beeston, W. Yorks. D 11
26 Beeston Regis A 5
43 Beeswing E 10
39 Beetham G 7
26 Beetley D 3
14 Began F 5
16 Begbroke C 5
24 Begdale E 6
12 Begelly F 5
21 Beggar's Bush F 8
21 Beguildy D 7
26 Beighton, Norf. E 7
32 Beighton, S. Yorks. B 2
47 Beith D 8
11 Bekesbourne C 10
26 Belaugh D 6
22 Belbroughton D 3
27 Belchamp Otten L 1
27 Belchamp St. Paul L 1
27 Belchamp Walter L 1
58 Belcherrie D 1
33 Belchford C 10
21 Belford C 12
45 Belford Mains C 12
58 Belhelvie F 7
58 Belhinnie E 2
18 Bell Bar C 3
35 Bell Busk B 7
22 Bell Heath D 3
58 Bellabeg F 1
50 Bellanoch H 5
36 Bellasize D 6
35 Belle Vue E 12
33 Belleau B 11
56 Bellehiglash F 7
40 Bellerby F 1
5 Bellever H 5
49 Bellhaven B 9
17 Bellingdon D 10
45 Bellingham E 7
46 Belloch F 2
46 Bellochantuy F 2
10 Bells Yew Green D 5
42 Bellsbank A 5
45 Bellshill, Northumb. C 12
47 Bellshill, Strathclyde C 12
48 Bellspool F 4
48 Bellsquarry C 3
42 Bellymore C 3
56 Belmaduthy D 2
24 Belmesthorpe D 1
34 Belmont, Lancs. F 5
47 Belmont, Strathclyde G 8
64 Belmont, Shetland Is. B 8
47 Belmore A 7
58 Belnacraig F 1
3 Belowda D 7
31 Belper E 11
31 Belper Lane End E 11
45 Belsay E 9
27 Belstead L 4
47 Belston G 9
4 Belstone F 5
4 Belstone Corner F 5
34 Belthorn E 6
11 Beltinge A 10
44 Beltingham G 6
32 Belton, Leics. H 2
23 Belton, Leics. B 11
36 Belton, Humber. F 6
32 Belton, Lincs. F 6
26 Belton, Norfolk E 8
32 Belvoir G 5
9 Bembridge G 8
49 Bemersyde F 8
8 Bemerton C 3
41 Bempton H 12
61 Ben Armine Lodge E 7
63 Ben Casgro D 5
27 Benacre G 8
57 Benalder Lodge L 1
43 Benbruie B 8
48 Bendameer A 5
50 Benderloch D 6
54 Bendronaig Lodge F 4
11 Benenden E 7
42 Benfield E 5
27 Benfield Green J 7
45 Benfieldside H 9
43 Bengall D 12
26 Bengate C 6
22 Bengeworth H 4
59 Benholm K 5
36 Beningbrough A 3
18 Benington, Herts. B 3
33 Benington, Lincs. E 11
33 Benington Sea End F 11
28 Benllech B 4
60 Benmore Lodge F 4
5 Bennacott G 2
46 Bennecarrigan G 4
33 Benniworth B 9
10 Benover C 6
17 Benson E 7
47 Benston H 10
59 Bent K 4
45 Benthall D 12
15 Bentham C 12
59 Benthoul G 5
9 Bentley, Hants. B 9
37 Bentley, Humber. D 8
36 Bentley, S. Yorks. G 3
22 Bentley, War. C 6
22 Bentley Heath D 5
4 Benton B 5
46 Benton Polliwilline H 2
44 Bentpath D 2
24 Bentwick F 4
4 Bentwitchen C 6
9 Bentworth B 8
42 Beoch, Dumf. & Gall. E 2
42 Beoch, Strathclyde B 6
22 Beoley E 4
55 Beoraidberg K 1
9 Bepton D 10
18 Berden A 5
5 Bere Alston J 3
5 Bere Ferrers J 3
7 Bere Regis G 11
2 Berepper G 4
26 Bergh Apton E 6
17 Berinsfield E 7
15 Berkeley D 10
17 Berkhamstead C 10
7 Berkley A 11
16 Berkshire, Co. F 5
22 Berkswell D 6
18 Bermondsey F 3
62 Bernisdale C 3
17 Berrick Salome E 7
61 Berriedale E 10
38 Berrier B 6
21 Berriew B 7
49 Berrington,
Northumb. E 12
21 Berrington, Salop. B 10
49 Berringtonlaw E 12
6 Berrow A 6
22 Berrow Green F 1
4 Berry Cross D 3
4 Berry Down Cross B 4
12 Berry Hill, Dyfed C 4
15 Berry Hill, Glos. C 9
5 Berry Pomeroy K 7
58 Berryhillock B 2
4 Berrynarbor A 4
18 Berry's Green H 4
43 Berryscaur B 12
59 Berrysloch H 3
29 Bersham E 12
20 Berthddu H 4
7 Berwick, Dorset G 8
10 Berwick, E. Sussex H 4
16 Berwick Bassett G 2
45 Berwick Hill F 10
8 Berwick St. James B 2
8 Berwick St. John D 1
7 Berwick St. Leonard C 12
49 Berwick-upon-Tweed D 12
29 Berwyn F 11
32 Bescaby G 5
34 Bescar F 3
32 Besford H 3
36 Bessacarr G 4
10 Bessels Green C 4
16 Bessels Leigh D 5
37 Bessingby A 9
26 Bessingham B 4
10 Best Beech Hill E 5
26 Besthorpe, Norf. F 4
32 Besthorpe, Notts. D 5
37 Beswick B 8
18 Betchworth C 1
20 Bethania, Dyfed F 1
28 Bethania, Gwynedd F 6
28 Bethanie E 5
28 Bethel, Gwynedd C 3
28 Bethel, Gwynedd D 5
29 Bethel, Gwynedd F 9
11 Bethersden D 8
12 Bethesda, Dyfed E 4
28 Bethesda, Gwynedd D 6
13 Bethlehem D 10
18 Bethnal Green F 4
30 Betley E 6
10 Betsham A 5
11 Betteshanger C 11
7 Bettiscombe F 7
30 Bettisfield G 3
30 Betton G 5
14 Bettws F 2
20 Bettws Bledrws G 2
12 Bettws Evan B 6
15 Bettws Newydd D 7
61 Bettyhill B 7
13 Betws F 9
21 Betws Cedewain C 7
28 Betws Garmon D 5
29 Betws Gwerfil Goch F 9
29 Betws-y-coed E 7
29 Betws-yn-Rhos C 8
12 Beulah, Dyfed B 6
20 Beulah, Powys G 5
32 Bevercotes C 4
37 Beverley C 8
15 Beverstone E 11
15 Bevington E 10
38 Bewaldeth B 4
44 Bewcastle F 4
22 Bewdley E 1
35 Bewerley A 10
37 Bewholme B 9
49 Bewlie G 8
10 Bexhill G 6
18 Bexley F 5
18 Bexleyheath F 5
24 Bexwell E 7
27 Beyton J 2
27 Beyton Green J 2
16 Bibury C 2
17 Bicester B 7
22 Bickenhill D 5
24 Bicker B 3
34 Bickerstaffe G 3
30 Bickerton, Ches. E 4
45 Bickerton, Northumb. C 8
36 Bickerton, N. Yorks. B 2
4 Bickingcott C 6
4 Bickington, Devon C 4
5 Bickington, Devon H 7
6 Bickleigh, Devon E 3
5 Bickleigh, Devon J 4
4 Bickleton C 4
30 Bickley Moss E 4
19 Bicknacre D 8
6 Bicknoller B 5
11 Bicknor B 7
8 Bickton, Hants. E 3
21 Bicton,
Heref. & Worc. F 10
21 Bicton, Salop D 8
21 Bicton, Salop A 10
10 Bidborough D 4
11 Biddenden D 7
11 Biddenden Green D 7
25 Biddenham K 1
15 Biddestone G 11
7 Biddisham A 7
23 Biddlesden H 9
45 Biddlestone B 8
31 Biddulph D 7
31 Biddulph Moor D 7
4 Bideford C 3
22 Bidford-on-Avon G 4
36 Bielby C 5
59 Bieldside G 6
8 Bierley, I.o.W. H 6
35 Bierley, W. Yorks. D 10
17 Bierton C 9
43 Big Corlae B 7
54 Big Sand B 1
5 Bigbury L 5
5 Bigbury-on-Sea L 5
37 Bigby F 8
34 Biggar, Lancs. A 1
48 Biggar, Strathclyde F 3
48 Biggarshiels Mains E 3
31 Biggin, Derby E 11
31 Biggin, Derby D 10
36 Biggin, N. Yorks. D 3
18 Biggin Hill H 4
25 Biggleswade L 3
9 Bighton C 7
9 Bignor E 11
64 Bigton F 7
3 Bilberry D 7
32 Bilborough F 3
6 Bilbrook B 4
36 Bilbrough C 3
32 Bilby B 4
27 Bildeston K 3
3 Billacott A 9
19 Billericay D 7
32 Billesdon B 10
22 Billesley F 5
24 Billingborough B 2
34 Billinge G 4
27 Billingford G 5
26 Billingford C 3
40 Billingham C 5
33 Billinghay E 8
36 Billingley G 2
9 Billinghurst C 12
21 Billingsley D 12
17 Billington, Beds. B 10
34 Billington, Lancs. D 6
26 Billockby D 7
40 Billy Row A 2
34 Bilsborrow C 4
33 Bilsby C 11
9 Bilsham F 11
11 Bilsington E 9
15 Bilson Green C 9
32 Bilsthorpe D 4
48 Bilston, Lothian C 5
22 Bilston, W. Midlands B 3
23 Bilstone B 7
11 Bilting C 9
45 Bilton, Northumb. B 10
37 Bilton, Humber. D 9
36 Bilton, N. Yorks. B 3
23 Bilton, W. Midlands E 8

45 Bilton Banks .... B 10
64 Bimbister .... C 2
37 Binbrook .... H 10
7 Bincombe .... H 10
61 Bindal .... H 9
7 Binegar .... A 9
17 Binfield .... G 9
17 Binfield Heath .... F 8
45 Bingfield .... F 8
32 Bingham .... F 4
7 Bingham's Melcombe . F 11
35 Bingley .... C 10
26 Binham .... B 3
8 Binley .... A 6
48 Binniehill .... B 1
40 Binsoe .... G 3
9 Binstead .... G 7
9 Binsted .... B 9
22 Binton .... G 5
26 Bintree .... C 3
21 Binweston .... B 8
19 Birch .... B 9
19 Birch Green .... B 9
31 Birch Vale .... B 8
26 Bircham Newton .... B 1
26 Bircham Tofts .... B 1
18 Birchanger .... B 5
21 Bircher .... F 10
57 Birchfield .... G 5
13 Birchgrove .... G 10
11 Birchington .... A 11
31 Birchover .... D 10
32 Bircotes .... A 3
22 Bird End .... C 4
25 Birdbrook .... L 8
9 Birdham .... F 9
23 Birdingbury .... E 8
15 Birdlip .... C 12
36 Birdsall .... A 6
22 Birdsgreen .... D 1
7 Birdsmoor Gate .... F 7
47 Birdston .... B 11
35 Birdwell .... G 12
15 Birdwood .... B 10
49 Birgham .... E 10
34 Birkacre .... F 4
40 Birkby .... E 3
34 Birkdale .... F 2
30 Birkenhead .... A 2
58 Birkenhills .... C 5
47 Birkenshaw, Strathclyde .... D 12
35 Birkenshaw, W. Yorks. .... D 10
59 Birkhall .... H 1
49 Birkhill, Borders .... E 8
48 Birkhill, Borders .... H 5
53 Birkhill, Tayside .... D 8
36 Birkin .... D 3
44 Birks .... E 6
43 Birkshaw .... C 9
21 Birley .... G 10
10 Birling, Kent .... B 5
45 Birling, Northumb. .... B 10
25 Birlingham .... H 3
22 Birmingham .... D 5
52 Birnam .... C 5
59 Birse .... H 3
59 Birsemore .... H 3
23 Birstall, Leics. .... A 9
35 Birstall, W. Yorks. .... E 11
35 Birstwith .... A 11
24 Birthorpe .... B 2
48 Birthwood .... F 3
21 Birtley, Heref. & Worc. E 9
45 Birtley, Northumb. .... E 7
45 Birtley, Tyne & Wear G 11
15 Birts Street .... A 11
23 Bisbrooke .... B 12
4 Bish Mill .... C 6
17 Bisham .... F 9
22 Bishampton .... G 3
40 Bishop Auckland .... B 2
37 Bishop Burton .... C 7
40 Bishop Middleham .... B 3
40 Bishop Monkton .... H 3
33 Bishop Norton .... A 7
15 Bishop Sutton .... H 9
35 Bishop Thornton .... A 10
36 Bishop Wilton .... B 6
33 Bishopbridge .... A 7
47 Bishopbriggs .... B 11
56 Bishopmill .... C 8
16 Bishops Cannings .... H 2
21 Bishop's Castle .... D 8
7 Bishop's Caundle .... E 10
15 Bishop's Cleeve .... B 12
21 Bishop's Frome .... G 12
18 Bishop's Green .... B 6
6 Bishop's Hull .... D 5
23 Bishop's Itchington .... F 7
6 Bishop's Lydeard .... C 5
4 Bishop's Nympton .... D 6
30 Bishop's Offley .... G 6
18 Bishop's Stortford .... B 5
9 Bishop's Sutton .... C 7
22 Bishop's Tatchbrook .... F 6
4 Bishop's Tawton .... C 4
9 Bishop's Waltham .... D 7
22 Bishop's Wood .... A 2
11 Bishopsbourne .... C 10
5 Bishopsteignton .... H 8
8 Bishopstoke .... D 6
13 Bishopston .... H 9
17 Bishopstone, Bucks. .... C 9
10 Bishopstone, E. Sussex H 4
21 Bishopstone, Heref. & Worcs. .... H 9
8 Bishopstone, Wilts. .... C 2
16 Bishopstone, Wilts. .... F 3
7 Bishopstrow .... B 11
6 Bishopswood .... E 6
15 Bishopsworth .... G 9
36 Bishopthorpe .... B 4
40 Bishopton, Dur. .... C 4
47 Bishopton, Strathclyde B 9
15 Bishpool .... E 7
15 Bishton .... F 7
15 Bisley, Glos. .... D 12
17 Bisley, Surrey .... H 10
34 Bispham .... C 2
2 Bissoe .... E 5
8 Bisterne Close .... F 4
33 Bitchfield .... G 7
4 Biteford .... D 2
4 Bittadon .... B 4
5 Bittaford .... K 5
26 Bittering Street .... D 2
21 Bitterley .... E 11
8 Bitterne .... E 6
23 Bitteswell .... D 8
17 Bix .... F 8
64 Bixter .... D 7
23 Blaby .... B 9
16 Black Bourton .... D 4
54 Black Bridge .... C 7
45 Black Callerton .... F 10
42 Black Clauchrie .... C 4
51 Black Corries .... B 10
50 Black Croft .... D 6
4 Black Dog .... E 7
45 Black Heddon .... E 9
51 Black Mount .... C 10
19 Black Notley .... B 7
13 Black Pill .... H 9
4 Black Torrington .... E 3
43 Blackacre .... C 11
49 Blackadder Bank .... D 11
5 Blackawton .... L 7
6 Blackborough .... E 4
24 Blackborough End .... D 8
10 Blackboys .... F 4
31 Blackbrook, Derby. .... E 11
34 Blackbrook, Merseyside .... G 4
30 Blackbrook, Staffs. .... F 6
49 Blackburn, Borders .... D 8
44 Blackburn, Borders .... D 3
58 Blackburn, Grampian .... F 6
34 Blackburn, Lancs. .... D 5
48 Blackburn, Lothian .... C 3
48 Blackburn, Strathclyde G 2
43 Blackcraig .... D 8
4 Blackditch Cross .... E 6
54 Blackdog .... F 7
35 Blacker Hill .... G 12
8 Blackfield .... F 6
44 Blackford, Cumb. .... G 2
7 Blackford, Som. .... A 7
7 Blackford, Som .... D 10
52 Blackford, Tayside .... F 4
31 Blackfordby .... H 11
8 Blackgang .... H 6
40 Blackhall Colliery .... A 5
45 Blackhall Mill .... G 9
10 Blackham .... D 4
49 Blackhaugh .... E 7
19 Blackheath, Essex .... B 10
27 Blackheath, Suff. .... H 7
9 Blackheath, Surrey .... B 11
22 Blackheath, W. Midlands .... D 3
58 Blackhill, Grampian .... B 8
58 Blackhill, Grampian .... C 8
62 Blackhill, Highland .... C 3
58 Blackhilllock .... C 1
44 Blackhills, Dumf. & Gall. .... F 1
56 Blackhills, Grampian .... D 8
15 Blackhorse .... F 10
48 Blackhopebyre .... E 6
16 Blackland .... G 1
43 Blacklaw .... A 11
35 Blackley .... G 7
52 Blacklunans .... A 6
21 Blackmarstone .... H 10
14 Blackmill .... F 3
9 Blackmoor .... C 9
4 Blackmoor Gate .... B 5
18 Blackmore .... D 6
25 Blackmore End, Essex M 8
18 Blackmore End, Hertfordshire .... B 2
48 Blackness .... A 3
9 Blacknest .... B 9
35 Blacko .... C 7
43 Blackpark .... C 10
34 Blackpool .... C 2
44 Blackpool Gate .... E 4
48 Blackridge .... C 2
14 Blackrock, Gwent .... C 5
15 Blackrock, Gwent .... E 8
34 Blackrod .... F 5
43 Blackshaw .... E 11
35 Blackshaw Head .... D 8
27 Blacksmith's Cnr. .... M 3
10 Blackstone .... F 1
17 Blackthorn .... B 7
27 Blackthorpe .... J 2
36 Blacktoft .... E 6
59 Blacktop .... G 6
2 Blackwater, Corn. .... E 4
17 Blackwater, Hants. .... H 9
8 Blackwater, I.o.W. .... G 6
6 Blackwater, Som. .... E 6
27 Blackwater, Suff. .... H 8
46 Blackwaterfoot .... G 4
31 Blackwell, Derby .... C 10
32 Blackwell, Derby .... D 2
40 Blackwell, Durham .... D 3
22 Blackwell, Heref. & Worc. .... E 3
6 Blackwell, Som. .... D 4
22 Blackwell, War. .... H 6
43 Blackwood, Dumf. & Gall. .... C 10
14 Blackwood, Gwent .... E 5
47 Blackwood, Strathclyde .... E 12
31 Blackwood Hill .... E 8
30 Blacon .... C 2
42 Bladnoch .... F 5
16 Bladon .... C 5
13 Blaen Celyn .... B 7
14 Blaen Dyryn .... A 3
12 Blaenannerch .... B 6
28 Blaennau-Dolwyddelan E 6
28 Blaenau Ffestiniog .... F 6
14 Blaenavon .... C 6
14 Blaenawey .... B 6
12 Blaenffos .... C 5
14 Blaengarw .... E 2
14 Blaengavenny .... B 6
14 Blaengwrach .... D 2
14 Blaengwynfi .... E 2
20 Blaenpennal .... F 2
20 Blaenplwyf .... E 1
12 Blaenporth .... B 6
12 Blaenwaun .... D 6
13 Blaen-y-Coed .... D 7
14 Blaerhondda .... D 3
6 Blagdon Hill .... D 5
15 Blagdon .... H 8
55 Blaich .... M 4
50 Blain .... A 4
14 Blaina .... D 5
58 Blair .... E 6
52 Blair Atholl .... A 4
52 Blair Drummond .... G 2
52 Blairadam .... H 6
48 Blairburn .... A 3
58 Blairdaff .... F 4
52 Blairgowrie .... C 6
52 Blairhall .... H 5
52 Blairingone .... G 5
52 Blairlogie .... G 3
60 Blairmore, Highland .... B 3
47 Blairmore, Strathclyde A 7
47 Blairnairn .... A 8
57 Blairnmarrow .... H 8
47 Blairquhosh .... A 10
46 Blair's Ferry .... B 5
47 Blairskaith .... B 10
15 Blaisdon .... C 10
22 Blakebrook .... D 2
22 Blakedown .... D 2
49 Blakelaw .... F 10
21 Blakemere .... H 9
15 Blakeney, Glos. .... D 10
26 Blakeney, Norfolk .... A 3
30 Blakenhall, Ches. .... E 6
22 Blakenhall, W. Midlands .... B 3
22 Blakenhall Heath .... B 4
22 Blakeshall .... D 2
23 Blakesley .... G 9
45 Blanchland .... H 8
35 Bland Hill .... B 10
7 Blandford Forum .... E 12
7 Blandford St. Mary ... F 12
47 Blanefield .... A 10
33 Blankney .... D 8
51 Blar a'Chaoruinn .... A 8
50 Blaran .... F 6
51 Blarghour .... F 7
55 Blarmachfoldach, Highland .... M 5
51 Blarmachfoldach, Highland .... A 8
8 Blashford .... E 3
23 Blaston .... C 11
24 Blatherwycke .... F 1
38 Blawith .... F 5
27 Blaxhall .... J 7
36 Blaxton .... G 4
45 Blaydon .... G 10
7 Bleadon .... A 7
11 Blean .... B 10
33 Bleasby, Lincs. .... B 8
32 Bleasby, Notts. .... E 4
53 Blebocraigs .... F 9
21 Bleddfa .... F 7
16 Bledington .... B 3
17 Bledlow .... D 8
17 Bledlow Ridge .... D 9
4 Blegberry .... C 1
49 Blegbie .... C 7
39 Blencarn .... B 9
43 Blencogo .... G 12
9 Blendworth .... E 8
43 Blennerhasset .... G 12
16 Bletchingdon .... B 6
10 Bletchingley .... C 2
17 Bletchley, Bucks. .... A 9
30 Bletchley, Salop. .... G 5
12 Bletherston .... E 4
25 Bletsoe .... J 1
16 Blewbury .... F 6
26 Blickling .... C 5
32 Blidworth .... E 3
32 Blidworth Bottoms .... E 3
44 Blindburn .... B 6
38 Blindcrake .... B 4
10 Blindley Heath .... C 2
49 Blinkbonny .... F 11
3 Blisland .... B 8
22 Bliss Gate .... E 1
8 Blissford .... E 3
23 Blisworth .... G 10
31 Blithbury .... H 9
31 Blithford .... H 9
43 Blitterlees .... F 11
27 Blo Norton .... G 3
16 Blockley .... A 3
26 Blofield .... E 6
26 Blofield Corner .... D 6
43 Bloomfield, Dumf. & Gall. .... D 10
49 Bloomfield, Borders .... G 8
31 Blore .... E 10
31 Blounts Green .... G 9
16 Bloxham .... A 5
33 Bloxholm .... E 8
22 Bloxwich .... B 3
7 Bloxworth .... G 12
35 Blubberhouses .... B 10
2 Blue Anchor, Corn. .... D 6
6 Blue Anchor, Somerset .... B 4
13 Blue Anchor, W. Glam. .... G 9
10 Bluebell Hill .... B 6
60 Blughasary .... F 3
34 Blundellsands .... G 2
26 Blundeston .... F 8
25 Blunham .... K 3
16 Blunsdon St. Andrew .. E 2
22 Bluntington .... E 2
25 Bluntisham .... H 5
3 Blunts .... C 10
37 Blyborough .... H 7
27 Blyford .... H 7
22 Blymhill .... A 2
45 Blyth, Northumb. .... E 11
32 Blyth, Notts. .... B 3
48 Blyth Bridge .... E 4
31 Blyth Marsh .... F 8
27 Blythburgh .... H 7
36 Blyton .... H 6
53 Boarhills .... F 10
9 Boarhunt .... E 7
16 Boars Hill .... D 6
10 Boarshead .... E 4
17 Boarstall .... C 7
4 Boasley Cross .... F 4
57 Boat of Garten .... H 5
56 Boath .... B 1
11 Bobbing .... B 7
22 Bobbington .... C 2
18 Bobbingworth .... C 5
56 Boblainy .... F 1
19 Bocking .... B 7
19 Bocking Churchstreet . A 7
3 Boconnoc .... D 8
58 Boddam, Grampian ... C 8
64 Boddam, Shetland Is. .. F 7
7 Bodden .... B 10
28 Bodedern .... B 3
29 Bodelwyddan .... C 9
21 Bodenham, Heref. & Worcs. ... G 10
8 Bodenham, Wilts. .... D 3
21 Bodenham Moor .... G 11
28 Boderwryd .... A 3
29 Bodfari .... C 10
28 Bodffordd .... C 4
28 Bodfuan .... F 3
26 Bodham Street .... B 4
10 Bodiam .... E 6
23 Bodicote .... H 8
3 Bodieve .... B 7
3 Bodinnick .... D 8
10 Bodle Street Grn. .... G 5
3 Bodmin .... C 8
29 Bodnant .... C 7
26 Bodney .... E 1
28 Bodorgan .... C 3
11 Bodsham Green .... D 9
28 Boduan .... F 3
3 Bodwen .... D 7
56 Bogallan .... E 2
58 Bogbrae .... D 8
49 Bogend, Borders ... D 10
47 Bogend, Strathclyde ... F 9
48 Boghall, Lothian .... C 5
48 Boghall, Lothian .... C 3
47 Boghall, Strathclyde .. H 9
58 Boghead, Grampian ... E 7
47 Boghead, Strathclyde . F 10
47 Boghead, Strathclyde . E 12
43 Bogknowe .... F 10
15 Bogmarsh .... A 8
58 Bogmoor .... A 1
59 Bogmuire .... K 4
58 Bogniebrae .... C 3
9 Bognor Regis .... F 11
58 Bograxie .... F 4
48 Bogsbank .... D 4
48 Bogside .... D 1
58 Bogton .... C 4
43 Bogue .... C 7
2 Bohortha .... F 6
55 Bohuntine .... L 7
3 Bokiddick .... C 7
40 Bolam, Durham .... C 2
45 Bolam, Northumb. .... E 9
5 Bolberry .... M 6
30 Bold Heath .... A 4
45 Boldon Colliery .... G 11
8 Boldre .... F 5
50 Boldron .... D 1
32 Bole .... B 5
31 Bolehill .... E 11
2 Boleigh .... G 2
49 Boleside .... F 7
52 Bolfracks .... B 3
6 Bolham .... E 3
6 Bolham Water .... E 5
2 Bolingey .... D 5
31 Bollington, Ches. .... B 8
30 Bollington, Ches. .... B 6
31 Bollington Cross .... C 8
10 Bolney .... F 1
25 Bolnhurst .... J 2
53 Bolshan .... B 11
32 Bolsover .... C 2
35 Bolsterstone .... G 11
15 Bolstone .... A 8
40 Boltby .... F 5
17 Bolter End .... E 9
39 Bolton, Cumbria .... C 8
34 Bolton, Manchester ... F 6
36 Bolton, Humber. .... B 5
49 Bolton, Lothian .... B 7
45 Bolton, Northumb. .... B 9
35 Bolton Abbey .... B 9
35 Bolton Bridge .... B 9
34 Bolton by Bowland ... B 6
39 Bolton-le-Sands .... H 7
38 Bolton Low Houses ... A 5
36 Bolton-on-Dearne ... G 2
40 Bolton-on-Swale .... E 3
36 Bolton Percy .... C 3
39 Bolton Town End .... H 7
44 Boltonfellend .... F 3
3 Bolventor .... B 9
30 Bomere Heath .... H 3
60 Bonar Bridge .... G 6
51 Bonawe Quarries .... D 7
37 Bonby .... F 8
12 Boncath .... C 5
44 Bonchester Bridge ... B 4
9 Bonchurch .... H 7
4 Bondleigh .... E 5
34 Bonds .... C 4
22 Bonehill .... B 5
48 Bo'ness .... A 3
52 Bonhard .... D 6
47 Bonhill .... A 9
22 Boningdale .... B 2
49 Bonjedward .... G 9
48 Bonkle .... D 1
48 Bonnington .... B 4
53 Bonnybank .... G 8
48 Bonnybridge .... A 1
58 Bonnykelly .... B 6
48 Bonnyrigg and Lasswade .... C 6
47 Bonnyton .... F 9
31 Bonsall .... D 11
15 Bont .... B 7
28 Bont Newydd .... F 6
28 Bontddu .... H 6
20 Bont-dolgadfan .... B 4
20 Bontnewydd, Dyfed ... F 2
28 Bont-newydd, Gwynedd .... D 4
20 Bontrhydgaled .... D 4
29 Bontuchel .... D 10
14 Bonvilston .... G 4
13 Bon-y-maen .... G 10
4 Boode .... B 4
30 Booley .... H 4
39 Boon .... E 8
41 Boosbeck .... C 7
4 Boot .... F 1
36 Booth .... D 5
35 Booth Wood .... E 9
33 Boothby Graffoe .... D 7
33 Boothby Pagnell .... G 7
34 Boothtown .... G 6
38 Bootle, Cumbria .... F 4
34 Bootle, Merseyside ... H 2
47 Boquhan .... A 10
21 Boraston .... E 11
9 Borden .... D 9
35 Bordley .... A 8
3 Bordon .... C 9
19 Boreham .... C 7
10 Boreham Street .... G 5
18 Borehamwood .... D 2
52 Boreland, Central ... D 1
43 Boreland, Dumf. & Gall. .... B 12
43 Boreland of Girthon ... F 7
62 Boreraig .... C 1
49 Borewell .... D 12
61 Borgie .... B 7
43 Borgue, Dumf. & Gall. G 7
61 Borgue, Highland ... E 10
27 Borley .... L 1
62 Bornaskitaig .... A 3
43 Borness .... G 7
10 Borough Green .... B 5
40 Boroughbridge .... H 4
30 Borras Head .... E 2
61 Borrobol Lodge .... E 8
32 Borrowash .... G 1
40 Borrowby .... F 4
38 Borrowdale .... D 5
59 Borrowfield .... H 6
20 Borth .... C 2
44 Borthwickbrae .... B 2
44 Borthwickshiels .... B 3
28 Borth-y-gest .... F 5
62 Borve .... C 4
63 Borve Lodge .... G 1
63 Borvemore .... G 1
39 Borwick .... H 7
21 Bosbury .... H 12
3 Boscastle .... A 8
8 Boscombe, Dorset ... G 3
8 Boscombe, Wilts. .... B 3
3 Boscoppa .... D 7
9 Bosham .... F 9
12 Bosherston .... G 3
2 Boskenna .... G 1
31 Bosley .... D 7
31 Bossall .... A 5
59 Bossholes .... H 6
3 Bossiney .... A 8
11 Bossingham .... C 10
6 Bossington .... A 3
30 Bostock Green .... C 5
24 Boston .... A 4
33 Boston Long Hedges . E 10
36 Boston Spa .... C 2
3 Boswinger .... F 7
2 Botallack .... F 1
18 Botany Bay .... D 3
58 Botary Mains .... C 2
23 Botcheston .... B 8
27 Botesdale .... H 3
45 Bothal .... D 10
32 Bothamsall .... C 4
43 Bothel .... H 12
7 Bothenhampton .... G 8
47 Bothwell .... D 12

17 Botley, Bucks. D 10
8 Botley, Hants. E 6
16 Botley, Oxon. C 6
17 Botolph Claydon B 8
10 Botolphs G 1
54 Bottacks D 8
37 Bottesford, Humber. F 7
32 Bottesford, Leics. F 5
25 Bottisham J 6
16 Bottlesford H 2
31 Bottom House E 9
34 Bottom O'th'Moor F 5
53 Bottomcraig E 8
35 Bottoms E 8
38 Bottongate A 5
4 Bottreaux Mill C 7
3 Botusfleming D 11
28 Botwnnog G 2
10 Bough Beech C 4
21 Boughrood H 7
21 Boughrood Brest H 7
15 Boughspring E 9
24 Boughton, Norfolk E 8
32 Boughton, Notts. C 4
11 Boughton Aluph C 9
23 Boughton E 11
11 Boughton Lees C 9
11 Boughton Malherbe C 7
10 Boughton Monchelsea C 6
11 Boughton Street B 9
41 Boulby C 8
21 Bouldon D 11
45 Boulmer B 11
12 Boulston F 3
58 Boultenstone F 2
32 Boultham C 6
25 Bourn K 4
24 Bourne D 2
25 Bourne End, Beds. L 1
17 Bourne End, Bucks. E 10
17 Bourne End, Herts. D 11
18 Bournebridge D 5
8 Bournemouth G 3
19 Bournes Green, Essex E 9
15 Bournes Green, Gloucestershire D 12
22 Bournheath E 3
45 Bournmoor H 11
22 Bournville D 4
16 Bourton, Oxon. E 3
7 Bourton, Dorset C 11
21 Bourton, Salop. C 11
23 Bourton on Dunsmore E 8
16 Bourton-on-the-Hill A 3
16 Bourton-on-the-Water A 3
44 Boustead Hill G 1
38 Bouth G 6
40 Bouthwaite H 2
17 Boveney F 10
14 Boverton G 3
5 Bovey Tracey H 7
17 Bovingdon D 11
17 Bovingdon Green E 9
18 Bovinger C 5
49 Bow, Borders E 7
4 Bow, Devon F 6
64 Bow, Orkney Is E 2
17 Bow Brickhill A 10
53 Bow of Fife F 8
20 Bow Street D 2
39 Bowbank C 11
40 Bowburn A 3
8 Bowcombe G 6
6 Bowd G 4
49 Bowden, Borders F 8
5 Bowden, Devon L 7
15 Bowden Hill H 12
39 Bowerdale E 9
30 Bowdon B 6
44 Bower E 6
7 Bower Hinton D 8
8 Bowerchalke D 2
15 Bowerhill H 12
61 Bowermadden B 11
31 Bowers G 7
19 Bowers Gifford E 7
52 Bowershall H 6
61 Bowertower B 11
39 Bowers D 12
34 Bowgreave C 4
49 Bowhill G 7
43 Bowhouse E 11
3 Bowithick A 9
34 Bowker's Green G 3
38 Bowland Bridge F 6
21 Bowley G 11
9 Bowlhead Green B 10
47 Bowling B 9
22 Bowling Green G 2
38 Bowmanstead F 5
44 Bowness-on-Solway G 1
38 Bowness-on-Windermere E 6
49 Bowsden E 12
61 Bowside Lodge B 8
48 Bowtrees A 2
15 Box, Glos. D 11
15 Box, Wilts. G 11
15 Boxbush C 10
16 Boxford, Berks. G 5
27 Boxford, Suffolk L 3
9 Boxgrove E 10
10 Boxley B 6
4 Box's Shop F 1
27 Boxted, Essex M 3
27 Boxted, Suffolk K 1
27 Boxted Cross M 3
25 Boxworth J 4
25 Boxworth End H 5
11 Boyden Gate B 11
31 Boylestone G 10
58 Boyndie A 4
41 Boynton H 11
7 Boys Hill E 10
5 Boyton, Cornwall G 2
27 Boyton, Suffolk K 7
8 Boyton, Wilts. B 1
18 Boyton Cross C 6
23 Bozeat F 12
38 Braaid H 2
27 Brabling Green J 6
11 Brabourne D 9
11 Brabourne Lees D 9
61 Brabstermire A 12
62 Bracadale D 3
24 Braceborough D 2
33 Bracebridge Heath C 7
33 Braceby G 7
35 Bracewell B 7
32 Brackenfield D 1
59 Brackenrigg K 5
38 Brackenthwaite, Cumbria C 4
44 Brackenthwaite, Cumbria H 1
9 Bracklesham F 9
55 Brackletter L 6
23 Brackley, Northants. H 9
46 Brackley, Strathclyde E 3
60 Brackloch E 3
17 Bracknell G 9
52 Braco F 3
58 Bracobrae B 3
26 Bracon Ash E 5
55 Bracora K 1
55 Bracorina K 1
31 Bradbourne E 10
40 Bradbury B 3
38 Bradda H 1
23 Bradden G 10
17 Bradenham D 9
16 Bradenstoke F 1
17 Bradfield, Berks. G 7
6 Bradfield, Devon E 4
27 Bradfield, Essex M 4
35 Bradfield, S. Yorks. H 11
27 Bradfield Combust J 2
30 Bradfield Green D 5
27 Bradfield Heath M 4
27 Bradfield St. Clair J 2
27 Bradfield St. George J 2
4 Bradford, Devon E 3
45 Bradford, Northum. D 11
35 Bradford, W. Yorks. D 10
7 Bradford Abbas E 9
15 Bradford Leigh H 11
4 Bradford Mill D 7
15 Bradford-on-Avon H 11
6 Bradford-on-Tone D 5
9 Brading G 7
30 Bradley, Clwyd E 2
31 Bradley, Derby. F 10
9 Bradley, Hants. B 7
37 Bradley, Humber. F 10
39 Bradley, N. Yorks. G 12
31 Bradley, Staffs. H 7
22 Bradley, W. Midlands C 3
30 Bradley Common F 4
22 Bradley Green F 3
31 Bradley in the Moors F 9
32 Bradmore G 3
7 Bradney B 7
6 Bradninch F 3
31 Bradnop E 8
7 Bradpole G 8
34 Bradshaw F 6
5 Bradstone H 3
30 Bradwall Green D 6
31 Bradwell, Derby. B 10
19 Bradwell, Essex B 8
26 Bradwell, Suffolk E 8
23 Bradwell, Bucks. H 11
16 Bradwell Grove C 3
19 Bradwell-on-Sea C 10
19 Bradwell Waterside C 10
4 Bradworthy E 2
4 Bradworthy Cross E 2
64 Brae C 7
60 Brae Doune G 5
60 Brae of Achnahaird E 2
55 Brae Roy Lodge K 7
56 Braeantra B 1
57 Braedownie M 8
43 Braefoot A 9
58 Braehead, Grampian F 7
42 Braehead, Dumf. & Gall. F 5
64 Braehead, Orkney Is. D 3
48 Braehead, Strathclyde D 2
48 Braehead, Strathclyde F 1
53 Braehead, Tayside B 11
61 Braehungie D 11
54 Braeintra F 2
60 Braelangwell Lodge G 6
57 Braemar K 7
61 Braemore, Highland D 10
54 Braemore, Highland B 6
47 Braeside B 7
51 Braeval G 12
40 Brafferton, Dur. C 3
40 Braverton, N. Yorks. H 4
23 Bradfield-on-the Green F 11
63 Bragar B 4
18 Bragbury End B 3
50 Braglenbeg E 6
34 Braides B 3
49 Braidshawrig D 8
48 Braidwood E 1
31 Brailsford F 11
45 Brainshaugh C 10
19 Braintree B 7
27 Braiseworth H 4
8 Braishfield D 5
38 Braithwaite, Cumb. C 5
36 Braithwaite, S. Yorks. F 4
32 Braithwell A 3
10 Bramber G 1
32 Bramcote F 2
9 Bramdean C 7
26 Bramerton E 6
18 Bramfield, Herts. B 3
27 Bramfield, Suffolk H 7
27 Bramford K 4
31 Bramhall B 7
33 Bramham C 2
36 Bramham Crossroads C 2
35 Bramhope C 11
9 Bramley, Surrey B 11
32 Bramley, S. Yorks. A 2
17 Bramley Green H 7
6 Brampford Speke F 3
25 Brampton, Cambs. H 3
44 Brampton, Cumb. G 4
39 Brampton, Cumb. C 9
15 Brampton, Heref. & Worc. A 7
32 Brampton, Lincs. B 6
36 Brampton, S. Yorks. G 2
27 Brampton, Suffolk G 7
15 Brampton Abbots B 9
23 Brampton Ash C 11
21 Brampton Bryan E 9
32 Brampton en le Morthen A 2
31 Bramshall G 9
8 Bramshaw E 4
9 Bramshott C 9
18 Bran End A 6
26 Brancaster A 1
26 Brancaster Staithe A 1
40 Brancepeth A 2
56 Branchill D 6
15 Brand Green B 10
56 Branderburgh C 8
37 Brandesburton B 9
27 Brandeston J 5
4 Brandis Corner E 3
26 Brandiston C 4
28 Brandingill C 4
40 Brandon, Durham A 3
32 Brandon, Lincs. E 6
45 Brandon, Northumb. A 8
27 Brandon, Suffolk G 1
23 Brandon, War. D 7
24 Brandon Creek F 7
26 Brandon Parva E 4
40 Brandsby H 6
37 Brandy Wharf G 8
2 Brane G 1
8 Branksome G 2
8 Branksome Park G 2
8 Bransbury B 6
32 Bransby C 6
6 Branscombe G 5
22 Bransford G 1
8 Bransgore F 3
22 Branson's Cross E 4
32 Branston, Leics. G 5
33 Branston, Lincs. C 7
31 Branston, Staffs. H 10
33 Branston Booths C 8
9 Branstone H 7
32 Brant Broughton E 6
44 Branteth E 1
27 Brantham M 4
38 Branthwaite, Cumb. C 3
38 Branthwaite, Cumb. B 5
37 Brantingham D 7
45 Branton, Northumb. A 8
36 Branton, S. Yorks. G 4
44 Branxholme B 3
49 Branxton F 11
49 Branxtonmoor F 11
31 Brassington E 11
10 Brasted C 3
10 Brasted Chart C 3
59 Brathens H 4
33 Bratoft D 11
32 Brattleby B 6
6 Bratton, Somerset B 3
8 Bratton, Wilts. A 1
5 Bratton Clovelly G 3
4 Bratton Fleming B 5
7 Bratton Seymour C 10
18 Braughing A 4
23 Braunston, Leics. A 11
23 Braunston, Northants. E 9
23 Braunstone B 9
4 Braunton B 4
12 Brawby, Dyfed E 2
41 Brawby, N. Yorks. G 7
61 Brawlbin B 10
17 Bray F 10
3 Bray Shop B 10
17 Bray Wick F 9
23 Braybrooke D 11
4 Brayford C 6
36 Brayton D 4
3 Brazacott A 9
62 Breabost C 3
11 Breach B 7
18 Breachwood Green B 2
63 Breaclete C 2
31 Breadsall F 12
15 Breadstone D 10
54 Breafield F 8
2 Breage G 3
54 Breakachy E 8
15 Bream D 9
8 Breamore D 3
15 Bream's Eaves D 9
6 Brean A 6
35 Brearton A 11
63 Breasclete C 3
32 Breaston G 2
13 Brechfa D 8
59 Brechin L 4
43 Breckonside A 9
62 Breckrey B 4
14 Brecon A 4
35 Bredbury H 8
11 Brede F 7
21 Bredenbury G 11
27 Bredfield K 6
11 Bredgar B 7
11 Bredhurst B 7
22 Bredicot G 3
15 Bredon A 12
22 Bredon's Norton H 3
21 Bredwardine H 9
32 Breedon on the Hill H 1
48 Breich C 2
36 Breighton D 5
21 Breinton H 10
21 Breinton Com. H 10
16 Bremhill G 1
51 Brenachoille G 7
10 Brenchley D 5
4 Brendon A 6
46 Brenfield A 3
63 Brenish D 1
45 Brenkley F 10
18 Brent E 2
27 Brent Eleigh K 2
6 Brent Knoll A 6
25 Brent Pelham M 5
18 Brentford F 2
18 Brentwood E 6
11 Brenzett E 8
22 Brereton A 4
30 Brereton Green D 6
30 Brereton Heath D 6
64 Bressay E 7
27 Bressingham G 4
31 Bretby H 11
23 Bretford D 7
22 Bretforton H 4
39 Bretherdale Head E 8
34 Bretherton E 4
6 Brett B 4
64 Brettabister D 7
27 Brettenham, Suff. K 3
27 Brettenhm, Norf. G 2
30 Bretton D 2
10 Brewer Street C 2
53 Brewlands Bridge A 7
22 Brewood A 2
56 Briach D 6
7 Briantspuddle G 11
18 Bricket Wood D 1
22 Bricklehampton H 3
38 Bride F 2
38 Bridekirk B 4
12 Bridell C 5
5 Bridestowe G 4
58 Brideswell D 3
5 Bridford G 7
11 Bridge, Kent C 10
2 Bridge, Cornwall E 4
25 Bridge End, Beds. K 1
24 Bridge End, Lincs. B 2
45 Bridge End, Northumb. B 9
40 Bridge Hewick H 4
58 Bridge of Alford F 3
52 Bridge of Allan G 3
56 Bridge of Avon F 7
51 Bridge of Awe E 7
51 Bridge of Balgie, Perth C 12
57 Bridge of Brown G 7
52 Bridge of Cally B 6
59 Bridge of Canny H 4
53 Bridge of Craigisla B 7
43 Bridge of Dee F 8
56 Bridge of Derrybeg F 8
58 Bridge of Don F 7
59 Bridge of Dun L 4
59 Bridge of Dye J 4
52 Bridge of Earn E 6
51 Bridge of Ericht B 12
59 Bridge of Feugh H 4
61 Bridge of Forss A 10
59 Bridge of Gairn H 1
51 Bridge of Gaur B 12
53 Bridge of Lintrathen B 7
59 Bridge of Murchalls H 6
55 Bridge of Oich J 7
51 Bridge of Orchy D 10
52 Bridge of Tilt A 4
64 Bridge of Waith D 1
64 Bridge of Walls D 6
47 Bridge of Weir C 9
4 Bridge Reeve E 5
21 Bridge Sollars H 9
27 Bridge Street K 2
30 Bridge Trafford C 3
25 Bridgefoot, Cambs. L 5
38 Bridgefoot, Cumb. B 3
7 Bridgehampton D 9
49 Bridgelands F 7
9 Bridgemary F 7
3 Bridgend, Corn. D 8
38 Bridgend, Cumbria D 6
43 Bridgend, Dumf. & Gall. A 11
12 Bridgend, Dyfed B 5
53 Bridgend, Fife F 8
58 Bridgend, Grampian C 5
58 Bridgend, Grampian D 3
58 Bridgend, Grampian E 6
58 Bridgend, Grampian D 1
54 Bridgend, Highland D 7
48 Bridgend, Lothian B 3
14 Bridgend, Mid Glam. F 2
50 Bridgend, Strathclyde H 6
59 Bridgend, Tayside K 3
4 Bridgerule F 1
21 Bridges C 9
3 Bridgetown, Corn. A 10
6 Bridgetown, Som. C 3
22 Bridgetown, Staffs. A 3
27 Bridgham G 3
21 Bridgnorth C 12
7 Bridgwater B 6
41 Bridlington H 12
7 Bridport G 8
15 Bridstow B 9
35 Brierfield D 7
15 Brierley, Glos. C 9
21 Brierley, Heref. & Worc. G 10
36 Brierley, S. Yorks. F 2
22 Brierley Hill C 3
40 Brierton B 5
14 Briery Hill C 5
51 Brig o' Turk G 12
37 Brigg F 8
59 Briggs of Criggie J 6
41 Briggswath D 9
38 Brigham, Cumb. B 3
37 Brigham, Humber. B 8
35 Brighouse E 10
8 Brighstone H 6
16 Brighthampton D 5
31 Brightgate D 11
10 Brightling F 5
19 Brightlingsea B 10
2 Brighton, Corn. D 6
10 Brighton, E. Sussex H 2
48 Brightons B 2
16 Brightwalton F 5
17 Brightwell, Oxon. E 7
27 Brightwell, Suffolk L 5
17 Brightwell Baldwin E 7
40 Brignall D 1
37 Brigsley G 10
39 Brigsteer F 7
23 Brigstock D 12
17 Brill, Bucks. C 7
2 Brill, Cornwall G 4
21 Brilley G 8
12 Brimaston D 3
21 Brimfield F 10
32 Brimington C 1
15 Brimpsfield C 12
16 Brimpton H 6
64 Brims E 1
15 Brimscombe D 11
30 Brimstage B 2
57 Brin G 2
55 Brinacory K 1
36 Brind D 5
64 Brindister, Shetland Is. D 6
64 Brindister, Shetland Is. E 7
34 Brindle E 5
31 Brindley Ford E 7
22 Brineton A 2
23 Bringhurst C 11
25 Brington H 2
26 Briningham B 3
33 Brinkhill C 10
25 Brinkley K 7
23 Brinklow D 8
16 Brinkworth F 1
34 Brinscall E 5
15 Brinsea H 7
32 Brinsley E 2
21 Brinsop H 10
32 Brinsworth A 1
26 Brinton B 3
64 Brinyan B 2
26 Brisley C 3
15 Brislington G 9
11 Brissenden Green D 8
15 Bristol G 9
26 Briston B 4
27 Britannia E 7
8 Britford C 3
29 Brithdir, Gwynedd H 7
14 Brithdir, Mid Glam. D 5
10 British Legion Village B 6
13 Briton Ferry G 10
17 Britwell Salome E 7
5 Brixham K 8
5 Brixton K 4
7 Brixton Deverill B 11
23 Brixworth E 10
16 Brize Norton C 4
16 Broad Blunsdon E 3
22 Broad Campden H 5
8 Broad Chalke C 2
6 Broad Clyst F 3
25 Broad Green, Beds. L 1
19 Broad Green, Essex B 8
22 Broad Green, Heref. & Worc. F 1
12 Broad Haven F 2
25 Broad Hill H 7
16 Broad Hinton F 2
16 Broad Laying H 5
22 Broad Marston G 5
38 Broad Oak, Cumb. F 4
13 Broad Oak, Dyfed E 9
11 Broad Oak, E. Sussex F 7
15 Broad Oak, Heref. & Worc. B 8
36 Broad Oak, N. Yorks. B 4
11 Broad Street B 7
19 Broad Street Green C 8
16 Broad Town F 2
35 Broadbottom H 8
9 Broadbridge E 9
9 Broadbridge Hth. C 12
12 Broadfield G 5
62 Broadford F 5
8 Broadford Bri. D 12
48 Broadgairhill H 5
44 Broadhaugh B 3
61 Broadhaven C 12
30 Broadheath A 6
7 Broadhembury F 5
5 Broadhempston J 7
11 Broadland Row F 7
13 Broadlay F 7
35 Broadley B 1
18 Broadley Com. C 4
49 Broadmeadows F 7
9 Broadmere A 7

12 Broadmoor **F 4**
10 Broadoak, E. Sussex **F 5**
11 Broadoak, Kent **B 10**
58 Broadrashes **B 2**
58 Broadsea **E 5**
11 Broadstairs **A 12**
8 Broadstone, Dorset **F 2**
21 Broadstone, Salop. **C 11**
16 Broadtown Lane **F 2**
22 Broadwas **G 1**
18 Broadwater, Herts. **B 2**
9 Broadwater, W. Sussex **F 12**
12 Broadway, Dyfed **F 6**
12 Broadway, Dyfed **F 2**
22 Broadway, Heref. & Worc. **H 4**
6 Broadway, Som. **E 6**
16 Broadwell, Glos. **A 3**
16 Broadwell, Oxon **D 3**
23 Broadwell, War. **F 8**
45 Broadwell House **H 7**
15 Broadwell Lane End **C 9**
7 Broadwey **H 10**
7 Broadwindsor **F 8**
4 Broadwood-Kelly **E 5**
5 Broadwoodwidger **G 3**
21 Brobury **H 9**
62 Brochel **D 5**
9 Brockbridge **D 7**
45 Brockdam **A 9**
27 Brockdish **G 5**
8 Brockenhurst **F 4**
48 Brocketsbrae **E 1**
27 Brockford Street **J 4**
23 Brockhall **F 9**
10 Brockham **C 1**
16 Brockhampton, Glos. **B 1**
15 Brockhampton, Heref. & Worc. **A 9**
7 Brockhampton Green **F 10**
35 Brockholes **F 10**
9 Brockhurst **F 7**
38 Brocklebank **A 5**
37 Brocklesby **F 9**
15 Brockley **H 8**
27 Brockley Green **K 1**
22 Brockton, Salop. **B 1**
21 Brockton, Salop. **B 8**
21 Brockton, Salop. **C 11**
15 Brockweir **D 8**
9 Brockwood **D 7**
15 Brockworth **C 12**
31 Brocton **H 8**
46 Brodick **F 5**
58 Brodiesord **B 3**
36 Brodsworth **F 3**
62 Brogaig **A 4**
25 Brogborough **L 1**
30 Broken Cross, Cheshire **C 6**
31 Broken Cross, Cheshire **C 7**
15 Brokenborough **E 12**
30 Bromborough **B 2**
27 Brome **H 4**
27 Brome Street **H 5**
27 Bromeswell **K 6**
43 Bromfield, Cumb. **G 12**
21 Bromfield, Salop. **E 10**
25 Bromham, Beds. **K 1**
16 Bromham, Wilts. **H 1**
18 Bromley **G 4**
11 Bromley Green **D 8**
10 Brompton, Kent **A 6**
41 Brompton, N. Yorks. **G 9**
40 Brompton, N. Yorks. **E 4**
21 Brompton Hall **C 8**
40 Brompton-on-Swale **E 2**
6 Brompton Ralph **C 4**
6 Brompton Regis **C 3**
15 Bromsash **B 9**
15 Bromsberrow **A 10**
22 Bromsgrove **E 3**
22 Bromyard **G 12**
21 Bromyard Downs **G 12**
28 Bronaber **G 6**
20 Bronant **F 2**
12 Brongest **C 6**
30 Bronington **F 4**
14 Bronllys **A 5**
13 Bronwydd Arms **E 7**
21 Bronydd **H 8**
12 Brook, Dyfed **F 6**
8 Brook, Hants. **C 5**
8 Brook, Hants. **E 4**
8 Brook, I.o.W. **H 5**
11 Brook, Kent **D 9**
9 Brook, Surrey **B 12**
9 Brook, Surrey **B 10**
25 Brook End **J 2**
8 Brook Hill **E 4**
18 Brook Street, Essex **E 6**
10 Brook Street, W. Sussex **E 2**
23 Brooke, Leics. **B 12**
26 Brooke, Norfolk **E 6**
15 Brookend **D 9**
47 Brookfield **C 9**
31 Brookhouse, Ches. **C 8**
34 Brookhouse, Lancs. **A 4**
31 Brookhouse Green **D 7**
11 Brookland **E 8**
43 Brooklands **D 9**
18 Brookmans Park **D 2**
21 Brooks **C 7**
17 Brookwood **H 10**
25 Broom, Beds. **L 3**
40 Broom, Durham **A 3**
22 Broom, War. **G 4**
8 Broom Hill **F 2**
52 Broom of Dalreoch **E 5**
49 Broomdykes **D 11**
22 Broome, Heref. & Worcs. **D 3**
26 Broome, Norfolk **F 6**
21 Broome, Salop. **D 9**
10 Broome Park **C 1**
30 Broomedge **B 5**
5 Broomer's Crn. **D 12**
19 Broomfield, Essex **C 7**
58 Broomfield, Grampian **D 7**
11 Broomfield, Kent **A 10**
11 Broomfield, Kent **C 7**
6 Broomfield, Som. **C 6**
48 Broomfield, Strathclyde **E 1**
36 Broomfleet **D 6**
17 Broomhall **G 10**
45 Broomhaugh **G 8**
45 Broomhill, Northumb. **C 10**
56 Broomhill, Highland **C 3**
57 Broomhill House **G 6**
26 Broomholm **B 6**
45 Broomhouse **C 11**
43 Broomhouses **C 12**
45 Broomley **G 8**
15 Brooms Green **A 10**
15 Broomsberrow Heath **A 10**
61 Brora **F 9**
21 Broseley **B 12**
22 Brotheridge Green **H 2**
49 Brotherstone **F 9**
33 Brothertoft **F 10**
36 Brotherton **E 3**
45 Brotherwick **C 10**
41 Brotton **C 7**
61 Broubster **B 10**
39 Brough, Cumbria **D 10**
31 Brough, Derby. **B 10**
61 Brough, Highland **A 11**
37 Brough, Humberside **D 7**
32 Brough, Notts. **D 5**
64 Brough, Orkney Is. **C 2**
64 Brough, Whalasay, Shetland Is. **C 8**
64 Brough, Yell, Shetland Is. **C 7**
64 Brough, Zetland, Shetland Is. **C 7**
64 Brough Lodge **B 8**
39 Brough Sowerby **D 10**
30 Broughall **F 4**
23 Broughton, Bucks. **H 12**
48 Broughton, Borders **F 4**
25 Broughton, Cambs. **G 4**
30 Broughton, Clwyd **D 2**
38 Broughton, Cumb. **B 3**
8 Broughton, Hants. **C 4**
37 Broughton, Humber. **F 7**
34 Broughton, Lancs. **D 4**
14 Broughton, Mid Glam. **G 2**
23 Broughton, Northants. **E 11**
41 Broughton, N. Yorks. **H 8**
35 Broughton, N. Yorks. **B 8**
64 Broughton, Orkney Is. **A 2**
23 Broughton, Oxon **H 7**
23 Broughton Astley **C 8**
38 Broughton Beck **G 5**
15 Broughton Com. **H 12**
16 Broughton Foggs **D 3**
15 Broughton Gifford **H 12**
22 Broughton Hackett **G 3**
38 Broughton in Furness **F 5**
38 Broughton Mills **F 4**
38 Broughton Moor **B 3**
64 Broughtown **B 4**
53 Broughty Ferry **D 9**
44 Browhouses **G 1**
9 Brown Candover **B 7**
31 Brown Edge **E 7**
58 Brownhill, Grampian **D 6**
30 Brownhill, Salop. **H 3**
53 Brownhills, Fife **F 10**
22 Brownhills, W. Midlands **B 4**
31 Brownlow Heath **D 7**
59 Brownmuir **K 5**
45 Brownridge **B 11**
15 Brown's Hill **D 12**
23 Brownsover **D 8**
5 Brownston **K 6**
45 Brownyside **A 9**
17 Brox **H 11**
41 Broxa **F 9**
18 Broxborune **C 4**
49 Broxburn, Lothian **B 9**
48 Broxburn, Lothian **B 4**
18 Broxted **A 6**
30 Broxton **E 3**
21 Broxwood **G 9**
10 Broyle Side **G 3**
61 Bruan **C 12**
57 Bruar Lodge **M 4**
63 Brue **B 4**
30 Bruera **D 3**
16 Bruern Abbey **B 4**
27 Bruisyard **J 6**
27 Bruisyard Street **J 6**
26 Brumby **F 6**
31 Brund **D 9**
26 Brundhall **E 6**
27 Brundish **H 5**
27 Brundish Street **H 6**
55 Brunery **M 1**
45 Brunswick Village **F 10**
23 Bruntingthorpe **C 9**
53 Brunton, Fife **E 8**
45 Brunton, Northumb. **A 10**
16 Brunton, Wilts. **H 3**
6 Brushford **D 3**
4 Brushford Barton **E 5**
7 Bruton **C 10**
7 Bryanston **F 12**
43 Brydekirk **E 12**
29 Brymbo **E 12**
7 Brympton **E 8**
29 Bryn, Clwyd **F 12**
13 Bryn, Dyfed **G 9**
34 Bryn, Manchester **G 4**
13 Bryn, W. Glam **H 11**
21 Bryn, Salop. **D 8**
14 Bryn Golau **E 3**
28 Bryn-Siencyn **D 4**
13 Brynamman **F 10**
13 Brynberian **C 4**
13 Brynbryddan **H 11**
14 Bryncethin **F 2**
28 Bryncir **F 4**
13 Bryn-coch **G 10**
28 Bryncroes **G 2**
20 Bryncrug **B 2**
29 Bryneglwys **E 10**
29 Brynford **C 11**
28 Bryngwran **B 3**
15 Bryngwyn, Gwent **C 7**
21 Bryngwyn, Powys **G 7**
12 Bryn-henllan **C 4**
13 Brynhoffnant **B 7**
34 Bryning **D 3**
14 Brynmawr **C 5**
14 Brynmenyn **F 2**
28 Bryn'refail **D 5**
14 Brynsadler **F 3**
29 Bryn-teg **E 12**
14 Bryn-y-Cae **F 3**
14 Bryn-y-gwenin **C 6**
29 Bryn-y-maen **C 7**
62 Bualintur **F 3**
23 Bubbenhall **E 7**
36 Bubwith **C 5**
48 Buccleuch **H 6**
42 Buchan **D 5**
47 Buchanan Castle **A 9**
51 Buchanan Smithy **H 11**
58 Buchanhaven **C 8**
52 Buchanty **D 4**
52 Buchlyvie **H 1**
58 Buchts **B 7**
44 Buckabank **H 2**
25 Buckden, Cambs. **H 3**
39 Buckden, N. Yorks. **G 11**
26 Buckenham **E 6**
6 Buckerell **F 5**
5 Buckfast **J 6**
5 Buckfastleigh **J 6**
53 Buckhaven **G 8**
49 Buckholm **E 7**
18 Buckhurst Hill **E 4**
58 Buckie **A 2**
17 Buckingham **A 8**
17 Buckinghamshire, Co. **C 8**
17 Buckland, Bucks. **C 9**
5 Buckland, Devon **L 5**
16 Buckland, Glos. **A 2**
25 Buckland, Herts. **M 5**
11 Buckland, Kent **D 11**
16 Buckland, Oxon **D 4**
10 Buckland, Surrey **C 1**
4 Buckland Brewer **D 3**
17 Buckland Com. **C 10**
7 Buckland Dinham **A 11**
4 Buckland Filleigh **E 3**
5 Buckland in the Moor **H 6**
5 Buckland Monachorum **J 4**
7 Buckland Newton **F 10**
6 Buckland St. Mary **E 6**
24 Bucklegate **B 4**
53 Bucklerheads **D 9**
8 Bucklers Hard **F 5**
27 Bucklesham **L 5**
29 Buckley **D 12**
30 Bucklow Hill **B 6**
32 Buckminster **H 6**
33 Bucknall, Lincs. **C 9**
31 Bucknall, Staffs. **E 7**
16 Bucknell, Oxon **B 6**
21 Bucknell, Salop. **E 9**
58 Buckpool **A 2**
4 Buck's Cross **D 2**
9 Bucks Green **C 12**
9 Bucks Horn Oak **B 9**
4 Buck's Mills **D 2**
7 Buckthorn Weston **D 10**
21 Buckton, Heref. & Worc. **E 9**
41 Buckton, Humberside **H 11**
45 Buckton, Northumb. **B 12**
25 Buckworth **H 2**
16 Bucklebury **G 6**
22 Budbrooke **F 6**
32 Budby **C 3**
4 Bude **E 1**
6 Budlake **F 3**
45 Budle **D 12**
6 Budleigh Salterton **H 4**
2 Budock Water **F 5**
30 Buerton **F 5**
23 Bugbrooke **F 10**
31 Buglawton **D 7**
3 Bugle **D 7**
36 Bugthorpe **A 5**
21 Buildwas **B 11**
47 Builstonend **E 9**
20 Builth Road **G 6**
20 Builth Wells **G 6**
17 Bulbourne **C 10**
24 Bulby **C 2**
32 Bulcote **F 4**
8 Bulford **B 3**
30 Bulkeley **E 4**
23 Bulkington, War. **D 7**
15 Bulkington, Wilts **H 12**
4 Bulkworthy **E 3**
28 Bull Bay **A 4**
8 Bull Hill **F 5**
40 Bullamoor **F 4**
17 Bullbrook **G 9**
58 Bullers of Buchan **D 8**
15 Bulley **B 11**
43 Bullgill **H 11**
15 Bullinghope **A 8**
8 Bullington, Hants. **B 6**
33 Bullington, Lincs. **B 8**
39 Bullpot Farm **G 9**
46 Bullwood **B 6**
27 Bulmer, Essex **L 2**
41 Bulmer, N. Yorks. **H 7**
27 Bulmer Tye **L 1**
18 Bulphan **E 6**
10 Bulverhythe **G 6**
58 Bulwark **C 7**
15 Bulwark Village **E 8**
32 Bulwell **F 3**
24 Bulwick **F 1**
18 Bumble's Green **C 4**
55 Bunacaimb **K 1**
55 Bunarkaig **L 6**
63 Bunaveneadar **F 2**
30 Bunbury **D 4**
56 Bunchrew **E 2**
9 Buncton **E 12**
55 Bundalloch **G 3**
50 Bunessan **E 1**
38 Bungalow Station **G 2**
26 Bungay **F 6**
57 Bunloit **G 1**
32 Bunny **G 3**
54 Buntait **F 8**
18 Buntingford **A 4**
26 Bunwell **F 4**
26 Bunwell Street **F 4**
31 Burbage, Derby **C 9**
23 Burbage, Leics. **C 8**
16 Burbage, Wilts. **H 3**
17 Burchett's Green **F 9**
8 Burcombe **C 2**
22 Burcot, Heref. & Worc. **E 3**
16 Burcot, Oxon **E 6**
17 Burcott **B 9**
36 Burdale **A 6**
27 Bures **M 2**
16 Burford, Oxon **C 4**
21 Burford, Salop. **F 11**
50 Burg **C 1**
10 Burgess Hill **F 2**
27 Burgh **K 5**
44 Burgh by Sands **G 2**
26 Burgh Castle **E 8**
10 Burgh Heath **B 1**
33 Burgh le Marsh **D 12**
58 Burgh Muir **E 5**
26 Burgh next Aylsham **C 5**
33 Burgh on Bain **B 9**
26 Burgh St. Margaret **D 7**
26 Burgh St. Peter **F 8**
16 Burghclere **H 6**
56 Burghead **C 7**
17 Burghfield **G 7**
17 Burghfield Com. **G 7**
21 Burghill **H 10**
36 Burghwallis **F 3**
10 Burham **B 6**
9 Buriton **D 9**
30 Burland **E 5**
3 Burlawn **C 7**
6 Burlescombe **E 4**
7 Burleston **G 11**
8 Burley, Hants. **F 3**
23 Burley, Leics. **A 12**
21 Burley Gate **H 11**
35 Burley in Wharfdale **C 10**
8 Burley Lodge **E 4**
8 Burley Street **F 3**
30 Burleydam **F 5**
21 Burlingjobb **G 8**
30 Burlow **F 4**
30 Burlton **H 3**
11 Burmarsh **E 9**
22 Burmington **H 6**
6 Burn, Devon **F 3**
43 Burn, Dumf. & Gall **B 10**
36 Burn, N. Yorks. **D 4**
34 Burn Naze **C 2**
52 Burn of Cambus **G 2**
35 Burnage **H 7**
31 Burnaston **G 11**
47 Burnbank **D 11**
47 Burnbrae **E 12**
36 Burnby **C 6**
35 Burncross **G 12**
39 Burneside **F 7**
64 Burness **A 4**
40 Burneston **G 3**
15 Burnett **H 10**
44 Burnfoot, Borders **A 3**
44 Burnfoot, Borders **B 2**
43 Burnfoot, Dumf. & Gall. **B 10**
44 Burnfoot, Dumf. & Gall. **D 2**
45 Burnfoot, Northumb. **B 8**
47 Burnfoot, Strathclyde **B 11**
32 Burngreave **A 1**
17 Burnham, Bucks. **F 10**
37 Burnham, Humberside **E 8**
17 Burnham Beeches **F 10**
26 Burnham Deepdale **A 1**
18 Burnham Green **B 3**
26 Burnham Market **A 1**
26 Burnham Norton **A 1**
26 Burnham Overy **A 1**
26 Burnham Thorpe **B 2**
6 Burnham-on-Sea **A 6**
19 Burnham-on-Crouch **D 9**
58 Burnhaven **C 8**
43 Burnhead, Dumf. & Gall. **C 10**
43 Burnhead, Dumf. & Gall. **B 9**
58 Burnhervie **F 5**
22 Burnhill Green **B 1**
45 Burnhope **H 10**
47 Burnhouse **D 8**
49 Burnhouse Mains **D 7**
41 Burniston **F 10**
35 Burnley **D 7**
49 Burnmouth, Borders **C 12**
43 Burnmouth, Dumf. & Gall. **A 9**
45 Burnopfield **G 10**
59 Burnroot **H 2**
35 Burnsall **A 9**
43 Burnside, Dumf. & Gall. **C 11**
52 Burnside, Fife **F 6**
56 Burnside, Grampian **F 5**
48 Burnside, Lothian **B 4**
64 Burnside, Shetland Is. **C 6**
47 Burnside, Strathclyde **H 10**
53 Burnside, Tayside **B 9**
53 Burnside of Dantrune **D 9**
19 Burnt Heath **A 10**
40 Burnt Houses **C 2**
35 Burnt Yates **A 11**
2 Burnthouse **F 5**
48 Burntisland **A 5**
47 Burnton, Strathclyde **H 8**
42 Burnton, Strathclyde **A 6**
47 Burnton, Strathclyde **H 10**
22 Burntwood **A 4**
9 Burpham, Surrey **A 11**
9 Burpham, W. Sussex **E 11**
45 Burradon, Northumb. **B 8**
45 Burradon, Tyne & Wear **F 11**
64 Burrafirth **A 8**
2 Burras **F 4**
64 Burravoe **C 7**
39 Burrells **C 9**
53 Burrelton **C 7**
4 Burridge, Devon **C 4**
9 Burridge, Hants. **E 7**
40 Burrill **F 3**
36 Burringham **F 6**
15 Burrington, Avon **H 8**
4 Burrington, Devon **D 5**
21 Burrington, Heref. & Worc. **E 10**
25 Borrough Green **K 7**
23 Burrough on the Hill **A 10**
6 Burrow, Devon **G 4**
6 Burrow, Somerset **B 3**
7 Burrow Bridge **C 7**
17 Burrowhill **H 10**
9 Burrows Cross **A 12**
13 Burry **H 8**
13 Burry Port **G 8**
13 Burrygreen **H 8**
34 Burscough **F 3**
34 Burscough Bridge **F 3**
36 Bursea **D 6**
36 Bursea Lane Ends **D 6**
37 Burshill **B 8**
8 Bursledon **E 6**
31 Burslem **E 7**
27 Burstall **L 4**
7 Burstock **F 7**
27 Burston, Norfolk **G 4**
31 Burston, Staffs. **G 8**
10 Burstow **D 2**
37 Burstwick **D 10**
39 Burtersett **F 11**
30 Burton, Cheshire **D 4**
39 Burton, Cumbria **G 8**
7 Burton, Dorest **G 10**
8 Burton, Dorset **G 3**
12 Burton, Dyfed **F 3**
33 Burton, Lincs. **C 7**
30 Burton, Merseyside **C 2**
45 Burton, Northumb. **D 12**
6 Burton, Somerset **B 5**
15 Burton, Wilts. **F 11**
37 Burton Agnes **A 9**
7 Burton Bradstock **G 8**
33 Burton Coggles **H 7**
37 Burton Contable **C 9**
23 Burton Dassett **G 7**
41 Burton Fleming **H 11**
30 Burton Green, Clwyd **D 2**
22 Burton Green, W. Midlands **E 6**
23 Burton Hastings **C 7**
39 Burton in Lonsdale **H 9**
32 Burton Joyce **F 4**
23 Burton Latimer **E 12**
32 Burton Lazars **H 5**
35 Burton Leonard **A 12**
32 Burton on the Wolds **H 3**
31 Burton-on-Trent **H 10**
23 Burton Overy **B 10**
24 Burton Pedwardine **A 2**
37 Burton Pidsea **D 10**
36 Burton Salmon **D 3**
36 Burton upon Stather **E 6**
34 Burtonwood **H 4**
30 Burwardsley **D 4**
21 Burwarton **D 11**
10 Burwash **F 5**
10 Burwash Common **F 5**
10 Burwash Weald **F 5**
25 Burwell, Cambs. **J 7**
33 Burwell, Lincs. **B 10**
28 Burwen **A 4**
64 Burwick **E 2**
25 Bury, Cambs. **G 4**
35 Bury, Manchester **F 7**
6 Bury, Somerset **C 3**
9 Bury, W. Sussex **E 11**
18 Bury Green **B 4**
27 Bury St Edmunds **J 2**
36 Burythorpe **A 6**
47 Busby **D 10**
41 Buscel **G 9**
16 Buscot **D 3**
59 Bush **L 5**
21 Bush Bank **G 10**
27 Bush Green **G 5**
22 Bushbury **B 3**
18 Bushey **D 1**
18 Bushey Heath **E 2**
15 Bushley **A 11**

16 Bushton F 2
64 Busta C 7
45 Buston Barns B 10
18 Butcher's Pasture B 6
15 Butcombe H 8
45 Buteland E 7
7 Butleigh C 8
7 Butleigh Wootton C 8
17 Butler's Cross C 9
22 Butlers Marston G 6
27 Butley K 7
30 Butt Green E 5
44 Butterburn F 5
36 Buttercrambe A 5
40 Butterknowle C 1
6 Butterleigh E 3
38 Buttermere, Cumb. D 4
16 Buttermere, Wilts. H 4
30 Butters Green E 6
35 Buttershaw D 10
52 Butterstone C 5
31 Butterton E 9
40 Butterwick, Dur. B 4
24 Butterwick, Lincs. A 5
41 Butterwick, N. Yorks. H 10
41 Butterwick, N. Yorks. G 7
21 Buttington B 8
23 Buttock's Booth F 11
22 Buttonoak D 1
8 Butt's Green C 4
8 Buttsash E 6
27 Buxhall J 3
49 Buxley D 10
10 Buxted F 4
31 Buxton, Derby C 9
26 Buxton, Norfolk C 5
26 Buxton Heath C 5
14 Bwlch B 5
29 Bwlchgwyn E 11
20 Bwlchllan F 1
28 Bwlchtocyn H 3
29 Bwlch-y-cibau H 11
29 Bwlch-y-ddâr H 11
13 Bwlchyfadfa B 8
20 Bwlch-y-ffridd C 6
12 Bwlch-y-groes C 6
20 Bwlch-y-sarnau E 6
43 Byeloch D 11
40 Byers Green B 2
23 Byfield G 8
17 Byfleet H 11
21 Byford H 9
25 Bygrave L 4
61 Bylbster B 11
29 Bylchau D 9
30 Byley C 6
13 Bynea G 9
36 Byram E 3
49 Byrewalls E 9
44 Byrness C 6
25 Bythorn H 2
21 Byton F 9
45 Bywell G 8
9 Byworth D 11
52 Cablea C 4
37 Cabourne G 9
58 Cabrach E 1
54 Cabule Ldoge C 5
6 Cadbury F 3
4 Cadbury Barton D 6
59 Caddam K 1
47 Cadder B 11
51 Cadderlie D 7
17 Caddington B 11
49 Caddonfoot F 7
10 Cade Street F 5
23 Cadeby, Leics. B 7
36 Cadeby, S. Yorks. G 3
6 Cadeleigh E 3
48 Cademuir F 5
44 Cadgillhead E 2
2 Cadgwith H 4
53 Cadham G 7
34 Cadishead H 6
13 Cadle G 9
16 Cadley, Wilts. G 3
8 Cadley, Wilts. A 4
17 Cadmore End E 8
8 Cadnam E 5
37 Cadney G 8
29 Cadole D 11
13 Cadoxton-Juxta-Neath G 11
60 Cadubh G 3
14 Caehopkin C 2
28 Caenthraw D 4
33 Caenby A 7
33 Caenby Corner A 7
13 Caeo C 10
12 Caer Farchell D 1
14 Caerau E 2
13 Cae'r-bryn F 9
28 Caerdeon H 6
28 Cae'r-geiliog B 3
29 Caergwrle D 12
29 Caerhun C 7
44 Caerlanrig C 2
14 Caerleon E 6
12 Caerlleon E 6
28 Caernarvon D 4
14 Caerphilly F 5
20 Caersws C 6
13 Caerwedros A 7
15 Caerwent E 8
29 Caerwys C 10
43 Cairn C 10
58 Cairnargat D 2
50 Cairnbaan H 5
58 Cairnbrogie E 6
49 Cairncross C 11
42 Cairnderry D 4
51 Carndow F 9
58 Cairness B 8
48 Cairneyhill A 3
42 Cairnfield G 5
58 Cairnfield House B 2
42 Cairngaan H 2
42 Cairngarroch G 1
43 Cairnhall C 10
58 Cairnhill D 4
58 Cairnie, Grampian C 2
59 Cairnie, Grampian G 5
58 Cairnorrie D 6
42 Cairnryan E 2
42 Cairnsmore E 5
47 Cairntable H 9
42 Cairnwhin B 3
54 Caiseachan D 6
26 Caister-on-Sea D 8
37 Caistor G 9
26 Caistor St. Edmund E 5
45 Caistron C 8
49 Caitha Bowland E 7
63 Calbost E 5
8 Calbourne G 6
33 Calceby C 11
22 Calchems Corner E 6
15 Calcot Farm E 11
17 Calcot Row G 7
56 Calcots Station C 8
11 Calcott B 10
38 Caldbeck A 6
40 Caldbergh G 1
25 Caldecote, Beds. L 3
25 Caldecote, Cambs. K 4
25 Caldecote, Cambs. G 2
23 Caldecott, Leics. C 12
25 Caldecott, Northants H 1
38 Calder, Cumb. E 3
49 Calder, Northumb. G 12
38 Calder Bridge E 3
35 Calder Grove E 11
61 Calder Mains B 10
34 Calder Vale C 4
47 Calderbank C 12
35 Calderbrook E 8
48 Caldercruix C 1
47 Caldermill E 11
47 Calderwood D 11
15 Caldicot E 8
49 Caldside E 9
40 Caldwell D 2
30 Caldy B 1
13 Caledfwlch D 10
13 Caledrhydiau B 8
64 Calfsound B 3
50 Calgary B 1
56 Califer D 6
48 California, Central B 2
26 California, Norf. D 8
27 California, Suff. L 5
5 California Cross K 6
31 Calke H 12
45 Callaly B 9
52 Callander F 1
63 Callanish D 3
21 Callaughton C 11
51 Callert House A 8
2 Callestick E 5
62 Calligarry H 5
3 Callington C 10
15 Callow A 8
22 Callow End G 2
22 Callow Hill, Heref. & Worcs. E 1
22 Callow Hill, Heref. & Worcs. F 4
16 Callow Hill, Wilts. F 1
17 Callowhill G 11
21 Callows Grave F 11
8 Calmore E 5
16 Calmsden C 1
16 Calne G 1
32 Calow C 1
8 Calshot F 6
3 Calstock C 11
16 Calstone Wellington G 1
26 Calthorpe B 5
39 Calthwaite A 7
35 Calton, N. Yorks. A 8
31 Calton, Staffs. E 9
30 Calveley D 4
31 Calver C 11
21 Calver Hill G 9
30 Calverhall F 5
6 Calverleigh E 3
35 Calverley C 10
23 Calverton, Bucks. H 11
32 Calverton, Notts. E 3
52 Calvine A 3
43 Calvo F 12
15 Cam D 10
62 Camascross G 6
50 Camasnacroise B 6
54 Camasterach E 1
62 Camastianavaig D 4
62 Camasunary F 4
56 Camault Muir F 1
64 Camb B 7
11 Camber F 8
17 Camberley H 9
18 Camberwell F 3
36 Camblesforth D 4
53 Cambo, Fife F 10
45 Cambo, Northumb. D 8
45 Cambois E 11
2 Camborne F 4
25 Cambridge, Cambs. J 5
15 Cambridge, Glos. D 10
25 Cambridgeshire Co. K 5
52 Cambus H 3
59 Cambus o'May G 2
52 Cambusbarron H 3
52 Cambuskenneth H 3
47 Cambuslang C 11
54 Cambussorray F 7
18 Camden E 3
18 Cameley H 9
3 Camelford A 8
48 Camelon A 2
9 Camelsdale C 10
56 Camerory F 6
7 Camerton, Avon A 10
38 Camerton, Cumb. B 3
52 Camghouran B 1
55 Camisky L 5
59 Cammachmore H 6
32 Cammeringham B 6
46 Campbeltown G 2
45 Camperdown F 11
53 Campmuir C 7
25 Camps Green L 7
36 Campsall F 3
27 Campsea Ashe K 6
25 Campton L 2
44 Camptown B 5
12 Camrose E 3
52 Camserney B 3
61 Camster C 11
55 Camus-luinie G 3
50 Camuschoirk A 5
60 Camusnagaul G 2
54 Camusteel E 1
52 Camusvrachan B 1
8 Canada D 4
59 Candacraig G 1
58 Candacraig House F 1
33 Candlesby C 11
59 Candy J 5
48 Candy Mill E 3
17 Cane End F 8
19 Canewdon D 9
18 Canfield End B 6
8 Canford Bottom F 2
8 Canford Magna F 2
61 Canisbay A 12
7 Cann D 12
7 Cann Common D 12
3 Cannaframe B 9
7 Cannards Grave B 9
54 Canncih F 7
6 Cannington B 6
22 Cannock A 3
22 Cannock Wood A 4
15 Cannop C 9
21 Canon Bridge H 10
21 Canon Pyon G 10
44 Canonbie E 2
23 Canons Ashby G 9
2 Canonstown F 2
11 Canterbury B 10
26 Cantley, Norfolk E 7
36 Cantley, S. Yorks. G 4
14 Canton G 5
56 Cantraybruich E 3
56 Cantraydoune E 3
56 Cantraywood E 3
39 Cantsfield H 8
19 Canvey F 8
33 Canwick C 7
2 Canworthy Water B 2
55 Caol M 5
55 Caonich K 4
10 Capel D 1
20 Capel-Bangor D 2
20 Capel Betws Lleucu G 2
28 Capel Carmel G 1
28 Capel Curig D 6
13 Capel Cynon B 7
13 Capel Dewi, Dyfed E 8
20 Capel Dewi, Dyfed D 2
13 Capel Dewi, Dyfed C 8
29 Capel Garmon E 7
13 Capel Gwyn E 8
13 Capel Gwynfe E 10
13 Capel Hendre F 9
13 Capel Isaac D 9
12 Capel Iwan C 6
11 Capel le Ferne D 11
14 Capel Llanilterne F 4
27 Capel St. Andrew K 7
27 Capel St. Mary L 4
20 Capel Seion D 2
20 Capel Trisant E 3
12 Capel Tygwydd C 6
28 Capel-côch B 4
28 Capel-gwyn C 3
13 Capel-lago C 9
28 Capel-uchaf E 4
29 Capelulo C 7
14 Capel-y-ffin A 6
30 Capenhurst C 2
39 Capenwray H 8
45 Capheaton E 8
48 Cappercleuch G 5
48 Capplegill H 4
5 Capton, Devon K 7
6 Capton, Somerset B 4
52 Caputh C 6
32 Car Colston F 4
2 Carbis Bay F 2
62 Carbost, Skye E 3
62 Carbost, Skye C 4
60 Carbreck B 4
32 Cârbrook A 1
26 Carbrooke E 3
32 Carburton C 3
3 Carclaze D 7
47 Carcluie H 8
36 Carcroft F 3
53 Cardenden H 7
21 Cardeston A 9
14 Cardiff G 5
12 Cardigan B 5
25 Cardington, Bedfordshire K 2
21 Cardington, Salop. C 10
3 Cardinham C 8
42 Cardorcan D 5
56 Cardow E 7
48 Cardrona F 6
47 Cardross B 8
43 Cardurnock F 12
24 Careby D 1
59 Careston L 3
12 Carew G 4
12 Carew Cheriton G 4
12 Carew Newton F 4
44 Carewoodrig C 3
15 Carey A 9
47 Carfin D 12
49 Carfrae B 8
43 Cargenbridge D 10
52 Cargill C 6
44 Cargo G 2
3 Cargreen C 11
49 Carham F 10
6 Carhampton B 3
2 Carharrack F 4
52 Carie A 1
8 Carisbrooke G 6
38 Cark G 6
3 Carkeel D 11
2 Carland Cross D 5
44 Carlatton Mill H 4
24 Carlby D 2
35 Carlecotes G 10
2 Carleen G 3
44 Carleton, Cumb. H 3
42 Carleton, Dumf. & Gall. H 5
35 Carleton, N. Yorks. B 8
26 Carleton Forehoe E 4
26 Carleton Rode F 4
2 Carlidnack G 5
41 Carlin How C 7
15 Carlingcott H 10
44 Carlisle G 2
48 Carlops D 4
63 Carloway C 3
25 Carlton, Beds. K 1
25 Carlton, Cambs. K 7
40 Carlton, Cleveland C 4
23 Carlton, Leics. B 7
40 Carlton, N. Yorks. F 6
40 Carlton, N. Yorks. G 1
36 Carlton, N. Yorks. E 4
32 Carlton, Notts. F 3
35 Carlton, S. Yorks. F 12
27 Carlton, Suffolk J 7
36 Carlton, W. Yorks. D 1
26 Carlton, Colville F 8
23 Carlton Curlieu B 10
40 Carlton Husthwaite G 5
40 Carlton in Cleveland E 5
32 Carlton in Lindrick B 3
40 Carlton Miniott G 4
32 Carlton Scroop F 6
32 Carlton-le-Moorland D 6
32 Carlton-on-Trent D 5
48 Carluke D 1
3 Carlyon Bay D 7
48 Carmacoup G 1
13 Carmarthen E 7
29 Carmel, Clwyd C 11
13 Carmel, Dyfed E 9
28 Carmel, Gwynedd E 4
28 Carmel, Gwynedd B 3
13 Carmel Chapel D 10
38 Carmel Fell F 6
63 Carminish H 1
59 Carmont J 5
47 Carmunnock D 11
47 Carmyle C 11
53 Carmyllie C 10
37 Carnaby A 9
55 Carnach, Highland L 1
55 Carnach, Highland G 4
63 Carnach, W. Isles G 3
61 Carnachy C 7
57 Carnachuin K 4
57 Carnaqheen K 8
53 Carnbee F 10
52 Carnbo G 5
55 Carndu G 3
47 Carnduff E 11
2 Carne F 6
47 Carnell F 9
14 Carnetown E 4
39 Carnforth H 7
55 Carn-gorm G 3
12 Carnhedryn Uchaf D 2
2 Carnhell Green F 3
63 Carnish D 1
2 Carnkie F 4
20 Carno C 5
55 Carnoch, Highland K 2
54 Carnoch, Highland F 7
54 Carnoch, Highland E 6
52 Carnock H 5
2 Carnon Downs F 5
53 Carnoustie D 10
48 Carnwath E 3
29 Carog E 7
62 Caroy D 2
39 Carperby F 12
32 Carr A 2
34 Carr Cross F 3
44 Carr Shield H 6
32 Carr Vale C 2
46 Carradale E 3
63 Carragrich G 3
57 Carrbridge G 5
35 Carrbrook G 8
28 Carreglefn A 3
12 Carregwen C 6
53 Carrick, Fife E 9
51 Carrick, Strathclyde H 9
48 Carriden A 3
34 Carrington, Manchester H 6
33 Carrington, Lincs. E 10
48 Carrington, Lothian C 6
29 Carrog F 10
48 Carron, Central A 2
56 Carron, Grampian E 8
47 Carron Bridge A 12
43 Carronbridge B 9
48 Carronshore A 2
47 Carrot E 10
15 Carrow Hill E 7
43 Carrutherstown D 11
40 Carrville A 3
46 Carsaig, Strathclyde A 2
50 Carsaig, Strathclyde E 3
42 Carscreugh F 3
46 Carse House C 2
42 Carsebuie E 4
42 Carsegown F 5
42 Carseriggan E 4
43 Carsethorn F 10
18 Carshalton G 3
31 Carsington E 11
46 Carskiey H 2
42 Carsluith F 6
42 Carsphairn B 6
48 Carstairs E 2
48 Carstairs Junction E 2
44 Carter Bar B 5
49 Carterhaugh G 7
8 Carter's Clay D 4
16 Carterton C 4
45 Carterway Heads H 8
3 Carthew D 7
40 Carthorpe G 3
45 Cartington C 8
48 Cartland E 1
38 Cartmel G 6
13 Carway F 8
7 Cary Fitzpaine D 9
63 Caryshader D 2
43 Carzield C 10
21 Cascob F 8
51 Cashlie C 12
8 Cashmoor E 1
16 Cassey Compton C 1
16 Cassington, Oxon C 5
7 Cassington, Som. B 7
40 Cassop A 4
24 Casswell's Bridge C 3
14 Castell-y-bwch E 6
39 Casterton G 8
26 Castle Acre D 1
23 Castle Ashby F 11
31 Castle Bank H 7
39 Castle Bolton F 12
22 Castle Bromwich C 5
24 Castle Bytham D 1
21 Castle Caereinion B 7
25 Castle Camps L 7
44 Castle Carrock G 4
7 Castle Cary C 10
15 Castle Combe F 11
32 Castle Donnington G 2
43 Castle Douglas E 8
16 Castle Eaton E 2
40 Castle Eden A 4
58 Castle Forbes F 4
21 Castle Frome H 12
17 Castle Green H 10
31 Castle Gresley H 11
49 Castle Heaton E 11
27 Castle Hedingham L 1
10 Castle Hill D 6
41 Castle Howard H 7
53 Castle Huntly D 8
42 Castle Kennedy F 2
12 Castle Morris D 3
44 Castle O'er D 1
21 Castle Pulverbatch B 9
24 Castle Rising C 8
56 Castle Stuart E 3
12 Castlebythe D 4
47 Castlecary B 12
48 Castlecraig, Borders E 4
56 Castlecraig, Highland C 4
43 Castlefairn C 8
36 Castleford E 2
48 Castlehill, Borders F 5
58 Castlehill, Grampian C 5
47 Castlehill, Strathclyde B 9
48 Castlehill, Strathclyde D 1
42 Castlemaddy C 6
12 Castlemartin G 3
43 Castlemilk D 12
15 Castlemorton A 11
45 Castleside H 9
23 Castlethorpe H 11
44 Castleton, Borders D 3
31 Castleton, Derby B 10
35 Castleton, Manchester F 7
14 Castleton, Gwent F 6
41 Castleton, N. Yorks D 7
46 Castleton, Strathclyde A 4
53 Castleton, Tayside C 8
7 Casteltown, Dorset H 7
61 Castletown, Highland A 11
56 Castletown, Highland E 3
38 Castletown, I.o.M. H 1
45 Castletown, Tyne & Wear G 11
35 Castley C 11
26 Caston F 2
24 Castor F 2
13 Caswell H 9
31 Cat and Fiddle Inn C 8
46 Catacol D 4
15 Catbrain F 9
15 Catbrook D 8
2 Catchall G 2
44 Catcleugh C 6
32 Catcliffe A 2
7 Catcott B 7
7 Catcott Burtle B 7
10 Caterham C 2
26 Catfield C 7
64 Catfirth D 7
18 Catford G 4
34 Catforth D 4

14 Cathays **F 5**
47 Cathcart **C 10**
14 Cathedine **B 5**
9 Catherington **E 8**
7 Catherston Leweston **G 7**
21 Catherton **E 12**
49 Cathpair **E 7**
43 Catlins **C 12**
57 Catlodge **K 2**
44 Catlowdy **E 3**
16 Catmore **F 5**
34 Caton **A 4**
5 Cator Court **H 5**
47 Catrine **G 10**
15 Cat's Ash **E 7**
10 Catsfield **G 6**
22 Catshill **E 3**
36 Cattal **B 2**
27 Cattawade **M 4**
34 Catterall **C 4**
40 Catterick **E 3**
40 Catterick Bridge **E 3**
40 Catterick Camp **E 2**
39 Catterlen **B 7**
59 Catterline **J 6**
36 Catterton **C 3**
9 Catteshall **B 11**
23 Catthorpe **D 9**
7 Cattistock **F 9**
26 Catton, Norfolk **D 5**
44 Catton, Northumb. **G 6**
40 Catton, N. Yorks **G 4**
37 Catwick **C 9**
25 Catworth **H 2**
16 Caulcott **B 6**
52 Cauldhame **H 1**
44 Cauldmill **B 4**
31 Cauldon **E 9**
44 Cauldside **E 3**
31 Cauldwell **H 11**
58 Cauldwells **B 5**
43 Caulkerbush **F 10**
7 Caundle Marsh **E 10**
22 Caunsall **D 2**
32 Caunton **D 5**
42 Causeway End **F 5**
58 Causewayend, Grampian **F 7**
48 Causewayend, Strathclyde **F 3**
52 Causewayhead, Central **H 3**
43 Causewayhead, Cumb. **F 12**
45 Causey Park Bri. **D 10**
39 Cautley **F 9**
27 Cavendish **K 1**
27 Cavenham **H 1**
17 Caversfield **B 7**
17 Caversham **G 8**
31 Caverswall **F 8**
36 Cavil **D 5**
56 Cawdor **E 4**
37 Cawkeld **B 8**
3 Cawsand **E 11**
26 Cawston **C 4**
41 Cawthorne **F 8**
35 Cawthorne **F 11**
24 Cawthorpe **C 2**
36 Cawood **C 3**
40 Cawton **G 6**
25 Caxton **J 4**
21 Caynham **E 11**
32 Caythorpe, Lincs. **E 6**
32 Caythorpe, Notts. **F 4**
41 Cayton **G 10**
61 Ceann-na-coille **C 7**
29 Cefn-Berain **C 9**
29 Cefn-Canol **G 11**
29 Cefn Coch **G 10**
14 Cefn Cribbwr **F 2**
14 Cefn Cross **F 2**
21 Cefn Einion **D 8**
14 Cefn Fforest **D 5**
15 Cefn Llaithan **B 7**
29 Cefn Mawr **F 12**
14 Cefn Rhigos **D 2**
29 Cefn-brith **E 8**
13 Cefn-bryn-brain **F 10**
14 Cefn-coed-y-cymmer **C 3**
29 Cefn-ddwysarn **F 9**
13 Cefneithin **F 9**
20 Cefngorwydd **H 5**
29 Cefn-y-bedd **E 12**
12 Cefn-y-pant **D 5**
13 Cellan **B 9**
31 Cellarhead **E 8**
39 Celleron **C 7**
28 Cemaes Bay **A 3**
20 Cemmaes **B 4**
20 Cemmaes Road **B 4**
12 Cenarth **C 6**
53 Ceres **F 9**
20 Cerist **D 5**
7 Cerne Abbas **F 10**
16 Cerney Wick **E 2**
28 Cerrigceinwen **C 4**
29 Cerrigydrudion **E 9**
26 Cess **D 7**
49 Cessford **G 10**
28 Ceunant **D 5**
15 Chaceley **A 11**
2 Chacewater **E 5**
17 Chackmore **A 8**
23 Chacombe **H 8**
22 Chad Valley **D 4**
22 Chadbury **G 4**
35 Chadderton **G 7**
31 Chaddesden **F 12**
22 Chaddesley Corbett **E 2**
16 Chaddleworth **F 5**
16 Chadlington **B 4**
23 Chadshunt **G 7**
32 Chadwell **H 5**
18 Chadwell St. Mary **F 6**
22 Chadwick End **E 5**
7 Chaffcombe **E 7**
5 Chagford **G 6**
10 Chailey **F 3**
24 Chainbridge **E 5**
10 Chainhurst **C 6**
8 Chalbury **E 2**
8 Chalbury Com. **E 2**
10 Chaldon **C 2**
7 Chaldon Herring or East Chaldon **H 11**
8 Chale **H 6**
8 Chale Green **H 6**
17 Chalfont St. Giles **E 10**
17 Chalfont St. Peter **E 11**
15 Chalford **D 12**
17 Chalford Com. **E 11**
17 Chalgrove **D 7**
10 Chalk **A 5**
4 Challacombe, Devon **B 6**
4 Challacombe, Devon **D 6**
42 Challoch **E 5**
11 Challock Lees **C 8**
17 Chalton, Beds. **B 11**
9 Chalton, Hants. **E 8**
17 Chalvey **F 10**
10 Chalvington **G 4**
48 Champany **B 3**
20 Chancery **E 1**
17 Chandler's Cross **D 11**
8 Chandler's Ford **D 6**
43 Chanlockfoot **B 8**
7 Chantry **B 10**
53 Chapel **H 7**
7 Chapel Allerton **A 7**
35 Chapel Allerton **C 11**
3 Chapel Amble **B 7**
23 Chapel Brampton **E 10**
30 Chapel Chorlton **F 6**
23 Chapel End **C 7**
22 Chapel Green **D 6**
36 Chapel Haddlesey **D 4**
58 Chapel Hill, Grampian **D 8**
15 Chapel Hill, Gwent **D 8**
33 Chapel Hill, Lincs. **E 9**
35 Chapel Hill, N. Yorks. **C 12**
21 Chapel Lawn **E 8**
39 Chapel le Dale **G 9**
49 Chapel Mains **E 8**
59 Chapel of Barras **J 6**
58 Chapel of Garioch **E 5**
42 Chapel Rossan **G 2**
16 Chapel Row, Berks. **G 6**
10 Chapel Row, E. Sussex **G 5**
33 Chapel St. Leonards **C 12**
38 Chapel Stile **E 5**
42 Chapeldonan **B 3**
31 Chapel-en-le-Frith **B 9**
47 Chapelhall **C 12**
43 Chapelhill, Dumf. & Gall. **B 11**
53 Chapelhill, Tayside **E 7**
52 Chapelhill, Tayside **D 5**
48 Chapelhope **G 5**
44 Chapelknowe **F 2**
38 Chapels **G 5**
4 Chapelton, Devon **C 5**
43 Chapelton, Dumf. & Gall. **G 8**
59 Chapelton, Grampian **J 5**
57 Chapelton, Grampian **H 5**
47 Chapelton, Highland **E 11**
53 Chapelton, Tayside **B 11**
57 Chapeltown, Grampian **G 8**
34 Chapeltown, Lancs. **F 6**
35 Chapeltown, S. Yorks. **G 12**
5 Chapmans Well **G 2**
7 Chapmanslade **B 11**
18 Chapmore End **B 3**
19 Chappel **A 9**
7 Chard **E 7**
6 Chardstock **F 6**
15 Charfield **E 10**
11 Charing **C 8**
8 Charing Cross **E 3**
11 Charing Heath **C 8**
22 Charingworth **H 5**
16 Charlbury **B 5**
15 Charlcombe **H 10**
16 Charlcutt **G 1**
22 Charlecote **F 6**
4 Charles **C 6**
43 Charlesfield **E 12**
53 Charleston **C 8**
59 Charlestown, Grampian **G 7**
8 Charlestown, Corn. **E 7**
7 Charlestown, Dorset **H 9**
48 Charlestown, Fife **A 3**
54 Charlestown, Highland **B 2**
56 Charlestown, Highland **E 2**
35 Charlestown, W. Yorks. **D 8**
56 Charlestown of Aberlour **E 8**
35 Charlesworth **H 9**
5 Charleton **L 6**
6 Charlinch **B 6**
18 Charlton, Herts. **A 2**
40 Charlton, Cleveland **D 6**
22 Charlton, Heref. & Worc. **H 4**
44 Charlton, Northumb. **D 6**
16 Charlton, Oxon **A 6**
9 Charlton, W. Sussex **E 10**
8 Charlton, Wilts. **A 3**
8 Charlton, Wilts. **D 3**
16 Charlton, Wilts. **H 2**
7 Charlton, Wilts. **D 12**
16 Charlton, Wilts. **E 1**
16 Charlton Abbots **B 1**
7 Charlton Adam **C 9**
7 Charlton Horethorne **D 10**
16 Charlton Kings **B 1**
7 Charlton Mackrell **C 8**
7 Charlton Marshall **F 12**
45 Charlton Mires **A 10**
7 Charlton Musgrove **C 10**
16 Charlton-on-Otmoor **C 6**
7 Charlton-on-the-Hill **F 12**
9 Charlwood, Hants. **C 8**
10 Charlwood, Surrey **D 1**
7 Charminster **G 10**
7 Charmouth **G 7**
17 Charndon **B 7**
16 Charney Bassett **E 5**
34 Charnock Richard **F 4**
27 Charsfield **J 5**
11 Chart Sutton **C 7**
17 Charter Alley **H 7**
49 Charterhouse, Borders **F 9**
7 Charterhouse, Som. **A 8**
16 Charterville Allotments **C 4**
11 Chartham **C 9**
11 Chartham Hatch **B 9**
8 Charton **A 5**
17 Chartridge **D 10**
17 Charvil **G 8**
23 Charwelton **G 8**
22 Chase Terrace **A 4**
22 Chasetown **A 4**
16 Chastleton **A 3**
4 Chasty **F 2**
34 Chatburn **C 6**
30 Chatcull **G 6**
10 Chatham **B 6**
45 Chathill **E 12**
10 Chattenden **A 6**
25 Chatteris **G 5**
27 Chattisham **L 4**
44 Chatto **A 6**
45 Chatton **C 12**
17 Chaul End **B 11**
4 Chawleigh **E 6**
25 Chawston **K 3**
9 Chawton **B 8**
31 Cheadle, Manchester **A 7**
31 Cheadle, Staffs. **F 8**
31 Cheadle Hulme **B 7**
18 Cheam **G 2**
17 Cheapside **G 10**
17 Chearsley **C 8**
31 Chebsey **G 7**
17 Checkendon **F 7**
30 Checkley, Cheshire **F 6**
21 Checkley, Heref. & Worc. **H 11**
31 Checkley, Staffs. **F 9**
27 Chedburgh **J 1**
7 Cheddar **A 8**
17 Cheddington **B 10**
31 Cheddleton **E 8**
6 Cheddon Fitzpaine **C 6**
26 Chedgrave **E 7**
7 Chedington **F 8**
27 Chediston **G 7**
16 Chedworth **C 2**
7 Chedzoy **B 7**
49 Cheeklaw **D 10**
35 Cheetham Hill **G 7**
4 Cheglinch **B 4**
4 Cheldon **E 6**
31 Chelford **C 7**
31 Chellaston **G 12**
25 Chellington **K 1**
22 Chelmarsh **C 1**
27 Chelmondiston **L 5**
31 Chelmorton **C 9**
19 Chelmsford **C 7**
18 Chelsea **F 3**
18 Chelsfield Village **G 5**
27 Chelsworth **K 3**
15 Cheltenham, Glos. **B 12**
14 Cheltenham, Gwent **C 5**
25 Chelveston **H 1**
15 Chelvey **G 8**
15 Chelwood **H 9**
10 Chelwood Com. **E 3**
10 Chelwood Gate **E 3**
21 Cheney Longville **D 9**
17 Chenies **D 11**
15 Chepstow **E 8**
16 Cherhill **G 1**
15 Cherington, Glos. **D 12**
22 Cherington, War. **H 6**
9 Cheriton, Hants. **C 7**
11 Cheriton, Kent **D 11**
4 Cheriton, Som. **A 6**
13 Cheriton, W. Glam. **H 8**
4 Cheriton Bishop **F 6**
5 Cheriton Cross **G 6**
6 Cheriton Fitzpaine **F 2**
12 Cheriton or Stackpole Elidor **G 3**
30 Cherrington **H 5**
37 Cherry Burton **C 7**
25 Cherry Hinton **K 6**
22 Cherry Orchard **G 2**
52 Cherrybank **E 6**
49 Cherrytrees **F 10**
17 Chertsey **G 11**
7 Cheselbourne **F 11**
17 Chesham **D 10**
17 Chesham Bois **D 10**
30 Cheshire, Co. **D 5**
18 Cheshunt **D 4**
22 Cheslyn Hay **A 3**
18 Chessington **H 2**
30 Chester **D 3**
45 Chester Moor **H 11**
7 Chesterblade **B 10**
32 Chesterfield **C 1**
22 Chesterfield **B 4**
48 Chesterhall **F 2**
48 Chesterhill **C 6**
45 Chester-le-Street **H 11**
44 Chesters, Borders **B 5**
49 Chesters, Borders **G 8**
24 Chesterton, Cambs. **F 2**
16 Chesterton, Oxon **B 6**
31 Chesterton, Staffs. **E 7**
44 Chesterwood **F 6**
11 Chestfield **B 10**
30 Cheswardine **G 6**
45 Cheswick **A 11**
45 Cheswick Bldgs. **A 11**
7 Chetnole **E 9**
6 Chettiscombe **E 3**
25 Chettisham **G 6**
8 Chettle **E 1**
21 Chetton **C 12**
30 Chetwynd Aston **H 6**
30 Chetwynd Park **H 6**
25 Cheveley **J 8**
10 Chevening **B 4**
27 Chevington **J 1**
45 Chevington Drift **C 11**
6 Chevithorne **E 3**
15 Chew Magna **H 9**
15 Chew Stoke **H 9**
15 Chewton Keynsham **H 9**
7 Chewton Mendip **A 9**
23 Chicheley **G 12**
9 Chichester **F 10**
7 Chickerell **H 9**
7 Chicklade **C 12**
21 Chickward **G 8**
9 Chidden **D 8**
9 Chiddingfold **C 11**
10 Chiddingly **G 4**
10 Chiddingstone **D 4**
10 Chiddingstone Causeway **C 4**
10 Chiddingstone Hoath **D 4**
7 Chideock **G 8**
6 Chidgley **C 4**
9 Chidham **F 9**
16 Chieveley **G 5**
18 Chignall St. James **C 6**
18 Chignall Smealy **C 6**
18 Chigwell **E 4**
18 Chigwell Row **E 5**
8 Chilbolton **B 5**
8 Chilcomb **C 6**
7 Chilcombe **G 9**
7 Chilcompton **A 9**
22 Chilcote **A 6**
7 Child Okeford **E 11**
16 Childrey **E 5**
30 Child's Ercall **H 5**
22 Childswickham **H 4**
30 Childwall **A 3**
18 Childwick Green **C 1**
7 Chilfrome **F 9**
9 Chilgrove **E 9**
11 Chilham **C 9**
8 Chilhampton **C 3**
4 Chilla **F 3**
5 Chillaton **H 3**
11 Chillenden **C 11**
8 Chillerton **H 6**
27 Chillesford **K 7**
45 Chillingham **C 12**
5 Chillington, Devon **L 7**
7 Chillington, Somerset **E 7**
8 Chilmark **C 1**
16 Chilson **B 4**
3 Chilsworthy, Corn. **B 11**
4 Chilsworthy, Devon **E 2**
7 Chilthorne Domer **D 8**
17 Chilton, Bucks. **C 8**
4 Chilton, Devon **E 7**
16 Chilton, Oxon **F 6**
40 Chilton, Durham **B 3**
9 Chilton Candover **B 7**
7 Chilton Cantelo **D 9**
16 Chilton Foliat **G 4**
40 Chilton Lane **B 3**
7 Chilton Polden **B 7**
27 Chilton Street **K 1**
6 Chilton Trinity **B 6**
32 Chilwell **G 2**
8 Chilworth, Hants. **D 5**
9 Chilworth, Surrey **A 11**
16 Chimney **D 4**
9 Chineham **A 8**
18 Chingford **E 4**
31 Chinley **B 9**
31 Chinley Head **B 9**
17 Chinnor **D 8**
30 Chipnall **G 6**
25 Chippenham, Cambs. **H 8**
15 Chippenham, Wilts. **G 12**
17 Chipperfield **D 11**
25 Chipping, Herts. **M 5**
34 Chipping, Lancs. **C 5**
22 Chipping Campden **H 5**
16 Chipping Norton **B 4**
15 Chipping Sodbury **F 10**
23 Chipping Warden **G 8**
6 Chipstable **D 4**
10 Chipstead, Kent **B 4**
10 Chipstead, Surrey **B 2**
21 Chirbury **C 8**
29 Chirk **F 12**
29 Chirk Green **F 12**
42 Chirmorie **D 3**
49 Chirnside **D 11**
49 Chirnsidebridge **D 11**
16 Chirton **H 2**
16 Chisbury **G 4**
7 Chiselborough **E 8**
16 Chiseldon **F 3**
35 Chiserley **D 9**
17 Chislehampton **D 7**
18 Chislehurst **G 4**
11 Chislet **B 11**
18 Chiswell Green **C 1**
18 Chiswick **F 2**
35 Chisworth **H 8**
11 Chitcombe **F 7**
9 Chithurst **D 9**
25 Chittering **H 6**
8 Chitterne **B 2**
4 Chittlehamholt **D 5**
4 Chittlehampton **C 5**
15 Chittoe **H 12**
5 Chivelstone **M 6**
17 Chobham **H 10**
49 Choicelee **D 10**
8 Cholderton **B 4**
17 Cholesbury **C 10**
45 Chollerford **F 7**
45 Chollerton **F 7**
17 Cholsey **E 7**
21 Cholstrey **F 10**
40 Chop Gate **E 6**
45 Choppington **E 10**
45 Chopwell **G 9**
30 Chorley, Cheshire **E 4**
34 Chorley, Lancs. **E 5**
21 Chorley, Salop. **D 12**
22 Chorley, Staffs. **A 4**
17 Chorleywood **E 11**
30 Chorlton **E 6**
35 Chorlton cum Hardy **H 7**
30 Chorlton Lane **E 3**
25 Chrishall **L 5**
24 Christchurch, Cambs. **F 6**
8 Christchurch, Dorset **G 3**
15 Christchurch, Gwent **E 7**
16 Christian Malford **F 1**
30 Christleton **D 3**
17 Christmas Com. **E 8**
7 Christon **A 7**
45 Christon Bank **A 10**
5 Christow **G 7**
9 Christ's Hospital **C 12**
47 Chryston **B 11**
5 Chudleigh **H 7**
5 Chudleigh Knighton **H 7**
4 Chulmleigh **E 6**
35 Chunal **H 9**
34 Church **D 6**
30 Church Aston **H 6**
23 Church Brampton **E 10**
31 Church Broughton **G 10**
9 Church Crookham **A 9**
31 Church Eaton **H 7**
25 Church End, Beds. **L 3**
19 Church End, Essex **A 7**
25 Church End, Essex **L 7**
17 Church End, Hants. **H 7**
17 Church End, Hertfordshire **C 12**
37 Church End, Lincs. **G 12**
18 Church End, London **E 3**
24 Church End, Norf. **E 5**
22 Church End, War. **C 6**
16 Church End, Wilts. **F 1**
16 Church Enstone **B 5**
36 Church Fenton **C 3**
6 Church Green **G 5**
31 Church Gresley **H 11**
16 Church Hanborough **C 5**
30 Church Hill **D 5**
41 Church House **E 7**
41 Church Houses **E 7**
8 Church Knowle **H 1**
32 Church Laneham **C 5**
23 Church Langton **C 10**
23 Church Lawford **D 8**
31 Church Lawton **E 7**
31 Church Leigh **G 9**
22 Church Lench **G 4**
30 Church Minshull **D 5**
21 Church Preen **C 11**
21 Church Pulverbatch **B 9**
21 Church Stoke **C 8**
23 Church Stowe **F 9**
10 Church Street, Kent **A 6**
27 Church Street, Suffolk **G 8**
21 Church Stretton **C 10**
14 Church Village **F 4**
32 Church Warsop **C 3**
15 Churcham **B 11**
15 Churchdown **B 12**
15 Churchend, Avon **E 10**
18 Churchend, Essex **B 6**
19 Churchend, Essex **E 10**
22 Churchfield **C 4**
15 Churchill, Avon. **H 7**
4 Churchill, Devon **B 5**
6 Churchill, Devon **F 6**
22 Churchill, Heref. & Worc. **G 3**
16 Churchill, Oxon **B4**
22 Churchill, Salop. **D 2**
6 Churchingford **E 5**
23 Churchover **D 8**
6 Churchstanton **E 5**
5 Churchstow **L 6**
38 Churchtown, Cumb. **A 6**
4 Churchtown, Dev. **F 2**
38 Churchtown, I.o.M. **G 2**
34 Churchtown, Lancs. **C 4**
34 Churchtown, Merseyside **E 3**
44 Churnsike Lodge **E 5**
5 Churston Ferrers **K 8**
9 Churt **B 10**
30 Churton **E 3**
35 Churwell **D 11**
8 Chute Standen **A 5**
28 Chwilog **F 4**
29 Cilcain **D 11**
13 Cilcennin **A 8**
13 Cilfrew **G 11**
14 Ciffnydd **E 4**
12 Cilgerran **C 5**
12 Cilgwyn **C 4**
13 Ciliau Aeron **A 8**
13 Cilmaengwyn **F 10**
20 Cilmery **G 5**

12 Cilrhedyn D 6
13 Cilsan E 9
29 Ciltalgarth F 8
12 Cilwendeg C 6
13 Cilybebyll F 10
13 Cilycwm C 11
15 Cinderford C 10
12 Cippyn B 5
16 Cirencester D 1
40 Citadilla E 2
28 City Dulas B 4
57 Clachaig, Highland H 6
46 Clachaig, Strathclyde A 6
62 Clachan, Highland E 5
50 Clachan, Strathclyde C 6
50 Clachan, Strathclyde F 5
51 Clachan, Strathclyde F 9
46 Clachan, Strathclyde D 3
47 Clachan of Campsie A 11
46 Clachan of Glendaruel A 5
50 Clachan-Seil F 5
46 Clachbreck B 3
59 Clachnabrain L 1
60 Clachtoll D 2
52 Clackmannan H 4
56 Clackmarras D 8
19 Clacton on Sea B 11
47 Cladance E 11
51 Cladich E 8
50 Claggan C 4
62 Claigan C 2
22 Claines F 2
60 Clais Charnach A 4
60 Claisfearn C 3
7 Clandown A 10
9 Clanfield, Hants. D 8
16 Clanfield, Oxon D 4
8 Clanville A 5
46 Claonaig D 4
35 Clap Gate B 12
11 Clap Hill D 9
8 Clapgate, Dorset F 2
13 Clapgate, Herts. A 4
25 Clapham, Beds. K 1
6 Clapham, Devon H 2
18 Clapham, London F 3
39 Clapham, N. Yorks. H 9
9 Clapham, W. Sussex E 12
49 Clappers D 12
38 Clappersgate E 6
7 Clapton, Somerset F 7
7 Clapton, Som. A 10
15 Clapton-in-Gordano G 8
16 Clapton on the Hill B 3
4 Clapworthy D 5
20 Clarach D 2
12 Clarbeston E 4
12 Clarbeston Road E 4
32 Clarborough B 4
27 Clare L 1
43 Clarebrand E 8
43 Clarencefield E 11
49 Clarilaw G 8
49 Clarilawmoor F 8
9 Clarken Green A 7
47 Clarkston D 10
61 Clashbuie B 7
61 Clashcoig G 7
58 Clashindarroch D 2
61 Clashmore G 7
60 Clashnessie D 2
57 Clashnoir G 8
52 Clathy E 5
58 Clatt E 3
20 Clatter C 5
8 Clatterford G 6
59 Clattering Bridge J 4
42 Clatteringshawes D 6
6 Clatworthy C 4
34 Claughton, Lancs. A 4
34 Claughton, Lancs. C 4
30 Claughton, Merseyside A 2
6 Clavelshay C 6
22 Claverdon F 5
15 Claverham H 8
25 Clavering M 6
22 Claverley C 2
15 Claverton H 11
14 Clawdd-coch F 4
29 Clawddnewydd E 10
39 Clawthorpe G 8
4 Clawton F 2
37 Claxby, Lincs. H 9
33 Claxby, Lincs. C 11
26 Claxton, Norfolk E 6
36 Claxton, N. Yorks. A 5
23 Clay D 9
27 Clay Common G 8
32 Clay Cross D 1
57 Claybokie K 6
23 Claybrooke Magna C 8
23 Claybrooke Parva C 8
23 Claydon, Oxon G 8
27 Claydon, Suffolk K 4
59 Clayfolds H 6
44 Claygate, Dumf. & Gall. E 2
10 Claygate, Kent D 6
17 Claygate, Surrey H 12
6 Clayhanger, Devon D 4
22 Clayhanger, W. Midlands B 4
6 Clayhidon E 5
11 Clayhill, E. Sussex F 7
8 Clayhill, Hants. E 5
58 Claymires E 7
32 Claypole E 6
31 Clayton, Staffs. F 7
36 Clayton, S. Yorks. F 2
10 Clayton, W. Sussex G 2
35 Clayton, W. Yorks. D 10
34 Clayton Green E 5
35 Clayton West F 11
34 Clayton-le-Moors D 6
34 Clayton-le-Woods E 4
32 Clayworth A 4
45 Cleadon G 12
5 Clearbrook J 4
15 Clearwell D 9
40 Cleasby D 3
64 Cleat E 2
40 Cleatlam C 1
38 Cleator D 3
38 Cleator Moor D 3
35 Cleckheaton E 10
21 Clee St. Margaret D 11
21 Cleedownton D 11
21 Cleehill E 11
21 Cleestanton D 11
37 Cleethorpes F 10
21 Cleeton St. Mary E 11
15 Cleeve, Avon H 8
17 Cleeve, Oxon F 7
16 Cleeve Hill A 1
22 Cleeve Prior G 4
15 Clehonger A 8
50 Cleigh E 6
52 Cleish G 6
48 Cleland D 1
50 Clenamacrie E 6
16 Clench Common H 3
24 Clenchwarton C 7
45 Clennell B 7
22 Clent D 3
21 Cleobury Mortimer E 12
21 Cleobury North D 11
56 Clephanton E 4
47 Clerkland E 9
49 Clerklands G 7
64 Clestran D 1
44 Cleuch Head B 4
43 Cleuchbrae D 11
44 Cleuchfoot E 2
43 Clecuhhead B 9
43 Cleuchheads C 12
43 Cleuchside D 12
16 Clevancy G 2
15 Clevedon G 7
40 Cleveland, Co. C 5
40 Cleveland Tontine Inn E 5
34 Cleveleys C 2
16 Cleverton F 1
14 Clevis G 2
7 Clewer A 8
26 Cley-next-the-Sea A 3
63 Cliasamol F 2
39 Cliburn C 8
9 Cliddesden A 7
50 Cliff A 4
11 Cliff End G 7
10 Cliff Woods A 6
53 Cliffburn C 11
19 Cliffe, Kent F 7
36 Cliffe, N. Yorks. D 4
40 Cliffe, N. Yorks. D 2
4 Clifford, Devon D 2
21 Clifford, Heref. & Worc. H 8
36 Clifford, W. Yorks. C 2
22 Clifford Chambers G 5
15 Clifford's Mesne B 10
11 Cliffsend B 12
15 Clifton, Avon G 9
25 Clifton, Beds. L 3
51 Clifton, Central D 10
39 Clifton, Cumbria C 8
31 Clifton, Derby F 10
22 Clifton, Heref. & Worc. G 2
34 Clifton, Lancs. D 4
48 Clifton, Lothian B 4
35 Cliton, N. Yorks B 10
36 Clifton, N. Yorks. B 4
45 Clifton, Northumb. E 10
32 Clifton, Notts. G 3
16 Clifton, Oxon A 6
36 Clifton, S. Yorks. G 3
22 Clifton Campville A 6
16 Clifton Hampden E 6
23 Clifton Reynes G 12
23 Clifton upon Dunsmore D 8
21 Clifton upon Teme F 12
11 Cliftonville A 12
9 Climping F 11
48 Climpy D 2
7 Clink A 11
35 Clint A 11
26 Clint Green D 3
49 Clintmains F 8
26 Clippesby D 7
24 Clipsham D 1
4 Clipston, Devon F 5
23 Clipston, Northants D 10
32 Clipston, Notts. G 4
32 Clipstone D 3
34 Clitheroe C 6
30 Clive H 4
64 Clivocast B 8
37 Clixby G 8
29 Clocaenog E 10
58 Clochan B 1
13 Clochyrie F 8
30 Clock Face A 4
49 Clockmill D 10
14 Clodock B 6
7 Cloford B 10
13 Cloigyn F 8
58 Clola C 7
25 Clophill L 2
25 Clopton G 2
27 Clopton Green K 1
38 Close Clark H 1
43 Closeburn B 9
43 Closeburnmill B 10
7 Closworth E 9
25 Clothall M 4
40 Clotherholme H 3
30 Clotton D 4
35 Clough F 9
35 Clough Foot E 8
41 Cloughton F 10
41 Cloughton Newlands F 10
64 Clousta D 6
58 Colva, Grampian E 2
59 Clova, Tayside K 1
39 Clove Lodge C 11
4 Clovelly D 2
49 Clovenfords F 7
58 Clovenstone F 5
56 Cloves D 7
51 Clovulin A 7
35 Clow Bridge D 7
32 Clowne C 2
55 Cluanie Inn H 4
55 Cluanie Lodge H 5
21 Cluddley A 11
63 Cluer H 2
21 Clun D 8
21 Clunbury D 9
56 Clune E 7
55 Clunes K 6
21 Clungunford E 9
58 Clunie, Grampian C 4
52 Clunie, Tayside C 6
21 Clunton D 9
53 Cluny H 7
57 Cluny Castle K 2
15 Clutton, Avon H 9
30 Clutton, Cheshire E 3
29 Clwyd, Co. E 10
14 Clydach, Gwent C 5
13 Clydach, W. Glam. G 10
13 Clydach Vale E 3
47 Clydebank B 10
12 Clydey C 6
16 Clyffe Pypard F 2
47 Clynder A 7
12 Clynderwen E 5
13 Clyne G 11
61 Clynelish F 8
28 Clynnog-fawr E 4
21 Clyro H 7
6 Clyst Honiton G 3
6 Clyst Hydon F 4
6 Clyst St. George G 3
6 Clyst St. Lawrence F 4
6 Clyst St. Mary G 3
28 Clywt-y-bont D 5
20 Cnwch Coch E 2
58 Coachford C 2
3 Coad's Green B 10
32 Coal Ashton B 1
21 Coalbrookdale B 12
14 Coalbrookvale C 5
48 Coalburn F 1
45 Coalburns G 9
39 Coalcleugh A 10
15 Coaley D 11
59 Coalford G 6
47 Coalhall G 9
19 Coalhill D 7
15 Coalpit Heath F 10
31 Coalpit Hill E 7
21 Coalport B 12
52 Coalsnaughton H 4
53 Coaltown of Balgonie G 8
53 Coaltown of Wemyss H 8
23 Coalville A 8
15 Coalway Lane End C 9
7 Coat D 8
47 Coatbridge C 12
47 Coatdyke C 12
16 Coate, Wilts. H 2
16 Coate, Wilts. F 3
24 Coates, Cambs. F 4
16 Coates, Glos. D 1
9 Coates, W. Sussex D 11
40 Coatham C 6
40 Coatham Mundeville C 3
43 Coatsgate A 11
4 Cobbaton C 5
15 Coberley C 12
10 Cobham, Kent A 5
17 Cobham, Surrey H 11
51 Cobleland H 12
21 Cobnash F 10
58 Coburty A 7
57 Cock Bridge H 8
19 Cock Clarks D 8
21 Cock Gate F 10
40 Cockayne E 6
25 Cockayne Hatley K 4
49 Cockburnspath B 10
49 Cockenzie and Port Seton B 7
34 Cockerham B 3
38 Cockermouth B 4
18 Cockernhoe B 1
40 Cockfield, Durham C 2
27 Cockfield, Suffolk K 2
9 Cocking D 10
5 Cockington J 8
7 Cocklake A 8
45 Cocklaw F 7
49 Cocklawfoot G 11
49 Cockles B 8
26 Cockley Clet E 1
58 Cockmuir D 4
17 Cockpole Green F 9
30 Cockshutt G 3
26 Cockthorpe A 3
6 Cockwood H 3
15 Cockyard A 7
3 Codda B 9
27 Coddenham K 4
30 Coddington, Ches. E 3
21 Coddington, Heref. & Worc. H 12
32 Coddington, Notts. E 5
8 Codford St. Mary B 1
8 Codford St. Peter B 1
18 Codicote B 2
9 Codmore Hill D 12
32 Codnor E 1
15 Codrington F 10
22 Codsall B 2
22 Codsall Wood B 2
15 Coed Morgan C 7
28 Coed Ystumgwern H 5
28 Coedana B 4
14 Coedely F 4
14 Coedkernew F 6
29 Coedpoeth E 12
21 Coedway A 9
13 Coed-y-bryn C 7
15 Coed-y-fedw C 7
14 Coed-yr-ynys B 5
14 Coelbren C 2
5 Coffinswell J 8
6 Cofton H 3
22 Cofton Hacket E 3
14 Cogan G 5
23 Cogenhoe F 11
19 Coggeshall B 8
19 Coggeshall Hamlet B 8
57 Coignafearn Lo. H 2
57 Coignafeuinternich H 3
57 Coignascallan H 3
59 Coilacreich H 1
57 Coilintuie J 6
51 Coillaig E 7
55 Coille Mhorgil J 5
62 Coillore D 3
57 Coire Bhachdaidh Lodge M 1
14 Coity F 3
60 Colaboll F 6
2 Colan D 6
6 Colaton Raleigh G 4
62 Colbost C 1
40 Colburn E 2
8 Colbury E 5
39 Colby, Cumbria C 9
38 Colby, I.o.M. H 1
26 Colby, Norfolk B 5
19 Colchester A 10
16 Cold Ash G 6
23 Cold Ashby D 10
15 Cold Ashton G 10
16 Cold Aston B 2
12 Cold Blow F 5
23 Cold Brayfield G 12
33 Cold Hanworth B 7
30 Cold Hatton H 5
45 Cold Hesleden H 12
35 Cold Hiendly F 12
23 Cold Higham G 10
40 Cold Kirby G 5
3 Cold Northcott A 9
19 Cold Norton D 8
23 Cold Overton A 11
39 Coldbeck E 9
60 Coldbackie B 6
10 Coldean G 2
5 Coldeast H 7
8 Colden Common D 6
27 Coldfair Green J 7
24 Coldham E 5
15 Coldharbour, Glos. D 8
10 Coldharbour, Kent C 4
58 Coldhome C 3
49 Coldingham C 11
52 Coldrain G 6
11 Coldred C 11
4 Coldridge E 6
49 Coldstream E 11
9 Coldwaltham D 11
58 Coldwells D 8
58 Coldwells Croft E 3
7 Cole C 10
18 Cole Green C 3
8 Cole Henley A 6
21 Colebatch D 8
6 Colebrook F 3
4 Colebrooke F 6
56 Coleburn D 8
37 Coleby, Humber. E 7
33 Coleby, Lincs. D 7
4 Coleford, Devon F 6
15 Coleford, Glos. C 9
7 Coleford, Som. A 10
8 Colehill F 2
10 Coleman's Hatch E 3
30 Colemere G 3
9 Colemore C 8
32 Coleorton H 1
15 Colerne G 11
16 Colesbourne C 1
25 Colesden K 2
17 Coleshill, Bucks. E 10
16 Coleshill, Oxon E 3
22 Coleshill, War. C 5
6 Colestocks F 4
10 Colgate E 1
47 Colgrain A 8
53 Colinsburhg G 9
48 Colinton C 5
46 Colintraive B 5
26 Colkirk C 2
63 Coll C 6
53 Collace D 7
64 Collafirth C 7
2 Collamoor Head B 2
5 Collaton L 4
5 Collaton St. Mary K 7
47 Collenan F 8
53 Collessie F 7
4 Colleton Mills D 5
18 Collier Row E 5
10 Collier Street C 6
18 Collier's End B 4
58 Collieston E 8
43 Collin D 11
8 Collingbourne Ducis A 4
8 Collingbourne Kingston A 4
35 Collingham C 12
21 Collington F 12
23 Collingtree G 11
34 Collins Green H 4
53 Colliston C 10
6 Colliton F 4
59 Collmuir G 3
58 Collynie D 6
24 Collyweston E 1
42 Colmonell C 3
25 Colmworth J 2
16 Coln Rogers C 2
16 Coln St. Aldwyn D 2
16 Coln St. Dennis C 2
57 Colnabaichin H 8
17 Colnbrook F 11
25 Colne, Cambs. H 5
35 Colne, Lancs. C 7
27 Colne Engaine M 2
26 Colney E 5
18 Colney Heath C 2
18 Colney Street D 2
45 Colpitts Grange G 8
58 Colpy D 4
48 Colquhar E 6
4 Colscott D 2
40 Colsterdale G 2
32 Colsterworth H 6
32 Colston Bassett G 4
56 Coltfield C 7
26 Coltishall D 6
38 Colton, Cumbria G 5
26 Colton, Norfolk D 4
36 Colton, N. Yorks. C 3
31 Colton, Staffs. H 9
35 Colton, W. Yorks D 12
21 Colva G 7
22 Colwall Green H 1
22 Colwall Stone H 1
45 Colwell E 8
31 Colwich H 8
14 Colwinston G 3
38 Colwith E 5
9 Colworth F 10
29 Colwyn Bay B 8
6 Colyford G 6
6 Colyton G 6
44 Comb D 6
16 Combe, Berks. H 5
21 Combe, Heref. & Worc. F 9
16 Combe, Oxon C 5
9 Combe Common B 10
21 Combe Moor F 9
6 Combe Florey C 5
4 Combe Martin A 5
6 Combe Raleigh F 5
6 Combe St. Nicholas E 6
5 Combebow G 4
5 Combeinteignhead J 8
30 Comberbach C 5
25 Comberton, Cambs. K 5
21 Comberton, Heref. & Worc. F 10
6 Combpyne G 6
31 Combridge F 9
22 Combrook G 6
31 Combs, Derby B 9
27 Combs, Suffolk K 3
6 Combwich B 6
59 Comers G 4
20 Comin Capel Betws G 2
20 Comins-coch Dyfed D 2
20 Comins-coch Powys B 4
58 Comisty C 3
14 Common Coed-y-paen D 6
3 Common Moor C 9
32 Common Side C 1
41 Commondale D 7
31 Compstall A 8
43 Compstonend F 7
16 Compton, Berks. F 6
5 Compton, Devon J 7
8 Compton, Hants. C 6
9 Compton, Surrey A 11
9 Compton, W. Sussex E 9
8 Compton, Wilts. A 3
7 Compton Abbas D 12
16 Compton Abdale C 2
16 Compton Bassett G 1
16 Compton Beauchamp E 4
7 Compton Bishop A 7
8 Compton Chamberlayne C 2
15 Compton Dando H 9
7 Compton Dundon C 8
15 Compton Greenfield F 9
7 Compton Martin A 8
7 Compton Pauncefoot D 10
7 Compton Valence G 9
52 Comrie, Fife H 5
52 Comrie, Tayside E 3
51 Conaglen House A 7
46 Conchra A 5
34 Conder Green B 3
16 Condicote A 3
47 Condorrat B 12
21 Condover B 10
27 Coney Weston G 3
9 Coneyhurst Com. D 12
41 Coneysthorpe H 7
35 Coneythorpe A 12
58 Confunderland F 3
3 Congdon's Shop B 10
43 Congeith E 9
23 Congerstone B 7
24 Congham C 8
31 Congleton D 7
28 Congl-y-wal F 6
15 Congresbury H 7
56 Conicavel D 5
33 Coningsby D 9
25 Conington, Cambs. J 4

25 Conington, Cambs. G 3
36 Conisbrough G 3
37 Conisholme H 11
38 Coniston, Cumbria E 5
37 Coniston, Humber. D 9
35 Coniston Cold B 7
39 Conistone H 12
29 Connah's Quay C 12
50 Connel D 6
47 Connel Park H 11
47 Connelbush H 12
2 Connor Downs F 3
56 Cononbridge D 1
35 Cononley B 8
53 Cononsyth C 10
31 Consall E 8
45 Consett H 9
40 Constable Burton F 2
2 Constantine G 4
2 Constantine Bay B 6
54 Contin D 8
49 Conundrum D 12
59 Conveth Mains K 5
56 Convinth F 1
29 Conwy B 7
11 Conyer B 8
27 Conyer's Green H 2
10 Cooden G 6
4 Cookbury E 3
17 Cookham F 10
17 Cookham Dean F 9
17 Cookham Rise F 9
22 Cookhill F 4
22 Cookley, Heref. & Worc. D 2
27 Cookley, Suffolk H 6
17 Cookley Green E 8
59 Cookney H 6
10 Cooksbridge G 3
18 Cooksmill Green C 6
9 Coolham D 12
10 Cooling, Kent A 6
19 Cooling, Kent F 7
10 Cooling Street A 6
2 Coombe, Cornwall D 6
4 Coombe, Cornwall E 1
6 Coombe, Devon D 4
6 Coombe, Wilts. A 3
8 Coombe Bissett C 3
15 Coombe Down H 11
15 Coombe Hay H 10
15 Coombe Hill B 12
7 Coombe Keynes H 11
10 Coombes G 1
12 Coombs F 4
56 Cooperhill D 6
10 Cooper's Corner C 4
10 Cooper's Green F 4
18 Coopersale Com. D 5
9 Cootham E 12
27 Copdock L 4
19 Copford Green B 9
64 Copister C 7
25 Cople K 2
40 Copley C 1
36 Copmanthorpe B 3
2 Coppathorne A 2
31 Coppenhall H 7
2 Copperhouse F 3
25 Coppingford G 3
7 Coppleridge D 11
4 Copplestone F 6
34 Coppull F 4
34 Coppull Moor F 4
10 Copsale F 1
34 Copster Green D 5
22 Copt Heath D 5
40 Copt Hewick H 4
23 Copt Oak A 8
10 Copthorne D 2
26 Copy's Green B 2
6 Copythorne E 5
45 Corbridge G 8
23 Corby C 12
33 Corby Glen H 7
21 Coreley E 11
17 Cores End E 10
6 Corfe D 6
8 Corfe Castle H 1
8 Corfe Mullen F 1
21 Corfton D 10
57 Corgariff J 8
9 Corhampton D 7
22 Corley D 6
22 Corley Ash C 6
22 Corley Moor D 6
48 Cormiston F 3
51 Cormonachan H 9
53 Cormuir A 8
57 Corndavon Lodge J 8
40 Cornforth B 3
58 Cornhill B 3
49 Cornhill-on-Tweed E 11
45 Cornhills E 8
35 Cornholme D 8
25 Cornish Hall End L 8
40 Cornsay A 2
40 Cornsay Colliery A 2
56 Corntown, Mid Glam. G 3
56 Corntown, Highland D 1
59 Corntulloch H 2
3 Cornwall, County C 8
16 Cornwell A 4
5 Cornwood K 5
5 Cornworthy K 7
55 Corpach M 5
26 Corpusty C 4
51 Corran, Highland A 7
55 Corran, Highland J 2
46 Corranbuie C 3
38 Corrany G 2
55 Corribeg L 4
46 Corrie E 5
43 Corrie Common C 12
46 Corriecravie G 4
54 Corriefeol E 6
55 Corriegour K 6
54 Corriemoillie C 7
60 Corriemulzie Lo G 4
57 Corrievorrie G 3
54 Corrieviuc E 6
55 Corrimony G 7
19 Corringham, Essex F 7
32 Corringham, Lincs. A 6
20 Corris B 3
51 Corrour Shooting Lodge A 11
51 Corrow G 9
62 Corry F 6
56 Corry of Ardnagrask E 1
46 Corrygills F 5
55 Corryhully L 3
60 Corrykinloch E 5
52 Corrymuckloch D 4
50 Corrynachenchy C 4
49 Corsbie E 8
7 Corscombe F 8
58 Corse, Grampian D 3
58 Corse, Grampian B 7
59 Corse House G 3
58 Corse of Kinnoir C 3
59 Corsebauld J 5
58 Corsehill B 7
42 Corsemalzie F 4
15 Corhsam G 11
59 Corsindae G 4
7 Corsley B 11
7 Corsley Heath B 11
47 Corsliehill C 9
43 Corsock D 8
15 Corston, Avon H 10
15 Corston, Wilts. F12
48 Corstorphine B 5
59 Cortachy Castle L 1
26 Corton, Suffolk F8
8 Corton, Wilts. B1
7 Corton Denham D 9
51 Coruanan Lodge A 8
29 Corwen F 10
7 Coryates H 9
5 Coryton, Devon G 3
19 Coryton, Essex F 7
23 Cosby C 9
22 Coseley C 3
23 Cosgrove H 11
9 Cosham F 8
12 Cosheston G 3
52 Coshieville B 3
32 Cossall F 2
23 Cossington A 9
64 Costa B 2
26 Costessey D 5
32 Costock H 3
32 Coston, Leics. H 6
26 Coston, Norfolk E 4
44 Cote C 1
30 Cotebrook D 4
44 Cotehill H 3
31 Cotes, Cumbria F 7
31 Cotes, Staffs. G 7
23 Cotesbach D 8
32 Cotgrave G 3
58 Cothall F 6
32 Cotham E 5
6 Cothelstone C 5
39 Cotherstone C 12
49 Cothill, Borders D 10
16 Cothill, Oxon D 6
6 Cotleigh F 5
32 Cotmanhay F 2
25 Coton, Cambs. J 5
23 Coton, Northants. E 10
31 Coton, Staffs. H 7
31 Coton, Staffs. G 8
31 Coton Clanford H 7
31 Coton in the Clay G 10
22 Coton in the Elms A 6
5 Cott K 6
34 Cottam, Lancs. D 4
32 Cottam, Notts. B 5
56 Cottartown F 6
25 Cottenham H 5
39 Cotterdale F 10
18 Cottered A 3
24 Cotterstock F 1
23 Cottesbrooke E 10
23 Cottesmore A 12
6 Cotteylands E 3
37 Cottingham, Humberside D 8
23 Cottingham, Northants. C 11
35 Cottingley C 9
17 Cottisford A 7
31 Cotton, Derby F 9
27 Cotton Suffolk J 4
25 Cotton End L 2
58 Cot-town, Grampian E 2
58 Cot-town, Grampian D 6
31 Cotwalton G 8
58 Cotwells B 5
3 Couchsmill D 8
15 Coughton, Heref. & Worc. B 9
22 Coughton, War. F 4
46 Coulaghailtro C 2
54 Coulags E 3
54 Couldoran E 2
54 Coulin Lodge D 4
59 Coull G 3
47 Coulport A 7
18 Coulsdon H 3
8 Coulston A 1
48 Coulter F 3
40 Coulton H 6
21 Cound B 11
40 Coundon, Durham B 3
22 Coundon, W. Midlands D 6
40 Coundon Grange B 2
39 Countersett F 11
23 Countesthorpe C 9
8 Countess B 3
6 Countess Wear G 3
4 Countisbury A 6
53 Coupar Angus C 7
49 Coupland F 12
6 Couple Cross B 3
46 Cour E 3
43 Courance C 11
17 Court Corner H 7
13 Court Henry E 9
55 Courteachan K 1
23 Courteenhall G 11
19 Courtsend E 10
6 Courtway C 5
48 Cousland C 6
10 Cousleywood E 5
46 Coustonn B 6
6 Cove, Devon D 3
9 Cove, Hampshire A 10
54 Cove, Highland A 2
47 Cove, Strathclyde A 7
59 Cove Bay G 7
27 Covehithe G 8
22 Coven A 3
25 Coveney G 6
37 Covenham St. Bartholomew H 11
37 Covenham St. Mary H 11
23 Coventry D 7
2 Coverack H 5
40 Coverham F 1
25 Covington H 2
22 Cow Honeybourne H 5
39 Cowan Bridge G 8
10 Cowbeech G 5
24 Cowbit D 4
14 Cowbridge, S. Glam. G 3
6 Cowbridge, Som. B 3
10 Cowden, Kent D 3
45 Cowden, Northumb. E 7
52 Cowdenbeath H 6
48 Cowdenburn D 5
8 Cowes F 6
40 Cowesby F 5
10 Cowfold F 1
52 Cowie, Central H 3
59 Cowie, Grampian J 6
45 Cowpen E 11
40 Cowpen Bewley C 5
31 Cowers Lane E 11
6 Cowley, Devon G 3
15 Cowley, Glos. C 12
18 Cowley, London F 1
16 Cowley, Oxon D 6
40 Cowling, N. Yorks. F 3
35 Cowling, N. Yorks. C 8
25 Cowlinge K 8
9 Cowplain E 8
39 Cowshill A 10
52 Cowstrandburn H 5
36 Cowthorpe B 2
17 Cox Green F 9
30 Coxbank F 5
31 Coxbench F 12
10 Coxheath C 6
11 Coxhill C 11
40 Coxhoe B 3
7 Coxley B 8
18 Coxtie Green D 5
40 Coxwold G 5
14 Coychurch F 3
47 Coylton G 9
57 Coylumbridge H 5
59 Coynach G 2
58 Coynachie D 2
14 Coytrahen F 2
54 Cozae Lodge F 6
22 Crabbs Cross F 4
10 Crabtree F 1
61 Crackaig F 9
39 Crackenthorpe C 9
2 Crackington Haven B 2
22 Crackley E 6
22 Crackley Bank A 1
39 Crackpot E 12
35 Cracoe A 8
6 Craddock E 4
22 Cradley G 1
22 Cradley Heath D 3
14 Cradoc A 3
3 Crafthole D 10
45 Cragend C 9
35 Cragg E 8
57 Craggan, Highland G 6
60 Craggan, Highland G 4
51 Craggan, Strathclyde H 10
56 Craggiemore F 3
45 Craghead H 10
58 Craibstone, Grampian F 6
58 Craibstone, Grampian B 2
53 Craichie B 10
43 Craig, Dumf. & Gall. D 7
43 Craig, Dumf. & Gall. E 8
54 Craig, Highland E 4
42 Craig, Strathcylde A 5
46 Craig Lodge B 5
14 Craig Penllyn F 3
13 Craig Trebanos G 10
52 Craiganour Lodge A 1
55 Craigard J 7
55 Craigbeg L 8
42 Craigcaffie E 2
13 Craig-cefn-parc G 10
58 Craigdam E 6
43 Craigdarrcoh, Dumf. & Gall. C 8
43 Craigdarroch, Strathclyde A 7
42 Craigdews D 6
54 Craigdhu F 8
58 Craigearn F 5
56 Craigellachie E 8
42 Craigencallie D 6
42 Craigencross E 1
48 Craigend, Strathclyde F 1
52 Craigend, Tayside E 6
47 Craigendoran A 8
42 Craigengillan A 5
42 Craigenrae C 4
47 Craigens G 10
59 Craiggiecat H 6
56 Craighead, Grampian F 8
48 Craighead, Strathclyde G 2
58 Craigie, Grampian F 6
47 Craigie, Strathclyde F 9
52 Craigie, Tayside C 6
43 Craigieburn A 11
48 Craiglockhart B 5
42 Craimalloch B 5
58 Craigmaud B 6
46 Craigmore C 6
59 Craigmoston K 4
30 Craignant G 1
42 Craigneil C 2
48 Craigneston C 8
47 Craigneuk D 12
50 Craignure D 4
59 Craigo L 4
52 Craigow F 6
53 Craigrothie F 8
53 Craigs G 7
59 Craigton, Grampian G 6
54 Craigton, Highland F 3
56 Craigton, Highland E 2
47 Craigton, Strathclyde D 10
53 Craigton, Tayside C 10
53 Craigton, Tayside B 8
61 Craigtown B 9
13 Craig-y-Duke G 10
14 Craig-y-nos C 2
44 Craik B 2
53 Crail F 11
49 Crailing G 9
49 Crailinghall G 9
36 Craiselound G 5
48 Cramalt G 5
36 Crambe A 5
45 Cramlington E 11
48 Cramond B 5
48 Cramond Bridge B 4
55 Cranachan L 7
30 Cranage C 6
31 Cranberry G 7
58 Cranbog F 7
8 Cranborne E 2
17 Cranbourne G 10
10 Cranbrook D 6
10 Cranbrook Com. D 6
35 Crane Moor G 11
25 Cranfield L 1
18 Cranford F 1
23 Cranford St. Andrew D 12
23 Cranford St. John D 12
15 Cranham, Glos. C 12
18 Cranham, London E 6
34 Crank G 4
9 Cranleigh B 12
8 Cranmore G 5
58 Cranna B 4
58 Crannach B 2
50 Crannich C 2
23 Cranoe C 11
27 Cransford J 6
49 Cranshaws C 9
38 Cranstal F 2
37 Cranswick B 8
2 Crantock D 5
33 Cranwell E 7
26 Cranwich F 1
26 Cranworth E 3
42 Cranyard H 2
5 Crapstone J 4
51 Crarae H 7
60 Crask Inn E 6
54 Crask of Aigas E 8
54 Craskie F 7
59 Craskins G 3
45 Craster A 10
27 Cratfield H 6
59 Crathes H 5
57 Crathie K 1
40 Crathorne D 5
21 Craven Arms D 10
45 Crawcrook G 9
48 Crawford G 2
48 Crawfordjohn G 2
43 Crawfordton B 9
47 Crawick H 12
8 Crawley, Hants. C 6
16 Crawley, Oxon C 4
10 Crawley, W. Sussex D 1
10 Crawley Down D 2
39 Crawleyside A 12
35 Crawshaw Booth E 7
59 Crawton J 6
39 Cray, N. Yorks. G 11
14 Cray, Powys B 2
18 Crayford F 5
40 Crayke H 6
19 Crays Hill E 7
17 Cray's Pond F 7
17 Crazies Hill F 9
50 Creach Bheinn Lodge E 4
4 Creacombe D 7
51 Creag a' Phuill G 8
51 Creagan C 7
46 Creagan Beag A 3
51 Creaguaineach Lo. A 10
23 Creaton E 10
44 Creca F 1
21 Credenhill H 10
4 Crediton F 7
42 Creebank D 4
42 Creebridge E 5
6 Creech Heathfield D 6
6 Creech St. Michael D 6
2 Creed E 6
18 Creekmouth F 5
42 Creeside C 4
27 Creeting St. Mary J 4
24 Creeton D 1
42 Creetown F 6
21 Cregerina G 7
51 Creggans G 8
38 Cregneish H 1
38 Creg-ny-Baa G 2
53 Creich E 8
14 Creigiau F 4
54 Crelevan F 7
3 Cremyll D 11
21 Cressage B 11
12 Cresselly F 4
17 Cressex E 9
19 Cressing B 8
12 Cresswell, Dyfed F 4
45 Cresswell, Northumb. D 11
31 Cresswell, Staffs. F 8
32 Creswell C 2
27 Cretingham J 5
46 Cretshengan C 2
21 Crew Green A 8
30 Crewe, Cheshire E 3
30 Crewe, Cheshire E 6
7 Crewkerne E 7
51 Crainlarich E 11
13 Cribyn B 8
28 Criccieth F 4
32 Crich, Derby E 12
48 Crichton C 6
15 Crick, Gwent E 8
23 Crick, Northants. E 9
20 Crickadarn H 6
7 Cricket Malherbie E 7
7 Cricket St. Thomas E 7
30 Crickheath H 2
14 Crickhowell B 5
16 Cricklade E 2
36 Cridling Stubbs E 3
52 Crieff E 3
21 Criggian A 8
35 Crigglestone E 11
58 Crimond B 8
58 Crimonmogate B 8
24 Crimplesham E 7
54 Crinaglack F 8
50 Crinan H 5
26 Cringleford E 3
12 Crinow F 5
8 Cripplestyle E 3
10 Cripp's Corner F 6
38 Croasdale C 3
7 Crock Street E 7
10 Crockenhill A 4
5 Crockernwell G 6
7 Crockerton B 11
43 Crocket or Ninemile Bar D 9
36 Crockey Hill B 4
10 Crockham Hill C 3
10 Crockhurst Street D 5
19 Crockleford Hth. A 10
14 Croes-Hywel C 6
14 Croeserw E 2
12 Croesgoch D 2
13 Croes-Ian C 7
28 Croesor F 6
13 Croesyceiliog E 7
14 Croes-y-mwyalch E 6
12 Croft, Dyfed C 5
23 Croft, Leics. C 8
34 Croft, Merseyside H 5
33 Croft, Lincs. D 12
40 Croft, N. Yorks. D 3
47 Croftamie A 9
47 Crofthead E 12
52 Croftmill C 3
35 Crofton, W. Yorks. E 12
16 Crofton, Wilts. H 4
58 Crofts of Belnagoak C 6
58 Crofts of Haddo D 6
58 Crofts of Hillbrae C 3
58 Crofts of Meikle Ardo D 6
58 Crofts of Savoch B 8
58 Crofts of Shanquhar D 3
13 Crofty G 8
50 Croggan E 4
44 Croglin H 4
60 Croick G 5
63 Croir C 2
56 Cromarty C 3
54 Cromasaig D 4
58 Cromblet D 5
57 Cromdale G 6
28 Cromer, Herts. A 3
26 Cromer, Norfolk A 5
31 Cromford E 11
15 Cromhall E 10
15 Cromhall Com. E 10
63 Cromore E 5
57 Cromra K 1
32 Cromwell D 5
47 Cronberry G 11
9 Crondall A 9
38 Cronk-y-Voddy G 2
30 Cronton A 4
39 Crook, Cumbria F 7
40 Crook, Durham B 2
56 Crook of Alves D 7
52 Crook of Devon G 5
34 Crooke F 4
47 Crookedholm F 9
48 Crookedstane H 2
32 Crookes B 1
16 Crookham, Berks. H 6
49 Crookham, Northumb. F 11
9 Crookham Village A 9
49 Crookham Westfield F 11

48 Crookhaugh G 4
49 Crookhouse G 10
39 Crooklands G 8
47 Crookston C 10
49 Crookston North Mains D 7
22 Croome Court H 2
23 Cropredy G 8
23 Cropston A 9
22 Cropthorne H 3
41 Cropton F 8
32 Cropwell Bishop G 4
32 Cropwell Butler F 4
47 Crosbie D 7
43 Crosby, Cumb. H 11
38 Crosby, I.o.M. G 2
36 Crosby, Humber. F 6
34 Crosby, Merseyside G 2
40 Crosby Court F 4
39 Crosby Garrett D 9
39 Crosby Ravensworth D 8
43 Crosby Villa H 11
7 Croscombe B 9
7 Cross A 7
15 Cross Ash B 7
10 Cross-at-Hand C 6
20 Cross Foxes Hotel A 3
27 Cross Green, Suffolk K 2
27 Cross Green, Suffolk K 3
13 Cross Hands, Dyfed F 9
12 Cross Hands, Dyfed F 4
35 Cross Hills C 9
21 Cross Houses B 11
10 Cross in Hand F 4
13 Cross Inn, Dyfed A 7
13 Cross Inn, Dyfed A 9
13 Cross Inn, Dyfed D 11
14 Cross Inn, Mid Glam F 4
10 Cross Keys, Kent C 4
15 Cross Keys, Wilts. G 11
2 Cross Lanes, Corn. G 4
30 Cross Lanes, Clwyd F 2
7 Cross Lanes, Dorset F 11
36 Cross Lanes, N. Yorks. A 3
63 Cross North Dell A 6
14 Cross Oak B 4
58 Cross of Jackson D 5
31 Cross o'th Hands F 11
27 Cross Street H 5
46 Crossaig D 3
63 Crossbost D 5
43 Crosscanonby H 11
26 Crossdale Street B 5
34 Crossens E 3
48 Crossford, Fife A 3
48 Crossford, Strathclyde E 1
24 Crossgate C 3
48 Crossgatehall C 6
52 Crossgates, Fife H 6
40 Crossgates, N. Yorks. H 2
20 Crossgates, Powys F 6
39 Crossgill, Cumb. A 9
34 Crossgill, Lancs. A 4
5 Crossgreen, Devon G 3
21 Crossgreen, Salop A 10
49 Crosshall E 10
12 Crosshands, Dyfed E 5
47 Crosshands, Strathclyde F 9
52 Crosshill, Fife G 6
42 Crosshill, Strathcylde A 4
47 Crosshill, Strathclyde G 9
47 Crosshouse F 9
44 Crossings E 3
14 Crosskeys E 5
61 Crosskirk A 10
38 Crosslands F 6
30 Crosslanes H 2
48 Crosslee G 6
47 Crosslees D 10
48 Crossleuch G 5
43 Crossmichael E 8
34 Crossmoor C 3
10 Crosspost F 1
59 Crossroads, Grampian H 5
47 Crossroads, Strathclyde F 9
35 Crossroads, W. Yorks. C 9
64 Cross-voe-sand C 6
15 Crossway, Heref. & Worc. A 9
15 Crossway, Gwent B 8
20 Crossway, Powys G 6
22 Crossway Green E 2
7 Crossways, Dorset G 11
21 Crossways, Powys E 7
12 Crosswell C 5
20 Crosswood E 2
39 Crosthwaite F 7
34 Croston E 4
26 Crostwick D 6
10 Crouch C 5
7 Crouch Hill E 10
8 Croucheston D 2
16 Croughton A 6
58 Crovie A 5
8 Crow F 3
35 Crow Edge G 10
15 Crow Hill B 9
2 Crowan F 4
10 Crowborough E 4
6 Crowcombe C 5
35 Crowden G 9
17 Crowell D 8
23 Crowfield, Northants. H 9
27 Crowfield, Suffolk J 5
10 Crowhurst, E. Sussex G 6
10 Crowhurst, Surrey C 3
10 Crowhurst Lane End C 3
24 Crowland D 3
2 Crowlas F 2
22 Crowle, Heref. & Worc. G 3
36 Crowle, Humber. F 5
63 Crowlista D 1
17 Crowmarsh Gifford E 7
2 Crown Town G 3
5 Crownhill K 4
26 Crownthorpe E 4
42 Crows F 4
2 Crows-an-wra G 1
17 Crowthorne H 9
30 Crowton C 4
22 Croxall A 5
37 Croxby G 9
40 Croxdale B 3
31 Croxden F 9
17 Croxley Green E 11
25 Croxton, Cambs. J 3
37 Croxton, Humber. F 8
27 Croxton, Norfolk G 2
30 Croxton, Staffs. G 6
32 Croxton Kerrial G 5
56 Croy, Highland E 4
47 Croy, Strathclyde B 12
4 Croyde B 3
4 Croyde Bay B 3
25 Croydon, Cambs. K 4
18 Croydon, London G 3
57 Crubenmore Lo. K 2
21 Cruckmeole A 9
58 Cruden Bay D 8
30 Crudington H 5
16 Crudwell E 1
21 Crug E 1
2 Crugmeer B 6
13 Crugybar C 10
54 Cruive F 8
63 Crulivig D 3
14 Crumlin D 5
3 Crumplehorn E 9
12 Crundale, Dyfed E 3
11 Crundale, Kent C 9
44 Crurie D 1
6 Cruwys Morchard E 2
16 Crux Easton H 5
13 Crwbin F 8
17 Cryers Hill D 9
12 Crymych D 5
13 Crynant F 11
54 Cuaig D 1
23 Cubbington E 7
2 Cubert D 5
17 Cublington B 9
10 Cuckfield F 2
7 Cucklington D 10
32 Cuckney C 3
17 Cuddesdon D 7
17 Cuddington, Bucks. C 8
30 Cuddington, Ches. C 4
30 Cuddington Heath F 3
34 Cuddy Hill C 4
18 Cudham H 4
7 Cudworth, Som. E 7
36 Cudworth, S. Yorks. F 2
12 Cuffern E 2
18 Cuffley D 3
63 Cuiashader A 6
56 Culbo D 2
56 Culbokie D 2
56 Culburnie E 1
56 Culcabock E 2
56 Culcairn C 2
56 Culcharry E 4
34 Culcheth H 5
58 Culdrain D 3
54 Culduie F 1
27 Culford H 1
39 Culgaith B 8
16 Culham E 6
46 Culinlongart H 2
60 Culkien D 2
60 Culkein Drumbeg D 3
15 Culkerton E 12
57 Cullachie G 5
58 Cullen A 3
45 Cullercoats F 12
56 Cullicudden C 2
54 Culligran F 7
35 Cullingworth D 9
50 Cullipool F 5
64 Cullivoe B 8
52 Culloch E 3
55 Cullochy J 7
6 Cullompton E 4
6 Culm Davy E 5
61 Culmaily G 8
42 Culmalzie F 5
21 Culmington D 10
6 Culmstock E 4
60 Culnacraig F 2
43 Culnaightrie F 8
62 Culnakncok B 4
42 Culquhirk F 5
60 Culrain G 6
48 Culross A 3
47 Culroy H 8
42 Culscadden G 5
59 Culsh H 1
42 Culshabbin F 4
64 Culswick D 6
58 Cultercullen E 7
42 Cults, Dumf. & Gall. G 5
58 Cults, Grampian D 3
59 Cults, Grampian G 6
52 Cultybraggan E 3
10 Culverstone Green B 5
33 Culverthorpe F 7
23 Culworth G 9
56 Culzie Lodge C 1
47 Cumberhead F 12
49 Cumberland Bower D 12
47 Cumbernauld B 12
33 Cumberworth C 12
38 Cumbria, Co. C 6
58 Cuminestown C 5
49 Cumledge D 10
44 Cummersdale H 2
43 Cummertrees E 12
56 Cummingstown C 7
47 Cumnock G 10
16 Cumnor D 5
44 Cumrew H 4
43 Cumrue C 11
43 Cumstone C 12
44 Cumwhinton H 3
44 Cumwhitton H 3
40 Cundall H 4
47 Cunninghamhead E 8
64 Cunnister B 7
53 Cupar F 8
53 Cupar Muir F 8
8 Cupernnam D 5
31 Curbar C 11
16 Curbridge, Oxon C 4
9 Curdbridge, Hants. E 7
22 Curdworth C 5
54 Curin D 7
6 Curland E 6
42 Currarie B 2
16 Curridge G 6
48 Currie C 4
7 Curry Mallet D 7
7 Curry Rivel D 7
10 Curtisden Green D 6
2 Cury G 4
58 Cushnie B 5
6 Cushuish C 5
21 Cusop H 8
64 Cusvie B 3
42 Cutcloy H 5
6 Cutcombe B 3
48 Cuthill B 6
22 Cutnall Green E 2
16 Cutsdean A 2
31 Cutthorpe C 11
17 Cuxham E 7
10 Cuxton A 6
37 Cuxwold G 9
29 Cwm, Clwyd C 10
14 Cwm, Gwent D 5
13 Cwm Capel G 8
20 Cwm-Cewydd A 4
12 Cwm Cych C 6
13 Cwm-Duad D 7
14 Cwm Ffrwd Oer D 6
20 Cwm Irfon G 4
13 Cwm-Mawr F 8
12 Cwm-Morgan D 6
29 Cwm-Penmachno E 7
14 Cwmaman D 3
13 Cwmann B 9
13 Cwmafon H 11
12 Cwmbach, Dyfed D 6
14 Cwm-bach, Mid. Glam. D 4
20 Cwm-bach, Powys G 6
21 Cwm-bach, Powys H 7
20 Cwmbelan D 5
14 Cwmbran E 6
20 Cwmbrwyno D 3
14 Cwmcarn E 5
15 Cwmcarvan D 8
12 Cwmcoy C 6
14 Cwmdare D 3
13 Cwmdu, Dyfed D 9
14 Cwm-du, Powys B 5
14 Cwmfelin, Mid Glam. D 4
14 Cwmfelin, Mid Glam. E 2
12 Cwmfelin Boeth E 5
14 Cwmfelinfach E 5
12 Cwmfelin-Mynach E 6
13 Cwmffrwd E 7
14 Cwmgiedd C 1
13 Cwmgors F 10
13 Cwmgwili F 9
13 Cwmifor D 10
13 Cwmisfael E 8
20 Cwmlline B 4
13 Cwmllyfri F 7
13 Cwmllynfell F 10
12 Cwmmiles E 5
14 Cwmparc E 3
13 Cwmpengraig C 7
14 Cwm-rhos B 5
13 Cwmsychpant B 8
14 Cwmtillery D 5
13 Cwmtwrch Isaf F 11
13 Cwmtwrch Uchaf F 11
14 Cwmwysg A 2
13 Cwm-y-glo F 9
14 Cwmyoy B 6
20 Cwmystwyth E 3
20 Cwrt B 2
13 Cwrtnewydd B 8
13 Cwrt-y-Cadno C 10
14 Cwrt-y-defaid F 1
14 Cwrt-y-gollen C 6
29 Cyffilliog D 10
29 Cymau E 12
14 Cymmer, Mid Glam. E 3
14 Cymmer, W. Glam. E 2
14 Cyncoed F 5
13 Cynghordy, Dyfed C 11
13 Cynghordy, W. Glam. G 10
13 Cynheidre F 8
14 Cynonville E 2
29 Cynwyd F 10
13 Cynwyl Elfed D 7
35 Dacre Banks A 10
23 Dadford H 10
23 Dadlington B 7
13 Dafen G 8
18 Dagenham F 5
16 Daglingworth D 1
17 Dagnall C 10
51 Dail D 8
42 Dailly B 3
57 Dail-na-mine Lo. M 3
53 Dairsie or Osnaburgh E 9
34 Daisy Hill G 5
51 Dalavich F 7
43 Dalbeattie E 9
63 Dalbeg B 3
47 Dalblair G 11
59 Dalbog K 3
38 Dalby H 1
61 Dalchalm F 9
51 Dalchenna G 8
52 Dalchonzie E 2
60 Dalchork F 6
55 Dalchreichart H 7
52 Dalchruin E 2
54 Dalchuirn F 3
56 Dalcross Station E 3
33 Dalderby D 9
32 Dale, Derby F 2
12 Dale, Dyfed F 2
64 Dale, Shetland Is. D 6
39 Dale Head D 7
32 Dalebank D 1
41 Dalehouse C 8
50 Dalelia A 5
57 Dalestie H 7
43 Dalfibble C 11
47 Dalfram G 11
61 Dalganachan C 10
47 Dalgarven E 8
48 Dalgety Bay A 4
47 Dalgig H 10
52 Dalginross E 3
52 Dalguise B 5
61 Dalhalvaig B 9
25 Dalham J 8
46 Dalinlongart A 6
48 Dalkeith C 6
52 Dall B 1
56 Dallas D 7
47 Dalleagles H 10
27 Dallinghoo K 5
10 Dallington, E. Sussex F 5
23 Dallington, Northants. F 10
39 Dalmain Dacre C 7
43 Dalmakerran B 8
51 Dalmally E 9
51 Dalmary H 12
42 Dalmellington A 6
48 Dalmeny B 4
48 Dalmeny Rows B 4
60 Dalmichy F 6
57 Dalmigavie Lodge G 3
56 Dalmore, Highland C 2
56 Dalmore, Highland B 1
63 Dalmore, W. Isles B 3
47 Dalmuir B 10
56 Dalmunach E 8
50 Dalnabreck A 4
57 Dalnacardoch Lo. M 3
57 Dalnahaitnach H 4
61 Dalnamain G 7
57 Dalnaspidal M 2
61 Dalnawillan Lo. C 10
51 Dalness B 9
61 Dalnessie E 7
52 Daloist A 3
52 Dalqueich G 6
42 Dalquhairn B 4
61 Dalreavoch F 7
52 Dalriach A 2
43 Dalry, Dumf. & Gall. C 7
47 Dalry, Strathclyde D 8
47 Dalrymple H 8
48 Dalserf D 1
44 Dalston H 2
43 Dalswinton C 10
43 Dlaton, Dumf. & Gall. D 12
34 Dalton, Lancs. F 4
45 Dalton, Northumb. F 9
45 Dalton, Northumb. G 7
40 Dalton, N. Yorks. G 4
40 Dalton, N. Yorks. D 1
32 Dalton, S. Yorks. A 2
40 Dalton Piercy B 5
38 Dalton-in-Furness H 5
45 Dalton-le-Dale H 12
40 Dalton-on-Tees D 3
46 Daltot A 3
42 Dalvadie F 2
52 Dalveich E 1
47 Dalvennan H 9
61 Dalvina Lodge C 7
43 Dalwhat B 8
57 Dalwhinnie L 2
6 Dalwood F 6
8 Damerham D 3
26 Damgate E 7
42 Damnaglaur H 2
48 Damside D 4
11 Danaway borden B 7
19 Danbury C 8
41 Danby D 7
40 Danby Wiske E 3
56 Dandaleith E 8
48 Danderhall B 6
18 Dane End B 3
23 DaneHills B 9
31 Danebridge D 8
10 Danehill E 3
34 Dangerous Corner F 4
40 Dan's Corner A 1
49 Danskine C 8
22 Danzey Green E 5
14 Daren—felen C 5
10 Darenth A 4
30 Daresbury B 4
36 Darfield G 2
11 Dargate B 9
45 Dargues D 7
3 Darite C 9
22 Darlaston C 3
35 Darley A 10
31 Darley Bridge D 11
22 Darlingscott H 6
40 Darlington D 3
30 Darliston G 4
32 Darlton C 5
32 Darnall A 1
56 Darnaway Castle D 5
47 Darnconner G 10
43 Darngarroch E 7
49 Darnick F 8
20 Darowen B 4
58 Darra C 5
4 Darracott, Corn D 1
4 Darracott, Devon B 3
45 Darras Hall F 9
36 Darrington E 3
27 Darsham H 7
10 Dartford A 4
5 Dartington J 6
5 Dartmeet H 5
5 Dartmouth K 7
35 Darton F 11
47 Darvel F 10
34 Darwen E 6
17 Datchet F 10
18 Datchworth B 3
18 Datchworth Green B 3
34 Daubill F 6
16 Dauntsey F 1
16 Dauntsey Green F 1
16 Dauntsey Lock F 1
30 Davenham C 5
23 Daventry F 9
20 David's Well E 6
48 Davidson's Mains B 5
56 Davidston C 3
3 Davidstow A 8
44 Davington C 1
58 Daviot, Grampian E 5
6 Daviot, Highland F 3
17 Davis Street G 9
58 Davoch of Grange C 2
35 Daw Cross B 11
10 Dawesgreen C 1
21 Dawley B 12
21 Dawley Bank B 12
5 Dawlish H 8
7 Dawlish Wake E 7
6 Dawlish Warren H 3
29 Dawn C 8
19 Daws Heath E 8
3 Daw's House A 10
24 Dawsmere C 5
38 Dawthwaitehead C 6
16 Daylesford B 3
29 Ddol C 10
44 Deadwater C 4
47 Deadwaters E 12
11 Deal C 12
38 Dean, Cumb C 3
4 Dean, Devon B 4
4 Dean, Devon B 5
5 Dean, Devon J 6
8 Dean, Dorset D 1
9 Dean, Hants D 7
7 Dean, Somerset B 10
5 Dean Prior J 6
31 Dean Row B 7
10 Dean Street C 6
44 Deanburnhaugh B 2
9 Deane A 7
60 Deanich Lodge H 5
8 Deanland D 2
48 Deans C 3
38 Deanscales C 3
23 Deanshanger Hill H 11
52 Deanston G 2
38 Dearham B 3
36 Dearne G 3
27 Debach K 5
25 Debden, Essex M 7
18 Debden Estate D 4
25 Debden Green M 7
27 Debenham J 5
48 Dechmont B 3
16 Deddington A 6
27 Dedham M 4
59 Deebank H 4
59 Deecastle H 2
23 Deene C 12
24 Deenethorpe F 1
17 Deepcut H 10
24 Deeping Gate E 3
24 Deeping St. James E 3
24 Deeping St. Nicholas D 3
58 Deerhill B 2
15 Deerhurst A 11
64 Deerness D 3
22 Defford H 3
14 Defynnog B 2
29 Deganwy B 7
40 Deighton, N. Yorks. E 4
35 Deighton, W. Yorks. E10
36 Deighton C 4
28 Deiniolen D 5
3 Delabole A 8
30 Delamere C 4
42 Delamford B 4
56 Delchirach F 7
58 Delfrigs E 7
57 Dell Lodge H 6
56 Delliefure F 6
57 Delnabo H 7
57 Delnadamph Lo J 8
57 Delnamer M 7
48 Deloraineshiel H 6
35 Delph F 8
45 Delves H 9
24 Dembleby B 1
36 Denaby Main G 3
43 Denbie Mains D 11
29 Denbigh D10
5 Denbury J 7
32 Denby F 1
35 Denby Dale F 11
16 Denchworth E 5
58 Denend D 3
25 Denford H 1
19 Dengie D 9
17 Denham, Bucks E 11

27 Denham, Suffolk **H 5**
27 Denham, Suffolk **J 1**
53 Denhead, Fife **F 9**
58 Denhead, Grampian **B 7**
58 Denhead, Grampian **E 7**
49 Denholm **G 8**
35 Denholme **D 9**
9 Denmead **E 8**
27 Dennington **H 6**
48 Denny **A 1**
10 Denny Bottom **D 4**
8 Denny Lodge **E 5**
48 Dennyloanhead **A 1**
35 Denshaw **F 8**
59 Denside **H 5**
27 Denston **K 1**
31 Denstone **F 9**
39 Dent **F 9**
39 Dent Station **F 10**
25 Denton, Cambs **G 2**
40 Denton, Durham **C 2**
10 Denton, E. Sussex **H 3**
11 Denton, Kent **C 11**
32 Denton, Lincs **G 6**
35 Denton, Manchester **H 8**
27 Denton, Norfolk **G 6**
35 Denton, N. Yorks **B 10**
23 Denton, Northants **F 11**
17 Denton, Oxon **D 7**
24 Denver **E 7**
45 Denwick **B 10**
45 Denwick Lane End **A 10**
26 Deopham **E 3**
26 Deopham Green **F 3**
4 Deptford, Devon **D 5**
4 Deptford, Devon **D 1**
18 Deptford, London **F 4**
8 Deptford, Wilts **B 2**
31 Derby **G 11**
38 Derbyhaven **H 1**
32 Derbyshire, Co **D11**
52 Derculich **B 4**
14 Deri **D 5**
20 Deri—Odwyn **F 2**
52 Derry **E 1**
15 Derry Hill **G 12**
50 Derryguaig **D 2**
11 Derringstone **C 10**
31 Derrington **H 7**
36 Derrythorpe **F 6**
24 Dersingham **C 8**
50 Dervaig **B 2**
29 Derwen **E 10**
13 Derwlwyn **C 9**
23 Desborough **D 11**
23 Desford **B 8**
45 Detchant **B 12**
11 Detling **B 7**
29 Deuddwr **H 11**
15 Devauden **D 8**
59 Devenick **G 7**
20 Devil's Bridge **E 3**
16 Devizes **H 1**
4 Devon, County **F 5**
48 Devonburn **E 1**
3 Devonport **D 11**
52 Devonside **G 4**
2 Devoran **F 5**
48 Dewar **D 6**
7 Dewlish **F 11**
15 Dewsall Court **A 8**
35 Dewsbury **E 11**
38 Dhoon **G 2**
38 Dhoor **F 2**
38 Dhowin **F 2**
9 Dial Post **D 12**
8 Dibden **E 5**
8 Dibden Purlieu **E 5**
27 Dickleburgh **G 4**
16 Didbrook **A 2**
16 Didcot **E 6**
25 Diddington **J 3**
21 Diddlebury **D 10**
15 Didley **A 7**
9 Didling **D 10**
15 Didmarton **F 11**
5 Didworthy **J 5**
60 Diebidale Lodge **H 5**
33 Digby **E 8**
62 Digg **A 4**
35 Diggle **F 9**
34 Digmoor **G 4**
18 Digswell Water **B 3**
13 Dihewid **A 8**
47 Dikeneuk **D 11**
26 Dilham **C 6**
31 Dilhorne **F 8**
48 Dillarburn **E 1**
25 Dillington **J 2**
45 Dilston **G 8**
7 Dilton Marsh **A 11**
21 Dilwyn **G 9**
48 Dinanrig **H 1**
12 Dinas, Dyfed **D 6**
12 Dinas, Dyfed **C 4**
28 Dinas, Gwynedd **G 3**
28 Dinas Dinlle **D 4**
20 Dinas Mawddwy **A 4**
14 Dinas Powis **G 5**
13 Dinasbach **C 11**
7 Dinder **B 9**
15 Dinedor **A 8**
15 Dinedor Cross **A 8**
15 Dingestow **C 7**
30 Dingle **B 2**
49 Dingleton **F 8**
23 Dingley **C 11**
56 Dingwall **D 1**
44 Dinlabyre **D 4**
44 Dinley **C 3**
59 Dinnet **H 2**
43 Dinning **C 9**
45 Dinnington, Northumb **F 10**
7 Dinnington, Som. **E 7**
28 Dinorwic **D 5**
40 Dinsdale Station **D 4**
17 Dinton, Bucks **C 8**
8 Dinton, Wilts **C 2**
42 Dinvin **F 1**
43 Dinwoodie Mains **C 11**
43 Dinwoodiegreen **C 11**
4 Dinworthy **D 2**
46 Dippen **F 3**
9 Dippenhall **A 9**
46 Dippin **G 5**
58 Dipple, Grampian **B 1**
42 Dipple, Strathclyde **A 3**
5 Diptford **K 6**
45 Dipton **H 9**
49 Dirleton **A 8**
21 Discoed **F 8**
32 Diseworth **H 2**
40 Dishforth **H 4**
31 Disley **B 8**
27 Diss **G 4**
20 Disserth **G 6**
38 Distington **C 2**
8 Ditchampton **C 2**
7 Ditcheat **C 9**
26 Ditchingham **F 6**
10 Ditchling **F 2**
15 Ditteridge **G 11**
5 Dittisham **K 7**
30 Ditton, Cheshire **B 3**
10 Ditton, Kent **B 6**
25 DittonGreen **J 8**
21 Ditton Priors **D 11**
57 Divach **G 1**
13 Divlyn **C 11**
16 Dixton, Glos **A 1**
15 Dixton, Gwent **C 8**
35 Dobcross **F 8**
3 Dobwalls **C 9**
5 Doccombe **G 6**
56 Dochfour House **F 2**
56 Dochgarroch **F 2**
26 Docking **B 1**
21 Docklow **G 11**
38 Dockray **C 6**
44 Dodburn **B 3**
18 Doddinghurst **D 6**
24 Doddington, Cambs. **F 5**
11 Doddington, Kent **B 8**
32 Doddington, Lincs. **C 6**
49 Doddington, Northumb **F 12**
21 Doddington, Salop. **E 11**
6 Doddiscombsleigh **H 2**
22 Dodford, Heref. and Worc **E 3**
23 Dodford, Northants. **F 9**
15 Dodington, Avon **F 10**
6 Dodington, Som **B 5**
30 Dodleston **D 2**
35 Dodworth **G 11**
32 Doe Lea **D 2**
6 DogVillage **G 3**
33 Dogdyke **E 9**
9 Dogmersfield **A 9**
20 Dolanog **A 6**
14 Dolau, Mid. Glam **F 3**
21 Dolau, Powys **F 7**
28 Dolbenmaen **F 4**
20 Dolfach **E 5**
20 Dol-ffanog **A 3**
20 Dol-for, Powys **B4**
20 Dol-for, Powys **D 6**
29 Dolgarrog **C 7**
28 Dolgellau **H 6**
13 Dolgerdd **B 7**
20 Dol-goch **B 2**
13 Dol-gran **D 8**
20 Dolhelfa **E 5**
61 Doll **F 8**
52 Dollar **G 4**
52 Dollarbeg **G 4**
21 Dolley Green **F 8**
21 Dolleycanney **G 7**
34 Dolphinholme **B 4**
48 Dolphinton **E 4**
4 Dolton **E 4**
29 Dolwen, Clwyd **C 8**
20 Dolwen, Powys **B 5**
29 Dolwyd **B 7**
29 Dolwyddelan **E 7**
20 Dol-y-bont **D 2**
20 Dolypandy **D 2**
36 Doncaster **G 4**
8 Donhead St. Andrew **D 1**
7 Donhead St. Mary **D 12**
52 Donibristle **H 6**
6 Doniford **B 4**
24 Donington, Lincs **B 3**
22 Donington, Salop **B 2**
33 Donington ON Bain **B 9**
24 Donington South Ing **B 3**
22 Donisthorpe **A 6**
17 Donkey Town **H 10**
44 Donkleywood **D 6**
16 Donnington, Berks. **G 6**
16 Donnington, Glos **A 3**
15 Donnington, Heref. and Worc. **A 10**
21 Donnington, Salop. **B 11**
21 Donnington, Salop. **A 12**
9 Donnington, W. Sussex **F 10**
21 Donnington Wood **A 12**
7 Donyatt **E 7**
47 Doonbank **H 9**
47 Doonfoot **G 8**
47 Doonholm **H 8**
57 Dorback Lodge **H 6**
7 Dorchester, Dorset **G 10**
17 Dorchester, Oxon **E 7**
22 Dordon **B 6**
31 Dore **B 11**
56 Dores **F 2**
32 Dorket Head **E 3**
10 Dorking **C 1**
10 Dormansland **D 3**
40 Dormanstown **C 6**
21 Dormington **H 11**
17 Dorney **F 10**
55 Dornie **G 3**
61 Dornoch **G 8**
44 Dornock **F 1**
61 Dorrery **B 10**
22 Dorridge **E 5**
33 Dorrington, Lincs **E 8**
21 Dorrington, Salop. **B 10**
7 Dorset, County **F 10**
22 Dorsington **G 5**
21 Dorstone **H 8**
17 Dorton **C 7**
55 Dorusduain **G 3**
54 Dosmuckeran **D 6**
22 Dosthill **B 6**
7 Dottery **G 8**
3 Doublebois **C 9**
46 Dougarie **F 4**
15 Doughton **E 12**
38 Douglas, I.o.M. **H 2**
48 Douglas, Strathclyde **F 1**
53 Douglas & Angus **D 9**
28 Douglas Hill **D 5**
48 Douglas Water **F 2**
48 Douglas West **F 1**
53 Douglastown **B 9**
7 Doulting **B 10**
64 Dounby **C 1**
52 Doune, Central **G 2**
55 Doune, Highland **J 1**
60 Doune, Highland **F 5**
42 Dounepark **B 3**
59 Douneside **G 2**
60 Dounie **G 6**
58 Dounie Park **B 4**
47 Doura **F 9**
5 Dousland **J 4**
31 Dove Holes **B 9**
38 Dovenby **B 3**
11 Dover **D 12**
27 Dovercourt **M 6**
22 Doverdale **F 2**
31 Doveridge **G 9**
52 Dowally **B 5**
34 Dowbridge **D 3**
16 Dowdeswell **B 1**
42 Dowhill **A 3**
14 Dowlais **D 4**
4 Dowland **E 4**
16 Down Ampney **D 2**
15 Down Hatherley **B 11**
4 Down St. Mary **E 6**
5 Down Thomas **L 4**
56 Downan, Grampian **F 7**
42 Downan, Strathclyde **C 2**
3 Downderry **D 10**
18 Downe **H 4**
15 Downend, Avon **G 9**
16 Downend, Berks **G 6**
9 Downend, I.o.W. **G 7**
53 Downfield **D 8**
3 Downgate **B 10**
25 Downham, Cambs. **G 6**
19 Downham, Essex **D 7**
34 Downham, Lancs **C 6**
49 Downham, Northumb. **F 11**
24 Downham Market **E 7**
7 Downhead, Som **D 9**
7 Downhead, Som **B 10**
52 Downhill **D 6**
34 Downholland Cross **F 2**
40 Downholme **E 1**
59 Downies **H 7**
17 Downley **E 9**
7 Downside, Som **A 10**
7 Downside, Som **B 9**
15 Downside, Avon **H 8**
17 Downside, Surrey **H 12**
8 Downton, Hants **G 4**
8 Downton, Wilts **D 3**
21 Downton on the Rock **E 9**
24 Dowsby **C 2**
45 Doxford **A 10**
15 Doynton **G 10**
14 Draethen **F 5**
48 Draffan **E 1**
9 Dragons Green **D 12**
36 Drakeholes **H 5**
5 Drakeland Corner **K 4**
47 Drakemyre **D 8**
22 Drake's Broughton **G 4**
22 Drakes Cross **D 4**
3 Drakewalls **C 11**
23 Draughton, Northants **D 11**
35 Draughton, N. Yorks. **B 9**
36 Drax **D 5**
16 Draycot Foliat **F 3**
23 Draycote **E 8**
32 Draycott, Derby **G 2**
16 Draycott, Glos **A 3**
7 Draycott, Som **A 8**
31 Draycott in the Clay **G 10**
31 Draycott in the Moors **F 8**
4 Drayford **E 6**
9 Drayton, Hants **E 8**
23 Drayton, Leics **C 11**
24 Drayton, Lincs **B 4**
26 Drayton, Norfolk **D 5**
16 Drayton, Oxon **E 6**
23 Drayton, Oxon **H 8**
22 Drayton, Salop **E 3**
7 Drayton, Som **D 7**
22 Drayton Bassett **B 5**
17 Drayton Beauchamp **C 10**
17 Drayton Parslow **A 9**
17 Drayton St. Leonard **D 7**
35 Drebley **A 9**
12 Dreenhill **F 3**
13 Dre-fach, Dyfed **B 8**
13 Drefach, Dyfed **C 7**
13 Drefach, Dyfed **F 8**
47 Dreghorn **F 8**
11 Drellingore **N 11**
49 Drem **A 8**
5 Drewsteignton **G 6**
33 Driby **C 11**
16 Driffield, Glos **D 2**
37 Driffield, Humber. **A 8**
38 Drigg **E 3**
35 Drighlington **D 11**
51 Drimfern **F 8**
58 Drimmies **E 5**
50 Drimnin **B 3**
50 Drimnin House **B 3**
7 Drimpton **F 7**
55 Drimsallie **L 3**
51 Drimsynie **G 9**
27 Drinkstone **J 3**
27 Drinkstone Green **J 3**
51 Drishaig **F 8**
48 Drochil **E 4**
31 Drointon **G 9**
22 Droitwich **F 2**
52 Dron **F 6**
32 Dronfield **B 1**
31 Dronfield Woodhouse **B 11**
47 Drongan **G 9**
53 Dronley **D 8**
14 Drope **G 4**
9 Droxford **D 7**
29 Druid **F 9**
43 Druidhall **B 9**
12 Druidston **E 2**
46 Druim **A 2**
55 Druimarbin **M 5**
51 Druimavuic **C 7**
54 Druimdhu **D 5**
46 Druimdrishaig **B 2**
54 Druimindarroch **F 8**
46 Druimyeon More **D 2**
58 Drum, Grampian **C 6**
56 Drum, Highland **D 2**
46 Drum, Strathclyde **B 4**
52 Drum, Tayside **G 5**
60 Drumbeg **D 3**
58 Drumblade **D 3**
58 Drumblair House **C 4**
42 Drumbuie, Dumf. & Gall. **C 6**
55 Drumbuie, Highland **G 2**
44 Drumburgh **G 1**
43 Drumburn **E 10**
47 Drumchapel **B 10**
56 Drumchardine **E 1**
47 Drumclog **E 11**
43 Drumcoltran **E 9**
56 Drumcroy **F 1**
43 Drumcruilton **A 9**
58 Drumdaig **F 3**
56 Drumdyre **D 2**
53 Drumeldrie **G 9**
48 Drumelzier **F 4**
62 Drumfearn **G 6**
47 Drumfork **G 10**
57 Drumgask **K 2**
53 Drumgley **B 9**
56 Drumguish, Highland **F 6**
57 Drumguish, Highland **J 4**
59 Drumhead, Grampian **H 4**
58 Drumhead, Grampian **F 7**
42 Drumjohn **B 6**
43 Drumlanrig Castle **B 9**
59 Drumlasie **G 4**
46 Drumlemble **G 2**
58 Drumligair **F 6**
59 Drumlithie **J 5**
42 Drummoddie **G 5**
56 Drummond **C 2**
42 Drummore **H 2**
57 Drumnadrochit **G 1**
59 Drumnagair **K 4**
58 Drumnagorrach **B 3**
57 Drumnahoy **F 4**
60 Drumnunie **F 3**
42 Drumpail **E 3**
43 Drumpark **D 9**
42 Drumrae **G 5**
43 Drumrash **D 7**
58 Drums **E 7**
47 Drumshang **H 7**
43 Drumstinchall **F 9**
59 Drumtochty Castle **J 4**
62 Drumuie **D 4**
57 Drumuillie **G 5**
52 Drumvaich **G 2**
42 Drumwalt **F 4**
58 Drumwhindle **D 7**
43 Drumwhirn **D 8**
29 Drury **D 12**
32 Dry Doddington **F 6**
25 Dry Drayton **J 5**
19 Dry Street **E 7**
39 Drybeck **D 9**
58 Drybridge Grampian **A 2**
47 Drybridge Strathclyde **F 8**
15 Drybrook **C 9**
49 Dryburgh **F 8**
43 Dryfesdale Gate **C 11**
48 Dryhope **G 5**
47 Drymen **A 9**
58 Drymuir **C 6**
62 Drynoch **E 3**
13 Dryslwyn **E 9**
60 Duag Bridge **G 4**
58 Dubford, Grampian **C 5**
58 Dubford, Grampian **A 5**
58 Dubiton **C 4**
60 Duchally **E 5**
43 Duchrae **C 7**
8 Duck Street **A 5**
30 Duckington **E 4**
16 Ducklington **C 4**
32 Duckmanton **C 2**
25 Duck's Cross **K 2**
25 Duddenhoe End **L 6**
48 Duddingston **B 6**
24 Duddington **E 1**
10 Duddleswell **E 3**
49 Duddo **E 12**
30 Duddon **D 4**
38 Duddon Bridge **F 4**
30 Dudleston **F 2**
30 Dudleston Heath **F 2**
45 Dudley, Northants. **F 10**
22 Dudley, W. Midlands **C 3**
12 Dudwells **E 3**
31 Duffield **F 11**
14 Duffryn **E 2**
58 Dufftown **D 1**
56 Duffus **C 7**
39 Dufton **C 9**
41 Duggleby **H 9**
62 Duisdalemore **G 6**
55 Duisky **M 4**
14 Dukestown **C 5**
35 Dukinfield **G 8**
56 Dularich **F 1**
28 Dulas **A 4**
58 Dulax **F 1**
7 Dulcote **B 9**
6 Dulford **F 4**
52 Dull **B 3**
47 Dullatur **B 12**
25 Dullingham **J 7**
57 Dulnain Bridge **G 5**
25 Duloe, Beds. **J 3**
3 Duloe, Cornwall **D 9**
56 Dulsie **E 5**
6 Dulverton **C 3**
18 Dulwich **G 3**
47 Dumbarton **B 9**
16 Dumbleton **A 1**
43 Dumcrieff **A 11**
58 Dumeath **D 2**
43 Dumfries **D 10**
47 Dumgoyne **A 10**
9 Dummer **B 7**
59 Dun **L 4**
63 Dun Carloway **C 3**
57 Dunachtonmore **J 4**
56 Dunain House **E 2**
52 Dunalastair **A 2**
46 Dunan, Strathclyde **B 6**
52 Dunan, Tayside **D 2**
51 Dunan, Tayside **B 11**
62 Dunan, Skye **E 5**
51 Dunans **H 7**
49 Dunbar **B 9**
61 Dunbeath **D 11**
50 Dunbeg **D 6**
52 Dunblane **G 3**
53 Dunbog **E 7**
6 Dunboll **B 6**
8 Dunbridge **C 5**
61 Duncansby Head **A 12**
58 Duncanston, Grampian **E 3**
56 Duncanston, Highland **D 2**
6 Dunchideock **G 2**
23 Dunchurch **E 8**
23 Duncote **G 10**
43 Duncow **C 10**
51 Duncraggan **G 12**
54 Duncraig College **F 2**
52 Duncrievie **F 6**
9 Duncton **D 11**
53 Dundee **D 9**
7 Dundon **C 8**
53 Dundonald, Fife **H 7**
47 Dundonald, Strathclyde **F 8**
60 Dundonnell Hotel **H 2**
60 Dundonnell **H 3**
43 Dundraw **G 12**
55 Dundreggan **H 7**
43 Dundrennan **G 8**
15 Dundry **H 8**
15 Dunduff **H 6**
59 Dunecht **G 5**
48 Dunfermline **A 4**
16 Dunfield **D 2**
35 Dunford Bridge **G 10**
7 Dunge **A 12**
36 Dungworth **H 1**
32 Dunham **C 5**
30 Dunham Town **B 6**
30 Dunham-on-the-Hill **C 3**
22 Dunhampton **E 2**
33 Dunholme **B 7**
52 Dunie **D 4**
53 Dunino **F 10**
48 Dunipace **A 1**
52 Dunira **E 2**
52 Dunkeld **C 5**
15 Dunkerton **H 10**
6 Dunkeswell **E 5**
11 Dunkirk **B 9**
10 Dunk's Green **C 5**
59 Dunlappie **K 3**
22 Dunley **E 1**
56 Dunlichity Lodge **F 2**
47 Dunlop **D 9**
57 Dunmaglass Lodge **G 2**
3 Dunmere **C 7**
52 Dunmore, Central **H 4**
46 Dunmore, Strathclyde **C 3**
11 Dunn Street **B 7**
61 Dunnet **A 11**
53 Dunnichen **B 10**
53 Dunninald **B 11**
52 Dunning **F 5**
37 Dunnington, Humberside **B 9**
36 Dunnington, N. Yorks. **B 4**
22 Dunnington, War **G 4**
35 Dunnockshaw **D 7**

59 Dunnottar Mains J 6
58 Dunnydeer E 4
50 Dunollie D 6
46 Dunoon B 6
42 Dunragit F 2
46 Dunrostan A 2
49 Duns D 10
16 Duns Tew A 5
24 Dunsby C 2
43 Dunscore C 9
36 Dunscroft F 4
40 Dunsdale C 6
17 Dunsden Green F 8
9 Dunsfold B 11
5 Dunsford G 7
53 Dunshelt F 7
58 Dunshillock C 7
41 Dunsley D 8
17 Dunsmore D 9
34 Dunsop Bridge B 5
17 Dunstable B 11
31 Dunstall H 10
6 Dunster B 3
33 Dunston, Lincs D 8
26 Dunston, Norfolk E 5
45 Dunston, Northumb. A 10
31 Dunston, Staffs H 8
45 Dunston, Tyne & Wear G 10
5 Dunstone H 6
36 Dunsville F 4
37 Dunswell D 8
48 Dunsyre E 3
44 Dunterley E 6
5 Dunterton H 2
16 Duntisbourne Abbots C 1
16 Duntisbourne Rouse D 1
7 Duntish F 10
47 Duntocher B 9
25 Dunton, Beds L 3
17 Dunton, Bucks B 9
26 Dunton, Norfolk C 2
23 Dunton Bassett C 9
10 Dunton Green B 4
18 Dunton Wayletts E 6
62 Duntulm A 3
47 Dunure H 7
47 Dunure Mains H 7
13 Dunvant H 9
62 Dunvegan C 2
27 Dunwich H 8
52 Dupplin Castle E 5
44 Durdar H 2
9 Durford D 9
40 Durham A 3
43 Durisdeer A 10
43 Durisdeermill A 9
6 Durleigh C 6
16 Durley, Wilts H 3
8 Durley, Hants D 6
9 Durley Street D 7
60 Durnamuck G 2
60 Durness A 5
58 Durno E 5
9 Durrington, W. Sussex F 12
8 Durrington, Wilts. B 3
15 Dursley D 10
6 Durston C 6
7 Durweston E 11
64 Dury D 7
23 Duston F 10
57 Duthil G 5
21 Dutlas E 7
18 Duton Hill A 6
3 Dutson A 10
30 Dutton B 4
25 Duxford L 6
28 Dwygyfylchi C 7
28 Dwyran D 4
58 Dyce F 6
45 Dye House G 7
12 Dyfed, Co D 6
12 Dyffryn, Dyfed E 6
12 Dyffryn, Dyfed C 3
14 Dyffryn, Mid. Glam. F 4
14 Dyffryn, S. Glam G 4
14 Dyffryn, W. Glam E 2
28 Dyffryn-Ardudwy H 5
14 Dyffryn Cellwen C 2
20 Dyffryn-castell D 3
4 Dyke, Devon D 2
24 Dyke, Lincs C 2
56 Dyke, Grampian D 5
49 Dykegatehead D 11
52 Dykehead, Central G 1
48 Dykehead, Strathclyde C 2
59 Dykehead, Tayside L 1
59 Dykelands K 5
53 Dykends A 7
58 Dykeside C 5
20 Dylife C 4
11 Dymchurch E 9
15 Dymock A 10
15 Dyrham G 10
53 Dysart H 8
29 Dyserth B 10
45 Eachwick F 9
34 Eagland Hill C 3
32 Eagle D 6
40 Eaglescliffe Junc D 4
38 Eaglesfield, Cumb B 3
44 Eaglesfield, Dumf. & Gall. F 1
47 Eaglesham D 10
24 Eaglethorpe F 2
38 Eairy H 1
23 Eakley Lanes G 11
32 Eakring D 4
36 Ealand F 6
18 Ealing F 2
39 Eamont Bridge B 7
35 Earby C 8
34 Earcroft E 6
21 Eardington C 12
21 Eardisland F 9
21 Eardisley G 8
21 Eardiston, Heref. & Worc. F 12
30 Eardiston, Salop H 2
25 Earith H 5
23 Earl Shilton B 8
27 Earl Soham J 5
31 Earl Sterndale C 9
27 Earl Stonham J 4
49 Earle G 12
17 Earley G 8
26 Earlham E 5
62 Earlish B 3
23 Earls Barton F 12
19 Earls Colne A 8
22 Earl's Croome H 2
27 Earl's Green J 3
22 Earlsdon D 6
53 Earlsferry G 9
58 Earlsford D 6
49 Earlston, Borders F 8
47 Earlston, Strathclyde F 9
22 Earlswood E 5
15 Earlswood Com. E 8
9 Earnley F 9
45 Earsdon, Northumb. D 10
45 Earsdon, Tyne & Wear F 11
26 Earsham F 6
36 Earswick A 4
9 Eartham E 10
38 Earystane H 1
40 Easby, N. Yorks. D 6
40 Easby, N. Yorks. E 2
50 Easdale F 5
9 Easebourne D 10
23 Easenhall D 8
9 Eashing B 11
17 Easington, Bucks. C 8
41 Easington, Cleveland C 7
40 Easington, Dur. A 4
37 Easington, Humberside E 11
45 Easington, Northumb. C 12
17 Easington, Oxon. D 7
40 Easington Colliery A 4
45 Easington Grange B 12
45 Easington Lane H 12
40 Easingwold H 5
11 Easole Street C 11
53 Eassie & Nevay C 8
14 East Aberthaw H 4
16 East Adderbury A 6
5 East Allington L 6
45 East Ancroft A 11
4 East Anstey C 7
40 East Appleton E 3
9 East Ashling E 9
58 East Auchronie F 6
41 East Ayton G 10
14 East Bank D 5
33 East Barkwith B 9
10 East Barming C 6
41 East Barnby D 8
18 East Barnet D 3
49 East Barns B 9
26 East Barsham B 2
26 East Beckham B 5
18 East Bedfont F 1
27 East Bergholt M 4
26 East Bilney D 3
49 East Blanerne D 11
10 East Blatchington H 4
7 East Bloxworth G 12
45 East Boldon G 11
8 East Boldre F 5
45 East Bolton A 9
47 East Brackenridge E 11
26 East Bradenham E 2
7 East Brent A 7
27 East Bridge J 7
32 East Bridgford F 4
45 East Brunton F 10
4 East Buckland C 5
6 East Budleigh H 4
64 East Burra E 7
64 East Burrafirth D 7
7 East Burton G 11
40 East Butsfield A 1
36 East Butterwick G 6
59 East Cairnbeg K 5
48 East Calder C 4
26 East Carleton E 5
23 East Carlton C 11
16 East Challow E 5
7 East Chelborough F 9
10 East Chiltington G 3
7 East Chinnock E 8
8 East Chisenbury A 3
9 East Clandon A 12
17 East Claydon B 8
15 East Clevedon G 7
61 East Clyne F 9
7 East Coker E 9
6 East Combe C 5
7 East Compton B 9
36 East Cottingwith C 5
8 East Cowes F 6
36 East Cowick E 4
40 East Cowton E 3
45 East Cramlington E 11
7 East Cranmore B 10
8 East Creech H 1
57 East Croachy G 2
46 East Darlochan G 2
8 East Dean, Hants C 4
9 East Dean, W. Sussex E 10
26 East Dereham D 3
45 East Ditchburn A 9
4 East Down B 5
32 East Drayton C 5
15 East Dundry H 9
45 East Edington E 10
15 East End, Avon G 8
8 East End, Dorset F 2
16 East End, Hants. H 5
9 East End, Hants. D 8
8 East End, Hants. F 5
18 East End, Herts A 4
37 East End, Humber. D 10
11 East End, Kent E 7
26 East End, Norfolk D 8
16 East End, Oxon C 5
8 East Erlestoke A 1
10 East Farleigh C 6
23 East Farndon D 10
36 East Ferry G 6
45 East Fleetham D 12
53 East Flisk E 8
49 East Fortune A 8
36 East Garforth D 2
16 East Garston F 5
16 East Ginge E 5
49 East Gordon E 9
16 East Grafton H 4
8 East Grimstead C 4
10 East Grinstead D 3
11 East Guldeford F 8
23 East Haddon E 10
16 East Hagbourne E 6
37 East Halton E 9
37 East Halton Skitter E 9
18 East Ham F 4
16 East Hanney E 5
19 East Hanningfield D 7
36 East Hardwick E 2
27 East Harling G 3
40 East Harlsey E 4
8 East Harnham C 3
7 East Harptree A 9
45 East Hartford E 11
9 East Harting D 9
7 East Hatch C 12
25 East Hatley K 4
52 East Haugh B 4
40 East Hauxwell F 2
53 East Haven D 10
24 East Heckington A 3
40 East Hedleyhope A 2
16 East Hendred E 5
41 East Heslerton G 9
10 East Hoathly F 4
7 East Horrington B 9
9 East Horsley A 12
45 East Horton C 11
7 East Huntspill B 7
17 East Hyde B 12
4 East Ilkerton A 6
16 East Ilsley F 6
33 East Keal D 11
16 East Kennett G 2
35 East Keswick C 12
47 East Kilbride D 11
58 East Kinharrachie D 7
33 East Kirkley D 10
41 East Knapton G 9
7 East Knighton H 11
4 East Knowstone D 7
7 East Knoyle C 12
7 East Lambrook D 7
11 East Langdon C 12
23 East Langton C 10
61 East Langwell F 7
9 East Lavant E 10
40 East Layton D 2
32 East Leake H 3
4 East Leigh E 6
49 East Learmouth F 11
26 East Lexham D 2
45 East Lilburn A 8
49 East Linton B 8
9 East Liss C 9
47 East Lockhead D 8
3 East Looe D 9
36 East Lound G 6
9 East Lovington E10
7 East Lulworth H 12
41 East Lutton H 9
7 East Lydford C 9
59 East Mains H 4
10 East Malling B 6
9 East Marden E 9
32 East Markham C 5
35 East Marton B 8
9 East Meon D 8
6 East Mere E 3
19 East Mersea C 10
17 East Molesey G 12
7 East Mordon G 12
43 East Morton, Dumf. & Gall. B 9
35 East Morton, W. Yorks. C 9
42 East Muntloch H 2
41 East Ness G 7
23 East Norton B 11
6 East Nynehead D 5
9 East Oakley A 7
5 East Ogwell J 7
7 East Orchard D 11
49 East Ord D 12
5 East Panson G 2
10 East Peckham C 5
7 East Pennard C 9
26 East Poringland E 6
5 East Portlemouth M 6
5 East Prawle M 6
9 East Preston F 12
6 East Quantoxhead B 5
45 East Rainton H 11
37 East Ravendale G 10
26 East Raynham C 2
32 East Retford B 4
35 East Rigton C 12
40 East Rounton E 4
26 East Rudham C 1
26 East Runton A 5
26 East Ruston C 6
49 East Saltoun C 7
44 East Scales F 1
16 East Shefford G 5
45 East Sleekburn E 11
26 East Somerton D 8
36 East Stockwith H 6
7 East Stoke, Dorset H 12
32 East Stoke, Notts. E 5
7 East Stour D 11
11 East Stourmouth B 11
4 East Stowford C 5
9 East Stratton B 7
11 East Studdal C 11
10 East Sussex, Co F 5
3 East Taphouse C 9
19 East Tilbury F 7
43 East Tinwald C 11
9 East Tistead C 8
33 East Torrington B 8
59 East Town J 5
26 East Tuddenham D 4
8 East Tytherley C 4
16 East Tytherton G 1
4 East Village E 7
24 East Walton D 8
4 East Warlington E 6
5 East Week G 5
8 East Wellow D 5
53 East Wemyss G 8
48 East Whitburn C 2
19 East Wick D 10
12 East Williamston F 4
24 East Winch D 8
9 East Wittering F 9
40 East Witton G 2
45 East Woodburn D 7
16 East Woodhay H 5
9 East Worldham B 9
26 East Wretham F 2
4 East Youlstone D 1
10 Eastbourne H 5
37 Eastburn B 7
18 Eastbury, Herts E 1
16 Eastbury, Berks F 4
11 Eastchurch A 8
15 Eastcombe D 12
18 Eastcote, London C 12
23 Eastcote, Northants G 10
22 Eastcote, W. Midlands D 5
4 Eastcott, Devon D 1
8 Eastcott, Wilts A 2
16 Eastcourt, Wilts. H 3
16 Eastcourt, Wilts. E 1
10 Eastdean H 4
19 Eastend E 9
57 Easter Aberchalder G 1
56 Easter Ardross B 2
56 Easter Balcroy E 4
57 Easter Balmoral K 8
57 Easter Boleskine G 1
56 Easter Brae C 2
15 Easter Compton F 9
54 Easter Crochail F 8
56 Easter Culbo D 2
59 Easter Davoch G 2
55 Easter Drummond H 8
52 Easter Dullater F 1
43 Easter Earshaig A 11
61 Easter Fearn H 7
44 Easter Fodderlee B 4
56 Easter Galcantray E 4
22 Easter Green D 6
48 Easter Happrew E 4
48 Easter Howgate C 5
49 Easter Howlaws E 10
56 Easter Kinkell D 1
49 Easter Langlee F 8
53 Easter Lednathie A 8
56 Easter Milton D 5
56 Easter Moniack E 1
56 Easter Muckovie E 3
53 Easter Ogil A 9
59 Easter Ord G 6
47 Easter Pencaitland B 7
64 Easter Quarff E 7
58 Easter Silverford A 5
64 Easter Skeld D 6
49 Easter Softlaw F 10
59 Easter Tillygarmond H 4
59 Easter Tulloch K 5
56 Easterfield E 3
9 Eastergate F 11
47 Easterhouse, Strathclyde C 11
48 Easterhouse, Strathclyde D 3
8 Easterton A 2
58 Eastertown, Grampian D 1
48 Eastertown, Strathclyde F 2
48 Eastertown, Strathclyde E 3
7 Eastertown, Som. A 7
58 Eastertown of Auchleuchries D 8
59 Eastfield, Grampian H 1
41 Eastfield, N. Yorks G 10
48 Eastfield, Strathclyde C 2
48 Eastfield, Strathclyde E 2
45 Eastfield Hall B 10
49 Eastfield of Lempitlaw F 10
39 Eastgate, Dur. A 11
26 Eastgate, Norfolk C 4
30 Eastham B 2
17 Easthampstead G 9
17 Eastheath G 9
4 East-the-Water C 3
21 Easthope C 11
19 Easthorpe, Essex B 9
32 Easthorpe, Notts. E 4
48 Easthouses C 6
4 Eastington, Devon E 6
15 Eastington, Glos. D 11
16 Eastington, Glos. C 2
16 Eastleach Martin D 3
16 Eastleach Turville D 3
4 Eastleigh, Devon C 4
8 Eastleigh, Hants D 6
11 Eastling B 8
45 Eastnook D 8
15 Eastnor A 10
36 Eastoft E 6
9 Eastoke F 8
25 Easton, Cambs H 2
44 Easton, Cumb. G 1
44 Easton, Cumb. F 3
5 Easton, Devon G 6
7 Easton, Dorset H 7
8 Easton, Hants. C 6
8 Easton, I.o.W. G 5
32 Easton, Leics. G 6
26 Easton, Norfolk D 4
7 Easton, Somerset A 8
27 Easton, Suffolk J 6
15 Easton, Wilts. G 12
15 Easton Grey E 12
15 Easton-in-Gordano G 8
23 Easton Maudit F 12
24 Easton-on-the-Hill E 1
16 Easton Royal H 3
24 Eastrea F 4
44 Eastriggs F 1
36 Eastrington D 5
11 Eastry C 11
33 Eastville E 11
32 Eastwell G 5
18 Eastwick C 4
19 Eastwood, Essex E 8
32 Eastwood, Notts F 2
23 Eathorpe E 7
30 Eaton, Cheshire D 4
31 Eaton, Cheshire D 7
32 Eaton, Leics B 4
32 Eaton, Leics G 5
26 Eaton, Norfolk E 5
16 Eaton, Oxon. D 5
21 Eaton, Salop C 9
21 Eaton, Salop. C 10
21 Eaton Bishop H 10
17 Eaton Bray B 10
21 Eaton Constantine B 11
17 Eaton Green B 10
25 Eaton Socon J 3
30 Eaton upon Tern H 5
41 Ebberston G 9
8 Ebbesbourne Wake D 2
14 Ebbw Vale C 5
45 Ebchester G 9
15 Ebdon H 7
6 Ebford G 3
15 Ebley D 11
22 Ebrington H 5
5 Ebsworthy Town G 4
16 Ecchinswell H 6
49 Ecclaw C 10
43 Ecclefechan D12
49 Eccles, Borders E 10
10 Eccles, Kent B 6
34 Eccles, Manchester G 6
21 Eccles Green H 9
26 Eccles Road F 3
49 Eccles Tofts E 10
32 Ecclesall B 1
35 Ecclesfield H 12
59 Ecclesgreig L 5
31 Eccleshall G 7
35 Eccleshill D 10
48 Ecclesmachan B 3
30 Eccleston, Ches. D 3
34 Eccleston, Lancs. E 4
34 Eccleston, Merseyside H 4
35 Eccup C 11
59 Echt G 5
49 Eckford G 9
22 Eckington H 3
23 Ecton F 11
31 Edale B 9
10 Edburton G 1
43 Edderside G 11
61 Edderton H 7
16 Eddington, Berks. G 4
11 Eddington, Kent A 10
4 Eddistone D 1
48 Eddleston E 5
47 Eddlewood D 12
49 Eden Hall F 10
10 Edenbridge C 3
35 Edenfield E 7
39 Edenhall B 8
24 Edenham C 2
31 Edensor C 11
51 Edentaggart H 10
36 Edenthorpe F 4
44 Edentown G 2
28 Edern F 2
7 Edgarley C 8
22 Edgbaston D 4
17 Edgcott, Bucks. B 8
6 Edgcott, Som. B 2
21 Edge B 9
15 Edge End C 9
30 Edge Green, Ches. E 3
27 Edge Green, Norf. G 3
30 Edge Hill A 2
30 Edgebolton H 4
26 Edgefield B 4
26 Edgefield Green B 6
30 Edgemond H 6
44 Edgerston B 5
44 Edges Green F 5
35 Edgeside E 7
15 Edgeworth D 12
4 Edgeworthy E 7
30 Edgmond H 6
30 Edgmond Marsh H 6
21 Edgton D 9
18 Edgware E 2
34 Edgworth E 6

52 Edinample E 1
62 Edinbain C 3
48 Edinburgh B 5
22 Edingale A 6
32 Edingley E 4
26 Edingthorpe B 6
49 Edington, Borders D 11
7 Edington, Som. B 7
8 Edington, Wilts. A 1
7 Edington Burtle B 7
7 Edingworth A 7
58 Edintore C 2
23 Edith Weston B 12
6 Edithmead A 6
17 Edlesborough B 10
45 Edlingham B 9
33 Edlington C 9
8 Edmondsham E 2
45 Edmondsley H 10
32 Edmondthorpe H 6
64 Edmonstone C 3
18 Edmonton E 3
45 Edmundbyers H 8
49 Ednam F 10
51 Edra F 11
49 Edrom D 11
30 Edstaston G 4
22 Edstone F 5
21 Edvin Loach G 12
32 Edwalton G 3
27 Edwardstone L 2
13 Edwinsford D 9
32 Edwinstowe D 3
25 Edworth L 3
21 Edwyn Ralph G 12
59 Edzell K 3
14 Efail Isaf F 4
28 Efailnewydd G 3
29 Efail-rhyd H 11
12 Efailwen D 5
29 Efenechtyd E 10
9 Effingham A 12
64 Effirth D 6
4 Efford F 8
11 Egerton, Kent C 8
34 Egerton, Manchester F 6
5 Eggbuckland K 4
17 Eggington B 10
40 Egglescliffe D 4
39 Eggleston C 12
17 Egham G 11
23 Egleton A 12
45 Eglingham A 9
3 Egloshayle C 7
3 Egloskerry A 9
14 Eglwys-Brewis G 3
29 Eglwysbach C 7
20 Eglwysfach C 3
12 Eglwyswrw C 5
32 Egmanton C 4
38 Egremont, Cumb D 3
30 Egremont, Merseyside A 2
41 Egton D 8
41 Egton Bridge E 8
17 Egypt F 10
19 Eight Ash Green A 9
50 Eignaig C 5
55 Eilanreach H 2
49 Eildon F 8
61 Eilean Darach H 3
56 Eileanach Lodge C 1
63 Eishken F 4
20 Elan Village F 5
15 Elberton E 9
5 Elburton K 4
52 Elcho E 6
16 Elcombe F 2
24 Eldernell F 4
15 Eldersfield A 11
40 Eldon B 3
42 Eldrick C 4
34 Eldroth A 6
35 Eldwick C 10
20 Elerch D 2
59 Elfhill J 5
45 Elford, Northumb. D 12
22 Elford, Staffs A 5
56 Elgin C 8
62 Elgol G 6
11 Elham D 10
53 Elie G 9
45 Elilaw B 8
28 Elim B 3
8 Eling E 5
62 Elishader B 4
45 Elishaw D 7
32 Elkesley C 4
16 Elkstone C 1
57 Ellan G 5
35 Elland E 10
46 Ellary B 2
31 Ellastone F 9
34 Ellel B 4
49 Ellemford C 10
31 Ellenhall G 7
9 Ellen's Green C 12
40 Ellerbeck E 4
41 Ellerby D 8
30 Ellerdine Heath H 5
6 Ellerhayes F 3
51 Elleric C 7
37 Ellerker D 7
36 Ellerton, Humber. C 5
40 Ellerton, N. Yorks. E 3
30 Ellerton, Salop H 6
17 Ellesborough C 9
30 Ellesmere G 2
30 Ellesmere Port C 3
8 Ellingham, Hants E 3
26 Ellingham, Norf. F 6
45 Ellingham, Northumb. E 12
40 Ellingstring G 2
25 Ellington, Cambs. H 3
45 Ellington, Northumb. D 11
9 Ellisfield B 8
23 Ellistown A 8
58 Ellon D 7
58 Ellonby B 6
37 Elloughton D 7
15 Ellwood C 9
24 Elm E 6
18 Elm Park E 5
22 Elmbridge E 2
25 Elmdon, Essex L 6
22 Elmdon, W. Midlands D 5
22 Elmdon Heath D 5
18 Elmers End G 4
23 Elmesthorpe C 8
9 Elmfield G 7
22 Elmhurst A 5
22 Elmley Castle H 3
22 Elmley Lovett E 2
15 Elmore C 11
15 Elmore Back C 10
4 Elmscott D 1
27 Elmsett K 3
19 Elmstead Market B 10
11 Elmstone B 11
15 Elmstone Hardwicke B 12
37 Elmswell, Humber. A 7
27 Elmswell, Suffolk J 3
32 Elmton C 2
60 Elphin F 3
48 Elphinstone B 6
59 Elrick G 6
42 Elrig G 4
51 Elrigbeag F 8
45 Elsdon D 7
35 Elsecar G 12
18 Elsenham A 5
16 Elsfield C 6
37 Elsham F 8
26 Elsing D 4
35 Elslack B 8
30 Elson G 2
48 Elsrickle E 3
9 Elstead B 10
9 Elsted D 9
32 Elston, Notts. E 5
8 Elston, Wilts B 2
4 Elstone D 5
37 Elstronwick D 10
25 Elstow K 2
18 Elstree D 2
34 Elswick C 3
25 Elsworth J 4
38 Elterwater E 5
18 Eltham F 4
25 Eltisley J 4
24 Elton, Cambs. F 2
30 Elton, Cheshire C 3
40 Elton, Cleveland C 4
31 Elton, Derby D 10
15 Elton, Glos. C 10
21 Elton, Heref. & Worc. E 10
32 Elton, Notts. F 5
48 Elvanfoot H 2
31 Elvaston G 12
27 Elveden G 1
11 Elvington, Kent C 11
36 Elvington, N. Yorks B 5
49 Elwartlaw E 10
40 Elwick, Cleveland B 5
45 Elwick, Northumb. B 12
30 Elworth D 6
6 Elworthy C 4
25 Ely, Cambs. G 6
14 Ely, S. Glam. G 5
23 Emberton G 12
44 Emblehope D 6
38 Embleton, Cumb B 4
40 Embleton, Dur B 4
45 Embleton, Northumb. A 10
61 Embo G 8
35 Embsay B 8
8 Emery Down E 4
35 Emley F 11
35 Emley Moor F 11
17 Emmbrook G 8
17 Emmington D 8
24 Emneth E 6
24 Emneth Hungate E 6
23 Empingham A 12
9 Empshott C 9
9 Emsworth E 9
63 Enaclete D 2
16 Enborne G 5
16 Enborne Row H 5
21 Enchmarsh C 10
7 Encombe H 12
23 Enderby B 8
39 Endmoor G 7
31 Endon E 7
31 Endon Bank E 8
18 Enfield D 3
8 Enford A 3
15 Engine Common F 10
17 Englefield G 7
17 Englefield Green G 10
15 English Bicknor C 9
30 English Frankton G 3
15 Englishcombe H 10
8 Enham Alamein A 5
6 Enmore C 6
38 Ennerdale Bridge D 3
43 Enoch B 9
52 Enochdu A 5
50 Ensay C 1
8 Ensbury F 2
21 Ensdon A 9
4 Ensis C 4
16 Enstone B 5
43 Enterkinfoot A 9
40 Enterpen E 5
22 Enville C 2
50 Eorabus E 1
63 Eoropie A 6
15 Epney C 11
32 Epperstone E 4
18 Epping D 4
18 Epping Green C 3
18 Epping Green C 4
18 Epping Upland C 4
40 Eppleby D 2
10 Epsom B 1
23 Epwell H 7
36 Epworth G 5
29 Erbistock F 12
55 Erbusaig G 1
54 Erchless Castle E 8
22 Erdington C 5
51 Eredine G 7
60 Eriboll B 5
48 Ericstane H 3
10 Eridge Green E 4
46 Erines B 4
25 Eriswell G 8
18 Erith F 5
33 Ermine C 7
5 Ermington K 5
26 Erpingham B 5
55 Errocht L 5
57 Errogie G 1
53 Errol E 7
47 Erskine B 9
42 Ervie E 1
27 Erwarton M 5
20 Erwood H 6
40 Eryholme D 3
29 Eryrys D 11
46 Escart C 3
40 Escomb B 2
36 Escrick C 4
13 Esgair D 7
20 Esgairgeiliog B 3
13 Esgerdawe C 9
40 Esh A 2
40 Esh Winning A 2
17 Esher H 12
45 Eshott C 10
35 Eshton B 8
54 Eskadale F 8
48 Eskbank C 6
38 Eskdale Green E 4
44 Eskdalemuir C 1
37 Eskham G 11
34 Esprick D 3
24 Essendine D 1
18 Essendon C 3
19 Essex, Co C 7
56 Essich F 2
22 Essington B 3
64 Eswick D 7
40 Eston C 6
49 Etal E 11
16 Etchilhampton H 2
10 Etchingham E 6
11 Etchinghill, Kent D 10
31 Etchinghill, Staffs H 8
53 Ethie Mains B11
17 Eton F 10
17 Eton Wick F 10
57 Etteridge K 3
22 Ettington G 6
24 Etton, Cambs. E 2
37 Etton, Humberside C 7
44 Ettrick H 5
48 Ettrickbridge G 6
31 Etwall G 11
27 Euston G 2
24 Euximoor Drove F 6
34 Euxton E 4
14 Evanstown E 3
56 Evanton C 2
33 Evedon E 8
61 Evelix G 7
21 Evenjobb F 8
17 Evenley A 7
16 Evenlode A 3
40 Evenwood C 2
40 Evenwood Gate C 2
64 Everbay C 4
7 Evercreech B 9
23 Everdon F 9
36 Everingham C 6
8 Everleigh A 3
41 Everley F 10
25 Eversholt M 1
7 Evershot F 9
17 Eversley H 8
17 Eversley Cross H 9
37 Everthorpe D 7
25 Everton, Beds K 3
8 Everton, Hants G 4
30 Everton, Merseyside A 2
32 Everton, Notts A 4
44 Evertown E 2
21 Evesbatch H 12
22 Evesham H 4
23 Evington B 10
35 Ewden Village G 11
10 Ewell B 1
11 Ewell Minnis D 11
17 Ewelme E 7
16 Ewen D 1
14 Ewenny G 2
33 Ewerby E 8
44 Eweslees C 2
11 Ewhurst Green F 7
9 Ewhurst, Surrey B 12
9 Ewhurst Green B 12
29 Ewloe D 12
4 Eworthy F 3
9 Ewshot A 9
15 Ewyas Harold B 7
4 Exbourne F 5
8 Exbury F 6
6 Exebridge D 3
40 Exelby F 3
6 Exeter G 3
6 Exford B 2
22 Exhall G 4
17 Exlade Street F 7
6 Exminster G 3
6 Exmouth H 4
64 Exnaboe F 7
25 Exning J 7
6 Exton, Devon H 3
9 Exton, Hants D 7
23 Exton, Leics. A 12
6 Exton, Somerset C 3
6 Exwick G 3
31 Eyam C 10
23 Eydon G 9
24 Eye, Cambs. E 3
21 Eye, Heref. & Worc. F 10
27 Eye, Suffolk H 4
49 Eyemouth C 12
25 Eyeworth L 4
11 Eyhorne Street C 7
27 Eyke K 6
25 Eynesbury J 3
62 Eynort E 3
10 Eynsford B 4
16 Eynsham C 5
7 Eype G 8
62 Eyre C 3
11 Eythorne C 11
29 Eyton, Clwyd F 12
21 Eyton,
Heref. & Worc. F 10
21 Eyton, Salop D 9
30 Eyton, Salop H 3
21 Eyton upon the Weald
Moors A 12
16 Faccombe H 5
40 Faceby E 5
28 Fachwen D 5
35 Facit E 7
30 Faddiley E 4
55 Faddoch G 3
41 Fadmoor F 7
31 Fagginton G 11
13 Fagwyr G 10
47 Fail F 9
15 Failand G 8
47 Failford G 9
35 Failsworth G 8
54 Fain B 5
6 Fair Oak, Devon D 4
8 Fair Oak, Hants. D 6
17 Fair Oak Green H 7
20 Fairbourne A 2
36 Fairburn D 2
22 Fairfield,
Heref. & Worc. H 4
22 Fairfield,
Heref. & Worc. E 3
16 Fairford D 3
43 Fairgirth F 9
47 Fairlie D 7
11 Fairlight G 7
11 Fairlight Cove G 7
6 Fairmile F 4
48 Fairmilehead C 5
49 Fairnilee F 7
30 Fairoak G 6
10 Fairseat B 5
19 Fairstead, Essex B 7
26 Fairstead, Norfolk C 6
10 Fairwarp E 3
4 Fairy Cross D 3
26 Fakenham C 2
49 Fala C 7
48 Falahill D 6
41 Falcon Inn E 10
33 Faldingworth B 8
15 Falfield E 10
27 Falkenham L 6
48 Falkirk A 2
53 Falkland F 7
44 Falla B 5
32 Fallgate D 1
52 Fallin H 3
49 Fallsidehill E 9
10 Falmer G 2
2 Falmouth F 5
44 Falnash B 2
41 Falsgrave F 10
44 Falside B 5
44 Falstone D 5
60 Fanagmore C 3
40 Fangdale Beck F 6
36 Fangfoss B 5
50 Fanmore C 2
54 Fannich Lodge C 6
49 Fans E 9
17 Far Bletchley A 9
22 Far Forest E 1
38 Far Sawrey F 6
24 Farcet F 3
21 Farden E 11
9 Fareham F 7
22 Farewell A 4
33 Farforth B 10
44 Farglow F 5
16 Faringdon E 4
34 Farington E 4
44 Farlam G 4
15 Farleigh, Avon G 8
10 Farleigh, Surrey B 3
7 Farleigh Hungerford A 11
9 Farleigh Wallop A 8
15 Farleigh Wick H 11
33 Farlesthorpe C 11
39 Farleton G 8
15 Farley, Avon G 7
31 Farley, Cheshire F 9
21 Farley, Salop B 9
8 Farley, Wiltshire C 4
9 Farley Green B 12
17 Farley Hill H 8
15 Farleys End C 11
40 Farlington H 6
21 Farlow D 11
29 Farm Yard D 7
15 Farmborough H 10
16 Farmcote A 2
13 Farmers C 10
43 Farmersfield C 9
16 Farmington C 2
16 Farmoor C 5
58 Farmtown C 3
16 Farnborough, Berks. F 5
9 Farnborough, Hants. A 10
18 Farnborough, London G 4
23 Farnborough, War. G 8
17 Farnborough Green H 9
9 Farncombe B 11
30 Farndon, Clwyd E 3
32 Farndon, Notts E 5
53 Farnell B 11
8 Farnham, Dorset E 1
18 Farnham, Essex A 5
35 Farnham, N. Yorks A 12
27 Farnham, Suffolk J 7
9 Farnham, Surrey B 9
17 Farnham Com F 10
18 Farnham Green A 5
17 Farnham Royal F 10
35 Farnhill C 9
6 Farningdon G 4
10 Farningham A 4
35 Farnley, N. Yorks B 11
35 Farnley, W. Yorks D 11
35 Farnley Tyas F 10
32 Farnsfield D 4
30 Farnworth, Ches. B 4
34 Farnworth, Manchester G 6
56 Farr, Highland F 2
57 Farr, Highland J 4
61 Farr, Highland B 7
56 Farr House F 2
7 Farrington Gurney A 9
35 Farsley D 10
23 Farthinghoe H 8
11 Farthingloe D 11
23 Farthingstone G 9
35 Fartown E 10
6 Farway G 5
54 Fasag D 3
50 Fascadale A 2
55 Fasnakyle G 7
59 Fasque K 4
55 Fassfern L 4
45 Fatfield H 11
58 Fattahead B 4
44 Faugh G 3
48 Fauldhouse C 2
44 Fauldie F 2
19 Faulkbourne B 8
7 Faulkland A 10
30 Faulsgreen G 4
11 Faversham B 9
56 Favillar F 8
45 Fawdon B 8
31 Fawfieldhead D 9
10 Fawkham Green B 5
16 Fawler B 5
16 Fawley, Berks F 5
17 Fawley, Bucks E 8
8 Fawley, Hants F 6
15 Fawley Chapel A 9
49 Fawside E 9
36 Faxfleet E 6
3 Faygate E 1
22 Fazeley B 5
40 Fearby G 2
56 Fearn B 4
60 Fearn Lodge H 6
52 Fearnan C 2
54 Fearnbeg D 1
30 Fearnhead A 5
54 Fearnmore D 1
22 Featherstone, Staffs. B 3
36 Featherstone,
W. Yorks. E 2
22 Feckenham F 4
56 Feddan D 5
19 Feering B 8
39 Feetham E 12
10 Felbridge D 3
26 Felbrigg B 5
10 Felcourt D 3
17 Felden D 11
21 Felhampton D 10
12 Felin-Wnda B 6
20 Felindre, Dyfed G 1
13 Felindre, Dyfed D 10
13 Felindre, Dyfed G 9
13 Felindre, Dyfed E 9
21 Felindre, Powys D 7
14 Felindre, Powys B 5
13 Felinfach, Dyfed A 8
14 Felin-fach, Powys A 4
13 Felinfoel G 8
13 Felingwm Isaf E 8
13 Felingwm Uchaf E 8
40 Felixkirk G 5
27 Felixstowe M 6
27 Felixstoweferry L 6
49 Felkington E 12
5 Felldownhead H 2
45 Felling G 11
38 Fellside B 5
25 Felmersham J 1
26 Felmingham C 6
9 Felpham F 11
27 Felsham J 2
19 Felstead B 7
18 Feltham G 1
26 Felthorpe D 5
21 Felton,
Heref. & Worc. G 11
45 Felton, Northumb. C 10
15 Felton, Somerset H 8
21 Felton Butler A 9
24 Feltwell F 8

25 Fen Ditton J 6
25 Fen Drayton H 4
22 Fen End E 6
35 Fenay Bridge F 10
35 Fence C 7
45 Fence Houses H 11
33 Fendike Corner D 11
56 Fendom B 4
24 Fengate F 3
45 Fenham B 12
45 Fenhamhill B 12
34 Feniscowles E 5
6 Feniton F 4
31 Fenny Bentley E 10
23 Fenny Compton G 7
23 Fenny Drayton B 7
17 Fenny Stratford A 10
45 Fenrother D 10
25 Fenstanton H 4
25 Fenton, Cambs. G 4
32 Fenton, Lincs C 6
32 Fenton, Notts E 6
31 Fenton, Staffs F 7
49 Fenton Barns A 8
49 Fenton Town F 12
49 Fentonhill F 12
45 Fenwick, Northumb. F 9
45 Fenwick, Northumb. B 12
36 Fenwick, N. Yorks E 4
47 Fenwick, Strathclyde E 9
46 Feochaig H 3
2 Feock F 5
62 Feriniquarrie C 1
50 Ferlochan D 6
59 Fern L 2
55 Fern Villa G 3
14 Ferndale E 3
8 Ferndown F 2
49 Ferneyhill F 10
16 Fernham E 4
10 Fernhill D 2
22 Fernhill Heath F 2
9 Fernhurst C 10
53 Fernie F 8
62 Fernilea E 3
31 Fernilee B 8
21 Ferny Common G 9
35 Ferrensby A 12
62 Ferrindonald G 6
9 Ferring F 12
25 Ferry Hill G 5
61 Ferry Point H 7
36 Ferrybridge E 3
53 Ferryden B 12
40 Ferryhill, Durham B 3
59 Ferryhill, Grampian G 7
40 Ferryhill Station B 3
13 Ferryside F 7
27 Fersfield G 4
55 Fersit L 7
57 Feshiebridge J 4
17 Fetcham H 12
58 Fetterangus C 7
59 Fettercairn K 4
35 Fewston B 10
13 Ffairfach E 9
20 Ffair-rhôs F 3
13 Ffaid-y-Brenin C 9
14 Ffawyddog B 5
28 Ffestiniog F 6
21 Fforddlas, Powys H 7
13 Fforest G 9
13 Fforest fach G 9
13 Fforest Goch G 10
13 Ffostrasol B 7
13 Ffos-y-ffin A 8
29 Ffrith E 12
21 Ffynnon Gynydd H7
13 Ffynnon-ddrain E 7
29 Ffynnongroew B 10
60 Fiag Bridge E 5
60 Fiag Lodge D 5
50 Fidden G 1
15 Fiddington, Glos A 12
6 Fiddington, Som B 5
7 Fiddleford E 11
18 Fiddlers Hamlet D 5
44 Fiddleton C 2
31 Field G 9
38 Field Broughton G 6
26 Field Dalling B 3
23 Field Head A 8
47 Fieldhead D 11
53 Fife, County G 7
58 Fife of Keith C 2
7 Fifehead Magdalen D 11
7 Fifehead Neville E 11
7 Fifehead St. Quinton E 11
17 Fifield, Berks F 10
16 Fifield, Glos. B 3
8 Fifield, Wilts A 3
8 Fifield Bavant D 2
8 Figheldean A 3
40 Fighting Cocks D 4
26 Filby D 8
41 Filey G 11
23 Filgrave G 12
16 Filkins D 3
4 Filleigh, Devon E 6
4 Filleigh, Devon C 5
32 Fillingham B 6
22 Fillongley C 6
15 Filton F 9
37 Fimber A 7
59 Finavon L 2
24 Fincham E 8
17 Finchampstead H 9
50 Fincharn G 6
9 Finchdean E 9
25 Finchingfield M 8
18 Finchley E 3
53 Fincraigs E 8
31 Findern G 11
56 Findhorn C 6
57 Findhorn Bridge G 4
58 Findochty A 2
59 Findon, Grampian H 7
9 Findon, W. Sussex E 12
56 Findon Mains D 2
59 Findrack House G 3
23 Finedon E 12
27 Fingal Street H 5
58 Fingask, Grampian E 5
52 Fingask, Tayside E 6
22 Fingerpost E 1
17 Fingest E 8
40 Finghall F 2
44 Fingland, Cumb G 1
47 Fingland, Dumf. & Gall. H 12
11 Finglesham C 12
19 Fingringhoe B 10
55 Finiskaig K 2
52 Finlarig D 1
17 Finmere A 7
51 Finnart B 12
43 Finniegill B 12
27 Finningham H 3
36 Finningley G 4
58 Finnygaud B 3
63 Finsbay H 2
18 Finsbury F 3
22 Finstall E 3
38 Finsthwaite F 6
16 Finstock C 4
64 Finstown C 2
43 Fintloch D 7
47 Fintry, Central A 11
58 Fintry, Grampian B 5
53 Fintry, Tayside D 9
50 Fionnphort F 1
40 Fir Tree B 2
32 Firbeck A 3
41 Firby, N. Yorks H 7
40 Firby, N. Yorks G 3
33 Firsby D 11
60 First Coast G 1
36 Fishlake F 4
43 Fishbeck C 11
9 Fishbourne, I.o.W. G 7
9 Fishbourne, W. Sussex F 10
40 Fishburn B 4
52 Fishcross H 4
58 Fisherford D 4
8 Fisher's Pond D 6
9 Fisherstreet C 11
56 Fisherton, Highland E 3
47 Fisherton, Strathclyde H 7
8 Fisherton de la Mere B 2
12 Fishguard C 3
15 Fishponds G 9
35 Fishpool, Manchester F 7
32 Fishpool, Notts E 3
24 Fishtoft A 5
33 Fishtoft Drove E 10
53 Fishtown of Usan B 12
49 Fishwick D 11
62 Fiskavaig E 2
33 Fiskerton, Lincs C 7
32 Fiskerton, Notts E 4
37 Fitling D 10
24 Fitten End D 5
8 Fittleton A 3
9 Fittleworth D 11
30 Fitz H 3
6 Fitzhead C 5
36 Fitzwilliam F 2
50 Fiunary C 3
15 Five Acres C 9
10 Five Ashes F 4
34 Five Lane Ends B 4
3 Five Lanes B 9
10 Five Oak Green D 5
9 Five Oaks C 12
63 Five Penny Borve A 5
63 Five Penny Ness A 6
13 Five Roads F 8
30 Fivecrosses C 4
7 Fivehead D 7
19 Flack's Green B 7
17 Flackwell Heath E 9
22 Fladbury G 3
64 Fladdabister E 7
31 Flagg C 10
41 Flamborough H 2
17 Flamstead C 11
9 Flansham F 11
35 Flappit Spring C 9
62 Flashader C 3
35 Flasby B 8
31 Flash C 8
17 Flaunden D 11
32 Flawborough F 5
36 Flawith A 3
15 Flax Bourton G 8
35 Flaxby A 12
15 Flaxley C 10
6 Flaxpool C 5
36 Flaxton A 4
23 Fleckney C 10
23 Flecknoe F 8
32 Fledborough C 5
7 Fleet, Dorset H 9
9 Fleet, Hants A 9
9 Fleet, Hants F 8
24 Fleet, Lincs C 5
33 Fleet Hargate H 11
45 Fleetham E 12
34 Fleetwood B 2
14 Flemingston G 3
47 Flemington, Strathclyde C 11
47 Flemington, Strathclyde E 12
27 Flempton H 1
38 Fletchertown A 4
10 Fletching F 3
44 Flex B 3
4 Flexbury E 1
9 Flexford A 10
38 Flimby B 3
10 Flimwell E 6
29 Flint C 11
29 Flint Mountain C 11
32 Flintham F 5
37 Flinton D 10
24 Flitcham C 8
25 Flitton L 2
4 Flitton Barton C 6
25 Flitwick M 1
36 Flixborough F 6
34 Flixton, Manchester H 6
41 Flixton, N. Yorks G 10
27 Flixton, Suffolk G 6
35 Flockton F 11
35 Flockton Green F 11
49 Flodden F 11
63 Flodabay H 2
62 Flodigarry Hotel A 4
24 Flood's Ferry F 5
38 Flookburgh H 6
26 Flordon F 5
23 Flore F 9
45 Flotterton C 8
35 Flouch Inn G 10
27 Flowton K 4
2 Flushing, Cornwall F 5
58 Flushing, Grampian C 8
6 Fluxton G 4
22 Flyford Flavell G 3
19 Fobbing E 7
58 Fochabers B 1
14 Fochriw D 4
36 Fockerby E 6
57 Fodderletter G 7
56 Fodderty D 1
7 Foddington C 9
20 Foel A 5
13 Foelgastell E 9
53 Foffarty C 9
36 Foggathorpe C 5
49 Fogo D 10
49 Fogorig E 10
60 Foindle C 3
53 Folda A 7
31 Fole F 9
23 Foleshill D 7
7 Folke E 10
11 Folkestone E 11
24 Folkingham B 2
10 Folkington H 4
24 Folksworth F 2
41 Folkton G 10
58 Folla Rule D 5
35 Follifoot B 12
4 Folly Gate F 4
14 Fonmon G 4
8 Fonthill Bishop C 1
7 Fonthill Gifford C 12
7 Fontmell Magna E 12
9 Fontwell E 10
31 Foolow C 10
18 Foots Cray G 5
58 Forbestown F 1
6 Forches Corner D 5
17 Ford, Bucks C 8
5 Ford, Devon L 7
4 Ford, Devon D 3
16 Ford, Glos. A 2
49 Ford, Northumb. F 12
21 Ford, Salop A 9
6 Ford, Somerset C 4
31 Ford, Staffs E 9
50 Ford, Strathclyde G 6
9 Ford, W. Sussex F 11
15 Ford, Wilts G 11
6 Ford Barton D 3
19 Ford End B 7
6 Ford Street D 5
10 Fordcombe D 4
52 Fordel F 6
52 Fordell H 6
21 Forden B 8
25 Fordham, Cambridgeshire H 7
19 Fordham, Essex A 9
24 Fordham, Norfolk E 7
22 Fordhouses B 3
8 Fordingbridge E 3
41 Fordon H 10
59 Fordoun K 5
19 Fordstreet A 9
16 Fordwells C 4
11 Fordwich B 10
58 Fordyce A 3
31 Forebridge H 8
9 Forest Green B 12
39 Forest Hall E 8
44 Forest Head G 4
17 Forest Hill C 7
51 Forest Lo., Highland C 10
57 Forest Lo., Highland H 6
52 Forest Lo., Tayside A 4
52 Forest Mill H 4
10 Forest Row D 3
32 Forest Town D 3
45 Forestburn Gate C 9
56 Foresterseat D 7
9 Forestside E 9
53 Forfar B 9
52 Forgandenny E 6
14 Forge Hammer E 6
14 Forge Side D 6
58 Forgie B 1
58 Forgieside B 1
58 Forglen House B 4
34 Formby F 2
26 Forncett End F 4
26 Forncett St. Mary F 4
26 Forncett St. Peter F 5
52 Forneth C 6
27 Fornham All Saints J 1
27 Fornham St. Martin H 2
56 Forres D 6
48 Forrestfield C 1
31 Forsbrook F 8
61 Forse D 11
61 Forsinain Farm C 9
61 Forsinard C 9
61 Forsinard Station C 8
7 Forston G 10
55 Fort Augustus J 7
56 Fort George D 3
55 Fort William M 5
47 Fortacres F 9
52 Forteviot E 5
48 Forth D 2
15 Forthampton A 11
52 Fortingall B 2
8 Forton, Hants B 6
34 Forton, Lancs B 4
21 Forton, Salop A 9
7 Forton, Somerset E 7
30 Forton, Staffs H 6
58 Fortrie C 4
56 Fortrose D 3
7 Fortuneswell H 7
17 Forty Green E 10
25 Forty Feet Bridge G 4
27 Forward Green J 4
16 Fosbury H 4
16 Foscot B 3
24 Fosdyke B 4
24 Fosdyke Bridge B 4
52 Foss A 3
16 Fossebridge C 2
18 Foster Street C 5
36 Fosterhouses F 4
31 Foston, Derby G 10
32 Foston, Lincs F 6
36 Foston, N.Yorks A 5
37 Foston on the Wolds B 8
33 Fotherby A 10
24 Fotheringhay F 2
64 Foubister D 3
10 Foul Mile F 5
49 Foulden, Borders D 11
26 Foulden, Norfolk E 1
56 Foulis Castle C 1
35 Foulridge C 7
26 Foulsham C 3
58 Fountainbleau, Grampian D 8
58 Fountainbleau, Grampian E 7
49 Fountainhall D 7
27 Four Ashes H 3
29 Four Crosses, Powys H 12
20 Four Crosses, Powys B 6
22 Four Crosses, Staffs. A 3
10 Four Elms C 3
6 Four Forks C 6
34 Four Gates F 5
24 Four Gates D 5
30 Four Lane Ends, Ches. D 4
39 Four Lane Ends, Cumbria F 8
34 Four Lane Ends, Lancashire B 4
36 Four Lane Ends, N. Yorks B4
2 Four Lanes F 4
9 Four Marks C 8
28 Four Mile Bridge B 2
11 Four Oaks, E. Sussex F 7
15 Four Oaks, Glos B 10
22 Four Oaks, W. Midlands D 6
22 Four Oaks, W. Midlands B 4
13 Four Roads, Dyfed F 8
38 Four Roads, I.o.M. H 1
10 Four Throws E 6
30 Fourlanes End D 6
45 Fourlaws E 7
45 Fourstones F 7
8 Fovant C 2
58 Foveran E 7
3 Fowey D 8
58 Fowlershill F 7
53 Fowlis D 8
52 Fowlis Wester E 4
25 Fowlmere L 5
15 Fownhope A 9
9 Fox Corner A 11
17 Fox Lane H 9
7 Foxcote A 10
38 Foxdale H 1
27 Foxearth L 1
38 Foxfield G 5
16 Foxham F 1
3 Foxhole D 7
41 Foxholes H 10
10 Foxhunt Green F 4
26 Foxley, Norfolk C 3
15 Foxley, Wilts F 12
31 Foxt E 9
25 Foxton, Cambs K 5
40 Foxton, Durham C 4
23 Foxton, Leics C 10
39 Foxup G 11
30 Foxwist Green C 5
21 Foxwood E 11
15 Foy A 9
57 Foyers G 1
7 Foys E 9
2 Fraddam F 3
2 Fraddon D 6
22 Fradley A 5
31 Fradswell G 8
37 Fraisthorpe A 9
10 Framfield F 4
26 Framingham Earl E 6
26 Framingham Pigot E 6
27 Framlingham J 6
7 Frampton, Dorset G 9
24 Frampton, Lincs B 4
15 Frampton Cotterell F 9
15 Frampton Mansell D 12
15 Frampton on Severn D 10
24 Frampton West End B 4
27 Framsden J 5
40 Framwellgate Moor A 3
22 Franche D 2
30 Frandley B 5
30 Frankby B 1
22 Frankley D 3
21 Frank's Bridge G 7
23 Frankton E 7
21 Frankwell, Salop A 10
10 Frant E 5
58 Fraserburgh A 7
19 Frating B 10
19 Frating Green B 10
3 Freathy D 11
32 Frecheville B 1
25 Freckenham H 8
34 Freckleton D 3
32 Freeby H 5
16 Freeland C 5
26 Freethorpe E 7
26 Freethorpe Com. E 7
24 Freiston A 5
4 Fremington, Devon C 4
40 Fremington, N. Yorks E 1
15 Frenchay F 9
5 Frenchbeer G 5
51 Frenich, Central G 11
52 Frenich, Tayside A 3
9 Frensham B 9
61 Fresgoe A 9
34 Freshfield F 2
8 Freshwater G 5
12 Freshwater East G 4
27 Fressingfield H 5
61 Freswick A 12
15 Fretherne C 10
26 Frettenham D 5
53 Freuchie F 7
12 Freystrop Cross F 3
7 Friar Waddon H 10
52 Friarton E 6
24 Friday Bridge E 6
10 Friday Street H 5
36 Fridaythorpe A 6
18 Friern Barnet E 3
33 Friesthorpe B 8
32 Frieston E 6
17 Frieth E 9
16 Frilford D 5
16 Frilsham G 6
17 Frimley H 9
17 Frimley Green H 10
10 Frindsbury A 6
24 Fring B 8
17 Fringford A 7
11 Frinsted B 7
19 Frinton B 12
53 Friockheim B 10
20 Friog A 2
32 Frisby on the Wreake H 4
33 Friskney E 11
10 Friston, E. Sussex H 4
27 Friston, Suffolk J 7
32 Fritchley E 1
33 Frith Bank E 10
21 Frith Common E 12
8 Fritham E 4
4 Frithelstock D 3
4 Frithelstock Stone D 3
17 Frithsden C 11
33 Frithville E 10
11 Frittenden D 7
26 Fritton, Norfolk F 5
26 Fritton, Norfolk E 7
16 Fritwell A 6
38 Frizington D 3
15 Frocester D 11
21 Frochas B 7
21 Frodesley B 10
37 Frodingham F 7
30 Frodsham B 4
49 Frogden G 10
31 Froggatt C 11
31 Froghall E 9
15 Frogland Cross F 9
5 Frogmore, Devon L 6
17 Frogmore, Hants H 9
23 Frolesworth C 8
7 Frome B 11
7 Frome St. Quintin F 9
21 Fromes Hill H 12
29 Fron, Clwyd D 10
13 Fron, Dyfed D 11
28 Fron, Gwynedd E 4
28 Fron, Gwynedd F 3
21 Fron, Powys B 8
20 Fron, Powys F 6
29 Fron Isaf F 12
29 Froncysyllte F 12
29 Fron-deg E 12
29 Frongoch F 8
28 Fron-oleu G 6
39 Frosterley A 12
64 Frotoft B 2
16 Froxfield G 4
9 Froxfield Green D 8
9 Froyle B 9
18 Fryerning D 6
41 Fryton H 7
32 Fulbeck E 6
25 Fulbourn K 6
16 Fulbrook C 4
36 Fulford, N. Yorks B 4
6 Fulford, Somerset C 5
31 Fulford, Staffs F 8
18 Fulham F 2
10 Fulking G 1

36 Full Sutton **B 5**
4 Fullaford **B 6**
47 Fullarton **F 8**
19 Fuller Street **B 7**
30 Fuller's Moor **E 4**
8 Fullerton **B 5**
33 Fulletby **C 10**
47 Fullwood **D 9**
17 Fulmer **F 10**
26 Fulmodestone **B 3**
33 Fulnetby **B 8**
37 Fulstow **G 11**
34 Fulwood, Lancs **D 4**
6 Fulwood, Som **D 5**
9 Funtington **E 9**
9 Funtley **E 7**
52 Funtullich **D 2**
64 Funzie **B 8**
6 Furley **F 6**
54 Furnace, Highland **C 3**
51 Furnace, Strathclyde **G 7**
22 Furnace End **C 6**
10 Furner's Green **E 3**
36 Furness **E 5**
31 Furness Vale **B 8**
18 Furneux Pelham **A 4**
17 Furze Platt **F 9**
7 Furzebrook **H 12**
4 Furzehill **B 6**
6 Fyfett **E 6**
18 Fyfield, Essex **C 6**
16 Fyfield, Glos. **D 3**
8 Fyfield, Hants **A 4**
16 Fyfield, Oxon **D 5**
16 Fyfield, Wilts **G 2**
41 Fylingthorpe **E 9**
58 Fyvie **D 5**
47 Gabroc Hill **D 9**
23 Gaddesby **A 10**
47 Gadgirth **G 9**
14 Gaer **B 5**
28 Gaerwen **C 4**
16 Gagingwell **B 5**
57 Gaick Lodge **L 3**
47 Gailes **F 8**
22 Gailey **A 3**
40 Gainford **C 2**
32 Gainsborough, Lincs. **A 5**
27 Gainsborough, Suff. **L 5**
25 Gainsfords End **L 8**
43 Gairloch, Dumf. & Gall. **D 11**
59 Gairloch, Grampian **G 5**
54 Gairloch, Highland **B 2**
55 Gairlochy **L 6**
52 Gairney Bank **G 6**
57 Gairnshiel Lodge **J 8**
39 Gaisgill **E 8**
44 Gaitsgill **H 2**
49 Galashiels **F 7**
23 Galby **B 10**
42 Galdenoch **E 3**
49 Galewood **F 12**
34 Galgate **B 4**
7 Galhampton **C 9**
43 Gallaberry **C 10**
50 Gallanach **E 5**
50 Gallanachmore **E 5**
50 Gallchoille **H 5**
22 Galley Common **C 6**
19 Galleyend **D 7**
19 Galleywood **D 7**
51 Gallin **C 12**
53 Gallowfauld **C 9**
22 Gallows Green, Heref. & Worc. **F 3**
31 Gallows Green, Staffs. **F 9**
17 Gallowtree Common **F 8**
55 Galltair **G 2**
5 Galmpton, Devon **K 7**
5 Galmpton, Devon **M 6**
40 Galphay **H 3**
47 Galston **F 10**
62 Galtrigill **C 1**
43 Galtway **G 8**
39 Gamblesby **A 8**
49 Gamelshiel **C 9**
25 Gamlingay **K 3**
4 Gammaton Moor **D 4**
40 Gammersgill **G 1**
58 Gamrie **A 5**
32 Gamston, Notts **C 4**
32 Gamston, Notts **F 3**
15 Ganarew **C 8**
50 Ganavan **D 6**
28 Ganllwyd **H 6**
59 Gannachy **K 3**
52 Gannochy **E 6**
30 Gannow Hill **G 2**
37 Ganstead **D 9**
41 Ganthorpe **H 7**
41 Ganton **G 10**
50 Gaodhail **D 3**
54 Garbat **C 8**
51 Garbhallt **H 7**
27 Garboldisham **G 3**
57 Garbole **G 3**
29 Garden City **C 12**
36 Garden Village **D 2**
58 Gardenstown **A 5**
64 Garderhouse **D 6**
37 Gardham **C 7**
7 Gare Hill **B 11**
51 Garelochhead **H 9**
63 Garenin **C 3**
16 Garford **E 5**
36 Garforth **D 2**
35 Gargrave **B 8**
52 Gargunnock **H 2**
28 Garizim **C 6**
42 Garlieston **G 5**
11 Garlinge Green **C 9**
59 Garlogie **G 5**
58 Garmond **B 5**
50 Garmony **D 4**
58 Garmouth **A 1**
28 Garn **G 2**
28 Garn-Dolbenmaen **F 4**
13 Garnant **F 10**
14 Garndiffaith **D 6**
39 Garnett Bridge **E 7**
47 Garnkirk **C 11**
14 Garnlydan **C 5**
13 Garnswllt **F 9**
14 Garn-yr-erw **C 5**
63 Garrabost **D 6**
57 Garragie **H 1**
2 Garras **G 4**
28 Garreg **F 5**
52 Garrick **F 3**
39 Garrigill **A 9**
40 Garriston **F 2**
43 Garroch **C 7**
42 Garrochtrie **H 2**
62 Garros **B 4**
52 Garrow **C 3**
47 Garryhorn **H 8**
39 Garsdale Head **F 10**
16 Garsdon **E 1**
31 Garshall Green **G 8**
17 Garsington **D 7**
34 Garstang **C 4**
30 Garston **B 3**
34 Garswood **G 4**
51 Gartachoil **H 12**
47 Gartcosh **C 11**
29 Garth, Clwyd. **F 11**
38 Garth, I.o.M. **H 2**
14 Garth, Mid. Glam. **E 2**
20 Garth, Powys **G 5**
20 Garth House **B 2**
14 Garth Place **E 5**
47 Garthamlock **C 11**
14 Garthbrengy **A 4**
59 Garthdee **G 7**
21 Garthmyl **C 7**
36 Garthorpe, Humber. **E 6**
32 Garthorpe, Leics **H 5**
58 Gartly **D 3**
51 Gartmore **H 12**
46 Gartnagrenach **C 3**
47 Gartness **A 10**
47 Gartocharn **A 9**
37 Garton **D 10**
37 Garton-on-the-Wolds **A 7**
61 Gartymore **E 9**
48 Garvald, Borders **D 6**
49 Garvald, Lothian **B 8**
57 Garvamore **K 1**
55 Garvan **M 3**
50 Garvard **H 1**
54 Garve **D 8**
26 Garvestone **E 3**
47 Garvock, Strathclyde **B 7**
59 Garvock, Tayside **K 5**
15 Garway **B 8**
63 Garynahine **D 3**
58 Gash of Philorth **A 7**
55 Gaskan **M 2**
7 Gaspar **C 11**
42 Gass **A 5**
43 Gasstown **D 10**
47 Gasswater **G 11**
15 Gastard **G 12**
27 Gasthorpe **G 3**
8 Gatcombe **H 6**
36 Gate Helmsley **B 5**
30 Gateacre **A 3**
39 Gatebeck **G 8**
36 Gateforth **D 3**
47 Gatehead **F 9**
44 Gatehouse, Northumb. **D 6**
52 Gatehouse, Tayside **B 4**
43 Gatehouse of Fleet **F 7**
43 Gatelawbridge **B 10**
26 Gateley **C 3**
40 Gatenby **F 3**
38 Gatesgarth **D 4**
49 Gateshaw **G 10**
45 Gateshead **G 10**
30 Gatesheath **D 3**
52 Gateside, Fife **F 6**
56 Gateside, Grampian **D 7**
47 Gateside, Strathclyde **D 8**
47 Gateside, Strathclyde **B 8**
53 Gateside, Tayside **C 9**
43 Gateslack **A 10**
34 Gathurst **F 4**
31 Gatley **A 7**
10 Gatton **C 3**
49 Gattonside **F 8**
20 Gaufron **F 5**
53 Gauldry **E 8**
24 Gaultree **E 6**
8 Gaunt's Common **F 2**
33 Gautby **C 9**
49 Gavinton **D 10**
58 Gawanhill **A 8**
35 Gawber **F 11**
17 Gawcott **A 8**
38 Gawthwaite **G 5**
23 Gaydon **G 7**
23 Gayhurst **G 11**
39 Gayle **F 11**
40 Gayles **D 1**
30 Gayton, Merseyside **B 1**
24 Gayton, Norfolk **D 8**
23 Gayton, Northants. **G 10**
31 Gayton, Staffs **G 8**
33 Gayton le Marsh **B 11**
33 Gayton le Wold **B 9**
24 Gayton Thorpe **D 8**
24 Gaywood **C 7**
25 Gazeley **J 8**
62 Geary **B 2**
56 Geddes House **D 4**
27 Gedding **J 2**
23 Geddington **D 12**
62 Gedintailor **E 4**
24 Gedney **C 5**
24 Gedney Broadgate **C 5**
24 Gedney Drove End **C 6**
24 Gedney Dyke **C 5**
24 Gedney Hill **D 8**
35 Gee Cross **H 8**
47 Geilston **F 6**
60 Geisgeil **C 3**
26 Geldeston **F 7**
29 Gell **C 8**
14 Gelli **E 3**
14 Gellideg **D 3**
14 Gelligaer **E 5**
28 Gellilydan **F 6**
13 Gellinudd **G 10**
29 Gellioedd **F 8**
52 Gellyburn **C 6**
43 Gelston **F 8**
37 Gembling **A 9**
42 Genoch Square **F 2**
22 Gentleshaw **A 4**
63 Geocrab **H 2**
4 George Nympton **D 6**
44 Georgefield **D 1**
4 Georgeham **B 3**
43 Georgetown, Dumf. & Gall. **D 10**
14 Georgetown, Gwent **C 5**
47 Georgetown, Strathclyde **C 9**
61 Georgmas Junction Station **B 11**
64 Georth **C 2**
28 Gerlan **C 6**
4 Germansweek **F 3**
2 Germoe **G 3**
2 Gerrans **F 6**
43 Gerranton **E 8**
17 Gerrards Cross **E 11**
63 Geshader **D 2**
27 Gestingthorpe **L 1**
21 Geuffordd **A 7**
43 Gibbshill **D 8**
33 Gibraltar **D 12**
15 Giddeahall **G 11**
18 Gidea Park **E 5**
5 Gidleigh **G 5**
49 Gifford **C 8**
53 Giffordtown **F 7**
35 Giggleswick **A 7**
36 Gilberdyke **D 6**
43 Gilchristland **B 10**
43 Gilcrux **H 12**
35 Gildersome **D 11**
32 Gildingwells **B 3**
40 Gilesgate Moor **A 3**
14 Gilfach **D 5**
14 Gilfach Goch **E 3**
13 Gilfachrheda **A 7**
41 Gillamoor **F 7**
43 Gillenbie **C 12**
43 Gillesbie **B 12**
40 Gilling East **G 6**
40 Gilling West **E 2**
7 Gillingham, Dorset **D 11**
11 Gillingham, Kent **A 7**
26 Gillingham, Norfolk **F 7**
61 Gillock **B 11**
31 Gillow Heath **D 7**
61 Gills **A 12**
10 Gill's Green **E 6**
48 Gilmanscleuch **G 6**
48 Gilmerton, Lothian **C 5**
52 Gilmerton, Tayside **E 4**
39 Gilmonby **D 12**
23 Gilmorton **C 9**
44 Gilsland **F 5**
44 Gilsland Spa **F 5**
49 Gilston **D 7**
14 Gilwern **C 6**
26 Gimingham **B 6**
27 Gipping **J 4**
33 Gipsey Bridge **E 10**
47 Girdle Toll **E 8**
64 Girlsta **D 7**
40 Girsby **D 4**
25 Girtford **K 3**
47 Girthill **E 7**
43 Girthon **F 7**
25 Girton, Cambs **J 5**
32 Girton, Notts **D 5**
42 Girvan **B 3**
42 Girvan Mains **B 3**
35 Gisburn **B 7**
63 Gisla **D 2**
26 Gisleham **F 8**
27 Gislingham **H 4**
27 Gissing **G 4**
6 Gittisham **F 5**
10 Givons Grove **C 1**
52 Glack **D 5**
56 Glackbea **F 1**
11 Gladdish **C 7**
21 Gladestry **G 8**
48 Gladhouse **D 6**
49 Gladsmuir **B 7**
31 Gladwin's Mark **D 11**
13 Glais **G 10**
41 Glaisdale **E 8**
43 Glaisters **D 8**
53 Glamis **B 8**
13 Glan Duar **C 8**
28 Glan-Dwyfach **F 4**
28 Glanaber **E 6**
13 Glanaman **F 10**
26 Glandford **B 3**
14 Glandwr **D 5**
12 Glandwr **D 5**
20 Glandyfi **C 3**
14 Glangrwyney **C 5**
21 Glanmule **C 7**
12 Glanryd **C 5**
14 Glan-ryd, Powys **C 1**
45 Glanton **B 9**
45 Glanton Pike **B 9**
7 Glanvilles Wootton **E 10**
29 Glan-y-don **B 11**
20 Glan-y-nant **D 5**
29 Glanyrafon **F 9**
28 Glan-y-Wern **G 5**
24 Glapthorn **F 1**
32 Glapwell **D 2**
57 Glas-allt Shiel **L 8**
21 Glasbury **H 7**
56 Glaschoil **F 6**
38 Glascoe **F 2**
29 Glascoed **C 9**
58 Glascoforest **F 5**
22 Glascote **B 6**
21 Glascwm **G 7**
51 Glasdrum **C 7**
29 Glasfryn **E 8**
47 Glasgow **C 10**
62 Glashvin **A 4**
28 Glasinfryn **C 5**
59 Glaslaw **J 6**
55 Glasnacardoch, Highland **L 1**
55 Glasnacardoch, Highland **K 1**
62 Glasnakille **G 5**
20 Glaspwll **C 3**
54 Glassburn **F 7**
42 Glasserton **H 5**
47 Glassford **E 12**
15 Glasshouse Hill **B 10**
35 Glasshouses **A 10**
53 Glasslie **G 7**
42 Glassoch **E 4**
44 Glasson, Cumb **G 1**
34 Glasson, Lancs **B 3**
39 Glassonby **A 8**
53 Glasterlaw **B 10**
23 Glaston **B 12**
7 Glastonbury **B 8**
47 Glastron **H 8**
25 Glatton **G 2**
34 Glazebury **G 5**
21 Glazely **D 12**
32 Gleadless Townend **B 1**
38 Gleaston **H 5**
46 Glecknabae **C 5**
43 Gledpark **F 7**
44 Gledsnest **B 3**
46 Glemanuilt **H 1**
27 Glemsford **K 1**
42 Glen, Dumf. & Gall. **F 6**
43 Glen, Dumf. & Gall. **D 9**
52 Glen, Tayside **E 6**
38 Glen Auldyn **G 2**
58 Glen Barry **B 3**
62 Glen Bernisdale **C 3**
57 Glen Clunie Lodge **L 7**
58 Glen Dronoch **C 4**
48 Glen House **F 6**
38 Glen Mona **G 2**
55 Glen Nevis House **M 5**
23 Glen Parva **B 9**
59 Glen Tanar House **H 2**
48 Glen Village **B 2**
38 Glen Vine **G 2**
55 Glenancross **K 1**
50 Glenaros House **C 3**
46 Glenbarr **F 2**
57 Glenbeg, Grampian **G 6**
50 Glenbeg, Highland **A 3**
59 Glenbervie **J 5**
47 Glenboig **C 12**
50 Glenborrodale **A 3**
51 Glenbranter **H 8**
48 Glenbreck **G 3**
55 Glenbrein Lodge **H 8**
62 Glenbrittle House **F 3**
58 Glenbuchat Lodge **F 1**
47 Glenbuck **F 12**
47 Glenburn **C 9**
59 Glencally **L 1**
60 Glencalvie Lodge **G 5**
60 Glencanisp Lodge **E 3**
47 Glencaple **E 10**
54 Glencarron Lodge **E 4**
53 Glencarse **E 7**
60 Glencassley Castle **F 5**
46 Glencloy **F 5**
51 Glencoe **B 8**
57 Glenconglass **G 7**
58 Glencraig **H 6**
50 Glencripesdale **B 4**
58 Glencuie **F 2**
59 Glendavan House **G 2**
49 Glendearg, Borders **F 8**
44 Glendearg, Dumf. & Gall. **C 1**
52 Glendevon **G 5**
55 Glendoe Lodge **H 8**
55 Glendoebeg **J 8**
53 Glendoik **E 7**
57 Glendoll Lodge **M 8**
53 Glenduckie **E 7**
59 Glendye Lodge **J 4**
52 Gleneagles Hotel **F 4**
55 Gleneig **H 2**
56 Glenernie **E 6**
51 Glenfalloch Farm **F 10**
52 Glenfarg **F 6**
59 Glenfenzie **G 1**
56 Glenferness House **E 5**
58 Glenfiddich Lodge **D 1**
23 Glenfield **B 9**
47 Glenfinart House **A 7**
55 Glenfinnan **L 3**
55 Glenfintaig Lodge **L 6**
52 Glenfoot **F 6**
55 Glenforslan **M 1**
51 Glenfyne Lodge **F 9**
43 Glengap **F 7**
47 Glengarnock **D 8**
52 Glengoulandie **B 3**
62 Glengrasco **D 4**
51 Glengyle **F 11**
42 Glengyre **E 1**
52 Glenhead, Tayside **G 4**
53 Glenhead Farm **A 7**
48 Glenhighton **F 4**
42 Glenhoise **E 5**
43 Glenholm **D 12**
43 Glenhoul **C 7**
50 Glenhurich **A 5**
48 Glenkerry **H 5**
43 Glenkiln **D 9**
58 Glenkindie **F 2**
48 Glenkirk **F 3**
56 Glenlatterach **D 7**
43 Glenlee **D 7**
57 Glenlia **H 1**
57 Glenlivet **G 7**
43 Glenlochar **E 8**
57 Glenlochsie **M 6**
46 Glenloig **F 4**
42 Glenluce **F 3**
54 Glenmarksie **D 7**
46 Glenmassan **A 6**
47 Glenmavis **C 12**
38 Glenmaye **G 1**
54 Glenmeanne **D 7**
43 Glenmidge **C 9**
38 Glenmooar **G 2**
50 Glenmore, Highland **A 3**
62 Glenmore, Highland **D 4**
50 Glenmore, Strathclyde **F 6**
57 Glenmore Lodge **H 5**
50 Glenmorven Cott. **B 3**
53 Glenmoy **A 9**
42 Glenmuck **A 6**
48 Glenochar **H 2**
53 Glenprosen Village **A 8**
59 Glenquiech **L 2**
48 Glenrath **F 5**
38 Glenridding **D 6**
46 Glenrisdell **D 4**
60 Glenrossal **F 5**
53 Glenrothes **G 7**
42 Glenruther **D 4**
50 Glensanda **C 5**
59 Glensaugh **J 4**
52 Glenshee **D 5**
43 Glenshimmeroch **C 7**
57 Glenshero **K 1**
47 Glenside, Strathclyde **D 7**
63 Glenside, W. Isles **E 5**
51 Glensluain **H 8**
46 Glenstriven **B 6**
55 Glensulaig **L 4**
48 Glentaggart **G 1**
33 Glentham **A 7**
48 Glentress, Borders **E 5**
48 Glentress, Borders **E 6**
57 Glentromie Lodge **K 3**
42 Glentrool Village **D 4**
38 Glentruan **F 2**
57 Glentruim House **K 2**
32 Glentworth **A 6**
55 Glenuig **M 1**
56 Glenurquhart **C 3**
43 Glenwhargen **A 8**
42 Glenwhilly **D 3**
48 Glespin **G 1**
64 Gletness **D 7**
15 Glewstone **B 9**
24 Glinton **E 3**
59 Glithno **H 6**
23 Glooston **C 11**
35 Glossop **H 9**
45 Gloster Hill **C 10**
15 Gloucester **C 11**
15 Gloucestershire, Co. **D 10**
64 Gloup **A 7**
2 Gloweth **E 5**
35 Glusburn **C 8**
61 Glutt Lodge **D 9**
2 Gluvian **C 6**
16 Glympton **B 5**
29 Glyn **D 7**
29 Glyn Ceiriog **F 11**
12 Glynarthen **B 6**
20 Glynbrochan **D 5**
14 Glyncoch **E 4**
14 Glyncorrwg **D 2**
10 Glynde **G 3**
10 Glyndebourne **G 3**
29 Glyndyfrdwy **F 10**
28 Glynllifon Park **E 4**
14 Glynneath **D 2**
14 Glyntaff **E 4**
13 Glynteg **C 7**
31 Gnosall **H 7**
31 Gnosall Heath **H 7**
23 Goadby **B 11**
32 Goadby Marwood **H 5**
11 Goat Lees **C 9**
16 Goatacre **F 1**
7 Goathill **E 10**
41 Goathland **E 8**
6 Goathurst **C 6**
10 Goathurst Com **C 4**
60 Gobernuisgach Lo. **C 5**
30 Gobowen **G 2**
9 Godalming **B 11**
11 Goddard's Green **E 7**
10 Godden Green **C 4**
6 Godford Cross **F 5**
25 Godmanchester **H 3**
7 Godmanstone **F 10**
11 Godmersham **C 9**
7 Godney **B 8**
2 Godolphin Cross **F 3**
13 Godre'r-graig **F 11**
8 Godshill, Hants **E 3**
9 Godshill, I.o.W. **H 7**

10 Godstone C 2
8 Godwinscroft F 3
14 Goetre D 6
18 Goff's Oak D 3
48 Gogar B 4
20 Gogfnan D 2
28 Golan F 5
3 Golant D 8
3 Golberdon C 10
34 Golborne G 5
35 Golcar E 9
24 Gold Hill, Cambs F 6
7 Gold Hill, Dorset E 11
15 Goldcliff F 7
16 Golden Balls D 6
10 Golden Cross G 4
10 Golden Green C 5
13 Golden Grove E 9
12 Golden Hill, Dyfed G 3
8 Golden Hill, Hants. F 4
9 Golden Pot B 8
15 Golden Valley B 12
31 Goldenhill E 7
18 Golders Green E 3
19 Goldhanger C 9
21 Golding B 11
25 Goldington K 2
41 Goldsborough, N. Yorks. D 8
36 Goldsborough, N. Yorks. B 2
2 Goldsithney G 3
30 Goldstone G 6
36 Goldthorpe G 3
4 Goldworthy D 3
56 Gollanfield D 4
40 Gollinglith Foot G 2
6 Golsoncott B 4
61 Golspie G 8
61 Golval B 9
8 Gomeldon C 3
35 Gomersal E 10
50 Gometra House C 1
9 Gomshall A 12
32 Gonalston E 4
64 Gonfirth D 7
18 Good Easter C 6
26 Gooderstone E 1
43 Goodhope B 11
4 Goodleigh C 5
36 Goodmanham C 6
11 Goodnestone, Kent C 11
11 Goodnestone, Kent B 9
15 Goodrich B 9
5 Goodrington K 8
12 Goodwick C 3
8 Goodworth Clatford B 5
23 Goodyers End D 7
36 Goole E 5
36 Goole Fields E 5
2 Goonbell E 4
2 Goonhavern D 5
10 Goose Green C 5
59 Goosecruives J 5
4 Gooseham D 1
5 Goosewell K 4
16 Goosey E 4
34 Goosnargh C 4
30 Goostrey C 6
22 Gorcott Hill E 4
28 Gorddinog C 6
49 Gordon E 9
61 Gordonbush F 8
58 Gordonstown, Grampian D 5
58 Gordonstown, Grampian B 3
48 Gorebridge C 6
24 Gorefield D 5
17 Goring F 7
9 Goring-by-Sea F 12
17 Goring Heath F 7
26 Gorleston-on-Sea E 8
22 Gornalwood C 3
3 Gorran Churchtown E 7
3 Gorran Haven E 7
44 Gorrenberry C 3
20 Gors E 2
16 Gorse Hill E 3
29 Gorsedd C 10
13 Gorseinon G 9
64 Gorseness C 2
31 Gorseybank E 11
13 Gorsgoch B 8
13 Gorslas F 9
15 Gorsley B 10
54 Gorstan D 7
55 Gorstanvorran M 2
30 Gorstella D 2
15 Gorsty Common A 8
35 Gorton G 7
27 Gosbeck K 5
24 Gosberton B 3
24 Gosberton Clough C 3
27 Gosfield M 1
21 Gosford F 10
49 Gosford House B 7
38 Gosforth, Cumb E 3
45 Gosforth, Tyne & Wear F 10
18 Gosmore A 2
9 Gosport F 7
64 Gossabrough C 8
45 Goswick B 12
32 Gotham G 3
16 Gotherington A 1
10 Goudhurst D 6
33 Goulceby B 9
47 Gourock B 7
58 Gourdas C 5
59 Gourdon K 6
47 Govan C 10
32 Goverton E 4
5 Goveton L 6
43 Govig F 1
14 Govilon C 6
36 Gowdall E 4
13 Gowerton G 9
52 Gowkhall H 5
36 Gowthorpe B 5
37 Goxhill, Humber. E 9
37 Goxhill, Humber. C 9
37 Goxhill Haven E 9
13 Goytre H 11
43 Gracefield C 9
49 Graden F 10
9 Graffham D 10
25 Grafham, Cambs H 3
9 Grafham, Surrey B 11
15 Grafton, Heref. & Worc A 8
21 Grafton, Heref. & Worc F 11
16 Grafton, Oxon D 4
30 Grafton, Salop H 3
36 Grafton, N. Yorks A 2
22 Grafton Flyford G 3
23 Grafton Regis G 11
23 Grafton Underwood D 12
11 Grafty Green C 7
29 Graianrhyd E 11
29 Graig C 7
29 Graig-fechan E 10
48 Graigmillar B 6
19 Grain F 9
37 Grainsby G 10
37 Grainthorpe G 11
2 Grampound E 6
2 Grampound Road E 6
17 Granborough B 8
32 Granby G 5
23 Grandborough E 8
52 Grandtully B 4
34 Grane E 6
38 Grange, Cumb. C 5
30 Grange, Merseyside B 1
40 Grange, N. Yorks. F 6
47 Grange, Strathclyde F 9
53 Grange, Tayside E 7
58 Grange Crossroads B 2
56 Grange Hall D 6
35 Grange Moor E 11
53 Grange of Lindores E 7
45 Grange Villa H 10
48 Grangehall E 2
31 Grangemill D 11
48 Grangemouth A 2
38 Grange-over-Sands G 6
48 Grangepans A 3
40 Grangetown, Cleveland C 6
14 Grangetown, S. Glam. G 5
37 Gransmoor A 9
12 Granston D 2
25 Grantchester K 5
32 Grantham G 6
58 Grantlodge F 5
48 Granton, Dumf. & Gall. H 3
48 Granton, Lothian B 5
57 Granton-on-Spey G 6
21 Grantsfield F 10
49 Grantshouse C 10
30 Grappenhall B 5
37 Grasby G 8
38 Grasmere D 6
35 Grasscroft G 8
30 Grassendale B 3
39 Grassholme C 11
35 Grassington A 9
45 Grasslees C 8
32 Grassmoor D 1
32 Grassthorpe C 5
8 Grateley B 4
31 Gratwich G 9
25 Graveley, Cambs. J 4
18 Graveley, Herts. A 2
22 Gravelly Hill C 5
11 Graveney B 9
10 Gravesend A 5
63 Gravir E 5
37 Grayingham G 7
39 Grayrigg E 8
18 Grays F 6
9 Grayshott C 10
9 Grayswood C 10
40 Graythorp B 5
17 Grazeley G 8
36 Greasbrough H 2
30 Greasby B 1
32 Greasley E 2
25 Great Abington K 6
25 Great Addington H 1
22 Great Alne F 5
34 Great Altcar F 2
18 Great Amwell C 4
39 Great Asby D 9
27 Great Ashfield H 3
40 Great Ayton D 6
19 Great Baddow C 7
15 Great Badminton F 11
25 Great Bardfield M 8
25 Great Barford K 2
22 Great Barr C 4
16 Great Barrington C 3
30 Great Barrow C 3
27 Great Barton J 2
41 Great Barugh G 7
45 Great Bavington E 8
27 Great Bealings K 5
16 Great Bedwyn H 4
19 Great Bentley B 11
23 Great Billing F 11
26 Great Bircham B 1
27 Great Blakenham K 4
39 Great Blencow B 7
30 Great Bolas H 5
9 Great Bookham A 12
23 Great Bourton H 8
23 Great Bowden C 11
25 Great Bradley K 8
19 Great Braxted G 8
27 Great Bricett K 3
17 Great Brickhill A 10
31 Great Bridgeford G 7
23 Great Brington F 10
19 Great Bromley A 10
40 Great Broughton D 5
30 Great Budworth B 5
40 Great Burdon B 5
19 Great Burstead E 7
40 Great Busby E 5
18 Great Canfield B 6
33 Great Carlton B 11
24 Great Casterton E 1
15 Great Chalfield H 11
11 Great Chart D 8
22 Great Chatwell A 1
25 Great Chesterfield L 6
8 Great Cheverall A 1
25 Great Chishill L 5
19 Great Clacton B 11
38 Great Clifton B 3
37 Great Coate F 10
22 Great Comberton H 3
44 Great Corby H 3
27 Great Cornard L 2
37 Great Cowden C 10
16 Great Coxwell E 4
40 Great Crakehall F 3
23 Great Cransley D 11
26 Great Cressingham E 1
34 Great Crosby G 2
31 Great Cubley F 10
23 Great Dalby A 10
23 Gt. Doddington F 12
6 Great Dorweeke F 3
15 Great Doward C 9
26 Great Dunham D 2
18 Great Dunmow B 6
8 Great Durnford B 3
18 Great Easton, Essex A 6
23 Great Easton, Leics. C 11
34 Great Eccleston C 3
41 Great Edstone G 7
26 Great Ellingham F 3
7 Great Elm A 10
25 Great Eversden K 5
40 Great Fencote F 3
27 Great Finborough J 3
26 Great Fransham D 2
17 Great Gaddesden C 11
25 Great Gidding G 2
36 Great Givendale B 6
27 Great Glenham J 6
23 Great Glen B 10
32 Great Gonerby F 6
15 Great Graig B 7
25 Great Gransden K 4
26 Great Green, Norf. F 6
27 Great Green, Suff. K 2
41 Great Habton G 8
24 Great Hale A 2
18 Great Hallingbury B 5
23 Great Harrowden E 12
34 Great Harwood D 6
17 Great Haseley D 7
37 Great Hatfield C 9
31 Great Haywood H 8
23 Great Heath D 7
36 Great Heck E 4
27 Great Henny L 2
15 Great Hinton H 12
26 Great Hockham F 2
19 Great Holland B 12
27 Great Horkesley M 3
25 Great Hormead M 5
35 Great Horton D 10
17 Great Horwood A 8
23 Great Houghton, Northants F 11
36 Great Houghton, S. Yorks. F 2
31 Great Hucklow B 10
37 Great Kelk A 8
17 Great Kimble D 9
17 Great Kingshill D 9
40 Great Langton F 3
19 Great Leighs B 7
37 Great Limber F 9
23 Great Linford H 12
27 Great Livermere H 2
31 Great Longstone C 10
45 Great Lumley H 11
22 Great Malvern G 2
27 Great Maplestead M 1
34 Great Marton D 2
26 Great Massingham C 1
26 Great Melton E 4
17 Great Milton D 7
17 Great Missenden D 10
34 Great Mitton C 6
11 Great Mongeham C 12
39 Great Musgrave D 10
30 Great Ness H 3
19 Great Oakley, Essex A 11
23 Great Oakley, Northants D 12
18 Great Offley A 1
39 Great Ormside C 9
44 Great Orton H 2
36 Great Ouseburn A 2
23 Great Oxendon D 10
18 Great Oxney Grn. C 6
26 Great Palgrave D 1
18 Great Parndon C 4
25 Great Paxton J 3
34 Great Plumpton D 3
26 Great Plumstead D 6
32 Great Ponton G 6
36 Great Preston D 2
25 Great Raveley G 4
16 Great Rissington B 3
16 Great Rollright A 4
12 Great Rudbaxton E 3
26 Great Ryburgh C 3
45 Great Ryle B 8
19 Great Saling A 7
39 Great Salkeld B 8
25 Great Sampford L 7
30 Great Sankey A 4
27 Great Saxham J 1
16 Great Shefford G 5
25 Great Shelford K 6
40 Great Smeaton E 4
26 Great Snoring B 2
16 Great Somerford F 1
40 Great Stainton C 3
19 Great Stambridge E 9
25 Great Staughton J 2
33 Great Steeping D 11
11 Great Stonar B 12
39 Great Strickland C 8
25 Great Stukeley H 3
33 Great Sturton C 9
30 Gt. Sutton, Ches. C 2
21 Gt. Sutton, Salop. D 10
45 Great Swinburne E 7
19 Great Tarpots E 7
16 Great Tew A 5
19 Great Tey A 9
25 Great Thurlow K 8
4 Great Torrington D 4
45 Great Tosson C 8
19 Great Totham C 8
37 Great Tows H 10
38 Great Urswick H 5
19 Great Wakering E 9
27 Great Waldingfield L 2
26 Great Walsingham B 2
19 Great Waltham C 7
18 Great Warley E 6
16 Great Washbourne A 1
27 Great Welnetham J 2
27 Great Wenham L 4
45 Great Whittington F 8
19 Great Whigborough B 9
25 Great Wilbraham J 6
8 Great Wishford C 2
15 Great Witcombe C 12
22 Great Witley E 1
16 Great Wolford A 3
23 Great Woolstone H 12
25 Great Wratting K 8
18 Great Wymondley A 2
22 Great Wyrley A 3
30 Great Wytheford H 4
26 Great Yarmouth E 8
27 Great Yeldham L 1
18 Greater London, Co. F 3
35 Greater Manchester, Co. G 7
24 Greatford D 2
31 Greatgate F 9
40 Greatham, Cleveland B 5
9 Greatham, Hants. C 9
9 Greatham, W. Sussex E 11
11 Greatstone-on-Sea F 9
23 Greatworth H 9
25 Green End K 2
36 Green Hammerton A 2
7 Green Ore A 9
10 Green Street Green A 5
19 Green Tye B 4
43 Greenbeck C 11
48 Greenburn C 2
38 Greendale E 4
7 Greendown A 9
45 Greendykes C 12
49 Greenend G 8
25 Greenfield, Beds. M 2
29 Greenfield, Clwyd B 11
55 Greenfield, Highland J 6
35 Greenfield, Manchester G 8
17 Greenfield, Oxon. E 8
18 Greenford F 1
48 Greengairs B 1
34 Greenhalgh D 3
16 Greenham, Berks. H 6
6 Greenham, Som. D 4
44 Greenhaugh D 6
43 Greenhead, Dunf. & Gal. C 10
44 Greenhead, Northumb. F 5
47 Greenhead, Strathclyde E 9
48 Greenhill, Central B 1
11 Greenhill, Kent A 10
47 Greenhills D 8
10 Greenhithe A 5
47 Greenholm F 10
39 Greenholme E 8
49 Greenhouse G 8
35 Greenhow Hill A 9
49 Greenknowe E 9
61 Greenland A 11
17 Greenlands F 8
49 Greenlaw, Borders E 9
58 Greenlaw, Grampian B 4
49 Greenlaw Walls E 12
43 Greenlea, Dumf. & Gal. D 11
47 Greenlea, Dumf. & Gal. A 7
52 Greenloaning F 3
47 Greenock B 8
38 Greenodd G 5
48 Greenrig E 1
43 Greenrow F 11
23 Greens Norton G 10
32 Greenscares F 3
48 Greenshields E 3
45 Greenside G 9
45 Greensidehill A 8
58 Greenskairs A 5
19 Greenstead Green A 8
18 Greensted Green D 5
64 Greenwall C 3
12 Greenway, Dyfed D 4
14 Greenway, S. Glam. G 4
18 Greenwich F 4
16 Greet A 1
21 Greete E 11
23 Greetham, Leics. A 12
33 Greetham, Lincs. C 10
35 Greetland E 9
7 Greinton C 7
23 Grendon, N'thants F 12
22 Grendon, War. B 6
22 Grendon Common B 6
21 Grendon Green G 11
17 Grendon Underwood B 8
5 Grenofen J 4
35 Grenoside H 11
30 Gresford E 2
26 Gresham B 5
62 Greshornish C 3
63 Gress C 6
26 Gressenhall D 3
26 Gressenhall Grn. D 3
39 Gressingham H 8
40 Greta Bridge D 1
44 Gretna F 2
44 Gretna Green F 1
16 Gretton, Glos. A 1
23 Gretton, N'thants C 12
21 Gretton, Salop. C 10
40 Grewelthorpe G 2
58 Grey Stone E 6
40 Greygarth H 2
13 Greynor F 9
48 Greyrigg, Central B 2
43 Greyrigg, Dumf. & Gall. C 11
38 Greysouthen B 3
39 Greystoke, Cumb. B 7
53 Greystoke, Tayside C 10
43 Greystone D 10
9 Greywell A 8
4 Gribbleford Bridge F 4
36 Gribthorpe D 5
50 Gribun D 2
5 Gridley Corner G 2
23 Griff C 7
14 Griffithstown D 6
39 Grigghall F 7
64 Grimbister C 2
34 Grimeford Village F 5
36 Grimethorpe F 2
22 Grimley F 2
47 Grimmet H 8
33 Grimoldby A 11
34 Grimsargh D 5
37 Grimsby F 10
23 Grimscote G 10
4 Grimscott E 1
63 Grimshader D 5
24 Grimsthorpe C 2
37 Grimston, Humber. D 10
32 Grimston, Leics. H 4
24 Grimston, Norfolk C 8
7 Grimstone G 9
5 Grinacombe Moor G 3
41 Grindale H 11
22 Grindle B 1
31 Grindleford B 11
34 Grindleton C 6
30 Grindley Brook F 4
31 Grindlow B 10
40 Grindon, Cleveland C 4
44 Grindon, Northumb. F 6
49 Grindon, Northumb. E 11
31 Grindon, Staffs. E 9
44 Grindon Hill F 6
49 Grindonrigg E 11
32 Gringley on the Hill A 4
44 Grinsdale G 2
30 Grinshill H 4
40 Grinton E 1
41 Gristhorpe G 11
26 Griston E 2
16 Grittenham F 1
15 Grittleton F 11
38 Grizebeck G 5
38 Grizedale F 6
64 Grobister C 4
23 Groby A 8
29 Groes, Clwyd D 9
13 Groes, W. Glam. H 11
14 Groesfaen F 4
28 Groesffordd F 2
29 Groesffordd C 7
29 Groesffordd Marli C 9
21 Groesllwyd A 7
46 Grogport E 3
29 Gronant B 10
10 Groombridge D 4
63 Grosebay H 2
15 Grosmont, Gwent B 7
41 Grosmont, N. Yorks. E 8
27 Groton L 2
7 Grove, Dorset H 7
16 Grove, Oxon. E 5
32 Grove, Notts. B 4
13 Grovesend G 9
54 Grudie D 7
60 Gruids F 6
60 Gruinard House G 1
50 Gruline House D 3
2 Grumbla G 1
27 Grundisburgh K 5
64 Grundsound E 7
64 Gruting D 6
64 Grutness F 7
28 Grwedog B 3
51 Gualachulain C 8
60 Gualin House B 4
53 Guard Bridge E 9
22 Guarlford H 2
52 Guay B 5

43 Gubhill **B 10**
11 Guestling Green **G 7**
11 Guestling Icklesham **F 7**
26 Guestwick **C 3**
34 Guide **E 6**
45 Guide Post **E 10**
25 Guilden Morden **L 4**
30 Guilden Sutton **C 3**
9 Guildford **A 11**
53 Guildtown **D 6**
23 Guilsborough **E 10**
21 Guilsfield **A 8**
11 Guilton **B 11**
47 Guiltreehill **H 8**
4 Guineaford **B 4**
55 Guisachan House **G 7**
40 Guisborough **D 6**
35 Guiseley **C 10**
26 Guist **C 3**
16 Guiting Power **B 2**
64 Gulberwick **E 7**
49 Gullane **A 7**
2 Gulval **F 2**
5 Gulworthy **H 3**
12 Gumfreston **G 4**
23 Gumley **C 10**
2 Gummow's Shop **D 6**
36 Gunby, Humber. **D 5**
32 Gunby, Lincs. **H 6**
9 Gundleton **C 7**
4 Gunn **C 5**
39 Gunnerside **E 11**
45 Gunnerton **F 7**
45 Gunnerton Fell **E 7**
36 Gunness **F 6**
3 Gunnislake **C 11**
64 Gunnista **D 7**
36 Gunthorpe, Humber. **G 6**
26 Gunthorpe, Norf. **B 3**
32 Gunthorpe, Notts. **F 4**
8 Gunville **G 6**
6 Gupworthy **C 3**
8 Gurnard **F 6**
7 Gurney Slade **A 9**
14 Gurnos **C 1**
8 Gussage All Saints **E 2**
8 Gussage St. Andrew **E 1**
8 Gussage St. Michael **E 1**
11 Guston **D 11**
64 Gutcher **B 8**
53 Guthrie **B 10**
24 Guy's Head **C 6**
7 Guy's Marsh **D 11**
24 Guyhirn **E 5**
45 Guyzance **C 10**
14 Gwaelod-y-garth **F 4**
29 Gwaenysgor **B 10**
28 Gwalchmai **C 3**
12 Gwastad **D 4**
13 Gwaun-cae-Gurwen **F 10**
12 Gwbert-on-Sea **B 5**
2 Gweek **G 4**
15 Gwehelog Com. **D 7**
20 Gwenddwr **H 6**
2 Gwennap **F 4**
14 Gwent, Co. **D 6**
2 Gwenter **H 4**
29 Gwernaffield **D 11**
21 Gwernaffel **E 8**
15 Gwernesney **D 7**
13 Gwernogle **D 8**
29 Gwernymynydd **D 11**
14 Gwern-y-Steeple **G 4**
30 Gwersyllt **E 2**
29 Gwespyr **B 10**
2 Gwinear **F 3**
2 Gwithian **F 3**
29 Gwddelwern **F 10**
13 Gwyddgrug **C 8**
29 Gwynfryn **E 11**
28 Gwynedd, Co. **E 5**
20 Gwystre **F 6**
29 Gwytherin **D 8**
29 Gyfelia **F 12**
29 Gyffin **C 7**
29 Gyffylliog **D 10**
21 Habberley **B 9**
63 Habost, W. Isles **E 4**
63 Habost, W. Isles **A 6**
37 Habrough **F 9**
24 Hacconby **C 2**
24 Haceby **B 1**
27 Hacheston **J 6**
32 Hackenthorpe **B 1**
26 Hackford **E 3**
40 Hackforth **F 3**
64 Hackland **C 2**
63 Hacklete **C 2**
23 Hackleton **G 11**
41 Hackness **F 10**
18 Hackney **E 4**
33 Hackthorn **B 7**
39 Hackthorpe **C 7**
18 Hacton **E 5**
49 Hadden **F 10**
17 Haddenham, Bucks. **C 8**
25 Haddenham, Cambs. **H 6**
49 Haddington, Lothian **B 8**
32 Haddington, Lincs. **D 6**
26 Haddiscoe **F 7**
58 Haddoch **C 3**
24 Haddon **F 2**
35 Hade Edge **G 10**
22 Hademore **A 5**
35 Hadfield **G 9**
18 Hadham Cross **B 4**
18 Hadham Ford **B 4**
19 Hadleigh, Essex **E 8**
27 Hadleigh, Suffolk **L 3**
21 Hadley **A 12**
31 Hadley End **H 10**
18 Hadley Wood **D 3**
10 Hadlow **C 5**
10 Hadlow Down **F 4**
30 Hadnall **H 4**
25 Hadstock **L 7**
45 Hadwin's Close **B 10**
22 Hadzor **F 3**
11 Haffenden Quarter **D 7**
20 Hafod **G 1**
29 Hafod-Dinbych **E 8**
20 Hafod-Peris **F 1**
35 Haggate **D 7**
44 Haggbeck **F 3**
45 Haggerston **B 11**
21 Hagley, Heref. & Worcs. **H 11**
22 Hagley, Heref. & Worcs. **D 3**
33 Hagworthingham **C 10**
34 Haigh, Manchester **F 5**
35 Haigh, S. Yorks. **F 11**
35 Haigh Moor **E 11**
34 Haighton Green **D 4**
25 Hail Weston **J 3**
38 Haile **D 3**
18 Hailey, Herts. **C 4**
16 Hailey, Oxon. **C 4**
10 Hailsham **G 5**
18 Hainault **E 4**
26 Hainford **D 5**
33 Hainton **B 9**
37 Haisthorpe **A 9**
32 Halam **E 4**
52 Halbeath **H 6**
6 Halberton **E 3**
61 Halcro **B 11**
30 Hale, Cheshire **B 3**
30 Hale, Manchester **B 6**
8 Hale, Hants. **D 3**
9 Hale, Surrey **A 10**
30 Hale Cliff **B 3**
30 Halebarns **B 6**
26 Hales, Norfolk **F 7**
30 Hales, Staffs. **G 6**
22 Halesowen **D 3**
27 Halesworth **H 7**
30 Halewood **B 3**
22 Halfrod, War. **H 6**
21 Halford, Salop. **D 10**
12 Halfpenny Furze **F 6**
22 Halfpenny Green **C 2**
16 Halfway, Berks. **G 5**
13 Halfway, Dyfed **D 11**
13 Halfway, Dyfed **D 10**
3 Halfway House, Cornwall **C 8**
6 Halfway House, Devon **G 4**
21 Halfway House, Salop. **A 9**
42 Halfway House, Dumf. & Gall. **E 4**
11 Halfway Houses **A 8**
35 Halifax **E 9**
47 Halket **D 9**
61 Halkirk **B 10**
29 Halkyn **C 11**
38 Hall Dunnerdale **F 5**
22 Hall Green **D 5**
21 Hall of the Forest **D 7**
38 Hall Waberthwaite **F 3**
10 Halland **F 4**
23 Hallaton **B 11**
7 Hallatrow **A 10**
44 Hallbankgate **G 4**
15 Hallen **F 8**
32 Hallfield Gate **D 1**
49 Halliburton **D 9**
62 Hallin **B 2**
10 Halling **B 6**
33 Hallington, Lincs. **B 10**
45 Hallington, Northumb. **E 8**
34 Halliwell **F 6**
32 Halloughton **E 4**
22 Hallow **F 2**
44 Hallrule **B 4**
49 Halls **B 9**
18 Hall's Green **A 3**
5 Hallsands **M 7**
43 Hallscaur **B 8**
24 Halltoft End **A 5**
49 Halltree **D 7**
3 Hallworthy **A 9**
48 Hallyne **E 5**
30 Halmer End **E 6**
15 Halmore **D 10**
48 Halmyre Mains **D 4**
9 Halnaker **E 10**
34 Halsall **F 2**
23 Halse, Northants. **H 9**
6 Halse, Somerset **C 5**
2 Halsetown **F 2**
37 Halsham **D 10**
4 Halsinger **B 4**
27 Halstead, Essex **M 1**
10 Halstead, Kent **B 4**
23 Halstead, Leics. **B 11**
7 Halstock **E 8**
38 Haltcliff Bridge **B 6**
33 Haltham **D 9**
17 Halton, Bucks. **C 9**
30 Halton, Cheshire **B 4**
29 Halton, Clwyd **F 12**
34 Halton, Lancs. **A 4**
45 Halton, Northumb. **F 8**
35 Halton, W. Yorks **D 12**
35 Halton East **B 9**
39 Halton, Gill **G 11**
33 Halton Holegate **D 11**
44 Halton Lea Gate **G 5**
34 Halton Park **A 4**
11 Halton Shields **F 8**
35 Halton West **B 7**
44 Haltwhistle **C 5**
26 Halvergate **E 7**
5 Halwell **K 6**
4 Halwill **F 3**
4 Halwill Junction **F 3**
6 Ham, Devon **F 6**
15 Ham, Glos. **D 10**
11 Ham, Kent **C 12**
18 Ham, London **G 2**
16 Ham, Wilts. **H 4**
15 Ham Green, Avon **G 8**
22 Ham Green, Heref. & Worcs. **F 4**
11 Ham Green, Kent **A 7**
10 Ham Hill **B 6**
11 Ham Street, Kent **E 8**
7 Ham Street, Som. **C 9**
8 Hamble **E 6**
17 Hambledon **E 8**
9 Hambledon, Hants. **E 8**
9 Hambledon, Surrey **B 11**
34 Hambleton, Lancs. **C 3**
36 Hambleton, N. Yorks. **D 3**
7 Hambridge **D 7**
9 Hambrook **E 9**
33 Hameringham **C 10**
25 Hamerton **G 2**
47 Hamilton **D 12**
9 Hammer **C 10**
9 Hammerpot **F 11**
18 Hammersmith **F 2**
22 Hammerwich **A 4**
18 Hammond Street **C 3**
7 Hammoon **E 11**
64 Hamnavoe, W. Burra **E 7**
64 Hamnavoe, Yell **C 7**
64 Hamnavoe, Zetland **C 6**
64 Hamnavoe, Zetland **C 7**
10 Hampden **H 5**
17 Hampden Row **D 9**
16 Hampnett **C 2**
36 Hampole **F 3**
8 Hampreston **F 2**
8 Hampshire, Co. **C 6**
18 Hampstead **E 3**
16 Hampstead Norris **F 6**
35 Hampsthwaite **A 11**
22 Hampton, Heref. & Worcs. **H 4**
18 Hampton, London **G 1**
22 Hampton, Salop. **D 1**
15 Hampton Bishop **A 9**
30 Hampton Heath **E 4**
22 Hampton in Arden **D 5**
22 Hampton Lovett **F 2**
22 Hampton Lucy **F 6**
22 Hampton on the Hill **F 6**
16 Hampton Poyle **C 6**
31 Hamstall Ridware **H 9**
8 Hamstead, I.o.W. **G 5**
22 Hamstead, W. Midlands **C 4**
16 Hamstead Marshall **H 5**
40 Hamsteels **A 2**
40 Hamsterley, Dur. **B 1**
45 Hamsterley, Dur. **G 9**
8 Hamworthy **G 1**
31 Hanbury, Staffs. **G 10**
22 Hanbury, Heref. & Worcs. **F 3**
30 Handbridge **D 3**
10 Handcross **E 2**
31 Handforth **B 7**
30 Handley **D 3**
22 Handsacre **A 4**
22 Handsworth **C 4**
17 Handy Cross, Bucks. **E 9**
4 Handy Cross, Devon **C 3**
31 Hanford **F 7**
8 Hanging Langford **B 2**
43 Hangingshaw, Dumf. & Gall. **C 11**
48 Hangingshaw, Strathclyde **E 2**
30 Hankelow **F 5**
16 Hankerton **E 1**
10 Hankham **G 5**
31 Hanley **E 7**
22 Hanley Castle **H 2**
21 Hanley Childe **F 12**
22 Hanley Swan **H 2**
21 Hanley William **F 12**
35 Hanlith **A 8**
30 Hanmer **F 3**
33 Hannah **B 12**
9 Hannington, Hants. **A 7**
23 Hannington, Northants. **E 11**
16 Hannington, Wilts. **E 3**
16 Hannington Wick **E 3**
23 Hanslope **G 11**
24 Hanthorpe **C 2**
18 Hanwell, London **F 2**
23 Hanwell, Oxon. **H 8**
18 Hanworth, Lond. **G 1**
26 Hanworth, Norf. **B 5**
48 Happendon **F 1**
26 Happisburgh **B 7**
26 Happisburgh Com. **C 7**
30 Hapsford **C 3**
34 Hapton, Lancs. **D 6**
26 Hapton, Norfolk **F 5**
6 Harberton **K 6**
5 Harbertonford **K 6**
11 Harbledown **B 10**
22 Harborne **D 4**
23 Harborough Magna **D 8**
45 Harbottle **C 7**
5 Harbourneford **J 6**
23 Harbury **F 7**
32 Harby, Leics. **G 5**
32 Harby, Notts. **C 6**
6 Harcombe, Devon **H 2**
6 Harcombe, Devon **G 5**
2 Harcourt **F 5**
35 Harden **C 9**
15 Hardenhuish **G 12**
43 Hardgate, Dumf. & Gall. **E 9**
59 Hardgate, Grampian **G 5**
43 Hardgrove **D 1**
9 Hardham **D 11**
26 Hardingham **E 3**
31 Hardings Wood **E 3**
23 Hardingstone **F 11**
7 Hardington **A 10**
7 Hardington Mandeville **E 8**
7 Hardington Marsh **E 8**
4 Hardisworthy **D 4**
8 Hardley **F 6**
26 Hardley Street **E 7**
18 Hardmonsworth **F 1**
39 Hardrow **F 11**
32 Hardstoft **D 2**
7 Hardway **C 10**
17 Hardwick, Bucks. **B 9**
25 Hardwick, Cambs. **J 5**
32 Hardwick, Lincs. **C 6**
26 Hardwick, Norf. **F 5**
23 Hardwick, Northants. **E 11**
16 Hardwick, Oxon. **D 5**
17 Hardwick, Oxon. **A 7**
32 Hardwick Grange **C 4**
15 Hardwicke, Glos. **B 12**
15 Hardwicke, Glos. **C 11**
21 Hardwicke, Heref. & Worcs. **H 8**
19 Hardy's Green **B 9**
6 Hare & Hounds Inn **G 5**
19 Hare Green **A 10**
17 Hare Hatch **F 9**
18 Hare Street, Essex **C 4**
18 Hare Street, Herts. **A 4**
10 Harebeating **G 5**
33 Hareby **D 10**
34 Hareden **B 5**
18 Harefield **E 1**
35 Harehills **D 11**
45 Harehope **A 9**
49 Harelaw, Borders **G 8**
48 Harelaw, Strathclyde **E 2**
47 Harelaw, Strathclyde **D 9**
59 Haremuir **K 5**
39 Haresceugh **A 8**
15 Harescombe **C 11**
15 Haresfield **C 11**
48 Hareshaw **C 1**
35 Harewood **C 12**
15 Harewood End **B 8**
36 Harewood Estate **F 3**
5 Harford, Devon **K 5**
26 Hargate **F 4**
31 Hargatewall **C 9**
30 Hargrave, Ches. **D 3**
25 Hargrave, Northants. **H 1**
27 Hargrave Green **J 1**
18 Haringey **E 3**
44 Harker **G 2**
27 Harkstead **M 5**
22 Harlaston **A 5**
58 Harlaw House **E 5**
32 Harlaxton **G 6**
35 Harle Syke **D 7**
28 Harlech **G 5**
21 Harlescott **A 10**
18 Harlesden **F 2**
27 Harleston, Norf. **G 5**
27 Harleston, Suffolk **J 3**
23 Harlestone **F 10**
21 Harley **B 11**
48 Harleyholm **F 2**
25 Harlington, Beds. **M 1**
18 Harlington, Lond. **F 1**
36 Harlington, S. Yorks. **G 3**
62 Harlosh **D 2**
18 Harlow **C 5**
45 Harlow Hill **F 9**
36 Harlthorpe **C 5**
25 Harlton **K 5**
8 Harman's Cross **H 1**
40 Harmby **F 2**
18 Harmer Green **B 3**
30 Harmerhill **H 3**
33 Harmston **D 7**
16 Harnhill **D 2**
18 Harold Hill **E 5**
12 Haroldston West **E 2**
64 Haroldswick **A 8**
40 Harome **G 6**
17 Harpenden **C 12**
49 Harper Ridge **E 11**
49 Harpertoun **E 10**
6 Harpford **G 4**
37 Harpham **A 8**
21 Harpley, Heref. & Worcs. **F 12**
26 Harpley, Norfolk **C 1**
23 Harpole **F 10**
17 Harpsden **F 8**
32 Harpswell **A 6**
31 Harpur Hill **C 9**
35 Harpurhey **G 7**
64 Harra **B 7**
44 Harraby **H 3**
4 Harracott **C 4**
62 Harrapool **F 6**
52 Harrietfield **D 5**
49 Harrietsfield **G 9**
11 Harrietsham **C 7**
38 Harrington, Cumb. **C 2**
33 Harrington, Lincs. **C 10**
23 Harrington, Northants. **D 11**
23 Harringworth **B 12**
31 Harriseahead **E 7**
35 Harrogate **B 12**
23 Harrold **F 12**
18 Harrow **E 2**
27 Harrow Street **L 3**
18 Harrow Weald **E 2**
3 Harrowbarrow **C 11**
3 Harrowbridge **B 9**
40 Harrowgate Village **C 3**
25 Harston, Cambs. **K 5**
32 Harston, Leics. **G 5**
36 Harswell **C 6**
40 Hart **B 5**
45 Hart Law **C 10**
45 Hartburn **D 9**
27 Hartest **K 1**
25 Hartford, Cambs. **H 4**
30 Hartford, Ches. **C 5**
19 Hartford End **B 7**
17 Hartfordbridge **H 8**
30 Harthill, Cheshire **E 4**
32 Harthill, S. Yorks. **B 2**
48 Harthill, Strathclyde **C 2**
31 Hartington **D 9**
4 Hartland **D 1**
22 Hartlebury **E 2**
40 Hartlepool **B 5**
39 Hartley, Cumbria **D 10**
10 Hartley, Kent **A 5**
10 Hartley, Kent **E 6**
45 Hartley, Northumb. **E 11**
10 Hartley Green **A 5**
17 Hartley Wespall **H 8**
17 Hartley Wintney **H 8**
11 Hartlip **B 7**
36 Harton, N. Yorks. **A 5**
21 Harton, Salop **D 10**
45 Harton, Tyne & Wear **G 12**
15 Hartpury **B 11**
35 Hartshead **E 10**
23 Hartshill **C 7**
31 Hartshorne **H 11**
38 Hartsop **D 6**
17 Hartwell, Bucks. **C 9**
23 Hartwell, Northants. **G 11**
35 Hartwith **A 11**
48 Hartwood **C 1**
49 Hartwoodburn **G 7**
49 Hartwoodmyres **G 7**
10 Harvel **B 5**
22 Harvington **G 4**
22 Harvington Cross **G 4**
16 Harwell **E 6**
27 Harwich **M 6**
39 Harwood, Dur. **B 10**
34 Harwood, Manchester **F 6**
45 Harwood, Northumb. **D 8**
41 Harwood Dale **F 9**
32 Harworth **A 3**
9 Hascombe **B 11**
23 Haselbech **D 10**
7 Haselbury Plucknett **E 8**
22 Haseley **E 6**
22 Haselor **F 5**
15 Hasfield **B 11**
12 Hasguard **F 2**
12 Hasguard Cross **F 2**
34 Haskayne **F 2**
27 Hasketon **K 5**
32 Hasland **C 1**
9 Haslemere **C 10**
34 Haslingden **E 6**
25 Haslingfield **K 5**
30 Haslington **E 6**
30 Hassall **D 6**
30 Hassall Green **D 6**
11 Hassell Street **C 9**
49 Hassendean **G 8**
26 Hassingham **E 6**
49 Hassington **E 10**
10 Hassocks **F 2**
31 Hassop **C 10**
61 Hastigrow **B 11**
11 Hastingleigh **D 9**
11 Hastings **G 7**
18 Hastingwood **C 5**
17 Hastoe **C 10**
40 Haswell **A 4**
40 Haswell Plough **A 4**
48 Haswellsykes **E 5**
9 Hatch **A 8**
6 Hatch Beauchamp **D 6**
18 Hatch End **E 1**
6 Hatch Green **D 6**
46 Hatchednize **E 10**
8 Hatchet Gate **F 5**
30 Hatchmere **C 4**
37 Hatcliffe **G 10**
21 Hatfield, Heref. & Worcs. **F 11**
22 Hatfield, Heref. & Worcs. **G 2**
18 Hatfield, Herts. **C 2**
36 Hatfield, S. Yorks. **F 4**
18 Hatfield Broad Oak **B 5**
18 Hatfield Heath **B 5**
19 Hatfield Peverel **C 8**
36 Hatfield Woodhouse **F 5**
16 Hatford **E 4**
8 Hatherden **A 5**
4 Hatherleigh **E 4**
32 Hathern **H 2**
16 Hatherop **D 3**
31 Hathersage **B 10**
35 Hathershaw **G 8**
30 Hatherton, Ches. **E 5**
22 Hatherton, Staffs. **A 3**
25 Hatley St. George **K 4**
3 Hatt **C 11**
9 Hattingley **B 8**
30 Hatton, Cheshire **B 4**
31 Hatton, Derby **G 10**
58 Hatton, Grampian **D 8**
33 Hatton, Lincs. **C 9**
18 Hatton, London **F 1**
21 Hatton, Salop. **C 10**
22 Hatton, War. **E 6**
58 Hatton Fintray **F 6**
30 Hatton Heath **D 3**
58 Hattoncrook **E 6**
25 Hauxton **K 5**
35 Haugh, Manchester **F 8**

18 Haultwick B 3
50 Haunn C 1
47 Haugh, Strathclyde G 10
49 Haugh Head G 12
58 Haugh of Glass D 2
43 Haugh of Urr E 9
33 Haugham B 10
47 Haughhead B 11
27 Haughley J 3
22 Haughley Green J 3
58 Haughs of Clinterty F 6
45 Haughterslaw A 9
32 Haughton, Notts. C 4
21 Haughton, Salop. A 11
21 Haughton, Salop. C 12
30 Haughton, Salop. G 2
31 Haughton, Staffs. H 7
45 Haughton Castle F 7
35 Haughton Green H 8
30 Haughton Moss E 4
22 Haunton A 6
45 Hauxley C 11
9 Havant F 8
21 Haven G 9
36 Havercroft F 2
12 Haverfordwest E 3
25 Haverhill L 8
38 Haverigg G 4
18 Havering E 5
18 Havering-atte-Bower E 5
23 Haversham H 11
38 Haverthwaite G 6
40 Haverton Hill C 5
29 Hawarden D 12
19 Hawbush Green B 8
13 Hawen B 7
39 Hawes F 11
22 Hawford F 2
44 Hawick B 3
31 Hawk Green B 8
7 Hawkchurch F 7
27 Hawkedon K 1
10 Hawkenbury D 5
7 Hawkeridge A 11
22 Hawkes End D 6
15 Hawkesbury F 10
15 Hawkesbury Upton F 11
45 Hawkhill B 10
10 Hawkhurst E 6
9 Hawkley C 8
6 Hawkridge C 2
34 Hawkshaw F 6
38 Hawkshead E 6
38 Hawkshead Hill E 6
48 Hawksland E 1
39 Hawkswick H 12
32 Hawksworth, Notts. E 5
35 Hawksworth, W. Yorks. C 10
18 Hawkwell E 8
10 Hawley A 4
17 Hawley H 9
16 Hawling B 2
40 Hawnby F 5
35 Haworth D 9
27 Hawstead J 1
40 Hawthorn, Dur. A 4
15 Hawthorn, Wilts. G 11
44 Hawthornside B 4
24 Hawthorpe C 2
32 Hawton E 5
36 Haxby A 4
36 Haxey G 5
10 Haxted D 3
21 Hay-on-Wye H 8
18 Hay Street A 4
12 Haycastle D 2
12 Haycastle Cross D 3
34 Haydock G 4
7 Haydon, Dorset E 10
45 Haydon, Northumb. F 7
45 Haydon Bridge G 7
16 Haydon Wick E 2
3 Haye C 10
18 Hayes, Kent G 4
18 Hayes, London F 1
31 Hayfield, Derby B 9
53 Hayfield, Fife H 7
47 Hayhill H 9
2 Hayle F 3
9 Hayling Island F 8
49 Haymount F 9
6 Hayne F 2
25 Haynes L 2
25 Haynes West End L 2
10 Haysden D 4
53 Hayshead C 11
43 Hayton, Cumb. G 11
44 Hayton, Cumb. G 3
59 Hayton, Grampian G 7
36 Hayton, Humber. C 6
32 Hayton, Notts. B 4
21 Hayton's Bent D 10
5 Haytor Vale H 6
10 Hayward's Heath F 2
32 Haywood Oaks E 3
31 Hazel Grove B 8
48 Hazelbank E 1
7 Hazelbury Bryan E 11
17 Hazeley H 8
22 Hazelslade A 4
53 Hazelton Walls E 8
31 Hazelwood F 11
17 Hazlemere E 10
45 Hazlerigg F 10
16 Hazleton B 2
45 Hazon C 10
24 Heacham B 8
8 Headbourne Worthy C 6
21 Headbrook G 8
11 Headcorn D 7
35 Headingley D 11
16 Headington C 6
40 Headlam C 2
22 Headless Cross F 4
9 Headley, Hants. C 9
16 Headley, Hants. H 6
10 Headley, Surrey C 1
9 Headley Down B 10
32 Headon C 5
47 Heads E 12
44 Heads Nook G 3
32 Heage E 1
39 Healaugh, N. Yorks. E 12
36 Healaugh, N. Yorks. B 3
4 Heale, Devon A 5
7 Heale, Somerset B 10
35 Healey, Lancs. E 7
45 Healey, Nothumb. G 8
40 Healey, N. Yorks. G 2
45 Healey Cote C 9
45 Healeyfield H 9
37 Healing F 10
2 Heamor G 2
32 Heanor F 2
4 Heanton Punchardon B 4
32 Heapham A 6
48 Hearthstane G 4
4 Heasley Mill C 6
62 Heast F 6
32 Heath C 2
17 Heath and Reach A 10
4 Heath Cross F 7
17 Heath End, Berks. H 7
9 Heath End, Surrey A 10
22 Heath End, W. Midlands B 4
22 Heath Hayes A 4
22 Heath Hill A 1
7 Heath House B 7
6 Heath Pault Cross C 3
22 Heath Town B 3
31 Heathcote D 10
23 Heather A 7
62 Heatherfield D 4
61 Heatherwood Park G 8
52 Heatheryhaugh B 6
43 Heathfield, Cumb. G 12
5 Heathfield, Devon H 7
10 Heathfield, East Sussex F 4
6 Heathfield, Som. D 5
47 Heathfield, Strathclyde C 8
43 Heathhall D 10
22 Heathton C 2
30 Heatley A 5
34 Heaton, Lancs. A 3
35 Heaton, Manchester H 7
31 Heaton, Staffs. D 8
35 Heaton, W. Yorks. D 10
34 Heaton's Bridge F 3
10 Heaverham B 4
6 Heavitree G 3
45 Hebburn G 11
35 Hebden A 9
35 Hebden Bridge D 8
30 Hebden Green D 5
12 Hebron, Dyfed D 5
45 Hebron, Northumb. D 10
43 Heck D 11
17 Heckfield H 8
27 Heckfield Green H 5
24 Heckington A 2
48 Hecklebirnie F 2
35 Heckmondwike E 10
16 Heddington G 1
16 Heddington Wick G 1
4 Heddon C 5
45 Heddon on the Wall F 9
26 Hedenham F 6
5 Hedge Cross G 4
8 Hedge End E 6
17 Hedgerley E 10
6 Hedging C 6
45 Hedley on the Hill G 9
22 Hednesford A 3
37 Hedon D 9
17 Hedsor E 10
21 Hedgon Hill G 11
45 Heiferlaw Bank A 10
40 Heighington, Dur. C 3
33 Heighington, Lincs. C 7
56 Heights of Brae D 1
54 Heights of Kinlochewe C 4
60 Heilam B 5
49 Heiton F 9
6 Hele, Devon F 3
4 Hele, Devon A 4
5 Hele, Devon G 2
6 Hele, Somerset D 5
47 Helensburgh A 8
47 Helentongate F 9
2 Helford G 5
2 Helford Passage G 5
26 Helhoughton C 2
25 Helions Bumpstead L 7
3 Helland C 8
3 Hellandbridge C 8
26 Hellesdon D 5
23 Hellidon F 8
35 Hellifield B 7
10 Helling G 4
26 Hellington E 6
45 Helm C 10
23 Helmdon H 9
27 Helmingham J 5
40 Helmington Row B 2
61 Helmsdale E 10
34 Helmshore E 6
40 Helmsley G 6
40 Helperby H 5
41 Helperthorpe H 9
24 Helpringham B 2
24 Helpston E 2
30 Helsby C 3
2 Helston G 4
3 Helstone B 8
39 Helton C 7
39 Helwith Bridge H 10
17 Hemel Hempstead D 11
36 Hemingbrough D 4
33 Hemingby C 9
36 Hemongfield G 2
25 Hemingford Abbots H 4
25 Hemingford Grey H 4
27 Hemingstone K 5
32 Hemington, Leics. G 2
25 Hemington, Northants. G 2
7 Hemington, Som. A 10
27 Hemley L 6
40 Hemlington D 5
22 Hempholme B 8
26 Hempnall F 5
26 Hempnall Green F 5
25 Hempstead, Essex L 7
10 Hempstead, Kent B 6
26 Hempstead, Norf. B 4
15 Hempsted C 11
26 Hempton, Norfolk C 2
16 Hempton, Oxon. A 5
26 Hemsby D 8
32 Hemswell A 6
36 Hemsworth F 2
6 Hemyock E 5
15 Henbury, Avon F 9
31 Henbury, Ches. C 7
4 Henderbarrow Corner F 3
18 Hendon, London E 2
45 Hendon, Tyne & Wear G 12
15 Hendre C 8
14 Hendreforgan E 3
12 Hendre-wen D 3
13 Hendy G 9
28 Heneglwys C 4
24 Hen-feddau D 6
15 Henfield, Avon F 10
10 Henfield, W. Sussex F 1
11 Hengherst D 8
14 Hengoed, Mid Glam. E 5
21 Hengoed, Powys G 8
30 Hengoed, Salop. G 2
27 Hengrave H 1
18 Henham A 5
45 Henhill E 12
21 Heniarth B 7
6 Henlade D 6
45 Henlaw C 11
7 Henley, Dorset F 10
21 Henley, Salop. D 10
7 Henley, Somerset C 8
27 Henley, Suffolk K 5
9 Henley, W. Sussex D 10
22 Henley-in-Arden E 5
17 Henley-on-Thames F 8
10 Henley Street A 5
29 Henllan, Clwyd C 9
13 Henllan, Dyfed C 7
13 Henllan Amgoed E 5
14 Henllys E 6
25 Henlow L 3
5 Hennock H 7
27 Henny Street L 2
29 Henryd C 7
12 Henry's Moat D 4
36 Hensall E 4
44 Henshaw G 6
38 Hensingham D 2
27 Heanstead G 8
7 Henstridge D 10
7 Henstridge Ash D 10
7 Henstridge Bowden D 10
17 Henton, Oxon. D 8
7 Henton, Som. B 8
7 Henstridge Marsh D 11
22 Henwick G 2
3 Henwood B 9
64 Heogan D 7
14 Heol Senni B 3
13 Heol-las G 10
14 Heol-y-Cyw F 3
45 Hepburn A 9
45 Hepple C 8
45 Hepple Whitefield C 8
45 Hepscott E 10
35 Hepstonstall D 8
27 Hepworth, Suff. H 3
35 Hepworth, W. Yorks. F 10
12 Herbrandston F 2
21 Hereford H 10
22 Hereford & Worcester, Co. F 2
48 Heriot D 6
49 Hermiston G 8
16 Hermitage, Berks. G 6
44 Hermitage, Borders C 3
7 Hermitage, Dorset F 10
44 Hermitage, Dumf. & Gall. E 9
9 Hermitage, W. Sussex F 9
13 Hermon, Dyfed D 10
12 Hermon, Dyfed D 5
28 Hermon, Gwynedd C 3
11 Herne B 10
11 Herne Bay A 10
4 Herner C 5
11 Hernhill B 9
3 Herodsfoot D 9
11 Heronden C 11
18 Herongate E 6
42 Heronsford C 2
17 Heronsgate E 11
9 Herriard B 8
26 Herringfleet F 8
25 Herring's Green L 2
27 Herringswell H 8
45 Herrington H 11
11 Hersden B 10
17 Hersham H 12
10 Herstmonceux G 5
8 Herston, Dorset H 2
64 Herston, Orkney Is. E 2
18 Hertford C 3
18 Hertford Heath C 3
18 Hertfordshire, Co. B 2
18 Hertingfordbury C 3
38 Hesket Newmarket A 6
34 Hesketh Bank E 3
34 Hesketh Lane C 5
34 Heskin Green F 4
40 Hesleden A 4
44 Hesleyside E 6
36 Heslington B 4
36 Hessay B 3
3 Hessenford D 10
27 Hessett J 2
47 Hessilhead D 9
37 Hessle E 8
34 Hest Bank A 3
18 Heston F 1
30 Heswall B 1
17 Hethe A 7
26 Hethersett E 5
44 Hethersgill F 3
49 Hethpool G 11
40 Hett B 3
35 Hetton A 8
45 Hetton Downs H 11
45 Hetton Law C 11
45 Hetton Steads B 11
45 Hetton-le-Hole H 11
45 Heugh F 9
58 Heugh-head F 1
27 Heveningham H 6
10 Hever D 4
39 Heversham G 7
26 Hevingham C 5
15 Hewelsfield D 9
15 Hewish, Avon H 7
7 Hewish, Somerset E 7
36 Heworth B 4
45 Hexham G 7
49 Hexpath E 9
10 Hextable A 4
5 Hexworthy H 5
19 Heybridge, Essex C 8
18 Heybridge, Essex D 6
19 Heydridge Basin C 8
5 Heybrook Bay L 4
25 Heydon, Cambs. L 5
26 Heydon, Norfolk C 4
33 Heydour F 7
34 Heysham A 3
35 Heyshaw A 10
9 Heyshott D 10
8 Heytesbury B 1
16 Heythrop A 4
35 Heywood, Manchester F 7
7 Heywood, Wilts. A 12
37 Hibaldstow G 7
36 Hickleton G 3
26 Hickling, Norfolk C 7
32 Hickling, Notts. G 4
26 Hickling Green C 7
22 Hidcote Bartrim H 5
36 High Ackworth E 2
45 High Angerton E 9
39 High Bankhill A 8
18 High Beach D 4
39 High Bentham H 9
4 High Bickington D 5
39 High Birkwith G 10
47 High Blantyre D 11
48 High Bonnybridge B 1
43 High Borgue F 7
35 High Bradley B 9
4 High Bray C 6
10 High Brooms D 5
4 High Bullen D 4
40 High Burton G 2
45 High Buston B 10
45 High Callerton F 10
36 High Catton B 5
45 High Church E 10
47 High Cleughearn E 11
16 High Cogges C 5
40 High Conniscliffe D 3
49 High Cross, Borders E 8
9 High Cross, Hants. C 8
18 High Cross, Herts. B 4
31 High Cross Bank H 11
47 High Duncryne A 9
18 High Easter B 6
40 High Ellington G 2
40 High Entercommon E 4
21 High Ercall A 11
40 High Etherley B 2
19 High Garrett A 7
40 High Grange B 2
22 High Green, Heref. & Worcs. H 2
26 High Green, Norf. E 4
35 High Green, S. Yorks. G 12
11 High Halden D 8
10 High Halstow A 6
7 High Ham C 8
38 High Harrington C 3
40 High Haswell A 4
30 High Hatton H 5
41 High Hawsker D 9
39 High Hesket A 7
40 High Hesleden A 5
35 High Hoyland F 11
37 High Hursley D 7
10 High Hurstwood E 4
41 High Hutton H 8
38 High Ireby B 5
40 High Kilburn G 5
31 High Lane, Manchester B 8
21 High Lane, Heref. & Worcs. F 12
18 High Laver C 5
30 High Legh B 5
40 High Leven D 5
15 High Littleton H 9
38 High Lorton C 4
41 High Marishes G 8
32 High Marnham C 5
36 High Melton G 3
45 High Mickley G 9
42 High Mindork F 4
41 High Mowthorpe H 9
38 High Newton G 6
45 High Newton by-the-Sea E 12
38 High Nibthwaite F 5
30 High Offley H 6
18 High Ongar D 5
22 High Onn A 2
42 High Pennyvenie A 6
18 High Roding B 6
38 High Row B 6
39 High Shaw F 11
40 High Skelding H 2
45 High Spen G 9
40 High Stoop A 1
3 High Street, Corn. D 7
27 High Street, Suff. K 7
27 High Street, Suff. K 2
27 High Street Green K 3
40 High Throston B 5
33 High Toynton C 10
45 High Trewhitt B 8
48 High Valleyfield A 3
45 High Warden F 7
38 High Wray E 6
18 High Wych C 5
17 High Wycombe E 9
32 Higham, Derby D 1
10 Higham, Kent A 6
35 Higham, Lancs. D 7
25 Higham, Suffolk J 8
27 Higham, Suffolk L 3
45 Higham Dykes E 9
25 Higham Ferrers H 1
25 Higham Gobion M 2
23 Higham on the Hill C 7
10 Higham Wood C 5
4 Highampton E 4
55 Highbridge, Highland L 6
6 Highbridge, Som. B 6
10 Highbrook E 2
35 Highburton F 10
7 Highbury A 10
44 Highchesters B 3
16 Highclere H 5
8 Highcliffe G 4
7 Higher Alham B 10
7 Higher Ansty F 11
6 Higher Ashton H 2
34 Higher Ballam D 2
2 Higher Boscaswell F 1
6 Higher Combe C 3
2 Higher Crackington B 2
34 Higher End G 4
30 Higher Heath G 4
29 Higher Kinnerton D 12
7 Higher Nyland D 10
34 Higher Penwortham D 4
31 Higher Poynton B 8
2 Higher Town C 2
30 Higher Walton, Ches. B 4
34 Higher Walton, Lancs. D 5
7 Higher Whatcombe F 11
30 Higher Whitley B 5
30 Higher Wych F 3
32 Highfield, S. Yorks. B 1
47 Highfield, Strathclyde D 8
45 Highfield, Tyne & Wear G 9
25 Highfields, Cambs. J 5
49 Highfields, Northumb. D 12
18 Highgate, London E 3
36 Highgate, N. Yorks. E 4
44 Highgreen Manor D 6
40 Highlands, Dur. C 2
58 Highlands, Grampian F 6
32 Highlane B 1
15 Highleadon B 11
9 Highleigh F 9
22 Highley D 1
17 Highmoor Cross F 8
15 Highmoor Hill E 8
15 Highnam Green B 11
4 Highridge D 6
11 Highsted B 8
27 Highstreet Green M 1
27 Hightae D 11
31 Hightown, Ches. D 7
43 Hightown, Dumf. & Gall. C 11
34 Hightown, Merseyside G 2
43 Hightown of Craigs D 11
2 Highway, Corn. E 4
16 Highway, Wilts. G 2
5 Highweek J 7
16 Highworth E 3
26 Hilborough E 1
32 Hilcote D 2
16 Hilcott H 2
10 Hilden Park C 4
10 Hildenborough C 4
25 Hildersham K 6
31 Hilderstone G 8
37 Hilderthorpe A 9
7 Hilfield F 9
24 Hilgay F 7
15 Hill, Avon E 9
4 Hill, Devon E 9
22 Hill, W. Midlands B 5
9 Hill Brow D 9
41 Hill Cottages E 7
34 Hill Dale F 4
33 Hill Dyke E 10
39 Hill End, Dur. B 12
52 Hill End, Fife H 5
15 Hill Gate B 8
9 Hill Head, Hants. F 7

45 Hill Head, Northumb. F 7
12 Hill Mountain F 3
52 Hill of Beath H 6
56 Hill of Fearn B 4
58 Hill of Maud Crofts B 2
31 Hill Ridware H 9
25 Hill Row H 5
8 Hill Top, Hants F 5
35 Hill Top, W. Yorks. F 12
8 Hill View F 1
36 Hillam D 3
39 Hillbeck D 10
38 Hillberry G 2
11 Hillborough A 10
8 Hillbourne G 2
58 Hillbrae E 5
8 Hillbutts F 1
53 Hillcairnie E 8
6 Hillcommon D 5
48 Hillend, Fife A 4
48 Hillend, Strathclyde E 3
15 Hillersland C 9
17 Hillesden A 8
15 Hillesley E 11
6 Hillfarance D 5
5 Hillhead, Devon K 8
58 Hillhead, Grampian E 5
45 Hillhead, Northumb. B 9
47 Hillhead, Strathclyde F 10
47 Hillhead, Strathclyde G 9
48 Hillhead, Strathclyde E 3
58 Hillhead of Auchentumb B 7
58 Hillhead of Cocklaw C 8
49 Hillhouse D 7
22 Hilliard's Cross A 5
18 Hillingdon F 1
24 Hillington C 8
23 Hillmorton E 8
59 Hillockhead, Grampian G 1
58 Hillockhead, Grampian F 2
9 Hillpound D 7
43 Hillside, Dumf. & Gall. C 12
59 Hillside, Grampian H 7
64 Hillside, Shetlands C 7
59 Hillside, Tayside L 4
8 Hillstreet D 5
64 Hillswick C 6
9 Hillway G 8
64 Hillwell F 7
16 Hilmarton G 1
15 Hilperton H 12
15 Hilperton Marsh H 11
9 Hilsea F 8
37 Hilston D 10
25 Hilton J 4
49 Hilton, Borders D 11
40 Hilton, Cleveland D 5
39 Hilton, Cumbria C 9
31 Hilton, Derby G 11
7 Hilton, Dorset F 11
40 Hilton, Durham C 2
58 Hilton, Grampian D 7
22 Hilton, Salop C 1
56 Hilton of Cadboll B 4
22 Himbleton F 3
22 Himley C 2
39 Hincaster G 7
16 Hinchwick A 2
23 Hinckley C 7
27 Hinderclay H 3
41 Hinderwell D 8
30 Hindford G 2
9 Hindhead C 10
34 Hindley, Manchester G 5
45 Hindley, Northumb. G 8
34 Hindley Green G 5
22 Hindlip F 2
26 Hindolveston C 3
7 Hindon C 12
26 Hindringham B 3
26 Hingham E 3
30 Hinstock H 5
27 Hintlesham L 4
15 Hinton, Avon G 10
8 Hinton, Hants. G 4
21 Hinton, Heref. & Worcs. H 9
23 Hinton, Northants. G 8
21 Hinton, Salop. B 9
9 Hinton Ampner C 7
7 Hinton Blewett A 9
15 Hinton Charterhouse H 11
22 Hinton Green H 4
23 Hinton-in-the-Hedge H 9
9 Hinton Marsh C 7
8 Hinton Martell E 2
22 Hinton on the Green H 4
16 Hinton Parva F 3
7 Hinton St. George E 7
7 Hinton St. Mary E 11
16 Hinton Waldrist D 5
21 Hints, Salop. E 11
22 Hints, Staffs. B 5
23 Hinwick F 12
11 Hinxhill D 9
25 Hinxton L 6
25 Hinxworth L 3
35 Hipperholme E 10
40 Hipswell E 2
12 Hiraeth E 5
59 Hirn G 5
29 Hirnant, Powys H 10
20 Hirnant, Powys E 4
45 Hirst D 11
36 Hirst Courtney E 4
29 Hirwaen D 10
14 Hirwaun D 3
4 Hiscott C 4
25 Histon J 5
27 Hitcham K 3
43 Hitchill E 12
18 Hitchin A 2
18 Hither Green F 4
4 Hittisleigh Cross F 6
36 Hive D 6
31 Hixon H 8
11 Hoaden B 11
15 Hoaldalbert B 7
31 Hoar Cross H 10
15 Hoarwithy A 8
11 Hoath B 10
21 Hobarris E 8
64 Hobbister D 2
18 Hobbs Cross D 5
44 Hobkirk B 4
45 Hobson G 10
32 Hoby H 4
26 Hockering D 4
32 Hockerton E 4
19 Hockley E 8
22 Hockley Heath E 5
17 Hockliffe A 10
25 Hockwold cum Wilton G 8
6 Hockworthy D 4
18 Hoddesdon C 4
34 Hoddlesden E 6
43 Hoddomcross D 12
12 Hodgeston G 4
30 Hodnet G 5
10 Hodsoll Street B 5
16 Hodson F 3
32 Hodthorpe C 3
9 Hoe, Hampshire D 7
26 Hoe, Norfolk D 3
9 Hoe Gate E 8
39 Hoff C 9
9 Hog Patch A 9
17 Hoggeston B 9
34 Hoghton E 5
31 Hognaston E 11
33 Hogsthorpe C 12
24 Holbeach C 5
24 Holbeach Bank C 5
24 Holbeach Clough C 4
24 Holbeach Drove D 4
24 Holbeach Hurn C 5
24 Holbeach St. Johns D 4
24 Holbeach St. Marks C 5
24 Holbeach St. Matthew B 5
32 Holbeck, Notts. C 3
35 Holbeck, W. Yorks. D 11
22 Holberrow Green F 4
5 Holbeton L 5
31 Holbrook, Derby F 12
27 Holbrook, Suffolk L 5
8 Holbury F 6
45 Holburn B 11
5 Holcombe, Devon H 8
34 Holcombe, Manchester E 6
7 Holcombe, Som. A 10
34 Holcombe Brook F 6
6 Holcombe Rogus D 4
23 Holcot E 11
34 Holden B 6
23 Holdenby E 10
8 Holdenhurst G 3
21 Holdgate C 11
33 Holdingham E 7
7 Holditch F 7
49 Holefield F 10
47 Holehouse D 8
15 Hole-in-the-Wall A 9
43 Holestane B 9
6 Holford B 5
38 Holker G 6
26 Holkham A 2
4 Hollacombe F 2
64 Holland, Papa Westray, Orkney Is. A 3
64 Holland, Stronsay, Orkney Is. C 4
33 Holland Fen E 9
19 Holland-on-Sea B 11
64 Hollandstoun A 4
44 Hollee F 1
27 Hollesley L 6
34 Hollingfare H 6
11 Hollingbourne C 7
10 Hollingrove F 6
31 Hollington, Derby F 10
10 Hollington, E. Sussex G 6
31 Hollington, Staffs. F 9
35 Hollingworth G 8
34 Hollins Lane B 4
31 Hollinsclough D 9
4 Hollocombe E 5
22 Hollow Court F 3
31 Hollow Meadows A 11
31 Holloway E 11
23 Hollowell E 10
44 Hollows E 2
30 Holly Bush F 3
24 Holly End E 6
22 Holly Green H 2
15 Hollybush, Heref. & Worcs. A 10
47 Hollybush, Strathclyde H 9
37 Hollym E 11
22 Hollywood D 4
44 Holm, Dumf. & Gall. C 1
63 Holm, W. Isles D 5
4 Holmacott C 4
35 Holmbridge F 10
9 Holmbury St. Mary B 12
3 Holmbush D 7
31 Holmcroft H 8
25 Holme, Cambs. G 3
39 Holme, Cumbria G 7
37 Holme, Humber. F 7
40 Holme, N. Yorks. G 4
32 Holme, Notts. D 5
35 Holme, W. Yorks. F 9
35 Holme Chapel D 7
26 Holme Hale E 2
15 Holme Lacy A 9
21 Holme Marsh G 9
24 Holme next the Sea A 8
37 Holme-on-the-Wolds C 7
32 Holme Pierrepont F 3
38 Holme St. Cuthbert A 3
36 Holme-on-Spalding Moor C 6
21 Holmer H 10
17 Holmer Green D 10
30 Holmes Chapel C 6
31 Holmesfield B 11
34 Holmeswood E 3
32 Holmewood D 2
35 Holmfirth F 10
43 Holmfoot B 9
47 Holmhead G 10
62 Holmisdal C 1
37 Holmpton E 11
38 Holmrook E 3
45 Holmside H 10
44 Holmwrangle H 4
5 Holne J 6
4 Holsworthy F 2
4 Holsworthy Beacon E 2
30 Holt, Clwyd E 3
22 Holt, Heref. & Worcs. F 2
8 Holt, Dorset F 2
26 Holt, Norfolk B 4
15 Holt, Wilts. H 11
9 Holt End, Hants. B 8
22 Holt End, Heref. & Worcs. E 4
22 Holt Heath F 2
8 Holt Wood E 2
36 Holtby B 4
33 Holton, Lincs. B 8
17 Holton, Oxon. G 7
7 Holton, Som. D 10
27 Holton, Suffolk H 7
8 Holton Heath G 1
37 Holton le Clay G 10
37 Holton le Moor G 8
27 Holton St. Mary L 4
10 Holtye D 3
7 Holwell, Dorset E 10
18 Holwell, Herts. A 2
32 Holwell, Leics. H 5
16 Holwell, Oxon. C 3
29 Holwick C 11
7 Holworth H 11
22 Holy Cross D 3
45 Holy Island B 12
9 Holybourne B 9
28 Holyhead B 2
31 Holymoorside C 11
17 Holyport F 10
45 Holystone C 8
47 Holytown C 12
25 Holywell, Cambs. H 4
29 Holywell, Clwyd C 11
2 Holywell, Corn. D 5
44 Holywell, Cumb. E 3
7 Holywell, Dorset F 9
45 Holywell, Northumb. F 11
35 Holywell Green E 9
6 Holywell Lake D 5
25 Holywell Row H 8
43 Holywood C 10
15 Hom Green B 9
49 Homebank E 10
49 Homebyres E 9
21 Homer B 11
27 Homersfield G 6
8 Homington D 3
11 Honey Hill B 10
16 Honey Street H 2
27 Honey Tye L 2
12 Honeyborough F 2
22 Honeybourne H 5
4 Honeychurch F 5
22 Honiley E 6
26 Honing C 6
26 Honingham D 4
32 Honington, Lincs. F 6
27 Honington, Suff. H 2
22 Honington, War. H 6
6 Honiton F 5
35 Honley F 10
10 Hoo A 6
22 Hoobrook E 2
35 Hood Green G 11
5 Hooe, Devon K 4
10 Hooe, E. Sussex G 6
10 Hooe Common G 6
12 Hook, Dyfed F 3
9 Hook, Hants. A 8
36 Hook, Humber. E 5
18 Hook, London G 2
16 Hook, Wilts. F 2
10 Hook Green, Kent A 5
10 Hook Green, Kent D 5
16 Hook Norton A 4
7 Hooke F 9
30 Hookgate G 6
4 Hookway F 7
10 Hookwood D 2
30 Hoole C 3
10 Hooley B 2
30 Hooton B 2
32 Hooton Levitt A 2
36 Hooton Pagnell F 3
36 Hooton Roberts G 3
64 Hoove D 7
24 Hop Pole D 3
31 Hope, Derby B 10
5 Hope, Devon M 5
29 Hope, Clwyd D 12
60 Hope, Highland B 5
21 Hope, Powys B 8
21 Hope, Salop. B 9
21 Hope Bagot E 11
21 Hope Bowdler C 10
15 Hope Mansell B 9
21 Hope under Dinmore G 10
56 Hopeman C 7
21 Hopesay D 9
36 Hopperton B 2
31 Hopton, Derby E 11
30 Hopton, Salop. G 4
31 Hopton, Staffs. H 8
26 Hopton, Suffolk E 8
27 Hopton, Suffolk G 3
21 Hopton Cangeford D 11
21 Hopton Castle E 9
21 Hopton Wafers E 11
21 Hoptonheath E 9
22 Hopwas B 5
22 Hopwood E 4
10 Horam F 4
24 Horbling B 2
35 Horbury E 11
40 Horden A 5
21 Horderley D 9
8 Hordle F 4
30 Hordley G 2
13 Horeb, Dyfed C 7
13 Horeb, Dyfed D 8
15 Horfield F 9
63 Horgabost G 1
27 Horham H 5
19 Horkesley Heath A 9
37 Horkstow E 7
23 Horley, Oxon. H 7
10 Horley, Surrey D 2
7 Hornblotton Grn. C 9
39 Hornby, Lancs. H 8
40 Hornby, N. Yorks. F 2
40 Hornby, N. Yorks. E 4
33 Horncastle C 9
18 Hornchurch E 5
19 Horncliffe D 11
49 Horndean, Borders D 11
9 Horndean, Hants. E 8
5 Horndon H 4
18 Horndon-on-the-Hill F 6
10 Horne D 2
6 Horner B 3
26 Horning D 6
23 Horninghold B 11
31 Horninglow H 10
25 Horningsea J 6
7 Horningsham B 11
26 Horningtoft C 2
3 Horningtops D 9
4 Horns Cross, Devon D 3
11 Horns Cross, E. Sussex F 7
44 Hornsby H 3
37 Hornsea B 9
37 Hornsea Burton B 9
18 Hornsey E 3
23 Hornton H 7
5 Horrabridge J 4
27 Horringer J 1
9 Horringford H 7
48 Horsburgh E 6
31 Horse Bridge E 8
8 Horsebridge C 5
22 Horsebrook A 2
15 Horsecastle H 7
21 Horsehay B 12
25 Horseheath K 7
39 Horsehouse G 12
17 Horsell H 10
30 Horseman's Grn. F 3
17 Horsenden D 9
26 Horsey C 8
26 Horsford D 5
35 Horsforth C 11
22 Horsham, Heref. & Worcs. F 1
10 Horsham, W. Sussex E 1
26 Horsham St. Faith D 5
33 Horsington, Lincs. C 9
7 Horsington, Som. D 10
32 Horsley, Derby F 1
15 Horsley, Glos. E 11
45 Horsley, Northumb. C 7
45 Horsley, Northumb. F 9
19 Horsley Cross A 11
32 Horsley Woodhouse F 1
19 Horsleycross St. A 11
49 Horsleyhill G 8
10 Horsmonden D 6
17 Horspath D 7
26 Horstead D 5
10 Horsted Keynes E 3
15 Horton, Avon F 10
17 Horton, Bucks. B 10
17 Horton, Bucks. F 11
8 Horton, Dorset E 2
35 Horton, Lancs. B 7
23 Horton, Northants. G 11
6 Horton, Somerset E 6
31 Horton, Staffs. D 8
16 Horton, Wilts. H 2
13 Horton, W. Glam. H 8
7 Horton Cross E 7
30 Horton Green E 3
8 Horton Heath D 6
39 Horton in Ribblesdale H 10
10 Horton Kirby A 4
34 Horwich F 5
31 Horwich End B 8
4 Horwood C 4
44 Hoscote B 2
32 Hose G 5
49 Hoselaw F 10
38 Hoses F 5
64 Hoswick E 7
37 Hotham D 7
11 Hothfield D 8
32 Hoton H 3
44 Hott D 6
64 Houbie B 8
30 Hough E 6
32 Hough-on-the-Hill F 6
32 Hougham F 6
25 Houghton, Cambs. H 4
44 Houghton, Cumb. G 2
12 Houghton, Dyfed F 3
8 Houghton, Hants. C 5
9 Houghton, W. Sussex E 11
25 Houghton Conquest L 2
30 Houghton Green A 5
17 Houghton Regis B 11
45 Houghton-le-Spring H 11
23 Houghton on the Hill B 10
41 Houlsyke D 7
8 Hound E 6
17 Hound Green H 8
49 Houndridge F 10
49 Houndslow E 9
6 Houndsmoor D 5
49 Houndwood C 11
8 Hounsdown E 5
18 Hounslow F 2
64 Housay C 8
59 House of Glenmuick H 1
58 Housieside E 6
47 Houston C 9
61 Houstry D 10
10 Hove H 2
32 Hoveringham E 4
26 Hoveton D 6
41 Hovingham H 7
44 How G 3
16 How Caple A 9
10 How Green C 4
38 How Head E 6
35 Howbrook G 11
49 Howburn F 10
49 Howden, Borders G 9
36 Howden, Humber. D 5
35 Howden Clough D 11
40 Howden-le-Wear B 2
39 Howe, Cumbria F 7
61 Howe, Highland B 12
26 Howe, Norfolk E 6
19 Howe Green D 7
58 Howe of Teucher C 5
19 Howe Street, Essex B 7
25 Howe Street, Essex M 8
33 Howell F 8
43 Howes E 12
20 Howey F 6
48 Howford F 6
48 Howgate, Lothian D 5
48 Howgate, Strathclyde F 2
45 Howick A 10
30 Howle H 5
15 Howle Hill B 9
25 Howlett End M 7
6 Howley E 6
49 Howliston D 7
49 Hownam G 10
49 Hownam Mains G 10
44 Howpasley B 2
37 Howsham, Humber. G 8
36 Howsham, N. Yorks. A 5
49 Howtel F 11
64 Howth D 2
15 Howton A 7
39 Howtown C 7
47 Howwood C 9
64 Hoxa E 2
27 Hoxne G 5
30 Hoylake A 1
35 Hoylake Nether G 12
35 Hoylake Swaine G 11
12 Hubberston F 2
24 Hubbert's Bridge A 4
36 Huby, N. Yorks. A 3
35 Huby, N. Yorks. B 11
15 Hucclecote C 12
11 Hucking B 7
32 Hucknall E 3
35 Huddersfield E 10
22 Huddington F 3
40 Hudswell E 2
36 Huggate B 6
2 Hugh Town D 2
17 Hughenden Valley D 9
21 Hughley C 11
4 Huish, Devon E 4
16 Huish, Wilts. H 2
6 Huish Barton B 4
6 Huish Champflower C 4
7 Huish Episcopi D 8
17 Hulcott B 9
31 Hulland F 11
31 Hulland Ward E 11
15 Hullavington F 12
19 Hullbridge D 8
31 Hulme End D 9
31 Hulme Walfield D 7
34 Hulton Lane Ends G 6
27 Hulver Street G 8
8 Hulverstone H 5
21 Humber Court G 11
37 Humberside Co. C 7
37 Humberston G 10
23 Humberstone B 10
49 Humbie C 7
37 Humbleton, Humber. D 10
49 Humbleton, Northumb. G 12
33 Humby G 7
49 Hume E 9
47 Humeston H 7
45 Humshaugh F 7
61 Huna A 12
34 Huncoat D 6
23 Huncote B 8
49 Hundalee G 9
39 Hunderthwaite C 12
33 Hundleby D 11
12 Hundleton G 3
25 Hundon K 8
9 Hundred Acres E 7
34 Hundred End E 3
21 Hundred House G 7

23 Hungarton **A 10**
34 Hunger Hill **F 5**
16 Hungerford, Berks. **G 4**
8 Hungerford, Hants. **E 3**
16 Hungerford Newton **G 5**
32 Hungerton **G 6**
62 Hunglader **A 3**
63 Hunisish **F 1**
41 Hunmanby **G 11**
23 Hunningham **E 7**
8 Hunny Hill **G 6**
18 Hunsdon **C 4**
36 Hunsingore **B 2**
35 Hunslett Carr **D 11**
39 Hunsonby **B 8**
61 Hunspow **A 11**
24 Hunstanton **B 8**
45 Hunstanworth **H 8**
27 Hunston, Suffolk **H 3**
9 Hunston, W. Sussex **F 10**
15 Hunstrete **H 9**
35 Hunsworth **D 10**
22 Hunt End **F 4**
41 Hunt Ho **E 7**
47 Hunter's Quay **B 7**
49 Huntershall **F 10**
47 Hunterston Works **D 7**
44 Huntford **B 5**
59 Hunthill Lodge **K 2**
25 Huntingdon **H 3**
22 Huntington **A 3**
27 Huntingfield **H 6**
21 Huntington, Heref. & Worcs. **G 8**
21 Huntington, Heref. & Worcs. **H 10**
36 Huntington, N. Yorks. **B 4**
52 Huntingtower Haugh **E 5**
15 Huntley, Glos. **B 10**
31 Huntley, Staffs **F 8**
58 Huntly **D 3**
49 Huntlywood **E 9**
10 Hunton, Kent **C 6**
40 Hunton, N. Yorks. **F 2**
17 Hunton Bridge **D 11**
30 Hunt's Cross **B 3**
6 Huntscott **B 3**
6 Huntsham **D 3**
6 Huntspill **B 6**
7 Huntworth **C 7**
40 Huntwick **B 2**
26 Hunworth **B 4**
7 Hurcott **E 7**
8 Hurdcott **C 3**
17 Hurley, Berks. **F 9**
22 Hurley, War. **C 9**
47 Hurlford **F 9**
64 Hurliness **E 1**
8 Hurn **F 3**
31 Hursdfield **C 8**
8 Hursley **D 6**
17 Hurst, Berks. **G 9**
35 Hurst, Manchester **G 8**
40 Hurst, N. Yorks. **E 1**
7 Hurst, Somerset **D 8**
10 Hurst Green, E. Sussex **E 6**
34 Hurst Green, Lancs. **C 6**
10 Hurst Green, Surrey **C 3**
10 Hurst Wickham **F 2**
8 Hurstbourne Priors **A 6**
8 Hurstbourne Tarrant **A 5**
21 Hurstley **G 9**
10 Hurstpierpoint **F 2**
21 Hurstway Com. **G 8**
9 Hurtmore **B 11**
40 Hurworth **D 3**
39 Hury **C 11**
62 Husabost Piers **C 1**
23 Husbands Bosworth **D 10**
25 Husborne Crawley **L 1**
40 Husthwaite **H 5**
32 Huthwaite **D 2**
33 Huttoft **C 12**
15 Hutton, Avon **H 7**
49 Hutton, Borders **D 11**
39 Hutton, Cumb. **C 7**
18 Hutton, Essex **D 6**
37 Hutton, Humber. **B 8**
34 Hutton, Lancs. **D 4**
41 Hutton Buscel **G 9**
40 Hutton Conyers **H 3**
39 Hutton End **A 7**
40 Hutton Hang **F 2**
40 Hutton Henry **B 4**
39 Hutton-in-the-Forest **B 7**
39 Hutton John **C 7**
41 Hutton-le-Hole **F 7**
40 Hutton Magna **D 2**
38 Hutton Roof, Cumb. **B 6**
39 Hutton Roof, Cumbria **G 8**
40 Hutton Rudby **E 5**
40 Hutton Sessay **H 5**
40 Hutton Village **D 6**
36 Hutton Wandesley **B 3**
4 Huxford **D 6**
6 Huxham **F 3**
30 Huxley **D 4**
64 Huxter **D 7**
30 Huyton **A 3**
38 Hycemoor **F 3**
15 Hyde, Glos. **D 12**
35 Hyde, Manchester **H 8**
17 Hyde Heath **D 10**
31 Hyde Lea **H 7**
9 Hydestile **B 11**
38 Hydro **F 2**
48 Hyndford **E 2**
21 Hyssington **C 8**
8 Hythe, Hants. **E 5**
11 Hythe, Kent **E 10**
7 Hythe, Somerset **A 8**
17 Hythe End **G 11**
58 Hythie **C 7**
58 Ianstown **A 2**
7 Ibberton **E 11**
31 Ible **D 11**
8 Ibsley **E 3**
23 Ibstock **A 7**
17 Ibstone **E 8**
8 Ibthorpe **A 5**
9 Ibworth **A 7**
15 Icelton **H 7**
26 Ickburgh **F 1**
18 Ickenham **E 1**
17 Ickford **C 7**
11 Ickham **B 11**
18 Ickleford **A 2**
25 Ickleton **L 6**
27 Icklingham **H 1**
25 Ickwell Green **L 3**
16 Icomb **B 3**
16 Idbury **B 3**
4 Iddesleigh **E 4**
6 Ide **G 2**
10 Ide Hill **C 4**
5 Ideford **H 8**
11 Iden **F 8**
10 Iden Green, Kent **D 6**
11 Iden Green, Kent **E 7**
35 Idle **C 10**
22 Idlicote **H 6**
58 Idoch **C 5**
13 Idole **E 7**
31 Idridgehay **E 11**
62 Idrigil **B 3**
12 Idstone **F 4**
53 Idvies **B 10**
10 Ifield **D 1**
9 Ifold **C 11**
10 Iford **G 3**
15 Ifton **E 8**
30 Ifton Heath **G 2**
30 Ightfield **F 5**
10 Ightham **B 5**
27 Iken **K 7**
31 Ilam **E 10**
7 Ilchester **D 8**
49 Ilderton **G 12**
18 Ilford **E 4**
4 Ilfracombe **A 4**
32 Ilkeston **F 2**
27 Ilketshall St. Andrew **G 6**
27 Ilketshall St. Margaret **G 2**
35 Ilkley **B 9**
35 Illingworth **D 9**
22 Illey **D 3**
2 Illogan **E 4**
2 Illogan Highway **E 4**
23 Illston on the Hill **B 10**
17 Ilmer **D 8**
22 Ilmington **H 5**
7 Ilminster **E 7**
5 Ilsington **H 6**
13 Ilston **H 9**
40 Ilton, N. Yorks. **G 2**
7 Ilton, Somerset **D 7**
46 Imachar **E 4**
37 Immingham **F 9**
37 Immingham Dock **E 9**
25 Impington **J 5**
55 Inbhireala or Strathossian Ho. **M 8**
30 Ince **C 3**
34 Ince Blundell **G 2**
34 Ince-in-Makerfield **G 5**
59 Inch **K 4**
54 Inchbae Lodge **C 8**
59 Inchbare **L 3**
58 Inchberry **B 1**
53 Incheoch **B 7**
54 Incheril **J 4**
60 Inchina **G 2**
47 Inchinnan **B 9**
60 Inchkinloch **C 6**
55 Inchlaggan **J 5**
56 Inchlumpie **B 1**
54 Inchmore **E 8**
59 Inchnabobart **J 1**
55 Inchnacardoch (Hotel) **H 7**
60 Inchnadamph **E 4**
57 Inchrory **J 7**
53 Inchture **D 7**
54 Inchvuilt **F 6**
52 Inchyra **E 6**
2 Indian Queens **D 6**
4 Indicott **B 4**
18 Ingatestone **D 6**
35 Ingbirchworth **G 10**
31 Ingestre **H 8**
32 Ingham, Lincs. **B 6**
26 Ingham, Norfolk **C 7**
27 Ingham, Suffolk **H 2**
24 Ingleborough, Norfolk **D 6**
39 Ingleborough, N. Yorks. **H 10**
31 Ingleby **G 12**
40 Ingleby Arncliffe **E 5**
40 Ingleby Cross **E 5**
40 Ingleby Greenhow **E 6**
15 Inglesbatch **H 10**
16 Inglesham **D 3**
60 Ingleton, Durham **C 2**
39 Ingleton, N. Yorks. **H 9**
34 Inglewhite **C 4**
45 Ingoe **F 8**
33 Ingoldmells **C 12**
33 Ingoldsby **G 7**
24 Ingoldsthorpe **B 8**
45 Ingram **A 8**
18 Ingrave **E 6**
35 Ingrow **C 9**
39 Ings **E 7**
15 Ingst **E 9**
26 Ingworth **C 5**
51 Inistrynich **E 8**
38 Injebreck **G 2**
22 Inkberrow **F 4**
16 Inkpen **H 4**
61 Inkstack **A 11**
46 Inellan **B 6**
48 Innerleithen **F 6**
53 Innerleven **G 8**
42 Innermessan **E 2**
42 Innerwell Fishery **G 6**
49 Innerwick, Lothian **B 10**
52 Innerwick, Tayside **B 1**
51 Innis Chonain **E 8**
51 Innischoarach **D 12**
58 Insch **E 4**
58 Inschtammack **C 2**
57 Insh **J 4**
57 Insh House **J 4**
51 Inshaig **B 7**
60 Inshore **A 4**
34 Inskip **C 3**
4 Instow **C 3**
57 Inver, Grampian **K 8**
56 Inver, Highland **B 4**
52 Inver, Tayside **C 5**
55 Inver Mallie **K 5**
55 Inverailort **L 1**
54 Inveralligin **D 2**
58 Inverllochy **A 8**
60 Inveran **G 6**
51 Inverary **G 8**
53 Inverarity **C 9**
51 Inverarnan **F 10**
54 Inverasdale **A 2**
54 Inverbain **D 2**
51 Inverbeg Hotel **H 10**
59 Inverbervie **K 6**
58 Inverboyndie **A 4**
60 Inverbroom **H 3**
60 Invercassley **F 5**
57 Invercauld House **K 7**
46 Inverchapel **A 6**
51 Invercharnan **C 8**
54 Inverchoran **E 6**
51 Invercreran **C 7**
57 Inverdruie **H 5**
58 Inverebrie **D 7**
57 Inveredrie **M 7**
57 Invereshie House **J 4**
48 Inveresk **B 6**
51 Inveresragan **D 7**
54 Inverewe House **B 2**
57 Inverey **K 6**
57 Inverfarigaig **G 1**
55 Invergarry **J 7**
52 Invergeldie **D 2**
55 Invergloy **L 6**
56 Invergordon **C 3**
53 Invergowrie **D 8**
55 Inverguseran **J 1**
52 Inverhadden **A 2**
58 Inverharroch **D 1**
51 Inverherive **E 10**
55 Inverie **J 1**
51 Inverinan **F 7**
55 Inverinate **G 3**
53 Inverkeilor **B 11**
48 Inverkeithing **A 4**
58 Inverkeithny **C 4**
47 Inverkip **B 7**
60 Inverkirkaig **E 2**
60 Inverlael **H 3**
60 Inverlael Lodge **H 3**
55 Inverlair **L 7**
51 Inverlochlarig **F 11**
51 Inverlochy **E 9**
59 Invermark Lodge **J 2**
55 Invermoriston **H 8**
58 Invernan House **F 1**
61 Invernaver **B 7**
56 Inverness **E 2**
58 Invernettie **C 8**
51 Invernoaden **H 8**
51 Inveroran Hotel **C 10**
60 Inverpolly Lodge **E 2**
58 Inverquhomery **C 8**
55 Inverroy **L 6**
50 Inversanda **B 7**
55 Invershiel **H 3**
60 Invershin **G 6**
60 Invershin Station **G 6**
61 Invershore **D 11**
55 Inverskilavulin **L 5**
51 Inversnaid Hotel **G 10**
58 Inverugie, Grampian **C 8**
56 Inverugie, Grampian **C 7**
51 Inveruglas **G 10**
57 Inveruglass **J 4**
58 Inverurie **E 5**
52 Invervar **B 2**
59 Invery House **H 4**
58 Inverythan **C 5**
4 Inwardleigh **F 4**
19 Inworth **B 8**
9 Iping **D 10**
5 Ipplepen **J 7**
18 Ippollits **A 2**
17 Ipsden **F 7**
31 Ipstones **E 8**
27 Ipswich **L 5**
30 Irby **G 2**
33 Irby in the Marsh **D 11**
37 Irby Upon Humber **G 9**
23 Irchester **E 12**
39 Ireby **H 9**
38 Ireleth **G 5**
39 Ireshopeburn **A 11**
34 Irlam **H 6**
33 Irnham **G 7**
15 Iron Acton **F 10**
21 Iron Bridge **B 12**
22 Iron Cross **G 4**
43 Ironmacannie **D 7**
32 Ironville **E 2**
26 Irstead **C 7**
23 Irthlingborough **E 12**
44 Irthington **G 3**
41 Irton **G 10**
47 Irvine **E 8**
44 Irvington **F 1**
61 Isauld **A 9**
64 Isbister, Orkney **C 2**
64 Isbister, Zetland **B 7**
64 Isbister, Zetland **C 8**
10 Isfield **F 3**
23 Isham **E 12**
50 Ishriff **D 4**
7 Isle Abbots **D 7**
7 Isle Brewers **D 7**
18 Isle of Dogs **F 4**
42 Isle of Whithorn **H 6**
25 Isleham **H 7**
62 Isleornsay **G 6**
43 Islesteps **D 10**
18 Isleworth **F 2**
32 Isley Walton **H 2**
18 Islington **E 3**
25 Islip, Northants. **G 1**
16 Islip, Oxon. **C 6**
63 Islivig **D 1**
18 Istead Rise **G 6**
8 Itchen **E 6**
9 Itchen Abbas **C 7**
9 Itchen Stoke **C 7**
9 Itchingfield **C 12**
15 Itchington **F 10**
26 Itteringham **C 4**
15 Itton Common **E 8**
38 Ivegill **A 6**
39 Ivelet **E 11**
17 Iver **F 11**
17 Iver Heath **F 11**
45 Iveston **H 9**
17 Ivinghoe **B 10**
17 Ivinghoe Aston **B 10**
21 Ivington **G 10**
21 Ivington Green **G 10**
10 Ivy Hatch **C 5**
5 Ivybridge **K 5**
11 Ivychurch **E 9**
11 Iwade **A 7**
7 Iwerne Courtney or Shroton **E 12**
7 Iwerne Minster **E 12**
27 Ixworth **H 2**
27 Ixworth Thorpe **H 2**
35 Jack Hill **B 10**
32 Jacksdale **E 2**
58 Jackstown **D 5**
2 Jacobstow **B 2**
4 Jacobstowe **F 5**
9 Jacobswell **A 11**
12 Jameston **G 4**
44 Jamestown, Dumf. & Gall. **C 1**
54 Jamestown, Highland **D 8**
47 Jamestown, Strathclyde **A 9**
45 Jarrow **F 11**
10 Jarvis Brook **E 4**
19 Jasper's Green **A 7**
48 Jawcraig **B 1**
19 Jaywick Sands **C 11**
17 Jealott's Hill **G 9**
40 Jeater Houses **F 4**
49 Jedburgh **G 9**
12 Jeffreyston **F 4**
56 Jemimaville **C 3**
13 Jersey Marine **H 10**
59 Jessiefield **G 6**
10 Jevington **H 4**
17 Jockey End **C 11**
30 Jodrell Bank **C 6**
35 John O'Gaunts **D 12**
61 John o'Groats **A 12**
38 Johnby **B 6**
10 John's Cross **F 6**
59 Johnshaven **K 6**
12 Johnston **F 3**
44 Johnstone, Dumf. & Gall. **C 1**
47 Johnstone, Strathclyde **C 9**
43 Johnstonebridge **B 11**
29 Johnstown, Clwyd **F 12**
13 Johnstown, Dyfed **E 7**
20 Joppa, Dyfed **F 1**
48 Joppa, Lothian **B 6**
17 Jordans **E 10**
12 Jordanston **D 3**
19 Jordons **E 8**
35 Jump **G 12**
8 Jumpers Green **G 3**
48 Juniper Green **B 5**
38 Jurby East **F 2**
38 Jurby West **F 2**
44 Justicetown **G 2**
39 Kaber **D 10**
58 Kaecloch **C 4**
48 Kaimes **C 5**
49 Kalemouth **G 9**
54 Kalnakill **D 1**
46 Kames, Strathclyde **B 5**
50 Kames, Strathclyde **F 5**
47 Kames, Strathclyde **G 11**
36 Keadby **F 6**
33 Keal Cotes **D 10**
34 Kearsley **G 6**
39 Kearstwick **G 8**
39 Kearton **E 12**
60 Kearvaig **A 4**
39 Keasden **H 9**
33 Keddington **A 10**
25 Kedington **K 8**
31 Kedleston **F 11**
49 Kedslie **E 8**
37 Keelby **F 9**
25 Keeley Green **L 1**
45 Keepershield **F 7**
12 Keeston **E 3**
15 Keevil **H 12**
32 Kegworth **G 2**
2 Kehelland **F 3**
58 Keig **F 3**
35 Keighley **C 9**
51 Keil **B 7**
52 Keilarsbrae **H 4**
58 Keilhill **B 5**
46 Keillmore **A 2**
52 Keillour **E 5**
7 Keinton Mandeville **C 9**
52 Keir House **G 3**
43 Keir Mill **B 9**
24 Keisby **C 1**
61 Keiss **B 12**
58 Keith **C 2**
58 Keithen **C 5**
35 Kelbrook **C 8**
33 Kelby **F 7**
39 Keld, Cumbria **D 8**
39 Keld, N. Yorks. **E 11**
41 Keldholme **F 7**
41 Keldy Castle **F 8**
36 Kelfield **C 4**
32 Kelham **E 5**
43 Kelhead **E 12**
50 Kellan **C 3**
56 Kellas, Grampian **D 7**
53 Kellas, Tayside **D 9**
5 Kellaton **M 7**
16 Kellaways **G 1**
39 Kelleth **E 9**
26 Kelling **A 4**
36 Kellingley **E 3**
36 Kellington **E 3**
40 Kelloe **B 4**
49 Kelloe Mains **D 11**
5 Kelly **H 3**
3 Kelly Bray **C 10**
23 Kelmarsh **D 10**
16 Kelmscot **D 3**
27 Kelsale **J 7**
30 Kelsall **C 4**
30 Kelsall Hill **C 4**
25 Kelshall **L 4**
43 Kelsick **F 12**
49 Kelso **F 10**
31 Kelstedge **D 11**
33 Kelstern **A 9**
29 Kelsterton **C 12**
15 Kelston **H 10**
43 Kelton **D 10**
43 Kelton Hill **F 8**
52 Kelty **H 6**
19 Kelvedon **B 8**
18 Kelvedon Hatch **D 6**
2 Kelynack **G 1**
53 Kemback **F 9**
22 Kemberton **B 1**
16 Kemble **D 1**
22 Kemerton **H 3**
15 Kemeys Commander **D 7**
58 Kemnay **F 5**
10 Kemp Town **H 2**
60 Kempie **B 5**
15 Kempley **A 10**
22 Kempsey **G 2**
16 Kempsford **D 3**
9 Kempshott **A 7**
25 Kempston **K 1**
25 Kempston Hardwick **L 1**
25 Kempston West End **K 1**
21 Kempton **D 9**
10 Kemsing **B 4**
11 Kemsley **A 8**
11 Kenardington **E 8**
21 Kenchester Sugwas **H 10**
16 Kencot **D 4**
39 Kendal **F 7**
15 Kenderchurch **A 7**
14 Kenfig **F 1**
14 Kenfig Hill **F 2**
22 Kenilworth **E 6**
51 Kenknock **D 11**
21 Kenley **B 11**
54 Kenmore, Highland **D 1**
51 Kenmore, Strathclyde **G 8**
52 Kenmore, Tayside **C 3**
15 Kenn, Avon **G 7**
6 Kenn, Devon **H 3**
63 Kennacley **G 3**
46 Kennacraig **C 3**
3 Kennards House **A 10**
44 Kennedy's Corner **E 1**
2 Kenneggy Downs **G 3**
4 Kennerleigh **E 7**
52 Kennet **H 4**
43 Kenneth Bank **E 10**
25 Kennett **H 8**
6 Kennford **G 3**
27 Kenninghall **G 3**
11 Kennington, Kent **D 9**
18 Kennington, London **F 3**
16 Kennington, Oxon. **D 6**
53 Kennoway **G 8**
47 Kennox **E 8**
25 Kennyhill **G 8**
36 Kennythorpe **A 6**
62 Kensaleyre **C 3**
18 Kensington **F 3**
17 Kensworth **B 11**
17 Kensworth Com. **B 11**
11 Kentl County **C 8**
10 Kent Street **C 5**
51 Kentallen **B 7**
15 Kentchurch **B 7**
25 Kentford **J 8**
6 Kentisbeare **E 4**
4 Kentisbury **B 5**
4 Kentisburyford **B 5**
39 Kentmere **E 7**
6 Kenton, Devon **H 3**
18 Kenton, London **E 2**
27 Kenton, Suffolk **J 5**
45 Kenton Bank Foot **F 10**
50 Kentra **A 4**

38 Kents Bank H 6
15 Kent's Green B 10
8 Kent's Oak D 5
45 Kentstone B 11
30 Kenwick G 3
2 Kenwyn E 5
60 Keoldale A 5
63 Keose E 5
55 Keppcoh G 3
46 Keprigan H 2
40 Kepwick F 5
49 Kerchesters F 10
23 Keresley D 7
15 Kerne Bridge B 9
54 Kernsary B 3
48 Kerrcleuch H 5
31 Kerridge C 8
2 Kerris G 2
21 Kerry C 7
46 Kerrylamont D 6
15 Kerry's Gate A 7
54 Kerrysdale B 2
46 Kerrytonlia D 6
32 Kersall D 4
6 Kersbrooke H 4
4 Kerscott C 5
47 Kerse D 8
27 Kersey L 3
63 Kershader E 4
44 Kershopefoot E 3
49 Kersmains F 9
22 Kersoe H 3
6 Kerswell F 4
22 Kerswell Green G 2
27 Kesgrave L 5
38 Keskadale C 4
27 Kessingland G 8
27 Kessingland Beach G 8
2 Kestle Mill D 5
18 Keston G 4
38 Keswick, Cumb. C 5
26 Keswick, Norfolk B 6
26 Keswick, Norfolk E 5
21 Ketley A 12
49 Kettelshiel D 9
23 Kettering D 12
26 Ketteringham E 5
53 Kettins C 7
27 Kettlebaston K 3
53 Kettlebridge F 8
22 Kettlebrook B 6
27 Kettlebrugh J 5
53 Kettlehill F 8
41 Kettleness D 8
31 Kettleshulme B 8
35 Kettlesing B 11
35 Kettlesing Bottom A 11
26 Kettlestone B 3
32 Kettlethorpe C 6
64 Kettletoft B 4
39 Kettlewell H 11
24 Ketton E 1
18 Kew F 2
14 Kewstoke H 6
35 Kexbrough F 11
32 Kexby, Lincs. B 5
36 Kexby, N. Yorks. B 5
31 Key Green D 7
11 Key Street B 7
23 Keyham B 10
8 Keyhaven G 5
37 Keyingham E 10
10 Keymer F 2
15 Keynsham G 9
33 Key's Toft D 12
25 Keysoe J 2
25 Keysoe Roe J 2
25 Keyston H 1
45 Kibblesworth G 10
23 Kibworth Beauchamp C 10
23 Kibworth Harcourt C 10
18 Kidbrooke F 4
22 Kiddemore Green A 2
22 Kidderminster D 2
16 Kiddington B 5
16 Kidlington C 6
17 Kidmore End F 8
30 Kidnal E 3
58 Kidrummy F 2
31 Kidsgrove E 7
39 Kidstones G 11
13 Kidwelly F 7
50 Kiel Crofts D 6
44 Kielder D 4
52 Kilbagie H 4
47 Kilbarchan C 9
62 Kilbeg H 6
46 Kilberry C 2
47 Kilbirnie D 8
50 Kilbride E 6
62 Kilbride, Highland F 5
50 Kilbride, Strathclyde E 6
32 Kilburn, Derby F 1
40 Kilburn, N. Yorks. G 5
59 Kilburn, Tayside K 1
23 Kilby C 9
48 Kilcadzow D 2
50 Kilchattan, Strathclyde H 1
46 Kilchattan, Strathclyde D 6
46 Kilchenzie G 2
50 Kilcheran D 5
50 Kilchoan, Highland A 2
55 Kilchoan, Highland K 2
50 Kilchoan, Strathclyde F 5
51 Kilchrenan E 7
53 Kilconquhar G 9
15 Kilcot B 10
56 Kilcoy E 1
47 Kilcreggan A 7
40 Kildale D 6
46 Kildalloig G 4
56 Kildary B 3
46 Kildavanan C 5
56 Kildermorie Lodge B 1
46 Kildonan G 5
61 Kildonan Lodge E 9
42 Kildrochat House F 2
35 Kildwick C 9
46 Kilfinan B 4
50 Kilfinichen E 2
55 Kilfinnan K 6
12 Kilgetty F 5
37 Kilham, Humber. A 8
49 Kilham, Northumb. F 11
42 Kilkerran A 4
4 Kilkhampton E 1
32 Killamarsh B 2
13 Killay H 9
50 Killbeg C 3
46 Killchianaig A 1
46 Killean E 2
47 Killearn A 10
46 Killellan H 2
56 Killen D 2
40 Killerby C 2
42 Killern F 6
55 Killichonan B 12
50 Killichronan C 3
55 Killiechonate L 6
52 Killiecrankie A 4
57 Killiehuntly K 4
50 Killiemor D 2
55 Killilan G 3
61 Killimster B 12
52 Killin D 1
57 Killin Lodge J 1
35 Killinghall A 11
39 Killington F 8
49 Killochyett E 7
55 Killunaig E 2
50 Killundine C 3
43 Killyleoch C 9
47 Kilmacolm B 8
50 Kilmahumaig H 5
50 Kilmalieu B 6
62 Kilmaluag A 4
53 Kilmany E 8
62 Kilmarie F 5
47 Kilmarnock F 9
53 Kilmaron Castle E 8
50 Kilmartin H 5
47 Kilmaurs E 9
50 Kilmelford F 6
7 Kilmersdon A 10
9 Kilmeston D 7
46 Kilmichael G 2
50 Kilmichael Glassary H 6
46 Kilmichael of
Inverlussa A 3
6 Kilmington, Devon F 6
7 Kilmington, Wilts. C 11
7 Kilmington Street C 11
56 Kilmorack E 1
62 Kilmore, Highland G 6
50 Kilmore, Strathclyde E 6
46 Kilmory, Arran G 4
50 Kilmory, Highland A 3
46 Kilmory, Strathclyde B 2
61 Kilmote F 9
62 Kilmuir, Highland A 3
62 Kilmuir, Highland C 2
56 Kilmuir, Highland B 3
56 Kilmuir, Highland E 2
46 Kilmun A 6
17 Kiln Green F 9
46 Kiln Hill F 4
45 Kiln Pit Hill H 8
10 Kilndown E 6
43 Kilness D 10
47 Kilnford F 8
36 Kilnhurst G 2
50 Kilninian C 1
50 Kilninver E 5
37 Kilnsea F 11
39 Kilnsey H 12
37 Kilnwick B 7
36 Kilnwick Percy B 6
50 Kiloran H 1
46 Kilpatrick G 4
15 Kilpeck A 7
61 Kilphedir E 9
36 Kilpin D 5
36 Kilpin Pike D 5
53 Kilrenny G 10
23 Kilsby E 9
53 Kilspindie E 7
47 Kilsyth B 12
41 Kilton, Cleveland C 7
6 Kilton, Somerset B 5
62 Kilvaxter A 3
6 Kilve B 5
32 Kilvington F 5
47 Kilwinning E 8
26 Kimberley, Norf. E 4
32 Kimberley, Notts. F 2
17 Kimble Wick C 9
45 Kimblesworth H 11
25 Kimbolton, Cambs. H 2
21 Kimbolton,
Heref. & Worcs. F 10
23 Kimcote C 9
7 Kimmeridge H 12
49 Kimmerston F 12
8 Kimpton, Hants. A 4
18 Kimpton, Herts. B 2
53 Kinalty A 9
61 Kinbrace D 8
55 Kinbreack K 4
52 Kinbuck G 3
47 Kincaidston G 8
53 Kincaple E 9
52 Kincardine, Fife H 4
60 Kincardine, Highland G 6
59 Kincardine O'Neil G 3
52 Kinclaven C 6
59 Kincorth G 7
56 Kincorth House D 6
57 Kincraig J 4
52 Kindallachan B 5
56 Kindrummond F 2
46 Kinerarach D 2
16 Kineton, Glos. B 2
23 Kineton, War. G 7
52 Kinfauns E 6
15 King Stanley D 11
50 Kingairloch Ho. B 6
46 Kingarth D 6
15 Kincoed D 7
33 Kingerby A 7
4 Kingford D 5
16 Kingham B 3
43 Kingholm Quay D 10
48 Kinghorn A 5
53 Kinglassie G 7
58 Kingoodie, Grampian E 6
53 Kingoodie, Tayside D 8
21 King's Acre H 10
31 Kings Bromley H 9
15 Kings Caple A 9
24 King's Cliffe F 1
22 King's Coughton F 4
22 Kings Heath D 4
17 Kings Langley D 11
24 King's Lynn D 7
39 King's Meaburn C 8
48 Kings Muir E 5
31 Kings Newton H 12
23 King's Norton, Leics. B 10
22 King's Norton,
W. Midlands D 4
4 King's Nympton D 6
21 King's Pyon G 10
25 Kings Ripton H 4
8 Kings Samborne C 5
7 King's Stag E 10
16 King's Sutton A 6
18 King's Walden B 2
11 Kings Wood C 7
8 Kings Worth C 6
3 Kingsand E 11
53 Kingsbarns F 10
5 Kingsbridge, Devon L 6
6 Kingsbridge, Som. C 3
62 Kingsburgh C 3
18 Kingsbury, London E 2
22 Kingsbury, War. C 6
7 Kingsbury Episcopi D 8
16 Kingsclere H 6
15 Kingscote E 11
4 Kingscott D 4
46 Kingscross G 5
7 Kingsdon D 8
11 Kingsdown C 12
52 Kingseat H 6
17 Kinsey C 4
10 Kingsfold D 1
59 Kingsford, Grampian G 6
22 Kingsford,
Heref & Worcs. D 2
47 Kingsford, Strathclyde E 9
27 Kingshall Street J 2
4 Kingsheanton B 4
52 Kingshouse E 1
51 Kinghouse Hotel B 10
5 Kingskerswell J 7
53 Kingskettle F 8
28 Kingsland, Gwynedd B 2
21 Kingsland,
Heref. & Worcs. F 10
30 Kingsley, Ches. C 4
9 Kingsley, Hants. B 9
31 Kingsley, Staffs. F 8
9 Kingsley Green C 10
31 Kingsley Holt F 9
53 Kingsmuir B 9
11 Kingsnorth D 9
22 Kingstanding C 4
5 Kingsteignton H 7
15 Kingsthorne A 8
23 Kingsthorpe F 11
25 Kingston, Cambs. K 4
5 Kingston, Devon L 5
7 Kingston, Dorset E 11
8 Kingston, Dorset H 1
58 Kingston, Grampian A 1
8 Kingston, Hants. F 3
8 Kingston, I.o.W. H 6
11 Kingston, Kent C 10
49 Kingston, Lothian A 8
9 Kingston, W. Sussex F 12
16 Kingston Bagpuize D 5
17 Kingston Blount D 8
10 Kingston by Sea H 1
7 Kingston Deverill C 11
16 Kingston Lisle E 4
10 Kingston near Lewes G 3
32 Kingston on Soar G 2
7 Kingston Russell G 9
6 Kingston St Mary C 6
15 Kingston Seymour H 7
37 Kingston upon Hull D 8
18 Kingston upon Thames G 2
18 Kingston Vale G 2
15 Kingstone,
Heref. & Worcs. A 7
7 Kingstone, Som. E 7
31 Kingstone, Staffs. G 9
44 Kingstown G 2
5 Kingswear K 7
22 Kingswinford C 2
15 Kingswood, Avon G 9
17 Kingswood, Bucks. B 8
15 Kingswood, Glos. E 10
21 Kingswood, Powys B 8
10 Kingswood, Surrey B 1
22 Kingswood, War. E 5
21 Kingswood Com. G 8
21 Kington,
Heref. & Worcs. G 8
22 Kington,
Heref. & Worcs. G 3
15 Kington Langley G 12
7 Kington Magna D 11
15 Kington St. Michael F 12
57 Kingussie J 3
7 Kingweston C 8
43 Kinharvie E 10
52 Kinkell Bridge E 4
58 Kinknockie, Grampian C 7
58 Kinknockie, Grampian E 7
44 Kinkry Hill E 3
22 Kinlet D 1
53 Kinloch, Fife F 7
62 Kinloch, Highland F 6
60 Kinloch, Highland D 4
52 Kinloch, Tayside C 6
53 Kinloch, Tayside C 7
62 Kinloch Castle H 3
55 Kinloch Hourn J 3
57 Kinloch Laggan K 1
60 Kinloch Lodge B 6
52 Kinloch Rannoch A 2
50 Kinlochan A 5
51 Kinlochard G 11
55 Kinlochbeoraid L 2
60 Kinlochbervie B 3
55 Kinlocheil L 4
51 Kinlochetive C 8
54 Kinlochewe D 4
51 Kinlochleven A 9
55 Kinlochmoidart M 1
55 Kinlochmorar K 2
51 Kinlochmore A 9
50 Kinlochspelve E 4
55 Kinloid L 1
56 Kinloss D 6
29 Kinmel Bay B 9
58 Kinmuck F 6
58 Kinnadie C 7
54 Kinnahaird D 8
59 Kinnaid Castle L 4
53 Kinnaird D 7
59 Kinneff K 6
43 Kinnelhead B 11
53 Kinnell B 10
30 Kinnerley H 2
21 Kinnersley,
Heref. & Worcs. G 9
22 Kinnersley,
Heref. & Worcs. H 2
21 Kinnerton F 8
52 Kinnesswood G 6
40 Kinninvie C 1
53 Kinnordy B 8
32 Kinoulton G 4
57 Kinrara J 4
52 Kinross G 6
53 Kinrossie D 7
21 Kinsham F 9
36 Kinsley F 2
8 Kinson F 2
63 Kintaravay E 3
16 Kintbury G 5
56 Kintessack D 6
52 Kintillo E 6
59 Kintocher G 3
21 Kinton,
Heref. & Worcs. E 9
30 Kinton, Salop. H 2
58 Kintore F 5
50 Kintra F 1
56 Kintrae C 7
50 Kintraw G 5
50 Kinuachdrach H 4
57 Kinveachy H 5
22 Kinver D 2
36 Kippax D 2
52 Kippen H 1
43 Kippford or Scaur F 9
10 Kipping's Cross D 5
64 Kirbister D 2
38 Kirby H 2
26 Kirby Bedon E 6
32 Kirby Bellars H 4
26 Kirby Cane F 7
19 Kirby Cross B 12
41 Kirby Grindalythe H 9
40 Kirby Hill, N. Yorks. E 2
40 Kirby Hill, N. Yorks. H 4
40 Kirby Knowle F 5
19 Kirby le Soken B 12
41 Kirby Misperton G 8
23 Kirby Muxloe B 8
35 Kirby Overblow B 12
26 Kirby Row F 7
40 Kirby Sigston F 4
36 Kirby Underdale A 6
40 Kirby Wiske G 4
9 Kirdford C 11
63 Kirivick C 3
61 Kirk B 11
36 Kirk Bramwith F 4
35 Kirk Deighton B 12
37 Kirk Ella D 8
32 Kirk Hallam F 2
36 Kirk Hammerton B 3
31 Kirk Ireton E 11
31 Kirk Langley F 11
40 Kirk Merrington B 3
38 Kirk Michael G 1
48 Kirk of Shotts C 1
36 Kirk Sandall F 4
36 Kirk Smeaton E 3
49 Kirk Yetholm G 11
64 Kirkabister E 7
43 Kirkandrews G 7
44 Kirkandrews on Eden G 2
44 Kirkbampton G 1
43 Kirkbank C 11
43 Kirkbean F 10
64 Kirkbrae A 2
44 Kirkbride, Cumb. G 1
43 Kirkbride,
Dumf. & Gall. C 9
53 Kirkbuddo C 9
48 Kirkburn, Borders F 5
37 Kirkburn, Humber. B 7
35 Kirkburton F 10
34 Kirkby, Merseyside G 3
33 Kirkby, Lincs. A 8
40 Kirkby, N. Yorks. E 5
40 Kirkby Fleetham F 3
33 Kirkby Green D 8
32 Kirkby in Ashfield E 2
24 Kirkby le Thorpe A 2
39 Kirkby Lonsdale G 8
35 Kirkby Malham A 7
23 Kirkby Mallory B 8
40 Kirkby Malzeard H 2
41 Kirkby Mills G 7
33 Kirkby on Bain D 9
39 Kirkby Stephen D 10
39 Kirkby Thore C 9
24 Kirkby Underwood C 2
36 Kirkby Wharf C 3
41 Kirkbymoorside F 7
53 Kirkcaldy H 7
44 Kirkcambeck F 4
43 Kirkcarswell G 8
42 Kirkcolm E 1
47 Kirkconnel H 12
43 Kirkconnell,
Dumf. & Gall. E 10
43 Kirkconnell,
Dumf. & Gall. F 7
42 Kirkcowan E 4
43 Kirkcudbright F 8
30 Kirkdale A 2
42 Kirkdale House F 6
49 Kirkdean E 4
48 Kirkfieldbank E 1
43 Kirkgunzeon E 9
34 Kirkham, Lancs. D 3
36 Kirkham, N. Yorks. A 5
35 Kirkhamgate E 11
45 Kirkharle E 8
45 Kirkheaton, Northumb. E 8
35 Kirkheaton,
W. Yorks. E 10
56 Kirkhill, Highland E 1
48 Kirkhill, Lothian C 5
59 Kirkhill, Tayside L 4
48 Kirkhope G 6
48 Kirkhouse F 6
62 Kirkibost, Highland F 5
63 Kirkibost, W. Isles C 3
53 Kirkinch C 8
42 Kirkinner F 5
47 Kirkintilloch B 11
39 Kirkland, Cumb. B 9
38 Kirkland, Cumb. C 3
43 Kirkland,
Dumf. & Gall. C 9
43 Kirkland,
Dumf. & Gall. C 11
47 Kirkland,
Dumf. & Gall. H 12
42 Kirkland,
Dumf. & Gall. G 5
43 Kirkland Guards G 12
43 Kirkland of Gelston F 8
40 Kirkleatham C 6
40 Kirklevington D 4
26 Kirkley F 8
45 Kirkley March E 9
32 Kirklington, Notts. D 4
40 Kirklington, N. Yorks. G 3
44 Kirklinton F 3
48 Kirkliston B 4
42 Kirkmaiden H 2
42 Kirkmichael,
Strathclyde A 4
52 Kirkmichael, Tayside A 6
47 Kirkmuirhill E 12
48 Kirknewton, Lothian C 4
49 Kirknewton,
Northumb. F 11
58 Kirkney D 3
39 Kirkoswald, Cumb. A 8
42 Kirkoswald,
Strathclyde A 3
43 KirkpatrickDurham D 8
44 Kirkpatrick-Fleming F 1
38 Kirksanton G 4
33 Kirkstead D 9
44 Kirkstile,
Dumf. & Gall. D 2
58 Kirkstile, Grampian D 3
58 Kirkston of Culsalmond D 4
61 Kirkstyle A 12
44 Kirkton, Borders B 4
43 Kirkton,
Dumf. & Gall. C 10
53 Kirkton, Fife E 8
58 Kirkton, Grampian C 6
58 Kirkton, Grampian E 4
58 Kirkton, Grampian F 6
58 Kirkton, Grampian F 4
58 Kirkton, Grampian C 4
56 Kirkton, Highland F 2
56 Kirkton, Highland C 3
54 Kirkton, Highland F 3
48 Kirkton, Strathclyde G 2
53 Kirkton, Tayside C 9
59 Kirkton, Tayside J 2
48 Kirkton Manor D 5
53 Kirkton of Airlie B 8
53 Kirkton of
Auchterhouse C 8
59 Kirkton of Balfour K 3
56 Kirkton of Barevan E 4
53 Kirkton of Collace D 7
53 Kirkton of Craig B 11
59 Kirkton of Durris H 5
58 Kirkton of Glenbuchat F 1
Kirkton of Glenisla A 7
53 Kirkton of Kingoldrum B 8
53 Kirkton of Largo G 9

52 Kirkton of Lethendy **C 6**
58 Kirkton of Logie Buchan **E 7**
59 Kirkton of Menmuir **L 3**
53 Kirkton of Monikie **C 10**
58 Kirkton of Oyne **E 4**
59 Kirkton of Skene **G 5**
53 Kirkton of Strathmartine **D 8**
53 Kirkton of Tealing **C 9**
53 Kirktonbarns **D 9**
58 Kirktown **B 8**
58 Kirktown of Alvah **B 4**
58 Kirktown of Auchterless **C 5**
58 Kirktown of Bourtie **E 5**
58 Kirktown of Deskford **B 2**
59 Kirktown of Fetteresso **J 6**
58 Kirktown of Mortlach **D 1**
58 Kirktown of Rayne **E 4**
58 Kirktown of Slains **E 8**
64 Kirkwall **D 2**
45 Kirkwhelpington **E 8**
37 Kirmington **F 9**
33 Kirmond le Mire **A 9**
47 Kirn **B 7**
43 Kirncleuch **B 12**
53 Kirriemuir **B 8**
26 Kirstead Green **F 6**
44 Kirtlebridge **F 1**
44 Kirtleton **E 1**
25 Kirtling **J 8**
25 Kirtling Green **K 8**
16 Kirtlington **B 6**
61 Kirtomy **B 7**
56 Kirton, Highland **D 3**
24 Kirton, Lincs. **B 4**
32 Kirton, Notts. **C 4**
27 Kirton, Suffolk **L 6**
24 Kirton End **B 4**
24 Kirton Holme **A 4**
37 Kirton in Lindsey **G 7**
23 Kislingbury **F 10**
23 Kites Hardwick **E 8**
6 Kittisford **D 4**
13 Kittle **H 9**
31 Kitts Moss **B 7**
59 Kittybrewster **G 7**
9 Kitwood **C 8**
4 Kiverley **D 4**
15 Kivernoll **A 8**
32 Kiveton Park **B 2**
60 Klibreck **D 6**
32 Knaith **B 5**
32 Knaith Park **B 5**
7 Knap Corner **D 11**
17 Knaphill **H 10**
6 Knapp, Somerset **D 6**
53 Knapp, Tayside **D 7**
58 Knaps of Auchlee **C 8**
26 Knapton, Norfolk **B 6**
36 Knapton, N. Yorks. **B 3**
21 Knapton Green **G 10**
25 Knapwell **J 4**
35 Knaresborough **A 12**
44 Knarsdale **H 5**
58 Knauchland **B 3**
40 Knayton **F 4**
18 Knebworth **B 3**
36 Knedlington **D 5**
32 Kneesall **D 4**
25 Kneesworth **L 4**
32 Kneeton **F 4**
13 Knelston **H 8**
27 Knettishall **G 3**
4 Knightacott **B 5**
23 Knightcote **G 7**
5 Knighton, Devon **L 4**
7 Knighton, Dorset **E 9**
23 Knighton, Leics. **B 9**
21 Knighton, Powys **E 8**
30 Knighton, Staffs. **F 6**
30 Knighton, Staffs. **G 6**
16 Knighton, Wilts. **G 4**
22 Knightsford Bridge **G 1**
21 Knill **F 8**
32 Knipton **G 5**
45 Knitsley **H 9**
31 Kniveton **E 10**
39 Knock, Cumbria **B 9**
58 Knock, Grampian **B 3**
62 Knock, Highland **G 6**
50 Knock, Strathclyde **D 3**
63 Knock, W. Isles **D 6**
60 Knockan **F 3**
56 Knockando **E 7**
57 Knockandhu **G 8**
60 Knockanrock **F 3**
61 Knockarthur **F 7**
56 Knockbain **D 2**
62 Knockbreck **B 2**
43 Knockbrex **G 7**
61 Knockdee **B 11**
42 Knockdolian Cas. **C 2**
42 Knockdon **B 5**
47 Knockendon **D 7**
46 Knockenkelly **G 5**
47 Knockentiber **E 9**
58 Knockespock Ho. **E 3**
42 Knockgardner **A 4**
42 Knockglass **F 1**
10 Knockholt **B 4**
55 Knockie Lodge **H 8**
30 Knockin **H 2**
47 Knockinlaw **E 9**
42 Knocklaugh **B 3**
43 Knocklearn **D 8**
42 Knocknain **E 1**
46 Knockrome **B 1**
53 Knockshannoch **A 7**
38 Knocksharry **G 1**
42 Knocksheen **C 6**
43 Knockvennie **D 8**
42 Knockycoid **D 3**
27 Knodishall **J 7**
7 Knole **D 8**
15 Knole Park **F 9**
30 Knolls Green **B 6**
30 Knolton **F 2**
8 Knook **B 1**
23 Knossington **A 11**
34 Knott End-on-Sea **B 2**
25 Knotting **J 1**
25 Knotting Green **J 1**
36 Knottingley **E 3**
39 Knotts **C 7**
30 Knotty Ash **A 3**
17 Knotty Green **E 10**
21 Knowbury **E 11**
42 Knowe **D 4**
43 Knowhead, Dumf. & Gall. **C 7**
58 Knowhead, Grampian **F 2**
45 Knowesgate **D 8**
47 Knoweside **H 7**
49 Knowetownhead **G 8**
27 Knowl Green **L 1**
17 Knowl Hill **F 9**
15 Knowle, Avon **G 9**
6 Knowle, Devon **H 4**
4 Knowle, Devon **F 6**
4 Knowle, Devon **B 4**
21 Knowle, Shrop. **E 11**
7 Knowle, Somerset **B 7**
22 Knowle, W. Midlands **D 5**
34 Knowle Green **C 5**
8 Knowlton, Dorset **E 2**
11 Knowlton, Kent **C 11**
58 Knowsie **B 8**
34 Knowsley **H 3**
6 Knowstone **D 7**
10 Knox Brdige **D 6**
21 Knucklas **E 8**
10 Knutsford **B 6**
31 Knypersley **E 7**
2 Kuggar **H 4**
55 Kyle of Lochalsh **G 1**
55 Kyleakin **G 1**
55 Kylerhea **G 2**
63 Kyles Scalpay **G 3**
63 Kyles Stockinish **H 2**
55 Kylesbeg **M 1**
55 Kylesknoydart **K 2**
60 Kylesku **D 3**
55 Kylesmorar **K 2**
60 Kylestrome **D 4**
57 Kyllachy House **G 3**
15 Kymin **C 8**
15 Kynaston **B 8**
21 Kynnersley **A 12**
21 Kyre Park **F 11**
63 Labost **B 4**
37 Laceby **F 10**
17 Lacey Green **D 9**
30 Lach Dennis **C 5**
63 Lackalee **H 2**
40 Lackenby **C 6**
27 Lackford **H 1**
15 Lacock **G 12**
23 Ladbroke **F 7**
10 Laddingford **C 6**
33 Lade Bank **E 11**
2 Ladock **E 6**
53 Ladybank, Fife **F 8**
42 Ladybank, Strathclyde **A 3**
3 Ladycross **A 10**
49 Ladyflat **D 10**
49 Ladykirk **E 11**
58 Ladyleys **E 6**
58 Ladysford **B 6**
43 Lag **C 9**
50 Laga **B 4**
50 Lagalochan **F 6**
42 Lagg, Strathclyde **B 1**
46 Lagg, Strathclyde **G 4**
52 Laggan, Central **F 1**
58 Laggan, Grampian **D 1**
55 Laggan, Highland **K 7**
57 Laggan, Highland **K 2**
42 Laggan, Strathclyde **C 2**
42 Laggan, Strathclyde **C 3**
57 Lagganlia **J 4**
42 Lagganmullan **F 6**
50 Lagganulva **C 2**
60 Laid **B 5**
60 Laide **G 1**
47 Laigh Braidley **E 10**
47 Laigh Brocklar **G 10**
47 Laigh Cleughearn **D 11**
47 Laigh Fenwick **E 9**
47 Laighmuir **E 9**
47 Laighstonehall **D 12**
43 Laight **B 9**
19 Laindon **E 7**
57 Laintachan **H 6**
60 Lairg **F 6**
60 Lairg Muir **F 6**
60 Lairg Station **F 6**
51 Lairigmor **A 8**
35 Laisterdyke **D 10**
39 Laithes **B 7**
8 Lake **B 3**
56 Lake of Moy **D 6**
38 Lake Side **F 6**
25 Lakenheath **G 8**
24 Lakesend **F 6**
17 Laleham **G 11**
14 Laleston **F 2**
48 Lamancha **D 5**
27 Lamarsh **L 2**
26 Lamas **C 5**
27 Lamb Corner **M 3**
64 Lambaness **B 4**
49 Lambden **E 10**
10 Lamberhurst **D 5**
10 Lamberhurst Quarter **D 5**
18 Lambeth **F 3**
32 Lambley, Notts. **F 3**
44 Lambley, Northumb. **G 5**
16 Lambourn **F 4**
18 Lambourne End **D 5**
10 Lambs Green **D 1**
12 Lambston **E 3**
3 Lamellion **C 9**
5 Lamerton **H 3**
45 Lamesley **G 10**
42 Lamford **B 6**
56 Lamington, Highland **B 3**
48 Lamington, Strathclyde **F 3**
46 Lamlash **F 5**
42 Lamloch **B 6**
38 Lamonby **B 6**
2 Lamorna **G 2**
2 Lamorran **E 6**
13 Lampeter **B 9**
12 Lampeter Velfrey **F 5**
12 Lamphey **G 4**
38 Lamplugh **C 3**
23 Lamport **E 11**
7 Lamyatt **C 10**
4 Lana, Devon **F 2**
4 Lana, Devon **E 2**
48 Lanark **E 2**
34 Lancashire, Co. **E 5**
34 Lancaster **A 4**
45 Lanchester **H 10**
6 Landacre **C 2**
25 Lanbeach **J 6**
4 Landcross **D 3**
59 Landerberry **G 5**
2 Landewednack **H 4**
8 Landford **D 4**
8 Landford Manor **D 4**
13 Landimore **H 8**
4 Landkey **C 5**
13 Landlore **G 10**
3 Landrake, Corn. **D 10**
6 Landrake, Devon **D 3**
12 Landshipping **F 4**
3 Landulph **D 11**
22 Landywood **B 3**
2 Lane **D 5**
17 Lane End, Bucks. **E 9**
38 Lane End, Cumb. **F 3**
9 Lane End, Hants. **D 7**
9 Lane End, Hants. **G 8**
10 Lane End, Kent **A 4**
40 Lane Ends **B 2**
31 Lane Head, Derby **C 10**
40 Lane Head, Dur. **D 1**
34 Lane Head, Manchester **G 5**
3 Laneast **A 9**
32 Laneham **C 5**
44 Lanehad **D 6**
35 Laneshawbridge **C 8**
32 Langar **G 4**
47 Langbank **B 8**
35 Langbar **B 9**
44 Langburnshiels **C 4**
35 Langcliffe **A 7**
41 Langdale End **F 9**
2 Langdon, Corn. **B 2**
3 Langdon, Corn. **A 10**
15 Langdon, Heref. & Worc. **A 11**
39 Langdon Beck **B 11**
19 Langdon Hills **E 7**
53 Langdyke **G 8**
19 Langenhoe **B 10**
25 Langford, Beds. **L 3**
6 Langford, Devon **F 4**
19 Langford, Essex **C 8**
32 Langford, Notts. **D 5**
16 Langford, Oxon **D 3**
6 Langford Budville **D 4**
25 Langford End **K 3**
27 Langham, Essex **M 3**
23 Langham, Leics. **A 11**
26 Langham, Norf. **B 3**
27 Langham, Suffolk **H 3**
34 Langho **D 6**
44 Langholm, Dumf. & Gall. **E 2**
48 Langholm, Strathclyde **F 3**
49 Langleeford **G 12**
17 Langley, Berks. **F 11**
31 Langley, Ches. **C 8**
8 Langley, Hants. **F 6**
18 Langley, Herts. **B 2**
11 Langley, Kent **C 7**
44 Langley, Northumb. **G 6**
6 Langley, Som. **C 4**
22 Langley, War. **F 5**
9 Langley, W. Sussex **C 9**
15 Langley Burrell **G 12**
10 Langley Green **D 1**
11 Langley Heath **C 7**
25 Langley Lower Green **M 5**
32 Langley Mill **E 2**
40 Langley Moor **A 3**
40 Langley Park **A 2**
26 Langley Street **E 7**
25 Langley Upper Green **M 5**
10 Langney **H 5**
32 Langold **B 3**
3 Langore **A 10**
7 Langport **D 7**
33 Langrick **E 9**
15 Langridge **G 10**
4 Langridge Ford **D 4**
43 Langrigg **G 12**
9 Langrish **D 8**
33 Langriville **E 10**
35 Langsett **G 10**
49 Langshaw **E 8**
47 Langside, Strathclyde **D 8**
52 Langside, Tayside **F 3**
64 Langskaill **A 2**
9 Langstone **F 8**
40 Langthorne, N. Yorks. **F 3**
40 Langthorpe, N. Yorks. **H 4**
39 Langthwaite **E 12**
41 Langtoft, Humberside **H 10**
24 Langtoft, Lincs. **D 2**
40 Langton, Dur. **C 2**
33 Langton, Lincs. **C 9**
33 Langton, Lincs. **C 11**
41 Langton, N. Yorks. **H 8**
33 Langton by Wragby **C 8**
10 Langton Green **D 4**
7 Langton Herring **H 9**
8 Langton Matravers **H 2**
4 Langtree **D 3**
39 Langwathby **B 8**
60 Langwell **G 5**
32 Langwith Junc. **C 3**
33 Langworth **C 8**
3 Lanivet **C 7**
3 Lank **B 8**
3 Lanlivery **D 8**
2 Lanner **F 4**
3 Lanreath **D 9**
52 Lanrick Castle **G 2**
3 Lansallos **E 9**
15 Lansdown, Avon **G 10**
16 Lansdown, Glos. **B 3**
3 Lanteglos Highway **D 8**
49 Lanton, Borders **G 9**
49 Lanton, Northumb. **F 11**
4 Lapford **E 6**
22 Lapley **A 2**
22 Lapworth **E 5**
50 Larachbeg **C 4**
48 Larbert **A 1**
43 Larbreck **D 9**
58 Largie **D 4**
46 Largiemore **A 4**
53 Largoward **F 9**
47 Largs **C 7**
46 Largymore **G 5**
10 Larkfield, Kent **B 6**
47 Larkfield, Strathclyde **B 7**
47 Larkhall **D 12**
8 Larkhill **B 3**
26 Larling **F 3**
51 Laroch **B 8**
44 Larriston **D 4**
39 Lartington **C 12**
59 Lary **G 1**
9 Lasham **B 8**
40 Laskill **F 6**
15 Lassington **B 11**
52 Lassodie **H 6**
41 Lastingham **F 7**
19 Latchingdon & Shoreham **D 8**
3 Latchley **B 11**
17 Latchmeregreen **H 7**
34 Lately Common **G 5**
23 Lathbury **H 11**
61 Latheron **D 11**
53 Lathockar **F 9**
53 Lathones **F 9**
17 Latimer **D 10**
38 Latterhead **C 4**
15 Latteridge **F 10**
7 Lattiford **D 10**
16 Latton **E 2**
58 Lauchintilly **F 5**
50 Laudale House **B 5**
49 Lauder **E 8**
12 Laugharne **F 6**
32 Laughterton **C 5**
10 Laughton, E. Sussex **G 4**
36 Laughton, Humber. **G 6**
23 Laughton, Leics. **C 10**
32 Laughton en le Morthen **A 2**
4 Launcells **E 1**
3 Launceston **A 10**
7 Launcherley **B 9**
17 Launton **B 7**
38 Laurel Bank **G 1**
59 Laurencekirk **K 5**
48 Laurieston, Central **A 2**
43 Laurieston, Dumf. & Gall. **E 7**
23 Lavendon **G 12**
27 Lavenham **K 2**
43 Laverhay **B 12**
14 Lavernock **G 5**
8 Laverstock **C 3**
8 Laverstoke **A 6**
16 Laverton, Glos. **A 2**
40 Laverton, N. Yorks. **H 2**
7 Laverton, Som. **A 11**
30 Lavister **D 2**
48 Law **D 1**
52 Lawers, Tayside **C 2**
52 Lawers, Tayside **E 3**
27 Lawford **M 4**
3 Lawhitton **A 10**
39 Lawkland **H 10**
21 Lawley **B 12**
31 Lawnhead **H 7**
12 Lawrenny **F 4**
27 Lawshall **K 2**
21 Lawton **F 10**
63 Laxay **E 4**
63 Laxdale **C 5**
38 Laxey **G 2**
27 Laxfield **H 6**
64 Laxfirth **D 7**
60 Laxford Bridge **C 4**
64 Laxo **C 7**
64 Laxobigging **C 7**
36 Laxton, Humber. **E 6**
24 Laxton, Northants. **F 1**
32 Laxton, Notts. **D 4**
35 Laycock **C 9**
19 Layer Breton **B 9**
19 Layer-de-la-Haye **B 9**
19 Layer Marney **B 9**
27 Layham **L 3**
16 Layland's Green **G 5**
7 Laymore **F 7**
21 Laysters Pole **F 11**
36 Laytham **C 5**
40 Lazenby **C 6**
39 Lazonby **A 8**
31 Lea, Derby **D 11**
15 Lea, Heref. & Worc. **B 10**
32 Lea, Lincs. **B 5**
21 Lea, Shropshire **B 9**
21 Lea, Shropshire **C 9**
15 Lea, Wilts. **F 12**
22 Lea Marston **C 5**
34 Lea Town **D 4**
39 Lea Yeat **F 10**
32 Leabrooke **E 1**
55 Leachachan **G 3**
56 Leachkin **E 2**
48 Leadburn **D 5**
18 Leaden Roding **C 6**
33 Leadenham **E 7**
49 Leaderfoot **F 8**
39 Leadgate, Cumb. **A 9**
45 Leadgate, Dur. **H 9**
45 Leadgate, Tyne & Wear **G 9**
48 Leadhills **H 2**
16 Leafield **C 4**
17 Leagrave **B 11**
40 Leake **F 4**
33 Leake Common Side **E 11**
33 Leake Hurn's End **E 11**
41 Lealholm **D 8**
62 Lealt **B 4**
23 Leamington **E 7**
23 Leamington Hastings **E 8**
22 Leamonsley **A 4**
45 Leamside **H 11**
51 Leanach **H 7**
55 Leanachan **L 6**
56 Leanaig **D 1**
46 Leargybreck **B 1**
39 Leasgill **G 7**
33 Leasingham **E 7**
40 Leasingthorne **B 3**
17 Leatherhead **H 12**
35 Leathley **B 11**
43 Leaths **E 8**
30 Leaton **H 3**
11 Leaveland **C 8**
36 Leavening **A 5**
18 Leaves Green **H 4**
18 Leavesden Green **D 1**
45 Leazes **G 10**
41 Lebberston **G 10**
16 Lechlade **D 3**
39 Leck **G 9**
8 Leckford **B 5**
61 Leckfurin **B 7**
16 Leckhampstead, Berks. **G 5**
23 Leckhampstead, Bucks. **H 10**
16 Leckhampstead Street **F 5**
16 Leckhampstead Thicket **F 5**
15 Leckhampton **B 12**
54 Leckie **C 5**
60 Leckmelm **G 3**
55 Leckroy **K 7**
14 Leckwith **G 5**
37 Leconfield **C 8**
50 Ledaig **D 6**
17 Ledburn **B 10**
15 Ledbury **A 10**
51 Ledcharrie **E 12**
21 Ledgemoor **G 9**
54 Ledgowan **D 5**
21 Ledicot **F 9**
60 Ledmore **F 4**
61 Lednagullin **B 8**
30 Ledsham, Ches. **C 2**
36 Ledsham, W. Yorks. **D 2**
36 Ledston **D 2**
16 Ledwell **A 5**
4 Lee, Devon **A 4**
8 Lee, Hampshire **D 5**
34 Lee, Lancashire **B 4**
30 Lee, Shropshire **G 3**
30 Lee Brockenhurst **G 4**
17 Lee Clump **D 10**
5 Lee Mill Bridge **K 5**
5 Lee Mill Estate **K 5**
5 Lee Moor **J 4**
9 Lee-on-the-Solent **F 7**
21 Leebotwood **C 10**
38 Leece **H 5**
11 Leeds, Kent **C 7**
35 Leeds, W. Yorks. **D 11**
2 Leedstown **F 3**
31 Leek **E 8**
22 Leek Wootton **E 6**
40 Leeming **F 3**
40 Leeming Bar **F 3**
31 Lees, Derby **F 11**
35 Lees, Manchester **G 8**
44 Lees Hill **F 4**
29 Leeswood **D 12**
30 Leftwich **C 5**
33 Legbourne **B 10**
49 Legerwood **E 8**
33 Legsby **B 8**
23 Leicester **B 9**
23 Leicestershire, Co. **B 9**
23 Leicester For. East. **B 8**
7 Leigh, Dorset **E 9**
15 Leigh, Glos. **B 11**
10 Leigh, Kent **C 4**
34 Leigh, Manchester **G 5**
21 Leigh, Shropshire **B 9**
10 Leigh, Surrey **C 1**
16 Leigh, Wiltshire **E 2**
22 Leigh, Heref. & Worc. **G 1**
19 Leigh Beck **F 8**
15 Leigh Delamere **F 12**
11 Leigh Green **E 8**
19 Leigh-on-Sea **E 8**

9 Leigh Park E 8
22 Leigh Sinton G 1
7 Leigh upon Mendip B 10
6 Leighland Chapel C 4
15 Leighterton E 11
40 Leighton, N. Yorks. G 2
21 Leighton, Powys B 8
21 Leighton, Salop B 11
7 Leighton, Som. B 10
25 Leighton Bromswold H 2
17 Leighton Buzzard B 10
59 Leightonhill L 4
15 Leighwoods G 9
21 Leinthall Earls F 10
21 Leinthall Starkes E 10
21 Leintwardine E 9
23 Leire C 8
60 Leirinmore A 5
27 Leiston J 7
53 Leitfie C 7
48 Leith B 5
49 Leitholm E 10
2 Lelant F 3
37 Lelley D 10
56 Lemlair D 1
45 Lemmington Hall B 9
49 Lempitlaw F 10
63 Lemreway F 5
18 Lemsford C 2
58 Lenabo C 8
22 Lenchwick G 4
42 Lendalfoot C 2
51 Lendrick G 12
11 Lenham C 7
11 Lenham Heath C 8
49 Lennel E 11
42 Lennies F 5
47 Lennoxtown B 11
17 Lent Rise F 10
24 Lenton C 1
26 Lenwade D 4
47 Lenzie B 11
58 Leochel-Cushnie F 3
21 Leominster F 10
15 Leonard Stanley D 11
8 Lepe F 6
62 Lephin C 1
51 Lephinchapel H 7
51 Lephinmore H 7
36 Leppington A 5
35 Lepton F 10
50 Lerags E 6
3 Lerryn D 8
64 Lerwick E 7
45 Lesbury B 10
53 Leslie, Fife G 7
58 Leslie, Grampian E 3
48 Lesmahagow E 1
2 Lesnewth B 2
26 Lessingham C 7
44 Lessonhall H 1
42 Leswalt E 1
18 Letchmore Heath D 2
25 Letchworth M 3
16 Letcombe Bassett F 5
16 Letcombe Regis E 5
53 Letham, Fife F 8
53 Letham, Tayside B 10
52 Letham, Tayside E 6
53 Letham Grange C 11
56 Lethen House D 5
57 Lethendryveole H 5
58 Lethenty D 5
27 Letheringham J 6
26 Letheringsett B 4
5 Lettaford G 6
64 Lettan A 4
54 Letterewe C 3
55 Letterfearn G 3
55 Letterfinlay K 6
55 Lettermorar K 1
50 Lettermore C 2
60 Letters H 3
48 Lettershaws G 2
12 Letterston D 3
57 Lettoch, Highland H 6
56 Lettoch, Highland F 6
21 Letton, Heref. & Worc. E 9
21 Letton, Heref. & Worc. H 9
18 Letty Green C 3
32 Letwell B 3
53 Leuchars E 9
56 Leuchars House C 8
63 Leurbost D 5
22 Levedale A 3
37 Leven, Humberside C 8
53 Leven, Fife G 8
46 Levencorroch G 5
39 Levens G 7
35 Levenshulme H 7
64 Levenwick F 7
63 Leverburgh H 1
24 Leverington D 5
16 Leverton, Berks. G 4
33 Leverton, Lincs. E 11
33 Leverton Outgate E 11
27 Levington L 5
41 Levisham F 8
55 Levishie H 8
16 Lew D 4
3 Lewannick B 9
5 Lewdown G 3
10 Lewes G 3
12 Leweston E 3
18 Lewisham G 3
57 Lewiston G 1
14 Lewistown E 3
17 Lewknor D 8
4 Leworthy B 5
63 Lews Castle D 5
11 Lewson Street B 8
5 Lewtrenchard G 3
3 Ley, Cornwall C 9
58 Ley, Grampian F 3
10 Leybourne B 5
40 Leyburn F 1
30 Leycett E 6
18 Leygreen B 2
17 Leyhill D 10
34 Leyland E 4
58 Leylodge F 5
58 Leys B 7
56 Leys Castle F 2
53 Leys of Cossans B 8
58 Leys of Dummuies D 3
11 Leysdown-on-Sea A 9
53 Leysmill B 10
18 Leyton E 4
18 Leytonstone E 4
3 Lezant B 10
54 Liatrie F 6
14 Libanus B 3
48 Liberton, Lothian B 5
48 Libberton, Strathclyde E 3
22 Lichfield A 5
22 Lickey E 3
22 Lickey End E 3
9 Lickfold D 10
50 Liddesdale B 5
16 Liddington F 3
25 Lidgate J 8
25 Lidlington L 1
16 Lidstone B 4
55 Lienassie G 3
53 Liff D 8
5 Lifton G 3
5 Liftondown G 2
23 Lighthorne G 7
17 Lightwater H 10
31 Lightwood F 7
23 Lilbourne D 9
49 Lilburn Hill G 12
45 Lilburn Tower A 8
25 Lilleshall A 1
16 Lilley, Berks. F 5
18 Lilley, Herts. A 1
49 Lilliesleaf G 8
23 Lillingstone Dayrell H 10
23 Lillingstone Lovell H 10
7 Lillington, Dorest E 9
23 Lillington, War. E 7
8 Lilliput G 2
6 Lilstock B 5
47 Lilybank B 8
34 Limbrick F 5
35 Limefield F 7
47 Limekilnburn D 12
48 Limekilns A 3
48 Limerigg B 1
8 Limestone H 6
44 Limestone Brae H 6
7 Limington D 8
26 Limpenhoe E 7
15 Limpley Stoke H 11
10 Limpsfield C 3
48 Linburn C 4
32 Linby E 3
9 Linchmere C 10
43 Lincluden D 10
33 Lincoln C 7
33 Lincolnshire, Co. D 8
22 Lincomb E 2
38 Lindal in Furness H 5
38 Lindale G 6
49 Lindean F 7
10 Lindfield E 2
9 Lindford C 9
53 Lindifferon E 8
35 Lindley E 10
35 Lindley Green B 11
53 Lindores E 7
21 Lindridge E 12
18 Lindsell A 6
27 Lindsey L 3
38 Linefoot B 3
19 Linford, Essex F 7
8 Linford, Hants. E 3
38 Lingague H 1
41 Lingdale D 7
21 Lingen F 9
10 Lingfield D 3
10 Lingfield Com. D 3
30 Lingley Green A 4
26 Lingwood E 7
44 Linhope, Borders C 2
45 Linhope, N'thumb. A 8
16 Linkenholt H 5
3 Linkinhorne B 10
64 Linklater E 2
53 Linktown H 7
21 Linley Green G 12
48 Linlithgow B 3
48 Linlithgow Bridge B 3
60 Linneraineach F 3
12 Linney G 2
43 Linns D 11
63 Linshader D 3
45 Linshiels B 7
60 Linsidemore G 6
17 Linslade B 10
27 Linstead Parva G 6
44 Linstock G 3
49 Linthaugh F 12
35 Linthwaite F 9
49 Lintlaw D 11
58 Lintmill A 3
49 Linton, Borders G 10
25 Linton, Cambs. K 7
22 Linton, Derby A 6
15 Linton, Heref. & Worc. B 9
10 Linton, Kent C 6
35 Linton, N. Yorks. A 8
35 Linton, W. Yorks. B 12
36 Linton-on-Ouse A 3
8 Linwood, Hants. E 3
33 Linwood, Lincs. B 8
47 Linwood, Strathclyde C 9
29 Lioc C 10
63 Lionel A 6
9 Liphook C 9
6 Liscombe C 2
3 Liskeard C 9
9 Liss C 9
9 Liss Forest C 9
37 Lisset A 9
33 Lissington B 8
14 Lisvane F 5
15 Liswerry F 7
26 Litcham D 2
23 Litchborough G 9
8 Litchfield A 6
34 Litherland G 2
25 Litlington, Camb. L 4
10 Litlington, E. Sussex H 4
25 Little Abington K 6
25 Little Addington H 1
25 Little Alne F 5
60 Little Assynt E 3
22 Little Aston B 4
8 Little Atherfield H 6
64 Little Ayre E 1
40 Little Ayton D 6
19 Little Baddow C 7
15 Little Badminton F 11
52 Little Ballinluig B 4
44 Little Bampton G 1
25 Little Bardfield M 8
25 Little Barford J 3
26 Little Barningham B 4
23 Little Barrington C 3
30 Little Barrow C 3
41 Little Barugh G 8
25 Little Bavington E 8
27 Little Bealings K 5
16 Little Bedwyn G 4
19 Little Bentley A 11
18 Little Berkhampsted C 3
23 Little Billing F 11
15 Little Birch A 8
27 Little Blakenham K 4
39 Little Blencow B 7
9 Little Bookham A 12
23 Little Bowden C 11
25 Little Bradley K 8
21 Little Brampton D 9
19 Little Braxted B 8
59 Little Brechin L 3
17 Little Brickhill A 10
23 Little Brington F 10
19 Little Bromley A 10
30 Little Budworth D 5
18 Little Burstead E 6
24 Little Bytham D 1
42 Little Cairnbrock E 1
33 Little Carlton, Lincs. B 11
32 Little Carlton, Notts. D 5
24 Little Casterton E 1
33 Little Cawthorpe B 10
17 Little Chalfont D 11
11 Little Chart D 8
7 Little Cheney G 9
25 Little Chesterford L 6
8 Little Cheverell A 2
25 Little Chishill L 5
19 Little Clacton B 11
38 Little Clifton B 3
58 Little Colp C 5
22 Little Comberton H 3
16 Little Compton A 4
27 Little Cornard L 2
21 Little Cowarne G 11
16 Little Coxwell E 4
40 Little Crakehall F 3
26 Little Cressingham E 2
34 Little Crosby G 2
23 Little Dalby A 11
21 Little Dawley B 12
58 Little Dens C 8
15 Little Dewchurch A 8
37 Little Driffield A 8
26 Little Dunham D 2
52 Little Dunkeld C 5
18 Little Dunmow B 6
18 Little Easton B 6
31 Little Eaton F 12
26 Little Ellingham E 3
7 Little Elm B 10
18 Little End D 5
25 Little Eversden K 5
27 Little Fakenham H 2
16 Little Faringdon D 3
40 Little Fencote F 3
36 Little Fenton D 3
26 Little Fransham D 2
17 Little Gaddesden C 11
15 Little Garway B 8
25 Little Gidding G 2
27 Little Glemham J 6
25 Little Gransden K 4
7 Little Green A 10
33 Little Grimsby A 10
60 Little Gruinard G 1
18 Little Hadham B 4
24 Little Hale B 2
18 Little Hallingbury B 5
17 Little Hampden D 9
23 Little Harrowden E 12
17 Little Haseley D 7
37 Little Hatfield C 9
12 Little Haven F 2
22 Little Hay B 5
31 Little Hayfield A 9
31 Little Haywood H 8
21 Little Hereford F 11
27 Little Horkesley M 2
18 Little Hormead A 4
10 Little Horsted F 3
35 Little Horton D 10
17 Little Horwood A 9
23 Little Houghton F 11
31 Little Hucklow B 10
34 Little Hulton G 6
23 Little Irchester E 12
37 Little Kelk A 8
17 Little Kimble C 9
17 Little Kingshill D 10
38 Little Langdale E 5
8 Little Langford C 2
58 Little Ledikin E 4
30 Little Leigh C 5
19 Little Leighs B 7
34 Little Lever F 6
23 Little Linford H 11
10 Little Londond, E. Sussex F 4
8 Little London, Hants. A 5
17 Little London, Hants. H 7
24 Little London, Lincs. C 5
35 Little London, W. Yorks. C 10
31 Little Longstone C 10
58 Little Lynturk F 3
22 Little Malvern H 1
27 Little Maplestead M 1
15 Little Marcle A 10
17 Little Marlow E 9
26 Little Massingham C 1
26 Little Melton E 5
12 Little Milford F 3
14 Little Mill D 6
17 Little Milton D 7
17 Little Missenden D 10
30 Little Ness H 3
30 Little Neston C 2
12 Little Newcastle D 3
40 Little Newsham C 1
19 Little Oakley, Essex A 12
23 Little Oakley, Northants. D 12
44 Little Orton G 2
36 Little Ouseburn A 2
25 Little Paxton J 3
2 Little Petherick B 6
42 Little Pinmore C 3
26 Little Plumstead D 6
32 Little Ponton G 6
4 Little Potheridge E 4
25 Little Raveley G 4
35 Little Ribson B 12
16 Little Rissington B 3
26 Little Ryburgh C 3
45 Little Ryle B 8
39 Little Salkeld B 8
8 Little Samborne C 5
25 Little Sampford M 7
17 Little Sandhurst H 9
27 Little Saxham J 1
54 Little Scatwell D 7
25 Little Shelford K 5
4 Little Silver, Devon F 7
6 Little Silver, Devon E 3
34 Little Singleton C 3
36 Little Smeaton E 3
26 Little Snoring B 2
15 Little Sodbury F 10
16 Little Somerford F 1
40 Little Stainton C 4
30 Little Stanney C 3
25 Little Staughton J 2
33 Little Steeping D 11
27 Little Stonham J 4
23 Little Stretton, Leics. B 10
21 Little Stretton, Shropshire C 10
39 Little Strickland C 8
25 Little Stukeley H 3
45 Little Swinburne E 8
49 Little Swinton E 11
16 Little Tew A 5
25 Little Thetford H 6
25 Little Thurlow K 8
18 Little Thurrock F 6
42 Little Torhouse F 5
4 Little Torrington D 4
45 Little Tosson C 8
19 Little Totham C 9
38 Little Town C 5
56 Little Urchany E 4
38 Little Urswick H 5
19 Little Wakering E 9
27 Little Waldingfield L 2
26 Little Walsingham B 2
19 Little Waltham C 7
18 Little Warley E 6
37 Little Weighton D 7
27 Little Welnetham J 2
21 Little Wenlock B 12
27 Little Whittingham Green H 6
45 Little Whittington F 8
25 Little Wilbraham J 6
8 Little Wishford B 2
22 Little Witley F 1
16 Little Wittenham E 6
16 Little Wolford A 3
23 Little Woolstone H 12
25 Little Wymington J 1
18 Little Wymondley A 2
22 Little Wyrley B 4
27 Little Yeldam L 1
64 Little-ayre C 6
41 Littlebeck E 9
35 Littleborough, Manchester F 8
32 Littleborough, Notts. B 5
11 Littlebourne B 10
7 Littlebredy G 9
25 Littlebury L 6
34 Littledale A 4
15 Littledean C 10
61 Littleferry G 8
4 Littleham, Devon D 3
6 Littleham, Devon H 4
9 Littlehampton F 11
5 Littlehempston J 7
45 Littlehoughton A 10
59 Littlemill, Grampian H 1
56 Littlemill, Highland E 5
45 Littlemill, Northumb. A 10
47 Littlemill, Strathclyde H 9
16 Littlemore D 6
31 Littleover G 11
25 Littleport G 7
25 Littleport Bridge G 7
11 Littlestone-on-Sea F 9
40 Littlethorpe H 3
30 Littleton, Ches. D 3
43 Littleton, Dumf. & Gall. F 7
8 Littleton, Hants. C 6
7 Littleton, Som. C 8
9 Littleton, Surrey A 11
17 Littleton, Surrey G 11
53 Littleton, Tayside D 7
15 Littleton Drew F 11
8 Littleton Panell A 2
15 Littleton upon Severn E 9
40 Littletown A 4
17 Littlewick Green F 9
15 Littleworth, Glos. D 11
16 Littleworth, Oxon D 4
22 Littleworth, Heref. & Worc. G 2
22 Littleworth, Staffs. A 4
31 Littleworth, Staffs. H 8
10 Littleworth, W. Sussex F 1
31 Litton, Derby C 10
39 Litton, N. Yorks. H 11
7 Litton, Som. A 9
30 Liverpool A 2
35 Liversedge E 10
41 Liverton, Cleveland D 7
5 Liverton, Devon H 7
48 Livingston C 3
29 Lixwm C 11
2 Lizard H 4
28 Llaingoch B 2
20 Llaithddu D 6
20 Llan B 4
14 Llan-Rumney F 5
28 Llanaber H 5
28 Llanaelhaearn F 3
13 Llanaeron A 8
20 Llanafan E 2
20 Llanafan-fawr G 5
20 Llanafan-fechan G 5
28 Llanallgo B 4
28 Llanarmon F 4
29 Llanarmon Dyffryn Ceiriog G 10
29 Llanarmon-yn-lal E 11
13 Llanarth, Dyfed A 7
15 Llanarth, Gwent C 7
13 Llanarthney E 8
29 Llanasa B 10
28 Llanbabo B 3
20 Llanbadarn Fawr D 2
20 Llanbadarn Fynydd E 6
21 Llanbadarn-y- garreg G 7
15 Llanbadoc D 7
28 Llanbadrig A 3
15 Llanbeder E 7
28 Llanbedr, Gwynedd H 5
14 Llanbedr, Powys B 6
21 Llanbedr, Powys H 7
29 Llanbedr-Dyffryn-Clwyd D 10
28 Llanbedr-goch B 4
28 Llanbedrog G 3
29 Llanbedr C 7
28 Llanberis D 5
14 Llanbethery G 4
20 Llanbister E 6
14 Llanblethian G 3
12 Llanboidy E 5
14 Llanbradach E 5
56 Llanbryde D 8
20 Llanbrynmair B 5
14 Llancadle G 4
14 Llancarfan G 4
15 Llancayo D 7
15 Llancloudy B 8
21 Llancoch E 7
14 Llandaff F 5
28 Llandanwg G 5
13 Llandarcy G 10
12 Llandawke F 6
28 Llanddaniel Fab C 4
13 Llanddarog E 8
20 Llanddeiniol E 1
28 Llanddeiniolen D 5
29 Llandderfel F 9
13 Llanddeusant, Dyfed E 11
28 Llanddeusant, Gwynedd B 3
14 Llanddew A 4
13 Llanddewi H 8
20 Llanddewi-Brefi G 2
15 Llanddewi Rhydderch C 7
12 Llanddewi Velfrey E 5
20 Llanddewi'r Cwm G 6
29 Llanddoget D 7
28 Llanddona B 5
12 Llanddowror F 6
29 Llanddulas B 8
28 Llanddyfnan B 4
14 Llandefaelog Fach A 4
14 Llandefaelog ter-graig A 4
14 Llandefalle A 4
28 Llandegai C 5
28 Llandegfan C 5
15 Llandegfedd E 7
29 Llandegla E 11
21 Llandegley F 7
13 Llandeilo E 9
20 Llandeilo Graban H 6
14 Llandeilo'r Fan A 2
12 Llandeloy D 2

15 Llandenny D 7
15 Llandevenny F 7
12 Llandewi Velfrey E 5
20 Llandewi Ystradenny E 6
12 Llandilo D 4
15 Llandinabo A 8
20 Llandinam D 6
12 Llandissilio E 5
15 Llandogo D 8
14 Llandough, S. Glam. G 5
14 Llandough, S. Glam. G 3
13 Llandovery D 11
14 Llandow G 3
20 Llandre, Dyfed D 2
13 Llandre, Dyfed C 10
29 Llandrillo F 9
29 Llandrillo-yn-Rhos B 7
20 Llandrindod Wells F 6
21 Llandrinio A 8
29 Llandudno B 7
29 Llandudno Junc. B 7
28 Llandwrog E 4
13 Llandybie E 9
13 Llandyfaelog F 7
13 Llandyfan E 9
13 Llandyfriog C 7
28 Llandyfrydog B 4
12 Llandygwydd C 6
29 Llandyrnog D 10
29 Llandysilio H 12
21 Llandyssil C 7
13 Llandyssul C 7
14 Llanedeyrn F 5
20 Llaneglwys H 6
20 Llanegryn B 2
13 Llanegwad E 8
28 Llaneilian A 4
29 Llanelian-y-Rhos C 8
29 Llanelidan E 10
14 Llanelieu A 5
14 Llanellen C 6
13 Llanelli, Dyfed G 8
14 Llanelli, Gwent C 5
28 Llanelltyd H 6
20 Llanelwedd G 6
28 Llanenddwyn H 5
28 Llanengan G 2
28 Llanerchymedd B 4
20 Llanerfyl A 6
28 Llanfachraeth B 3
29 Llanfachreth H 7
28 Llanfaelog C 3
28 Llanfaelrhys G 2
15 Llanfaenor C 7
28 Llanfaes, Gwynedd C 5
14 Llanfaes, Powys B 4
28 Llanfaethlu B 3
28 Llanfalgan D 4
28 Llanfair G 5
20 Llanfair-Caereinion B 6
20 Llanfair-Clydogau G 2
29 Llanfair Dyffryn Clwyd E 10
12 Llanfair Nant-Gwyn C 5
29 Llanfair Talhaiarn C 8
21 Llandfair Waterdine E 8
28 Llanfairfechan C 6
28 Llanfairpwllgwngyll C 5
28 Llanfairynghornwy A 3
28 Llanfair-yn- Neubwll C 2
12 Llanfallteg E 5
12 Llanfallteg West E 5
20 Llanfaredd G 6
20 Llanfarian E 2
29 Llanfechain H 11
28 Llanfechell A 3
20 Llanfendigaid B 1
29 Llanferres D 11
28 Llanfflewyn A 3
28 Llanfigael B 3
20 Llanfihangel A 6
14 Llanfihangel Crucorney B 6
29 Llanfihangel Glyn Myfyr E 9
14 Llanfihangel Nant Bran A 3
21 Llanfihangel Rhydithon F 7
15 Llanfihangel Rogiet F 8
14 Llanfihangel Tal-y-llyn A 4
13 Llanfihangel ar-arth C 8
21 Llanfihangel-nant-Melan G 7
13 Llanfihangel-uwch-Gwili E 8
20 Llanfihangel-y-Creuddyn E 2
28 Llanfihangel yn Nhowyn C 3
20 Llanfihangel y Pennant B 2
28 Llanfihangel-y-pennant F 5
28 Llanfihangel-y-traethau G 5
14 Llanfilo A 4
14 Llanfoist C 6
29 Llanfor G 8
14 Llanfrechfa E 6
28 Llanfrothen F 5
14 Llanfrynach B 4
29 Llanfwrog, Clwyd D 10
28 Llanfwrog, Gwynedd B 2
29 Llanfyllin H 10
29 Llanfynydd, Clwyd E 12
13 Llanfynydd, Dyfed D 9
12 Llanfyrnach D 6
20 Llangadfan A 6
13 Llangadog, Dyfed D 10
13 Llangadog, Dyfed F 7
29 Llangadwaladr, Clwyd G 11
28 Llangadwaladr, Gwynedd C 3
28 Llangaffo C 4
13 Llangain E 7
20 Llangammarch Wells H 5
14 Llangan G 3
15 Llangarron B 8
14 Llangasty-Tal-y- Ilyn B 5
13 Llangathen E 9
14 Llangattock C 5
15 Llangattock Lingoed B 7
14 Llangattock nigh Usk C 6
15 Llangattock Vibon-Avel C 8
29 Llangedwyn H 11
28 Llangefni C 4
14 Llangeinor F 2
28 Llangeinwen D 4
20 Llangeitho F 2
13 Llangeler C 7
20 Llangelynin B 1
13 Llangendeirne F 8
13 Llangennech G 9
13 Llangennith H 7
14 Llangenny C 6
29 Llangernyw C 8
28 Llangian G 2
13 Llangiwg F 10
13 Llangloffan D 3
12 Llanglydwen D 5
28 Llangoed B 5
12 Llangoedmor B 5
29 Llangollen F 11
12 Llangolman D 5
14 Llangorse B 4
15 Llangoven D 8
29 Llangower G 8
13 Llangranog B 6
28 Llangristiolus C 4
15 Llangrove B 8
15 Llangua B 7
21 Llangunllo E 7
13 Llangunnor E 8
20 Llangurig D 5
29 Llangwm, Clwyd F 9
12 Llangwm, Dyfed F 3
15 Llangwm, Gwent D 7
15 Llangwm-isaf D 7
28 Llangwnnadl G 2
29 Llangwyfan D 10
28 Llangwyfanisaf C 3
28 langwyllog B 4
20 Llangwyryfon E 2
20 Llangybi, Dyfed G 2
15 Llangybi, Gwent E 7
28 Llangybi, Gwynedd F 4
13 Llangyfelach G 10
20 Llangynfelyn C 2
29 Llangynhafal D 10
14 Llangynidr B 5
12 Llangynin E 6
13 Llangynllo C 7
13 Llangynog, Dyfed E 7
29 Llangynog, Powys H 9
14 Llangynwyd E 2
14 Lanhamlach B 4
14 Llanharan F 3
14 Llanharry F 3
15 Llanhennock E 7
14 Llanhilleth D 5
20 Llanidloes D 5
28 Llaniestyn G 2
21 Llanigan H 7
20 Llanilar E 2
14 Llanilid F 3
14 Llanilterne F 4
15 Llanishen, Gwent D 8
14 Llanishen, S. Glam. F 5
13 Llandllawddog D 8
28 Llanllechid C 5
20 Llanllugan B 6
21 Llanllwchaiarn C 7
13 Llanllwch E 7
28 Llanllyfni E 4
15 Llanllywel D 7
13 Llanmadoc H 8
14 Llanmaes G 3
15 Llanmartin E 7
21 Llanmerewig C 7
14 Llanmihangel G 3
12 Llanmiloe F 6
13 Llanmorlais G 8
29 Llannefydd C 9
13 Llannon F 9
28 Llannor F 3
20 Llanon F 1
13 Llanpumsaint D 7
20 Llanreithan D 2
29 Llanrhaeadr D 10
29 Llanrhaeadr-ym-Mochnant H 10
13 Llanrhidian H 8
29 Llanrhos B 7
28 Llanrhyddlad A 3
20 Llanrhystyd E 1
12 Llanrian D 2
28 Llanrug D 5
29 Llanrwst D 7
12 Llansadurnen F 6
13 Llansadwrn, Dyfed D 10
28 Llansadwrn, Gwynedd C 5
13 Llansaint F 7
13 Llansamlet G 10
29 Llansannan D 8
14 Llansannor G 3
14 Llansantffraed B 5
20 Llansantffraed Cwmdeuddwr F 5
20 Llansantffraed-in-Elvel G 6
20 Llansantffraid F 1
29 Llansantffraid Glan Conway C 7
29 Llansantffraid-ym-Mechain H 11
13 Llansawel C 9
29 Llansilin G 11
15 Llansoy D 7
14 Llanspyddid B 3
12 Llanstadwell F 3
13 Llanstephan F 7
12 Llanteg F 5
14 Llanthony B 6
15 Llantilio Crossenny C 7
14 Llantilio Pertholey C 6
12 Llantood C 5
28 Llantrisant B 3
15 Llantrisant, Gwent E 7
14 Llantrisant, Mid Glam. F 4
14 Llantrithyd G 4
14 Llantwit Fardre F 4
14 Llantwit-Major G 3
29 Llanuwchllyn G 8
15 Llanvaches E 7
15 Llanvair Discoed E 8
15 Llanvapley C 7
15 Llanvetherine C 7
14 Llanveynoe A 6
15 Llanvihangel Gobion C 7
14 Llanvihangel Pontymoel D 6
15 Llanvihangel Ystern-Llewern C 7
15 Llanwarne B 8
29 Llanwddyn H 9
14 Llanwenarth C 6
14 Llanwenog B 8
15 Llanwern E 7
12 Llanwinio D 6
12 Llanwnda, Dyfed C 3
28 Llanwnda, Gwynedd D 4
13 Llanwnen B 8
20 Llanwnog C 6
13 Llanwrda D 10
20 Llanwrin B 3
20 Llanwrthwl F 5
20 Llanwrtyd H 4
20 Llanwrtyd Wells H 4
20 Llanwyddelan B 6
30 Llanyblodwel H 1
13 Llanybri F 7
13 Llanybyther C 8
12 Llanycefn E 4
12 Llanychaer Birdge C 3
29 Llanymawddwy H 8
30 Llanymynech H 1
28 Llanynghenedl B 3
29 Llanynys D 10
30 Llan-y-pwll E 2
20 Llanyre F 6
28 Llanystumdwy F 4
14 Llanywern A 4
12 Llawhaden E 4
30 Llawnt G 1
20 Llawr-y-glyn C 5
30 Llay E 2
14 Llechfaen A 4
12 Llechryd, Dyfed C 5
14 Llechryd, Mid Glam. C 4
29 Llechrydau G 11
13 Llethrid H 8
20 Lledrod E 2
13 Llidiadnenog C 9
29 Llidiardau F 8
29 Llidiart-y-parc F 10
28 Llithfaen F 3
29 Llong D 12
21 Llowes H 7
20 Llundain-fach G 1
14 Llwydcoed D 3
13 Llwyncelyn A 8
13 Llwyn Dafydd B 7
21 Llwynderw, Powys B 7
20 Llwynderw, Powys D 5
12 Llwyn-drain D 6
20 Llwyngwril A 2
13 Llwynhendy G 9
29 Llwyn-mawr G 11
14 Llwyn-on C 3
20 Llwyn-y-groes G 2
14 Llwyn-y-pia E 3
30 Llynclys H 1
28 Llynfaes B 3
20 Llysdinam F 6
29 Llysfaen C 8
14 Llyswen A 4
14 Llysworney G 3
12 Llys-y-fran E 4
14 Llywel A 2
20 Llywernog D 3
49 Loanend D 12
48 Loanhead, Lothian C 5
47 Loanhead, Strathclyde D 9
48 Loanhead, Strathclyde F 3
58 Loanhead of Fedderate C 6
47 Loans F 8
45 Loansdean E 10
4 Lobb B 3
61 Loch Choire Lodge D 7
42 LochHead G 4
60 Loch Loyal Lo. C 6
55 Lochailort L 2
50 Lochaline C 4
42 Lohans F 2
43 Locharbriggs D 10
43 Locharwoods E 11
60 Lochassynt Lodge D 3
51 Lochawe E 8
50 Lochbuie E 3
57 Lochcallater L 7
54 Lochcarron F 3
61 Lochdhu Lodge C 9
51 Lochdochart Ho. E 11
50 Lochdon D 5
54 Lochdrum B 6
46 Lochead, Strathclyde B 3
46 Lochead, Strathclyde A 5
52 Lochearnhead E 1
53 Lochee D 8
43 Lochend, Dumf. & Gall. F 9
52 Lochend, Fife H 6
56 Lochend, Highland F 2
61 Lochend, Highland A 11
43 Locherben B 10
43 Lochfoot D 9
50 Lochgair H 6
57 Lochgarthside H 1
47 Lochgate F 11
53 Lochgelly H 7
46 Lochgilphead A 4
51 Lochgoilhead G 9
56 Loch-hill C 8
47 Lochhill H 11
56 Lochindorb Lo. F 5
47 Lochingirrcoh H 11
60 Lochinver E 3
54 Lochluichart C 7
48 Lochlycoch F 2
43 Lochmaben C 11
60 Lochmore Lodge D 4
52 Lochore G 6
46 Lochranza D 4
47 Lochridge E 9
58 Lochs Crofts B 1
59 Lochside, Grampian L 5
56 Lochside, Highland D 4
61 Lochside, Highland D 8
60 Lochstack Lodge C 4
61 Lochstrathy C 8
59 Lochton H 5
59 Lochton of Leys H 4
53 Lochty, Fife F 10
59 Lochty, Tayside L 3
50 Lochuisge B 5
43 Lochurr C 8
47 Lochwinnoch C 8
43 Lochwood B 11
55 Lochy Bridge M 5
3 Lockengate D 7
43 Lockerbie C 12
16 Lockeridge G 3
8 Lockerley C 4
15 Locking H 7
16 Lockinge E 5
37 Lockington, Humber. B 7
32 Lockington, Leics. G 2
30 Lockleywood G 5
8 Lock's Heath E 6
41 Lockton F 8
23 Loddington, Leics. B 11
23 Loddington, Northants. D 11
5 Loddiswell L 6
26 Loddon F 6
25 Lode J 6
7 Loders G 8
59 Lodges G 5
9 Lodsworth D 10
40 Lofthouse, N. Yorks. H 1
35 Lofthouse, W. Yorks. E 12
41 Loftus C 7
47 Logan G 10
42 Logan Mains G 2
30 Loggerheads G 6
60 Loggie G 3
59 Logie Coldstone G 2
53 Logie, Fife E 7
53 Logie, Fife E 9
56 Logie Hill B 3
58 Logie Newton D 4
59 Logie Pert L 4
52 Logiealmond Lo. D 4
52 Logierait B 5
12 Login E 5
25 Lolworth J 5
54 Lonbain D 1
36 Londesborough C 6
18 London F 3
3 London Apprentice E 7
18 London Colney D 2
40 Londonderry F 3
33 Londonthorpe F 7
54 Londubh B 2
60 Lone C 4
15 Long Ashton G 9
32 Long Bennington F 5
7 Long Bredy G 9
23 Long Buckby E 9
32 Long Clawson G 4
8 Long Common E 6
31 Long Compton, Staffordshire H 7
16 Long Compton, Warwickshire A 4
17 Long Crendon C 8
8 Long Crichel E 1
17 Long Ditton G 12
36 Long Drax D 5
32 Long Duckmanton C 2
32 Long Eaton G 2
30 Long Green C 3
16 Long Hanborough C 5
48 Long Hermiston B 4
23 Long Itchington F 7
23 Long Lawford D 8
7 Long Load D 8
17 Long Marston, Herts. C 9
36 Long Marston, N. Yorks. B 3
22 Long Marston, Warwick G 5
39 Long Marton C 9
27 Long Melford K 2
15 Long Newnton E 12
40 Long Newton D 4
35 Long Preston A 7
37 Long Riston C 9
36 Long Sandall F 4
25 Long Stanton All Saints J 5
25 Long Stanton St. Michael J 5
26 Long Stratton F 5
23 Long Street G 11
9 Long Sutton, Hants. A 9
24 Long Sutton, Lincs. C 5
7 Long Sutton, Som. D 8
21 Long Waste A 11
32 Long Whatton H 2
18 Long Wittenham E 6
47 Longbar D 8
45 Longbenton F 11
16 Longborough A 3
22 Longbridge, War. F 6
22 Longbridge, W. Midlands D 3
7 Longbridge Deverill B 11
54 Longbridgemuir E 11
7 Longburton E 10
44 Longbyre F 5
42 Longcastle G 5
31 Longcliffe E 10
16 Longcot E 4
49 Longcroft, Borders D 8
48 Longcroft, Central A 1
17 Longcross H 10
21 Longden B 10
22 Longdon A 4
22 Longdon Green A 4
21 Longdon upon Tern A 11
6 Longdown G 2
2 Longdowns F 4
45 Longdyke B 10
10 Longfield A 5
10 Longfield Hill A 5
31 Longford, Derby F 10
15 Longford, Glos. B 11
18 Longford, London F 1
30 Longford, Salop G 5
23 Longford, W. Midlands D 7
53 Longforgan D 8
49 Longformacus D 9
45 Longframlington C 9
8 Longham, Dorset F 2
26 Longham, Norf. D 2
58 Longhill B 7
45 Longhirst D 10
15 Longhope B 10
45 Longhorsley D 9
45 Longhoughton B 10
38 Longlands B 5
16 Longlane, Berks. G 6
31 Longlane, Derby F 11
15 Longlevens B 11
22 Longley Green G 1
58 Longmanhill A 5
9 Longmoor Camp C 9
56 Longmorn D 8
49 Longnewton G 8
15 Longney C 11
49 Longniddry B 7
31 Longnor D 9
21 Longnot B 10
8 Longparish B 6
34 Longridge, Lancs. D 5
48 Longridge, Lothian C 2
48 Longriggend B 1
31 Longsdon E 8
58 Longside C 8
30 Longslow G 5
8 Longstock B 5
3 Longstone B 7
25 Longstowe K 4
24 Longthorpe F 3
34 Longton, Lancs. E 4
31 Longton, Staffs F 7
44 Longtown, Cumb. F 2
14 Longtown, Heref. & Worc. A 6
21 Longville in the Dale C 11
15 Longwell Green G 10
17 Longwick D 8
45 Longwitton D 9
21 Longwood B 11
16 Longworth D 5
49 Longyester C 8
62 Lonmore D 2
10 Loose C 6
17 Loosley Row D 9
58 Lootcherbrae B 3
8 Lopcombe Corner C 4
7 Lopen E 8
30 Loppington G 3
45 Lorbottle B 8
45 Lorbottle Hall B 8
9 Lordington E 9
44 Lordsgate F 3
43 Lorg B 7
32 Loscoe E 2
56 Lossiemouth C 8
30 Lostock Gralam C 5
30 Lostock Green C 5
34 Lostock Junction F 5
3 Lostwithiel D 8
61 Lothbeg F 9
35 Lothersdale C 8
61 Lothmore F 9
7 Lottisham C 9
17 Loudwater E 10
32 Loughborough H 3
13 Loughor G 9
23 Loughton, Bucks. H 11
18 Loughton, Essex D 4
21 Loughton, Salop D 11
24 Lound, Lincs. D 2
32 Lound, Notts. B 4
26 Lound, Suffolk E 8
31 Lount H 12
33 Louth B 10
35 Love Clough D 7
9 Lovedean E 8
8 Lover D 4
36 Loversall G 4
18 Loves Green C 6
40 Lovesome Hill E 4
12 Loveston F 4
7 Lovington C 9
42 Low Ardwell G 2
39 Low Bentham H 9
35 Low Bradfield H 11

35 Low Bradley B 9
38 Low Braithwaite A 6
45 Low Brunton F 7
36 Low Burnham G 5
40 Low Burton G 3
45 Low Buston B 10
36 Low Catton B 5
40 Low Coniscliffe D 3
42 Low Craighead A 3
44 Low Cranecleugh D 5
44 Low Crosby G 3
41 Low Dalby F 8
40 Low Dinsdale D 4
36 Low Eggborough E 3
40 Low Ellington G 2
40 Low Etherley B 2
44 Low Geltbridge G 4
47 Low Grange H 8
22 Low Habberley D 2
7 Low Ham C 8
45 Low Hedgeley A 9
39 Low Hesket A 7
45 Low Hesleyhurst C 9
41 Low Hutton H 8
42 Low Knockbrex E 5
31 Low Leighton B 8
38 Low Lorton C 4
42 Low Malzie F 4
41 Low Marishes G 8
32 Low Marnham C 5
41 Low Mill F 7
45 Low Morsley H 11
45 Low Newton-by-the-Sea A 10
44 Low Row, Cumb. G 4
38 Low Row, Cumb. B 6
39 Low Row, N. Yorks. E 12
42 Low Salchrie E 1
37 Low Santon F 7
47 Low Shawsburn D 12
26 Low Street C 6
26 Low Thurlton E 7
48 Low Torry A 3
45 Low Town C 9
40 Low Worsall D 4
38 Low Wray E 6
38 Lowca C 2
32 Lowdham F 4
30 Lowe G 4
6 Lower Aisholt C 5
7 Lower Ansty F 11
6 Lower Ashton H 2
17 Lower Assendon F 8
63 Lower Bayble D 6
10 Lower Beeding E 1
24 Lower Benefield F 1
7 Lower Bockhampton G 10
23 Lower Boddington G 8
2 Lower Boscaswell F 1
9 Lower Bourne B 10
22 Lower Brailes H 6
62 Lower Breakish F 6
22 Lower Broadheath F 2
15 Lower Bullingham A 8
25 Lower Caldecote K 3
15 Lower Cam D 10
14 Lower Chapel A 4
8 Lower Chicksgrove C 1
8 Lower Chute A 4
10 Lower Cokeham H 1
31 Lower Crossings B 9
35 Lower Cumberworth F 11
34 Lower Darwen E 6
25 Lower Dean H 2
54 Lower Diabaig D 2
10 Lower Dicker G 4
21 Lower Dinchope D 10
61 Lower Dounreay A 9
21 Lower Down D 9
2 Lower Drift G 2
36 Lower Dunsforth A 2
8 Lower Everleigh A 3
15 Lower Failand G 8
9 Lower Farringdon C 8
38 Lower Foxdale G 1
12 Lower Freystrop F 3
9 Lower Froyle B 9
60 Lower Gledfield G 6
10 Lower Green, Kent D 5
26 Lower Green, Norf. B 3
27 Lower Hacheston J 6
62 Lower Halistra B 2
11 Lower Halstow A 7
11 Lower Hardres C 10
56 Lower Hempriggs C 7
21 Lower Hergest G 8
16 Lower Heyford B 6
10 Lower Higham A 6
30 Lower Hordley G 3
10 Lower Horsebridge G 4
51 Lower Kinchrackine E 8
7 Lower Kingcombe F 9
10 Lower Kingswoood C 1
30 Lower Kinnerton D 2
15 Lower Langford H 8
53 Lower Largo G 9
31 Lower Leigh G 8
57 Lower Lenie G 1
20 Lower Llanfadog F 5
4 Lower Loxhore B 5
15 Lower Lydbrook C 9
21 Lower Lye F 9
14 Lower Machen E 5
15 Lower Maes-coed A 7
19 Lower Mayland D 9
62 Lower Milovaig C 1
22 Lower Moor G 3
18 Lower Nazeing C 4
52 Lower Oakfield H 6
62 Lower Ollach D 4
14 Lower Penarth G 5
22 Lower Penn C 2
8 Lower Pennington G 5
30 Lower Peover C 6
35 Lower Place F 8
22 Lower Quinton G 5
21 Lower Rochford F 11
16 Lower Seagry F 1
63 Lower Shader A 5
25 Lower Shelton L 1
17 Lower Shiplake F 8
23 Lower Shuckburgh F 8
16 Lower Slaughter B 3
15 Lower Stanton St. Quintin F 12
11 Lower Stoke A 7
26 Lower Street B 6
22 Lower Strensham H 3
17 Lower Sundon A 11
8 Lower Swanwick E 6
16 Lower Swell B 3
62 Lower Tote B 4
12 Lower Town C 3
23 Lower Tysoe H 7
9 Lower Upham D 7
6 Lower Vexford C 5
34 Lower Walton H 5
7 Lower Waterston G 10
7 Lower Weare A 7
21 Lower Welson G 8
30 Lower Whitley B 5
9 Lower Wield B 8
17 Lower Winchendon C 8
17 Lower Woodend E 9
8 Lower Woodford C 3
22 Lower Wyche H 1
23 Lowesby A 10
26 Lowestoft F 8
26 Lowestoft End F 8
38 Loweswater C 4
10 Lowfield Heath D 2
34 Logwill, Lancs. A 5
39 Lowgill, Cumbria E 8
25 Lowick, Northants. G 1
45 Lowick, Northumb. B 11
38 Lowick Green G 5
14 Lowlands E 6
22 Lowsonford E 5
39 Lowther C 8
37 Lowthorpe A 8
34 Lowton, Manchester G 5
6 Lowton, Som. D 5
34 Lowton Common G 5
6 Loxbeare E 3
9 Loxhill B 11
4 Loxhore B 5
22 Loxley G 6
7 Loxton A 7
9 Loxwood C 11
60 Lubachoinnich G 5
60 Lubcroy F 4
23 Lubenham C 10
51 Lubnaclach A 11
54 Lubriach B 7
6 Luccombe B 3
9 Luccombe Village H 7
45 Lucker D 11
3 Luckett B 11
15 Luckington F 11
53 Lucklawhill E 9
6 Luckwell Bridge B 2
21 Lucton F 10
37 Ludborough H 10
12 Ludchurch F 5
35 Luddenden E 9
35 Luddenden Foot E 9
10 Luddesdown B 5
36 Luddington, Humberside E 6
22 Luddington, War. G 5
25 Luddington in the Brook G 2
21 Ludford E 10
33 Ludford A 9
17 Ludgershall B 7
8 Ludgershall A 4
2 Ludgvan F 2
26 Ludham D 7
21 Ludlow E 10
37 Ludney G 11
7 Ludwell D 12
40 Ludworth A 4
4 Luffincott F 2
47 Lugar G 10
49 Lugate E 7
49 Luggate Burn B 8
47 Luggiebank B 12
47 Lugton D 9
21 Lugwardine H 11
62 Luib E 5
51 Luib Hotel E 12
51 Luibeilt A 9
21 Lulham H 9
22 Lullington, Derby A 6
7 Lullington, Som. A 11
22 Lulsey G 1
15 Lulsgate Bottom H 8
35 Lumb E 9
35 Lumbutts E 8
36 Lumby D 3
47 Lumloch B 11
59 Lumphanan G 3
52 Lumphinnans H 6
49 Lumsdaine B 11
58 Lumsden E 2
53 Lunan B 11
53 Lunanhead B 9
52 Luncarty D 6
37 Lund, Humberside B 7
36 Lund, N. Yorks. D 4
51 Lundavra A 8
58 Lunderton C 8
55 Lundie, Highland H 5
53 Lundie, Tayside D 8
53 Lundin Links G 9
50 Lungar (Hotel) G 5
64 Lunna C 7
64 Lunning C 7
13 Lunnon H 9
10 Lunsford B 6
10 Lunsford's Cross G 6
34 Lunt G 2
21 Luntley G 9
6 Luppitt F 5
35 Lupsett E 11
39 Lupton G 8
9 Lurgashall C 10
56 Lurgmore F 1
33 Lusby C 10
51 Luss H 10
62 Lusta C 2
5 Lustleigh H 6
21 Luston F 10
59 Luthermuir K 4
53 Luthrie E 8
17 Luton, Beds. B 12
5 Luton, Devon H 8
10 Luton, Kent A 6
23 Lutterworth D 9
5 Lutton, Devon K 5
24 Lutton, Lincs. C 5
25 Lutton, Northants. G 2
6 Luxborough B 3
3 Luxulyan D 7
61 Lybster D 11
21 Lydbury North D 9
11 Lydd F 9
11 Lydd-on-Sea F 9
11 Lydden D 11
23 Lyddington B 12
17 Lyde Green H 8
6 Lydeard St. Lawrence C 4
5 Lydford G 4
35 Lydgate E 8
21 Lydham C 9
16 Lydiard Millicent F 2
34 Lydiate G 2
7 Lydlinch E 10
15 Lydney D 9
15 Lydstep G 4
22 Lye D 3
15 Lye Cross H 8
17 Lye Green, Bucks. D 10
10 Lye Green, E. Sussex E 4
16 Lyford E 5
47 Lylestone, Strathclyde E 8
49 Lylestone, Borders D 8
11 Lymbridge Green D 10
7 Lyme Regis G 7
11 Lyminge D 10
8 Lymington F 4
9 Lyminster F 11
30 Lymm B 5
8 Lymore G 4
11 Lympne E 10
6 Lympsham A 6
6 Lympstone H 3
57 Lynaberack K 3
57 Lynachlaggan J 4
6 Lynch B 3
26 Lynch Green E 4
57 Lynchat J 3
8 Lyndhurst E 4
23 Lyndon B 12
48 Lyne, Borders E 5
17 Lyne, Surrey G 11
15 Lyne Down A 9
57 Lyne of Gorthleck H 1
58 Lyne of Skene F 5
30 Lyneal G 3
62 Lynedale House C 3
16 Lyneham, Oxon B 4
16 Lyneham, Wilts. F 1
44 Lyneholm D 1
44 Lyneholmeford F 4
57 Lynmore G 6
45 Lynemouth D 11
64 Lyness E 1
26 Lyng, Norfolk D 4
7 Lyng, Somerset C 7
4 Lynmouth A 6
11 Lynsted B 8
4 Lynton A 6
7 Lyon's Gate F 10
21 Lyonshall G 9
8 Lytchett Matravers G 1
8 Lytchett Minster G 1
61 Lyth B 11
34 Lytham D 3
34 Lytham St Anne's D 2
41 Lythe D 8
64 Lythes E 3
63 Maaruig F 3
2 Mabe Burnthouse F 5
43 Mabie D 10
33 Mablethorpe B 12
48 Macbiehill D 4
31 Macclesfield C 7
31 Macclesfield For. C 8
58 Macduff A 4
14 Machen E 5
46 Machrihanish G 1
50 Machrins H 1
20 Machynlleth B 3
31 Mackworth F 11
49 Macmerry B 7
52 Madderty E 4
48 Maddiston B 2
9 Madehurst E 11
30 Madeley, Staffs. F 6
30 Madeley Heath F 6
25 Madingley J 5
21 Madley H 9
22 Madresfield G 2
2 Madron F 2
28 Maenaddwyn B 4
12 Maenclochog D 4
14 Maendy G 3
28 Maentwrog F 6
13 Maen-y-groes A 7
30 Maer F 6
29 Maerdy, Clwyd F 9
13 Maerdy, Dyfed D 10
15 Maerdy, Gwent B 7
14 Maerdy, Mid Glam. D 3
30 Maesbrook Green H 2
30 Maesbury H 2
30 Maesbury Marsh H 2
12 Maesgwynne E 5
29 Maeshafn D 11
13 Maesllyn C 7
20 Maesmynis H 6
14 Maesteg E 2
13 Maestir B 9
13 Maestwynog C 10
13 Maesybont E 9
13 Maesycrugiau C 8
14 Maes-y-cwmmer E 5
13 Maesymeillion B 7
18 Magdalen Laver C 5
58 Maggieknockater C 1
10 Magham Down G 5
34 Maghull G 3
15 Magor F 7
7 Maiden Bradley B 11
45 Maiden Law H 10
7 Maiden Newton F 9
12 Maiden Wells G 3
5 Maidencombe J 8
48 Maidencotes G 2
17 Maidenhead F 10
39 Maidenhill B 7
42 Maidens A 3
17 Maiden's Green G 9
33 Maidenwell B 10
23 Maidford G 9
17 Maid's Moreton A 8
10 Maidstone C 6
23 Maidwell D 10
64 Mail E 7
14 Maindee E 6
61 Mains, Highland F 8
47 Mains, Strathclyde D 11
52 Mains, Tayside B 6
42 Mains of Airies E 1
59 Mainsof Allardice K 6
59 Mains of Altries H 6
58 Mains of Annochie C 7
53 Mains of Ardestie D 10
58 Mains of Arnage D 7
58 Mains of Auchindachy C 2
58 Mains of Auchmedden A 6
53 Mains of Balgavies B 10
53 Mains of Ballindarg B 9
59 Mains of Balnakettle K 4
58 Mains of Birness D 7
56 Mains of Bunachton F 2
58 Mains of Cairnborrow D 2
58 Mains of Cardno A 7
58 Mains of Crichie C 7
56 Mains of Dalvey F 7
59 Mains of Drum G 5
58 Mains of Drummuir C 2
56 Mains of Drynie E 2
58 Mains of Edingight B 3
58 Mains of Esslemont E 7
59 Mains of Glenfarquhar J 5
59 Mains of Haulkerton K 5
58 Mains of Inkhorn D 7
58 Mains of Keithfield D 6
58 Mains of Kirkhall F 6
58 Mains of Logie B 8
59 Mains of Melgund L 3
56 Mains of Newhall C 3
59 Mains of Thornton K 4
52 Mains of Throsk H 3
56 Mains of Tore D 2
58 Mains of Towie C 5
61 Mains of Ulbster C 12
53 Mains of Usan B 12
40 Mainsforth B 3
43 Mainsriddle F 10
21 Mainstone D 8
15 Maisemore B 11
5 Malborough M 6
18 Malden Rushett H 2
19 Maldon C 8
35 Malham A 8
55 Mallaig K 1
55 Mallaigvaig K 1
48 Malleny Mills C 4
52 Malling G 1
28 Malltraeth C 3
20 Mallwyd A 4
15 Malmesbury F 12
4 Malmsmead A 7
30 Malpas, Cheshire E 3
2 Malpas, Corn. E 5
14 Malpas, Gwent E 6
51 Malt Land F 8
40 Maltby, Cleveland D 5
32 Maltby, S. Yorks. A 3
33 Maltby le Marsh B 11
11 Maltman's Hill D 8
41 Malton H 8
22 Malvern Link G 1
22 Malvern Wells H 1
21 Mamble E 12
14 Mamhilad D 6
2 Manaccan G 5
21 Manafon B 7
5 Manaton H 6
33 Manby B 11
22 Mancetter C 6
35 Manchester G 7
29 Mancot D 12
55 Mandally J 7
24 Manea F 6
42 Maneight A 6
40 Manfield D 2
64 Mangaster C 7
63 Mangersta D 1
44 Mangertton D 3
15 Mangotsfield G 10
12 Manian Fawr B 5
63 Manish H 2
30 Manley C 4
14 Manmoel D 5
16 Manningford Bohune H 2
16 Manningford Bruce H 2
35 Manningham D 10
10 Mannings Heath E 1
8 Mannington F 2
27 Manningtree M 4
59 Mannofield G 6
12 Manorbier G 4
12 Manorbier Newton G 4
49 Manorhill F 9
12 Manorowen C 3
43 Mansfield B 9
13 Manselfield H 9
21 Mansell Gamage H 9
21 Mansell Lacy H 9
39 Mansergh G 8
47 Mansfield, Strathclyde H 11
32 Mansfield, Notts. D 3
32 Mansfield Woodhouse D 3
38 Mansriggs G 5
7 Manston, Dorset E 11
11 Manston, Kent B 12
8 Manswood E 2
24 Manthorpe, Lincs. D 2
32 Manthorpe, Lincs. F 6
37 Manton, Humber. G 7
23 Manton, Leics. B 12
16 Manton, Wilts. G 3
37 Manton Warren F 7
18 Manuden A 5
50 Maolachy F 6
7 Maperton D 10
17 Maple Cross E 11
32 Maplebeck D 4
17 Mapledurham F 7
9 Mapledurwell A 8
10 Maplehurst F 1
10 Maplescombe B 4
31 Mapleton E 10
32 Mapperley F 2
32 Mapperley Park F 3
7 Mapperton, Dorset F 12
7 Mapperton, Dorset F 8
22 Mappleborough Green E 4
37 Mappleton C 10
35 Mapplewell F 12
7 Mappowder F 10
57 Mar Lodge K 7
2 Marazion G 2
30 Marbury F 4
24 March, Cambs. F 5
48 March, Strathclyde H 3
16 Marcham D 5
30 Marchamley G 4
43 Marchbankwood B 11
47 Marchburn H 11
31 Marchington G 9
31 Marchington Woodlands G 9
30 Marchwiel E 2
8 Marchwood E 5
28 Marchros H 3
14 Marcross G 3
21 Marden, Heref. & Worc. H 10
10 Marden, Kent D 6
16 Marden, Wilts. H 2
18 Marden Ash D 5
10 Marden Beech D 6
10 Marden Thorn D 6
14 Mardy C 6
7 Mare Green D 7
17 Marefield, Bucks. E 9
23 Marefield, Leics. A 11
33 Mareham le Fen D 10
33 Mareham on the Hill C 10
32 Marehey E 1
10 Maresfield F 3
37 Marfleet D 9
30 Marford E 2
13 Margam H 11
7 Margaret Marsh D 11
18 Margaret Roding C 6
18 Margaretting D 6
11 Margafe A 12
46 Margnaheglish F 5
24 Marham D 8
4 Marhamchurch F 1
24 Marholm E 2
28 Mariandyrys B 5
28 Marianglas B 4
4 Mariansleigh D 6
59 Marionburgh G 5
62 Marishader B 4
63 Mariveg E 5
43 Marjoriebanks C 11
43 Mark, Dumf. & Gall. F 7
42 Mark, Strathclyde D 2
7 Mark, Somerset A 7
7 Mark Causeway B 7
10 Mark Cross E 5
10 Markbeech D 4
33 Markby B 12
31 Markeaton F 11
23 Market Bosworth B 7
24 Market Deeping E 2
30 Market Drayton G 5
23 Market Harborough C 10
8 Market Lavington A 2
23 Market Overton A 12
33 Market Rasen A 8
33 Market Stainton B 9
26 Market Street C 6
36 Market Weighton C 6
27 Market Weston G 3
23 Markfield A 8
14 Markham D 5
32 Markham Moor C 4
53 Markinch G 8
35 Markington A 10

49 Markle B 8
19 Marks Tey B 9
15 Marksbury H 10
17 Markyate C 11
48 Marlage D 1
16 Marlborough G 3
21 Marlbrook, Heref. & Worc. G 10
22 Marlbrook, Heref. & Worc. E 3
22 Marlcliff G 4
5 Marldon J 7
27 Marlesford J 6
30 Marley Green F 4
45 Marley Hill G 10
8 Marley Mount F 4
49 Marleyknowe F 12
26 Marlingford E 4
12 Marloes F 1
17 Marlow, Bucks. E 9
21 Marlow, Heref. & Worc. E 9
17 Marlow Bottom E 9
10 Marlpit Hill C 3
32 Marlpool F 2
7 Marnhull D 11
58 Marnoch C 3
31 Marple A 8
36 Marr G 3
61 Marrel E 9
40 Marrick E 1
12 Marros F 5
45 Marsden, Tyne & Wear G 12
35 Marsden, W. Yorks. F 9
39 Marsett F 11
6 Marsh, Devon E 6
6 Marsh, Somerset C 4
16 Marsh Baldon D 6
16 Marsh Benham G 5
17 Marsh Gibbon B 7
6 Marsh Green, Devon G 4
10 Marsh Green, Kent D 3
21 Marsh Green, Shropshire A 11
6 Marsh Street B 3
18 Marshall's Heath B 2
26 Marsham C 5
34 Marshaw B 5
11 Marshborough B 11
21 Marshbrook C 10
37 Marshchapel G 11
15 Marshfield, Avon G 11
14 Marshfield, Gwent F 6
2 Marshgate B 2
32 Marshland B 1
34 Marshside E 2
7 Marshwood F 7
40 Marske E 1
40 Marske-by-the-Sea C 6
30 Marston, Ches. C 5
21 Marston, Heref. & Worc. G 9
32 Marston, Lincs. F 6
16 Marston, Oxon C 6
22 Marston, Staffs. A 2
31 Marston, Staffs. G 8
16 Marston, Wilts. H 1
22 Marston Green D 5
7 Marston Magna D 9
16 Marston Meysey D 2
31 Marston Montgomery F 10
25 Marston Moretaine L 1
31 Marston on Dove G 11
23 Marston St. Lawrence H 8
21 Marston Stannett G 11
23 Marston Trussell D 10
15 Marstow B 9
17 Marsworth C 10
16 Marten H 4
30 Marthall C 6
26 Martham D 8
8 Martin, Hants. D 2
11 Martin, Kent C 12
33 Martin, Lincs. D 8
8 Martin Drove End D 2
22 Martin Hussingtree F 2
4 Martinhoe A 5
4 Martinhoe Cross A 6
30 Martinscroft A 5
44 Martinshouse B 3
7 Martinstown G 10
27 Martlesham K 6
12 Martletwy F 4
22 Martley F 1
7 Martock D 8
31 Marton, Ches. C 7
40 Marton, Cleveland D 5
37 Marton, Humber. C 9
32 Marton, Lincs. B 5
41 Marton, N. Yorks. G 7
36 Marton, N. Yorks. A 2
21 Marton, Salop B 8
23 Marton, War. E 7
40 Marton le Moor H 4
40 Marton-in-the- Forest H 6
8 Martyr Worthy C 6
17 Martyr's Green H 11
43 Marwhirn B 8
64 Marwick C 1
4 Marwood Middle B 4
5 Mary Tavy H 4
54 Marybank D 8
56 Maryburgh D 1
59 Maryculter G 6
49 Marygold C 10
58 Maryhill, Grampian C 6
47 Maryhill, Strathclyde B 10
59 Marykirk L 4
56 Marypark F 7
38 Maryport, Cumb. B 3
42 Maryport, Dumf. & Gall. H 2
53 Maryton, Tayside B 8
53 Maryton, Tayside B 11
59 Marywell, Grampian H 3
59 Marywell, Grampian G 7
53 Marywell, Tayside C 11
40 Masham G 2
45 Mason F 10
32 Mastin Moor C 2
59 Mastrick G 6
18 Matching C 5
18 Matching Green C 5
18 Matching Tye C 5
45 Matfen F 8
10 Matfield D 5
15 Mathern E 8
22 Mathon H 1
12 Mathry D 2
26 Matlaske B 5
31 Matlock D 11
31 Matlock Bath D 11
15 Matson C 11
38 Matterdale End C 6
32 Mattersey A 4
32 Mattersey Thorpe A 4
17 Mattingley H 8
26 Mattishall D 4
26 Mattishall Burgh D 4
58 Mattocks C 9
47 Mauchline G 10
58 Maud C 7
13 Maudsland D 7
16 Maugersbury B 3
38 Maughold G 3
54 Mauld F 8
25 Maulden L 2
39 Maulds Meaburn D 8
40 Maunby F 4
21 Maund Bryan G 11
6 Maundown C 4
26 Mautby D 8
22 Mavesyn Ridware A 4
33 Mavis Enderby D 10
22 Maw Green B 4
43 Mawbray G 11
52 Mawcarse G 6
34 Mawdesley F 4
14 Mawdlam F 1
2 Mawgan G 4
2 Mawla E 4
2 Mawnan G 5
2 Mawnan Smith G 5
24 Maxey E 2
22 Maxstroke C 6
49 Maxton, Borders F 8
11 Maxton, Kent D 11
49 maxwellheugh F 10
42 Maxwellston B 4
43 Maxwellstown D 10
5 Maxworthy G 1
31 May Bank E 7
13 Mayals H 9
47 Maybole H 8
17 Maybury H 11
10 Mayfield, E. Sussex E 5
48 Mayfield, Lothian C 6
31 Mayfield, Staffs. F 10
17 Mayford H 10
19 Mayland D 9
10 Maynard's Green F 5
15 Maypole, Gwent C 8
2 Maypole, Is. of Scilly D 2
26 Maypole Green F 7
64 Maywick E 7
4 Mead D 1
15 Meadgate H 10
17 Meadle D 9
47 Meadowfoot E 11
21 Meadowtown B 8
39 Meal Bank F 8
37 Meals G 11
38 Mealsgate A 4
7 Meare B 8
6 Meare Green D 6
47 Mearns D 10
23 Mears Ashby E 11
23 Measham A 7
10 Meath Green D 2
39 Meathop G 7
63 Meavag G 3
5 Meavy J 4
23 Medbourne C 11
45 Medburn F 9
4 Meddon D 2
32 Meden Valley C 3
17 Medmenham F 9
45 Medomsley H 9
9 Medstead B 8
22 Meer End E 6
31 Meerbrook D 8
33 Meers Bridge B 12
25 Meesden M 5
4 Meeth E 4
44 Megdale C 1
48 Meggethead G 4
12 Meidrim E 6
21 Meifod A 7
53 Meigle C 7
43 Meikle Barncleugh D 10
43 Meikle Beoch D 9
47 Meikle Carco H 12
47 Meikle Earnock D 12
59 Meikle Fiddes J 5
52 Meikle Forter A 6
46 Meikle Grenach C 6
47 Meikle Hareshaw E 11
47 Meikle Ittington E 7
56 Meikle Kildrummie D 4
49 Meikle Pinkerton B 9
59 Meikle Strath K 4
58 Meikle Tarty E 7
58 Meikle Wartle D 5
43 Meikleholm C 11
47 Meiklelaught E 7
52 Meikleour C 6
58 Meikleton C 3
28 Meillteyrn G 2
43 Meinbank D 12
13 Meinciau F 8
31 Meir Heath F 8
63 Melbost D 6
63 Melbost Borve A 5
25 Melbourn L 5
31 Melbourne, Derby H 12
36 Melbourne, Humberside C 5
48 Melbourne, Strathclyde E 4
7 Melbury Abbas D 12
7 Melbury Bubb F 9
7 Melbury Osmond E 9
7 Melbury Sampford F 9
64 Melby D 6
25 Melchbourne J 1
7 Melcombe Regis H 10
5 Meldon, Devon G 4
45 Meldon, N'thumb. E 9
25 Meldreth L 5
58 Meldrum House E 6
50 Melfort F 5
55 Melgarve K 8
29 Meliden B 10
14 Melin Court D 2
20 Melin-byrhedin C 4
29 Melin-y-coed D 7
20 Melin-y-grug B 6
29 Melin-y-wig E 9
39 Melkinthorpe C 8
44 Melkridge G 5
15 Melksham H 12
54 Mellanguan A 2
46 Melldalloch B 4
39 Melling, Lancs. H 8
34 Melling, Merseyside G 3
34 Melling Mount G 3
27 Mellis H 4
60 Mellon Charles G 1
60 Mellon Udrigle G 1
31 Mellor, Manchester A 8
34 Mellor, Lancs. D 5
34 Mellor Brook D 5
7 Mells A 10
39 Melmerby, Cumb. B 8
40 Melmerby, N. Yorks. G 4
40 Melmerby, N. Yorks. G 1
7 Melplash F 8
49 Melrose F 8
64 Melsetter E 1
40 Melsonby D 2
35 Meltham F 9
35 Meltham Mills F 10
37 Melton, Humber. D 7
27 Melton, Suffolk K 6
26 Melton Constable B 3
32 Melton Mowbray H 5
37 Melton Ross F 8
36 Meltonby B 6
54 Melvaig A 1
21 Melverley A 9
61 Melvich B 8
6 Membury F 6
58 Memsie A 7
59 Memus L 2
3 Menabilly E 8
28 Menai Bridge C 5
27 Mendham G 6
27 Mendlesham J 4
27 Mendlesham Green J 4
3 Menheniot C 10
43 Mennock A 9
35 Menston C 10
52 Menstrie G 3
36 Menthorpe D 5
17 Mentmore B 10
55 Meoble L 2
21 Meole Brace A 10
9 Meonstroke D 7
10 Meopham B 5
10 Meopham Green B 5
10 Meopham Station A 5
25 Mepal G 5
25 Meppershall L 2
21 Merbach H 8
30 Mere, Cheshire B 6
7 Mere, Wilts. C 11
34 Mere Brow E 3
35 Mereclough D 7
11 Meresborough B 7
34 Mereside D 2
30 Meretown H 6
10 Mereworth C 5
59 Mergie H 5
22 Meriden D 6
62 Merkadale E 3
43 Merkland D 8
60 Merkland Lodge D 5
12 Merlin's Bridge F 3
30 Merrington H 3
12 Merrion G 3
7 Merriot E 8
5 Merrivale H 4
9 Merrow A 11
44 Merrylaw C 2
3 Merrymeet C 10
34 Merseyside, Co. H 3
11 Mersham D 9
10 Merstham C 2
9 Merston F 10
8 Merstone H 6
2 Merther E 6
13 Merthyr E 7
14 Merthyr Cynog A 3
14 Merthyr Mawr F 2
14 Merthyr Tydfil D 4
14 Merthyr Vale D 4
4 Merton, Devon E 4
18 Merton, London G 3
26 Merton, Norfolk F 2
17 Merton, Oxon B 7
44 Mervinslaw B 5
4 Meshaw D 6
19 Messing B 9
37 Messingham G 7
27 Metfield G 6
33 Metheringham D 8
53 Methil G 8
28 Methlem G 1
35 Methley D 12
58 Methlick D 6
52 Methven E 5
24 Methwold F 8
24 Methwold Hythe F 8
26 Mettingham F 6
26 Metton B 5
3 Mevagissey E 7
36 Mexborough G 3
61 Mey A 12
16 Meysey Hampton D 2
63 Miavaig C 2
58 Michael Muir D 6
15 Michaelchurch B 8
14 Michaelchurch Escley A 6
21 Michaelchurch-on-Arrow G 8
14 Michaelston-le-Pit G 5
14 Michaelston-super-Ely G 4
14 Michaelstone-y-Fedw F 6
3 Michaelstow B 8
8 Michelmersh C 5
27 Mickfield J 4
30 Mickle Trafford C 3
36 Micklebring H 3
41 Mickleby D 8
10 Mickleham C 1
31 Mickleover G 11
44 Micklethwaite H 1
39 Mickleton, Dur. C 12
22 Mickleton, Glos. H 5
35 Mickletown D 12
40 Mickley G 3
45 Mickley Square G 9
58 Mid Ardlaw A 7
59 Mid Beltie G 4
59 Mid Cairncross J 2
48 Mid Calder C 3
61 Mid Clyth D 11
56 Mid Coul E 3
58 Mid Cowbog B 6
54 Mid Crochail F 7
47 Mid Drumloch D 11
14 Mid Glamorgan, Co. E 4
48 Mid Hartwood C 3
43 Mid Laggan D 8
9 Mid Lavant E 10
54 Mid Mains F 8
46 Mid Sannox E 5
54 Mid Strom F 2
46 Mid Thundergay E 4
64 Mid Walls D 6
64 Mid Yell B 7
64 Midbea A 2
17 Middle Assendon F 8
16 Middle Aston A 6
16 Middle Barton B 5
7 Middle Chinnock E 8
59 Middle Drums L 3
58 Middle Essie B 8
32 Middle Handley B 1
17 Middle Claydon B 8
22 Middle Littleton G 4
12 Middle Mill D 2
49 Middle Ord D 12
33 Middle Rasen A 8
52 Middle Rigg F 5
15 Middle Street D 11
23 Middle Tysoe H 7
8 Middle Wallop B 4
8 Middle Winterslow C 4
8 Middle Woodford C 3
43 Middlebie D 12
57 Middlebridge M 4
49 Middlefield D 10
43 Middlegill A 11
40 Middleham F 2
21 Middlehope D 10
7 Middlemarsh E 10
58 Middlemuir House E 7
40 Middlesbrough C 5
39 Middleshaw, Cumb. F 8
43 Middleshaw, Dumf. & Gall. D 12
44 Middlesknowes B 6
40 Middlesmoor H 1
40 Middlestone B 3
40 Middlestone Moor B 3
35 Middlestown E 11
49 Middlethird E 9
31 Middleton, Derby E 11
31 Middleton, Derby D 10
27 Middleton, Essex L 2
58 Middleton, Grampian E 6
35 Middleton, Manchester F 7
8 Middleton, Hants. B 6
21 Middleton, Heref. & Worc. E 11
34 Middleton, Lancs. A 3
48 Middleton, Lothian D 6
24 Middleton, Norf. D 8
41 Middleton, N. Yorks. G 8
35 Middleton, N. Yorks. B 10
25 Middleton, Northants. C 11
45 Middleton, Northumberland E 9
45 Middleton, Northumb. B 12
21 Middleton, Salop E 11
30 Middleton, Salop G 2
47 Middleton, Strathclyde E 8
27 Middleton, Suffolk H 7
52 Middleton, Tayside F 6
52 Middleton, Tayside B 6
22 Middleton, War. B 5
13 Middleton, W. Glam. H 7
35 Middleton, W. Yorks. D 11
23 Middleton Cheney H 8
31 Middleton Green G 8
49 Middleton Hall G 12
40 Middleton-in- Leven D 5
39 Middleton-in-Teesdale C 11
58 Middleton of Rora C 8
9 Middleton-on-Sea F 11
21 Middleton on the Hill F 11
37 Middleton-on-the-Wolds B 7
40 Middleton One Row D 4
21 Middleton Priors C 11
40 Middleton Quernhow G 3
40 Middleton St. George D 4
21 Middleton Scriven D 12
16 Middleton Stoney B 6
40 Middleton Tyas E 3
21 Middletown A 8
30 Middlewich D 6
27 Middlewood Green J 4
47 Middleyard F 10
7 Middlezoy C 7
40 Middridge C 3
15 Midford H 10
34 Midge Hall E 4
44 Midgeholme G 5
35 Midgeley F 11
16 Midgham G 6
35 Midgley D 9
35 Midhopestones G 11
9 Midhurst D 10
49 Midlem G 8
48 Midlock G 2
7 Midsomer Norton A 10
60 Midtown B 6
54 Midtown Brae A 2
58 Midtown of Buchromb C 1
33 Midville E 11
43 Miefield F 7
61 Migdale G 7
59 Migvie G 2
7 Milborne Port D 10
7 Milborne St. Andrew F 11
7 Milborne Wick D 10
45 Milbourne E 9
50 Milbuie H 1
39 Milburn B 9
15 Milbury Heath E 10
40 Milby H 4
16 Milcombe A 5
27 Milden K 3
25 Mildenhall, Suff. H 8
16 Mildenhall, Wilts. G 3
16 Mile Elm G 1
19 Mile End, Essex A 9
26 Mile End, Suffolk F 6
21 Milebrook E 8
26 Mileham D 2
15 Miles End C 9
30 Miles Green E 6
21 Miles Hope F 11
52 Milesmark H 5
49 Milfield F 12
31 Milford, Derby F 12
4 Milford, Devon D 1
31 Milford, Staffs. H 8
9 Milford, Surrey B 11
8 Milford, Wilts. C 3
12 Milford Haven F 4
8 Milford on Sea G 4
47 Milhall D 10
15 Milkwall C 9
8 Milkwell D 1
35 Mill Bank E 9
31 Mill Brow A 8
27 Mill Common G 7
17 Mill End, Bucks. F 9
25 Mill End, Cambs. G 4
17 Mill End, Herts. E 11
25 Mill End, Herts. M 4
18 Mill Green, Essex D 6
27 Mill Green, Suffolk L 3
18 Mill Hill E 2
39 Mill Houses H 8
9 Mill Lane A 9
58 Mill of Ardo, Grampian E 7
58 Mill of Ardo, Grampian D 6
58 Mill of Carden E 4
58 Mill of Culfork F 2
59 Mill of Gellan G 3
47 Mill of Haldane A 9
59 Mill of Monquich H 6
58 Mill of Muiresk C 4
58 Mill of Pot C 5
59 Mill of Uras J 6
26 Mill Street D 3
38 Millbeck C 5
64 Millbounds B 3
58 Millbreck C 7
58 Millbrex C 6
9 Millbridge B 10
25 Millbrook, Beds. L 1
3 Millbrook, Corn. D 11
4 Millbrook, Devon C 6
8 Millbrook, Hants. E 5
47 Millburn F 9
5 Millcombe L 7
11 Millcorner F 7
31 Milldale E 10
59 Millden Lodge J 3
53 Milldens B 10
48 Millerhill B 6
31 Miller's Dale C 10
31 Millers Green E 11
47 Millerston C 11
59 Millfield H 2
30 Millgreen G 5
21 Millhalf H 8
6 Millhayes E 5
49 Millheugh, Borders G 9
47 Millheugh, Strathclyde D 12
39 Millholme F 8

38 Millhouse, Cumb. **B 6**
46 Millhouse, Strathclyde **B 4**
35 Millhouse Green **G 11**
43 Millhousebridge **C 11**
32 Millhouses **B 1**
43 Milliganton **C 10**
47 Millikenpark **C 9**
36 Millington **B 6**
31 Millmeece **G 7**
38 Millom **G 4**
3 Millpool **C 8**
46 Millport **D 6**
43 Millquarter **C 7**
31 Millthorpe **C 11**
39 Millthrop **F 9**
59 Milltimber **G 6**
53 Millton **C 8**
57 Millton of Auchriachan **H 7**
58 Milltown, Grampian **F 2**
58 Milltown, Grampian **F 7**
59 Milltown, Grampian **G 4**
58 Milltown, Grampian **C 3**
32 Milltown, Derby **D 1**
4 Milltown, Devon **B 4**
59 Milltown, Tayside **K 5**
52 Milltown of Aberdalgie **E 5**
58 Milltown of Auchindoun **D 1**
59 Milltown of Campfield **G 4**
58 Milltown of Craigston **B 5**
56 Milltown of Edinvillie **F 8**
58 Milltown of Minnes **E 7**
58 Milltown of Towie **F 2**
47 Millwell **D 11**
53 Milnacraig **B 7**
52 Milnathort **G 6**
43 Milne **B 12**
47 Milngavie **B 10**
43 Milnmark **C 7**
35 Milnrow **F 8**
39 Milnthorpe **G 7**
21 Milson **E 11**
11 Milstead **B 7**
8 Milston **B 3**
14 Milton, Avon **H 6**
25 Milton, Cambs. **J 6**
51 Milton, Central **G 12**
44 Milton, Cumb. **G 4**
31 Milton, Derby **G 11**
43 Milton, Dumf. & Gall. **C 9**
43 Milton, Dumf. & Gall. **D 9**
42 Milton, Dumf. & Gall. **F 3**
12 Milton, Dyfed **G 4**
58 Milton, Grampian **E 1**
58 Milton, Grampian **A 3**
61 Milton, Highland **C 12**
57 Milton, Highland **H 5**
57 Milton, Highland **G 1**
56 Milton, Highland **D 2**
56 Milton, Highland **E 1**
56 Milton, Highland **B 3**
54 Milton, Highland **E 1**
16 Milton, Oxon **E 6**
16 Milton, Oxon **A 5**
7 Milton, Som. **D 8**
42 Milton, Strathclyde **B 4**
42 Milton, Strathclyde **A 3**
47 Milton, Strathclyde **B 9**
59 Milton, Tayside **J 2**
52 Milton, Tayside **A 6**
7 Milton Abbas **F 11**
5 Milton Abbot **H 3**
48 Milton Bridge **C 5**
25 Milton Bryna **M 1**
7 Milton Clevedon **C 10**
58 Milton Coldwells **D 7**
4 Milton Damerel **E 3**
16 Milton End **D 2**
25 Milton Ernest **K 1**
30 Milton Green **D 3**
16 Milton Hill **E 6**
23 Milton Keynes **H 12**
16 Milton Lilbourne **H 3**
23 Milton Malsor **G 10**
52 Milton Morenish **D 1**
58 Milton of Ardlethen **D 6**
59 Milton of Auchinhove **G 3**
57 Milton of Auchriaclan **H 7**
53 Milton of Balgonie **G 8**
47 Milton of Campsie **B 11**
58 Milton of Cushnie **F 3**
59 Milton of Dillavaird **J 5**
56 Milton of Farr **F 2**
58 Milton of Fishrie **B 5**
58 Milton of Lesmore **E 2**
59 Milton of Logie **G 2**
59 Milton of Murtle **G 6**
58 Milton of Noth **E 2**
46 Milton of Smerby **G 2**
59 Milton of Tullich **H 1**
7 Milton on Stour **C 11**
11 Milton Regis **B 7**
16 Milton under Wychwood **B 4**
5 Miltoncombe **J 4**
56 Miltonduff **D 7**
42 Miltonise **D 3**
6 Milverton **D 4**
31 Milwich **G 8**
51 Minard **H 7**
15 Minchinhampton **D 12**
49 Mindrum **F 11**
49 Mindrummill **F 11**
6 Minehead **B 3**
29 Minera **E 12**
16 Minety **E 1**
28 Minffordd **F 5**
50 Mingarrypark **A 4**
33 Miningsby **D 10**
3 Minions **C 9**
47 Minishant **H 8**
42 Minnigaff **E 5**
58 Minnonie **B 5**
38 Minorca **G 2**
44 Minsca **E 1**
36 Minskip **A 2**
8 Minstead **E 4**
11 Minster, Kent **B 11**
11 Minster, Kent **A 8**
16 Minster Lovell **C 4**
45 Minsteracres **G 8**
21 Minsterley **B 9**
15 Minsterworth **C 11**
7 Minterne Magna **F 10**
33 Minting **C 9**
58 Mintlaw **C 7**
49 Minto **G 8**
21 Minton **C 9**
12 Minwear **F 4**
22 Minworth **C 5**
64 Mirbister **C 1**
38 Mirehouse **D 2**
61 Mireland **B 12**
35 Mirfield **E 10**
15 Miserden **C 12**
14 Miskin, Mid Glam. **F 4**
14 Miskin, Mid Glam. **D 4**
36 Misson **H 5**
36 Misterton, Notts. **H 5**
7 Misterton, Som. **E 8**
23 Misterton, War. **D 9**
27 Mistley **M 4**
18 Mitcham **G 3**
15 Mitcheldean **B 9**
4 Mitcheldever **B 6**
15 Mitchel Troy **C 8**
2 Mitchell **D 6**
15 Mitcheltroy Com. **C 8**
45 Mitford **D 10**
2 Mithian **E 4**
22 Mitton **A 2**
17 Mixbury **A 7**
31 Mixon **D 9**
53 Moanzie **E 8**
44 Moat **F 3**
30 Mobberley **B 6**
21 Moccas **H 9**
29 Mochdre, Clwyd **B 7**
20 Mochdre, Powys **D 6**
42 Mochrum **G 4**
10 Mockbeggar, Kent **C 6**
10 Mockbeggar, Kent **A 6**
38 Mockerkin **C 3**
5 Modbury **K 5**
31 Moddershall **G 8**
61 Modsarie **B 7**
29 Moelfre, Clwyd **G 11**
28 Moelfre, Gwynedd **B 4**
43 Moffat **A 11**
25 Moggerhanger **K 2**
60 Moin House **B 6**
22 Moira **A 6**
11 Molash **C 9**
62 Mol-chlach **G 4**
29 Mold **D 11**
35 Moldgreen **F 10**
18 Molehill Green **A 5**
37 Molescroft **C 8**
45 Molesden **E 9**
25 Molesworth **H 2**
4 Molland **C 7**
4 Molland Cross **C 6**
30 Mollington, Ches. **C 2**
23 Mollington, Oxon **G 8**
47 Mollinsburn **B 12**
19 Molting Green **B 9**
13 Monachty **A 8**
51 Monachylemore **F 11**
46 Monamore Bridge **F 5**
54 Monar Lo. **F 6**
21 Monaughty **F 8**
59 Monboddo House **J 5**
51 Monevechadan **G 9**
27 Moneyden **J 5**
52 Moneydie **D 5**
43 Moniaive **C 8**
53 Monifieth **D 9**
53 Monikie **C 9**
53 Monimail **F 8**
12 Monington **C 5**
35 Monk Bretton **F 12**
36 Monk Fryston **D 3**
17 Monk Sherborne **H 7**
27 Monk Soham **J 5**
45 Monk-Wearmouth **G 12**
21 Monkhide **H 11**
21 Monkhopton **C 11**
21 Monkland **G 10**
4 Monkleigh **D 3**
14 Monknash **G 3**
4 Monkokehampton **E 5**
45 Monkridge **D 7**
27 Monks Eleigh **K 3**
10 Monk's Gate **E 1**
31 Monks' Heath **C 7**
23 Monks Kirby **D 8**
17 Monks Risborough **D 9**
58 Monkshill **D 5**
6 Monksilver **C 4**
22 Monkspath Street **D 5**
15 Monkswood **D 7**
6 Monkton, Devon **F 5**
12 Monkton, Dyfed **G 3**
11 Monkton, Kent **B 11**
6 Monkton, Som. **C 6**
47 Monkton, Strathclyde **G 8**
15 Monkton Coombe **H 11**
7 Monkton Deverill **B 11**
15 Monkton Farleigh **H 11**
6 Monkton Heathfield **D 6**
8 Monkton Up Wimborne **E 2**
7 Monkton Wyld **F 7**
47 Monktonhill **F 8**
9 Monkwood **C 8**
15 Monmouth **C 8**
15 Monmouth Cap **B 7**
21 Monnington on Wye **H 9**
53 Monorgan **D 8**
42 Monreith **G 4**
42 Monreith Mains **G 4**
7 Montacute **E 8**
58 Montcoffer House **B 4**
21 Mountford **A 9**
21 Montford Bridge **A 9**
58 Montgarrie **F 3**
21 Montgomery **C 8**
47 Montgreenan **E 8**
53 Montrave **F 8**
59 Montrose **L 5**
8 Monxton **B 5**
31 Monyash **D 10**
58 Monymusk **F 4**
52 Monzie, Tayside **E 4**
57 Monzie, Tayside **M 5**
47 Moodiesburn **B 11**
35 Moor Allerton **C 11**
8 Moor Crichel **E 2**
36 Moor Monkton **B 3**
56 Moor of Granary **D 6**
38 Moor Row **D 3**
11 Moor Street **B 7**
33 Moorby **D 10**
8 Moordown **G 3**
30 Moore **B 4**
15 Moorend **D 10**
16 Moorends **F 5**
8 Moorgreen **E 6**
31 Moorhall **C 11**
21 Moorhampton **H 9**
44 Moorhouse, Cumb. **G 2**
32 Moorhouse, Notts. **D 5**
7 Moorlinch **C 7**
41 Moorsholm **D 7**
5 Moorshop **H 4**
33 Moorside, Lincs. **D 9**
8 Moortown, Hants. **F 3**
8 Moortown, I.o.W. **H 6**
37 Moortown, Lincs. **G 8**
55 Morar **K 1**
24 Morborne **F 2**
4 Morchard Bishop **E 6**
23 Morcott **B 12**
30 Morda **G 2**
7 Morden, Dorest **G 12**
18 Morden, London **G 2**
15 Mordiford **A 9**
49 Mordington Mains **D 12**
40 Mordon **C 3**
21 More **C 9**
6 Morebath **D 3**
49 Morebattle **G 10**
34 Morecambe **A 3**
7 Morecombelake **G 7**
60 Morefield **G 3**
39 Moreland **C 8**
5 Moreleigh **K 6**
52 Morenish **D 1**
38 Moresby **C 2**
8 Morestead **D 6**
7 Moreton, Dorest **G 11**
18 Moreton, Essex **C 5**
30 Moreton, Merseyside **A 1**
17 Moreton, Oxon **D 8**
16 Moreton-in-Marsh **A 3**
21 Moreton Jeffries **G 11**
22 Moreton Morrell **F 6**
21 Moreton on Lugg **H 10**
23 Moreton Pinkney **G 9**
30 Moreton Say **G 5**
15 Moreton Valence **C 11**
5 Moretonhampstead **G 6**
13 Morfa **F 9**
28 Morfa'Bychan **F 5**
14 Morfa Glas **D 2**
28 Morfa-Nefyn **F 2**
8 Morgan's Vale **D 4**
32 Morley, Derby **F 1**
40 Morley, Dur. **B 2**
35 Morley, W. Yorks. **D 11**
31 Morley Green **B 7**
26 Morley St. Botolph **E 4**
26 Morning Thorpe **F 5**
48 Morningside, Lothian **B 5**
48 Morningside, Strathclyde **D 1**
45 Morpeth **D 10**
31 Morrey **H 10**
43 Morrington **C 9**
25 Morris Green **M 8**
42 Morriston, Strathclyde **A 3**
13 Morriston, W. Glam. **G 10**
26 Morston **A 3**
4 Mortehoe **B 3**
32 Morthen **A 2**
17 Mortimer **H 7**
17 Mortimer West End **H 7**
21 Mortimer's Cross **F 9**
18 Mortlake **F 2**
15 Morton, Avon **E 9**
44 Morton, Cumb. **H 2**
32 Morton, Derby **D 1**
24 Morton, Lincs. **C 2**
32 Morton, Lincs. **A 5**
26 Morton, Norf. **D 4**
32 Morton, Notts. **E 4**
30 Morton, Salop **H 2**
22 Morton Bagot **F 4**
40 Morton-on-Swale **F 3**
40 Morton Tinmouth **C 2**
2 Morvah **F 1**
3 Morval **D 9**
55 Morvich **G 3**
61 Morvich Lodge **F 8**
21 Morville **C 12**
4 Morwenstow **D 1**
32 Mosbrough **B 2**
44 Moscow, Cumb. **F 4**
47 Moscow, Strathclyde **E 9**
38 Mosedale **B 6**
35 Moselden Height **F 9**
22 Moseley, Heref. & Worc. **F 2**
22 Moseley, W. Midlands **D 4**
29 Moss, Clywd **E 12**
50 Moss, Highland **A 4**
36 Moss, S. Yorks. **F 4**
34 Moss Bank **G 4**
17 Moss End **G 9**
56 Moss of Barmuckity **D 8**
58 Mossat **F 2**
64 Mossbank **C 7**
44 Mossburnford **A 5**
43 Mossdale **D 7**
47 Mossend **C 12**
38 Mosser **C 4**
47 Mossgiel **F 9**
49 Mosshouses **E 8**
31 Mossley, Ches. **D 7**
35 Mossley, Manchester **G 8**
30 Mossley Hill **B 3**
44 Mosspeeble **D 2**
46 Moss-side **D 4**
58 Mosstodloch **B 1**
7 Mosterton **F 8**
29 Mostyn **B 11**
7 Motcombe **D 11**
5 Mothecombe **L 5**
47 Motherwell **D 12**
18 Mottingham **G 4**
8 Mottisfont **C 5**
8 Mottistone **H 5**
35 Mottram in Longdendale **H 8**
31 Mottram St. Andrew **B 7**
30 Mouldsworth **C 4**
52 Moulin **A 4**
52 Moulinearn **B 4**
17 Moulsford **F 7**
23 Moulsoe **H 12**
30 Moulton, Ches. **C 5**
24 Moulton, Lincs. **C 4**
26 Moulton, Norf. **E 7**
40 Moulton, N. Yorks. **E 3**
23 Moulton, Northants **E 11**
14 Moulton, S. Glam. **G 4**
25 Moulton, Suffolk **J 8**
24 Moulton Chapel **D 4**
25 Moulton St. Michael **F 5**
24 Moulton Seas End **C 4**
57 Moulzie **L 8**
44 Mounces **D 5**
58 Mounie Castle **E 5**
3 Mount **C 8**
2 Mount Ambrose **E 4**
27 Mount Bures **M 2**
2 Mount Hawke **E 4**
48 Mount Lothian **D 5**
49 Mount Pleasant, Borders **D 10**
31 Mount Pleasant, Derbyshire **E 11**
14 Mount Pleasant, Mid Glam. **D 4**
8 Mount Pleasant, Hampshire **F 4**
17 Mount Pleasant, Hampshire **H 7**
22 Mount Pleasant, Heref. & Worc. **F 3**
27 Mount Pleasant, Suffolk **G 8**
8 Mount Sorrel **D 2**
35 Mount Tabor **D 9**
45 Mountain **B 8**
14 Mountain Ash **D 4**
48 Mountain Cross **E 4**
12 Mountain Water **E 3**
48 Mountbenger **G 6**
58 Mountblairy **B 4**
10 Mountfield **F 6**
56 Mountgerald **D 1**
2 Mountjoy **D 6**
18 Mountnessing **D 6**
15 Mounton **E 8**
58 Mountsolie **B 7**
23 Mountsorrel **A 9**
2 Mousehole **G 2**
43 Mouswald **D 11**
31 Mow Cop **D 7**
49 Mowhaugh **G 10**
23 Mowsley **C 10**
59 Mowtie **H 6**
55 Moy, Highland **L 5**
55 Moy, Highland **L 8**
56 Moy, Highland **F 3**
56 Moy Hall **F 3**
56 Moy House **D 6**
55 Moy Lodge **L 8**
55 Moyle **H 3**
8 Moyles Court **E 3**
12 Moylgrove **C 5**
46 Muasdale **E 2**
15 Much Birch **A 8**
21 Much Cowarne **H 11**
15 Much Dewchurch **A 8**
18 Much Hadham **B 4**
34 Much Hoole **E 3**
15 Much Marcle **A 10**
21 Much Wenlock **B 11**
59 Muchalls **H 6**
7 Muchelney **D 8**
3 Muchlarnick **D 9**
54 Muchrachd **F 6**
56 Muckernich **D 2**
42 Muckfoot **C 3**
19 Mucking **F 7**
7 Muckleford **G 9**
30 Mucklestone **F 6**
30 Muckleton **H 4**
58 Muckletown **E 3**
22 Muckley Corner **B 4**
33 Muckton **B 10**
60 Mudale **D 6**
4 Muddiford **B 4**
10 Muddles Green **G 4**
8 Mudeford **G 3**
7 Mudford **D 9**
7 Mudgley **B 8**
47 Mugdock **B 10**
62 Mugeary **D 4**
31 Mugginton **F 11**
45 Muggleswick **H 9**
61 Muie **F 7**
57 Muir **K 6**
54 Muir of Fairburn **D 8**
58 Muir of Fowlis **F 3**
56 Muir of Ord **E 1**
58 Muirden **B 4**
48 Muirfoot **D 2**
53 Muirhead, Fife **E 9**
53 Muirhead, Fife **G 7**
59 Muirhead, Grampian **L 5**
47 Muirhead, Strathclyde **B 11**
53 Muirhead, Tayside **D 8**
48 Muirhouses, Lothian **A 3**
47 Muirkirk **G 11**
47 Muirmill **A 12**
53 Muirsdrum **C 10**
55 Muirshearlich **L 5**
59 Muirskie **H 6**
58 Muirtack, Grampian **C 5**
58 Muirtack, Tayside **D 7**
56 Muirton, Highland **C 3**
59 Muirton, Tayside **L 4**
52 Muirton, Tayside **E 6**
54 Muirton Mains **D 8**
52 Muirton of Ardblair **C 6**
52 Muirtown **F 4**
58 Muiryfold **C 5**
43 Muiryhill **A 9**
39 Muker **E 11**
26 Mulbarton **E 5**
58 Mulben **C 1**
41 Mulgrave **D 8**
2 Mullion **H 4**
55 Mullochbuie **L 1**
13 Mumbles **H 9**
33 Mumby **C 12**
21 Munderfield Row **G 12**
21 Munderfield Stocks **G 12**
26 Mundesley **B 6**
26 Mundford **F 1**
26 Mundham **F 6**
19 Mundon Hill **D 8**
55 Munerigie **J 6**
60 Mungasdale **G 2**
38 Mungrisdale **B 6**
56 Munlochy **D 2**
47 Munnoch **E 7**
21 Munsley **H 12**
21 Munslow **D 10**
21 Munslow Aston **D 10**
5 Murchington **G 6**
17 Murcott **C 7**
61 Murkle **A 11**
55 Murlaggan, Highland **K 4**
55 Murlaggan, Highland **L 7**
48 Murrayfield, Lothian **B 5**
52 Murrayfield, Tayside **D 5**
43 Murraythwaite **D 12**
24 Murrow **E 5**
17 Mursley **A 9**
59 Murthil **L 2**
52 Murthly **C 6**
52 Murthly Castle **C 5**
39 Murton, Cumbria **C 9**
45 Murton, Dur. **H 12**
49 Murton, Northumb. **E 12**
36 Murton, N. Yorks. **B 4**
40 Murton Grange **F 5**
6 Musbury **G 6**
41 Muscoates **G 7**
48 Musselburgh **B 6**
32 Muston, Leics. **F 5**
41 Muston, N. Yorks. **G 11**
22 Mustow Green **E 2**
43 Mutehill **G 7**
27 Mutford **G 8**
52 Muthill **E 4**
6 Mutterton **F 4**
21 Muxton **A 12**
61 Mybster **B 11**
13 Myddfai **D 11**
30 Myddle **H 3**
13 Mydroilyn **B 8**
2 Mylor Bridge **F 5**
12 Mynachlog-ddu **D 5**
21 Myndtown **C 9**
20 Mynydd-bach, Dyfed **E 8**
15 Mynydd-bach, Gwent **E 8**
13 Mynyddygarreg **F 7**
28 Myntho **G 3**
58 Myre of Bedlam **C 6**
59 Myrebird **G 5**
9 Mytchett **A 10**
35 Mytholmroyd **E 9**
34 Mythop **D 2**
40 Myton-on-Swale **H 4**
36 Naburn **C 4**
11 Nackington **C 10**
27 Nacton **L 5**
37 Nafferton **A 8**
7 Nailbridge **C 9**
15 Nailsea **G 8**
23 Nailstone **A 7**
15 Nailsworth **D 11**
56 Nairn **D 4**
10 Nalderswood **D 1**
2 Nancegollan **F 3**
2 Nancledra **F 2**
9 Nanhurst **B 11**
29 Nannerch **C 11**
32 Nanpantan **H 2**
3 Nanpean **D 7**
3 Nanstallon **C 7**
28 Nant Peris **D 5**
14 Nant-ddu **C 3**

13 Nanteris A 7
13 Nantgaredig E 8
14 Nantgarw F 4
20 Nant-glas F 5
29 Nantglyn D 9
20 Nantgwyn E 5
28 Nantlle E 4
30 Nantmawr H 1
20 Nantmel F 6
28 Nantmor F 5
30 Nantwich E 5
13 Nantybai C 11
14 Nant-y-Bwch C 5
14 Nant-y-cafn D 2
13 Nant-y-ffin D 9
14 Nantyffyllon E 2
14 Nantyglo C 5
21 Nant-y-Meichiaid A 7
14 Nant-y-moel E 3
28 Nant-y-pandy C 6
17 Naphill D 9
35 Nappa B 7
23 Napton on the Hill F 8
12 Narberth E 4
23 Narborough, Leics. B 8
24 Narborough, Norf. D 8
3 Narkurs D 10
50 Narrachan F 6
28 Nasareth E 4
23 Naseby D 10
17 Nash, Bucks. A 8
21 Nash, Heref. & Worc. F 8
15 Nash, Gwent F 7
21 Nash, Salop E 11
24 Nassington F 2
18 Nasty B 4
4 Natcott D 2
39 Nateby, Cumbria D 10
34 Nateby, Lancs. C 3
39 Natland F 7
27 Naughton K 3
16 Naunton, Glos. B 2
22 Naunton, Heref. & Worc. H 2
22 Naunton, Beauchamp G 3
54 Naust B 2
33 Navenby D 7
18 Navestock Heath D 5
18 Navestock Side D 5
61 Navidale E 10
41 Nawton G 7
27 Nayland M 3
19 Naze Park B 12
18 Nazeing C 4
8 Neacroft F 3
64 Neap D 7
38 Near Sawrey F 6
40 Neasham D 4
13 Neath G 11
13 Neath Abbey G 10
31 Neather Heage E 12
26 Neatishead C 6
20 Nebo, Dyfed F 1
28 Nebo, Gwynedd A 4
28 Nebo, Gwynedd E 4
29 Nebo, Gwynedd E 7
26 Necton E 2
60 Nedd D 3
27 Nedging K 3
27 Nedging Tye K 3
27 Needham G 5
27 Needham Market K 4
25 Needingworth H 4
31 Needlewood H 10
21 Neen Savage E 12
21 Neen Sollars E 12
21 Neenton D 11
28 Nefyn F 3
47 Neilston D 9
23 Neithrop H 8
21 Nelly Andrews Green A 8
35 Nelson, Lancs. C 7
14 Nelson, Mid Glam. E 4
45 Nelson Village E 10
48 Nemphlar E 1
15 Nempnett Thrubwell H 8
39 Nenthall A 10
39 Nenthead A 10
49 Nenthorn F 9
29 Nercwys D 11
47 Nerston D 11
35 Nesfield B 9
49 Nesbit F 12
30 Ness C 2
30 Nesscliffe H 3
30 Neston, Ches. B 2
15 Neston, Wilts. G 11
31 Nether Alderley C 7
49 Nether Blainslie E 8
31 Nether Booth B 10
49 Nether Brotherstone D 7
32 Nether Broughton H 4
39 Nether Burrow H 8
44 Nether Cassock C 1
7 Nether Cerne F 10
59 Nether Contlaw G 6
43 Nether Craigenputtock C 9
58 Nether Crimond E 6
48 Nether Dalgliesh H 5
58 Nether Dallachy A 1
6 Nether Exe F 3
48 Nether Fingland H 2
58 Nether Glasslaw B 6
43 Nether Gribton D 10
53 Nether Handwick C 8
36 Nether Haugh G 2
23 Nether Hayford F 10
44 Nether Hindhope B 6
48 Nether Howcleugh H 3
39 Nether Kellet H 7
58 Nether Kinmundy C 8
47 Nether Kirkton D 9
32 Nether Langwith C 3
58 Nether Leask D 8
47 Nether Newton E 10
31 Nether Padley B 11
58 Nether Park B 7
59 Nether Pitforthie J 6
36 Nether Poppleton B 3
40 Nether Silton F 5
6 Nether Stowey B 5
59 Nether Thaneston K 4
53 Nether Urquhart F 7
8 Nether Wallop B 5
22 Nether Whitacre C 6
48 Nether Whitecleuch G 1
16 Nether Worton A 5
8 Netheravon A 3
58 Netherbrae B 5
48 Netherburn E 1
7 Netherbury F 8
44 Netherby, Cumb. F 2
35 Netherby, N. Yorks. C 11
4 Nethercott B 4
15 Netherend D 9
10 Netherfield F 6
8 Netherhampton C 3
49 Netherhowden D 7
43 Netherlaw G 8
59 Netherley H 6
43 Nethermill, Dumf. & Gall. C 11
58 Nethermill, Grampian D 8
58 Nethermills C 3
43 Nethermiln A 11
58 Nethermuir C 7
47 Netherplace D 10
22 Netherseal A 6
16 Netherstreet H 1
43 Netherthird, Dumf. & Gall. F 8
47 Netherthird, Strathclyde G 10
35 Netherthong F 10
45 Netherwitton D 9
47 Netherwood F 11
47 Netherton, Central A 10
5 Netherton, Devon J 8
6 Netherton, Hants. H 5
22 Netherton, Heref. & Worc. H 3
34 Netherton, Merseyside G 2
45 Netherton, Northumb. B 8
47 Netherton, Strathclyde D 12
59 Netherton, Tayside L 3
52 Netherton, Tayside B 6
22 Netherton, W. Midlands C 3
35 Netherton, W. Yorks. F 10
35 Netherton, W. Yorks. F 11
64 Nethertown, Highland F 2
38 Nethertown, Cumb. D 2
57 Nethy Bridge G 6
8 Netley E 6
8 Netley Marsh E 5
17 Nettlebed E 8
7 Nettlebridge A 10
7 Nettlecombe, Dorset G 8
9 Nettlecombe, I.o.W. H 7
6 Nettlecombe, Som. C 4
17 Nettleden C 11
33 Nettleham C 7
10 Nettlestead C 6
10 Nettlestead Green C 5
9 Nettlestone G 8
45 Nettlesworth H 10
37 Nettleton, Lincs. G 9
15 Nettleton, Wilts. F 11
5 Netton, Devon L 4
8 Netton, Wilts B 3
20 Neuadd B 6
20 Neuadd-ddu E 5
19 Nevendon E 7
12 Nevern C 4
43 New Abbey E 10
58 New Aberdour A 6
18 New Addington H 4
9 New Alresford C 7
53 New Alyth B 7
32 New Annesley E 2
10 New Ash Green B 5
18 New Barnet D 3
18 New Base G 6
49 New Belses G 8
45 New Berwick A 9
23 New Bilton E 8
33 New Bolingbroke D 10
23 New Bradwell H 11
32 New Brampton C 1
40 New Brancepeth A 2
43 New Bridge, Dumf. & Gall. D 10
36 New Bridge, Humberside E 4
29 New Brighton, Clwyd D 11
30 New Brighton, Merseyside A 2
32 New Brinsley E 2
26 New Buckenham F 4
58 New Byth B 6
26 New Catton E 5
32 New Clipstone D 3
26 New Costessey D 5
43 New Cowper G 12
20 New Cross E 2
47 New Cumnock H 11
58 New Deer C 6
45 New Delaval E 11
17 New Denham F 11
2 New Downs E 4
23 New Duston F 10
36 New Earswick B 4
36 New Edlington G 3
56 New Elgin D 8
37 New Ellerby C 9
22 New End F 4
30 New Ferry B 2
36 New Fryston D 2
43 New Galloway D 7
2 New Grimsby D 2
45 New Haggerston B 11
45 New Hartley E 11
12 New Hedges G 5
45 New Herrington H 11
35 New Hey F 8
16 New Hinksey D 6
26 New Holkham B 2
37 New Holland E 8
38 New Hotel E 5
32 New Houghton, Derbyshire D 2
26 New Houghton, Norfolk C 1
39 New Houses H 10
39 New Hutton F 8
10 New Hythe B 6
13 New Inn, Dyfed C 8
15 New Inn, Gwent D 8
39 New Inn, N. Yorks. H 10
21 New Invention E 8
54 New Kelso E 3
58 New Kendal E 6
45 New Lambton H 11
48 New Lanark E 2
34 New Lane F 3
33 New Leake D 11
58 New Leeds B 7
34 New Longdon E 4
42 New Luce E 3
49 New Mains, Lothian A 8
48 New Mains, Strathclyde F 1
59 New Mains of Ury J 6
18 New Malden G 2
40 New Marske C 6
30 New Marton G 2
35 New Mill, W. Yorks F 10
16 New Mill, Wilts. H 3
2 New Mills, Corn. D 6
31 New Mills, Derby B 8
20 New Mills, Powys B 6
8 New Milton F 4
27 New Mistley M 4
12 New Moat D 4
45 New Mousen C 12
32 New Ollerton C 4
58 New Pitsligo B 6
2 New Polzeath B 6
47 New Prestwick G 8
13 New Quay A 7
21 New Radnor F 7
39 New Rent B 7
45 New Ridley G 9
11 New Romney F 9
36 New Rossington G 4
20 New Row E 3
8 New Sarum C 3
52 New Sauchie H 4
52 New Scone E 6
63 New Shawbost B 4
45 New Shoreston D 12
47 New Stevenston C 12
8 New Swanage H 2
63 New Tolsta B 6
17 New Town, Berks. G 7
8 New Town, Dorset E 3
7 New Town, Dorset D 11
10 New Town, E. Sussex F 3
17 New Town, Hants. H 7
49 New Town, Lothian B 7
16 New Town, Wilts. G 4
14 New Tredegar D 5
63 New Valley C 5
37 New Waltham G 10
25 New Wimpole K 4
49 New Winton B 7
16 New Yatt C 5
33 New York, Lincs. E 9
45 New York, Tyne & Wear F 11
64 Newark A 4
24 Newark, Cambs. E 3
32 Newark, Notts. E 5
48 Newarthill C 1
48 Newbattle C 6
39 Newbiggin, Cumb. B 7
44 Newbiggin, Cumbria H 4
38 Newbiggin, Cumbria H 5
39 Newbiggin, Cumbria B 8
39 Newbiggin, Dur. B 11
45 Newbiggin, Dur. H 9
45 Newbiggin, Northumb. G 8
49 Newbiggin, N. Yorks. F 11
39 Newbiggin, N. Yorks. G 12
45 Newbiggin-by-the Sea D 11
39 Newbiggin on Lune E 9
49 Newbigging, Borders D 8
48 Newbigging, Strathclyde E 3
59 Newbigging, Tayside K 1
32 Newbold, Derby C 1
32 Newbold, Leics. H 1
23 Newbold on Avon D 8
22 Newbold on Stour G 6
22 Newbold Pacey F 6
23 Newbold Verdon B 8
24 Newborough, Cambs. E 3
28 Newborough, Gwynedd D 4
31 Newborough, Staffordshire H 10
23 Newbottle, Northants H 8
45 Newbottle, Tyne & Wear H 11
27 Newbourn L 6
29 Newbridge, Clwyd F 12
2 Newbridge, Corn. F 1
3 Newbridge, Corn. C 10
12 Newbridge, Dyfed D 3
14 Newbridge, Gwent E 5
8 Newbridge, Hants. E 4
8 Newbridge, I.o.W. G 6
48 Newbridge, Lothian B 4
15 Newbridge-on-Usk E 7
20 Newbridge on Wye F 6
45 Newbrough F 7
48 Newburgh, Borders G 6
53 Newburgh, Fife E 7
58 Newburgh, Grampian B 7
58 Newburgh, Grampian E 7
40 Newburgh Priory G 5
49 Newburn, Northumb. E 11
45 Newburn, Tyne & Wear G 10
16 Newbury G 5
39 Newby, Cumbria C 8
40 Newby, N. Yorks. D 5
41 Newby, N. Yorks. F 10
39 Newby, N. Yorks. H 9
38 Newby Bridge G 6
44 Newby East G 3
44 Newby West H 2
40 Newby Wiske F 4
15 Newcastle, Gwent C 7
21 Newcastle, Salop D 8
12 Newcastle Emlyn C 6
31 Newcastle-under-Lyme F 7
45 Newcastle upon Tyne F 10
44 Newcastleton D 3
12 Newchapel, Dyfed C 6
31 Newchapel, Staffs. E 7
10 Newchapel, Surrey D 2
13 Newchurch, Dyfed E 7
15 Newchurch, Gwent E 8
9 Newchurch, I.o.W. H 7
11 Newchurch, Kent E 9
35 Newchurch, Lancs. C 7
35 Newchurch, Lancs. E 7
21 Newchurch, Powys G 7
31 Newchurch, Staffs. H 10
6 Newcott E 6
10 Newdigate D 1
17 Newell Green G 9
11 Newenden E 7
15 Newent B 10
15 Newerne D 9
43 Newfield, Dumf. & Gall. E 12
43 Newfield, Dumf. & Gall. E 9
40 Newfield, Dur. B 2
45 Newfield, Dur. H 10
56 Newfield, Highland B 3
9 Newfound A 7
12 Newglae E 2
26 Newgate A 3
18 Newgate Street C 3
64 Newgord A 8
48 Newhall, Borders F 6
30 Newhall, Ches. F 5
31 Newhall, Derby H 11
56 Newhallpoint C 3
18 Newham, London F 4
45 Newham, Northumb. E 12
45 Newham Hall D 12
10 Newhaven H 3
31 Newhaven House D 10
41 Newholm D 8
48 Newhouse C 1
45 Newhouses E 8
10 Newick F 3
11 Newingreen D 10
11 Newington, Kent B 7
11 Newington, Kent D 10
32 Newington, Notts. A 4
17 Newington, Oxen D 7
21 Newington, Salop D 9
15 Newland, Glos. C 9
22 Newland, Heref. & Worc. G 2
37 Newland, Humber. D 8
36 Newland, N. Yorks. E 5
6 Newland, Som. B 2
53 Newlandhead C 9
44 Newlands, Borders D 3
43 Newlands, Dumf. & Gall. C 10
56 Newlands, Grampian E 8
45 Newlands, Northumb. G 9
61 Newlands of Geise A 10
2 Newlyn G 2
58 Newmachar F 6
48 Newmains D 1
25 Newmarket, Suff. J 7
63 Newmarket, W. Isles C 5
44 Newmill, Borders B 3
2 Newmill, Corn. F 2
58 Newmill, Grampian B 2
59 Newmill of Inshewan L 2
35 Newmillerdam F 12
48 Newmills, Fife A 3
15 Newmills, Gwent D 8
56 Newmills, Highland C 2
48 Newmills, Lothian C 4
58 Newmills of Boyne B 3
52 Newmiln D 6
47 Newmilns F 10
15 Newnham, Glos. C 10
9 Newnham, Hants. A 8
25 Newnham, Herts. L 3
11 Newnham, Kent B 8
23 Newnham, Northants F 9
21 Newnham Bridge E 11
53 Newpark F 9
4 Newport, Devon C 4
12 Newport, Dyfed C 4
25 Newport, Essex M 6
15 Newport, Glos. E 10
14 Newport, Gwent F 6
61 Newport, Highland E 10
36 Newport, Humber. D 6
8 Newport, I.o.W. G 6
26 Newport, Norfolk D 8
30 Newport, Salop H 6
53 Newport-on-Tay D 9
23 Newport Pagnell H 12
12 Newport Sands C 4
9 Newpound Com. C 11
2 Newquay D 5
52 Newrow H 4
58 Newseat D 4
34 Newsham, Lancs. D 4
40 Newsham, N. Yorks. D 1
40 Newsham, N. Yorks. G 4
36 Newsholme, Humberside D 5
35 Newsholme, Lancs. B 7
35 Newsholme, W. Yorks. C 9
49 Newstead, Borders F 8
45 Newstead, Northumb. E 12
32 Newstead, Notts. E 2
36 Newthorpe D 3
49 Newton, Borders G 8
25 Newton, Cambs. K 5
30 Newton, Ches. C 3
30 Newton, Ches. C 4
30 Newton, Ches. D 4
35 Newton, Ches. G 8
40 Newton, Cleveland D 6
38 Newton, Cumbria H 5
32 Newton, Derby D 2
7 Newton, Dorset E 11
43 Newton, Dumf. & Gall. B 12
58 Newton, Grampian C 8
56 Newton, Grampian C 7
15 Newton, Heref. & Worc. A 7
21 Newton, Heref. & Worc. G 10
61 Newton, Highland C 12
56 Newton, Highland E 3
56 Newton, Highland C 3
56 Newton, Highland E 1
60 Newton, Highland D 4
34 Newton, Lancs. D 2
34 Newton, Lancs. D 3
39 Newton, Lancs. H 8
34 Newton, Lancs. B 6
24 Newton, Lincs. B 1
48 Newton, Lothian B 4
14 Newton, Mid Glam. G 2
24 Newton, Norfolk D 5
26 Newton, Norfolk D 1
23 Newton, Northants. D 12
45 Newton, Northumb. B 8
45 Newton, Northumb. G 8
32 Newton, Notts. F 4
6 Newton, Som. B 5
31 Newton, Staffs. H 9
48 Newton, Strathclyde F 2
27 Newton, Suffolk L 2
52 Newton, Tayside D 4
23 Newton, War. D 8
13 Newton, W. Glam. H 9
36 Newton, W. Yorks. D 2
8 Newton, Wilts. D 4
5 Newton Abbot J 7
43 Newton Arlosh F 12
40 Newton Aycliffe C 3
40 Newton Bewley C 5
23 Newton Blossomville G 12
25 Newton Bromswold J 1
23 Newton Burgoland A 7
33 Newton by Toft B 7
5 Newton Ferrers L 4
26 Newton Flotman F 5
23 Newton Harcourt B 9
58 Newton House E 4
34 Newton-le-Willows, Lancashire H 4
40 Newton-le-Willows, N. Yorkshire F 2
36 Newton Kyme C 2
17 Newton Longville A 9
47 Newton Mearns D 10
40 Newton Morrell D 3
41 Newton Mulgrave D 8
12 Newton Mountain F 3
50 Newton of Ardtoe A 4
52 Newton of Balcanquhal F 6
53 Newton of Falkland F 7
58 Newton of Murcar F 7
60 Newton of Ochtow G 5
52 Newton of Pitcairns F 5
36 Newton-on-Ouse A 3
41 Newton-on-Rawcliffe F 8
45 Newton-on-the-Moor C 10
32 Newton on Trent C 5
6 Newton Poppleford G 4
17 Newton Purcell A 7
22 Newton Regis A 6
39 Newton Reigny B 7
49 Newton St. Boswells F 8
4 Newton St. Cyres F 7
26 Newton St. Faith D 5
15 Newton St. Loe H 10
4 Newton St. Petrock E 3
31 Newton Solney H 11
8 Newton Stacey B 6
42 Newton Stewart E 5
8 Newton Toney B 4
4 Newton Tracey C 4
47 Newton upon Ayr G 8
36 Newton upon Derwent B 5
9 Newton Valence C 8
43 Newtonairds D 9
58 Newtongarry Croft D 3
48 Newtongrange C 6
59 Newtonmill L 3
57 Newtonmore J 3
31 Newtown, Ches. B 8
30 Newtown, Ches. E 5
2 Newtown, Corn. G 4
44 Newtown, Cumb. G 2
44 Newtown, Cumb. G 3
39 Newtown, Cumbria C 7
4 Newtown, Devon C 6

8 Newtown, Dorset G 2
15 Newtown, Glos. A 12
15 Newtown, Glos. D 10
56 Newtown, Grampian C 7
8 Newtown, Hants. D 4
9 Newtown, Hants. D 7
8 Newtown, Hants. E 4
9 Newtown, Hants. E 7
16 Newtown, Hants. H 6
21 Newtown, Heref. & Worc. G 10
21 Newtown, Heref. & Worc. H 11
55 Newtown, Highland J 7
38 Newtown, I.o.M. H 2
8 Newtown, I.o.W. G 5
34 Newtown, Lancs. E 4
45 Newtown, Northumb. A 8
45 Newtown, Northumb. C 8
49 Newtown, Northumb. F 12
20 Newtown, Powys C 6
30 Newtown, Salop G 3
31 Newtown, Staffs. D 7
31 Newtown, Staffs. D 9
7 Newtown, Wilts. C 12
23 Newtown Linford A 8
48 Newtown of Covington E 3
58 Newtown of Melrose A 5
53 Newtyle C 8
12 Neyland F 3
15 Nibley F 10
64 Nibon C 6
6 Nicholashayne E 5
13 Nicholaston H 8
44 Nickie's Hill F 4
35 Nidd A 11
59 Nigg, Grampian G 7
56 Nigg, Highland C 4
56 Nigg Station B 4
6 Nightcott D 2
18 Nine Ashes D 6
48 Nine Mile Burn D 4
44 Ninebanks H 6
10 Ninfield G 6
8 Ningwood G 5
49 Nisbet G 9
43 Nithside D 10
8 Niton H 6
30 No Man's Heath, Cheshire E 4
22 No Man's Heath, Warwickshire A 6
2 No Man's Land, Cornwall C 6
4 No Man's Land, Devon E 7
18 Noak Hill E 5
48 Noblehouse D 5
21 Nobold A 10
23 Nobottle F 10
33 Nocton D 8
16 Noke C 6
12 Nolton E 2
12 Nolton Haven E 2
30 Noneley G 3
11 Nonington C 11
39 Nook G 8
30 Norbury, Ches. E 4
31 Norbury, Derby F 9
21 Norbury, Salop C 9
30 Norbury, Staffs. H 6
64 Norby D 6
24 Nordelph E 7
35 Norden F 7
8 Norden H 1
21 Nordley C 12
16 Nore Marsh F 2
26 Norfolk, Co. D 4
49 Norham E 11
30 Norley C 4
8 Norley Wood F 5
24 Norman Cross F 3
36 Normanby, Humber. E 6
41 Normanby, N. Yorks. G 7
33 Normanby-by- Spital A 7
37 Normanby le Wold H 9
9 Normandy A 10
10 Norman's Bay G 6
6 Norman's Green F 4
8 Normansland D 4
31 Normanton, Derbyshire G 11
32 Normanton, Leics. F 5
32 Normanton, Lincs. F 6
32 Normanton, Notts. E 4
36 Normanton, W. Yorks. E 2
23 Normanton le Heath A 7
32 Normanton on Soar H 2
32 Normanton on the Wolds G 3
32 Normanton on Trent C 5
34 Normoss C 2
9 Norney B 10
15 Norrington Com. H 12
31 Norris Hill H 11
32 North Anston B 2
16 North Aston A 6
58 North Atrochie D 7
8 North Baddesley D 5
51 North Ballachulish B 8
7 North Barrow C 9
26 North Barsham B 2
19 North Benfleet E 7
9 North Bersted F 10
49 North Berwick A 8
8 North Boarhunt E 7
5 North Bovey G 6
47 North Brackenridge E 12
7 North Bradley A 12
5 North Brentor H 4
7 North Brewham C 10
4 North Buckland B 4
26 North Burlingham D 7
7 North Cadbury D 9
32 North Carlton, Lincolnshire B 6
32 North Carlton, Notts. B 3
46 North Carrine H 2
36 North Cave D 6
16 North Cerney C 1
9 North Chapel C 11
8 North Charford D 3
45 North Charlton A 10
7 North Cheriton D 10
7 North Chideock G 8
36 North Cliffe C 6
32 North Clifton C 5
37 North Coates G 11
33 North Cockerington A 10
7 North Coker E 9
32 North Collingham D 5
10 North Common F 3
14 North Cornelly F 2
50 North Corry B 5
58 North Cottown F 5
26 North Cove F 8
43 North Cowshaw C 11
40 North Cowton E 3
27 North Crawley H 12
18 North Cray G 5
26 North Creake B 2
7 North Curry D 7
37 North Dalton B 7
3 North Darley B 10
35 North Deighton B 12
47 North Drumboy D 10
36 North Duffield C 5
33 North Elkington A 10
26 North Elmham C 3
36 North Elmsall F 3
15 North End, Avon G 11
15 North End, Avon H 7
17 North End, Bucks. A 9
17 North End, Bucks. E 8
7 North End, Dorset D 11
18 North End, Essex B 6
9 North End, Hants. F 8
16 North End, Hants. H 5
37 North End, Humberside D 10
24 North End, Lincs. B 3
45 North End, Northumb. C 9
6 North End, Som. D 6
9 North End, W. Sussex E 12
54 North Erradale B 1
6 North Esworthy D 2
19 North Fambridge D 8
62 North Fearns D 5
46 North Feorline F 4
37 North Ferriby E 7
37 North Frodingham B 8
63 North Galson A 5
64 North Gluss C 7
6 North Gorley E 3
58 North Gorrachie B 5
26 North Green F 5
44 North Greenhill F 4
41 North Grimston H 8
10 North Halling B 6
47 North Halls F 11
9 North Hayling F 9
45 North Hazelrigg C 12
9 North Heath D 12
3 North Hill B 9
16 North Hinksey D 6
10 North Holmwood C 1
47 North Hourat D 8
5 North Huish K 6
32 North Hykeham D 6
12 North Johnston F 3
37 North Kelsey G 8
56 North Kessock E 2
37 North Killingholme E 9
40 North Kilvington G 4
23 North Kilworth D 9
58 North Kinmundy F 6
58 North Kirkton C 8
33 North Kyme E 8
10 North Lancing G 1
17 North Lee C 9
40 North Lees H 3
23 North Luffenham B 12
16 North Leigh C 5
32 North Leverton with Habblesthorpe B 5
22 North Littleton G 4
27 North Lopham G 3
45 North Lyham C 12
9 North Marden D 9
17 North Marston B 8
48 North Middleton, Lothian C 6
49 North Middleton, Northumb. G 12
4 North Molton C 6
58 North Monkshill C 5
41 North Moor H 12
16 North Moreton E 6
9 North Mundham F 10
32 North Muskham D 5
37 North Newbald C 7
23 North Newington H 7
16 North Newnton H 2
6 North Newton C 6
15 North Nibley E 10
9 North Oakley A 7
18 North Ockendon E 6
40 North Ormesby C 5
33 North Ormsby A 10
40 North Otterington F 4
37 North Owersby H 8
7 North Perrott E 8
6 North Petherton C 6
3 North Petherwin A 10
26 North Pickenham E 1
22 North Piddle G 3
7 North Poorton F 8
6 North Quarme C 3
48 North Queensferry A 4
4 North Radworthy C 6
33 North Rauceby F 7
35 North Rigton B 11
31 North Rode D 7
64 North Roe B 7
24 North Runcton D 7
64 North Sandwick B 8
38 North Scale H 4
32 North Scarle D 6
45 N. Seaton Colliery D 11
63 North Shawbost B 4
50 North Shian C 6
45 North Shields F 11
19 North Shoebury E 9
34 North Shore D 2
34 North Shortcleugh H 2
38 North Side, Cumb. B 2
24 North Side, Cambs. E 4
41 North Skelton C 7
37 North Somercotes G 12
40 North Stainley G 3
39 North Stainmore D 10
15 North Stoke, Avon G 10
17 North Stoke, Oxon F 7
9 North Stoke, W. Sussex E 11
17 North Street, Berks. G 7
9 North Street, Hants. C 8
45 North Sunderland D 12
4 North Tamerton F 2
4 North Tawton F 5
37 North Thoresby G 10
8 North Tidworth A 4
45 North Togston C 10
63 North Tolsta B 6
26 North Tuddenham D 3
45 North Walbottle F 10
26 North Walsham C 6
9 North Waltham B 7
9 North Warnborough A 9
59 North Water Bri. L 4
61 North Watten B 11
18 North Weald Bassett D 5
32 North Wheatley B 5
15 North Wick H 9
5 North Whilborough J 7
33 North Willingham A 8
32 North Wingfield D 1
32 North Witham H 6
7 North Wootton, Dorset E 10
24 North Wootton, Norfolk C 7
7 North Wootton, Somerset B 9
15 North Wraxall G 11
16 North Wroughton F 3
45 North Yardhope C 7
40 North Yorkshire, Co. F 5
40 Northallerton F 4
4 Northam, Devon C 3
8 Northam, Hants. E 6
23 Northampton F 11
23 Northamptonshire, County E 11
18 Northaw D 3
24 Northborough Peakirk E 3
11 Northbourne C 12
8 Northbrook B 6
17 Northchurch C 10
5 Northcott G 2
23 Northend G 7
49 Northfield, Borders C 11
59 Northfield, Grampian G 6
22 Northfield, W. Midlands D 4
10 Northfleet A 5
11 Northiam F 7
25 Northill K 3
9 Northington B 7
33 Northlands E 10
16 Northleach C 2
6 Northleigh G 5
4 Northlew F 4
16 Northmoor D 5
6 Northmoor Green or Moorland C 6
53 Northmuir B 8
9 Northney F 9
18 Northolt E 1
29 Northop C 11
29 Northophall C 12
24 Northorpe, Lincs. B 3
24 Northorpe, Lincs. D 2
37 Northorpe, Lincs. G 7
7 Northover, Som. B 8
7 Northover, Som. D 8
35 Northowram D 10
8 Northport G 1
26 Northrepps B 5
63 Northton H 1
64 Northtown D 3
45 Northumberland, County D 8
15 Northway, Glos. A 12
6 Northway, Som. C 5
30 Northwich C 5
15 Northwick F 9
24 Northwold F 8
8 Northwood, I.o.W. G 6
18 Northwood, Lond. E 1
30 Northwood, Salop G 3
25 Northwood End L 2
15 Northwood Green C 10
30 Northwood, Ches. B 4
40 Norton, Cleveland C 5
15 Norton, Glos. B 11
15 Norton, Gwent B 7
22 Norton, Heref. & Worc. G 2
22 Norton, Heref. & Worc. G 4
8 Norton, I.o.W. G 5
41 Norton, N. Yorks. H 8
23 Norton, Northants. F 9
32 Norton, Notts. C 3
21 Norton, Powys F 8
21 Norton, Salop A 11
22 Norton, Salop B 1
21 Norton, Salop D 10
36 Norton, S. Yorks. F 3
27 Norton, Suffolk J 3
15 Norton, Wilts. F 12
8 Norton Bavant B 1
31 Norton Bridge G 7
22 Norton Canes A 4
21 Norton Canon H 9
32 Norton Disney D 6
22 Norton East A 4
7 Norton Ferris C 11
6 Norton Fitzwarren D 5
8 Norton Green G 5
15 Norton Hawkfield H 9
18 Norton Heath D 6
30 Norton in Hales C 6
31 Norton in the Moors E 7
23 Norton Juxta Twycross A 7
40 Norton-le-Clay H 4
22 Norton Lindsey F 6
15 Norton Malreward H 9
7 Norton St. Philip A 11
7 Norton sub Hamdon E 8
26 Norton Subcourse F 7
32 Norton Woodseats B 1
32 Norwell D 5
32 Norwell Woodhouse D 5
26 Norwich E 5
64 Norwick A 8
32 Norwood B 2
10 Norwood Hill D 1
23 Noseley B 10
5 Noss Mayo L 4
40 Nosterfield G 3
55 Nostie G 2
16 Notgrove B 2
14 Nottage F 1
32 Nottingham F 3
32 Nottinghamshire, County D 4
35 Notton, W. Yorks. F 12
15 Notton, Wilts. G 12
19 Nounsley C 8
22 Noutard's Green E 2
21 Nox A 9
17 Nuffield E 7
57 Nuide K 3
36 Nun Monkton A 3
36 Nunburnholme B 6
32 Nuncargate E 2
23 Nuneaton C 7
16 Nuneham Courtenay D 6
49 Nunlands D 12
38 Nunnery Howe H 2
7 Nunney B 10
41 Nunnington G 7
45 Nunnykirk D 9
37 Nunsthorpe F 10
40 Nunthorpe D 5
8 Nunton C 3
40 Nunwick H 3
43 Nunwood D 10
8 Nursling D 5
9 Nutbourne F 9
9 Nutbourne D 12
10 Nutfield C 2
32 Nuthall F 2
25 Nuthampstead M 5
10 Nuthurst E 1
10 Nutley, E. Sussex E 3
9 Nutley, Hants. B 7
36 Nutwell G 4
9 Nyetimber F 10
9 Nyewood D 9
4 Nymet Rowland E 6
4 Nymet Tracey F 6
15 Nympsfield D 11
6 Nynehead D 5
7 Nythe C 7
9 Nyton E 10
11 Oad Street B 7
23 Oadby B 9
31 Oakamoor F 9
48 Oakbank C 4
14 Oakdale D 5
6 Oake D 5
22 Oaken B 2
34 Oakenclough B 4
21 Oakengates A 12
29 Oakenholt C 12
40 Oakenshaw, Dur. A 2
35 Oakenshaw, W. Yorks. D 10
8 Oakfield, Hants. C 5
6 Oakford, Devon D 3
13 Oakford, Dyfed A 8
6 Oakfordbridge D 3
31 Oakgrove C 8
23 Oakham A 12
9 Oakhanger C 9
7 Oakhill B 9
25 Oakington J 5
29 Oaklands D 7
15 Oakle Street C 10
25 Oakley, Beds. K 1
17 Oakley, Bucks. C 7
8 Oakley, Dorset F 2
52 Oakley, Fife H 5
9 Oakley, Hants. A 7
27 Oakley, Suffolk H 5
17 Oakley Green F 10
20 Oakleypark D 5
15 Oakridge Lynch D 12
16 Oaksey E 1
22 Oakthorpe A 6
40 Oaktree Hill E 4
45 Oakwood, Northumb. F 8
49 Oakwood, Borders G 7
9 Oakwoodhill B 12
35 Oakworth C 9
11 Oar B 9
16 Oare, Berks. G 6
6 Oare, Som. B 2
16 Oare, Wilts. H 3
6 Oareford B 2
33 Oasby F 7
59 Oathlaw M 2
55 Oban, Highland K 2
50 Oban, Strathclyde E 6
58 Obliston B 1
7 Oborne D 10
56 Obsdale C 2
30 Occlestone Green D 5
27 Occold H 5
52 Ochil Hills Hosp. F 6
47 Ochiltree G 10
52 Ochtermuthill E 3
42 Ochtrelure F 2
32 Ockbrook G 2
17 Ockham H 11
50 Ockle A 3
21 Ocle Pychard H 11
9 Ocley B 12
41 Octon H 10
7 Odcombe E 8
15 Odd Down H 10
39 Oddendale D 8
22 Oddingley F 3
16 Oddington, Glos. B 3
16 Oddington, Oxon C 6
25 Odell J 1
64 Odie B 4
9 Odiham A 9
8 Odstock C 3
23 Odstone A 7
23 Offchurch F 7
22 Offenham G 4
45 Offerton G 11
10 Offham, E. Sussex G 3
10 Offham, Kent B 5
30 Offley Marsh G 6
25 Offord Cluny J 3
25 Offord D'Arcy J 3
27 Offton K 4
6 Offwell F 5
16 Ogbourne Maizey G 3
16 Ogbourne St. Andrew G 3
16 Ogbourne St. George G 3
45 Ogle E 9
14 Ogmore G 2
14 Ogmore-by-Sea G 2
14 Ogmore Vale E 3
7 Okeford Fitzpaine E 11
4 Okehampton F 5
59 Old Aberdeen G 7
9 Old Alresford C 7
53 Old Balkello C 8
45 Old Berwick A 9
52 Old Blair A 4
33 Old Bolingbroke D 10
31 Old Brampton C 11
43 Old Bridge of Urr E 8
26 Old Buckenham F 4
16 Old Burghclere H 6
40 Old Byland G 6
37 Old Clee F 10
6 Old Cleeve B 4
43 Old Clouden D 9
29 Old Colwyn B 8
43 Old Craighouse C 12
42 Old Dailly B 3
32 Old Dalby H 4
58 Old Deer C 7
36 Old Denaby G 3
49 Old Dryburn E 12
36 Old Edlington G 3
40 Old Eldon B 3
37 Old Ellerby C 9
24 Old Fletton F 3
36 Old Goole E 5
37 Old Hall F 10
19 Old Heath B 10
10 Old Heathfield F 5
25 Old Hurst H 4
39 Old Hutton F 8
2 Old Kea E 5
47 Old Kilpatrick B 9
18 Old Knebworth B 2
26 Old Lakenham E 5
38 Old Laxey G 2
33 Old Leake E 11
45 Old Lyham C 12
41 Old Malton H 8
36 Old Micklefield D 2
8 Old Milton G 4
22 Old Milverton E 6
47 Old Monkland C 12
19 Old Montsale D 10
45 Old Mousen C 12
8 Old Netley E 6
27 Old Newton J 4
43 Old Orchardton F 9
48 Old Philpstoun B 3
40 Old Quarrington A 3
32 Old Radford F 3
21 Old Radnor F 8
58 Old Rattray B 8
58 Old Rayne E 4
11 Old Romney E 9
52 Old Scone D 6
36 Old Snydale E 2
15 Old Sodbury F 10
33 Old Somerby G 7
23 Old Stratford H 11
30 Old Swan A 3
39 Old Tebay E 8
40 Old Thirsk G 4
39 Old Town, Cumb. A 7
39 Old Town, Cumbria G 8
2 Old Town, Is. of Scilly D 2
45 Old Town, Northumb. D 7

32 Old Tupton D 1
25 Old Warden L 2
25 Old Weston H 2
17 Old Windsor G 10
11 Old Wives Lees C 9
17 Old Woking H 11
60 Oldany D 3
22 Oldberrow F 5
4 Oldborough E 6
21 Oldbury, Salop C 12
22 Oldbury, War. C 6
22 Oldbury, W. Midlands C 3
15 Oldbury on the Hill E 11
15 Oldbury-upon-Severn E 9
14 Oldcastle, Gwent B 6
14 Oldbury, Mid Glam. F 2
32 Oldcotes A 3
22 Oldfield, Heref. & Worc. F 2
35 Oldfield, W. Yorks. C 8
7 Oldford A 11
35 Oldham G 8
49 Oldhamstocks B 10
15 Oldland G 10
58 Oldmeldrum E 6
58 Oldnoth D 3
21 Oldpark A 12
60 Oldshore Beg B 3
60 Oldshore More B 3
40 Oldstead G 5
58 Oldtown of Ord B 4
14 Oldway H 9
4 Oldways End D 7
58 Oldwhat C 6
48 Oliver G 4
8 Oliver's Battery C 6
64 Ollaberry C 7
30 Ollerton, Ches. C 6
32 Ollerton, Notts. C 4
30 Ollerton, Salop H 5
20 Olmarch G 2
23 Olney G 12
22 Olton D 5
15 Olveston F 9
22 Ombersley F 2
32 Ompton D 4
44 Once Brewed F 6
38 Onchan H 2
31 Onecote E 9
15 Onen C 7
18 Ongar D 5
24 Onger Hill C 7
21 Onibury D 10
51 Onich A 7
14 Onllwyn C 2
21 Ongar Street F 9
30 Onneley F 6
9 Onslow Village A 11
47 Onthank E 9
35 Openshaw G 7
32 Openwoodgate E 1
54 Opinan, Highland C 1
60 Opinan, Highland G 1
49 Orange Lane E 10
62 Orbost D 2
33 Orby C 12
46 Orcadia C 6
4 Orchard Hill C 3
6 Orchard Portman D 6
8 Orcheston B 2
15 Orcop B 8
15 Orcop Hill A 8
62 Ord G 5
64 Ordale A 8
58 Ordens B 4
58 Ordhead F 4
59 Ordie G 2
58 Ordiequish B 1
32 Ordsall B 4
11 Ore G 7
30 Orford, Cheshire A 5
21 Oreton, Salop D 12
27 Orford, Suffolk K 7
8 Organford G 1
64 Orgill D 1
22 Orgreave A 5
64 Orkney, Co. C 2
11 Orlestone E 8
21 Orleton, Heref. & Worc. F 10
21 Orleton, Heref. & Worc. F 12
23 Orlingbury E 12
40 Ormesby C 5
26 Ormesby St. Margaret D 8
26 Ormesby St. Michael D 8
60 Ormiscaig G 1
49 Ormiston B 7
38 Ormely Hall F 2
50 Ormsaigbeg A 2
50 Ormsaigmore A 2
46 Ormsary House B 2
34 Ormskirk F 3
63 Orosay F 5
64 Orphir D 2
18 Orpington G 5
34 Orrell, Merseyside G 2
34 Orrell, Manchester G 4
34 Orrell Post G 4
53 Orrock H 7
18 Orsett F 6
18 Orsett Heath F 6
22 Orslow A 2
32 Orston F 5
38 Orthwaite B 5
39 Orton, Cumbria D 8
23 Orton, Northants. D 11
24 Orton Longueville F 3
22 Orton on the Hill B 6
58 Orton Station B 1
24 Orton Waterville F 3
25 Orwell K 5
34 Osbaldeston D 5
36 Osbaldwick B 4
23 Osbaston B 7
24 Osbournby B 2
61 Osclay D 11
30 Oscroft D 4
62 Ose D 2
32 Osgathorpe H 2
33 Osgodby, Lincs. A 8
36 Osgodby, N. Yorks. D 4
41 Osgodby, N. Yorks. G 10
62 Oskaig D 5
50 Oskamuil D 2
31 Osmaston F 10
7 Osmington H 10
7 Osmington Mills H 10
35 Osmondthorpe D 12
40 Osmotherley E 5
11 Ospringe B 8
35 Ossett E 11
32 Ossington D 5
19 Ostend D 9
40 Oswaldkirk G 6
34 Oswaldtwistle D 6
30 Oswestry G 2
40 Otford B 4
11 Otham C 7
7 Othery C 7
27 Otley, Suffolk K 5
35 Otley, W. Yorks. C 10
46 Otter Ferry A 4
8 Otterbourne D 6
45 Otterburn, Northumb. D 7
35 Otterburn, N. Yorks. A 7
45 Otterburn Camp C 7
2 Otterham B 2
6 Otterhampton B 6
17 Ottershaw H 11
64 Otterswick B 7
6 Otterton H 4
6 Ottery St. Mary G 5
11 Ottinge D 10
37 Ottingham E 10
39 Oughtershaw G 11
43 Oughterside H 12
35 Oughtibridge H 11
40 Oulston H 6
44 Oulton, Cumb. H 1
26 Oulton, Norfolk C 4
31 Oulton, Staffs. G 7
26 Oulton, Suffolk F 8
35 Oulton, W. Yorks. D 12
26 Oulton Broad F 8
26 Oulton Street C 5
25 Oundle G 1
39 Ousby B 8
61 Ousdale E 10
25 Ousden J 8
36 Ousefleet E 6
45 Ouston, Dur. H 10
45 Ouston, Northumb. F 9
44 Ouston, Northumb. H 6
38 Out Gate E 6
37 Out Newton E 11
34 Out Rawcliffe C 3
45 Outchester C 12
64 Outertown D 1
39 Outhgill E 10
35 Outlane E 9
24 Outwell E 6
8 Outwick D 3
10 Outwood, Surrey D 2
35 Outwood, W. Yorks. E 12
35 Ovenden D 9
49 Ovenscloss F 7
25 Over, Cambs. H 5
30 Over, Cheshire D 5
15 Over, Glos. F 9
7 Over Compton E 9
48 Over Dalgleish H 5
31 Over Haddon D 10
43 Over Hazlefield G 8
39 Over Kellet H 7
16 Over Kiddlington B 5
16 Over Norton A 4
40 Over Silton F 5
6 Over Stowey B 5
7 Over Stratton E 8
30 Over Tabley B 6
8 Over Wallop B 4
22 Over Whitacre C 6
49 Over Whitton G 10
32 Over Woodhouse C 2
64 Overbister B 4
22 Overbury H 3
58 Overhall C 5
7 Overleigh C 8
22 Oversley Green F 4
30 Overpool C 3
22 Overseal A 6
58 Overside B 8
11 Oversland B 9
23 Overstone E 11
26 Overstrand B 5
23 Overthorpe H 8
30 Overton, Ches. C 4
30 Overton, Clwyd F 2
43 Overton, Dumf. & Gall. E 10
58 Overton, Grampian F 6
58 Overton, Grampian D 7
8 Overton, Hants. A 6
34 Overton, Lancs. A 3
36 Overton, N. Yorks. B 3
21 Overton, Salop E 10
47 Overton, Strathclyde D 8
13 Overton, W. Glam. H 8
29 Overton Bridge F 12
30 Overton Green D 6
48 Overtown, Strathclyde D 1
39 Overtown, Lancs. H 8
16 Overtown, Wilts. F 3
58 Overtown of Memsie B 7
26 Overy Staithe A 1
17 Oving, Bucks. B 8
9 Oving, W. Sussex F 10
10 Ovingdean H 2
45 Ovingham G 9
40 Ovington, Durham D 2
27 Ovington, Essex L 1
9 Ovington, Hants. C 7
26 Ovington, Norfolk E 2
45 Ovington, Northumb. G 9
8 Ower D 5
7 Owermoigne H 11
31 Owler Bar B 11
32 Owlerton A 1
17 Owlswick C 8
33 Owmby-by-Spital B 7
8 Owslebury D 6
23 Owston, Leics. A 11
36 Owston, S. Yorks. F 3
36 Owston Ferry G 6
37 Owstwick D 10
32 Owthorpe G 4
24 Oxborough E 8
33 Oxcombe C 10
38 Oxen Park F 5
39 Oxenholme F 8
35 Oxenhope D 9
49 Oxenrig E 11
16 Oxenton A 1
16 Oxenwood H 4
16 Oxford D 6
4 Oxford Cross B 3
16 Oxfordshire, Co. C 5
18 Oxhey D 1
22 Oxhill G 6
22 Oxley B 2
19 Oxley Green C 9
49 Oxnam G 9
17 Oxshott H 12
35 Oxspring G 11
10 Oxted C 3
49 Oxton, Borders D 7
32 Oxton, Notts. E 3
36 Oxton, N. Yorks. C 3
13 Oxwich H 8
13 Oxwich Green H 8
60 Oykel Bridge G 5
58 Oyne E 4
13 Oystermouth H 9
7 Packers Hill E 10
23 Packington A 7
22 Packington Park D 5
53 Padanaram B 9
17 Padbury A 8
18 Paddington F 3
11 Paddlesworth D 10
10 Paddock Wood D 5
56 Paddockhaugh D 8
44 Paddockhole E 1
30 Paddolgreen G 4
35 Padfield G 9
30 Padgate A 5
35 Padiham D 7
29 Padog E 8
35 Padside A 10
2 Padstow B 6
17 Padworth G 7
40 Page Bank B 3
9 Pagham F 10
19 Paglesham E 9
63 Paible G 1
5 Paignton K 8
23 Pailton D 8
21 Painscastle H 7
45 Painshawfield G 9
15 Painswick C 12
11 Painter's Forstal B 8
47 Paisley C 9
58 Paithnick B 2
26 Pakefield F 8
27 Pakenham J 2
29 Pale G 9
10 Palehouse Com. F 4
8 Palestine B 4
17 Paley Street G 9
42 Palgowan C 5
27 Palgrave G 4
11 Palmarsh E 10
18 Palmers Green E 3
43 Palnackie F 9
42 Palnure E 5
32 Palterton C 2
17 Pamber End H 7
17 Pamber Green H 7
17 Pamber Heath H 7
8 Pamphill F 1
25 Pampisford K 6
7 Panborough B 8
53 Panbride D 10
4 Pancrasweek E 2
29 Pandy, Clwyd G 11
15 Pandy, Gwent B 7
20 Pandy, Gwynedd B 2
20 Pandy, Powys B 5
29 Pandy Tudor D 8
19 Panfield A 7
17 Pangbourne F 7
43 Panlands C 11
35 Pannal B 11
59 Pannancih H 1
30 Pant H 1
20 Pant Mawr D 4
28 Pant-glas, Gwynedd E 4
21 Pantglas, Salop C 8
13 Pantgwyn, Dyfed D 9
12 Pantgwyn, Dyfed B 6
13 Pant-lasau G 10
33 Panton B 9
20 Pant-perthog B 3
20 Pant-y-dwr E 5
21 Pant-y-ffrid B 7
13 Pantyffynnon F 9
14 Pantygasseg D 5
15 Pant y Goitre C 7
12 Pantymenyn D 5
29 Pantymwyn D 11
14 Pant-yr-awel E 3
26 Panxworth D 6
38 Papcastle B 3
49 Papple B 8
32 Papplewick E 3
25 Papworth Everard J 4
25 Papworth St. Agnes J 4
3 Par D 8
34 Parbold F 4
7 Parbrook C 9
29 Parc G 8
12 Parcllyn B 6
38 Pardshaw C 3
27 Parham J 6
43 Park, Dumf. & Gall. B 10
59 Park, Grampian G 5
50 Park, Strathclyde C 6
17 Park Corner, Berks. F 9
10 Park Corner, E. Sussex D 4
40 Park End, Cleveland C 5
45 Park End, Northumb. E 7
9 Park Gate E 7
44 Park Nook F 4
58 Parkdargue C 4
38 Parkend, Cumb. A 5
15 Parkend, Glos. D 9
27 Parkeston M 5
30 Parkgate, Ches. B 1
43 Parkgate, Dumf. & Gall. C 11
10 Parkgate, Surrey D 1
48 Parkgatestone F 4
4 Parkham D 3
4 Parkham Ash D 2
56 Parkhead F 8
58 Parkhill House F 6
15 Parkhouse D 8
8 Parkhurst G 6
13 Parkmill H 9
59 Parkneuk K 5
30 Parkside E 3
8 Parkstone G 2
8 Parley Cross F 2
4 Parracombe B 5
30 Parrah Green F 6
31 Parsley Hay D 10
24 Parson Drove E 5
19 Parson's Heath A 10
47 Partick C 10
34 Partington H 6
33 Partney C 11
38 Parton, Cumb. C 2
43 Parton, Dumf. & Gall. E 8
15 Parton, Glos. B 12
10 Partridge Green F 1
31 Parwich E 10
23 Passenham H 11
9 Passfield C 9
26 Paston B 6
4 Patchacott F 3
10 Patcham G 2
9 Patching E 12
4 Patchole B 5
15 Patchway F 9
35 Pateley Bridge A 10
19 Paternoster Heath B 9
52 Path of Condie F 5
7 Pathe C 7
53 Pathead, Fife H 8
48 Pathead, Lothian C 6
47 Pathhead H 11
52 Pathstruie F 5
47 Patna H 9
16 Patney H 2
38 Patrick G 1
40 Patrick Brompton F 2
34 Patricroft G 6
37 Patrington E 10
11 Patrixbourne C 10
38 Patterdale D 6
44 Pattieshill F 3
22 Pattingham B 2
23 Pattishall G 10
19 Pattiswick Green B 8
2 Paul G 2
23 Paulerspury G 10
37 Paull E 9
7 Paulton A 10
45 Pauperhaugh C 9
25 Pavenham K 1
6 Pawlett B 6
49 Pawston F 11
22 Paxford H 5
49 Paxton D 12
6 Payhembury F 4
35 Paythorne B 7
10 Peacehaven H 3
31 Peak Dale C 9
31 Peak Forest B 9
58 Peaknowe B 4
55 Peanmeanach L 1
59 Pearsie L 1
10 Pearsons Green D 6
10 Pease Pottage E 1
7 Peasedown St. John A 10
16 Peasemore F 5
27 Peasenhall H 7
9 Peaslake B 12
11 Peasmarsh F 7
49 Peaston Bank C 7
53 Peat Inn F 9
58 Peathill A 7
23 Peatling Magna C 9
23 Peatling Parva C 9
21 Peaton D 10
27 Pebmarsh M 2
22 Pebworth G 5
35 Peckett Well D 8
30 Peckforton E 4
18 Peckham F 3
23 Peckleton B 8
44 Pedderhill F 3
11 Pedlinge E 10
22 Pedmore D 3
7 Pedwell C 8
48 Peebles E 5
38 Peel G 1
9 Peel Common F 7
11 Peening Quarter E 7
25 Pegsdon M 2
45 Pegswood D 10
62 Peinaha B 4
62 Peinchorran E 4
62 Peinlich B 3
62 Peinmore C 4
12 Pelcomb Cross E 3
19 Peldon B 9
22 Pelsall B 4
45 Pelton H 10
45 Pelton Fell H 10
43 Pelutho G 12
3 Pelynt D 9
13 Pemberton, Dyfed G 8
34 Pemberton, Manchester G 4
13 Pembrey G 7
21 Pembridge G 9
12 Pembroke G 3
12 Pembroke Dock G 3
10 Pembury D 5
13 Pen Rhiwfawr F 10
13 Pen-Sarn E 7
7 Pen Selwood C 11
15 Penalt C 8
12 Penally G 5
15 Penalt A 9
3 Penare F 7
14 Penarth G 5
20 Pen-bont-rhyd-y-beddau D 2
12 Penbryn B 6
13 Pencader C 8
13 Pen-cae A 7
28 Pencaenewydd F 3
28 Pencarnisiog C 3
13 Pencarreg C 8
14 Pencelli B 4
13 Penclawdd G 9
14 Pencoed F 3
15 Pencoid B 8
21 Pencombe G 11
15 Pencraig, Heref. & Worc. B 9
29 Pencraig, Powys G 9
2 Pendeen F 1
14 Penderyn C 3
12 Pendine F 6
34 Pendlebury G 6
34 Pendleton, Lancs. C 6
35 Pendleton, Manchester G 7
15 Pendock A 11
3 Pendoggett B 7
7 Pendomer E 8
14 Pendoylan G 4
14 Pendre F 2
20 Penegoes B 3
12 Penfeidir D 2
13 Pen-ffordd, Dyfed C 8
12 Pen-ffordd, Dyfed E 4
14 Pengam D 5
18 Penge G 3
3 Pengelly A 8
14 Pengenffordd A 5
3 Pengover Green C 10
14 Pen-groes oped D 6
2 Penhale H 4
2 Penhalurick F 4
16 Penhill E 2
15 Penhow E 7
10 Penhurst F 6
20 Peniarth B 2
48 Penicuik C 5
13 Peniel E 8
62 Penifiler D 4
46 Peninver G 4
28 Penisar-waum D 5
35 Penistone G 11
30 Penketh A 4
42 Penkill B 3
42 Penkiln G 6
22 Penkridge A 3
30 Penley F 3
13 Penllergaer G 9
28 Pen-llyn, Gwynedd B 3
14 Penllyn, S. Glam. G 3
29 Penmachno E 7
13 Penmaen H 8
28 Penmaenen C 6
28 Penmaenmawr C 6
28 Penmaenpool H 6
29 Penmaenrhos B 8
14 Penmark G 4
28 Penmon B 6
50 Penmore Mill B 1
28 Penmorfa F 5
28 Penmynydd C 4
17 Penn E 10
17 Penn Street E 10
20 Pennal B 3
58 Pennan A 6
29 Pennant, Clwyd G 9
13 Pennant, Dyfed A 8
29 Pennant, Gwynedd D 7
20 Pennant, Powys C 4
29 Pennant-Melangell H 9
13 Pennard H 9
21 Pennerley C 9
38 Pennington, Cumb. G 5
8 Pennington, Hants. G 4
14 Pennorth B 4
38 Penny Bridge G 5
24 Penny Hill C 5
50 Pennyghael E 3
47 Pennyglen H 7
50 Pennygown C 3
4 Pennymoor E 7

45 Pennywell G 11
12 Penparc, Dyfed B 5
12 Penparc, Dyfed D 2
20 Penparcau D 2
14 Penpelleni D 6
3 Penpillick D 8
3 Penpoint B 8
2 Penpol F 5
43 Penpont, Dumf. & Gall. B 9
14 Penpont, Powys A 3
12 Penrherber C 6
12 Penrhiw C 6
14 Penrhiwceiber E 4
13 Penrhiw-goch E 9
13 Penrhiwllan C 7
13 Penrhiwpal B 7
15 Penrhos, Gwent C 7
28 Penrhos, Gwynedd G 3
14 Penrhos, Powys C 1
28 Penrhos,garnedd C 5
28 Penrhyn A 3
29 Penrhyn Bay B 7
20 Penrhyn-coch D 2
28 Penrhyndeudraeth F 5
29 Penrhynside B 7
13 Penrice H 8
12 Penrieth C 6
39 Penrith B 7
2 Penrose C 6
38 Penruddock B 6
2 Penryn F 5
29 Pensarn B 9
22 Pensax E 1
30 Pensby B 1
15 Pensford H 9
45 Penshaw H 11
10 Penshurst D 4
3 Pensilva C 10
49 Penston B 7
3 Pentewan E 7
28 Pentir D 5
2 Pentire D 5
2 Pentireg B 6
12 Pentlepoir F 5
27 Pentlow L 1
24 Pentney D 8
8 Penton Mewsey A 5
28 Pentraeth B 5
29 Pentre, Clwyd D 10
29 Pentre, Clwyd F 12
14 Pentre, Mid Glam. E 3
21 Pentre, Powys B 8
21 Pentre, Powys C 8
20 Pentre, Powys D 6
21 Pentre, Salop A 9
29 Pentre Bagillt C 11
28 Pentre Berw C 4
20 Pentre Dolau-Honddu H 5
13 Pentre Gwenlais E 9
28 Pentre Gwynffryn G 5
29 Pentre Halkyn C 11
29 Pentre-Isaf C 8
14 Pentre Meyrick G 3
13 Pentrebach, Dyfed B 9
14 Pentrebach, Mid Glam. D 4
14 Pentre-bach, Powys A 2
13 Pentrebach, W. Glam. F 9
21 Pentrebeirdd A 7
29 Pentre-bont E 7
13 Pentre-cagal C 7
29 Pentre-celyn E 10
13 Pentre-cwrt C 7
29 Pentre-dwfr F 11
13 Pentre-dwr G 10
13 Pentrefelin, Dyfed E 9
28 Pentrefelin, Gwynedd A 4
29 Pentrefoelas E 8
12 Pentre-galar D 5
13 Pentregat B 7
20 Pentre-llwyn-llwyd G 5
14 Pentre-poeth F 6
13 Pentre'r-felin, Dyfed B 9
28 Pentre'r felin, Gwynedd F 5
14 Pentrer-felin, Powys A 3
29 Pentre-tafarn-y-fedw D 7
13 Pentre-ty-gwyn C 11
29 Pentre-uchaf C 10
32 Pentrich E 1
8 Pentridge D 2
15 Pen-twyn, Gwent C 8
14 Pentwyn, Mid Glam. D 4
14 Pentyrch F 4
14 Penuchadre G 2
20 Penuwch F 2
3 Penwithick Stents D 7
16 Penwood H 5
14 Penwylit C 2
29 Pen-y-bont, Clwyd H 11
13 Penybanc, Dyfed E 9
13 Pen-y-banc, Dyfed F 9
21 Penybont, Powys F 7
29 Pen-y-bont-fawr H 10
12 Pen-y-bryn C 5
29 Pen-y-cae, Clwyd F 12
14 Peb-y-cae, Powys C 2
15 Pen-y-cae-mawr E 7
15 Pen-y-clwdd D 7
14 Pen-y-coedcae F 4
12 Penycwm E 2
14 Pen-y-fai F 2
29 Penyffordd D 12
29 Pen-y-garnedd H 10
14 Penygraig E 3
13 Penygroes, Dyfed F 9
12 Penygroes, Dyfed C 5
28 Penygroes, Gwynedd E 4
14 Pen-y-groes, S. Glam. F 5
28 Pen-y-groeslon G 2
28 Pen-y-Gwyrd E 6
14 Penyrheol E 5
14 Pen-yr-Heolgerrig D 4
14 Penyrynys B 2
28 Penysarn A 4
29 Pen-y-stryt E 11
14 Penywaun D 3
2 Penzance G 2
22 Peopleton G 3
30 Peover Heath C 6
9 Peper Harow B 10
30 Peplow H 5
45 Peppermoor B 10
47 Perceton E 8
59 Percie H 3
58 Percyhorner A 7
45 Perkinsville H 10
2 Perranarworthal F 5
2 Perranporth D 5
2 Perranuthnoe G 3
2 Perranwell F 5
2 Perranwell Station F 5
2 Perranzabuloe D 5
25 Perry J 2
22 Perry Barr C 4
18 Perry Green B 4
10 Perry Street A 5
22 Pershore G 3
25 Pertenhall J 2
52 Perth E 6
22 Perton B 2
7 Pertwood C 12
5 Peter Tavy H 4
24 Peterborough F 3
54 Peterburn B 1
21 Peterchurch H 9
59 Petercutter G 6
58 Peterhead C 8
40 Peterlee A 4
18 Peter's Green B 2
4 Peters Marland E 3
9 Petersfield D 9
14 Peterstone Wentlooge F 6
14 Peterston-super-Ely G 4
15 Peterstow B 9
4 Petrockstowe E 4
11 Pett G 7
27 Pettaugh J 5
53 Petterden C 9
48 Pettinain E 2
27 Pettistree K 6
6 Petton, Devon D 4
30 Petton, Salop G 3
18 Petts Wood G 4
58 Petty D 5
48 Pettycur A 5
58 Pettymuck E 6
9 Petworth D 11
10 Pevensey H 5
10 Pevensey Bay H 5
16 Pewsey H 3
17 Pheasants E 9
17 Pheasant's Hill E 9
4 Philham D 1
49 Philiphaugh G 7
2 Phillack F 3
2 Philleigh F 6
48 Phil-stoun B 3
15 Phocle Green B 9
17 Phoenix Green H 8
57 Phones K 3
38 Phurt F 2
38 Pica C 3
17 Piccott's End C 11
36 Pickburn F 3
41 Pickering G 8
8 Picket Piece A 5
8 Picket Post E 3
40 Pickhill G 4
21 Picklescott B 10
53 Pickletillem E 9
30 Pickmere C 5
6 Pickney C 5
4 Pickwell, Devon B 3
23 Pickwell, Leics. A 11
24 Pickworth, Lincs. B 1
24 Pickworth, Leics. D 1
30 Picton, Cheshire C 3
40 Picton, N. Yorks. D 4
10 Piddinghoe H 3
17 Piddington, Bucks. E 9
23 Piddington, Northants. G 11
17 Piddington, Oxon B 7
7 Piddlehinton F 10
7 Piddletrenhide F 10
25 Pidley H 4
40 Piercebridge D 2
64 Pierowall A 2
45 Pigdon D 9
31 Pikehall D 10
18 Pilgrims Hatch D 6
32 Pilham A 6
15 Pill G 8
3 Pillaton C 10
22 Pillerton Hersey G 6
22 Pillerton Priors G 6
21 Pilleth F 8
8 Pilley, Hants. F 5
35 Pilley, S. Yorks. G 12
4 Pillhead C 3
34 Pilling B 3
34 Pilling Lane B 3
15 Pillowell D 9
7 Pillwell D 11
44 Pilmuir, Borders B 3
59 Pilmuir, Grampian H 5
15 Pilning F 9
31 Pilsbury D 9
7 Pilsdon F 7
31 Pilsley, Derby C 11
32 Pilsley, Derby D 2
25 Pilton, Northants. G 1
23 Pilton, Leics. B 12
7 Pilton, Somerset B 9
13 Pilton Green H 8
7 Pimperne E 12
24 Pinchbeck C 3
24 Pinchbeck Bars C 3
24 Pinchbeck West C 3
42 Pinclanty C 3
34 Pinfold F 3
6 Pinhoe G 3
17 Pinkneys Green F 9
22 Pinley Green E 5
42 Pinminnoch B 3
42 Pinmoee B 3
42 Pinmore Mains C 3
6 Pinn G 4
18 Pinner E 1
22 Pinvin G 3
42 Pinwherry C 3
32 Pinxton E 2
21 Pipe and Lyde H 10
30 Pipe Gate F 6
22 Pipehill A 4
56 Piperhill E 4
3 Pipers Pool A 9
23 Pipewell D 11
4 Pippacott B 4
14 Pipton A 5
17 Pirbright H 10
49 Pirnie G 9
46 Pirnmill E 4
22 Pirton, Heref. & Worc. G 2
18 Pirton, Herts. A 2
17 Pishill E 8
28 Pistyll F 3
52 Pitagowan A 3
58 Pitblae A 7
53 Pitcairlie Farm F 7
52 Pitcairn B 4
52 Pitcairngreen D 5
56 Pitcalnie C 4
58 Pitcaple E 5
17 Pitch Green D 8
9 Pitch Place A 11
15 Pitchcombe D 11
17 Pitchcott B 8
21 Pitchford B 10
7 Pitcombe C 10
53 Pitcorthie F 10
49 Pitcox B 9
59 Pitdrichie J 5
58 Pitfichie F 4
53 Pitfour Castle E 7
53 Pitkevy G 7
53 Pitlessie F 8
53 Pitlochry A 4
58 Pitmachie E 4
57 Pitmain J 3
58 Pitmedden E 6
6 Pitminster D 5
53 Pitmuies B 10
58 Pitmunie F 4
52 Pitnacree B 4
7 Pitney C 8
53 Pitroddie E 7
53 Pitscottie F 9
19 Pitsea E 7
23 Pitsford E 11
17 Pitstone C 10
17 Pitstone Green C 10
59 Pittarrow K 5
56 Pittendreich D 7
61 Pittenraill F 7
53 Pittenweem G 10
40 Pittington A 3
58 Pittodrie E 4
8 Pitton C 4
10 Pittswood C 5
58 Pittulie A 7
40 Pity Me, Durham A 3
45 Pity Me, Northumb. E 7
27 Pixey Green H 5
10 Pixham C 1
21 Pixley H 12
41 Place Newton H 9
58 Plaidy B 5
12 Plain Dealings E 4
48 Plains C 1
6 Plainsfield C 5
21 Plaish C 10
9 Plaistow C 11
10 Plaistow Street D 3
8 Plaitford D 4
29 Plas Newydd F 11
44 Plashetts D 5
16 Plastow Green H 6
29 Plas-yn-Cefn C 9
10 Platt B 5
34 Platt Bridge G 5
45 Plawsworth H 11
10 Plaxtol C 5
17 Play Hatch F 8
11 Playden F 8
27 Playford K 5
2 Playing Place E 5
15 Playley Green A 10
21 Plealey B 9
52 Plean H 3
53 Pleasance F 7
34 Pleasington E 5
32 Pleasley D 2
44 Plenmeller G 5
18 Pleshey B 6
54 Plockton F 2
63 Plocrapool G 3
21 Ploughfield H 9
49 Ploughlands E 10
21 Plowden D 9
21 Ploxgreen B 9
11 Pluckley D 8
11 Pluckley Thorne D 8
43 Plumbland H 12
30 Plumley C 6
10 Plumpton G 2
39 Plumptonfoot A 7
10 Plumpton Green F 2
39 Plumpton Head B 7
39 Plumpton B 7
26 Plumstead B 4
32 Plumtree G 3
32 Plungar B 5
7 Plush F 10
13 Plwmp B 7
5 Plymouth K 4
5 Plympton K 4
5 Plympton St. Maurice K 3
5 Plymstock K 4
6 Plymtree F 4
40 Pockley G 6
36 Pocklington B 6
24 Pode Hole C 3
7 Podimore D 9
23 Podington F 12
30 Podmore G 6
24 Pointon B 2
8 Pokesdown G 3
42 Polbae D 4
60 Polbain F 2
3 Polbathic D 10
48 Polbeth C 3
43 Poldean B 11
58 Poldullie Bridge F 1
35 Pole Moor E 9
25 Polebrook G 2
10 Polegate G 5
30 Polelane Ends B 5
22 Polesworth B 6
60 Polglass F 2
3 Polgooth E 7
9 Poling F 11
9 Poling Corner E 11
3 Polkerris D 8
60 Polla B 5
36 Pollington E 4
50 Polloch A 5
47 Pollockshaws C 10
47 Pollokshields C 10
43 Polmaddie C 7
54 Polmaily F 8
3 Polmassick E 7
47 Polmont B 2
48 Polmoody H 4
47 Polnessan H 9
55 Polnish L 1
9 Polperro E 9
3 Polruan E 8
7 Polsham B 8
43 Polskeoch A 8
27 Polstead L 3
6 Poltimore G 3
48 Polton C 5
49 Polwarth D 10
3 Polyphant B 9
2 Polzeath B 6
24 Pondersbridge F 4
9 Pondtail A 9
2 Ponsanooth F 5
5 Ponsworthy H 6
13 Pont-Antwn F 8
29 Pont Cyfyngf D 7
13 Pont Hentry F 8
20 Pont-Llogel A 6
28 Pont Pen-y-benglog D 6
28 Pont Rhyd-goch D 6
20 Pont-Robert A 6
13 Pont Yates F 8
13 Pontamman F 9
14 Pont ar Hydfer B 2
13 Pontardawe G 10
13 Pontardulais G 9
13 Pontargothi E 8
13 Pont-ar-llechau E 10
13 Pontarsais D 8
29 Pontblyddyn D 12
14 Pontbren Llwyd D 3
36 Pontefract E 2
45 Ponteland F 10
20 Ponterwyd D 3
27 Pontesbury B 9
21 Pontesford B 9
29 Pontfadog F 11
12 Pontfaen, Dyfed D 4
14 Pont-faen, Powys A 3
13 Pontgarreg B 7
14 Ponthir E 6
12 Ponthirwaun B 6
14 Pont-llan-fraith E 5
13 Pontlliw G 9
14 Pontlottyn D 4
28 Pontlyfni E 4
14 Pontneddfechan D 2
14 Pontnewydd E 6
20 Pontrhydfendigaid F 3
13 Pontrhydyfen G 11
20 Pontrhydygroes E 3
14 Pontrhydyrun E 6
15 Pontrilas B 7
28 Pont-rug D 4
10 Ponts Green F 5
13 Pontshaen B 8
15 Pontshill B 9
14 Pontsticill C 4
13 Pont-tywely C 7
13 Pontyberem F 8
29 Pont-y-bodkin D 12
29 Pont y Clogwyn E 8
14 Pontyclun F 4
14 Pontycymer E 2
12 Pontyglazier C 5
14 Pont-y-gwaith E 3
29 Ponty-y-pant E 7
14 Pontypool D 6
14 Pontypool Road D 6
14 Pontypridd E 4
12 Pont-yr-hafod D 3
21 Pont-ysgawrhyd A 7
14 Pontywaun E 5
8 Pooksgreen E 5
2 Pool, Cornwall E 4
21 Pool Heref. & Worc. H 10
6 Pool, Som. D 3
35 Pool, W. Yorks C 11
34 Pool Hey F 2
21 Pool Head G 11
52 Pool of Muckhart G 5
21 Pool Quay A 8
27 Pool Street L 1
8 Poole G 2
30 Poole Green E 5
16 Poole Keynes E 1
31 Poolend D 8
54 Poolewe B 2
39 Pooley Bridge C 7
15 Poolhill A 10
32 Poolsbrook C 2
38 Poortown G 1
10 Pootings C 3
17 Popeswood G 9
9 Popham B 7
18 Poplar F 4
8 Porchfield G 6
54 Porin D 7
2 Porkellis F 4
6 Porlock B 2
6 Porlock Weir B 2
53 Port Allen E 7
50 Port Appin C 6
46 Port Bannatyne C 6
44 Port Carlisle G 1
40 Port Clarence C 5
28 Port Dinorwic C 5
46 Port Driseach B 5
58 Port Elphinstone F 5
38 Port Erin H 1
58 Port Erroll D 8
13 Port Eynon H 8
47 Port Glasgow B 8
54 Port Henderson B 1
3 Port Isaac B 7
46 Port Lamont B 6
42 Port Logan H 2
41 Port Mulgrave C 8
52 Port of Menteith G 1
63 Port of Ness A 6
3 Port Quin B 7
50 Port Ramsay C 6
38 Port St. Mary H 1
51 Port Sonachan E 7
30 Port Sunlight B 2
13 Port Talbot H 10
13 Port Tennant H 10
42 Port William G 4
46 Portachoillan D 3
46 Port an Eilein B 5
46 Portavadie B 4
15 Portbury G 8
9 Portchester F 7
47 Portencross D 7
7 Portesham H 9
58 Portessie A 2
38 Port e Vullen G 3
12 Portfield Gate E 3
5 Portgate G 3
58 Portgordon A 1
61 Portgower E 9
14 Porth E 4
2 Porth Mellin H 4
2 Porth Navas G 5
3 Porthallow, Corn. D 9
2 Porthallow, Corn G 5
14 Porthcawl G 1
2 Porthcothan Bay C 6
2 Porthcurno G 1
28 Porthdafarch B 2
12 Porthgain D 2
2 Porthilly B 6
14 Porthkerry H 4
2 Porthleven G 3
28 Porthmadog F 5
2 Porthmeor F 2
11 Portholland F 7
2 Porthoustock G 5
2 Porthowann E 4
3 Porthpean D 7
13 Porthyrhyd, Dyfed E 8
13 Porthyrhyd, Dyfed C 10
51 Portincaple H 9
36 Portington D 6
51 Portinnisherrich F 7
38 Portinscale C 5
15 Portishead G 8
58 Portknockie A 2
59 Portlethen H 7
2 Portloe F 6
61 Portmahomack H 9
28 Portmeirion F 5
3 Portmellon E 7
8 Portmore F 5
62 Port na Long E 3
63 Portnaguran C 6
55 Portnaluchaig K 1
60 Portnancon B 5
51 Portnellan, Central E 11
51 Portnellan, Central F 11
50 Portnocroish C 6
48 Portobello B 6
8 Porton B 3
42 Portpatrick F 1
2 Portreath E 4
62 Portree D 4
47 Portrye D 7
2 Portscatho F 6
9 Portsea F 8
61 Portskerra A 8
15 Portskewett E 8
10 Portslade, Surrey G 1
10 Portslade, Surrey G 2
42 Portslogan F 1
9 Portsmouth, Hants F 8
35 Portsmouth, W. Yorks E 7
58 Portsoy A 3
8 Portswood E 6
50 Portuairk A 2
60 Portvasgo A 6
63 Portvoller C 6

63 Portway, Heref. & Worc. A 8
22 Portway, War. E 4
3 Portwrinkle D 10
42 Portyerrock H 5
2 Postbridge H 5
17 Postcombe D 8
11 Postling D 10
26 Postwick E 6
59 Potarch H 3
47 Poteath D 7
44 Potholm D 2
17 Potsgrove A 10
24 Pott Row C 8
31 Pott Shrigley B 8
17 Potten End C 11
41 Potter Brompton G 10
26 Potter Heigham D 7
18 Potter Street C 5
33 Potterhanworth D 7
33 Potterhanworth Booths C 8
16 Potterne H 1
16 Potterne Wick H 1
18 Potters Bar D 3
22 Potters Cross D 2
23 Potterspury H 11
40 Potto E 5
25 Potton K 3
4 Poughill, Corn E 1
4 Poughill, Devon E 7
16 Poulshot H 1
30 Poulton, Ches. D 3
16 Poulton, Glos. D 2
34 Poulton-Le-Fylde C 2
14 Pound F 1
22 Pound Bank E 1
10 Pound Green, E. Sussex F 4
8 Pound Green, I.o.W. G 5
10 Pound Hill D 2
41 Poundland, Dumf. & Gall. C 9
42 Poundland, Strathclyde C 3
17 Poundon B 7
10 Poundsbridge D 4
5 Poundsgate J 6
2 Poundstock A 2
53 Pourie D 9
45 Powburn A 9
6 Powderham H 3
7 Powerstock G 8
43 Powfoot E 12
53 Powgavie E 7
22 Powick G 2
4 Powler's Piece D 2
52 Powmill G 5
20 Powys, Co E 6
7 Poxwell H 11
17 Poyle F 11
10 Poynings G 1
7 Poyntington D 10
31 Poynton B 8
30 Poynton Green H 4
27 Poys Street H 6
12 Poyston Cross E 3
27 Poystreet Green J 3
2 Praa Sands G 3
62 Prabost E 4
18 Pratt's Bottom H 5
11 Pratt'sHeath H 7
2 Praze F 3
2 Praze-an-Beeble F 3
2 Predannack Wollas H 4
30 Prees G 4
34 Preesall B 2
34 Preesall Park C 2
12 Prendergast E 3
45 Prendwick B 8
13 Pren-gwyn C 7
28 Prenteg F 5
30 Prenton B 2
30 Prescot A 3
30 Prescott H 3
49 Pressen F 11
30 Pressgreen G 4
29 Prestatyn B 10
31 Prestbury, Ches. C 7
15 Prestbury, Glos. B 12
21 Presteigne F 8
21 Presthope C 11
7 Prestleigh B 9
49 Preston, Borders D 10
5 Preston, Devon H 7
7 Preston, Dorset H 10
10 Preston, E. Sussex G 2
27 Preston, Essex K 2
15 Preston, Glos A 10
16 Preston, Glos D 2
18 Preston, Herts A 2
37 Preston, Humber. D 9
11 Preston, Kent B 9
11 Preston, Kent B 11
34 Preston, Lancs D 4
45 Preston, Northumb. E 12
48 Preston, Lothian B 6
49 Preston, Lothian B 8
16 Preston, Wilts F 1
22 Preston Bagot E 5
17 Preston Bissett A 7
6 Preston Bowyer D 5
30 Preston Brockhurst H 4
30 Preston Brook B 4
9 Preston Candover B 7
23 Preston Capes G 9
17 Preston Crowmarsh E 7
3 Preston Gubbals H 4
22 Preston on Stour G 5
30 Preston on the Hill B 4
21 Preston on Wye H 9
7 Preston Plucknett E 8
21 Preston upon the Weald Moors A 12
21 Preston Wynne H 11
43 Prestonmill F 10
48 Prestonpans B 6
40 Preston-under-Scar F 1
35 Prestwich G 7
47 Prestwick, Northumb. F 10
47 Prestwick, Strathclyde G 8
17 Prestwood D 9
14 Price Town E 3
25 Prickwillow G 7
7 Priddy A 8
39 Priest Hulton H 7
44 Priesthaugh C 3
47 Priesthill C 10
47 Priestland F 10
21 Priestweston C 8
23 Primethorpe C 8
24 Primrose Hill, Cambs. F 5
32 Primrose Hill, Notts. D 2
41 Primrose Valley G 8
49 Primrosehill, Borders D 10
17 Primrosehill, Herts D 11
49 Primsidemill G 10
12 Princes Gate F 5
17 Princes Risborough D 9
23 Princethorpe E 7
5 Princetown, Devon H 5
14 Princetown, Mid Glam. C 4
49 Printonan E 10
29 Prion D 10
21 Priors Frame H 11
23 Priors Hardwick G 8
23 Priors Marston F 8
21 Priorslee A 12
21 Priory Wood H 8
15 Priston H 10
19 Prittlewell E 8
9 Privett C 8
4 Prixford B 4
2 Probus E 6
43 Prospect G 12
58 Protstonhill A 6
45 Prudhoe G 9
51 Ptarmigan Lodge G 10
51 Pubil C 11
15 Publow H 9
18 Puckeridge B 4
7 Puckington D 7
15 Pucklechurch G 10
8 Pucknall D 5
30 Puddington, Ches. C 2
4 Puddington, Devon E7
26 Puddledock F 4
7 Puddletown G 10
21 Pudlestone F 11
35 Pudsey D 11
9 Pulborough D 12
30 Puleston H 6
30 Pulford D 2
7 Pulham E 10
27 Pulham Market G 5
27 Pulham St. Margaret G 5
25 Pulloxhill M 2
48 Pumpherston B 3
43 Pumplaburn B 12
13 Pumpsaint C 10
12 Puncheston D 3
7 Puncknoll G 9
19 Punnett's Town F 5
9 Purbrook E 8
44 Purdomstone E 1
8 Purewell G 3
18 Purfleet F 5
7 Puriton B 7
19 Purleigh D 8
17 Purley, Berks F 7
18 Purley, London H 3
25 Purls Bridge G 6
7 Purse Caundle D 10
21 Purslow D 9
36 Purston Jaglin E 2
7 Purtington E 7
15 Purton, Glos D 10
16 Purton, Wilts E 2
16 Purton Stoke E 2
49 Purvishaugh E 8
23 Pury End H 10
16 Pusey D 4
4 Putford D 2
15 Putley A 9
18 Putney F 2
4 Putsborough B 3
17 Puttenham, Bucks. C 9
9 Puttenham, Surrey A 10
15 Puxton H 7
13 Pwll G 8
12 Pwllcrochan G 3
28 Pwlldefaid H 1
14 Pwllgloyw A 3
28 Pwllheli G 3
15 Pwllmeyric E 8
12 Pwlltrap E 6
13 Pwll-y-glaw H 11
21 Pydew B 7
32 Pye Bridge E 2
15 Pye Corner, Gwent F 7
18 Pye Corner, Herts C 4
22 Pye Green A 3
10 Pyecombe G 2
8 Pyle, I.o.W. H 6
14 Pyle, Mid Glam. F 2
7 Pylle B 9
25 Pymore G 6
17 Pyrford H 11
14 Pyrgad C 4
17 Pyrton E 8
23 Pytchley E 12
4 Pyworthy F 2
21 Quabbs D 7
24 Quadring B 3
17 Quainton B 8
8 Quarley B 4
31 Quarndon, Derby F 11
23 Quarndon, Leics. A 9
47 Quarrier's Homes C 8
24 Quarrington A 2
40 Quarrington Hill A 4
42 Quarry Bank C 3
30 Quarrybank D 4
58 Quarryburn A 6
56 Quarrywood C 7
47 Quarter D 12
22 Quat C 1
22 Quatford C 1
40 Quebec A 2
15 Quedgeley C 11
25 Queen Adelaide G 7
15 Queen Charlton H 9
4 Queen Dart D 7
7 Queen Oak C 11
10 Queen Street D 6
11 Queenborough in Sheppey A 8
7 Queens Camel D 9
30 Queens Head G 2
30 Queen's Park E 2
35 Queensbury D 9
29 Queensferry, Clwyd C 12
48 Queensferry, Lothian B 4
34 Queenstown D 2
47 Queenzieburn B 11
16 Quemerford G 1
64 Quendale F 7
25 Quendon M 6
23 Queniborough A 10
16 Quenington D 2
34 Quernmore A 4
3 Quethiock C 10
27 Quidenham G 3
8 Quidhampton, Hants. A 6
8 Quidhampton, Wilts. C 3
58 Quilquox D 6
38 Quine's Hill H 2
50 Quinish House B 2
23 Quinton G 11
2 Quintrel Downs D 5
49 Quixwood C 10
4 Quoditch F 3
52 Quoig E 3
48 Quothquan E 3
64 Quoys D 7
62 Rassay House (Hotel) D 5
4 Rabscott C 6
30 Raby B 2
28 Rachub C 5
28 Rackenford C 5
4 Rackenford D 7
9 Rackham E 11
26 Rackheath Com. D 6
43 Racks D 11
64 Rackwick, Orkney D 1
64 Rackwick, Orkney A 2
31 Radbourne G 11
34 Radcliffe, Manchester F 6
45 Radcliffe, Northumb. C 11
32 Radcliffe on Soar G 2
32 Radcliffe on Trent F 4
17 Radclive A 7
16 Radcot D 4
56 Raddery D 3
23 Radford Semele F 7
7 Radpole H 10
18 Radlett D 2
16 Radley D 6
17 Radnage D 8
7 Radstock A 10
23 Radstone H 9
23 Radway G 7
30 Radway Green E 6
25 Radwell J 1
25 Radwinter L 7
14 Radyr F 5
48 Raecleugh H 3
63 Raerinish D 5
60 Raffin D 2
56 Rafford D 6
32 Ragdale H 4
53 Ragfield F 10
15 Raglan D 7
32 Ragnall C 5
34 Rainford G 4
18 Rainham, Essex F 5
11 Rainham, Kent B 7
30 Rainhill A 4
30 Rainhill Stoops A 4
31 Rainow C 8
40 Rainton H 4
32 Rainworth D 3
39 Raisbeck D 9
44 Raise H 5
36 Raisthorpe A 6
53 Rait D 7
56 Raitcastle D 5
33 Raithby, Lincs. C 10
33 Raithby, Lincs. B 10
9 Rake C 9
11 Ram Lane C 8
62 Ramasaig D 1
3 Rame, Corn. E 11
2 Rame, Corn. F 4
7 Rampisham F 9
34 Rampside A 1
25 Rampton, Cambs. H 5
32 Rampton, Notts. B 5
35 Ramsbottom E 7
16 Ramsbury G 4
61 Ramscraigs D 10
9 Ramsdean D 8
17 Ramsdell H 7
16 Ramsden C 4
19 Ramsden Bellhouse E 7
19 Ramsden Heath D 7
25 Ramsay, Cambs. G 4
27 Ramsey, Essex M 5
38 Ramsey, I.o.M. G 2
19 Ramsay Island C 9
25 Ramsay St. Mary's G 4
48 Ramseycleuch H 5
11 Ramsgate B 12
26 Ramsgate Street B 4
40 Ramsgill H 1
45 Ramshaw H 8
44 Ramshope C 6
31 Ramshorn F 9
5 Ramsley G 5
9 Ramsnest Com. C 11
32 Ranby B 4
33 Rand B 8
15 Randwick D 11
47 Ranfurly C 9
31 Rangemore H 10
15 Rangeworthy F 10
47 Rankinston H 9
9 Ranmore Com. A 12
34 Rann E 6
38 Rannerdale C 4
51 Rannoch Station B 11
55 Ranochan L 2
6 Ranscombe B 3
32 Ranskill A 4
31 Ranton H 7
26 Ranworth D 7
64 Rapness B 3
55 Rarsaidh H 2
43 Rascarre G 9
46 Rashfield A 6
58 Rashiereive E 7
40 Raskelf H 5
14 Rassau C 5
35 Rastrick E 10
55 Ratagan H 3
23 Ratby B 8
23 Ratcliffe Culey B 7
23 Ratcliffe on the Wreake A 9
58 Rathen B 7
53 Rathillet E 8
35 Rathmell A 7
48 Ratho B 4
48 Ratho Station B 4
58 Rathven A 2
23 Ratley G 7
21 Ratlinghope C 9
61 Rattar A 11
5 Rattery K 6
27 Rattlesden J 3
53 Rattray C 7
38 Raughton Head A 6
25 Raunds H 1
49 Ravelaw D 11
36 Ravenfield H 3
38 Ravenglass F 3
26 Raveningham F 7
41 Ravenscar E 10
47 Ravenscraig B 7
38 Ravensdale G 2
25 Ravensden K 2
32 Ravenshead E 3
30 Ravensmoor E 5
23 Ravensthorpe E 8
23 Ravenstone, Bucks. G 11
23 Ravenstone, Leics. A 7
39 Ravenstonedale E 9
48 Ravenstruther E 2
40 Ravensworth D 2
41 Raw E 9
49 Rawburn D 9
36 Rawcliffe, Humber. E 5
36 Rawcliffe, N. Yorks. B 4
36 Rawcliffe Bridge E 5
35 Rawdon C 11
36 Rawmarsh G 2
22 Rawnsley A4
19 Rawreth E 8
6 Rawridge F 5
47 Raws E 9
35 Rawtenstall E 7
47 Rawyards C 12
58 Raxton D 6
27 Raydon L 3
45 Raylees D 7
19 Rayleigh E 8
7 Raymond's Hill F 7
19 Rayne B 7
25 Reach J 7
34 Read D 6
17 Reading G 8
11 Reading Street E 8
39 Reagill C 8
61 Rearquhar G 7
23 Rearsby A 10
61 Reaster A 11
45 Reaveley A 8
64 Reawick D 6
61 Reay B 9
11 Reculver A 11
6 Red Ball E 4
44 Red Dial H 1
22 Red Hill G 2
5 Red Post J 7
34 Red Rock F 5
12 Red Roses F 5
45 Red Row C 10
31 Red Street E 7
28 Red Wharf B 5
12 Redberth G 4
17 Redbourn C 12
37 Redbourne G 7
18 Redbridge E 4
30 Redbrook, Clwyd F 4
15 Redbrook, Gwent C 8
11 Redbrook Street D 8
56 Redburn, Highland E 5
56 Redburn, Highland C 1
44 Redburn, Northumb. G 6
40 Redcar C 8
56 Redcastle, Highland E 1
53 Redcastle, Tayside B 11
15 Redcliffe Bay G 7
47 Redcraig G 9
49 Redden F 10
48 Redding B 2
48 Reddingmuirhead B 2
35 Reddish H 8
22 Redditch E 4
47 Reddochbraes F 12
27 Redenhall G 6
44 Redesdale Camp C 6
45 Redesmouth E 7
53 Redford, Tayside C 10
59 Redford, Tayside K 5
48 Redfordgreen H 6
27 Redgrave G 3
59 Redheugh L 2
15 Redhill, Avon H 8
58 Redhill, Grampian D 4
59 Redhill, Grampian G 5
10 Redhill, Surrey C 2
46 Redhouse C 3
27 Redisham G 7
15 Redland, Avon G 9
64 Redland, Orkney C 2
27 Redlingfield H 5
25 Redlodge Warren H 8
8 Redlynch, Dorset D 4
7 Redlynch, Som. C 10
39 Redmain B 4
15 Redmarley D'Abitot A 10
40 Redmarshall C 4
32 Redmile G 5
40 Redmire F 1
3 Redmoor D 8
59 Redmyre K 5
30 Rednal G 2
49 Redpath F 8
54 Redpoint C 1
2 Redruth E 4
48 Redscarhead E 5
15 Redwick, Avon F 8
15 Redwick, Gwent F 7
40 Redworth C 3
25 Reed L 5
26 Reedham E 7
36 Reedness E 6
49 Reedy Loch D 11
63 Reef C 2
33 Reepham, Lincs. C 7
26 Reepham, Norf. C 4
40 Reeth E 1
38 Regaby F 2
56 Rehaurie E 5
61 Reidhbreac G 7
60 Reiff E 2
10 Reigate C 1
41 Reighton H 11
41 Reighton Gap G 11
58 Reisque E 6
61 Reiss B 12
2 Rejerrah D 5
2 Releath F 4
43 Relief D 12
2 Relubbus F 3
56 Relugas E 5
17 Remenham F 8
17 Remenham Hill F 9
52 Remony C 3
32 Rempstone H 3
16 Rendcomb C 1
27 Rendham J 6
47 Renfrew C 10
25 Renhold K 2
32 Renishaw B 2
45 Rennington A 10
47 Renton B 9
39 Renwick A 8
26 Repps D 7
31 Repton G 11
55 Reraig G 2
53 Rescobie B 10
50 Resipole A 4
56 Resolis C 2
14 Resolven D 2
55 Resourie M 2
49 Reston C 11
2 Retew D 6
19 Rettendon D 7
19 Rettendon Place D 7
50 Reudle C 1
33 Revesby D 10
8 Rew Street G 6
6 Rewe F 3
27 Reydon G 8
26 Reymerston E 3
12 Reynalton F 4
13 Reynoldston H 8
3 Rezare B 10
15 Rhadyr D 7
13 Rhandirmwyn C 11
20 Rhayader F 5
60 Rhegreanoch E 3
56 Rheindown E 1
50 Rhemore C 3
62 Rhenetra C 3
29 Rhewl, Clwyd D 10
29 Rhewl, Clwyd F 11
60 Rhicarn E 2
60 Rhiconich B 4
56 Rhicullen C 3
60 Rhidorroch G 3
60 Rhidorroch Old Lodge G 4
28 Rhid-y-sarn F 6
61 Rhifail C 7
14 Rhigos D 3
60 Rhimichie B 4
56 Rhinduie E 1
60 Rhiroy G 3
28 Rhiwbryfdir F 6
14 Rhiwderyn F 6
29 Rhiwlas, Clwd G 11
28 Rhiwlas, Gwynedd D 5
29 Rhiwlas, Gwynedd F 8
6 Rhode C 6
11 Rhodes Minnis D 10
32 Rhodesia B 3
12 Rhodiad D 1
14 Rhoose H 4
13 Rhos, Dyfed C 7
13 Rhos, W. Glam. G 10

13 Rhosamman F 10
28 Rhoscolyn C 2
12 Rhoscrowther G 3
29 Rhosesmor C 11
12 Rhosfach D 5
28 Rhos-fawr B 4
28 Rhosgadfan D 4
28 Rhosgoch, Gwynedd A 3
21 Rhosgoch, Powys H 7
12 Rhos-hill C 5
28 Rhos-lan F 4
20 Rhoslefain B 1
29 Rhosllanerchrugog F 12
13 Rhosmaen E 9
28 Rhos-meirch B 4
28 Rhosneigr C 3
29 Rhos-on-Sea B 8
13 Rhossili H 7
12 Rhosson D 1
28 Rhostryfan D 4
30 Rhostyllen E 2
28 Rhosybol A 4
29 Rhos-y-gwaliau G 9
28 Rhos-y-llan F 2
46 Rhu, Strathclyde C 3
47 Rhu, Strathclyde A 7
54 Rhu Noa C 4
29 Rhualt C 10
46 Rhubodach B 5
30 Rhuddall Heath D 4
29 Rhuddlan B 9
4 Rhude Cross E 1
60 Rhue G 2
21 Rhulen G 7
46 Rhunahaorine E 2
28 Rhyd, Gwynedd F 6
20 Rhyd, Powys B 5
28 Rhyd-Ddu E 5
29 Rhyd-Lydan E 8
13 Rhydargaeau D 8
14 Rhydberry A 3
13 Rhydcymerau C 9
22 Rhydd H 2
13 Rhydding G 10
13 Rhyddlan C 8
29 Rhyd-leos G 11
13 Rhydlewis B 7
28 Rhydlios G 1
20 Rhydlydan C 6
13 Rhydlydan C 6
13 Rhydowen C 8
20 Rhydrosser F 1
21 Rhydspence H 8
29 Rhydtalog E 11
28 Rhydwyn A 3
29 Rhyd-y-croesau G 11
28 Rhydyeclafdy G 3
14 Rhydyfelin E 4
20 Rhydyfelin D 2
13 Rhydyfro F 10
21 Rhyd-y-groes B 8
29 Rhydymain H 7
14 Rhyd-y-meirch D 6
29 Rhydymwyn D 11
20 Rhyd-yr-onmen B 2
20 Rhyfud F 2
29 Rhyl B 9
14 Rhymney D 4
53 Rhynd, Fife E 9
52 Rhynd, Tayside E 6
58 Rhynie E 2
39 Ribblehead G 10
34 Ribbleton D 4
34 Ribby D 3
34 Ribchester D 5
60 Ribigill B 6
37 Riby F 9
37 Riby Cross Roads F 9
36 Riccall C 4
47 Riccarton F 9
21 Richards Castle E 10
17 Richings Park F 11
18 Richmond, London F 2
40 Richmond, N. Yorks. E 2
54 Rickarton H 5
27 Rickinghall Inferior H 3
27 Rickinghall Superior H 3
25 Rickling M 6
25 Rickling Green A 5
17 Rickmansworth E 11
44 Riddings, Cumb. E 3
32 Riddings, Derby E 2
4 Riddlecombe E 5
35 Riddlesden C 9
8 Ridge, Dorset G 1
8 Ridge, Hants. D 5
18 Ridge, Herts. D 2
8 Ridge, Wilts. C 1
10 Ridge Green C 2
22 Ridge Lane C 6
20 Ridgebourne F 6
15 Ridgehill H 8
32 Ridgeway B 1
21 Ridgeway Cross H 12
25 Ridgewell L 8
10 Ridgewood F 3
25 Ridgemont L 1
45 Riding Mill G 8
10 Ridley, Kent B 5
44 Ridley, Northumb. G 6
30 Ridley Green E 4
23 Ridlington, Leics. B 11
26 Ridlington, Norf. B 6
45 Ridsdale E 7
52 Riechip B 5
52 Riemore B 5
60 Rienachait D 2
40 Rievaulx G 6
55 Rifern K 2
47 Rigfoot D 9
44 Rigg F 1
47 Riggend B 12
47 Righead F 10
39 Rigmaden Park G 8
33 Rigsby C 11
48 Rigside F 2
35 Rigton Hill C 12
22 Rileyhill A 5
3 Rilla Mill B 10
41 Rillington H 8
35 Rimington C 7
7 Rimpton D 9
61 Rimsdale C 7
37 Rimswell D 10
12 Rinaston D 3
43 Ringford F 8
31 Ringinglow B 11
26 Ringland D 4
10 Ringles Cross F 3
10 Ringmer G 3
5 Ringmore, Devon J 8
5 Ringmore, Devon L 5
56 Ringorm E 8
24 Ring's End E 5
27 Ringsfield G 7
27 Ringsfield Corner G 7
17 Ringshall, Bucks. C 10
27 Ringshall, Suffolk K 3
27 Ringshall Stocks K 4
24 Ringstead, Norf. B 8
25 Ringstead, Northants. H 1
8 Ringwood F 3
11 Ringwould C 12
58 Ringmore F 2
64 Rinnigill E 2
2 Rinsey G 3
10 Ripe G 4
32 Ripley, Derby E 1
8 Ripley, Hants. F 3
35 Ripley, N. Yorks. A 11
17 Ripley, Surrey H 11
37 Riplingham D 7
40 Ripon H 3
24 Rippingale C 2
22 Ripple, Heref. & Worcs. H 2
11 Ripple, Kent C 12
35 Ripponden E 9
21 Risbury G 11
37 Risby, Humberside F 7
27 Risby, Suffolk J 1
14 Risca E 6
37 Rise C 9
24 Risegate C 3
33 Riseholme C 7
25 Riseley, Beds. J 1
17 Riseley, Berks. H 8
27 Rishangles H 4
34 Rishton D 6
35 Rishworth E 9
32 Risley G 2
40 Risplith H 3
60 Rispond A 5
16 Rivar H 4
19 Rivenhall End B 8
25 River Bank H 6
10 Riverhead B 4
34 Rivington F 5
4 Roachill D 7
23 Roade G 11
44 Roadhead F 4
48 Roadmeetings D 1
61 Roadside, Highland B 11
47 Roadside, Strathclyde H 10
59 Roadside of Catterline J 6
59 Roadside of Kinneff K 6
6 Roadwater B 4
62 Roag D 2
42 Roan of Craigoch A 4
44 Roansgreen E 3
14 Roath F 5
43 Roberthill D 12
44 Roberton, Borders B 3
48 Roberton, Strathclyde F 2
10 Robertsbridge F 6
35 Roberttown E 10
12 Robeston Cross F 2
12 Robeston Wathen E 4
35 Robin Hood D 11
31 Robin Hood Inn C 11
41 Robin Hood's Bay E 9
4 Roborough D 4
30 Roby A 3
34 Roby Mill F 4
31 Rocester F 9
12 Roch E 2
12 Roch Gate E 2
35 Rochdale F 7
3 Roche D 7
10 Rochester, Kent A 6
44 Rochester, Northumb. C 6
10 Rochford E 8
2 Rock, Cornwall B 6
45 Rock, Northumb. A 10
22 Rock, Heref. & Worcs. E 1
9 Rock, W. Sussex E 12
30 Rock Ferry B 2
22 Rock Hill E 3
6 Rockbeare G 4
44 Rockcliffe, Cumb. G 2
43 Rockcliffe, Dumf. & Gall. F 9
15 Rockfield, Gwent C 8
61 Rockfield, Highland H 9
8 Rockford E 3
15 Rockhampton E 9
26 Rockheath D 6
21 Rockhill D 8
23 Rockingham C 12
26 Rockland All Saints F 3
26 Rockland St. Mary E 6
26 Rockland St. Peter F 3
16 Rockley G 3
44 Rockliffe Cross G 2
17 Rockwell End E 9
6 Rockwell Green D 5
15 Rodborough D 11
15 Rodbourne, Wilts. F 2
15 Rodbourne, Wilts. F 12
16 Rodbourne Cheney E 2
21 Rodd F 8
49 Roddam G 12
49 Roddam Rigg G 12
7 Rodden H 9
7 Rode A 11
30 Rode Heath D 6
31 Rodeheath C 7
63 Rodel H 1
21 Roden A 11
6 Rodhuish B 4
21 Rodington A 11
15 Rodley C 10
15 Rodmarton D 12
10 Rodmell G 3
11 Rodmersham B 8
7 Rodney Stoke A 8
31 Rodsley F 10
6 Rodway B 6
7 Rodwell H 7
35 Roecliffe A 12
18 Roehampton G 2
64 Roesound C 7
10 Roffey E 1
61 Rogart F 7
9 Rogate D 9
14 Rogerstone E 6
47 Rogerton D 11
15 Rogiet E 8
26 Rollesby D 7
23 Rolleston, Leics. B 10
32 Rolleston, Notts. E 5
31 Rolleston, Staffs. G 10
37 Rolston C 10
11 Rolvenden E 7
11 Rolvenden Layne E 7
39 Romaldkirk C 12
26 Roman Hill F 8
40 Romanby F 4
48 Romannobridge E 4
4 Romansleigh D 6
62 Romesdal C 3
18 Romford E 5
31 Romiley A 8
8 Romsey D 5
22 Romsley, Salop. D 1
22 Romsley, Salop. D 3
38 Ronague H 1
41 Rookdale H 9
39 Rookhope A 11
8 Rookley H 6
7 Rooks Bridge A 7
6 Rook's Nest C 4
37 Roos D 10
48 Rootpark D 2
9 Ropley C 8
9 Ropley Dean C 7
33 Ropsley G 7
58 Rora C 8
58 Rorandle F 4
21 Rorrington B 8
2 Rose D 5
4 Rose Ash D 7
10 Rose Hill F 3
10 Roseacre, Kent C 6
34 Roseacre, Lancs. C 3
48 Rosebank D 1
45 Rosebrough C 12
12 Rosebush D 4
2 Rosecare B 2
41 Rosedale Abbey F 7
45 Roseden A 8
58 Rosehearty A 7
30 Rosehill G 5
56 Roseisle C 7
12 Rosemarket F 3
56 Rosemarkie D 3
6 Rosemary Lane E 5
53 Rosemount C 7
2 Rosenannon C 6
2 Rosewarne F 3
48 Rosewell C 5
40 Roseworth C 4
2 Roseworthy F 3
39 Rosgill D 8
55 Roshven L 1
62 Roskhill D 2
38 Rosley A 6
48 Roslin C 5
31 Rosliston H 11
47 Rosneath A 7
43 Ross, Dumf. & Gall. G 7
45 Ross, Northumb. B 12
15 Ross-on-Wye B 9
30 Rossett D 2
52 Rossie Ochill F 6
36 Rossington G 4
56 Rosskeen C 2
47 Rossland B 9
61 Roster C 11
30 Rostherne B 6
38 Rosthwaite D 5
31 Roston F 10
2 Rosudgeon G 3
48 Rosyth A 4
45 Rothbury C 9
23 Rotherby A 10
10 Rotherfield E 4
17 Rotherfield Greys F 8
17 Rotherfield Peppard F 8
32 Rotherham A 2
23 Rothersthorpe F 10
17 Rotherwick H 8
56 Rothes E 8
46 Rothesay C 6
58 Rothiebrisbane D 5
58 Rothienorman D 5
64 Rothiesholm C 4
45 Rothill B 9
23 Rothley A 9
58 Rothmaise D 4
37 Rothwell, Lincs. G 9
23 Rothwell, Northants. D 11
35 Rothwell, W. Yorks. D 12
37 Rotsea B 8
59 Rottal K 1
10 Rottingdean H 3
38 Rottington D 2
43 Roucan D 11
8 Roud H 6
31 Rough Close F 8
11 Rough Common B 10
31 Rough Hay H 10
26 Rougham C 1
27 Rougham Green J 2
55 Roughburn L 7
35 Roughlee C 7
22 Roughley B 5
44 Roughsike E 3
33 Roughton, Lincs. D 9
26 Roughton, Norf. B 5
22 Roughton, Salop. C 1
47 Roughwood D 8
17 Round Oak H 7
7 Roundham E 7
35 Roundhay C 12
43 Roundstonefoot A 12
9 Roundstreet Com. C 12
16 Roundway H 1
22 Rous Lench G 4
6 Rousdon G 6
16 Rousham B 6
47 Routdaneburn D 7
37 Routh C 8
61 Rovie Lodge F 7
3 Row, Cornwall B 8
39 Row, Cumbria F 7
44 Rowanburn E 2
51 Rowardennan Hotel H 10
31 Rowarth A 8
16 Rowde H 1
29 Ro-wen C 7
44 Rowfoot G 5
19 Rowhedge B 10
9 Rowhook C 12
22 Rowington E 5
31 Rowland C 10
9 Rowland's Castle E 9
45 Rowland's Gill G 10
9 Rowledge B 9
37 Rowley, Humber. D 7
21 Rowley, Salop. B 8
22 Rowley Regis C 3
15 Rowlstone B 7
9 Rowly B 11
22 Rowney Green E 4
8 Rownhams D 5
17 Rowsham B 9
31 Rowsley D 11
33 Rowston E 8
30 Rowton, Ches. D 3
30 Rowton, Salop. H 5
49 Roxburgh F 9
49 Roxburgh Newtown F 9
37 Roxby, Humber. E 7
41 Roxby, N. Yorks. D 7
25 Roxton K 3
18 Roxwell C 6
34 Royal Oak G 3
55 Roybridge L 6
18 Roydon, Essex C 4
27 Roydon, Norfolk G 4
24 Roydon, Norfolk C 8
25 Royston, Herts. L 5
35 Royston, S. Yorks. F 12
35 Royton F 8
29 Ruabon F 12
2 Ruan High Lanes F 6
2 Ruan Lanihorne E 6
2 Ruan Minor H 4
15 Ruardean C 9
15 Ruardean Woodside C 9
22 Ribery D 3
39 Ruckcroft A 8
21 Ruckhall Com. H 10
11 Ruckinge E 9
33 Ruckland B 10
21 Ruckley B 10
40 Rudby D 5
45 Rudchester F 9
32 Ruddington G 3
15 Rudford B 11
7 Rudge A 11
15 Rudgeway F 9
9 Rudgwick C 12
15 Rudhall B 9
14 Rudry F 5
41 Rudston H 11
31 Rudyard D 8
49 Ruecastle G 8
34 Rufford F 3
36 Rufforth B 3
45 Ruffside H 8
23 Rugby E 8
31 Rugeley H 9
56 Ruilick E 1
6 Ruishton D 6
18 Ruislip E 1
18 Ruislip Common E 1
44 Ruletownhead B 4
49 Rumbletonlaw E 9
52 Rumblingbridge G 5
27 Rumburgh G 6
2 Rumford C 6
14 Rumney F 5
52 Runacraig F 1
30 Runcorn B 4
9 Runcton F 10
24 Runcton Holme E 7
5 Rundlestone H 4
9 Runfold A 10
26 Runhall E 4
26 Runham D 7
6 Runnington D 5
19 Runsell Green C 8
41 Runswick D 8
57 Runtaleave M 8
19 Runwell D 7
17 Ruscombe F 9
56 Rosehaugh House D 2
19 Rush Green B 11
15 Rushall, Heref. & Worcs. A 9
27 Rushall, Norfolk G 5
22 Rushall, W. Midlands B 4
8 Rushall, Wilts. A 3
27 Rushbrooke J 2
21 Rushbury C 10
25 Rushden, Herts. M 4
25 Rushden, Northants. J 1
27 Rushford G 2
10 Rushlake Green F 5
27 Rushmere G 8
27 Rushmere St. Andrew. K 5
27 Rushmere Street K 5
9 Rushmoor, Surrey B 10
8 Rushmore, Wilts. D 1
22 Rushock E 2
35 Rusholme H 7
30 Rushton, Ches. D 4
23 Rushton, Northants. D 11
21 Rushton, Salop. B 11
31 Rushton Spencer D 8
22 Rushwick G 2
40 Rushyford B 3
52 Ruskie G 1
33 Ruskington E 8
43 Rusko F 7
38 Rusland F 6
10 Rusper D 1
15 Ruspidge C 9
10 Russell's Green G 6
17 Russell's Water E 8
9 Rustington F 11
41 Ruston G 9
37 Ruston Parva A 8
41 Ruswarp D 9
49 Rutherford F 9
47 Rutherglen C 11
3 Ruthernbridge C 7
29 Ruthin D 10
59 Ruthrieston G 7
49 Ruthven, Borders E 10
58 Ruthven, Grampian C 3
56 Ruthven, Highland F 4
57 Ruthven, Highland J 3
53 Ruthven, Tayside B 7
53 Ruthven House B 8
2 Ruthvoes D 6
43 Ruthwell E 11
15 Ruxton Green B 8
30 Ruyton Eleven Towns H 3
45 Ryal F 8
7 Ryall G 7
10 Ryarsh B 5
38 Rydal E 6
9 Ryde G 7
4 Rydon F 2
11 Rye F 8
11 Rye Foreign F 7
11 Rye Harbour F 8
43 Ryemuir D 11
24 Ryhall D 1
37 Ryhill, Humber. E 10
36 Ryhill, W. Yorks. F 2
45 Ryhope H 12
33 Ryland B 7
35 Rylstone A 8
7 Ryme Intrinseca E 9
49 Ryslaw E 10
36 Ryther C 3
15 Ryton, Glos. A 10
41 Ryton, N. Yorks. H 8
21 Ryton, Salop. B 10
22 Ryton, Salop. B 1
45 Ryton, Tyne & Wear G 9
23 Ryton-on-Dunsmore E 7
34 Sabden C 6
18 Sacombe B 3
45 Sacriston H 10
40 Sadberge C 4
46 Saddell F 3
23 Saddington C 10
24 Saddle Bow D 7
8 Saddle Heath E 3
39 Sadgill E 7
25 Saffron Walden L 6
12 Sageston G 4
26 Saham Hills E 2
26 Saham Toney E 2
30 Saighton D 3
50 Sailean C 6
49 St. Abbs C 11
2 St. Agnes, Corn. E 4
2 St. Agnes, Is. of Scilly D 2
18 St. Albans C 2
2 St. Allen E 5
53 St. Andrews E 10
14 St. Andrews Major G 5
34 St. Anne's D 2
43 St. Ann's B 11
3 St. Ann's Chapel, Cornwall C 11
5 St. Ann's Chapel, Devon L 5
2 St. Anthony G 5
10 St. Anthony's Hill H 5
15 St. Arvans E 8
29 St. Asaph C 9
14 St. Athan G 3
3 St. Austell D 7
7 St. Bartholomew's Hill D 12
38 St. Bees D 2
3 St. Blazey D 8
3 St. Blazey Gate D 7
49 St. Boswells F 8
3 St. Breock C 7
3 St. Breward B 8
15 St. Briavels D 9

12 St. Brides F 2
14 St. Brides Major G 2
15 St. Brides Netherwent E 7
14 St. Bride's-super- Ely G 4
14 St. Bride's Wentlooge F 6
5 St. Budeaux K 3
2 St. Buryan G 1
15 St. Catherine G 11
51 St. Catherines G 8
12 St. Clears E 6
3 St. Cleer C 9
2 St. Clement E 5
3 St. Clether A 9
46 St. Colmac C 5
2 St. Columb Major C 6
2 St. Columb Minor C 5
2 St. Columb Road D 6
58 St. Combs A 8
27 St. Cross South Elmham G 6
49 St. Cuthberts E 11
53 St. Cyrus A 12
12 St. David's, Dyfed D 1
52 St. David's, Tayside E 4
2 St. Day E 4
6 St. Decumans B 4
2 St. Dennis D 6
15 St. Devereux A 7
12 St. Dogmaels B 5
12 St. Dogwells D 3
3 St. Dominick C 11
14 St. Donats G 3
16 St. Edith's Marsh H 1
3 St. Endellion B 7
2 St. Enoder D 6
2 St. Erme E 5
3 St. Erney D 10
2 St. Erth F 3
2 St. Ervan C 6
3 St. Ewe E 7
14 St. Faggans F 4
58 St. Fergus B 8
52 St. Fillans E 2
12 St. Florence G 4
2 St. Gennys B 2
29 St. George C 9
15 St. George's, Avon H 7
14 St. George's, S. Glam. G 4
3 St. Germans D 10
4 St. Giles in the Wood D 4
5 St. Giles on the Heath G 2
20 St. Harmon E 5
40 St. Helen Auckland C 2
26 St. Helena D 5
9 St. Helens, I.o.W. G 7
34 St. Helens, Merseyside G 4
2 St. Hilary, Corn. F 3
14 St. Hilary, S. Glam. G 3
10 Saint Hill D 3
14 St. Illtyd D 5
12 St. Ishmael's F 2
2 St. Issey C 6
3 St. Ive C 10
3 St. Ive Cross C 10
25 St. Ives, Cambs. H 4
2 St. Ives, Corn. F 2
8 St. Ives, Dorset F 3
27 St. James South Elmham G 6
8 St. Joan á Gores Cross A 2
3 St. John D 11
22 St. John's, Heref. & Worcs. G 2
38 St. John's, I.o.M. G 1
4 St. John's Chapel, Devon C 4
39 St. John's Chapel, Durham A 11
24 St. John's Fen End D 6
24 St. John's Highway D 6
38 St. Judas F 2
2 St. Just G 1
2 St. Just Lane F 6
58 St. Katherines D 5
2 St. Keverne G 5
3 St. Kew B 7
3 St. Kew Highway B 7
3 St. Keyne D 9
3 St. Lawrence, Corn. C 7
19 St. Lawrence, Essex C 9
9 St. Lawrence, I.o.W. H 7
17 St. Leonards, Bucks. C 10
8 St. Leonards, Dorset F 3
11 St. Leonards, E. Sussex G 7
2 St. Levan G 1
14 St. Lythans G 4
3 St. Mabyn B 7
6 St. Margaret D 4
27 St. Margaret, South Elmham G 6
15 St. Margarets, Heref. & Worcs. A 7
18 St. Margarets, Hertfordshire C 4
11 St. Margaret's at Cliffe D 12
64 St. Margaret's Hope E 2
38 St. Mark's H 1
3 St. Martin D 9
52 St. Martins, Tayside D 6
30 St. Martin's, Salop G 2
2 St. Martin's Green G 4
8 St. Mary Bourne A 6
14 St. Mary Church G 3
18 St. Mary Cray G 5
11 St. Mary in the Marsh E 9
18 St. Marylebone F 3
64 St. Marys D 3
11 St. Mary's Bay E 9
15 St. Mary's Grove G 8
19 St. Mary's Hoo F 8
15 St. Maughans C 8
2 St. Mawes F 5
2 St. Mawgan C 6
3 St. Mellion C 11
14 St. Mellons F 6
2 St. Merryn B 6
3 St. Mewan E 7
3 St. Michael Caerhays E 7
2 St. Michael Penkevil E 6
27 St. Michael, South Elmham G 6
11 St. Michaels, Kent E 7
21 St. Michaels, Heref. & Worcs. F 11
34 St. Michaels on Wyre C 3
3 St. Minver B 7
53 St. Monans G 10
3 St. Neot C 9
25 St. Neots J 3
2 St. Newlyn East D 5
12 St. Nicholas, Dyfed C 2
14 St. Nicholas, S. Glam. G 4
11 St. Nicholas at Wade A 11
52 St. Ninians H 3
26 St. Olaves E 8
19 St. Osyth B 11
15 St. Owen's Cross B 8
18 St. Pancras F 3
18 St. Paul's Cray G 5
18 St. Paul's Walden B 2
11 St. Peters A 12
12 St. Petrox G 3
47 St. Quivox G 8
2 St. Stephen D 6
3 St. Stephens, Corn. A 10
3 St. Stephens, Corn. D 11
3 St. Teath B 7
3 St. Tudy B 8
12 St. Twynnells G 3
3 St. Veep D 8
53 St. Vigeans C 11
3 St. Wenn C 7
15 St. Weonards B 8
22 Saintbury H 5
51 Salachail B 8
5 Salcombe M 6
6 Salcombe Regis G 5
19 Salcott C 9
35 Sale H 7
22 Sale Green F 3
33 Saleby B 11
10 Salehurst F 6
20 Salem, Dyfed D 2
13 Salem, Dyfed D 9
28 Salem, Gwynedd E 5
50 Salen, Highland A 4
50 Salen, Mull, Strathclyde C 3
34 Salesbury D 5
23 Salford, Beds. H 12
35 Salford, Manchester G 7
16 Salford, Oxon. A 4
22 Salford Priors G 4
10 Salfords C 2
26 Salhouse D 6
52 Saline H 5
8 Salisbury C 3
26 Sall C 4
51 Sallachan A 7
55 Sallachy, Highland G 3
60 Sallachy, Highland F 6
33 Salmonby C 10
43 Salmond's Muir C 10
21 Salop, Co. B 10
16 Salperton H 7
25 Salph End K 2
48 Salsburgh C 1
31 Salt G 8
3 Saltash D 11
56 Saltburn C 3
41 Saltburn-by-the Sea C 7
32 Saltby H 6
47 Saltcoats E 7
35 Salterforth C 7
24 Salters Lode E 7
30 Satterswall D 5
33 Saltfleet A 11
33 Saltfleetby St. Clement A 11
33 Saltfleetby St. Peter A 11
33 Saltfleetby All Saints A 11
15 Saltford G 10
37 Salthaugh Grange E 10
26 Salthouse A 4
36 Saltmarshe E 6
30 Saltney D 3
41 Salton G 7
4 Saltren's D 3
45 Saltwick E 10
11 Saltwood D 10
9 Salvington F 12
22 Salwarpe F 2
7 Salway Ash F 8
22 Sambourne F 4
30 Sambrook H 6
34 Samlesbury D 5
34 Samlesbury Bottoms D 5
6 Sampford B 4
6 Sampford Arundel D 5
4 Sampford Courtenay F 5
6 Sampford Peverell E 4
5 Sampford Spinney H 4
19 Samuel's Corner E 9
49 Samuelston B 7
54 Sanachan F 2
51 Sanahole G 7
2 Sancreed G 1
37 Sancton C 7
64 Sand D 7
36 Sand Hutton A 5
38 Sand Side G 5
55 Sandaig, Highland J 1
55 Sandaig, Highland H 1
35 Sandal Magna E 12
38 Sandale A 5
30 Sandbach D 6
46 Sandbank A 6
8 Sandbanks G 2
58 Sandend A 3
18 Sanderstead H 3
15 Sandford, Avon H 7
39 Sandford, Cumbria D 9
4 Sandford, Devon F 7
8 Sandford, Dorset G 1
9 Sandford, I.o.W. H 7
30 Sandford, Salop H 2
47 Sandford, Strathclyde E 12
16 Sandford-on- Thames D 6
7 Sandford Orcas D 9
16 Sandford St. Martin B 5
58 Sandfordhill C 8
64 Sandgarth C 3
11 Sandgate E 10
58 Sandhaven A 7
42 Sandhead G 2
47 Sandhill H 9
45 Sandhoe F 8
44 Sandholm D 3
36 Sandholme, Humber. D 6
24 Sandholme, Lincs. B 4
17 Sandhurst, Berks. H 9
15 Sandhurst, Glos. B 11
11 Sandhurst, Kent E 7
10 Sandhurst Cross E 6
40 Sandhutton G 4
32 Sandiacre G 2
33 Sandilands B 12
30 Sandiway C 5
16 Sandleigh D 6
10 Sandling B 6
64 Sandness D 6
19 Sandon, Essex C 7
25 Sandon, Herts. M 4
31 Sandon, Staffs. G 8
9 Sandown H 7
3 Sandplace D 9
18 Sandridge, Herts. C 2
15 Sandridge, Wilts. H 12
41 Sandsend D 8
64 Sandside D 1
61 Sandside Hotel A 9
64 Sandsound D 7
36 Sandtoft F 5
11 Sandway, Kent C 7
6 Sandway, Som. C 2
22 Sandwell C 4
38 Sandwick, Cumbria C 6
64 Sandwick, Orkney Is. E 2
63 Sandwick, Highland D 5
64 Sandwick, Shetland Is. E 7
38 Sandwith D 2
25 Sandy K 3
30 Sandy Bank G 4
10 Sandy Cross F 5
12 Sandy Haven F 2
16 Sandy Lane, Wilts. G 1
35 Sandy Lane, W. Yorks. D 9
29 Sandycroft D 12
43 Sandyford, Dumf. & Gall. B 12
47 Sandyford, Strathclyde G 9
38 Sandygate F 2
43 Sandyhills F 9
34 Sandylands A 3
4 Sandymoor Cross F 3
5 Sandypark G 6
44 Sandysike F 2
49 Sandystones G 8
15 Sandyway B 8
60 Sangobeg A 5
50 Sanna A 2
47 Sanquhar H 12
38 Santon Bridge E 4
27 Santon Downham G 1
23 Sapcote C 8
21 Sapey Common F 12
27 Sapiston H 2
15 Sapperton, Glos. D 12
33 Sapperton, Lincs. G 7
24 Saracen's Head C 4
61 Sarclet C 12
12 Sardis F 3
12 Sardis Mountain F 5
8 Sarisbury E 6
28 Sarn, Gwynedd G 2
14 Sarn, Mid Glam. F 2
21 Sarn, Powys C 7
12 Sarnau, Dyfed B 6
13 Sarnau, Dyfed D 8
29 Sarnau, Gwynedd F 9
14 Sarnau, Powys A 3
21 Sarnau, Powys A 8
28 Sarn-bach H 2
21 Sarnesfield G 9
13 Saron, Dyfed C 7
13 Saron, Dyfed F 9
28 Saron, Gwynedd D 5
17 Sarratt D 11
11 Sarre B 11
16 Sarsden B 4
8 Sarson B 4
38 Sartfield F 2
40 Satley A 1
4 Satterleigh D 5
38 Satterthwaite F 6
17 Satwell F 8
58 Sauchen F 4
53 Saucher D 7
59 Sauchieburn K 4
47 Sauchrie H 8
30 Saughall C 2
44 Saughtree C 4
45 Saughtrees E 3
15 Saul C 10
32 Saundby A 5
12 Saundersfoot F 5
17 Saunderton D 9
17 Saunderton Lee D 9
4 Saunton B 3
33 Sausthorpe C 11
60 Saval F 6
31 Saverley Green F 8
50 Savory C 4
18 Sawbridgeworth B 5
41 Sawdon G 9
32 Sawley, Derby G 2
34 Sawley, Lancs. C 6
25 Sawston K 6
25 Sawtry G 3
32 Saxby, Leics. H 5
33 Saxby, Lincs. B 7
37 Saxby All Saints E 7
32 Saxelby H 4
32 Saxilby C 6
26 Saxingham B 3
26 Saxlingham Nethergate F 5
27 Saxmundham J 7
25 Saxon Street J 8
32 Saxondale F 4
27 Saxtead J 6
27 Saxtead Green J 6
26 Saxthorpe C 4
36 Saxton C 3
10 Sayers Common F 2
48 Scabcleuch H 5
40 Scackleton H 6
63 Scadabay H 3
32 Scaftworth A 4
41 Scagglethorpe H 8
50 Scalasaig H 1
36 Scalby, Humber. D 6
41 Scalby, N. Yorks. F 10
23 Scaldwell E 11
44 Scaleby G 3
44 Scalebyhill G 3
38 Scales, Cumb. C 6
38 Scales, Cumbria H 5
34 Scales, Lans. D 3
39 Scales Houses A 8
32 Scalford H 5
41 Scaling D 7
50 Scallastle D 4
64 Scalloway E 7
62 Scalpay House E 5
55 Scamadale K 1
55 Scamodale M 2
41 Scampston H 8
33 Scampton B 7
56 Scaniport F 2
64 Scapa D 2
64 Scar A 4
39 Scar End B 11
63 Scarastavore H 1
41 Scarborough F 10
43 Scarbrae C 9
32 Scarcliffe C 2
35 Scarcroft C 12
54 Scardroy D 6
61 Scarfskerry A 11
40 Scargill D 1
34 Scarisbrick F 3
26 Scarning D 2
32 Scarrington F 4
34 Scarth Hill F 3
37 Scartho G 10
64 Scarwell C 1
56 Scatraig F 3
64 Scatsta C 7
37 Scawby G 7
37 Scawby Brook F 7
36 Scawsby G 3
40 Scawton G 6
10 Scayne's Hill F 3
14 Scethrog B 4
47 Schaw G 9
31 Scholar Green E 7
35 Scholes, W. Yorks. F 10
35 Scholes, W. Yorks. E 10
36 Scholes, W. Yorks. D 2
40 School Aycliffe C 3
35 Scissett F 11
12 Scleddau D 3
26 Sco Ruston C 6
27 Scole G 4
59 Scolly's Cross J 4
12 Scolton E 3
62 Sconser E 4
53 Scoonie G 8
50 Scoor F 2
33 Scopwick D 8
60 Scoraig G 2
37 Scorborough C 8
47 Scorrieholm F 12
2 Scorrier E 4
5 Scorriton J 6
40 Scorton E 3
34 Scot Lane End F 5
44 Scotby G 3
40 Scotch Corner E 2
34 Scotforth A 4
33 Scothern B 7
45 Scots' Gap D 8
33 Scots Hole D 8
56 Scotsburn B 3
61 Scotscalder Sta. B 10
53 Scotscraig D 9
44 Scotsdike F 2
59 Scotston, Grampian K 5
52 Scotston, Tayside C 4
50 Scotstown A 5
45 Scotswood G 10
53 Scottas J 1
36 Scotter G 6
36 Scotterthorpe G 6
37 Scotton, Lincs. G 7
40 Scotton, N. Yorks. F 2
35 Scotton, N. Yorks. A 12
49 Scoughall A 8
26 Scoulton E 3
60 Scourie C 3
60 Scourie More C 3
64 Scousburgh F 7
61 Scrabster A 10
49 Scraesburgh G 9
33 Scrafield C 10
45 Scrainwood B 8
33 Scramblesby B 10
24 Scrane End A 5
23 Scraptoft B 10
26 Scratby D 8
36 Scrayingham A 5
24 Scredington B 2
6 Screedy D 4
43 Screel F 9
33 Scremby C 11
49 Scremerston D 12
32 Screveton F 4
61 Scriberscross F 8
33 Scrivelsby D 9
35 Scriven A 12
43 Scroggs C 12
32 Scrooby A 4
31 Scropton G 10
33 Scrub Hill E 9
40 Scruton F 3
37 Sculcoates D 8
26 Sculthorpe B 2
37 Scunthorpe F 7
13 Scurlage H 8
26 Sea Palling C 7
7 Seaborough F 8
30 Seacombe A 2
33 Seacroft, Lincs. D 12
35 Seacroft, W. Yorks. D 12
48 Seafield, Lothian C 3
47 Seafield, Strathclyde G 8
10 Seaford H 4
34 Seaforth G 2
63 Seaforth Head E 4
45 Seaham H 12
45 Seahouses D 12
10 Seal B 4
30 Sealand C 2
9 Seale A 10
41 Seamer, N. Yorks. G 10
40 Seamer, N. Yorks. D 5
47 Seamill E 7
37 Searby G 8
11 Seasalter B 9
38 Seascale E 3
33 Seathorne D 12
38 Seathwaite, Cumb. D 5
38 Seathwaite, Cumb. F 5
38 Seatoller D 5
3 Seaton, Corn. D 10
38 Seaton, Cumb. B 3
6 Seaton, Devon G 6
45 Seaton, Dur. H 12
23 Seaton, Leics. B 12
37 Seaton, Humber. B 9
45 Seaton, Northumb. E 11
45 Seaton Burn F 10
40 Seaton Carew B 5
45 Seaton Delaval E 11
36 Seaton Ross C 6
45 Seaton Sluice E 11
58 Seatown, Grampian A 3
58 Seatown, Grampian A 2
7 Seatown, Dorset G 7
40 Seave Green E 6
9 Seaview G 8
43 Seaville F 12
7 Seavington St. Mary E 7
7 Seavington St. Michael E 7
19 Seawick Sands C 11
14 Sebastopol E 6
38 Sebergham A 6
22 Seckington A 6
60 Second Coast G 1
39 Sedbergh F 9
15 Sedbury E 9
39 Sedbusk F 11
22 Sedgeberow H 4
32 Sedgebrook F 6
40 Sedgefield B 4
24 Sedgeford B 8
7 Sedgehill C 12
22 Sedgley C 2
39 Sedgwick F 7
10 Sedlescombe F 6
15 Seend H 12
15 Seende Cleeve H 12
17 Seer Green E 10
26 Seething F 6
34 Sefton G 2
45 Seghill F 11
31 Seighford H 7
63 Seilebost G 2
22 Seisdon C 2
30 Selattyn G 1
9 Selborne C 9
36 Selby D 4
9 Selham D 10
49 Selkirk G 7
15 Sellack B 9
38 Sellafield Station E 3
64 Sellafirth B 7
11 Sellindge D 9
11 Sellindge Lees D 9
11 Selling B 9
15 Sells Green H 12
22 Selly Oak D 4
10 Selmeston G 4
18 Selsdon H 4
15 Selsey D 11
10 Selsfield Common E 2
39 Selside H 10
11 Selstead D 10
32 Selston E 2
6 Selworthy B 3
64 Semblister D 6
27 Semer K 3
15 Semington H 12
7 Semley D 12
9 Send A 11
9 Sendmarsh A 11
14 Senghenydd E 4
2 Sennen G 1
2 Sennen Cove G 1
14 Sennybridge B 3
43 Senwick Ho. G 7

40 Sessay **H 5**
24 Setchey **D 7**
8 Setley **F 5**
64 Settascarth **C 2**
64 Setter, Bressay Shetland Is. **E 7**
64 Setter, Zetland Shetland Is. **D 7**
35 Settle **A 7**
45 Settlingstones **F 7**
41 Settrington **H 8**
6 Seven Ash **C 5**
18 Seven Kings **E 4**
14 Seven Sisters **C 2**
16 Seven Springs **B 1**
16 Seven Wells **A 2**
16 Sevenhampton, Glos. **B 1**
16 Sevenhampton, Wilts. **E 3**
10 Sevenoaks **C 4**
10 Sevenoaks Weald **C 4**
15 Severn Beach **F 8**
22 Severn Stoke **H 2**
11 Sevington, Kent **D 9**
15 Sevington, Wilts. **F 11**
25 Sewards End **L 7**
41 Sewerby **H 12**
2 Seworgan **G 4**
32 Sewstern **H 6**
10 Seyning **G 1**
17 Shabbington **C 7**
23 Shackerstone **A 7**
27 Shadingfield **G 7**
9 Shackleford **B 10**
40 Shadforth **A 4**
11 Shadoxhurst **D 8**
27 Shadwell, Norfolk **G 2**
35 Shadwell, W. Yorks. **C 12**
7 Shaftesbury **D 12**
36 Shafton **F 2**
16 Shalbourne **H 4**
8 Shalcombe **G 5**
9 Shalden **B 8**
5 Shaldon **J 8**
8 Shalfleet **G 5**
19 Shalford, Essex **A 7**
9 Shalford, Surrey **A 11**
19 Shalford Green **A 7**
4 Shallowford **B 6**
11 Shalmsford Street **C 9**
23 Shalstone **H 9**
46 Shalunt **B 5**
9 Shamley Green **B 11**
43 Shancastle **C 9**
47 Shandon **A 7**
56 Shandwick **B 4**
23 Shangton **C 10**
45 Shankhouse **E 11**
9 Shanklin **H 7**
46 Shannochie **G 5**
53 Shanzie **B 7**
39 Shap **D 8**
8 Shapwick, Dorset **F 1**
7 Shapwick, Som. **B 7**
32 Shardlow **G 2**
22 Shareshill **B 3**
35 Sharlston, W. Yorks. **E 12**
36 Sharlston, W. Yorks. **E 2**
11 Sharnal Street **A 7**
17 Sharnbrook **J 1**
23 Sharnford **C 8**
34 Sharoe Green **D 4**
40 Sharow **H 3**
25 Sharpenhoe **M 2**
45 Sharperton **C 8**
15 Sharpness **D 10**
10 Sharpthorne **E 3**
26 Sharrington **B 3**
22 Shatterford **D 1**
5 Shaugh Prior **J 4**
7 Shave Cross **F 7**
30 Shavington **E 6**
16 Shaw, Berks. **G 6**
35 Shaw, Lancs. **F 8**
15 Shaw, Wilts. **H 12**
34 Shaw Green **E 4**
35 Shaw Mills **A 11**
30 Shawbury **H 4**
45 Shawdon Hill **B 9**
23 Shawell **D 9**
8 Shawford **D 6**
35 Shawforth **E 7**
43 Shawhead **D 9**
43 Shawhill **E 12**
47 Shawwood **G 10**
40 Shawton **D 11**
7 Shear Cross **B 11**
43 Shearington **E 11**
23 Shearsby **C 9**
4 Shebbear **E 3**
30 Shebdon **H 6**
61 Shebster **B 9**
9 Shedfield **E 7**
31 Sheen **D 9**
21 Sheephouse **H 7**
15 Sheepscombe **C 12**
5 Sheepstor **J 4**
4 Sheepwash, Devon **E 4**
4 Sheepwash, Devon **C 7**
45 Sheepwash, Northumb. **D 10**
15 Sheepway **G 8**
23 Sheepy Magna **B 7**
23 Sheepy Parva **B 7**
18 Sheering **C 5**
11 Sheerness **A 8**
9 Sheet, Hants. **D 9**
21 Sheet, Salop **E 10**
32 Sheffield **B 1**
25 Shefford **L 2**
16 Shefford Woodlands **G 4**
60 Sheigra **B 3**
43 Sheillahill **F 8**
21 Sheinton **B 11**
21 Shelderton **E 9**
31 Sheldon, Derby **C 10**
6 Sheldon, Devon **E 5**
22 Sheldon, War. **D 5**
11 Sheldwich **B 9**
35 Shelf **D 10**
27 Shelfhanger **G 4**
22 Shelfield, W. Midlands **B 4**
22 Shelfield, War. **F 5**
32 Shelford **F 4**
49 Shellacres **E 11**
18 Shelley, Essex **C 5**
35 Shelley, W. Yorks. **F 10**
16 Shellingford **E 4**
18 Shellow Bowells **C 6**
22 Shelsley Beauchamp **F 1**
21 Shelsley Walsh **F 12**
32 Shelthorpe **H 3**
26 Shelton, Norfolk **F 5**
25 Shelton, Northants. **H 1**
32 Shelton, Notts. **F 5**
21 Shelton, Salop **A 10**
21 Shelve **C 9**
21 Shelwick **H 10**
21 Shelwick Green **H 10**
56 Shenachie **F 4**
18 Shenfield **D 6**
23 Shenington **H 7**
18 Shenley **D 2**
17 Shenley Brook End **A 9**
23 Shenley Church End **H 11**
15 Shenmore **A 7**
57 Shennach **G 6**
42 Shennanton **E 4**
22 Shenstone, Heref. & Worcs. **E 2**
22 Shenstone, Staffs. **B 4**
57 Shenval **G 8**
24 Shepeu Stow **D 4**
23 Shephall **B 3**
18 Shepherd's Bush **F 2**
17 Shepherd's Green **F 8**
24 Shepherd's Port **B 7**
11 Shepherdswell **C 11**
35 Shepley **F 10**
15 Shepperdine **E 9**
17 Shepperton **G 11**
17 Shepperton Grn. **G 11**
25 Shepreth **K 5**
32 Shepshed **H 2**
7 Shepton Beauchamp **D 7**
7 Shepton Mallet **B 9**
7 Shepton Montague **C 10**
10 Shepway **C 6**
40 Sheraton **B 5**
7 Sherborne, Dorset **E 10**
16 Sherborne, Glos. **C 3**
9 Sherborne St. John **A 8**
22 Sherbourne **F 6**
40 Sherburn, Dur. **A 3**
41 Sherburn, N. Yorks. **G 9**
40 Sherburn Hill **A 4**
36 Sherburn in Elmet **D 3**
9 Shere **A 12**
26 Shereford **C 2**
8 Sherfield English **D 4**
17 Sherfield on Loddon **H 7**
5 Sherford **L 6**
36 Sheriff Hutton **A 3**
26 Sheringham **A 4**
23 Sherington **G 12**
24 Shernborne **B 8**
22 Sherriffhales **A 1**
8 Sherrington **B 1**
15 Sherston **F 11**
4 Sherwood Green **D 4**
63 Sheshader **C 6**
47 Shettleston **C 11**
34 Shevington **F 4**
34 Shevington Moor **F 4**
3 Sheviock **D 10**
55 Shewglie **G 8**
52 Shian **C 3**
49 Shidlaw **F 10**
43 Shiel, Dumf. & Gall. **A 8**
43 Shiel, Dumf. & Gall. **D 7**
55 Shiel Bridge **H 3**
45 Shiel Dykes **B 9**
54 Shieldaig **C 2**
48 Shieldhill, Central **B 2**
43 Shieldhill, Dumf. & Gall. **C 10**
43 Shieldhill, Dumf. & Gall. **C 11**
47 Shieldmuir **D 12**
50 Shielfoot **A 4**
58 Shielhill, Grampian **B 8**
59 Shielhill, Tayside **L 2**
47 Shieloans **F 11**
16 Shifford **D 5**
22 Shifnal **A 1**
45 Shilbottle **B 10**
44 Shilburn Haugh **D 5**
40 Shildon **C 3**
47 Shillford **D 9**
6 Shillingford, Devon **D 3**
17 Shillingford, Oxon. **E 7**
6 Shillingford Abbot **G 2**
6 Shillingford St. George **G 2**
7 Shillingstone **E 11**
25 Shillington **M 2**
45 Shillmoor **B 7**
63 Shiltenish **E 4**
16 Shilton, Oxon. **C 4**
23 Shilton, War. **D 7**
7 Shilvinghampton **H 9**
27 Shimpling, Norf. **G 4**
27 Shimpling, Suffolk **K 2**
27 Shimpling Street **K 2**
40 Shincliffe **A 3**
40 Shincliffe Colliery **A 3**
45 Shiney Row **H 11**
17 Shinfield **G 8**
59 Shinfur **J 2**
43 Shinnelhead **B 8**
5 Shinner's Bridge **J 7**
60 Shinness **E 6**
10 Shipbourne **C 5**
26 Shipdham **E 3**
7 Shipham **A 8**
5 Shiphay **J 8**
17 Shiplake **F 8**
48 Shiplaw **D 5**
45 Shipley, Northumb. **A 9**
22 Shipley, Salop **C 2**
9 Shipley, W. Sussex **D 12**
35 Shipley, W. Yorks. **C 10**
10 Shipley Bridge **D 2**
26 Shipmeadow **F 7**
15 Shippea Hill Sta. **G 7**
16 Shippon **D 6**
22 Shipston on Stour **H 6**
16 Shipton, Glos. **B 1**
36 Shipton, N. Yorks **A 3**
21 Shipton, Salop. **C 11**
8 Shipton Bellinger **B 4**
7 Shipton Gorge **G 8**
9 Shipton Green **F 9**
15 Shipton Moyne **E 12**
16 Shipton-on-Cherwell **B 6**
16 Shipton-under-Wychwood **B 4**
36 Shiptonthorpe **C 6**
17 Shirburn **E 8**
34 Shirdley Hill **F 2**
22 Shire Oak **B 4**
32 Shirebrook **C 3**
32 Shiregreen **A 1**
15 Shirehampton **F 8**
45 Shiremoor **F 11**
15 Shirenewton **E 8**
32 Shireoaks **B 3**
4 Shirewell Cross **B 5**
21 Shirl Heath **F 10**
32 Shirland **D 1**
31 Shirley, Derby **F 10**
8 Shirley, Hants. **E 5**
22 Shirley, W. Midlands **D 5**
9 Shirrell Heath **E 7**
4 Shirwell **B 5**
46 Shishkine **F 4**
21 Shobdon **F 9**
4 Shobrooke **F 7**
30 Shocklach **E 3**
19 Shoeburyness **E 9**
11 Sholden **C 12**
8 Sholing **E 6**
21 Shoot Hill **A 9**
4 Shop, Cornwall **D 1**
2 Shop, Cornwall **B 6**
27 Shop Street **H 5**
44 Shopford **F 4**
18 Shoreditch **F 3**
10 Shoreham **B 4**
10 Shoreham-by-Sea **G 1**
56 Shoremill **C 3**
49 Shoresdean **E 12**
49 Shoreswood **E 12**
56 Shoretown **D 2**
16 Shornecote **E 1**
10 Shorne Ridgeway **A 6**
22 Short Heath, Leics. **A 6**
22 Short Heath, W. Midlands **B 3**
22 Short Heath, W. Midlands **C 4**
5 Shortacombe **G 4**
10 Shortgate **G 4**
2 Shortlanesend **E 5**
47 Shortlees **F 9**
15 Shortwood **G 10**
8 Shorwell **H 6**
7 Shoscombe **A 10**
30 Shotatton **H 2**
26 Shotesham **F 6**
19 Shotgate **E 7**
45 Shotley Bridge **H 9**
27 Shotley Gate **M 5**
27 Shotley Street **M 5**
45 Shotleyfield **H 9**
11 Shottenden **C 9**
9 Shottermill **C 10**
22 Shottery **G 5**
23 Shotteswell **H 8**
27 Shottisham **L 6**
31 Shottle **E 11**
29 Shotton, Clwyd **C 12**
40 Shotton, Durham **A 4**
49 Shotton, Northumb. **F 11**
40 Shotton Colliery **A 4**
48 Shotts **C 1**
30 Shotwick **C 2**
38 Shoughlaige-e-Caine **G 1**
56 Shougle **D 8**
24 Shouldham **E 8**
24 Shouldham Thorpe **E 8**
22 Shoulton **F 2**
10 Shover's Green **E 5**
21 Shrawardine **A 9**
22 Shrawley **F 2**
17 Shreding Green **F 11**
22 Shrewley **E 5**
21 Shrewsbury **A 10**
8 Shrewton **B 2**
9 Shripney **F 10**
16 Shrivenham **E 3**
26 Shropham **F 3**
19 Shrub End **B 9**
21 Shucknall **H 11**
25 Shady Camps **L 7**
63 Shulishader **C 6**
38 Shundraw **C 5**
15 Shurdington **B 12**
17 Shurlock Row **G 9**
61 Shurrery Lodge **B 10**
6 Shurton **B 5**
22 Shustoke **C 6**
22 Shut End **C 2**
4 Shute, Devon **F 8**
6 Shute, Devon **F 6**
23 Shutford **H 7**
15 Shuthonger **A 12**
23 Shutlanger **G 10**
22 Shuttington **B 6**
32 Shuttlewood **C 2**
43 Sibbaldbie **C 12**
23 Sibbertoft **D 10**
21 Sibdon Carwood **D 9**
23 Sibford Ferris **H 7**
23 Sibford Gower **H 7**
27 Sible Hedingham **M 1**
33 Sibsey **E 10**
24 Sibson, Cambs. **F 2**
23 Sibson, Leics. **B 7**
32 Sibthorpe **F 5**
27 Sicklesmere **J 2**
35 Sicklinghall **B 12**
6 Sid **G 5**
6 Sidbury, Devon **G 5**
21 Sidbury, Salop **D 12**
18 Sidcup **G 5**
38 Siddick **B 2**
31 Siddington, Ches. **C 7**
16 Siddington, Glos. **D 1**
22 Sidemoor **E 3**
6 Sidford **G 5**
9 Sidlesham **F 10**
10 Sidley **G 6**
10 Sidlowbridge **C 1**
6 Sidmouth **H 4**
5 Sigford **H 6**
14 Siggingston **G 3**
37 Sigglesthorne **C 9**
17 Silchester **H 7**
23 Sileby **A 9**
38 Silecroft **G 4**
20 Silian **G 1**
24 Silk Willoughby **A 2**
35 Silkstone **G 11**
35 Silkstone Com. **G 11**
43 Silloth **F 11**
58 Sillyearn **B 3**
13 Siloh **C 10**
41 Silpho **F 9**
35 Silsden **C 9**
25 Silsoe **M 2**
25 Silver End, Beds. **L 2**
19 Silver End, Essex **B 8**
11 Silver Street **B 7**
48 Silverburn **C 5**
39 Silverdale, Lancs. **H 7**
31 Silverdale, Staffs. **F 7**
23 Silverstone **H 10**
6 Silverton **F 3**
21 Silvington **D 11**
45 Simonburn **F 7**
6 Simonsbath **B 1**
34 Simonstone **D 6**
49 Simprim **E 11**
23 Simpson, Bucks. **H 12**
12 Simpson, Dyfed **E 2**
49 Sinclair's Hill **D 10**
47 Sinclairston **H 9**
40 Sinderby Quernhow **G 4**
45 Sinderhope **H 7**
17 Sindlesham **G 8**
44 Singdean **C 4**
17 Singleborough **A 8**
34 Singleton, Lancs. **C 3**
9 Singleton, W. Sussex **E 10**
10 Singlewell or Ifield **A 5**
30 Singret **F 2**
58 Sinnahard **F 2**
41 Sinnington **G 7**
22 Sinton Green **C 2**
18 Sipson **F 1**
14 Sirhowy **C 5**
11 Sissinghurst **D 7**
49 Sisterpath **E 10**
15 Siston **G 10**
2 Sithney **G 3**
11 Sittingbourne **B 8**
58 Sittyton **E 6**
22 Six Ashes **C 2**
32 Six Hills **H 4**
25 Six Mile Bottom **J 7**
31 Six Roads End **G 10**
33 Sixhills **B 9**
27 Sizewell **J 8**
61 Skail **C 7**
64 Skail, Egilsay, Orkney Is. **B 3**
64 Skaill, Mainland, Orkney Is. **D 3**
64 Skaill, Mainland, Orkney Is. **C 1**
47 Skares **H 10**
59 Skateraw, Grampian **H 7**
49 Skateraw, Lothian **B 10**
62 Skeabost **C 3**
40 Skeeby **E 2**
23 Skeffington **B 11**
37 Skeffling **E 11**
32 Skegby **D 2**
33 Skegness **D 12**
61 Skelbo **G 8**
36 Skelbrooke **F 3**
24 Skeldyke **B 4**
32 Skellingthorpe **C 6**
64 Skellister **D 7**
36 Skellow **F 3**
35 Skelmanthorpe **F 11**
34 Skelmersdale **F 4**
58 Skelmonae **D 6**
47 Skelmorlie **C 7**
58 Skelmuir **C 7**
61 Skelpick **B 7**
39 Skelton, Cumb. **B 7**
40 Skelton, Cleveland **C 6**
36 Skelton, Humber. **E 5**
36 Skelton, N. Yorks. **B 3**
40 Skelton, N. Yorks. **E 1**
40 Skelton, N. Yorks. **H 4**
38 Skelwirth Bridge **E 6**
64 Skelwick **A 3**
33 Skendleby **C 11**
58 Skene House **F 5**
15 Skenfrith **B 8**
37 Skerne **B 8**
46 Skeroblingarry **G 2**
61 Skerray **B 7**
60 Skerricha **C 4**
34 Skerton **A 4**
23 Sketchley **C 7**
13 Sketty **H 9**
13 Skewen **G 10**
40 Skewsby **H 6**
26 Skeyton **C 5**
60 Skiag Bridge **E 4**
33 Skidbrooke **A 11**
37 Skidby **D 8**
63 Skigersta **A 6**
6 Skilgate **D 3**
32 Skillington **H 6**
43 Skinburness **F 12**
62 Skinidin **C 1**
41 Skinningrove **C 7**
46 Skipness **D 4**
37 Skipsea **B 9**
37 Skipsea Brough **B 9**
35 Skipton **B 8**
40 Skipton-on-Swale **G 4**
36 Skipwith **C 4**
24 Skirbeck **A 4**
48 Skirling **E 3**
17 Skirmett **E 8**
36 Skirpenbeck **A 5**
39 Skirwith, Cumb. **B 8**
39 Skirwith, N. Yorks. **H 9**
61 Skirza **A 12**
44 Skitby **F 3**
62 Skulamus **F 6**
60 Skullomie **B 6**
57 Skye of Curr **G 5**
35 Slack **D 8**
31 Slackhall **B 9**
58 Slackhead **A 2**
43 Slacks **C 11**
58 Slacks of Cairnbanno **C 6**
15 Slad **D 12**
4 Slade **B 4**
18 Slade Green **F 5**
36 Slade Hooton **H 3**
3 Sladesbridge **C 7**
44 Slaggyford **H 5**
34 Slaidburn **B 6**
59 Slains Park **K 6**
49 Slainsfield **E 12**
35 Slaithwaite **F 9**
45 Slaley **G 8**
48 Slamannan **B 1**
17 Slapton, Bucks. **B 10**
5 Slapton, Devon **L 7**
23 Slapton, Northants. **G 9**
54 Slattadale **C 3**
35 Slattcks **F 7**
10 Slaugham **E 1**
30 Slaughter Hill **E 6**
3 Slaughterbridge **A 8**
15 Slaughterford **G 11**
23 Slawston **C 11**
9 Sleaford, Hants. **B 9**
24 Sleaford, Lincs. **A 2**
39 Sleagill **C 8**
21 Sleap **A 11**
21 Sleapford **A 11**
15 Sledge Green **A 11**
37 Sledmere **A 7**
44 Sleetbeck **E 3**
39 Sleightholme **D 11**
41 Sleights **D 8**
8 Slepe **G 1**
4 Slerra **D 2**
61 Slickly **A 12**
46 Sliddery **G 4**
62 Sligachan **E 4**
51 Sligrachan **H 9**
15 Slimbridge **D 10**
31 Slindon, Staffs. **G 7**
9 Slindon, W. Sussex **E 11**
9 Slinfold **C 12**
28 Sling **D 5**
41 Slingsby **H 7**
58 Slioch **D 3**
17 Slip End, Beds. **B 11**
25 Slip End, Herts. **L 4**
26 Slipper's Bottom **D 6**
23 Slipton **D 12**
31 Slitting Mill **H 9**
57 Slochd **G 4**
57 Slochnacraig **M 7**
50 Slockavullin **H 5**
43 Slogarie **E 7**
33 Sloothby **C 12**
17 Slough **F 10**
6 Slough Green **D 6**
57 Sluggan **G 4**
34 Slyne **A 4**
49 Smailholm **F 9**
10 Small Dole **G 1**
11 Small Hythe **E 7**
35 Smallbridge **F 8**
26 Smallburgh **C 6**
58 Smallburn, Grampian **D 8**
47 Smallburn, Strathclyde **G 11**
32 Smalley **F 1**
10 Smallfield **D 2**
18 Smallford **C 2**
43 Smallholm **D 11**
6 Smallridge **F 6**
8 Smannel **A 5**
39 Smardale **D 9**
11 Smarden **D 7**
6 Smeatharpe **E 5**

11 Smeeth, Kent **D 9**
24 Smeeth, Norfolk **E 6**
23 Smeeton Westerby **C 10**
35 Smelthouses **A 10**
61 Smerral **D 11**
22 Smethwick **C 4**
31 Smisby **H 12**
34 Smith Green **B 4**
17 Smith Harefield **E 11**
44 Smithfield **F 3**
6 Smithincott **E 4**
18 Smith's Green **B 6**
54 Smithstown **B 2**
56 Smithtown **E 3**
32 Smithy Houses **E 1**
45 Snableazes **B 10**
43 Snade **C 9**
21 Snailbeach **B 9**
25 Snailwell **H 7**
41 Snainton **G 9**
36 Snaith **E 4**
31 Snake Inn **A 9**
27 Snape, Suffolk **J 7**
40 Snape, N. Yorks. **G 3**
34 Snape Green **F 3**
27 Snape Street **J 7**
23 Snarestone **A 7**
33 Snarford **B 7**
11 Snargate **E 8**
11 Snave **E 9**
21 Snead **C 8**
41 Sneaton **D 9**
41 Sneatonthorpe **E 9**
33 Snelland **B 8**
31 Snelston **F 10**
24 Snettisham **B 8**
45 Snitter **C 8**
33 Snitterby **A 7**
22 Snitterfield **F 5**
21 Snitton **E 11**
21 Snodhill **H 8**
10 Snodland **B 6**
11 Snowdown **C 11**
16 Snowshill **A 2**
5 Soar, Devon **M 6**
13 Soar, Dyfed **D 9**
14 Soar, Powys **A 3**
9 Soberton **D 7**
9 Soberton Heath **E 7**
40 Sockburn **E 4**
25 Soham **H 7**
12 Solbury **F 2**
4 Soldon Cross **E 2**
9 Soldridge **C 8**
10 Sole Street **A 5**
11 Solestreet **C 9**
22 Solihull **D 5**
21 Sollers Dilwyn **G 9**
15 Sollers Hope **A 9**
34 Sollom **E 3**
7 Solway Ash **F 8**
12 Solva **E 2**
7 Solway Ash **F 8**
44 Solwaybank **E 1**
23 Somerby, Leics. **A 11**
37 Somerby, Lincs. **F 8**
32 Somercotes **E 2**
8 Somerford **G 3**
16 Somerford Keynes **E 1**
9 Somerley **F 9**
26- Somerleyton **F 8**
31 Somersal Herbert **G 10**
33 Somersby **C 10**
6 Somerset, Co. **C 6**
25 Somersham, Cambs. **H 5**
27 Somersham, Suff. **K 4**
16 Somerton, Oxon. **A 6**
7 Somerton, Som. **C 8**
27 Somerton, Suffolk **K 1**
10 Sompting **G 1**
17 Sonning **G 8**
17 Sonning Common **F 8**
17 Sonning Eye **F 8**
59 Sootywells **K 5**
8 Sopley **F 3**
15 Sopworth **F 11**
44 Sorbie, Dumf. & Gall. **D 2**
42 Sorbie, Dumf. & Gall. **G 5**
45 Sorbietrees **E 3**
61 Sordale **B 10**
47 Sorn **G 10**
47 Sornbeg **F 10**
48 Sornfallow **F 2**
47 Sornhill **F 10**
50 Soroba Farm **E 6**
61 Sortat **B 12**
33 Sotby **B 9**
17 Sotwell **E 7**
30 Soudley **G 6**
29 Soughton **D 11**
17 Soulbury **A 9**
39 Soulby **D 9**
16 Souldern **A 6**
25 Souldrop **J 1**
64 Sound, Zetland, Shetland Is. **D 7**
64 Sound, Zetland, Shetland Is. **E 7**
49 Sourhope **G 11**
64 Sourin **B 12**
5 Sourton **G 4**
38 Soutergate **G 5**
26 South Acre **D 1**
5 South Allington **M 7**
52 South Alloa **H 4**
9 South Ambersham **D 10**
32 South Anston **B 2**
17 South Ascot **G 10**
8 South Baddesley **F 5**
51 South Ballachulish **A 7**
42 South Balloch **B 4**
7 South Barrow **C 9**
28 South Beach **G 3**
48 South Bellsdyke **A 2**
19 South Benfleet **E 7**
9 South Bersted **F 10**
36 South Bramwith **F 4**
33 South Brent **K 6**
7 South Brewham **C 10**
52 South Bridge-end **E 3**
45 South Broomhill **C 10**
26 South Burlingham **E 7**
7 South Cadbury **D 9**
42 South Cairn **E 1**
33 South Carlton **C 7**
46 South Carrine **H 2**
37 South Cave **D 7**
16 South Cerney **D 2**
7 South Chard **F 7**
45 South Charlton **A 9**
7 South Cheriton **D 10**
36 South Cliffe **D 6**
32 South Clifton **C 5**
36 South Cockerington **A 11**
32 South Collingham **D 5**
14 South Cornelly **F 1**
27 South Cove **G 8**
51 South Creagan **C 7**
26 South Creake **B 1**
23 South Croxton **A 10**
62 South Cuil **B 3**
37 South Dalton **C 7**
10 South Darenth **A 4**
63 South Dell **A 6**
58 South Denmore **F 7**
46 South Druimachro **E 2**
36 South Duffield **D 5**
33 South Elkington **A 10**
36 South Elmsall **F 3**
17 South End, Berks. **G 7**
17 South End, Bucks. **B 9**
34 South End, Cumb. **A 1**
37 South End, Humber. **E 9**
54 South Erradale **C 1**
19 South Fambridge **D 8**
16 South Fawley **F 5**
46 South Feorline **G 4**
37 South Ferriby **E 7**
58 South Fornet **F 5**
63 South Galson **A 5**
46 South Garrochty **D 6**
14 South Glamorgan, Co. **G 4**
10 South Godstone **C 2**
8 South Gorley **E 3**
58 South Gorrachie **B 5**
19 South Green, Essex **E 7**
11 South Green, Kent **B 7**
46 South Hall **B 5**
19 South Hanningfield **D 7**
9 South Harting **D 9**
9 South Hayling **F 8**
45 South Hazelrigg **C 11**
17 South Heath **D 10**
10 South Heighton **H 3**
40 South Hetton **A 4**
36 South Hiendley **F 2**
3 South Hill, Corn. **B 10**
7 South Hill, Som. **D 8**
16 South Hunksey **D 6**
4 South Hole **D 1**
41 South Holme **G 7**
10 South Holmwood **D 1**
18 South Hornchurch **F 5**
47 South Hourat **D 8**
32 South Hykeham **D 6**
45 South Hylton **G 11**
37 South Kelsey **G 8**
37 South Killingholme **F 9**
47 South Kilrusken **D 7**
40 South Kilvington **G 4**
23 South Kilworth **D 9**
36 South Kirkby **F 2**
59 South Kirktown **G 5**
33 South Kyme **E 9**
10 South Lancing **H 1**
16 South Leigh **C 5**
32 South Leverton **B 5**
47 South Limmerhaugh **G 11**
22 South Littleton **G 4**
27 South Lopham **H 3**
23 South Luffenham **B 12**
10 South Malling **G 3**
16 South Marston **E 3**
49 South Middleton **G 12**
36 South Milford **D 3**
5 South Milton **L 6**
18 South Mimms **D 2**
4 South Molton **C 6**
16 South Moreton **E 6**
9 South Mundham **F 10**
32 South Muskham **E 5**
37 South Newbald **D 7**
16 South Newington **A 5**
8 South Newton **C 2**
32 South Normanton **E 2**
18 South Norwood **G 3**
10 South Nutfield **C 2**
18 South Ockendon **F 6**
33 South Ormsby **C 10**
40 South Otterington **F 4**
33 South Owersby **A 8**
18 South Oxhey **E 1**
7 South Perrott **F 8**
7 South Petherton **D 8**
3 South Petherwin **B 10**
26 South Pickenham **E 1**
5 South Pool **M 6**
4 South Radworthy **C 6**
33 South Rauceby **F 7**
26 South Raynham **C 2**
33 South Reston **B 11**
24 South Runcton **E 7**
32 South Scarle **D 6**
63 South Shawbost **B 3**
45 South Shields **F 12**
34 South Shore **D 2**
37 South Skirlaugh **C 9**
33 South Somercotes **A 11**
35 South Stainley **A 1**
18 South Stifford **F 6**
15 South Stoke, Avon **H 10**
17 South Stoke, Oxon. **F 7**
9 South Stoke, W. Sussex **E 11**
11 South Street, Kent **B 9**
18 South Street, London **H 4**
10 South Street E. Sussex **F 3**
4 South Tawton **F 5**
33 South Thoresby **C 11**
8 South Tidworth **A 4**
9 South Town **B 8**
26 South Walsham **D 7**
9 S. Warnborough **A 8**
18 South Weald **E6**
17 South Weston **D 8**
5 South Wheatley, Corn. **G 1**
32 South Wheatley, Notts. **B 5**
7 South Widcombe **A9**
23 South Wigston **B 9**
33 South Willingham **B 9**
32 South Wingfield **E 1**
32 South Witham **H 6**
8 South Wonston **B 6**
19 South Woodham Ferrers **D 6**
24 South Wootton **C 7**
15 South Wraxall **H 11**
36 South Yorkshire, Co. **G 2**
4 South Zeal **F 5**
18 Southall **F1**
16 Southam, Glos **B1**
23 Southam, War **F 7**
8 Southampton **E 5**
10 Southborough **E 5**
8 Southbourne, Dorset **G 3**
9 Southbourne, W. Sussex **E 9**
26 Southburgh **E 3**
37 Southburn **B 7**
19 Southchurch **E 9**
4 Southcott, Devon **D 3**
16 Southcott, Wilts **H 3**
44 Southdean **B 5**
10 Southease **G 5**
46 Southend, Strathclyde **H 2**
16 Southend, Wilts **G 3**
19 Southend-on-Sea **E 8**
14 Southerndown **G 2**
43 Southerness **F 10**
49 Southernknowe **G 11**
24 Southery **F 7**
41 Southfield **G 7**
10 Southfleet **A 5**
18 Southgate, London **E 3**
24 Southgate, Norfolk **B 8**
26 Southgate, Norfolk **C 4**
13 Southgate, W. Glam **H 9**
25 Southill **L 3**
6 Southleigh **G 5**
19 Southminister **D 9**
45 Southmoor **B 10**
25 Southoe **J 3**
27 Southolt **H 5**
24 Southorpe **E 2**
35 Southowram **E 10**
34 Southport **E 2**
26 Southrepps **B 6**
33 Southrey **D8**
16 Southrop **D 3**
9 Southrope **D 8**
9 Southsea **F 8**
64 Southtown **E 3**
18 Southwark **E 3**
9 Southwater **D 12**
7 Southway **B 8**
7 Southwell, Dorset **H 7**
32 Southwell, Notts **E 4**
45 Southwick, Tyne & Wear **G 12**
9 Southwick, Hants **E 8**
24 Southwick, Northants **F 1**
10 Southwick, W. Sussex **G 1**
7 Southwick, Wilts **A 11**
27 Southwold **H 8**
26 Southwood, Norf **E 7**
7 Southwood, Som. **C 9**
49 Soutra Mains **C 7**
63 Soval Lodge **D 4**
40 Sowerby, N. Yorks. **G 4**
35 Sowerby, W. Yorks. **E 9**
35 Sowerby Bridge **E 9**
38 Sowerby Row **A 6**
6 Sowton **G 3**
44 Spadeadam Farm **F 4**
24 Spalding **C 3**
36 Spaldington **D 5**
25 Spaldwick **H 2**
53 Spalefield **F 10**
32 Spalford **C 5**
24 Spanby **B 2**
26 Sparham **D 4**
38 Spark Bridge **G 5**
7 Sparkford **D 9**
31 Sparklow **D 9**
5 Sparkwell **K 4**
31 Sparrowpit **B 9**
8 Sparsholt, Hants. **C 6**
16 Sparsholt, Oxon **E 4**
45 Spartylea **H 7**
41 Spaunton **F 7**
6 Spaxton **C 6**
55 Spean Bridge **L 6**
8 Spearywell **C 4**
43 Speddoch **C 9**
16 Speen, Berks. **G 5**
17 Speen, Bucks. **D 9**
41 Speeton **H 11**
30 Speke **B 3**
10 Speldhurst **D 4**
18 Spellbrook **B 5**
16 Spelsbury **B 4**
14 Spelter **E 2**
17 Spencers Wood **G 8**
40 Spennithorne **F 2**
40 Spennymoor **B 3**
22 Spetchley **G 2**
7 Spetisbury **F 12**
27 Spexhall **G 7**
58 Spey Bay **A 1**
57 Spey Bridge **J 4**
57 Speybridge **G 6**
56 Speyview **E 8**
33 Spilsby **D 11**
45 Spindlestone **D 11**
32 Spinkhill **B 2**
23 Spinney Hills **B 9**
61 Spinningdale **G 7**
33 Spital in the Street **A 7**
45 Spitalford **A 10**
10 Spithursthurst **F 3**
49 Spittal, Dumf. & Gall. **E 5**
42 Spittal, Dumf. & Gall. **F 4**
12 Spittal, Dyfed **E 3**
61 Spittal, Highland **B 10**
49 Spittal, Lothian **B 7**
49 Spittal, Northumb. **D 12**
36 Spittal, Humberside **B 5**
59 Spittal of Glenmuick **J 1**
57 Spittal of Glenshee **M 7**
59 Spittalburn **J 4**
52 Spittalfield **C 6**
26 Spixworth **D 5**
3 Splatt **A 9**
10 Splayne's Green **F 3**
35 Spofforth **B 12**
29 Spon Green **D 12**
32 Spondon **G 1**
26 Spooner Row **F 4**
26 Sporle **D 2**
49 Spott **B 9**
49 Spottiswoode **D 8**
23 Spratton **E 10**
9 Spreakley **B 9**
4 Spreyton **F 6**
33 Spridlington **B 7**
38 Spring Valley **H 2**
47 Springburn **C 10**
63 Springcotrie **D 3**
44 Springfield, Dumf. & Gall. **F 2**
53 Springfield, Fife **F 8**
56 Springfield, Grampiam **D 6**
22 Springfield, W. Midlands **D 4**
22 Springhill **B 3**
43 Springholm **E 9**
44 Springkell **E 1**
47 Springside **E 8**
32 Springthorpe **A 6**
45 Springwell **G 11**
32 Springthorpe **A 6**
45 Springwell **G 11**
37 Sproatley **D 9**
30 Sproston Green **C 6**
36 Spotbrough **G 3**
27 Sproughton **L 4**
49 Sprouston **F 10**
26 Sprowston **D 6**
32 Sproxton, Leics. **H 6**
40 Sproxton, N. Yorks **G 6**
30 Spurstow **E 4**
57 Sronlairig Lodge **J 1**
57 Sronpadruig **L 3**
35 Stackhouse **A 7**
12 Stackpole **G 3**
35 Stacksteads **E 7**
5 Staddiscombe **K 4**
36 Staddlethorpe **E 6**
17 Stadhampton **D 7**
39 Staffield **A 8**
62 Staffin **A 4**
31 Stafford **H 8**
31 Staffordshire, Co **H 8**
49 Stagehall **E 7**
24 Stag's Holt **E 5**
25 Stagsden **K 1**
25 Stagsden W. End **K 1**
35 Stainburn **B 11**
32 Stainby **H 6**
35 Staincross **F 12**
17 Staines **G 11**
33 Stainfield, Lincs. **C 8**
24 Stainfield, Lincs. **C 2**
39 Stainforth, N. Yorks. **H 10**
36 Stainforth, S. Yorks. **F 4**
34 Staining **D 2**
35 Stainland **E 9**
41 Stainsacre **D 9**
40 Stainton, Cleveland **D 5**
39 Stainton, Cumb. **B 7**
39 Stainton, Cumbria **G 7**
40 Stainton, Dur **C 1**
40 Stainton, N. Yorks. **F 1**
32 Stainton, S. Yorks. **A 3**
33 Stainton by Langworth **B 8**
37 Stainton le Vale **H 9**
38 Stainton with Adgarley **H 5**
41 Staintondale **E 10**
38 Stair, Cumb. **C 5**
47 Stair, Strathclyde **G 9**
41 Staithes **C 8**
34 Stake Pool **B 3**
45 Stakeford **D 11**
7 Stalbridge **D 10**
7 Stalbridge Weston **E 10**
26 Stalham **C 7**
26 Stalham Green **C 7**
11 Stalisfield Green **C 6**
39 Stalling Busk **G 11**
37 Stallingborough **F 9**
34 Stalmine **C 3**
35 Stalybridge **G 8**
25 Stambourne **L 8**
24 Stamford, Lincs **E 1**
45 Stamford, Northumb. **A 10**
36 Stamford Bridge **B 5**
45 Stamfordham **F 9**
38 Stanah **C 6**
18 Stanborough **C 2**
17 Stanbridge, Beds. **B 10**
8 Stanbridge, Dorset **F 2**
35 Stanbury **C 9**
47 Stand **C 12**
48 Standburn **B 2**
22 Standeford **A 3**
11 Standen **D 7**
7 Standerwick **A 11**
9 Standford **C 9**
34 Standish **F 4**
16 Standlake **D 5**
8 Standon, Hants. **C 6**
18 Standon, Herts **B 4**
30 Standon, Staffs. **G 6**
18 Standon Massey **D 6**
27 Standwell Green **H 4**
48 Stane **C 2**
26 Stanfield **C 2**
25 Stanford, Beds. **L 3**
11 Stanford, Kent **D 10**
21 Stanford Bishop **G 12**
22 Stanford Bridge **F 1**
16 Stanford Dingley **G 6**
19 Stanford le Hope **F 7**
23 Stanford on Avon **D 9**
32 Stanford on Soar **H 3**
21 Stanford on Teme **F 12**
18 Stanford Rivers **D 5**
16 Stanford the Vale **E 4**
10 Stanford's End **D 3**
24 Stranground **F 3**
26 Stanhoe **B 1**
39 Stanhope **A 12**
23 Stanion **C 12**
52 Stank **F 1**
32 Stanley, Derby **F 1**
45 Stanley, Dur. **H 10**
31 Stanley, Staffs. **E 8**
32 Stanley, Tayside **D 6**
16 Stanley, Wilts **G 1**
35 Stanley, W. Yorks. **E 12**
32 Stanley Common **F 1**
21 Stanley Hill **H 12**
10 Stanmer **G 2**
16 Stanmore, Berks. **F 6**
8 Stanmore, Hants. **C 6**
18 Stanmore, London **E 2**
44 Stannersburn **D 5**
45 Stannington, Northumb. **E 10**
31 Stannington, S. Yorks **A 11**
21 Stansbatch **F 9**
27 Stansfield **K 1**
31 Stanshope **E 9**
27 Stanstead **K 1**
18 Stanstead Abbots **C 4**
27 Stanstead Street **K 1**
10 Stansted **B 5**
18 Stansted Mountfitchet **A 5**
31 Stanton, Derby **H 11**
16 Stanton, Glos **A 2**
14 Stanton, Gwent **B 6**
45 Stanton, Northumb. **D 9**
31 Stanton, Staffs. **F 9**
27 Stanton, Suffolk **H 3**
31 Stanton by Bridge **G 12**
15 Stanton by Dale **F 2**
15 Stanton Drew **H 9**
16 Stanton Fitzwarren **E 3**
16 Stanton Harcourt **D 5**
32 Stanton Hill **D 2**
31 Stanton in Peak **D 11**
21 Stanton Lacy **E 10**
21 Stanton Long **C 11**
32 Stanton on the Wolds **G 3**
15 Stanton Prior **H 10**
16 Stanton St. Bernard **H 2**
17 Stanton St. John **C 7**
15 Stanton St. Quintin **F 12**
27 Stanton Street **J 3**
23 Stanton under Bardon **A 8**
30 Stanton upon Hine Heath **H 4**
15 Stanton Wick **H 9**
30 Stanwardine in the Fields **H 3**
19 Stanway, Essex **B 9**
16 Stanway, Glos. **A 2**
17 Stanwell **G 11**
17 Stanwell Moor **G 11**
25 Stanwick **H 1**
41 Stape **F 8**
8 Stapehill **F 2**
30 Stapeley **E 5**
31 Stapenhill **H 11**
11 Staple, Kent **B 11**
6 Staple, Somerset **B 4**
6 Staple Cross, Devon **D 4**
10 Staple Cross, E. Sussex **F 6**
6 Staple Fitzpaine **D 6**
15 Staple Hill **G 9**
10 Staplefield **E 2**
25 Stapleford, Cambs. **K 6**
18 Stapleford, Heref. & Worc. **B3**
32 Stapleford, Leics. **H 5**
32 Stapleford, Lincs **D 6**
32 Stapleford, Notts. **F 2**
8 Stapleford, Wilts. **B 2**
18 Stapleford Abbotts **D 5**
18 Stapleford Tawney **D 5**
16 Staplegrove **D 6**
6 Staplehay **D 5**
10 Staplehurst **D 6**
8 Staplers **G 6**
44 Stapleton, Cumb. **F 3**
21 Stapleton, Heref. & Worc. **F 9**
23 Stapleton, Leics. **B 8**

40 Stapleton, N. Yorks. **D 3**
21 Stapleton, Salop **B 10**
7 Stapleton, Som **D 8**
44 Stapleton Grange **F 1**
6 Stapley **E 5**
25 Staploe **J 2**
12 Star, Dyfed **C 6**
53 Star, Fife **G 8**
15 Star, Somerset **H 7**
39 Starbottom **H 11**
6 Starcross **H 3**
64 Starkigarth **E 7**
25 Starlings Green **M 6**
27 Starston **G 5**
39 Starforth **D 12**
15 Startley **F 12**
7 Stathe **C 7**
32 Stathern **G 5**
40 Station Town **B 4**
25 Staughton Green **J 2**
25 Staughton Highway **J 2**
15 Staunton, Glos. **C 9**
15 Staunton, Glos. **A 11**
31 Staunton Harold Hall **H 12**
32 Staunton in the Vale **F 5**
21 Staunton on Arrow **F 9**
21 Staunton on Wye **H 9**
38 Staveley, Cumbria **G 6**
39 Staveley, Cumbria **E 7**
32 Stavely, Derby **C 2**
35 Staveley, N. Yorks. **A 12**
5 Staverton, Devon **J 7**
15 Staverton, Glos. **B 12**
23 Staverton, Northants. **F 9**
15 Staverton, Wilts **H 11**
15 Staverton Bridge **B 12**
7 Stawell **B 7**
5 Stawford **G 3**
6 Stawley **D 4**
61 Staxigoe **B 12**
41 Staxton **G 10**
20 Staylittle **C 4**
34 Staynall **C 2**
32 Staythorpe **E 5**
40 Stean **H 1**
40 Stearsby **H 6**
6 Steart **B 6**
18 Stebbing **B 6**
64 Stebbligrind **D 7**
9 Stedham **D 10**
45 Steel Rigg **E 8**
44 Steele Road **D 4**
21 Steen's Bridge **G 11**
9 Steep **D 9**
7 Steeple, Dorset **H 12**
19 Steeple, Essex **D 9**
7 Steeple Ashton **A 12**
16 Steeple Aston **B 6**
16 Steeple Barton **B 5**
25 Steeple Bumpstead **L 8**
17 Steeple Claydon **A 8**
25 Steeple Gidding **G 2**
15 Steeple Langford **B 2**
25 Steeple Morden **L 4**
35 Steeton **C 9**
62 Stein **C 2**
58 Steinmanhill **C 5**
45 Stelling Hall **F 8**
11 Stelling Minnis **C 10**
3 Stenalees **D 7**
48 Stenhousemuir **A 2**
64 Stenness **C 6**
62 Stenscholl **A 4**
31 Stenson **G 11**
64 Stenswall **D 7**
49 Stenton **B 9**
12 Stepaside **F 5**
43 Stepends **C 9**
18 Stepney **F 4**
25 Steppingley **M 1**
47 Stepps **C 11**
27 Sternfield **J 7**
16 Stert **H 1**
25 Stetchworth **J 7**
18 Stevenage **B 2**
47 Stevenston **E 7**
9 Steventon, Hants. **A 7**
16 Steventon, Oxon. **E 5**
25 Stevington **K 1**
25 Stewarby **L 1**
46 Stewarton, Strathclyde **G 2**
47 Stewarton, Strathclyde **E 9**
17 Stewkley **B 9**
33 Stewton **B 10**
12 Steynton **F 4**
4 Stibb **E 1**
4 Stibb Cross **D 3**
16 Stibb Green **H 3**
26 Stibbard **C 3**
24 Stibbington **F 2**
49 Stichill **F 9**
3 Sticker **E 7**
33 Stickford **D 10**
4 Sticklepath, Devon **F 5**
6 Sticklepath, Som. **E 6**
33 Stickney **D 10**
26 Stiffkey **A 3**
18 Stifford **F 6**
22 Stifford's Bridge **G 1**
10 Stile Bridge **C 6**
36 Stillingfleet **C 4**
40 Stillington, Cleveland **C 4**
40 Stillington, N. Yorks. **H 6**
24 Stilton **F 3**
15 Stinchcombe **D 10**
7 Stinsford **G 10**
21 Stirchley **B 12**
61 Stirkoke House **C 12**
52 Stirling, Central **H 3**
38 Stirling, Grampian **C 8**
19 Stisted **A 8**
16 Stitchcombe **G 3**
2 Stithians **F 4**
56 Stittenham **B 2**
23 Stivichall **D 7**
33 Stixwould **D 9**
48 Stobo **F 4**
7 Stoborough **H 12**
7 Stoborough Grn. **H 12**
44 Stobs Castle **B3**
49 Stobswood, Borders **D 9**
45 Stobswood,
Northumb. **D 10**
48 Stobwood **D 2**
19 Stock **D 7**
22 Stock Wood **F 3**
58 Stockbridge, Grampian **C 8**
8 Stockbridge, Hants. **C 5**
43 Stockbridgehill **D 12**
47 Stockbriggs **F 12**
11 Stockbury **B 7**
16 Stockcross **G 5**
38 Stockdale Wath **A 6**
23 Stockerston **B 11**
9 Stockholm **B 11**
47 Stockiemuir **A 10**
18 Stocking Pelham **A 4**
23 Stockingford **C 7**
6 Stockland **F 6**
6 Stockland Bristol **B 6**
4 Stockleigh English **E 7**
4 Stockleigh Pomeroy **F 7**
16 Stockley **G 1**
7 Stocklinch **E 7**
31 Stockport **A 7**
35 Stocksbridge **G 11**
45 Stocksfield **G 9**
21 Stockton,
Heref. & Worcs. **F 10**
26 Stockton, Norfolk **F 7**
21 Stockton, Salop **B 8**
22 Stockton, Salop **B 1**
23 Stockton, War. **F 8**
8 Stockton, Wilts. **B 1**
30 Stockton Heath **B 5**
40 Stocktonon-Tees **C 4**
22 Stockton on Teme **F 1**
36 Stockton-on-the-
Forest **B 4**
11 Stodmarsh **B 11**
26 Stody **B 4**
60 Stoer **D 2**
7 Stoford, Som. **E 9**
8 Stoford, Wilts. **C 2**
6 Stogumber **C 4**
6 Stogursey **B 5**
4 Stoke, Devon **D 1**
8 Stoke, Hants. **A 5**
9 Stoke, Hants **F 8**
11 Stoke, Kent **A 7**
27 Stoke, Suffolk **L 5**
7 Stoke Abbott **F 4**
23 Stoke Albany **C 11**
27 Stoke Ash **H 4**
32 Stoke Bardolph **F 4**
21 Stoke Bliss **F 12**
23 Stoke Bruerne **G 10**
25 Stoke-by-Clare **L 8**
27 Stoke-by-Nayland **L 3**
6 Stoke Canon **F 3**
8 Stoke Charity **B 6**
8 Stoke Climsland **B 10**
21 Stoke Cross **G 11**
17 Stoke D'Abernon **H 12**
25 Stoke Doyle **G 1**
23 Stoke Dry **B 12**
21 Stoke Edith **H 11**
8 Stoke Farthing **D 2**
24 Stoke Ferry **E 8**
5 Stoke Fleming **L 7**
5 Stoke Gabriel **K 7**
15 Stoke Gifford **F 9**
23 Stoke Golding **B 7**
23 Stoke Goldington **G 11**
17 Stoke Green **F 10**
17 Stoke Hammond **A 9**
26 Stoke Holy Cross **E 5**
21 Stoke Lacy **G 11**
16 Stoke Lyne **A 6**
17 Stoke Mandeville **C 9**
18 Stoke Newington **E 3**
31 Stoke-on-Trent **F 7**
15 Stoke Orchard **A 12**
6 Stoke Pero **B 2**
17 Stoke Poges **F 10**
21 Stoke Prior,
Heref. & Worcs. **G 10**
22 Stoke Prior,
Heref. & Worcs. **E 3**
4 Stoke Rivers **C 5**
32 Stoke Rochford **G 6**
17 Stoke Row **F 8**
7 Stoke St. Gregory **D 7**
7 Stoke St. Mary **D 6**
7 Stoke St. Michael **B 10**
21 Stoke St. Milborough **D 11**
7 Stoke sub Hamdon **D 8**
17 Stoke Talmage **D 7**
7 Stoke Trister **C 10**
30 Stoke upon Tern **G 5**
30 Stoke Wake **F 11**
7 Stokeford **G 12**
32 Stokeham **C 5**
5 Stokeinteignhead **J 8**
17 Stokenchurch **D 8**
5 Stokenham **L 7**
21 Stokesay **D 10**
26 Stokesby **D 1**
40 Stokesley **D 5**
6 Stolford **B 5**
7 Ston Easton **A 9**
17 Stone, Bucks. **C 8**
15 Stone, Glos. **E 10**
22 Stone, Heref. & Worc. **E 2**
10 Stone,Kent **A 4**
32 Stone, S. Yorks **A 3**
11 Stone, Staffs. **G 7**
7 Stone Allerton **A 7**
24 Stone Bridge Corner **E 4**
35 Stone Chair **D 10**
4 Stone Cross, Devon **C 5**
11 Stone Cross, Kent **D 9**
10 Stone Cross, W. Sussex **H 5**
39 Stone House **G 10**
10 Stone Street **C 4**
26 Stonebridge, Norf. **B 6**
22 Stonebridge,
W. Midlands **D 5**
32 Stonebroom **D 1**
10 Stonecrouch **E 6**
15 Stone-edge Batch **G 8**
37 Stoneferry **D 8**
47 Stonefield **D 11**
46 Stonefield Castle Hotel **B 4**
44 Stonegarthside **E 3**
10 Stonegate, E. Sussex **E 5**
41 Stonegate, N. Yorks **D 8**
58 Stonegate Crofts **D 8**
41 Stonegrave **G 7**
44 Stonehaugh **E 6**
59 Stonehaven **J 6**
5 Stonehouse, Devon **K 3**
43 Stonehouse,
Dumf. & Gall. **E 9**
15 Stonehouse, Glos. **D 11**
44 Stonehouse,
Northumb. **G 5**
47 Stonehouse,
Strathclyde **E 12**
23 Stoneleigh **E 7**
25 Stonely **J 2**
19 Stone's Green **A 11**
32 Stonesby **H 5**
16 Stonesfield **B 5**
38 Stonethwaite **D 5**
8 Stoney Cross **E 4**
31 Stoney Middleton **C 10**
23 Stoney Stanton **C 8**
7 Stoney Stoke **C 10**
7 Stoney Stratton **B 10**
21 Stoney Stretton **A 9**
48 Stoneyburn, Lothian **C 2**
48 Stoneyburn,
Strathclyde **G 2**
23 Stoneygate **B 9**
19 Stoneyhills **D 9**
42 Stoneykirk **F 2**
58 Stoneywood **F 6**
27 Stonham Aspal **J 4**
17 Stonor **E 8**
23 StontonWyville **C 10**
4 Stony Cross, Devon **C 4**
22 Stony Cross,
Heref. & Worc. **G 1**
23 Stony Stratford **H 11**
4 Stoodleigh, Devon **C 5**
6 Stoodleigh, Devon **D 3**
9 Stopham **D 11**
17 Stopsley **B 12**
30 Storeton **B 2**
35 Storiths **B 9**
63 Stornoway **D 5**
22 Storridge **G 1**
9 Storrington **E 12**
39 Storth **G 7**
36 Storwood **C 5**
56 Stotfield **C 8**
25 Stotford **L 3**
21 Stottesdon **D 12**
23 Stoughton, Leics **B 9**
9 Stoughton, Surrey **A 11**
9 Stoughton, W. Sussex **E 9**
55 Stoul **K 1**
22 Stourlton **G 3**
7 Stour Provost **D 11**
7 Stour Row **D 11**
22 Stourbridge **D 2**
7 Stourpaine **E 12**
22 Stourport-on- Severn **E 2**
22 Stourton, Staffs **D ,**
22 Stourton, War **H 6**
7 Stourton, Wilts. **C 11**
7 Stourton Caundle **E 10**
64 Stove **B 3**
27 Stoven **G 7**
49 Stow, Borders **E 7**
32 Stow, Lincs. **B 6**
24 Stow Bardolph **E 7**
26 Stow Bedon **F 3**
25 Stow cum Quy **J 6**
25 Stow Longa **H 2**
19 Stow Maries **D 8**
16 Stow-on-the-Wold **B 3**
24 Stowbridge **E 7**
21 Stowe, Salop **E 8**
31 Stowe-by-Chartley **H 8**
15 Stowe Green **D 9**
7 Stowell **D10**
27 Stowlangtoft **H 3**
27 Stowmarket **J 3**
11 Stowting **D 10**
27 Stowupland **J 4**
46 Straad **C 5**
57 Straanruie **H 6**
59 Strachan **H 4**
51 Strachur **G 8**
27 Stradbroke **H 5**
25 Stradishall **K 8**
24 Stradsett **E 8**
32 Stragglethorpe **E 6**
43 Strahanna **B 7**
42 Straid **C 2**
43 Straith **C 9**
42 Straiton **A 5**
58 Stralock, Grampian **E 6**
52 Straloch, Tayside **A 5**
31 Stramshall **G 9**
59 Stranathro **H 6**
48 Strand **G 2**
47 Strandhead **G 9**
38 Strang **H 2**
41 Stranghow **D 7**
59 Stranog **H 6**
42 Stranraer **E 1**
20 Strata Florida **F 3**
17 Stratfield Mortimer **H 7**
17 Stratfield Saye **H 8**
17 Stratfield Turgis **H 8**
18 Stratford **F 4**
27 Stratford St. Andrew **J 6**
27 Stratford St. Mary **M 3**
8 Stratford sub Castle **C 3**
8 Stratford Tony **C 2**
22 Stratford-upon- Avon **G 5**
52 Strathallan Castle **F 4**
55 Strathan, Highland **K 3**
60 Strathan, Highland **E 2**
60 Strathan, Highland **A 6**
47 Strathaven **E 12**
47 Strathblane **B 10**
54 Strathcarron **E 3**
50 Strathcoil **D 4**
61 Strathcoul **B 10**
58 Strathdon **F 1**
60 Strathkanaird **F 3**
53 Strathkinness **F 9**
57 Strathmashie Ho **K 2**
53 Strathmiglo **F 7**
61 Strathmore, Lo. **C 10**
54 Strathpeffer **D 8**
54 Strathrannoch **B 8**
54 Strathvaich Lo **B 7**
61 Strathy **A 8**
61 Strathy Inn **A 8**
52 Strathyre **E 1**
4 Stratton, Corn **E 1**
7 Stratton, Dorset **G 10**
16 Stratton, Glos. **D 1**
17 Stratton Audley **B 7**
7 Stratton-on-the-
Fosse **A 10**
16 Stratton St. Margaret **E 3**
26 Stratton St. Michael **F 5**
26 Stratton Strawless **C 5**
53 Stravithie **F 10**
10 Streat **F 2**
18 Streatham **G 3**
17 Streatley, Beds **A 11**
17 Streatley, Berks. **F 7**
7 Street, Somerset **C 8**
41 Street, Yorks **E 7**
30 Street Dinas **F 2**
11 Street End, Kent **C 10**
9 Street End, W. Sussex **F 10**
36 Street Houses **C 3**
57 Street of Kincardine **H 5**
22 Streethay **A 5**
36 Streethouse **E 2**
40 Streetlam **E 3**
22 Streetly **B 4**
21 Strefford **D 10**
32 Strelley **F 2**
36 Strensall **A 4**
6 Stretcholt **B 6**
5 Strete **L 7**
25 Strethall **L 6**
25 Stretham **H 6**
30 Stretton, Cheshire **B 5**
30 Stretton, Cheshire **E 3**
32 Stretton, Derby **D 1**
23 Stretton, Leics. **A 12**
22 Stretton, Staffs. **A 2**
31 Stretton, Staffs. **G 11**
22 Stretton en le Field **A 6**
21 Stretton Grandison **H 11**
23 Stretton-on- Dunsmore **E 7**
22 Stretton on Fosse **H 6**
21 Stretton Sugwas **H 10**
23 Stretton-under- Fosse **D 8**
58 Strichen **B 7**
6 Stringston **B 5**
23 Strixton **F 12**
15 Stroat **E 9**
54 Stromeferry **F 2**
54 Stromemore **F 2**
64 Stromness **D 1**
51 Stronachlachar **F 11**
55 Stronchreggan **M 4**
60 Stronchrubie **E 4**
63 Strond **H 1**
55 Strone, Highland **L 5**
57 Strone, Highland **G 1**
47 Strone, Strathclyde **A 7**
51 Strone, Strathclyde **H 10**
55 Stronenaba **L 6**
57 Stronetoper **K 4**
51 Stronmilchan **E 8**
50 Strontian **A 5**
50 Strontoiller **E 6**
51 Stronuich **C 12**
10 Strood **A 6**
10 Strood Green **C 1**
15 Stroud, Glos. **D 11**
9 Stroud, Hants. **D 8**
19 Stroud Green **E 8**
17 Stroude **G 11**
32 Stroxton **G 6**
62 Struan **D 3**
33 Strubby **B 11**
26 Strumpshaw **E 6**
54 Struy **F 8**
58 Stuartfield **C 7**
38 Stub Place **F 3**
9 Stubbington **F 7**
35 Stubbins **E 7**
11 Stubbs Cross **D 8**
44 Stubbyknowe **F 2**
8 Stubhampton **E 1**
34 Stubshaw Cross **G 5**
32 Stubton **E 6**
51 Stuckgowan **G 10**
51 Stuckindroin **F 10**
8 Stuckton **E 3**
17 Stud Green **F 9**
45 Studdon **H 7**
39 Studfold **E 9**
17 Studham **C 11**
8 Studland **H 2**
17 Studley, Oxon **C 7**
22 Studley, War. **F 4**
16 Studley, Wilts **G 1**
25 Stump Cross **L 6**
25 Stuntney **G 7**
10 Stunts Green **G 5**
31 Sturbridge **G 7**
25 Sturmer **L 8**
7 Sturminster Com. **E 11**
8 Sturminster Marshall **F 1**
7 Sturminster Newton **E 11**
11 Sturry **B 10**
37 Sturton **G 7**
32 Sturton by Stow **B 6**
32 Sturton le Steeple **B 5**
27 Stuston **H 4**
27 Stutton, Suffolk **M 4**
36 Stutton, N. Yorks. **C 3**
31 Styal **B 7**
32 Styrrup **A 3**
58 Succoth, Grampian **D 2**
51 Succoth, Highland **G 10**
21 Suckley **G 12**
25 Sudborough **G 1**
27 Sudbourne **K 7**
15 Sudbrook, Gwent **F 8**
33 Sudbrook, Lincs. **F 7**
33 Sudbrooke **C 7**
18 Sudbury, Derby **G 10**
18 Sudbury, London **E 2**
27 Sudbury, Suffolk **L 2**
56 Suddie **D 2**
15 Sudgrove **D 12**
26 Suffield, Norfolk **B 5**
41 Suffield, N. Yorks. **F 10**
27 Suffolk, County **J 4**
30 Sugnall **G 6**
61 Suisgill **E 9**
62 Suisnish **E 5**
38 Sulby **G 2**
23 Sulgrave **H 9**
17 Sulham **G 7**
17 Sulhamstead **G 7**
17 Sulhamstead Abbots **G 7**
62 Sulishaderbeg **D 4**
9 Sullington **E 12**
64 Sullom **C 7**
14 Sully **G 5**
29 Summer Hill **E 12**
35 Summerbridge **A 10**
2 Summercourt **D 6**
40 Summerhouse **C 2**
15 Summerleaze **F 7**
35 Summerseat **F 7**
16 Summertown **C 6**
35 Summit, Lancs **F 8**
35 Summit, Lancs **E 8**
17 Sunbury on Thames **G 11**
43 Sundaywell **C 9**
38 Sunderland, Cumb **B 4**
34 Sunderland, Lancs **B 3**
45 Sunderland,
Tyne & Wear **G 12**
40 Sunderland Bridge **A 3**
48 Sundhope **G 6**
17 Sundon Park **B 11**
10 Sundridge **C 4**
50 Sunipol **B 1**
37 Sunk Island **E 10**
17 Sunningdale **G 10**
17 Sunninghill **G 10**
16 Sunningwell **D 6**
40 Sunniside, Dur. **A 2**
45 Sunniside,
Tyne & Wear **G 10**
38 Sunny Bank **F 5**
56 Sunnyhillock **D 4**
52 Sunnylaw **G 3**
10 Sunnyside **D 3**
8 Sunton **A 4**
49 Sunwick **D 11**
18 Surbiton **G 2**
38 Surby **H 1**
24 Surfleet **C 3**
24 Surfleet Seas End **C 4**
26 Surlingham **E 6**
10 Surrey, County **C 2**
26 Sustead **B 5**
36 Susworth **G 6**
4 Sutcombe **E 2**
64 Sutherland **E 2**
26 Suton **E 4**
56 Sutors of Cromarty **C 4**
33 Sutterby **C 11**
24 Sutterton **B 4**
25 Sutton, Beds. **K 3**
17 Sutton, Berks. **F 11**
25 Sutton, Cambs. **G 5**
24 Sutton, Cambs. **F 2**
12 Sutton, Dyfed **E 3**
11 Sutton, Kent **C 12**
18 Sutton, London **H 3**
34 Sutton, Merseyside **H 4**
26 Sutton, Norfolk **C 7**
32 Sutton, Notts. **B 4**
32 Sutton, Notts. **F 5**
16 Sutton, Oxon **C 5**
22 Sutton, Salop **C 1**
30 Sutton, Salop. **G 5**
7 Sutton, Som **C 9**
36 Sutton, S. Yorks **F 3**
30 Sutton, Staffs. **H 6**
27 Sutton, Suffolk **K 6**
10 Sutton, Surrey **B 12**
9 Sutton, W. Sussex **E 11**
23 Sutton Basset **C 11**
10 Sutton at Hone **A 4**
15 Sutton Benger **F 12**
32 Sutton Bonington **H 2**
24 Sutton Bridge **C 6**

23 Sutton Cheney **B 7**
23 Sutton Coldfield **B 5**
16 Sutton Courteney **E 6**
24 SuttonCrosses **C 5**
40 Sutton Grange **H 3**
9 Sutton Green **A 11**
21 Sutton Hill **B 12**
40 Sutton Howgrave **G 3**
32 Sutton in Ashfield **D 2**
35 Sutton-in-Craven **C 8**
23 Sutton in the Elms **C 8**
31 Sutton Lane Ends **C 8**
21 Sutton Maddock **B 12**
7 Sutton Mallet **C 7**
8 Sutton Mandeville **C 1**
7 Sutton Montis **D 9**
37 Sutton-on-Hull **D 9**
33 Sutton on Sea **B 12**
36 Sutton-on-the-Forest **A 4**
31 Sutton on the Hill **G 11**
32 Sutton on Trent **D 5**
24 Sutton St. Edmund **D 5**
24 Sutton St. James **D 5**
21 Sutton St. Michael **H 10**
21 Sutton St. Nicholas **H 10**
8 Sutton Scotney **B 6**
22 Sutton-under-Brailes **H 6**
40 Sutton-under-Whitestonecliffe **G 5**
36 Sutton upon Derwent **B 5**
11 Sutton Valence **C 7**
7 Sutton Veny **B 11**
7 Sutton Waldron **E 12**
15 Sutton Wick **H 9**
33 Swaby **B 11**
31 Swadlincote **H 11**
26 Swaffham **E 1**
25 Swaffham Bulbeck **J 7**
25 Swaffham Prior **J 7**
26 Swafield **B 6**
40 Swainby **E 5**
21 Swainshill **H 10**
26 Swainsthorpe **E 5**
15 Swainswick **G 10**
23 Swalcliffe **H 7**
11 Swalecliffe **A 10**
37 Swallow **G 9**
8 Swallowcliffe **C 1**
17 Swallowfield **H 8**
32 Swallownest **B 2**
45 Swalwell **G 10**
30 Swan Green **C 6**
8 Swanage **H 2**
64 Swanbister **D 2**
17 Swanbourne **A 9**
63 Swanibost **A 6**
37 Swanland **D 7**
10 Swanley **A 4**
10 Swanley Village **A 4**
9 Swanmore **D 7**
23 Swannington, Leics. **A 7**
26 Swannington, Norf. **D 4**
10 Swanscombe **A 5**
13 Swansea **H 10**
26 Swanton Abbott **C 6**
26 Swanton Morley **D 3**
26 Swanton Novers **B 3**
32 Swanwick **E 1**
24 Swarby **B 1**
26 Swardeston **E 5**
31 Swarkestone **G 12**
45 Swarland **C 10**
45 Swarland Estate **C 10**
9 Swarraton **B 7**
24 Swaton **B 2**
25 Swavesey **H 5**
8 Sway **F 4**
33 Swayfield **H 7**
8 Swaythling **D 6**
21 Sweet Green **F 12**
4 Sweetham **F 7**
39 Sweetholme **C 8**
49 Sweethope **E 9**
3 Sweethouse **C 8**
27 Swefling **J 6**
23 Swepstone **A 7**
16 Swerford **A 5**
30 Swettenham **C 6**
40 Swetton **H 2**
27 Swilland **K 5**
36 Swillington **D 2**
4 Swimbridge **C 5**
4 Swimbridge Newland **C 5**
16 Swinbrook **C 4**
32 Swinderley **D 6**
15 Swindon, Glos. **B 12**
22 Swindon, Staffs. **C 2**
16 Swindon, Wilts **F 3**
37 Swine **D 9**
36 Swinefleet **E 5**
15 Swineford **G 10**
25 Swineshead, Beds. **J 2**
24 Swineshead, Lincs. **B 3**
24 Swineshead Bridge **A 3**
61 Swiney **D 11**
23 Swinford, Leics. **D 9**
16 Swinford, Oxon **C 5**
11 Swingfield Minnis **D 10**
11 Singfield Street **D 11**
47 Swinhill **D 12**
45 Swinhoe **E 12**
37 Swinhope **G 9**
64 Swining **C 7**
40 Swinithwaite **F 1**
44 Swinnie **A 5**
31 Swinscoe **E 9**
44 Swinside Hall **A 5**
24 Swinstead **C 1**
49 Swinton, Borders **E 11**
34 Swinton, Manchester **G 6**
41 Swinton, N. Yorks. **H 7**
40 Swinton, N. Yorks. **G 2**
36 Swinton, S. Yorks. **G 2**
49 Swinton Quarter **E 11**
49 Swintonmill **E 10**
23 Swithland **A 9**
56 Swordale, Highland **C 1**
63 Swordale, W. Isles **D 6**
55 Swordland **K 2**
61 Swordly **B 7**
30 Sworton Heath **B 5**
20 Swydd-ffynnon **F 3**
31 Swynnerton **G 7**
7 Swyre **G 8**
20 Sychnant **E 5**
20 Sychtyn **B 5**
15 Syde **C 12**
17 Sydenham **D 8**
5 Sydenham Damerel **H 3**
26 Syderstone **B 1**
7 Sydling St. Nicholas **F 10**
16 Sydmonton **H 6**
32 Syerston **E 5**
35 Syke **F 8**
36 Sykehouse **E 4**
34 Sykes **B 5**
64 Symbister **D 8**
47 Symington, Strathclyde **F 8**
48 Symington, Strathclyde **F 3**
15 Symonds Yat **C 9**
7 Symondsbury **G 8**
13 Synod Inn **B 7**
49 Synton Parkhead **G 7**
61 Syre **C 7**
16 Syreford **B 1**
23 Syresham **H 9**
23 Syston, Leics **A 9**
32 Syston, Lincs. **F 6**
22 Sytchampton **F 2**
23 Sywell **E 11**
54 Taagan **C 4**
47 Tackhouse **E 11**
16 Tackley **B 6**
26 Tacolneston **F 4**
36 Tadcaster **C 3**
31 Taddington **C 10**
4 Taddiport **D 4**
17 Tadley **H 7**
25 Tadlow **K 4**
23 Tadmarton **H 7**
15 Tadwick **G 10**
10 Tadworth **B 1**
14 Tafarnau-bach **C 4**
29 Tafarn-gelyn **D 11**
12 Tafarn-y-bwlch **D 4**
14 Taffs Well **F 5**
20 Tafolwern **B 4**
29 Tai **D 7**
29 Tai-bach, Clwyd **G 10**
13 Taibach, W. Glam **H 11**
29 Tai-mawr **F 9**
61 Tain, Highland **A 11**
56 Tain, Highland **B 3**
29 Tainant **F 12**
13 Tairgwaith **F 10**
28 Tai'r-lon **E 4**
18 Takeley **B 5**
18 Takeley Street **B 5**
14 Talachddu **A 4**
29 Talacre **B 10**
6 Talaton **F 4**
12 Talbenny **F 2**
14 Talbot Green **F 4**
8 Talbot Village **G 2**
20 Talerddig **B 5**
13 Talgarreg **B 7**
14 Talgarth **A 5**
20 Taliesin **C 2**
62 Talisker **E 3**
31 Talke **E 7**
44 Talkin **G 4**
48 Talla Linnfoots **G 4**
54 Talladale **C 3**
38 Tallantire **B 3**
29 Tallard **G 8**
30 Tallarn Green **F 3**
13 Talley **D 9**
24 Tallington **E 2**
60 Talmine **B 6**
13 Talog **D 7**
20 Talsarn, Dyfed **G 1**
14 Talsarn, Dyfed **B1**
28 Talsarnau **G 5**
2 Talskiddy **C 6**
28 Talwrn, Gwynedd **C 4**
29 Talwrn, Clwyd **E 12**
20 Talybont, Dyfed **C 2**
28 Tal-y-bont, Gwynedd **H 5**
28 Tal-y-bont,Gwynedd **C 5**
29 Tal-y-bont, Gwynedd **C 7**
14 Talybont, Powys **B 4**
29 Tal-y-cafn **C 7**
15 Tal-y-coed **C 7**
14 Tal-y-garn **F 4**
20 Tal-y-llyn, Gwynedd **A 3**
14 Tal-y-llyn, Powys **B 4**
18 Tal-y-sarn **E 4**
14 Talywain **D 6**
20 Tal-y-wern **B 4**
40 Tame **D 5**
5 Tamerton Foliot **K 3**
34 Tameside **G 8**
22 Tamworth **A 8**
39 Tan Hill **E 11**
12 Tancredston **D 2**
11 Tanden **D 8**
47 Tandlemuir **C 8**
10 Tandridge **C 3**
45 Tanfield **G 10**
45 Tanfield Lea **H 10**
8 Tangley **A 5**
9 Tangmere **E 10**
64 Tankerness **D 3**
35 Tankersley **G 12**
28 Tan-lan **F 5**
61 Tannach **C 12**
59 Tannachie **J 5**
59 Tannadice **L 2**
27 Tannington **H 5**
31 Tansley **D 11**
31 Tansley Knoll **D 11**
24 Tansor **F 2**
45 Tantobie **H 10**
40 Tanton **D 5**
40 Tanworth in Arden **E 5**
28 Tan-y-bwlch **F 6**
29 Tan-y-fron **D 9**
20 Tan-y-graig, Dyfed **E 3**
28 Tan-y-graig, Gwynedd **F 3**
28 Tan-y-grisiau **F 6**
12 Tan-y-groes **B 6**
29 Tan-y-pistyll **G 10**
17 Taplow **F 10**
46 Tarbert, Strathclyde **A 1**
46 Tarbert, Strathclyde **C 4**
63 Tarbert, W. Isles **G 2**
55 Tarbet, Highland **K 2**
60 Tarbet, Highland **C 3**
51 Tarbet, Strathclyde **G 10**
47 Tarbolton **G 9**
47 Tarbrax **D 3**
30 Tarbuck Green **A 3**
44 Tarcoon **E 2**
22 Tardebigge **E 3**
59 Tarfside **J 2**
59 Tarland **G 2**
34 Tarleton **E 3**
34 Tarlscough **F 3**
15 Tarlton **D 12**
34 Tarnbrook **B 5**
30 Tarporley **D 4**
6 Tarr **C 4**
8 Tarrant Crawford **F 1**
8 Tarrant Gunville **E 1**
8 Tarrant Hinton **E 1**
8 Tarrant Keyneston **F 1**
8 Tarrant Launceston **E 1**
8 Tarrant Monkton **E 1**
8 Tarrant Rawston **E 1**
8 Tarrant Rushton **E 1**
61 Tarrel **H 9**
10 Tarring Neville **H 3**
21 Tarrington **H 11**
62 Tarskavaig **G 5**
58 Tarves **D 6**
54 Tarvie **D 8**
30 Tarvin **D 4**
26 Tasburgh **F 5**
21 Tasley **C 12**
16 Taston **B 5**
31 Tatenhill **H 10**
43 Tath Hill **B 11**
39 Tatham **H 8**
33 Tathwell **B 10**
17 Tatling End **E 11**
10 Tatsfield **B 3**
30 Tattenhall **D 3**
26 Tatterford **C 2**
26 Tattersett **C 1**
33 Tattershall **D 9**
33 Tattershall Bridge **E 9**
33 Tattershall Thorpe **D 9**
27 Tattingstone **L 4**
27 Tattingstone Whitehorse **L 4**
6 Tatworth **F 6**
58 Tauchers **C 1**
6 Taunton **D 6**
26 Taverham **D 5**
12 Tavernspite **F 5**
5 Tavistock **H 3**
4 Taw Green, Devon **E 5**
4 Taw Green, Devon **F 5**
4 Tawstock **C 4**
31 Taxal **B 8**
47 Tayburn **E 10**
51 Taychreggan **E 7**
46 Tayinloan **E 2**
52 Taymouth Castle **C 3**
51 Taynafead **F 8**
15 Taynton, Glos. **B 10**
16 Taynton, Oxon **C 3**
51 Taynuilt **D 7**
53 Tayport **D 9**
46 Tayvallich **A 2**
33 Tealby **A 8**
62 Teangue **G 6**
39 Tebay **E 8**
17 Tebworth **A 10**
4 Tedburn St. Mary **F 7**
16 Teddington, Glos. **A 1**
18 Teddington, London **G 2**
21 Tedstone Delamere **F 12**
21 Tedstone Wafre **F 12**
23 Teeton **E 10**
8 Teffont Evias **C 1**
8 Teffont Magna **C 2**
12 Tegryn **D 6**
23 Teigh **A 12**
5 Teigngrace **H 7**
5 Teignmouth **H 8**
56 Teindland **D 8**
44 Teindside **B 3**
21 Telford **B 12**
10 Telham **G 6**
7 Tellisford **A 11**
10 Telscombe **H 3**
43 Templand **C 11**
3 Temple, Cornwall **B 8**
13 Temple Bar, Dyfed **B 8**
13 Temple Bar, Dyfed **E 9**
48 Temple, Lothian **D 6**
22 Temple Balsall **E 5**
7 Temple Cloud **A 9**
11 Temple Ewell **D 11**
22 Temple Grafton **G 5**
16 Temple Guiting **A 2**
36 Temple Hirst **E 4**
32 Temple Normanton **C 1**
39 Temple Sowerby **C 8**
7 Templecombe **D 10**
53 Templehall **H 7**
6 Templeton, Devon **E 2**
12 Templeton, Dyfed **F 4**
4 Tempelton Bridge **E 7**
25 Tempsford **K 3**
24 Ten Mile Bank **F 7**
21 Tenbury Wells **F 11**
12 Tenby **G 5**
19 Tendring **B 11**
19 Tendring Green **A 11**
64 Tenston **C 1**
11 Tenterden **E 7**
42 Terally **G 2**
19 Terling **B 7**
30 Ternhill **G 5**
2 Terras **D 6**
43 Terregles **D 10**
17 Terrick **C 9**
41 Terrington **H 7**
24 Terrington St. Clement **D 6**
24 Terrington St. John **D 6**
10 Teston **C 6**
8 Testwood **E 5**
15 Tetbury **E 12**
15 Tetbury Upton **E 12**
30 Tetchill **G 3**
4 Tetcott **F 2**
33 Tetford **C 10**
37 Tetney **G 10**
37 Tetney Lock **G 11**
17 Tetsworth **D 8**
22 Tettenhall **B 2**
58 Teuchan **D 8**
58 Teuchar **C 5**
53 Teuchatcroft **B 9**
32 Teversal **D 2**
25 Teversham **J 6**
44 Teviothead **C 2**
59 Tewel **J 6**
18 Tewin **B 3**
15 Tewkesbury **A 12**
11 Teynham **B 8**
11 Teynham Street **B 8**
35 Thackley **C 10**
38 Thackthwaite, Cumb. **C 4**
38 Thackthwaite, Cumb. **C 6**
9 Thakeham **D 12**
17 Thame **D 8**
17 Thames Ditton **G 12**
11 Thanington **B 10**
48 Thankerton **F 2**
26 Tharston **F 5**
16 Thatcham **G 6**
34 Thatto Heath **H 4**
25 Thaxted **M 7**
62 The Aird **C 3**
21 The Bage **H 8**
43 The Barony, Dumf. & Gall. **C 11**
64 The Barony, Orkney **B 1**
31 The Blythe **G 9**
62 The Braes **E 4**
21 The Broad **F 10**
14 The Bryn **D 6**
15 The Camp **C 12**
17 The City **D 8**
15 The Cleaver **A 8**
8 The Common **C 4**
21 The Corner **D 10**
60 The Craigs **G 5**
38 The Cronk **F 2**
47 The Den **D 8**
24 The Engine **E 4**
44 The Fauld **F 2**
44 The Flatt **E 4**
11 The Forstal **C 7**
38 The Green, Cumbria **G 4**
7 The Green, Wilts **C 12**
43 The Grove **D 10**
49 The Hardens **D 10**
9 The Haven **C 12**
27 The Heath **L 2**
10 The Hermitage **C 1**
46 The Highland Hotel **A 5**
38 The Hill **G 4**
38 The Howe **H 1**
19 The Hythe **B 10**
43 The Lake **G 7**
11 The Leacon **E 8**
17 The Lee **D 10**
38 The Lhen **B 8**
21 The Marsh **C 8**
45 The Middles **H 10**
10 The Moor **E 6**
61 The Mound **G 8**
47 The Murray **D 11**
64 The Ness **A 8**
59 The Neuk **H 5**
15 The Oval **H 10**
15 The Pill **F 8**
58 The Pole of Itlaw **B 4**
21 The Pound **E 7**
15 The Quarry **D 10**
12 The Rhos **F 4**
9 The Sands **B 10**
44 The Scare **F 3**
16 The Slade **G 6**
11 The Stocks **E 8**
19 The Stone **C 9**
17 The Throat **G 9**
2 The Towans **F 3**
21 The Vauld **G 10**
22 The Wyke **B 1**
40 Theakston **G 3**
37 Thealby **E 7**
17 Theale, Berks. **G 7**
7 Theale, Somerset **B 8**
17 Theale Green **G 7**
37 Thearne **C 8**
27 Theberton **J 7**
23 Theddingworth **D 10**
33 Theddlethorpe All Saints **A 11**
33 Theddlethorpe St. Helen **A 11**
4 Thelbridge Cross **E 7**
27 Thelnetham **G 3**
30 Thelwall **B 5**
26 Themelthorpe **C 4**
23 Thenford **H 8**
25 Therfield **L 4**
27 Thetford **G 2**
18 Theydon Bois **D 4**
15 Thickwood **G 11**
33 Thimbleby, Lincs. **C 9**
40 Thimbleby, N. Yorks. **F 5**
29 Thingwall **B 11**
40 Thirkleby **G 5**
40 Thirlby **G 5**
49 Thirlestane **E 8**
38 Thirlspot **C 5**
40 Thirn **G 2**
40 Thirsk **G 4**
37 Thirtleby **D 9**
38 Thistlebottom **A 5**
34 Thistleton, Lancs. **C 3**
32 Thistleton,Leics. **H 6**
25 Thistley Green **H 8**
36 Thixendale **A 6**
45 Thockrington **E 8**
24 Tholomas Drove **E 5**
40 Tholthorpe **H 5**
12 Thomas Chapel **F 4**
39 Thomas Close **A 7**
58 Thomastown **D 3**
26 Thompson **F 2**
56 Thomshill **D 8**
10 Thong **A 5**
39 Thoralby **F 12**
32 Thoresby **C 4**
33 Thoresway **G 9**
37 Thorganby, Lincs. **G 9**
36 Thorganby, N. Yorks. **C 5**
41 Thorgill **E 7**
27 Thorington **H 7**
27 Thorington Street **L 3**
35 Thorlby **B 8**
18 Thorley, Herts. **B 5**
8 Thorley, I.o.W. **G 5**
18 Thorley Street, Herts. **B 5**
8 Thorley Street, I.o.W. **G 5**
40 Thormanby **H 5**
11 Thorn **F 7**
40 Thornaby-on-Tees **C 5**
26 Thornage **B 4**
17 Thornborough, Bucks. **A 8**
40 Thornborough, N. Yorks. **G 3**
15 Thornbury, Avon **E 9**
4 Thornbury, Devon **E 3**
21 Thornbury, Heref. & Worc. **F 11**
23 Thornby **E 10**
31 Thorncliff **D 8**
7 Thorncombe **F 7**
9 Thorncombe Street **B 11**
25 Thorncote Green **K 3**
8 Thorncross **H 6**
27 Thorndon **H 4**
4 Thorndon Cross **F 4**
6 Thorne, Somerset **D 4**
36 Thorne, S. Yorks. **F 5**
35 Thorner **C 12**
24 Thorney, Cambs. **E 4**
32 Thorney, Notts. **C 6**
7 Thorney, Somerset **D 7**
37 Thorney Crofts **E 9**
8 Thorney Hill **F 4**
58 Thorneybank **D 4**
6 Thornfalcon **D 6**
7 Thornford **E 9**
44 Thorngrafton **F 6**
7 Thorngrove **C 7**
37 Thorngumbald **D 9**
24 Thornham **A 8**
27 Thornham Magna **H 4**
27 Thornham Parva **H 4**
24 Thornhaugh **E 2**
52 Thornhill, Central **G 2**
38 Thornhill, Cumb. **D 3**
31 Thornhill, Dumf. & Gall. **B 9**
8 Thornhill, Hants. **E 6**
14 Thornhill, Mid Glam. **F 5**
35 Thornhill, W. Yorks. **E 11**
37 Thornholme **A 9**
49 Thornielaw **F 8**
49 Thornington **F 11**
40 Thornley, Dur. **A 4**
40 Thornley, Dur. **B 1**
47 Thornliebank **D 10**
25 Thorns **K 8**
35 Thornseat **H 11**
31 Thornsett **B 8**
38 Thornthwaite, Cumb. **C 5**
35 Thornthwaite, N. Yorks. **A 10**
17 Thornton, Bucks. **A 8**
40 Thornton, Cleveland **D 5**
12 Thornton, Dyfed **F 2**
53 Thornton, Fife **G 7**
36 Thornton, Humber. **C 5**
34 Thornton, Lancs. **C 2**
23 Thornton, Leics. **A 8**
33 Thornton, Lincs. **C 9**
34 Thornton, Merseyside **G 2**
49 Thornton, Northumb. **E 12**
53 Thornton, Tayside **C 9**
35 Thornton, W. Yorks. **D 9**
37 Thornton Curtis **E 8**
18 Thornton Heath **G 3**
30 Thornton Hough **B 2**
35 Thornton in Craven **B 8**
39 Thornton in Lonsdale **H 9**
40 Thornton-le-Beans **F 4**
36 Thornton-le-Clay **A 5**
41 Thornton-le-Dale **G 8**

37 Thornton le Moor, Lincolnshire **G 8**
40 Thornton-le-Moor, N. Yorks. **F 4**
30 Thornton-le-Moors **C 3**
40 Thornton-le-Street **G 4**
47 Thornton Mains **E 12**
36 Thornton Moor **A 4**
39 Thornton Rust **F 12**
40 Thornton Steward **F 2**
40 Thornton Watlass **G 3**
47 Thorntonhall **D 10**
49 Thorntonloch **B 10**
49 Thorntonpark **E 12**
18 Thornwood Com **C 5**
49 Thorndykes **E 9**
38 Thornythwaite **C 6**
32 Thoroton **F 5**
36 Thorp Arch **C 2**
27 Thorp Green **K 2**
31 Thorpe, Derby **E 10**
37 Thorpe, Humberside **B 7**
33 Thorpe, Lincs **B 12**
26 Thorpe, Norf. **F 7**
35 Thorpe, N. Yorks. **A 9**
32 Thorpe, Notts. **E 5**
17 Thorpe, Surrey **G 11**
27 Thorpe Abbotts **G 5**
32 Thorpe Acre **H 2**
36 Thorpe Arch **B 2**
32 Thorpe Arnold **H 5**
36 Thorpe Audlin **F 3**
41 Thorpe Bassett **H 8**
19 Thorpe Bay **E 9**
23 Thorpe by Water **C 12**
22 Thorpe Constantine **A 6**
26 Thorpe End Garden Village **D 6**
35 Thorpe Hesley **G 12**
36 Thorpe in Balne **F 4**
32 Thorpe in the Fallows **B 6**
23 Thorpe Langton **C 10**
40 Thorpe Larches **C 4**
19 Thorpe-le-Soken **B 11**
36 Thorpe le Street **C 6**
23 Thorpe Malsor **D 11**
23 Thorpe Mandeville **H 9**
26 Thorpe Market **B 5**
27 Thorpe Morieux **K 2**
32 Thorpe on the Hill **D 6**
26 Thorpe St. Andrew **D 6**
33 Thorpe St. Peter **D 11**
32 Thorpe Salvin **B 2**
23 Thorpe Satchville **A 10**
40 Thorpe Thewles **C 4**
36 Thorpe Underwood **A 3**
25 Thorpe Waterville **G 1**
26 Thorpe Willoughby **D 3**
27 Thorpeness **J 8**
19 Thorrington **B 10**
7 Thorverton **F 3**
27 Thrandeston **H 4**
25 Thrapston **G 1**
38 Threapland **A 4**
30 Threapwood **F 3**
42 Threave **A 4**
10 Three Bridges **D 2**
2 Three Burrows **E 4**
11 Three Chimneys **D 7**
14 Three Cocks **A 5**
13 Three Crosses **H 9**
10 Three Cups Corner, **F 5**
40 Three Gates, Cleveland **B 5**
7 Three Gates, Dorset **E 9**
24 Three Holes **E 6**
8 Three Legged Cross **E 3**
11 Three Oaks **G 7**
49 Threeburnford **D 7**
24 Threekingham **B 2**
10 Threelag Cross **E 6**
31 Threelows **E 9**
17 Threemile Cross **G 8**
2 Threemilestone **E 5**
49 Threepwood **E 8**
38 Threlkeld **C 6**
35 Threshfield **A 8**
26 Thrigby **D 7**
39 Thringarth **C 11**
32 Thringstone **H 2**
40 Thrintoft **F 3**
25 Thriplow **K 5**
24 Throckenholt **E 5**
25 Throcking **M 4**
45 Throckley **F 9**
22 Throckmorton **G 3**
45 Throphill **D 9**
45 Thropton **C 8**
43 Throughgate **C 9**
5 Throwleigh **G 5**
11 Throwley **C 8**
11 Throwley Forstal **C 8**
32 Thrumpton **G 2**
61 Thrumster **C 12**
37 Thrunscoe **F 10**
45 Thrunton **B 9**
7 Thrupe **B 9**
15 Thrupp, Glos. **D 11**
16 Thrupp, Oxon **C 6**
5 Thrushelton **G 3**
18 Thrushesbush **C 5**
23 Tsington **A 10**
8 Thruxton, Hants. **B 4**
15 Thruxton, Heref. & Worc. **A 7**
36 Thrybergh **H 3**
23 Thurcaston **A 9**
32 Thurcroft **A 2**
4 Thurdon **E 2**
26 Thurgarton, Norf. **B 5**
32 Thurgarton, Notts. **E 4**
35 Thurgoland **G 11**
23 Thurlaston, Leics. **B 8**
23 Thurlaston, War. **E 8**
6 Thurlbear **D 6**
24 Thurlby, Lincs. **D 2**
32 Thurlby, Lincs. **D 6**
25 Thurleigh **J 2**
5 Thurlestone **L 5**
6 Thurloxton **C 6**
32 Thurlston **G 1**
35 Thurlstone **G 11**
26 Thurlton **F 7**
23 Thurmaston **A 9**
23 Thurnby **B 10**
26 Thurne **D 7**
11 Thurnham, Kent **B 7**
34 Thurnham, Lancs. **B 3**
26 Thurning, Norf. **C 4**
25 Thurning, Northants. **G 2**
36 Thurnscoe **G 2**
44 Thursby **H 2**
26 Thursford Green **B 3**
9 Thursley **B 10**
61 Thurso **A 10**
61 Thurso East **A 10**
30 Thurstaston **B 1**
27 Thurston **J 2**
44 Thurstonfield **G 2**
35 Thurstonland **F 10**
26 Thurton **E 6**
31 Thurvaston **F 11**
26 Thuxton **E 3**
27 Thwaite, Suffolk **H 4**
39 Thwaite, N. Yorks. **E 11**
26 Thwaite St. Mary **F 6**
41 Thwing **H 10**
52 Tibbermore **E 5**
43 Tibbers **B 9**
15 Tibberton, Glos. **B 10**
22 Tibberton, Heref. & Worc. **F 3**
30 Tibberton, Salop **H 5**
26 Tibenham **F 4**
32 Tibshelf **D 2**
37 Tibthorpe **B 7**
10 Ticehurst **E 6**
9 Tichborne **C 7**
9 Tichfield **F 7**
24 Tickencote **E 1**
15 Tickenham **G 8**
32 Tickhill **A 3**
21 Ticklerton **C 10**
31 Ticknall **H 12**
37 Tickton **C 8**
22 Tidbury Green **E 4**
16 Tidcombe **H 4**
17 Tiddington, Oxon **D 7**
22 Tidington, War. **F 6**
10 Tidebrook **E 5**
3 Tideford **D 10**
3 Tideford Cross **D 10**
15 Tidenham **E 9**
31 Tideswell **C 10**
17 Tidmarsh **G 7**
22 Tidmington **H 6**
8 Tidpit **D 2**
12 Tiers Cross **F 3**
23 Tiffield **G 10**
58 Tifty **D 5**
59 Tigerton **L 3**
54 Tighchuig **F 8**
52 Tighnablair **E 3**
46 Tighnabruaich **B 5**
51 Tigh-na-criche **G 8**
60 Tighnafiline **G 1**
5 Tigley **K 6**
25 Tilbrook **H 2**
18 Tilbury **F 6**
17 Tilehurst **G 7**
9 Tilford **B 10**
10 Tilgale **E 2**
58 Tillathrowie **D 2**
30 Tilley **G 4**
52 Tillicoultry **G 4**
19 Tillingham **D 10**
21 Tillington, Heref. & Worc. **H 10**
9 Tillington, W. Sussex **D 11**
21 Tillington Com **H 10**
59 Tillyarblet **L 3**
59 Tillybardine **K 2**
58 Tillycorthie **E 7**
59 Tillydrine House **H 4**
58 Tillyfar **E 7**
58 Tillyfourie **F 4**
58 Tillygreig **E 6**
58 Tillyminnate **D 2**
11 Tilmanstone **C 11**
32 Tiln **B 4**
24 Tilney All Saints **D 7**
24 Tilney High End **D 7**
24 Tilney St. Lawrence **D 7**
8 Tilshead **A 2**
30 Tilstock **F 4**
30 Tilston **E 3**
30 Tilstone Fearnall **D 4**
17 Tilsworth **B 10**
23 Tilton on the Hill **B 10**
15 Tiltups End **E 11**
33 Timberland **D 8**
31 Timbersbrook **D 7**
6 Timberscombe **B 3**
35 Timble **B 10**
49 Timpendean **G 9**
30 Timperley **A 6**
15 Timsbury, Avon **H 10**
8 Timsbury, Hants. **D 5**
63 Timsgarry **D 2**
27 Timworth Green **H 2**
7 Tincleton **G 11**
44 Tindale **G 4**
17 Tingewick **A 7**
35 Tingley **D 11**
25 Tingrith **M 1**
5 Tinhay **G 3**
48 Tinnis **F 6**
35 Tinshill **C 11**
3 Tintagel **A 7**
15 Tintern Parva **D 8**
7 Tintinhull **D 8**
35 Tintwistle **G 9**
43 Tinwald **C 11**
24 Tinwell **E 1**
4 Tippacott **A 6**
58 Tipperty, Grampian **E 7**
58 Tipperty, Grampian **B 4**
24 Tipp's End **F 6**
8 Tiptoe **F 4**
22 Tipton **C 3**
6 Tipton St. John **G 4**
19 Tiptree **B 9**
20 Tarabad **H 4**
50 Tirghoil **E 1**
15 Tirley **A 11**
14 Tirphil **D 4**
39 Tirril **C 7**
60 Tirryside **F 6**
8 Tisbury **C 1**
9 Tisman's Com **C 12**
31 Tissington **E 10**
4 Titchberry **C 1**
25 Titchmarsh **G 1**
26 Titchwell **A 1**
32 Tithby **F 4**
45 Titlington **B 9**
21 Titley **F 9**
10 Titsey **C 3**
31 Tittensor **F 7**
26 Tittleshall **C 2**
15 Tittups End **E 11**
30 Tiverton, Ches. **D 4**
6 Tiverton, Devon **E 3**
6 Tiverton Junction **E 4**
27 Tivetshall St. Margaret **G 4**
27 Tivetshall St. Mary **G 4**
22 Tividale **C 3**
6 Tivington **B 3**
31 Tixall **H 8**
24 Tixover **E 1**
64 Toab **D 3**
31 Toadmoor **E 12**
50 Tobermory **B 2**
50 Toberonochy **G 5**
63 Tobson **C 2**
58 Tocher **D 4**
16 Tockenham **F 2**
16 Tockenham Wick **F 1**
34 Tockholes **E 5**
15 Tockington **F 9**
36 Tockwith **B 3**
7 Todber **D 11**
17 Toddington, Beds. **A 11**
16 Toddington, Glos. **A 1**
22 Todenham **H 6**
53 Todhall **E 8**
44 Todhills **G 2**
35 Todmorden **E 8**
49 Todrig **G 7**
32 Todwick **B 2**
23 Toft, Cambs. **K 5**
24 Toft, Lincs. **D 2**
40 Toft Hill **B 2**
26 Toft Monks **F 7**
33 Toft Next Newton **A 7**
49 Toftbarns **G 8**
26 Toftrees **C 2**
61 Tofts **A 12**
26 Toftwood Com **D 3**
45 Togston **C 10**
55 Toigal **K 1**
62 Tokavaig **G 5**
17 Tokers Green **F 8**
36 Toll Bar **F 3**
22 Toll End **C 3**
58 Toll of Birness **D 7**
6 Tolland **C 4**
8 Tollard Royal **D 1**
7 Toller Fratrum **F 9**
7 Toller Porcorum **F 9**
32 Tollerton, Notts. **G 3**
36 Tollerton, N. Yorks. **A 3**
19 Tollesbury **C 9**
19 Tolleshunt D'Arcy **C 9**
19 Tolleshunt Major **C 9**
56 Tollie **D 1**
63 Tolmachan **F 2**
7 Tolpuddle **G 11**
63 Tolstachaolais **C 3**
57 Tolvah **J 4**
10 Tolworth **B 1**
57 Tomatin **G 4**
57 Tombain **J 4**
56 Tombreck **F 2**
55 Tomchrasky **H 6**
55 Tomdoun **J 5**
56 Tomich, Highland **E 1**
55 Tomich, Highland **G 7**
56 Tomich, Highland **C 3**
60 Tomich, Highland **F 6**
57 Tomintoul, Grampian **K 7**
57 Tomintoul, Grampian **H 7**
57 Tomintoul, Highland **G 2**
58 Tomnaven **D 2**
57 Tomnavoulin **G 8**
52 Tomphibil **B 3**
44 Tomishielburn **E 2**
14 Ton **D 6**
14 Ton-Pentre **E 3**
10 Tonbridge **C 5**
14 Tondu **F 2**
20 Ton-fanau **B 1**
22 Tong, Salop **A 2**
63 Tong, W. Isles **C 5**
35 Tong, W. Yorks. **D 10**
35 Tong Street **D 10**
32 Tonge **H 2**
9 Tongham **A 10**
43 Tongland **F 8**
60 Tongue **B 6**
60 Tongue House **B 6**
14 Tongwynlais **F 5**
13 Tonna **G 11**
14 Ton-teg **F 4**
18 Tonwell **B 3**
14 Tonypandy **E 3**
14 Tonyrefail **E 3**
16 Toot Baldon **D 6**
18 Toothill **D 5**
35 Top of Hebers **F 7**
40 Topcliffe **H 4**
26 Topcroft **F 6**
26 Topcroft Street **F 5**
25 Toppesfield **L 8**
34 Toppings **F 6**
6 Topsham **G 3**
57 Torbain **H 7**
46 Torbeg, Arran I. **F 4**
59 Torbeg, Grampian **G 1**
61 Torboll **G 7**
56 Torbreck **F 3**
5 Torbryan **J 7**
55 Torcastle **L 5**
5 Torcross **L 7**
57 Torcroy **J 3**
55 Torcuileainn **J 2**
56 Tore **D 2**
55 Torgyle Bridge **H 7**
46 Torinturk **C 3**
32 Torksey **B 5**
55 Torlundy **M 5**
15 Tormarton **F 11**
42 Tormitchell **B 3**
46 Tormore **F 4**
56 Tornagrain **E 3**
57 Tornahaish **J 8**
59 Tornaveen **G 4**
57 Torness **G 1**
40 Toronto **B 2**
38 Torpenhow **A 4**
48 Torphichen **B 2**
59 Torphins **G 4**
3 Torpoint **D 11**
5 Torquay **J 8**
49 Torquhan **E 7**
62 Torran **C 5**
47 Torrance **B 11**
50 Torraneidhinn **B 3**
50 Torrans **E 2**
47 Torranyard **E 8**
5 Torre, Devon **J 8**
6 Torre, Somerset **B 4**
54 Torridon **D 3**
54 Torridon House **D 2**
62 Torrin **F 5**
61 Torrisdale **B 7**
34 Torrisholme **A 3**
55 Torrlaoighseach **H 3**
60 Torrobole **F 6**
58 Torry, Grampian **D 2**
59 Torry, Grampian **G 7**
48 Torryburn **A 3**
58 Torterston **C 8**
43 Torthorwald **D 11**
9 Tortington **F 11**
62 Torvaig **D 4**
38 Torver **F 5**
48 Torwood **A 1**
32 Torworth **B 4**
4 Tosberry **D 1**
54 Toscaig **F 1**
25 Toseland **J 3**
34 Tosside **B 6**
50 Tostarie **C 1**
27 Tostock **J 3**
62 Totaig, Highland **C 1**
55 Totaig, Highland **G 2**
62 Totardor **D 3**
62 Tote **C 3**
61 Totegan **A 8**
8 Totland **G 5**
31 Totley **B 11**
7 Totnell **E 9**
5 Totnes **K 7**
62 Totscore **B 3**
18 Tottenham **E 3**
24 Tottenhill **D 7**
18 Totteridge **E 2**
17 Totternhoe **B 10**
34 Tottington **F 6**
8 Totton **E 5**
17 Touchen-end **F 9**
6 Toulton **C 5**
56 Toulvaddie **B 4**
54 Tournaig **B 2**
58 Toux **C 7**
40 Tow Law **A 1**
46 Toward **C 6**
46 Toward Quay **C 6**
23 Towcester **G 10**
2 Towednack **F 2**
18 Tower Hamlets **F 4**
10 Tower Hill **E 1**
17 Towersey **D 8**
58 Towie **F 2**
58 Towiemore **C 1**
39 Town End **G 7**
34 Town Green **G 3**
10 Town Row **E 4**
27 Town Street **G 1**
49 Town Yetholm **G 10**
43 Townfoot **B 10**
43 Townhead, Dumf. & Gall. **C 10**
43 Townhead, Dumf. & Gall. **G 8**
59 Townhead, Grampian **K 5**
45 Townhead, Northumb. **F 7**
42 Townhead, Strathclyde **A 3**
47 Townhead of Aber **A 9**
47 Townhead of Gree **E 9**
43 Town head of Greenlaw **E 8**
52 Townhill **H 6**
16 Townsend, Oxon **E 5**
7 Townsend, Som. **A 8**
2 Townshend **F 3**
36 Towthorpe **A 4**
36 Towton **C 3**
29 Towyn **B 9**
33 Toynton All Saints **D 11**
33 Toynton Fen Side **D 11**
33 Toynton St. Peter **D 11**
10 Toy's Hill **C 3**
47 Trabboch **G 9**
47 Trabboch Mains **G 9**
47 Trabbochburn **G 9**
2 Traboe **G 4**
56 Tradespark **D 4**
35 Trafford Park **H 7**
55 Traigh House **K 1**
14 Trallong **A 3**
49 Tranent **B 7**
30 Tranmere **A 2**
61 Trantlebeg **C 8**
61 Trantlemore **B 8**
45 Tranwell **E 10**
13 Trapp **E 10**
49 Traprain **B 8**
48 Traquair **F 6**
17 Traveller's Rest **B 10**
35 Trawden **C 8**
14 Trawscoed **A 4**
28 Trawsfynydd **G 6**
13 Tre-Herbert **B 9**
14 Trelaw **E 3**
34 Treales **D 3**
28 Trearddur Bay **B 2**
62 Treaslane **C 3**
14 Trebanog **E 3**
13 Trebanos **G 10**
3 Trebartha **B 9**
3 Trebarwith **A 7**
2 Trebetheric **B 6**
6 Treborough **C 3**
2 Trebudannon **D 6**
3 Trebullett **B 10**
3 Treburley **B 10**
3 Trebyan **C 8**
14 Trecastle **A 2**
14 Trecenydd **F 5**
12 Trecwn **D 3**
14 Trecynon **D 3**
30 Tredaule **B 9**
12 Tre-ddiog **D 2**
14 Tredegar **C 5**
22 Tredington **H 6**
2 Tredizzick **B 6**
14 Tredomen **A 4**
12 Tredrissi **C 4**
14 Tredustan **A 5**
2 Treen **G 1**
32 Treeton **A 2**
12 Trefasser **C 2**
28 Trefdraeth **C 3**
14 Trefecca **A 5**
20 Trefeglwys **C 5**
20 Trefenter **E 2**
12 Treffgarne **E 3**
12 Treffgarne Owen **D 2**
12 Treffynnon, Dyfed **D 2**
14 Trefil **C 4**
20 Trefilan **G 1**
29 Trefnant **C 10**
30 Trefonen **G 1**
28 Trefor **B 3**
14 Treforest Industrial Estate **F 4**
29 Trefriw **D 7**
29 Tref-y-nant **F 12**
3 Tregadillet **A 10**
28 Tregaian **B 4**
15 Tregare **C 7**
20 Tregaron **F 2**
28 Tregarth **C 5**
3 Tregeare **A 9**
29 Tregeiriog **G 11**
28 Tregele **A 3**
2 Tregeseal **F 1**
12 Treglemais **D 2**
2 Tregonetha **C 6**
2 Tregony **E 6**
3 Tregoss **D 7**
2 Tregowris **G 5**
14 Tregoyd **A 5**
13 Tre-groes **C 7**
2 Tregurrian **C 5**
20 Tregynon **C 6**
14 Trehafod **E 4**
14 Treharris **E 4**
14 Treherbert **D 3**
3 Trekenner **B 10**
3 Treknow **A 7**
3 Trelash **A 9**
2 Trelassick **D 6**
29 Trelawnyd **B 10**
12 Trelach **D 6**
12 Tre-lech-a'r-Betws **D 6**
12 Treleddyd fawr **D 1**
14 Trelewis **E 4**
3 Treligga **A 7**
3 Trelights **B 7**
3 Trelill **B 7**
2 Trelissick **F 5**
15 Trelleck **D 8**
15 Trelleck Grange **D 8**
29 Trelogan **B 10**
28 Tremadog **F 5**
3 Tremail **A 8**
12 Tremain **B 6**
3 Tremaine **A 9**
3 Tremar **C 9**
3 Trematon **D 11**
29 Tremeirchion **C 10**
3 Tremore **C 7**
2 Trenance, Corn. **C 5**
2 Trenance, Corn. **C 6**
2 Trenance, Corn. **H 4**
3 Trenarren **E 7**

21 Trench A 12
2 Trenear F 4
3 Treneglos A 9
3 Trenewan D 9
2 Trengune B 2
7 Trent Nether Compton D 2
31 Trentham F 7
4 Trentishoe A 5
14 Treoes F 3
14 Treorchy E 3
3 Trequite B 7
20 Tre'r-ddol C 2
3 Trerule Foot D 10
12 Tresaith B 6
3 Tresayes D 7
22 Trescott B 2
2 Trescowe G 3
15 Tresham E 11
2 Tresillian E 6
12 Tresinwen C 2
2 Treskinnick Cross A 2
3 Tresmeer A 9
2 Tresparrett B 2
2 Tresparrett Posts B 2
52 Tressait A 3
64 Tresta, Zetland B 8
64 Tresta, Zetland D 7
32 Treswell B 5
2 Trethosa D 6
3 Trethurgy D 7
12 Tretio D 1
15 Tretire B 8
14 Tretower B 5
29 Treuddyn D 11
3 Trevadlock B 9
3 Trevalga A 8
30 Trevalyn D 3
3 Trevanson B 7
2 Trevarren D 6
2 Trevarrian C 5
3 Trevarrick E 7
12 Trevaughan, Dyfed E 5
13 Trevaughan, Dyfed E 7
2 Trevellas D 4
3 Trevelmond C 9
2 Treverva F 5
14 Trevethin D 6
3 Trevigro C 10
12 Trevine D 2
3 Trevivian A 9
2 Trevone B 6
28 Trevor F 3
2 Trevose B 6
3 Trewarmett A 8
3 Trewassa A 8
2 Trewellard F 1
3 Trewen A 9
2 Trewennack G 4
21 Trewern A 8
3 Trewethern B 7
3 Trewetha B 7
3 Trewidland D 9
12 Trewilym C 5
2 Trewint B 2
2 Trewithian F 6
3 Trewoon D 7
2 Treyarnon Bay B 6
9 Treyford D 9
35 Triangle E 9
8 Trickett's Cross F 3
44 Triermain F 4
40 Trimdon B 4
40 Trimdon Colliery B 4
40 Trimdon Grange B 4
26 Trimingham B 6
27 Trimley St. Mary L 6
27 Trimley St. Martin L 6
22 Trimpley D 1
13 Trimsaran F 8
52 Trinafour A 2
14 Trinant D 5
17 Tring C 10
17 Tring Wharf C 10
6 Trinity, Devon F 3
59 Trinity, Tayside L 4
6 Triscombe C 5
55 Trislaig M 5
2 Trispen E 5
45 Tritlington D 10
52 Trochry C 5
14 Troedrhiw D 4
13 Troedyraur B 7
13 Troed-y-rhiw B 8
47 Troon, Strathclyde F 8
2 Troon, Cornwall F 4
43 Troqueer D 10
51 Trossachs Hotel G 12
27 Trostan H 2
10 Trottiscliffe B 5
9 Trotton D 9
45 Troughend D 7
38 Troutbeck, Cumbria C 6
38 Troutbeck, Cumbria E 6
38 Troutbeck Bridge E 6
15 Trow Green D 9
32 Troway B 1
15 Trowbridge H 11
32 Trowell F 2
15 Trowle Common H 11
17 Trowley Botton C 11
49 Trows F 9
26 Trowse Newton E 5
7 Trudoxhill B 10
6 Trull D 6
62 Trumpan B 2
21 Trumpet H 12
25 Trumpington K 6
6 Trumps E 4
26 Trunch B 6
2 Truro E 5
3 Truscott A 10
6 Trusham H 2
31 Trusley G 11
33 Trusthorpe B 12
22 Trysull C 2
16 Tubney D 5
5 Tuckenhay K 7
2 Tuckingmill F 4
25 Tuddenham, Suff. H 8
27 Tuddenham, Suff. K 5
10 Tudeley D 5
40 Tudhoe B 3
15 Tudorville B 9
28 Tudweiliog G 2
9 Tuesley B 11
15 Tuffley C 11
12 Tufton D 4
23 Tugby B 11
21 Tugford D 11
45 Tughall E 12
57 Tulchan M 7
52 Tullibardine F 4
52 Tullibody H 3
51 Tullich, Central D 12
57 Tullich, Highland G 2
54 Tullich, Highland E 3
51 Tullich, Strathclyde F 8
56 Tullich Muir B 3
52 Tulliemet B 5
59 Tullo' of Benholm K 5
58 Tulloch House D 5
55 Tulloch L 7
52 Tullochan D 1
53 Tullochgorm H 7
57 Tullochmacarrick J 8
58 Tullochs C 2
59 Tullochvenus G 3
52 Tullybannocher E 2
53 Tullyfergus B 7
53 Tullymurdoch B 7
58 Tullynessle F 3
13 Tumble F 9
33 Tumby D 9
33 Tumby Woodside D 9
18 Tumford C 4
52 Tummel Bridge A 3
10 Tunbridge Wells D 5
15 Tunley H 10
37 Tunstall, Humber. D 10
11 Tunstall, Kent B 7
39 Tunstall, Lancs. H 8
40 Tunstall, N. Yorks. F 2
31 Tunstall, Staffs. E 7
27 Tunstall, Suffolk K 6
45 Tunstall,
Tyne & Wear H 12
26 Tunstall St. Mary E 7
9 Tunworth A 8
21 Tupsley H 10
31 Tupton D 12
23 Tur Langton C 10
17 Turgis Green H 8
53 Turin B 10
16 Turkdean B 2
15 Turleigh Freshford H 11
15 Turnastone A 7
42 Turnberry A 3
31 Turnditch F 11
10 Turner's Hill E 2
7 Turners Puddle G 11
48 Turnhouse B 4
7 Turnworth E 11
58 Turriff C 5
34 Turton Bottoms F 6
49 Turvelaws F 12
23 Turvey G 12
17 Turville E 8
17 Turville Heath E 8
23 Turweston H 9
48 Tushielaw G 6
31 Tutbury G 10
22 Tutnall E 3
15 Tutshill E 8
26 Tuttington C 5
17 Tutts Clump G 7
3 Tutwell B 11
32 Tuxford C 4
64 Twatt, Orkney Is. C 1
64 Twatt, Shetland Is. D 7
47 Twechar B 11
48 Tweeddaleburn D 5
49 Tweedmouth D 12
48 Tweedshaws H 3
48 Tweedsmuir G 4
2 Twelveheads E 5
30 Twemlow Green C 6
24 Twenty C 3
15 Twerton H 10
18 Twickenham G 2
15 Twigworth B 11
10 Twineham F 1
15 Twinhoe H 10
27 Twinstead L 2
27 Twinstead Green L 2
4 Twitchen, Devon B 4
4 Twitchen, Devon C 7
21 Twitchen, Salop D 9
5 Two Bridges H 5
31 Two Dales D 11
22 Two Gates B 5
4 Two Pots B 4
23 Twycross B 7
17 Twyford, Berks G 9
17 Twyford, Bucks B 7
31 Twyford, Derby G 11
8 Twyford, Hants D 6
23 Twyford, Leics. A 10
26 Twyford, Norf. C 3
15 Twyford Com A 8
13 Twyn Llanan E 11
14 Twyncarno C 4
43 Twynholm F 7
15 Twyning A 12
13 Twyn-mynydd F 10
15 Twyn-y-Sheriff D 7
23 Twywell D 12
28 Ty-Hen G 1
21 Tyberton H 9
13 Tycroes, Dyfed F 9
28 Ty-croes, Gwynedd C 3
29 Tycrwyn H 10
24 Tydd Gote D 5
24 Tydd St. Giles D 5
24 Tydd St. Mary D 5
29 Tyddyninco G 9
19 Tye Green, Essex B 7
25 Tye Green, Essex L 7
12 Ty-hen E 6
34 Tyldesley G 6
11 Tyler Hill B 10
17 Tylers Green, Bucks. E 10
10 Tyler's Grn., Surrey C 2
14 Tylorstown E 3
20 Tylwch D 5
29 Ty-nant, Clwyd F 9
29 Ty-nant, Gwynedd H 8
20 Tyncwm D 4
51 Tyndrum E 10
7 Tyneham H 12
45 Tyne & Wear, Co. F 10
48 Tynehead C 6
45 Tynemouth F 11
14 Tynewydd D 3
49 Tyninghame B 8
50 Tynribbie C 6
43 Tynron B 9
20 Tynswydd F 2
29 Ty'n-y-ffridd G 10
28 Ty'n-y-gongl B 4
29 Ty'n-y-groes C 7
28 Tyn-y-pwll B 4
29 Tyn-y-Wern G 10
23 Tyringham G 12
4 Tythecott D 3
14 Tythegston F 2
15 Tytherington, Avon E 10
31 Tytherington, Ches C 7
7 Tytherington, Som. B 11
8 Tytherington, Wilts. B 1
7 Tytherleigh F 7
3 Tywardreath D 8
3 Tywardreath Highway D 8
29 Tywyn B 7
20 Tywyn Mer B 2
54 Uags F 1
27 Ubbeston Green H 6
15 Ubley H 8
40 Uckerby E 3
10 Uckfield F 4
15 Uckington B 12
47 Uddingston C 11
48 Uddington F 1
11 Udimore F 7
58 Udny Green E 6
47 Udston E 12
47 Udstonhead E 12
16 Uffcott F 2
6 Uffculme E 4
24 Uffington, Lincs. E 2
16 Uffington, Oxon E 4
21 Uffington, Salop A 10
24 Ufford, Cambs. E 2
27 Ufford, Suffolk K 6
23 Ufton F 7
17 Ufton Green G 7
17 Ufton Nervet G 7
46 Ugadale F 3
5 Ugborough K 5
27 Uggeshall G 7
41 Ugglebarnby D 9
18 Ugley A 5
41 Ugthorpe D 8
62 Uig, Skye C 1
62 Uig, Skye B 3
46 Uig, Strathclyde A 6
62 Uigshader D 4
50 Uisken F 1
61 Ulbster C 12
33 Ulceby, Humberside F 8
33 Ulceby, Lincs. C 11
33 Ulceby Cross C 11
37 Ulceby Skitter F 9
11 Ulcombe C 7
38 Uldale B 5
15 Uley D 11
45 Ulgham D 10
60 Ullapool G 3
22 Ullenhall E 5
15 Ullenwood C 12
36 Ulleskelf C 3
23 Ullesthorpe C 8
32 Ulley B 2
21 Ullingswick G 11
62 Ullinish D 2
38 Ullock C 3
8 Ullwell H 2
38 Ulpha F 4
37 Ulrome B 9
64 Ulsta C 7
49 Ulsoon G 9
50 Ulva House D 2
38 Ulverston G 5
43 Ulzieside A 8
62 Umachan C 5
4 Umberleigh D 5
60 Unapool D 4
36 Uncleby A 6
44 Under Burnmouth E 3
10 Under River C 4
39 Underbarrow F 7
36 Undercliffe D 10
47 Underhills F 9
64 Underhoull A 8
32 Underwood E 2
15 Undy F 7
64 Unifirth D 6
59 Union Croft H 6
38 Union Mills H 2
32 Unstone C 1
32 Unstone Green C 1
44 Unthank, Cumb. H 2
39 Unthank, Cumb. A 8
39 Unthank, Cumb. B 7
49 Unthank, Northumb. E 12
39 Unthank End B 7
7 Up Cerne F 10
6 Up Exe F 3
15 Up Hatherley B 12
34 Up Holland G 4
9 Up Marden E 9
9 Up Nately A 8
8 Up Somborne C 5
7 Up Sydling F 9
8 Upavon A 3
11 Upchurch A 7
4 Upcott, Devon E 4
21 Upcott,
Heref. & Worc. G 8
6 Upcott, Somerset D 3
48 Uphall B 3
48 Uphall Station B 3
4 Upham, Devon E 7
9 Upham, Hants D 7
21 Uphampton,
Heref. & Worc. F 9
22 Uphampton,
Heref. & Worc. F 2
14 Uphill H 6
47 Uplawmoor D 9
15 Upleadon B 10
40 Upleatham C 6
11 Uplees B 8
7 Uploders G 8
6 Uplowman E 4
6 Uplyme G 6
18 Upminster E 6
6 Upottery E 5
71 Uppat F 8
21 Upper Affcott D 10
60 Upper Ardchronie G 6
22 Upper Arley D 1
17 Upper Arncott B 7
23 Upper Astrop H 8
60 Upper Badcall C 3
63 Upper Barvas B 5
17 Upper Basildon F 7
63 Upper Bayble D 6
10 Upper Beeding G 1
24 Upper Benefield F 1
22 Upper Bentley E 3
58 Upper Boddam E 4
23 Upper Boddington G 8
20 Upper Borth D 2
9 Upper Bourne B 9
58 Upper Boyndie A 6
22 Upper Brailes H 6
62 Upper Breakish F 6
21 Upper Breinton H 10
32 Upper Broughton H 4
16 Upper Bucklebury G 6
8 Upper Burgate D 3
59 Upper Burnhaugh H 6
25 Upper Caldecote L 3
8 Upper Canterton E 4
23 Upper Catesby F 8
20 Upper Chapel H 6
6 Upper Cheddon C 6
8 Upper Chicksgrove C 1
14 Upper Church Village F 4
8 Upper Chute A 4
8 Upper Clatford B 5
43 Upper Clifton F 10
28 Upper Clynnog F 4
63 Upper Coll C 5
42 Upper Craigenbay D 6
35 Upper Cumberworth F 10
14 Upper Cwmbran E 6
58 Upper Dallachy A 1
43 Upper Dalveen A 9
25 Upper Dean H 1
35 Upper Denby F 11
44 Upper Denton G 4
56 Upper Derraid F 6
54 Upper Diabaig D 2
10 Upper Dicker G 4
61 Upper Dournreay A 9
50 Upper Druimfin B 2
31 Upper Elkstone D 9
31 Upper End C 9
56 Upper Ethie C 3
15 Upper Framilode C 10
22 Upper Gornal C 3
25 Upper Gravenhurst L 2
16 Upper Green H 5
15 Upper Grove Com B 9
9 Upper Hale A 10
62 Upper Halistra B 2
17 Upper Halliford G 11
10 Upper Halling B 6
23 Upper Hambleton A 12
11 Upper Hardress Court C 10
10 Upper Hartfield E 3
36 Upper Haugh G 2
21 Upper Heath D 11
26 Upper Hellesdon D 5
36 Upper Helmsley A 5
21 Upper Hergest G 8
23 Upper Heyford,
Northants F 10
16 Upper Heyford, Oxon B 6
21 Upper Hill G 10
44 Upper Hindhope B 6
35 Upper Hopton E 10
10 Upper Horsebridge G 5
31 Upper Hulme D 8
16 Upper Inglesham D 3
57 Upper Inverbrough G 4
53 Upper Kenley F 10
13 Upper Killay H 9
58 Upper Kinkell E 5
58 Upper Knaven C 6
56 Upper Knockando E 7
16 Upper Lambourn F 4
15 Upper Langford H 8
31 Upper Leigh F 8
59 Upper Lochton H 4
22 Upper Longdon A 4
61 Upper Lybster D 11
15 Upper Lydbrook C 9
21 Upper Lye F 9
62 Upper Milovaig C 1
16 Upper Minety E 1
35 Upper Moor Side D 11
15 Upper Morton E 9
58 Upper Mulben B 1
44 Upper Mumble E 2
49 Upper Nisbet G 9
17 Upper North Dean D 9
52 Upper Obney C 5
62 Upper Ollach E 4
22 Upper Penn C 3
36 Upper Poppleton B 3
57 Upper Port G 6
22 Upper Quinton G 5
8 Upper Ratley D 5
21 Upper Rochford F 11
42 Upper Rusko E 6
55 Upper Sandaig H 2
21 Upper Sapey F 12
46 Upper Scoulag C 6
16 Upper Seagry F 1
63 Upper Shader B 5
25 Upper Shelton L 1
26 Upper Sheringham A 4
48 Upper Side D 6
47 Upper Skelmorlie C 7
16 Upper Slaughter B 3
51 Upper Sonachan E 8
15 Upper Soudley C 10
15 Upper Stanton Drew H 9
25 Upper Stondon M 3
23 Upper Stowe F 10
8 Upper Street, Hants. D 3
26 Upper Street, Norf. D 7
22 Upper Strensham H 3
17 Upper Sundon A 11
16 Upper Swell B 3
26 Upper Tasburgh F 5
31 Upper Tean F 8
52 Upper Tillyrie F 6
62 Upper Tote B 4
15 Upper Town, Avon H 8
21 Upper Town,
Heref. & Worc. G 11
23 Upper Tysoe H 7
16 Upper Upham F 3
10 Upper Upnor A 6
23 Upper Wardington G 8
23 Upper Weald H 11
23 Upper Weedon F 9
9 Upper Wield B 7
17 Upper Winchendon C 8
8 Upper Woodford B 3
58 Upper Woodhead F 4
9 Upper Wootton A 7
22 Upper Wyche H 1
44 Upperby H 2
35 Uppermill G 8
58 Uppertack of
Gressiehill B 6
35 Upperthong F 10
59 Upperton, Grampian K 5
9 Upperton, W. Sussex D 11
64 Uppertown F 2
21 Uppington A 11
40 Upsall F 5
18 Upshire D 4
11 Upstreet B 11
17 Upton, Berks F 10
24 Upton, Cambs. E 2
25 Upton, Cambs. G 3
30 Upton, Cheshire C 3
4 Upton, Cornwall E 1
6 Upton, Devon F 4
8 Upton, Dorset G 1
7 Upton, Dorset H 11
8 Upton, Hants. D 5
32 Upton, Lincs. B 6
30 Upton, Merseyside A 1
26 Upton, Norfolk D 7
23 Upton, Northants. F 10
32 Upton, Notts. C 5
32 Upton, Notts. E 4
8 Upton, Notts. A 5
16 Upton, Oxon E 6
6 Upton, Somerset C 3
7 Upton, Somerset D 8
22 Upton, War. F 5
36 Upton, W. Yorks. F 3
15 Upton Bishop B 9
15 Upton Cheyney G 10
21 Upton Cressett C 12
9 Upton Grey A 8
4 Upton Hellions F 7
8 Upton Lovel B 1
21 Upton Magna A 11
7 Upton Noble B 10
6 Upton Pyne F 3
15 Upton St. Leonards C 11
7 Upton Scudamore A 12
22 Upton Snodsbury G 3
22 Upton upon Severn H 2
22 Upton Warren E 3
9 Upwaltham E 10
25 Upware H 6
24 Upwell E 6
7 Upwey H10
25 Upwood G 4
64 Urafirth C 6
56 Urchal E 3
16 Urchfont H 2
64 Ure C 6
63 Urgha Beag G 3
40 Urlay Nook D 4
34 Urmston H 6
56 Urquhart, Grampian C 8
56 Urquhart, Highland D 1
40 Urra E 6

56 Urray **D 1**
40 Ushaw Moor **A 3**
15 Usk **D 7**
37 Usselby **H 8**
56 Ussie **D 1**
64 Ustaness **D 7**
45 Usworth **G 11**
35 Utley **C 9**
4 Uton **F 7**
37 Utterby **H 10**
31 Uttoxeter **G 9**
28 Uwchmynydd **H 1**
18 Uxbridge **F 1**
64 Uyeasound **B 8**
12 Uzmaston **F 3**
12 Vachelich **D 1**
28 Valley **B 2**
3 Valley Truckle **A 8**
62 Valtos, Skye **B 4**
63 Valtos, W. Isles **C 2**
20 Van **D 5**
19 Vange **E 7**
14 Varteg Hill **D 6**
62 Vatten **D 2**
14 Vaynor **C 4**
13 Velindre, Dyfed **C 7**
12 Velindre, Dyfed **C 4**
14 Velindre, Powys **A 5**
6 Vellow **B 4**
64 Vementry **D 6**
64 Veness **B 3**
6 Venn Ottery **G 4**
21 Vennington **A 9**
4 Venny Tedburn **F 7**
9 Ventnor **H 7**
16 Vernham Dean **H 4**
16 Vernham Street **H 4**
12 Verwig **B 5**
8 Verwood **E 2**
2 Veryan **F 6**
6 Vicarage **G 5**
38 Vickerstown **H 4**
3 Victoria, Corn. **D 7**
14 Victoria, Gwent **D 5**
64 Vidlin **C 7**
10 Vinehall Street **F 6**
10 Vine's Cross **F 5**
15 Viney Hill **D 9**
17 Virginia Water **G 10**
5 Virginstow **G 3**
7 Vobster **A 10**
64 Voe **C 7**
15 Vowchurch **A 7**
64 Voy **C 1**
40 Wackerfield **C 2**
26 Wacton **F 5**
22 Wadborough **G 3**
17 Waddesdon **B 8**
37 Waddingham **G 7**
34 Waddington Lancs. **C 6**
33 Waddington, Lincs. **D 7**
3 Wadebridge **B 7**
6 Wadeford **E 6**
25 Wadenhoe **G 1**
18 Wadesmill **B 4**
10 Wadhurst **E 5**
31 Wadshelf **C 11**
31 Wadsley **A 11**
32 Wadsley Bridge **A 1**
15 Wadswick **G 11**
36 Wadworth **G 3**
29 Waen **D 10**
29 Waen Fach **H 11**
33 Wainfleet All Saints **D 12**
33 Wainfleet Bank **D 11**
45 Wainfordrigg **C 7**
32 Waingroves **E 1**
2 Wainhouse Corner **B 2**
10 Wainscott **A 6**
35 Wainstalls **D 9**
39 Waitby **D 10**
35 Wakefield **E 12**
24 Wakerley **F 1**
19 Wakes Colne **A 9**
27 Walberswick **H 8**
9 Walberton **E 11**
45 Walbottle **F 10**
44 Walby **G 3**
24 Walcot, Lincs. **B 2**
33 Walcot, Lincs. **E 8**
21 Walcot, Salop **A 11**
21 Walcot, Salop **D 9**
22 Walcot, War. **F 5**
16 Walcot, Wilts. **F 3**
23 Walcote **D 9**
26 Walcott **B 7**
39 Walden Head **G 12**
36 Walden Stubbs **E 3**
10 Walderslade **B 6**
9 Walderton **E 9**
7 Walditch **G 8**
31 Waldley **F 9**
45 Waldridge **H 10**
27 Waldringfield **L 6**
10 Waldron **F 4**
32 Wales **B 2**
33 Walesby, Lincs. **A 8**
32 Walesby, Notts. **C 4**
15 Walford, Heref. & Worc. **B 9**
21 Walford, Heref. & Worc. **E 9**
30 Walford, Salop **H 3**
30 Walford Heath **H 3**
30 Walgherton **E 5**
23 Walgrave **E 11**
8 Walhampton **F 5**
35 Walk Mill **D 7**
34 Walkden **G 6**
45 Walker **G 11**
34 Walker Fold **C 5**
48 Walkerburn **F 6**
32 Walkeringham **A 5**
32 Walkerith **A 5**
18 Walkern **A 3**
21 Walker's Green **H 10**
53 Walkerton **G 7**
8 Walkford **G 4**
5 Walkhampton **J 4**
37 Walkington **C 8**
32 Walkley **A 1**
45 Wall, Northumb. **F 7**
22 Wall, Staffs. **B 4**
44 Wall Bowers **G 4**
21 Wall under Heywood **C 10**
43 Wallaceton **C 9**
42 Wallacetown **A 4**
30 Wallasey **A 2**
38 Wallend, Cumbria **G 5**
19 Wallend, Kent **F 8**
17 Wallingford **E 7**
9 Wallington, Hants. **E 7**
25 Wallington, Herts **M 4**
18 Wallington, London **H 3**
9 Walliswood **B 12**
64 Walls **D 6**
45 Wallsend **F 11**
38 Wallthwaite **C 6**
48 Wallyford **B 6**
11 Walmer **C 12**
34 Walmer Bridge **E 3**
35 Walmersley **F 7**
22 Walmley **C 5**
27 Walpole **H 7**
24 Walpole Crosskeys **D 6**
24 Walpole Highway **D 6**
24 Walpole Island **D 6**
24 Walpole St. Andrew **D 6**
24 Walpole St. Peter **D 6**
22 Walsall **B 4**
22 Wallsall Wood **B 4**
35 Walsden **E 8**
23 Walsgrave on Sowe **D 7**
27 Walsham le Willows **H 3**
34 Walshaw **F 6**
35 Walshford **B 12**
24 Walsoken **D 6**
48 Walston **E 3**
18 Walsworth **A 2**
17 Walter's Ash **D 9**
14 Walterston **G 4**
15 Walterstone **B 7**
11 Waltham, Kent **C 9**
37 Waltham, Humber. **G 10**
18 Waltham Abbey **D 4**
9 Waltham Chase **E 7**
18 Waltham Cross **D 4**
18 Waltham Forest **E 4**
32 Waltham on the Wolds **H 2**
17 Waltham St. Lawrence **F 9**
18 Walthamstow **E 3**
23 Walton, Bucks. **H 12**
24 Walton, Cambs **E 3**
44 Walton, Cumb. **G 3**
32 Walton, Derby **C 1**
23 Walton, Leics **C 9**
21 Walton, Powys **F 8**
30 Walton, Salop **H 4**
7 Walton, Som. **C 8**
27 Walton, Suffolk **L 6**
22 Walton, War. **G 6**
36 Walton, W. Yorks. **B 2**
35 Walton, W. Yorks. **E 12**
15 Walton Cardiff **A 12**
7 Walton Elm **D 11**
12 Walton East **E 4**
15 Walton-in-Gordano **G 7**
34 Walton-Le-Dale **D 4**
17 Walton-on-Thames **G 12**
34 Walton on the Hill, Merseyside **H 3**
31 Walton-on-the-Hill, Staffordshire **H 8**
10 Walton on the Hill, Surrey **C 1**
19 Walton on the Naze **B 12**
32 Walton on the Wolds **H 3**
15 Walton Park **G 7**
31 Walton upon Trent **H 10**
12 Walton West **F 2**
29 Walwen **C 11**
45 Walwick **F 7**
45 Walwick Grange **F 7**
40 Walworth **C 3**
12 Walwyn's Castle **F 2**
6 Wambrook **E 6**
43 Wamphraygate **B 12**
44 Wampool **H 1**
9 Wanborough, Surrey **A 10**
16 Wanborough, Wilts **F 3**
48 Wandel **G 2**
45 Wandon **C 11**
18 Wandsworth **F 3**
45 Wandylaw **A 9**
27 Wangford **G 8**
23 Wanlip **A 9**
48 Wanlockhead **H 2**
10 Wannock **H 4**
24 Wansford, Cambs. **F 2**
37 Wansford, Humber. **B 8**
18 Wanstead **E 4**
7 Wanstrow **B 10**
15 Wanswell **D 10**
16 Wantage **E 5**
15 Wapley **F 10**
23 Wappenbury **E 7**
23 Wappenham **H 9**
36 Warcop **D 9**
10 Warbleton **F 5**
9 Warblington **E 8**
17 Warborough **E 7**
25 Warboys **G 4**
34 Warbreck **C 2**
2 Warbstow **B 2**
30 Warburton **A 5**
27 Ward Green **J 4**
11 Warden **A 9**
23 Wardington **G 8**
48 Wardlaw, Borders **H 5**
47 Wardlaw, Strathclyde **E 8**
30 Wardle, Ches. **E 5**
35 Wardle, Lancs. **E 8**
23 Wardley **B 11**
31 Wardlow **C 10**
45 Wardon **F 7**
25 Wardy Hill **G 6**
18 Ware, Herts. **C 4**
11 Ware, Kent **B 11**
8 Wareham **G 1**
11 Warehorne **E 8**
45 Waren Mill **C 12**
45 Warenford **C 12**
45 Warenton **C 12**
18 Wareside **B 4**
25 Waresley, Cambs. **K 3**
22 Waresley, Heref. & Worc. **E 2**
17 Warfield **G 9**
5 Warfleet **L 7**
24 Wargate **C 3**
17 Wargrave **F 9**
26 Warham All Saints **A 3**
26 Warham St. Mary **A 2**
45 Wark, Northumb **E 7**
49 Wark, Northumb. **E 11**
4 Warkleigh **D 5**
23 Warkton **D 12**
23 Warkwork, Bucks. **H 8**
45 Warkworth, Northumb. **B 10**
40 Warlaby **F 4**
35 Warland **E 8**
3 Warleggan **C 8**
22 Warley **C 3**
10 Warlingham **B 2**
35 Warmfield **E 12**
30 Warmingham **D 5**
9 Warminghurst **D 12**
24 Warmington, Cambs. **F 2**
23 Warmington, War. **G 7**
7 Warminster **B 11**
11 Warmlake **C 7**
15 Warmley **G 10**
15 Warmley Tower **G 10**
36 Warmsworth **G 3**
7 Warmwell **H 11**
22 Warndon **F 2**
9 Warnford **D 8**
10 Warnham **E 1**
9 Warningcamp **E 11**
10 Warninglid **E 1**
31 Warren, Ches. **C 7**
12 Warren, Dyfed **G 3**
5 Warren House Inn **H 5**
17 Warren Row **F 9**
11 Warren Street **C 8**
23 Warrington, Bucks. **G 12**
30 Warrington, Ches. **A 5**
8 Warsash **E 6**
31 Warslow **D 9**
32 Warsop **C 3**
32 Warsop Vale **C 3**
36 Warter **B 6**
40 Warthermarske **G 2**
36 Warthill **B 4**
10 Wartling **G 5**
32 Wartnaby **H 4**
34 Warton, Lancs. **D 3**
39 Warton, Lancs. **H 7**
45 Warton, Northumb. **C 8**
22 Warton, War. **B 6**
44 Warwick, Cumb. **G 3**
22 Warwick, War. **F 6**
44 Warwick Bridge **G 3**
22 Warwickshire, Co. **F 6**
44 Warwicksland **E 3**
64 Wasbister **B 2**
38 Wasdale Head **D 4**
16 Wash Common **H 5**
3 Washaway **C 7**
5 Washbourne **K 7**
31 Washerwall **E 8**
6 Washfield **E 3**
40 Washfold **E 1**
6 Washford **B 4**
4 Washford Pyne **E 7**
33 Washingborough **C 7**
45 Washington, Tyne & Wear **G 11**
9 Washington, W. Sussex **E 12**
17 Wasing **H 7**
40 Waskerley **A 1**
22 Wasperton **F 6**
40 Wass **G 6**
6 Watchet **B 4**
16 Watchfield, Oxon **E 3**
7 Watchfield, Som. **B 7**
39 Watchgate **E 8**
43 Watchhill **G 12**
38 Watendlath **D 5**
5 Water, Devon **H 6**
35 Water, Lancs. **E 7**
18 Water End, Herts. **C 2**
36 Water End, Humber. **C 6**
24 Water Newton **F 2**
22 Water Orton **C 5**
17 Water Stratford **A 7**
14 Water Street **F 1**
38 Water Yeat **F 5**
25 Waterbeach **J 6**
44 Waterbeck **E 1**
26 Waterden **B 2**
17 Waterend **C 11**
31 Waterfall **E 9**
35 Waterfoot, Lancs. **E 7**
47 Waterfoot, Strath **D 10**
8 Waterford, Hants. **G 5**
18 Waterford, Herts. **B 3**
38 Waterhead, Cumb. **E 6**
43 Waterhead, Dumf. & Gall. **B 12**
43 Waterhead, Dumf. & Gall. **C 8**
47 Waterford, Strath **H 10**
59 Waterhead, Tayside **K 2**
48 Waterheads **D 5**
40 Waterhouses, Dur **A 5**
31 Waterhouses, Staffs. **E 9**
33 Watering Dyke Houses **B 7**
10 Wateringbury **C 6**
64 Wateringhouse **E 2**
15 Waterlane **D 12**
32 Waterloo, Derby **D 1**
8 Waterloo, Dorset **G 2**
12 Waterloo, Dyfed **G 3**
34 Waterloo, Merseyside **G 2**
26 Waterloo, Norf. **D 5**
62 Waterloo, Skye **F 6**
48 Waterloo, Strathclyde **D 1**
52 Waterloo, Tayside **C 5**
6 Waterloo Cross **E 4**
9 Waterlooville **E 8**
48 Watermeetings **H 2**
17 Waterperry **C 7**
6 Waterrow **D 4**
30 Waters Upton **H 5**
9 Watersfield **E 11**
44 Waterside, Cumb. **H 1**
58 Waterside Grampian **E 7**
42 Waterside, Strathclyde **A 5**
47 Waterside Strathclyde **E 9**
47 Waterside, Strathclyde **B 11**
17 Waterstock **D 7**
12 Waterston **F 3**
18 Watford, Herts. **D 1**
23 Watford, Northants. **E 9**
40 Wath, N. Yorks. **G 3**
40 Wath, N. Yorks. **H 2**
38 Wath Brow **D 3**
36 Wath upon Dearne **G 2**
15 Watley's End **F 9**
24 Watlington, Norf. **D 7**
17 Watlington, Oxon **E 8**
32 Watnall Chaworth **F 2**
61 Watten **B 11**
27 Wattisfield **H 3**
27 Wattisham **K 3**
21 Wattlesborough Heath **A 9**
37 Watton, Humberside **B 8**
26 Watton, Norf. **E 2**
18 Watton-at-Stone **B 3**
47 Wattston **B 12**
14 Wattstown **E 3**
55 Wauchan **L 3**
20 Waun Fawr **D 2**
13 Waunarlwydd **G 9**
28 Waunfawr **D 5**
14 Waunlwyd **D 5**
23 Wavendon **H 12**
44 Waverbridge **H 1**
30 Waverton, Ches. **D 3**
44 Waverton, Cumb. **H 1**
37 Wawne **C 8**
26 Waxham **C 7**
37 Waxholme **D 11**
6 Way Village **E 3**
10 Wayfield **B 6**
7 Wayford **F 7**
7 Waytown **F 8**
6 Weacombe **B 5**
16 Weald **D 4**
18 Wealdstone **E 2**
35 Weardley **C 11**
7 Weare **A 7**
4 Weare Giffard **D 3**
39 Wearhead **A 11**
39 Weasdale **E 9**
26 Weasenham All Saints **C 1**
26 Weasenham St. Peter **C 1**
30 Weaverham **C 5**
41 Weaverthorpe **H 9**
22 Webheath **E 4**
15 Webton **A 7**
58 Wedderlairs **D 6**
49 Wedderlie **D 9**
23 Weddington **C 7**
16 Wedhampton **H 2**
7 Wedmore **A 8**
22 Wednesbury **C 3**
22 Wednesfield **B 3**
17 Weedon **B 9**
23 Weedon Bec **F 9**
23 Weedon Lois **G 9**
22 Weeford **B 5**
4 Week, Devon **C 4**
4 Week, Devon **D 6**
4 Week St. Mary **F 1**
8 Weeke **C 6**
23 Weekely **D 12**
37 Weel **C 8**
19 Weeley **B 11**
19 Weeley Heath **B 11**
52 Weem **B 3**
21 Weeping Cross, Shropshire **A 10**
31 Weeping Cross, Staffs. **H 8**
27 Weeting **G 1**
34 Weeton, Lancs. **D 3**
35 Weeton, N. Yorks. **B 11**
49 Weetwoodhill **F 12**
35 Weir **F 7**
15 Weirend **B 9**
32 Welbeck Abbey **C 3**
26 Welborne **E 4**
33 Welbourn **E 7**
41 Welburn, N. Yorks. **G 7**
41 Welburn, N. Yorks **H 7**
40 Welbury **E 4**
33 Welby **F 7**
25 Welches Dam **G 6**
4 Welcombe **D 1**
23 Weldon **C 12**
16 Welford, Berks. **G 5**
23 Welford, Northants. **D 9**
22 Welford-on-Avon **G 5**
23 Welham **C 11**
18 Welham Green **C 2**
9 Well, Hants. **A 9**
33 Well, Lincs. **C 11**
40 Well, N. Yorks. **G 3**
7 Well Bottom **E 12**
17 Well End **E 9**
10 Well Hill **B 4**
6 Well Town **E 3**
22 Welland **H 2**
53 Wellbank **C 9**
43 Welldale **E 12**
22 Wellesbourne **G 6**
40 Wellfields **A 4**
59 Wellford **L 2**
18 Welling **F 5**
23 Wellingborough **E 12**
26 Wellingham **C 2**
33 Wellingore **E 7**
38 Wellington, Cumb. **E 3**
21 Wellington, Heref. & Worc. **H 10**
21 Wellington, Salop **A 12**
6 Wellington, Som. **D 5**
21 Wellington Heath **H 12**
21 Wellington Marsh **H 10**
15 Wellow, Avon **H 10**
8 Wellow, I.o.W. **G 5**
32 Wellow, Notts. **D 4**
7 Wells **B 9**
26 Wells-next-the-Sea **A 2**
58 Wells of Ytham **D 4**
23 Wellsborough **B 7**
5 Wellswood **J 8**
52 Wellwood **H 6**
24 Welney **F 6**
4 Welsford **D 1**
15 Welsh Bicknor **C 9**
30 Welsh Frankton **G 2**
12 Welsh Hook **D 3**
15 Welsh Newton **B 8**
14 Welsh St. Donats **G 4**
30 Welshampton **G 3**
21 Welshpool **B 8**
7 Welton, Avon **A 10**
38 Welton, VB. **A 6**
37 Welton, Humberside **D 7**
33 Welton, Lincs. **B 7**
23 Welton, Northants **E 9**
33 Welton le Marsh **C 11**
33 Welton le Wold **B 10**
37 Welwick **E 11**
18 Welwyn **B 2**
18 Welwyn Garden City **C 2**
30 Wem **G 4**
6 Wembdon **C 6**
18 Wembley **E 2**
5 Wembury **L 4**
4 Wembworthy **E 5**
47 Wemyss Bay **B 7**
25 Wendens Ambo **L 6**
16 Wendlebury **B 6**
26 Wendling **D 2**
17 Wendover **C 9**
2 Wendron **G 4**
25 Wendy **K 4**
27 Wenhaston **H 7**
25 Wennington, Cambs. **G 3**
39 Wennington, Lancs. **H 8**
18 Wennington, London **F 5**
31 Wensley, Derby. **D 11**
40 Wensley, N. Yorks. **F 1**
36 Wentbridge **E 3**
21 Wentor **C 9**
25 Wentworth, Cambs. **G 6**
35 Wentworth, S. Yorks **G 12**
14 Wenvoe **G 4**
21 Weobley **G 9**
21 Weobley Marsh **G 9**
24 Wareham **E 8**
22 Wergs **B 2**
28 Wern, Gwynedd **F 5**
14 Wern, Powys. **C 4**
13 Wernffrwd **H 8**
15 Wernyrheolydd **C 7**
24 Werrington, Cambs. **E 3**
3 Werrington, Corn. **A 10**
31 Werrington, Suffolk **E 8**
30 Wervin **C 3**
34 Wesham **D 3**
32 Wessington **D 1**
57 West Aberchalder **G 1**
26 West Acre **D 1**
16 West Adderbury **A 5**
6 West Adsborough **C 6**
49 West Allerdean **E 12**
45 West Allotment **F 11**
5 West Alvington **L 6**
8 West Amesbury **B 3**
4 West Anstey **C 7**
4 West Ash **D 2**
33 West Ashby **C 9**
9 West Ashling **E 9**
7 West Ashton **A 12**
40 West Auckland **C 2**
41 West Ayton **G 10**
59 West Balhagarty **K 5**
6 West Bagborough **C 5**
33 West Barkwith **B 8**
41 West Barnby **D 8**
49 West Barns **B 9**
42 West Bar **G 4**
26 West Barsham **B 2**
7 West Bay **G 8**
26 West Beckham **B 4**
17 West Bedfont **G 11**
45 West Benridge **D 10**
19 West Bergholt **A 9**
7 West Bexington **H 9**
24 West Bilney **D 8**
49 West Blackadder **D 11**

10 West Blatchington G 2
48 West Bold F 6
45 West Boldon G 11
43 West Bowhill D 12
35 West Bowling D 10
26 West Bradenham E 2
34 West Bradford C 6
7 West Bradley C 9
35 West Bretton F 11
32 West Bridgford G 3
22 West Bromwich C 4
47 West Browncastle E 11
4 West Buckland, Devon C 5
6 West Buckland, Som. D 5
64 West Burrafirth D 6
9 West Burton, W. Sussex E 11
39 West Burton, N. Yorks F 12
40 West Butsfield A 1
36 West Butterwick G 6
17 West Byfleet H 11
49 West Byres C 7
26 West Caister D 8
48 West Calder C 3
7 West Camel D 9
58 West Cannahars E 7
36 West Carr F 5
47 West Cauldcoats E 11
7 West Chaldon H 11
16 West Challow E 4
7 West Chelborough F 9
45 West Chevington C 10
9 West Chiltington D 12
9 West Chiltington Common D 12
7 West Chinnock E 8
8 West Chisenbury A 3
9 West Clandon A 11
11 West Cliffe D 12
61 West Clyne F 9
61 West Clyth D 11
7 West Coker E 8
7 West Compton, Dorset G 9
7 West Compton, Som. B 9
36 West Cowick E 4
7 West Cranmore B 10
27 West Creeting Grn. J 4
57 West Croftmore H 5
13 West Cross H 9
59 West Cullerley G 5
44 West Curthwaite H 2
46 West Darlochan G 2
8 West Dean, Hants. C 4
9 West Dean, Sus. E 10
24 West Deeping E 2
30 West Derby A 3
24 West Dereham E 7
45 West Ditchburn A 9
4 West Down B 4
18 West Drayton, London F 1
32 West Drayton, Notts. C 4
45 West Edington E 9
37 West Ella D 8
15 West End, Avon G 8
17 West End, Berks. G 9
28 West End, Gwynedd G 3
8 West End, Hants. E 6
18 West End, Herts C 3
37 West End, Humber. D 7
37 West End, Lincs. G 11
26 West End, Norf. D 8
48 West End, Strathclyde E 2
17 West End, Surrey H 10
8 West End, Wilts. D 1
45 West Fallodon A 10
10 West Farleigh C 6
30 West Felton H 2
10 West Firle G 3
16 West Ginge E 5
13 West Glamorgan, Co. G 10
16 West Grafton H 3
17 West Green H 8
8 West Grimstead D 4
10 West Grinstead F 1
36 West Haddlesey D 3
23 West Haddon E 9
16 West Hagbourne E 6
22 West Hagley D 3
44 West Hall F 4
32 West Hallam F 2
37 West Halton E 7
18 West Ham F 4
16 West Hanney E 5
19 West Hanningfield D 7
36 West Hardwick E 2
8 West Harnham C 3
7 West Harptree A 9
45 West Harrington H 11
40 West Hartlepool B 5
6 West Hatch D 6
15 West Hay H 8
24 West Head E 7
61 West Helmsdale E 9
16 West Hendred E 5
41 West Heslerton H 9
15 West Hill, Avon G 8
6 West Hill, Devon. G 4
10 West Hoathly E 2
7 West Holme H 12
49 West Hopes C 8
18 West Horndon E 6
7 West Horrington A 9
9 West Horsley A 12
45 West Horton C 11
11 West Hougham D 11
6 West Huntspill B 6
17 West Hyde E 11
11 West Hythe E 10
16 West Ilsley F 6
9 West Itchenor F 9
33 West Keal D 10
16 West Kennett G 2
47 West Kilbride E 7
10 West Kingsdown B 5
15 West Kington F 11
58 West Kinharrachie D 7
58 West Kinnernie F 5
30 West Kirby B 1
41 West Knapton H 9
7 West Knighton G 10
7 West Knoyle C 11
45 West Kyloe B 11
7 West Lambrook D 7
11 West Langdon C 11
61 West Langwell F 7
9 West Lavington, W. Sussex D 10
8 West Lavington, Wiltshire A 2
40 West Layton D 2
32 West Leake G 3
49 West Learmouth F 11
26 West Lexham D 1
36 West Lilling A 4
45 West Linkhall A 10
48 West Linton D 4
9 West Liss C 9
15 West Littleton G 11
3 West Looe D 9
6 West Luccombe B 2
7 West Lulworth H 11
41 West Lutton H 9
7 West Lydford C 9
45 West Lyham C 12
7 West Lyng C 7
24 West Lynn D 7
45 West Mains, Northumb. B 12
47 West Mains, Strathclyde D 8
48 West Mains, Strathclyde D 2
10 West Malling B 5
22 West Malvern G 1
9 West Marden E 9
32 West Markham C 4
37 West Marsh F 10
35 West Marton B 8
9 West Meon D 8
19 West Mersea C 10
22 West Midlands, Co. C 4
7 West Milton G 8
11 West Minster A 8
17 West Molesey G 12
8 West Moors F 2
7 West Morden G 12
49 West Morrison F 8
41 West Ness G 7
37 West Newton, Humberside C 9
24 West Newton, Norfolk C 8
5 West Ogwell J 7
7 West Orchard E 11
16 West Overton G 2
8 West Parley F 2
5 West Panson G 2
10 West Peckham C 5
45 West Pelton H 10
7 West Pennard B 9
2 West Pentire D 5
6 West Porlock B 2
4 West Putford D 2
6 West Quantoxhead B 5
45 West Rainton H 11
33 West Rasen A 8
26 West Raynham C 2
40 West Rounton E 4
25 West Row H 8
26 West Rudham C 1
26 West Runton A 5
49 West Saltoun C 7
4 West Sandford F 7
64 West Sandwick B 7
40 West Scrafton G 1
48 West Sidewood D 3
43 West Skelston C 9
45 West Sleekburn E 11
26 West Somerton D 7
7 West Stafford G 10
36 West Stockwith H 6
9 West Stoke E 9
39 West Stonesdale E 11
7 West Stoughton A 7
7 West Stour D 11
11 West Stourmouth B 11
27 West Stow H 1
16 West Stowell H 2
60 West Strathan B 6
8 West Stratton B 6
11 West Street C 8
40 West Summer Side G 2
10 West Sussex, Co. E 1
40 West Tanfield G 3
3 West Taphouse C 8
46 West Tarbert C 3
49 West Third F 9
45 West Thirston C 10
9 West Thorney F 9
18 West Thurrock F 6
9 West Tisted C 8
52 West Tofts D 6
33 West Torrington B 8
15 West Town, Avon G 8
15 West Town, Avon H 8
9 West Town, Hants F 8
21 West Town, Heref. & Worc. F 10
8 West Tytherley C 4
16 West Tytherton G 1
24 West Walton D 6
24 West Walton Highway D 6
4 West Warlington E 6
53 West Wemyss H 8
15 West Wick H 7
25 West Wickham, Cambs. K 7
18 West Wickham, London G 4
12 West Williamston F 4
8 West Willow D 4
27 West Winch D 7
8 West Winterslow C 4
9 West Wittering F 9
40 West Witton F 1
45 West Woodburn D 7
16 West Woodhay H 5
7 West Woodlands B 11
9 West Worldham B 9
25 West Wratting K 7
17 West Wycombe E 9
64 West Yell C 7
35 West Yorkshire, Co. D 10
4 Westacott C 5
11 Westbere B 10
32 Westborough F 6
8 Westbourne, Dorset G 2
9 Westbourne, W. Sussex E 9
16 Westbrook G 5
17 Westbury, Bucks. A 7
21 Westbury, Salop A 9
7 Westbury, Wilts. A 12
7 Westbury Leigh A 12
15 Westbury on Trym G 9
15 Westbury-on-Severn C 10
7 Westbury-sub-Mendip A 8
34 Westby D 3
9 Westcatt A 12
19 Westcliff on Sea E 8
7 Westcombe B 10
16 Westcote B 3
17 Westcott, Bucks B 8
6 Westcott, Devon F 4
16 Westcott Barton B 5
10 Westdean H 4
57 Wester Aberchalder G 1
52 Wester Balgedie G 6
48 Wester Causewayend C 3
52 Wester Clunie A 4
49 Wester Essenside G 7
58 Wester Fintray F 6
60 Wester Greenyards G 6
48 Wester Happrew E 4
49 Wester Housebryres F 8
56 Wester Milton D 5
53 Wester Newburn G 9
48 Wester Ochiltree B 3
49 Wester Pencaitland C 7
64 Wester Quarff E 7
56 Wester Rarichie B 4
64 Wester Skeld D 6
54 Wester Slumbay F 3
61 Westerdale, Highland C 10
41 Westerdale, N. Yorks E 7
27 Westerfield K 5
9 Westergate F 10
10 Westerham C 3
45 Westerhope F 10
15 Westerleigh F 10
64 Westermill E 3
40 Westerton, Dur. B 3
58 Westerton, Grampian C 3
53 Westerton, Tayside B 11
9 Westerton, W. Sussex E 10
58 Westertown C 3
38 Westfield, Cumb. B 2
11 Westfield, E. Sussex F 7
58 Westfield, Grampian E 7
22 Westfield, Heref. & Worc. G 1
61 Westfield, Highland B 10
26 Westfield, Norf. D 3
45 Westfield, Northumb. D 12
7 Westfields F 10
52 Westfields of Rattray C 6
39 Westgate, Dur. A 11
36 Westgate, Lincs. F 5
26 Westgate, Norf. B 3
11 Westgate on Sea A 11
44 Westgillsyke F 2
27 Westhall G 7
7 Westham, Dorset H10
10 Westham, E. Sussex H 5
7 Westham, Som. B 7
9 Westhampnett E 10
58 Westhaugh E 4
7 Westhay B 8
34 Westhead F 3
17 Westheath H 9
21 Westhide H 11
59 Westhill G 6
21 Westhope, Heref. & Worc. G 10
21 Westhope, Salop D 10
24 Westhorpe, Lincs. B 3
27 Westhorpe, Suff. H 3
34 Westhoughton G 5
39 Westhouse H 9
32 Westhouses D 2
10 Westhumble C 1
4 Westleigh, Devon C 3
6 Westleigh, Devon D 4
34 Westleigh, Gtr. Manchester G 5
27 Westleton H 7
21 Westley, Salop B 9
27 Westley, Suffolk J 1
25 Westley Waterless K 7
17 Westlington C 8
44 Westlinton G 2
11 Westmarsh B 11
10 Westmeston G 2
18 Westmill A 4
18 Westminster F 3
53 Westmuir B 8
64 Westness B 2
43 Westnewton, Cumb. G 12
49 Westnewton, Northumb. F 11
15 Weston, Avon H 10
30 Weston, Ches. E 6
30 Weston, Ches. B 4
6 Weston, Devon F 5
6 Weston, Devon G 5
7 Weston, Dorset H 7
9 Weston, Hants. D 8
21 West, Heref. & Worcs G 9
18 Weston, Herts. A 3
24 Weston, Lincs. C 4
35 Weston, N. Yorks. B 10
23 Weston, Northants G 9
32 Weston, Notts. C 5
21 Weston, Salop C 11
21 Weston, Salop E 9
30 Weston, Salop G 4
31 Weston, Staffs. G 8
48 Weston, Strathclyde E 3
7 Weston Bampfylde D 9
21 Weston Beggard H 11
23 Weston by Welland C 11
25 Weston Colville K 7
31 Weston Coyney F 8
23 Weston Favell F 11
25 Weston Green K 7
22 Weston Heath A 1
24 Weston Hills C 4
15 Weston-in-Gordano G 8
30 Weston Jones H 6
26 Weston Longville D 4
30 Weston Lullingfields H 3
22 Weston-on-Avon G 5
16 Weston-on-the-Grn B 6
9 Weston Patrick B 8
30 Weston Rhyn G 1
15 Weston Road G 8
22 Weston Sudedge H 5
14 Weston-super-Mare H 6
17 Weston Turville C 9
15 Weston under Penyard B 9
23 Weston under Wetherley E 7
23 Weston Underwood, Bucks G 12
31 Weston Underwood, Derbyshire F 11
32 Weston Upon Trent G 1
22 Weston-under-Lizard A 2
15 Westonbirt E 11
25 Westoning M 1
7 Westonzoyland C 7
36 Westow A 5
7 Westport, Som. D 7
46 Westport, Strathclyde G 2
16 Westridge Green F 6
48 Westrigg C 2
49 Westruther D 9
24 Westry F 5
32 Westville E 2
38 Westward, Cumbria A 5
45 Westward, Durham G 9
4 Westward Ho C 3
44 Westwater E 1
11 Westwell, Kent C 8
16 Westwell, Oxon C 3
11 Westwell Leacon C 8
25 Westwick, Cambs. J 5
40 Westwick, Dur. D 1
6 Westwood, Devon F 4
47 Westwood, Strath. D 11
15 Westwood, Wilts. H 11
36 Westwoodside G 5
40 Wether Cote F 6
44 Wetheral H 3
35 Wetherby B 12
27 Wetherden J 3
27 Wetheringsett J 4
25 Wethersfield M 8
64 Wethersta C 7
27 Wetherup Street J 4
31 Wetley Rocks E 8
30 Wettenhall D 5
31 Wetton E 9
37 Wetwang A 7
30 Wetwood G 6
16 Wexcombe H 4
17 Wexham Street F 10
26 Weybourne A 4
27 Weybread G 5
17 Weybridge H 11
9 Weycroft F 6
61 Weydale A 10
8 Weyhill B 5
7 Weymouth G 7
17 Whaddon, Bucks. A 9
25 Whaddon, Cambs. K 4
15 Whaddon, Glos. C 11
8 Whaddon, Wilts. C 3
39 Whale C 7
32 Whaley C 2
31 Whaley Bridge B 8
32 Whaley Thorns C 3
34 Whalley D 6
45 Whalton E 9
24 Whaplode C 4
24 Whaplode Drove D 4
24 Whaplode St. Catherine D 4
39 Wharfe H 10
34 Wharles D 3
45 Wharmley F 7
35 Wharncliffe Side H 11
36 Wharram-le-Street A 6
30 Wharton, Ches. D 5
21 Wharton, Heref. & Worc. G 10
40 Whashton E 2
39 Whasset G 7
22 Whatcote H 6
22 Whateley B 6
27 Whatfield K 3
10 Whatlington F 6
31 Whatstandwell E 11
32 Whatton F 5
42 Whauphill G 5
26 Wheatacre F 8
18 Wheathampstead C 2
21 Wheathill D 11
9 Wheatley, Hants. B 9
17 Wheatley, Oxon. D 7
40 Wheatley Hill A 4
35 Wheatley Lane C 7
22 Wheaton Aston A 2
6 Wheddon Cross B 3
58 Wheedlemont E 2
17 Wheeler's Green G 8
9 Wheelerstreet B 11
30 Wheelock D 6
30 Wheelock Heath D 6
34 Wheelton E 5
59 Wheen K 1
36 Wheldrake C 4
16 Whelford D 3
38 Whelpo A 5
40 Whenby H 6
27 Whepstead J 1
27 Wherstead L 5
8 Wherwell B 5
31 Wheston C 10
10 Whetsted C 5
23 Whetstone B 9
16 Whichford A 4
38 Whicham, Cumb. G 4
45 Whickham, Tyne & Wear G 10
5 Whiddon Down G 6
53 Whigstreet C 9
23 Whilton F 9
4 Whimble F 2
6 Whimple F 4
26 Whimpwell Green C 7
26 Whinburgh E 3
49 Whinkerstones E 10
43 Whinnie Liggate F 8
58 Whinnyfold D 8
8 Whippingham G 6
17 Whipsnade B 11
6 Whipton G 3
23 Whissendine A 11
26 Whissonsett C 2
17 Whistley Green G 9
23 Whiston, Northants. F 11
30 Whiston, Merseyside A 3
32 Whiston, S. Yorks. A 2
22 Whiston, Staffs. A 2
31 Whiston, Staffs. F 9
38 Whitbeck G 3
21 Whitbourne G 12
22 Whitbourne Ford F 1
48 Whitburn, Lothian C 2
45 Whitburn, Tyne & Wear G 12
45 Whitburn Colliery G 12
58 Whitby, Cheshire C 3
41 Whitby, N. Yorks. D 9
44 Whitcastles D 1
15 Whitchurch, Avon G 9
17 Whitchurch, Bucks. B 9
5 Whitchurch, Devon H 4
12 Whitchurch, Dyfed D 2
8 Whitchurch, Hants. A 6
15 Whitchurch, Heref. & Worc. C 8
17 Whichurch, Oxon F 7
30 Whitchurch, Salop F 4
14 Whitchurch, S. Glam. F 5
7 Whitchurch Canonicorum G 7
17 Whitchurch Hill F 7
7 Whitcombe G 10
21 Whitcott Keysett D 8
34 White Chapel C 4
34 White Coppice E 5
6 White Cross, Avon A 9
6 White Cross, Devon. G 4
7 White Lackington F 10
22 White Ladies Aston G 3
13 White Mill E 8
19 White Notley B 8
33 White Pit B 11
18 White Roding C 5
21 White Stone H 11
17 White Waltham F 9
56 Whiteacen E 8
22 Whiteacre Heath C 5
55 Whitebridge H 8
15 Whitebrook D 8
49 Whiteburn E 8
42 Whitecairn F 3
58 Whitecairns F 7
48 Whitecastle E 3
48 Whitecraig B 6
15 Whitecroft D 9
42 Whitecrook F 3
48 Whitecross, Central B 2
3 Whitecross, Corn. B 7
61 Whiteface G 7
46 Whitefarland E 4
42 Whitefaulds A 4
35 Whitefields, Manchester G 7
52 Whitefield, Tayside D 6
6 Whitefirld, Som. C 4
58 Whiteford E 5
6 Whitehall, Devon E 5
64 Whitehall, Orkney B 4
44 Whitehaugh B 3
38 Whitehaven C 2
43 Whitehill, Dumf. & Gall. D 12
58 Whitehill, Grampian B 3
9 Whitehill, Hants. C 9
58 Whitehills, Grampian A 4
58 Whitehouse, Grampian F 4
16 Whitehouse, Strathclyde C 3
49 Whitekirk A 8
59 Whiteknowes G 3
7 Whitelackington E 7
49 Whitelaw D 11

49 Whitelee F 8
36 Whiteley E 3
9 Whiteley Bank H 7
31 Whiteley Green B 8
17 Whiteley Village H 11
10 Whitemans Green E 2
56 Whitemire D 5
3 Whitemoor D 7
8 Whitenap D 5
8 Whiteparish D 4
58 Whiterashes E 6
15 Whiteshill D 11
48 Whiteside, Lothian C 2
44 Whiteside, Northumb. F 5
10 Whitesmith G 4
6 Whitestaunton E 6
4 Whitestone, Devon A 4
4 Whitestone, Devon F 7
59 Whitestone, Grampian H 4
58 Whitestones B 6
15 Whiteway C 12
6 Whiteway House H 2
34 Whitewell B 5
5 Whiteworks J 5
56 Whitewreath D 8
15 Whitfield, Avon E 10
48 Whitfield, Borders D 4
11 Whitfield, Kent D 11
23 Whitfield, Northants. H 9
44 Whitefield, Northumb. G 6
29 Whitford, Clwyd B 10
6 Whitford, Devon G 6
36 Whitgift E 6
31 Whitgreave G 7
42 Whithorn G 5
46 Whiting Bay G 5
24 Whitington E 8
12 Whitland E 5
47 Whitletts G 8
15 Whitley, Wilts. H 12
45 Whitley Bay F 11
45 Whitley Chapel G 7
35 Whitley Lower E 11
22 Whitlock's End D 4
15 Whitminster D 11
31 Whitmore F 7
6 Whitnage E 4
21 Whitney H 8
38 Whitrigg, Cumb. A 4
44 Whitrigg, Cumb. G 1
44 Whitriggs B 4
8 Whitsbury D 3
4 Whitsleigh Barton D 4
49 Whitsome D 11
49 Whitsomehill D 11
15 Whitson F 7
11 Whitstable A 9
4 Whitstone F 1
45 Whittingham B 9
21 Whittingslow D 9
32 Whittington, Derby. C 1
16 Whittington, Glos. B 1
22 Whittington, Heref. & Worc. G 2
39 Whittington, Lancs. H 8
30 Whittington, Salop G 2
22 Whittington, Staffs A 5
22 Whittington, Staffs. D 2
34 Whittle-le-Woods E 5
23 Whittlebury H 10
24 Whittlesey F 4
25 Whittlesford K 6
34 Whittlestone Head E 6
49 Whitton, Borders G 10
40 Whitton, Cleveland C 4
37 Whitton, Humber. E 7
45 Whitton, Northumb. C 9
21 Whitton, Powys F 8
21 Whitton, Salop E 11
27 Whitton, Suffolk K 4
16 Whittonditch G 4
45 Whittonstall G 9
16 Whitway H 6
32 Whitwell, Derby. C 3
18 Whitwell, Herts. B 2
9 Whitwell, I.o.W. H 7
23 Whitwell, Leics. A 12
40 Whitwell, N. Yorks. E 3
41 Whitwell-on-the- Hill H 7
23 Whitwick A 8
36 Whitwood E 2
35 Whitworth E 7
30 Whixal G 4
36 Whixley A 2
22 Whoberly D 6
40 Whorlton, Dur. D 1
40 Whorlton, N. Yorks. E 5
44 Whygate E 6
21 Whyle F 11
10 Whyteleafe B 2
15 Wibdon E 9
23 Wibtoft C 8
11 Wichling B 8
15 Wick, Avon G 10
8 Wick, Dorset G 3
22 Wick, Heref. & Worc. H 3
61 Wick, Highalnd C 12
14 Wick, Mid Glam. G 3
6 Wick, Som. B 5
7 Wick, Som. D 7
9 Wick, W. Sussex F 11
6 Wick, Wilts. D 3
17 Wick Hill H 9
15 Wick St. Lawrence H 7
25 Wicken, Cambs. H 7
23 Wicken, Northants. H 10
25 Wicken Bonhunt M 6
33 Wickenby B 8
22 Wichenford F 1
32 Wickersley A 2
19 Wickford E 7
16 Wickham, Berks. G 5
9 Wickham, Hants. E 7
19 Wickham Bishops C 8
16 Wickham Heath G 5
27 Wickham Market K 6
27 Wickham St. Paul L 1
27 Wickham Skeith H 4
27 Wickham Street, Suffolk H 4
27 Wickham Street, Suffolk K 1
11 Wickhambreaux B 10
25 Wickhambrook K 8
22 Wickhamford H 4
26 Wickhampton E 7
26 Wicklewood E 4
26 Wickmere B 5
10 Wickstreet G 4
15 Wickwar E 10
25 Widdington M 6
45 Widdrington C 10
45 Widdrington Sta. D 10
45 Wide Open F 10
5 Widecombe in the Moor H 6
3 Widegates D 10
2 Widemouth A 2
64 Widewall E 2
19 Widford, Essex C 7
18 Widford, Hertford B 4
17 Widmer End D 9
32 Widmerpool G 4
30 Widnes B 4
6 Widworthy F 5
34 Wigan F 5
8 Wigbeth E 2
6 Wiggaton G 5
24 Wiggenhall St. Germans D 7
24 Wiggenhall St. Mary Magdalen D 7
24 Wiggenhall St. Mary the Virgin D 7
24 Wiggenhall St. Peter D 7
17 Wigginton, Herts. C 10
36 Wigginton, N. Yorks A 4
16 Wigginton, Oxon A 5
22 Wigginton, Staffs. A 6
16 Wigginton Heath A 5
35 Wiggleworth A 7
44 Wiggonby H 1
9 Wiggonholt D 11
36 Wighill B 3
8 Wight, Isle of, Co. G 6
26 Wighton B 2
8 Wigley D 5
21 Wigmore, Heref. & Worc. E 9
11 Wigmore, Kent B 7
32 Wigsley C 6
25 Wigsthorpe G 1
23 Wigston Magna B 9
24 Wigtoft B 4
44 Wigton H 1
42 Wigtown F 5
35 Wigtwizzle G 11
35 Wike C 12
23 Wilbarston C 11
36 Wilberfoss B 5
25 Wilburton H 6
26 Wilby, Norfolk F 3
23 Wilby, Northants E 12
27 Wilby, Suffolk H 5
16 Wilcot H 2
30 Wilcott H 2
15 Wilcrick E 7
31 Wildboarclough C 8
25 Wilden, Beds. K 2
22 Wilden, Heref & Worc. E 2
8 Wildhern A 5
36 Wildsworth G 6
32 Wilford F 3
30 Wilkesley F 5
61 Wilkhaven H 9
48 Wilkieston C 4
6 Willand E 4
30 Willaston, Ches. B 2
30 Willaston, Ches. E 5
23 Willen H 12
22 Willenhall, W. Midlands B 3
23 Willenhall, W. Midlands E 7
37 Willerby, Humber. D 8
41 Willerby, N. Yorks. G 10
22 Willersey H 4
21 Willersley H 8
11 Willesborough D 9
18 Willesden E 2
4 Willesleigh C 5
23 Willey Leics D 8
21 Willey, Salop C 12
9 Willey Green A 11
23 Williamscot H 8
18 Willian A 2
18 Willingale C 6
4 Willingcott B 4
10 Willingdon H 5
25 Willingham, Cambs. H 5
32 Willingham, Lincs. B 6
25 Willington, Beds. K 2
31 Willington, Derby. G 11
40 Willington, Dur. B 2
22 Willington, War. H 6
30 Willington Corner D 4
36 Willitoft D 5
6 Williton B 4
44 Willmontswick G 6
33 Willoughby, Lincs. C 11
23 Willoughby, War. E 8
32 Willoughby on the Wolds H 4
23 Willoughby Waterleys C 9
32 Willoughton A 6
19 Willows Green B 7
15 Willsbridge G 10
5 Willsworthy H 4
22 Wilmcote F 5
6 Wilmington, Devon F 5
10 Wilmington, Kent A 4
10 Wilmington, E. Sussex H 4
31 Wilmslow B 7
22 Wilnecote B 6
34 Wilpshire D 5
35 Wilsden D 9
33 Wilsford, Lincs. F 7
8 Wilsford, Wilts. B 3
16 Wilsford, Wilts H 2
25 Wilshamstead L 2
35 Wilsill A 10
10 Wilsley Pound D 6
15 Wilson, Heref. & Worc. B 9
32 Wilson, Leics. H 1
48 Wilsontown D 2
24 Wilsthorpe D 2
17 Wilstone C 10
44 Wilton, Borders B 3
40 Wilton, Cleveland C 6
38 Wilton, Cumb. D 3
16 Wilton, Hants. H 4
15 Wilton, Heref. & Worc B 9
41 Wilton, N. Yorks G 8
8 Wilton, Wilts. C 3
16 Wiltshire, Co. G 2
25 Wimbish L 7
25 Wimbish Green M 7
18 Wimbledon G 2
24 Wimblington F 5
8 Wimborne Minster F 1
8 Wimborne St. Giles E 2
24 Wimbotsham E 7
25 Wimpole Lodge K 4
22 Wimpstone G 5
7 Wincanton C 10
9 Winchfield A 9
30 Wincham C 5
48 Winchburgh B 4
16 Winchcombe Al
11 Winchelsea F 8
11 Winchelsea Beach F 8
8 Winchester C 6
10 Winchet Hill D 6
17 Winchmore Hill E 10
31 Wincle D 8
38 Windermere E 6
23 Winderton H 7
17 Windlesham H 10
31 Windley F 11
31 Windmill B 10
10 Windmill Hill, E. Sussex G 5
6 Windmill Hill, Som. E 6
16 Windrush C 3
44 Windshielknowe C 4
17 Windsor G 10
15 Windsoredge D 11
47 Windy Yet D 9
59 Windyedge H 6
53 Windygates G 8
49 Windywalls F 10
10 Wineham F 1
37 Winestead E 10
35 Winewall C 8
27 Winfarthing G 4
15 Winford, Avon H 8
9 Winford, I.o.W. H 7
21 Winforton H 8
7 Winfrith Newburgh H 11
17 Wing, Bucks. B 9
23 Wing, Leics. B 12
40 Wingate A 4
34 Wingates, Manchester F 5
45 Wingates, Northumb. D 9
32 Wingerworth C 1
17 Wingfield, Beds B 11
27 Wingfield, Suffolk H 5
7 Wingfield, Wilts. A 11
11 Wingham B 11
11 Wingmore C 10
17 Wingrave B 9
32 Winkburn D 4
17 Winkfield G 9
17 Winkfield Row G 10
17 Winkfield Street G 10
31 Winkhill E 9
4 Winkleigh E 5
40 Winksley H 3
8 Winkton F 3
45 Winlaton G 10
45 Winlaton Mill G 10
61 Winless B 12
34 Winmarleigh B 3
8 Winnall, Hants. C 6
15 Winnall, Heref. & Worc. A 7
2 Winnard's Perch C 6
17 Winnersh G 8
38 Winscales C 3
15 Winscombe H 7
30 Winsford, Ches. D 5
6 Winsford, Som. C 3
7 Winsham F 7
31 Winshill H 11
13 Winsh-wen G 10
39 Winskill B 8
9 Winslade A 8
15 Winsley H 11
17 Winslow A 8
16 Winson C 2
8 Winsor E 5
38 Winster, Cumbria F 6
31 Winster, Derby. D 11
40 Winston, Dur. D 2
27 Winston, Suff. J 5
15 Winstone C 12
4 Winswell E 4
7 Winterborne Clenston F 11
7 Winterborne Herringston G 10
7 Winterborne Houghton F 11
7 Winterborne Kingston F 11
7 Winterborne Monkton G 10
7 Winterborne Stickland F 11
7 Winterborne Whitechurch F 11
7 Winterborne Zelston F 12
15 Winterbourne, Avon F 9
16 Winterbourne, Berks. G 5
7 Winterbourne Abbas G 9
16 Winterbourne Bassett G 2
8 Winterbourne Dauntsey C 3
15 Winterbourne Down F 10
8 Winterbourne Earls C 3
8 Winterbourne Gunner C 3
16 Winterbourne Monkton G 2
7 Winterbourne Steepleton G 9
8 Winterbourne Stoke B 2
35 Winterburn A 8
48 Wintercleugh H 2
37 Winteringham E 7
30 Winterley E 6
35 Wintersett F 12
44 Wintershields F 4
8 Winterslow C 4
37 Winterton E 7
26 Winterton-on-Sea D 8
33 Winthorpe, Lincs. D 12
32 Winthorpe, Notts. E 5
39 Winton, Cumbria D 10
8 Winton, Dorset G 2
40 Winton, N. Yorks. F 4
41 Wintringham H 9
25 Winwick, Cambs. G 2
34 Winwick, Cheshire H 5
23 Winwick, Northants. E 9
31 Wirksworth E 11
30 Wirswall F 4
24 Wisbech E 6
24 Wisbech St. Mary E 5
9 Wisborough Green C 11
47 Wishaw, Strathclyde D 12
22 Wishaw, War. C 5
17 Wisley H 11
33 Wispington C 9
27 Wissett G 6
21 Wistanstow D 10
30 Wistanswick G 5
30 Wistaston E 5
30 Wistaston Green E 5
25 Wistow, Cambs. G 4
12 Wiston, Dyfed E 4
36 Wistow, N. Yorks. D 4
48 Wiston, Strathclyde F 2
34 Wiswell C 6
25 Witcham G 6
8 Witchampton E 1
25 Witchford G 6
19 Witham B 8
7 Witham Friary B 11
24 Witham on the Hill D 2
33 Withcall B 10
10 Witherenden Hill E 5
4 Witheridge E 7
23 Witherley B 7
33 Withern B 11
37 Withernsea D 11
37 Withernwick C 9
27 Withersdale Street G 6
25 Withersfield K 7
39 Witherslack G 7
3 Withiel C 7
6 Withiel Florey C 3
16 Withington, Glos. C 1
21 Withington, Heref. & Worc. H 11
35 Withington, Manchester H 7
21 Withington, Salop A 11
31 Withington, Staffs. G 9
30 Withington Green C 6
21 Withington Marsh H 11
6 Withleigh E 3
34 Withnell E 5
23 Withybrook D 8
6 Withycombe B 3
6 Withycombe Raleigh H 4
10 Withyham E 4
6 Withypool C 2
9 Witley B 11
27 Witnesham K 5
16 Witney C 5
24 Wittering E 2
11 Wittersham E 7
22 Witton, Heref. & Worc. F 2
59 Witton, Tayside K 3
45 Witton Gilbert H 10
40 Witton le Wear B 2
40 Witton Park B 2
6 Wiveliscombe C 4
9 Wivelrod B 8
10 Wivelsfield F 2
10 Wivelsfield Green F 2
19 Wivenhoe B 10
19 Wivenhoe Cross B 10
26 Wiveton A 3
19 Wix A 11
22 Wixford G 4
25 Wixoe L 8
17 Woburn A 10
23 Woburn Sands H 12
17 Woking H 11
17 Wokingham G 9
5 Wolborough J 7
37 Wold Newton, Humberside G 10
41 Wold Newton, Humberside H 10
10 Woldingham C 3
48 Wolfclyde F 3
24 Wolferton C 7
52 Wolfhill D 6
12 Wolf's Castle D 3
12 Wolfsdale E 3
49 Woll G 7
23 Wollaston, Northants. F 12
21 Wollaston, Salop A 9
30 Wollerton G 5
31 Wolseley H 9
40 Wolsingham A 1
31 Wolstanton E 7
23 Wolston E 7
16 Wolvercote C 6
22 Wolverhampton B 2
22 Wolverley, Heref. & Worc. D 2
30 Wolverley, Salop G 3
23 Wolverton, Bucks. H 11
16 Wolverton, Hants H 6
22 Wolverton, War. F 5
16 Wolverton Com H 6
15 Wolvesnewton D 8
23 Wolvey C 8
40 Wolviston C 5
41 Wombleton G 7
22 Wombourn C 2
36 Wombwell G 2
11 Womenswold C 11
36 Womersley E 3
9 Wonersh B 11
5 Wonsan G 5
17 Wooburn E 10
17 Wooburn Green E 10
26 Wood Dalling C 4
25 Wood End, Beds. K 1
25 Wood End, Beds. K 2
18 Wood End, Herts. A 3
22 Wood End, War. B 6
22 Wood End, War. E 4
33 Wood Enderby D 10
18 Wood Green E 3
22 Wood Hayes B 3
26 Wood Norton C 3
25 Wood Walton G 3
4 Woodacott E 3
39 Woodale G 12
26 Woodbastwick D 6
32 Woodbeck B 5
7 Woodbridge, Dorset. E 10
27 Woodbridge, Suff. K 6
32 Woodborough, Notts. E 3
16 Woodborough, Wilts. H 2
6 Woodbury, Devon G 4
7 Woodbury, Som. B 9
6 Woodbury Salterton G 4
15 Woodchester D 11
11 Woodchurch E 8
6 Woodcombe B 3
17 Woodcote, Oxon. F 7
22 Woodcote, Salop A 1
8 Woodcott A 6
15 Woodcroft E 8
8 Woodcutts D 1
25 Wooditton J 8
16 Woodeaton C 6
38 Woodend, Cumb. F 4
59 Woodend, Grampian H 3
48 Woodend, Strathclyde F 2
23 Woodend, Northants. G 9
8 Woodfalls D 3
44 Woodfield, Dumf. & Gall. F 1
47 Woodfield, Strathclyde G 8
10 Woodfield, Surrey B 1
4 Woodford, Corn. E 1
15 Woodford, Glos. E 10
31 Woodford, Manchester B 7
18 Woodford, London E 4
25 Woodford, Northants. H 1
7 Woodford, Som B 9
23 Woodford Halse G 9
26 Woodgate, Norf. D 3
22 Woodgate, Heref. & Worc. E 3
9 Woodgate, W. Sussex F 10
8 Woodgreen D 3
49 Woodhall, Lothian B 9
45 Woodhall, Northumb. B 9
39 Woodhall, N. Yorks. F 12
32 Woodhall, S. Yorks B 2
33 Woodhall Spa D 9
17 Woodham H 11
19 Woodham Ferrers D 8
19 Woodham Mortimer C 8
19 Woodham Walter C 8
53 Woodhaven D 9
35 Woodhead, Derby G 9
58 Woodhead, Grampian D 5
58 Woodhead House C 5
49 Woodheads E 8
15 Woodhill, Avon G 8
22 Woodhill, Salop D 1
56 Woodholme D 2
45 Woodhorn D 11
45 Woodhorn Demesne D 11
32 Woodhouse, Derby B 1
23 Woodhouse, Leics. A 9
35 Woodhouse, W. Yorks. D 11
23 Woodhouse Eaves A 8
5 Woodhuish K 8
25 Woodhurst H 4
10 Woodingdean G 2
5 Woodland, Devon J 7
40 Woodland, Dur. C 1
58 Woodland, Grampian E 6
58 Woodland, Grampian F 6
8 Woodlands, Dorset E 2
43 Woodlands, Dumf. & Gall. D 11
59 Woodlands, Grampian H 5
8 Woodlands, Hants. E 4
56 Woodlands, Highland D 1
17 Woodlands Park F 9

16 Woodlands St. Mary G 4
31 Woodlane H 10
5 Woodleigh L 6
35 Woodlesford D 12
17 Woodley, Berks. G 8
35 Woodley, Manchester H 8
16 Woodmancote, Glos. A 1
16 Woodmancote, Glos. C 1
9 Woodmancote, W. Sussex E 9
9 Woodmancott B 7
37 Woodmansey C 8
9 Woodmansgreen C 10
10 Woodmansterne B 2
8 Woodminton D 2
11 Woodnesborough B 11
24 Woodnewton F 1
34 Woodplumpton D 4
26 Woodrising E 3
10 Wood's Green E 5
30 Woodseaves, Salop G 5
30 Woodseaves, Staffs. H 6
16 Woodsend F 3
32 Woodsetts B 3
7 Woodsford G 11
17 Woodside, Berks. G 10
43 Woodside, Dumf. & Gall. D 11
53 Woodside, Fife F 9
59 Woodside, Grampian G 7
49 Woodside, Northants. E 12
53 Woodside, Tayside C 7
59 Woodside of Arbeadie H 5
44 Woodslee F 2
16 Woodstock B 5
12 Woodstock Cross D 4
12 Woodstock Slop D 4
32 Woodthorpe, Derby. C 2
32 Woodthorpe, Leics. H 3
26 Woodton F 6
4 Woodtown, Devon. C 3
4 Woodtown, Devon. D 3
59 Woodtown, Grampian K 3
34 Woodvale F 2
31 Woodville H 11
8 Woodyates D 2
21 Woofferton F 10
7 Wookey B 8
7 Wookey Hole A 9
7 Wool H 11
4 Woolacombe B 3
11 Woolage Green C 11
15 Woolaston D 9
7 Wollavington B 7
9 Woolbeding D 10
6 Woolbrook G 5
6 Woolcotts C 3
35 Wooldale F 10
49 Wooler G 12
4 Woolfardisworthy E 7
48 Woolfords Cotts D 3
8 Woolgarston H 2
17 Woolhampton G 7
15 Woolhope A 9
7 Woolland F 11
15 Woollard H 9
4 Woollaton E 3
4 Woolley, Corn. D 1
15 Woolley, Avon G 10
25 Woolley, Cambs. H 3
35 Woolley, S. Yorks. F 11
18 Woolmer Green B 3
22 Woolmere Green F 3
27 Woolpit J 3
27 Woolpit Green J 3
23 Woolscott E 8
4 Woolsery D 2
45 Woolsington F 10
21 Woolstaston C 10
32 Woolsthorpe, Lincs. G 5
32 Woolsthorpe, Lincs. H 6
30 Woolston, Cheshire A 5
5 Woolston, Devon L 6
8 Woolston, Hants. E 6
21 Woolston, Salop D 9
30 Woolston, Salop H 2
5 Woolston Green J 6
16 Woolstone E 4
30 Woolton B 3
16 Woolton Hill H 5
27 Woolverstone L 5
7 Woolverton A 11
18 Woolwich F 4
21 Woonton G 9
45 Wooperton A 8
49 Wooplaw E 7
30 Woore F 6
25 Wootton, Beds. L 1
8 Wootton, Hants. F 4
37 Wootton, Humber. E 8
11 Wootton, Kent C 11
23 Wootton, Northants. F 11
16 Wootton, Oxon. B 5
16 Wootton, Oxon. D 6
21 Wootton, Salop E 10
31 Wootton, Staffs. F 9
31 Wootton, Staffs. G 7
16 Wootton Bassett F 2
9 Wootton Bridge G 7
9 Wootton Com. G 7
6 Wootton Courtenay B 3
7 Wootton Fitzpaine G 7
16 Wootton Rivers H 3
9 Wootton St. Lawrence A 7
22 Wootton Wawen F 5
22 Worcester G 2
22 Wordsley C 2
22 Worfield C 1
64 Work C 3
38 Workington B 2
32 Worksop B 3
37 Worlaby F 8
16 World's End, Berks. F 6
9 World's End, Hants. E 8
15 Worle H 7
30 Worleston E 5
26 Worlingham F 7
25 Worlington H 8
27 Worlingworth H 5
27 Wormald Green A 11
15 Wormbridge A 7
24 Wormegay D 8
15 Wormelow Tump A 8
31 Wormhill C 9
53 Wormiehills C 11
27 Wormingford M 2
17 Worminghall C 7
16 Wormington A 1
7 Worminster B 9
48 Wormiston E 5
53 Wormit E 9
23 Wormleighton G 8
18 Wormley, Herts. C 4
9 Wormley, Surrey B 10
11 Wormshill B 7
21 Wormsley H 9
9 Worplesdon A 11
35 Worral H 11
35 Worsbrough G 12
34 Worsley G 6
26 Worstead C 6
25 Worsted Lodge K 6
35 Worsthorne D 7
34 Worston C 6
5 Worswell L 4
11 Worth, Kent C 12
10 Worth, W. Sussex D 2
8 Worth Matravers H 1
27 Wortham H 4
21 Worthen B 9
30 Worthenbury F 3
26 Worthing, Norf. D 3
9 Worthing, W. Sussex F 12
32 Worthington H 1
6 Worthy A 2
9 Worting A 7
35 Wortley, S. Yorks. G 11
35 Wortley, W. Yorks. D 11
16 Worton H 1
27 Wortwell G 6
5 Wotter J 4
9 Wotton A 12
15 Wotton-under-Edge E 11
17 Wotton Underwood C 8
23 Woughton on the Green H 12
10 Wouldham B 6
27 Wrabness M 5
58 Wraes D 3
4 Wrafton C 4
33 Wragby, Lincs. B 8
36 Wragby, W. Yorks. E 2
37 Wragholme G 11
26 Wramplingham E 4
36 Wrangbrook F 3
58 Wrangham, Grampian D 4
49 Wrangham, Northumb. F 12
33 Wrangle E 11
33 Wrangle Com. E 11
33 Wrangle Lowgate E 11
6 Wrangway D 5
6 Wrantage D 6
37 Wrawby F 8
15 Wraxall, Avon G 8
7 Wraxall, Dorset. F 9
7 Wraxhall, Som. C 9
39 Wray H 8
5 Wrayland H 7
17 Wraysbury G 11
34 Wrea Green D 3
39 Wreay, Cumb. C 7
44 Wreay, Cumb. H 3
9 Wrecclesham B 9
45 Wrekenton G 11
41 Wrelton F 8
30 Wrenbury E 4
26 Wreningham F 4
27 Wrentham G 8
35 Wrenthorpe E 11
21 Wrentnall B 9
36 Wressle D 5
25 Wrestlingworth K 4
24 Wretton F 8
30 Wrexham E 2
30 Wrexham Industrial Estate E 2
22 Wribbenhall E 2
34 Wrightlington Bar F 4
30 Wrinehill E 6
15 Wrington H 8
7 Writhlington A 10
19 Writtle C 7
21 Wrockwardine A 11
36 Wroot G 5
10 Wrotham B 5
10 Wrotham Heath B 5
16 Wroughton F 3
22 Wroxall E 6
21 Wroxeter B 11
9 Wroxhall H 7
26 Wroxham D 6
23 Wroxton H 7
31 Wyaston F 10
24 Wyberton B 4
25 Wyboston K 3
30 Wybunbury E 5
10 Wych Cross E 3
22 Wychbold F 3
22 Wychnor A 5
22 Wychnor Bridges A 5
9 Wyck B 9
40 Wycliffe D 1
17 Wycombe Marsh E 10
25 Wyddial M 5
11 Wye C 9
11 Wyerstone H 3
27 Wyerstone Street H 3
15 Wyesham C 8
7 Wyke, Dorset D 11
21 Wyke, Salop B 12
9 Wyke, Surrey A 10
35 Wyke, W. Yorks. D 10
7 Wyke Champflower C 10
7 Wyke Regis H 7
16 Wyke Rissington B 3
41 Wykeham, N. Yorks. H 8
41 Wykeham, N. Yorks. G 9
32 Wykeham Moor C 6
30 Wykey H 3
45 Wylam G 9
22 Wylde Green C 5
14 Wyllie E 5
8 Wylye B 2
9 Wymering E 8
32 Wymeswold H 3
25 Wymington J 1
32 Wymondham, Leics. H 6
26 Wymondham, Norf. E 4
14 Wyndham E 3
7 Wynford Eagle G 9
40 Wynyard Forest C 4
22 Wyre Piddle G 3
32 Wysall G 3
22 Wythall E 4
16 Wytham C 6
38 Wythburn D 6
31 Wythenshawe A 7
25 Wyton H 4
32 Wyville G 6
54 Wyvis Lodge B 8
36 Yaddlethorpe F 6
8 Yafford H 6
40 Yafforth F 4
5 Yalberton K 7
10 Yalding C 6
16 Yanworth C 2
36 Yapham B 6
9 Yapton F 11
33 Yarburgh A 10
6 Yarcombe E 6
4 Yard D 6
4 Yard Gate C 6
22 Yardley D 5
23 Yardley Gobion H 11
23 Yardley Hastings F 12
21 Yardro F 8
21 Yarkhill H 11
31 Yarlet G 7
7 Yarlington C 10
40 Yarm D 4
8 Yarmouth G 5
4 Yarnacott C 5
7 Yarnbrook A 12
31 Yarnfield G 7
4 Yarnscombe D 4
16 Yarnton C 6
21 Yarpole F 10
48 Yarrow G 6
48 Yarrow Feus G 6
21 Yarsop H 9
24 Yarwell F 2
15 Yate F 10
17 Yateley H 9
16 Yatesbury G 2
16 Yattendon G 6
15 Yatton, Avon H 7
15 Yatton, Heref. & Worc. A 9
21 Yatton, Heref. & Worc. F 9
15 Yatton Keynell G 12
9 Yaverland H 7
37 Yawthorpe H 7
26 Yaxham D 3
24 Yaxley, Cambs. F 3
27 Yaxley, Suffolk H 4
21 Yazor H 9
35 Yeadon C 10
39 Yealand Conyers H 7
39 Yealand Redmayne H 7
5 Yealmpton K 4
40 Yearby C 6
40 Yearsley H 6
30 Yeaton H 3
31 Yeaveley F 10
49 Yeavering F 12
16 Yelford D 4
25 Yelling J 4
11 Yelsted B 7
23 Yelvertoft E 9
5 Yelverton, Devon J 4
26 Yelverton, Norfolk E 6
7 Yenston D 10
4 Yeo Mill C 7
4 Yeoford F 6
3 Yeolmbridge A 10
7 Yeovil D 9
7 Yeovil Marsh D 9
7 Yeovilton D 9
12 Yerbeston F 4
12 Yerbeston Mountain F 4
64 Yesnaby C 1
49 Yetholm Mains F 11
45 Yetlington B 8
7 Yetminster E 9
47 Yett, Strathclyde G 9
47 Yett, Strathclyde C 12
6 Yettington H 4
52 Yetts of Muckhart G 5
28 Yffor F 3
25 Yielden J 1
48 Yieldshields D 2
18 Yiewsley F 1
20 Ynys F 2
20 Ynys Tachwedd C 2
14 Ynys-boeth E 4
14 Ynysbwl E 4
14 Ynysddu E 5
14 Ynyshir E 4
13 Ynstawe G 10
39 Yockenthwaite G 11
21 Yockleton A 9
36 Yokefleet E 6
47 Yoker C 10
58 Yonder Bognie C 3
36 York B 3
17 York Town H 9
11 Yorkletts B 9
39 Yockenthwaite G 11
21 Yockleton A 9
36 Yokefleet E 6
47 Yoker C 10
58 Yonder Bognie C 3
36 York B 3
17 York Town H 9
11 Yorkletts B 9
15 Yorkley D 9
48 Yorkeston D 6
4 Youldonmoor Cross E 2
31 Youlgreaves D 10
36 Youlthorpe B 5
36 Youlton A 3
19 Young's End B 7
31 Yoxall H 10
27 Yoxford H 7
20 Ysbytty Cynfyn D 3
29 Ysbyty Ifan E 8
20 Ysbyty Ystwyth E 3
29 Ysceifog C 10
13 Yspitty G 9
13 Ystalyfera F 11
14 Ystrad E 3
13 Ystrad Aeron A 8
20 Ystrad Meurig F 3
14 Ystradfellte C 3
13 Ystradffin B 11
14 Ystradgynlais C 1
14 Ystrad-mynach E 5
13 Ystradowen, Dyfed F 10
14 Ystradowen, S. Glam. G 3
20 Ystumtuen D 3
58 Ythsie D 6
4 Zeal Monachorum F 6
7 Zeals C 11
2 Zelah D 5
2 Zennor F 2
64 Zetland, Co. D 7

INDEX TO LONDON MAPS

ABBREVIATIONS

App. – *Approach*
Av. – *Avenue*
Bdy. – *Broadway*
Bldg. – *Building(s)*
Br. – *British*
Bri. – *Bridge*
Ch. – *Church*
Cl. – *Close*
Cnr. – *Corner*
Coll. – *College*
Con. – *Convent*
Cres. – *Crescent*
Ct. – *Court*
Dri. – *Drive*
Ex. – *Exchange*
F.C. – *Football Club*
Gdns. – *Gardens*
Gro. – *Grove*
Gt. – *Great*
Ho. – *House*
Hosp. – *Hospital*
Hot. – *Hotel*
Inst. – *Institute*
La. – *Lane*
Lit. – *Little*
Min. – *Ministry*
Mkt. – *Market*
Mt. – *Mount*
Mus. – *Museum*
Nat. – *National*
Nth. – *North*
Pal. – *Palace*
Pk. – *Park*
Ol. – *Place*
Pol. – *Police*
Poly. – *Polytechnic*
Pr. – *Prince*
R.C. – *Roman Catholic*
Rd. – *Road*
Sanct. – *Sanctuary*
Sch. – *School*
Soc. – *Society*
Sq. – *Square*
St. – *Street, Saint*
Sta. – *Station*
Sth. – *South*
Ter. – *Terrace*
Th. – *Theatre*
Wk. – *Walk*
Yd. – *Yard*

The normal abbreviations for the London Postal Districts have been used throughout, e.g., NW10.

73 Abbey Gdns ..... C 3
73 Abbey Gdns Mews C 3
79 Abbey Orchard St. D 7
73 Abbey Pl. .... C 3
73 Abbey Rd. .... B 3
80 Abbey St. .... D 4
67 Abbey Wood .... G 12
80 Abbots La. .... B 4
76 Abchurch La. .... H 3
73 Abercorn Close .. C 4
73 Abercorn Pl. ..... C 3
73 Aberdeen Place .. E 5
80 Aberdour St. ..... E 3
77 Abingdon Rd. ..... D 1
79 Abingdon St. ..... D 8
77 Abingdon Villas .. E 1
68 Abridge .... A 1
67 Abridge Rd. ..... A 12
73 Acacia Gdns. .... B 5
73 Acacia Pl. .... B 5
73 Acacia Rd. ...... B 5
67 Academy Rd. ... H 11
70 Acre La. .... B 6
70 Acre La., Carshalton .... F 5
66 Acton .... F 3
66 Acton Central Sta. G 3
66 Acton La. .... F 3
66 Acton (Main Line) Sta. .... F 3
66 Acton Park ..... G 3
75 Acton St. ...... D 9
66 Acton Town Sta. . G 2
75 Adam St. .... J 9
77 Adam Eve Mews . D 2
74 Adams Row ..... J 4
71 Addington ...... F 8
71 Addington G.C. ... F 8
71 Addington Palace G.C. .... F 8
71 Addington Rd., Sanderstead ... G 7
71 Addington Rd., W. Wickham .. E 9
80 Addington Square . J 2
79 Addington St. ... C 10
71 Addington Village Rd. .... F 8
71 Addiscombe ..... E 7
71 Addiscombe Rd. . E 7
71 Addiscombe Sta. . E 7
69 Addlestone ...... F 2
66 Adelaide Rd. ..... E 5
75 Adelaide St. ...... J 8
75 Adelphi Ter. ...... J 9
75 Adelphi Theatre ... J 9
76 Adler St. .... G 6
79 Admiralty .... B 8
79 Admiralty Arch .. B 8
73 Adpar St. .... F 5
74 Æolian Hall ...... H 5
75 Agar St. .... J 8
75 Agdon St. .... E 12
77 Airways Terminal (Europe) .... E 3
78 Airways Terminal . F 4
79 Alaska St. .... B 11
71 Albany Park Sta. C 12
80 Albany Rd. ...... H 3
74 Albany St. ...... C 5
74 Albermarle St. .... J 5
78 Albert Bridge .... J 1
78 Albert Bridge Rd. . J 1
77 Albert Court ..... D 4
79 Albert Embank. ... F 9
78 Albert Gate ...... C 3
77 Albert Memorial . C 4
77 Albert Place ..... D 3
67 Albert Rd. ...... G 11
74 Albert St. .... B 5
74 Albert Ter. ...... A 3
74 Albert Ter. Mews . A 3
79 Alberta St. ...... G 12
75 Albery Theatre .... J 8
73 Albion Close ..... H 6
73 Albion Gate ..... H 6
73 Albion Mews ..... H 6
73 Albion St. .... H 6
67 Aldborough Hatch .... C 12
67 Aldborough Rd. . C 12
80 Aldbridge St. ..... G 4
66 Aldenham Park .. A 2
66 Aldenham Res. ... A 2
65 Aldenham Rd., Bushey .... A 5
66 Aldenham Rd., Watford .... A 2
74 Aldenham St. .... C 7
76 Aldermanbury .... G 2
80 Alderminster Rd. .. F 6
78 Alderney St. ...... F 5
67 Aldersbrook .... D 10
67 Aldersbrook Rd. D 10
75 Aldersgate St. ... F 13
78 Aldford St. .... A 3
76 Aldgate .... H 4
76 Aldgate High St. . G 5
75 Aldwych .... H 9
75 Aldwych Theatre . H 9
65 Alexander Ave. .. D 6
77 Alexander Place .. E 6
77 Alexander Square. E 6
73 Alexander St. .... G 2
77 Alexandra Gate .. C 5
66 Alexandra Place .. C 6
66 Alexandra Park .. C 6
66 Alexandra Park Rd. .... C 6
80 Alexis St. .... E 6
74 Alfred Mews ...... F 7
74 Alfred Place ...... F 7
73 Alfred Rd. .... F 1
80 Alice St. .... E 3
76 Alie St. .... H 6
70 All England Lawn Tennis Club ... C 4
70 All Saints Rd. .... E 4
75 All Saints St. ..... B 9
66 All Souls Ave. .... E 4
77 Allen St. .... D 1
76 Allhallows La. .... J 2
75 Allingham Ter. ... B 13
78 Allington St. ..... D 5
73 Allitsen Rd. ...... B 6
74 Allsop Place ..... E 3
66 Allum La. .... A 2
80 Alma Grove ...... F 6
73 Alma Sq. .... C 4
66 Alperton .... E 2
77 Alpha Place ...... H 6
80 Alsace Rd. .... G 3
80 Alscot Rd. .... E 5
80 Alvey St. .... F 3
75 Ambassadors Th. H 8
79 Ambergate St. ... G 12
73 Amberley Rd. .... E 2
70 Amberwood Rise . E 3
78 Ambrosden Av. .. E 6
79 Amelia St. ...... F 13
67 Amhurst Park ... D 7
74 Ampthill Sq. ..... C 6
80 Amina Way ...... E 6
75 Ampton St. ...... D 9
75 Amwell St. ...... D 11
78 Anderson St. ...... F 2
73 Andover Pl. ...... C 2
71 Anerley Rd. ...... D 7
71 Anerley Sta. ...... D 7
70 Angel Hill .... E 4
67 Angel Rd. .... B 8
67 Angel Road Sta. .. B 8
75 Angel St. .... G 13
76 Anglesea St. ...... E 7
77 Ann La. .... J 4
77 Ansdell St. .... D 3
77 Ansdell Ter. ...... D 2
77 Anselm Rd. ...... H 1
66 Apex Corner ..... B 3
78 Apple Tree Yard . A 7
76 Appleby St. ...... B 5
76 Appolo St. .... F 4
78 Apsley House ..... C 4
78 Apsley Way ...... C 4
71 Aquarius G.C. ..... B 8
79 Aquinas St. ..... B 11
80 Arch St. .... E 1
79 Archbishop's Pk. D 10
74 Archer St. .... H 7
74 Archery Close .... H 2
66 Archway Rd. ...... D 6
68 Ardleigh Green .. C 3
68 Ardleigh Green Rd. .... C 3
77 Argyll Rd., W8 ... D 1
66 Argyle Rd., W13 .. F 1
75 Argyle Square .... D 9
74 Argyll St., W1 .... H 6
75 Argyle St. WC1 .. D 9
66 Arkley .... A 4
66 Arkley La. .... A 4
76 Arlington Av. .... B 2
74 Arlington Rd. .... B 5
76 Arlington Sq. .... B 2
78 Arlington St. ..... B 6
75 Arlington Way .. C 11
77 Armadale Rd. ..... J 1
75 Arne St. .... H 9
76 Arnold Circus .... D 5
72 Arnolds La. ...... C 3
66 Arnos Grove Sta. . B 6
80 Arnside St. .... H 2
67 Arsenal F.C. ...... E 7
73 Artesian Rd. ...... H 1
76 Arthur St. .... J 3
76 Artillery Ground . E 2
76 Artillery La. ...... F 4
78 Artillery Row ..... D 7
73 Arts Theatre ..... H 8
75 Arundel St. ..... H 10
72 Ash .... F 5
73 Ashbridge St. .... E 6
77 Ashburn Gdns. ... E 3
77 Ashburn Mews ... E 3
77 Ashburn Place .... F 3
75 Ashby St. .... D 12
69 Ashford Hospital . B 3
69 Ashford La. ...... D 3
69 Ashford Manor G.C. .... C 3
69 Ashford Rd, Feltham .... C 4
69 Ashford Rd, Laleham .... D 3
69 Ashley Rd., Walton .... E 4
74 Ashland Place ..... F 3
69 Ashley Park ...... E 4
78 Ashley Place ..... E 6
70 Ashley Rd., Epsom .... G 3
73 Ashmill St. .... F 6
79 Ashmole St. ..... H 10
70 Ashtead .... H 2
70 Ashtead Common G 1
70 Ashtead Park .... H 2
70 Ashtead Sta. ..... H 1
73 Ashworth Rd. .... D 3
77 Astell St. .... G 6
65 Aston Rd. .... B 4
77 Astwood Mews .... F 3
77 Atherstone Mews . E 4
79 Atterbury St. ...... F 8
75 Attneave St. ..... D 10
79 Auckland St. ..... G 9
78 Audley St. .... B 4
76 Audrey St. .... B 6
74 Augustus St. ..... C 5
79 Aulton Pl. .... G 11
76 Austin St. .... D 5
76 Austin Friars ..... G 3
79 Austral St. ...... E 12
75 Australia House . H 10
75 Ave Maria La. .. H 12
76 Avebury Estate ... D 6
76 Avebury St. ...... A 3
68 Aveley .... G 4
68 Aveley Rd. .... E 4
79 Aveline St. ...... G 10
80 Avely St. .... F 3
76 Avenue, The EC3 H 4
70 Avenue, The SW4 B 5
69 Avenue, The Sunbury .... D 5
66 Avenue Rd. N14 .. A 6
73 Avenue Rd. NW8 B 6
68 Avenue Rd, Bexleyheath ... H 1
74 Avery Row .... H 5
71 Averyhill Rd. ..... B 11
80 Avon Place ...... C 2
80 Avondale Square . G 6
79 Avonmouth St. .. D 13
74 Aybrook St. .... F 3
80 Aylesbury Rd. .... G 3
75 Aylesbury St. ... E 12
78 Aylesford St. ..... G 7
80 Ayres St. .... C 1
76 Bache's St. .... D 3
76 Back Church La. . H 6
75 Back Hill .... E 11
68 Back La. .... G 5
80 Bacon Gr. .... E 5
76 Bacon St. .... E 6
72 Badger's Mount .. G 1
80 Bagshot St. ...... G 4
75 Bainbridge St. .... G 8
74 Baker St. .... F 3
74 Baker's Mews ..... G 3
75 Baker's Row .... E 11
80 Balaclava Rd. ..... F 6
74 Balcombe St. ..... E 2
74 Balderton St. ..... H 4
76 Baldwin St. ...... D 2
75 Baldwin Ter. .... B 13
75 Baldwin's Gdns. . F 11
65 Baldwin's La. .... A 4
80 Balfour St. .... E 2
68 Balgores La. ..... C 3
70 Balham .... B 5
70 Balham High Rd. . C 5
70 Balham Hill ...... B 5
70 Balham Sta. ...... B 5
66 Ballards La. ...... C 5
67 Balls Pond Rd. ... E 7
76 Baltic Shipping Exchange ...... G 4
76 Baltic St. .... E 1
67 Banbury Res. .... C 8
80 Bank End .... A 2
76 Bank of England . G 3
75 Bankruptcy Court .... H 10
79 Bankside .... A 13
79 Bankside Power Station .... A 13
76 Banner St. .... E 2
70 Banstead .... G 4
70 Banstead Downs . G 4
70 Banstead Downs G.C. .... G 4
70 Banstead Hospital G 4
70 Banstead Rd. ..... G 3
70 Banstead Road South .... F 5
76 Barbican .... F 1
75 Barbican Sta. ... F 13
75 Barford St. ...... B 11
79 Barge House St. . A 11
71 Baring Rd. .... C 9
76 Baring St. .... A 2
73 Bark Place .... J 2
67 Barking .... E 11
67 Barking Park .... E 11
67 Barking Rd. ..... F 10
67 Barking Sta. .... E 11
67 Barkingside ..... C 11
77 Barkston Gdns. ... F 2
75 Barlett Court .... G 11
67 Barley La. ...... D 12
80 Barlow St. .... F 3
66 Barn Hill Park ... D 2
74 Barnby St. .... C 6
72 Barnehurst .... A 1
70 Barnes .... A 3
70 Barnes Bridge .... A 3
70 Barnes Bridge Sta. A 3
70 Barnes Common . A 3
70 Barnes Sta. .... A 3
66 Barnet .... B 4
66 Barnet Bypass .... A 3
66 Barnet Gate ...... A 3
76 Barnet Grove .... D 6
66 Barnet La, Elstree A 2
66 Barnet La, Totteridge ..... A 4
66 Barnet Rd. .... A 3
66 Barnet Way ...... A 3
70 Barnetwood La. .. H 1
80 Barnham St. ..... C 4
75 Barnsbury Estate .... B 10
75 Barnsbury Rd. .. B 11
75 Baron St. .... B 11
76 Baroness Rd. .... C 5
79 Baron's Place ... C 11
74 Barrett St. .... H 4
73 Barrie St. .... H 4
73 Barrow Hill Rd. .. C 6
67 Barrowell Green . B 7
75 Barter St. .... G 9
75 Bartholomew Cl. F 13
76 Bartholomew La. . G 3
80 Bartholomew St. . E 3
78 Basil St. .... D 2
76 Basing Place ..... C 4
76 Basinghall Av. ... G 2
76 Basinghall St. .... G 2
75 Bastwick St. .... E 13
72 Bat Ball Sta. ...... H 2
75 Batchelor St. .... B 11
65 Batchworth ...... B 3
65 Batchworth Hth. . B 4
65 Batchworth Heath Hill .... B 4
74 Bateman St. ...... H 7
76 Bateman's Row .. D 4
75 Bath Ct. .... E 11
65 Bath R., Cranford ...... H 5
65 Bath Rd., Colnbrook ..... H 2
76 Bath St. .... D 2
80 Bath Ter. .... D 1
66 Bathurst Gdns. .... F 4
73 Bathurst Mews ... H 5
73 Bathurst St. ..... H 5
70 Battersea .... A 5
77 Battersea Bridge ... J 5
70 Battersea Bridge Rd. .... A 5
70 Battersea Park ... A 5
70 Battersea Park Rd. A 5
70 Battersea Rise .... B 5
80 Battle Bridge La. . B 3
75 Battle Bridge Rd. . C 8
75 Battlebridge Basin B 9
76 Batty St. .... G 7
76 Baxendale St. .... C 6
74 Bayham St. ...... B 6
65 Bayhurst Wood .. C 3
74 Bayley St. .... F 7
79 Baylis Rd. .... C 11
66 Bayswater .... F 5
73 Bayswater Rd. .... J 4
80 Beaconsfield Rd. . G 3
68 Beacontree Hth. .. D 1
74 Beak St. .... H 6
72 Bean .... C 4
80 Bear Gdns. .... A 1
79 Bear La. .... B 12
75 Bear St. .... J 8
74 Beatty St. .... B 5
78 Beauchamp Place D 2
75 Beauchamp St. .. F 11
78 Beaufort Gdns. ... D 2
77 Beaufort St. ...... H 5
74 Beaumont Mews . F 4
74 Beaumont Place . E 6
74 Beaumont St. ..... F 4
71 Beckenham ...... D 8
71 Beckenham Hill Rd. .... C 9
71 Beckenham Hill Sta. .... C 9
71 Beckenham Junc. Sta. .... D 8
71 Beckenham Place Park .... C 9
71 Beckenham Place Foxgrove G.C. . C 9
71 Beckenham Rd. .. D 8
67 Beckton .... F 11
80 Beckway St. .... F 3
68 Becontree .... D 1
68 Becontree Ave. ... D 1
68 Becontree Sta. .... E 1
80 Bedale St. .... B 2
70 Beddington .... F 6
70 Beddington Cnr .. E 5
70 Beddington La. .. E 6
70 Beddington Lane Sta. .... E 5
70 Beddington Park . E 5
71 Beddlestead La. .. H 9
69 Bedfont Rd. ...... B 3
69 Bedford Rd, Feltham .... C 4
75 Bedford Av. ...... G 7
74 Bedford College .. D 3
77 Bedford Gdns. ... B 2
70 Bedford Hill ..... C 5
75 Bedford Place .... F 8
75 Bedford Row .... F 10
75 Bedford Square ... F 7
75 Bedford St. .... J 8
75 Bedford Way ..... E 8
75 Bedfordbury ...... J 8
68 Bedford's Park ... B 3
72 Bedonwell Rd. ... A 1
71 Beech Farm Rd. .. H 9
76 Beech St. .... F 1
72 Beechen Wood .... F 1
72 Beechenlea La. ... D 2
78 Beeston Place .... D 5
78 Belgrave Mews North .... D 3
78 Belgrave Mews South .... D 4
78 Belgrave Mews West .... D 3
78 Belgrave Place ... D 4
78 Belgrave Rd. ...... F 6
78 Belgrave Square .. D 3
66 Belgravia .... G 5
75 Belgrove St. ...... C 8
68 Belhus Park .... F 4
76 Bell La. .... G 5
73 Bell St. .... F 6
76 Bell Wharf La. .... J 2
75 Bell Yard .... H 11
71 Belle Grove Rd. . A 11
71 Bellingham ...... C 8
71 Bellingham Rd. .. C 9
66 Belmont .... C 1
66 Belmont G.C. .... C 1
70 Belmont Rise ..... F 4
70 Belmont Sta. ...... F 4
68 Belvedere .... G 2
79 Belvedere Rd. ... B 10
75 Bemerton St. ..... A 9
75 Benjamin St. .... F 12
70 Benhill Av. .... F 4
70 Benhill Rd. .... E 5

68 Bennet Castle La. E 1
74 Bentinck St. ...... G 4
68 Beredens La. ...... C 5
78 Berkeley Hotel ... B 5
74 Berkeley Mews ... G 3
74 Berkeley Square ... J 5
78 Berkeley St. ...... A 5
67 Bermondsey ..... G 8
80 Bermondsey Leather Market .... C 3
80 Bermondsey St. .. C 4
80 Bermondsey Wall East .... C 7
80 Bermondsey Wall West .... C 6
75 Bernard St. ...... E 8
74 Berners Mews .... G 6
74 Berners Place .... G 6
75 Berners Rd. ..... B 12
74 Berners St. ...... G 6
75 Berry St. .... E 12
79 Berryfield Rd. ... G 13
70 Berrylands Sta. ... D 2
71 Berry's Green Rd. H11
71 Berry's Hill ..... G 11
68 Berwick Pond Rd. E 3
74 Berwick St. ...... H 6
79 Bessborough Gdns. G 7
79 Bessborough Pl. .. G 7
69 Bessborough Res. D 5
78 Bessborough St. .. G 7
71 Bethlehem Royal Hospital .... E 8
67 Bethnal Green ... E 8
76 Bethnal Green Rd. E 5
67 Bethnal Green Sta. F 8
80 Bethwin Rd. ...... J 1
72 Betsham .... C 5
75 Betterton St. ..... G 9
71 Beulah Hill ...... C 7
76 Bevan St. .... B 2
76 Bevenden St. ..... C 3
80 Bevington St. .... D 7
76 Bevis Marks ...... G 4
72 Bexley .... B 1
71 Bexley Heath G,C. .... B 12
72 Bexley Hospital .. C 1
71 Bexley La. ...... C 12
71 Bexley Rd.SE9 .. B 11
72 Bexley Rd.Erith .. A 1
72 Bexley Sta. .... B 1
72 Bexleyheath ...... B 1
80 Bianca Rd. .... H 6
80 Bibury Close ..... H 4
74 Bickenhall St. .... F 3
71 Bickley .... D 10
75 Bidborough St. ... D 8
73 Biddulph Rd. .... D 2
71 Biggin Hill ..... H 10
71 Biggin Hill Airport .... G 10
67 Billet Rd.E17 ..... C 8
68 Billet Rd., Chadwell Heath C 1
77 Billing Place ...... J 3
77 Billing Rd. .... J 3
77 Billing St. .... J 3
76 Billingsgate Market. J 3
76 Billiter St. .... H 4
77 Bina Gdns. .... F 3
68 Bind La. .... C 4
74 Bingham Place .... F 3
71 Bingham Rd.Sta. . E 7
74 Binney St. .... H 4
72 Birches, The ...... F 2
76 Birchin La. .... H 3
72 Birchwood Rd. ... C 1
74 Bird St. .... H 4
78 Birdcage Walk ... C 7
80 Bird-in-Bush Rd. .. J 6
80 Birdlip Close ...... J 4
74 Birkbeck Coll. ... E 7
71 Birkbeck Sta. .... D 8
75 Birkenhead St. ... C 9
66 Bishops Ave. The . D 5
73 Bishop's Bridge Rd. .... G 3
79 Bishop's Ter. .... E 11
70 Bishopsford Rd. .. E 4
76 Bishopsgate ...... G 4
69 Bittams La. ...... E 2
67 Black Horse La. ... C 8
67 Black Horse Rd. Sta. .... C 8
73 Black Lion Gate ... J 3
65 Black Park .... E 1
79 Black Prince Rd. F 10
76 Blackall St. ...... E 3
66 Blackbird Hill .... D 3
74 Blackburnes Mews J 3
71 Blackfen .... B 11
71 Blackfen Rd. ..... B 11
75 Blackfriars Bridge J 12
75 Blackfriars La. .. H 12
79 Blackfriars Rd. .. C 12
75 Blackfriars Sta. .. H 12
71 Blackheath .... A 9
67 Blackheath Hill .. H 9
67 Blackheath Rd. ... H 9
71 Blackheath Royale G.C. .... B 10
78 Blacklands Ter. ... F 2
67 Blackwall .... F 9
67 Blackwall Reach . G 9
67 Blackwell Tunnel . G 9
80 Blackwood St. ... G 2
67 Blake Hall ...... D 10
80 Blake's Rd. .... J 4
74 Blandford Estate . E 1
74 Blandford Square E 1
74 Blandford St. .... G 3
77 Blantyre St. .... J 4
71 Blendon Rd. .... B 12
80 Blendon Row ..... F 2
73 Blenheim Rd. .... B 4
73 Blenheim Ter. .... B 3
75 Bletchley St. ..... C 2
77 Blithfield St. ..... E 2
73 Blomfield Rd. ..... F 3
76 Blomfield St. ..... G 3
73 Blomfield Vil. ..... F 3
78 Bloomfield Ter. ... F 4
66 Bloomsbury .... F 6
75 Bloomsbury Sq. ... F 9
75 Bloomsbury St. .. G 8
75 Bloomsbury Way . G 8
76 Blossom St. ...... E 4
69 Blundell La. ...... G 6
75 Boadicea St. ..... B 9
69 Board La. .... C 6
70 Bolingbroke Grove. B 5
74 Bolsover St. .... F 5
70 Bolters La. .... G 4
79 Bolton Cres. ...... J 12
77 Bolton Gdns. ..... F 3
78 Bolton St. .... B 5
77 Boltons, The ..... G 3
79 Bondway .... H 9
76 Bonhill St. .... E 3
79 Bonnington Sq. .. H 9
76 Boot St. .... D 3
67 Borders La. ..... A 11
66 Borehamwood .... A 3
72 Borough Green .. H 5
80 Borough High St. C 2
80 Borough Market . B 2
79 Borough Poly. .. D 12
79 Borough Rd. .... D 12
79 Borrett Rd. ..... G 13
73 Boscobel St. ...... E 5
80 Boss St. .... C 5
67 Bostall Hill Rd. . G 12
67 Bostall Woods .. H 12
66 Boston Manor ... G 1
66 Boston Manor Sta. G 1
74 Boston Place ..... E 2
66 Boston Rd. .... G 1
75 Boswell Ct. .... F 9
75 Boswell St. .... F 9
78 Botanic Gdns. .... H 2
69 Botleys .... E 1
69 Botley's Hosp. ... E 2
76 Botolph La. ...... J 3
67 Bounces Rd. ..... B 8
80 Boundary La. .... H 2
71 Boundary Rd. .... G 9
79 Boundary Row .. C 11
76 Boundary St. ..... D 5
66 Bounds Green Rd. C 6
74 Bourdon St. ...... J 5
66 Bourne, The ..... B 6
66 Bourne Hill ...... B 6
78 Bourne St. .... F 3
73 Bourne Ter. .... F 2
68 Bournebridge .... A 2
68 Bournebridge La. A 2
75 Bouverie St. ..... H 11
67 Bow .... F 9
67 Bow Bridge ...... F 9
67 Bow Common .... F 9
76 Bow La. .... H 2
67 Bow Rd. .... F 9
75 Bow St. .... H 9
66 Bowes Park Sta. .. C 6
80 Bowles Rd. .... H 6
75 Bowling Green La. E 11
79 Bowling Green St. H 11
76 Bowling Green Walk .... D 3
76 Boyd St. .... H 6
79 Boyfield St. ..... C 12
76 Brackley St. .... F 1
79 Brad St. .... B 11
73 Braden St. .... E 2
79 Braganza St. .... G 12
76 Braham St. .... G 5
80 Braidwood St. .... B 4
68 Bramble La. ..... E 4
77 Bramerton St. .... H 6
77 Bramham Gdns. .. F 2
66 Bramley Rd. ..... A 6
71 Brampton Rd. ... A 12
76 Branch Place ..... A 3
70 Brand Drive ..... D 3
80 Brandon St. ...... F 2
72 Brands Hatch ..... F 4
72 Brands Hatch Motor Racing Circuit .. F 4
71 Brasted Hill ..... H 12
71 Brasted La. ..... H 12
67 Bravel La. ...... B 12
78 Bray Place .... F 2
76 Bread St. .... H 1
65 Breakspear Rd. N. C 3
65 Breakspear Rd. S. D 3
75 Bream's Buildings G 11
75 Brechin Place ..... F 4
66 Brecknock Rd. ... E 6
77 Bremner Rd. ..... D 4
74 Brendon St. ...... G 1
66 Brent .... D 2
66 Brent Reservoir .. D 3
66 Brent Sta. .... D 4
66 Brent St. .... C 4
66 Brentford .... G 2
70 Brentford Central Sta. .... A 1
66 Brentford F.C. ... H 2
68 Brentwood .... B 6
68 Brentwood Bypass B 5
68 Brentwood Rd. ... D 3
68 Brentwood Warley Sta. .... B 5
78 Bressenden Place . D 5
69 Bretlands .... E 2
74 Brewer St. .... H 7
76 Brick La. .... E 5
78 Brick St. .... B 4
75 Bride La. .... H 12
78 Bride St. .... E 5
75 Bridewell Place .. H 12
74 Bridford Mews .... F 5
69 Bridge Rd. Chertsey .... E 2
69 Bridge Rd. Esher . D 6
70 Bridge Rd. Chessington .... F 2
79 Bridge St. .... C 8
79 Bridgefoot ...... G 8
73 Bridgeman St. .... C 6
66 Bridgewater Rd. ... E 2
75 Bridgewater Sq. . F 13
74 Bridgeway St. .... C 7
74 Bridle Lane ...... H 6
65 Bridle Rd. .... D 5
76 Bridport Place ... B 3
67 Bridport Rd. .... B 7
73 Bridstow Place ... G 1
70 Brighton Rd. Coulsdon ...... H 5
70 Brighton Rd. Croydon .... G 6
70 Brighton Rd. Sutton .... F 4
70 Brigstock Rd. .... D 6
67 Brimsdown Sta. .. A 8
75 Briset St. .... F 12
73 Bristol Gdns. ...... F 3
73 Bristol Mews ..... E 3
75 Britannia St. ..... C 9
75 British Council .. F 10
75 British Medical Association .... D 8
75 British Museum ... F 8
77 Britten St. .... G 6
75 Britton St. .... F 12
70 Brixton .... A 6
70 Brixton Hill ...... B 6
70 Brixton Prison ... B 6
79 Brixton Rd. ...... J 11
70 Brixton Sta. ...... B 6
67 Broad La.N15 .... C 8
72 Broad La. Dartford ...... C 2
67 Broad Mead Rd. C 10
79 Broad Sanctuary . D 8
76 Broad Street Sta. .. F 3
77 Broad Walk, The . C 3
74 Broadcasting House .... G 5
73 Broadley St. .... F 5
73 Broadley Ter. .... E 6
74 Broadstone Place. . F 3
78 Broadway, SW1 .. D 7
70 Broadway, SW19 . C 4
65 Broadway, Southall .... G 5
74 Broadwick St. .... H 6
80 Brockham St. .... D 2
66 Brockley Hill ..... B 2
71 Brockley Rise .... B 8
71 Brockley Rd. ..... B 8
71 Brockley Sta. ..... A 8
70 Brockwell Park ... B 6
80 Brockworth Close . J 4
75 Bromfield St. .... B 11
71 Bromley .... D 9
67 Bromley, Tower Hamlets .... F 9
67 Bromley-by-Bow .. F 9
71 Bromley Common E 10
71 Bromley Hill ..... C 9
71 Bromley North Sta. .... D 9
71 Bromley Rd.SE6 . C 9
71 Bromley Rd. Beckenham .... D 9
71 Bromley Rd. Chislehurst ... D 11
71 Bromley South Sta. D 9
66 Brompton .... G 5
77 Brompton Cemetery H 2
77 Brompton Hospital F 5
78 Brompton Place .. D 2
77 Brompton Square D 6
77 Brompton Rd. ... E 6
66 Brondesbury Park E 4
66 Brondesbury Park Sta. .... E 4
66 Brondesbury Sta. . E 4
80 Bronti Close ..... G 2
79 Brook Drive .... E 11
71 Brook Fever Hospital ...... A 10
66 Brook Green ..... G 4
73 Brook Mews North H 4
74 Brook St. .... H 4
75 Brooke St. ...... F 11
69 Brooklands Rd. ... F 3
74 Brook's Mews .... H 5
66 Brookshill .... B 1
70 Broom Rd. .... C 1
66 Broomfield Park . B 6
72 Broomfield Wood . F 4
74 Brown Hart Gdns. H 4
74 Brown St. .... G 2
71 Brownhill Rd. .... B 9
75 Brownlow Mews E 10
80 Browning St. ...... F 2
75 Brownlow St. ... F 10
69 Brox .... F 2
68 Broxhill Rd. ...... B 3
74 Broxwood Way .. B 1
67 Bruce Castle Park C 7
67 Bruce Grove Sta. . C 7
76 Brune St. .... F 5
73 Brunel Estate ..... F 1
65 Brunel University . F 3
75 Brunswick Centre E 8
75 Brunswick Cl. Estate .... D 12
80 Brunswick Court . C 4
77 Brunswick Gdns. . B 2
66 Brunswick Park .. B 6
76 Brunswick Place .. D 3
75 Brunswick Square E 9
76 Brushfield St. ..... F 4
74 Bruton La .... J 5
74 Bruton Place ...... J 5
74 Bruton St. .... J 5
74 Bryanston Mews East .... G 2
74 Bryanston Mews West .... G 2
74 Bryanston Place .. G 2
74 Bryanston Square G 2
74 Bryanston St. .... H 2
68 Bryant Ave. ...... C 3
76 Buckfast St. ...... D 6
67 Buckhurst Hill .. B 10
71 Buckhurst Rd. .. H 11
78 Buckingham Gate D 6
78 Buckingham Palace C 5
78 Buckingham Palace Gdns .... C 5
78 Buckingham Palace Rd. .... E 5
78 Buckingham Place D 6
79 Buckingham St. .. A 9
76 Buckland St. ..... C 3
76 Buckle St. .... G 6
76 Bucklersbury ..... H 2
75 Bucknall St. ...... G 8
71 Bug Hill .... H 8
67 Bugsby's Reach . G 10
79 Bulinga St. .... F 8
68 Bull La. .... D 2
74 Bulstrode St. ..... G 4
76 Bunhill Fields .... E 2
76 Bunhill Row ..... E 2
72 Bunker's Hill La. .. F 5
80 Burbage Close ... D 2
79 Burdett St. ...... D 11
70 Burgh Heath ..... H 4
70 Burgh Heath Rd. . G 3
75 Burgh St. .... B 13
69 Burhill G.C. ...... F 4
75 Burleigh St. ...... H 9
71 Burling La. ..... H 11
74 Burlington Arcade .... J 6
74 Burlington Gdns. .. J 6
73 Burne St. .... F 6
77 Burnsall St. ...... G 6
71 Burnt Ash La. .... C 9
66 Burnt Oak .... C 3
66 Burnt Oak Sta. ... C 3
71 Burntash Hill .... B 9
71 Burntash Rd. ..... B 9
70 Burntwood La. SW17 .... C 5
71 Burntwood La. Coulsdon ...... H 7
79 Burrell St. .... B 12
78 Burton Court .... G 2
80 Burton Grove .... G 3
75 Burton St. .... D 8
69 Burtons Rd. ...... C 5
73 Burwood Place ... G 6
69 Burwood Rd. ..... F 4
76 Bury Court ...... G 4
75 Bury Place .... G 8
76 Bury St. EC3 ..... G 4
67 Bury St. N9 ...... A 7
78 Bury St. SW1 .... B 6
65 Bury St. Ruislip .. D 4
77 Bury Walk .... F 6
67 Bury Wood ..... A 10
76 Busby St. .... E 6
67 Bush Hill .... A 7
67 Bush Hill G.C. ... A 7
76 Bush La. .... H 2
65 Bushey .... A 6
65 Bushey Hall G.C. A 5
66 Bushey Heath .... A 1
70 Bushey Rd. ...... D 3
65 Bushey & Oxhey Sta. .... A 5
67 Bushill Park ...... A 7
67 Bushill Park Sta. . A 7
69 Bushy Park ...... D 6
77 Bute St. .... F 5
76 Buttesland St. .... D 3
72 Button St. .... D 2
68 Butts La. .... D 3
71 Buxton La. .... H 7
76 Buxton St. .... E 6
69 Byfleet .... G 3
69 Byfleet Rd. ...... G 4
69 Byfleet & New Haw Sta. .... F 3
74 Byng Place .... E 7
76 Byward St. .... J 4
78 Bywater St. .... F 2
73 Cabbel St. .... G 6
76 Cable St. .... H 6
71 Cackets La. ..... G 11
80 Cadbury Way .... E 6
80 Cadiz St. .... G 2
78 Cadogan Gdns. .. E 2
78 Cadogan Gate ... E 3
78 Cadogan La. ..... E 3
78 Cadogan Pier .... H 1
78 Cadogan Place ... E 3
78 Cadogan Square . E 2
78 Cadogan St. .... F 2
67 Cadogan Ter. .... E 9
76 Caesar St. .... C 4
80 Caldew St. .... J 2
77 Cale St. .... F 6
75 Caledonia St. .... C 9
75 Caledonian Rd. .. B 9
66 Caledonian Rd. & Barnsbury Sta. . E 6
77 Callow St. .... H 4
80 Calmington Rd. .. H 4
75 Calshot St. .... B 9
75 Calthorpe St. .... E 10
76 Calvert Av. ...... D 4
76 Calvin St. .... E 5
71 Camberwell ...... A 7
79 Camberwell New Rd. .... J 11
80 Camberwell Rd. ... J 2
75 Cambridge Circus H 8
74 Cambridge Gate . D 5
67 Cambridge Heath Sta. .... F 8
67 Cambridge Park E11 .... D 10
70 Cambridge Park Twickenham ... B 1
77 Cambridge Place . D 3
70 Cambridge Rd. ... D 2
73 Cambridge Sq. ... G 6
78 Cambridge St. ..... F 5
74 Cambridge Ter. .. D 5
66 Camden .... E 6
74 Camden High St. . B 5
66 Camden Rd. ..... E 6
74 Camden St. ...... A 6
66 Camden Town ... E 6
77 Camera Place .... H 4
76 Camlet St. .... D 5
75 Camley St. .... B 7
76 Camomile St. .... G 4
77 Campden Grove . C 1
77 Campden Hill ... C 1
77 Campden Hill Rd. C 1
77 Campden St. ..... B 2
66 Camrose Ave .... C 2
79 Canada House ... A 8
80 Canal St. .... H 3
70 Cane Hill Hospital H 5
67 Cann Hall ...... D 10
77 Canning Place .... D 3
67 Canning Town .. F 10
67 Canning Town Sta. F 9
76 Cannon St. .... H 2
76 Cannon Street Sta. J 2
78 Cannon Row ...... C 8
76 Canon St. .... A 1
67 Canonbury ...... E 7
67 Canonbury Sta. .. E 7
66 Canons Park ..... B 2
66 Canon's Park Sta. C 2
67 Capel Rd. .... E 10
73 Capland St. ...... E 5
74 Capper St. .... E 6
74 Carburton St. ..... F 5
73 Cardigan Rd. .... D 1
79 Cardigan St. .... G 11
74 Cardington St. ... D 6
71 Carey La. .... G 1
75 Carey St. .... G 10
76 Carlisle Av. ...... H 4
79 Carlisle La. ..... D 10
78 Carlisle Place .... E 6
74 Carlisle St. .... G 7
74 Carlos Place ...... J 4
74 Carlow St. .... B 5
66 Carlton Ave. East D 2
78 Carlton Gdns. .... B 7
73 Carlton Hill ...... B 3
79 Carlton House Ter. B 7
73 Carlton Vale ..... C 1
77 Carlyle Square ... G 5
77 Carlyle's House .. H 6
75 Carmelite St. .... H 11
74 Carnaby St. ...... H 6
75 Carnegie St. ..... B 10
73 Caroline Place .... J 2
78 Caroline Ter. ..... F 3
65 Carpenters Park .. B 5
65 Carpenters Park Sta. .... B 5
67 Carpenters Rd. ... E 9
78 Carriage Drive East J 4
78 Carriage Drive Nth. H 4
78 Carriage Rd., ... C 2
79 Carroun Rd. ..... J 10
70 Carshalton .... E 5
70 Carshalton Beeches Sta. .... F 5
70 Carshalton Ho. ... F 5
70 Carshalton on the Hill .... F 5
70 Carshalton Rd. Wallington ..... F 5
70 Carshalton Rd. Woodmansterne G 5

75 Carter La. ....H 13
80 Carter Place ......G 1
79 Carter St. ....G 13
78 Carteret St. ......D 7
75 Carthusian St. ...F 13
75 Carting La. ....J 9
75 Cartwright Gdns. D 8
76 Cartwright St......J 6
65 Cassiobury Park . A 4
76 Casson St. ....F 6
73 Castellain Rd. .... E 3
70 Castelnau .... A 3
66 Castle Bar Park Sta. ....F 1
75 Castle Baynard St. ....H 13
66 Cat Hill .... A 5
80 Catesby St.........F 3
71 Catford .... B 9
71 Catford Bridge ... B 8
71 Catford Hill ...... B 8
71 Catford Sta....... B 8
77 Cathcart Rd. ..... H 3
78 Catherine Place .. D 6
75 Catherine St. .....H 9
74 Cato St. .... G 1
80 Cator St. ....J 5
69 Catos Hill .... E 6
75 Catton St. .... G 9
79 Causton St. ....F 7
77 Cavaye Place ..... G 4
73 Cavendish Av. ... C 5
73 Cavendish Cl. .... C 5
78 Cavendish Hotel . B 6
74 Cavendish Place .. G 5
66 Cavendish Rd. NW6 .... E 4
70 Cavendish Rd. SW12 .... B 5
74 Cavendish Square G 5
76 Cavendish St. .... C 2
78 Caversham St. ...H 2
78 Caxton Hall ...... D 7
78 Caxton St. .... D 7
76 Cayton St. .... D 2
70 Caesar's Camp ... C 3
79 Cenotaph .... C 8
79 Centaur St. ..... D 10
75 Central Criminal Court .... G 12
71 Central Hill ...... C 7
68 Central Park ..... D 2
70 Central Rd. ...... D 4
75 Central St. ......D 13
68 Chadwell Heath .. D 1
68 Chadwell Hth. La. D 1
75 Chadwell St. .... C 11
78 Chadwick St...... E 7
74 Chagford St. ..... E 2
65 Chalfont Common B 1
65 Chalfont Park .... C 1
65 Chalfont St. Peter C 1
66 Chalk Farm Rd... E 6
70 Chalk La. .... G 3
71 Chalky Hill .....G 11
74 Chalton St. ...... C 7
76 Chamber St. .....H 6
80 Chambers St. .... C 6
76 Chambord St. .... D 5
78 Chancel St. B12
75 Chancery La. ... G 10
75 Chandos Place ....J 8
74 Chandos St. ...... G 5
75 Chantry St. ..... B 13
80 Chapel Court .... C 2
67 Chapel End ...... C 9
75 Chapel Market .. B 11
73 Chapel Side ....J 2
73 Chapel St.NW1 ...F 6
78 Chapel St. SW1 .. D 4
79 Chapter Rd. .....G 13
78 Chapter St. ....F 7
79 Charing Cross Pier B 9
75 Charing Cross Rd. H 8
79 Charing Cross Sta. A 9
73 Charlbert St. ..... B 6
73 Charles La. ...... B 6
76 Charles Square ... D 3
78 Charles St. .... B 4
78 Charles II St...... A 7
80 Charleston St. ....F 2
74 Charlotte Mews ...F 6
76 Charlotte Rd. .... D 4
74 Charlotte St. .....F 6
75 Charlotte Ter. ... B 10
67 Charlton ....G 10
67 Charlton F.C. ....G 10
69 Charlton La. ..... D 4
67 Charlton Park ...H 10
75 Charlton Place .. B 12
67 Charlton Rd.SE7 H 10
69 Charlton Rd. Shepperton .... D 4
67 Charlton Way .... H 9
78 Charlwood Place ..F 6
78 Charlwood St. ... G 6
71 Charmwood La.. F 12
74 Charrington St. .. B 7
76 Chart St. .... D 3
75 Charterhouse .... F 12
75 Charterhouse Sq. F 13
75 Charterhouse St. F 12
66 Chase Rd. .... A 6
66 Chase Side .... A 6
80 Chatham St. ..... E 3
70 Cheam ....F 4
70 Cheam Rd. ....F 3
70 Cheam Sta. ....F 4
76 Cheapside ....H 2
78 Chelsea Barracks . G 4
78 Chelsea Bridge ...H 4
78 Chelsea Bridge Rd. G 4
78 Chelsea Embank.. H 2
77 Chelsea Hospital for Women .... G 5
77 Chelsea Manor Gdns. .... C 6
77 Chelsea Manor St. G 6
77 Chelsea Park Gdns. H5
77 Chelsea Polytechnic .... G 5
78 Chelsea Reach ... H 3
77 Chelsea Square ... G 5
71 Chelsfield Hill ... F 12
71 Chelsfield La. Orpington .... E 12
72 Chelsfield La. Orpington ......F 1
71 Chelsfield Rd. ... E 12
71 Chelsfield Sta.... F 12
71 Chelsfield Village F 12
71 Chelsham ....H 8
71 Chelsham Ct. Rd. H 9
71 Chelsham Rd. ....H 8
78 Cheltenham Ter. ..F 2
75 Cheney Rd. ...... C 8
74 Chenies Mews .... E 7
74 Chenies St. ....F 7
77 Cheniston Gdns. . D 2
73 Chepstow Cres. .. H 1
73 Chepstow Place .. H 1
73 Chepstow Rd. .... G 1
73 Chepstow Villas .. H 1
76 Chequer St. ...... E 2
68 Chequers Rd. .... B 3
76 Cherbury St. ..... C 3
69 Chertsey .... E 2
69 Chertsey Bridge .. E 3
69 Chertsey G.C. .... D 2
69 Chertsey La. ..... D 2
69 Chertsey Rd. Byfleet .... G 3
69 Chertsey Rd. Feltham .... C 4
69 Chertsey Rd. Shepperton .... E 3
78 Chesham Mews .. D 3
78 Chesham Place ... D 3
78 Chesham St. ...... E 3
76 Cheshire St. ...... E 6
70 Chessington ....F 2
70 Chessington Nth. Sta. ....F 2
70 Chessington Rd....F 2
70 Chessington South Sta. ....F 2
70 Chessington Zoological Gdns. F 1
78 Chester Close .... D 4
74 Chester Gate ..... D 5
74 Chester Mews .... D 4
74 Chester Place .... C 5
74 Chester Rd. ...... D 4
78 Chester Row ......F 3
78 Chester Square ... E 4
78 Chester St. .... D 4
74 Chester Terrace .. D 5
79 Chester Way .... F 11
78 Chesterfield Gdns. B 4
78 Chesterfield Hill .. A 4
78 Chesterfield St.... B 4
77 Cheval Place ..... D 6
71 Chevening Park . H 12
77 Cheyne Gdns. .... H 6
77 Cheyne Hospital . H 6
77 Cheyne Row .....H 6
77 Cheyne Walk ....H 6
79 Chicheley St. .... C 10
73 Chichester Rd. ....F 3
78 Chichester St. .... G 6
76 Chicksand St. .....F 6
67 Chigwell .... B 11
67 Chigwell La. .... A 11
67 Chigwell Rise ... B 11
67 Chigwell Rd. .... C 10
67 Chigwell Row ... B 12
68 Childerditch La... D 6
77 Child's Place ......F 2
77 Child's St. ....F 2
70 Chiltern Rd. ....F 4
74 Chiltern St. ....F 3
76 Chilton St. .... E 6
73 Chilworth Mews . H 4
73 Chilworth St. .... H 4
70 Chingford .... B 9
67 Chingford Hatch . B 9
67 Chingford La.... B 10
67 Chingford Mount Rd. .... B 9
67 Chingford Rd. ... C 9
73 Chippenham Mews E 1
73 Chippenham Rd. . E 1
70 Chipstead ....H 5
70 Chipstead Valley Rd. ....H 5
71 Chislehurst .....D 11
71 Chislehurst Common ..... C 11
71 Chislehurst G.C. C 11
71 Chislehurst Rd. Bromley ...... D 10
71 Chislehurst Rd. Orpington .... E 11
71 Chislehurst Sta. . D 10
71 Chislehurst West C 10
76 Chiswell St. ....F 2
66 Chiswick .... G 3
70 Chiswick Bridge .. A 2
66 Chiswick High Rd. .... G 3
70 Chiswick House .. A 3
66 Chiswick Park Sta. .... G 3
70 Chiswick Sta. .... A 2
66 Chiswick Steps ... H 3
74 Chitty St. ....F 6
65 Chorleywood Rd. A 3
66 Christchurch Ave. C 1
70 Christchurch Rd. . B 6
78 Christchurch St... G 2
76 Christian St. ..... H 7
76 Christina St. ..... E 4
76 Christopher St.....F 3
80 Chumleigh St. .... H 4
68 Church Elm La. .. E 2
66 Church End ...... C 4
72 Church Hill, Dartford ...... C 2
67 Church Hill, Loughton ..... A 11
69 Church Hill, Pyrford .... H 2
66 Church Hill Rd. .. A 5
79 Church House .... D 9
71 Church La. .... H 9
71 Church Rd. SE19 . D 7
70 Church Rd. SW19 C 4
69 Church Rd. Addlestone .....F 2
69 Church Rd. Ashford .... C 3
69 Church Rd. Byfleet .... G 3
71 Church Rd. Chelsfield ..... F 12
68 Church Rd. Noak Hill ...... A 3
65 Church Rd. Northolt .... E 5
72 Church Rd. Sutton-at-Hone .... C 3
70 Church Rd. Teddington .... C 1
73 Church St. NW8 ..F 5
67 Church St. Edmonton ..... B 7
67 Church St. Enfield A 7
70 Church St. Epsom .... G 3
69 Church St. Walton .... E 4
78 Churchill Gardens Estate .... G 6
78 Churchill Gardens Rd. .... G 5
74 Churchill Hotel .. G 3
75 Churchway ...... D 7
79 Churchyard Row E 12
78 Churton St. ....F 6
73 Circus Rd. .... C 5
75 City Garden Row C 13
75 City of London School .... H 12
75 City Rd. EC1 .... C 12
76 City Rd. EC1 ..... D 3
76 City Road Basin .. C 1
75 City University .. D 12
77 City & Guilds College .... D 5
74 Civil Service Commission ....J 6
78 Clabon Mews .... E 2
73 Clanricarde Gdns. .J 2
70 Clapham .... A 6
70 Clapham Common B 5
70 Clapham Common North Side ..... B 5
70 Clapham Common South Side ..... B 5
66 Clapham Junc. Sta. ....H 5
70 Clapham Park Rd. .... B 6
70 Clapham Rd. ..... A 6
70 Clapham Sta. .... A 6
67 Clapton Common D 8
67 Clapton Sta. ..... D 8
75 Claremont Close C 11
75 Claremont Square C 11
74 Clarence Gate .... E 3
74 Clarence Gardens D 5
78 Clarence House .. C 6
73 Clarendon Gate .. H 6
73 Clarendon Gdns. . E 4
74 Clarendon Grove . C 7
73 Clarendon Place .. H 6
78 Clarendon St. .... G 5
77 Clareville Grove ...F 4
77 Clareville Mews ...F 4
77 Clareville St. ......F 4
78 Clarges Mews .... B 5
78 Clarges St. .... B 5
74 Claridge's Hotel .. H 4
78 Claverton St. ..... G 6
74 Clay St. ....F 3
67 Claybury Hosp. . C 11
70 Claygate ....F 1
67 Clayhall .... C 11
67 Clayhall Av. .... C 11
67 Clayhall Park ... C 11
79 Claylands Place ..J 10
79 Claylands Rd. ....J 10
79 Clayton St. ......H 11
79 Cleaver Square .. G 11
79 Cleaver St. ...... G 11
72 Clement St. ...... C 2
76 Clement's La. .... H 3
79 Cleopatra's Needle .... A 9
76 Clere Place .... E 3
76 Clere St. .... E 3
75 Clerkenwell Close E 11
75 Clerkenwell Green E 12
75 Clerkenwell Rd. . E 11
73 Cleveland Gdns. . H 3
78 Cleveland Row ... B 6
73 Cleveland Square . H 3
74 Cleveland St. ......F 6
73 Cleveland Terrace G 4
75 Clifford Inn ..... G 11
74 Clifford St. ....J 5
73 Clifton Gdns. .... E 3
73 Clifton Hill ...... B 3
73 Clifton Place ..... H 5
73 Clifton Rd. .... E 4
76 Clifton St. ....F 3
73 Clifton Villas ......F 3
80 Clink St. .... A 2
74 Clipstone Mews ...F 6
74 Clipstone St. ......F 5
67 Clissold Park ..... D 7
78 Cliveden Place ... E 3
76 Cloak La. ....H 2
71 Clock House Sta. . D 8
69 Clockhouse La. .. C 3
75 Cloth Fair ...... F 13
75 Cloudesley Place B 11
75 Cloudesley Rd. .. B 11
75 Cloudesley Sq. .. A 11
75 Cloudesley St. ... B 11
76 Club Row .... D 5
80 Cluny Pl. .... D 4
77 Coalbrookdale Gt. C 5
76 Coate St. .... C 7
76 Cobb St. .... G 5
69 Cobham .... G 5
69 Cobham Park ....H 5
69 Cobham Rd. .....H 6
72 Cobham Terr. Rd. B 4
69 Cobham & Stoke D'Abernon Sta. H 5
80 Cobourg Rd. .....H 5
74 Cobourg St. ...... D 6
73 Cochrane St. ..... C 5
76 Cock Hill .... G 4
75 Cock La. .... G 12
66 Cockfosters ...... A 5
66 Cockfosters Sta... A 6
79 Cockspur St. ..... B 8
76 Code St. .... E 6
79 Coin St. .... B 11
77 Colbeck Mews ....F 3
68 Colchester Rd. ... C 3
72 Coldblow Maypole B 1
70 Coldharbour La. SE5 .... B 6
65 Coldharbour La. Hayes .... G 5
70 Cole Park .... B 1
80 Cole St. .... D 2
75 Colebrooke Row B 12
80 Colegrove Rd. .....J 6
77 Coleherne Mews . G 2
77 Coleherne Rd..... G 2
80 Coleman Rd. ....J 4
76 Coleman St. ...... G 2
75 Coley St. .... E 10
65 Colham Green ....F 4
66 Colin Deep La.... C 3
66 Colindale .... C 3
66 Colindale Av. .... C 3
66 Colindale Sta. .... C 3
75 Coliseum Theatre .J 8
76 College Hill ...... H 2
75 College of Arms . H 13
74 College Place ..... A 6
71 College Rd.SE21 . B 7
71 College Rd. Bromley .... D 9
72 College Rd. Dartford ...... D 1
70 College Rd. Epsom .... G 3
76 College St. .... H 2
68 Collier Row ...... C 2
68 Collier Row La. .. C 2
68 Collier Row Rd... C 2
75 Collier St. .... C 9
70 Collier's Wood ... C 5
77 Collingham Gdns. .F 3
77 Collingham Place .F 2
77 Collingham Rd. ...F 3
79 Collinson St. .... C 13
65 Colnbrook ....H 2
65 Colnbrook Bypass ....H 2
79 Colnbrook St. ... D 12
65 Colney Butts ..... A 5
66 Colney Hatch .... B 5
66 Colney Hatch La. C 6
79 Colombo St. .... B 12
75 Colonnade .... E 8
76 Columbia Rd. .... D 5
74 Colville Place ....F 7
80 Colwyn Gr. ....F 2
72 Colyer La. .... A 1
76 Commercial Rd... G 6
76 Commercial St. ...F 5
67 Commercial Way . H 8
66 Common Rd. ..... B 1
70 Commonside East D 5
70 Commonside West D 5
75 Compton St. .... E 12
79 Concert Hall Approach .... B 10
73 Conduit Mews ... H 4
73 Conduit Place .... H 5
74 Conduit St. .... H 5
80 Congreve St. ......F 4
74 Connaught Place . H 2
74 Connaught Sq. ... H 2
73 Connaught St. ... H 6
79 Cons St. .... C 11
78 Constitution Hill . C 5
80 Content St. ....F 2
69 Convent Rd. ..... C 4
74 Conway St. ...... E 6
79 Cooks Rd. ......H 12
70 Coombe Hill G.C. C 2
70 Coombe La. ..... D 3
70 Coombe Rd., Kingston ...... D 2
70 Coombe Rd. New Malden ....D 3
71 Coombe Rd. Sta. . E 7
70 Coombe Wood G.C. .... C 2
75 Coomb's St. ..... C 13
80 Cooper's Rd. ..... G 5
72 Cooper's Wood .. G 4
77 Cope Place .... D 1
75 Copenhagen St. .. A 9
79 Copperfield St. .. C 13
70 Copse Hill .... D 3
65 Copse Wood ..... C 4
69 Copsem La. ....F 6
76 Copthall Av. ..... G 3
76 Copthall Court ... G 3
75 Coptic St. .... G 8
79 Coral St. .... C 11
75 Coram St. .... E 8
75 Coram's Field Playground .... E 9
76 Corbet Place ......F 5
68 Corbets Tey ...... E 4
68 Corbets Tey Rd... E 4
74 Cork St. ....J 6
76 Corn Exchange ... H 4
76 Cornhill ....H 3
77 Cornwall Gdns. .. E 3
79 Cornwall Rd. ... B 11
76 Coronet St. ...... D 3
75 Corporation Row E 11
76 Corsham St. ..... D 3
79 Cosser St. .... D 10
73 Cosway St. ....F 6
80 Cotham St. ....F 2
77 Cottage Place .... D 6
78 Cottage Walk .... D 3
70 Cottenham Park . D 3
70 Cottenham Park Rd. .... D 3
77 Cottesmore Gdns. D 3
79 Cottington St.... F 12
70 Coulsdon ....H 6
70 Coulsdon Court G.C. .... G 6
70 Coulsdon La. .... H 5
70 Coulsdon North Sta. .... G 6
70 Coulsdon Rd. .... H 6
78 Coulson St. F2
79 County Hall ..... C 9
80 County St. .... E 2
71 Court La. B7
79 Courtenay St. ... G 10
77 Courtfield Gdns. ..F 2
77 Courtfield Rd. ....F 3
75 Convent Garden . H 9
79 Covent Garden Market ....H 8
74 Coventry St. ......J 7
80 Cowan St. .... H 4
75 Cowcross St. .... F 12
65 Cowley ....F 3
79 Cowley St. .... D 8
76 Cowper St. .... D 3
70 Craddocks Av. ... H 2
80 Crail Row ....F 3
74 Cramer St. ....F 4
79 Crampton St. ... F 13
75 Cranbourn St. ....H 8
67 Cranbrook Rd... C 11
65 Cranford .... H 4
65 Cranford La...... H 5
68 Cranham .... D 5
74 Cranleigh St. ..... C 6
77 Cranley Gdns. ... G 4
77 Cranley Mews .....F 4
77 Cranley Place .....F 5
76 Cranwood St. .... D 3
73 Craven Hill Gdns H3
79 Craven St. .... B 8
73 Craven Terrace ... H 4
74 Crawford Place .. G 1
74 Crawford St. ......F 2
72 Crayford .... A 2
72 Crayford Rd. ..... B 2
76 Creechurch La.... H 4
75 Creed La. ....H 12
67 Creekmouth .... F 12
76 Cremer St. .... C 5
77 Crescent Place ... E 6
75 Crescent Row ... E 13
77 Cresswell Gdns ...F 3
77 Cresswell Place ... G 4
75 Crestfield St. ..... C 9
66 Cricklewood ..... E 4
66 Cricklewood La. . D 4
66 Cricklewood Sta. . E 4
80 Crimscott St...... E 4
75 Crinan St. .... B 9
78 Cringle St. ....J 6

76 Cripplegate Institute ....F 1
74 Criterion Theatre ..J 7
72 Crockenhill ...... E 1
71 Crofton Heath .. E 10
71 Crofton Park Sta. B 8
71 Crofton Rd...... E 11
71 Croham Hurst G.C. ....F 7
71 Croham Rd. ......F 7
75 Cromer St. .... D 9
73 Crompton St. .... E 4
77 Cromwell Cres. ...F 1
77 Cromwell Gdns... E 5
77 Cromwell Mews .. E 5
77 Cromwell Place .. E 5
77 Cromwell Rd. SW5 & SW7........... E 3
69 Cromwell Rd. Hounslow ..... B 6
76 Crondall St....... C 3
76 Cropley St........ B 2
80 Crosby Row ..... C 3
76 Crosby Square ... G 4
68 Cross La. .... D 3
70 Crossdeep .... C 1
76 Crosswall .... H 5
66 Crouch End ...... D 6
66 Crouch Hill ...... D 6
66 Crouch Hill Sta... D 6
68 Crow La. .... D 2
70 Crown Dale ...... C 6
75 Crown Office Row .... H 11
80 Crown St..........J 2
74 Crowndale Rd.... B 6
65 Croxley Green ... A 4
65 Croxley Green Sta. A 4
65 Croxley Sta....... A 4
71 Croxted Rd....... B 7
71 Croydon .... E 7
70 Croydon La. ...... G 5
71 Croydon Rd. SE20 .... D 7
71 Croydon Rd. Beckenham .... D 8
71 Croydon Rd. Bromley ...... E 10
71 Croydon Rd. Chelsham ...... H 9
70 Croydon Rd. Croydon .... E 6
70 Croydon Rd. Mitcham ...... D 5
80 Crucifix La....... C 4
75 Cruden St. .... B 12
75 Cruickshank St. . C 10
76 Crutched Friars .. H 4
71 Crystal Palace F.C. D 7
71 Crystal Palace Sta. C 7
71 Crystal Palace Park C 7
75 Cubit St. .... D 10
70 Cuddington G.C.. G 4
71 Cudham .... G 11
71 Cudham La. Cudham ...... G 11
71 Cudham La. Green Street Green .. F 11
71 Cudham La. Horns Green .... H 11
71 Cudham Rd. .... G 11
78 Culford Gdns. ....F 2
76 Culham St........ H 4
75 Culpepper St. ... B 11
74 Culross St. ....J 3
73 Culworth St. ..... C 6
74 Cumberland Gate H 2
74 Cumberland Hotel H 3
74 Cumberland Market .... D 5
78 Cumberland St. .. G 5
74 Cumberland Ter . C 5
75 Cumming St..... C 10
80 Cunard St. .... H 3
78 Cundy St..........F 4
73 Cunningham Pl... E 5
79 Cureton St. ....F 8
80 Curlew St. .... C 5
75 Cursitor St. ..... G 11
76 Curtain Rd. ...... E 4
80 Curtis St. .... E 5
80 Curtis Way ...... E 5
78 Curzon Gate ..... B 4
78 Curzon St. .... B 4
76 Custom House ....J 4
67 Custom House Sta. .... F 10
79 Cut, The .... C 11
73 Cuthbert St........F 5
76 Cutler St. .... G 4
75 Cynthia St....... C 10
74 Cypress Place .....F 6
75 Cyrus St......... D 12
78 Dacre St. .... D 7
68 Dagenham .... E 2
68 Dagenham Av. ... E 1
68 Dagenham Dock Sta. ....F 1
68 Dagenham Heathway Sta. .... E 1
68 Dagenham Rd.... D 2
68 Dagenham Park .. B 4
75 Dallington St. ... E 12
67 Dalston .... E 7
67 Dalston Junc. Sta. E 7
67 Dalston La. ...... E 8
72 Daltons Rd. ...... E 1
75 Dame St. .... B 13
75 Danbury St...... B 12
75 Dane St. ....F 9
72 Danson Park .... B 12
79 Danson Rd.SE17 G 13
71 Danson Rd. Bexley Heath .... B 12
79 Dante Rd. ...... F 12
77 Danvers St. ...... H 5
74 D'Arblay St. ..... H 6
72 Darenth .... C 3
72 Darenth Rd. ..... B 3
72 Dartford .... B 2
72 Dartford G.C. ... C 2
72 Dartford Heath .. B 2
72 Dartford-Purfleet Tunnel .... A 3
72 Dartford Rd. Dartford ...... B 2
72 Dartford Rd. Hextable ...... C 2
66 Dartmouth Park Hill .... D 6
71 Dartmouth Rd. .. C 8
78 Dartmouth St. ... D 7
80 Dartnell Rd. ..... H 4
80 Darwin St. ....F 3
65 Datchet .... H 1
80 Date St........... G 2
76 Davenant St. ......F 6
73 Daventry St. ......F 6
80 Davey St. .... H 5
71 Davidson Rd. .... E 7
74 Davies Mews ..... H 4
74 Davies St......... H 4
66 Dawes Rd. .... H 4
80 Dawes St. ....F 3
65 Dawley Rd. ...... G 4
67 Daws Hill .... A 9
73 Dawson Place .... H 1
71 Days La. .... B 11
79 De Laune St. ... G 12
77 De Vere Gdns. ... D 3
74 De Walden St. ....F 4
80 Deacon St. .... E 1
80 Deacon Way ..... E 1
76 Deal St. ....F 6
79 Dean Bradley St. . E 8
78 Dean Farrar St. .. D 7
79 Dean Ryle St. .... E 8
79 Dean Stanley St. . E 8
74 Dean St. .... H 7
78 Deanery St. ...... B 4
80 Dean's Buildings ..F 3
75 Dean's Court ... H 13
66 Dean's La. .... B 3
79 Dean's Yard ..... D 8
66 Deansbrook Rd. . B 3
67 Debden Sta...... A 11
80 Decima St. .... D 4
70 Deer Park .... D 4
79 Defence, Ministry of .... B 8
65 Delaford Park .....F 2
73 Delamere Terrace .F 3
74 Delancey St. ..... B 5
73 Delaware Rd. .... E 2
75 Delhi St. .... A 9
78 Denbigh Place ....F 6
78 Denbigh St. ....F 6
65 Denham .... D 2
65 Denham Aerodrome .... C 2
74 Denman St. ....J 7
75 Denmark Grove. B 11
71 Denmark Hill .... B 7
71 Denmark Hill Sta. A 7
75 Denmark St. ..... G 8
70 Denning Avenue ..F 6
68 Dennises La. ..... E 4
79 Denny Crescent . F 11
79 Denny St. .... F 11
78 Denyer St. ....F 2
67 Deptford .... H 8
67 Deptford Sta. .... H 9
76 Derbyshire St..... D 7
76 Dereham Place ... D 4
74 Dering St. .... H 5
71 Derry Downs ... E 12
77 Derry St. .... D 2
73 Desborough Cl. ...F 3
80 Deverell St. ...... E 2
75 Devonia Rd. ..... B 12
67 Devons Rd. ....F 9
74 Devonshire Close .F 5
74 Devonshire Mews South ....F 4
74 Devonshire Mews West ....F 4
74 Devonshire Place ..F 4
74 Devonshire Plce. Mews ....F 4
76 Devonshire Row . G 4
76 Devonshire Square G 4
74 Devonshire St. ....F 4
73 Devonshire Ter... H 4
75 Dewey Rd....... B 11
77 Dial Walk, The .. C 3
74 Diana Place ...... E 5
80 Dickens Square .. D 2
75 Dignum St. ..... B 11
78 Dilke St. .... H 2
76 Dingley Place .... D 2
76 Dingley Rd. ...... D 1
76 Diss St. .... C 5
76 Distaff La. .... H 1
79 Distin St. .... F 11
70 Ditton Hill .... E 1
65 Ditton Park ...... G 1
70 Ditton Rd. .... E 2
76 Dock St. ....J 6
80 Dockhead .... C 6
80 Dockley Rd. ..... D 6
79 Doddington Gr.. G 12
79 Dolben St. ...... B 12
79 Dolland St. ..... G 10
66 Dollis Hill La..... D 4
66 Dollis Hill Sta. ... E 3
78 Dolphin Square .. G 7
75 Dombey St. ....F 9
75 Dominion St. .....F 3
80 Domville Grove .. G 5
75 Donegal St. ..... C 10
78 Donne Place ..... E 1
79 Doon St. .... B 10
78 Dorchester Hotel . B 4
74 Doric Way .... D 7
70 Dorking Rd. ..... G 2
75 Dorrington St. .. F 11
74 Dorset Close ......F 2
76 Dorset Estate .... C 5
78 Dorset Mews ..... D 4
78 Dorset Place ......F 7
75 Dorset Rise ..... H 12
70 Dorset Rd.SW19 . D 4
79 Dorset Rd.SW8 ...J 9
74 Dorset Square .... E 2
74 Dorset St. ....F 3
75 Doughty Mews .. E 10
75 Doughty St. ..... E 10
78 Douglas St. ....F 7
77 Douro Place ..... D 3
77 Dove Mews ....F 4
76 Dove Row .... H 4
77 Dovehouse St. ... G 5
70 Dover House Rd.. B 3
78 Dover St. .... A 5
76 Dowgate Hill .... H 2
78 Down St. .... B 4
71 Downe .... G 10
71 Downham Estate . C 9
71 Downham Way .. C 9
79 Downing St. ..... C 8
70 Downs Rd. Epsom G 3
70 Downs Rd. Sutton G 4
72 Downs Rd. Swanscombe ... C 6
72 Downs Wood .... G 6
69 Downside .... H 5
69 Downside Rd. .... H 5
79 Draco St. .... H 13
75 Drake St. ....F 9
76 Drant St. ....F 5
79 Draper St. ...... E 13
76 Drapers Hall .... G 3
78 Draycott Avenue .F 1
78 Draycott Place ....F 2
78 Draycott Terrace ..F 2
77 Drayson Mews ... C 2
77 Drayton Gdns.... G 4
66 Drayton Green ....F 1
67 Drive, The ...... D 11
80 Druid St. .... C 5
74 Drummond Cres. C 7
74 Drummond St.... D 6
75 Drury La. .... H 9
75 Dryden St. .... H 9
76 Drysdale St....... D 4
76 Ducal St. .... D 5
77 Duchess of Bedford's Walk .... C 1
74 Duchess St. ....F 5
75 Duchess Theatre . H 9
79 Duchy St. .... B 11
65 Ducks Hill .... C 4
65 Ducks Hill Rd. ... C 4
66 Dudden Hill La... E 3
76 Dufferin St. ...... E 2
78 Duke of York St. . A 6
78 Duke of York's H.Q. ....F 3
75 Duke of York's Th. J 8
78 Duke St. SW1 .... A 6
74 Duke St. W1 ..... H 4
80 Duke Street Hill .. B 3
77 Duke's La. .... C 2
76 Duke's Place ..... G 4
75 Duke's Rd. .... D 7
71 Dulwich .... B 7
71 Dulwich College . C 7
71 Dulwich Common B 7
71 Dulwich Park ... B 7
71 Dulwich Village .. B 7
71 Dulwich Wood Pk. C 7
71 Dulwich & Sydenham Hill .......G.C. C 7
76 Dunbridge St..... E 7
75 Duncan St....... B 12
75 Duncan Terrace . B 12
76 Dunloe St. .... C 5
80 Dunlop Place .... E 6
68 Dunning's La..... D 6
74 Dunraven St...... H 3
70 Dunstans Hill .....F 4
76 Dunston Rd. ..... A 5
72 Dunton Green ... H 1
80 Dunton Rd. ....F 5
78 Duplex Ride ..... C 3
76 Durant St. .... C 6
67 Durants Park .... A 8
70 Durham Rd. ..... D 3
79 Durham St. ..... G 10
73 Durham Terrace . G 2
66 Durnsford Rd. N11 .... C 6
70 Durnsford Rd. SW19 .... C 4
78 Dyley St. .... E 3
75 Dyott St. .... G 8
76 Dysart St......... E 3
75 Eagle St. ....F 9
76 Eagle Wharf Rd. . B 2
66 Ealing ....F 2
66 Ealing Broadway Sta. ....F 2
66 Ealing Common .. G 2
66 Ealing Common Sta. .... G 2
66 Ealing G.C. ....F 1
66 Ealing Rd. Brentford ...... G 2
65 Ealing Rd. Greenford ..... E 6
66 Ealing Rd. Wembley ...... E 2
73 Eamont St........ B 6
77 Eardley Cres. .... G 1
80 Earl Rd. ....F 5
76 Earl St. ....F 3
75 Earlham St. ...... H 8
77 Earl's Court ..... G 1
77 Earl's Court Gdns. F 2
77 Earl's Court Rd... E 1
77 Earl's Court Sq. .. G 2
77 Earl's Court Sta. ..F 2
67 Earl's Path ...... A 10
77 Earl's Walk ...... E 1
70 Earlsfield Rd. .... B 4
70 Earlsfield Sta. .... B 4
75 Earlstoke St. ... D 12
75 Earnshaw St...... G 8
66 East Acton ...... G 3
66 East Acton Sta. ...F 3
66 East Barnet ..... A 6
69 East Bedfont ..... B 4
71 East Croydon Sta. E 7
71 East Dulwich .... B 7
71 East Dulwich Rd. B 7
71 East Dulwich Sta. B 7
66 East End Rd. ..... C 5
70 East Ewell ....F 4
66 East Finchley .... C 5
66 East Finchley Sta. C 5
71 East Hall Rd. ... E 12
67 East Ham .... F 11
75 East Harding St. G 11
72 East Hill, Dartford ...... B 3
70 East Hill, SW18 .. B 4
67 East India Dock Rd. ....F 9
80 East La. .... D 6
66 East La., Wembley D 2
69 East Moseley .... D 6
70 East Putney Sta... B 4
76 East Rd. .... D 3
71 East Rochester Way .... B 12
70 East Sheen .... B 2
70 East Sheen Gate .. B 2
76 East Smithfield ....J 6
80 East St. SE17......F 4
70 East St., Epsom .. G 3
76 East Tenter St. ... H 6
67 East Wickham .. H 12
73 Eastbourne Mews G 4
73 Eastbourne Ter... G 4
65 Eastbury .... B 4
74 Eastcastle St...... G 6
76 Eastcheap .... H 3
65 Eastcote .... D 6
65 Eastcote La. ..... E 5
65 Eastcote Rd. ..... D 4
67 Eastern Avenue . D 10
68 Eastern Avenue East .... C 2, C 3
68 Eastern Avenue West .... C 1
68 Easthall La. ....F 3
67 Eastham Manor Way .... F 11
75 Eastham Dental Hospital ...... D 10
75 Easton St........ D 11
69 Eastworth .... E 2
69 Eastworth Rd. ... E 2
78 Eaton Gate ...... E 3
78 Eaton La. .... D 5
78 Eaton Mews North E 3
78 Eaton Mews South E 4
78 Eaton Mews West E 4
78 Eaton Place ...... E 3
78 Eaton Row ...... D 4
78 Eaton Square .... E 4
78 Eaton Terrace .... E 3
76 Ebenezer St. ..... D 2
76 Ebor St. .... E 5
78 Ebury Bridge ......F 4
78 Ebury Bridge Rd.. G 4
78 Ebury Mews ..... E 4
78 Ebury Mews East. E 4
78 Ebury Square .....F 4
78 Ebury St. .... E 4
78 Eccleston Bridge . E 5
78 Eccleston Mews .. D 4
78 Eccleston Square ..F 5
78 Eccleston Street Mews ....F 5
78 Eccleston Place ... E 5
73 Edbrooke Rd. .... E 1
71 Eden Park .... D 8
70 Edge Hill Rd. .....F 6
77 Edge St. .... B 2
66 Edgware .... B 3
66 Edgware Rd., NW2 .... D 3
66 Edgware Rd.NW9 C 3
73 Edgware Rd. W2 ..F 5
78 Edinburgh Gate .. C 2
77 Edith Grove ....J 4
77 Edith Terrace .....J 3
80 Edmund St. ....J 3
70 Eel Pie Is. .... B 1
70 Effra Rd. .... B 6
77 Egerton Crescent . E 6
77 Egerton Gardens . E 6
77 Egerton Place .... E 6
77 Egerton Terrace .. E 6
69 Egham .... C 1
80 Elba Place .... E 2
71 Elder Rd. .... C 7
76 Elder St. .... E 4
77 Eldon Rd. .... D 3
76 Eldon St. ....F 3
80 Elephant Rd. ..... E 1
80 Elephant & Castle Sta. .... E 1
73 Elgin Avenue .... D 2
75 Elia Mews ...... C 12
75 Elia St. .... C 12
78 Elizabeth Bridge ....F 5
78 Elizabeth St. ..... E 4
76 Ellen St. .... H 6
79 Elliott's Row .... E 12
78 Ellis St. .... E 3
65 Elm Avenue ...... D 5
68 Elm Park .... D 3
77 Elm Park Gdns. .. G 5
77 Elm Park La...... G 4
77 Elm Park Rd. SW3 .... H 4
77 Elm Place .... G 5
75 Elm St. .... E 10
75 Elm Tree Cl. ..... C 5
73 Elm Tree Rd...... C 5
71 Elmers End ...... D 8
73 Elms Mews ....J 4
71 Elmstead .... C 10
71 Elmstead La..... C 10
71 Elmstead Wood . C 10
69 Elmwood Avenue C 5
73 Elnathan Mews .. E 3
66 Elstree .... A 2
66 Elstree Aerodrome .... A 1
66 Elstree Hill South .... A 2
66 Elstree Rd., Bushey .... A 1
66 Elstree Rd., Stanmore .... B 2
66 Elstree & Borehamwood Sta. .... A 2
80 Elsted St. ....F 3
71 Eltham .... B 10
71 Eltham Bypass .. C 10
71 Eltham Common A 10
71 Eltham Hill ..... B 10
71 Eltham Park .... B 11
71 Eltham Park Sta. B 10
71 Eltham Rd. ...... B 9
80 Eltham St. ....F 2
71 Eltham Warren G.C. .... B 11
71 Eltham West Hall Sta. .... B 10
66 Elthorne Heights ..F 1
77 Elvaston Mews ... D 4
77 Elvaston Place ... D 4
70 Elvers Way ...... H 3
78 Elverton St. ...... E 7
76 Elwin St......... C 6
75 Ely Place........ F 11
78 Elystan Place ......F 2
77 Elystan St. ....F 6
78 Embankment Gdns. .... H 3
69 Ember La. .... E 6
75 Emerald St. ..... F 10
68 Emerson Park .... D 3
80 Emerson St....... A 1
78 Emery Hill St..... E 6
77 Emperor's Gate .. E 3
66 Empire Pool ..... E 2
75 Endell St. .... G 8
67 Endlebury Rd. ... B 9
74 Endsleigh Gdns... D 7
74 Endsleigh Place .. E 7
74 Endsleigh St. ..... D 7
71 Endwell Rd. ..... A 8
67 Enfield .... A 7
67 Enfield Chase Sta. A 7
67 Enfield G.C. ..... A 7
66 Enfield Rd. ...... A 6
67 Enfield Town Sta. A 7
74 Enford St. ....F 2
80 Enid St. .... D 6
77 Ennismore Gdns.. D 6
77 Ennismore Gardens Mews .... D 5
77 Ennismore Mews . D 6
77 Ennismore St. .... D 6
76 Ensign St. ....J 6
79 Environment, Dept. of ...... B 13
70 Epsom .... G 2
70 Epsom Common . G 2
70 Epsom District Hospital .... G 2
70 Epsom Downs Race Course .... H 3
70 Epsom Downs Sta. G 3
70 Epsom G.C. ..... G 3
70 Epsom La. .... H 3
70 Epsom Rd., Croydon .... E 6

70 Epsom Rd., Ewell G 3
70 Epsom Rd., Leatherhead ... H 1
70 Epsom Rd., Morden .... E 4
67 Epping Forest .... A 10, C 9
67 Epping New Rd.. A 10
76 Epworth St. .... E 3
79 Erasmus St. .... F 8
79 Erbisham Dr. .... H 9
72 Erith .... A 2
68 Erith Marshes .... G 1
68 Erith Reach ...... G 2
68 Erith Rd. Belvedere ...... G 2
68 Erith Rd., Northumberland Heath .... H 2
74 Eros .... J 7
76 Errol St. .... E 2
69 Esher .... F 6
69 Esher Common ... F 6
69 Esher La. .... E 6
69 Esher Rd. .... F 5
69 Esher Sta. .... E 6
80 Esmeralda Rd. .... F 7
73 Essendine Rd. .... D 1
75 Essex Rd. .... A 12
77 Essex St. .... H 10
77 Essex Villas ...... D 1
77 Eustace Rd. ...... J 1
74 Euston Centre .... E 5
74 Euston Square ... D 7
74 Euston Sta. .... D 6
74 Euston Station Colonnade ..... D 7
74 Euston Rd. .... E 6
74 Euston St. .... D 6
74 Euston Tower ..... E 6
77 Evelyn Gdns. .... G 4
67 Evelyn St. .... G 8
75 Everilda St. ...... A 10
74 Eversholt St. ..... C 6
70 Ewell .... F 3
70 Ewell Bypass ...... F 3
70 Ewell East Sta. .... F 3
70 Ewell West Sta. ... F 3
79 Ewer St. .... B 13
75 Exeter St. .... H 9
77 Exhibition Rd. ... D 5
75 Exmouth Market D 11
80 Exon St. .... F 4
79 Exton St. .... B 11
72 Eynsford .... E 3
75 Eyre Street Hill .. E 11
76 Ezra St. .... C 6
69 Faggs Rd. .... B 4
80 Fair St. .... C 4
76 Fairchild St. ..... E 4
71 Fairchildes Rd. ... G 9
76 Fairclough St. .... H 7
80 Faircombe St. ..... C 7
73 Fairlop Pl. .... D 5
67 Fairlop Sta. ...... C 11
67 Fairmead Rd. .... A 10
69 Fairmile .... G 5
69 Fairmile La. ..... G 5
70 Fairoak La. .... G 1
72 Fairseat .... G 5
71 Falconwood Sta. B 11
76 Falkirk St. .... C 4
65 Falling La. .... F 3
80 Falmouth Rd. .... E 2
76 Fann St. .... E 1
76 Fanshaw St. ...... C 4
71 Farleigh .... G 8
71 Farleigh Court Rd. G 8
71 Farley Rd. .... F 7
77 Farm La. SW6 ..... J 1
70 Farm La., Epsom H 2
74 Farm St. .... J 4
79 Farmers Rd. ..... J 12
71 Farnborough ... F 11
71 Farnborough Bypass .... F 11
71 Farnborough Common ..... E 10
79 Farnham Place .. B 13
79 Farnham Royal . G 10
72 Farningham ..... E 3
72 Farningham Rd. . D 3
72 Farningham Rd. & Sutton-at-Hone Sta. .... D 3
72 Farningham Wood D 2
75 Farringdon Rd. . E 11
75 Farringdon Sta. . F 12
75 Farringdon St. .. G 12
76 Fashion St. .... F 5
79 Faunce St. .... G 12
77 Fawcett St. .... H 3
72 Fawkham Green . E 4
71 Featherbed La. .... F 8
76 Featherstone St. .. E 2
69 Feltham .... C 4
69 Feltham Rd. ..... C 4
69 Felthamhill ...... C 5
69 Felthamhill Rd. .. C 4
80 Felton Rd. .... C 6
68 Fen La. .... E 6
67 Fencepiece Rd. .. B 11
76 Fenchurch Avenue H 4
76 Fenchurch Bldgs. . H 4
76 Fenchurch St. .... H 4
76 Fenchurch Street Sta. .... H 5
80 Fendall St. .... D 4
79 Fentiman Rd. ..... J 9
75 Fernsbury St. ... D 11
77 Fernshaw Rd. ..... J 3
67 Ferry La. N17 .... C 8
68 Ferry La., Rainham F 2
75 Fetter La. .... G 11
71 Fickleshole ...... G 9
75 Field Court ..... F 10
65 Field End Rd. .... D 5
75 Field Place ...... C 11
75 Field St. .... C 9
76 Fieldgate St. ..... G 7
75 Fife Ter. .... B 10
72 Filston La. .... G 2
77 Finborough Rd. .. H 3
76 Finch La. .... H 3
66 Finchley .... C 5
66 Finchley Cent. Sta. C 5
66 Finchley G.C. .... B 4
73 Finchley Pl. ...... B 4
66 Finchley Rd. ..... E 5
73 Finchley Rd. ..... B 4
66 Finchley Rd. ..... D 4
66 Finchley Road & Frognall Sta. ... E 5
79 Finck St. .... D 10
67 Finsbury .... F 7
76 Finsbury Circus ... F 3
75 Finsbury Estate . D 12
67 Finsbury Park .... D 7
67 Finsbury Park Sta. D 7
76 Finsbury Pavement F 3
76 Finsbury Square .. F 3
76 Finsbury St. ...... F 2
79 Fire Brigade H.Q. . F 9
67 Firs La. .... B 7
78 First St. .... E 1
70 Firtree Rd. .... G 4
76 Fish Street Hill .... J 3
75 Fisher St. .... F 9
73 Fisherton St. ..... E 5
76 Fishmongers' Hall . J 3
79 Fitzalan St. ...... E 10
74 Fitzhardinge St. .. G 3
66 Fitzjohn's Avenue E 5
78 Fitzmaurice Place A 5
74 Fitzroy Square ... E 6
74 Fitzroy St. .... E 6
75 Flaxman Terrace . D 8
75 Fleet La. .... G 12
75 Fleet St. .... H 11
79 Fleming Rd. .... H 12
76 Fleur de Lis St. ... E 4
80 Flint St. .... F 3
80 Flinten St. .... F 4
78 Flood St. .... G 1
77 Flood Walk ...... G 6
75 Floral St. .... H 8
76 Florida St. .... D 7
77 Flower Walk, The C 4
76 Flower & Dean St. F 5
76 Fochelle St. ...... D 5
74 Foley St. .... F 6
76 Folgate St. .... F 4
71 Foots Cray .... C 12
71 Foots Cray La. .. C 12
71 Foots Cray Rd. .. B 10
76 Forbes St. .... H 6
69 Ford Bridge Rd. .. C 3
69 Fordbridge Rd. .. D 4
76 Fore St. EC2 ...... F 2
67 Fore St. N18 ..... B 8
65 Fore St., Ruislip .. C 5
79 Foreign Office ... C 8
67 Forest Gate ..... E 10
71 Forest Hill .... C 7
71 Forest Hill Sta. ... C 8
67 Forest Hospital . B 10
67 Forest La. .... E 10
67 Forest Rd. E17 ... C 9
67 Forest Rd., Ilford C 12
70 Forest Rd., Sutton E 4
67 Forest Side ...... A 10
73 Formosa St. .... E 3
76 Fornier St. .... F 5
74 Forest St. .... G 2
76 Forston St. .... B 2
80 Fort Rd. .... F 6
66 Fortis Green Rd. . C 5
66 Fortress Rd. ..... E 6
66 Fortune Green Rd. E 4
76 Fortune St. ...... E 2
66 Forty Avenue .... D 2
66 Forty La. .... D 3
76 Foster La. .... G 1
74 Foubert's Place .. H 6
77 Foulis Terrace .... F 5
75 Fox Court ...... F 11
69 Fox Hill Rd. ...... F 1
66 Fox La. .... B 6
68 Foxburrow Wood A 1
69 Foxoak Hill .... F 4
73 Frampton St. .... E 5
78 Francis St. .... E 6
78 Franklin's Row .. G 3
79 Frazier St. ...... C 11
80 Frean St. .... D 6
75 Frederick St. ..... D 9
80 Fremantle St. ..... F 4
69 French St. .... D 5
80 Frensham St. ..... H 6
80 Friary Rd. .... J 7
75 Friday St. .... H 13
75 Friend St. .... C 12
74 Friends House ... D 7
66 Friern Barnet .... B 5
74 Frith St. .... H 7
71 Frith Wood ...... G 8
75 Frome St. .... B 13
68 Front La. .... D 4
66 Fryent Way ...... D 2
70 Fulham F.C. ..... A 3
70 Fulham Palace ... A 4
66 Fulham Palace Rd. H 4
70 Fulham Rd. SW6 . A 4
77 Fulham Rd. SW10 G 5
76 Fuller St. .... D 6
65 Fulmer .... E 1
69 Fulwell G.C. ..... C 5
75 Furnival St. ..... G 11
70 Furze Hill .... H 4
66 Furzehill Rd. ..... A 3
78 Fynes St. .... E 7
80 Gainsford St. .... C 5
68 Gale St. .... E 1
71 Gallery Rd. ...... B 7
72 Galley Hill .... B 5
67 Galliard Rd. ..... A 8
67 Gallions Reach .. G 11
68 Gallows Corner .. C 3
79 Gambia St. ..... B 12
70 Gander Green La. E 4
74 Ganton St. .... H 6
67 Gants Hill Sta. .. D 11
74 Garbutt Place ..... F 4
73 Garden Rd. ...... C 4
79 Garden Row ..... D 12
76 Garden Walk .... D 4
76 Garlick Hill ...... H 2
75 Garnault Place .. D 11
70 Garratt La. ...... C 4
76 Garrett St. .... E 1
75 Garrick St. .... H 8
75 Garrick Theatre ... J 8
70 Garth Rd. .... E 3
73 Garway Rd. ...... H 2
76 Gascogne Place ... D 5
79 Gasholder Place . G 10
69 Gaston Bridge Rd. D 4
75 Gate St. .... G 9
73 Gateforth St. ..... E 6
67 Gates Corner ... C 10
78 Gatliff Rd. .... G 4
79 Gaunt St. .... D 13
79 Gayfere St. .... E 8
79 Gaywood St. .... E 12
79 Gaza St. .... G 12
75 Gee St. .... E 13
76 Geffrye Museum C 14
76 Geffrye St. .... B 5
75 General Post Office .... G 13
77 Geological Mus... E 5
80 George Row ..... C 6
74 George St. .... G 2
74 George Yard ..... H 4
65 George V Avenue C 6
79 Geraldine Mary Harmsworth Pk. E 11
79 Geraldine St. ..... E 12
68 Gerpins La. ...... E 4
75 Gerrard Rd. ...... B 12
74 Gerrard St. ...... H 7
65 Gerrards Cross ... D 1
79 Gerridge St. ..... D 11
77 Gertrude St. ..... H 4
79 Gibson Rd. ...... F 10
68 Gidea Park ...... C 3
68 Gidea Park Sta. .. C 3
75 Gilbert Place ..... G 8
79 Gilbert Rd. ..... F 11
74 Gilbert St. .... H 4
72 Gildenhill Rd. .... D 3
78 Gillingham St. ... E 5
77 Gilston Rd. ...... G 4
75 Giltspur St. ..... G 12
66 Gladstone Park .. E 3
79 Gladstone St. ... D 12
78 Glasgow Ter. .... G 6
79 Glass Hill St. .... C 13
74 Glasshouse St. .... J 6
79 Glasshouse Walk . G 9
75 Glasshouse Yard E 13
77 Glebe Place ...... H 6
77 Gledhow Gdns. ... F 3
80 Glengall Rd. ..... H 6
80 Glengall Terrace . H 5
74 Glentworth St. ... E 2
67 Globe Rd. .... F 8
80 Globe St. .... D 2
80 Globe Theatre, SE1 E 3
74 Globe Theatre, W1 H 7
74 Globe Yard ...... H 5
74 Gloucester Avenue A 4
74 Gloucester Gate .. B 4
73 Gloucester Mews . H 4
73 Gloucester Mews West .... H 4
74 Gloucester Place .. F 2
74 Gloucester Place Mews .... G 3
77 Gloucester Rd. ... E 3
73 Gloucester Square H 5
78 Gloucester St. .... G 6
73 Gloucester Terrace G 3
77 Gloucester Walk . C 1
75 Gloucester Way . D 11
79 Glyn St. .... G 9
77 Godfrey St. ...... G 6
79 Goding St. .... G 9
75 Godson St. ...... B 11
71 Godstone Rd. .... H 7
76 Golden La. ...... E 1
75 Golden La. Est. . E 13
74 Golden Square ... H 6
66 Golders Green ... D 4
66 Golders Green Rd. D 4
66 Golders Green Sta. D 5
66 Goldhawk Rd. ... G 4
74 Goldington Crcs. . B 7
74 Goldington St. ... B 7
75 Goldman St. .... H 13
73 Goldney Rd. ...... E 1
76 Goldsmiths Hall . G 1
76 Goldsmiths Row . B 6
74 Goodge Place ..... F 6
74 Goodge St. .... F 6
76 Goodman St. .... H 6
76 Goodmans Yard . H 5
67 Goodmayes ..... D 12
67 Goodmayes Hospital ...... D 12
67 Goodmayes La. . D 12
75 Goods Way ...... B 8
75 Goose Yd. ...... C 11
76 Gopsall St. .... B 3
77 Gordon Place .... C 2
75 Gordon Square .. E 7
74 Gordon St. .... E 7
72 Gore Hill .... C 3
77 Gore St. .... D 4
71 Gorse Rd. .... E 12
68 Goresbrook Rd... E 1
76 Gorsuch St. ..... C 5
74 Gosfield St. .... F 5
66 Gospel Oak Sta... E 6
76 Gosset St. .... D 6
75 Goswell Rd. ..... D 12
75 Goswell Terrace . D 12
76 Goulston St. ..... G 5
75 Gough Square .. G 11
75 Gough St. .... E 10
74 Gower Mews ...... F 7
74 Gower Place ..... E 7
74 Gower St. .... E 7
76 Gowers Walk .... H 6
76 Gracechurch St... H 3
74 Grafton Mews ... E 6
74 Grafton Place .... D 7
74 Grafton St. .... J 5
74 Grafton Way ..... E 6
67 Graham Rd. ..... E 8
75 Graham St. ..... C 13
78 Graham Terrace .. F 3
76 Granby St. .... D 6
74 Granby Terrace .. C 6
70 Grandstand Rd. .. H 3
80 Grange, The ..... D 5
67 Grange Hill ..... B 11
67 Grange Park Sta . A 7
80 Grange Rd. SE1 .. D 4
71 Grange Rd. SE25 . D 7
76 Grange St. .... B 3
80 Grange Walk .... D 4
80 Grange Yard ..... D 5
71 Grangewood ..... D 7
75 Grantbridge St. . B 12
73 Grantully Rd. .... D 2
74 Granville Place ... H 3
73 Granville Rd. .... C 1
75 Granville Square D 10
75 Grape St. .... G 8
76 Gravel La. E1 .... G 5
67 Gravel La., Abridge ...... A 12
72 Gravesend G.C. .. C 6
79 Gray St. .... C 11
68 Grays .... H 6
75 Gray's Inn Gardens ...... F 10
75 Grays Inn Rd. .... D 9
71 Grays Rd. .... H 11
69 Great Bookham Common ...... H 6
67 Great Cambridge Rd. .... A 8
74 Great Castle St. .. G 5
74 Great Central St. .. F 2
74 Great Chapel St. . G 7
70 Great Chertsey Rd. A 2
79 Great College St. . D 8
74 Great Cumberland Place .... H 2
80 Great Dover St. .. D 2
76 Great Eastern St. . E 4
79 Great George St. . C 8
79 Great Guildford St. .... B 13
75 Great James St. . F 10
74 Great Marlborough St. .... H 6
66 Great North Rd. . A 5
66 Great North Way C 4
75 Great Ormond St. . F 9
75 Great Percy St. .. C 10
79 Great Peter St. ... D 8
74 Great Portland St. . F 5
74 Great Pulteney St. H 6
75 Great Queen St. .. G 9
75 Great Russell St. . G 8
76 Great St. Helens .. G 4
79 Great Scotland Yd. B 8
79 Great Smith St. .. D 8
69 Great South West Rd. .... B 4
79 Great Suffolk St. C 13
75 Great Sutton St. . E 12
76 Great Swan Alley G 3
70 Great Tattenhams .... H 3
74 Great Titchfield St. F 6
76 Great Tower St. ... J 4
68 Great Warley .... C 5
69 Great West Rd. .. A 5
76 Great Winchester St. .... G 3
74 Great Windmill St. .... H 7
68 Great Wood ..... A 1
72 Great Wood ..... G 6
72 Greatness .... H 2
76 Greatorex St. ..... F 6
75 Greek St. .... H 7
65 Green, The .... G 5
72 Green Court ..... E 1
67 Green Dragon La. A 7
80 Green Hundred Rd. .... H 7
71 Green La. SE9 .. C 11
70 Green La. SW16 .. D 6
69 Green La., Addlestone .... E 2
68 Green La., Goodmayes .... D 1
69 Green La., Hatton B 5
67 Green La., Ilford D 12
70 Green La., Morden E 4
65 Green La., Northwood .... B 4
69 Green La., Shepperton .... D 4
67 Green Lanes, N4 & N16 .... B 7, D 7
78 Green Park ...... C 5
72 Green Rd. .... C 3
74 Green St. W1 .... H 3
72 Green St., Dartford C 3
67 Green St., Newham ...... E 10
69 Green St., Sunbury D 4
72 Green Street Green, Dartford ...... C 4
71 Green Street Green, Farnborough . F 11
75 Green Terrace ... D 11
70 Green Wrythe La. E 5
73 Greenberry St. ... C 6
78 Greencoat Place .. E 6
78 Greencoat Row .. E 6
76 Greenfield Rd. ... G 7
65 Greenford .... F 6
66 Greenford Avenue F 1
65 Greenford Green . E 6
65 Greenford Rd. .... F 6
65 Greenford Sta. ... E 6
66 Greenhill .... D 1
72 Greenhithe .... B 4
74 Greenwell St. ..... E 5
67 Greenwich .... H 9
67 Greenwich High Rd. .... H 9
67 Greenwich Park .. H 9
67 Greenwich Reach G 9
67 Greenwich Sta. ... H 9
79 Greet St. .... B 11
73 Grendon St. ...... E 6
77 Grenville Place ... E 3
75 Grenville St. ..... E 9
76 Gresham St. ..... G 2
74 Gresse St. .... G 7
75 Greville St. ...... F 11
78 Greycoat Place ... E 7
78 Greycoat St. ..... E 7
76 Greyeagle St. ..... E 5
76 Grimsby St. ...... E 6
73 Grittleton Rd. .... E 1
78 Groom Place .... D 4
78 Grosvenor Bridge H 5
78 Grosvenor Cres... C 4
78 Grosvenor Crescent Mews .... C 3
78 Grosvenor Gdns.. D 5
74 Grosvenor Hill .... J 5
74 Grosvenor House Hotel .... J 3
80 Grosvenor Park ... J 1
78 Grosvenor Place . D 4
78 Grosvenor Rd. ... H 6
74 Grosvenor Square H 4
74 Grosvenor St. .... H 5
80 Grosvenor Terrace H 1
73 Grove End Rd. ... C 4
71 Grove Park ..... C 10
71 Grove Park Hospital ...... C 10
67 Grove Rd. E2 ..... F 8
67 Grove Rd. E18 .. C 10
70 Grove Rd., Mitcham ...... D 5
67 Grove Rd., Romford ..... D 12
67 Grovegreen Rd. .. D 9
68 Gubbins La. ..... C 4
69 Guildford Rd. ..... F 2
76 Guildhall .... G 2
78 Guildhouse St. .... F 6
75 Guilford St. ...... E 9
79 Gundulf St. ..... F 10
66 Gunnersbury ..... G 3
66 Gunnersbury Ave. G 2
66 Gunnersbury Park G 2
77 Gunter Grove ..... J 3
75 Gutter La. ...... G 13
80 Guy St. .... C 3
80 Guy's Hospital ... C 2
71 Gypsey Hill Sta... C 7
76 Haberdasher St. .. C 3
70 Hackbridge ...... E 5
67 Hackney .... E 8
67 Hackney Downs . E 8
67 Hackney Downs Sta. .... E 8
67 Hackney Marsh .. E 8
76 Hackney Rd. ..... C 5
67 Hackney Wick ... E 9
68 Hacton La. ...... E 4

76 Hadrian Estate ... **C 7**
76 Haggerston Park . **B 6**
76 Haggerston Rd. .. **A 5**
67 Hainault ... **C 12**
67 Hainault Estate . **B 12**
68 Hainault Forest .. **B 1**
67 Hainault Rd., Chigwell ... **B 11**
67 Hainault Rd., Hainault ... **C 12**
76 Halcomb St. ... **B 4**
67 Hale End ... **B 9**
78 Half Moon St. ... **B 5**
77 Halford Rd. ... **H 1**
68 Halfway Reach ... **F 2**
71 Halfway St. ... **B 11**
70 Haling Park Rd. ... **F 6**
78 Halkin Place ... **D 3**
78 Halkin St. ... **D 4**
73 Hall Gate ... **D 4**
67 Hall La.E4 ... **B 9**
68 Hall La., Upminster ... **D 4**
68 Hall La. ... **D 6**
73 Hall Place, W2 ... **F 5**
72 Hall Place, Bexley **B 1**
73 Hall Rd.NW8 ... **D 4**
71 Hall Rd., Eltham **B 10**
75 Hall St. ... **C 12**
68 Hall Wood, Brentwood ... **B 6**
72 Hall Wood, Fairseat ... **G 6**
74 Hallam St. ... **F 5**
73 Hallfield Estate .. **G 3**
69 Halliford Rd. ... **D 4**
78 Halsey St. ... **E 2**
72 Halstead ... **G 1**
70 Ham ... **C 1**
70 Ham Common ... **C 2**
70 Ham Cross ... **C 2**
70 Ham Gate ... **C 2**
70 Ham House ... **B 1**
73 Hamilton Close .. **D 4**
73 Hamilton Gdns. .. **C 4**
78 Hamilton Place .. **B 4**
73 Hamilton Terrace **C 3**
66 Hammersmith ... **G 4**
66 Hammersmith Bri. **G 4**
66 Hammersmith Rd. **G 4**
74 Hampden Way ... **B 6**
65 Hampermill La. .. **A 5**
66 Hampstead ... **E 5**
66 Hampstead Heath **D 5**
66 Hampstead Heath Sta. ... **E 5**
66 Hampstead La. ... **D 5**
66 Hampstead Ponds **E 5**
74 Hampstead Rd. .. **C 6**
69 Hampton ... **D 6**
73 Hampton Cl. ... **D 1**
69 Hampton Court Bridge ... **D 6**
70 Hampton Court G.C. ... **D 1**
70 Hampton Court Palace ... **D 1**
70 Hampton Court Park ... **D 1**
69 Hampton Court Rd. ... **D 6**
69 Hampton Court Way ... **E 6**
69 Hampton Rd., Feltham ... **C 5**
69 Hampton Rd., Twickenham ... **C 6**
79 Hampton St. ... **F 13**
70 Hampton Wick .. **D 1**
71 Hamsey Green ... **G 8**
76 Hanbury St. ... **F 5**
75 Handel St. ... **E 8**
69 Hangar Hill ... **F 4**
66 Hanger Hill ... **F 2**
66 Hanger La. ... **F 2**
66 Hanger Lane Sta. .. **F 2**
80 Hankey St. ... **D 3**
79 Hanover Gdns. .. **H 10**
74 Hanover Gate ... **D 1**
74 Hanover Square .. **H 5**
74 Hanover St. ... **H 5**
74 Hanover Terrace . **D 2**
74 Hanover Terrace Mews ... **D 2**
78 Hans Crescent ... **D 2**
78 Hans Place ... **D 2**
78 Hans Rd. ... **D 2**
78 Hans St. ... **D 2**
74 Hanson St. ... **F 6**
74 Hanway Place ... **G 7**
74 Hanway St. ... **G 7**
66 Hanwell ... **G 1**
69 Hanworth ... **C 5**
69 Hanworth Park .. **C 5**
69 Hanworth Rd., Hanworth ... **C 5**
69 Hanworth Rd., Hounslow ... **B 6**
73 Harbet Rd. ... **F 5**
74 Harcourt St. ... **F 1**
77 Harcourt Terrace . **G 3**
69 Hardwick La. ... **E 2**
75 Hardwick St. ... **D 11**
80 Hardwide St. ... **C 4**
69 Hare Hill ... **F 2**
70 Hare La. ... **F 1**
68 Hare Street ... **C 3**
65 Harefield ... **C 3**
65 Harefield Hospital **C 3**
65 Harefield Place G.C. ... **D 3**
65 Harefield Rd. ... **B 3**
74 Harewood Avenue **E 1**
68 Harewood Hall La. **E 4**
74 Harewood Place .. **H 5**
73 Harewood Row ... **F 6**
66 Harlesden ... **E 3**
66 Harlesden Sta. ... **F 3**
77 Harley Gdns. ... **G 4**
74 Harley Place ... **G 4**
74 Harley St. ... **F 4**
79 Harleyford Rd. ... **H 9**
79 Harleyford St. ... **H 11**
65 Harlington ... **H 4**
65 Harlington Rd. ... **F 4**
69 Harlington Road East ... **B 5**
65 Harmondsworth . **H 3**
65 Harmondsworth La. ... **H 3**
79 Harmsworth St. . **G 12**
68 Harold Hill ... **B 3**
79 Harold Place ... **G 10**
68 Harold Wood ... **C 4**
80 Harper Rd. ... **D 2**
75 Harper St. ... **F 9**
67 Harringay Stadium **D 7**
67 Harringay Stadium Sta. ... **D 7**
67 Harringay West Sta. ... **D 7**
77 Harrington Gdns. . **F 3**
77 Harrington Rd. .. **E 5**
74 Harrington Square **B 6**
74 Harrington St. ... **C 6**
75 Harrison St. ... **D 9**
66 Harrow ... **C 1**
66 Harrow on the Hill **D 1**
66 Harrow on the Hill Sta. ... **D 1**
76 Harrow Place ... **G 4**
73 Harrow Rd.W9 ... **F 1**
71 Harrow Rd., Chelsham ... **G 8**
66 Harrow Rd., Wembley ... **E 2**
66 Harrow School ... **D 1**
66 Harrow Weald ... **C 1**
66 Harrow & Wealdstone Sta. ... **C 1**
74 Harrowby St. ... **G 2**
76 Hart St. ... **H 4**
72 Hartley ... **E 5**
72 Hartley Wood ... **D 5**
65 Hartsbourne G.C. **B 6**
76 Harvey St. ... **A 3**
65 Harvil Rd. ... **D 3**
78 Hasker St. ... **E 2**
67 Haslebury Rd. ... **B 7**
65 Haste Hill G.C. .. **C 4**
75 Hastings St. ... **D 8**
65 Hatch End ... **C 6**
65 Hatch End Sta. ... **C 6**
67 Hatch La. ... **B 9**
69 Hatchord Park ... **H 4**
76 Hatfield St. ... **E 1**
79 Hatfields ... **B 12**
73 Hatherley Grove . **G 2**
69 Hatton ... **B 4**
69 Hatton Cross Sta. **B 4**
75 Hatton Garden .. **F 11**
69 Hatton Rd. ... **B 4**
73 Hatton St. ... **E 5**
75 Hatton Wall ... **F 11**
75 Havelock St. ... **A 9**
68 Havering ... **D 3**
68 Havering Park ... **B 2**
68 Havering Rd. ... **B 2**
68 Havering-atte-Bower ... **B 2**
66 Haverstock Hill .. **E 5**
75 Haverstock St. .. **C 13**
72 Hawley ... **C 3**
72 Hawley Rd. ... **C 3**
71 Hawsted La. ... **F 12**
74 Hay Hill ... **J 5**
70 Haydon's Rd.Sta. **C 4**
65 Hayes ... **G 4**
71 Hayes, Bromley .. **E 9**
71 Hayes Common .. **E 9**
65 Hayes End ... **F 4**
71 Hayes Lane, Beckenham ... **D 9**
71 Hayes La., Bromley **E 9**
70 Hayes La., Coulsdon ... **H 6**
73 Hayes Place ... **F 6**
65 Hayes Rd. ... **G 5**
65 Hayes & Harlington Sta. ... **G 4**
79 Hayles St. ... **E 12**
65 Hayling Rd. ... **B 5**
74 Haymarket ... **J 7**
75 Haymarket Theatre **J 7**
80 Haymerle Rd. ... **H 6**
75 Hayne St. ... **F 13**
80 Hays La. ... **B 3**
78 Hay's Mews ... **A 4**
75 Hayward's Place **E 12**
71 Hazel Wood ... **G 11**
75 H.Q.S. Wellington **J 10**
78 Headfort Place ... **D 4**
70 Headley Rd. ... **H 2**
65 Headstone ... **C 6**
66 Headstone Drive . **C 1**
65 Headstone La. ... **C 6**
65 Headstone La. Sta. **C 6**
76 Hearn St. ... **E 4**
72 Heath La. ... **C 2**
68 Heath Park ... **D 3**
68 Heath Park Rd. .. **D 3**
69 Heath Rd. ... **B 6**
69 Heath Row ... **F 3**
68 Heath Way ... **E 1**
66 Heathbourn Rd. .. **B 1**
75 Heathcote St. ... **D 9**
69 Heathrow Airport London ... **A 3**
72 Heaverham ... **H 4**
74 Heddon St. ... **J 6**
67 Hedge La. ... **B 7**
68 Hedgemans Rd. .. **E 1**
79 Heiron St. ... **H 13**
75 Hemingford Rd. . **A 10**
76 Hemming St. ... **E 7**
75 Hemsworth St. ... **B 4**
77 Hemus Place ... **G 6**
66 Hendon ... **C 4**
66 Hendon Central Sta. ... **D 4**
66 Hendon G.C. ... **C 4**
66 Hendon Way ... **D 4**
66 Hendon Wood La. **A 3**
80 Hendre Rd. ... **F 4**
76 Heneage ... **F 6**
76 Heneage La. ... **G 4**
77 Henniker Mews .. **H 4**
74 Henrietta Place .. **G 4**
75 Henrietta St. ... **J 9**
76 Henriques St. ... **H 7**
80 H.M.S. *Belfast* .. **B 4**
75 H.M.S. *Chrysanthemum* **J 11**
75 H.M.S. *Discovery* . **J 10**
75 H.M.S. *President* . **J 11**
75 Herbal Hill ... **E 11**
75 Herbrand St. ... **E 8**
79 Hercules Rd. ... **D 10**
77 Hereford Square .. **F 4**
73 Hereford Rd. ... **G 1**
76 Hereford St. ... **E 6**
75 Hermes St. ... **C 10**
75 Hermit St. ... **C 12**
80 Hermitage Wall .. **B 7**
71 Herne Hill ... **B 7**
70 Herne Hill Sta. ... **B 6**
79 Herrick St. ... **F 8**
69 Hersham ... **F 5**
69 Hersham Rd. ... **E 5**
69 Hersham Sta. ... **E 5**
67 Hertford Rd. ... **A 8**
78 Hertford St. ... **B 4**
71 Heseirs Hill ... **H 9**
71 Heseirs Rd. ... **H 9**
77 Hesper Mews ... **F 2**
65 Heston ... **H 5**
65 Heston Rd. ... **H 5**
71 Hewitts Rd. ... **F 12**
72 Hextable ... **D 2**
79 Heyford Avenue .. **J 9**
80 Heygate St. ... **F 1**
78 Hide Place ... **F 7**
66 High Barnet Sta. . **A 4**
75 High Holborn ... **G 10**
66 High Rd. N2 ... **C 5**
67 High Rd. N17 ... **C 7**
66 High Rd. N20 ... **A 5**
66 High Rd. NW10 .. **E 3**
69 High Rd., Byfleet . **G 3**
67 High Rd., Chigwell ... **B 11**
72 High Rd., Dartford ... **C 2**
65 High Rd., Eastcote **D 5**
67 High Rd., Ilford . **D 12**
67 High Rd., Leytonstone ... **D 9**
67 High Rd., Loughton ... **A 10**
71 High Rd., Orpington ... **E 11**
67 High Rd., Woodford Bridge ... **C 10**
67 High Rd., Woodford Green ... **B 10**
67 High St. E11 ... **D 10**
67 High St. E15 ... **F 9**
66 High St. N8 ... **C 6**
67 High St. SE15 ... **H 8**
70 High St. SE27 ... **C 6**
70 High St. SW18 ... **B 4**
70 High St., Merton, Sw19 ... **D 4**
70 High St. SW19 ... **C 4**
68 High St., Aveley .. **G 4**
70 High St., Banstead **G 4**
71 High St., Beckenham ... **D 8**
71 High St., Bexley Heath ... **A 12**
65 High St., Bushey . **A 6**
70 High St., Carshalton ... **F 5**
71 High St., Croydon **E 7**
70 High St., Epsom .. **G 2**
69 High St., Feltham **C 4**
65 High St., Harlington ... **G 4**
66 High St., Harrow . **C 1**
68 High St., Hornchurch ... **D 3**
69 High St., Hounslow **A 6**
70 High St., New Malden ... **D 3**
67 High St., Ponders End ... **A 8**
65 High St., Rickmansworth **A 3**
69 High St., Shepperton ... **E 4**
71 High St., Sidcup . **C 12**
69 High St., Stanwell **B 3**
70 High St., Sutton .. **F 4**
70 High St., Teddington ... **C 1**
69 High St., Walton . **E 4**
65 High St., Watford **A 5**
71 High St., West Wickham ... **E 8**
70 High St., Colliers Wood ... **C 5**
67 High St. North .. **E 10**
67 High St. South . **F 11**
67 Higham Hill ... **C 8**
67 Highams Park ... **B 9**
67 Highams Park, Hale End Sta. ... **B 9**
67 Highbury ... **E 7**
67 Highbury & Islington Sta. ... **E 7**
66 Highgate ... **D 6**
66 Highgate G.C. ... **D 5**
66 Highgate Ponds . **D 5**
66 Highgate Rd. ... **E 6**
66 Highgate Sta. ... **D 6**
66 Highgate Wood .. **D 6**
76 Highway, The ... **J 7**
66 Highwood Hill ... **B 3**
77 Hildyard Rd. ... **H 1**
66 Hilfield La. ... **A 1**
66 Hilfield Reservoir **A 1**
65 Hill End ... **B 3**
65 Hill End Rd. ... **C 3**
73 Hill Rd. ... **C 4**
78 Hill St. ... **A 4**
77 Hillgate Place ... **B 2**
77 Hillgate St. ... **B 2**
65 Hillingdon ... **E 4**
65 Hillingdon G.C. ... **F 3**
65 Hillingdon Heath . **F 4**
65 Hillingdon Hill ... **F 3**
65 Hillingdon Rd. ... **E 3**
65 Hillingdon Sta. ... **E 4**
79 Hillingdon St. ... **H 13**
67 Hillreach ... **G 10**
71 Hilly Fields ... **B 8**
78 Hilton Hotel ... **B 4**
70 Hinchley Wood .. **E 1**
74 Hinde St. ... **G 4**
71 Hither Green ... **B 9**
78 Hobart Place ... **D 4**
77 Hobury St. ... **H 4**
76 Hocker St. ... **D 5**
68 Hoe La. ... **A 1**
67 Hoe Street ... **D 9**
66 Hogarth House .. **H 3**
77 Hogarth Rd. ... **F 2**
71 Hogtrough Hill . **H 11**
78 Holbein Mews ... **F 3**
78 Holbein Place ... **F 3**
75 Holborn ... **G 11**
75 Holborn Circus . **G 11**
75 Holborn Viaduct **G 12**
75 Holborn Viaduct Sta. ... **G 12**
68 Holden's Wood .. **C 5**
66 Holders Hill ... **C 4**
66 Holders Hill Rd. . **C 4**
75 Holford Gdns. .. **C 10**
66 Holland Avenue .. **G 4**
66 Holland Rd. ... **G 4**
77 Holland Rd. ... **C 1**
74 Hollen St. ... **G 7**
74 Holles St. ... **G 5**
67 Hollow Pond ... **D 9**
66 Holloway Rd. ... **D 6**
76 Holloway St. ... **G 6**
72 Hollows Wood ... **F 1**
70 Holly La. ... **H 4**
77 Hollywood Rd. ... **H 3**
71 Holmwood Park **F 10**
79 Holyoake Rd. ... **F 12**
80 Holyrood St. ... **B 4**
76 Holywell La. ... **E 4**
76 Holywell Row ... **E 3**
79 Home Office ... **C 8**
72 Home Rd. ... **C 2**
74 Homer Row ... **F 1**
74 Homer St. ... **F 1**
67 Homerton ... **E 8**
67 Homerton High St. **E 8**
67 Homerton Rd. ... **E 8**
79 Hone Parade ... **E 10**
66 Honeypot La. ... **C 2**
71 Honor Oak Park . **B 8**
71 Honor Oak Park Sta. ... **B 8**
71 Honor Oak & Forest Hill G.C. ... **B 8**
70 Hook ... **E 2**
72 Hook Green, Meopham ... **E 6**
72 Hook Green, Southfleet ... **C 5**
72 Hook Green ... **E 6**
72 Hook Green ... **C 5**
72 Hook Green Rd. . **C 2**
71 Hook La., Bexley Hth. ... **B 11**
68 Hook La., Stapleford Abbotts ... **A 2**
70 Hook Rise ... **E 2**
70 Hook Rd., Chessington ... **E 2**
70 Hook Rd., Epsom **G 2**
70 Hook Rd., Horton **F 2**
71 Hookwood Rd. . **G 12**
76 Hooper St. ... **H 6**
76 Hopetown St. ... **F 6**
74 Hopkins St. ... **H 7**
79 Hopton St. ... **A 12**
80 Hopwood Rd. ... **H 3**
76 Horatio St. ... **C 6**
66 Horn La. ... **G 3**
66 Hornchurch ... **D 3**
68 Hornchurch Marshes ... **F 2**
68 Hornchurch Rd. .. **D 3**
68 Hornchurch Stadium ... **E 4**
71 Horns Green ... **H 11**
67 Horns Rd. ... **D 11**
66 Hornsey ... **D 6**
66 Hornsey La. ... **D 6**
66 Hornsey Rise ... **D 6**
66 Hornsey Rd. ... **D 6**
77 Hornton Place ... **C 2**
77 Hornton St. ... **C 1**
79 Horse Guards ... **B 8**
79 Horseferry Rd. ... **E 7**
79 Horseguards Av. . **B 8**
80 Horselydown La. . **B 5**
66 Horsenden Hill ... **E 1**
80 Horsley St. ... **H 2**
77 Hortensia Rd. ... **J 3**
70 Horton, Ewell ... **F 2**
69 Horton, Staines .. **A 1**
70 Horton Hospital . **G 2**
72 Horton Kirby ... **D 3**
70 Horton La. ... **G 2**
69 Horton Rd., Horton ... **A 1**
69 Horton Rd., Stanwell ... **B 2**
75 Hosier La. ... **G 12**
69 Hospital Bridge Rd. ... **B 6**
74 Hospital for Nervous Diseases ... **G 4**
75 Hospital for Sick Children ... **E 9**
73 Hospital of St. John ... **C 5**
79 Hotspur St. ... **F 11**
75 Houghton St. ... **H 10**
76 Houndsditch ... **G 4**
69 Hounslow ... **A 6**
69 Hounslow Central Sta. ... **B 6**
69 Hounslow East Sta. **B 6**
69 Hounslow Heath . **B 5**
69 Hounslow Rd. ... **C 5**
69 Hounslow Sta. ... **B 6**
69 Hounslow West Sta. ... **A 5**
79 Houses of Parliament ... **D 9**
70 Howell Hill ... **G 3**
78 Howick Place ... **E 6**
74 Howland St. ... **F 6**
73 Howley Place ... **F 4**
76 Hows St. ... **B 5**
67 Hoxton ... **E 7**
76 Hoxton Square ... **D 4**
76 Hoxton St. ... **B 4**
74 Hugh Mews ... **F 5**
78 Hugh St. ... **F 5**
78 Hudsons Pl. ... **E 5**
76 Hull St. ... **D 1**
80 Humphrey St. ... **G 5**
79 Hungerford Railway Bridge ... **B 9**
74 Huntley St. ... **E 7**
65 Huntsmoor Park .. **F 3**
74 Huntsworth Mews **E 2**
76 Hunton St. ... **E 6**
70 Hurlingham House **A 4**
69 Hurst Rd., Molesey **D 5**
71 Hurst Rd., Sidcup **B 12**
66 Hyde, The ... **C 3**
78 Hyde Park Barracks ... **C 3**
78 Hyde Park Corner **C 4**
73 Hyde Park Cres. .. **H 6**
73 Hyde Park Gdns. . **H 5**
73 Hyde Park Gdns. Mews ... **H 5**
77 Hyde Park Gate .. **D 4**
78 Hyde Park Hotel . **C 2**
73 Hyde Park Square ... **H 6**
73 Hyde Park St. ... **H 6**
76 Hyde Rd. ... **B 3**
79 Hythe ... **C 2**
69 Hythe End ... **C 1**
65 Ickenham ... **D 4**
76 Idol La. ... **J 4**
77 Ifield Rd. ... **H 3**
72 Ightham ... **H 5**
73 Ilchester Gdns. .. **D 11**
67 Ilford ... **E 11**
67 Ilford Football Club ... **D 11**
67 Ilford G.C. ... **D 11**
67 Ilford La. ... **E 11**
79 Iliffe St. ... **F 13**
76 Imber St. ... **B 2**
77 Imperial College . **D 5**
77 Imperial College of Science ... **D 5**
77 Imperial College Rd. **D 4**
65 Imperial Drive ... **D 6**
75 Imperial Hotel ... **F 8**
77 Imperial Institute . **D 5**

79 Imperial War Museum ...... E 11
76 India St. .... H 5
74 Ingestre Place .... H 6
75 Inglebert St. ..... C 11
68 Ingrave .... B 6
68 Ingrave Green .... B 6
74 Inner Circle ...... D 3
77 International Hotel E 2
73 Inverness Place ... H 3
73 Inverness Terrace H 3
73 Inverness Terrace Gate .... J 3
80 Inville Rd. .... G 3
76 Ironmonger La. .. G 2
76 Ironmonger Row . D 1
76 Ironmonger St. ... D 2
76 Ironmonger's Hall . F 1
75 Irving St. .... J 8
79 Isabella St. ...... B 12
69 Island Barn Res... E 6
67 Isle of Dogs ...... G 9
70 Isleworth .... B 1
70 Isleworth Sta. .... A 1
67 Islington .... E 7
75 Islington Green . B 12
75 Islington High St. B 12
72 Istead Rise .... C 6
65 Iver .... F 2
65 Iver Heath .... E 2
65 Iver La. .... F 2
77 Iverna Court ..... D 2
77 Iverna Gdns. ..... D 2
66 Iverson Rd. ...... E 4
78 Ives St. .... E 1
74 Ivor Place .... E 2
76 Ivy St. .... B 4
72 Ivyhouse La. ..... H 1
77 Ixworth Place .... F 6
71 Jackass La. ..... F 10
80 Jacob St. .... C 6
71 Jail La. .... G 10
80 Jamaica Rd. ..... D 6
75 James St. WC2 ... H 9
74 James St. W1 .... G 4
77 Jameson St. ...... B 2
80 Jardin St. .... H 4
77 Jay Mews .... D 4
78 Jermyn St. .... A 6
73 Jerome Crescent . E 6
76 Jerome St. .... F 5
69 Jersey Rd. .... A 6
76 Jewry St. .... H 5
79 Joan St. .... B 12
75 Jockey's Fields .. F 10
65 Joel St. .... C 5
75 John Adam St. .... J 9
75 John Carpenter St. .... H 12
76 John Fisher St. .... J 6
79 John Islip St. ..... F 8
74 John Princess St. . G 5
79 John Ruskin St. .. J 13
75 John St. .... E 10
79 Jonathan St. ...... F 9
75 John's Mews .... E 10
72 Joyce Green Hosp. A 3
72 Joyce Green La... A 3
72 Joyden's Wood .. C 1
67 Jubilee Park ..... A 8
78 Jubilee Place ..... G 1
75 Judd St. .... D 8
73 Junction Mews ... G 6
66 Junction Rd. ..... D 6
77 Justice Walk ..... H 6
79 Juxon St. .... E 10
67 Katherine Rd. ... E 10
76 Kay St. .... B 6
75 Kean St. .... H 9
75 Keeley St. .... G 9
77 Kelso Place ...... D 2
75 Kemble St. .... H 9
77 Kempsford Gdns. G 2
79 Kempsford Rd. . F 12
69 Kempton Park Race Course .... C 5
72 Kemsing .... H 3
73 Kendal Street .... H 6
71 Kenley .... H 7
79 Kennings Way .. G 12
79 Kennington Grove .... H 10
79 Kennington La. . G 10
79 Kennington Oval H 10
79 Kennington Park H 11
79 Kennington Park Gdns. .... H 12
79 Kennington Park Place .... H 12
79 Kennington Park Rd. .... G 12
79 Kennington Rd. . E 11
74 Kenrick Place ..... F 3
66 Kensal Green ..... F 4
66 Kensal Green Sta. . F 4
77 Kensington Church St. .... B 2
77 Kensington Court C 3
77 Kensington Court Place .... D 3
77 Kensington Gdns. B 3
73 Kensington Gardens Square .... H 2
77 Kensington Gate . D 3
77 Kensington Gore . C 4
77 Kensington High St. .... D 1
77 Kensington Mall . B 2
77 Kensington Palace B 2
77 Kensington Palace Barracks ...... C 2
77 Kensington Palace Gdns. .... B 2
77 Kensington Palace Green .... C 2
73 Kensington Park Rd. .... J 1
77 Kensington Place . B 2
77 Kensington Rd. .. C 3
77 Kensington Square D 2
66 Kensington & Chelsea .... G 4
71 Kent House Sta... D 8
76 Kent St. .... B 5
74 Kent Terrace ..... D 2
66 Kentish Town .... E 6
66 Kentish Town Sta. E 6
66 Kenton .... D 2
66 Kenton La. ...... C 2
66 Kenton Rd. ...... C 2
75 Kenton St. .... E 8
77 Kenway Rd. ...... F 2
66 Kenwood .... D 5
71 Keston .... F 10
71 Keston Mark .... E 10
70 Kew .... A 2
66 Kew Bridge ...... G 2
70 Kew Bridge Rd. .. A 2
66 Kew Bridge Sta. .. G 2
70 Kew Gardens Sta. A 2
70 Kew Palace ...... A 2
70 Kew Rd. .... A 2
80 Keyse Rd. .... E 5
75 Keystone Crescent C 9
79 Keyworth St. .... D 12
71 Kidbrooke .... A 9
71 Kidbrooke Sta. .. A 10
66 Kilburn .... E 4
66 Kilburn High Rd. Sta. .... E 5
73 Kilburn Park Rd. . D 1
66 Kilburn Sta. ...... E 4
73 Kildare Terrace .. G 2
75 Killick St. .... C 9
79 King Charles St. . C 8
79 King Edward St. G 13
79 King Edward Walk .... D 11
67 King George V Dock .... G 11
69 King George VI Res. .... B 2
67 King George's Res. A 9
79 King James St. .. D 12
76 King John's Court E 4
75 King Sq. Estate .. D 13
76 King St. EC2 ..... G 2
78 King St. SW1 .... B 6
75 King St. WC2 .... H 8
66 King St. W6 ..... G 3
76 King William St. .. J 3
80 King & Queen St. . F 2
69 Kingfieldgreen ... H 1
80 Kinglake St. ..... G 4
74 Kingly St. .... H 6
76 King's Arms Yard G 2
79 King's Bench St. . C 12
75 King's Bench Walk .... H 11
75 King's College .. H 10
75 King's Cross Rd. D 10
75 King's Cross Sta. . C 8
67 King's Head Hill . A 9
80 King's Head Yard B 3
75 King's Mews .... F 10
80 King's Place ...... D 1
78 King's Rd. SW1 .. E 4
77 King's Rd. SW3 .. G 6
67 King's Rd., Chingford ..... B 9
78 King's Scholars' Passage .... E 6
74 King's Terrace ... B 6
66 Kingsbury .... C 3
66 Kingsbury Green . D 3
66 Kingsbury Rd. ... D 3
66 Kingsbury Sta. ... D 2
72 Kingsdown .... F 4
65 Kingshill Avenue .. F 5
67 Kingsland .... E 7
76 Kingsland Rd. .... C 4
69 Kingsley Rd. ..... A 6
73 Kingsmill Terrace B 5
70 Kingston Bridge .. D 1
70 Kingston Bypass . D 3
70 Kingston Gate ... C 2
70 Kingston Hill .... C 2
65 Kingston Lane .... F 3
70 Kingston Rd. SW15 .... B 3
70 Kingston Rd. SW20 .... D 4
70 Kingston Rd., Leatherhead ... H 1
70 Kingston Rd., New Malden ... D 2
69 Kingston Rd., Staines .... C 3
70 Kingston Rd., Teddington .... C 1
70 Kingston Rd., Tolworth .... F 3
70 Kingston upon Thames .... D 2
70 Kingston Vale .... C 2
75 Kingsway .... G 9
70 Kingswood Sta. .. H 4
78 Kinnerton St. .... C 3
80 Kipling St. .... C 3
79 Kipton St. .... D 3
80 Kirby Grove ..... C 3
75 Kirby St. .... F 11
71 Kirkdale .... C 7
78 Kirtling St. .... J 6
79 Kirwyn Way ..... J 13
80 Kitson Rd. .... J 2
71 Kitto Rd. .... A 8
77 Knaresborough Place .... F 2
70 Knight's Hill ..... C 6
69 Knights Res. ..... D 5
78 Knightsbridge .... C 2
69 Knipp Hill .... G 5
77 Knivet Rd. .... J 1
71 Knockholt ...... H 12
71 Knockholt Main Rd. .... H 11
71 Knockholt Pound G 12
71 Knockholt Rd. .. G 12
71 Knockholt Sta. .. F 12
69 Knowle Green ... C 2
74 Knox St. .... F 2
77 Kynance Mews ... E 3
77 Kynance Place ... D 3
76 Laburnham St. ... B 5
76 Lackington St. .... F 3
66 Ladbroke Grove .. F 4
80 Lafone St. .... C 5
69 Laleham .... D 3
69 Laleham Rd., Shepperton .... D 3
69 Laleham Rd., Staines .... C 2
76 Lamb Passage .... E 2
76 Lamb St. .... F 5
80 Lamb Walk ...... C 4
70 Lambeth .... B 6
79 Lambeth Bridge .. E 9
79 Lambeth High St. E 9
79 Lambeth Hospital F 12
79 Lambeth Palace .. E 9
79 Lambeth Palace Rd. .... D 9
79 Lambeth Pier .... E 9
79 Lambeth Rd. .... E 10
76 Lambeth St. ...... H 6
79 Lambeth Walk .. E 10
75 Lamb's Conduit .. E 9
69 Lammas La. ...... F 6
77 Lamont Rd. ...... H 4
69 Lampton .... A 6
69 Lampton Rd. .... A 6
73 Lanark Place ..... E 4
73 Lanark Rd. ...... D 3
73 Lancaster Gate .... J 4
78 Lancaster House . C 6
73 Lancaster Mews .. H 4
75 Lancaster Place ... J 9
79 Lancaster St. .... C 12
73 Lancaster Terrace H 5
78 Lancelot Place ... D 2
74 Lancing St. ...... D 7
75 Land Registry Office .... G 10
70 Landor Rd. ...... A 6
73 Langford Place ... B 4
74 Langham Place ... G 5
74 Langham St. ...... F 5
65 Langley .... G 1
79 Langley La. ...... H 9
71 Langley Park, Eden Park ..... E 9
65 Langley Park, Slough .... F 1
71 Langley Park G.C. E 9
75 Langley St. .... H 8
70 Langley Vale ..... H 3
75 Langton Close .. D 10
77 Langton St. .... J 4
73 Lanhill Rd. ...... E 1
67 Lansdowne Rd. .. C 8
79 Lant St. .... C 13
70 Latchmere Rd. ... A 5
71 Lathams Rd. ...... F 9
80 Latona Rd. ...... H 6
79 Laud St. .... G 9
73 Lauderdale Rd. .. D 2
77 Launceston Place . D 3
68 Launders La. ...... F 3
76 Laurence Pountney La. .... J 3
67 Lausanne Rd. .... H 8
70 Lavender Hill .... B 5
77 Laverton Place .... F 2
79 Lavington St. ... B 13
75 Lavinia Grove ... B 9
80 Law St. .... D 3
79 Lawn La. .... H 9
70 Lawn Rd. .... H 1
66 Lawrence St. NW7 B 3
77 Lawrence St. SW3 H 6
71 Layhams Rd. ..... G 9
75 Laystall St. ..... E 10
70 Layton Rd. ...... F 1
67 Lea Bridge ...... D 8
67 Lea Bridge Rd. ... D 8
67 Lea Bridge Sta. ... D 8
67 Lea Valley Rd. ... A 9
76 Leadenhall Market H 3
76 Leadenhall St. .... H 4
79 Leake St. ...... C 10
71 Leas Rd. .... H 8
75 Leather La. ..... F 11
70 Leatherhead Bypass .... H 1
70 Leatherhead Common ...... H 1
70 Leatherhead G.C. G 1
70 Leatherhead Rd., Chessington .... F 1
70 Leatherhead Rd., Leatherhead ... H 1
80 Leathermarket St. C 3
71 Leaves Green ... G 10
71 Leaves Green Rd. F 10
71 Ledgers Rd. ...... H 8
71 Lee .... B 9
71 Lee High Rd. ..... B 9
71 Lee Rd. .... A 9
75 Leeke St. .... C 9
74 Lees Place .... H 3
71 Leesons Rd. ..... D 11
75 Leicester Square ... J 7
80 Leigh Hunt St. ... C 1
70 Leigham Court Rd. C 6
73 Leinster Gdns. ... H 3
73 Leinster Mews .... J 4
73 Leinster Pl. ...... H 3
73 Leinster Rd. ...... C 1
73 Leinster Square .. H 2
73 Leinster Ter. ...... J 3
76 Leman St. .... H 6
78 Lennox Gdns. .... E 2
78 Lennox Gardens Mews .... E 2
76 Leonard St. ...... E 3
79 Leopold Walk .... G 9
80 Leroy St. .... E 4
68 Lessness Heath ... G 2
76 Lever St. .... D 1
71 Lewisham .... B 8
71 Lewisham High St., B 9
71 Lewisham Rd. .... A 9
79 Lewisham St. .... C 7
77 Lexham Gdns. ... E 2
77 Lexham Mews ... E 1
74 Lexington St. .... H 6
67 Ley St. .... D 11
76 Leyden St. .... G 5
67 Leyton .... D 9
67 Leyton High Rd. . D 9
67 Leyton Marshes .. D 8
67 Leyton Midland Road Sta. ...... D 9
67 Leytonstone High Rd. Sta. .... D 9
67 Leytonstone Rd. . E 9
69 Liberty La. .... F 2
79 Library St. ...... D 12
74 Lidlington Place .. C 6
76 Ligonier St. ...... D 5
73 Lilestone St. ..... E 6
66 Lillie Rd. .... H 4
78 Lillington Gardens Estate .... F 7
76 Lime St. .... H 4
67 Limehouse .... F 9
67 Limehouse Reach G 9
77 Limerston St. .... H 4
71 Limpsfield Rd. ... G 7
67 Lincoln Rd. ...... A 7
78 Lincoln St. .... F 2
75 Lincoln's Inn .... G 10
75 Lincoln's Inn Fields .... G 10
73 Linden Gdns. ..... J 1
75 Lindsey St. ...... F 13
74 Linhope St. ...... E 2
80 Linsey St. .... E 6
76 Linton St. .... B 2
74 Lisle St. .... H 7
73 Lisson Green Estate .... E 6
73 Lisson Grove ..... E 6
73 Lisson St. .... F 6
74 Little Albany St. .. D 5
77 Little Boltons, The G 3
75 Little Britain .... G 13
65 Little Bushey La. . A 6
78 Little Chester St. . D 4
74 Little Edward St. . C 5
66 Little Ealing ..... G 2
68 Little Gaynes La. . E 4
79 Little George St... C 8
65 Little Green La. .. A 4
74 Little Marlborough St. .... G 6
75 Little New St. ... G 11
65 Little Oxhey La... B 5
74 Little Portland St. G 6
75 Little Russell St. .. G 8
78 Little St. James's St. B 6
76 Little Trinity La. . H 2
70 Little Woodcote .. G 5
70 Little Woodmansterne La. .... G 5
69 Littleton .... D 3
69 Littleton La. ..... D 3
80 Liverpool Grove . G 2
75 Liverpool Rd. ... B 11
76 Liverpool St. ..... G 3
76 Liverpool Street Sta. .... F 4
74 Livonia St. .... H 6
76 Lizard St. .... D 2
80 Llewellyn St. ..... C 6
75 Lloyd Baker St. . D 10
75 Lloyd Square ... D 10
75 Lloyd St. .... C 11
76 Lloyd's Avenue .. H 4
76 Lloyd's Buildings . H 3
75 Lloyd's Row .... D 12
71 Loampit Hill ..... A 8
69 Lock La. .... H 3
66 Locket Rd. .... C 1
71 Locksbottom ... E 10
67 Lockwood Res. .. C 8
67 Lodge Avenue .. E 12
71 Lodge La. .... F 9
73 Lodge Rd. .... D 5
80 Loftie St. .... C 7
77 Logan Mews ..... E 1
77 Logan Place ..... E 1
79 Lollard Place .... F 11
79 Lollard St. ...... F 10
79 Loman St. ...... C 13
75 Lombard La. .... H 11
76 Lombard St. ..... H 3
80 London Bridge ... A 3
80 London Bridge Station .... B 3
80 London Bridge St. B 3
74 London Clinic ... E 4
74 London College of Music .... H 6
79 London College of Printing ...... E 12
67 London Fields Sta. E 8
74 London Planetarium ... E 3
79 London Rd. SE1 D 12
71 London Rd. SE23 B 7
68 London Rd., Aveley .... G 4
72 London Rd., Badger's Mount .... G 1
65 London Rd., Batchworth .... B 3
70 London Rd., Croydon .... E 6
72 London Rd., Dunton Green .... H 1
67 London Rd., Enfield .... A 7
70 London Rd., Hackbridge .... E 5
70 London Rd., Kingston ...... D 2
70 London Rd., Mitcham ...... D 5
70 London Rd., Morden .... D 4
70 London Rd., Norbury .... D 6
68 London Rd., Romford ...... D 2
68 London Rd., Shenfield ...... A 6
69 London Rd., Staines .... C 3
66 London Rd., Stanmore ...... B 2
72 London Rd., Swanscombe ... B 4
68 London Rd., W. Thurrock ... H 5
75 London School of Economics .... H 10
70 London School of Hygiene .... F 7
70 London Scottish G.C. .... C 3
76 London St. EC3 .. H 4
73 London St. W2 ... G 5
69 London St., Chertsey .... E 2
68 London Tilbury Rd. .... G 4, G 5
76 London Wall ..... G 3
75 London Weather Centre .... G 10
75 Long Acre ...... H 8
70 Long Ditton ..... E 1
65 Long Elmes ...... C 6
70 Long Grove Hospital .... F 2
70 Long Grove Rd. ... F 2
75 Long La. EC1 ... F 13
80 Long La. SE1 ..... C 3
71 Long La., Bexley Heath .... A 12
71 Long La., Croydon D 8
69 Long La., Staines . B 3
65 Long La., Uxbridge E 4
77 Long Ridge Rd. ... F 1
76 Long St. .... C 5
80 Long Walk .... D 4
77 Long Water, The . B 5
75 Long Yard .... E 9
67 Longbridge Rd. . E 11
80 Longcroft Rd. .... H 4
70 Longdown Road North .... G 3
72 Longfield .... D 5
72 Longfield Hill .... D 6
72 Longfield Rd. .... D 5
65 Longford .... H 3
74 Longford St. ..... E 5
71 Longlands ...... C 11
67 Longleigh La. ... H 12
80 Longley St. .... F 6
66 Longmore Avenue A 5
78 Longmore St. ..... F 6
67 Longwood Gdns. C 11
73 Lord Hills Bridge . G 2
73 Lord Hills Rd. .... F 2
79 Lord North St. .... E 8
73 Lord's Cricket Ground .... D 5
67 Lordship La. N17 . C 7
71 Lordship La. SE22 B 7
67 Lordship Rd. ..... D 7
75 Lorenzo St. ..... C 10
79 Lorrimore Rd. .. H 13

79 Lorrimore Square **H 13**
76 Lothbury **G 3**
73 Loudon Rd. **B 4**
65 Loudwater La. **A 3**
79 Loughborough St. **G 10**
70 Loughborough Junc. Sta. **A 6**
67 Loughton **A 11**
67 Loughton Way **A 10**
76 Lovat La. **J 3**
76 Love La. EC2 **G 2**
70 Love La., Morden **E 4**
80 Lovegrove St. **G 7**
78 Lowdnes Cl. **D 4**
71 Lower Addiscombe Rd. **E 7**
70 Lower Ashtead **H 1**
68 Lower Bedford Rd. **C 2**
78 Lower Belgrave St. **E 4**
67 Lower Clapton Rd. **E 8**
67 Lower Edmonton **B 8**
69 Lower Feltham **C 4**
69 Lower Green **E 6**
69 Lower Green Rd. **E 6**
78 Lower Grosvenor Place **D 5**
79 Lower Marsh **C 11**
70 Lower Morden La. **E 4**
70 Lower Mortlake Rd. **B 2**
70 Lower Richmond Rd. **A 3**
67 Lower Rd. **G 8**
78 Lower Sloane St. **F 3**
69 Lower Sunbury Rd. **D 5**
71 Lower Sydenham **C 8**
71 Lower Sydenham Sta. **C 8**
76 Lower Thames St. **J 3**
72 Lowfield St. **B 3**
66 Lowlands Rd. **D 1**
78 Lowndes Place **D 3**
78 Lowndes Square **D 3**
78 Lowndes St. **D 3**
77 Lucan Place **F 6**
80 Lucey Way **E 6**
75 Ludgate Circus **H 12**
75 Ludgate Hill **H 12**
76 Luke St. **E 3**
72 Lullingstone Castle **F 2**
72 Lullingstone Park **F 1**
74 Lumley St. **H 4**
71 Lunghurst Rd. **H 8**
78 Lupus St. **G 6**
79 Luscombe Way **J 8**
71 Lusted La. **H 10**
73 Luton St. **E 5**
74 Luxborough St. **F 3**
71 Luxted Rd. **G 10**
78 Lyall Gdns. **E 3**
78 Lyall St. **E 3**
80 Lydney Close **J 4**
80 Lynton Rd. **F 6**
73 Lyons Place **E 5**
80 Lytham St. **G 2**
66 Lyttelton Rd. **C 5**
75 Mabledon Place **D 8**
75 Macclesfield Rd. **D 13**
73 Mackennal St. **B 6**
75 Macklin St. **G 9**
80 Macks Rd. **E 6**
74 Mackworth St. **C 6**
80 Macleod St. **G 2**
65 Mad Bess Wood **C 4**
74 Madame Tussaud's **E 3**
74 Maddox St. **H 5**
80 Madron St. **F 4**
80 Magdalen St. **B 4**
79 Magee St. **H 11**
80 Maguire St. **C 5**
73 Maida Avenue **F 4**
73 Maida Vale **D 3**
75 Maiden La. **J 9**
71 Maidstone Rd. **C 12**
76 Maidstone St. **B 6**
71 Main Rd., Biggin Hill **H 10**
71 Main Rd., Sidcup **C 11**
72 Main Rd., Sutton-at-Hone **D 3**
78 Makins St. **F 1**
70 Malden **E 3**
70 Malden Manor Sta. **E 3**
70 Malden Rd., Cheam **F 4**
70 Malden Rd., New Malden **D 3**
70 Malden Rushett **G 1**
70 Malden Way **E 3**
74 Malet Place **E 7**
74 Malet St. **E 7**
78 Mall, The **B 7**
77 Mallord St. **H 5**
73 Mallory St. **E 6**
76 Mallow St. **E 2**
80 Malt St. **H 6**
75 Malta St. **D 12**
80 Maltby St. **D 5**
73 Malvern Mews **D 1**
73 Malvern Rd. **D 1**
67 Manchester Rd. **G 9**
74 Manchester Square **G 4**
74 Manchester St. **G 3**
80 Manciple St. **D 3**
74 Mandeville Place **G 4**
75 Manette St. **H 7**
71 Manor Avenue **A 8**
70 Manor Hospital **G 2**
67 Manor Park **E 11**
79 Manor Place **G 13**
67 Manor Rd. N16 **D 7**
67 Manor Rd. Buckhurst Hill **A 10**
68 Manor Rd., Hainault **B 1**
70 Manor Rd., Mitcham **D 5**
70 Manor Rd., Wallington **F 5**
67 Manor Rd., Woodford Bridge **B 11**
70 Manor Rd. North **E 1**
77 Manresa Rd. **G 6**
76 Mansell St. **H 5**
67 Mansfield Hill **B 9**
74 Mansfield St. **F 5**
76 Mansfield St. **C 7**
71 Mansion, The **B 12**
76 Mansion House **H 2**
76 Mansion House Place **H 2**
77 Manson Place **F 4**
75 Mantell St. **B 11**
72 Maplescombe **F 3**
70 Marble Hill Park **B 1**
75 Marchmont Ter. **E 8**
80 Marcia Rd. **F 4**
74 Margaret St. **G 6**
77 Margaretta Ter. **H 6**
75 Margery St. **D 11**
76 Mark La. **H 4**
76 Mark St. **E 3**
78 Market Mews **B 4**
74 Market Place **G 6**
78 Markham Square **G 2**
78 Markham St. **G 2**
67 Markhouse Rd. **D 9**
68 Marks Gate **C 1**
68 Marks Gate Rd. **C 1**
76 Marlborough Av. **A 6**
73 Marlborough Gate **J 5**
80 Marlborough Grove **G 6**
78 Marlborough Ho. **B 7**
73 Marlborough Hill **B 4**
73 Marlborough Pl. **B 4**
78 Marlborough Rd. **B 6**
77 Marlborough St. **F 6**
74 Marle St. **F 6**
77 Marloes Rd. **E 2**
70 Marlpit La. **H 6**
66 Marsh La., Highwood Hill **B 3**
66 Marsh La., Stanmore **B 2**
65 Marsh Rd. **C 5**
67 Marsh Side **B 8**
74 Marshall St. **H 6**
80 Marshalsea Rd. **C 2**
79 Marsham St. **E 8**
79 Marsland Rd. **G 13**
75 Mart St. **H 9**
76 Martin La. **H 3**
69 Martindale Rd. **B 5**
78 Marriet Walk **D 2**
70 Martin Way **D 4**
76 Mary St. **A 2**
74 Mary Terrace **B 5**
67 Maryland Sta. **E 9**
73 Marylands Rd. **E 1**
66 Marylebone **F 6**
73 Marylebone Flyover **F 5**
74 Marylebone High St. **F 4**
74 Marylebone La. **G 4**
74 Marylebone Mews **G 4**
74 Marylebone Rd. **F 2**
74 Marylebone Sta. **E 2**
74 Marylebone St. **F 4**
79 Marylee Way **F 10**
68 Mascalls La. **B 5**
80 Mason St. **E 3**
71 Masons Hill **D 9**
80 Massinger St. **F 4**
79 Mathew Parker St. **D 8**
75 Matilda St. **A 10**
78 Maunsel St. **E 7**
80 Mawbey Place **G 6**
69 Maybury **H 1**
67 Mayesbrook Park **E 12**
66 Mayfair **G 6**
78 Mayfair Hotel **A 5**
78 Mayfair Place **B 5**
75 Maygood St. **B 10**
68 Mayney Rd. **C 2**
71 Maypole Rd. **F 12**
66 Mays La. **A 4**
67 Maze Hill Sta. **H 9**
79 Mead Row **D 11**
79 Meadcroft Rd. **H 12**
79 Meadow Mews **J 10**
79 Meadow Rd. **J 9**
80 Meadow Row **E 1**
74 Meard St. **H 7**
75 Mecklenburg Place **E 9**
75 Mecklenburg Sq. **E 9**
75 Medical College of St. Bartholomew's **E 13**
78 Medway St. **E 7**
75 Melbourne Pl. **H 10**
74 Melbury Terrace **E 2**
74 Melcombe Place **E 2**
74 Melcombe St. **E 2**
70 Melfort Rd. **D 6**
73 Melina Place **D 4**
80 Melior St. **C 3**
80 Menshaw St. **E 2**
72 Meopham **E 6**
72 Meopham Green **E 6**
72 Meopham Sta. **D 6**
79 Mepham St. **B 10**
75 Mercer St. **H 8**
76 Mercers Hall **H 2**
76 Merchant Taylor's Hall **H 3**
75 Meredith St. **D 12**
75 Merlin St. **D 11**
80 Mermaid Court **C 2**
75 Mermaid Theatre **H 12**
80 Merrick Square **D 2**
80 Merrow St. **G 3**
65 Merry Hill **B 6**
65 Merryhill Rd. **A 6**
70 Merton Park Sta. **D 4**
70 Merton Rd., SW18 **B 4**
70 Merton Rd., SW19 **C 4**
79 Methley St. **G 11**
78 Metropolitan Police H.Q. **D 7**
69 Metropolitan Police Training School **E 6**
79 Metropolitan Tabernacle **E 12**
79 Meymott St. **B 12**
76 Micawber St. **C 1**
77 Micklethwaite Rd. **H 1**
75 Middle St. **F 13**
75 Middle Temple La. **H 11**
74 Middlesex Hosp. **F 6**
76 Middlesex St. **G 5**
71 Midfield Way **D 12**
75 Midland Rd. **C 8**
77 Milborne Grove **G 4**
69 Milbourne La. **F 6**
72 Mildmay Forest **G 1**
76 Mildmay Miss. Hosp. **D 5**
67 Mile End Rd. **F 8**
69 Miles La. **G 5**
79 Miles Street **H 8**
75 Milford La. **H 10**
76 Milk St. **G 2**
66 Mill Hill **B 3**
66 Mill Hill (Broadway) Sta. **B 3**
66 Mill Hill East Sta. **C 4**
66 Mill Hill G.C. **A 3**
69 Mill La., Chertsey **D 2**
68 Mill La., Dagenham **G 4**
76 Mill Row **B 4**
80 Mill St. SE1 **C 6**
74 Mill St. W1 **H 5**
78 Millbank **E 8**
79 Millbank Barracks **F 8**
74 Miller St. **B 5**
67 Millers La. **B 12**
75 Millman St. **E 10**
67 Millwall **G 9**
67 Millwall Dock **G 9**
67 Millwall F.C. **H 8**
77 Milmans St. **J 5**
78 Milner St. **E 2**
69 Milton Park **C 1**
76 Milton St. **F 2**
79 Milverton St. **G 11**
80 Mina Rd. **G 4**
76 Mincing La. **H 4**
78 Minerva Mews **E 4**
80 Minnow St. **F 4**
76 Minories **H 5**
80 Mint St. **C 1**
76 Mintern St. **B 3**
70 Mitcham **D 5**
70 Mitcham Common **D 5**
70 Mitcham G.C. **D 5**
70 Mitcham Junc. Sta. **D 5**
70 Mitcham La. **C 5**
70 Mitcham SW17 **C 5**
70 Mitcham Rd., Croydon **E 6**
70 Mitcham Sta. **D 5**
76 Mitchell St. **D 1**
71 Mitchley Av. **G 7**
71 Mitchley Hill **G 7**
79 Mitre Rd. **C 11**
76 Mitre St. **H 4**
66 Moat Mount **A 3**
69 Molesey Rd. **E 5**
74 Molyneux St. **G 2**
79 Monck St. **E 7**
77 Moncorio Gdns. **D 5**
79 Monckton St. **E 11**
73 Monmouth Rd. **H 2**
75 Monmouth St. **H 8**
80 Monnow Rd. **F 6**
80 Montagu Close **B 2**
74 Montagu Mansions **F 3**
74 Montagu Mews North **F 2**
74 Montagu Mews South **G 2**
74 Montagu Mews West **G 2**
74 Montagu Place **G 2**
74 Montagu Row **F 3**
74 Montagu Square **G 2**
74 Montagu St. **G 3**
75 Montagu Place **F 8**
67 Montagu Rd. **B 8**
75 Montagu St. **F 8**
75 Montclare St. **D 5**
79 Montford Place **G 11**
77 Montpelier Place **D 6**
77 Montpelier Square **D 6**
77 Montpelier St. **D 6**
77 Montpelier Walk **D 6**
66 Montrose Avenue **C 3**
78 Montrose Place **D 4**
76 Monument St. **J 3**
76 Moor La. EC2 **F 2**
68 Moor La., Hornchurch **C 5**
65 Moor La., Rickmansworth **B 3**
70 Moor La., Surbiton **F 2**
65 Moor Park G.C. **B 4**
65 Moor Park Sta. **B 4**
78 Moore St. **E 2**
76 Moorfields **F 2**
76 Moorfields Eye Hosp. **D 2**
65 Moorfields Rd. **D 3**
76 Moorgate **G 2**
73 Moorhouse Rd. **G 1**
76 Mora Place **D 2**
72 Morants Ct. Rd. **H 1**
70 Morden **E 4**
70 Morden G.C. **E 4**
70 Morden Hall Rd. **D 4**
70 Morden Park **E 4**
70 Morden Rd. **D 4**
70 Morden Road Halt **D 4**
70 Morden South Sta. **D 4**
70 Morden Sta. **D 4**
80 Morecambe St. **F 2**
75 Moreland St. **D 13**
78 Moreton Place **G 6**
78 Moreton St. **G 6**
78 Moreton Terrace **G 6**
80 Morgan's La. **B 4**
71 Morland Rd. **E 7**
79 Morley St. **D 11**
74 Mornington Cres. **C 6**
74 Mornington Place **B 5**
74 Mornington St. **B 5**
74 Mornington Ter. **B 5**
80 Morocco St. **C 4**
78 Morpeth Ter. **E 6**
73 Morshead Rd. **D 2**
74 Mortimer St. **G 6**
70 Mortlake **B 2**
70 Mortlake Rd. **A 2**
74 Morwell St. **G 7**
73 Moscow Rd. **J 2**
78 Mossop St. **E 1**
70 Mostyn Rd. **D 4**
78 Motcomb St. **D 3**
70 Motspur Park **D 3**
71 Mottingham **C 10**
71 Mottingham Rd. **C 10**
75 Mount Pleasant, WC1 **E 10**
65 Mount Pleasant, Southall **F 6**
74 Mount Row **J 4**
74 Mount Royal Hotel **H 3**
72 Mount Rd. **B 4**
74 Mount St. **J 4**
65 Mount Vernon Hospital **B 4**
74 Moxon St. **F 3**
76 Mulberry St. **G 6**
77 Mulberry Walk **H 5**
70 Mulgrave Rd. **F 4**
74 Munster Square **D 5**
80 Munton Rd. **E 2**
75 Muriel St. **B 10**
79 Murphy St. **D 11**
76 Murray Grove **C 2**
75 Museum of London **F 13**
75 Museum St. **G 8**
66 Muswell Hill **C 6**
66 Muswell Hill G.C. **C 6**
66 Muswell Hill Park Rd. **C 6**
75 Myddleton Passage **C 11**
75 Myddleton Square **C 11**
75 Myddleton St. **D 11**
68 Nags Head La. **C 4**
67 Nags Head Rd. **A 8**
76 Napier Grove **B 2**
71 Nash **F 9**
72 Nash Street **D 6**
74 Nassau St. **F 6**
74 National Dental Hospital **F 5**
79 National Film Theatre **B 10**
79 National Gallery **A 8**
74 National Heart Hospital **F 4**
77 National History Museum **E 5**
75 National Hospital **E 9**
67 National Maritime Museum **H 9**
79 National Theatre **B 10**
76 Navarre St. **D 5**
68 Navestock Common **A 3**
75 Neal St. **H 8**
66 Neasden **E 3**
66 Neasden Sta. **E 3**
80 Neate St. **H 4**
80 Neckinger **D 5**
76 Nelson Gdns. **C 7**
75 Nelson Place **C 12**
69 Nelson Rd. **B 6**
79 Nelson Square **C 12**
75 Nelson Terrace **C 12**
79 Nelson's Column **A 8**
66 Nether St. **C 4**
66 Netherland Rd. **A 5**
77 Netherton Grove **H 4**
74 Netley St. **D 6**
77 Nevern Place **F 1**
77 Nevern Square **F 1**
77 Neville St. **G 5**
77 Neville Ter. **G 5**
71 New Addington **F 9**
72 New Ash Green **E 5**
72 New Barn **D 5**
71 New Barn La., Cudham **H 11**
72 New Barn La., Swanley Village **D 2**
71 New Beckenham **C 8**
71 New Beckenham Sta. **C 8**
74 New Bond St. **H 5**
75 New Bridge St. **H 12**
76 New Broad St. **G 3**
74 New Burlington St. **H 6**
74 New Cavendish St. **F 5**
76 New Change **H 1**
67 New Charlton **G 10**
80 New Church Rd. **J 2**
75 New Compton St. **H 8**
67 New Cross Gate Sta. **H 8**
67 New Cross Rd. **H 8**
67 New Cross Stadium **H 8**
67 New Cross Sta. **H 9**
72 New Cut **H 1**
65 New Denham **E 3**
71 New Eltham **C 10**
75 New Fetter La. **G 11**
69 New Haw **F 3**
69 New Haw Rd. **F 3**
76 New Inn St. **E 4**
76 New Inn Yard **E 4**
80 New Kent Rd. **E 2**
70 New King's Rd. **A 4**
70 New Malden **D 3**
70 New Malden G.C. **D 3**
76 New North Place **E 4**
76 New North Rd. **B 2**
67 New North Rd., Hainault **B 12**
75 New North St. **F 9**
75 New Oxford St. **G 8**
79 New Palace Yard **C 8**
74 New Quebec St. **H 3**
78 New Ride **C 2**
67 New Rd. E4 **B 9**
65 New Rd., Croxley Green **A 4**
68 New Rd., Dagenham **F 2**
69 New Rd., Littleton **D 4**
69 New Rd., W. Molesey **D 6**
75 New Row **J 8**
66 New Southgate **B 6**
66 New Southgate & Friern Barnet Sta. **B 6**
75 New Square **G 10**
76 New St. **G 4**
75 New Wharf Rd. **B 9**
71 New Years La. **G 11**
69 Newark La. **H 2**
74 Newburgh St. **H 6**
79 Newburn St. **G 10**
67 Newbury Park **D 11**
75 Newbury St. **F 13**
73 Newcastle Place **F 5**
77 Newcombe St. **B 2**
80 Newcomen St. **C 2**
73 Newcourt St. **C 6**
80 Newent Close **J 4**
75 Newgate St. **G 13**
67 Newham **F 10**
67 Newham Way **F 10**
79 Newington Butts. **F 12**
79 Newington Causeway **D 13**
74 Newman Passage **G 7**
74 Newman St. **G 6**
75 Newport Place **H 8**
79 Newport St. **F 10**
75 Newton Grove **B 3**
73 Newton Rd. **G 2**
75 Newton St. **G 9**
76 Nicholas La. **H 3**
79 Nicholson St. **B 12**
76 Nicoll St. **B 6**
70 Nightingale La. **B 5**
67 Nightingale Rd., Edmonton **A 8**
70 Nightingale Rd., Wallington **E 5**
76 Nile St. **C 2**
80 Nile Terrace **G 5**
78 Nine Elms La. **J 7**
68 Noak Hill **B 3**
68 Noak Hill Rd. **B 3**

76 Noble St. .... G 1
65 Nockhill Wood ... C 2
67 Noel Park .... C 7
75 Noel Rd. .... B 12
74 Noel St. .... G 6
70 Nonsuch Park .....F 3
70 Norbiton .... D 2
70 Norbiton Sta. .... D 2
70 Norbury .... D 6
70 Norbury Cres..... D 6
70 Norbury Hill ..... D 6
73 Norfolk Cres. .... G 6
73 Norfolk Place .... G 5
79 Norfolk Row .... E 10
73 Norfolk Rd. .... A 5
73 Norfolk Square .. G 5
76 Norman St. ...... D 1
66 North Acton Sta. ..F 3
74 North Audley St. . H 3
66 North Circular Rd. .... C 5
66 North Circular Rd. NW2 .... D 3
66 North Circular Rd. NW10 .... E 2
67 North Circular Rd., Wood Green ... B 7
71 North Cray ..... C 12
72 North Cray Rd. .. C 1
74 North Crescent ....F 7
75 North Down St. .. C 9
70 North Cheam .... E 4
66 North Ealing Sta. ..F 2
71 North End, Croydon .... E 7
72 North End, Erith . A 2
71 North End La. .. F 10
66 North End Rd., NW11 .... D 5
66 North End Rd., W14 .... G 4
66 North End Way .. D 5
66 North Finchley ... B 5
74 North Gower St. . D 6
65 North Harrow Sta. D 6
66 North Hill .... D 6
65 North Hyde ...... G 5
65 North Hyde La. .. H 5
75 North Mews .... E 10
66 North Middlesex G.C. .... B 5
67 North Middlesex Hospital .... B 7
68 North Ockendon . E 5
65 North Orbital Rd. C 2
73 North Ride ....J 4
66 North Rd. N6 .... D 6
68 North Road, Purfleet .... G 4
68 North Rd., Romford ...... B 2
74 North Row .... H 3
70 North Sheen Sta. . B 2
68 North St. .... C 2
70 North Sugden Rd. E 1
76 North Tenter St... H 5
77 North Terrace .... E 6
65 North View ...... D 5
66 North Wembley Sta. .... E 2
74 North West Poly . A 5
66 North Western Av. A 1
73 North Wharf Rd. . G 5
67 North Woolwich G 11
67 North Woolwich Rd. .... G 10
76 Northampton Rd. E 11
75 Northampton Sq. D 12
70 Northborough Rd. D 6
75 Northburgh St... E 12
66 Northfields Av. .. G 2
66 Northfields Sta. .. G 2
72 Northfleet .... B 6
75 Northington St. . F 10
65 Northolt .... E 5
65 Northolt Aerodrome .... E 4
65 Northolt Park .... E 6
65 Northolt Park Sta. E 6
65 Northolt Rd. ..... E 6
71 Northover Rd. ... C 9
76 Northumberland Alley .... H 4
79 Northumberland Av. .... B 8
72 Northumberland Heath .... A 1
67 Northumberland Park Sta. ...... C 8
73 Northumberland Place .... G 1
79 Northumberland St. .... A 8
73 Northwick Close . E 5
66 Northwick Park Hospital .... D 1
66 Northwick Park Sta. .... D 1
73 Northwick Terrace E 4
65 Northwood ...... B 4
65 Northwood G.C. . C 4
65 Northwood Hills Sta. .... C 5
65 Northwood Rd. .. C 3
76 Norton Folgate ...F 4
76 Norwich Rd. ..... A 6
75 Norwich St. ..... G 11
71 Norwood .... C 7
65 Norwood Green .. G 6
71 Norwood Junc. Sta. .... D 7
70 Norwood Rd. SE27 C 6
65 Norwood Rd., Southall .... G 5
66 Notting Hill ....F 4
77 Notting Hill Gate A 1
74 Nottingham Place .F 3
74 Nottingham St. ....F 3
74 Nottingham Ter. . E 3
73 Nugent Terrace .. C 4
71 Nunhead .... A 8
71 Nunhead La. ...... A 7
80 Nursery Row ......F 2
74 Nutford Place ..... G 2
76 Nuttall St. .... B 4
69 Oak Avenue ..... C 5
73 Oak Tree Rd. .... D 5
79 Oakden St. .... E 11
70 Oaken La. ....F 1
65 Oakend Wood ... C 1
72 Oakfield La. ...... C 2
73 Oakington Rd. ... E 1
66 Oakleigh Park .... A 5
66 Oakleigh Park South .... B 5
66 Oakleigh Park Sta. A 5
75 Oakley Crescent . C 12
77 Oakley Gdns. .... H 6
80 Oakley Place ..... G 5
74 Oakley Square ... B 6
77 Oakley St. .... H 6
67 Oakwood Hill ... A 11
66 Oakwood Park ... A 6
66 Oakwood Sta. .... A 6
79 Oar St. .... B 13
76 Oat La. .... G 1
69 Oatlands Av. ......F 4
69 Oatlands Chase .. E 4
69 Oatlands Drive ... E 4
69 Oatlands Park .... E 4
79 Occupation Rd. . G 13
68 Ockendon Rd. ... E 5
69 Ockham Common H 4
69 Ockham La. ..... H 3
69 Ockham Park .... H 3
79 Offley Rd. ....J 11
74 Ogle St. ....F 6
67 Okehampton Cres. .... H 12
75 Old Bailey ...... G 12
74 Old Bond St. ......J 6
76 Old Broad St. .... G 3
77 Old Brompton Rd. F 3
74 Old Burlington St. .J 6
76 Old Castle St. .... G 5
74 Old Cavendish St. G 5
67 Old Church Rd. E4 B 9
68 Old Church Rd., Romford .... D 2
77 Old Church St. ... G 5
74 Old Compton St. . H 7
70 Old Coulsdon .... H 6
77 Old Court Place .. C 2
70 Old Deer Park ... A 1
71 Old Farleigh Rd. . G 8
67 Old Ford Rd. .... E 8
75 Old Gloucester St. .F 9
80 Old Jamaica Rd. . D 6
76 Old Jewry .... G 2
80 Old Kent Rd. ......F 4
69 Old La. .... H 4
73 Old Marylebone Rd. .... G 6
76 Old Montague St. .F 6
76 Old Nichol St. .... E 5
79 Old Paradise St. . E 10
78 Old Park La. ..... B 4
78 Old Pye St. .... D 7
74 Old Quebec St. ... H 3
79 Old Queen St. .... C 7
65 Old Redding ..... B 6
72 Old Rd. .... B 1
67 Old Royal Observatory ... H 9
75 Old Seacoal La. . G 12
76 Old St. .... D 3
79 Old Vic Theatre . C 11
69 Old Woking Rd... G 2
74 Oldbury St. ....F 4
65 Oldfield La. ....F 6
70 Oldfield Rd. ...... E 4
80 Olmar St. .... H 6
80 Olney Rd. .... H 1
66 Olympia .... G 4
80 Omeara St. .... B 2
75 Omega Pl. .... C 9
77 Ongar Rd. .... H 1
77 Onslow Gdns. .....F 4
77 Onslow Square ....F 5
79 Ontario St. ...... D 13
79 Opal St. .... F 12
74 Open Air Theatre D 3
75 Orange St. ....J 7
77 Oratory, The ..... E 6
80 Orb St. ....F 2
74 Orchard St. ...... H 3
73 Orchardson St. ... E 5
75 Orde Hall St. ......F 9
73 Ordnance Hill .... B 5
67 Orient Football Club .... D 9
73 Orme Court ....J 2
73 Orme La. ....J 2
73 Orme Square ......J 2
73 Orme Square Gate J 2
78 Ormond Yard .... A 6
78 Ormonde Gate ... G 2
76 Ormsby St. .... B 5
71 Orpington ...... E 12
71 Orpington Bypass, Orpington ..... E 12
71 Orpington Bypass, St. Paul's Cray D 12
71 Orpington Rd. .. D 11
73 Orsett Mews ..... G 3
79 Orsett St. .... F 10
73 Orsett Terrace .... G 3
76 Orsman Rd. ...... A 4
76 Osborn St. .... G 6
66 Osidge La. .... A 6
73 Oslo Ct. .... C 6
74 Osnaburgh St. .... E 5
73 Ossington St. ......J 2
80 Ossory Rd. .... H 6
74 Ossulston St. ..... C 7
70 Osterley .... A 1
66 Osterley La. ...... G 1
65 Osterley Park .... G 6
69 Osterley Park Ho. A 6
79 Oswin St. .... E 12
72 Otford .... H 2
72 Otford La. .... G 1
69 Ottershaw ....F 2
79 Otto St. .... H 12
70 Ottways La. ...... H 1
74 Outer Circle B 2, D 2, C 4
75 Outram St. .... A 9
70 Outwood La. ...... H 4
79 Oval Cricket Ground, The .... H 10
74 Oval Rd. .... A 4
79 Oval Way .... G 10
71 Ovenden Rd. .... H 12
78 Ovington Gdns. .. D 1
78 Ovington Square . E 2
78 Ovington St. ..... E 2
74 Oxendon St. ......J 7
74 Oxford Circus .... G 5
65 Oxford Rd. ...... D 1
73 Oxford Square ... H 6
74 Oxford St. .... G 6
65 Oxhey .... A 5
65 Oxhey Drive ..... B 5
65 Oxhey La. ... A 5, B 6
71 Oxlea Wood .... A 11
69 Oxshott .... G 6
69 Oyster La. .... G 3
75 Packington Sq. .. B 13
75 Packington St. .. A 13
66 Paddington ....F 5
73 Paddington General Hospital ....F 1
73 Paddington Green .F 5
73 Paddington Recreation Ground .... C 2
73 Paddington Sta. .. G 4
74 Paddington St. ....F 3
68 Padnall Corner ... C 1
79 Page St. .... E 7
80 Page's Walk ...... E 4
75 Paget St. .... C 12
67 Painters Rd. ..... C 12
75 Pakenham St. ... D 10
73 Palace Court ......J 2
77 Palace Gate ...... D 3
77 Palace Gardens Mews .... B 2
77 Palace Gdns. Terr. B 2
77 Palace Green ..... B 2
75 Palace Hotel ..... H 9
71 Palace Parade .... C 7
70 Palace Rd. .... B 6
78 Palace St. .... D 6
75 Palace Theatre ... H 8
76 Palissy St. .... D 5
78 Pall Mall .... B 7
79 Pall Mall East .... A 7
74 Palladium Theatre H 6
78 Palmer St. .... D 7
66 Palmer's Green ... B 6
67 Palmers Green Southgate Sta. . C 7
67 Palmerston Rd... B 10
70 Pampisford Rd. ...F 6
76 Pancras La. ...... H 2
75 Pancras Rd. ...... B 7
74 Panton St. ....J 7
78 Parade, The ....J 3
78 Paradise Walk .... H 2
70 Parchmore Rd. ... D 6
80 Pardoner St. ..... D 3
76 Parfett St. .... G 7
79 Paris Garden .... B 12
67 Park Avenue ..... A 7
74 Park Crescent .... E 5
74 Park Crescent Mews East .... E 5
74 Park Crescent Mews West .... E 4
68 Park Farm Rd. ... E 4
71 Park Hill Rd. .... B 12
71 Park Hospital .... B 9
78 Park La. W1 ..... B 4
70 Park La., Ashtead H 2
67 Park La., Tottenham .... C 8
78 Park Lane Hotel .. B 5
78 Park Place .... B 6
73 Park Place Villas ..F 4
74 Park Rd. NW1 ... D 1
70 Park Rd., Banstead G 4
71 Park Rd., Fickleshole .... G 9
69 Park Rd., Stanwell B 3
70 Park Rd., Teddington .... C 1
69 Park Rd., Twickenham ... C 6
66 Park Royal ....F 2
66 Park Royal Sta. ...F 2
70 Park Side .... C 3
74 Park Square East . E 5
74 Park Square West E 4
80 Park St. SE1 ...... B 2
74 Park St. W1 ....J 3
74 Park Village East . B 5
74 Park Village West B 5
77 Park Walk .... H 4
73 Park West Place .. G 6
65 Park Wood ...... C 4
75 Parker St. .... G 9
80 Parker's Row .... C 6
75 Parkfield St. .... B 11
72 Parkfield Wood .. E 4
80 Parkhouse St. .....J 3
71 Parklangley ...... D 9
74 Parkway .... A 5
65 Parkway, The .... G 5
66 Parliament Hill ... E 5
79 Parliament Square C 8
79 Parliament St. .... C 8
76 Parr St. .... B 2
79 Parry St. .... H 9
68 Parsloes Avenue .. E 1
68 Parsloes Park .... E 1
66 Parson St. .... C 4
69 Parvis Rd. .... G 3
79 Pascal St. ....J 8
79 Pasley Rd. ...... G 13
78 Passmore Terrace .F 3
75 Patent Office .... G 11
77 Pater St. .... D 1
75 Paternoster Sq. .. G 13
76 Paton St. .... D 1
76 Paul St. .... E 3
77 Paulton's Square . H 5
77 Paultons St. ...... H 5
73 Paveley St. .... D 6
78 Pavilion Rd. ..... D 2
68 Pea La. .... E 5
78 Peabody Avenue . G 5
76 Peace St. .... E 7
79 Peacock St. ..... F 13
75 Pear Tree Court . E 11
75 Pear Tree St. .... D 13
79 Pearman St. ..... D 11
69 Pears Rd. .... A 6
76 Pearson St. .... B 5
71 Peckham .... A 7
80 Peckham Hill St. ..J 6
80 Peckham Park Rd. J 6
71 Peckham Rd. ..... A 7
71 Peckham Rye .... B 7
71 Peckham Rye Com. B 7
71 Peckham Rye Park B 7
71 Peckham Rye Sta. A 7
76 Pedley St. .... E 6
77 Peel St. .... B 2
76 Peerless St. .... D 2
77 Pelham Crescent ..F 6
77 Pelham Place ......F 5
77 Pelham St. .... E 5
79 Pelier St. .... H 13
73 Pembridge Gdns. ..J 1
73 Pembridge Place . H 1
73 Pembridge Rd. ....J 1
73 Pembridge Square .J 1
73 Pembridge Villas . H 1
78 Pembroke Close .. C 4
77 Pembroke Place .. D 1
77 Pembroke Rd. W8 E 1
65 Pembroke Rd., Ruislip .... D 4
77 Pembroke Square E 1
77 Pembroke Villas .. E 1
70 Pen Ponds .... B 2
73 Penfold Place .....F 5
73 Penfold St. .... E 5
71 Penge .... C 7
71 Penge East Sta. ... C 8
71 Penge West Sta. .. C 7
71 Penhill Rd. ...... B 12
76 Penn St. .... A 3
80 Pennack Rd. ..... H 5
77 Pennant Mews ... E 2
76 Pennington St. ....J 7
79 Penrose Grove .. G 13
79 Penrose St. ...... G 13
74 Penryn St. .... B 7
79 Penton Place .... G 13
75 Penton Rise ..... C 10
75 Penton St. ...... B 10
75 Pentonville Rd. .. C 10
77 Penywern Rd. .....F 2
80 Pepler Rd. .... G 5
70 Pepys Rd. .... D 3
76 Pepys St. .... H 4
75 Percival St. ..... D 12
75 Percy Circus .... C 10
73 Percy Rd. NW6 ... C 1
69 Percy Rd., Hampton ...... C 6
69 Percy Rd., Twick. B 6
74 Percy St. .... G 7
66 Perivale .... E 2
78 Perkins Rents .... D 7
71 Perry Hill .... C 8
71 Perry St. .... C 11
77 Peter Pan Statue .. A 5
74 Peter St. .... H 7
75 Peters La. .... F 12
70 Petersham .... B 2
77 Petersham La. .... D 3
77 Petersham Mews . E 4
77 Petersham Place .. D 4
74 Peto Place .... E 5
76 Petticoat Square .. G 5
71 Petts Wood ..... D 11
71 Petts Wood Rd. . D 11
78 Petty France ..... D 6
76 Petyward ....F 1
80 Phelp St. .... H 2
77 Philbeach Gdns. ...F 1
67 Philip La. .... C 7
77 Phillimore Gdns. . D 1
77 Phillimore Place .. D 1
77 Phillimore Walk .. D 1
76 Phillipp St. .... B 4
76 Philpot La. .... H 3
76 Phipp St. .... E 4
75 Phoenix Place ... E 10
74 Phoenix Rd. ...... C 7
75 Phoenix St. ...... H 8
78 Piccadilly .... B 5
74 Piccadilly Circus ..J 7
74 Piccadilly Hotel ...J 6
74 Piccadilly Theatre .J 7
75 Pickard St. ...... C 13
71 Pickford La. ..... A 12
71 Pickhurst La. .... E 9
80 Pickwick St. ...... C 1
74 Picton Place ...... G 4
68 Pike La. .... E 5
75 Pilgrim St. ...... H 12
80 Pilgrimage St. .... D 2
68 Pilgrims Hatch ... A 5
71 Pilgrims Way, Knockholt .... H 12
72 Pilgrims Way, Otford .... H 2
78 Pimlico Garden .. H 7
78 Pimlico Rd. ....F 4
76 Pinchin St. .... H 6
76 Pindar St. ....F 4
73 Pindock Mews ... E 3
75 Pine St. .... E 11
66 Pinkham Way .... C 6
65 Pinner .... C 5
65 Pinner Green ..... C 5
65 Pinner Hill G.C... C 5
65 Pinner Hill Rd. ... C 5
65 Pinner Rd. .... D 6
76 Pitfield St. .... C 3
77 Pitt St. .... C 1
78 Pitts Head Mews . B 4
67 Plaistow .... F 10
71 Plaistow La. ..... D 10
67 Plaistow Sta. .... F 10
72 Platt .... H 5
74 Platt St. .... B 7
74 Plender St. .... B 6
69 Plough La. .... H 5
76 Plough Yard ..... E 4
75 Plum Tree Court G 12
76 Plumbers Row ... G 6
67 Plumstead ...... G 11
67 Plumstead Common ..... H 11
67 Plumstead Common Rd. .... H 11
67 Plumstead High St. .... G 12
67 Plumstead Marshes ...... G 12
67 Plumstead Rd. .. G 11
67 Plumstead Sta. .. G 11
73 Plympton St. ..... E 6
69 Pointers Rd. ..... H 4
80 Poiter St. .... D 3
72 Pol Hill .... G 1
74 Poland St. .... H 6
66 Police College .... C 3
76 Pollard Row ..... D 7
74 Pollen St. .... H 5
74 Polygon Rd. ..... C 7
74 Polytechnic of London ....F 3
67 Pomeroy St. ...... H 8
77 Pond Place ....F 6
67 Ponders End ..... A 8
79 Ponsonby Place ...F 9
79 Ponsonby Terrace .F 8
78 Pont St. .... E 2
76 Poole St. .... B 2
80 Pope St. .... D 4
67 Poplar ....F 9
67 Poplar High St. ...F 9
73 Poplar Place ......J 2
73 Porchester Gdns. . H 3
73 Porchester Place .. H 6
73 Porchester Rd. ... G 2
73 Porchester Square G 3
73 Porchester Square Mews .... G 3
73 Porchester Terrace H 3
73 Porchester Terrace Gate ....J 3
73 Porchester Terrace North .... G 3
80 Porlock St. .... C 3
68 Porters Avenue ... E 1
73 Porteus Rd. ....F 4
71 Portland Rd. ..... D 7
80 Portland St. ...... G 3
74 Portman Close ... G 3
74 Portman Hotel ... G 3
74 Portman Mews S. H 3
74 Portman Square .. G 3
74 Portman St. ...... H 3
69 Portmore Park Rd. E 3
70 Portnalls Rd. ..... H 5
75 Portpool La. .... F 11
74 Portsea Place ..... H 2

69 Portsmouth Rd. Esher F 6
70 Portsmouth Rd., Thames Ditton E 1
69 Portsmouth Rd., Wisley H 3
75 Portsmouth St. G 10
76 Portsoken St. H 5
75 Portugal St. H 10
74 Post Office Tower F 6
65 Potter St. C 5
80 Potter's Fields B 4
65 Potterstreet Hill B 5
76 Poultrey H 2
71 Pound La. G 12
71 Poverest Rd. D 11
69 Powdermill La. B 5
76 Pownall Rd. A 6
69 Poyle A 2
70 Poynders Rd. B 6
73 Praed St. G 5
74 Pratt Mews A 6
74 Pratt St. A 6
79 Pratt Walk E 10
71 Pratt's Bottom F 12
76 Prebend St. A 1
76 Prescot St. H 6
66 Preston D 2
66 Preston Rd. D 2
66 Preston Rd. Sta. D 2
65 Prestwick Rd. B 5
79 Price's St. B 12
75 Prideaux Place D 10
79 Prima Rd. J 11
66 Primrose Hill E 5
66 Primrose Hill Sta. E 5
76 Primrose St. F 4
74 Prince Albert Rd. B 2
75 Prince Charles Theatre H 7
77 Prince Consort Rd. D 4
77 Prince of Wales Gate C 6
74 Prince of Wales Theatre J 7
67 Prince Regents La. F 10
76 Princelet St. F 5
70 Princes Coverts G 1
77 Prince's Gdns. D 5
77 Prince's Gate C 5
77 Prince's Gate Mews D 5
73 Princes Mews H 2
72 Princes Rd. B 2
73 Princes Square H 2
76 Princes St. G 2
77 Princess Beatrice Hospital G 2
73 Princess Rd. C 1
75 Princeton St. F 10
80 Prioress St. E 3
70 Priory La. B 3
66 Priory Rd. C 6
77 Priory Walk G 4
76 Pritchards Rd. B 7
80 Priter Rd. D 6
75 Procter St. F 9
75 Provence St. B 13
76 Provost St. C 2
69 Pryford Rd. G 2
75 Public Record Office G 11
75 Public Trustee Office G 9
76 Pudding La. EC3 J 3
67 Pudding La., Chigwell A 12
75 Puddle Dock H 12
72 Puddledock La. C 1
80 Purbrook St. D 4
76 Purcell St. B 4
74 Purchese Rd. C 7
68 Purfleet G 4
68 Purfleet Bypass G 4
68 Purfleet Rd. G 4
70 Purley G 6
71 Purley Downs G 7
71 Purley Downs G.C. G 7
71 Purley Downs Rd. G 7
71 Purley Oaks Sta. F 7
80 Purley Rd. J 7
70 Purley Way E 6
70 Putney B 3
70 Putney Bridge A 4
70 Putney Bridge Rd. B 4
70 Putney Heath B 3
70 Putney High St. B 4
70 Putney Hill B 4
70 Putney Sta. B 4
69 Pyrcroft E 2
69 Pyrford H 2
69 Pyrford Common Rd. H 2
68 Pyrgo Park B 3
76 Quaker St. E 5
79 Queen Alexandra Military Hospital F 8
74 Queen Anne Mews G 5
74 Queen Anne St. G 4
78 Queen Anne's Gate D 7
77 Queen Elizabeth College C 1
79 Queen Elizabeth Hall B 10
70 Queen Elizabeth Hospital H 4
80 Queen Elizabeth St. C 5
69 Queen Elizabeth II Res. E 5
69 Queen Mary Res. D 3
74 Queen Mary's Gardens D 3
71 Queen Mary's Hospital C 12
70 Queen Mary's Hospital for Children F 5
75 Queen Square F 9
76 Queen St. EC4 H 2
78 Queen St. W1 B 5
78 Queen Victoria Memorial C 6
75 Queen Victoria St. H 13
74 Queen's College G 4
73 Queen's Gdns. H 4
77 Queen's Gate D 4
77 Queen's Gate Gdns E 4
77 Queen's Gate Mews D 4
77 Queen's Gate Place E 4
77 Queen's Gate Place Mews E 4
77 Queen's Gate Ter. D 4
73 Queen's Grove A 5
75 Queen's Head St. A 12
73 Queen's Mews H 2
66 Queen's Park Rangers F.C. G 4
66 Queen's Park Sta. F 4
67 Queen's Rd. SE15 H 8
70 Queen's Rd., Richmond B 2
70 Queens Rd., Teddington C 1
69 Queens Rd., Weybridge F 4
67 Queen's Rd., Peckham Sta. H 8
70 Queen's Rd. Sta. A 5
80 Queen's Row H 2
73 Queen's Terrace B 5
74 Queen's Theatre H 7
66 Queen's Wood D 6
77 Queensberry Way E 5
73 Queensborough Ter. H 3
76 Queensbridge Rd. B 6
66 Queensbury C 2
77 Queensbury Place E 4
70 Queensmere Rd. C 4
78 Queenstown Rd. J 4
73 Queensway H 3
75 Quick St. C 12
80 Quilp St. C 2
76 Quilter St. C 6
77 Racton Rd. H 1
77 Radley Mews E 2
73 Radnor Mews H 5
73 Radnor Place H 6
80 Radnor Rd. J 6
76 Radnor St. D 2
78 Radnor Walk G 2
71 Rag Hill H 10
80 Railway Approach B 3
76 Railway Place H 4
75 Railway St. C 9
80 Rainbow St. J 4
68 Rainham F 3
68 Rainham Marshes F 3
68 Rainham Rd. E 2
73 Rainsford St. G 6
75 Raleigh St. B 13
78 Ralston Gate G 2
80 Ralph St. D 2
74 Ramillies Place H 6
74 Ramillies St. H 6
78 Rampayne St. G 7
76 Ramsey St. D 6
79 Randall Road F 9
79 Randall Row F 9
70 Randalls Rd. H 1
73 Randolph Avenue D 3
73 Randolph Crescent E 3
73 Randolph Gdns. C 2
73 Randolph Mews E 4
73 Randolph Rd. E 4
73 Ranelagh Bridge G 3
78 Ranelagh Gardens G 4
78 Ranelagh Grove F 4
67 Rangers Rd. A 10
73 Ranston St. F 6
78 Raphael St. C 2
74 Rathbone Place G 7
74 Rathbone St. G 7
71 Ravensbourne Sta. D 9
66 Ravenscourt Park G 3
66 Ravenscourt Pk. Sta. G 4
76 Ravenscroft St. C 5
79 Ravensdon St. G 11
76 Ravey St. E 4
78 Rawlings St. F 2
75 Rawstorne St. D 12
75 Ray St. E 11
65 Rayners La. D 6
70 Raynes Park D 3
70 Raynes Park Sta. D 3
76 Rector St. A 1
69 Rectory La., Byfleet G 3
67 Rectory La., Loughton A 11
70 Rectory La., Mitcham C 5
70 Rectory La., Sutton G 5
67 Rectory Rd.,Sta. E 8
70 Red La. F 1
80 Red Lion Row H 2
75 Red Lion Square F 9
75 Red Lion St. F 10
71 Red Lodge Rd. E 9
74 Red Place H 3
73 Redan Place H 2
67 Redbridge C 12
67 Redbridge La. D 10
67 Redbridge Sta. D 10
78 Redburn St. G 2
76 Redchurch St. E 5
77 Redcliffe Gdns. G 3
77 Redcliffe Mews G 3
77 Redcliffe Place H 3
77 Redcliffe Rd. G 4
77 Redcliffe Square G 2
77 Redcliffe St. H 3
80 Redcross Way C 2
73 Rede Pl. H 1
78 Redesdale St. G 2
77 Redfield La. E 2
69 Redhill Rd. G 4
74 Redhill St. C 5
80 Redmead La. B 6
77 Reece Mews F 4
68 Reede Rd. E 2
79 Reedworth St. F 11
76 Rees St. A 2
74 Reeves Mews J 4
74 Regal La. A 4
76 Regan Way C 4
78 Regency St. E 7
74 Regent Palace Hotel J 6
75 Regent Square D 9
74 Regent St. H 6
74 Regent's Park C 3
74 Regent's Park Barracks C 5
66 Regent's Park Rd. N3 C 4
74 Regent's Park Rd. NW1 A 4
76 Regents Row A 6
70 Reigate Avenue E 4
70 Reigate Rd. G 3
75 Remington St. C 12
75 Remnant St. G 9
73 Rendall Mews F 6
79 Renfrew Rd. F 12
79 Rennie St. A 12
80 Rephidim St. D 3
77 Reston Place D 3
80 Reveroy Rd. F 6
78 Rex Place A 4
75 Rheidol Terrace B 13
76 Rhoda St. D 5
78 Richard's Place E 1
65 Richings Park G 2
70 Richmond B 2
70 Richmond Bridge B 1
70 Richmond Gate B 2
70 Richmond G.C. C 2
74 Richmond Mews H 7
70 Richmond Park B 2
70 Richmond Park Public G.C. B 3
70 Richmond Rd. C 2
79 Richmond Terrace C 8
77 Rickett St. H 1
71 Ricketts Hill Rd. H 10
65 Rickmansworth A 3
65 Rickmansworth Rd., Croxley Green A 4
65 Rickmansworth Rd., Harefield C 3
70 Riddlesdown Rd. G 6
71 Riddlesdown Sta. G 7
67 Ridge Avenue A 7
70 Ridge Rd. E 4
72 Ridge Wood F 6
74 Ridgmount Gdns. F 7
74 Ridgmount St. F 7
67 Ridgeway B 9
70 Ridgway C 3
74 Riding House St. G 6
80 Riley Rd. D 4
77 Riley St. J 5
73 Ring, The H 4
69 Ripley H 3
68 Ripple Rd. E 1
75 Risinghill St. B 10
79 Rita Rd. J 9
75 Ritchie St. B 11
78 Ritz Hotel B 6
75 River St. C 11
79 Riverwalk Gdns. G 8
76 Rivington St. D 4
74 Robert Adam St. G 3
74 Robert Mews D 6
74 Robert St. D 5
76 Roberta St. D 6
70 Robin Hood Gate C 3
70 Robin Hood Way C 3
78 Rochester Row E 6
78 Rochester St. E 7
71 Rochester Way, SE9 A 10
72 Rochester Way Bexley B 1
75 Rockcliffe St. C 12
80 Rockingham St. E 1
67 Roding La. E18 C 10
67 Roding La., Buckhurst Hill B 11
67 Roding Lane South C 10
67 Roding Valley B 10
74 Rodmarton St. G 3
80 Rodney Place E 2
80 Rodney Rd. F 2
75 Rodney St. B 10
70 Roehampton B 3
70 Roehampton Gate B 3
70 Roehampton G.C. B 3
70 Roehampton Vale C 3
75 Roger St. E 10
77 Roland Gdns. G 4
77 Roland Way G 4
80 Rolls Rd. F 5
72 Roman Villa Rd. C 3
68 Romford D 2
68 Romford G.C. C 3
68 Romford Rd., Aveley F 4
68 Romford Rd., Chadwell Heath D 1
68 Romford Rd., Chigwell Row B 1
67 Romford Rd., Ilford D 11
67 Romford Rd., Stratford E 10
75 Romilly St. H 7
79 Romney St. SW1 E 8
72 Romney St. Kent G 3
76 Rood La. H 4
74 Roosevelt Memorial H 4
76 Ropemaker St. F 2
80 Roper La. C 4
76 Ropley St. C 6
77 Rosary Gdns. F 4
76 Roscoe St. E 2
80 Rose Alley A 1
70 Rose Hill E 4
68 Rose La. C 1
75 Roseberry Avenue E 11
78 Rosemoor St. F 2
71 Rosendale Rd. B 7
75 Rosoman St. D 11
74 Rossmore Rd. E 1
79 Rotary St. D 12
67 Rotherhithe G 8
67 Rotherhithe New Rd. G 8
67 Rotherhithe St. G 8
80 Rothsay St. D 3
78 Rotten Row C 2
77 Round Pond B 3
70 Roundshaw F 6
67 Roundway, The C 7
79 Roupell St. B 11
65 Rousebarn La. A 4
69 Row Hill F 2
69 Row Town F 2
70 Rowan Rd. D 6
80 Rowcross St. G 5
76 Rowland St. F 7
66 Rowley Bank A 3
66 Rowley La. A 3
66 Roxeth D 1
65 Roxeth Green Av. D 6
77 Roxley Pl. H 1
74 Royal Academy of Arts J 6
74 Royal Academy of Music E 4
66 R.A.F. Museum C 3
67 Royal Albert Dock G 11
77 Royal Albert Hall C 4
79 Royal Army Medical College F 8
78 Royal Automobile Club B 7
78 Royal Avenue G 2
70 Royal Botanical Gardens A 2
77 Royal Cancer Hospital F 5
77 Royal College of Art D 5
77 Royal College of Music D 5
74 Royal College of Physicians E 5
77 Royal College of Science D 5
75 Royal College of Surgeons G 10
74 Royal College St. B 7
75 Royal Courts of Justice H 10
74 Royal Ear Hospital E 7
76 Royal Exchange H 3
79 Royal Eye Hospital D 12
79 Royal Festival Hall B 10
75 Royal Free Hospital, N1 A 11
75 Royal Free Hospital, WC1 D 10
77 Royal Geographical Society C 5
78 Royal Horticultural Society Hall E 7
78 Royal Hospital G 3
78 Royal Hospital Road G 3
74 Royal Institute of British Architects F 5
73 Royal Lancaster Hotel H 5
78 Royal Mews, The D 5
67 Royal Military Academy H 11
69 Royal Military School of Music B 6
76 Royal Mint St. J 5
67 Royal Naval College G 9
75 Royal Opera House H 9
79 Royal Rd. H 12
74 Royal Society J 6
79 Royal St. D 10
74 Royal Veterinary College A 7
67 Royal Victoria Dock G 10
79 Royal Waterloo Hospital B 10
70 Royal Wimbledon G.C. C 3
74 Royle St. H 6
65 Royston Park B 6
67 Ruckholt Rd. E 9
73 Rudolf Rd. C 2
76 Rufus St. D 4
70 Rugby Union Football Ground B 1
65 Ruislip D 4
65 Ruislip Common C 4
65 Ruislip Gardens Sta. E 5
65 Ruislip G.C. D 4
65 Ruislip Lido C 4
65 Ruislip Manor Sta. D 5
65 Ruislip Rd. F 6
74 Rupert St. H 7
68 Rush Green D 2
68 Rush Green Rd. D 2
70 Rushett La. G 1
71 Rushey Green B 8
71 Rushmore Hill Rd. G 12
79 Rushworth St. C 12
71 Ruskin Park B 7
75 Russell Hotel E 8
66 Russell La. B 5
75 Russell Square F 8
75 Russell St. H 9
80 Rust Square J 2
78 Rutherford St. E 7
77 Rutland Gdns. C 6
77 Rutland Gate C 6
77 Rutland Mews D 6
77 Rutland St. D 6
69 Ruxbury Rd. E 2
70 Ruxley La. F 2
69 Rydens Rd. E 5
78 Ryder St. B 6
73 Ryders Terrace B 3
71 Rye La. A 7
74 Sackville St. J 6
75 Saffron Hill F 11
75 Saffron St. F 11
79 Sail St. E 10
77 St. Alban's Grove D 3
74 St. Alban's St. J 7
76 St. Alphage Gdn. F 2
75 St. Andrew St. G 11
75 St. Andrew's Gdns. D 10
75 St. Andrew's Hill H 12
67 St. Ann's Rd. N15 D 7
69 St. Ann's Rd., Chertsey E 2
79 St. Ann's St. D 7
73 St. Ann's Terrace B 5
78 St. Barnabas St. F 4
75 St. Bartholomew's Hospital G 12
66 St. Bernard's Hanwell Hospital G 1
76 St. Botolph St. G 5
75 St. Bride St. G 12
75 St. Chad St. C 9
75 St. Chad's Place C 9
76 St. Clare St. H 5
75 St. Clement Dane's Church H 10
76 St. Clement's Church H 3
75 St. Clement's La. H 10
75 St. Cross St. F 11
71 St. Denham Hill C 7
76 St. Dunstan's Hill J 4
74 St. Edmund's Ter. B 2
79 St. Gabriel St. E 12
74 St. George St. H 5
69 St. George's Av. F 4
79 St. George's Cathedral D 11
79 St. George's Circus D 12
78 St. George's Drive F 5
75 St. George's Gdns. D 9
69 St. George's Hill G.C. F 4
78 St. George's Hospital C 4
79 St. George's Rd. D 12
78 St. George's Square G 7
80 St. George's Way H 4
75 St. Giles High St. G 8
75 St. Helena St. D 11
76 St. Helen's Place G 4
70 St. Helier E 5
70 St. Helier Avenue E 4
70 St. Helier Hospital E 4
70 St. Helier Sta. E 4

67 St. Jame's Street Sta. ... D 8
74 St. James's Terrace Mews ... B 2
78 St. James's ... B 6
70 St. James's Drive . B 5
78 St. James's Palace B 6
78 St. James's Park .. C 7
78 St. James's Place . B 6
80 St. James's Rd. SE16 ... E 7
71 St. James's Rd., Croydon ... E 7
75 St. James's Row . E 12
78 St. James's Square B 7
78 St. James's St. ... B 6
75 St. John St. ... D 12
70 St. John's Hill ... B 5
75 St. John's La. ... F 12
75 St. John's Square E 12
67 St. John's Sta. ... H 9
66 St. John's Wood .. F 5
73 St. John's Wood Barracks ... B 5
73 St. John's Wood High St. ... C 5
73 St. John's Wood Park ... A 5
73 St. John's Wood Rd. ... D 5
73 St. John's Wood Terrace ... B 6
80 St. Katherine's Way ... B 6
67 St. Leonard St. ... F 9
76 St. Leonard's Hospital ... B 4
78 St. Leonard's Ter. G 2
78 St. Loo Avenue .. H 2
77 St. Luke's Hospital G 6
77 St. Luke's St. ... G 6
79 St. Margaret St. .. D 8
70 St. Margarets ... B 1
79 St. Margaret's Church ... D 8
75 St. Mark's Hospital ... C 13
75 St. Martins in the Fields Church ... J 8
75 St. Martin's La. ... J 8
75 St. Martin's le Grand ... G 13
79 St. Martin's Place A 8
75 St. Martin's St. ... J 8
75 St. Martin's Theatre H 8
77 St. Mary Abbots Hospital ... E 2
76 St. Mary at Hill ... J 3
76 St. Mary Axe ... G 4
71 St. Mary Cray ... D 12
76 St. Mary-le-Bow Church ... H 2
79 St. Mary's Gdns. E 11
73 St. Mary's Hospital W2 ... G 5
68 St. Mary's La. D 4, D 5
70 St. Mary's Rd. ... E 1
73 St. Mary's Terrace . F 4
79 St. Mary's Walk . E 11
78 St. Matthew St. ... D 7
76 St. Matthew's Row D 6
73 St. Michael's St. . G 5
71 St. Mildred's Rd. . B 9
79 St. Oswald Place G 10
74 St. Pancras Gardens ... B 7
74 St. Pancras Hospital ... B 7
75 St. Pancras Sta. .. C 8
74 St. Pancras Way .. A 7
76 St. Paul St. ... B 1
75 St. Paul's Cath. .. H 13
75 St. Paul's Churchyard ... H 13
71 St. Paul's Cray .. D 12
71 St. Paul's Cray Rd. ... D 11
75 St. Paul's Pier ... J 12
67 St. Paul's Rd. ... E 7
79 St. Paul's Terrace H 12
71 St. Paul's Wood Hill ... D 11
76 St. Peter's Avenue C 6
76 St. Peter's Close .. C 7
69 St. Peter's Hosp. . E 2
75 St. Peter's St. ... B 12
73 St. Petersburgh Mews ... J 2
73 St. Petersburgh Pl. .. J 2
76 St. Philip Way ... A 2
66 St. Quinton Av ... F 4
73 St. Stephen's Gdns. G 1
77 St. Stephen's Hospital ... H 4
65 St. Thomas Drive C 5
80 St. Thomas St. ... B 3
79 St. Thomas's Hospital ... D 9
79 Salamanca St. ... F 9
73 Sale Place ... G 6
73 Salem Rd. ... H 2
75 Salisbury Court . H 12
74 Salisbury Place ... F 2
73 Salisbury St. ... E 6
66 Salmon St. ... D 3
71 Salmons La. ... H 7
73 Samford St. ... E 5
79 Sancroft St. ... F 10
80 Sanctuary St. ... C 2
71 Sanderstead ... G 7
71 Sanderstead Hill . G 7
71 Sanderstead Rd. ... F 7
71 Sanderstead Sta. .. F 7
71 Sandhurst Rd. ... B 9
75 Sandland St. ... F 10
69 Sandown Park Race Course ... E 6
75 Sandwich St. ... D 8
68 Sandy La., Dagenham ... G 4
69 Sandy La., Esher . G 5
70 Sandy La., Twickenham ... D 1
70 Sandy Lane South . F 6
65 Sandy Lodge G.C. B 4
65 Sandy Lodge La. . B 4
65 Sandy Lodge Rd. . B 4
76 Sandy Row ... F 4
70 Sandycombe Rd. . A 2
71 Sangley Rd. ... B 9
75 Sans Walk ... E 12
75 Sardinia St. ... G 9
79 Saunders St. ... E 10
76 Savage Gdns. ... H 4
74 Saville Row ... J 6
75 Savoy Hill ... J 9
75 Savoy Place ... J 9
75 Savoy St. ... J 9
75 Savoy Theatre ... J 9
79 Sawyer St. ... C 13
71 Scadbury Park .. C 11
74 Scala St. ... F 6
76 Scarborough St. .. H 5
80 Scarsdale Rd. ... H 4
77 Scarsdale Villas .. E 1
76 Scawfell St. ... B 5
69 School La. ... F 2
75 School of Arts & Crafts ... F 9
77 Science Museum . D 5
76 Sclater St. ... E 5
79 Scoresby St. ... B 12
71 Scotshall La. ... G 9
73 Scott Ellis Gdns. . D 5
80 Scott Lidgett Cres. D 6
71 Scotts La. ... D 9
71 Scotts Lodge ... H 11
80 Scovell Rd. ... D 1
66 Scratchwood ... A 3
66 Scrubs La. ... F 4
76 Scrutton St. ... E 3
72 Scudders Hill ... D 4
75 Seacoal La. ... G 12
77 Seagrave Rd. ... H 1
72 Seal ... H 3
80 Searles Rd. ... E 3
80 Sears St. ... J 2
75 Sebastian St. ... D 12
79 Secker St. ... B 11
80 Sedan Way ... F 3
78 Sedding St. ... F 3
71 Sedlescombe Rd. . H 1
76 Seething La. ... J 4
75 Sekforde St. ... E 12
76 Selby St. ... E 7
71 Selhurst ... D 7
71 Selhurst Rd. ... D 7
79 Sellow Mews ... F 10
74 Selous St. ... A 6
71 Selsdon ... F 8
71 Selsdon Park G.C. G 7
71 Selsdon Park Rd. .. F 8
71 Selsdon Rd. ... F 7
71 Selsdon Sta. ... F 7
71 Selsdon Wood ... G 8
78 Semley Place ... F 4
75 Senate House ... F 8
73 Senior St. ... F 2
75 Serle St. ... G 10
77 Serpentine, The .. B 6
77 Serpentine Bridge B 5
78 Serpentine Rd. ... B 2
80 Setchell Rd. ... E 5
80 Setchell Way ... E 5
76 Settles Rd. ... G 7
75 Seven Dials ... H 8
67 Seven Kings ... D 12
67 Seven Sisters Rd. . D 7
67 Seven Sisters Sta. . C 7
71 Sevenoaks Rd. .. F 12
69 Severnhills Rd. ... F 4
78 Seville St. ... C 3
73 Sevington St. ... E 2
75 Seward St. ... D 13
67 Sewardstone Rd. . A 9
67 Sewardstonebury . A 9
74 Seymour Hall ... G 2
74 Seymour Mews ... G 3
74 Seymour Place ... G 2
74 Seymour St. ... H 2
77 Seymour Walk ... H 4
80 Shad Thames ... C 5
74 Shaftesbury Av. .. H 7
76 Shaftesbury St. ... C 2
77 Shalcomb St. ... H 4
80 Shand St. ... C 4
76 Shap St. ... B 5
79 Sharsted St. ... G 12
71 Shaw La. ... H 7
78 Shawfield St. ... G 2
70 Sheen Common .. B 2
70 Sheen Rd. ... B 2
69 Sheerwater Rd. ... G 2
77 Sheffield Terrace . B 2
77 Sheldrake Place .. C 1
71 Shelleys Hill ... H 11
75 Shelton St. ... H 8
68 Shenfield ... A 6
76 Shenfield St. ... C 4
66 Shenley Rd. ... A 2
78 Shepherd Market . B 5
78 Shepherd St. ... B 4
76 Sheperdess Pl. ... D 2
76 Shepherdess Walk C 2
66 Shepherd's Bush . G 4
66 Shepherd's Bush Rd. ... G 4
66 Shepherds Hill ... D 6
69 Shepperton ... E 4
69 Shepperton Rd. .. D 3
74 Sheraton St. ... H 7
76 Sherborne La. ... H 3
71 Sherwood Park Av. ... B 12
74 Sherwood St. ... J 6
68 Ship La., Aveley .. G 4
72 Ship La., Dartford D 3
76 Shipton St. ... C 6
71 Shire La. ... F 10, F 11
72 Shirehall Rd. . C 2, C 3
73 Shirland Rd. ... E 2
71 Shirley ... E 8
71 Shirley Park G.C. E 7
71 Shirley Rd. ... E 8
75 Shoe La. ... G 11
67 Shooter's Hill ... H 11
67 Shooter's Hill G.C. ... H 11
67 Shooter's Hill Rd. H 10
67 Shoreditch ... E 7
76 Shoreditch High St. E 4
76 Shoreditch Park .. B 2
72 Shoreham ... G 2
80 Shorncliffe Rd. ... G 5
79 Short St. ... C 11
71 Shortlands ... D 9
75 Short's Gdns. ... H 8
71 Shortlands G.C. .. D 9
71 Shortlands Rd. ... D 9
71 Shortlands Sta. ... D 9
74 Shouldham St. ... G 2
73 Shrewsbury Mews G 1
73 Shrewsbury Rd. .. G 1
73 Shroton St. ... F 6
71 Sidcup ... C 11
71 Sidcup Bypass ... C 11
71 Sidcup G.C. ... C 12
71 Sidcup Hill ... C 12
71 Sidcup Rd. ... C 11
74 Siddons La. ... E 2
79 Sidford Place ... E 10
75 Sidmouth St. ... D 9
70 Sidmouth Wood . B 2
79 Silex St. ... C 12
76 Silk St. ... F 2
67 Silver St. ... B 7
67 Silver Street Sta. .. B 7
70 Silver Thorne Rd. A 5
67 Silvertown ... G 10
67 Silvertown Way . F 10
80 Silvester St. ... C 2
76 Singer St. ... D 3
71 Single St. ... G 11
65 Sipson ... H 4
65 Sipson Rd. ... G 4
69 Sixth Cross Rd. .. C 5
71 Skeet Hill La. ... E 12
71 Skibbs La. ... E 12
79 Skin Mkt.Pl. ... A 13
76 Skinner La. ... H 2
75 Skinner St. ... D 11
76 Skinners Hall ... H 2
72 Slade Green ... A 2
77 SlaidburnSt. ... J 4
71 Slines New Rd. ... H 8
71 Slines Oak Rd. ... H 8
75 Slingsby Place ... H 8
78 Sloane Avenue ... F 1
78 Sloane Court East. G 3
78 Sloane Court West G 3
78 Sloane Gardens ... F 3
78 Sloane Square ... F 3
78 Sloane St. ... D 2
78 Sloane Terrace ... F 3
65 Slough ... G 1
79 Smith Square ... E 8
78 Smith St. ... G 2
78 Smith Terrace ... G 2
70 Smitham Sta. ... G 6
75 Smithfield Central Market ... F 12
75 Smithfield St. ... G 12
80 Smyrk's Rd. ... G 4
67 Snaresbrook ... C 10
67 Snaresbrook Rd. . C 9
75 Snow Hill ... G 12
76 Snowden St. ... F 4
80 Snowfields ... C 3
66 Soho ... F 6
74 Soho Square ... G 7
74 Soho St. ... G 7
73 Somers Cres. ... H 6
73 Somers Mews ... G 6
66 Somers Town ... F 6
75 Somerset House . H 10
80 Sondes St. ... H 3
66 South Acton Sta. . G 3
79 South Africa House ... A 8
74 South Audley St. .. J 4
67 South Bermondsey Sta. ... G 8
77 South Bolton Gdns. G 3
77 South Carriage Rd. C 5
74 South Crescent ... F 7
70 South Croydon ... F 6
71 South Croydon Sta. ... F 7
71 South Croxted Rd. C 7
72 South Darenth ... D 3
66 South Ealing Rd. . G 2
66 South Ealing Sta. . G 2
78 South Eaton Place E 4
71 South Eden Park . D 8
71 South End, SE9 . B 11
77 South End, W8 ... D 2
71 South End, Croydon ... F 7
68 South End Rd. ... E 3
77 South End Row .. D 2
66 South Greenford Halt ... F 1
66 South Hampstead Sta. ... E 5
65 South Harrow ... D 6
66 South Herts G.C. . A 5
68 South Hornchurch ... E 3
66 South Kenton Sta. D 2
79 South Lambeth Rd. H 9
70 South La. ... E 3
70 South Merton Sta. D 4
74 South Molton La. H 4
74 South Molton St. . H 4
71 South Norwood .. D 7
71 South Norwood Hill ... D 7
68 South Ockendon .. F 5
65 South Oxhey ... B 5
77 South Parade ... G 5
67 South Park Drive E 12
76 South Place ... F 3
65 South Ruislip Sta. E 5
68 South Stifford ... H 5
78 South St., W1 ... A 4
72 South Street, Meopham ... F 6
67 South St., Ponders End ... A 8
68 South St., Romford D 2
76 South Tenter St. .. H 5
77 South Terrace ... E 6
67 South Tottenham Sta. ... D 7
68 South Weald ... B 4
68 South Weald Common ... A 4
73 South Wharf Rd. . G 5
67 South Woodford Sta. ... C 10
65 Southall ... G 5
65 Southall Green .. G 6
65 Southall La. ... H 5
75 Southampton Bldgs. ... G 10
75 Southampton Place G 9
75 Southampton Row F 9
75 Southampton St. .. J 9
67 Southampton Way H 7
71 Southborough, Bromley ... D 10
70 Southborough, Surbiton ... E 2
71 Southborough La. D 10
71 Southborough Rd. D 10
67 Southbury Rd. ... A 7
70 Southcroft Rd. ... C 5
71 Southend ... C 9
67 Southend Rd. E18 C 10
68 Southend Rd., Romford ... C 4
75 Southern St. ... B 9
70 Southfields Sta. .. B 4
72 Southfleet ... C 5
66 Southgate ... A 6
67 Southwark ... G 7
76 Southwark Bridge . J 2
79 Southwark Bridge Rd. ... C 13
80 Southwark Cathedral ... B 2
67 Southwark Park .. G 8
80 Southwark Park Rd. ... E 6
79 Southwark St. ... B 13
77 Southwell Gdns. .. E 3
73 Southwick Mews . G 5
73 Southwick Place .. H 6
73 Southwick St. ... G 6
71 Spa Hill ... C 7
80 Spa Rd. ... E 5
66 Spaniards Rd. ... D 5
65 Sparrowsherne ... A 6
77 Spear Mews ... F 1
76 Spelman St. ... F 6
75 Spencer St. ... D 12
78 Spenser St. ... D 6
69 Spinney Hill ... F 2
68 Spital La. ... B 5
76 Spital Square ... F 4
76 Spital St. ... E 6
67 Spitalfields ... F 8
76 Spitalfields Market F 5
78 Sprimont Place ... F 2
79 Spring Gdns. ... B 8
70 Spring Grove ... A 1
73 Spring St. ... H 5
67 Springfield Park .. D 8
73 Springfield Rd. ... A 3
71 Spur Rd. ... E 12
80 Spurgeon St. ... D 2
69 Squires Bridge Rd. D 3
68 Squirrels Heath .. C 3
68 Squirrels Heath Rd. C 4
76 Squirries St. ... D 6
75 Stacey St. ... H 8
73 Stafford Cl. ... D 1
78 Stafford Place ... D 6
73 Stafford Rd. NW6 C 1
70 Stafford Rd., Beddington ... F 6
78 Stafford St. ... A 5
77 Stafford Terrace .. D 1
66 Stag La. ... C 3
78 Stag Place ... D 6
69 Staines ... C 2
69 Staines Bridge ... C 2
69 Staines Central Sta. C 2
69 Staines La. ... D 2
69 Staines Reservoirs B 3
69 Staines Rd., Hounslow ... B 5
69 Staines Rd., Laleham ... D 2
69 Staines Road East D 5
69 Staines Rd., West . C 4
77 Stamford Bridge Stadium ... J 2
66 Stamford Brook Sta. ... G 3
67 Stamford Hill ... D 7
67 Stamford Hill Sta. D 7
79 Stamford St. ... B 11
77 Stanford Rd. ... D 3
77 Stanhope Gdns. .. E 4
78 Stanhope Gate ... B 4
77 Stanhope Mews East ... E 4
77 Stanhope Mews West ... E 4
74 Stanhope Place ... H 2
74 Stanhope Place Gate ... H 2
78 Stanhope Row ... B 4
74 Stanhope St. ... D 6
73 Stanhope Terrace H 5
70 Stanley Park Rd. .. F 5
70 Stanley Rd. ... C 1
75 Stanley Passage .. C 8
66 Stanmore ... B 2
66 Stanmore Hill ... B 1
66 Stanmore Sta. ... B 2
79 Stannary St. ... G 11
71 Stanstead Rd. ... B 8
72 Stansted ... F 5
76 Stanway St. ... C 4
69 Stanwell ... B 3
69 Stanwell New Rd. C 2
69 Stanwell Rd., Staines ... C 3
69 Stanwell Rd., W. Bedfont ... B 4
69 Stanwellmoor ... B 2
80 Stanworth St. ... D 5
80 Staple St. ... D 3
68 Stapleford Abbotts ... A 2
66 Staples Corner ... D 4
73 Star St. ... G 5
70 Star & Garter Home ... B 2
72 Star Hill Rd. ... H 1
74 Starcross St. ... D 6
69 Station Avenue ... E 4
68 Station La. ... D 3
67 Station Rd. ... A 9
69 Station Rd., Addlestone ... E 3
66 Station Rd., Harrow ... C 1
65 Station Rd., Hayes G 4
66 Station Rd., New Barnet ... A 5
71 Station Rd., Orpington ... E 11
71 Station Rd., Sidcup ... C 11
75 Stationers' Hall . G 12
80 Stead St. ... F 2
79 Steedman St. ... F 13
69 Steels La. ... G 6
74 Stephen St. ... G 7
74 Stephenson Way . D 6
67 Stepney ... F 8
67 Stepney East Sta. .. F 8
77 Sterling St. ... D 6
80 Sterry St. ... C 2
76 Steward St. ... F 4
77 Stewart's Grove ... F 5
68 Stifford ... G 6
68 Stifford Rd. ... G 4
78 Stillington St. ... E 6
76 Stock Exchange .. G 3
65 Stockley Rd. ... G 4
70 Stockwell Rd. ... A 6
69 Stoke D'Abernon H 5
67 Stoke Newington . D 7
67 Stoke Newington Rd. ... E 7
67 Stoke Newington Sta. ... D 7
69 Stoke Rd. ... G 5
72 Stone ... B 4
75 Stone Buildings . G 10
72 Stone Crossing Halt ... B 4
66 Stone Grove ... B 2
72 Stone Marshes ... A 3
66 Stonebridge Park Sta. ... E 2
70 Stonecot Hill ... E 4
75 Stonecutter St. .. G 12
69 Stonehill Rd. ... F 1

71 Stonehouse La., Orpington .... F 12
68 Stonehouse La., W. Thurrock ... G 4
70 Stoneleigh Sta. .... F 3
80 Stones End St. ... D 1
76 Stoney La. .... G 4
80 Stoney St. .... B 2
72 Stony Corner .... D 6
79 Stopford Rd. .... G 13
74 Store St. .... F 7
79 Storey's Gate .... D 8
74 Stourcliffe St. .... G 2
68 Straight Rd. ...... C 3
75 Strand .... J 9
75 Strand Theatre ... H 9
67 Stratford .... E 9
67 Stratford New Town .... E 9
74 Stratford Place ... H 4
77 Stratford Rd. ..... E 1
67 Stratford Sta. .... E 9
73 Strathearn Place .. H 5
80 Strathnairn St. .... F 7
78 Stratton St. ...... B 5
70 Strawberry Hill G.C. .... C 1
70 Strawberry Hill Sta. .... C 1
70 Strawberry Vale .. C 1
66 Streatfield Rd. ... C 2
70 Streatham .... C 6
70 Streatham Common ...... C 6
70 Streatham Common North .... C 6
70 Streatham Common Sta. .... C 5
70 Streatham High Rd. .... C 6
70 Streatham Hill ... B 6
70 Streatham Hill Sta. C 6
70 Streatham Rd. ... D 5
70 Streatham Sta. ... C 6
75 Streatham St. .... G 8
70 Streatham Vale ... C 6
70 Street, The .... H 2
66 Stroud Green Rd. D 7
69 Stroude .... D 1
78 Strutton Ground . D 7
76 Strype St. .... G 5
73 Stuart Rd. .... D 1
68 Stubbers La. ..... E 4
75 Stukeley St. ...... G 9
79 Sturgeon Rd. .... G 13
76 Stutfield St. ..... H 7
70 Sudbrook Park ... C 2
66 Sudbury G.C. .... E 2
66 Sudbury Hill Sta. . E 1
66 Sudbury Hill & Harrow Sta. ... E 1
66 Sudbury Town Sta. E 2
66 Sudbury & Harrow Rd. Sta. .... E 2
75 Sudeley St. ...... C 12
79 Sudrey St. .... C 13
76 Suffolk La. .... J 2
80 Suffolk St. SE1 ... C 1
79 Suffolk St. SW1 ... A 7
80 Sultan St. .... J 1
70 Summer Rd. ..... D 1
66 Summers La. ..... B 5
77 Sumner Place ..... F 5
80 Sumner Rd. .... J 5
79 Sumner St. ...... B 13
76 Sun St. .... F 13
69 Sunbury .... D 4
69 Sunbury Sta. ..... D 4
73 Sunderland Ter. .. G 2
71 Sundridge Hill Rd. .... H 12
71 Sundridge Park G.C. .... C 10
71 Sundridge Park Sta. .... D 9
72 Sundridge Rd. .... H 1
68 Sunnings La. ..... E 4
70 Surbiton .... E 2
70 Surbiton G.C. .... E 1
73 Surrendale Place . E 2
80 Surrey Gr. .... G 4
79 Surrey Row ..... C 12
80 Surrey Square ..... F 4
75 Surrey St. ...... H 10
80 Surrey Terrace ... F 4
73 Sussex Gardens .. H 5
73 Sussex Place ..... H 5
73 Sussex Square .... H 5
78 Sussex St. .... G 5
73 Sutherland Avenue .... E 2
73 Sutherland Place . G 1
78 Sutherland St. .... G 5
80 Sutherland Walk . G 2
70 Sutton .... F 4
72 Sutton-at-Hone .. D 3
72 Sutton at Hone Rd. C 2
68 Sutton Avenue ... D 3
70 Sutton Common Rd. .... E 4
70 Sutton Common Sta. .... E 4
69 Sutton La., Hounslow ..... A 5
70 Sutton La., Sutton G 4
74 Sutton Row ...... G 7
70 Sutton Sta. .... F 4
65 Swakeleys .... E 4
74 Swallow St. .... J 6
80 Swan Mead ...... E 4
80 Swan St. .... D 2
78 Swan Walk ...... H 2
72 Swancombe Marshes .... A 5
76 Swanfield St. ...... D 5
72 Swanley .... D 2
72 Swanley La. ...... D 2
72 Swanley Village .. D 2
72 Swanley Village Rd. .... D 2
72 Swanscombe ..... B 5
72 Swanscombe Halt B 5
72 Swanscombe Park C 5
80 Sweeney Crescent D 5
75 Swinton St. ...... D 9
66 Swiss Cottage Sta. E 5
76 Swithin's Hall .... H 2
71 Sydenham .... C 7
71 Sydenham Hill Sta. C 7
71 Sydenham Rd. ... C 8
71 Sydenham Sta. ... C 8
77 Sydney Place ...... F 5
77 Sydney St. .... G 6
78 Symon St. .... F 3
70 Syon La. .... A 1
70 Syon Lane Sta. ... A 1
70 Syon House ...... A 1
80 Tabard St. .... D 2
76 Tabernacle St. .... E 3
78 Tachbrook St. ...... F 6
73 Talbot Rd. .... G 1
73 Talbot Square .... H 5
80 Talbot Yard ...... B 2
75 Tallis St. .... H 11
77 Tamworth St. .... H 1
68 Tank La. .... G 4
80 Tanner St. .... C 4
76 Taplow St. .... C 2
79 Tarver Rd. ...... G 13
79 Tate Gallery ...... F 8
71 Tatsfield .... H 10
71 Tatsfield La. .... H 10
70 Tattenham Corner Rd. .... H 3
70 Tattenham Corner Sta. .... H 3
70 Tattenham Way .. H 4
80 Tatum St. .... F 3
74 Taunton Place ... E 2
75 Tavistock Place .. E 8
75 Tavistock Square . E 8
75 Tavistock St. ...... H 9
74 Taviton St. .... E 7
76 Teale St. .... B 7
70 Teddington ...... C 1
78 Tedworth Square . G 2
75 Temple, The .... H 11
75 Temple Avenue . H 11
75 Temple Bar ..... H 11
75 Temple Gardens H 11
75 Temple Place .... H 10
70 Templeton Rd. ...... G 2
77 Templeton Place .. F 1
79 Tenison Way .... B 10
80 Tennis St. .... C 2
65 Tentelow La. ..... G 6
78 Terminus Place ... E 5
69 Terrace Rd. ...... E 5
77 Thackeray St. .... D 2
70 Thames Ditton ... E 1
70 Thames Ditton Sta. E 1
75 Thames Water Authority ...... D 11
68 Thamesmead ..... G 1
76 Thanet St. .... D 8
75 Thavies Inn ..... G 11
74 Thayer St. .... G 4
75 Theatre Royal ... H 9
79 Theed St. .... B 11
66 Theobald St., Borehamwood . A 2
80 Theobald St., Southwark ..... E 2
75 Theobald's Rd. .... F 9
78 Thirleby Rd. ..... E 6
77 Thistle Gr. .... G 4
69 Thistlecroft .... F 5
79 Thomas Doyle St. D 12
80 Thomas More St. . A 6
80 Thorburn Square .. F 6
76 Thoresby St. ..... C 1
68 Thorndon Park .. C 6
68 Thorndon Park G.C. .... C 6
65 Thorney La. ...... F 2
79 Thorney St. ...... E 8
73 Thorngate Rd. ... E 2
70 Thornton Heath .. D 6
74 Thornton Place ... F 2
70 Thornton Rd. .... E 6
69 Thorpe .... D 2
69 Thorpe Park ..... D 2
69 Thorpe Rd., Chertsey .... D 2
69 Thorpe Rd., Staines .... C 2
80 Thrale St. .... B 2
76 Thrawl St. .... G 5
76 Threadneedle St. . H 3
74 Three Kings Yard H 4
80 Three Oak La. ... C 5
76 Throgmorton Av. G 3
76 Throgmorton St. . G 3
79 Thrush St. ...... G 13
80 Thurland Rd. .... D 6
77 Thurloe Place .... E 5
77 Thurloe Square .. E 5
77 Thurloe St. .... E 5
80 Thurlow St. ...... G 3
76 Thurtle Rd. ...... B 5
70 Tibbetts Corner .. B 4
78 Tilney St. .... B 4
79 Tinworth St. ...... F 9
73 Titchborne Row .. H 6
74 Titchfield Rd. .... B 2
78 Tite St. .... H 2
79 Tiverton St. ..... D 13
76 Token House Yd. . G 3
66 Tollington Park Rd. .... D 6
74 Tolmers Square .. D 6
65 Tolpits La. .... A 4
70 Tolworth .... E 2
70 Tolworth Rise .... E 2
70 Tolworth Rd. .... E 2
67 Tomswood Hill . C 11
75 Tonbridge St. .... D 8
80 Tooley St. .... B 4
70 Tooting Bec Rd. .. C 5
70 Tooting Bec Sta. . C 5
70 Tooting Common C 5
70 Tooting Graveney C 5
70 Tooting Graveney Common ...... C 5
70 Tooting High St. . C 5
70 Tooting Sta. ..... C 5
79 Topaz St. .... E 10
75 Topham St. ..... E 11
77 Tor Gdns. .... C 1
73 Torquay St. .... F 2
75 Torrens St. ...... C 12
74 Torrington Place .. F 7
67 Tottenham .... C 7
74 Tottenham Court Rd. .... F 6
67 Tottenham Hale .. C 8
67 Tottenham Hale Sta. .... C 8
67 Tottenham Hotspur F.C. .... C 8
66 Tottenham La. ... D 6
74 Tottenham St. ..... F 6
66 Totteridge .... A 4
66 Totteridge La. .... B 4
66 Totteridge & Whetstone Sta. . B 5
79 Toulmin St. ..... C 13
76 Tower, The .... J 5
80 Tower Bridge .... B 5
76 Tower Bridge Approach ...... J 5
80 Tower Bridge Rd. D 4
67 Tower Hamlets .... F 8
76 Tower Hill .... J 5
75 Tower St. .... H 8
69 Town La. .... B 3
71 Townley Rd. .... B 12
80 Townsend St. ..... F 3
73 Townshend Rd. .. B 6
76 Toynbee St. ...... G 5
79 Tracey St. .... F 11
79 Trade, Dept. of ... D 7
80 Trafalgar Avenue H 5
67 Trafalgar Rd. .... G 9
79 Trafalgar Square . A 8
80 Trafalgar St. ..... G 3
73 Transept St. .... F 6
67 Traps Hill .... A 11
70 Traps La. .... D 3
79 Treasury .... C 8
75 Treaty St. .... B 9
77 Trebovir Rd. ...... F 1
77 Tregunter Rd. .... G 3
73 Tresham Crescent D 6
79 Treveris St. ..... B 12
78 Trevor Place ..... D 1
78 Trevor Square .... D 2
78 Trevor St. .... C 2
79 Trigon Rd. .... J 10
80 Trinity Church Sq. D 2
76 Trinity House .... H 5
70 Trinity Rd. .... B 5
76 Trinity Square .... J 4
80 Trio Pl. .... D 2
80 Trothy Rd. .... F 7
74 Triton Square .... E 5
72 Trottiscliffe ...... G 6
78 Tryon St. .... F 2
71 Tubbenden La. .. E 11
70 Tudor Drive ..... E 4
69 Tudor Rd. .... C 6
75 Tudor St. .... H 11
66 Tufnell Park Rd. . E 6
79 Tufton St. .... E 8
70 Tulse Hill .... B 6
70 Tulse Hill Sta. .... C 6
76 Turin St. .... D 6
78 Turk's Row ...... G 3
66 Turnham Green Sta. .... G 3
75 Turnmill St. ..... F 12
67 Turnpike La. ..... C 7
69 Twickenham ..... B 6
70 Twickenham Bridge .... B 1
70 Twickenham Park .... B 1
70 Twickenham Rd., Teddington .... C 1
69 Twickenham Rd., Twickenham ... C 5
74 Tyburn Way ..... H 2
80 Tyers Gate .... C 4
79 Tyers St. .... G 9
79 Tyers Terrace ... G 10
79 Tysoe St. .... D 11
78 Udall St. .... F 6
79 Ufford St. .... C 12
76 Underwood Rd. ... F 6
76 Underwood St. ... C 2
76 Union Square .... B 1
79 Union St. .... B 12
76 Union Walk ...... C 4
74 University College E 7
74 University College Hospital .... E 6
75 University of London .... F 8
74 University St. .... E 6
80 Unwin Close ..... H 6
73 Upbrook Mews .. H 4
68 Upminster .... D 4
68 Upminster Bridge Sta. .... D 4
68 Upminster G.C. .. D 4
68 Upminster Rd., Rainham .... F 3
68 Upminster Rd., Upminster ..... D 4
67 Upney .... E 12
67 Upney La. ...... E 11
67 Upney Sta. ...... E 12
78 Upper Belgrave St. D 4
74 Upper Berkeley St. G 2
74 Upper Brook St. ... J 3
77 Upper Cheyne Row .... H 6
67 Upper Clapton ... D 8
67 Upper Clapton Rd. D 8
67 Upper Edmonton B 8
71 Upper Elmer End E 8
74 Upper Grosvenor St. .... J 3
79 Upper Ground .. A 11
69 Upper Halliford Halt .... D 4
69 Upper Halliford Rd. .... D 4
74 Upper Harley St. . E 4
66 Upper Holloway Sta. .... D 6
79 Upper Marsh .... D 10
74 Upper Montagu St. F 2
70 Upper Norwood .. D 6
77 Upper Phillimore Gdns. .... C 1
68 Upper Rainham Rd. .... D 3
70 Upper Richmond Rd., East Sheen ..... B 2
70 Upper Richmond Rd., Putney .... B 3
75 Upper St. Martins La. .... H 8
75 Upper St. .... B 12
69 Upper Sunbury Rd. D 5
71 Upper Sydenham . C 7
76 Upper Thames St. H 2
70 Upper Tooting Rd. C 5
67 Upper Walthamstow .. C 9
71 Upper Warlington Sta. .... H 7
71 Upper Wickham La. .... A 12
74 Upper Wimpole Street .... F 4
67 Upton .... E 10
67 Upton La. ...... E 10
67 Upton Park Sta. . E 10
71 Upton Rd. ...... B 12
80 Urlwin St. .... H 1
65 Uxbridge .... E 3
66 Uxbridge Rd., Acton .... G 3
69 Uxbridge Rd., Feltham .... C 5
65 Uxbridge Rd., Harefield ...... D 3
65 Uxbridge Rd., Hatch End ..... C 6
66 Uxbridge Rd., Hanwell .... G 1
65 Uxbridge Rd., Hayes End ...... F 4
65 Uxbridge Rd., Maple Cross ... B 2
65 Uxbridge Rd., Southall .... F 5
66 Uxbridge Rd., Stanmore ...... B 1
77 Uxbridge St. ..... B 2
77 Vale, The SW3 ... H 5
66 Vale, The W3 ..... G 3
73 Vale Close .... D 3
68 Valence Avenue .. D 1
79 Valentine Place .. C 11
67 Valentines Park . D 11
76 Vallance Rd. ..... E 7
78 Vandon St. .... D 6
76 Vandy St. .... E 3
77 Vanston Place ..... J 1
74 Varndell St. ...... D 6
80 Vauban St. .... E 5
75 Vaudeville Theatre .... J 9
79 Vauxhall Bridge .. G 7
78 Vauxhall Bridge Rd. .... E 6
79 Vauxhall Grove .. H 9
79 Vauxhall Park .... H 9
79 Vauxhall Sta. .... G 8
79 Vauxhall St. ..... G 10
73 Venables St. ...... F 5
71 Verdant La. ...... B 9
74 Vere St. .... H 4
75 Vernon Rise ..... C 10
75 Verulam St. ..... F 11
71 Vesta Rd. .... A 8
76 Vestry St. .... C 3
69 Vicarage Farm Rd. A 5
77 Vicarage Gate .... B 2
67 Vicarage La. Chigwell ...... B 11
68 Vicarage La., South Weald .... B 4
69 Vicarage Rd. ..... C 4
78 Victoria Coach Sta. F 4
67 Victoria Dock Rd. F 10
70 Victoria Drive .... B 4
79 Victoria Embankment .. B 9
79 Victoria Embankment Gdns. .... A 9
73 Victoria Gate ..... J 5
77 Victoria Grove ... D 3
78 Victoria Hospital . H 3
78 Victoria Palace Theatre .... D 5
67 Victoria Park .... E 8
67 Victoria Park Rd. E 8
66 Victoria Rd. NW10 .... F 3
77 Victoria Rd. W8 .. D 3
68 Victoria Rd., Romford ...... D 2
65 Victoria Rd., Ruislip .... D 5
78 Victoria Square .. D 5
80 Victory Place ..... E 2
80 Victory Square .... J 3
78 Victoria Sta. ..... E 5
78 Victoria St. ...... D 6
77 Victoria & Albert Museum .... E 5
74 Vigo St. .... J 6
72 Vigo Village ...... G 6
80 Villa St. .... G 3
67 Village Way, Enfield .... A 7
65 Village Way, Harrow .... D 5
79 Villiers St. .... A 9
76 Vince St. .... D 3
78 Vincent Square ... E 7
79 Vincent St. .... F 7
75 Vincent Terrace . B 12
75 Vine Hill .... E 11
80 Vine La. .... B 4
76 Vine St. .... H 5
73 Violet Hill .... C 4
79 Virgil St. .... D 10
79 Victoria Tower Gardens .... D 9
76 Virginia Rd. ...... D 5
69 Virginia Water Sta. D 1
75 Viscount St. ..... F 13
80 Wadding St. ...... F 2
70 Waddington ..... H 6
70 Waddon .... E 6
70 Waddon Marsh Halt .... E 6
67 Wadham Rd. ..... C 9
80 Waite St. .... H 5
75 Wakefield St. .... D 9
75 Wakley St. ...... C 12
76 Walbrook .... H 2
79 Walcot Square .. E 11
70 Waldgrave Rd. ... C 1
71 Waldram Park Rd. B 8
77 Walham Grove .... J 1
74 Wallace Collection ..... G 3
67 Wallend .... E 11
77 Wallgrave Rd. ..... F 2
70 Wallington .... F 5
79 Walnut Tree Wk. E 11
78 Walpole St. .... F 2
73 Walterton Rd. .... D 1
67 Waltham Forest .. C 9
67 Walthamstow .... D 8
67 Walthamstow Avenue .... C 9
67 Walthamstow Central Sta. .... C 9
67 Walthamstow Marshes .... D 8
67 Walthamstow Queen's Rd. Sta. .... C 9
69 Walton Bridge ... E 4
70 Walton Downs ... H 3
78 Walton Place ..... D 2
69 Walton Rd. ...... D 5
78 Walton St. .... E 1
69 Walton-upon-Thames .... E 5
67 Walworth .... G 7
80 Walworth Place .. G 2
80 Walworth Rd. ..... F 1
80 Wansey St. .... F 1
67 Wanstead .... D 10
67 Wanstead Flats . D 10
67 Wanstead G.C. .. D 10
67 Wanstead Park .. D 10
67 Wanstead Park Sta. .... E 10
67 Wanstead Sta. ... D 10
70 Wandsworth ..... B 4
70 Wandsworth Bridge .... A 4
70 Wandsworth Bridge Rd. .... A 4
70 Wandsworth Common ...... B 5

70 Wandsworth Common Sta. B 5
70 Wandsworth Prison B 5
79 Wandsworth Rd. H 8
70 Wandsworth Rd. Sta. A 6
70 Wandsworth Town Sta. B 4
67 Wapping G 8
80 Wapping High St. B 6
74 Wardour St. H 7
70 Warham Rd. F 6
79 Warham St. J 12
68 Warley Barracks B 5
68 Warley Rd. C 4, C 5
71 Warlingham H 8
75 Warner St. E 11
76 Warner Place C 6
68 Warren La., W. Thurrock G 5
69 Warren La., Woking H 2
71 Warren Rd. F 11, F 12
74 Warren St. E 6
73 Warrington Cres. E 3
73 Warwick Avenue E 3
73 Warwick Crescent F 3
73 Warwick Estate F 2
79 Warwick House St. B 7
75 Warwick Lane, EC4 G 12
68 Warwick La., Rainham F 4
73 Warwick Place F 3
67 Warwick Res. D 8
77 Warwick Rd. F 1
78 Warwick Row D 5
78 Warwick Square F 6
74 Warwick St. J 6
78 Warwick Way F 5
71 Wash Pond Rd. H 9
67 Water La. D 12
67 Waterden Rd. E 9
75 Watergate H 12
70 Waterhouse La. H 4
75 Waterloo Bridge J 10
75 Waterloo Pier J 10
78 Waterloo Place B 7
79 Waterloo Rd. C 11
79 Waterloo Sta. C 10
66 Waterlow Park D 6
76 Waterson St. D 4
69 Watersplash Rd. D 3
65 Watford A 5
66 Watford Bypass A 2
65 Watford F.C. A 5
65 Watford Heath A 5
65 Watford High St. Sta. A 5
66 Watford Rd., Harrow E 1
65 Watford Rd., Rockmansworth A 3
66 Watford Way, NW4 C 4
66 Watford Way, Edgware B 2
65 Watford West Sta. A 4
66 Watling Avenue C 3
76 Watling St. EC4 H 1
72 Watling St., Swanscombe C 4
72 Watling St. B 1
71 Watts La. D 11
73 Waverley Place B 4
78 Waverton St. B 4
79 Waxwell Terrace D 10
68 Weald Park A 4
66 Wealdstone C 1
76 Weaver St. E 6
80 Weaver's La. B 4
80 Webb St. E 4
79 Webber Row D 11
79 Webber St. C 12
74 Welbeck St. G 4
74 Welbeck Way G 4
74 Weigh House St. H 4
75 Weirs Passage D 8
72 Well Hill F 1
76 Wellclose Square H 6
80 Weller St. C 1
71 Welling A 12
71 Welling Way A 11
78 Wellington Arch C 4
78 Wellington Barracks D 6
73 Wellington Pl. C 5
73 Wellington Rd. C 5
69 Wellington Rd. South B 5
76 Wellington Row D 6
78 Wellington Square G 2
75 Wellington St. H 9
74 Wells Mews G 6
74 Wells Rise B 2
74 Wells St. G 6
80 Wells Way H 3
80 Welsford St. F 6
66 Wembley E 2
66 Wembley Central Sta. E 2
66 Wembley Hill Sta. E 2
66 Wembley Stadium E 2
76 Wenlock Basin C 1
76 Wenlock Rd. C 1
76 Wenlock St. C 2
68 Wennington F 3
68 Wennington Marshes G 3
68 Wennington Rd. F 3
76 Wentworth St. G 5
74 Werrington St. C 7
76 Wesley's Chapel E 3
66 West Acton Sta. F 2
69 West Bedfont B 3
69 West Byfleet G 2
69 West Byfleet G.C. G 2
69 West Byfleet Sta. G 2
75 West Central St. G 8
71 West Common Rd. E 9
77 West Cromwell Rd. F 1
71 West Croydon Sta. E 7
65 West Drayton G 3
65 West Drayton Rd. F 4
65 West Drayton & Yiewsley Sta. G 3
71 West Dulwich Sta. C 7
66 West Ealing Sta. F 1
78 West Eaton Place E 3
69 West End, Esher F 6
65 West End, Southall F 5
66 West End La. E 5
65 West End Rd. D 4, E 5
70 West Ewell F 3
67 West Ferry Rd. G 9
66 West Finchley Sta. B 5
67 West Green C 7
67 West Green Rd. C 7
69 West Grove F 5
78 West Halkin St. D 3
67 West Ham F 10
67 West Ham F.C. E 10
67 West Ham Park E 10
67 West Ham Stadium F 10
66 West Hampstead Sta. E 5
65 West Harrow D 6
66 West Heath, NW3 D 5
68 West Heath, SE2 H 1
72 West Hill B 2
68 West Horndon Sta. D 6
67 West India Docks G 9
71 West Kent G.C. G 11
77 West Mall A 1
66 West Middlesex G.C. F 1
69 West Molesey D 6
71 West Norwood C 7
70 West Norwood Sta. C 6
70 West Park Hospital G 2
78 West Rd. G 3
65 West Ruislip Sta. D 4
75 West Smithfield F 12
79 West Square E 12
75 West St. H 8
70 West Sutton Sta. F 4
76 West Tenter St. H 5
68 West Thurrock H 5
68 West Thurrock Marshes H 5
71 West Wickham E 9
71 West Wood La. B 11
73 Westbourne Bridge G 3
73 Westbourne Cres. H 4
73 Westbourne Gdns. G 2
73 Westbourne Gate J 5
73 Westbourne Grove H 2
73 Westbourne Park Rd. G 1
66 Westbourne Park Sta. F 4
73 Westbourne Park Villas G 2
73 Westbourne St. H 5
73 Westbourne Ter. G 4
73 Westbourne Ter. Rd. F 3
74 Westbury Hotel J 5
67 Westcombe Park Sta. H 10
79 Westcott Rd. H 12
69 Westend La. F 5
71 Westerham Rd. F 10
66 Western Avenue, Greenford F 1
65 Western Avenue, Uxbridge E 4
77 Western Hospital H 2
70 Western Rd., Mitcham D 5
65 Western Rd., Southall G 5
77 Westgate Terrace H 3
71 Westhall Rd. H 7
71 Westhorne Av. B 10
76 Westland Place D 2
70 Westmead Rd. F 5
66 Westminster G 6
79 Westminster Abbey D 8
79 Westminster Bridge C 9
79 Westminster Bridge Rd. D 11
78 Westminster Chapel D 6
79 Westminster Hall D 8
79 Westminster Hospital E 8
79 Westminster Pier C 9
78 Westminster R.C. Cathedral E 6
79 Westminster School D 8
78 Westminster Theatre D 5
78 Westmoreland Place G 5
80 Westmoreland Rd. SE17 H 2
80 Westmorland Rd. SE17 G 4
71 Westmoreland Rd., Bromley D 9
74 Westmoreland St. F 4
78 Westmoreland Ter. G 5
70 Weston Green E 1
70 Weston Green Rd. E 1
75 Weston Rise C 10
80 Weston St. C 3
73 Westway F 3
72 Westwood C 5
71 Westwood Hill C 7
77 Wetherby Gdns. F 3
77 Wetherby Place F 4
69 Weybridge E 4
69 Weybridge Rd. E 3
69 Weybridge Sta. F 3
74 Weymouth Mews F 5
76 Weymouth Ter. B 5
74 Weymouth St. F 4
68 Whalebone La. C 1
68 Whalebone La. South D 1
75 Wharf Rd. C 13
75 Wharfdale Rd. B 9
75 Wharton St. D 10
79 Wheatsheaf La. J 8
76 Wheler St. E 5
66 Whetstone B 5
75 Whetstone Park G 10
75 Whidborne St. D 9
67 Whipps Cross D 9
75 Whiskin St. D 12
76 Whiston Rd. B 5
76 Whitby St. E 5
66 Whitchurch La. C 2
75 Whitcomb St. J 7
76 White Church Lane G 6
66 White City Stadium F 4
75 White Conduit St. B 11
79 White Hall Place B 8
67 White Hart La. N17 C 7
68 White Hart La., Collier Row C 2
67 White Hart Lane Sta. C 7
80 White Hart Yard B 2
65 White Hill B 4
72 White Hill La. F 6
71 White Horse Hill C 10
78 White Horse St. B 5
76 White Kennett St. G 4
75 White Lion Hill H 13
70 White Lodge B 2
67 Whitechapel F 8
76 Whitechapel High St. G 5
76 Whitechapel Rd. G 6
76 Whitecross St. E 2
71 Whitefoot La. C 9
75 Whitefriars St. H 11
79 Whitehall B 8
79 Whitehall Court B 8
79 Whitehall Gdns. B 8
67 Whitehall Rd. B 9
79 Whitehall Theatre B 8
79 Whitehart St. G 11
78 Whiteheads Grove F 1
71 Whitehorse Rd. D 7
69 Whiteley Village F 4
80 White's Grounds C 4
76 White's Row F 5
74 Whitfield Place E 6
74 Whitfield St. F 6
79 Whitgift St. F 9
76 Whitmore Rd. A 3
78 Whittaker St. F 3
79 Whittlesey St. B 11
69 Whitton B 6
65 Whitton Avenue E 6
69 Whitton Rd. B 6
71 Whyteleafe H 7
71 Whyteleafe Rd. H 7
71 Whyteleafe South Sta. H 7
67 Wick Rd. E 8
67 Wickham La. H 12
71 Wickham Rd. SE4 A 8
71 Wickham Rd., Beckenham D 8
71 Wickham Rd., Croydon E 8
79 Wickham St. G 10
71 Wickham Way D 9
75 Wicklow St. C 9
76 Widegate St. F 4
73 Widley Rd. D 1
71 Widmore Rd. D 10
67 Wightman Rd. D 7
74 Wigmore Hall G 4
74 Wigmore Place G 5
74 Wigmore St. G 4
78 Wilbraham Place E 3
67 Wilbury Way B 7
75 Wild Court G 9
75 Wild St. A 9
71 Willersley Av. B 11
66 Willesden E 3
66 Willesden Green E 4
66 Willesden Green Sta. E 4
66 Willesden Junc. Sta. F 3
66 Willesden La. E 4
67 William Girling Res. B 8
78 William Mews C 3
74 William Rd. D 5
78 William St. C 3
75 William IV St. J 8
67 Willoughby La. C 8
71 Willow Grove C 10
78 Willow Place E 6
76 Willow St. D 3
80 Willow Walk E 4
65 Willowbank E 3
80 Willowbrook Rd. J 5
76 Wilmer Gdns. B 4
70 Wilmerhatch La. H 2
72 Wilmington C 2
75 Wilmington Square D 11
76 Wilson St. F 3
76 Wiltshire Row A 3
78 Wilton Crescent D 3
78 Wilton Mews D 4
78 Wilton Place C 3
78 Wilton Rd. E 5
78 Wilton Row C 3
76 Wilton Square A 2
78 Wilton St. D 4
78 Wilton Terrace D 3
70 Wimbledon C 4
70 Wimbledon Chase D 4
70 Wimbledon Common C 3
70 Wimbledon G.C. C 3
70 Wimbledon Hill Rd. C 4
70 Wimbledon Park C 4
70 Wimbledon Park G.C. C 4
70 Wimbledon Park Rd. B 4
70 Wimbledon Park Sta. C 4
70 Wimbledon Stadium C 4
70 Wimbledon Sta. C 4
76 Wimbolt St. C 6
76 Wimbourne St. B 2
74 Wimpole Mews F 4
74 Wimpole St. G 4
78 Winchester St. G 5
80 Winchester Walk B 2
67 Winchmore Hill A 7
79 Wincott St. F 11
66 Windmill La. G 1
74 Windmill St. F 7
79 Windmill Walk C 11
76 Windsor Terrace C 2
74 Winfield House C 1
68 Wingletye La. D 4
70 Winkworth Rd. G 4
73 Winsland Mews G 5
73 Winsland St. G 5
74 Winsley St. G 6
69 Wisley G 3
69 Wisley Common H 3
69 Wisley La. G 3
69 Woburn Hill E 3
75 Woburn Place E 8
75 Woburn Square E 8
69 Woking H 1
71 Woldingham Rd. H 8
80 Wolseley St. C 6
65 Wolsey Way B 4
65 Wood End, Hayes F 4
65 Wood End, S. Harrow E 6
67 Wood Grange Park Sta. E 10
66 Wood Green C 6
66 Wood Green Sta. C 6
66 Wood La. W12 F 4
68 Wood La. Becontree E 1
68 Wood La., Dagenham E 3
66 Wood La., Stanmore B 2
67 Wood St. E17 C 9
76 Wood St. EC2 G 2
66 Wood St., Barent. A 4
67 Wood Street Sta. C 9
75 Woodbridge St. E 12
73 Woodchester Sq. F 2
70 Woodcote Grove Rd. G 6
70 Woodcote La. G 5
70 Woodcote Park G.C. G 5
70 Woodcote Park G.C. (R.A.C.) H 3
70 Woodcote Rd. F 5
78 Woodfall St. G 2
70 Woodfield La. H 2
67 Woodford C 10
67 Woodford Bridge B 10
67 Woodford Green B 10
67 Woodford New Rd. C 9
67 Woodford Wells B 10
69 Woodham G 2
69 Woodham La. G 2
69 Woodham Park H 6
72 Woodlands G 3
69 Woodlands La. H 6
70 Woodmansterne G 5
70 Woodmansterne La. G 5
70 Woodmansterne Rd. F 5
70 Woodmansterne Sta. G 5
65 Woodridings C 6
74 Woods Mews J 3
76 Woodseer St. F 6
71 Woodside E 7
66 Woodside Avenue C 5
66 Woodside Park Sta. B 5
80 Woodstaplers Way E 6
70 Woodstock La. E 1
74 Woodstock St. H 4
69 Woodthorpe Rd. C 3
80 Wooler St. G 3
67 Woolwich G 11
67 Woolwich Arsenal Sta. G 11
67 Woolwich Church St. G 11
67 Woolwich Common H 10
67 Woolwich Dockyard Sta. G 11
67 Woolwich Reach G 11
67 Woolwich Rd. SE7 G 10
68 Woolwich Rd. W. Heath G 1
79 Wootton St. B 11
70 Worcester Park E 3
70 Worcester Park Sta. E 3
79 Worgan St. G 9
77 World's End Pass. J 4
66 Wormwood Scrubs F 3
76 Wormwood St. G 4
73 Woronzow Rd. A 5
70 Worple Rd. SW19 D 3
69 Worple Rd., Staines D 2
76 Worship St. E 3
69 Wraysbury B 1
69 Wraysbury Res. B 2
75 Wren St. E 10
80 Wright's Buildings E 4
77 Wright's La. D 2
72 Wrotham H 5
72 Wrotham Heath H 6
72 Wrotham Heath G.C. H 6
72 Wrotham Hill Park G 5
72 Wrotham Rd. C 6, D 6
70 Wrythe, The E 5
70 Wrythe La. E 5
74 Wybert St. D 5
75 Wyclif St. D 12
66 Wyke Green G.C. G 1
73 Wymering Rd. D 2
75 Wynatt St. D 12
74 Wyndham Place F 2
74 Wyndham St. F 2
75 Wyndham's Theatre J 8
75 Wynford Rd. B 10
77 Wynnstay Gdns. D 1
74 Wythburn Place G 2
79 Wyvil Rd. J 8
80 Yalding Rd. E 6
65 Yeading F 5
65 Yeading La. F 5
77 Yeoman's Row E 6
65 Yiewsley F 4
74 York Bridge E 3
75 York Buildings J 9
74 York Gate E 3
77 York House Place C 2
79 York Rd. C 10
74 York St. F 2
74 York Terrace E 4
75 York Way B 9
76 Yorkton St. C 6
77 Young St. C 2
74 Zoological Gardens B 3